Blain

15 GENERATIONS OF
Whipples

Descendants of
Matthew Whipple of Ipswich, Massachusetts
Abt 1590-1647

• AN AMERICAN STORY •

Volume III

WRITTEN AND COMPILED BY
Blaine Whipple

GATEWAY PRESS, INC.
Baltimore, MD   2007

Copyright © 2007 by
Blaine Whipple
All rights reserved.

Permission to reproduce in any form
must be secured from the author.

Please direct all correspondence and book orders to:
Blaine Whipple
236 N.W. Sundown Way
Portland, OR 97229-6575

Library of Congress Control Number 2007940931

ISBN Four Volume Set 978-0-9801022-4-6
ISBN Volume III 978-0-9801022-2-2

Published for the author by
Gateway Press, Inc.
3600 Clipper Mill Rd., Suite 260
Baltimore, MD 21211-1953

www.gatewaypress.com

Printed in the United States of America

CONTENTS

Foreword by Jana Sloan Broglin, CG		vi
Author's Preface		viii
Illustrations		x
1.	First There Was England	1
2.	Essex County and Bocking, England	31
3.	The Whipples of Bocking	48
4.	Sea Voyage to New England	99
5.	Then There Was New England	115
6.	Ipswich and Hamilton, Mass.	159
7.	Matthew Whipple and Anne Hawkins	196
8.	The Joseph Whipple Family	220
9.	Jonathan Whipple and Frances Edwards	231
10.	Francis Whipple and Abigail Lamson	250
11.	Benjamin Whipple and Hepzibah Crosby	309
12.	Nehemiah Whipple and Sarah Robert	354
13.	Enoch Whipple and Catharine Shaw	373
14.	Lucien Ransom Whipple and Sarah Sheward	407
15.	James Ezekiel Whipple and Ellen Thompson	447
16.	Lucien Blaine Whipple and Lillian Neva Lefebre Lucien Blaine Whipple and Pearl Julia Scott	533 561
17.	Robert Blaine Whipple and Ines Mae Peterson	690
18.	Blaine Scott Whipple and Lorna Jo Zoerink	925

Appendix I.
    Whipple English Records 1397-1663   958

Appendix II.
    Will of Matthew Whipple of Ipswich, Mass.   1016
    Inventory of Matthew Whipple Estate   1017
    Sale of Matthew Whipple's Home to John Annibal   1019
    Will of Jonathan Whipple of Westborough, Mass.   1020
    Will of Francis Whipple of Westborough, Mass.   1022

Appendix III.
    The Whipple Flag   1025
    The Whipple Museum of the History of Science   1027

Appendix IV.
    Whipple Soldiers and Sailors in the Revolutionary War   1032
    Massachusetts   1032
    New Hampshire   1049
    Vermont   1057
    Rhode Island   1061
    Connecticut   1064
    Virginia   1065
    Biography of General William Whipple of N.H.   1067
    Biography of Commodore Abraham Whipple of R.I.   1075

Appendix V.
    Ancestors of Spencer B. and Turner C. Whipple   1096

Appendix VI.
    Historical Origin of the Coats of Arms   1128

Appendix VII.   Dates, Names, and Relationships   1133
    Common or Cannon Law Relationship Chart   1137

Appendix VIII.
    Which John Whipple Is Your Ancestor?   1140
    Biography of "Elder" John Whipple of Ipswich, Mass.   1141
    Biography of Captain John Whipple of Providence, R.I.   1166

Appendix IX.
    Some Whipples Who Have Been Published   1189

Appendix X.
    Proposed Ancestors of Matthew Whipple of
    Bocking, England   1208

Genealogy Preface	G 1
Genealogy	G 4
Genealogy Appendix I.	
John Hawkins Family of Bocking, England	G 1520
Genealogy Appendix II.	
Dane and Faulkner Families of Andover, Mass.	G 1520
Descendants of Francis Dane	G 1525
Descendants of Edmund Faulkner	G 1530
Dane Family Members Accused of Witchcraft	G 1544
Indictment of Abigail (Dane) Faulkner in 1692	G 1548
Genealogy Appendix III.	
Thomas Crosby to Hepzibah (Crosby) Whipple	G 1569
Genealogy Appendix IV.	
West, Clingman, LeFebre, Ruhl Families	G 1596
Genealogy Appendix V.	
Scott, Hamel, Dolan, Darmody Families	G 1610
Genealogy Appendix VI.	
Drotzman, Remund, Guerrero Families	G 1677
Genealogy Appendix VII.	
Peterson, Bartruff, Steele, Zoerink Families	G 1700
Genealogy Appendix VIII.	
Jasperson Family	G 1820
Genealogy Appendix IX.	
McPherson, Mauro, Giambanis Families	G 1834
Genealogy Appendix X.	
Vital Records of Whipples in Ipswich, Mass.	G 1850
Index to Genealogy	G 1857
Index to History	2627
Bibliography	2653
Errata	2723

15 GENERATIONS OF
Whipples

Volume III

ELEVENTH GENERATION

4890. **Arthur Vinton**[11] **Getchell** (Alice Leiby[10] **Coombs**, Joseph Jackson[9], Andrew[8], Ebenezer[7], Elisabeth[6] **Pratt**, Hannah[5] **Kennedy**, Elizabeth[4] **Annable**, Anne[3] **Whipple**, Matthew[2], Matthew[1])[1] was born in Dorchester, Suffolk Co., Mass. 11 February 1888 and died in a taxi on his way from the bank to his office 6 March 1969 in Boston, Suffolk Co., Mass., at 81 years of age. He married **Alice Montgomery** in Boston 8 April 1914. Alice,[2] daughter of Malcolm **Montgomery** and Elsie **Macdonald**, was born in Middleborough, Plymouth Co., Mass. 22 September 1888 and died in 1984 in Charlton, Worcester Co., Mass., at 95 years of age. Arthur was President of Addison C. Getchell & Son, Law Printers. The firm edited and printed briefs for cases on appeal in the state and federal courts. He was also Professor of Law at Suffolk Law School and President of Portia Law School (later named New England School of Law). It was the first law school in the country for women. He was a Deacon, Superintendent of the Church School, and Lay Preacher of the Eliot Church in Roxbury.

Arthur Vinton **Getchell** and Alice **Montgomery** had the following child:
+   5757   i.   Anne Montgomery[12] **Getchell** born 14 September 1918.

4897. **Martha Anne**[11] **Young** (Ruth Ann[10] **Cross**, William[9], Jesse[8], Stephen[7], Sarah[6] **Boardman**, Thomas[5], Elizabeth[4] **Perkins**, Elizabeth[3] **Whipple**, Matthew[2], Matthew[1])[3] was born in Clarksville, Coos Co., N.H. 14 October 1871 and died 15 June 1941 in Canaan, Grafton Co., Vt., at 69 years of age. She married twice. (1) **Frank Lewis Owen** in Clarksville 6 Setember 1892. Frank,[4] son of Ethan L. **Owen** and Elvira Bundy **Trask**, was born in Colebrook, Coos Co., N.H. 17 March 1867 and died 8 February 1898 in Stewartstown, Coos Co., N.H., at 30 years of age. (2) **Albion Watts.**

Martha Anne **Young** and Frank Lewis **Owen** had the following children born in Clarksville:
     5758   i.   Gerald Edmund[12] **Owen**[5] 1 July 1894 and died 3 March 1978 at 83 years of age. He married an unnamed person and had three children; no details provided on wife or children.
+   5759   ii.   Addie Ruth **Owen** 17 October 1895.
     5760   iii. Ruth **Owen**[6] 13 March 1897 and died there 23 September 1897, at less than 1 year of age.

{ G 844 }

4898. **Eunice**[11] **Schenck** (Eunice Porter[10] **Wood,** Phebe Smith[9] **Whipple,** Stephen[8], Jonathan[7], Capt. Stephen[6], John[5], Matthew[4], Lt. John[3], Matthew[2], Matthew[1])[7] was born in Cleveland, Cuyahoga Co., Ohio 22 February 1879 and died 15 August 1972 in Ft. Lauderdale, Broward Co., Fla., at 93 years of age. She married **Henry Richard Ahrens**. Henry,[8] son of Richard William **Ahrens** and Emma **Wetzel,** was born in Cleveland 14 December 1879 and died 3 March 1963 in Ft. Lauderdale, at 83 years of age.

Eunice **Schenck** and Henry Richard **Ahrens** had the following child:
+   5761   i.   Henry Richard[12] **Ahrens** Jr. born 11 June 1907.

4899. **Ferne Catherine**[11] **Patterson** (Proctor[10], Phebe Smith[9] **Whipple,** Stephen[8], Jonathan[7], Capt. Stephen[6], John[5], Matthew[4], Lt. John[3], Matthew[2], Matthew[1])[9] was born in Chicago, Cook Co., Ill. 22 September 1889 and died 20 June 1968 in Cleveland, Cuyahoga Co., Ohio, at 78 years of age. She married **John Beverly Jones** in Cleveland 30 September 1913. He was born in Montreal, Canada 5 January 1880 and died 6 October 1955 in Cleveland, at 75 years of age.[10]

Ferne Catherine **Patterson** and John Beverly **Jones** had the following children:
+   5762   i.   Proctor Patterson[12] **Jones** born 25 May 1916.
     5763   ii.   Ferne Beverly **Jones**[11] born in Lakewood, Cuyahoga Co., Ohio 19 June 1917.

4902. **Walter**[11] **Whipple** (Stephen Lovett[10], Stephen[9], Jonathan[8], Jonathan[7], Capt. Stephen[6], John[5], Matthew[4], Lt. John[3], Matthew[2], Matthew[1])[12] was born in Salem, Essex Co., Mass. 18 July 1879 and died 22 September 1955 in Boston, Suffolk Co., Mass., at 76 years of age. He married **Alice Lillian Reeves** in September 1903. Alice,[13] daughter of John H. **Reeves** and Emma B. **Lovejoy,** was born in Salem 24 August 1880 and died in May 1947 in Nashua, Hillsborough Co., N. H., at 66 years of age.

Walter **Whipple** and Alice Lillian **Reeves** had the following children:
+   5764   i.   Winthrop[12] **Whipple** born in 1904.
+   5765   ii.   Kenneth **Whipple** born 31 May 1906.
+   5766   iii. Martha **Whipple** born 22 March 1915.

4903. **Augusta**[11] **Whipple** (Stephen Lovett[10], Stephen[9], Jonathan[8], Jonathan[7], Capt. Stephen[6], John[5], Matthew[4], Lt. John[3], Matthew[2], Matthew[1])[14] was born in Salem, Essex Co., Mass. 20 October 1881 and died 23 December 1959 in Lyme, New London Co., Conn., at 78 years of age. She married **Will Samuel Taylor** 19 June 1912. Will,[15] son of Henry Clarence Clifton **Taylor** and Emmaline **White,** was born in Ansonia, New Haven Co., Conn. 27 November 1881 and died in December 1968 in New London, New London Co., Conn., at 87 years of age. Will's mother was born in Norway and his grandfather Samuel **Taylor,** in England. Augusta qualified for membership in the Colonial Dames of America.

Augusta **Whipple** and Will Samuel **Taylor** had the following children:
+ 5767 i. Virginia Augusta[12] **Taylor** born 6 August 1913.
+ 5768 ii. Carol Ashby **Taylor** born 14 January 1921.

4904. **Paul**[11] **Whipple** (Stephen Lovett[10], Stephen[9], Jonathan[8], Jonathan[7], Capt. Stephen[6], John[5], Matthew[4], Lt. John[3], Matthew[2], Matthew[1])[16] was born in Salem, Essex Co., Mass. 4 November 1885 and died 29 June 1974 in Lexington, Middlesex Co., Mass., at 88 years of age. He married **Marion E. Green** 2 October 1915. Marion,[17] daughter of Charles H. **Green** was born in Spencer, Worcester Co., Mass. 2 December 1891 and died 15 March 1987 in Lexington, at 95 years of age. Paul and Marion are buried in Harmony Grove Cemetery, Salem.

Paul **Whipple** and Marion E. **Green** had the following children:
  5769 i. Lawrence[12] **Whipple**.[18]
  5770 ii. Paul Trumbull **Whipple**[19] born in Arlington, Middlesex Co, Mass. 13 February 1917. Paul was graduated from the Lexington High School and Wentworth Institute of Technology in 1938 and began work as a Mechanical Engineering Draftsman and later became a Production Control Supervisor for Grant Gear, Inc., a manufacturer of geared speed reducers. He retired after 39 years with the company. He lived on the old Green (his mother's family) homestead in Spencer.

4905. **Charles Augustus**[11] **Whipple** (Charles Lewis[10], Stephen[9], Jonathan[8], Jonathan[7], Capt. Stephen[6], John[5], Matthew[4], Lt. John[3], Matthew[2], Matthew[1])[20] was born 2 April 1889 and married **Mary B. Lane**.

Charles Augustus **Whipple** and Mary B. **Lane** had the following children born in Massachusetts:
  5771 i. Roger Lane[12] **Whipple**[21] in March 1913 and died there in May 1913 at approximately 3 months of age.
+ 5772 ii. Charles Lewis **Whipple** II 8 May 1914.
  5773 iii. Richard Lane **Whipple**[22] 21 September 1915 and married Victoria **Eldridge** 10 May 1940.

5774 iv. Mary Elizabeth **Whipple**[23] and married James Woodberry **Smith Jr.** 9 June 1989.

5775 v. Louise Abbott **Whipple**[24] 22 August 1920 and married Lt. Samuel D. **Howarth** 22 January 1944.

4906. **John Whitmore**[11] **Whipple** (Sidney[10], John Hitchings[9], John[8], Jonathan[7], Capt. Stephen[6], John[5], Matthew[4], Lt. John[3], Matthew[2], Matthew[1])[25] was born 5 February 1884 and married **Emma Hunt** who was born 4 January 1886.[26]

John Whitmore **Whipple** and Emma **Hunt** had the following children:

5776 i. Evelyn Augusta[12] **Whipple**[27] born 7 March 1906 and died 10 August 1988 at 82 years of age.

+ 5777 ii. Jeanette R. **Whipple** born 24 December 1907.

4915. **Joanna Evans**[11] **Keyes** (Charles Evans[10], George Everett[9], Mary Alden[8] **Gould**, Benjamin[7], Martha[6] **Gilbert**, Esther[5] **Perkins**, Serg. John[4], Elizabeth[3] **Whipple**, Matthew[2], Matthew[1])[28] was born in Mankato, Jewell Co., Kans. 12 March 1889 and died 2 August 1981 in Enid, Garfield Co., Okla., at 92 years of age. She married **Joseph (Fred) Frederick Dose** in Kiefer Creek, Creek Co., Okla. 12 June 1924. Joseph,[29] son of Josiah Frederick **Dose** and Josephine **Beckit**, was born in Marianna, Lee Co., Ark. 18 September 1883 and died of a massive heart attack 1 July 1973 in Enid, at 89 years of age. Josiah was born at Oldensworth, Germany 12 January 1841. Joseph worked as a ranch hand before joining the Sinclair Prairie Oil Co. at Kiefer. He was a 33rd degree Mason and Order of the Rose Croix. Anna was educated at Kansas State Agricultural College at Manhattan, Riley Co., Oklahoma State University, and Kansas State Teachers College at Pittsburgh, Crawford Co. She was a teacher and school Principal for 30 years in Kansas and Oklahoma. She retired from teaching upon the birth of her first born and resumed teaching when her second child, Dorothy Irene, was graduated from high school. Her second retirement was at age 70. She was a life-long member of the Methodist Episcopal Church and taught Sunday School classes to both children and adults. She was a 50-year member of the Order of Eastern Star, holding all of the chapter offices and was active in the Adult Ladies' Study Club until she moved from Garber, Garfield Co., Okla. to the Methodist Golden Age Home in Enid. A series of strokes had weakened her heart and she needed the help the Home could offer. She died seven months later of congestive heart failure at age 90. Joanna and Joseph are buried at Garber.

Joanna Evans **Keyes** and Joseph Frederick **Dose** had the following children:
+   5778   i.   Ralph Kenneth[12] **Dose** born 14 July 1925.
+   5779   ii.   Dorothy Irene **Dose** born 8 May 1928.

4916. **George Everett**[11] **Keyes** (Charles Evans[10], George Everett[9], Mary Alden[8] **Gould**, Benjamin[7], Martha[6] **Gilbert**, Esther[5] **Perkins**, Serg. John[4], Elizabeth[3] **Whipple**, Matthew[2], Matthew[1])[30] was born in Mankato, Jewell Co., Kans. 18 March 1890 and died 11 November 1967 in Topeka, Shawnee Co., Kans., at 77 years of age. He married twice. (1) **Lua Pearl Homan** in Columbus, Cherokee Co., Kans. 25 May 1918. Pearl,[31] daughter of Matthew Douglas **Homan** and Melissa Jane **Neill**, was born in Mercer Co., Mo. 26 December 1893 and died 20 October 1960 in Topeka, at 66 years of age. (2) **Isabel Earl** in Topeka in January 1962. She died there in February 1990.[32] George was a Postal Service employee in Topeka and a Bookkeeper in Oklahoma before moving to Topeka.

George Everett **Keyes** and Lua Pearl **Homan** had the following children:
+   5780   i.   Dorothy Gene[12] **Keyes** born 18 September 1920.
     5781   ii.   Helen Marie **Keyes**[33] born in Sapulpa, Creek Co., Okla. 18 February 1922.

4917. **Eunice Britt**[11] **Keyes** (Charles Evans[10], George Everett[9], Mary Alden[8] **Gould**, Benjamin[7], Martha[6] **Gilbert**, Esther[5] **Perkins**, Serg. John[4], Elizabeth[3] **Whipple**, Matthew[2], Matthew[1])[34] was born in Mankato, Jewell Co., Kans. 23 January 1894 and died 26 October 1959 in Chickasha, Grady Co., Okla., at 65 years of age. She married **John Jasper Bayles** in Manhattan, Riley Co., Kans., 12 May 1917. John,[35] son of Benjamin Bolton **Bayles** and Ella Julia **Cowell**, was born in Manhattan 13 November 1890 and died 16 December 1979 in Oklahoma City, Oklahoma Co., Okla., at 89 years of age. He was buried in Chickasha. John's mother was born at Islington Parish, Middlesex, England 23 July 1860. He was graduated from Kansas State Agricultural College at Manhattan in 1915 with a BS in Agronomy. He held several positions in the Kansas Agricultural Extension Service before becoming Superintendent of a new Agricultural Experiment Station at Balmorhea, Reeves Co., Tex. The station began experimenting with crops to support farming but later shifted its emphasis to support the state's cattle industry. He remained in that job until his retirement in 1955 at which time he and Eunice moved to Chickasha. Eunice attended normal school and was teaching at Rocky Ford School, a one-room school, when she met John. Over the years she became the unofficial hostess to the many officials who came to inspect the Texas Experiment Station. She and her husband were co-teachers of a Youth Sunday School class at the Methodist Church in Chickasha.

{ G 848 }

Eunice Britt **Keyes** and John Jasper **Bayles** had the following children:
- \+ 5782 i. Lawrence Gordon[12] **Bayles** born 31 August 1918.
- \+ 5783 ii. George Vincent **Bayles** born 7 March 1920.
- \+ 5784 iii. John Junior **Bayles** born 6 July 1922.
- \+ 5785 iv. Ruth Alene **Bayles** born 27 November 1924.

4920. **Burt Byron**[11] **Thomas** (Ambrose[10], Dilla[9] **Beeman**, Daniel[8], Lydia[7] **Cogswell**, Samuel[6], Hannah[5] **Browne**, Judith[4] **Perkins**, Elizabeth[3] **Whipple**, Matthew[2], Matthew[1])[36] was born in Dowagiac, Cass. Co., Mich. 16 November 1865 and died 2 April 1942 in Clearwater, Pinellas Co., Fla., at 76 years of age. He married **Effa Isabelle Brock** in Green Mountain, Tama Co., Iowa 31 August 1887. Effa,[37] daughter of James Kerr **Brock** and Laura Jane **Somers**, was born in Green Mountain 16 September 1867 and died 6 February 1953 in Clearwater, at 85 years of age.

Burt Byron **Thomas** and Effa Isabelle **Brock** had the following children:
- \+ 5786 i. Dilman Kar[12] **Thomas** born 3 September 1888.
- \+ 5787 ii. Eva Dillie **Thomas** born 21 July 1909.

4921. **Col. John Calvin**[11] **Coolidge** (Sarah Almeda[10] **Brewer**, Sally[9] **Brown**, Israel Putnam[8], Adam[7], Adam[6], Jacob[5], Judith[4] **Perkins**, Elizabeth[3] **Whipple**, Matthew[2], Matthew[1])[38] was born in Plymouth, Windsor Co., Vt. 31 March 1844 and died there 18 March 1926, at 81 years of age. He married twice. (1) **Victoria Josephine Moor** 6 May 1868. Victoria,[39] daughter of Hiram Dunlop **Moor** and Abigail **Franklin**, was born in Pinney Hollow, Vt. 14 March 1846 and died 14 March 1885 in Plymouth, at 39 years of age. (2) **Caroline Brown** 9 September 1891. She was born in Plymouth 22 January 1857 and died 19 May 1920 in Plymouth, at 63 years of age.[40] Colonel Coolidge was a Vermont Justice of the Peace, politician, farmer, and storekeeper.

Col. John Calvin **Coolidge** and Victoria Josephine **Moor** had the following children born in Plymouth:
- \+ 5788 i. Pres. John Calvin[12] **Coolidge** 4 July 1872.
- 5789 ii. Abigail Gratia **Coolidge**[41] in 1875 and died in 1890 at 15 years of age.

4922. **Walter Frederick**[11] **Ellis** (Frederick Orin[10], Mary Phillips[9] **Brown**, Aaron[8], John[7], John[6], Jacob[5], Judith[4] **Perkins**, Elizabeth[3] **Whipple**, Matthew[2], Matthew[1])[42] was born in S. Royalston, Worcester Co., Mass. 4 April 1876 and died 9 August 1939 in Longmeadow, Hampden Co., Mass., at 63 years of age. Buried at Swampscott, Essex Co., Mass. He married **Florence Hirt** 17 November 1905.

{ G 849 }

Walter Frederick **Ellis** and Florence **Hirt** had the following child:

    5790   i.   Sidonia[12] **Ellis**[43] married Charles G. **Blumenhauer**.

4923. **Dr. Robert Hale**[11] **Ellis** (Frederick Orin[10], Mary Phillips[9] **Brown**, Aaron[8], John[7], John[6], Jacob[5], Judith[4] **Perkins**, Elizabeth[3] **Whipple**, Matthew[2], Matthew[1])[44] was born in Swampscott, Essex Co., Mass. 27 April 1878 and died 15 March 1963 in Portland, Multnomah Co., Oreg., at 84 years of age. He married **Blanche Eloise Day** in Portland 10 February 1909. She was born in Sacramento, Sacramento Co., Calif. 2 February 1879 and died 9 September 1949 in Portland, at 70 years of age.[45]

Dr. Robert Hale **Ellis** and Blanche Eloise **Day** had the following children born in Portland:

    5791   i.   Henry Day[12] **Ellis**[46] 1 January 1911.
    5792   ii.   Robert Hale **Ellis** Jr.[47] 19 December 1914 and died abt 1980 in Portland. He served with the Army Corps of Engineers 1942-46.
+   5793   iii.   Frederick Eugene **Ellis** 26 August 1916.
+   5794   iv.   Elizabeth Eleanor **Ellis** 8 November 1917.

4924. **Anna Hale**[11] **Ellis** (Frederick Orin[10], Mary Phillips[9] **Brown**, Aaron[8], John[7], John[6], Jacob[5], Judith[4] **Perkins**, Elizabeth[3] **Whipple**, Matthew[2], Matthew[1])[48] was born in Braintree, Norfolk Co., Mass. 3 June 1883 and died 30 December 1963 in Winter Park, Orange Co., Fla., at 80 years of age. Buried at Swampscott, Mass. She married **William Oliver Wise** in Braintree 10 September 1912. He was born in Lancaster, Worcester Co., Mass. 22 March 1884 and died 8 September 1971 in Ithaca, Tompkins Co., N.Y., at 87 years of age.[49]

Anna Hale **Ellis** and William Oliver **Wise** had the following children:

+   5795   i.   Robert E.[12] **Wise** born 26 December 1913.
+   5796   ii.   Miriam **Wise** born 17 November 1916.
+   5797   iii.   William Oliver **Wise** Jr. born 24 July 1919.

4925. **Miriam**[11] **Ellis** (Frederick Orin[10], Mary Phillips[9] **Brown**, Aaron[8], John[7], John[6], Jacob[5], Judith[4] **Perkins**, Elizabeth[3] **Whipple**, Matthew[2], Matthew[1])[50] was born in Braintree, Norfolk Co., Mass. 18 May 1888 and died 7 December 1986 in Weymouth, Norfolk Co., Mass., at 98 years of age. She married **Joseph Leszkiewicz** in Braintree 23 September 1919. He was born in Vilna, Poland (now Russia) 22 October 1893. Son of John **Leszkiewicz** and Agatha **Jacewicz**, he died 7 January 1978 in Braintree, at 84 years of age.[51]

Miriam **Ellis** and Joseph **Leszkiewicz** had the following children:

      5798   i.   Mary[12] **Leszkiewicz**[52] born in 1921 and died 29 March 1976 at 54 years of age. She married Robert **Jones.**

+   5799   ii.   Rosamond **Leszkiewicz** born in 1922.

      5800   iii. Elizabeth **Leszkiewicz**[53] born in 1923 and married (__) **Kirkpatrick.**

+   5801   iv. Wanda Ellis **Leszkiewicz** born 23 November 1924.

      5802   v.   John **Leszkiewicz**[54] was born in 1925 and married twice; no details provided.

4927. **Ione**[11] **Andrews** (Henry[10], Caleb[9], Molly[8] **Burnham**, Capt. Westley[7], Westley[6], Elizabeth[5] **Perkins**, Jacob[4], Elizabeth[3] **Whipple**, Matthew[2], Matthew[1])[55] was born in Essex, Essex Co., Mass. 9 August 1853 and died 17 July 1907 in Beverly, Essex Co., Mass., at 53 years of age. She married **George William Bragdon** in Lynn, Essex Co., Mass. 9 May 1868. George was 21, Ione 15 when they married. George,[56] son of George Frost **Bragdon** and Fannie Elizabeth **Woodbury**, was born in Beverly 3 March 1848 and died there 7 July 1911, at 63 years of age. Buried at Central Cemetery, Beverly.

Ione **Andrews** and George William **Bragdon** had the following children:

+   5803   i.   George Henry[12] **Bragdon** born in 1868.

      5804   ii.   Arthur Ellsworth **Bragdon**[57] born in Essex 21 September 1870 and died there in 1942 at 71 years of age. Buried in Essex. He married Elizabeth Anne **Crafts.**

+   5805   iii. Fannie Woodberry **Bragdon** born 28 December 1872.

+   5806   iv. Charles William **Bragdon** born 11 January 1876.

      5807   v.   Leonard Leslie **Bragdon**[58] born in Beverly 27 March 1881 and died there 10 May 1891 at 10 years of age.

      5808   vi. James Frederick **Bragdon**[59] born in Beverly 24 December 1887 and died 27 September 1914 at 26 years of age.

4928. **Hattie Leslie**[11] **Andrews** (Henry[10], Caleb[9], Molly[8] **Burnham**, Capt. Westley[7], Westley[6], Elizabeth[5] **Perkins**, Jacob[4], Elizabeth[3] **Whipple**, Matthew[2], Matthew[1])[60] was born in Essex, Essex Co., Mass. 18 January 1865 and died 7 February 1919 at 54 years of age. She married **Charles Henry Butman** in Essex 23 November 1884. Charles,[61] son of Ancil Kimball **Butman** and Elsie Ann **Morse**, was born 7 November 1859.

Hattie Leslie **Andrews** and Charles Henry **Butman** had the following children:

  5809 i. Fannie[12] **Butman**[62] born 12 July 1891 and died the day after birth.

  5810 ii. Ione Leslie **Butman**[63] born 19 August 1894 and died by suicide. She married Elliott **Melanson** in 1916.

  5811 iii. Raymond Hanson **Butman**[64] born 6 December 1897.

4929. **Emma Louise**[11] **Andrews** (Henry[10], Caleb[9], Molly[8] **Burnham**, Capt. Westley[7], Westley[6], Elizabeth[5] **Perkins**, Jacob[4], Elizabeth[3] **Whipple**, Matthew[2], Matthew[1])[65] was born in Essex, Essex Co., Mass. 17 August 1867 and died there 25 January 1959, at 91 years of age. She married **Charles Gilman Low** in Essex 19 September 1883. Charles,[66] son of Reuben Smith **Low** and Martha Jane **Brooks**, was born in Leominster, Worcester Co., Mass. 18 January 1860 and died 11 June 1922 in Essex, at 62 years of age. Both are buried at the Spring Street Cemetery.

Emma Louise **Andrews** and Charles Gilman **Low** had the following children born in Essex:

+ 5812 i. Emma Louise[12] **Low** 7 April 1884.

  5813 ii. Lester Brooks **Low**[67] 6 November 1886 and died there 25 July 1903, at 16 years of age.

  5814 iii. Althine Frances **Low**[68] 9 September 1890 and died in 1990 in Beverly, Essex Co., Mass. at 99 years of age.

  5815 iv. Eleanor Woodbury **Low**[69] 19 September 1893 and died 8 December 1897 in Beverly, at 4 years of age.

+ 5816 v. Ardelle **Low** 14 November 1899.

+ 5817 vi. Ceciline **Low** 20 December 1905.

+ 5818 vii. Elston Brooks **Low** 8 December 1908.

4930. **Henry Ward**[11] **Andrews** (Henry[10], Caleb[9], Molly[8] **Burnham**, Capt. Westley[7], Westley[6], Elizabeth[5] **Perkins**, Jacob[4], Elizabeth[3] **Whipple**, Matthew[2], Matthew[1])[70] was born in Essex, Essex Co., Mass. 17 February 1870 and died there in 1920, at 50 years of age. He married **Minnie Foster Hibbard** 23 November 1896. Minnie,[71] daughter of Martin **Hibbard** and Alice **Wilmington**, was born 14 December 1878 and died 1967 at 88 years of age. Buried at Spring Street Cemetery, Essex.

Henry Ward **Andrews** and Minnie Foster **Hibbard** had the following children born in Essex:

  5819 i. Henry[12] **Andrews**[72] 27 August 1897 and died the day of birth.

+ 5820 ii. Henry Foster **Andrews** 27 December 1899.

            5821   iii.   Burton Elwell **Andrews**[73] 30 January 1904 and married Laura (__).

4931. **Frank Albert**[11] **Andrews** (Henry[10], Caleb[9], Molly[8] **Burnham**, Capt. Westley[7], Westley[6], Elizabeth[5] **Perkins**, Jacob[4], Elizabeth[3] **Whipple**, Matthew[2], Matthew[1])[74] was born in Essex, Essex Co., Mass. 27 December 1874 and died 8 January 1953 in Woodville, Middlesex Co., Mass., at 78 years of age. He married **Lavinia Wells Goddard** in Ipswich, Essex Co., Mass. 31 March 1897. Lavinia,[75] daughter of John Calvin **Goddard** and Lavinia **Wells**, was born in South Branch, Kings, New Brunswick, Canada 14 October 1872 and died 8 October 1952 in Woodville, at 79 years of age. Both are buried at Evergreen Cemetery, Hopkinton, Middlesex Co., Mass.

Frank Albert **Andrews** and Lavinia Wells **Goddard** had the following children born in Essex:

+   5822   i.   Edna Frances[12] **Andrews** 10 February 1898.
+   5823   ii.   Viola Alberta **Andrews** 14 February 1901.
      5824   iii.   Elsie Lavinia **Andrews**[76] 20 August 1903 and died 5 March 1935 in Hopkinton, at 31 years of age. Buried at Evergreen Cemetery, Woodville.
+   5825   iv.   Jean Dorothy **Andrews** 7 August 1907.
+   5826   v.   Frank Sydney **Andrews** 18 May 1911.

4934. **David Edward**[11] **Mears** (Sallie Maria[10] **Andrews**, Caleb[9], Molly[8] **Burnham**, Capt. Westley[7], Westley[6], Elizabeth[5] **Perkins**, Jacob[4], Elizabeth[3] **Whipple**, Matthew[2], Matthew[1])[77] was born in Essex, Essex Co., Mass. 17 June 1863 and died there 29 December 1954, at 91 years of age. He married **Helene Sophie Briand** in Essex 3 March 1889. Helene,[78] daughter of Edward **Briand** and Adele **Forgeron**, was born in Arichat, Nova Scotia, Canada 26 August 1870 and died 31 March 1964 in Essex, at 93 years of age.

David Edward **Mears** and Helene Sophie **Briand** had the following children born in Essex:

      5827   i.   Lucy A.[12] **Mears**[79] 2 October 1889 and died 31 August 1941 at 51 years of age. She married Rufus **Hatch**.
+   5828   ii.   Edward Francis **Mears** Sr. 9 October 1893.

4936. **Robert Francis**[11] **Andrews** (Levi Smalley[10], Noah[9], John[8], Joanna[7] **Burnham**, Westley[6], Elizabeth[5] **Perkins**, Jacob[4], Elizabeth[3] **Whipple**, Matthew[2], Matthew[1])[80] was born, probably in England 20 June

1866 and died 13 September 1901 in Rio de Janeiro, Brazil, at 35 years of age. He married **Isabella Jane Robinson**. Isabella,[81] daughter of Samuel **Robinson** and Sarah **Shell**, was born in Rio de Janeiro 4 June 1871 and died there 18 June 1966, at 95 years of age.

Robert Francis **Andrews** and Isabella Jane **Robinson** had the following children:

	5829	i.	Violet Margaret[12] **Andrews**[82] born in Rio de Janeiro 19 June 1891 and died there 12 February 1911, at 19 years of age. She married Carlos Germack **Passolo** in Rio de Janeiro 14 May 1910.
	5830	ii.	Lawrence Sefton **Andrews**[83] born in Vitoria, Brazil 9 May 1894 and died 11 October 1947 in Rio de Janeiro, at 53 years of age.
+	5831	iii.	Leslie Francis **Andrews** born 13 March 1896.
	5832	iv.	Frederick Lumley **Andrews** born 24 March 1898.[84]

4937. **Florence**[11] **Andrews** (Levi Smalley[10], Noah[9], John[8], Joanna[7] **Burnham**, Westley[6], Elizabeth[5] **Perkins**, Jacob[4], Elizabeth[3] **Whipple**, Matthew[2], Matthew[1])[85] was born in Rio de Janeiro, Brazil in February 1871 and died abt 1953 in Philadelphia, Philadelphia City Co., Penn. She married **Alexander Leslie**. Alexander, son of Charles Mitchell Smith **Leslie**, was born abt 1870.[86]

Florence **Andrews** and Alexander **Leslie** had the following children:

+	5833	i.	Levi Charles Smalley[12] **Leslie** born 11 February 1892.
+	5834	ii.	Herbert **Leslie** born 25 November 1893.
	5835	iii.	Alexander **Leslie** Jr.[87] born in Macacos, Rio de Janeiro in 1895 and married Margaret (__).
+	5836	iv.	Eleanor **Leslie** born 6 February 1897.
	5837	v.	William H. **Leslie**[88] born in 1899 and died in January 1903 in Philadelphia, at 3 years of age.

4938. **Evelyn**[11] **Andrews** (Levi Smalley[10], Noah[9], John[8], Joanna[7] **Burnham**, Westley[6], Elizabeth[5] **Perkins**, Jacob[4], Elizabeth[3] **Whipple**, Matthew[2], Matthew[1])[89] was born in Rio de Janeiro, Brazil in 1873 and died in 1932 in Yverdon-les-bains, Switzerland, at 59 years of age. She married **Hermann Hinderer**, maybe in Grandson, Switzerland.

Evelyn **Andrews** and Hermann **Hinderer** had the following children:

	5838	i.	Henry[12] **Hinderer**.[90]
	5839	ii.	Peter **Hinderer**.[91]

5840 iii. David **Hinderer**.[92]
5841 iv. Florence **Hinderer**.[93]
5842 v. May **Hinderer**.[94]

4939. **Lucinda Rivers**[11] **Andrews** (Levi Smalley[10], Noah[9], John[8], Joanna[7] **Burnham**, Westley[6], Elizabeth[5] **Perkins**, Jacob[4], Elizabeth[3] **Whipple**, Matthew[2], Matthew[1])[95] was born in Corbridge, Northumberland, England 4 April 1877 and died in Rio de Janeiro, Brazil. She married **Charles Arnold Hents** in in St. Paul's Church, London, England in 1897. Charles,[96] son of Charles **Hents** and Elizabeth **Booth**, was born in Quincy, Gladsen Co., Fla. 24 September 1870 and died 3 June 1947 in Rio de Janeiro, at 76 years of age.

Lucinda Rivers **Andrews** and Charles Arnold **Hents** had the following children:

+ 5843 i. Margaret Ruth[12] **Hents** born 14 June 1898.
  5844 ii. Doris **Hents**[97] born 28 July 1900 and died 22 March 1907 in Rio de Janeiro, at 6 years of age.
  5845 iii. (Daughter) **Hents**[98] was born abt 1904 and died at birth.
  5846 iv. Lucy Elizabeth **Hents**[99] born in Rio de Janeiro 8 January 1912 and married Carl Ward **Faber** in Toronto, York, Ontario, Canada, 6 January 1932.

4940. **Dennis Rivers**[11] **Andrews** (Levi Smalley[10], Noah[9], John[8], Joanna[7] **Burnham**, Westley[6], Elizabeth[5] **Perkins**, Jacob[4], Elizabeth[3] **Whipple**, Matthew[2], Matthew[1])[100] was born in Rio de Janeiro, Brazil 17 July 1878 and died there 24 April 1929, at 50 years of age. He married **Cicely Harriet Alice Smith** in Rio de Janeiro 3 September 1904. Cicely,[101] daughter of George **Smith** and Alice **Bowditch**, was born in Dorking, Surrey Co., England 23 May 1886 and died 1959 in Liverpool, England, at 73 years of age.

Dennis Rivers **Andrews** and Cicely Harriet Alice **Smith** had the following children:

+ 5847 i. Margaret Alice[12] **Andrews** born 7 June 1905.
  5848 ii. Lucinda Rivers **Andrews**[102] born in Juiz de Fora, Brazil 4 May 1907 and married George Edward **Fox** in Rio de Janeiro 8 November 1929. He was born, probably in England, in 1901 and died 8 December 1977 in Rio de Janeiro, at 76 years of age.[103]
+ 5849 iii. John Rivers **Andrews** born in 1910.

4947. **Frances Archer**[11] **McCandlish** (Randolph Walke[10], Eliza Whipple[9] **Putnam**, Douglas[8], Elizabeth[7] **Perkins**, Dr. Elisha[6], Dr. Joseph[5], Joseph[4], Elizabeth[3] **Whipple**, Matthew[2], Matthew[1])[104] was born in Chicago, Cook Co., Ill. 24 October 1924 and married **Frank Louis Strand** in St. Augustine's Church in Wilmette, Lake Co., Ill, 26 December 1948. The marriage certificate mistakenly gives the marriage year as 1949. Frank,[105] son of Peter Jensen **Strand** and Dagmar Christine Augusta **Rasmussen**, was born in Skien, Norway 22 April 1925 and died 28 January 2000 while on vacation in Savannah, Chatham Co., Ga., at 74 years of age.

Frances Archer **McCandlish** and Frank Louis **Strand** had the following children:

+ 5850   i.   Frances Archer[12] **Strand** born 15 July 1950.
+ 5851   ii.   Robert William **Strand** born 7 December 1951.
   5852   iii.   Elizabeth Whipple **Strand**[106] born in Evanston, Cook Co., Ill. 20 January 1954 and died 30 March 1998 in East Stroudsburg, Penn., at 44 years of age.
+ 5853   iv.   Susan Holt **Strand** born 12 November 1956.
   5854   v.   Katherine Dagmar **Strand**[107] born in Evanston, 28 May 1960.

4948. **Pres. Franklin Delano**[11] **Roosevelt** (James[10], Mary Rebecca[9] **Aspinwall**, Susan[8] **Howland**, Lydia[7] **Bill**, Lydia[6] **Huntington**, Hannah[5] **Perkins**, Jabez[4], Elizabeth[3] **Whipple**, Matthew[2], Matthew[1])[108] was born in Hyde Park, Dutchess Co., N.Y. 30 January 1882 and died 12 April 1945 in Warm Springs, Meriwether Co., Ga., at 63 years of age. He was buried 15 April 1945 in Hyde Park. He married **Anna Eleanor Roosevelt** in New York, N.Y. 17 March 1905. They were fifth cousins once removed. Eleanor,[109] daughter of Elliott **Roosevelt** and Anna Rebecca **Hall**, was born in New York, N.Y. 12 October 1884 and died there 7 November 1962, at 78 years of age.

Franklin earned an AB from Harvard College in 1903 and studied law at the Columbia Law School in New York City. He was admitted to the New York Bar in 1907 and entered politics, being elected to the State Senate in 1910 and 1912. He was appointed Assistant Secretary of the Navy by President Woodrow Wilson in 1913 and was nominated for Vice President by the Democratic National Convention in San Francisco 6 July 1920 with James Cox as the Presidential Nominee. They lost in November. He was elected Governor of New York in 1928

Franklin Delano Roosevelt, thrirty-second President of The United States.

ANCESTORS OF AMERICAN PRESIDENTS

Matthew WHIPPLE, d. 1618/9, Bocking, Essex, England = Joan ——

John WHIPPLE (1596-1669) of Ipswich, Mass.
= Susanna —— (STACY or CLARK)

Matthew WHIPPLE, d. 1647, Ipswich, Mass.
= Anne HAWKINS

John WHIPPLE, Jr.
= Martha REYNER

Mary WHIPPLE
= Simon STONE, Jr.

Elizabeth WHIPPLE = Jacob PERKINS

Susannah WHIPPLE
= John LANE

Mary STONE
= Comfort STARR

Judith PERKINS
= Nathaniel BROWN

Jabez PERKINS
= Hannah LATHROP

John LANE, Jr.
= Katherine WHITING

Comfort STARR, Jr.
= Elizabeth PELLEY

Jacob BROWN
= Sarah BURNHAM

Hannah PERKINS
= Joshua HUNTINGTON

Susanna LANE
= Nathaniel DAVIS

Comfort STARR (III)
= Judith COOPER

Adam BROWN
= Esther PARKMAN

Lydia HUNTINGTON
= Ephraim BILL

Nathaniel DAVIS, Jr.
= Lydia HARWOOD

Sarah STARR
= Jabez FRANKLIN

Adam BROWN, Jr.
= Priscilla PUTNAM

Lydia BILL
= Joseph HOWLAND

Mary DAVIS
= John MOOR

Luther FRANKLIN
= Priscilla PINNEY

Israel Putnam BROWN
= Sally BRIGGS

Susan HOWLAND
= John ASPINWALL, Jr.

Hiram D. MOOR = Abigail FRANKLIN

Sally BROWN
= Israel C. BREWER

Mary Rebecca ASPINWALL
= Isaac ROOSEVELT

Sarah Almeda BREWER
= Calvin Galusha COOLIDGE

James ROOSEVELT
= Sara DELANO

Victoria Josephine MOOR = John Calvin COOLIDGE

(John) Calvin COOLIDGE (Jr.)
1872-1933
30th U.S. President
= Grace Anna GOODHUE

Franklin Delano ROOSEVELT
1882-1945
32nd U.S. President
= (Anna) Eleanor ROOSEVELT

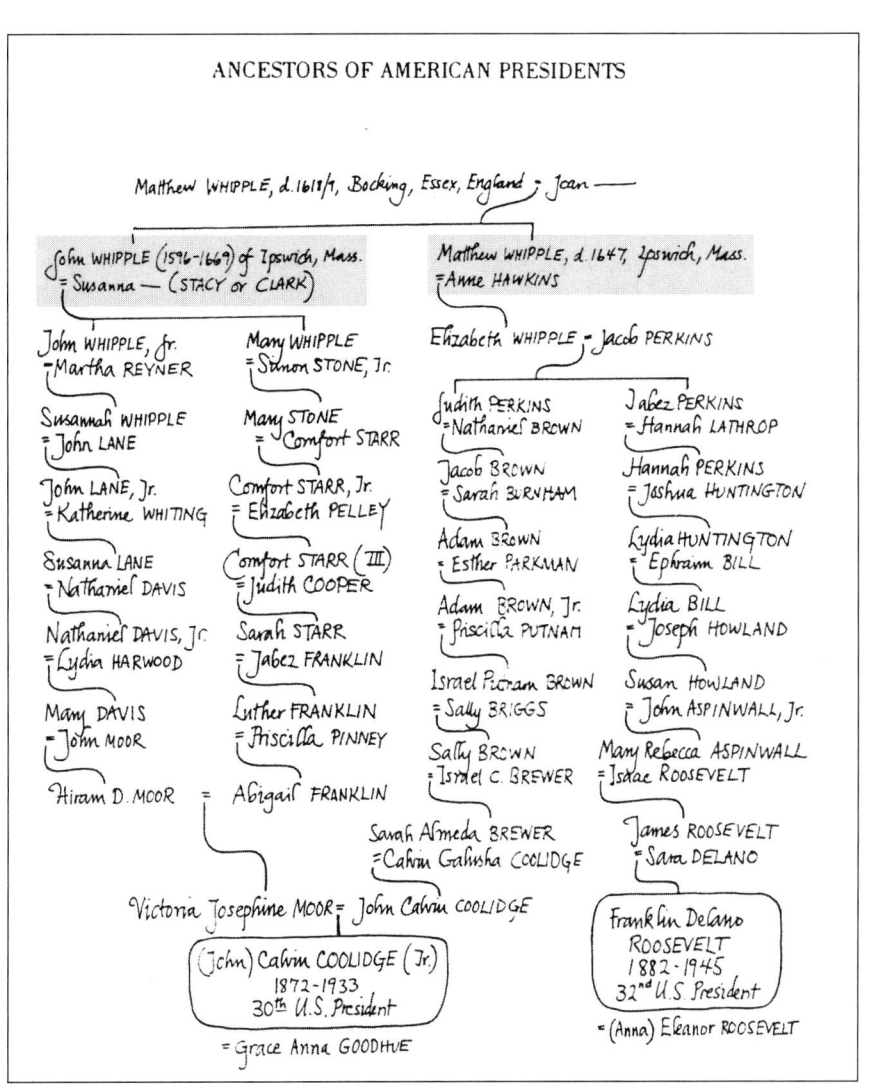

Permission to use sketch given by Gary Boyd Roberts, New England Historic Genealogical Society, Boston.

and 1930 and won the Democratic nomination for President at the Democratic National Convention in Chicago, Ill. 1 July 1932. He and his running mate, John Nance Garner, won the election with 472 electoral votes to 59 for Herbert Hoover, the Republican incumbent. The popular vote was 22,809,638 to 15,758,901

The country was in a major depression at the time but Roosevelt convinced the nation that "the only thing we have to fear is fear itself." His administration developed legislation, known as "The New Deal" to provide relief and jobs for the unemployed. It didn't end the depression but had an important psychological effect by convincing people that the

Administration was taking action to end it. As a result, he easily won reelection in 1936, defeating Alfred Landon of Kansas by the largest margin ever won up to that time—27,752,869 to 16,674,665 and 523 to 8.

During his second term the war in Europe became an additional worry and he stretched presidential prerogative to the limit in supporting the Allies. He won an unprecedented third term in 1940 beating Wendell L. Wilkie 27,307,819 to 22,321,018 and 449 to 82. After the Japanese surprise attack on Pearl Harbor 7 December 1941, he blossomed as a wartime leader and in 1944 the nation paid him an extraordinary honor by electing him to a fourth term. Sen. Harry S Truman of Missouri was his running mate. He beat Gov. Thomas E. Dewey of New York 25,605,585 to 22,014,745 and 432 to 99. By the time of his inauguration 20 January 1945, the nation's war effort had been organized with great effect and the Allies were dominant in the air, at sea, and on land.

He left for the Yalta Conference to meet with Winston Churchill, Prime Minister of England, and Joseph Stalin, leader of the Soviet Union, 22 January and returned to Washington, D.C. 28 February. He addressed Congress on the Conference 1 March and went to the Little White House at Warm Springs, Ga. where he died suddenly 12 April of cerebral hemorrhage. He was the seventh president to die in office, having served longer than other president. His only book was *The Happy Warrior, Alfred E. Smith* (1928).

President Roosevelt was related to the wife of Pres. James Monroe whose mother was an Aspinwall. He was a fourth cousin once removed of Pres. Ulysses Grant through the Delano family and through his maternal grandmother's family, a seventh cousin once removed to his war time colleague, Prime Minister Winston Churchill.[110]

Pres. Franklin Delano **Roosevelt** and Anna Eleanor **Roosevelt** had the following children:

+   5855   i.   Anna Eleanor[12] **Roosevelt** born 3 May 1906.
+   5856   ii.   Congressman James **Roosevelt** born 23 December 1907.
     5857   iii.   Franklin Delano **Roosevelt**III born in New York, N.Y. 18 March 1909 and died there 8 November at almost 9 months of age.
+   5858   iv.   Elliott **Roosevelt** born 23 September 1910.
+   5859   v.   Franklin Delano **Roosevelt** Jr. born 17 August 1914.
+   5860   vi.   John Aspinwall **Roosevelt** born 13 March 1916.

4949. Esther Myrtle[11] **Smith** (Julia Ann[10] **Stevens**, Melissa Esther[9] **Jones**, Mariah B.[8] **Ayers**, Lovica[7] **Stanton**, Lovica[6] **Gates**, Charity[5] **Perkins**, Jabez[4], Elizabeth[3] **Whipple**, Matthew[2], Matthew[1])[112] was born in

Port Huron, St. Clair Co., Mich. 22 June 1875 and died there 8 January 1936, at 60 years of age. She married twice. (1) **George Edward Bradley** in Sarnia, Lambton Co., Ontario, Canada, 29 June 1895. George,[113] son of George James **Bradley** and Mary Ann **Hannon**, was born in Port Huron 18 June 1873 and died there 7 January 1901 at 27 years of age. (2) **Charles McIntosh Wheelihan** in Sarnia 13 March 1907. Charles,[114] son of Nicholas W. **Wheelihan** and Mary Ann **Moore**, was born in Grove Mills, Ontario, Canada in 1879 and died in 1941 in Port Huron, at 62 years of age.

Esther Myrtle **Smith** and George Edward **Bradley** had the following children:

+ 5861 i. Hazel Georgia[12] **Bradley** born 27 March 1896.
 5862 ii. Olive B. **Bradley**[115] born in Port Huron, 11 August 1898 and died there 5 August 1899, at almost 1 year of age.

Esther Myrtle **Smith** and Charles McIntosh **Wheelihan** had the following children born in Port Huron:

 5863 iii. Harold McDermond **Wheelihan**[116] 21 June 1903 and died there 20 July 1958, at 55 years of age. He married twice. (1) Mable **Spooner** in 1925. (2) Bessie **Truitt**.
 5864 iv. Myrtle Emma **Wheelihan**[117] 31 July 1905 and died 10 December 1985 in Marysville, St. Clair Co., Mich., at 80 years of age.
 5865 v. James McIntosh **Wheelihan**[118] 5 October 1909 and died there in 1949, at 39 years of age.
 5866 vi. David Nicholas Alexander **Wheelihan**[119] 5 October 1909 and died there 11 March 1984, at 74 years of age.
 5867 vii. Gailord Alvah **Wheelihan**[120] 19 November 1911 and died there 4 September 1983, at 71 years of age.
 5868 viii. Julia Esther **Wheelihan**[121] 27 November 1914.
 5869 ix. Frank Alexander **Wheelihan**[122] 3 April 1917 and died there 13 October 1985, at 68 years of age.

4955. **Edwin Ralph**[11] **Huse** (Luther Richards[10], Thomas[9], Robert[8], John[7], Elizabeth[6] **Hale**, Anna[5] **Short**, Sarah[4] **Whipple**, Lt. John[3], Matthew[2], Matthew[1])[123] was born in Clark Co., Mo. 5 July 1865 and died 3 April 1942 in Indianapolis, Marion Co., Ind., at 76 years of age. He married **Julia Agnes Bennett** in Clark Co. 19 September 1888. Julia,[124] daughter of Richard **Bennett** and Sarah **Ryan**, was born in Clark Co., 30 September 1867 and died 24 September 1946 in Indianapolis, at 78 years of age.

Edwin Ralph **Huse** and Julia Agnes **Bennett** had the following children:

    5870 i. Rena G.[12] **Huse**[125] born in Clark Co. 28 October 1889 and died there 14 September 1891, at almost 2 years of age.

    5871 ii. Frank P. **Huse**[126] born in Clark Co. 17 July 1891 and died in Indianapolis. He married Eva **Tinder** in Hamilton Co., Ind., 19 July 1913.

    5872 iii. Richard LeRoy **Huse**[127] born in Clark Co. 26 February 1893 and died in Indianapolis. He married Mabel **Andrews** 28 May 1913.

    5873 iv. William Murray **Huse**[128] born in Clark Co. 7 November 1894 and died in Indianapolis. He married Edna E. **Jones** 25 March 1918.

    5874 v. James Alva **Huse**[129] born in Clark Co. 23 March 1896 and died in 1936 in South Bend, Saint Joseph Co., Ind., at 40 years of age. He married Lusa **Butler**.

    5875 vi. Floyd E. **Huse**[130] born in Clark Co. 10 April 1898 and died 21 December 1900 in Indianapolis, at 2 years of age.

+   5876 vii. Joseph Harold **Huse** born 17 July 1899.

    5877 viii. Glenn B. **Huse**[131] born in Indianapolis 7 November 1901 and died there. He married an unnamed person 31 January 1923.

    5878 ix. Floyd T. **Huse**[132] born in Indianapolis 1 October 1904 and died there 26 December 1904, at less than 3 months of age.

    5879 x. Grace Mary **Huse**[133] born in Indianapolis 6 October 1905 and married E. Richard **Biggins** in South Bend, 2 December 1939.

    5880 xi. Howard E. **Huse**[134] born in Indianapolis 3 February 1909 and died 23 April 1930 at 21 years of age.

    5881 xii. Dorothy J. **Huse**[135] born in Indianapolis 13 April 1911.

4963. **John Godfrey**[11] **Whipple** (William Orland[10], William Ward[9], John[8], John[7], Capt. John[6], Hannah[5], John[4], Lt. John[3], Matthew[2], Matthew[1])[136] was born in Moundsville,[137] Ill. 5 March 1882 and died 19 August 1948 in Greeley, Weld Co., Colo., at 66 years of age. He married **Ola Bull** in August 1906. Ola,[138] daughter of Charles **Bull** and Medora **Hayden**, was born in Smith Center, Smith Co., Kans. 26 May 1886 and died 19 November 1974 in Hemet, Riverside Co., Calif., at 88 years of age.

John Godfrey **Whipple** and Ola **Bull** had the following child:

+   5882 i. Paul Warren[12] **Whipple** born 21 January 1915.

4964. **Helen Loveland**[11] **Patch** (Robert Charles[10], William Johnson[9], John[8], Joseph[7], Hannah[6] **Whipple**, Hannah[5], John[4], Lt. John[3], Matthew[2], Matthew[1]) birth date unknown, married **Albert William Simson**.[139]

Helen Loveland **Patch** and Albert William **Simson** had the following child:

+   5883   i.   Elizabeth Ann[12] **Simson**.

4968. **Henry King**[11] **McHarg Jr.** (Henry King[10], Martha Whipple[9] **Patch**, Martha[8] **Safford**, Martha[7] **Whipple**, John[6], Capt. John[5], John[4], Lt. John[3], Matthew[2], Matthew[1])[140] was born in New York, N.Y. 30 October 1883 and died 10 July 1943 in Miami, Dade Co. Florida. He married three times. (1) **Laura Whiting Brown** in Roanoke, Roanoke Co., Va., 15 August 1906. They were divorced in 1908. (2) **Jane Vandergrift Craven** in Salem, Salem Co., N.J., 15 March 1911. They were divorced in 1933. (3) **Grace Corbett** in 1934. Henry was a rail road executive and is buried at Arlington National Cemetery.

Henry King **McHarg** Jr. and Jane Vandergrift **Craven** had the following children:

+   5884   i.   Jane Craven[12] **McHarg** born 10 March 1912.
      5885   ii. Henry King **McHarg** III[141] born in New York, N.Y. 8 August 1913.
      5886   iii. Esterbelle **McHarg**[142] born in New York, N.Y. 8 August 1916.

4970. **Albert**[11] **Whipple** (Albert Lawrence[10], John Henry[9], John[8], Lt. Edward[7], John[6], Capt. John[5], John[4], Lt. John[3], Matthew[2], Matthew[1])[143] birth date unknown, died in 1952 in Swampscott, Essex Co., Mass., at 67 years of age. He married an unnamed person.

Albert **Whipple** had the following child:

      5887   i.   Howard[12] **Whipple**[144] who died in 1975 at 65 years of age.

4981. **Raymond Arthur**[11] **Whipple** (Arthur Eli[10], John Henry[9], John[8], Lt. Edward[7], John[6], Capt. John[5], John[4], Lt. John[3], Matthew[2], Matthew[1])[145] was born in Hamilton, Essex Co., Mass. in 1903 and died in 1985 at 82 years of age. He married **Ruth Boyles Perley**. Ruth,[146] daughter of Alvin **Perley** and Jennie **Smith**, was born in 1905. He was Superintendent of the Hamilton Water Department and a member of the Fire Department.

Raymond Arthur **Whipple** and Ruth Boyles **Perley** had the following children:

+   5888   i.   Shirley Anne[12] **Whipple** born in 1928.
      5889   ii. Alvin Perley **Whipple**[147] born in 1930 and married Elaine May **Mood** in 1956. Elaine,[148] daughter of Ernest **Mood** and May **Jeff**, was born in 1934

5890 iii. Raymond Arthur **Whipple** Jr.[149] born in 1937 and married Donna Louise **Sennott** in 1963. She is the daughter of Donald **Sennott** and Marie **Urquart**.

4982. **Francis Henry**[11] **Whipple** (Arthur Eli[10], John Henry[9], John[8], Lt. Edward[7], John[6], Capt. John[5], John[4], Lt. John[3], Matthew[2], Matthew[1])[150] was born in Hamilton, Essex Co., Mass. in 1904 and died there in 1975, at 71 years of age. He married twice. (1) **Iola Patten** in 1929. (2) **Alva Louise Richard** in 1939. He was a policeman and the Town clerk.

Francis Henry **Whipple** and Iola **Patten** had the following child born in Hamilton:
5891 i. Barbara Frances[12] **Whipple**[151] in 1930 and died in 1987. She married twice. (1) Henry C. **Jackson Jr.**, the son of Henry C. **Jackson** and Charlotte (__). (2) George **Kasnie**.

4983. **Chester Francis**[11] **Whipple** (Arthur Eli[10], John Henry[9], John[8], Lt. Edward[7], John[6], Capt. John[5], John[4], Lt. John[3], Matthew[2], Matthew[1])[152] was born in Hamilton, Essex Co., Mass. in 1907 and died in 1972 at 65 years of age. He married twice. (1) **Hope Buzzell** in 1930. (2) **Alice M. Krotchie**.

Chester Francis **Whipple** and Hope **Buzzell** had the following child born in Hamilton:
5892 i. Nancy Jane[12] **Whipple**[153] in 1940 and married Charles Lefferts **Pulford Jr.** in 1961. Charles,[154] son of Charles Lefferts **Pulford** and Mildred M. (__), was born in 1937.

4985. **Gladys Sevelyn**[11] **Whipple** (Arthur Eli[10], John Henry[9], John[8], Lt. Edward[7], John[6], Capt. John[5], John[4], Lt. John[3], Matthew[2], Matthew[1])[155] was born in Hamilton, Essex Co., Mass. in 1909 and died in 1991, at 82 years of age. She married **George Wahlquist Peterson** in 1931. George,[156] son of Carol **Peterson** and Ebba (__), was born in 1909.

Gladys Sevelyn **Whipple** and George Wahlquist **Peterson** had the following child:
5893 i. Sandra Whipple[12] **Peterson**[157] born in 1939 and married Roger **Daly** in 1959. They were divorced in 1985. Roger is the son of James **Daly** and Evelyn **Rose**.

4986. **Theodore Laurence**[11] **Wanstall** (Lura Amelia[10] **Whipple**, John Henry[9], John[8], Lt. Edward[7], John[6], Capt. John[5], John[4], Lt. John[3],

Matthew[2], Matthew[1])[158] was born 16 July 1909 and died 12 May 1991 in Bethel, Windsor Co., Vt., at 81 years of age. Buried in Fairview Cemetery. He married twice. (1) **Lydia F. Flint** in Swampscott, Essex Co., Mass. 16 September 1936. She was born 8 January 1909 and died in 1970 in Nahant, Essex Co., Mass., at 61 years of age.[159] (2) **Virginia M. McPhee** in Bethel or Hanover, Grafton Co., N.H. 11 December 1972.

Theodore Laurence **Wanstall** and Lydia F. **Flint** had the following children:
+   5894   i.   Cynthia Adele[12] **Wanstall** born 20 September 1938.
      5895   ii.   Stephen Foster **Wanstall**[160] born 2 August 1943 and married Lynda (__) 27 November 1964.

4987. **Elmer**[11] **Wanstall** (Lura Amelia[10] **Whipple**, John Henry[9], John[8], Lt. Edward[7], John[6], Capt. John[5], John[4], Lt. John[3], Matthew[2], Matthew[1])[161] was born 2 June 1914 and died 13 June 1997 in Ketchikan, Ketchikan Gateway Borough, Alaska, at 83 years of age. He married twice. (1) **Susan Thompson** in Bellows Falls, Windham Co., Vt., 2 July 1940. Susan,[162] daughter of George Horace **Thompson** and Marion **Williams**, was born in Bellows Falls 10 July 1917 and died 2 July 1988 in Kennebunk, York Co., Maine, at 70 years of age. Buried in the Thompson family plot in the cemetery of Immanuel Episcopal Church in Bellows Falls. They were divorced in Bellows Falls. (2) **Beverly Yost** in Peoria, Peoria Co., Ill. 4 February 1950. She was born in South Bend, Saint Joseph Co., Ind. 5 August 1925 and was living in Las Vegas, Clark Co., Nev. in the late 1990s.[163] Elmer was graduated from Dartmouth College in 1936, served in the Naval Reserves during WWII. His rank was Lieutenant and he was the Intelligence and Navigation Officer on the *U.S.S. Guam* in the Pacific theatre. Following the war he was a Branch Manager for a finance company and a Loan Officer in a bank in South Bend. He retired in 1975 and moved to Ketchikan in 1984. He was cremated and his remains scattered over the inland passage waters near Juneau, Juneau Borough, Alaska.

Elmer **Wanstall** and Susan **Thompson** had the following child:
+   5896   i.   George Elmer[12] **Wanstall** born 16 April 1941.

Elmer **Wanstall** and Beverly **Yost** had the following children:
      5897   ii.   Karen Lynn **Wanstall**[164] born in Chicago, Cook Co., Ill. 12 November 1950 and married Thomas **Haig** in South Bend in August 1975. They were divorced in Las Vegas in 1990.
+   5898   iii.   Bruce Eric **Wanstall** born 18 February 1952.

{ G 863 }

4988. **Laura Barker**[11] **Wanstall** (Lura Amelia[10] **Whipple**, John Henry[9], John[8], Lt. Edward[7], John[6], Capt. John[5], John[4], Lt. John[3], Matthew[2], Matthew[1])[165] was born 9 June 1917 and died 7 December 1993 in Lewiston, Androscoggin Co., Maine, at 76 years of age. She married **Edward Murray Spence Jr.** 9 July 1939. He was born in Swampscott, Essex Co., Mass. 4 November 1914 and died 15 December 1975 in Lewiston, at 61 years of age.[166]

Laura Barker **Wanstall** and Edward Murray **Spence** Jr. had the following children:

- \+ 5899 i. Robert Edward[12] **Spence** born 5 June 1940.
- \+ 5900 ii. Donald Arthur **Spence** born 14 February 1943.
-   5901 iii. Carol **Spence**[167] born 8 June 1948 and died 12 February 1949 at less than 1 year of age.
-   5902 iv. Wendy Kathryn **Spence**[168] born 20 September 1950 and married Kenneth Arthur **Philbrick** in Lewiston 9 August 1972. He was born 24 June 1949.[169]

4989. **Gertrude Louise**[11] **Wanstall** (Lura Amelia[10] **Whipple**, John Henry[9], John[8], Lt. Edward[7], John[6], Capt. John[5], John[4], Lt. John[3], Matthew[2], Matthew[1])[170] was born 30 June 1919 and married **Robert Kelley** 16 November 1941. He was born 19 July 1919 and died 27 March 1967 at 47 years of age.[171]

Gertrude Louise **Wanstall** and Robert **Kelley** had the following children:

- \+ 5903 i. Robert[12] **Kelley** born 28 November 1941.
- \+ 5904 ii. David **Kelley** born 2 August 1944.
- \+ 5905 iii. Dianne **Kelley** born 11 November 1946.
- \+ 5906 iv. Madelaine **Kelley** born 11 November 1946.
- \+ 5907 v. Patricia **Kelley** born 1 March 1953.

4991. **Richard Randolph**[11] **Whipple** (Guy Montrose[10], John Francis[9], Daniel[8], William[7], William[6], Capt. John[5], John[4], Lt. John[3], Matthew[2], Matthew[1])[172] was born in 1905 and married twice. (1) **Evelyn Ogborn** who was born in 1906 and died in 1945 at 39 years of age.[173] (2) **Dorothy Ogborn**. His wives were sisters.

Richard Randolph **Whipple** and Evelyn **Ogborn** had the following children:

- \+ 5908 i. Richard Ogborn[12] **Whipple** born in 1930.
- \+ 5909 ii. Cornelia Jane **Whipple** born in 1933.
-   5910 iii. John Hood **Whipple**[174] born in 1942 and married Frances Vaughan **Lowman** in 1966. She was born in 1944.[175]

4992. **Guy Montrose**[11] **Whipple Jr.** (Guy Montrose[10], John Francis[9], Daniel[8], William[7], William[6], Capt. John[5], John[4], Lt. John[3], Matthew[2], Matthew[1])[176] was born in 1915 and married **Eleanor Faye Scudder** in 1939.

Guy Montrose **Whipple** Jr. and Eleanor Faye **Scudder** had the following children:

    5911   i.   Brent[12] **Whipple**[177] who married twice. (1) JoAnn **Ashmore** in 1967. (2) Susan **Campbell** in 1983.

+   5912   ii.   Bryan Randolph Rogers **Whipple** born 1 March 1940.

5000. **William S.**[11] **Whipple** (Herman M.[10], William Stark[9], John[8], Charles[7], Benjamin[6], Capt. John[5], John[4], Lt. John[3], Matthew[2], Matthew[1])[178] was born in Goffstown, Hillsborough Co., N.H. 10 May 1909 and died 17 December 1956 in Manchester, Hillsborough Co., N.H., at 47 years of age. He married **Ann Daily Revere** in Goffstown 29 May 1935. Ann,[179] daughter of George William **Revere** and Flora Mae **Daily**, was born in Braintree, Norfolk Co., Mass. 24 January 1914 and married (2) **Williard Chapman Pratt** 5 September 1957.

William S. **Whipple** and Ann Daily **Revere** had the following child:

+   5913   i.   William Stark[12] **Whipple** Jr. born 30 September 1945.

5004. **Earle C.**[11] **Whipple** (George H.[10], Amos Woodbury[9], John[8], Charles[7], Benjamin[6], Capt. John[5], John[4], Lt. John[3], Matthew[2], Matthew[1])[180] was born in Barnstead, Belknap Co., N.H. 18 August 1896 and married **Violet Talbot** 1 July 1925. Violet,[181] daughter of George **Talbot** and Alice Ada (__), was born in Truro, Nova Scotia, Canada 19 April 1898. Earle was graduated from the U. of N. H. in 1918.

Earle C. **Whipple** and Violet **Talbot** had the following children:

+   5914   i.   Gayle[12] **Whipple** born 15 June 1926.
+   5915   ii.   Janet **Whipple** born 16 June 1930.

5005. **Stanley I.**[11] **Whipple** (George H.[10], Amos Woodbury[9], John[8], Charles[7], Benjamin[6], Capt. John[5], John[4], Lt. John[3], Matthew[2], Matthew[1])[182] was born in Goffstown, Hillsborough Co., N.H. 19 December 1897 and died 6 April 1985 at 87 years of age. He married **Mildred Imogene Johnson** in Goffstown 16 October 1920. Mildred,[183] daughter of Moses **Johnson** and Carrie (__), was born in Manchester, Hillsborough Co., N.H. 17 February 1898 and died 10 July 1986 at 88 years of age. Stanley worked for the New England Telephone and Telegraph Co. for over 40 years.

Stanley I. **Whipple** and Mildred Imogene **Johnson** had the following children:
+ 5916 i. Donald I.[12] **Whipple** born 29 December 1921.
+ 5917 ii. Richard Earle **Whipple** born 18 July 1923.

5006. **Olive E.**[11] **Whipple** (George H.[10], Amos Woodbury[9], John[8], Charles[7], Benjamin[6], Capt. John[5], John[4], Lt. John[3], Matthew[2], Matthew[1])[184] was born in Goffstown, Hillsborough Co., N.H. 19 February 1900 and died 15 July 1985 at 85 years of age. She married **Willard L. Litchfield**. He was born in Manchester, Hillsborough Co., N.H. 17 February 1898 and died bef 1985.[185] Williard was a Captain in the Scituate, Plymouth Co., Mass. Fire Department. Olive was graduated from the Normal School at Keene, Cheshire Co., N.H. in 1922 with a degree in Elementary Education. She taught in Gorham, Coos Co., N.H. and Hingham, Plymouth Co., Mass. and lived in North Scituate for 55 years.

Olive E. **Whipple** and Willard L. **Litchfield** had the following children:
+ 5918 i. Nancy[12] **Litchfield** born 20 July 1932.
+ 5919 ii. Carol **Litchfield** born 19 July 1934.
+ 5920 iii. Thaddeus **Litchfield** born 4 July 1935.
+ 5921 iv. Willard **Litchfield** born 28 February 1941.

5009. **Norris**[11] **Corey** (Emma L.[10] **Whipple**, Amos Woodbury[9], John[8], Charles[7], Benjamin[6], Capt. John[5], John[4], Lt. John[3], Matthew[2], Matthew[1])[186] was born in Manchester, Hillsborough Co., N.H. 21 June 1894 and married **Mary Riddle**.

Norris **Corey** and Mary **Riddle** had the following child:
5922 i. Norma[12] **Corey**.[187]

5030. **Merle Everett**[11] **Packard** (Horace Sherman[10], Ebenezer James[9], Hosea[8], Dea. Zenas[7], Mary[6] **Perkins**, Dorothy[5] **Whipple**, Matthew[4], Lt. John[3], Matthew[2], Matthew[1])[188] was born in Holbrook, Norfolk Co., Mass. 19 July 1895 and died 10 September 1972 at 77 years of age. He married **Amelia Julia Rose Preskins** in Salem Depot,[189] N.H., 28 April 1923. Amelia,[190] daughter of William **Preskins** and Louise M. **Kulesus**, was born in Boston, Suffolk Co., Mass. 20 September 1903.

Merle Everett **Packard** and Amelia Julia Rose **Preskins** had the following children:
+ 5923 i. Lila Lee[12] **Packard** born 30 September 1924.

  5924 ii. Kathleen Lorraine **Packard**[191] born in Haverhill, Essex Co., Mass. 22 October 1925 and died 23 June 1989 in West Palm Beach, Palm Beach Co., Fla., at 63 years of age. She married Anthony T. **Guliano** in Barrington, Bristol Co., R.I. They had three children; no details provided.

5031. **Lewis Grant**[11] **Whipple** (William Lewis[10], Heman[9], David[8], Eleazer[7], Eleazer[6], Nathan[5], Matthew[4], Lt. John[3], Matthew[2], Matthew[1]) birth date unknown, died 4 January 1961.[192] He married **Elsie May Hunnewell** in Solon, Somerset Co., Maine, 1 September 1898. She died in 1969.

Lewis Grant **Whipple** and Elsie May **Hunnewell** had the following children:
+ 5925 i. Elizabeth Rebecca[12] **Whipple**.
  5926 ii. William Heman **Whipple** married Lillian **Pezel** in 1928 anddied in 1969 in Wichita, Sedgwick Co., Kans.[193]

5036. **Jessie M.**[11] **Washburn** (Lillian Jane[10] **Corson**, Jane[9] **Whipple**, John[8], Eleazer[7], Eleazer[6], Nathan[5], Matthew[4], Lt. John[3], Matthew[2], Matthew[1])[194] was born in Bingham, Somerset Co., Maine 29 August 1890 and married twice. (1) **William Lampher Hamilton** 8 April 1909 who was born in Greenville, Piscataquis Co., Maine 9 April 1884. They were divorced in Seattle, King Co., Wash., 16 December 1932. He is buried in Seattle's Calvary Cemetery. (2) **Clifford Keif**.

Jessie M. **Washburn** and William Lampher **Hamilton** had the following children:
+ 5927 i. Inez Eunice[12] **Hamilton** born 9 October 1909.
  5928 ii. Henry **Hamilton**[195] born in Bingham in 1911 and died in 1988 in Los Angeles, Los Angeles Co., Calif., at 77 years of age. Buried in Bingham Village Cemetery.

5037. **Caroline May**[11] **Campbell** (Lewis Cass[10], Lydia[9] **Averill**, Gideon[8], Bethia[7] **Whipple**, Zebulon[6], Samuel[5], Cyprian[4], Lt. John[3], Matthew[2], Matthew[1])[196] was born in Florence, Marion Co., Kans. 10 May 1881 and died 13 May 1937 in Port Orchard, Kitsap Co., Wash., at 56 years of age. She married **Walter Enos Smith** 8 July 1904. Walter,[197] son of Madison Elihu **Smith** and Maria Jane **Mitchell**, was born in Nunda, Mc Henry Co., Ill. 30 June 1878 and died 4 February 1960 in Seattle, King Co., Wash., at 81 years of age.

Caroline May **Campbell** and Walter Enos **Smith** had the following child:
+ 5929 i. Julia Mabel[12] **Smith** born 21 July 1917.

5046. **William Madison**[11] **Reighard** (Ada[10] **Whipple**, George W.[9], John Russell[8], Zebulon[7], Zebulon[6], Samuel[5], Cyprian[4], Lt. John[3], Matthew[2], Matthew[1])[198] was born in Crestline, Crawford Co., Ohio 11 November 1918. He married **Helene Dorothy Wolpert** in Detroit, Wayne Co., Mich., 4 November 1945. Helene,[199] daughter of Herman F. **Wolpert** and Wilhelmine Elise **Dasenbrock**, was born 23 December 1923.

William Madison **Reighard** and Helene Dorothy **Wolpert** had the following children:
- \+ 5930 i. Lynn Ellen[12] **Reighard** born 5 December 1951.
- \+ 5931 ii. Joan Elise **Reighard** born 5 March 1954.

5049. **Maude Belle**[11] **Kennison** (America Martha Jane[10] **Walker**, Calvin Augustus[9], Lydia[8] **Whipple**, Zebulon[7], Zebulon[6], Samuel[5], Cyprian[4], Lt. John[3], Matthew[2], Matthew[1])[200] was born in New Hartford, Butler Co., Iowa 10 October 1879 and died 30 May 1937 in Hartford Beach, Roberts Co., S. Dak. at 57 years of age. Buried in Woodlawn Cemetery, Sioux Falls, Minnehaha Co., S. Dak. She married twice. (1) **John Lafayette Shannon** in New Hartford 2 February 1895. John,[201] son of John A. **Shannon** and Elizabeth **Fisher**, was born in Clarksville, Butler Co. Iowa 23 January 1870 and died 7 January 1933 in Minneapolis, Hennepin Co., Minn., at 62 years of age. Buried at Lynwood Cemetery, Clarksville. Maude and John were divorced in Black Hawk Co., Iowa, 6 January 1915. (2) **George Thomas**.

Maude Belle **Kennison** and John Lafayette **Shannon** had the following children:
- \+ 5932 i. Eva Muryl[12] **Shannon** born 28 July 1896.
-     5933 ii. Flora Glee **Shannon**[202] born in 1909 and died the year of birth.
-     5934 iii. Mable May **Shannon**[203] born in Waterloo, Black Hawk Co., Iowa 1 May 1910 and died 15 February 1998 at 87 years of age. She married three times. (1) Bernard **Cone**. (2) Donald **Givler**. (3) John **Ross**.

5053. **Ned Ernest**[11] **Walker** (Charles Guy[10], Luther Martin[9], Lydia[8] **Whipple**, Zebulon[7], Zebulon[6], Samuel[5], Cyprian[4], Lt. John[3], Matthew[2], Matthew[1])[204] was born in Redbird, Holt Co., Nebr. 14 June 1921 and married **Rita Marie Foltz** in Papillion,[205] Nebr., 6 December 1945. Rita,[206] daughter of William **Foltz** and Elfrieda **Homan**, was born 7 June 1914.

Ned Ernest **Walker** and Rita Marie **Foltz** had the following children:
- 5935 i. Dean Charles[12] **Walker** born in Omaha, Douglas Co., Nebr. 16 December 1946.[207]
- 5936 ii. Joan Marie **Walker**[208] born in Omaha 14 January 1948 and married Terry **Mayah** 3 June 1966. He is the son of Hubert **Mayah**.

5054. **Naomi Frances**[11] **Walker** (Charles Guy[10], Luther Martin[9], Lydia[8] **Whipple**, Zebulon[7], Zebulon[6], Samuel[5], Cyprian[4], Lt. John[3], Matthew[2], Matthew[1])[209] was born in Louisville, Cass Co., Nebr. 4 July 1924 and married **Max Eugene Eckert** 12 September 1944. He was born 2 December 1924.[210]

Naomi Frances **Walker** and Max Eugene **Eckert** had the following children born in Omaha, Douglas Co., Nebr.:
- 5937 i. Bryan Eugene[12] **Eckert** 8 February 1953.[211]
- 5938 ii. Max Douglas **Eckert** 7 July 1954.[212]
- 5939 iii. Boyd Lee **Eckert** 22 August 1957.[213]

5055. **Betty Gene**[11] **Walker** (Charles Guy[10], Luther Martin[9], Lydia[8] **Whipple**, Zebulon[7], Zebulon[6], Samuel[5], Cyprian[4], Lt. John[3], Matthew[2], Matthew[1])[214] was born in Louisville, Cass Co., Nebr. 31 July 1927 and married **Carl Merwin Engelking** in Lincoln, Lancaster Co., Nebr., 17 June 1948. Carl[215] son of William Augustus **Engelking** and Lydia Elfreda **Myler**.

Betty Gene **Walker** and Carl Merwin **Engelking** had the following children born in Ohmaha, Douglas Co., Nebr.:
- 5940 i. Lana Elaine[12] **Engelking** 24 March 1949.[216]
- 5941 ii. Richard William **Engelking** 14 August 1950.[217]
- 5942 iii. Lori Ellen **Engelking** 10 June 1960.[218]

5056. **William Luther**[11] **Thornton** (Clara May[10] **Walker**, Luther Martin[9], Lydia[8] **Whipple**, Zebulon[7], Zebulon[6], Samuel[5], Cyprian[4], Lt. John[3], Matthew[2], Matthew[1])[219] was born in South Omaha, Douglas Co., Nebr. 14 November 1895 and married **Irene (__)**.

William Luther **Thornton** and Irene (__) had the following children:
- 5943 i. Betty Jean[12] **Thornton** born in S. Dakota 9 January 1931.[220]
- 5944 ii. James Donald **Thornton** born in S. Dakota 18 March 1941.[221]

5057. **Alfred Raymond**[11] **Thornton** (Clara May[10] **Walker**, Luther Martin[9], Lydia[8] **Whipple**, Zebulon[7], Zebulon[6], Samuel[5], Cyprian[4], Lt. John[3], Matthew[2], Matthew[1])[222] was born in Nebraska 12 September 1897 and died 4 September 1960 in Omaha, Douglas Co., Nebr., at 62 years of age. He married **Essie May Underwood** 9 May 1940. Essie,[223] daughter of Tom **Underwood** and Middie **Williams**, was born in Tuscaloosa, Tuscaloosa Co., Ala. 12 February 1917.

Alfred Raymond **Thornton** and Essie May **Underwood** had the following children born in Nebraska City, Otoe Co., Nebr:
  5945 i. (Infant)[12] **Thornton**[224] 3 December 1943 and died there 4 December 1945, at 2 years of age.
  5946 ii. Janice Marie **Thornton** in January 1948.[225]

5059. **Jessie May**[11] **Thornton** (Clara May[10] **Walker**, Luther Martin[9], Lydia[8] **Whipple**, Zebulon[7], Zebulon[6], Samuel[5], Cyprian[4], Lt. John[3], Matthew[2], Matthew[1])[226] was born in Norfolk, Madison Co., Nebr. 28 May 1900 and married **Emil Augustus Frank** in Sioux City, Woodbury Co., Iowa, 17 January 1924. Emil,[227] son of Christoph **Frank** and Katherine **Janssen**, was born in Otoe Co., Nebr. 9 June 1899.

Jessie May **Thornton** and Emil Augustus **Frank** had the following children:
+ 5947 i. Ernin Emil[12] **Frank** born 16 January 1925.
+ 5948 ii. Clara Katherine **Frank** born 14 September 1934.

5061. **Goldie Helen**[11] **Thornton** (Clara May[10] **Walker**, Luther Martin[9], Lydia[8] **Whipple**, Zebulon[7], Zebulon[6], Samuel[5], Cyprian[4], Lt. John[3], Matthew[2], Matthew[1])[228] was born in Burton, Keya Paha Co., Nebr. 24 December 1905 and married **William F. Graham** in Glennwood, Mills Co., Iowa, 2 September 1924. William,[229] son of August **Graham**, was born in Otoe Co., Nebr. 6 December 1892.

Goldie Helen **Thornton** and William F. **Graham** had the following children:
+ 5949 i. Doris Irene[12] **Graham** born 26 December 1925.
+ 5950 ii. Betty Mae **Graham** born 7 September 1928.

5063. **Donald Kenneth**[11] **Thornton** (Clara May[10] **Walker**, Luther Martin[9], Lydia[8] **Whipple**, Zebulon[7], Zebulon[6], Samuel[5], Cyprian[4], Lt. John[3], Matthew[2], Matthew[1])[230] was born in Gregory, Gregory Co., S. Dak. 24 August 1911 and married **Leona Halpin** in San Francisco, San Francisco Co., Calif., 7 May 1947. Leona,[231] daughter of John Patrick **Halpin** and Margaret **Gray**, was born in Greeley, Greeley Co., Nebr. 24 March 1918.

Donald Kenneth **Thornton** and Leona **Halpin** had the following child born in San Francisco:

    5951   i.   Ronald John[12] **Thornton** 21 March 1948.[232]

5064. **Clara Edith Marie**[11] **Thornton** (Clara May[10] **Walker**, Luther Martin[9], Lydia[8] **Whipple**, Zebulon[7], Zebulon[6], Samuel[5], Cyprian[4], Lt. John[3], Matthew[2], Matthew[1])[233] was born in Gregory, Gregory Co., S. Dak. 7 November 1913 and married **Harold Haberman** 3 April 1943.

Clara Edith Marie **Thornton** and Harold **Haberman** had the following children born in Oregon:

    5952   i.   Harold Everett[12] **Haberman** 24 February 1946.[234]
    5953   ii.   Jimmie Donald **Haberman** 4 November 1949.[235]

5065. **Andrew Jackson**[11] **Whipple II** (Andrew Bina[10], Andrew Jackson[9], Zebulon[8], Zebulon[7], Zebulon[6], Samuel[5], Cyprian[4], Lt. John[3], Matthew[2], Matthew[1])[236] was born in Gidings, Ashtabula Co. Ohio 22 August 1886 and died 19 October 1969 in Conneaut, Ashtabula Co., Ohio, at 83 years of age. He married **Florence Julia Stentz** in Dunkirk, Chautaugua Co., N.Y. 14 September 1907. Florence,[237] daughter of Lewis **Stentz** and Cora May **Barnes**, was born in Medina, Medina Co., Ohio 2 December 1889 and died 8 June 1989 in Bossier City,[238] La., at 99 years of age. Andrew retired from the Bessemer and Lake Erie Railroad where he was a Switchman and later Yard Foreman. He was a Conneaut City Councilman for several terms and the City Safety Service Director. He ran a grocery store in the early 1930s.

Andrew Jackson **Whipple** II and Florence Julia **Stentz** had the following children:

    5954   i.   Marguerite Eileen[12] **Whipple**[239] born in Conneaut 22 September 1909 and died 1 June 1969 in Dayton, Montgomery Co., Ohio, at 59 years of age. She was a Second Lieut. in WWII in the Army Medical Corps serving as a physical therapist (Oct. 1944 to Feb. 1946). She earned a degree from Ohio University at Miami and spent her life's work in physical therapy.
+   5955   ii.   Lewis Dale **Whipple** born 4 August 1930.

5066. **Paul Darius**[11] **Whipple** (Andrew Bina[10], Andrew Jackson[9], Zebulon[8], Zebulon[7], Zebulon[6], Samuel[5], Cyprian[4], Lt. John[3], Matthew[2], Matthew[1])[240] was born in Denmark, Ashtabula Co., Ohio 2 January 1892 and died 22 February 1962 in Conneaut, Ashtabula Co., Ohio, at 70 years of age. He married **Hazel Marie Risley** in 1912. Hazel,[241] daughter of Philip James **Risley** and Agnes Levina **Salisbury**, was born in Conneaut 18 April 1896 and died there 2 February 1991, at 94 years of age.

Paul Darius **Whipple** and Hazel Marie **Risley** had the following children:
- \+ 5956 i. Graedon[12] **Whipple**.
- \+ 5957 ii. Sherman **Whipple**.
- \+ 5958 iii. Phyllis Martha **Whipple**.
- \+ 5959 iv. Paul Darius **Whipple** Jr. born 17 March 1924.

5067. **Alfred Arner**[11] **Whipple** (Andrew Bina[10], Andrew Jackson[9], Zebulon[8], Zebulon[7], Zebulon[6], Samuel[5], Cyprian[4], Lt. John[3], Matthew[2], Matthew[1])[242] was born in Denmark, Ashtabula Co., Ohio 14 October 1898 and died 18 April 1942 in Conneaut, Ashtabula Co., Ohio, at 43 years of age. He married **Anna Northrup**.

Alfred Arner **Whipple** and Anna **Northrup** had the following children:
- 5960 i. Anadair[12] **Whipple**.[243]
- 5961 ii. Mary Lou **Whipple**.[244]

5068. **Lillian Estella**[11] **Whipple** (Andrew Bina[10], Andrew Jackson[9], Zebulon[8], Zebulon[7], Zebulon[6], Samuel[5], Cyprian[4], Lt. John[3], Matthew[2], Matthew[1])[245] was born in Conneaut, Ashtabula Co., Ohio 20 December 1904 and married **Charles Frank Risley** in Cleveland, Cuyahoga Co., Ohio 11 November 1928.

Lillian Estella **Whipple** and Charles Frank **Risley** had the following child:
- 5962 i. Gary[12] **Risley**.[246]

5075. **Ida Adelle**[11] **Whipple** (Russel Loring[10], Josiah Loring[9], Josiah Russell[8], Zebulon[7], Zebulon[6], Samuel[5], Cyprian[4], Lt. John[3], Matthew[2], Matthew[1])[247] was born in River Falls, Pierce Co., Wisc. 29 March 1887 and died 31 January 1968 in Kansas City, Jackson Co., Mo., at 80 years of age. She married **William Jackson Canaday** in Hennepin Co., Minn. 5 November 1906. William,[248] son of Cornelius Scott **Canaday** and Nancy Jane **Bass**, was born in Urbana, Champaign Co., Ill. 15 April 1881 and died 20 January 1972 in Kansas City, at 90 years of age.

Ida Adelle **Whipple** and William Jackson **Canaday** had the following children:
- 5963 i. Raymond Loring[12] **Canaday**[249] born in Omaha, Douglas Co., Nebr. in November 1907 and died 13 April 1933 in

			Pecos, Reeves Co., Tex., at 25 years of age.
+	5964	ii.	Kenneth William Russel **Canaday** born 10 February 1909.
	5965	iii.	Edith Ortensia **Canaday**[250] born in Minneapolis, Hennepin Co., Minn. in 1911 and died in 1930 in Kansas City, at 19 years of age.
	5966	iv.	Ruby **Canaday**[251] born in Minneapolis in 1920 and died there in 1926, at 6 years of age.
	5967	v.	(Daughter) **Canaday** born in Minneapolis in 1922 and died the year of birth.[252]

5086. **Stella Sybile**[11] **Corwin** (Laura Marie[10] **Whipple**, Henry Frederick[9], Josiah Russell[8], Zebulon[7], Zebulon[6], Samuel[5], Cyprian[4], Lt. John[3], Matthew[2], Matthew[1])[253] was born in Beaver Township, Butler Co., Iowa 13 March 1904 and married **George Reinhardt** in Eldora, Hardin Co., Iowa 23 April 1923. George,[254] son of Carl **Reinhardt** and Bertha Ann **Schade**, was born in Rockensuess, Hessen, Germany 24 August 1879 and died 23 December 1943 in Independence, Buchanan Co., Iowa, at 64 years of age. Buried at Cedar Falls, Black Hawk Co., Iowa.

Stella Sybile **Corwin** and George **Reinhardt** had the following child:

+	5968	i.	Esther Laura[12] **Reinhardt** born 9 January 1925.

5088. **Glen**[11] **Butterfield** (Caroline[10] **Cobb**, Julia[9] **Whipple**, William[8], Zebulon[7], Zebulon[6], Samuel[5], Cyprian[4], Lt. John[3], Matthew[2], Matthew[1])[255] was born in Walnut Grove, Knox Co., Nebr. 23 April 1889 and married **Laura Ann Smith** 23 September 1909. Laura,[256] daughter of George Spencer **Smith** and Christina **Butzier**, was born in Moorland, Webster Co., Iowa 29 September 1888.

Glen **Butterfield** and Laura Ann **Smith** had the following children:

	5969	i.	Berneice[12] **Butterfield** born in Venus, Antelope Co., Nebr. 27 June 1914 and died in infancy.[257]
+	5970	ii.	Irma **Butterfield** born 16 July 1916.
+	5971	iii.	Orma Jeanne **Butterfield** born 24 November 1929.

5093. **Arthur Waterman**[11] **Whipple** (Arthur[10], Zebulon[9], Henry[8], Joseph[7], Zebulon[6], Samuel[5], Cyprian[4], Lt. John[3], Matthew[2], Matthew[1])[258] was born in 1894 and had the following child:

	5972	i.	Constance[12] **Whipple**[259] and married (__) Swan.

5094. **Stanley Paterson**[11] **Whipple** (Arthur[10], Zebulon[9], Henry[8], Joseph[7], Zebulon[6], Samuel[5], Cyprian[4], Lt. John[3], Matthew[2],

Matthew¹)²⁶⁰ was born in Providence, Providence Co., R.I 5 December 1896 and married **Helen Borden** in 1925.

Stanley Paterson **Whipple** and Helen **Borden** had the following children:
    5973   i.   Barbara Frances¹² **Whipple**²⁶¹ born 21 July 1925.
    5974   ii. Elizabeth Borden **Whipple**²⁶² born 11 November 1928.

5095. **Harvey Abbott¹¹ Whipple** (Arthur¹⁰, Zebulon⁹, Henry⁸, Joseph⁷, Zebulon⁶, Samuel⁵, Cyprian⁴, Lt. John³, Matthew², Matthew¹)²⁶³ was born in Providence, Providence Co., R.I. 5 December 1896 and died 11 November 1955, at 58 years of age. He married **Marion Raybold**.

Harvey Abbott **Whipple** and Marion **Raybold** had the following children:
+   5975   i.   Richard Raybold¹² **Whipple** born 5 May 1924.
+   5976   ii.   Shirley Virginia **Whipple** born 9 April 1927.
+   5977   iii. Harvey Abbott **Whipple** II born 5 July 1928.
+   5978   iv. Kingsley Allan **Whipple** born 20 February 1932.
+   5979   v.   Christopher David **Whipple** born 13 June 1968.

5096. **Hazel Susan¹¹ Sanford** (Norman N.¹⁰, Diantha⁹ **Jones**, Oliver⁸, Polly⁷ **Whipple**, Zebulon⁶, Samuel⁵, Cyprian⁴, Lt. John³, Matthew², Matthew¹)²⁶⁴ was born in Lind, Adams Co., Wash. 11 June 1902 and married **Orra Gus Spencer** in Seattle, King Co., Wash. in 1922. He was born in Lapeer, Lapeer Co., Mich. 27 October 1884 and died 20 January 1943 in Shelton, Mason Co., Wash., at 58 years of age.²⁶⁵

Hazel Susan **Sanford** and Orra Gus **Spencer** had the following child:
+   5980   i.   Josephine Elizabeth¹² **Spencer** born 17 October 1924.

5101. **Charles¹¹ Whipple** (William T.¹⁰, Tallman⁹, William⁸, David⁷, Samuel⁶, Samuel⁵, Cyprian⁴, Lt. John³, Matthew², Matthew¹)²⁶⁶ was born in La Crosse, La Crosse Co., Wisc. abt 1894 and died there 9 April 1933, at 38 years of age.²⁶⁷ He married **Elizabeth Catharine (__)** in Winona, Winona Co., Minn. 17 September 1917. She was born in Black River Falls, Jackson Co., Wisc. 26 September 1895 and died 23 November 1928 at 33 years of age.²⁶⁸ Buried in Oak Grove Cemetery. Charles' working career was with the railroad. He was a Foreman in the Burlington Roundhouse in LaCrosse and later worked for the Milwaukee Road. He was buried in the Oak Grove Cemetery with members of the North LaCrosse Masonic Lodge No. 163 in charge at the cemetery.

{ G 874 }

Charles **Whipple** and Elizabeth Catharine **(__)** had the following children born in La Crosse:
    5981   i.   Doris[12] **Whipple**.[269]
    5982   ii. Ira **Whipple**.[270]

5107. **Asher Porter**[11] **Whipple** (George Washington[10], Jonathan Jones[9], Joseph[8], David[7], Samuel[6], Samuel[5], Cyprian[4], Lt. John[3], Matthew[2], Matthew[1])[271] was born in 1873 and died in 1928 at 55 years of age. He married an unnamed person.

Asher Porter **Whipple** had the following children:
    5983   i.   Ward R.[12] **Whipple**[272] born 11 March 1912.
    5984   ii. Ruth **Whipple**[273] born 1919, married (__) **Cross**.

5109. **Oran Porter**[11] **Whipple** (Joseph Walter[10], Jonathan Jones[9], Joseph[8], David[7], Samuel[6], Samuel[5], Cyprian[4], Lt. John[3], Matthew[2], Matthew[1])[274] was born in Jefferson, Greene Co., Iowa 14 March 1870 and died 27 September 1947 in Carmen, Alfalfa Co., Okla., at 77 years of age. He married **Myrtle Bell Robertson** in Trinidad, Las Animas Co., Colo. 31 December 1899. Myrtle,[275] daughter of Miles Berry **Robertson** and Roxana Morningglory **Gandy**, was born in Laredo, Webb Co., Tex. 17 May 1881 and died 3 March 1951 in Carmen, at 69 years of age. Oran was a professional photographer. He served in the Spanish American War with the New Mexico Volunteers.

Oran Porter **Whipple** and Myrtle Bell **Robertson** had the following children:
+   5985   i.   Grace Irene[12] **Whipple** born 5 May 1901.
    5986   ii. Clyde Joseph **Whipple**[276] born in Ludlow, Pueblo Co., Colo. 1 December 1902 and died 20 April 1982 in San Jose, Santa Clara Co., Calif., at 79 years of age. He married Eunice E. **Moran** 18 October 1923.
    5987   iii. Blanch May **Whipple**[277] born in Columbus, Cherokee Co., Kans. 11 February 1905.
    5988   iv. Oran Paul **Whipple**[278] born in Longton, Elk Co., Kans. 4 July 1907 and died in 1978 in Florida, at 70 years of age. He married Delores **Balog** 21 April 1934.
    5989   v. Earl Emerson **Whipple**[279] born in Ordway, Crowley, Colo. 23 December 1910 and died in 1979 in Johnson, Stanton Co., Kans., at 68 years of age. He married Erma **(__)**.
    5990   vi. Nina Belle Elnora **Whipple**[280] born in Ordway 11 March 1913 and married twice. (1) John **Smith** 17 November 1931. (2) Cecil **Bird**.

5991 vii. Betty Louise **Whipple**[281] born in Wellington, Sumner Co., Kans. 13 May 1922 and married Glen **McClure** 8 February 1946.

5992 viii. Bessie Lorraine **Whipple**[282] born in Wellington 13 May 1922 and married twice. (1) Thayer **Sheriff** 26 March 1943. (2) Monty **Stokes.**

5993 ix. Helen Jean **Whipple**[283] born in Wichita, Sedgwick Co., Kans. 31 December 1925 and married Frank **Shockley** 3 February 1949.

5121. **Henry Learned**[11] **Whipple** (Dr. Alfred Augustus[10], Henry Francisco[9], Joseph[8], David[7], Samuel[6], Samuel[5], Cyprian[4], Lt. John[3], Matthew[2], Matthew[1])[284] was born in Salamanca, Cattaraugus Co., N.Y 6 January 1871 and died 3 June 1947 in Riverside, Riverside Co., Calif., at 76 years of age. He married **Alice Reed** in Illinois. She died 3 November 1939.[285] Henry was a dentist and in his later years managed the Riverside Inn.

Henry Learned Whipple. (Courtesy Richard H. Whipple, Greensboro, N.C.

Henry Learned **Whipple** and Alice **Reed** had the following children:

5994 i. Henry Reed[12] **Whipple**[286] born 23 April 1894 and died in 1970 in Philadelphia, Philadelphia City Co., Penn., at 76 years of age.

+ 5995 ii. Grace **Whipple** born 20 August 1896.

5123. **Merritt Pendell**[11] **Whipple** (Dr. Alfred Augustus[10], Henry Francisco[9], Joseph[8], David[7], Samuel[6], Samuel[5], Cyprian[4], Lt. John[3], Matthew[2], Matthew[1])[287] was born in Mansfield or Salamanca, Cattaraugus Co., N.Y 22 April 1875 and died 3 October 1936 in Rochester, Monroe Co., N.Y., at 61 years of

Estella May (Durfee) Whipple with daughter Helen and son Paul. Photo courtesy of Karen (Whipple) Thomas of Hamden, Conn.

{ G 876 }

age. He married **Estella May Durfee** in Quincy, Adams Co., Ill. or Boulder, Boulder Co., Colo. 19 September 1900. Estella,[288] daughter of Edwin **Durfee** and Mary **Thayer**, was born in Quincy 16 January 1876 and died 6 March 1963 in Rochester, at 87 years of age.

Merritt Pendell **Whipple** and Estella May **Durfee** had the following children:

+	5996	i.	Arthur Paul[12] **Whipple** born 17 July 1901.
	5997	ii.	Helen Estelle **Whipple**[289] born in Rochester 18 December 1905 and died there 1 February 1979, at 73 years of age.
+	5998	iii.	Virginia Dallas **Whipple** born 25 June 1907.
+	5999	iv.	Ralph Alfred **Whipple** born 10 July 1909.

Merritt Pendell Whipple. (Courtesy Richard H. Whipple, Greensboro, N.C.

5125. **William**[11] **Whipple** (Dr. Alfred Augustus[10], Henry Francisco[9], Joseph[8], David[7], Samuel[6], Samuel[5], Cyprian[4], Lt. John[3], Matthew[2], Matthew[1])[290] was born in Quincy, Adams Co., Ill. 10 August 1886 and died 10 January 1967 in North Platte, Lincoln Co., Nebr., at 80 years of age. He married **Dora Cecile Byron** in Chicago, Cook Co., Ill. 9 October 1909. Dora,[291] daughter of Pierre Joachim **Biron** and Elnette May **Johnson**, was born in Sault Ste. Marie, Chippewa Co., Mich. 3 September 1888 and died of abdominal cancer in North Platte 14 December 1952, at 64 years of age. She lived in Sault Ste. Marie until age 12 when she moved with her widowed mother to Chicago where she completed her schooling. She was baptized by her grandfather Joachim **Biron**, founder of the First Baptist Church of Sault Ste. Marie, and volunteered in the church's children and young people's activities all her life. She was also a member of Signet Chapter 55 of the Order of Eastern Star in North Platte. Her funeral services were at the Maloney, Cox & Kuhns Chapel in North Platte with her son Rev. L. Byron Whipple officiating.

William worked as a Sears-Roebuck & Co. Correspondent in Chicago. The family also lived in Maywood, Cook Co., Ill before William was drafted in 1918 to do farm work in Nebraska. The family moved to North Platte from Kearney, Buffalo Co., where he began work for the Union Pacific as a Railroad Clerk in 1942, retiring in 1958. He was a member of the First Baptist Church, Inter Church Reserve, Platte Valley Lodge No.

{ G 877 }

32 Accepted and Free Masons, Signet Chapter No. 55 Order of the Eastern Star, and the Brotherhood of Railway and Steamship Clerks. The family genealogist, he died of hypostatic pneumonia which resulted from a fall on ice.

William **Whipple** and Dora Cecile **Byron** had the following children:

   6000 i. Elnette Cecile[12] **Whipple**[292] born in Chicago 25 July 1910.[293] As a baby it was believed Elnette had spinal meningitis but her grand father determined she was not getting the proper energy from her food and developed a formula that corrected this problem. She was 8 when the family moved to Red Cloud, Webster Co., Nebr. and she and the other children thrived on farm life and in country schools. She was graduated from Glenvil, Clay Co., Nebr. High School and from Barnes School of Commerce in Denver, Denver Co., Colo. After passing the federal Civil Service exam she began work in Washington, D.C. She retired after 35 years in government working in Washington, Philadelphia, and Red Bank, Monmouth Co., N.J. She then moved to North Platte to be near family. She never married.

   6001 ii. Rev. Lydia Elizabeth **Whipple**[294] born in Chicago 2 June 1911 and died 15 April 1965 in Cambridge, Middlesex Co., Mass., at 53 years of age. She married **Rev. Chester Wood** in Newton Center, Norfolk Co., Mass. 3 May 1942. He died in June 1961 in Templeton, Worcester Co., Mass. A former resident of Boston, Chester was Pastor of Bethany Baptist Church in Showhegan,[295] Maine at the time of their marriage.[296] Lydia attended Kearney State Teachers College, Kearney, Buffalo Co., Nebr. and earned a B.A. degree from the Baptist Missionary Training School of Chicago in 1936. She became Pastor of the First Baptist Church at Gildford, Hill Co., Mont. and Interim Pastor of the Weston, Saunders Co., Nebr. Baptist Church before entering Andover-Newton Seminary of Newton, Middlesex Co., Mass. where she received a degree of Master of Religious Education in 1941 and a Bachelor of Arts in Divinity from the same Seminary in 1946. She was ordained Pastor of the community churches of Croydon, Croydon Flat, and North Newport, all in Sullivan Co., N.H., in January 1942. Nine ministers participated in the laying on of hands as her brother, Rev. L. Byron Whipple of Springfield, Hampden Co., Mass.,

Lydia E. (Whipple) Wood 1942.

gave the ordination prayer, invoking divine leadership and blessing. She was a member of the Templeton, Worcester Co., Mass. Historical Society, the Templeton Village Improvement Assn., and an honorary member of the Templeton Woman's Club. She died in Mount Auburn Hospital, Cambridge, following open heart surgery. She was buried on 19 April in the Pine Grove Cemetery at Templeton.[297]

+ 6002 iii. Rev. Leroy Byron **Whipple** born 8 January 1913.
+ 6003 iv. William **Whipple** Jr. born 31 December 1916.
+ 6004 v. Alfreda Louise **Whipple** born 4 January 1918.
+ 6005 vi. Marian Learned **Whipple** born 25 April 1920.

5140. **Burdette D.**[11] **Whipple** (James Spencer[10], Henry Francisco[9], Joseph[8], David[7], Samuel[6], Samuel[5], Cyprian[4], Lt. John[3], Matthew[2], Matthew[1])[298] was born in Salamanca, Cattaraugus Co., N.Y 4 April 1878 and died there 17 January 1964, at 85 years of age. He married **Laura S. Vreeland** in Salamanca 27 November 1901 or 22 November 1902. Laura,[299] daughter of E. B. **Vreeland**, was born in 1882 and died in August 1914 in Salamanca, at 32 years of age. Burdette was graduated from the Albany, N.Y. Law School in 1903, admitted to practice law at Rochester, Monroe Co., N.Y. and spent his entire career practicing in Salamanca, originally in partnership with his father. Following his father's death, he practiced solo. He served as Justice of the Peace, United States Commissioner, Salamanca City Judge and as a Captain in Co. W, 164th Regiment, New York National Guard, during WWI. He was living in December 1957.

Burdette D. **Whipple** and Laura S. **Vreeland** had the following children born in Salamanca:

    6006 i. James Vreeland[12] **Whipple**[300] 7 June 1904 and died there 8 August 1914, at 10 years of age.
+ 6007 ii. Elizabeth Olive **Whipple** 31 January 1909.

5141. **Dr. Willis Walton**[11] **Whipple** (James Spencer[10], Henry Francisco[9], Joseph[8], David[7], Samuel[6], Samuel[5], Cyprian[4], Lt. John[3], Matthew[2], Matthew[1])[301] was born in New York State 16 February 1882 and died in August 1956 at 74 years of age. He married **Wilhelmina Edith Sander** 7 October 1908. She was born in 1880 and died in 1964, at 84 years of age.[302] Both buried at Wildwood Cemetery, Salamanaca. Willis was graduated from the U. of Michigan in 1906 and earned a degree in Denistry at the New York School of Denistry. He was practicing in Salamanca in April 1941.

Dr. Willis Walton **Whipple** and Wilhelmina Edith **Sander** had the following children born in Salamanca:
- 6008 i. Vivian Olive[12] **Whipple**[303] 15 February 1910 and married an unnamed person.
- \+ 6009 ii. Dean Sander **Whipple** born 10 June 1913.
- \+ 6010 iii. Walton **Whipple**.

5148. **Ara Leroy**[11] **Whipple** (Willis Walton[10], Henry Francisco[9], Joseph[8], David[7], Samuel[6], Samuel[5], Cyprian[4], Lt. John[3], Matthew[2], Matthew[1])[304] was born in Salamanca, Cattaraugus Co., N.Y 13 April 1886 and died 30 August 1948 in Toronto, York, Ontario, Canada, at 62 years of age. He married **Lucy May Prosser** in Georgina Isles, Ontario, Canada 17 June 1908. Lucy,[305] daughter of Rev. J. H. **Prosser**, was born 25 August 1886 and died 7 February 1958 at 71 years of age. Ara began working for the Erie Railroad as a young man and retired as a passenger train Conductor. His funeral service was held in Meadville, Crawford Co., Penn. and he was buried in the Wildwood Cemetery, Salamanca. The family had a summer home at Kezwich, Ontario, Canada. Kezwich is 60 miles north of Toronto.

Ara Leroy **Whipple** and Lucy May **Prosser** had the following child:
- \+ 6011 i. Rev. John Walton[12] **Whipple** born 21 August 1909.

5151. **Clinton Albert**[11] **Whipple** (Seth Andrew[10], David Spencer[9], Joseph[8], David[7], Samuel[6], Samuel[5], Cyprian[4], Lt. John[3], Matthew[2], Matthew[1])[306] was born in Wattsburg, Erie Co., Penn. 17 April 1897 and died in 1964 in Erie, Erie Co., Penn., at 67 years of age.

Clinton Albert **Whipple** had the following child:
- 6012 i. Marjorie[12] **Whipple**[307] born in Erie 15 July 1940.

5156. **Edith Adelia**[11] **Hobart** (Edwin Whipple[10], Sarah[9] **Whipple**, Samuel[8], David[7], Samuel[6], Samuel[5], Cyprian[4], Lt. John[3], Matthew[2], Matthew[1])[308] was born in Sharon Township, Washtenaw Co., Mich. 19 February 1879 and married **Walter Davenport Rowe** in Grass Lake, Jackson Co., Mich. 26 June 1901. He was born in 1874 and died in 1946, at 72 years of age.[309]

Edith Adelia **Hobart** and Walter Davenport **Rowe** had the following children:
- 6013 i. Helen[12] **Rowe**.[310]
- 6014 ii. Ruth **Rowe**.[311]
- 6015 iii. Hobart **Rowe**.[312]

5157. **Earl Parker**[11] **Hobart** (Edwin Whipple[10], Sarah[9] **Whipple**, Samuel[8], David[7], Samuel[6], Samuel[5], Cyprian[4], Lt. John[3], Matthew[2], Matthew[1])[313] was born in Sharon Township, Washtenaw Co., Mich. 20 July 1880 and died in October 1955 in Detroit, Wayne Co., Mich., at 75 years of age. He married **Julia M. Chase** of Toledo, Lucas Co., Ohio.

Earl Parker **Hobart** and Julia M. **Chase** had the following children:

  6016 i. Russell Parker[12] **Hobart**[314] born in 1908 and died in 1962, at 54 years of age.
  6017 ii. Lawrence Chase **Hobart** born in 1909.[315]

5158. **Inez May**[11] **Hobart** (Edwin Whipple[10], Sarah[9] **Whipple**, Samuel[8], David[7], Samuel[6], Samuel[5], Cyprian[4], Lt. John[3], Matthew[2], Matthew[1])[316] was born in Sharon Township, Washtenaw Co., Mich. 22 December 1881 and married **George Clayton McGee** in Grass Lake, Jackson Co., Mich. 8 September 1907. He was born in 1858 and died in 1950, at 92 years of age.[317]

Inez May **Hobart** and George Clayton **McGee** had the following children:

+ 6018 i. Eleanor[12] **McGee** born 13 July 1908.
  6019 ii. Nellie **McGee**.[318]
  6020 iii. George Clayton **McGee** Jr.[319]
  6021 iv. Florence Irene **McGee**[320] born abt 1920 and died in 1922 at 2 years of age.

5159. **Vera Grace**[11] **Hobart** (Edwin Whipple[10], Sarah[9] **Whipple**, Samuel[8], David[7], Samuel[6], Samuel[5], Cyprian[4], Lt. John[3], Matthew[2], Matthew[1])[321] was born in Sharon Township, Washtenaw Co., Mich. 22 December 1881 and married **Maurice Shirley Douglas** in Grass Lake, Jackson Co., Mich., 2 September 1903. She was born in 1873 and died in 1955, at 82 years of age.[322] She was living in Flat Rock, Ind. in 1969.

Vera Grace **Hobart** and Maurice Shirley **Douglas** had the following children:

  6022 i. Catherine[12] **Douglas**.[323]
  6023 ii. John **Douglas**.[324]
  6024 iii. Edwin **Douglas**.[325]
  6025 iv. Robert **Douglas**.[326]
  6026 v. Margaret **Douglas**.[327]
  6027 vi. James **Douglas**.[328]
  6028 vii. Alice **Douglas**.[329]

5160. **Ella Sarah**[11] **Hobart** (Edwin Whipple[10], Sarah[9] **Whipple**, Samuel[8], David[7], Samuel[6], Samuel[5], Cyprian[4], Lt. John[3], Matthew[2],

Matthew[1])330 was born in Grass Lake, Jackson Co., Mich. 7 September 1886 and married **Walter Lloyd Finton** 16 February 1910. He was born in 1886 and died in 1963, at 77 years of age.[331] She was living at Jackson, Jackson Co., Mich. in 1969.

Ella Sarah **Hobart** and Walter Lloyd **Finton** had the following children:
    6029   i.   Walter[12] **Finton**.[332] He died during WWII.
    6030   ii.   Robert **Finton**.[333] He was a surgeon in Jackson in 1969.
    6031   iii.   Max **Finton**.[334] He was a retired physician living in Traverse Bay, Houghton Co., Mich. in 1969.

5161. **Delia Lucile[11] Hobart** (Edwin Whipple[10], Sarah[9] **Whipple**, Samuel[8], David[7], Samuel[6], Samuel[5], Cyprian[4], Lt. John[3], Matthew[2], Matthew[1])335 was born in Grass Lake, Jackson Co., Mich. 15 August 1892 and married **Edmund Frank Robinson** there 19 May 1915. She was living on Francisco Road in Grass Lake in 1969.

Delia Lucile **Hobart** and Edmund Frank **Robinson** had the following children:
    6032   i.   Horace[12] **Robinson**.[336]
    6033   ii.   Louella May **Robinson** and married Woodrow **Artz**.[337]

5165. **Walter Henry[11] Whipple** (Watson H.[10], William[9], Samuel[8], David[7], Samuel[6], Samuel[5], Cyprian[4], Lt. John[3], Matthew[2], Matthew[1])338 was born in Medina, Orleans Co., N.Y. 7 October 1897 and died there 18 April 1985, at 87 years of age. He married **Martha Mary Rands** 6 May 1917. Martha,[339] daughter of James Henry **Rands** and Annie **Bickle**, was born in Medina 8 November 1895 and died there 5 March 1990, at 94 years of age. Both are buried in Boxwood Cemetery.

Walter Henry **Whipple** and Martha Mary **Rands** had the following children:
+   6034   i.   Robert Hugh[12] **Whipple** born 15 November 1923.
+   6035   ii.   James Watson **Whipple** born 27 July 1927.

5168. **Hugh Scott[11] Whipple** (Francis Henry[10], William[9], Samuel[8], David[7], Samuel[6], Samuel[5], Cyprian[4], Lt. John[3], Matthew[2], Matthew[1])340 was born in Medina, Orleans Co., N.Y. 19 December 1895 and died there 7 September 1978, at 82 years of age. He married **Helene Eleanore Doty** in Evanston, Cook Co., Ill. 7 October 1922. Helene,[341] daughter of Marshall Lloyd **Doty** Sr. and Dora Lanning **Jones**, was born in Oak Park Cook Co., Ill. 16 January 1896 and died 21 August 1986 in Medina, at 90 years of age. Hugh was a Sales Manager for a food machinery manufacturer.

Hugh Scott **Whipple** and Helene Eleanore **Doty** had the following children:
- + 6036 i. David Doty[12] **Whipple** born 26 December 1923.
- + 6037 ii. Scott Lloyd **Whipple** born 31 December 1925.

5178. **Doris**[11] **Coulter** (Doris[10] **Whipple**, Edwin[9], Samuel[8], David[7], Samuel[6], Samuel[5], Cyprian[4], Lt. John[3], Matthew[2], Matthew[1])[342] was born 20 March 1921 and married **James Mample**.

Doris **Coulter** and James **Mample** had the following child:
- 6038 i. Murray[12] **Mample**.[343]

5179. **Izobel**[11] **Coulter** (Doris[10] **Whipple**, Edwin[9], Samuel[8], David[7], Samuel[6], Samuel[5], Cyprian[4], Lt. John[3], Matthew[2], Matthew[1])[344] was born 11 October 1922 and married twice. (1) **Rod Tiernan**. (2) **Lester Scully**.

Izobel **Coulter** and Rod **Tiernan** had the following child:
- 6039 i. James[12] **Tiernan**.[345]

Izobel **Coulter** and Lester **Scully** had the following child:
- + 6040 ii. John Michael **Scully** born 5 July 1960.

5182. **Zady**[11] **Harvey** (Annis Cleveland[10] **Whipple**, Edwin[9], Samuel[8], David[7], Samuel[6], Samuel[5], Cyprian[4], Lt. John[3], Matthew[2], Matthew[1])[346] was born 26 March 1918 and married **Hermanus Kriel**.

Zady **Harvey** and Hermanus **Kriel** had the following children:
- 6041 i. Hermanus[12] **Kriel** Jr. born 26 June 1946.[347]
- 6042 ii. Hans **Kriel** born 1 October 1948.[348]

5184. **Ralph Howard**[11] **Whipple** (Colby Favelle[10], Isaac[9], Hiram[8], David[7], Samuel[6], Samuel[5], Cyprian[4], Lt. John[3], Matthew[2], Matthew[1])[349] was born in Cleveland, Cuyahoga Co., Ohio 4 September 1883 and died 6 July 1957 in West Palm Beach, Palm Beach Co., Fla., at 73 years of age. He married **Elizabeth Bertine Miller**. Elizabeth,[350] daughter of Albertus Russ **Miller** and Christine **McLennan**, was born in Cleveland 5 July 1891 and died 25 June 1973 in West Palm Beach, at 81 years of age.

Ralph Howard **Whipple** and Elizabeth Bertine **Miller** had the following children:
- + 6043 i. Ruth Janis[12] **Whipple** born 10 August 1913.
- + 6044 ii. Genevieve Eynon **Whipple** born 23 June 1918.

5189. **Ernest B.**[11] **Hardy** (Lucy Ann[10] **Harriman**, Joel George[9], Lucy[8] **Ray**, Jonathan[7], Amos[6], Hannah[5] **Goodale**, Sarah[4] **Whipple**, Joseph[3], Matthew[2], Matthew[1])[351] was born in Benton, Scott Co., Mo. 5 January 1872 and died 7 June 1922, at 50 years of age. He married **Susie Idell**.

Ernest B. **Hardy** and Susie **Idell** had the following children:

  6045 i.   Lewis Berton[12] **Hardy**.[352]
  6046 ii.   Thomas **Hardy**.[353]
  6047 iii. Ralph **Hardy**.[354]
  6048 iv.   Christopher **Hardy**.[355]
  6049 v.   Charles **Hardy**.[356]
  6050 vi.   Alta Mae **Hardy**.[357]
  6051 vii. Myrtle **Hardy**.[358]
  6052 viii. Frances Louise **Hardy**.[359]

5191. **Annie Grace**[11] **Hardy** (Lucy Ann[10] **Harriman**, Joel George[9], Lucy[8] **Ray**, Jonathan[7], Amos[6], Hannah[5] **Goodale**, Sarah[4] **Whipple**, Joseph[3], Matthew[2], Matthew[1])[360] was born in Clarksville, Coos Co., N.H. 1 July 1882 and died 7 December 1941 in Clarksville, at 59 years of age. She married twice. (1) **George Edwin Ricker** 19 November 1903. He was born 12 May 1874 and died 23 September 1948 in Clarksville, at 74 years of age.[361] (2) **Earl Parker** bef 1936.

Annie Grace **Hardy** and George Edwin **Ricker** had the following children born in Clarksville:

     6053 i.   Edwin Sanford[12] **Ricker**[362] 25 April 1905.
  + 6054 ii.   Annie Mae **Ricker** 26 January 1907.
  + 6055 iii. Arthur Walter **Ricker** 12 April 1909.
  + 6056 iv.   Freeman Otis **Ricker** 10 February 1913.
     6057 v.   Moses Almon **Ricker**[363] 22 May 1913 and died there 22 May 1929, at 16 years of age.
     6058 vi.   Georgie Walice **Ricker**[364] 18 April 1916 and died in 1983, at 67 years of age.
  + 6059 vii. Lucy Ann **Ricker** 28 July 1918.
     6060 viii. Jimmie Edwin **Ricker**[365] 8 October 1919.
     6061 ix.   Henry Thomas **Ricker**[366] 31 July 1921.
     6062 x.   Edna Josephine **Ricker**[367] 12 July 1924.

5194. **Gilbert Ray**[11] **Eno** (Rosina Bell[10] **Harriman**, Joel George[9], Lucy[8] **Ray**, Jonathan[7], Amos[6], Hannah[5] **Goodale**, Sarah[4] **Whipple**, Joseph[3], Matthew[2], Matthew[1])[368] was born in Iowa abt 1875.

Gilbert Ray **Eno** and Bessie (__) had the following children:
- 6063   i.   Kent D.[12] **Eno**[369] born c 1905.
- 6064   ii.   Vivian **Eno**[370] born c 1908.
- 6065   iii. Gerald H. **Eno**[371] born c 1910.
- 6066   iv.   Virginia **Eno**[372] born c 1912.
- 6067   v.   Woodrow **Eno**[373] born c 1916.
- 6068   vi.   Leon **Eno**[374] born c Oct. 1919.

5195. **Fred Eugene**[11] **Eno** (Rosina Bell[10] **Harriman**, Joel George[9], Lucy[8] **Ray**, Jonathan[7], Amos[6], Hannah[5] **Goodale**, Sarah[4] **Whipple**, Joseph[3], Matthew[2], Matthew[1])[375] was born abt 1879 and married Marie J. (__).

Fred Eugene **Eno** and Marie J. (__) had the following child:
- 6069   i.   Harold Gordon[12] **Eno**.[376]

5196. **Delwin Gordon**[11] **Eno** (Rosina Bell[10] **Harriman**, Joel George[9], Lucy[8] **Ray**, Jonathan[7], Amos[6], Hannah[5] **Goodale**, Sarah[4] **Whipple**, Joseph[3], Matthew[2], Matthew[1])[377] was born in Canton, Lincoln Co., S. Dak. abt 1882 and married **Effie Kienhoff** abt 1908.

Delwin Gordon **Eno** and Effie **Kienhoff** had the following children:
- 6070   i.   Keith Harriman[12] **Eno**.[378]
- 6071   ii.   Carroll F. **Eno**.[379]
- 6072   iii. Delwin Gordon **Eno** Jr.[380] born abt 1916.

5197. **Mabel Dot**[11] **Eno** (Rosina Bell[10] **Harriman**, Joel George[9], Lucy[8] **Ray**, Jonathan[7], Amos[6], Hannah[5] **Goodale**, Sarah[4] **Whipple**, Joseph[3], Matthew[2], Matthew[1])[381] was born 22 February 1885 and died in October 1977 in Alameda, Alameda Co., Calif., at 92 years of age. She married (__) **Groth**.

Mabel Dot **Eno** and (__) **Groth** had the following child:
- 6073   i.   Ina Bell[12] **Groth**[382] died in December 1989.

5198. **Lynn Harold**[11] **Harriman** (Daniel S.[10], Joel George[9], Lucy[8] **Ray**, Jonathan[7], Amos[6], Hannah[5] **Goodale**, Sarah[4] **Whipple**, Joseph[3], Matthew[2], Matthew[1])[383] was born in Warner, Merrimack Co., N.H. 8 May 1892 and died 31 May 1918, at 26 years of age. He was a Lieutenant with the Army's 101st (Co. A) Infantry and was killed in France during WWI. He married **Anna M. Johnson** in Warner 9 March 1914. She was born in South Sutton, Merrimac Co., N.H. abt 1893.[384]

Lynn Harold **Harriman** and Anna M. **Johnson** had the following child:
> 6074   i.   Byron Lynn[12] **Harriman** born in Manchester, Hillsborough Co., N.H. 31 March 1916.[385]

5199. **Charles Mayland**[11] **Harriman** (Daniel S.[10], Joel George[9], Lucy[8] **Ray**, Jonathan[7], Amos[6], Hannah[5] **Goodale**, Sarah[4] **Whipple**, Joseph[3], Matthew[2], Matthew[1])[386] was born in Warner, Merrimack Co., N.H. 2 May 1894 and died 15 January 1964 in Homestead, Miami-Dade Co., Fla., at 69 years of age. He married **Edith Maude Smith** in Warner 12 November 1917. She was born 7 March 1895 and died in February 1983 in Port Arthur, Jefferson Co., Tex., at 87 years of age.[387] Buried in Pine Grove Cemetery, Warner.

Charles Mayland **Harriman** and Edith Maude **Smith** had the following children:
> +   6075   i.   Mayland Earl[12] **Harriman** born 1 November 1921.
>   6076   ii.   Donald Boyd **Harriman**[388] born in Warner 6 February 1924 and died 16 October 1947 in Laconia, Belknap Co., N.H., at 23 years of age. Buried in Pine Grove Cemetery, Warner.

5203. **Ruby Edna**[11] **Harriman** (George Dearborn[10], Joel George[9], Lucy[8] **Ray**, Jonathan[7], Amos[6], Hannah[5] **Goodale**, Sarah[4] **Whipple**, Joseph[3], Matthew[2], Matthew[1])[389] was born in Warner, Merrimac Co., N.H. 9 February 1905 and died 17 November 1984 in Delphi, Carroll Co., Ind., at 79 years of age. She married twice. (1) **Ernest Lester Davis** in Warner 14 September 1926. They were divorced in 1942. Ernest,[390] son of Edward B. **Davis** and Ida May **Carson**, was born in Perry Township, Clinton Co., Ind. 24 July 1900. He married (2) **Velma Ruth Scowden** in August 1943 and died 2 June 1972 in Boca Raton, Palm Beach Co., Fla., at 71 years of age. Buried in the I.O.O.F. Cemetery, Tippecanoe Township, Carroll Co. Ernest served in Germany during WWI. He managed the telephone company at Clarks Hill, Tippecanoe Co., Ind. beginning in 1929. The family later moved to Frankfort, Clinton Co., Ind. where Ernest learned the dry cleaning business and in 1939 Ernest and Ruby founded Carroll Cleaners in Delphi. (2) **Floyd Addison Sigman** 10 November 1947. Floyd,[391] son of Samuel **Sigman** and Mary **Withrow**, was born in Lafayette, Tippecanoe Co., Ind. 20 June 1911. Ruby was an orphan at 15; her mother died when she was 12 and father when she was 15.

Ruby Edna **Harriman** and Ernest Lester **Davis** had the following children:
> +   6077   i.   Phyllis Jean[12] **Davis** born 22 July 1930.

6078 ii. James Ray **Davis**[392] born in Perry Township 31 March 1932 and married June Darlene **Phillips** in Delphi 25 October 1951. June,[393] daughter of Clyde **Phillips** and Stella **Richardson**, was born in Carroll Co. 5 June 1932. James was in the U.S. Army stationed in Germany during the Korean War.

+ 6079 iii. Richard Lee **Davis** born 20 April 1935.

5205. **Fred Carlos**[11] **Wiggins** (George Henry[10], Louisa[9] **Harriman**, Lucy[8] **Ray**, Jonathan[7], Amos[6], Hannah[5] **Goodale**, Sarah[4] **Whipple**, Joseph[3], Matthew[2], Matthew[1])[394] was born in Bremer Co., Iowa in February 1869 and died 10 May 1967 in Canton, Lincoln Co., S. Dak., at 98 years of age. Buried in Forest Hill Cemetery. He married **Mary (__)** who was born in Wisconsin in March 1866.[395]

Fred Carlos **Wiggins** and Mary (__) had the following child:

6080 i. Henry[12] **Wiggins**[396] born in Lincoln Co., S. Dak. in November 1898.

5213. **Fredrick V.**[11] **Morgan** (Nehemiah[10], Samuel[9], Betsey[8] **Whipple**, Nehemiah[7], Benjamin[6], Francis[5], Jonathan[4], Joseph[3], Matthew[2], Matthew[1])[397] was born in Sweden, Oxford Co., Maine abt 1857 and died there abt 1901. Buried in Bates Cemetery, Johnsburg, Warren Co., N.Y. He married **Cora Adeline Morehouse**. Cora,[398] daughter of Wesley D. **Morehouse** and Charlotte "Lottie" **Treadwell**, was born in Sweden abt 1860.

Fredrick V. **Morgan** and Cora Adeline **Morehouse** had the following children:

+ 6081 i. Grace Elenore[12] **Morgan** born 29 June 1884.
  6082 ii. Fredrick N. **Morgan**[399] born in Sweden abt 1887 and died the year of birth.
  6083 iii. Mrytle Emeline **Morgan**[400] born in Sweden 20 September 1889 and died 8 May 1959 at 69 years of age. She married Nathan William **Davis.**
  6084 iv. Emma **Morgan**[401] born in Sweden 20 September 1891.
  6085 v. Jane **Morgan**[402] born 2 April 1893 and married Ray **Van-Husen**.
  6086 vi. Harry Robinson **Morgan**[403] born 19 August 1898 and married (__) **Pryce.**
  6087 vii. Bertram V. **Morgan**[404] born 19 August 1898.

5222. **Charles Russel**[11] **Norton** (Judge James Carmont[10], Harriet Whipple[9] **Carpenter**, Anner[8] **Whipple**, Nehemiah[7], Benjamin[6], Francis[5], Jonathan[4], Joseph[3], Matthew[2], Matthew[1])[405] was born in Highland Co., Ohio 9 August 1855 and died 7 April 1937 in Covina, Los Angeles Co., Calif., at 81 years of age. He married **Augusta Brown** in Evansville, Vanderburgh Co., Ind. 28 February 1882. Augusta,[406] daughter of David W. **Brown** and Mary Jane **Forsythe**, was born in Perry Co., Ind. 29 November 1856 and died 2 January 1938 in Puenta, Los Angeles Co., Calif., at 81 years of age. Charles farmed in Kansas before moving his family to California where he owned a walnut orchard in Puente.

Charles Russel **Norton** and Augusta **Brown** had the following children born in Marquette, McPherson Co., Kans.:

        6088   i.   Charles Owen[12] **Norton**[407] 8 February 1883.
+   6089   ii. James Newton **Norton** 8 March 1885.
+   6090   iii. Mary **Norton** 28 November 1886.
+   6091   iv. Hugh Russell **Norton** 14 December 1888.
        6092   v.   Mildred **Norton**[408] 20 August 1891.
+   6093   vi. Walter Emmet **Norton** 27 June 1893.
        6094   vii. Louise **Norton**[409] 21 July 1894.

5228. **Amy**[11] **Norton** (Judge James Carmont[10], Harriet Whipple[9] **Carpenter**, Anner[8] **Whipple**, Nehemiah[7], Benjamin[6], Francis[5], Jonathan[4], Joseph[3], Matthew[2], Matthew[1])[410] was born in Highland Co., Ohio in 1867 and married **Will Bean** there bef 25 December 1889.

Amy **Norton** and Will **Bean** had the following child:

        6095   i.   Waldo[12] **Bean**.[411]

5232. **Angeline**[11] **McKinley** (William Henry[10] McKinley, Angeline[9] **Whipple**, Enoch[8], Nehemiah[7], Benjamin[6], Francis[5], Jonathan[4], Joseph[3], Matthew[2], Matthew[1])[412] was born in Green Hill, Warren Co., Ind. 22 October 1877 and died 6 October 1959 in Vinton, Benton Co., Iowa, at 81 years of age. She married **Willard B. Franklin** in Benton Co. 31 October 1905. Willard,[413] son of Col. John **Franklin** and Emaline **Collier**, was born in Green Hill 21 October 1882 and died 8 February 1960 in Vinton, at 77 years of age. Both are buried in Section 18 Maplewood Cemetery, Vinton. Angeline was named after her grandmother Angeline Whipple. Willard, a Vinton barber, was also a first cousin to Harley Franklin who married Angeline's sister, Janette. Angeline and Willard were active in the United Brethren Church.

Angeline **McKinley** and Willard B. **Franklin** had the following children born in Vinton:

+ 6096 i. John Dorwin[12] **Franklin** 22 September 1906.
+ 6097 ii. Dorothy Marguerite **Franklin** 19 November 1907.
+ 6098 iii. Laura Charlotte **Franklin** 29 May 1909.
+ 6099 iv. Sylvia Fae **Franklin** 24 February 1912.

6100 v. William Woodrow **Franklin**[414] 1 July 1913. He married twice. (1) Margaret Schultz **Cass** 1 February 1958. Margaret,[415] daughter of Paula Sophia **Eickman,** was born in Germany 16 February 1915 and died 17 September 1987 at 72 years of age. (2) June **Raymar** in California in January 1988. She died 26 August 1998.[416] William was a WWII Naval veteran who settled in California following the war and became a sports writer and avid bowler. He was a writer, editor, researcher, innovator, speaker, publicist, historian, bowling tournament official, promoter and as a member of the ABC and ABC Hall of Fame Boards of Directors. He was Secretary-treasurer of the California State Bowling Assn. and was inducted into the ABC Bowling Hall of Fame in Corpus Christi, Nuecee Co., Tex. in 1992.

5233. **James Hiram**[11] **McKinley** (William Henry[10], Angeline[9] **Whipple**, Enoch[8], Nehemiah[7], Benjamin[6], Francis[5], Jonathan[4], Joseph[3], Matthew[2], Matthew[1])[417] was born in Cedar Township, Benton Co., Iowa 26 February 1879 and died 8 January 1954 in Portland, Multnomah Co., Oreg., at 74 years of age. He married **Pearl Leona Dudley** in Benton Co. 22 January 1908. Pearl,[418] daughter of John Franklin **Dudley** and Janette **Vorce,** was born 19 November 1884 and died 24 August 1958 in Portland, at 73 years of age. Both are buried at Riverview Mausoleum, Portland. James had a harrowing experience in May of 1900 when he was working for Mrs. John Powers south of Vinton, Benton Co., Iowa. He was driving a spirited horse when four men accosted him. He tried to outrun them but after being shot at—four bullets passed through the buggy top—he stopped and was robbed.[419]

James Hiram **McKinley** and Pearl Leon **Dudley** had the following children:

6101 i. Emmet Carleton[12] **McKinley**[420] born in Benton Co. 22 March 1909 and died there 26 March, at 4 days of age. Buried in Vinton's Maplewood Cemetery.
+ 6102 ii. LaVon Elizabeth **McKinley** born 12 March 1911.
6103 iii. Mildred Janette **McKinley**[421] born in Benton Co. in 1914 and died there 4 March 1915, at 1 year of age. Buried in Maplewood Cemetery.

6104   iv.   Harold William **McKinley**[422] born in Vinton 20 September 1917 and died there 3 April 1918, at less than seven months of age. Buried at Maplewood Cemetery.

5234. **Janette**[11] **McKinley** (William Henry[10], Angeline[9] **Whipple**, Enoch[8], Nehemiah[7], Benjamin[6], Francis[5], Jonathan[4], Joseph[3], Matthew[2], Matthew[1])[423] was born in Cedar Township, Benton Co., Iowa 29 September 1880 and died 4 July 1957 in Portage, Porter Co., Ind., at 76 years of age. Buried in McCool Cemetery. She married **Rev. Harley W. Franklin** in Brandon, Buchanan Co., Iowa, 24 February 1904. Harley,[424] son of Thomas **Franklin** and Sophronia **Martin**, was born in Independence, Warren Co. Ind. 8 September 1872 and died 17 March 1951 in Portage, at 78 years of age. Harley was Pastor at a little white community church in what was then Crisman but later became a part of Portage. He officiated at the wedding ceremonies of daughters Nina, Bernie, Estella, Frances, and Naomi at that church. Janette attended Valparaiso College in Valparaiso, Porter Co., Indiana and met her future husband there. She taught school near her parent's home before marrying. Some of her younger siblings were her students. Harley was a Pastor for several United Brethern churches in northern Indiana before retiring in Portage. When Harley was ill, Janette delivered his sermons. She was a member of the Women's Christian Temperance Union.

Janette **McKinley** and Rev. Harley W. **Franklin** had the following children:

6105   i.   Charlotte Marian[12] **Franklin**[425] born in Independence 5 January 1905 and died there 20 May 1905, at less than 5 months of age.

6106   ii.   Charlotte Marian **Franklin**[426] born in Independence in January 1905 and died there in June 1905, at less than 6 months of age.

+ 6107   iii.   Nina Eileen **Franklin** born 26 January 1906.

6108   iv.   Bernie Elizabeth **Franklin**[427] born in Independence 14 August 1907 and married Harold **Peyton** in Gary, Lake Co., Ind. 18 June 1948. Harold,[428] son of John **Peyton** and Mary **Doroughty**, was born in Clinton, Vermillion Co., Ind. 8 August 1899 and died 18 June 1989 in Portage, at 89 years of age. Harold was a widower when he married Bernie. His first wife and a daughter were killed in an auto-train accident. He also had a son Dale Harold **Peyton**, born 18 May 1937, who married Elaine **Zerr** 24 Dec. 1980. Bernie and Harold lived most of their married life in Portage. They had no children.

	+	6109	v.	Estella Eleanor **Franklin** born 7 January 1911.
	+	6110	vi.	Frances Freda **Franklin** born 27 July 1912.
	+	6111	vii.	Naomi Ruth **Franklin** born 9 July 1917.
		6112	viii.	Esther Janette **Franklin**[429] born in Albion, Noble Co., Ind. 6 August 1921 died 2 days after birth.

5236. **William Archibald**[11] **McKinley** (William Henry[10], Angeline[9] **Whipple**, Enoch[8], Nehemiah[7], Benjamin[6], Francis[5], Jonathan[4], Joseph[3], Matthew[2], Matthew[1])[430] was born in Cedar Township, Benton Co., Iowa 13 September 1885 and died 12 November 1934 in Vinton, Benton Co., Iowa, at 49 years of age. He married **Sarah Shaffer** in Brandon, Buchanan Co., Iowa 7 January 1914. Sarah,[431] daughter of George B. **Shaffer** and Alice **Edgeton**, was born in Brandon 3 November 1894 and died 30 September 1970 in Independence, Buchanan Co., Iowa, at 75 years of age. Buried at Brandon. In addition to the children listed below, they had two sons who died in infancy – one was born in 1918, the other in 1921. They also raised Glen and Betty Lucille **Dewitt,** children of Clayton and Ella **(Smith) Dewitt:** Glen, born 6 Jan. 1921, married Ruth **Mrstik**. He died in September 1984 and is buried in Cedar Memorial Park, Cedar Rapids, Linn Co., Iowa. Betty, born 27 September 1925 at Cedar Rapids, married David Dorin **DeLancey** 6 May 1951.

William Archibald **McKinley** and Sarah **Shaffer** had the following children born in Vinton:

		6113	i.	Charlotte Alice[12] **McKinley**[432] born 7 July 1915 and died in infancy.
	+	6114	ii.	Merton George **McKinley** born 16 March 1916.
		6115	iii.	Virginia Alice **McKinley**[433] born in 26 November 1928 and died there 3 days later.
		6116	iv.	Virgil Ellis **McKinley**[434] 26 November 1928 and died 4 days later.

5237. **Grover Cleveland**[11] **McKinley** (William Henry[10], Angeline[9] **Whipple**, Enoch[8], Nehemiah[7], Benjamin[6], Francis[5], Jonathan[4], Joseph[3], Matthew[2], Matthew[1])[435] was born in Cedar Township, Benton Co., Iowa 1 December 1886 and died 4 May 1944 at home on his farm near Walker, Linn Co., Iowa, at 57 years of age. He married **Pauline Hoffman** in Marion, Linn Co., Iowa 22 November 1916. Pauline,[436] daughter of Fred **Hoffman** and Delilah **Goings**, was born in Grant Township, Linn Co., Iowa 6 February 1897 and died 21 August 1966 in Linn Co., at 69 years of age. She was buried at Walker. Grover was named for Grover Cleveland, 22nd President of the U.S. He and Pauline farmed near the Linn, Benton, and Buchanan county line. In addition to the children listed, they had a daughter born 9 January 1919 and a son born 4 July 1925 who died in infancy. When he was 14, Grover fell on a pitchfork at the family farm in Harrison township. Three tines entered his body some eight inches.[437]

Grover Cleveland **McKinley** and Pauline **Hoffman** had the following children:

+ 6117 i. Clifford Hoffman[12] **McKinley** born 9 July 1917.
+ 6118 ii. Elizabeth Emily **McKinley** born 29 April 1920.
+ 6119 iii. Bernard Laverne **McKinley** born 23 November 1928.

5238. **John Carlysle**[11] **McKinley** (William Henry[10], Angeline[9] **Whipple**, Enoch[8], Nehemiah[7], Benjamin[6], Francis[5], Jonathan[4], Joseph[3], Matthew[2], Matthew[1])[438] was born in Cedar Township, Benton Co., Iowa 1 November 1888 and died 17 November 1920 in Cedar Rapids, Linn Co., Iowa, at 32 years of age. Buried at Garrison, Benton Co., Iowa. He married **Mary Luella Hardinger** in Garrison 4 March 1914. Mary,[439] daughter of Charley C. **Hardinger** and Ida May **Covert**, was born 9 March 1894 and died 21 January 1975 in Texas, at 80 years of age. Known as Carl, he and Mary farmed near Garrison. He served in WWI (no details provided). Just before his death, he became seriously ill with ulcers which were not treated properly, causing a premature death. Mary moved the family to Waterloo, Black Hawk Co., Iowa to live with her mother and became Assistant Manager of Black's Tea Room. Then she became a housekeeper for George Kurtz whom she married.

John Carlysle **McKinley** and Mary Luella **Hardinger** had the following children:

+ 6120 i. William Harry[12] **McKinley** born 15 August 1915.
6121 ii. George Gilman **McKinley**[440] born in Garrison 5 November 1917 and married twice. (1) Virginia Lucille **Baum** in Kohoka, Clark Co., Mo. 29 April 1944. Virginia, daughter of William **Baum** and Edith **York**, was born 4 June 1919 and died 15 August 1976 in Cedar Rapids, at 57 years of age. She was buried in Garrison. (2) Ruth **Conrad** 22 June 1979. George and Virginia moved to Cedar Rapids in 1938 where both worked for Collins Radio Co. They had no children.
+ 6122 iii. Dean Carlysle **McKinley** born 11 April 1920.

5239. **Lura**[11] **McKinley** (William Henry[10], Angeline[9] **Whipple**, Enoch[8], Nehemiah[7], Benjamin[6], Francis[5], Jonathan[4], Joseph[3], Matthew[2], Matthew[1])[441] was born in Cedar Township, Benton Co., Iowa 29 August

1890 and died 26 October 1975 in Perry, Dallas Co., Iowa, at 85 years of age. She married **Charles Arthur Shaffer** in Benton Co. 3 December 1912. Charles,[442] son of George B. **Shaffer** and Alice **Edgeton**, was born in Brandon, Buchanan Co., Iowa 24 September 1889 and died 2 September 1971 in Waterloo, Black Hawk Co., Iowa, at 81 years of age. Both are buried at Brandon. Neither Lura or Arthur ever lived more than 10 miles from their birthplace. They farmed until 1945 and both worked at Rath Meat Packing Co., Waterloo. Lura's brother William Archibald married Sarah Shaffer, Arthur's sister. Lura was Secretary-Treasurer of the McKinley family reunions (1936-74) and maintained a photo book of McKinley family descendants'. She was President of the Brandon United Methodist Women's Group three times and at the time of her death held the longevity record for membership in the church.

Lura **McKinley** and Charles Arthur **Shaffer** had the following children:

    6123   i.   Zella Arleen[12] **Shaffer**[443] born in Hartford, Warren Co., Iowa 21 September 1915 and died 12 November 1961 in Waterloo, Black Hawk Co., Iowa, at 46 years of age. Buried at Brandon. She married Fay P. **Thompson** 13 May 1945. Fay,[444] son of V. **Thompson** and Edna **Bickner**, was born 30 December 1914. Arleen was President of the United Methodist Women and a member of the Linden Methodist Church in Waterloo.

+   6124   ii.   Charles Russell **Shaffer** born 27 June 1920.
+   6125   iii.   Gail Carlysle **Shaffer** born 2 August 1930.

5240. **Edward Torrence**[11] **McKinley** (William Henry[10], Angeline[9] **Whipple**, Enoch[8], Nehemiah[7], Benjamin[6], Francis[5], Jonathan[4], Joseph[3], Matthew[2], Matthew[1])[445] was born in Cedar Township, Benton Co., Iowa 8 May 1892 and died 31 May 1967 in Vinton, Benton Co., Iowa, at 75 years of age. He married **Sarah Louise Peck** in Brandon, Buchanan Co. Iowa, 8 April 1914. Sarah,[446] daughter of Theodore **Peck** and Katie M. **Albert**, was born in Brandon 28 August 1895 and died 7 June 1975 in Vinton, at 79 years of age. She was buried at Brandon.

Edward Torrence **McKinley** and Sarah Louise **Peck** had the following children:

+   6126   i.   Donald Everett[12] **McKinley** born 30 December 1914.
+   6127   ii.   Marjorie Bernice **McKinley** born 26 December 1916.
+   6128   iii.   Tracy Eugene **McKinley** born 23 July 1918.
+   6129   iv.   Robert Cecil **McKinley** born 22 December 1919.
+   6130   v.   Ila Mae **McKinley** born 4 July 1922.

5241. **Merton Wallace**[11] **McKinley** (William Henry[10], Angeline[9] **Whipple**, Enoch[8], Nehemiah[7], Benjamin[6], Francis[5], Jonathan[4], Joseph[3], Matthew[2], Matthew[1])[447] was born in Cedar Township, Benton Co., Iowa 13 May 1895 and died 21 February 1964 in Cedar Rapids, Linn Co., Iowa, at 68 years of age. He married twice. (1) **Marian Lucille Hoffman** in Benton Co. 10 June 1925. Marian,[448] daughter of Fred **Hoffman** and Delilah **Goings**, was born in Grant Township., Linn Co., Iowa 27 May 1898 and died 6 February 1979 in Olewein, Fayette Co., Iowa, at 80 years of age. Both are buried in Vinton's Maplewood Cemetery. They were were divorced in Iowa, abt 1940. (2) **Leota Lodge Woodford** in Iowa 13 May 1948. She died 26 November 1987 in Cedar Rapids.[449] Merton attended Cornell College in Mt. Vernon, Linn Co., Iowa and was ordained a Methodist Minister in 1925. He was a Pastor for about 15 years in several northeastern Iowa communities. He began a new career in social work in 1946 and served as the Social Welfare Director for Benton, Union, and Freemont counties, all in Iowa, until his retirement in 1960.

Merton Wallace **McKinley** and Marian Lucille **Hoffman** had the following children:
+ 6131 i.   Belva Jean[12] **McKinley** born 4 December 1929.
+ 6132 ii. Evelyn Lee **McKinley** born 2 January 1932.

5242. **Elizabeth**[11] **McKinley** (William Henry[10], Angeline[9] **Whipple**, Enoch[8], Nehemiah[7], Benjamin[6], Francis[5], Jonathan[4], Joseph[3], Matthew[2], Matthew[1])[450] was born in Cedar Township, Benton Co., Iowa 1 September 1897 and died 19 December 1979 in Vinton, Benton Co., Iowa, at 82 years of age. She is buried in Evergreen Cemetery. She married three times. (1) **Carl Clarence Wood** in Vinton 7 August 1917. Carl,[451] son of Jesse H. **Wood** and Ida **Baker**, was born in De Witt, Saline Co., Nebr. 10 October 1893 and died 2 July 1936 in Vinton, at 42 years of age. Carl and his cousin Vern Wood were in the auto repair business in Brandon, Buchanon Co., Iowa until his marriage to Lizzy when he began farming north of town. The family moved to his grandparent's farm (Nicholas and Jane Wood) north of the Prairie Creek church in 1924 where he farmed until March 1930 when they moved to a farm four miles southeast of Vinton. He broke a leg in a haying accident and died of gangrene a week later. (2) **George Tyler** in Emmetsburg, Palo Alto Co., Iowa, 27 July 1940. He died 17 November 1952 in Vinton.[452] (3) **Henry Hinz** in Vinton 11 July 1953. He died there 15 November 1959.[453]

Libby had three stillborn children between 1918-22. No birth certificates were issued. Following Carl's death, Libby moved with Doris, 13, Mardene, 11, and Jack, 7, to Vinton where she was employed in the laundry at the State School for the Blind. Her initial wage was $37.50 monthly for a seven-day work week. She got every seventh Sunday off. She was a member of Vinton's Wesley Methodist Church. Her second husband George was a widower whose first wife died in childbirth. Her third husband Henry was also a widower. Libby outlived her third husband by 20 years and died of a heart attack.

Elizabeth **McKinley** and Carl Clarence **Wood** had the following children:
+   6133   i.   Doris Eileen[12] **Wood** born 26 February 1923.
+   6134   ii.   Mardene Dot **Wood** born 16 September 1924.
+   6135   iii.   Jack Edward **Wood** born 22 February 1929.

5253. **Eliza May**[11] **Scott** (Frances A.[10] **Gardner**, Eliza Roxana[9] **Whipple**, Enoch[8], Nehemiah[7], Benjamin[6], Francis[5], Jonathan[4], Joseph[3], Matthew[2], Matthew[1])[454] birth date unknown, married **Franklin P. Brown** in Benton Co., Iowa 14 February 1901. He was the son of W. H. **Brown**. Prior to marriage, Eliza was a traveling agent for a Muscatine, Muscatine Co., Iowa tea and coffee firm. She and Franklin were married at the home of her brother Holland, Rev. Hector C. Leland of the Baptist Church, officiating. The newlyweds settled on a farm in Monroe Township.[455]

Eliza May **Scott** and Franklin P. **Brown** had the following children:
   6136   i.   Clifford[12] **Brown**.[456]
   6137   ii.   William **Brown**.[457]
   6138   iii.   Donald **Brown**.[458]
   6139   iv.   Annola **Brown**.[459]

5254. **Will**[11] **Scott** (Frances A.[10] **Gardner**, Eliza Roxana[9] **Whipple**, Enoch[8], Nehemiah[7], Benjamin[6], Francis[5], Jonathan[4], Joseph[3], Matthew[2], Matthew[1])[460] birth date unknown.

Will **Scott** had the following children:
   6140   i.   Raymond[12] **Scott**.[461]
   6141   ii.   Luella **Scott**.[462]

5256. **Hiram Harper**[11] **Scott** (Frances A.[10] **Gardner**, Eliza Roxana[9] **Whipple**, Enoch[8], Nehemiah[7], Benjamin[6], Francis[5], Jonathan[4], Joseph[3], Matthew[2], Matthew[1])[463] birth date unknown, married **Lola Belle Edwards** and died at age 72. Lola,[464] daughter of Albert Thornton **Edwards** and Martha Jane **Brewer**, was 103 when she died at the home of her daughter Gladys (Scott) **Fassett**. No vital statistics provided on either.

Hiram Harper **Scott** and Lola Belle **Edwards** had the following children:

    6142   i.   Ruth[12] **Scott**.[465] She was living in 1988
    6143   ii.   Archie **Scott**.[466]
    6144   iii.   Lester **Scott**.[467]
    6145   iv.   Gladys **Scott** married (__) **Fassett**.[468]
    6146   v.   Dortha **Scott**.[469]
    6147   vi.   Josephine **Scott**.[470] He was living in 1988
    6148   vii.   Robert **Scott**.[471] He was living in 1988.
    6149   viii.   Glenn **Scott**[472] He was living in 1988
    6150   ix.   Pauline **Scott**.[473] She was living in 1988

5265. Rev. Raymond Viles[11] **Kearns** (Dr. Archibald Jackson[10], Eliza Roxana[9] **Whipple**, Enoch[8], Nehemiah[7], Benjamin[6], Francis[5], Jonathan[4], Joseph[3], Matthew[2], Matthew[1])[474] was born in Loup City, Sherman Co., Nebr. 22 May 1889 and died 28 September 1972 in Denver, Denver Co., Colo., at 83 years of age.

He married **Marguerite Bradley Webster** in Bellevue, Sarpy Co., Nebr., 4 August 1914. Marguerite,[475] daughter of George H. **Webster** and Georgia Ann **Bradley**, was born in New Haven, New Haven Co., Conn. 23 November 1888 and died 26 February 1977 in Denver, at 88 years of age. The memorization of great literature and the Bible was an important part of Ray and his brother Arch's (see below) home schooling. After completing household chores they gained work experience with local craftsmen. They attended the eighth grade and high school in Loop City and were graduated from Bellevue College of Omaha, Douglas Co., and the McCormick Theological Seminary (Presbyterian) in Chicago, Cook Co., Ill. Ray was Pastor of Presbyterian churches in Pekin, Tazewell Co., Ill, Fremont, Dodge Co., Nebr., and Salina, Salina Co., Kans. He was Associate Secretary of the Division of Evangelism of the Presbyterian Church, USA, for a number of years before accepting his last call as Associate Pastor of the Montview Boulevard Presbyterian Church of Denver. He was awarded an honorary Doctor of Divinity degree from Nebraska's Hastings College.

Rev. Raymond Viles **Kearns** and Marguerite Bradley **Webster** had the following child:

  +   6151   i.   Rev. Raymond Viles[12] **Kearns** born 6 September 1915.

5266. Rev. Archibald Jackson[11] **Kearns** (Dr. Archibald Jackson[10], Eliza Roxana[9] **Whipple**, Enoch[8], Nehemiah[7], Benjamin[6], Francis[5], Jonathan[4], Joseph[3], Matthew[2], Matthew[1])[476] was born in Loup City, Sherman Co., Nebr. 11 February 1891 and died 13 March 1970 in Portland, Multnomah Co., Oreg., at 79 years of age. He married **Grace Gordon Searight** 17 July

1917. Grace,[477] daughter of Harry Augustus **Searight** and Cyndisa **Gordon**, was born 3 July 1892 and died 23 October 1977 in Pasadena, Los Angeles Co., Calif., at 85 years of age. Arch served as Pastor of Presbyterian churches in Howard, Elk Co., Kans.; Alliance, Box Butte Co., Tekemah, Burt Co., and Laurel, Cedar Co., Nebr.; Missiouri Valley, Harrison Co., Iowa; Rocky Ford, Otero Co., Colo.; and Estacada, Clackamas Co., Oreg. He was responsible for the rebuilding of the church in Missouri Valley after it was destroyed by fire at the beginning of the Great Depression. He later accepted administrative assignments for the Board of National Missions, Presbyterian Church, USA, establishing new congregations in South Dakota and Oregon. His last call was as Associate Pastor of Westminister Presbyterian Church of Portland from 1952 until his retirement in 1960. Following an extended trip to the Middle East—Lebanon, Syria, Jordan, and the West Bank, and Jerusalem—he presented numerous historical lectures in churches in the Portland area. Huron College, Beadle Co., South Dakota, honored him with a Doctor of Divinity Degree. Rev. Kearns and Grace are buried at Riverview Cemetery, Portland.

Rev. Archibald Jackson **Kearns** and Grace Gordon **Searight** had the following children:

- 6152 i. (Infant)[12] **Kearns**[478] born in Howard, Elk Co., Nebr. 2 July 1918 and died the day of birth
- \+ 6153 ii. Lt. Col. Archibald Gordon **Kearns** born 16 August 1919.
- \+ 6154 iii. Rev. Paul Searight **Kearns** born 2 August 1921.
- \+ 6155 iv. Rev. Robert Harry **Kearns** born 27 December 1923.
- \+ 6156 v. Donald Raymond **Kearns** Ph.D. born 27 June 1930.

5270. **Milo Robert**[11] **Whipple** (William Perry[10], Cyrenius Thomas[9], Enoch[8], Nehemiah[7], Benjamin[6], Francis[5], Jonathan[4], Joseph[3], Matthew[2], Matthew[1])[479] was born in Benton Co., Iowa 13 March 1884 and died 24 July 1935 in Cedar Rapids, Linn Co., Iowa, at 51 years of age. He married **Lois Jeanette Fry** in Van Horn, Benton Co., Iowa 20 November 1906.[480] Jeanette, daughter of U.S. **Fry** and Clara **Dammon**, was born in Van Horn 31 October 1884 and died 10 November 1971 in Cedar Rapids, at 87 years of age. Both are buried at Cedar Memorial Cemetery, Cedar Rapids. Jeanette entered the millinery business in March 1903 when she purchased the business of Jones and Dexter in Vinton, Benton Co., Iowa. She upgraded the merchandise with buying trips to Chicago, Ill. and moved the business to the Black Building three doors west of the People's Savings Bank.[481]

Obituary: Jeanette Fry Whipple, Methwick Manor, widow of Milo R. Whipple, died Wednesday (10 Nov. 1971) following a short illness. A

Marriage License and Certificate of Marriage for Milo A. Whipple and Lois Jeanette Fry dated 17 and 22 November 1906 at Vinton, Iowa

Cedar Rapids resident for 60 years, she had been housemother for the Phi Gamma Delta Fraternity at the U. of Iowa, Iowa City, Johnson Co., Iowa. Mrs. Whipple was a member of the First Presbyterian Church, the Woman's Chapel Society and the Cedar Rapids Woman's Club. Surviving are a daughter, Mrs. Joseph Buss, and a son, William P. Whipple, both of Cedar Rapids; four grandchildren, five great grand children; and two sisters, Nelda Echternacht, Estherville, Emmett Co., Iowa and Bertha Acherman, Cedar Rapids. Services: Turner Chapel East. Burial: Cedar Memorial Cemetery.[482]

    Milo was graduated from Vinton High School in June 1902 and gave an oration on "The Vinton Public Library" on class day exercises. He was a guard on the basketball team, in the cast of the Thanksgiving play, "Tante's Thanksgiving," and in the Senior Class play, a farce, "The Heavenly Twins." He played the part of Vaughn in the play "School" presented at the Watson Opera House June 5th and 6th 1901. He attended Iowa College at Grinnell, Poweshkiek Co., and in January 1904 moved to Des Moines, Polk Co., Iowa where he was Clerk of the Senate Insurance Committee chaired by his father. He spent a month in the fall of 1905 in Oklahoma Indian Territory visiting his cousin Clifford Shortess. He was affiliated with the Albert & Whipple Real Estate Agency in Vinton in

{ G 898 }

1907 and in October 1908 joined the North British Mercantile Fire Insurance Co. as a Special Agent. His assigned territory was northwestern Iowa requiring him to travel frequently. He was a member of the Board of Directors of the Vinton schools in 1910. He remained in the insurance profession until his death.

Obituary:

WAS ONE OF FOREMOST INSURANCE MEN IN STATE

Milo R. Whipple, 319 Linden Terrace S.E., one of Iowa's foremost insurance men died at St. Luke's Hospital at 7 a.m. Wednesday (July, 24 1935). He had suffered a heart attack Saturday evening, the night before he was to have left for a vacation trip in northern Minnesota. Mr. Whipple was 51 years old, having been born at Vinton, March 13, 1884. He attended Grinnell College and returned to Vinton to establish a General Insurance Agency. He remained there several years, coming to Cedar Rapids in 1912. Mr. Whipple became associated with W.K. Wisner in a general agency here and several years later established his own agency.

He rapidly assumed a position of leadership in his field and was active in the business and civic life of the community. He was a member of the Chamber of Commerce and prominent in the various undertakings of that organization. During the World War (I) he was a Co-director of Red Cross in Linn county. Mr. Whipple had served as President of state and local insurance men's organizations. He was a Mason, a member of the Elks Club, of which he was Chairman of the Board of Trustees, and of the First Presbyterian Church. He is survived by his widow, the former Jeanette Fry of Van Horne, whom he married on Nov. 20, 1906; two children, William Perry and Dorothy; his stepmother, Mrs. W.P. Whipple of Vinton; a half-sister, Mrs. Louis P. Tobin of Vinton, and an aunt, Mrs. Cora Kellogg of Vinton. Mr. Whipple's father was W.P. Whipple who was a prominent Vinton attorney and State Senator.

MANY ATTEND RITES FOR MILO WHIPPLE

In a setting made beautiful by the floral tributes of his many friends, funeral services for Milo R. Whipple, prominent insurance man, were held Friday afternoon at Turner's Chapel. Attending the services in a body were Mr. Whipple's friends and associates in the fire underwriters organization here and members of the Elks Club. Other attending the services filled the chapel to capacity, many being seated on the lawn outside where loudspeakers were installed.[483] The 1910 federal census for Vinton listed Milo R., age 26, married 3 years to Jeanette F., age 26, living at 809 Iowa St. They then had no children. He was a fire insurance agent. They owned their home which was mortgaged. Jeanette was born in Iowa, her father in Pennsylvania and her mother in Germany.

Milo Robert **Whipple** and Lois Jeanette **Fry** had the following children:
+ 6157   i.   William Perry[12] **Whipple** born 1 November 1913.
  6158   ii. Dorothy Louise **Whipple**[484] born in Cedar Rapids 18 July 1916 and married Joseph **Buss.** They had three children: Thomas, born in Cedar Rapids 25 August 1939 and died abt 1957; James Loren born in Cedar Rapids 11 February 1942; and Janet born in Cedar Rapids in July 1943 and married (__) **Metolak.**

5272. **Virginia K.**[11] **Whipple** (William Perry[10], Cyrenius Thomas[9], Enoch[8], Nehemiah[7], Benjamin[6], Francis[5], Jonathan[4], Joseph[3], Matthew[2], Matthew[1])[485] was born in Vinton, Benton Co., Iowa 17 October 1902 and died there 25 October 1955, at 53 years of age. Buried at Evergreen Cemetery. She married twice. (1) **Louis P. Tobin**, an attorney in Vinton. (2) **John Casey**.

Virginia K. **Whipple** and Louis P. **Tobin** had the following children:
  6159   i.   Janet[12] **Tobin** born in Vinton and married Carl J. **Goetz.**[486]
+ 6160   ii. Mary Virginia **Tobin** born 11 November 1928.

5275. **Maude Maree**[11] **Whipple** (Milo Enoch[10], Cyrenius Thomas[9], Enoch[8], Nehemiah[7], Benjamin[6], Francis[5], Jonathan[4], Joseph[3], Matthew[2], Matthew[1])[487] was born in Benton Co., Iowa 6 September 1885[488] and died of uremia and heart disease 15 October 1968 in Allegan, Allegan Co., Mich., at 83 years of age.[489] She died at the Allegan Health Center and was buried in Oakwood Cemetery.[490] She married twice. (1) **Charles Ellsworth Frederick** who was born in Johnson City, Johnson Co., Iowa 4 May 1880. Charles,[491] son of Stephen **Frederick** and Almeda **McMaden**, died 8 June 1917 in Iowa City, Johnson Co., Iowa, at 37 years of age. He was a carpenter and died from a fall off a roof. He was buried in Vinton, Benton Co., Iowa. (2) **Thomas Jefferson Andrus Jr.** in Groton, Caledonia Co., Vt. 19 November 1919. Thomas,[492] son of Thomas Jefferson **Andrus** and Alice L. **Wenn**, was born in Humbird, Clark Co., Wisc. 15 July 1884 and died 6 April 1972 in Allegan, at 87 years of age. After Charles died, Maude moved with her family to Glendive, Dawson Co., Mont. to be near her parents where she met her second husband Thomas. When her parents moved to Groton about 1921 Maude and her family moved with them. Thomas followed later and he and Maude were married in Groton. Maude and Thomas and their family later moved to Michigan and she was living in Dunningville, Allegan Co., Mich. at the time of her father's death in 1934.

Maude Maree **Whipple** and Charles Ellsworth **Frederick** had the following children:

    6161   i.   Maree Louella[12] **Frederick**[493] was born in Seattle, King Co., Wash. 30 January 1909 and died 29 January 1975 in Allegan, at 65 years of age. She married Carl William **Thomas** in Allegan 22 May 1929.

+ 6162   ii.   Charles Stephan **Frederick** born 21 September 1910.

    6163 iii.   Laura Gertrude **Frederick**[494] born in Lincoln, Lancaster Co., Nebr. 2 December 1911 and died 28 January 1912 at less than 2 months of age.

    6164 iv.   Leva Lucille **Frederick**[495] born in Onawa, Monona Co., Iowa 25 December 1914 and died 28 February 1989 in Allegan, at 74 years of age. Buried at Cheshire Township., Allegan Co. She married Earl M. **Thomas** in Dennard, Van Buren Co., Ark. 15 July 1933.

    6165 v.   Charlotte Grace **Frederick**[496] born in Vinton, 9 November 1916 and died 10 June 1983 at 66 years of age. She married Edward **Rumsey** 18 March 1935.

Maude Maree **Whipple** and Thomas Jefferson **Andrus** Jr. had the following children:

    6166 vi.   Alice Louise **Andrus**[497] born in Groton 20 October 1920 and married Kenneth **Meiser** 23 March 1978.

    6167 vii.   Florence Irene **Andrus**[498] born in Groton 16 April 1922 and married John **Krcatovich** 25 October 1952.

    6168 viii.   Elgie Jeanette **Andrus**[499] born in Groton 21 April 1924 and married John **Gerry** 8 December 1951.

    6169 ix.   Thomas Jefferson **Andrus** II[500] born in Allegan 15 April 1927 and married Jacqueline **Frost** 5 September 1947.

+ 6170 x.   James Dudley **Andrus** born 5 August 1929.

5277. **Carl Thornton**[11] **Whipple** (Selmon Thomas[10], Cyrenius Thomas[9], Enoch[8], Nehemiah[7], Benjamin[6], Francis[5], Jonathan[4], Joseph[3], Matthew[2], Matthew[1])[501] was born in Benton Co., Iowa 9 March 1886 and died there 20 July 1951, at 65 years of age. He married **Sarah Esther Mossman** in Vinton, Benton Co., Iowa 27 March 1907.[502] Esther,[503] daughter of B. F. **Mossman**, was born in Benton Co. in 1886 and died there 7 December 1962, at 76 years of age. Both are buried at Evergreen Cemetery, Vinton. Carl and Esther were married at 4:30 p.m. at the home of the bride's mother. Rev. Clinton officiated. The groom's parents hosted a reception the following evening with about 55 in attendance. Esther was a school teacher. The couple began housekeeping on the Butler farm six miles northwest of Vinton.[504] The 1910 federal census for Cedar township, Benton Co., Iowa listed Carl, age 24, married for 3 years to Esther S. Mossman, age 28. Their children were Frank, 2, and George T., 1 month. He was working a rented farm.

Carl Thornton **Whipple** and Sarah Esther **Mossman** had the following children born in Benton County:

    6171   i.   Wayne[12] **Whipple**[505] died in his teens from a broken back caused by an auto accident. He is buried at Evergreen Cemetery.

    6172   ii.   Ethol **Whipple**[506] He married three times. (1) Gladys **Dickson**. (2) Ruth (__). No details provided on his third marriage. It is believed he had four children with Ruth and one with his third wife. He died in California.

+   6173   iii.   Virginia **Whipple**.
+   6174   iv.   Frank **Whipple** in 1908.
+   6175   v.   George **Whipple** 30 March 1910.

5278. **Callie Catherine**[11] **Whipple** (Selmon Thomas[10], Cyrenius Thomas[9], Enoch[8], Nehemiah[7], Benjamin[6], Francis[5], Jonathan[4], Joseph[3], Matthew[2], Matthew[1])[507] was born in Benton Co., Iowa 27 April 1887 and died 13 January 1981 at 93 years of age. She married **Howard Lewis Catlin** in Vinton, Benton Co., Iowa 8 July 1908.[508] The 8 p.m. wedding took place at the home of the bride's parent. Callie was a school teacher.[509] Howard,[510] son of James Edwin **Catlin** and Melissa Ann **Hughey,** was born in Van Horn, Benton Co., Iowa 29 August 1884 and died 20 December 1958 in Independence, Buchanan Co., Iowa, at 74 years of age. He farmed near Vinton, operated two "rent" farms near Jesup, Buchanan Co., Iowa and eventually purchased and worked his own farm southeast of Jesup. He died of a stroke and is buried at the Garden of Memories Cemetery in Waterloo, Black Hawk Co., Iowa.

After Howard's death Callie moved to Jesup and later to Independence. She passed on stories told her about her Whipple grandparents. She said her great grandfather Enoch was 6' tall, weighed 200 pounds and "could jump over anything he could stand under." His wife Catharine Shaw was a tiny Scotchwoman who could stand under her husband's outstretched arm. She was a first cousin of Commodore Oliver H. Perry and heard the fighting at the battle of Lake Erie from her home in New York state. Grandpa Cyrenius was not a tall man but was very strong. He could load a 280 pound barrel of salt in a wagon by himself. Great grandpa William Cline liked his daughter-in-law's cooking, Anna Cleland (Edwards) Whipple, and would frequently walk to the farm and stay for dinner. "We children always hated to see him come," Callie said "because if we didn't do things to please him, he would hook us around the neck with his cane."

Callie said when she was about 12, she helped grandma Whipple (Nancy Jane) get dinner and supper when grandpa had extra hired help. After the evening dishes were done, grandma paid me a dollar — as much as a working man earned in a day. Before I left grandpa asked if grandma had paid me and I proudly showed him my dollar. "That isn't enough for a girl who has worked as hard as you have," he said and exchanged the dollar for a five dollar bill, equal to a week's wage for the men helpers.

Callie Catherine **Whipple** and Howard Lewis **Catlin** had the following children born in Benton County:

      6176   i.   (Daughter)[12] **Catlin**[511] in January 1909 stillborn.

      6177   ii. Howard Lewis **Catlin** Jr.[512] 22 October 1910 and died 2 days later. Buried at Vinton's Maplewood Cemetery.

+   6178   iii. Anna Catherine **Catlin** 24 October 1913.

+   6179   iv. Elsie Laurel **Catlin** 8 July 1916.

+   6180   v. Ruby Aileen **Catlin** 30 June 1920.

5280. **William Walter**[11] **Whipple** (Selmon Thomas[10], Cyrenius Thomas[9], Enoch[8], Nehemiah[7], Benjamin[6], Francis[5], Jonathan[4], Joseph[3], Matthew[2], Matthew[1])[513] was born in Benton Co., Iowa 23 December 1889 and died 12 February 1972 in Vinton, Benton Co., Iowa, at 82 years of age. He married **Lola Ruth Grayson** in Vinton 11 January 1911. She was born 25 September 1891 and died 26 October 1975 in Vinton, at 84 years of age.[514] Both are buried in Vinton's Maplewood Cemetery. Bill farmed south of Vinton and then owned and operated a billiard parlor in town. He was a City Street Commissioner and retired from the Rock Island Railroad.

William Walter **Whipple** and Lola Ruth **Grayson** had the following children born in Benton County:

+   6181   i.   Anna Jeanette[12] **Whipple** 1 March 1913.

      6182   ii. Lucille Elvira **Whipple**[515] 14 June 1914 and died 8 June 2002 in Cedar Rapids, Linn Co., Iowa, at 87 years of age.[516] She married Russell **Schroeder** in Canton, Lincoln Co., S. Dak., 14 November 1964. Obituary: Lucille E. "Peg" Whipple Schroeder, 86, of Cedar Rapids, died Sat. June 8, 2002, in Mercy Hallmar Residential Care after a short illness. Graveside services were held Friday 21 June at Mount Calvary Cemetery. Cedar Memorial Funeral Home was in charge of arrangements. Lucille, born June

14 in Vinton. was a 1933 graudate of Vinton High School, was the daughter of William W. and Lola Grayson Whipple. She married Russell Schroeder on Nov. 14, 1964 in Canton, S.D. Lucille worked at the Elks Club in Cedar Rapids and began her career at Link-Belt Speeder Co. of Cedar Rapids in 1947 and worked there until her retirement. She enjoyed bowling, cooking, canning from her garden, sewing, and all type of needle work. Lucille also enjoyed fishing and card games with her husband, parents, and family. She was preceded in death by her parents; her husband Russell, in 1995; sisters, Marjorie Whipple and A. Jeanette Kalvig and her husband Leander (Lee); brother William (Bill) C. Whipple and his wife Frances; and a niece Janet L. Kalvig.[517]

  6183 iii. Marjorie **Whipple**[518] in 1918 and died of pneumonia the year of birth.

+ 6184 iv. William Clarence **Whipple** 9 October 1919.

5282. **Harrison Lincoln**[11] **Whipple** (Selmon Thomas[10], Cyrenius Thomas[9], Enoch[8], Nehemiah[7], Benjamin[6], Francis[5], Jonathan[4], Joseph[3], Matthew[2], Matthew[1])[519] was born in Benton Co., Iowa 21 January 1893 and died 1 November 1957 in Vinton, Benton Co., Iowa, at 64 years of age. He married twice. (1) **Clara Arvilla Rundall** 15 December 1915. (2) **Clara M. Ellerman** in Vinton 22 December 1922. She was born in Davenport, Scott Co., Iowa 14 May 1894 and died 18 December 1974 in Vinton, at 80 years of age. Buried at Maplewood Cemetery.[520] She married (2) **(__) Shipley**. (3) **(__) Stieger**. She had sons Marvin and Roy with Mr. Stieger. Harrison farmed in his younger years before joining the Benton Couty Highway Maintenance Department. He was Shop Foreman at the time of his retirement. He is buried at Maplewood Cemetery.

Harrison Lincoln **Whipple** and Clara M. **Ellerman** had the following child:
+ 6185 i. Richard Ellerman[12] **Whipple** born 4 July 1928.

5283. **Edward Clelland**[11] **Whipple** (Selmon Thomas[10], Cyrenius Thomas[9], Enoch[8], Nehemiah[7], Benjamin[6], Francis[5], Jonathan[4], Joseph[3], Matthew[2], Matthew[1])[521] was born in Benton Co., Iowa 5 December 1894 and died 19 October 1968 in Fairbank, Buchanan Co., Iowa, at 73 years of age. He married **Frances Edna Wakefield** in Vinton, Benton Co. 17 February 1915. Frances,[522] daughter of William Lewis **Wakefield** and Eliza Ann **Van Dyke**, was born in Vinton 29 October 1896 and died 10 July 1993 in Cedar Falls, Black Hawk Co., Iowa, at 96 years of age. The youngest of seven children, she was educated in the Vinton schools and was active in the Elk Run #5 School District PTA. She moved to Waterloo, Black Hawk Co., Iowa after her husband's death where she was active in the Kimball Avenue United Methodist Church and was a volunteer at Schoitz Hospital, Scattergood Circle of Kings Daughters, and Esther Circle of her church. She was a resident of the Western Home in Cedar Falls (1989-93.)

Ed ran a dairy in Waterloo in his early years then farmed for many years until his death caused by a tractor accident near Fairbank, Buchanan Co., Iowa. He was combining soybeans on the day of his death. When he didn't return home his wife went to look for him and found him pinned between the tipped-over tractor and the combine. Death was attributed to a head concussion caused by striking his head on the back of the combine. His memorial service was at the Chapel of Memories West at Waterloo. Funeral services were at the Dunkerton, Black Hawk Co., Iowa United Methodist Church. Both Ed and Frances are buried in the Garden of Memories Cemetery in Waterloo.

Edward Clelland **Whipple** and Frances Edna **Wakefield** had the following children:
+ 6186 i. Jean Earlene[12] **Whipple** born 14 May 1925.
+ 6187 ii. Jack Clelland **Whipple** born 9 August 1927.

5284. **Anna Bessie**[11] **Whipple** (Selmon Thomas[10], Cyrenius Thomas[9], Enoch[8], Nehemiah[7], Benjamin[6], Francis[5], Jonathan[4], Joseph[3], Matthew[2], Matthew[1])[523] was born in Benton Co., Iowa 31 July 1896 and died 21 January 1983 in Carbondale, Jackson Co., Ill., at 86 years of age. She married **Guy Laird Britt** in Vinton, Benton Co., Iowa, 16 November 1916. He was born in Coggon, Linn Co., Iowa 27 April 1895 and died 17 March 1976 in Benton Co., at 80 years of age.[524] Both are buried in Vinton's Evergreen Cemetery. Guy was a farmhand working for Howard Catlin in his youth. He eventually was employed by the Benton County Maintenance Department and rose to Assistant County Engineer.

Anna Bessie **Whipple** and Guy Laird **Britt** had the following children:
6188 i. Bonnie Mae[12] **Britt**[525] born in Vinton 13 January 1918 and married Clarence **Bilderback** in Richmond Heights, Saint Louis Co., Mo. 19 July 1953. He was born in Jackson Co., Ill. 19 October 1912 and died 20 October 1988 in Missouri, at 76 years of age.[526] Buried in Evergreen Cemetery, Ava, Jackson Co., Ill.
+ 6189 ii. Robert Clarence **Britt** born 6 October 1919.

+ 6190 iii. Patricia Ann **Britt** born 13 October 1927.
+ 6191 iv. Donald Lewis **Britt** born 21 May 1929.

5285. **Eugene Harold**[11] **Whipple** (Selmon Thomas[10], Cyrenius Thomas[9], Enoch[8], Nehemiah[7], Benjamin[6], Francis[5], Jonathan[4], Joseph[3], Matthew[2], Matthew[1])[527] was born in Benton Co., Iowa 24 February 1901 and died 23 April 1961 in Arcata, Humboldt Co., Calif., at 60 years of age. He married **Marie Edna Walter** in Vinton, Benton Co., Iowa 8 March 1923. She was born 8 March 1905 and died 10 February 1984 in Orovada, Humboldt Co., Nev., at 78 years of age.[528] Gene was a farmhand in his youth then learned the barber trade and was a barber in Vinton until moving to Walla Walla, Walla Walla Co., Wash. and later to Arcata, where he worked in a lumber mill. After his death, Marie moved to Orovada and after her death, Gene's body was moved from Arcata and reinterred with Marie at Orovada.

Eugene Harold **Whipple** and Marie Edna **Walter** had the following children:
+ 6192 i. George Walter[12] **Whipple** born 23 February 1924.
+ 6193 ii. Jacquelyn Ann **Whipple** born 31 January 1928.
+ 6194 iii. Rosemary **Whipple** born 5 May 1936.
+ 6195 iv. Carolyn Marie **Whipple** born 3 August 1945.

5286. **Martha Josephine Esther**[11] **Whipple** (Selmon Thomas[10], Cyrenius Thomas[9], Enoch[8], Nehemiah[7], Benjamin[6], Francis[5], Jonathan[4], Joseph[3], Matthew[2], Matthew[1])[529] was born in Benton Co., Iowa 12 February 1903 and died 11 December 2002 in Des Moines, King Co., Wash., at 99 years of age. She married **James Glenn Gordon** in Vinton, Benton Co., Iowa 24 December 1925. Glenn,[530] son of Louis Phillip **Gordon** and Mabel Eva Lena **Ridenour**, was born in Garrison, Benton Co., Iowa 12 December 1903 and died 7 February 1990 in Seattle, King Co., Wash., at 86 years of age.

In July of 1997 when she was 94, Martha wrote her granddaughter Jennifer Greer of Tucson, Pima Co., Ariz. of her remembrances of Christmas when she was a little girl. She wrote of the anticipation and preparations for Santa's arrival. The family lived on a farm in a large house a mile from Vinton and her father had planted a double row of spruce trees on the west side of their lower orchard. By the time she was old enough to remember, they had grown to Christmas tree size. A tree was cut the morning before Christmas and placed beside the fireplace and decorated with strung popcorn, some ornaments and real candles in little "pinch-on" holders. The candles were lit just before the children's bedtime and they sang Jingle Bells and other Christmas songs and hymns while father kept his eyes on the burning candles. There were 13 children so there wasn't

{ G 906 }

room for everyone to hang a stocking on the mantle so each child had a box to place on a chair. Cookies and milk were left for Santa before they went to bed. In the morning there was a special gift for each child, candy, mixed unshelled nuts, and an orange and a banana, the only time of the year they ever had this fruit. Martha remembers a gift of a little China tea set with a Christmas design that she kept for years.

She remembered being assigned chores at an early age, the first one was to provide kindling for "mama's" cook stove. She and brother Gene were jointly responsible for this chore. When they were older the two of them were responsible for "ranking" the firewood cut by the older boys. Ranking meant to stack it neatly by size in the basement fuel room. All the kids shared in the housework and were organized in pairs — two to set the table, two to remove the dirty dishes, two to wash and dry them, etc. They had a croquet court in the yard, long rope swings, and horses to ride. Martha remembers the day "Papa" came home with the first Edison phonograph and later a piano to replace an old-fashioned organ. She remembers celebrations on the 4th of July and other holidays. Papa always had fireworks on the 4th and Mama made a huge freezer of ice cream. The neighbors always came for the evening fireworks display. She remembers when the threshing bees came to their farm. It was a day of excitement for kids and of hard work for adults, both men and women. The big steam engine would turn into their lane followed by a water wagon and neighbors with hay racks — like a parade to the kids. It was set up in the feeding pasture about halfway between the barn and the field. The neighbors would go into the fields with their hay racks and collect the shocked grain and bring it to the thresher which would separate the grain from the straw. The water wagon was adjacent to the thresher's engine to provide the steam for the power to run the machine. Two wagons with side boards caught the grain and a blower blew the straw into stacks. While the men were involved in this work, the women were preparing food for the crew. Wash stands, combs, brushes, mirrors, and whisk brushes were set up outside so the men could clean up before entering the dining room to eat.

Her father died when she was nine and she remembers being called to his bedside to repeat the Lord's Prayer with him. He died a short time later.

Martha lived at the Wesley Retirement Home in Des Moines, Wash. for many years and died in her sleep at the Wesley Convalesant Home two months and a day before her 100th birthday.

Martha Josephine Esther **Whipple** and James Glenn **Gordon** had the following children:
+   6196   i.   Colleen Lou^{12} **Gordon** born 24 February 1929.
+   6197   ii.   Jo Anne **Gordon** born 27 March 1933.

5287. **Clara Adalene**[11] **Whipple** (Selmon Thomas[10], Cyrenius Thomas[9], Enoch[8], Nehemiah[7], Benjamin[6], Francis[5], Jonathan[4], Joseph[3], Matthew[2], Matthew[1])[531] was born in Benton Co., Iowa 7 December 1906 and died 11 May 1996 in Vinton, Benton Co., Iowa, at 89 years of age.[532] She married **Lyle Thomas Gallaher** in the Little Brown Church in Nashua, Chickasaw Co., Iowa, 12 June 1929. Lyle,[533] son of J. Albert **Gallaher** and Katharine Adelia **Ball**, was born in Jefferson, Greene Co., Iowa 2 October 1907 and died 18 March 2002 in Muscatine, Muscatine Co., Iowa, at 94 years of age. His entire working life (44.5 years) was with the Vinton post office. He retired in 1973 as Assistant Postmaster and moved to Bickford Cottage, Muscatine after Clara's death. Lyle died following a brief illness. Services were Thursday March 21 March at Phillips Funeral Home Chapel, Vinton by the Rev. Rose Blank. Both are buried in Evergreen Cemetery. He was survived by sons Thomas L. of Muscatine and David L. and wife Kathy of Joice, Worth Co., Iowa; five grandchildren, two step grandchildren; five great-grandchildren; and four step-great-grandchildren.

Clara Adalene **Whipple** and Lyle Thomas **Gallaher** had the following children born in Vinton:
+ 6198   i.   Thomas Lee[12] **Gallaher** 25 March 1933.
+ 6199   ii. David Lyle **Gallaher** 25 May 1936.

5288. **Cyrenius Albert**[11] **Whipple** (Selmon Thomas[10], Cyrenius Thomas[9], Enoch[8], Nehemiah[7], Benjamin[6], Francis[5], Jonathan[4], Joseph[3], Matthew[2], Matthew[1])[534] was born in Benton Co., Iowa 20 May 1908 and died of a stroke 20 December 1950 in Traer, Tama Co., Iowa, at 42 years of age. Buried in Buckingham Cemetery. He married **Martha Marie Halupnik** in Clear Lake, Cerro Gordo Co., Iowa, 6 July 1938. Martha,[535] daughter of Louis William **Halupnik** and Blanche Marie **Sevcik**, was born in Traer 27 March 1915. Rene worked for the Dollar Steamship Line, traveled around the world, and spent some time in the Orient and Italy before returning to Traer where he owned and operated the Pleas-U Cafe. Later he was a route man for the Curtiss Candy Co, and then an auto salesman for Cavalier Motor Co. in Traer.

Cyrenius Albert **Whipple** and Martha Marie **Halupnik** had the following children:
+ 6200   i.   Judith Ann[12] **Whipple** born 31 March 1939.
+ 6201   ii. Robert Mark **Whipple** born 25 October 1948.

5289. **Nellie Jeanette**[11] **Whipple** (Selmon Thomas[10], Cyrenius Thomas[9], Enoch[8], Nehemiah[7], Benjamin[6], Francis[5], Jonathan[4], Joseph[3], Matthew[2],

Matthew[1])[536] was born in Benton Co., Iowa 20 January 1911 and died 2 June 1966 in Belmond, Wright Co., Iowa, at 55 years of age. She married **Donald Andrew Faris** in Washington, Washington Co., Iowa 1 April 1931. He was born in Keota, Keokuk Co., Iowa 8 October 1908 and died in May 1979 in Vinton, Benton Co., Iowa, at 70 years of age.[537] Buried in Section 18, Maplewood Cemetery. Nell's body was moved from Belmond to Maplewood Cemetery and buried next to Donald.

Don coached girls basketball at the following Iowa towns: Steamboat Rock, Wellsburg, Olin, Belmond, and Seymour. His team won the State Championship in 1947. He was Superintendent of Schools at Belmond at the time of his retirement. After Nell's death, Don was married two more times, divorcing his second wife (name not provided). His third wife was Juanita **Trinder.**

Nellie Jeanette **Whipple** and Donald Andrew **Faris** had the following children:
+ 6202 i. Donald Wayne[12] **Faris** born 10 January 1933.
+ 6203 ii. James Russell **Faris** born 17 October 1935.
+ 6204 iii. John Mark **Faris** born 5 September 1947.

5293. **Lucien Blaine**[11] **Whipple** (James Ezekiel[10], Lucien Ransom[9], Enoch[8], Nehemiah[7], Benjamin[6], Francis[5], Jonathan[4], Joseph[3], Matthew[2], Matthew[1])[538] was born in Eugene, Vermilion Co., Ind. 22 June 1883 and died 27 August 1954 in Dresden, Weakley Co., Tenn., at 71 years of age. His death certificate was altered by Court Order on September 22, 1954, File C-26755, to correct his birth year to be 1883, not 1885 as originally shown. He was initially buried in Tracy, Lyon County, Minn. and later re-interred in Evergreen Cemetery, Vinton, Benton Co., Iowa.

He married twice. (1) **Lillian Neva LeFebre** 18 December 1908. When they were married both were affiliated with a traveling theater company, Blaine as an actor and Lillian in the costume department. They were married by a Justice of the Peace at the courthouse in Beatty, Kans. Lillian,[539] daughter of Henry **LeFebre** and Helen Margarite **Ruhl**, was born in Chicago, Cook Co., Ill. 20 November 1888 and died 30 April 1941 in Cedar Rapids, Linn Co., Iowa, at 52 years of age. Buried at Oak Hill Cemetery. Blaine and Lillian were divorced March 16, 1926 in Cedar Rapids. She married (2) **Charles Harold Zastera**, a drug store owner in Cedar Rapids, in Vinton in July 1928. Lillian's father was a French-Canadian and she attended a convent school for part of her early education. After her parents divorced, her mother married **Gustav E. Kloss** and the family lived in Mexico for five years (most of her teen years) where her stepfather was an electricial engineeer for a large silver mine. Their community had one other American family and a large population of Chinese. Lillian taught English to the Chinese children.

Blaine married (2) **Pearl Julia Scott** in Albion, Boone Co., Nebr. 21 September 1927. Witnesses were Jack and Bonnie Maie Krall of Oshkosh, Wisc. Blaine's residence was Chicago, Cook Co., Ill., Pearl's was Minot, Ward Co., N. Dak. Pearl,[540] daughter of Benoni **Scott** and Ellen "Nellie" **Dolan**, was born in Hamel, Hennepin County, Minn. 29 August 1905 and died 1 April 1988 in Glencoe, McLeod Co., Minn., at 82 years of age.

Obituary: Pearl Julia (Scott) Whipple of Glencoe died April 1 at the Glencoe Area Health Center following a long illness. She was born Aug. 29, 1905 in Hamel, Minn., daughter of Benoni and Ellen (Dolan) Scott. She married Blaine Whipple in Albion, Neb. Sept. 21, 1927.

In her younger years, she was a beautician in Minot. Her husband worked for and published several newspapers in the Dakotas and Minnesota, including Tracy, Watertown, and Renville. After the death of her husband, she was office manager of weekly newspapers in LeMars, Plymouth Co., Iowa, and Marshall, Lyon Co., Minn. She lived in Appleton, Swift Co., Minn. for some years and worked in a department store there. She moved to Glencoe in 1983 to be near her daughter and son-in-law Nancy and Don Jasperson. She was a member of the First Congregational Church in Glencoe.

She is survived by her sons, Blaine (wife Ines) of Portland, Oreg., and Richard of Eagan; daughters, Patricia Drotzman of Yankton, S.Dak., Mary McPherson (husband Bill) of Littleton, Mass; brothers L.J. Scott (wife Irene) of Minneapolis, Bill (wife Ruth) of Kansas City, Mo., Arthur (wife Josephine) of Underwood, N.Dak., Gordon (wife Kay) of Underwood, Donald (wife Florence) of Underwood; and sisters Edwidge Bjorlie of Minot, N.Dak., Clara Gunderson (husband Gunder) of Turtle Lake, N.Dak., and Alice Johnson (husband Burnell) of Underwood.

She was preceded in death by her parents, her husband, daughter Nancy; brothers, John and Robert; and sister Margaret. Blaine and Pearl are buried in Lot 23, Block L, in the Evergreen Cemetery in Vinton, Iowa along with Blaine's parents James E. and Ellen (Thompson) Whipple.[541]

Lucien Blaine **Whipple** and Lillian Neva **LeFebre** had the following children:
- 6205   i.   Helen[12] **Whipple**[542] born prematurely at St. Lukes Hospital in Kansas City, Jackson Co., Mo. 20 August 1909 and died the day of birth. The medical attendant was Dr. H.F. Mather.
- +   6206   ii.   Ellen Elaine **Whipple** born 6 August 1910.
- +   6207   iii.   James Earl **Whipple** born 29 October 1911.

Lucien Blaine **Whipple** and Pearl Julia **Scott** had the following children:
- + 6208 iv. Patricia Ellen **Whipple** born 1 February 1929.
- + 6209 v. Robert Blaine **Whipple** born 22 February 1930.
- + 6210 vi. Nancy Jane **Whipple** born 5 January 1932.

6211 vii. Richard Earl **Whipple**[543] born in Underwood, McLean Co., N. Dak. 12 September 1933 at 10:45 p.m. at home. F.E. Anderson, M.D. attending physician. He was baptized in Underwood 11 November 1933 at St. Bonaventure Catholic Church. His uncle Arthur Scott was his godfather, Alice Stadick his godmother. Dick was graduated from Tracy, Lyon Co., Minn. High School in June 1951 and attended Mankato State Teachers College in Mankato, Blue Earth Co., Minn for a quarter before joining the U.S. Navy 20 February 1952. He served almost 12 years before his discharge at Charleston, Charleston Co., S.C. 29 November 1963, the Monday following Pres. John F. Kennedy's assassination. After recruit training at Great Lakes, Illinois, he attended the Hospital Corps School after which he was assigned duty

Dick, Blaine, and Ines Whipple at Dick's Minneapolis home in June 1971.

Brian Drotzman and Bob Steele at their Uncle Dick's Minneapolis home in 1971.

Dick, High School graduation. All photographs courtesy of Blaine Whipple.

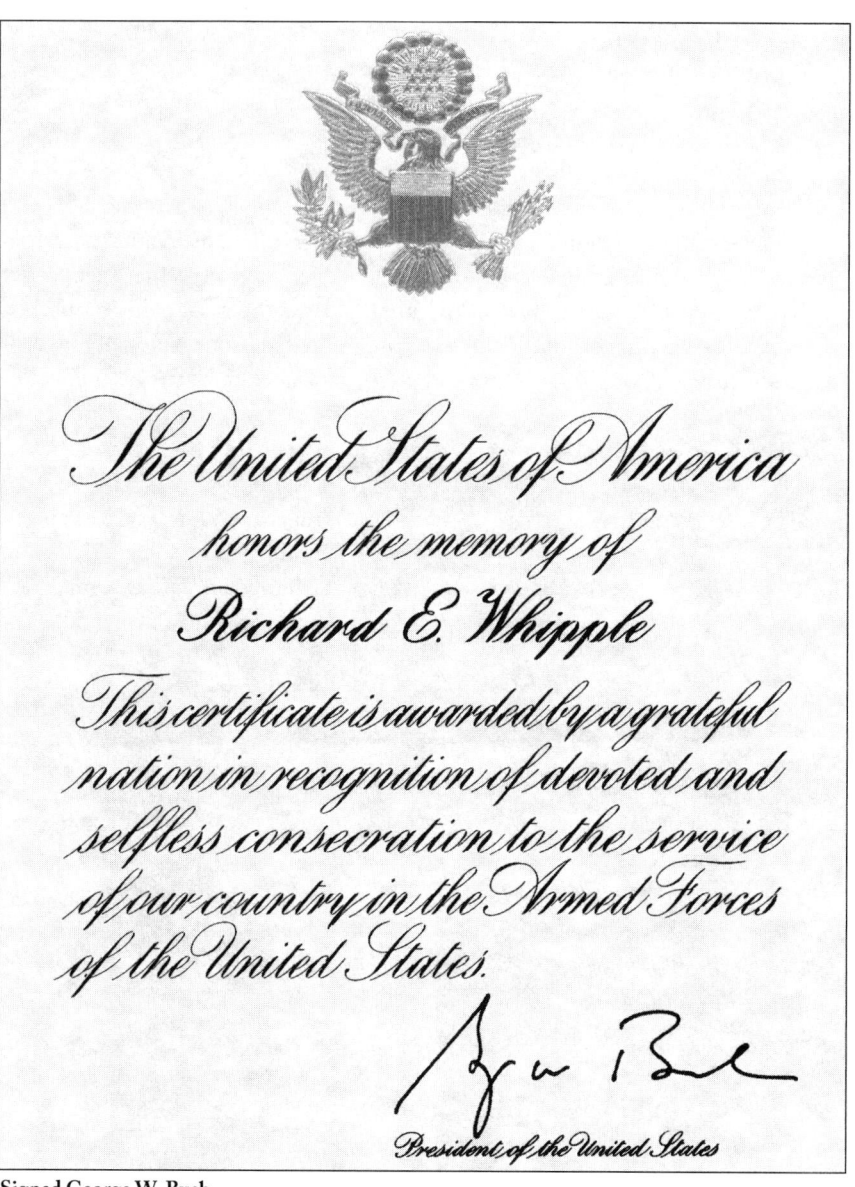

> The United States of America honors the memory of
>
> Richard E. Whipple
>
> This certificate is awarded by a grateful nation in recognition of devoted and selfless consecration to the service of our country in the Armed Forces of the United States.
>
> *President of the United States*

Signed George W. Bush.

with the Fleet Marine Corps at Camp Pendleton, San Diego Co., Calif. A tour of duty with the 3rd Battalion, 9th Marines 3rd Marine Division in Japan, was followed by duty at the Naval Medical Unit at Tripler Army Hospital, Honolulu, Oahu, Hawaii. His brother Blaine was stationed at the Barber's Point Naval Air Station on Oahu during part of this time and they returned to the States together to attend their father's funeral in the summer of 1954. From April 1958 to April 1960, Dick attended the Advanced Hospital Corps School in Portsmouth, Portsmouth City Area Co., Va. and the Basic Nuclear Power

School and Radiation Control & Health Physics School at New London, New London Co., Conn. after which he took Advanced Nuclear Power Training at Nuclear Power Training Unit at both Idaho Falls, Bonneville Co., Idaho and West Milton, Saratoga Co., N.Y. He served aboard the frigate USS Bainbridge (DLGN-25) from May 1962 to November 1963. During this period its home ports were Boston-Newport, R.I., New Jersey, Norfolk, Va., and Charleston, S.C. with duty in Spain, France, Italy, Greece, Lebanon, and Turkey. Following his discharge with the rank of Chief Hospital Corpsman, he enrolled at the U. of Minnesota (Minneapolis campus) graduating with a degree in Pharmacy in 1968. His first six years following graduation were with Walgreens at pharmacies at Edina, New Hope, and Minneapolis, all in Hennepin Co., Minn. He then spent six years with Daytons City Center Pharmacy in Minneapolis followed by 16 years at Campus Drugs in Stadium Village and Dinkytown adjacent to the U. of Minnesota campus in Minneapolis. He joined Synder Pharmacies in South Minneapolis in 1997 and retired in July 2004. He lived in Eagen, Dakota Co., a suburb of St. Paul, Ramsey Co. and died 18 May 2005 in a Minneapolis hospital. His ashes are buried in the Whipple lot, (Lot 23, Block 4) Evergreen Cemetery, Vinton, Iowa.

Dick, 15 August 2004.

Care deeply
Give freely
Think kindly
Act gently
And be at peace with the world...

This is the spirit of Dick.

September 12, 1933 - May 18, 2005

Dick Whipple. Photos courtesy of Michael J. Drotzman.

+ 6212 viii. Mary Ann **Whipple** born 8 December 1937.

5297. **Frank**[11] **Fultz** (Anna M.[10] **Whipple**, Lucien Ransom[9], Enoch[8], Nehemiah[7], Benjamin[6], Francis[5], Jonathan[4], Joseph[3], Matthew[2], Matthew[1])544 was born in Eugene, Vermilion Co., Ind. in 1882 and died there in 1957, at 75 years of age. Buried in Lot 22 in the Eugene Cemetery. He married **Maude Alle** in Eugene in 1907. She was born in 1882 and died in 1956 in Eugene, at 74 years of age.545 Frank was the first Rural Free

Delivery Carrier in Cayuga, Vermilion Co., Ind. when the route was established in 1903. The route had 112 houses in its 20 mile radius. He resigned in 1908.[546]

Frank **Fultz** and Maude **Alle** had the following child:
+   6213   i.   Donna[12] **Fultz**.

5300. **Suzie**[11] **Fultz** (Anna M.[10] **Whipple**, Lucien Ransom[9], Enoch[8], Nehemiah[7], Benjamin[6], Francis[5], Jonathan[4], Joseph[3], Matthew[2], Matthew[1])[547] was born, probably in Eugene, Vermilion County, Ind., in 1890 and probably died there in 1934 at 44 years of age. She married **Clarence Holtz** in Eugene in 1913. He was born in 1889 and died in 1961 at 72 years of age.[548]

Suzie **Fultz** and Clarence **Holtz** had the following children:
    6214   i.   Bert[12] **Holtz**.[549]
    6215   ii.   Eugene **Holtz**.[550]
    6216   iii.   Ned **Holtz**[551] was married and had four children. No further details provided.
+   6217   iv.   Betty Lou **Holtz** born in 1921.

5301. **Clara Belle**[11] **Fultz** (Anna M.[10] **Whipple**, Lucien Ransom[9], Enoch[8], Nehemiah[7], Benjamin[6], Francis[5], Jonathan[4], Joseph[3], Matthew[2], Matthew[1])[552] was born in Eugene, Vermilion Co., Ind. in 1892 and married **Arthur George Watson** there in 1912.[553] He was born in 1890 and died in 1958 at 68 years of age.[554] Clara was a 1910 graduate of Cayuga, Vermilion Co., Ind. High School.

Clara Belle **Fultz** and Arthur George **Watson** had the following children:
    6218   i.   Donald[12] **Watson**[555] and died at 15 months of age.
+   6219   ii.   Lee William **Watson** born 6 January 1913.
+   6220   iii.   Annabelle **Watson** born 14 October 1914.
+   6221   iv.   Helen Virginia **Watson** born 26 December 1919.

5302. **Mayme**[11] **Fultz** (Anna M.[10] **Whipple**, Lucien Ransom[9], Enoch[8], Nehemiah[7], Benjamin[6], Francis[5], Jonathan[4], Joseph[3], Matthew[2], Matthew[1])[556] was born in Eugene, Vermilion Co., Ind. in 1894 and married twice. (1) **Paul Spindan** in 1915. (2) **Garrah Dillman** in 1927.

Mayme **Fultz** and Paul **Spindan** had the following child:
    6222   i.   Guy[12] **Spindan**.[557]

5304. Rex[11] **Fultz** (Anna M.[10] **Whipple**, Lucien Ransom[9], Enoch[8], Nehemiah[7], Benjamin[6], Francis[5], Jonathan[4], Joseph[3], Matthew[2], Matthew[1])[558] was born in Eugene, Vermilion Co., Ind. in 1902 and died in January 1980 in Indiana, at 77 years of age. He married **Jewel Bright** in Eugene in 1930.[559] Rex was a 1917 and Jewell a 1915 graduate of Cayuga, Vermilion Co., Ind. High School.

Rex **Fultz** and Jewel **Bright** had the following children:
    6223 i. Emma Lou[12] **Fultz**.[560]
    6224 ii. Sally Sue **Fultz**.[561]

5305. Cora[11] **Fultz** (Anna M.[10] **Whipple**, Lucien Ransom[9], Enoch[8], Nehemiah[7], Benjamin[6], Francis[5], Jonathan[4], Joseph[3], Matthew[2], Matthew[1]) was born in Eugene, Vermilion Co., Ind. in 1902 and married **Francis M. (Joe) Pierson** 2 December 1922.[562] Cora was a 1922 graduate of Cayuga, Vermilion Co., Ind. High School. The Pierson family was living in Markham, Cook Co., Ill. in the 1960s.

Cora **Fultz** and Francis M. (Joe) **Pierson** had the following child:
+   6225 i. Marianne[12] **Pierson.**

5309. Ella Agnes[11] **Burgess** (Ellen[10] **Whipple**, Manley Nehemiah[9], Abraham[8], Nehemiah[7], Benjamin[6], Francis[5], Jonathan[4], Joseph[3], Matthew[2], Matthew[1])[563] was born in Ottawa, Putnam Co., Ohio 13 July 1871 and died 5 December 1947 in Colton, San Bernardino Co., Calif., at 76 years of age. She married **Albert Sylvester Sneary** in Livingston Co., Mo. 24 June 1896. He was born in Ottawa 27 October 1869 and died 23 March 1956 in Colton, at 86 years of age.[564] Ella and Albert were a part of the Oklahoma land rush when the Cherokee Strip was opened for settlement.

Ella Agnes **Burgess** and Albert Sylvester **Sneary** had the following children:
    6226 i. Verna May[12] **Sneary**[565] born in Ohio 5 August 1897 and died 16 November 1981 in Woodward, Woodward Co., Okla., at 84 years of age.
    6227 ii. Veral Faye **Sneary**[566] born in Arnett, Day Co., Okla. Territory 9 June 1902 and died there 3 December 1905, at 3 years of age. Buried in Gage Cemetery, Ellis Co., Okla.
+   6228 iii. Vivian Ray **Sneary** born 25 December 1904.
+   6229 iv. Veta Grace **Sneary** born 29 December 1907.
    6230 v. Verleta Edith **Sneary**[567] born in Ellis Co. 5 January 1911 and died 16 June 1958 in Long Beach, Los Angeles Co., Calif., at 47 years of age. She married Bill **Murphy** in California.

5314. **William**[11] **Burgess** (Ellen[10] **Whipple**, Manley Nehemiah[9], Abraham[8], Nehemiah[7], Benjamin[6], Francis[5], Jonathan[4], Joseph[3], Matthew[2], Matthew[1])[568] was born in Ottawa, Putnam Co., Ohio 21 August 1881 and died in Chillicothe, Livingston Co., Mo., at 92 years of age. He married **Amelia Mamie Jacob** in Troy, Lincoln Co., Mich. 25 November 1909. Amelia,[569] daughter of John Oswald **Jacob** and Emma Louisa **Engelbrecht**, was born in Warsaw, Hancock Co., Ill. 11 February 1888 and died 8 February 1982 in Chillicothe, at 93 years of age. Willie adopted the name of William J. as an adult. He is buried in the Edgewood Cemetery, Chillicothe.

William **Burgess** and Amelia Mamie **Jacob** had the following children:

+ 6231 i.   Glenn William[12] **Burgess** born 13 November 1910.
+ 6232 ii.   Harold Wright **Burgess** born 6 June 1912.
+ 6233 iii. Marjorie Ellen **Burgess** born 18 November 1914.
+ 6234 iv.   Dorothy Emma **Burgess** born 25 February 1917.
+ 6235 v.   Arthur Pershing **Burgess** born 12 May 1919.
+ 6236 vi.   Doris Fern **Burgess** born 21 February 1922.
+ 6237 vii. Helen Marie **Burgess** born 5 October 1924.
+ 6238 viii. John Francis **Burgess** born 9 October 1929.

5315. **Harry**[11] **Burgess** (Ellen[10] **Whipple**, Manley Nehemiah[9], Abraham[8], Nehemiah[7], Benjamin[6], Francis[5], Jonathan[4], Joseph[3], Matthew[2], Matthew[1])[570] was born in Ottawa, Putnam Co., Ohio 14 October 1883 and died 2 November 1970 in Chillicothe, Livingston Co., Mo., at 87 years of age. He married **Ethel Smith** in Chula, Livingston Co., Mo., 8 April 1915.

Harry **Burgess** and Ethel **Smith** had the following children born in Chula:

  6239 i.   Hazel Fenelle[12] **Burgess**[571] 15 May 1918 and married Ivan **Bigelow**.
  6240 ii. Nina Deloris **Burgess**[572] 1 August 1920 and married Raymond **Girdner**.

5318. **Carrie Emily**[11] **Whipple** (Alphonso[10], Horatio[9], Nathan[8], Nehemiah[7], Benjamin[6], Francis[5], Jonathan[4], Joseph[3], Matthew[2], Matthew[1])[573] was born in Madison, Lake Co., Ohio 3 November 1871 and died 16 August 1932 in Cleveland, Cuyahoga Co., Ohio, at 60 years of age. She married twice. (1) **Marcus Smith Van Dyke** in Madison 10 March 1889. (2) **J. F. Donahue** 4 January 1915.

Carrie Emily **Whipple** and Marcus Smith **Van Dyke** had the following children:

+ 6241 i. Lavine[12] **Van Dyke** born 3 January 1890.

| + | 6242 | ii. | Carroll Marcus **Van Dyke** born 21 May 1894. |
| + | 6243 | iii. | Ethel **Van Dyke** born 24 September 1896. |

5319. **Ira Orren**[11] **Whipple** (Alphonso[10], Horatio[9], Nathan[8], Nehemiah[7], Benjamin[6], Francis[5], Jonathan[4], Joseph[3], Matthew[2], Matthew[1])[574] was born in Madison, Lake Co., Ohio 15 January 1874 and died 31 July 1944 at 70 years of age. He married **Emma Laura Keener** 15 July 1896. She was born in Germany 12 March 1873 and died 28 December 1943, at 70 years of age.[575]

Ira Orren **Whipple** and Emma Laura **Keener** had the following children:
	6244	i.	Ford[12] **Whipple**[576] born in 1897.
+	6245	ii.	Stella Emma **Whipple** born 28 October 1898.
+	6246	iii.	Carl Wright **Whipple** born 21 May 1902.
+	6247	iv.	Irene May **Whipple** born 10 March 1907.
+	6248	v.	Lucy Freida **Whipple** born 28 August 1912.

5321. **Eli Albert**[11] **Whipple** (Alphonso[10], Horatio[9], Nathan[8], Nehemiah[7], Benjamin[6], Francis[5], Jonathan[4], Joseph[3], Matthew[2], Matthew[1])[577] was born in Madison, Lake Co., Ohio 16 February 1879 and married **Iva Pethtel** 6 November 1907. She was the daughter of Solomon **Pethtel** and Lydia A. (__).

Eli Albert **Whipple** and Iva **Pethtel** had the following children:
+	6249	i.	Joseph Albert[12] **Whipple** born 7 August 1908.
+	6250	ii.	Oren Arthur **Whipple** born 24 July 1910.
+	6251	iii.	Richard Eldsworth **Whipple** born 25 June 1912.
	6252	iv.	Horace Hudson **Whipple**[578] born 15 March 1914 and died 11 January 1979 at 64 years of age. He married Agnes Eileen **Shaughnessy** 7 May 1955.
+	6253	v.	Warren Harding **Whipple** born 31 October 1920.

5322. **Julia Mary**[11] **Whipple** (Alphonso[10], Horatio[9], Nathan[8], Nehemiah[7], Benjamin[6], Francis[5], Jonathan[4], Joseph[3], Matthew[2], Matthew[1])[579] was born in Madison, Lake Co., Ohio 13 June 1880 and married twice. (1) **O. J. Elton** 2 May 1899. (2) **Claude Mixter**.

Julia Mary **Whipple** and O. J. **Elton** had the following child:
| | 6254 | i. | Grant[12] **Elton**.[580] |

5323. **James Ford**[11] **Whipple** (Alphonso[10], Horatio[9], Nathan[8], Nehemiah[7], Benjamin[6], Francis[5], Jonathan[4], Joseph[3], Matthew[2],

Matthew[1])[581] was born in Madison, Lake Co., Ohio 23 February 1882 and married **Sally Pethtel** 7 December 1905. She was born in St. Marys, Pleasants Co., W. Va. 11 July 1882.[582]

James Ford **Whipple** and Sally **Pethtel** had the following children:
- \+ 6255 i. Florence Ilene[12] **Whipple** born 25 November 1906.
- 6256 ii. Carl Ford **Whipple**[583] born in Madison 16 December 1908 and died there 14 March 1949, at 40 years of age. He married Nina **Teachout**.
- \+ 6257 iii. Rollah Henry **Whipple** born 20 September 1910.
- \+ 6258 iv. Dorothy Dorene **Whipple** born 18 June 1912.
- \+ 6259 v. Grace Geraldine **Whipple** born 22 February 1914.
- \+ 6260 vi. Elsie Madge **Whipple** born 23 August 1916.
- \+ 6261 vii. Ray Wendell **Whipple** born 12 September 1918.
- 6262 viii. Betty Jean **Whipple**[584] born in Madison 8 August 1921 and married William **Schaffer** 27 October 1950.

5324. **Roxey Alamanda**[11] **Whipple** (Alphonso[10], Horatio[9], Nathan[8], Nehemiah[7], Benjamin[6], Francis[5], Jonathan[4], Joseph[3], Matthew[2], Matthew[1])[585] was born in Madison, Lake Co., Ohio 30 March 1884 and died 26 November 1945 in Mt. Dora, Lake Co., Fla., at 61 years of age. She married **LaVerne Leigh Greeley** 9 August 1913. He was born in Riceville, Crawford Co., Penn. 17 May 1872 and died 9 August 1946 in Lake Gem, Fla., at 74 years of age.[586]

Roxey Alamanda **Whipple** and LaVerne Leigh **Greeley** had the following child:
- \+ 6263 i. Veda Louise[12] **Greeley** born 14 June 1915.

5325. **Nathan Wilson**[11] **Whipple** (Alphonso[10], Horatio[9], Nathan[8], Nehemiah[7], Benjamin[6], Francis[5], Jonathan[4], Joseph[3], Matthew[2], Matthew[1])[587] was born in Madison, Lake Co., Ohio 21 June 1886 and died 21 December 1986 in Fallbrook, San Diego Co., Calif., at 100 years of age. He married **Florence Eva Brown** in Madison 19 July 1913. She was born in Martins Ferry, Belmont Co., Ohio 18 April 1892 and died 2 November 1964 in Madison, at 72 years of age.[588] Wilson was diagnosed with cancer of the liver 15 November 1986 at the hospital in Painesville, Lake Co., Ohio and returned to California to die.

Nathan Wilson **Whipple** and Florence Eva **Brown** had the following children:
- \+ 6264 i. Wallace Eugene[12] **Whipple** born 28 August 1914.

+	6265	ii.	Russell Elwood **Whipple** born 20 March 1916.
+	6266	iii.	Kenneth Elman **Whipple** born 4 January 1918.
+	6267	iv.	Sheldon Ray **Whipple** born 10 April 1926.
+	6268	v.	Roy Curwood **Whipple** born 29 April 1928.

5327. **Royal Howard**[11] **Whipple** (Alphonso[10], Horatio[9], Nathan[8], Nehemiah[7], Benjamin[6], Francis[5], Jonathan[4], Joseph[3], Matthew[2], Matthew[1])[589] was born in Madison, Lake Co., Ohio 12 April 1892 and died 7 August 1966 in Lansing, Ingham Co., Mich., at 74 years of age. He married **Grace Frisinger** 14 August 1913. She died 30 October 1947.[590]

Royal Howard **Whipple** and Grace **Frisinger** had the following children:
	6269	i.	Marjori[12] **Whipple**[591] married Joe **O'Dell**.
	6270	ii.	Reola **Whipple**[592] married Bruce **Smith**.
+	6271	iii.	R. Douglas **Whipple** born 27 September 1917.

5328. **Jessie**[11] **Brown** (Henry Whipple[10], Miranda[9] **Whipple**, Nathan[8], Nehemiah[7], Benjamin[6], Francis[5], Jonathan[4], Joseph[3], Matthew[2], Matthew[1])[593] was born in Rockford, Winnebago Co., Ill. 19 March 1865 and died 17 October 1951 in Moline, Rock Island Co., Ill., at 86 years of age. She married twice. (1) **William Ashton** in Monrovia, Calif. (2) **Walter Ransom Beddoes**. Walter was the son of Samuel Thomas **Beddoes** and Margaret **Meyers**. Jessie is buried in Greenwood Cemetery at Rockford.

Jessie **Brown** and William **Ashton** had the following children born in Monrovia:
	6272	i.	Ada[12] **Ashton**[594] in 1888 and died 16 June 1893 in Rockford, at 4 years of age.
	6273	ii.	Mary **Ashton**[595] in 1889 and married Orrin **Lillie**.
	6274	iii.	Elsie **Ashton**[596] in 1892 and married Roy **Abbots**.

Jessie **Brown** and Walter Ransom **Beddoes** had the following children:
+	6275	iv.	Lillian Isabelle **Beddoes** born 11 November 1896.
	6276	v.	Thomas **Beddoes**[597] born in Rockford 26 November 1899.
	6277	vi.	Kathryn **Beddoes**[598] born in Rockford 8 January 1907.

5340. **Gladys Marguerite**[11] **Olds** (Ransom Eli[10], Sarah[9] **Whipple**, Nathan[8], Nehemiah[7], Benjamin[6], Francis[5], Jonathan[4], Joseph[3], Matthew[2], Matthew[1])[599] was born in Lansing, Ingham Co., Mich. 15 January 1892 and married **Bruce Anderson** 17 October 1914. They were divorced in 1931.

Gladys Marguerite **Olds** and Bruce **Anderson** had the following children:
  6278 i. R. E. Olds[12] **Anderson** born 23 August 1916[600] and died in February 2003. He married Barbara **Piatt**.[601]
  6279 ii. Peggy Dunn **Anderson** born 7 July 1918[602] and married James **Wortz**.[603]

5341. Bernice Estelle[11] **Olds** (Ransom Eli[10], Sarah[9] **Whipple**, Nathan[8], Nehemiah[7], Benjamin[6], Francis[5], Jonathan[4], Joseph[3], Matthew[2], Matthew[1])[604] was born in Lansing, Ingham Co., Mich. 16 April 1894 and married **Clarence Sage Roe** there 19 December 1917.

Bernice Estelle **Olds** and Clarence Sage **Roe** had the following children:
  6280 i. Edward Olds[12] **Roe** born 20 August 1918.[605]
  6281 ii. John Woodward **Roe** born 20 December 1921.[606]
  6282 iii. Bernice Rosan **Roe** born 2 December 1927.[607]
  6283 iv. Arnim Sage **Roe** born 18 September 1930.[608]

5344. Henry A.[11] **Watkins** (Henry[10], Moses[9], Lois[8] **Mills**, Hepzibah[7] **Whipple**, Benjamin[6], Francis[5], Jonathan[4], Joseph[3], Matthew[2], Matthew[1])[609] was born in Potsdam, St. Lawrence Co., N.Y. 26 November 1860 and died 16 August 1915 at 54 years of age. He married **Carrie Emily Moore** in 1879. Carrie,[610] daughter of Darius Alonzo **Moore** and Emily **Beebe**, was born in DeKalb, St. Lawrence Co., N.Y. 12 May 1865 and died 1 April 1927 at 61 years of age.

Henry A. **Watkins** and Carrie Emily **Moore** had the following children:
+ 6284 i. Frederick[12] **Watkins** born 7 March 1894.
  6285 ii. (Child) **Watkins**[611] born bef 1897 and died bef 1897.
  6286 iii. (Child) **Watkins**[612] born bef 1897 and died bef 1897.
  6287 iv. Leslie Lawrence **Watkins**[613] born in Potsdam 30 December 1897 and died 17 December 1964 in Ithaca, Tompkins Co., N.Y., at 66 years of age. Buried in East Lawn Cemetery. He married Mildred **Potter**. No children born to this union.

5348. Winnifred L.[11] **Milland** (Phebe Jane[10] **Whipple**, Cyrus Avery[9], Ithamar[8], Rev. Benjamin[7], Benjamin[6], Francis[5], Jonathan[4], Joseph[3], Matthew[2], Matthew[1])[614] was born 15 August 1872 and married **Samuel M. Cozad** 23 September 1890.

Winnifred L. **Milland** and Samuel M. **Cozad** had the following children:
  6288 i. Esther L.[12] **Cozad**.[615]
  6289 ii. Webster M. **Cozad**.[616]

5351. **Cora**[11] **Remley** (Lydia Lucelia[10] **Whipple**, Cyrus Avery[9], Ithamar[8], Rev. Benjamin[7], Benjamin[6], Francis[5], Jonathan[4], Joseph[3], Matthew[2], Matthew[1])[617] birth date unknown, married **George Robinson**.

Cora **Remley** and George **Robinson** had the following child:
- 6290   i.   Frank Ithamar[12] **Robinson**.[618]

5353. **Effie Leora**[11] **Whipple** (Daniel Franklin[10], Cyrus Avery[9], Ithamar[8], Rev. Benjamin[7], Benjamin[6], Francis[5], Jonathan[4], Joseph[3], Matthew[2], Matthew[1])[619] was born 24 May 1859 and married **Frank Dana** 21 September 1881.

Effie Leora **Whipple** and Frank **Dana** had the following children:
- 6291   i.   Jay Lynn[12] **Dana**.[620]
- 6292   ii.   Hazel Augusta **Dana**.[621]
- 6293   iii.   Donald Whipple **Dana**[622] born 19 June 1882.
- 6294   iv.   Lee Howard **Dana**[623] born 19 November 1885.
- 6295   v.   Clyde Adelburt **Dana**[624] born 2 March 1893.

5354. **Anna Irene**[11] **Whipple** (Daniel Franklin[10], Cyrus Avery[9], Ithamar[8], Rev. Benjamin[7], Benjamin[6], Francis[5], Jonathan[4], Joseph[3], Matthew[2], Matthew[1])[625] was born in Marion, Linn Co., Iowa 7 July 1861 and married **W. Nathan Hunt** 9 June 1881. He was born 2 October 1856.[626]

Anna Irene **Whipple** and W. Nathan **Hunt** had the following children:
- 6296   i.   Sarah Irene[12] **Hunt**[627] born 19 October 1882.
- 6297   ii.   Ethel Leora **Hunt**[628] born 2 August 1884.
- 6298   iii.   Clara Alice **Hunt**[629] born 28 September 1888.
- 6299   iv.   Hubert Nathan **Hunt**[630] born 9 June 1891.
- 6300   v.   Lawrence Wilbur Hayes **Hunt**[631] born 25 August 1900.

5355. **Lurella**[11] **Whipple** (Daniel Franklin[10], Cyrus Avery[9], Ithamar[8], Rev. Benjamin[7], Benjamin[6], Francis[5], Jonathan[4], Joseph[3], Matthew[2], Matthew[1])[632] was born 3 May 1865 and married **Lewis Mead Lowe** 20 April 1886. Her given name may have been spelled Lurilia.

Lurella **Whipple** and Lewis Mead **Lowe** had the following children:
- 6301   i.   Lillian Mable[12] **Lowe**[633] born 8 May 1887.
- 6302   ii.   Lowell Mead **Lowe**[634] born 30 November 1894.
- 6303   iii.   Leland Ithamar **Lowe**[635] born 12 July 1901.
- 6304   iv.   Dorothy Whipple **Lowe**[636] born 12 April 1904.

5357. **William Levi**[11] **Whipple** (Ithamar Cyrus[10], Cyrus Avery[9], Ithamar[8], Rev. Benjamin[7], Benjamin[6], Francis[5], Jonathan[4], Joseph[3], Matthew[2], Matthew[1])[637] was born in Marion, Linn Co., Iowa 23 December 1864 and died 11 January 1939 in Whittier, Los Angeles Co., Calif., at 74 years of age. He married **Helen Elizabeth McCrum** in Mifflin, Penn. 11 September 1888. She died in Whittier. William was a Cashier at the Stockgrowers' Bank and like his father active in the Baptist Church. He moved his family from Cheyenne, Laramie Co., Wyo. to Seattle, King Co., Wash. in 1917. His mother moved with them.

William Levi **Whipple** and Helen Elizabeth **McCrum** had the following children born in Cheyenne:

- 6305 i. William Gerald[12] **Whipple**[638] 29 April 1891 and died there 9 December 1898, at 7 years of age.
- 6306 ii. Marjorie Helen **Whipple**[639] 25 November 1894 and married Alvin Axel **Peterson** in Whittier 23 September 1922. He was born 5 October 1898 and died 18 March 1948 in Seattle, at 49 years of age.
- 6307 iii. Donald McCrum **Whipple**[640] 28 September 1897 and died 25 June 1955 in Whittier, at 57 years of age.
- 6308 iv. Edith Margaret **Whipple**[641] 23 July 1910 and married Donovan Frederick **Gouldin** in Whittier 13 October 1929. He was born 4 August 1908.

5358. **Mary Lillian**[11] **Whipple** (Ithamar Cyrus[10], Cyrus Avery[9], Ithamar[8], Rev. Benjamin[7], Benjamin[6], Francis[5], Jonathan[4], Joseph[3], Matthew[2], Matthew[1])[642] was born in Cheyenne, Laramie Co., Wyo. 10 July 1869 and died 22 August 1943 in Kansas City, Jackson Co., Mo., at 74 years of age. She married **George W. Johnson II** in Cheyenne 7 May 1889. He was born in Leavenworth, Leavenworth Co., Kans. 7 May 1866 and died 9 June 1931 in Kansas City, at 65 years of age.[643] Buried in

Mary Lillian (Whipple) and George Johnson. Photo courtesy of Marge and George Chandler.

Mount Muncie Cemetery. After completing school in Leavenworth at 17, he attended a business college in Kansas City and then worked at the First National Bank in Leavenworth until advised by his doctor to seek a less confining occupation. He moved to Cheyenne in 1887 and worked in a hardware store. He moved back to Leavenworth after his marriage but shortly thereafter moved to Kansas City where he was an Iron Broker and Rental Agent for a large office building. He began a business manufacturing iron products in 1898. His company built fire escapes, elevator gates, and fire doors. He moved into his own building at 209-11 W. 17th St. in the spring of 1902 and expanded the business. He was one of the pioneer manufacturers in Kansas City and the company became nationally known.

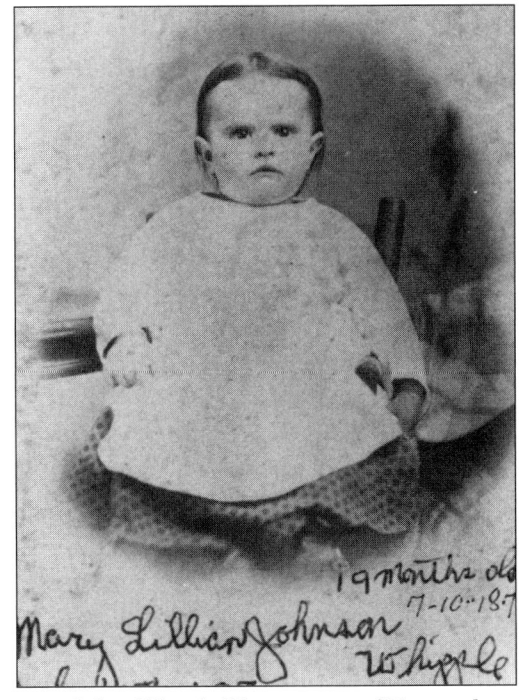

Mary Lillian Whipple. Photo courtesy of Marge and George Chandler.

Mary Lillian **Whipple** and George W. **Johnson** II had the following children born in Kansas City:

	6309	i.	George Harold[12] **Johnson**[644] 26 April 1891 and died there 2 December 1896, at 5 years of age.
	6310	ii.	Ralph Ithamar **Johnson**[645] 11 July 1895 and married Thelma Irene **Ferring** in Kansas City 28 June 1924. She was born in Council Bluffs, Pottawattamie Co., Iowa 12 October 1896.[646]
+	6311	iii.	Florence B. **Johnson** 4 January 1899.
	6312	iv.	Laura Grace **Johnson** 3 December 1901 and died in Carmel, Calif. 19 November 1960. She married George Walter **Vaughn** in Kansas City 28 August 1924.[647] He married (2) Katherine T. **Straub** in Mt. Dora, Lake Co., Fla. 29 December 1962.
	6313	v.	Robert Eugene **Johnson**[648] 7 March 1909 and died there 10 May 1936, at 27 years of age. He married Alice Blanche **Johnson** in Kansas City 30 June 1930.

6314 vi. Clarence Whipple **Johnson**[649] 15 May 1911 and died there 24 August 1963, at 52 years of age. He married twice. (1) Catherine **Chapman** in Kansas City. She died there 26 March 1955.[650] (2) Mildred Wilson **Casisky** in Kansas City.

5362. **Fred J.**[11] **Hart** (John P.[10], Florina H.[9] **Whipple**, Ithamar[8], Rev. Benjamin[7], Benjamin[6], Francis[5], Jonathan[4], Joseph[3], Matthew[2], Matthew[1])[651] was born in North Fairhaven, Cayuga Co., N.Y. 22 December 1880 and died 2 May 1955 in Pico Rivera, Los Angels Co., Calif., at 74 years of age. He married twice. (1) **Florence Frances Marks** in Auburn, Cayuga Co., N.Y. 15 September 1909. Florence,[652] daughter of William James **Marks** and Frances Hannah **Hitchcock**, was born in Auburn 25 March 1890 and died 9 March 1945 in Los Angeles, Los Angeles Co., Calif., at 54 years of age. (2) **Letha Minca Padgett** in Las Vegas, Clark Co., Nev. 8 September 1945. She was born in Natoma, Osborne Co., Kans. 12 October 1899 and died 2 October 1968 in Long Beach, Los Angeles Co., Calif., at 68 years of age.[653] Fred and his two wives were buried in the Sunnyside Mausoleum, Long Beach., Calif.

Fred J. **Hart** and Florence Frances **Marks** had the following children:

6315 i. Virginia Arlene[12] **Hart**[654] born in Syracuse, Onodaga Co., N.Y. 2 December 1910 and died 2 March 1941 in Compton, Los Angeles Co., Calif., at 30 years of age. Buried in Long Beach, Los Angeles Co., Calif., Sunnyside Mausoleum. She married William R. **Grant** in Cayuga Co., N.Y.

+ 6316 ii. Frederick Allan **Hart** born 18 January 1922.

6317 iii. Barbara Thayer **Hart**[655] born in South Gate, Los Angeles Co., Calif. 19 November 1933 and married Arlen **Helton**.

5368. **Ella Maude**[11] **Keeler** (Eliza Jane[10] **Whipple**, Daniel F.[9], Ithamar[8], Rev. Benjamin[7], Benjamin[6], Francis[5], Jonathan[4], Joseph[3], Matthew[2], Matthew[1])[656] was born in Erie, Erie Co., Penn. 5 February 1879 and died in 1972, at 93 years of age. She married **John Henry Morse**. He was born in 1886 and died in in the flu epidemic in 1918 in Erie, at 32 years of age.[657] Buried in Golden Cemetery, Erie. Ella married three times. John was her second husband. No information provided on the other two.

Ella Maude **Keeler** and John Henry **Morse** had the following child:

+ 6318 i. Wilma Mildred Martha[12] **Morse** born 22 May 1908.

5369. **Clayton J.**[11] **Whipple** (William Lemuel[10], Francis Jackson[9], Ithamar[8], Rev. Benjamin[7], Benjamin[6], Francis[5], Jonathan[4], Joseph[3], Matthew[2], Matthew[1])[658] was born in Auburn, Cayuga Co., N.Y. 23 April 1873 and died of scarlet fever 15 July 1912 in Yonkers, Westchester Co., N.Y., at 39 years of age. Buried in Oakland Cemetery in Yonkers. He married **Ida Ruth Elms** in Milwaukee, Milwaukee Co., Wisc. 3 June 1896. Ida,[659] daughter of George B. **Elms** and Helen Esther **Delancy**, was born in Pentwater, Oceans Co., Mich. 30 October 1871 and died 27 April 1947 in Hollywood, Los Angeles Co., Calif., at 75 years of age. She married (2) **Lucius Cannon** in 1914.

Clayton J. **Whipple** and Ida Ruth **Elms** had the following children:

    6319   i.   Sherman Elms[12] **Whipple**[660] born 29 June 1897 and died 25 March 1979 in Yonkers at 81 years of age. After his mother married Lucius **Cannon,** Sherman assumed Cannon as a surname. It is not known whether he was legally adopted.

    6320   ii.   Helen Esther **Whipple**[661] born in Chicago, Cook Co., Ill. 12 August 1899 and died 6 July 1912 in Yonkers, at 12 years of age. Buried in Oakland Cemetery.

+   6321   iii.   Leslie A. **Whipple** born 2 April 1903.

5370. **Leslie "Lula" Grace**[11] **Whipple** (William Lemuel[10], Francis Jackson[9], Ithamar[8], Rev. Benjamin[7], Benjamin[6], Francis[5], Jonathan[4], Joseph[3], Matthew[2], Matthew[1])[662] was born in Raymond, Blackhawk Co., Iowa 19 August 1880. She married **Albert Eads** in June 1906.

Lula Grace **Whipple** and Albert **Eads** had the following children:

    6322   i.   Harold W.[12] **Eads**[663] born in 1907.
    6323   ii.   Robert H. **Eads**.[664]
    6324   iii.   Mildred **Eads**.[665]

5378. **Bruce**[11] **Hotchkiss** (Jennie Evalina[10] **Whipple**, Francis Jackson[9], Ithamar[8], Rev. Benjamin[7], Benjamin[6], Francis[5], Jonathan[4], Joseph[3], Matthew[2], Matthew[1])[666] was born in Cussewago, Crawford Co., Penn. 19 May 1880 and married **Clara Hofman** 18 June 1906. She was born 17 May 1883.

Bruce **Hotchkiss** and Clara **Hofman** had the following children:

    6325   i.   Robert Bruce[12] **Hotchkiss**[667] born 13 July 1910.
    6326   ii.   Jeannette Mary **Hotchkiss**[668] born 19 May 1918.
    6327   iii.   Carolyn May **Hotchkiss**[669] born 16 February 1923.

5379. **Gertrude M.**[11] **Hotchkiss** (Jennie Evalina[10] **Whipple**, Francis Jackson[9], Ithamar[8], Rev. Benjamin[7], Benjamin[6], Francis[5], Jonathan[4], Joseph[3], Matthew[2], Matthew[1])[670] was born 12 April 1890 and married **John M. Ralston** 15 September 1915. He was born 5 April 1889.[671]

Gertrude M. **Hotchkiss** and John M. **Ralston** had the following children:

      6328   i.   Paul Hotchkiss[12] **Ralston**[672] born 5 March 1917.
      6329   ii. Pauline Louise **Ralston**[673] born 5 March 1917.
      6330   iii. Helen Marie **Ralston**[674] born 25 May 1919.

5381. **Sylvia May**[11] **Whipple** (Marcus Erastus[10], Francis Jackson[9], Ithamar[8], Rev. Benjamin[7], Benjamin[6], Francis[5], Jonathan[4], Joseph[3], Matthew[2], Matthew[1])[675] was born in Cussewago, Crawford Co., Penn. 22 April 1890 and died 18 April 1979 in Edinboro, Erie Co., Penn., at 88 years of age. She married **Brady James Skelton** in Edinboro 14 June 1921. He died 1 November 1951. Buried in Skelton Cemetery, Venanoo, Penn. She was his second wife. Brady brought 11 other children to the marriage.[676]

Sylvia May **Whipple** and Brady James **Skelton** had the following children:

      6331   i.   (Child)[12] **Skelton**[677] born in Edinboro 11 June 1922.
+   6332   ii. Mable Jeannette **Skelton** born 11 June 1922.
+   6333   iii. James John **Skelton** born 2 February 1924.
+   6334   iv. Paul Mark **Skelton** born 16 October 1926.

5382. **Dr. Raymond Orson**[11] **Whipple** (Marcus Erastus[10], Francis Jackson[9], Ithamar[8], Rev. Benjamin[7], Benjamin[6], Francis[5], Jonathan[4], Joseph[3], Matthew[2], Matthew[1])[678] was born in Cussewago, Crawford Co., Penn. either 4 March or 25 April 1892 and died 7 May 1966 in Myerstown, Lebanon Co., Penn., at 74 years of age. He married **Georgianna Mitchell** in Conneaut, Ashtabula Co., Ohio 24 June 1916. She was born in Cambridge Springs, Crawford Co., Penn. 25 June 1890 and died 16 November 1971 in Annville, Lebanon Co., Penn. at 81 years of age.[679] Both are buried in Grandview Memorial Park, Annville. He was a veterinarian.

Dr. Raymond Orson **Whipple** and Georgianna **Mitchell** had the following children:

      6335   i.   Donald Perry[12] **Whipple**[680] born 26 June 1917 and died 6 July 1979 at 62 years of age. He married Jane Aline **Reese** 22 June 1940.
+   6336   ii. Margaret Jane **Whipple** born 5 November 1919.

5385. **Carl Era**[11] **Whipple** (Marcus Erastus[10], Francis Jackson[9], Ithamar[8], Rev. Benjamin[7], Benjamin[6], Francis[5], Jonathan[4], Joseph[3], Matthew[2], Matthew[1])[681] was born in Edinboro, Erie Co., Penn. 31 July 1903 and married **Marion Elder Robbins** in Westfield, Chautaugua Co., N.Y. 20 September 1924. Marion,[682] daughter of James Louis **Robbins** and Lena Raeburn **Lichtenberger**, was born in Franklin, Penn. 13 March 1904 and died 31 July 1994 in Fairfax, Fairfax City Area Co., Va., at 90 years of age. Buried in Sandy Lake, Mercer Co., Penn.

Carl earned a master's degree from Penn State and a Ph.D. in Education from the U. of Pittsburgh, Allegheny Co., Penn. He was principal of Keith Junior High School in Altoona, Blair Co. and Superintendent of Schools at Warren, Penn. where he was Chairman of the Housing Authority from 1970-95. The American Baptist Churches of Pennsylvania and Delaware presented him with their church and community award for outstanding leadership and contributions to strengthen the ministry of the church.

Carl E. Whipple. Photos courtesy of Nancy (Whipple) Ebland.

Marion E. (Robbins) Whipple.

Carl Era **Whipple** and Marion Elder **Robbins** had the following children:
+ 6337 i. Capt. Caryll Robbins[12] **Whipple** born 12 October 1927.
+ 6338 ii. Nancy Louise **Whipple** born 5 June 1931.

5387. **Bessie Belle**[11] **Whipple** (Cephus Galusha[10], Samuel Elijah[9], Ithamar[8], Rev. Benjamin[7], Benjamin[6], Francis[5], Jonathan[4], Joseph[3], Matthew[2], Matthew[1])[683] was born in New Boston, Mercer Co., Ill. 18 May 1870 and died 1 December 1945 in Fort Smith, Sebastian Co., Ark., at 75 years of age. She married **Allen Burton Yantis** 20 June 1889.[684] He was born 5 November 1860 and died 25 August 1943 at 82 years of age.[685]

{ G 927 }

Bessie Belle **Whipple** and Allen Burton **Yantis** had the following children born in Niobrara, Knox Co., Nebr.:

    6339   i.   Grey Allen[12] **Yantis**[686] June 1890 and died unmarried 4 March 1921 at 30 years of age.[687]

+   6340   ii.   Helen Marjorie **Yantis** 22 June 1891.

    6341   iii.   Mildred Grace **Yantis**[688] 2 December 1894 and She married (__) **Langford**.[689]

5388. Gordon Lofland[11] **Whipple** (Cephus Galusha[10], Samuel Elijah[9], Ithamar[8], Rev. Benjamin[7], Benjamin[6], Francis[5], Jonathan[4], Joseph[3], Matthew[2], Matthew[1])[690] was born in Keithsburg, Mercer Co., Ill. 30 January 1872 and died 22 July 1944 in Omaha, Douglas Co., Nebr., at 72 years of age. He married **Carrie Erma Conley** in Perry, Dallas Co., Iowa 6 June 1896.

Gordon Lofland **Whipple** and Carrie Erma **Conley** had the following child:

    6342   i.   Elizabeth[12] **Whipple**.[691]

5390. Florence Elsie[11] **Whipple** (Cephus Galusha[10], Samuel Elijah[9], Ithamar[8], Rev. Benjamin[7], Benjamin[6], Francis[5], Jonathan[4], Joseph[3], Matthew[2], Matthew[1])[692] was born in Muscatine, Muscatine Co., Iowa 7 September 1875 and died 18 March 1953 in Lynch, Boyd Co., Nebr., at 77 years of age. She married **Dr. Guy Bentley Ira** in Omaha, Douglas Co., Nebr. 10 April 1898. Guy,[693] son of Dr. George Wesly **Ira** and Mary Beatta **Hobbs**, was born in Greenwood, Lawrence Co., S. Dak. 22 July 1873 and died 15 February 1961 in Lynch, at 87 years of age. Both were buried in L'Eau qui Court Cemetery, Niobrara, Knox Co., Nebr. Guy attended Freemont, Dodge Co., Nebr. Normal School for a year before completing three years of pre-med at the U. of Nebraska. He was graduated from Physicians & Surgeons Medical School of St. Louis, Independence Co., Mo. in 1890 and after a year's practice in Newburn, Jersey Co., Ill., began a 50-year practice at Lynch where his patients came from several surrounding counties. He was also doctor for the Chicago and Northwestern Railway which went through Lynch enroute to the Dakotas. Guy served in the Army Medical Corps during WWI (1917-19) in base hospitals just behind the front lines

He grew up on the Santee Indian Reservation near Niobrara where his father was the government doctor. Florence studied music at Bellview College in Nebraska. After her marriage, she became active in church work, directing the choir and the children's program for many years.

Florence Elsie **Whipple** and Dr. Guy Bentley **Ira** had the following children:
- \+   6343   i.   Dr. Gordon Henry[12] **Ira** born 7 March 1899.
- \+   6344   ii.   Naomi Grace **Ira** born 19 October 1900.

5391. **Charles Clifford**[11] **Whipple** (Cephus Galusha[10], Samuel Elijah[9], Ithamar[8], Rev. Benjamin[7], Benjamin[6], Francis[5], Jonathan[4], Joseph[3], Matthew[2], Matthew[1])[694] was born in Muscatine, Muscatine Co., Iowa 21 July 1881 and died 29 February 1972 in Tacoma, Pierce Co., Wash., at 90 years of age. He married **Grace Isabel Marshall** in Niobrara, Knox Co., Nebr. 2 October 1906. She was born in Mound City, Holt Co., Mo. 4 October 1885 and died 6 January 1979 in Tacoma, at 93 years of age.[695]

Charles Clifford **Whipple** and Grace Isabel **Marshall** had the following children:
- \+   6345   i.   Marshall Lofland[12] **Whipple** born 15 July 1909.
- \+   6346   ii.   Murray Douglas **Whipple** born 16 August 1912.
- \+   6347   iii.   Grey Gordon **Whipple** born 18 May 1914.
- \+   6348   iv.   Sherman Guy **Whipple** born 16 November 1919.
- \+   6349   v.   Lawrence Jerome **Whipple** born 19 March 1928.

5397. **Mary Etta**[11] **Bills** (George Dudley[10], Daniel F.[9], Elizabeth[8] **Whipple**, Rev. Benjamin[7], Benjamin[6], Francis[5], Jonathan[4], Joseph[3], Matthew[2], Matthew[1])[696] was born in Oak Park, Cook Co., Ill. 31 December 1881 and died 29 May 1925 in River Forest, Cook Co., Ill., at 43 years of age. She married **Arthur Henley Symons** in Oak Park 22 December 1904. Arthur,[697] son of John **Symons** and Ellen **Henley**, was born in Spiceland, Henry Co., Ind. 24 June 1871 and died 31 January 1956 in River Forest, at 84 years of age. Mary and Arthur were buried in Chicago's Oakwood Cemetery. Arthur began his working life as a Clerk in a steel mill at Lawrence, Douglas Co., Kans. in 1898 and founded and became President of Symons Clamp and Manufacturing Co. in 1911. He made many improvements on tools used by contractors. His associations included Sigma Chi, the Quaker Club, and the Republican party.

Mary Etta **Bills** and Arthur Henley **Symons** had the following children:
- \+   6350   i.   Helen Henley[12] **Symons** born 29 June 1906.
- \+   6351   ii.   John Griffith **Symons** born 16 September 1911.
- \+   6352   iii.   Sara Leigh **Symons** born 30 October 1917.

5398. **Robert Carman**[11] **Bills Sr.** (Charles Brownell[10], Daniel F.[9], Elizabeth[8] **Whipple**, Rev. Benjamin[7], Benjamin[6], Francis[5], Jonathan[4], Joseph[3], Matthew[2], Matthew[1])[698] birth date unknown, married **Rozalia Schwilk**.

Robert Carman **Bills** Sr. and Rozalia **Schwilk** had the following child:
+ 6353 i. Robert Carman[12] **Bills** Jr.

5410. **Hepsey Leoline**[11] **Whipple** (Cyrus Hanchett[10], Solomon[9], David[8], Rev. Benjamin[7], Benjamin[6], Francis[5], Jonathan[4], Joseph[3], Matthew[2], Matthew[1])[699] was born 2 December 1870 and married **William Andrew Stidd** 1 January 1894. He was born 4 April 1870 and died 3 March 1928 at 57 years of age.[700]

Hepsey Leoline **Whipple** and William Andrew **Stidd** had the following children:
+ 6354 i. Colvin W.[12] **Stidd** born 3 March 1895.
+ 6355 ii. Gregory Wright **Stidd** born 26 November 1896.
  6356 iii. Mary Louise **Stidd**[701] born 25 November 1900 and died in May 1902 at 1 year of age.
+ 6357 iv. Lorraine Lee **Stidd** born 31 May 1905.
  6358 v. William Andrew **Stidd** Jr.[702] born 14 August 1907.

5412. **Carlton Gregory**[11] **Whipple** (Cyrus Hanchett[10], Solomon[9], David[8], Rev. Benjamin[7], Benjamin[6], Francis[5], Jonathan[4], Joseph[3], Matthew[2], Matthew[1])[703] was born in Chicago, Cook Co., Ill. 27 September 1875 and died there 4 November 1936, at 61 years of age. He married **Laura Louise Booth** 18 May 1903. Laura,[704] daughter of John Stephen **Booth** and Capitola Ann **Smith**, was born in Lime Springs, Howard Co., Iowa 31 March 1878 and died 17 November 1963 in Los Angeles, Los Angeles Co., Calif., at 85 years of age.

Carlton Gregory **Whipple** and Laura Louise **Booth** had the following children:
+ 6359 i. Jean Carlton[12] **Whipple** born 5 May 1905.
+ 6360 ii. Gregory Booth **Whipple** born 3 April 1908.

5414. **Mabel Lura**[11] **Hoxie** (Lucina Jeanette[10] **Whipple**, Solomon[9], David[8], Rev. Benjamin[7], Benjamin[6], Francis[5], Jonathan[4], Joseph[3], Matthew[2], Matthew[1])[705] was born 26 August 1876 and married **Frank R. Asquith** 7 September 1898.

Mabel Lura **Hoxie** and Frank R. **Asquith** had the following children:
  6361 i. Helen Mae[12] **Asquith**[706] born 6 May 1905 and married William **Love** 24 June 1930. He was born 26 September 1905.[707]
  6362 ii. Homer Hoxie **Asquith**[708] born 13 November 1906.

5415. **Charles Ray**[11] **Hoxie** (Lucina Jeanette[10] **Whipple**, Solomon[9], David[8], Rev. Benjamin[7], Benjamin[6], Francis[5], Jonathan[4], Joseph[3], Matthew[2], Matthew[1])[709] was born 7 January 1880 and married **Ada Little** 3 July 1903. She was born 25 May 1882.[710]

Charles Ray **Hoxie** and Ada **Little** had the following children:
    6363   i.   Charles[12] **Hoxie**[711] born 27 July 1912.
    6364   ii. Gordon **Hoxie**[712] born 18 March 1920.

5416. **Maude Luella**[11] **Hoxie** (Lucina Jeanette[10] **Whipple**, Solomon[9], David[8], Rev. Benjamin[7], Benjamin[6], Francis[5], Jonathan[4], Joseph[3], Matthew[2], Matthew[1])[713] was born 4 May 1884 and died 21 November 1939 at 55 years of age. She married **Samuel S. Scott** 23 September 1903. He was born 17 May 1880 and died 6 March 1938 at 57 years of age.[714]

Maude Luella **Hoxie** and Samuel S. **Scott** had the following children:
+   6365   i.   Beatrice Eleanor[12] **Scott** born 23 July 1906.
    6366   ii. Winston Hoxie **Scott**[715] born 26 August 1910.
    6367   iii. Everett Hoxie **Scott**[716] born 2 March 1913.
    6368   iv. Betty Jean **Scott**[717] born 1 March 1921.
    6369   v. Charles Hoxie **Scott**[718] born 21 March 1924.

5418. **Minnie Margie**[11] **Goodenow** (Arminda Rose[10] **Deriar**, Fannie[9] **Whipple**, Jonathan[8], Rev. Benjamin[7], Benjamin[6], Francis[5], Jonathan[4], Joseph[3], Matthew[2], Matthew[1])[719] was born in Elk Creek Township, Erie Co., Penn. 28 February 1870 and died 2 January 1955 in Cambridge Springs, Crawford Co., Penn., at 84 years of age. She married **Charles Otho Stuntz** 6 April 1892. Charles,[720] son of Ezra Fletcher **Stuntz** and Jane Ann **Stitt**, was born in Erie Co. 15 April 1864 and died there 25 October 1943, at 79 years of age. Both buried in Hope Cemetery near Wellsburg, Erie Co., Penn.

Minnie Margie **Goodenow** and Charles Otho **Stuntz** had the following children:
+   6370   i.   Frederick Harold[12] **Stuntz** born 14 December 1893.
+   6371   ii. Homer Ezra **Stuntz** born 5 August 1895.
+   6372   iii. Gertrude **Stuntz** born 28 January 1900.
+   6373   iv. Paul Edmund **Stuntz** born 17 May 1906.

5424. **Eva Mae**[11] **Kline** (Ada Della[10] **Whipple**, Jonathan[9], Nathan[8], Rev. Benjamin[7], Benjamin[6], Francis[5], Jonathan[4], Joseph[3], Matthew[2], Matthew[1])[721] birth date unknown, married **Marle Hall**.

{ G 931 }

Eva Mae **Kline** and Marle **Hall** had the following children:
- 6374 i. Beatrice[12] **Hall**.[722]
- 6375 ii. Marle **Hall** Jr.[723]
- 6376 iii. Marjorie **Hall**[724] and married Chester M. **Eisaman**.
- 6377 iv. Betty Gayle **Hall**[725] and maried Donald G. **Steva**.

5428. **Orlan Milo**[11] **Herrick** (Albert Eugene[10], Berthier H.[9], Melinda[8] **Whipple**, Moses[7], Capt. Thomas[6], Francis[5], Jonathan[4], Joseph[3], Matthew[2], Matthew[1])[726] was born in East Pharsalia, Chenango Co., N.Y. 8 October 1877 and died 19 June 1955 in Jacksonville, Duval Co., Fla., at 77 years of age. He married **Belle Anna Grant**. Belle,[727] daughter of James Eugene **Grant** and Elsie Anna **Breed**, was born in East Pharsalia 18 November 1880 and died 17 August 1956 in Norwich, Chenanago Co., N. Y., at 75 years of age.

Orlan Milo **Herrick** and Belle Anna **Grant** had the following children:
- 6378 i. Archie Leo[12] **Herrick**.[728]
- 6379 ii. Berthier Eugene **Herrick**.[729]
- + 6380 iii. Freda Grant **Herrick** born 9 April 1904.

5430. **Hazel Marie**[11] **Bisbee** (George Ensign[10], Martha Melissa[9] **Herrick**, Melinda[8] **Whipple**, Moses[7], Capt. Thomas[6], Francis[5], Jonathan[4], Joseph[3], Matthew[2], Matthew[1])[730] was born in Boone, Boone Co., Iowa 13 January 1897 and died there in February 1972, at 75 years of age. Buried in Linwood Cemetery, plot E11. She married **Albert William Olson** abt 1917. Albert was the son of Carl **Olson** and Sophia **Johanson**.[731]

Hazel Marie **Bisbee** and Albert William **Olson** had the following children born in Boone:
- + 6381 i. Errol Bisbee[12] **Olson** 19 August 1918.
- + 6382 ii. Joyce Marie **Olson** 17 August 1920.
- 6383 iii. Darwin Lavern **Olson**[732] 27 July 1923 and died unmarried 28 May 1994 in Chicago, Cook Co., Ill., at 70 years of age.

5431. **William Burdette**[11] **Perkins** (Marissa Parmelia[10] **Dean**, Martha Putnam[9] **Whipple**, Duick[8], Charles[7], Francis[6], Francis[5], Jonathan[4], Joseph[3], Matthew[2], Matthew[1])[733] birth date unknown, married **Mary Agnes Bigony** in 1882. Mary,[734] daughter of Reuben **Bigony**, was born in Maryland. Mary's parents migrated from the Alsace Lorain area of France to Maryland. In addition to the 10 children listed below, William and Mary had two other daughters, given names not provided. They were Mrs. Leon Gibson of Westfield, Tioga Co., Penn. and Mrs. James Burt of Ulysses, Potter Co., Penn.

William Burdette **Perkins** and Mary Agnes **Bigony** had the following children:

    6384   i.   Guy[12] **Perkins**.[735]
    6385   ii.   Samuel **Perkins**.[736]
    6386   iii.   Phillip **Perkins**.[737]
    6387   iv.   Burdette **Perkins**.[738]
    6388   v.   Paul **Perkins**.[739]
    6389   vi.   Lewis **Perkins**.[740]
    6390   vii.   Reuben **Perkins**.[741]
    6391   viii.   Penn **Perkins**.[742]
    6392   ix.   Mary **Perkins**.[743]
    6393   x.   Dorothy **Perkins**.[744]

5433. **Manson Burdell**[11] **Perkins** (Marissa Parmelia[10] **Dean**, Martha Putnam[9] **Whipple**, Duick[8], Charles[7], Francis[6], Francis[5], Jonathan[4], Joseph[3], Matthew[2], Matthew[1])[745] was born in Sweeden Hill, Potter Co. Penn. in 1852 and died in 1916 at 64 years of age. He married **Carrie Roberts** in Sweeden Hill in 1882. Carrie,[746] daughter of Ben Franklin **Roberts** and Delila **Chase**, was born in Sweden Valley 25 December 1866 and died in June 1956 in Arcade, Wyoming Co., N.Y., at 89 years of age.

Manson Burdell **Perkins** and Carrie **Roberts** had the following children:

        6394   i.   Lee[12] **Perkins**.[747]
+   6395   ii.   Glenn Alonzo **Perkins** born 22 April 1884.
        6396   iii.   Grace **Perkins**[748] born in Sweeden Hill in 1886. She married twice. (1) James **Fassett**. (2) Rev. William **Freeman.**

5434. **Edith May**[11] **Whipple** (Martin Duick[10], Charles Jay[9], Duick[8], Charles[7], Francis[6], Francis[5], Jonathan[4], Joseph[3], Matthew[2], Matthew[1])[749] was born in Westfield, Tioga Co., Penn. 26 June 1884 and married **Richard G. Carr** 1 June 1905. He was born 3 April 1882 and died 25 October 1960 in Pleasantville, Atlantic Co., N.J., at 78 years of age.[750]

Edith May **Whipple** and Richard G. **Carr** had the following children:

+   6397   i.   Elsie Cecelia[12] **Carr** born 9 March 1906.
+   6398   ii.   Ruth Genevieve **Carr** born 4 June 1913.
        6399   iii.   Richard Whipple **Carr**[751] born in Spartansburg, Crawford Co., Penn. 3 February 1916 and died there 23 October 1919, at 3 years of age.
        6400   iv.   Robert Gene **Carr**[752] born in Atlantic City, Atlantic Co., N.J. 28 October 1921.

6401   v.   Eleanor Catherine **Carr**[753] born in Farmington, N. J. 30 September 1924 and married Charles **Hall** 11 October 1942.

5437. Barbara Grace[11] **Whipple** (Addison Willard[10], Charles Jay[9], Duick[8], Charles[7], Francis[6], Francis[5], Jonathan[4], Joseph[3], Matthew[2], Matthew[1])[754] was born in Andrew Settlement, Penn. 28 March 1893 and died 24 August 1971 in Elmira, Chemung Co., N.Y., at 78 years of age. She married **James Ira Van Auken** in Elmira 23 August 1911. He was born in Wyalusing, Penn. 28 October 1890 and died 12 July 1966 in Elmira, at 75 years of age.[755]

Barbara Grace **Whipple** and James Ira **Van Auken** had the following child:
+ 6402   i.   Mildred Grace[12] **Van Auken** born 27 December 1912.

5438. Charles Lewis[11] **Whipple** (Addison Willard[10], Charles Jay[9], Duick[8], Charles[7], Francis[6], Francis[5], Jonathan[4], Joseph[3], Matthew[2], Matthew[1])[756] was born in Andrew Settlement, Penn. 14 December 1895 and married **Amelia Mary Neal** 23 April 1919. She was born 25 June 1897 and died 8 July 1974 at 77 years of age.[757]

Charles Lewis **Whipple** and Amelia Mary **Neal** had the following children:
6403   i.   Marjorie Amelia[12] **Whipple**[758] born in Elmira, Chemung Co., N.Y. 4 July 1921 and died 3 August 1973 at 52 years of age. She married William **Cowan** 23 July 1943.
6404   ii. Charles Donald **Whipple**[759] born in Elmira 30 May 1927.

5441. Malcolm Monteith[11] **Whipple** (Warner F.[10], Frank H.[9], Warner Wright[8], Levi[7], Francis[6], Francis[5], Jonathan[4], Joseph[3], Matthew[2], Matthew[1])[760] was born in LaSalle, La Salle Co., Ill. 27 February 1925 and married **Doris Ann Baker** in Peru, La Salle Co. 17 June 1949. Doris,[761] daughter of William Hunka **Baker** and Vida **Weberling**, was born in Peru 23 February 1926 and died 19 July 2001 at Utica, La Salle Co. at 75 years of age. Buried at Waltham Cemetery, six miles north of Utica. Doris was graduated from the Oberlin Conservatory in 1948 and taught at Northland College in Wis-

Malcolm Monteith Whipple. Photo courtesy of Malcolm M. Whipple.

consin before her marriage. Malcolm was graduated from the U. of Illinois in 1950 where he majored in Agricultural Economics. He worked for the Agricultural Extension Service at Bloomington, McLean Co., Ill. for two years before beginning his farming career. He retired in 1989.

Malcolm Monteith **Whipple** and Doris Ann **Baker** had the following children:
- \+ 6405 i. Malcolm Monteith[12] **Whipple** Jr. born 9 July 1950.
- \+ 6406 ii. William Warner **Whipple** born 15 January 1953.
- 6407 iii. Mark Douglas **Whipple**[762] born in LaSalle 24 July 1954. He earned a degree from Northern Illinois University, DeKalb, De Kalb Co., Ill. in 1976 and did graduate work at the U. of Iowa (1977-78). He worked at Mercy and Resurection Hospitals and for the American Red Cross in Chicago, Cook Co., for several years and is now Marketing Manager for Shwab STEPS Industrial Rehabilitation Clinic, Naperville, Ill (1999).
- \+ 6408 iv. Gregory Baker **Whipple** born 11 August 1959.
- \+ 6409 v. Beth Ann **Whipple** born 20 November 1961.

5444. **Warner William**[11] **Whipple** (Warner Ernest[10], Eugene Warner[9], Warner Wright[8], Levi[7], Francis[6], Francis[5], Jonathan[4], Joseph[3], Matthew[2], Matthew[1])[763] was born in Duluth, St. Louis Co., Minn. 28 February 1914 and died there in 1958, at 44 years of age. He married **Victoria Blanchard**. She died 7 December 1979.[764] Warner served on PT boats in the South Pacific during WWII.

Warner William **Whipple** and Victoria **Blanchard** had the following child:
- \+ 6410 i. Warner Michael[12] **Whipple** born 20 May 1945.

5446. **Charlotte Louise**[11] **Hopkins** (Laura Edna[10] **Whipple**, Eugene Warner[9], Warner Wright[8], Levi[7], Francis[6], Francis[5], Jonathan[4], Joseph[3], Matthew[2], Matthew[1])[765] was born in Chicago, Cook Co., Ill. 22 January 1906 and died there 9 March 1979 at 73 years of age. She married **Luke William Doyle** in Chicago 21 June 1930. He was born in Chicago in December 1905 and died there 29 July 1982 at 76 years of age.[766]

Charlotte Louise **Hopkins** and Luke William **Doyle** had the following children:
- \+ 6411 i. Ruth Ann[12] **Doyle** born 10 May 1933.
- \+ 6412 ii. Thomas Luke **Doyle** born 16 September 1936.

5448. **Floyd Clendenen**[11] **Jones** (Edith[10] **Clendenen**, Josephine[9] **Whipple**, Warner Wright[8], Levi[7], Francis[6], Francis[5], Jonathan[4], Joseph[3], Matthew[2], Matthew[1])[767] was born in Los Angeles, Co., Calif. 25 December 1906 and died there. He married **Elsie Neff** of Allentown, Lehigh Co., Penn. in Los Angeles, Co. She married twice, once to an an unnamed person.[768]

Floyd Clendenen **Jones** and Elsie **Neff** had the following child:
+ 6413 i. Robert[12] **Jones**.

5449. **Mary Allen**[11] **Whipple** (Dr. Allen Oldfather[10], Rev. William Levi[9], Francis Rice[8], Levi[7], Francis[6], Francis[5], Jonathan[4], Joseph[3], Matthew[2], Matthew[1])[769] was born in New York, N.Y. 2 June 1913 and died of heart failure 25 June 1990 in Pasadena, Los Angeles Co., Calif., at 77 years of age. She married **Dr. Richard J. Bing** in Riverdale, Bronx Co., N.Y. 2 June 1938. Richard,[770] son of Berhard **Bing** and Lilli **Aischberg**, was born in Nuremberg, Bavaria, Germany 12 October 1909. Dr. Bing's extensive educational background began at the Universities of Vienna, Munich, and Berlin which he attended from 1929-1934. He received two M.D. degrees: U. of Munich in 1934 and U. of Bern, Switzerland in 1935. He did his Internship at Presbyterian Hospital in New York City 1938-39; his Residency at Johns Hopkins Hospital in Baltimore, Baltimore City Co., 1942-43; and served in the Army Medical Corp. 1943-45 achieving the rank of Lieutenant Colonel.

His teaching appointments include Instructor in Physiology at New York University and Columbia University, New York City; Assistant Professor of Surgery and Assistant Surgeon and Associate Professor of Surgery and Assistant Professor of Medicine at Johns Hopkins Medical School; Professor of Medicine, Professor of Clinical Physiology, and Director of Cardiac Clinic, Medical College, University of Alabama; Director, Washington University Medical Services VA Hospital and Professor of Medicine, Washington University School of Medicine, St. Louis; Professor of Medicine and Chair of the Dept. of Medicine, Wayne State University School of Medicine, Detroit, Professor of Medicine, University of Southern California and Director of Experimental Cardiology and Scientific Development, Huntington Medical Research Institutes and Hutington Memorial Hospital, Pasadena, Los Angeles Co., Calif. 1969–present.

His honors include the Presidential Citation from the American College of Cardiology; Honorary Doctor of Humane Letters, Johns Hopkins University; Honorary Doctorate of Science from the U. of Dusseldorf and the U. of Bologna; Research Achievement Award from the American

Heart Assn.; Distinguished Scientist Award from the American College of Cardiology; the Lindbergh Research Award from the Charles A. Lindbergh Foundation; the Claude Bernard Medal, U. of Montreal, Québec, Canada; the Los Angeles County Heart Association Award; and many others.

Dr. Bing is a former editor-in-chief of *The Journal of Molecular and Cellular Cardiology*, past Editorial Board member, *American Journal of Cardiology*, Editorial Board member of the *Journal of Cardiovascular Research*, and Editor-in-Chief of the *Journal of Applied Cardiology*.

He is also author of *Cardiology: The Evolution of the Science and the Art* and is a member of a variety of medical associations and physiological societies, both national and international.

Mary Allen **Whipple** and Dr. Richard J. **Bing** had the following children:
- \+ 6414 i. Barbara[12] **Bing**.
- \+ 6415 ii. John Whipple Ernst **Bing** born 28 October 1939.
- \+ 6416 iii. Julianne Whipple **Bing** born 14 December 1943.
- 6417 iv. William Whipple **Bing**[771] born 12 February 1947 and married Delores **Main** in Mason City, Cerro Gordo Co., Iowa, 12 August 1972. She was born 20 February 1948.[772]

5450. **Allen Oldfather**[11] **Whipple Jr.** (Dr. Allen Oldfather[10], Rev. William Levi[9], Francis Rice[8], Levi[7], Francis[6], Francis[5], Jonathan[4], Joseph[3], Matthew[2], Matthew[1])[773] was born in New York, N.Y. 13 December 1915 died 8 April 1963 in Princeton, Mercer Co., N.J., at 47 years of age. He married twice. (1) **Clement Brown** in Pensacola, Escambia Co., Fla. 4 July 1941. Clement,[774] daughter of Charles Marshall **Brown** and Mary **Botchford**, was born in Pittsburgh, Allegheny Co., Penn. 24 September 1919. They were divorced in 1949. She married (2) **Hugh Wheeler Sanford Jr** in Delray, Palm Beach Co., Fla. 21 June 1957. (2) **Laura Hewitt**. They were married in the 1950s and lived for a while in Fort Pierce, St. Lucie Co., Fla.

Allen Oldfather **Whipple** Jr. and Clement **Brown** had the following children:
- \+ 6418 i. Foster Neales[12] **Whipple** born 26 October 1944.
- 6419 ii. Allen Oldfather **Whipple** III[775] born at Columbia Presbyterian Hospital in New York, N.Y. 24 January 1946. The family home was Wilton, Fairfield Co., Conn. He never married.
- 6420 iii. Clement **Whipple**[776] born in Wilton in 1948 and died in infancy of polio. His siblings Allen and Foster survived the disease.

{ G 937 }

5453. **George Whipple**[11] **Clark** (Margaret Holmes[10] **Whipple**, Rev. William Levi[9], Francis Rice[8], Levi[7], Francis[6], Francis[5], Jonathan[4], Joseph[3], Matthew[2], Matthew[1])[777] was born in Evanston, Cook Co., Ill. 31 August 1928 and married twice. (1) **Elizabeth Kister** in Cambridge, Middlesex Co., Mass. in December 1954. Elizabeth,[778] daughter of Marion **Kister** and Hanna **Silber**, was born in Warsaw, Poland 27 July 1930. They were divorced in 1972. (2) **Charlotte Huston Reischer** in Brookline, Norfolk Co., Mass. 28 January 1978. Charlotte is the daughter of Charles **Huston** and Geneva **Holmes**.[779] She married (1) **Otto Reischer** and they had four children: Bridget, Blair, Sybil, and Electa.

George earned an AB at Harvard in 1949; a Ph. D at the Massachusetts Institute of Technology (MIT) in 1952 and taught physics at MIT from 1952 to 1997. He became a Professor Emeritus at MIT in 1998. He is a member of the National Academy of Science and the American Academy of Arts and Science.

George Whipple **Clark** and Elizabeth **Kister** had the following children:
- 6421 i. Dr. Katherine Marion Whipple[12] **Clark**[780] born in Boston, Suffolk Co., Mass. 13 May 1958. She earned an AB degree at Brown University, Providence, Providence Co., R. I. and an MD degree from Mt. Sinai Medical School and works in family medicine in Beacon, Dutchess Co., N. Y.
- 6422 ii. Jacqueline Whipple Kister **Clark**[781] born 22 May 1960.

5457. **Allen Whipple**[11] **Clark** (Eunice Fulton[10] **Whipple**, Rev. William Levi[9], Francis Rice[8], Levi[7], Francis[6], Francis[5], Jonathan[4], Joseph[3], Matthew[2], Matthew[1])[782] was born in Harvey, Cook Co., Ill. 31 December 1936 and married **Ann Eila Davison** in Madison, Dane Co., Wisc. 19 June 1966. Ann, daughter of Teppo **Davison** and Catherine **Dinwiddie**, earned an BS (1961) and a Ph.D. (1965) at the U. of Wisconsin, Madison. He became a Professor Emeritus of Anatomy at the University on January 14, 1999.

Allen Whipple **Clark** and Ann Eila **Davison** had the following children born in Madison:
- 6423 i. Robert Davison[12] **Clark**[783] 17 January 1970 and married Mary Eliot **Kennedy** in Pittsburgh, Allegheny Co., Penn., in July 2002. Mary[784] daughter of Thomas Joseph **Kennedy** and Mary **Peirson**, was born in Malaga, Spain 2 June 1965. Robert earned a BA degree form the U. of California, Berkely in 1996 and a JD from the U. of Wisconsin, Madison in 2001. He is a staff attorney for the United Steelworkers of America in Pittsburgh.

6424 ii. Amy **Clark**[785] born in Madison 19 February 1974 and earned a BS in Botany & Genetics from the U. of Wisconsin in 1997 and is a Laboratory Director of NeoClone Biotechnology, Madison. (2002)

5461. **Leslie Edwards**[11] **Holland** (Joseph Lester[10], Mary Henrietta[9] **Green**, Edwards Whipple[8], Stephen Whipple[7], Luci[6] **Whipple**, Edwards[5], Jonathan[4], Joseph[3], Matthew[2], Matthew[1])[786] was born in Worcester, Worcester Co., Mass. 3 May 1921 and married **Rose Inez Morang** in Auburn, Worcester Co., Mass. 13 April 1959. Rose,[787] daughter of George W. **Morang** and Ethel M. **Webb**, was born in Worcester 15 October 1924 and died there 26 January 1991 at 66 years of age. She married (1) **(__) Kelly**. Buried in Hope Cemetery. Leslie, an Army veteran of World War II (1942-5), was an Engineer and Inventor. He was living in retirement in Worcester in 1998 and was legally blind and deaf. Rose had sons Karl and Robert **Kelly** with her first husband.

Leslie Edwards **Holland** and Rose Inez **Morang** had the following children born in Worcester:

6425 i. Elaine Frances Kielinen[12] **Holland**[788] 6 October 1946 and died of cancer 20 January 1995 at 48 years of age. She married twice. (1) An unnamed person. (2) Ellwood V. **Lovely**.

6426 ii. George L. **Holland**[789] 2 February 1948.

6427 iii. Darlene Eva **Holland**[790] 1 July 1949 and died there of cancer 28 August 1995 at 46 years of age. She married three times. (1) Chet **Allison**. (2) Roger **Thuet**. (3) Wayne **Norton**.

6428 iv. Wendy Mae **Holland**[791] 19 December 1951.

6429 v. James Stephen **Holland**[792] 6 April 1959.

6430 vi. Starr Melody **Holland**[793] 18 June 1961.

6431 vii. Todd Lance **Holland**[794] 18 May 1969.

5462. **Orace Thomas**[11] **Holland** (Joseph Lester[10], Mary Henrietta[9] **Green**, Edwards Whipple[8], Stephen Whipple[7], Luci[6] **Whipple**, Edwards[5], Jonathan[4], Joseph[3], Matthew[2], Matthew[1])[795] was born in Worcester, Worcester Co., Mass. 24 September 1923 and married **Alice Hunt** there in January 1948. Alice,[796] daughter of John A. **Hunt** and Gertrude Isabel **Wright**, was born 24 July 1928.

Orace Thomas **Holland** and Alice **Hunt** had the following children born in Worcester:

    6432   i.   Thomas[12] Robert **Holland**[797] 30 December 1949 and married Claudia (__).

    6433   ii.   Marilyn Louise **Holland**[798] 27 July 1952 and married Robert **Rousseau**.

    6434   iii.   Karen Elizabeth **Holland**[799] 14 May 1958.

    6435   iv.   Carol Ann **Holland**[800] 13 September 1959.

    6436   v.   Bonnie Jeanne **Holland**[801] 5 October 1963.

5463. **Robert Edwin**[11] **Holland** (Joseph Lester[10], Mary Henrietta[9] **Green**, Edwards Whipple[8], Stephen Whipple[7], Luci[6] **Whipple**, Edwards[5], Jonathan[4], Joseph[3], Matthew[2], Matthew[1])[802] was born in Worcester, Worcester Co., Mass. 29 January 1926 and married twice. (1) Ruth **Bruno** in Worcester in 1947. (2) D. **Brockney** in 1960.

Robert Edwin **Holland** and Ruth **Bruno** had the following child:

+   6437   i.   Bernard George[12] **Holland** born 29 July 1948.

5465. **Luva Marion**[11] **Nichols** (Bertrand Fayette[10], Catherine[9] **Whipple**, Joel[8], Edmund Rice[7], Jonathan[6], Edwards[5], Jonathan[4], Joseph[3], Matthew[2], Matthew[1])[803] was born in Miles Pond, Essex Co., Vt. 5 May 1904 and died 2 January 1965 in St. Petersburg, Pinellas Co., Fla., at 60 years of age. She married **Edward Alfred Powers** in Springfield, Hampden Co., Mass. 26 October 1922. Edward,[804] son of Michael Louis **Powers** and Johanna **Whalen**, was born in Orange, Franklin Co., Mass. 31 July 1896 and died 21 July 1948 in Springfield, at 51 years of age. Both are buried in the Hillcrest Cemetery, Springfield.

Luva Marion **Nichols** and Edward Alfred **Powers** had the following children:

+   6438   i.   Edward Nichols[12] **Powers** born 5 June 1923.

+   6439   ii.   Shirley Luva **Powers** born 21 February 1925.

+   6440   iii.   William Roy **Powers** born 19 February 1926.

+   6441   iv.   Roy Clifford **Powers** born 29 September 1928.

+   6442   v.   Robert Alfred **Powers** born 9 March 1932.

5472. **John Stevens**[11] **Whipple** (Herbert Foster[10], Simeon Foster[9], Simeon R.[8], Joel Green[7], Jonathan[6], Edwards[5], Jonathan[4], Joseph[3], Matthew[2], Matthew[1])[805] was born in Lowell, Middlessex Co., Mass. 24 June 1909[806] and died 15 November 1977 in Marblehead, Essex Co., Mass., at 68 years of age. He married **Mary Natalie Lynch** in Salem, Essex Co., Mass. 15 April 1939. Natalie,[807] daughter of James **Lynch** and Margaret J.

White, was born in Cambridge, Middlesex Co., Mass. 6 May 1911. John earned an A.B. from Dartmouth (1930), an LL.B from Harvard (1933) and was a partner in the Boston, Mass. law firm of Peabody & Arnold. He lived in Marblehead from 1939 until his death. He was active in local government and was Secretary, later Commodore, of the Corinthian Yacht Club in Marblehead. He is buried in Waterside Cemetery, Marblehead.

John Stevens **Whipple** and Mary Natalie **Lynch** had the following children born in Marblehead:

  6443 i. James Foster[12] **Whipple**[808] 1 September 1940. He earned an A.B. from Yale (1962) and an LL.B from Harvard (1965). He was Assistant Vice President and Counsel, Liberty Mutual Insurance Co., Boston when he retired in 1995. He was living in Boston in 1999.

  6444 ii. John Emery **Whipple**[809] 21 January 1943. He earned an A.B. from Georgetown (1964) and an A.M. from Duke (1969). He worked for the Internal Revenue Service in Boston and is a Past Chairman of the Board of Selectmen in Marblehead. He was ordained as a Deacon by Cardinal and Archbishop Bernard Law in Boston 14 Sept. 1996. He was assigned to serve Our Lady, Star of the Sea Church, in Marblehead. Deacons are akin to assistant priests and work part-time nights and weekends without pay.

+ 6445 iii. Jeremy Alfred **Whipple** 13 August 1950.

5473. **James Beaumont**[11] **Whipple** (Herbert Foster[10], Simeon Foster[9], Simeon R.[8], Joel Green[7], Jonathan[6], Edwards[5], Jonathan[4], Joseph[3], Matthew[2], Matthew[1])[810] was born in Lowell, Middlesex Co., Mass. 31 May 1913[811] and died at Massachusetts General Hospital 17 November 1988 in Boston, Suffolk Co., Mass., at 75 years of age. Buried in Waterside Cemetery, Marblehead, Essex Co., Mass. He married **Florence Corkum** in Waban, Middlesex Co., Mass. 3 September 1946. She was born in Everett, Middlesex Co., Mass. 29 October 1919.[812] James earned an A.B at Dartmouth and a Ph.D. at Case Western Reserve in Cleveland, Cuyahoga Co., Ohio. He lived in Cleveland and Chicago for many years before returning to Massachusetts where he worked for many years at the Massachusetts Center for the Study of Liberal Education for Adults. He served on the Planning Committee for Bunker Hill Community College of Charlestown, Suffolk Co., before it opened in 1973; became one of its Administrators and eventually a Professor of American History. He lived in Marblehead the final 25 years of his life. He was in a Boston hospital recuperating from a serious auto accident when he suffered a fatal heart attack.

James Beaumont **Whipple** and Florence **Corkum** had the following children:

  6446 i. Jonathan Beaumont[12] **Whipple**[813] born 25 April 1957 and married Martha **Day** in 1989.[814] Jonathan was living in Fairfield, Jefferson Co., Iowa in 1999. He and Martha Day were separated in 1992.

  6447 ii. Judith Helen **Whipple**[815] born 26 May 1959 and married Paul **Leef** in Marblehead 13 October 1985.[816] They were living in Charlottesville, Charlottesville City Co., Va. in 1991.

5474. **Emery Stevens**[11] **Whipple** (Herbert Foster[10], Simeon Foster[9], Simeon R.[8], Joel Green[7], Jonathan[6], Edwards[5], Jonathan[4], Joseph[3], Matthew[2], Matthew[1])[817] was born in Lowell, Middlesex Co., Mass. 13 June 1915 and died of cancer 1 January 1989 in Honolulu, Oahu, Hawaii, at 73 years of age. He married **Nellie Ellen (Quinn) Smith** 15 June 1958. Nellie,[818] daughter of Charles Clark **Quinn** and Georgia Belle **Culpepper**, was born in Texas City, Galveston Co., Tex. 13 March 1923 and died 20 December 1987 in Miami, Dade Co., Fla., at 64 years of age. They were divorced abt 1968. Emery retired from the U.S. Marine Corps as a sergeant in 1960. He was stationed at Kaneohe Marine Corps Base, Hawaii at time of retirement. The ashes of both Emery and Nell were scattered off Kaena Point on the leeward side of Oahu near Waianae, Hawaii.

Emery Stevens **Whipple** and Nellie Ellen (Quinn) **Smith** had the following children:

+ 6448 i. Elizabeth Faith[12] **Whipple** born 25 October 1959.

  6449 ii. Clark Saunders **Whipple**[819] born in Honolulu 19 November 1960 and died 1 December 1990 at 30 years of age. He married an unnamed person in Miami 14 February 1986. His ashes were spread off Kaena Point near Waianae, Hawaii in March 1992.

5475. **Victoria Smith**[11] **Whipple** (Sidney Beaumont[10], Simeon Foster[9], Simeon R.[8], Joel Green[7], Jonathan[6], Edwards[5], Jonathan[4], Joseph[3], Matthew[2], Matthew[1])[820] was born 25 October 1917[821] and died in January 1984 in South Carolina, at 66 years of age. She married **William J. McKennan** December 1940.

Victoria Smith **Whipple** and William J. **McKennan** had the following children:

  6450 i. William W.[12] **McKennan**[822] born 28 November 1942.

  6451 ii. John Bradley **McKennan**[823] born 26 August 1944.

  6452 iii. David **McKennan**[824] born abt 1947.

5479. **Howard Rickard**[11] **Staples** (Arthur[10], Ella Melissa[9] **Whipple**, Chandler[8], Samuel[7], John[6], Edwards[5], Jonathan[4], Joseph[3], Matthew[2], Matthew[1])[825] was born 9 October 1920 and married **Maribelle Peckinpah**.

Howard Rickard **Staples** and Maribelle **Peckinpah** had the following child:
    6453   i.   Nancy[12] **Staples**.[826]

5480. **Ruth Adelaide**[11] **Staples** (Arthur[10], Ella Melissa[9] **Whipple**, Chandler[8], Samuel[7], John[6], Edwards[5], Jonathan[4], Joseph[3], Matthew[2], Matthew[1])[827] was born 29 March 1924 and married **Russell R. Kletzing**.

Ruth Adelaide **Staples** and Russell R. **Kletzing** had the following child:
    6454   i.   Craig[12] **Kletzing**.[828]

5481. **Marian Idelle**[11] **Beam** (Virginia Idelle[10] **Whipple**, Allen Lavier[9], Chandler[8], Samuel[7], John[6], Edwards[5], Jonathan[4], Joseph[3], Matthew[2], Matthew[1])[829] was born in Detroit, Wayne Co., Mich. 6 February 1931 and married **Peter James Kurapka IX** in Detroit 9 July 1955. Peter,[830] son of Peter James **Kurapka** VIII and Geraldine **Jayne**, was born in Gate City, Scott Co., Va. 12 August 1932. He earned two degrees from Washington and Lee University: a B.A. in 1953 and an L.L.B. in 1955. He was in the Armed Forces from January 1956 to July 1959, serving in the 318th U.S. Army Security Agency and was stationed in Germany. He held the rank of Specialist 5th class. Marian was graduated from the U. of Michigan with an A.B. degree in 1952 and earned a M.S. in Library Science from Western Reserve University in 1954.

Marian Idelle **Beam** and Peter James **Kurapka** IX had the following children:
    6455   i.   Peter James[12] **Kukrapka** X[831] born at a U.S. Army Hospital in Nuernburg, Germany 14 September 1958 and died there there 3 days later. Buried in Detroit.
+   6456 ii. Virginia Idelle **Kurapka** born 30 December 1959.
    6457 iii. David James **Kurapka**[832] born in Catonsville, Baltimore Co., Md. 9 April 1962 and married Carol Beth **Emert** in Washington, D.C. 21 October 1994. Carol,[833] daughter of Lee **Emert** and Joyce (__), was born in Germantown, Ohio 10 December 1964. David and Carol live in Oakland, Alameda Co., California where he was a speech writer for Robert Rubin, Secretary of the Treasury in 1999, and Carol was a reporter for the *San Francisco Chronicle* in 1999. David was graduated with a BA degree from the University of the South, Sewanne, Franklin Co., Tenn. in 1984. Carol is a graduate of Harvard.

5484. **Martha Lou**[11] **Simmons** (Allen Burdette[10], Mary Annette[9] **Whipple**, Chandler[8], Samuel[7], John[6], Edwards[5], Jonathan[4], Joseph[3], Matthew[2], Matthew[1])[834] was born 2 September 1946 and married **Billy Ray Denny** 14 September 1963.

Martha Lou **Simmons** and Billy Ray **Denny** had the following children:
    6458   i.   David Allen[12] **Denny**[835] born 15 April 1964.
    6459   ii. Sherrie Lynn **Denny**[836] born 20 March 1965.

5485. **John Leonard**[11] **Whipple** (Leonard Langford[10], Samuel Dexter[9], Allen Benedict Chaffee[8], Samuel[7], John[6], Edwards[5], Jonathan[4], Joseph[3], Matthew[2], Matthew[1])[837] was born in El Segundo, Los Angeles Co., Calif. 19 February 1938 and married **Patricia Anne Bacon** in Palos Verdes Estates, Los Angeles Co., Calif. 1 June 1963. Patricia,[838] daughter of James **Bacon** and Loretta **Othick**, was born in San Diego, San Diego Co., Calif. 9 August 1938. John was graduated from Yale in 1959.

John Leonard **Whipple** and Patricia Anne **Bacon** had the following children:
    6460   i.   Jeffrey William[12] **Whipple**[839] born in Phoenix, Maricopa Co., Ariz. 11 November 1967.
    6461   ii. Richard William **Whipple**[840] born in Phoenix 11 November 1967 and married Holly McFarlan **Hayes** in Ocho Rios, Jamaica 28 July 1999. Holly,[841] daughter of Ernest Thomas **Hayes** Jr. and Sandra Dawn **Daniels**, was born in Cumberland Co., No. Carolina 4 May 1963.
+   6462 iii. Elizabeth Dee **Whipple** born 10 August 1970.

5487. **Helen Marie**[11] **Chaffee** (Lyman Walter[10], Lyman Bruce[9], Lyman Edward[8], Mary[7] **Whipple**, John[6], Edwards[5], Jonathan[4], Joseph[3], Matthew[2], Matthew[1]) was born in Wellsville, Allegany Co., N.Y. 13 July 1925 and married **Richard F. Chandler** of Wellsville there in Ocober 1946. Richard is the son of Robert **Chandler** and Clara **Malby**.[842]

Helen Marie **Chaffee** and Richard F. **Chandler** had the following child born in Wellsville:
    6463   i.   Carrie Chaffee[12] **Chandler**[843] 13 August 1962.

5488. **Christine Winifred**[11] **Chaffee** (Lyman Walter[10], Lyman Bruce[9], Lyman Edward[8], Mary[7] **Whipple**, John[6], Edwards[5], Jonathan[4], Joseph[3], Matthew[2], Matthew[1])[844] was born in Wellsville, Allegany Co., N.Y. 8 September 1928 and and married **John J. Rapoza Jr.** of Yerington, Lyon

Co., Nevada in San Francisco, San Francisco Co., Calif. in December 1950. John is the son of John **Rapoza** and Marie **Borge**.[845]

Christine Winifred **Chaffee** and John J. **Rapoza** Jr. had the following children born in Mountain View, Santa Clara Co., Calif.:
- 6464 i. Jerome[12] **Rapoza**[846] 29 December 1951.
- 6465 ii. Christina Marie **Rapoza**[847] 11 August 1958.

5489. **Marilyn Janet**[11] **Chaffee** (Harold Bruce[10], Lyman Bruce[9], Lyman Edward[8], Mary[7] **Whipple**, John[6], Edwards[5], Jonathan[4], Joseph[3], Matthew[2], Matthew[1])[848] was born 31 March 1933 and married **George Ostrander** in Angelica, Allegany Co., N.Y. 17 July 1954. George,[489] son of George **Ostrander** and Florence **Wells**, was born in Almond, Allegany Co., N.Y. 7 March 1930.

Marilyn Janet **Chaffee** and George **Ostrander** had the following children:
- 6466 i. George Robert[12] **Ostrander** III[850] born 8 June 1955.
- 6467 ii. Katherine Dianne **Ostrander**[851] born 10 November 1958.
- 6468 iii. David Chaffee **Ostrander**[852] born 7 September 1961.
- 6469 iv. Joel Hunter **Ostrander**[853] born 8 July 1964.

5490. **Dianna Ruth**[11] **Chaffee** (Harold Bruce[10], Lyman Bruce[9], Lyman Edward[8], Mary[7] **Whipple**, John[6], Edwards[5], Jonathan[4], Joseph[3], Matthew[2], Matthew[1])[854] was born 20 January 1938 and married **Ralph Stanley Casperson Jr.** in Angelica, Allegany Co., N.Y. 28 June 1958. Ralph,[855] son of Ralph **Casperson** and Ruby **Brent**, was born in Rochester, Monroe Co., N.Y. 4 March 1935.

Dianna Ruth **Chaffee** and Ralph Stanley **Casperson** Jr. had the following children born in Batavia, Genesse Co., N. Y.:
- 6470 i. Rebecca Elaine[12] **Casperson**[856] 22 October 1960.
- 6471 ii. Stephen James **Casperson**[857] 28 March 1964.

5493. **Lillian Alice**[11] **Bess** (Lillian Belle[10] **Whipple**, Charles H.[9], Solomon[8], Russell[7], Solomon[6], Joseph[5], John[4], Joseph[3], Matthew[2], Matthew[1])[858] was born in Catherine, Schyler Co., N.Y. 29 September 1892 and died 6 February 1971 in Houston, Harris Co., Tex., at 78 years of age. She married **Lehman Sadler** in Black Creek, Allegany Co., N. Y. 8 June 1912. Lehman,[859] son of Uriah **Sadler** and Emma **Peasley**, was born in Gold, Ulysses Township., Potter Co., Penn. 23 April 1886 and died 3 November 1965 in Pasadena, Harris Co., Tex., at 79 years of age.

{ G 945 }

Lillian Alice **Bess** and Lehman **Sadler** had the following children:

+ 6472 i. Leon Delbert[12] **Sadler** born 10 November 1913.
+ 6473 ii. Lloyd Allen **Sadler** born 5 April 1916.
+ 6474 iii. Fredrick Henry **Sadler** born 26 April 1918.
+ 6475 iv. Everett Robert **Sadler** born 23 November 1920.
    6476 v. Leona Mae **Sadler**[860] born 14 April 1922 and married Donald W. **Freeman** 14 March 1946.
+ 6477 vi. Lillian Bessie **Sadler** born 10 April 1925.
+ 6478 vii. Gladys Gertrude **Sadler** born 15 August 1931.
+ 6479 viii. Kenneth Paul **Sadler** born 7 August 1933.
    6480 ix. Stanley Eugene **Sadler**[861] born 10 June 1936.
+ 6481 x. Eugene Richard **Sadler** born 26 April 1938.

5500. **Guy Burke**[11] **Whipple** (Orrin[10], Orrin Frank[9], Ira Martin[8], Elijah[7], Jeremiah[6], Joseph[5], John[4], Joseph[3], Matthew[2], Matthew[1])[862] was born in Ohio in 1878 and died there in 1927, at 49 years of age. Buried at Springdale Cemetery, Reilly Township., Butler Co., Ohio. He married **Christina Desher**. She was born in 1876 and died in 1935 at 59 years of age.[863]

Guy Burke **Whipple** and Christina **Desher** had the following child:
    6482 i. Guy Floyd[12] **Whipple**[864] died in 1905 in Ohio. Buried at the Springdale Cemetery.

5506. **Ladie Ellen**[11] **Smith** (Ruby Sophronia[10] **Whipple**, William[9], Ira Martin[8], Elijah[7], Jeremiah[6], Joseph[5], John[4], Joseph[3], Matthew[2], Matthew[1])[865] was born in Kansas 21 January 1880 and died 11 January 1975 in Oklahoma, at 94 years of age. Buried in Wier,[866] Okla. She married **Charles Andrew Ward** in Milan, Summer Co., Kansas 9 September 1898.[867]

Ladie Ellen **Smith** and Charles Andrew **Ward** had the following children:
    6483 i. Katie Cord[12] **Ward**.[868]
    6484 ii. Willis Dowell **Ward**.[869]
    6485 iii. Bessie Erma **Ward**.[870]
    6486 iv. Theodore Isaac **Ward**.[871]
    6487 v. Sylvia Thelma **Ward**.[872]
    6488 vi. George Franklin **Ward**[873] born 11 August 1898.
    6489 vii. Sadie Ellen **Ward**[874] born in Medford, Grant Co., Okla. 19 July 1902 and died 28 October 1971 in Ontario, San Bernardino Co., Calif., at 69 years of age.
    6490 viii. Andrew Daniel **Ward**[875] born 11 July 1904.
    6491 ix. Dolly May **Ward**[876] born 10 August 1919 and died 6 days later.

6492 x. Lester Luroy **Ward**[877] born 19 April 1921 and died 2 April 1922 at almost 1 year of age.

6493 xi. Roy Edward **Ward**[878] born 24 March 1924 and died 1 November 1981 at 57 years of age.

5508. **Mary Elizabeth**[11] **Smith** (Ruby Sophronia[10] **Whipple**, William[9], Ira Martin[8], Elijah[7], Jeremiah[6], Joseph[5], John[4], Joseph[3], Matthew[2], Matthew[1])[879] was born in Anthony, Harper Co., Kansas 6 March 1886 and died 3 June 1969 in Afton, Ottawa Co., Oklahoma, at 83 years of age.[880] Her obituary stated she moved from Kingfisher, Kingfisher Co., Okla. to Afton 20 years prior to death. Funeral arrangements were with James Thomas Funeral Director. She was buried close by her mother, **Ruby Whipple Smith Ward,** in the Southwest City, Missouri Cemetery. There is a marker on her grave. She married three times. (1) **Orange Riley Sproat** in Anthony 17 January 1906. Their marriage license is dated 17 Jan. 1906 and is found in Book E., Page 70, Records of Harper Co., Kansas. Orange[881] son of Cochran **Sproat** and Maria **Riley**, was born in Loudon, Fayette Co., Illinois 26 January 1855 and died 8 October 1915 in Beecher City, Effingham Co., Illinois, at 60 years of age. (2) **James Westley Redington** abt 1916. James,[882] son of John **Redington** and Cordelia (__), was born in Kansas 23 March 1885 and died in December 1963 in Alaska, at 78 years of age. (3) **Herman Redington** aft 1917. He was born in Kingfisher 22 September 1897 and died in December 1984 at 87 years of age.[883] Buried in Fairland Cemetery, Fairland, Ottawa Co., Oklahoma.

Mary Elizabeth **Smith** and James Westley **Redington** had the following children:

+ 6494 i. Ray[12] **Redington.**
+ 6495 ii. Joe **Redington** born 1 February 1917.

Mary Elizabeth **Smith** and Herman **Redington** had the following child:
6496 iii. Hazel **Redington.**[884]

Mary Elizabeth **Smith** and Orange Riley **Sproat** had the following children:
+ 6497 iv. Richard H. **Sproat** Sr. born 12 June 1904.
+ 6498 v. Edna Pearl **Sproat** born 29 July 1907.
+ 6499 vi. Mildred Elizabeth **Sproat** born 25 March 1910.
  6500 vii. Fred Riley **Sproat**[885] born in 1913 and died abt 1972.
+ 6501 viii. Everett Leander (**Sproat**) **Richards** born 25 June 1915.

5509. **Sara Jane**[11] **Ward** (Ruby Sophronia[10] **Whipple**, William[9], Ira Martin[8], Elijah[7], Jeremiah[6], Joseph[5], John[4], Joseph[3], Matthew[2],

Matthew[1])[886] was born in Caldwell, Sumner Co., Kans. 30 September 1889 and died 30 July 1965 in Williamsfield, Knox Co., Ill., at 75 years of age. She married **Roy Otis Thompson** in Buffalo, Dallas Co., Mo. 28 February 1909. Roy,[887] son of Charles **Thompson** and Mary **Franklin**, was born in Lee Township, Brown Co., Ill. 8 May 1889 and died 6 June 1969 in Galesburg, Knox Co., Ill., at 80 years of age.

Sara Jane **Ward** and Roy Otis **Thompson** had the following children:
   6502 i. Charles[12] **Thompson**[888] born in Buffalo 8 December 1909 and died there in June 1911, at 1 year of age.
+ 6503 ii. Virgil Ray **Thompson** born 2 February 1911.
+ 6504 iii. Dorothy Louise **Thompson** born in 1913.
+ 6505 iv. Donald Louis **Thompson** born in 1913.
+ 6506 v. Theodore **Thompson** born in 1920.
+ 6507 vi. Gladys Eileen **Thompson** born in 1923.
+ 6508 vii. Albert Leroy **Thompson** born in 1930.
+ 6509 viii. Robert Lee **Thompson** born in 1939.

5510. Laura Alice[11] **Ward** (Ruby Sophronia[10] **Whipple**, William[9], Ira Martin[8], Elijah[7], Jeremiah[6], Joseph[5], John[4], Joseph[3], Matthew[2], Matthew[1])[889] was born in Kansas 7 April 1891 and died 7 March 1970 in Ridgeway, Ouray Co., Colo., at 78 years of age. She married twice. (1) **(__) Buckley**. (2) **(__) Butner**.

Laura Alice **Ward** and (__) **Buckley** had the following children:
   6510 i. James[12] **Buckley** born in 1911.[890]
   6511 ii. Vonley **Buckley** born in 1913.[891]

5512. Cora A.[11] **Ward** (Ruby Sophronia[10] **Whipple**, William[9], Ira Martin[8], Elijah[7], Jeremiah[6], Joseph[5], John[4], Joseph[3], Matthew[2], Matthew[1])[892] was born in Kansas in August 1893 and died in 1975 in Knoxville, Knox Co., Ill., at 81 years of age. She married twice. (1) **Herbert Newton Smith**. (2) **William Rick**.

Cora A. **Ward** and Herbert Newton **Smith** had the following children:
+ 6512 i. Ruby Gertrude[12] **Smith** born in 1918.
   6513 ii. Helen Elizabeth **Smith**[893] born in 1919 and married (__) **Stubblebean**.
+ 6514 iii. Hazel Eileen **Smith** born in 1920.

5514. James Eugene[11] **Ward** (Ruby Sophronia[10] **Whipple**, William[9], Ira Martin[8], Elijah[7], Jeremiah[6], Joseph[5], John[4], Joseph[3], Matthew[2],

Matthew[1])[894] was born in Medford, Grant Co., Okla. 5 October 1902 and died 8 April 1945 in Houston, Harris Co., Tex., at 42 years of age. He married **Gracie Mae Bocox** in Galesburg, Knox Co., Ill. 23 November 1921. Gracie,[895] daughter of Samuel **Bocox** and Susan **Henry**, was born in Randall, Knox Co, Ill. 4 June 1904 and died 4 January 1988 in Houston, at 83 years of age. Gracie was James' second wife. No information provided on the first wife.

James Eugene **Ward** and Gracie Mae **Bocox** had the following children:
+ 6515 i. Samuel Alfred[12] **Ward** born 28 July 1922.
+ 6516 ii. Phyllis Marie **Ward** born 18 February 1924.
+ 6517 iii. James Eugene **Ward** II born 4 November 1926.
+ 6518 iv. Merle Frederick **Ward** born 13 October 1927.
+ 6519 v. Peggy Joyce **Ward** born 1 July 1931.

5515. **William Thomas**[11] **Teague** (Eunice Augusta[10] **Whipple**, William[9], Ira Martin[8], Elijah[7], Jeremiah[6], Joseph[5], John[4], Joseph[3], Matthew[2], Matthew[1])[896] was born in Napa, Napa Co., Calif. 10 July 1878 and died of cancer 31 August 1958 in Sarasota, Sarasota Co., Fla., at 80 years of age. He married **Bertie Mae Bardo** in Oakland, Alameda Co., Calif. 24 April 1902. Bertie,[897] daughter of Levi **Bardo** and Jane **Miller**, died 13 March 1966 in East Orange, Essex Co., N.J. William was educated at San Jose State University and was an Executive Vice President with A. T. & T.

William Thomas **Teague** and Bertie Mae **Bardo** had the following children:
+ 6520 i. Allan Leonard[12] **Teague** born 30 October 1903.
+ 6521 ii. Roland Bardo **Teague** born 29 June 1907.
+ 6522 iii. Burton William **Teague** born 12 October 1912.

5516. **Arthur**[11] **Teague** (Eunice Augusta[10] **Whipple**, William[9], Ira Martin[8], Elijah[7], Jeremiah[6], Joseph[5], John[4], Joseph[3], Matthew[2], Matthew[1])[898] was born in Saratoga, Santa Clara Co., Calif. 6 August 1882[899] and died 8 September 1942 in San Mateo, San Mateo, Co., Calif., at 60 years of age. He married **Mary Christie McLean** in San Francisco, San Francisco Co., Calif. 7 April 1912. Mary,[900] daughter of William **McLean** and Selina **Pomroy**, died 10 January 1938 in San Mateo. She immigrated to California from Hawaii in 1904. Both are buried in the Pescadero, San Mateo Co., Calif. Cemetery.

Arthur **Teague** and Mary Christie **McLean** had the following children:
+ 6523 i. Ethel Virginia[12] **Teague** born 24 April 1913.
+ 6524 ii. Elsie May **Teague** born 18 May 1914.

+ 6525 iii. James Frederick **Teague** born 13 January 1917.
6526 iv. Marjorie Louise **Teague** born in Redwood City, San Mateo Co., Calif. 5 February 1922 and married twice. (1) Charles P. **Porth** abt 1944 who died 8 March 1962 in Palo Alto, Santa Clara Co., Calif.[901] (2) Lloyd **Schneider** aft 1962.

5520. **Eunice May**[11] **Teague** (Eunice Augusta[10] **Whipple**, William[9], Ira Martin[8], Elijah[7], Jeremiah[6], Joseph[5], John[4], Joseph[3], Matthew[2], Matthew[1])[902] was born in Pescadero, San Mateo Co., Calif. 29 May 1896[903] and died 20 June 1967 in Redwood City, San Mateo Co., Calif., at 71 years of age.[904] She married **Harry Emmons Dearborn** in Pescadero 17 June 1917.[905] Harry,[906] son of Henry **Dearborn** and Lillie **Hobbs**, died 4 August 1949 in Truckee, Placer Co., Calif. Harry attended Polytechnic Engineering College and was an automobile dealer. Eunice and Harry are buried in Pescadero.

Eunice May **Teague** and Harry Emmons **Dearborn** had the following child:
+ 6527 i. Janet Anne[12] **Dearborn** born 23 January 1935.

5521. **Nancy**[11] **Rice** (Ellen Boise[10] **Leland**, Alonzo[9], Jasper[8], Lydia[7] **Sherman**, Mary[6] **Whipple**, Lieut. James[5], Deacon James[4], Joseph[3], Matthew[2], Matthew[1])[907] was born in Mount Idaho, Idaho Co., Idaho 9 May 1874 and died 30 September 1946 in Grangeville, Idaho Co., Idaho, at 72 years of age. She married **Francis Marion F. Bowman** in Grangeville 30 November 1890. Francis,[908] son of George Lewis **Bowman** and Mary **McLean**, was born in Arbor Hill,[909] Va. 9 August 1856 and died 1 May 1927 in Grangeville, at 70 years of age.

Nancy **Rice** and Francis Marion F. **Bowman** had the following child:
+ 6528 i. Lawrence Francis[12] **Bowman** born 22 January 1895.

5522. **Mabel Frances**[11] **Reynolds** (Helen[10] **Butterfield**, Elizabeth S.[9] **Reynolds**, Sarah W.R.[8] **Leland**, Thankful[7] **Sherman**, Mary[6] **Whipple**, Lieut. James[5], Deacon James[4], Joseph[3], Matthew[2], Matthew[1])[910] was born in San Rafael, Marin Co., Calif. 5 October 1875 and died there in November 1934, at 59 years of age. She married **William Peter Treanor** who was born in San Francisco, San Francisco Co., Calif. 25 September 1867 and died 9 September 1911 Fairfax, Marin Co., Calif., at 43 years of age.[911] Borh are buried in Mt. Tamalpais Cemetery, San Rafael.

Mabel Frances **Reynolds** and William Peter **Treanor** had the following child:
+ 6529 i. Grace[12] **Treanor** born 5 May 1895.

5532. **Marion Helena**[11] **Hill** (Ovid[10], Mary Ann[9] **Ayres**, Diademia[8] **Whipple**, Oliver[7], Lt. James[6], Lieut. James[5], Deacon James[4], Joseph[3], Matthew[2], Matthew[1])[912] was born in North Brookfield, Worcester Co., Mass. 22 August 1875 and died at the home of her daughter Henrietta Osborn Maury 10 June 1956 in Vineyard Haven, Dukes Co., Mass., at 80 years of age. She married **Walter Strong Osborn** in Edgartown, Dukes Co., Mass. 22 March 1900. He was born in Edgartown 25 October 1859 and died there 17 May 1928, at 68 years of age.[913]

Marion Helena **Hill** and Walter Strong **Osborn** had the following child born in Edartown:

    6530   i.   Elizabeth[12] **Osborn**[914] 3 October 1915 and married Henry Kyle **Ward** 26 August 1939. He was born 17 September 1909.[915]

5534. **William Vinet**[11] **Whipple** (Vinet A.[10], Adolphus Perley[9], Elijah Drury[8], Perley[7], Lt. James[6], Lieut. James[5], Deacon James[4], Joseph[3], Matthew[2], Matthew[1])[916] was born 14 January 1879 and died 12 September 1910 in Weaverville, Trinity Co., Calif., at 31 years of age. He married **Mabel E. Rafter** in Minneapolis, Hennepin Co., Minn., 28 September 1898.

William Vinet **Whipple** and Mabel E. **Rafter** had the following child born in Minneapolis:

    6531   i.   Ariel[12] **Whipple**[917] 4 November 1903 and died 1 February 1989 in Mercer Island, King Co., Wash., at 85 years of age. She married Wilbur Warren **Holes** in Minneapolis 28 February 1925.

5541. **Lewis Erwin**[11] **Whipple** (Harrison Leland[10], Alonzo Brigham[9], Edmund[8], Perley[7], Lt. James[6], Lieut. James[5], Deacon James[4], Joseph[3], Matthew[2], Matthew[1])[918] was born in Natick, Middlesex Co., Mass. 26 March 1882 and died there 17 July 1959, at 77 years of age. He married **Lizzie Emma Dight** in West Springfield, Hampden Co., Mass. 15 August 1906. She was the daughter of Alexander **Dight**.[919] Lewis was a manufacturer. His biography appears in Vol. 48 of the *National Cyclopaedia of American Biography*, 1965, 453. He was executor of the will of his uncle Charles Ayer, the noted portrait painter. (See Charles Ayer in Generation 10.)

Lewis Erwin **Whipple** had the following child:

    6532   i.   Dorothy[12] **Whipple**.[920]

Lewis Erwin **Whipple** and Lizzie Emma **Dight** had the following child born in Natick:
>   6533   ii.   Dorothy Dight **Whipple**[921] 7 June 1908 and married Alvin Wesley **Crain**.

5552. **Francis John**[11] **Whipple** (Fancis Looby[10], Lysander Greenlief[9], Edmund[8], Perley[7], Lt. James[6], Lieut. James[5], Deacon James[4], Joseph[3], Matthew[2], Matthew[1])[922] was born in Orange, New South Wales (NSW), Australia 31 May 1900 and died 22 February 1978 in Stratchfield, NSW, at 77 years of age. He married **Olive Catherine Bond** in April 1927.[923] She died 9 August 1990 in Australia. Francis was a career Army Officer with service in Australia and Japan. He was with the War Crimes Tribunal, British Commonwealth Occupation Forces, Kure, Japan during his final years of service.

Francis John **Whipple** and Olive Catherine **Bond** had the following children:
> +   6534   i.   William Edmund[12] **Whipple** born 16 March 1928.
> +   6535   ii.   Olwyn Dianne **Whipple** born 24 September 1931.

5554. **Leander Edmund**[11] **Whipple** (Fancis Looby[10], Lysander Greenlief[9], Edmund[8], Perley[7], Lt. James[6], Lieut. James[5], Deacon James[4], Joseph[3], Matthew[2], Matthew[1])[924] was born in Orange, New South Wales (NSW), Australia 4 April 1903 and died there 25 November 1989, at 86 years of age. He married **Millicent Gwendoline Oates** in Orange. Millicent,[925] daughter of William H. **Oates** and Elizabeth Jane **Richards**, was born in Guyong, NSW 5 April 1899 and died 28 June 1993 in Orange, at 94 years of age. Edmund was a farmer.

Leander Edmund **Whipple** and Millicent Gwendoline **Oates** had the following children:
> +   6536   i.   Jill Colleen[12] **Whipple** born 16 August 1929.
> +   6537   ii.   William Warwick **Whipple** born 19 September 1932.

5556. **Reginald Joseph**[11] **Whipple** (Fancis Looby[10], Lysander Greenlief[9], Edmund[8], Perley[7], Lt. James[6], Lieut. James[5], Deacon James[4], Joseph[3], Matthew[2], Matthew[1])[926] was born in Orange, New South Wales (NSW), Australia 12 May 1907 and died 8 January 1944 in Concord, NSW, at 36 years of age. He married twice. (1) **Merle Milner Armstrong** in Waverley, NSW 6 August 1927. Merle,[927] daughter of Alexander Milner **Armstrong** and Dinah Francis Euphemia **Davies**, was born in Nagga, NSW 24 October 1909 and died 1 March 1935 in Orange, at 25 years of age. She is buried at Waverley. (2) **Elizabeth Florence Howard**

in Australia in 1938. Reginald served in the Australian Air Force and after discharge worked as a motor mechanic. He is buried in the Rockwood War Cemetery, NSW.

Reginald Joseph **Whipple** and Merle Milner **Armstrong** had the following child:
+ 6538 i. Dr. Reginald Thomas Milner[12] **Whipple** born 21 January 1931.

5560. **William**[11] **Whipple** (Lt. Col. Charles William[10], Maj. Gen. Amiel Weeks[9], David[8], David[7], James[6], Deacon Jacob[5], Deacon James[4], Joseph[3], Matthew[2], Matthew[1])[928] was born in Cold Springs,[929] N.Y. 27 January 1880 and died 27 September 1962 in Baton Rouge, East Baton Rouge Parish, La., at 82 years of age. He married **Genevieve Liddell Randolph** 1 June 1905. Genevieve,[930] daughter of Moses Liddell **Randolph** and Jane Gustine **Conner**, was born in Bayou Goula, Iberville Parish, La. 29 March 1879 and died 20 December 1958 in Kenner, Jefferson Parish, La., at 79 years of age. William had hoped to follow the family's military tradition and sought but was unsuccessful in obtaining an appointment to The Army Military Academy at West Point, N.Y. and became a Professor at Louisana State University. He helped his son Walter get an appointment to the Naval Academy at Annapolis, Ann Arundel Co., Maryland. Son William, Jr. wanted to attend the Massachusetts Institute of Technology and earn a chemical engineering degree. But his father was able to get him offers of appointment to both West Point and Annapolis and he gave up the idea of MIT and went to West Point, not wanting to follow too closely in his brother's footsteps.

William **Whipple** and Genevieve Liddell **Randolph** had the following children:
+ 6539 i. Rear Adm. Walter Jones[12] **Whipple** born 22 March 1906.
+ 6540 ii. Brig. Gen. William **Whipple** born 4 February 1909.
+ 6541 iii. Jane Randolph **Whipple** born 16 September 1910.
+ 6542 iv. Genevieve Liddell **Whipple** born 29 September 1913.
  6543 v. John Randolph **Whipple**[931] born 12 October 1917 and died 11 June 1995 at 77 years of age. He married twice. (1) Terry **Thomas**. (2) Docia **Kent**. John was a Captain of Engineers in WWII.

5561. **Sherburne**[11] **Whipple** (Lt. Col. Charles William[10], Maj. Gen. Amiel Weeks[9], David[8], David[7], James[6], Deacon Jacob[5], Deacon James[4], Joseph[3], Matthew[2], Matthew[1])[932] was born 2 May 1881 and married **Carloyn Richards Bailey** in 1905. He was graduated from The Army Military

Academy at West Point, N.Y. and served against the Moros in the Philippines.[933] For services at the front in WWI he received the Distinguished Service Medal and the French Legion d'Honneur.

Sherburne **Whipple** and Carloyn **Richards Bailey** had the following children:

+   6544   i.   Sherburne[12] **Whipple** Jr.
       6545   ii.   Jack **Whipple**[934] died of diabetes abt 1946.
+   6546   iii.   Sarah Bailey **Whipple** born 13 October 1915.

5562. **Annette Bailey**[11] **Whipple** (Lt. Col. Charles William[10], Maj. Gen. Amiel Weeks[9], David[8], David[7], James[6], Deacon Jacob[5], Deacon James[4], Joseph[3], Matthew[2], Matthew[1])[935] was born 21 August 1883 and married **Arthur Morris Collens**. He was Chairman of the Board of the Phoenix Mutual Life Insurance Company in Hartford, Hartford Co., Conn.

Annette Bailey **Whipple** and Arthur Morris **Collens** had the following children:

       6547   i.   Arthur Morris[12] **Collens** Jr.[936]
       6548   ii.   William L. **Collens**[937] was a Navy Lieutenant stationed on a munitions vessel in the Pacific during WWII.
+   6549   iii.   Katherine C. **Collens** born in 1907.

5563. **Eleanor Sherburne**[11] **Whipple** (Lt. Col. Charles William[10], Maj. Gen. Amiel Weeks[9], David[8], David[7], James[6], Deacon Jacob[5], Deacon James[4], Joseph[3], Matthew[2], Matthew[1])[938] was born in New York, N.Y. 13 May 1887 and died there 13 January 1983, at 95 years of age. She married **Col. Francis Russell Stoddard** 8 November 1909. Francis,[939] son of Francis Russell **Stoddard** Sr. and Mary Frances **Baldwin**, was born in Boston, Suffolk Co., Mass. 27 July 1877 and died 11 October 1957 in New York City, at 80 years of age. Francis, a partner in the New York City law firm of Hamlin, Hubbell, Davis, Hunt, and Farley, specialized in banking and insurance law. He served in the New York State Assembly (1912-15). He was a veteran of the Spanish-American War, the Mexican Border War, and WWI (Major, 17th Division). He was a Colonel commanding 533d C.A. (1923-24) and served as Military Aide to Mayor Fiorello H. La Guardia during WWII. He wrote and published *The Stoddard Family* in 1912.

Eleanor Sherburne **Whipple** and Col. Francis Russell **Stoddard** had the following children born in New York City:

       6550   i.   Margery Peperrell[12] **Stoddard**[940] 29 December 1910. Unmarried.

  6551 ii. Howland Bradford **Stoddard**[941] 22 May 1912 and died 9 September 1977 at 65 years of age. He married Rose **Fillmore** in Ellsworth, Hancock Co., Maine 16 August 1947. Howard was Inspector General of the 35th Division in Germany and the 15th Army during WWII.

  6552 iii. Anna Bailey **Stoddard**[942] 20 March 1914 and died 24 October 1988 in New York, City, at 74 years of age. She married twice. (1) Renwick Washington **Hurry** in New York City 5 December 1936. (2) Stanley **Frame** in New York City.

  6553 iv. Dudley Wentworth **Stoddard**[943] born in Plymouth, Plymouth Co., Mass. 23 October 1915. Unmarried. Dudley was a combat infantryman in the 8th Division and was wounded during the attack on Cologne, Germany in WWII.

  6554 v. Frances LeBaron **Stoddard**[944] 8 December 1922 and married Edward Delaney **Dunn Jr.** in New York City 12 April 1946.

5564. Gertrude Mead[11] **Henry** (Abbie Howard[10] **Whipple**, George Alonzo[9], David[8], David[7], James[6], Deacon Jacob[5], Deacon James[4], Joseph[3], Matthew[2], Matthew[1])[945] was born 1 July 1878 and married **Edwin Bradley Mead** 13 February 1902.

Gertrude Mead **Henry** and Edwin Bradley **Mead** had the following children:

  6555 i. Eleanor[12] **Mead**[946] born 30 November 1902.
  6556 ii. Ruth **Mead**[947] born 28 January 1907.

5567. John Park[11] **Henry** (Abbie Howard[10] **Whipple**, George Alonzo[9], David[8], David[7], James[6], Deacon Jacob[5], Deacon James[4], Joseph[3], Matthew[2], Matthew[1])[948] was born 28 December 1888 and married **Dorothy L. Perry** in New York, N.Y. 14 October 1914.

John Park **Henry** and Dorothy L. **Perry** had the following child:

  6557 i. Catherine[12] **Henry**[949] born 13 August 1917.

5568. Jack Van Horn[11] **Whipple** (George Amiel[10], George Alonzo[9], David[8], David[7], James[6], Deacon Jacob[5], Deacon James[4], Joseph[3], Matthew[2], Matthew[1])[950] was born 9 October 1896 and married **Josephine Naomi Knipe** 10 September 1924. She was born 22 November 1900.[951]

Jack Van Horn **Whipple** and Josephine Naomi **Knipe** had the following child:

+ 6558 i. George Amiel[12] **Whipple** II born 2 June 1929.

5569. **Dorothy Vermilyea**[11] **Whipple** (George Amiel[10], George Alonzo[9], David[8], David[7], James[6], Deacon Jacob[5], Deacon James[4], Joseph[3], Matthew[2], Matthew[1])[952] was born 22 November 1900 and married **Ewan Clague** in Wisconsin 29 May 1923.

Dorothy Vermilyea **Whipple** and Ewan **Clague** had the following children:
- 6559   i.   Whipple[12] **Clague**[953] born 28 May 1930 and died in January 1931 at about 7 months of age.
- 6560   ii.   Ann Vermilyea **Clague**[954] born 27 October 1931.
- 6561   iii.   Llewllynn **Clague**[955] born 25 August 1936.

5570. **David Ethen**[11] **Whipple** (Charles E.[10], David M.[9], Mathew A.[8], David[7], James[6], Deacon Jacob[5], Deacon James[4], Joseph[3], Matthew[2], Matthew[1])[956] was born in Huron, Beadle Co., S. Dak. 2 March 1883 and died 14 October 1954 in Boise, Ada Co., Idaho, at 71 years of age. Buried in Morris Hill Cemetery. He married **Nellie Vay Hatcher** in Ontario, Malheur Co., Oreg. 22 April 1909. Nellie,[957] daughter of Harvey Arthur **Hatcher** and Louiana Bell **Williams**, was born in Zan Zandt, Whatcom Co., Wash. 12 February 1892 and died 10 March 1971 in Stockton, San Joaquin Co., Calif., at 79 years of age.

David Ethen **Whipple** and Nellie Vay **Hatcher** had the following children:
- \+   6562   i.   Arthur Harvey[12] **Whipple** born 12 December 1910.
- \+   6563   ii.   Orval Aaron **Whipple** born 6 July 1912.
- 6564   iii.   Harrison R. **Whipple**[958] born in Washington State 6 March 1918 and died 31 January 1977 in Eugene, Lane Co., Oreg., at 59 years of age.

5574. **James Fenton**[11] **Whipple** (Oscar M.[10], James Madison[9], James[8], James[7], James[6], Deacon Jacob[5], Deacon James[4], Joseph[3], Matthew[2], Matthew[1])[959] was born 5 February 1891 and died in 1974 at 83 years of age. He married twice. (1) **Florence Parshall** 18 March 1915. She was born 28 November 1894.[960] (2) **Madeline Harriet Schoemar** 23 October 1919. She was born 10 July 1894 and died in 1959 at 64 years of age.[961]

James Fenton **Whipple** and Madeline Harriet **Schoemar** had the following children:
- 6565   i.   Elsie May[12] **Whipple**[962] born 10 July 1924 and married Lewis James **Schiffner** in 1947.
- 6566   ii.   Janice Mary **Whipple**[963] born 1 May 1930 and was living in Stony Creek, Warren Co., N.Y. in 1993.

5575. **Martha Flora**[11] **Whipple** (Oscar M.[10], James Madison[9], James[8], James[7], James[6], Deacon Jacob[5], Deacon James[4], Joseph[3], Matthew[2], Matthew[1])[964] was born 27 July 1892 and died 13 October 1986 in Springfield, Otsego Co., N.Y., at 94 years of age. She married **Grover C. Thayer** 3 July 1915. He was born in 1886 and died 18 March 1965 in Springfield, at 78 years of age.[965] They owned and operated Thayer's Boat Livery on Otsego Lake, Springfield. Martha's birth year may have been 1893.

Martha Flora **Whipple** and Grover C. **Thayer** had the following children:
- 6567 i. William Oscar[12] **Thayer**[966] born in New York State in 1916 and died in 1984 at 68 years of age.
- 6568 ii. Rufus James **Thayer**[967] born in New York State in 1918.

5578. **Walter Ralph**[11] **Whipple** (William Isaac[10], Isaac Truax[9], James[8], James[7], James[6], Deacon Jacob[5], Deacon James[4], Joseph[3], Matthew[2], Matthew[1])[968] was born in Webster City, Hamilton Co., Iowa 28 February 1905 and died there 1 December 1982, at 77 years of age. He married **Harriett Idelia Fisher** in Webster City. Harriett,[969] daughter of Myron Alpheus **Fisher** and Alta Lucretia **Myers**, was born 5 May 1907 and died 31 October 1966 in Webster City, at 59 years of age.

Walter Ralph **Whipple** and Harriett Idelia **Fisher** had the following child:
- \+ 6569 i. George David[12] **Whipple** born 22 February 1937.

5588. **Minnie Grace**[11] **Whipple** (Fred G.[10], Obed[9], Obed[8], Thomas[7], Col. Moses[6], Deacon Jacob[5], Deacon James[4], Joseph[3], Matthew[2], Matthew[1])[970] was born in Glenburn, Shasta Co., Calif. 18 August 1883 and died 31 May 1981 at 97 years of age. She married **John Henry Creighton** in California. He was born in Glenburn.[971]

Minnie Grace **Whipple** and John Henry **Creighton** had the following children:
- \+ 6570 i. Burnette[12] **Creighton** born 16 June 1907.
- \+ 6571 ii. Evelyn Adelle **Creighton** born 30 December 1911.

5591. **Harry Meryl**[11] **Whipple** (Fred G.[10], Obed[9], Obed[8], Thomas[7], Col. Moses[6], Deacon Jacob[5], Deacon James[4], Joseph[3], Matthew[2], Matthew[1])[972] was born in Glenburn, Shasta Calif., Calif. 14 October 1897 and died 11 June 1986 at 88 years of age. He married **Georga Elmina Lee**. She was born in Bieber, Lassen Co., Calif.[973]

Harry Meryl **Whipple** and Georga Elmina **Lee** had the following child:
+ 6572   i.   Virginia Lee[12] **Whipple** born 28 July 1920.

5592. **Lois Philena**[11] **Whipple** (Fred G.[10], Obed[9], Obed[8], Thomas[7], Col. Moses[6], Deacon Jacob[5], Deacon James[4], Joseph[3], Matthew[2], Matthew[1])[974] was born in Glenburn, Shasta Co., Calif. 7 May 1900 and died 11 February 1997 in Petaluma, Sonoma Co., Calif., at 96 years of age.[975] She married **Homer Dewitt Hildebrant** in Glenburn 16 August 1925. Homer,[976] son of Jacob Elmer **Hildebrant** and Mary Ann **Hunt**, was born in Woodland, Yolo Co., Calif. 25 November 1897 and died 28 November 1974 in San Rafael, Marin Co., Calif., at 77 years of age. Lois and her mother both died on 11 February 30 years apart. Lois was two months 27 days shy of her 97th birthday and her mother was 12 days shy of her 104th.

Lois Philena **Whipple** and Homer Dewitt **Hildebrant** had the following children:
+ 6573   i.   Sylvia Ruth[12] **Hildebrant** born 29 March 1927.
+ 6574   ii. Harold Homer **Hildebrant** born 13 October 1930.

5600. **Laura Alexander**[11] **Gardiner** (Mary Powers[10] **Cooper**, Laurel[9] **Whipple**, David[8], Aaron[7], Col. Moses[6], Deacon Jacob[5], Deacon James[4], Joseph[3], Matthew[2], Matthew[1])[977] was born in Croydon, Sullivan Co., N.H. 14 January 1863 and died 17 February 1920 in New York State, at 57 years of age. She married **John Gilkison Whytlaw** in New York, N.Y. 12 March 1889. John,[978] son of Robert **Whytlaw** and Mary **Gilkison**, was born in Glasgow, Scotland 11 March 1861 and died 26 May 1927 in New York, N.Y., at 66 years of age. Both were buried in Claremont, Sullivan Co., N.H.

John began his working career at age 16 in a gingham mill in Glasgow owned by his father. He worked 12 hours a day six days a week. When he was 26 he sailed from Liverpool, England for the United States on the Cunard's passenger ship, *Oregon*. They left 6 March 1886 and on the 14th just off Sandy Hook, N. J. were involved in a collision which ripped three holes in the side of the *Oregon* causing it to sink. Fortunately there were vessels in the immediate area and all passengers and crew were safely transferred without loss of life. In a letter to his father written 16 March, John provided details of the ordeal but concluded "I am quite prepared to cross the Atlantic again as often as circumstances may demand but I can never forget the 14th day of March 1886."[979]

John was General Sales Manager for his father's mill and as such traveled widely. He eventually left the firm and in partnership with a Mons. Requeral of France owned and operated a weaving mill (named Tissages de Peissy) in Liege, Belgium. When the Germans captured Liege during

WWI, they confiscated the weaving equipment taking it to Germany and burned the mill. Mons. Requeral died before the war ended, leaving the business to John. His claim to the Reparations Commission was never honored. The estimated loss exceed a million dollars. John was operated on at the Mayo Clinic in Rochester, Olmsted Co., Minn. in the fall of 1926 for cancer of the pancreas. He was given six months to live and returned to New York City where he died.

After being graduated from Smith College, Laura attended the Sorbonne in Paris working in charcoals while her mother studied poreclain painting in Dresden, Germany. Laura met her future husband aboard ship as they were returning from Germany. Laura died of "ether pneumonia" following a goitre operation.

Laura Alexander **Gardiner** and John Gilkison **Whytlaw** had the following children:

      6575   i.   John Gilkison[12] **Whytlaw** Jr.[980] born 23 February 1890 and married Phyllis Palmer.

+   6576   ii.   Graeme Gardiner **Whytlaw** born 13 January 1897.

      6577   iii. Mary Gardiner **Whytlaw**[981] born 13 December 1898.

5612. **Elizabeth**[11] **Damon** (Sarah Ann[10] **Barton**, Adeline[9] **Whipple**, David[8], Aaron[7], Col. Moses[6], Deacon Jacob[5], Deacon James[4], Joseph[3], Matthew[2], Matthew[1])[982] was born in Boston, Suffolk Co., Mass. 13 October 1864 and died 7 January 1958 in Hamden, New Haven Co., Conn., at 93 years of age. She married **Gardner Irving Jones**. Gardner,[983] son of William Thompson **Jones** and Sarah Aurelia **Everett**, was born in Melrose, Middlesex Co., Mass. 12 August 1869 and died 13 February 1936 in Brookline, Norfolk Co., Mass., at 66 years of age.

Elizabeth was educated at the Boston Girls Latin School. She was a member of the Daughters of Founders and Patriots, Daughters of Colonial Wars, Daughters of American Colonists, National Society of Women Descendants of Ancient and Honorable Artillery Co., Daughters of the American Revolution, and National Society of New England Women. She traces her paternal line back to **John Damon,** baptized 25 June 1620 in Reading, England; married **Abagail Aherman;** died in 1708. Elizabeth was elected to annual membership in the New England Historic Genealogical Society 2 January 1940.

Elizabeth **Damon** and Gardner Irving **Jones** had the following children born in West Newton, Mass:

      6578   i.   Damon Everett[12] **Jones**[984] 1 December 1899 and married Barbara **Reineer** 27 October 1927. She was born in Santa

Barbara, Santa Barbara Co., Calif. 7 November 1900.[985] Damon was a graduate of Williams College in Williamstown, Berkshire Co., Mass. in 1921.

6579 ii. Marguerite **Jones**[986] 9 February 1902 and married Daniel Stewart **Pope Jr.** 16 June 1927. He was born in Yonkers, Westchester Co., N. Y. 22 July 1904.[987] Marguerite was graduated from Vassar College, Poughkeepsie, Dutchess Co., N.Y. in 1924.

5614. **Fay**[11] **Whipple** (Henry Chandler[10], David C.[9], David[8], Aaron[7], Col. Moses[6], Deacon Jacob[5], Deacon James[4], Joseph[3], Matthew[2], Matthew[1])[988] was born in Enfield, Grafton Co., N.H. 22 June 1880 and married **Grace Mae Louise Barrett** in Bristol, Grafton Co., N.H. 17 September 1903. She was born in York Beach, York Co., Maine 20 April 1881 and died 13 October 1918 in Bristol, at 37 years of age.[989]

Fay **Whipple** and Grace Mae Louise **Barrett** had the following child:

6580 i. Ruth Elizabeth[12] **Whipple**[990] born in Hamstead, N.Y. 11 October 1904.

5617. **Ashley Plummer**[11] **Whipple** (Henry Chandler[10], David C.[9], David[8], Aaron[7], Col. Moses[6], Deacon Jacob[5], Deacon James[4], Joseph[3], Matthew[2], Matthew[1])[991] was born in Bristol, Grafton Co., N.H. 16 April 1891 and married **Margaret Sargent** there 30 June 1914. She was born 6 March 1895.[992]

Ashley Plummer **Whipple** and Margaret **Sargent** had the following children born in Bristol:

6581 i. Barbara[12] **Whipple**[993] 21 April 1915.
6582 ii. Chandler Sargent **Whipple**[994] 19 April 1920.

5618. **Florence**[11] **Brewer** (Margaret Perritt[10] **Whipple**, David C.[9], David[8], Aaron[7], Col. Moses[6], Deacon Jacob[5], Deacon James[4], Joseph[3], Matthew[2], Matthew[1])[995] was born 2 December 1876 and married **Jo Tuttle Emery** in Montclair, Essex Co., N.J. 28 September 1904.

Florence **Brewer** and Jo Tuttle **Emery** had the following children:

6583 i. Jo Tuttle[12] **Emery** Jr.[996] born in Glen Ridge, Essex Co., N.J. 30 May 1906 and died there 2 days later
6584 ii. Margaret **Emery**[997] born 19 December 1907.
6585 iii. Grace **Emery**[998] born 15 October 1912.
6586 iv. Jean **Emery**[999] born 6 August 1918.

{ G 960 }

5619. **Orton**[11] Brewer (Margaret Perritt[10] **Whipple**, David C.[9], David[8], Aaron[7], Col. Moses[6], Deacon Jacob[5], Deacon James[4], Joseph[3], Matthew[2], Matthew[1])[1000] was born in Enfield, Grafton Co., N.H. 8 August 1878 and married **Natalie Grovesteen** in Brooklyn, N.Y. 18 January 1905. She was born in New York, N.Y.[1001]

Orton **Brewer** and Natalie **Grovesteen** had the following children:
- 6587 i. Natalie Grovesteen[12] **Brewer**[1002] born in Montclair, Essex Co., N.J. 2 February 1906.
- 6588 ii. John Slayback **Brewer**[1003] born in Glen Ridge, Essex Co., N.J. 25 May 1910.
- 6589 iii. Edward Slayback **Brewer**[1004] born in Glen Ridge 1 May 1917.

5620. **Hilton C.**[11] Brewer (Margaret Perritt[10] **Whipple**, David C.[9], David[8], Aaron[7], Col. Moses[6], Deacon Jacob[5], Deacon James[4], Joseph[3], Matthew[2], Matthew[1])[1005] was born in Glen Ridge, Essex Co., N.J. 9 March 1883 and married **Grace I. Burley** in Cranford, Union Co., N.J. 1 October 1913. She was born in New York, N.Y. 26 November 1887.

Hilton C. **Brewer** and Grace I. **Burley** had the following children:
- 6590 i. Bernice[12] **Brewer**[1006] born 30 January 1915.
- 6591 ii. Mary Elizabeth **Brewer**[1007] born 15 April 1921.

5621. **Frank Dodge**[11] Brewer (Margaret Perritt[10] **Whipple**, David C.[9], David[8], Aaron[7], Col. Moses[6], Deacon Jacob[5], Deacon James[4], Joseph[3], Matthew[2], Matthew[1])[1008] was born in Glen Ridge, Essex Co., N.J. 2 October 1885 and married **Amy M. Brown** in Montclair, Essex Co., N.J. 3 April 1913. She was born in Montclair 28 November 1886.[1009]

Frank Dodge **Brewer** and Amy M. **Brown** had the following children born in Glen Ridge:
- 6592 i. Russell Brown[12] **Brewer**[1010] 19 August 1915.
- 6593 ii. Chandler Rittenhouse **Brewer**[1011] 13 September 1922.

5623. **Dr. George Hoyt**[11] **Whipple** (Dr. Ashley Cooper[10], Dr. Solomon M.[9], David[8], Aaron[7], Col. Moses[6], Deacon Jacob[5], Deacon James[4], Joseph[3], Matthew[2], Matthew[1])[1012] was born in Ashland, Grafton Co., N.H. 28 August 1878 and died 1 February 1976 in Rochester, Monroe Co., N.Y., at 97 years of age. He married **Katharine Ball Waring** 24 June 1914. A Nobel Prize winner in physiology and medicine in 1934, George was two when his father died. His well-read mother was a believer in education and enrolled him in Phillips Academy, Andover, Essex Co., Mass. in

1892 and upon graduation (1896) he enrolled at Yale University, graduating in 1900. One of his Yale professors, Lafayette B. Mendel, a young research biochemist, was a major influence on his later career. Financial considerations required George to teach at Dr. Holbrook's Military School in Ossining, Westchester Co., N.Y. for a year before enrolling at Johns Hopkins University (then the nation's premier Medical School) from which he was graduated in 1905.

Dr. George H. Whipple.

Following graduation from Johns Hopkins his other great mentor, William H. Welch, offered him a position as as Assistant in Pathology. During his nine years (1905-14) at Johns Hopkins, except for 1907 when he was a Pathologist at the Ancon Hospital, Panama Canal Zone, he studied the pathology of tuberculosis and pancreatic disease. The result of his autopsy of a physician whose illness had baffled prominent internists was a paper on intestinal lipodystrophy (Whipple's disease). He published an important paper on backwater fever (a severe form or complication of malaria) following his year in Panama studying tropical diseases. He financed postgraduate study in Heidelberg, Germany and Vienna, Austria with funds saved while in Panama. His study of bile pigments began in 1908 and led to his interest in the body's manufacture of the oxygen-carrying hemoglobin, an important element in the production of bile pigments.

He joined the staff of the U. of California in San Francisco in 1914 (Dean of the Medical School 1920-21) where he taught research medicine and began a study on how bile pigments were affected by diets. Experimenting with dogs, he found that liver was one of the best foods for the production of new, hemoglobin-filled red blood cells. This discovery gave George R. Minot (1885-1950), a Harvard Hematologist, and his assistant, William R. Murphy, the idea of using a liver diet to treat pernicious anemia in humans, a previously incurable and fatal disease. For this work, Whipple, Minot, and Murphy were awarded the 1934 Nobel Prize in Medicine or Physiology.

Whipple became Dean of the School of Medicine and Dentistry at the U. of Rochester (1921-53) and Professor of Pathology (1921-55). His design of the new Medical School combined the Medical Center and University Hospital and became standard for this type of integrated facility. He retired as Dean at age 75 but retained the Professorship of Pathology until 1955. His last and most sophisticated scientific study was of the body's methods for storing and releasing proteins which he summarized in his only book, *The Dynamic Equilibruim of Body Proteins* (1956).

During his career he authored more than 200 publications on anemia, pigment metabolism, blood plasma proteins, bile salt metabolism, liver injury and repair, and related subjects. The "Papers of George Hoyt Whipple" are in the Edward G. Miner Library at the U. of Rochester Medical Center (the 83 document boxes occupy 99 linear feet in the Archives). Devoted mostly to his role as a scientist and educator, they span the period 1915-76 and are an invaluable source on one of the major figures in 20th century American Pathology. President John F. Kennedy presented him the Distinguished Federal Civilian Service Award in 1963.

The Whipple family home at 4 Pleasant St., Ashland, Grafton Co., N.H. is now the Whipple House Museum and is open from June through Labor Day. It features information about him, his family, and the area. Of particular interest is the Glidden Toy Museum which has over 1,000 items.

For a full account of his work and achievements see: *George Hoyt Whipple and His Friends* by George Washington Corner (1963); "George Hoyt Whipple (1879-1976)," by Leon Miller, published in the *Biographical Memoirs* of the National Academy of Sciences, 1995, 66:372-93; and Dr. Whipple's own "Autobiographical Sketch," published in *Perspectives in Biology & Medicine*, 1959, 2:253-89.

Peter Darling of Philadelphia, Penn shared the following story about Dr. Whipple which he believes has never been told outside his family. It involves Peter's father who died at age 83 in 2000.

"My father was very poor growing up. He arrived at Medical School with the first semester's tuition covered, but beyond that, had no idea how he was going to pay for the remainder of his medical training. Early in the spring semester, as he tells the story, he simply ran out of money. In telling the story, he said he was standing in an anatomy lab in the middle of a procedure, and finally admitted defeat. With only 37 cents in his pocket he decided to drop Medical School, hitchhike home to Williamstown, Mass. and get a job. He concluded that although he gave it a good try, he was never going to be a doctor.

"That very afternoon he was summoned to Dean Whipple's office. The Dean asked him how he was doing. Father said fine except he had run out of money and had to leave school. Dean Whipple then informed him he had found a private patient who needed blood and was willing to pay for two pints. That money, and subsequent sales, made the difference, enabled my father to survive, and to complete his first year of Medical School. He saved enough from his summer job that year to pay for his second year.

"He eventually became a surgeon and was the first board-certified surgeon in the town where I grew up. He fathered five kids, was Chief of Surgery for years at our local hospital, and became an outstanding surgeon and a pillar of the medical community. According to him, none of this would have happened had not George Hoyt Whipple, around 1938, spotted potential in him as a medical student and pulled some strings to alow him to make enough money to survive." E-mail to the author from Peter Darling dated 28 Dec. 2000.

Photos courtesy of Blaine Whipple.

Dr. George Hoyt **Whipple** and Katharine Ball **Waring** had the following children:
  6594 i. Barbara[12] **Whipple**[1013] married John **Schilling**.
+ 6595 ii. Dr. G. Hoyt **Whipple** born abt 1917.

5625. **Dorothy**[11] **Whipple** (Sherman Leland[10], Dr. Solomon M.[9], David[8], Aaron[7], Col. Moses[6], Deacon Jacob[5], Deacon James[4], Joseph[3], Matthew[2], Matthew[1])[1014] was born in Brookline, Norfolk Co., Mass. 27 July 1894 and married twice. (1) **Russell Thurston Fry** in August 1917. (2) **Carl W. Illig**.

Dorothy **Whipple** and Russell Thurston **Fry** had the following children:
  6596 i. Louise Fay[12] **Fry** born 22 August 1918.[1015]
  6597 ii. Russell T. **Fry** born 15 April 1920.[1016]
  6598 iii. Margaret Rogers **Fry** born 11 August 1921.[1017]
  6599 iv. Sylvia **Fry** born 23 October 1922.[1018]
  6600 v. Dorothy Deane **Fry** born 8 December 1923.[1019]

5626. **Katharyn Carlton**[11] **Whipple** (Sherman Leland[10], Dr. Solomon M.[9], David[8], Aaron[7], Col. Moses[6], Deacon Jacob[5], Deacon James[4], Joseph[3], Matthew[2], Matthew[1])[1020] was born in Brookline, Norfolk Co., Mass. 30 November 1895 and died 10 January 1990 in Plymouth, Plymouth Co., Mass., at 94 years of age.

She married **Lothrop Withington** in Plymouth 24 June 1916. Lothrop,[1021] son of David Little **Withington** and Marietta **Dennettpaul**, was born in Escondido, San Diego Co., Calif. 23 August 1889 and died 5 November 1967 in Plymouth, at 78 years of age. Lothrop earned two degrees at Harvard: a BA in 1911 and an LL.B. in 1914. He began the practice of law in September 1914 with the Boston firm of Whipple, Sears & Ogden. He served in Europe in WWI as an Army Lieutenant in Chemical Warfare Service and was in the Meuse-Argonne offensive and with the Army of Occupation in Germany. He returned to the United States in May 1919 and rejoined the Whipple law firm.

He descends from Henry Withington of Leigh, Co. Lancaster, England and Dorchester, Suffolk Co., Mass. Henry was baptized in the parish of Leigh 22 February 1589/90, son of George and Margaret **Withington,** and died at Dorchester, 2 February 1666/67. Henry married (1) at Leigh in September 1615, Anne **Leech** who was buried at Leigh 26 Sept. 1621; (2) at Leigh 20 Sept. 1622, Elizabeth **Smith** who died at Dorchester 16 February 1660; (3) at Dorchester in June 1676 Margery **(Turner) Paul** who died at Dorchester 20 May 1676. Margery was the widow of Richard Paul of Taunton.[1022] Katharyn Whipple was a graduate of the Chestnut Hill School and of Miss Wright's School in Philadelphia, Philadelphia City

{ G 965 }

Co., Penn. She and her husband were founding members of the Plymouth Yacht Club, the Plymouth Country Club, and the Eel River Beach Club and she was a long time member of the Plymouth Antiquarian Society, the Pilgrim Society, and the Jordan Hospital Club. Dedicated to many causes, she was instrumental in saving the 17th century Bishop House in downtown Plymouth when it was threatened by a developer's bulldozer. She helped bring the Mayflower II to Plymouth Harbor 13 June 1955, was involved with Plimouth Plantation from its inception, and was a volunteer at Children's Hospital. She had 35 grandchildren and 37 great grandchildren at time of death.

Katharyn Carlton **Whipple** and Lothrop **Withington** had the following children:

+ 6601 i. Lothrop[12] **Withington** Jr. born 16 February 1917.
   6602 ii. Sherman Whipple **Withington**[1023] born 2 April 1918 and died 10 August 1936 in Plymouth, at 18 years of age.
+ 6603 iii. Marietta Louise **Withington** born 12 February 1920.
   6604 iv. Richard Fay **Withington**[1024] born 26 October 1922 and married Katharyn **Driscoll** in West Roxbury, Suffolk Co., Mass.
   6605 v. Karkilie **Withington**[1025] born 21 October 1923 and married Henry H. **Atkins**.
+ 6606 vi. Anne Platt **Withington** born 26 September 1926.
+ 6607 vii. Paul **Withington** born 7 November 1927.
   6608 viii. Dennet **Withington**[1026] born 26 March 1938 and married twice. (1) Agnes **Richardson**. (2) Marjorie Anne **Beagle**.
+ 6609 ix. Nathan Noyes **Withington** born 29 June 1940.

5627. **Sherman Leland**[11] **Whipple Jr.** (Sherman Leland[10], Dr. Solomon M.[9], David[8], Aaron[7], Col. Moses[6], Deacon Jacob[5], Deacon James[4], Joseph[3], Matthew[2], Matthew[1])[1027] was born in Brookline, Norfolk Co., Mass. 21 February 1898 and died 16 June 1967 in Cleveland, Cuyahoga Co., Ohio, at 69 years of age. He married **Margaret Cassandra Jones** 15 April 1919. Sherman was President of Wiggin Terminals, Inc. at the time of his death from heart surgery. He had held the position since 1939 and was regarded as one of the most progressive terminal operators on the Atlantic coast. He advocated containerized shipping and was instrumental in introducing it on the Boston waterfront. His firm operated terminal facilities on Castle Island, South Boston, and in Charleston. Mass. He was Treasurer of Piers Operating Company which ran the Army Base from 1934-39. He maintained a home in Plymouth, Plymouth Co., and an apartment on Memorial Drive, Cambridge, Middlesex Co., Mass.

A graduate of Westminster School, Simsbury, Hartford Co., Conn., he volunteered with the American Field Service Ambulance Corps in France before the U.S. entered World War I. No ambulances were available when he arrived in France so he joined the French Army. He returned home when the U.S. entered the war and trained recruits at Camp Lee, Va. He served as President of the Foreign Commerce Club and of the Traffic Club of New England and was a member of the World Trade Center, the American Warehousemen's Assn., the Massachusetts Warehousemen's Assn., and the Propeller Club of Boston. A part owner of Boston's Locke-Ober Restaurant, he was a member of the Greater Boston Chamber of Commerce and of the Algonquin Club. As a member of the Plymouth Yacht Club, he was well-known in yachting circles and cruised the New England coast in his swordfishing craft, *Scuttlebutt*.[1028]

Sherman Leland **Whipple** Jr. and Margaret Cassandra **Jones** had the following children:
+ 6610 i. Sherman Leland[12] **Whipple** III born 4 April 1920.
+ 6611 ii. Paul Jones **Whipple** born 15 August 1922.
+ 6612 iii. Margaret Louise **Whipple** born 22 October 1926.

5628. **Sarah Whipple**[11] **Drew** (Rubie Jane[10] **Whipple**, Barnabas Cooper[9], David[8], Aaron[7], Col. Moses[6], Deacon Jacob[5], Deacon James[4], Joseph[3], Matthew[2], Matthew[1])[1029] was born in Croydon, Sullivan Co., N.H. 10 September 1888[1030] and died in July 1966 in California, at 77 years of age. Buried in Topsham, Sagadahoc Co., Maine. She married **Irving Edward Alexander** in Topsham 14 June 1913.

Sarah Whipple **Drew** and Irving Edward **Alexander** had the following child:
6613 i. Edward Lawson Drew[12] **Alexander**[1031] born in Lexington, Le Sueur Co., Maine 20 October 1925.

5629. **Mabel Alice**[11] **Drew** (Rubie Jane[10] **Whipple**, Barnabas Cooper[9], David[8], Aaron[7], Col. Moses[6], Deacon Jacob[5], Deacon James[4], Joseph[3], Matthew[2], Matthew[1])[1032] was born in Merrimac, Essex Co., Mass. 7 May 1890 and married **Alfred Howard Crowe** in Topsham, Sagadahoc Co., Maine, 25 November 1911.

Mabel Alice **Drew** and Alfred Howard **Crowe** had the following child:
+ 6614 i. Joseph Drew[12] **Crowe** born 18 March 1915.

5630. **Christine Louise**[11] **Drew** (Rubie Jane[10] **Whipple**, Barnabas Cooper[9], David[8], Aaron[7], Col. Moses[6], Deacon Jacob[5], Deacon James[4], Joseph[3], Matthew[2], Matthew[1])[1033] was born in Merrimac, Essex Co.,

{ G 967 }

Mass. 22 March 1892 and died in 1966 in California, at 74 years of age. She married **Walter Elvin Tirrell** in Springvale, York Co., Maine, 18 September 1913.

Christine Louise **Drew** and Walter Elvin **Tirrell** had the following child:
    6615   i.   Elvin Drew[12] **Tirrell**[1034] born in Lewiston, Androscoggin Co., Maine 12 March 1931.

5631. **Harlon Whitney**[11] **Drew** (Rubie Jane[10] **Whipple**, Barnabas Cooper[9], David[8], Aaron[7], Col. Moses[6], Deacon Jacob[5], Deacon James[4], Joseph[3], Matthew[2], Matthew[1])[1035] was born in Merrimac, Essex Co., Mass. 8 March 1894 and died in 1965 in Massachusetts, at 71 years of age. He married **Fredacia Marie Orr** in Portland, Cumberland Co., Maine 14 May 1919.

Harlon Whitney **Drew** and Fredacia Marie **Orr** had the following child born in Portland:
    6616   i.   Harlon Whitney[12] **Drew** Jr.[1036] 20 March 1921.

5632. **Isabel**[11] **Drew** (Rubie Jane[10] **Whipple**, Barnabas Cooper[9], David[8], Aaron[7], Col. Moses[6], Deacon Jacob[5], Deacon James[4], Joseph[3], Matthew[2], Matthew[1])[1037] was born in Merrimac, Essex Co., Mass. 21 April 1896 and died in March 1948 at 51 years of age. She married **Percy A. Quimby** in Portland, Cumberland Co., Maine 28 January 1918.

Isabel **Drew** and Percy A. **Quimby** had the following children born in Portland:
  +   6617   i.   Richard Francis[12] **Quimby** 2 May 1918.
        6618   ii.   Anna Isabel **Quimby**[1038] 23 November 1919.

5633. **Pauline Bryant**[11] **Drew** (Rubie Jane[10] **Whipple**, Barnabas Cooper[9], David[8], Aaron[7], Col. Moses[6], Deacon Jacob[5], Deacon James[4], Joseph[3], Matthew[2], Matthew[1])[1039] was born in West Newbury, Essex Co., Mass. 13 May 1898 and married **Dr. Charles Howard Gordon** in Portland, Cumberland Co., Maine 16 June 1924. He was born 11 July 1894 and died in 1958 at 63 years of age.[1040]

Pauline Bryant **Drew** and Dr. Charles Howard **Gordon** had the following child:
  +   6619   i.   Ruth Anne[12] **Gordon** born 10 January 1928.

5643. **Ralph Jonathan**[11] **Whipple** (Aaron Mason[10], Barnabas Cooper[9], David[8], Aaron[7], Col. Moses[6], Deacon Jacob[5], Deacon James[4], Joseph[3],

Matthew[2], Matthew[1])[1041] was born in Sunapee, Sullivan Co., N.H. 29 October 1901 and died 29 May 1983 in Lake Wales, Polk Co., Fla., at 81 years of age. He married **Emma C. Eastman** 24 December 1931. Emma,[1042] daughter of Orville G. **Eastman** and Clara M. **Jennings**, was born in Unity, Sullivan Co., N.H. 27 December 1913 and died 16 February 1999 in Newport, Sullivan Co., N.H., at 85 years of age. Emma was a home care giver to the elderly in New London, an aid at the Newport Hospital, and a 50-year member of the Grange on the state and national level. After Ralph's death, she moved to the Newbury-Sutton, Merrimac Co., N.H. area and settled in Warner, Merrimac Co., N.H. in 1994. Her graveside services were held at Millwood Cemetery, Sutton, 5 June 1999.

Ralph was a resident of South Sutton for 42 years where he operated a trucking business for 15 years. Previous to that he spent 28 years as a truckman for the Kearsarge Reel Corp. of Bradford, Merrimac Co., N.H. He also served as Sutton's Chief of Police for 15 years. He was active in the Grange, serving as Master of both the Sutton and Pomona Grange and as a State Grange Deputy for 10 years. He was also a member and Past Master of St. Peter Lodge, F & AM in Bradford. After semi-retiring in 1975, he and Emma began wintering in Lake Wales and they moved there in 1982 where he was active in the production of the Passion Play. He was buried in Millwood Cemetery. St. Peter Lodge held Masonic committal services.

Ralph Jonathan **Whipple** and Emma C. **Eastman** had the following children born in New Hamphire:

>6620   i.   Ralph Jonathan[12] **Whipple** Jr.[1043] was living in Suncook, Merrimac Co., N.H. in May 1983.
>6621   ii.   Edgar A. **Whipple**.[1044]
>6622   iii. Marjorie Avis **Whipple**[1045] 2 January 1933 and married (__) **Gove**. They were living in Wilmont, Merrimac Co., N.H. in May 1983.
>6623   iv.   Betty Lou **Whipple**[1046] 13 April 1934 and married (__) **Moore**. They were living in Concord, Merrimac Co.,N.H. in May 1983.
>6624   v.   Veda May **Whipple**[1047] 1 February 1936 and married (__) **Hosmer**. They were living in Bradford, Merrimac Co., N.H. in May 1983.
>6625   vi.   Claire Ann **Whipple**[1048] 13 January 1938 and died 2 October 1997 at 59 years of age. She married (__) **Heman**. They were living in Manchester, Hillsborough Co., N.H. in May 1983.
>6626   vii. Elaine Emma **Whipple**[1049] 7 October 1950 and married (__) **Tracy**. They were living in Springfield, Windsor Co., Vt. in May 1983.

5644. **Perley Arthur**[11] **Whipple** (Aaron Mason[10], Barnabas Cooper[9], David[8], Aaron[7], Col. Moses[6], Deacon Jacob[5], Deacon James[4], Joseph[3], Matthew[2], Matthew[1])[1050] was born in Sunapee, Sullivan Co., N.H. 10 February 1904 and died 12 June 1981 in Prescott, Yavapai Co., Ariz., at 77 years of age. He married twice. (1) **Bernice L. Connors** 9 May 1924. (2) **Avis Harriet Corwell** in Newport, Sullivan Co., N.H. 31 December 1934. Avis,[1051] daughter of George **Corwell** and Cora **Ball**, was born in Newport 22 June 1920 and died 20 August 1985 in Westmoreland, Cheshire Co., N.H., at 65 years of age. A longtime resident of Croydon, Sullivan Co., N.H. Avis worked at Sportwell Shoe Co. for many years. Perley attended Colby Academy in New London, Merrimac Co., N.H. and lived in Croydon where he was a cutter for a local shoe business. Upon retirement he moved to Prescott in November 1979 where he died after a brief illness. Both were buried at the Croydon Flat Cemetery.

Perley Arthur **Whipple** and Bernice L. **Connors** had the following child:
 6627 i. Perley Arthur[12] **Whipple** Jr.[1052] born in New Hampshire 11 December 1924 and was living in Lancaster, Coos Co., N.H. in 1985.

Perley Arthur Whipple and Avis Harriet Corwell had the following children:
+ 6628 ii. George Aaron **Whipple** born 14 August 1935.
+ 6629 iii. Donald Edwin **Whipple** born 19 August 1938.
+ 6630 iv. Martha Avis **Whipple** born 7 November 1953.

5645. **Veda May**[11] **Whipple** (Aaron Mason[10], Barnabas Cooper[9], David[8], Aaron[7], Col. Moses[6], Deacon Jacob[5], Deacon James[4], Joseph[3], Matthew[2], Matthew[1])[1053] was born in Sunapee, Sullivan Co., N.H. 25 January 1906 and died 2 February 1992 in Keene, Cheshire Co., N.H., at 86 years of age. She married **Paul Burgum Wright** in Newport, Sullivan Co., N.H. 6 February 1925. Paul,[1054] son of Caleb **Wright** and Florence **Burgum**, was born in Keene 25 May 1906 and died 11 November 1997 in Westmoreland, Cheshire Co., N.H., at 91 years of age. Veda graduated with the class of 1923 from Colby College, New London, Merrimac Co., N.H. and taught in a 1-room school for a year before marrying Paul. Paul was in construction work and the family lived in New London, Sullivan, Cheshire Co., Stoddard, Cheshire Co., and Keene. He also worked for Arthur Whitcomb, Inc. in Swanzey, Cheshire Co., N.H. and for Frank W. Whitcomb, Inc. in North Walpole, Cheshire Co., N.H. They moved back to Keene for good in 1987. A member of the Baptist Church, Veda died at Westwood Health Care Center and Paul died at the Maplewood Nursing Home. Both were buried in the family lot at East Sullivan Cemetery.

Veda May **Whipple** and Paul Burgum **Wright** had the following children:
- + 6631 i. Virginia May[12] **Wright** born 4 February 1925.
-   6632 ii. (Child) **Wright**[1055] born in Newport abt 1928 and died the year of birth.
- + 6633 iii. Everett Whipple **Wright** born 17 February 1930.
- + 6634 iv. Lawrence Blaine **Wright** born 3 January 1932.
- + 6635 v. Barbara Newton **Wright** born 14 October 1933.
- + 6636 vi. Charles Burgum **Wright** born 16 October 1936.

5652. Ruth Mildred[11] **Whipple** (Edgar J.[10], Darwin[9], Harvey[8], Aaron[7], Col. Moses[6], Deacon Jacob[5], Deacon James[4], Joseph[3], Matthew[2], Matthew[1])[1056] was born in Edgewood, Delaware Co., Iowa 2 September 1896 and died 18 August 1987 in Austin, Mower Co., Minn., at 90 years of age. She married **N. John Jensen** in Chester, Howard Co., Iowa 21 February 1924. John,[1057] son of Jens Soren **Jensen** and Karen Sophia **Nielsen**, was born in Cedar Falls, Black Hawk Co., Iowa 19 August 1893 and died in September 1963 in Minneapolis, Hennepin Co., Minn., at 70 years of age. Ruth was a homemaker and a music teacher. Both are buried in Chester Hill Cemetery.

Ruth Mildred **Whipple** and N. John **Jensen** had the following children:
-   6637 i. Marilyn Marie[12] **Jensen**[1058] born in Cresco, Howard Co., Iowa 26 April 1931 and died the day of birth
- + 6638 ii. Mary Lou **Jensen** born 29 October 1932.

5653. Raymond J.[11] **Whipple** (Edgar J.[10], Darwin[9], Harvey[8], Aaron[7], Col. Moses[6], Deacon Jacob[5], Deacon James[4], Joseph[3], Matthew[2], Matthew[1])[1059] was born in Edgewood, Delaware Co., Iowa 4 February 1902 and died 16 February 1974 in Anaheim, Orange Co., Calif., at 72 years of age. He married **Elsie Loretta Daws** in Chester, Howard Co., Iowa, 17 May 1923. She was born in 1902 and died in 1992 at 90 years of age.[1060] Both are buried at Angel's Lawn, Santa Ana, Orange Co., Calif.

Raymond J. **Whipple** and Elsie Loretta **Daws** had the following children:
- + 6639 i. Shirley Yvonne[12] **Whipple** born 20 September 1924.
- + 6640 ii. Robert Ray **Whipple** born 7 February 1929.

5654. William Joseph[11] **Brown** (Eva De Etta[10] **McMillin**, Elsie Elvira[9] **Whipple**, Tyler B.[8], Moses[7], Col. Moses[6], Deacon Jacob[5], Deacon James[4], Joseph[3], Matthew[2], Matthew[1])[1061] was born in Grand Forks, Grand Forks Co., N. Dak. 12 February 1890 and died there 13 February 1946, at 56 years of age. He married **Mabel Caroline Brenden** in Grand

Forks 20 August 1920. Mabel,[1062] daughter of Hans Hansen **Brenden** and Anne **Moe**, was born in Olewein, Fayette Co., Iowa 21 February 1894 and died 26 May 1964 in Grand Forks, at 70 years of age.

William Joseph **Brown** and Mabel Caroline **Brenden** had the following children:
- + 6641 i. Frank Addison[12] **Brown** born 19 May 1921.
- + 6642 ii. Elsie Ann **Brown** born 31 March 1927.
- + 6643 iii. Barbara Jean **Brown** born 15 March 1930.

5657. **Ivan Herbert**[11] **Northfield** (Jennie Viola[10] **McMillin**, Elsie Elvira[9] **Whipple**, Tyler B.[8], Moses[7], Col. Moses[6], Deacon Jacob[5], Deacon James[4], Joseph[3], Matthew[2], Matthew[1])[1063] was born in Minneapolis, Hennepin Co., Minn. 31 May 1891 and died 4 April 1986 in Duluth, Saint Louis Co., Minn., at 94 years of age. He married **Estella Marie Goering** in Duluth 19 November 1919. She was born in Duluth 29 December 1891 and died there 22 June 1969, at 77 years of age.[1064]

Ivan Herbert **Northfield** and Estella Marie **Goering** had the following children born in Duluth:
- + 6644 i. Jocelyn Marie[12] **Northfield** 3 December 1922.
- 6645 ii. John Whipple **Northfield**[1065] 21 May 1929.

5658. **Vida Adaline**[11] **Northfield** (Jennie Viola[10] **McMillin**, Elsie Elvira[9] **Whipple**, Tyler B.[8], Moses[7], Col. Moses[6], Deacon Jacob[5], Deacon James[4], Joseph[3], Matthew[2], Matthew[1])[1066] was born in Minneapolis, Hennepin Co., Minn. 3 October 1900 and married **George V. Erickson** in Lake City, Wabasha Co., Minn. 16 August 1922. He was born in Lake City 22 February 1891 and died there 18 October 1960, at 69 years of age.[1067]

Vida Adaline **Northfield** and George V. **Erickson** had the following children born in Lake City:
- 6646 i. Lois Jane[12] **Erickson**[1068] 3 December 1925 and married Paul **Powell** there 16 August 1947.
- 6647 ii. Elizabeth Henrietta **Erickson**[1069] 17 March 1927 and married Melvin Frank **Leonard** in Oak Park, Cook Co., Ill. 15 October 1949.
- 6648 iii. Charles Ivan **Erickson**[1070] 18 November 1929 and married Joann Lea **Kingsbury** in Olivia, Renville Co., Minn. 21 August 1954.

{ G 972 }

5659. **George Leon**[11] **Whipple** (William E.[10], John P.[9], Alexander[8], James[7], Col. Moses[6], Deacon Jacob[5], Deacon James[4], Joseph[3], Matthew[2], Matthew[1])[1071] was born in Westborough, Worcester Co., Mass. 19 February 1900 and died 10 December 1992 in Weatherly, Carbon Co., Penn., at 92 years of age. He married **Mildred Jean Hentz** of Weatherly 20 July 1949. George was a member of the Weatherly School Authority for 30 years and in 1991 was awarded Weatherly's Gold Cane honoring the oldest resident.

George Leon **Whipple** and Mildred Jean **Hentz** had the following children born in Weatherly:

6649 i. Robert William[12] **Whipple**[1072] 11 April 1950. He has two sons and resides in Birdsboro, Berks Co., Penn.

6650 ii. Todd David **Whipple**[1073] 8 August 1953. He has three sons and resides in Williamstown, Gloucester Co., N. J.

6651 iii. Barry Keith **Whipple**[1074] 23 March 1955 and married Robbie Ann **Sneed** of Sevierville, Franklin Co., Tenn. 11 November 1984.

5660. **Frances Elizabeth**[11] **Whipple** (Howard Thompson[10], George Jacob[9], Harvey[8], Jacob[7], Col. Moses[6], Deacon Jacob[5], Deacon James[4], Joseph[3], Matthew[2], Matthew[1])[1075] was born in Orange, Essex Co., N.J. 17 March 1917 and married **William Rulon Williamson Jr.** in Suitland,[1076] Md. 20 December 1941. William,[1077] son of William Rulon **Williamson** and Carolee **Churchill**, was born in West Hartford, Hartford Co., Conn. 2 October 1919. He was an officer in the Air Force during WWII assigned to the Air Force Flight Control Center in Washington, D.C. After the war he was an actuary with the Metropolitan Life Insurance Co. in New York City. Betty attended Wells College, Aurora, N. Y. before transferring to The George Washington University in Washington, D.C where she was graduated in 1939 with a degree in Political Science. Following graduation she worked for *TIME* Magazine until moving to Chicago, Cook Co., Ill. where Bill was trained for his Air Force commission. While in Chicago, Betty worked for the University of Chicago helping to formulate the early SAT college entrance exams. When Bill was assigned to Washington, she worked for the Office of War Information helping authors get their material past the strict censorship imposed at that time. After the war Betty became a homemaker and returned to work to help pay for tuition after their daughters reached college age She worked for the Rockerfeller Foundation in its Informations Services Department until July 1973 when she joined the Editorial Research Department of *The Reader's Digest*. She retired in 1980.

Frances Elizabeth **Whipple** and William Rulon **Williamson** Jr. had the following children:
- 6652 i. Katherine Elizabeth[12] **Williamson** born 23 August 1948.
- 6653 ii. Carolee Joan **Williamson**[1078] born 2 August 1952 and married Jerry **Tomlinson** in Sausalito, Marin Co., Calif. 31 December 1986. She attended the U. of Colorado at Boulder, Boulder Co., and Sonoma State University, Sonoma, Sonoma Co., Calif.

5662. **Mary**[11] **Whipple** (Dr. Edward Gove[10], George Jacob[9], Harvey[8], Jacob[7], Col. Moses[6], Deacon Jacob[5], Deacon James[4], Joseph[3], Matthew[2], Matthew[1])[1079] was born in Rochester, Monroe Co., N.Y. 4 August 1913 and married **Donald R. Clark**. He was born 18 May 1913 and died in 1984 at 71 years of age.[1080]

Mary **Whipple** and Donald R. **Clark** had the following children born in Rochester:
- 6654 i. Saralyn Thompson[12] **Clark**[1081] 6 May 1939.
- 6655 ii. Donald **Clark** Jr.[1082] 12 May 1941.
- 6656 iii. Mary Allison **Clark**[1083] 19 January 1947.

5663. **De Forest T.**[11] **Whipple** (Dr. Edward Gove[10], George Jacob[9], Harvey[8], Jacob[7], Col. Moses[6], Deacon Jacob[5], Deacon James[4], Joseph[3], Matthew[2], Matthew[1])[1084] was born in Rochester, Monroe Co., N.Y. 4 May 1916 and married **Agnes H. Kennedy** of New York City. She was born 29 November 1922.[1085] Dee served with the U.S. Army in Italy in 1943-44.

De Forest T. **Whipple** and Agnes H. **Kennedy** had the following children:
- 6657 i. William Thompson[12] **Whipple**[1086] born 26 October 1948.
- 6658 ii. Diane King **Whipple**[1087] born 7 August 1950.
- 6659 iii. Charles De Forest **Whipple**[1088] born in March 1952.

5664. **Frances**[11] **Whipple** (Dr. Edward Gove[10], George Jacob[9], Harvey[8], Jacob[7], Col. Moses[6], Deacon Jacob[5], Deacon James[4], Joseph[3], Matthew[2], Matthew[1])[1089] was born in Rochester, Monroe Co., N.Y. 4 May 1916 and married John G. **Kissane**. He was born 14 October 1913.[1090]

Frances **Whipple** and John G. **Kissane** had the following children:
- 6660 i. Gail[12] **Kissane**[1091] born 5 November 1942.
- 6661 ii. Edward De Forest **Kissane**[1092] born 26 June 1944.
- 6662 iii. John G. **Kissane** Jr.[1093] born 11 November 1946.

5665. **Sarah Thompson**[11] **Ames** (Frances Meigs[10] **Whipple**, George Jacob[9], Harvey[8], Jacob[7], Col. Moses[6], Deacon Jacob[5], Deacon James[4], Joseph[3], Matthew[2], Matthew[1])[1094] was born 25 April 1914 and married twice. (1) **Schnell Williams** 7 July 1939 who died two months later on 8 September 1939.[1095] (2) **Howard W. Rymers** 21 February 1942 who was born 16 January 1907.

Sarah Thompson **Ames** and Howard W. **Rymers** had the following children:
- 6663 i. Nancy Willard[12] **Rymers**[1096] born 17 May 1943.
- 6664 ii. Robert Wilbur **Rymers**[1097] born 26 August 1945.
- 6665 iii. John W. **Rymers**[1098] born 28 November 1947.

5673. **James Blair**[11] **Whipple** (George Harvey[10], Fred Harvey[9], Harvey[8], Jacob[7], Col. Moses[6], Deacon Jacob[5], Deacon James[4], Joseph[3], Matthew[2], Matthew[1])[1099] was born in Canon City, Fremont Co., Colo. 7 June 1920 and married **Alice Pearson** in Marion, Crittenden Co., Ark. 1 May 1943. Alice,[1100] daughter of George W. **Pearson** and Edith **Case**, was born in Evanston, Cook Co., Ill. 21 March 1923. James served in the Army during WWII from May 1942 to March 1946. He was a salesman before retiring.

James Blair **Whipple** and Alice **Pearson** had the following children:
- 6666 i. Katherine Nell[12] **Whipple**[1101] born in Denver, Denver Co., Colo. 17 October 1948 and married Jerry **Boren** in Colorado Springs, El Paso Co., Colo. 17 September 1982.
- 6667 ii. Margaret Jo **Whipple**[1102] born in Canon City 2 April 1950.
- 6668 iii. William Harvey **Whipple**[1103] born in Canon City 23 June 1952 and died 2 days after birth.
- 6669 iv. John Pearson **Whipple**[1104] born in Canon City 24 June 1953 and married an unnamed person in Las Vegas, Clark Co., Nev. 28 October 1984.
- + 6670 v. Carolyn Case **Whipple** born 2 November 1960.

5677. **Charles Franklin**[11] **Whipple** (Louis Whiting[10], Charles Crary[9], Oliver[8], Jacob[7], Col. Moses[6], Deacon Jacob[5], Deacon James[4], Joseph[3], Matthew[2], Matthew[1])[1105] was born in Chasley, Wells Co., N. Dak. 3 October 1912 and died 1 April 1981 in Fessenden, Wells Co., N. Dak., at 68 years of age. He married **Magdalene Marie Bambush** in Harvey, Wells Co., N. Dak. in June 1941. Magdalene, daughter of John **Bambush** and Susan **(__)**, was born 15 June 1918.

Charles Franklin **Whipple** and Magdalene Marie **Bambush** had the following children:

        6671   i.   Karen[12] **Whipple**[1106] born in Harvey 25 April 1942.
+   6672   ii.   Galen Charles **Whipple** born 10 May 1944.

5682. **Irene Alice**[11] **Whipple** (Louis Whiting[10], Charles Crary[9], Oliver[8], Jacob[7], Col. Moses[6], Deacon Jacob[5], Deacon James[4], Joseph[3], Matthew[2], Matthew[1])[1107] was born in Chasley, Wells Co., N. Dak. 11 March 1921 and married **Clarence Edward Arnold** in Jacksonville, Onslow Co., N.C. 4 May 1944. He was born in Los Angeles, Los Angeles Co., Calif. 16 November 1921 and died 30 June 1963 in Arcadia, Los Angeles Co., Calif., at 41 years of age.[1108]

Irene Alice **Whipple** and Clarence Edward **Arnold** had the following children:

+   6673   i.   Michael Henry[12] **Arnold.**
        6674   ii. Patricia Rene **Arnold.**[1109]

5695. **Hiram Lindsay**[11] **Haven** (John Sherman[10], George Pomroy[9], Capt. Moses[8], Rev. Jacob[7], Jerusha[6] **Whipple**, Deacon Jacob[5], Deacon James[4], Joseph[3], Matthew[2], Matthew[1])[1110] was born in Somerville, Middlesex Co., Mass. 5 June 1890 and married **Lillian Helen Harmon** 4 November 1915. She was born 23 January 1892.[1111] The family was living in Hollis, Queens Co., N.Y. in 1930.

Hiram Lindsay **Haven** and Lillian Helen **Harmon** had the following children:

        6675   i.   Roger Lindsay[12] **Haven**[1112] born 7 February 1927.
        6676   ii. Sherman White **Haven**[1113] born 21 February 1931 and died in April 1933 at 2 years of age.

5702. **Jessie Eudora**[11] **Smith** (John Wenzel[10], Angeline[9] **Wenzel**, Mehitable[8] **Haven**, Abner[7], Jerusha[6] **Whipple**, Deacon Jacob[5], Deacon James[4], Joseph[3], Matthew[2], Matthew[1])[1114] was born 11 February 1867 and married **Pulaski Robinson Woodman** in September 1888.

Jessie Eudora **Smith** and Pulaski Robinson **Woodman** had the following children:

        6677   i.   Marion[12] **Woodman**[1115] born 26 June 1890.
        6678   ii.   Ralph Smith **Woodman**[1116] born 30 March 1892.
        6679   iii. Rodney Canfield **Woodman**[1117] born 11 June 1894 and married Mildred Dodge **Kimball** 29 November 1917.

5703. **Emma Lucretia**[11] **Smith** (John Wenzel[10], Angeline[9] **Wenzel**, Mehitable[8] **Haven**, Abner[7], Jerusha[6] **Whipple**, Deacon Jacob[5], Deacon James[4], Joseph[3], Matthew[2], Matthew[1])[1118] was born 7 November 1868 and married **George Pease Lord** 30 June 1896.

Emma Lucretia **Smith** and George Pease **Lord** had the following children:
    6680 i. George Pease[12] **Lord** Jr.[1119] born 1 February 1901.
    6681 ii. Samuel Smith **Lord**[1120] born 25 January 1904.

5704. **Alice Corinna**[11] **Smith** (Charles Elbridge[10], Angeline[9] **Wenzel**, Mehitable[8] **Haven**, Abner[7], Jerusha[6] **Whipple**, Deacon Jacob[5], Deacon James[4], Joseph[3], Matthew[2], Matthew[1])[1121] was born 21 October 1861 and died 28 February 1905 at 43 years of age. She married **George Emmons** 21 October 1880.

Alice Corinna **Smith** and George **Emmons** had the following children:
 + 6682 i. Addie Corinna[12] **Emmons** born 24 July 1881.
    6683 ii. Celia Josephine **Emmons**[1122] born 17 October 1883 and died 13 December 1884 at 1 year of age.
    6684 iii. Alice Leonard **Emmons**[1123] born 1 October 1884 and married William Arthur **McBride** 20 June 1908.
    6685 iv. Rollin Charles **Emmons**[1124] born in August 1886 and died 13 August 1888 at 1 year of age.
    6686 v. Madeline Adel **Emmons**[1125] born 31 July 1888 and married Leslie W. **Marsh** 2 November 1910.
    6687 vi. Pearl Imogene **Emmons**[1126] born 6 June 1891 and married Raymond S. **Willey** 24 August 1911.
    6688 vii. Blanch Elward **Emmons**[1127] born 1 July 1892 and married Charles Thomas **Butler** 19 April 1916.
    6689 viii. Grace Sherman **Emmons**[1128] born in November 1894 and died 20 March 1895 at less than 4 months of age.

5706. **Walter Nye**[11] **Smith** (Charles Elbridge[10], Angeline[9] **Wenzel**, Mehitable[8] **Haven**, Abner[7], Jerusha[6] **Whipple**, Deacon Jacob[5], Deacon James[4], Joseph[3], Matthew[2], Matthew[1])[1129] was born 6 August 1867 and married twice. (1) **Charlotte McFaun** who died 14 September 1898.[1130] (2) **Clara L. Mathias** 11 December 1901.

Walter Nye **Smith** and Charlotte **McFaun** had the following child:
    6690 i. Clarence Lester[12] **Smith**[1131] born 2 May 1892. He was graduated from the Massachusetts Institute of Technology in 1915 with an B.S. degree.

Walter Nye **Smith** and Clara L. **Mathias** had the following child:
    6691   ii.   Charlotte **Smith**[1132] born 2 November 1904 and died 23 May 1912 at 7 years of age.

5707. **Lester Earle**[11] **Smith** (Charles Elbridge[10], Angeline[9] **Wenzel**, Mehitable[8] **Haven**, Abner[7], Jerusha[6] **Whipple**, Deacon Jacob[5], Deacon James[4], Joseph[3], Matthew[2], Matthew[1])[1133] was born 11 April 1872 and married **Sarah Belle Drury**.

Lester Earle **Smith** and Sarah Belle **Drury** had the following child:
    6692   i.   Alice Josephine[12] **Smith**[1134] born 20 August 1895.

5708. **Dana Fairbanks**[11] **Smith** (Charles Elbridge[10], Angeline[9] **Wenzel**, Mehitable[8] **Haven**, Abner[7], Jerusha[6] **Whipple**, Deacon Jacob[5], Deacon James[4], Joseph[3], Matthew[2], Matthew[1])[1135] was born 24 August 1876 and married **Abbie W. F. Bicknell** 6 April 1898.

Dana Fairbanks **Smith** and Abbie W. F. **Bicknell** had the following children:
    6693   i.   Sherman Dana[12] **Smith**[1136] born 20 December 1903.
    6694   ii.   Ida Louise **Smith**[1137] born 19 August 1905.

5709. **Helen Jackson**[11] **Smith** (Gorham Fairbanks[10], Angeline[9] **Wenzel**, Mehitable[8] **Haven**, Abner[7], Jerusha[6] **Whipple**, Deacon Jacob[5], Deacon James[4], Joseph[3], Matthew[2], Matthew[1])[1138] was born in Weymouth, Norfolk Co., Mass. 5 February 1882 and married **Walter Allen Wakefield** 30 September 1909.

Helen Jackson **Smith** and Walter Allen **Wakefield** had the following children:
    6695   i.   Walter Allen[12] **Wakefield** Jr.[1139] born in Passaic, Passaic Co., N.J. 2 August 1910.
    6696   ii.   Gorham Elliott **Wakefield**[1140] born 14 June 1911.

5716. **Fred Morton**[11] **Wenzel** (Dana Morton[10], Charles Haven[9], Mehitable[8] **Haven**, Abner[7], Jerusha[6] **Whipple**, Deacon Jacob[5], Deacon James[4], Joseph[3], Matthew[2], Matthew[1])[1141] was born 3 November 1884 and married **Mary L. Dunbar** 10 November 1923.

Fred Morton **Wenzel** and Mary L. **Dunbar** had the following child:
    6697   i.   Fred Herbert[12] **Wenzel**[1142] born in Ashland, Norfolk Co., Mass. 28 May 1924 and died 18 March 1926 at almost 2 years of age.

{ G 978 }

5721. **Dallas**[11] **Anderson** (Daisy Lovey[10] **Jordan**, Imogene[9] **Haven**, Abner[8], Abner[7], Jerusha[6] **Whipple**, Deacon Jacob[5], Deacon James[4], Joseph[3], Matthew[2], Matthew[1])[1143] was born 1 August 1910 and died 7 November 1972 at 62 years of age. She married **Maurice Blackman.**

Dallas **Anderson** and Maurice **Blackman** had the following child:
- 6698 i. Jane[12] **Blackman**.[1144]

5723. **Gilbert Haven**[11] **Jordan II** (Gilbert Haven[10], Imogene[9] **Haven**, Abner[8], Abner[7], Jerusha[6] **Whipple**, Deacon Jacob[5], Deacon James[4], Joseph[3], Matthew[2], Matthew[1])[1145] was born in Mohawk, Herkimer Co., N.Y. 4 September 1934 and married **Mary Margaret Coates** in San Diego, San Diego Co., Calif. 16 February 1956. Mary,[1146] daughter of Clarence Wade **Coates** and Doris Marie **Brown**, was born in Jackson Co., Mo. 14 June 1936..

Gilbert Haven **Jordan** II and Mary Margaret **Coates** had the following children:
- 6699 i. Mark Andrew[12] **Jordan**[1147] born in Phoenix, Maricopa Co., Ariz. 13 June 1957 and married Anita **Short** in San Diego 10 December 1983.
- 6700 ii. Carl Alan **Jordan**[1148] born in San Diego 13 August 1960 and married Cindy **Thompson** in El Cajon, San Diego Co., Calif. 3 December 1999.
- + 6701 iii. Craig Alan **Jordan** born 13 August 1960.
- 6702 iv. Amy Jo **Jordan**[1149] born in San Diego 26 March 1967.

5724. **Doris Elaine**[11] **Jordan** (Roland[10], Imogene[9] **Haven**, Abner[8], Abner[7], Jerusha[6] **Whipple**, Deacon Jacob[5], Deacon James[4], Joseph[3], Matthew[2], Matthew[1])[1150] was born in Plattsburgh, Clinton Co., N.Y. 9 June 1934 and married **Charles McHarg** 25 June 1957.

Doris Elaine **Jordan** and Charles **McHarg** had the following children:
- 6703 i. David[12] **McHarg**[1151] born in Troy, Rensselaer Co., N.Y. 10 July 1958.
- 6704 ii. Teresa **McHarg**[1152] born in Balltown,[1153] Maine 4 December 1959.
- 6705 iii. Catherine **McHarg**[1154] born in Washingtonville, Orange Co., N.Y. 15 December 1963.
- 6706 iv. Michele **McHarg**[1155] born in Washingtonville 23 March 1969.

5725. **Nancy Jean**[11] **Jordan** (Roland[10], Imogene[9] **Haven**, Abner[8], Abner[7], Jerusha[6] **Whipple**, Deacon Jacob[5], Deacon James[4], Joseph[3], Matthew[2], Matthew[1])[1156] was born in Plattsburgh, Clinton Co., N.Y. 10 June 1941 and married **Thomas Rowland Delux** in Palos Verdes, Los Angeles Co., Calif. 22 July 1966. He was born in Corning, N.Y. 1 May 1941.[1157]

Nancy Jean **Jordan** and Thomas Rowland **Delux** had the following children:
- 6707 i. Shelley Lynne[12] **Delux**[1158] born in Ilion, Herkimer Co, N.Y. 14 April 1969.
- 6708 ii. Christopher Rowland **Delux**[1159] born in New Haven, New Haven Co., Conn. 4 October 1971.

5727. **John Wright**[11] **Upson** (Marjory Alexander[10] **Wright**, Charles Baker[9], Susanna Whipple[8] **Baker**, Edward[7], Susannah[6] **Whipple**, Deacon Jacob[5], Deacon James[4], Joseph[3], Matthew[2], Matthew[1])[1160] was born in New York, N.Y. 16 October 1928 and married twice. (1) **Diane Marie (Dee) Tiangco** 6 October 1954. Diane is the daughter of Raymond V. **Dee** and Grace **Phillips**.[1161] (2) **Joan (Smith) Duryea** 26 August 1972. She is the daughter of Robert **Smith**.[1162] John owned a printing business and operated a Vermont transit bus station.

John Wright **Upson** and Diane Marie (Dee) **Tiangco** had the following child:
- + 6709 i. William Hazlett[12] **Upson** II born 9 May 1955.

5731. **Wallace Lowell**[11] **Whitney** (Harry Erwin[10], Eli Harrison[9], William Flanagan[8], Moses[7], Jemima[6] **Whipple**, Deacon Jacob[5], Deacon James[4], Joseph[3], Matthew[2], Matthew[1])[1163] was born in Tuolumne, Tuolomne Co., Calif 12 October 1918 and died 3 February 1998 in Chico, Butte Co., Calif., at 79 years of age. He married **Ruth Katharine Hilburn** in Las Vegas, Clark Co., Nev. 30 May 1942. Ruth,[1164] daughter of George **Hilburn** and Bernice **Young**, was born in Tampa, Hillsborough Co., Fla. 5 June 1919.

Wallace Lowell **Whitney** and Ruth Katharine **Hilburn** had the following children:
- + 6710 i. Cicely Ann[12] **Whitney** born 3 July 1943.
- + 6711 ii. Dale Craig **Whitney** born 16 December 1945.
- + 6712 iii. David Leroy **Whitney** born 3 February 1949.

5732. **Marion Burnett**[11] **Fitch** (William Herbert[10], Henry H.[9], Lucretia Lavinia[8] **Hurd**, Nathan[7], Ruth[6] **Labree**, Ruth[5] **Putnam**, Ruth[4] **Whipple**, Joseph[3], Matthew[2], Matthew[1])[1165] was born in Evansville, Vanderburgh Co.,

Ind. 9 March 1898 and died there 4 January 1976, at 77 years of age. She married **Earl J. Hyatt**, son of John Young **Hyatt** and Helen Frances **Richards**.

Marion Burnett **Fitch** and Earl J. **Hyatt** had the following child:
+   6713   i.   Marjorie Jean[12] **Hyatt** born 2 July 1923.

5733. **Gladys Eloise**[11] **Fitch** (William Herbert[10], Henry H.[9], Lucretia Lavinia[8] **Hurd**, Nathan[7], Ruth[6] **Labree**, Ruth[5] **Putnam**, Ruth[4] **Whipple**, Joseph[3], Matthew[2], Matthew[1])[1166] was born in Princeton, Gibson Co., Ind. 26 September 1911 and died 26 March 1989 in Lithonia, DeKalb Co., Ga., at 77 years of age. She married **Miles Matthew Becker** in Terre Haute, Vigo Co., Ind. 2 June 1930. Miles,[1167] son of Charles Matthew **Becker** and Helga **Ericksen**, was born in Chicago, Cook Co., Ill. 2 March 1909 and died 17 February 1968 in Blue Island, Cook Co., Ill., at 58 years of age. Gladys and Miles are buried in St. Mary's Cemetery, Chicago.

Gladys Eloise **Fitch** and Miles Matthew **Becker** had the following child:
+   6714   i.   Barbara Patricia[12] **Becker** born 7 September 1932.

5737. **Helen**[11] **Fitch** (George Paul[10], Henry H.[9], Lucretia Lavinia[8] **Hurd**, Nathan[7], Ruth[6] **Labree**, Ruth[5] **Putnam**, Ruth[4] **Whipple**, Joseph[3], Matthew[2], Matthew[1])[1168] was born abt 1909 and died in 1978 in Kushequa, McKean Co., Penn., at 69 years of age. She married **(__) Yingling**.

Helen **Fitch** and (__) **Yingling** had the following child:
       6715   i.   Paul[12] **Yingling**.[1169]

5739. **Helen**[11] **Reed** (Ora J.[10], Sylvester P.[9], Lydia[8] **Hurd**, Nathan[7], Ruth[6] **Labree**, Ruth[5] **Putnam**, Ruth[4] **Whipple**, Joseph[3], Matthew[2], Matthew[1])[1170] was born in Melrose, Middlesex Co., Mass. 23 July 1899 and died 10 February 1997 in Bangor, Penobscot Co., Maine, at 97 years of age. She married **Herman O. Faust** in Manchester, Hillsborough Co., N.H. 14 August 1929. Herman,[1171] son of Rudolph **Faust** and Hermine **Sauer**, was born in Boston, Suffolk Co., Mass. 31 July 1901 and died 10 May 1985 in Seminole, Pinnelas Co., Fla., at 83 years of age.

Helen **Reed** and Herman O. **Faust** had the following children:
+   6716   i.   Marguerite[12] **Faust** born 1 April 1931.
+   6717   ii.   Charles Allen **Faust** born 15 November 1933.

5743. **Janet Ruth**[11] **Walthers** (Edward William[10], Sarah Martha[9] **Whitcomb**, Walter Scott[8], Roxelane[7] **Putnam**, Bailey[6], Timothy[5], Ruth[4] **Whipple**, Joseph[3], Matthew[2], Matthew[1])[1172] was born in Wisconsin 2 March 1927 and married **Lloyd Francis Bursek** in Manitowoc, Manitowoc Co., Wisc. 2 October 1954. Lloyd,[1173] son of John **Bursek** and Pauline **Hoverson**, was born 8 April 1918 and died 17 January 1983 in Manitowoc, at 64 years of age. Lloyd, an accountant, was an Army Captain during WWII.

Janet Ruth **Walthers** and Lloyd Francis **Bursek** had the following children:
+ 6718 i. Nan Ellen[12] **Bursek** born 17 July 1957.
+ 6719 ii. Sue Ann **Bursek** born 20 May 1960.

5746. **Patricia Jean**[11] **Knudsen** (Inez Lillian[10] **Ammermann**, Anna Lydia[9] **Whitcomb**, Walter Scott[8], Roxelane[7] **Putnam**, Bailey[6], Timothy[5], Ruth[4] **Whipple**, Joseph[3], Matthew[2], Matthew[1])[1174] was born in Iron River, Iron Co., Mich. 28 October 1922 and married twice. (1) **Robert E. Skinner** in Bessemer, Gogebic Co., Mich. 26 October 1946. He was born in Minneapolis, Hennepin Co., Minn. in February 1916 and died in January 1978 in Birmingham, Talladaga Co., Ala., at 61 years of age.[1175] He was the adopted son of R. M. and E. Skinner. (2) **Kenneth G. Hamister** in Rocky River, Cuyahoga Co., Ohio 28 September 1968.[1176] They lived in Elyria, Lorain Co., Ohio (1998) where he practiced law before retiring.

Patricia Jean **Knudsen** and Robert E. **Skinner** had the following child born in Minneapolis:
6720 i. Anne Louise[12] **Skinner**[1177] 29 April 1951 and married Stanley J. **Glad** 22 May 1976.

5747. **Bjarne McDonald**[11] **Knudsen** (Inez Lillian[10] **Ammermann**, Anna Lydia[9] **Whitcomb**, Walter Scott[8], Roxelane[7] **Putnam**, Bailey[6], Timothy[5], Ruth[4] **Whipple**, Joseph[3], Matthew[2], Matthew[1])[1178] was born in Iron River, Iron Co., Mich. 15 January 1929 and married **Bess Peel**. Bess, daughter of Claude **Peel** and Mae (__), was born in Fannin Co., Tex. 12 June 1926 and died 4 March 1987 in Dallas, Dallas Co., Tex., at 60 years of age. Bjarne served in the Army during the Korean War and was living in Corinth, Denton Co., Tex. in 1998 where he was an Insurance Adjuster.

Bjarne McDonald **Knudsen** and Bess **Peel** had the following child:
6721 i. David[12] **Knudsen**[1179] born in San Angelo, Tom Green Co., Tex. 2 October 1961 and married Sandra (__) in 1979.

5748. **Virginia Coe**[11] **Miller** (Georgianna Lucille[10] **Ammermann**, Anna Lydia[9] **Whitcomb**, Walter Scott[8], Roxelane[7] **Putnam**, Bailey[6], Timothy[5], Ruth[4] **Whipple**, Joseph[3], Matthew[2], Matthew[1])[1180] was born in Iron River, Iron Co., Mich. 12 September 1918 and married **John Stevens Blankenhorn** in San Marino, Los Angeles Co., Calif. 24 January 1942. John,[1181] son of David F. **Blankenhorn** and Emma **Peterson**, was born in Pasadena, Los Angeles Co., Calif. 31 August 1913. He was a location manager in the motion picture industry.

Virginia Coe **Miller** and John Stevens **Blankenhorn** had the following children:
+ 6722 i. Virginia Stevens[12] **Blankenhorn** born 25 May 1947.
  6723 ii. Amanda Porter **Blankenhorn**[1182] born in Pasadena 5 June 1952 and married three times. (1) Dennis Louis **Navone** 20 September 1974. (2) Kent Curtis **Noye** in Pasadena 3 May 1980. (3) John **Young** in Grass Valley, Nevada Co., Calif. in 1990. Amanda was a travel agent in Grass Valley. (1998).

5749. **Peggy Jean**[11] **Miller** (Georgianna Lucille[10] **Ammermann**, Anna Lydia[9] **Whitcomb**, Walter Scott[8], Roxelane[7] **Putnam**, Bailey[6], Timothy[5], Ruth[4] **Whipple**, Joseph[3], Matthew[2], Matthew[1])[1183] was born in Los Angeles, Los Angeles Co., Calif. 3 May 1921 and married **Richard Howard Singer** there 28 September 1946. Richard,[1184] son of Howard **Singer** and Christine **Stindle**, was born in Racine, Racine Co., Wisc. 10 October 1918. He was a Flight Engineer for the U.S. Navy during WWII and worked as an Engineering Designer after his discharge. Betty was a Navigation Instructor in the U.S. Navy during WWII.

Peggy Jean **Miller** and Richard Howard **Singer** had the following children:
+ 6724 i. Stephen Howard[12] **Singer** born 10 January 1953.
+ 6725 ii. Andrew Porter **Singer** born 25 January 1955.

5751. **Robert**[11] **Rhodes** (Patricia Athey[10] **Ammermann**, Anna Lydia[9] **Whitcomb**, Walter Scott[8], Roxelane[7] **Putnam**, Bailey[6], Timothy[5], Ruth[4] **Whipple**, Joseph[3], Matthew[2], Matthew[1])[1185] was born in Pasadena, Los Angeles Co., Calif. 11 January 1931 and married **Carolyn (__)**.

Robert **Rhodes** and Carolyn (__) had the following child:
  6726 i. Jamie[12] **Rhodes**.[1186]

5752. **Douglas Duane**[11] **Deal** (Lynn Lee[10], Ettie Laura[9] **Coykendall**, Laura Emeline[8] **Putnam**, Hiram[7], Bailey[6], Timothy[5], Ruth[4] **Whipple**, Joseph[3], Matthew[2], Matthew[1])[1187] was born in Tacoma, Pierce Co., Wash. 19 March 1924 and married three times. (1) **Maude Ellen Harris** in Houston, Harris Co., Tex. 18 February 1946. She was born in Houston 22 November 1926.[1188] They were divorced 1 July 1964. (2) **Carol Jean Henderson** in Reno, Washoe Co., Nev. 12 September 1964. She was born in Holtville, Imperial Co., Calif. 18 November 1929.[1189] They were divorced in Oakland, Alameda Co., Calif. (3) **Shirley Faye August** in Concord, Contra Costa Co., Calif. 25 August 1979. She was born in Concord 9 October 1934.

Douglas Duane **Deal** and Maude Ellen **Harris** had the following children born in Berkeley, Alameda Co., Calif:

- 6727 i. Kirk Harris[12] **Deal**[1190] 23 June 1949 and died 2 March 1995 in Miami Beach, Dade Co., Fla., at 45 years of age. His ashes were scattered in the Atlantic Ocean off Miami, Dade County, Fla. He married **Sandra Sue Allen** in Miami 3 July 1979.
- 6728 ii. Debra Diane **Deal**[1191] 13 February 1951 and married Douglas **Kagawa** in Berkeley 19 June 1976.
- 6729 iii. Karen Louise **Deal**[1192] 16 December 1952 and married twice. (1) Stephen Henry **Lewis** in Reno 29 July 1972. (2) **Lee Gallegos** in Rodeo, Contra Costa Co., Calif. 23 May 1981.

Douglas Duane **Deal** and Carol Jean **Henderson** had the following children:

- 6730 iv. Michael Patrick **Deal**[1193] born in Salem, Mannington Township, Salem Co., N.J. 26 January 1952 and married Deborah Ann **Van Nest** in Reno 10 April 1971. Michael was adopted by Douglas and Carol on 9 January 1969.
- 6731 v. Patrick Joseph **Deal**[1194] born in Berkeley 7 December 1955 and married Lucinda Diane **Bowen** in Hayward, Alameda Co., Calif. 31 January 1975. Patrick was adopted by Douglas and Carol on 9 January 1969.

5754. **Helen Gertrude**[11] **Deal** (Koli Horace[10], Ettie Laura[9] **Coykendall**, Laura Emeline[8] **Putnam**, Hiram[7], Bailey[6], Timothy[5], Ruth[4] **Whipple**, Joseph[3], Matthew[2], Matthew[1])[1195] was born in Ceresco, Calhoun Co., Mich. 1 May 1912 and married **William Peder Thomte** in Decatur, Van Buren Co., Mich. 18 May 1935. William,[1196] son of Bernt **Thomte** and Marne **Arnesen**, was born in Oslo, Norway 19 July 1907 and died 20 December 1987 in Colorado Springs, El Paso Co., Colo., at 80 years of age.

Helen Gertrude **Deal** and William Peder **Thomte** had the following children born in Chicago, Cook Co., Ill.:

    6732   i.   Thomas Deal[12] **Thomte**[1197] 24 June 1943 and married Theresa **Perkins**. No children born to this union.

    6733   ii.   Robert Graham **Thomte**[1198] 2 October 1945 and married Pam **Marholz**. No children born to this union.

    6734   iii.   Nancy Lee **Thomte**[1199] 18 July 1947.

    6735   iv.   William Bertram **Thomte**[1200] 1 October 1949 and married Debbie **Witek**. No children born to this union.

    6736   v.   Richard Deal **Thomte**[1201] 23 October 1951 and married Pam **Faust**. No children born to this union.

5755. **Dorothy Mae**[11] **Deal** (Koli Horace[10], Ettie Laura[9] **Coykendall**, Laura Emeline[8] **Putnam**, Hiram[7], Bailey[6], Timothy[5], Ruth[4] **Whipple**, Joseph[3], Matthew[2], Matthew[1])[1202] was born in Kalamazoo, Kalamazoo Co., Mich. 17 May 1919 and died 17 July **1996** in Gobles, Van Buren Co., Mich., at 77 years of age. She married **Leland Glea Sherburne Sr.** in Chicago, Cook Co., Ill. 28 January 1939. Leland,[1203] son of Sherman Lewis **Sherburne** and Linda Adeline **Pollack,** was born 30 April 1918 and died 20 August 1960 in Paw Paw, Van Buren Co., Mich., at 42 years of age. Buried in Decatur, Van Buren Co., Mich.

Dorothy Mae **Deal** and Leland Glea **Sherburne** Sr. had the following children:

  + 6737   i.   Leland Glea[12] **Sherburne** Jr. born 3 July 1939.

  + 6738   ii.   James Lewis **Sherburne** born 16 October 1941.

  + 6739   iii.   Douglas Bernard **Sherburne** born 30 November 1942.

      6740   iv.   Steven Deal **Sherburne**[1204] born in Paw Paw 17 July 1947 and died 21 March 1961 in Decatur, at 13 years of age. Buried in Harrison Cemetery, Decatur.

5756. **Louise Elizabeth**[11] **Deal** (Kirk James[10], Ettie Laura[9] **Coykendall**, Laura Emeline[8] **Putnam**, Hiram[7], Bailey[6], Timothy[5], Ruth[4] **Whipple**, Joseph[3], Matthew[2], Matthew[1])[1205] was born in Kalamazoo, Kalamazoo Co., Mich. 25 October 1919 and married **Franklin Wilbur Smith** there 15 July 1941. Franklin,[1206] son of William **Smith** and Maude **Briggs**, was born in Perrinton, Gratiot Co., Mich. 10 February 1916 and died 30 March 1969 in St. Johns, Clinton Co., Mich., at 53 years of age.

Louise Elizabeth **Deal** and Franklin Wilbur **Smith** had the following children:

+ 6741 i. Alan Franklin[12] **Smith** born 26 January 1943.
+ 6742 ii. Kirk Wells **Smith** born 17 September 1946.
    6743 iii. Gordon Paul **Smith**[1207] born in Owosso, Shiawassee Co., Mich. 28 May 1948 and died 25 May 1995 in Ft. Lauderdale, Broward Co., Fla., at 46 years of age. He married Christine **Wasserman** in Muskegon, Muskegon Co., Mich. 10 June 1980. She was born in Muskegon.[1208]
+ 6744 iv. Sue Lynn **Smith** born 19 February 1951.
+ 6745 v. Dwight David **Smith** born 6 August 1952.
+ 6746 vi. Franklin Wilbur **Smith** born 17 February 1962.

ENDNOTES, GENERATION ELEVEN

1. and 2. Chaffee to Whipple, *2 Letters*.
3. through 6. Dodge to Whipple, *Letter, 6 April 1993*.
7. and 8. Ahrens to Whipple, *Letter, 25 May 1990*.
9. through 11. Proctor Patterson Jones to Blaine Whipple. letter dated 21 May 1991 & 16 Feb. 1997 at 3625 Sacramento St., San Francisco, Calif. 94118-1914 in possession of Whipple at 236 NW Sundown Way, Portland, OR 97229 (2004). (Hereafter Jones to Whipple, *Letter 05/21/1991 & 01/16/1997*).
12. and 13. Martha Whipple Davis to Blaine Whipple. Letter dated 26 March 1989 at 6 Reservoir St., Nashua, NH 03060. In possession of Whipple (2004.) Pedigree and family group sheets provided. (Hereafter Davis to Whipple, *Letter, 26 March 1989*).
14. through 15. Carlisle to Whipple, *Ltr, 20 March 1989*.
16. Ibid.; and P. T. Whipple, *3 Letters*.
17. P. T. Whipple, *3 Letters*.
18. John A. Whipple to Blaine Whipple. Letters dated 28 June 1995 and 8 Sept. 1998 at 7404 Curly Leaf Cove, Austin, Texas 78750-8312. In possession of Whipple (2004). (Hereafter J.A. Whipple, *2 Letters*).
19. P. T. Whipple, *3 Letters*.
20. through 24. C.L. Whipple to Whipple, *Letter, 2 May 1989*.
25. and 26. Kyle to Whipple, *2 Letters*.
27. H.Whipple to B. Whipple, *Letter, 04/20/1993*.
28. through 32. Bayles to Whipple, *2 letters*.
33. Dorothy Gene Keyes Sudikas to Blaine Whipple. Letter dated 8 June 1998 at 5412 44th St., Lubbock, Texas 79414-1324. In possession of Whipple (2004). (Hereafter Sudikas to Whipple, *Letter, 8 June 1998*).
34. and 35. Bayles to Whipple, *2 letters*.
36. and 37. Kelly to Whipple, *Letter, 17 May 1999*.
38. through 41. Burke's, *Presidential Families*, 472 and 473.
42. through 54. Wise to Whipple, *3 Letters*.
55. through 79. Storey to Whipple, *5 letters*.
80. through 103. Keener to Whipple, *Letters 30 May & 6 June 2000*.
104. through 107. Putnam-Whipple, *Family Group Sheet*.
108. Burke's, *Presidential Families*, 489-506.
109. Ibid., 504.
110. Ibid., 489-506.
111. Ibid., 504.
112. through 122. Workman to Whipple, *Letter, 26 April 1998*.
123. through 135. Huse to Whipple, *2 Letters*.
136. P. Whipple to B. Whipple, *Letter, 3 Jan. 1989*.
137. Author unable to find a town with this name, hence no county is named.
138. P. Whipple to B. Whipple, *Letter, 3 Jan. 1989*.
139. Bills to Whipple, *Letter, Nov. 1995*.
140. through 142. H. Byington to Whipple, *2 Letters*.
143. and 144. Wanstall to Whipple, *4 Letters*.
145. through 147. Adams to Whipple, *3 Letters*.
148. Wanstall to Whipple, *4 Letters*.
149. and 150. Adams to Whipple, *3 Letters*.
151. Wanstall to Whipple, *4 Letters*.
152. Adams to Whipple, *3 Letters*.

153. and 154. Wanstall to Whipple, *4 Letters*.
155. Adams to Whipple, *3 Letters*; and Wanstall to Whipple, *4 Letters*.
156. through 171. Wanstall to Whipple, *4 Letters*.
172. through 177. Bryan Whipple to B. Whipple, *3 letters*.
178. Goffstown, N. H, *History-Genealogy*, 2:552; and J. Whipple to Whipple, *Letter, 11 July 1989*.
179. J. Whipple to Whipple, *Letter, 11 July 1989*.
180. through 187. D. Whipple to B. Whipple, *Letter, 9 Feb. 1989*.
188. Woodworth to Whipple, *3 Letters*.
189. Author unable to find a town with this name, hence no county is named.
190. and 191. Woodworth to Whipple, *3 Letters*.
192. through 195. Dorian to Whipple, *Letter, 21 Aug. 2000*.
196. and 197. Ross to Whipple, *2 Letters*.
198. and 199. Reighard to Whipple, *2 Letters*.
200. through 203. John Lafayette Shannon-Maude Belle Kennison Family Group Sheet, supplied 2 July 1998 by Kathie Walsh, 218 Cape Way, Geneva, Ill. 60134. This sheet cites Butler Co, Iowa marriage records, Black Hawk Co, Iowa divorce records, 1895 Iowa state census, 1900 federal census, Black Hawk, Co., State of South Dakota death records, Minnesota certificate of death, and Maude Thomas' obituary. (Hereafter Shannon-Kennison, *Family Group Sheet*).
204. Henry Whipple, 2:41, 43, and 45.
205. Author unable to find a town with this name, hence no county is named.
206. through 235. Henry Whipple, 2:41, 43, and 45.
236. and 237. L. Whipple to Whipple, *7 Letters*.
238. Author unable to find a town with this name, hence no county is named.
239. and 240. L. Whipple to Whipple, *7 Letters*.
241. David Lee Whipple to Blaine Whipple. Letter dated 9 May 1994 at Children's Hospital Medical Center of Akron, Radiography School, One Perkins Square, Akron, Ohio 44308-1062. In possession of Whipple (2004). Provided extensive genealogical charts. No documentation noted. (Hereafter D.L. Whipple to Whipple, *Letter, 9 May 1994*).
242. L. Whipple to Whipple, *7 Letters*.
243. and 244. D.L. Whipple to Whipple, *Letter, 9 May 1994*.
245. L. Whipple to Whipple, *7 Letters*.
246. D.L. Whipple to Whipple, *Letter, 9 May 1994*.
247. through 252. Canaday to Whipple, *Various e-mail messages*.
253. and 254. Newcomer to Whipple, *Letter 14 April 1993*.
255. through 257. Henry Whipple, 2:36.
258. through 260. Joseph Whipple, *Family Bible*.
261. and 265. Matthais-Whipple, *Pedigree*.
266. Wm. T. Whipple obit., *The LaCrosse Morning Tribune*.
267. Obituary of Charles Whipple, *The LaCrosse Morning Tribune*, LaCrosse, Wisc. (10 April 1933), page 11. (Hereafter Charles Whipple obit., *The LaCrosse Morning Tribune*).
268. Elizabeth Catharine Whipple, *The LaCrosse Morning Tribune*, LaCrosse, Wisc. (24 November 1928), page 7.
269. and 270. Charles Whipple obit., *The LaCrosse Morning Tribune*, page 11..
271. through 273. Thomas to Whipple, *Letter, 24 Jan. 2000*.
274. through 283. Talmud-Whipple, *Family Group Sheets*.
284. through 288. E. Whipple to B. Whipple, *Various Letters*.
289. Mrs. John R. Boyd (Virginia Whipple) to Blaine Whipple. Letter dated 22 March 1989 at 222 North Marion, Apt. 3F, Oak Park, Ill. 60302. In possession of Whipple (2004). Enclosures included family group sheets. (Hereafter Whipple to B. Whip-

ple, *Letter, 22 March 1989*).
290. through 292. E. Whipple to B. Whipple, *Various Letters*.
293. Elnette Cecile Whipple, Birth Certificate Registered No. 74668, 1 May 1941, Bureau of Vital Statistics, Chicago, Ill.
294. E. Whipple to B. Whipple, *Various Letters*.
295. Author unable to find a town with this name, hence no county is named.
296. E. Whipple to B. Whipple, *Various Letters*.
297. *Malden Evening News*, Malden, Mass. 8 Jan. 1942 and *The Gardner News*, Gardner, Mass., 17 April 1965.
298. Genealogy, *Western NY*, 262; Thomas to Whipple, *Letter, 24 Jan. 2000*; and Ms. Gertrude J. Augie, Historian, City of Salamanca, N.Y. to Blaine Whipple. Letter dated 31 July 1990 at 109 N. Buffalo St., Apt. 54, Springville, N.Y. 14141. In possession of Whipple (2004). (Hereafter Augie to Whipple, *Letter 07/31/1990*).
299. Genealogy, *Western NY*, 262; and Thomas to Whipple, *Letter, 24 Jan. 2000*.
300. Genealogy, *Western NY*, 262; Tombstone Inscription, Wildwood Cemetery, Salamanca, Cattaraugus Co., N.Y.; and Thomas to Whipple, *Letter, 24 Jan. 2000*.
301. Genealogy, *Western NY*, 262; and Thomas to Whipple, *Letter, 24 Jan. 2000*.
302. Thomas to Whipple, *Letter, 24 Jan. 2000*.
303. Genealogy, *Western NY*, 262; and Thomas to Whipple, *Letter, 24 Jan. 2000*.
304. Genealogy, *Western NY*, 261; and Burroughs, *Burroughs Ancestors*.
305. Burroughs, *Burroughs Ancestors*.
306. and 307. M. Whipple to B. Whipple, *Letter 10 Dec. 1988*.
308. through 337. Henry Whipple, 2:28 and 29.
338. through 341. C. Whipple to B. Whipple, *3 Letters*.
342. and 343. Henry Whipple, 2:32.
344. Ibid., 2:32; and Patricia (Molina) Scully to Blaine Whipple. E-mail dated 26 March 2000 at scully@rsvl.net, mailing address 312 Grove St., Roseville, Calif. 95678. In possession of Whipple (2004.). (Hereafter Scully to Whipple, *E-Mail, 26 Mar. 2000*).
345. through 348. Henry Whipple, 2:32.
349. and 350. Avery-Whipple, *Pedigree Chart*.
351. through 396. Moore to Whipple, *Letter 2 May 1994*.
397. through 404. Joseph Duell, 1199 Bay Rd., Lake George, N. Y. 12845-4618, Letter dated 24 May 2004 including Samuel Morgan I - Betsey Whipple Family Group Sheets and extensive citations from a variety of Vermont genealogical published sources. In possession of Whipple (2004). (Hereafter Duell to Whipple, *Letter, 24 May 2002.*)
405. through 411. Prescott to Whipple, *7 letters*.
412. and 413. Orr to Whipple, *13 Letters*.
414. and 415. Crawford to Whipple, *4 Letters*.
416. through 424. Orr to Whipple, *13 Letters*.
425. Frances F. Horner to Blaine Whipple. Letters dated 30 June 1989; 6 April 1993; 3 Jan. & 16 Jan. 1996 at 5859 Susan Dr. E., Indianapolis, Ind. 46250-1826. In possession of Whipple (2004.) Family group sheets provided. (Hereafter Horner to Whipple, *4 Letters*).
426. Crawford to Whipple, *4 Letters*.
427. and 428. Orr to Whipple, *13 Letters*.
429. Horner to Whipple, *4 Letters*.
430. through 436. Orr to Whipple, *13 Letters*.
437. *Eagle*, Clinton, Iowa, 12 October 1900.
438. and 439. Orr to Whipple, *13 Letters*.
440. Dr. Dean C. McKinley, Chiropractor, to Blaine Whipple. Letters dated 11 June 1989, 26 Nov. 1995, 24 Sept. 1996, 20 Jan. 2001, and 24 Feb. 2004 at P. O. Box 663,

Alto, N. M. 88312. In possession of Whipple (2004). Includes Family Group Sheets. (Hereafter D. McKinley to Whipple, *5 Letters*).

441. through 449. Orr to Whipple, *13 Letters*.
450. and 451. Doris E. Hintze to Blaine Whipple. Letter dated 28 Nov. 1995 at 1900 6th Ave., #203, Rock Island, Ill. 61201-8138. In possession of Whipple (2004). (Hereafter Hintze to Whipple, *Letter 28 Nov. 1995*).
452. and 453. Orr to Whipple, *13 Letters*.
454. Randazzo to Whipple, *E-mail, 25 Oct. 01*.
455. *Vinton Eagle*, (Vinton, Iowa) 15 May 1894, 22 Feb. 1901.
456. through 473. Mrs. Gladys Fossett to Blaine Whipple. Letter dated 2 Aug. 1998 at 412 E. 10th St., Vinton, Iowa 52349. In possession of Whipple (2004). (Hereafter Fossett to Whipple.)
474. Kearns to Whipple, *Letter, 4 Aug. 1987*; and Kearns - Whipple, *Family Group Sheets*.
475. Kearns to Whipple, *Letter, 4 Aug. 1987*.
476. through 478. Kearns - Whipple, *Family Group Sheets*.
479. W.P. Whipple to B. Whipple, *3 Letters*.
480. Milo Robert Whipple & Lois Jeanette Fry, Marriage License Register, 20 Nov. 1906, Book I, District Court, Benton Co., Iowa: 166.
481. *Eagle*, Vinton, Iowa, 6 March, 9 June, 28 Aug. 1903.
482. Cedar Rapids *Gazette*, Cedar Rapids, Iowa, 11 Nov. 1971.
483. Ibid., July 24 and 27, 1935.
484. through 486. W.P. Whipple to B. Whipple, *3 Letters*.
487. Barr-Whipple, *Family Group Sheets*.
488. Benton Co., Iowa, *Biographical Album*, 312.
489. R. Wheeler, *Church Records*.
490. Informant for the Certificate of Death was Thomas J. Andrus, Sr., Rt. 5, Allegan, Mich, 49010.
491. B. Naydine Ziegler to Blaine Whipple. Letters dated 17 and 26 March 1989 at 2510 Williams St., Bellingham, Wash. 98225. In possession of Whipple (2004.) Extensive Family Group Sheets provided. Documentation included death certificates for Charles E. Frederick and Maude Whipple, obituaries, and other printed articles. (Hereafter Ziegler to Whipple, *2 Letters*).
492. Barr-Whipple, *Family Group Sheets*.
493. Ibid.; and Ziegler to Whipple, *2 Letters*.
494. and 495. Barr-Whipple, *Family Group Sheets*; and Ziegler to Whipple, *2 Letters*.
496. through 500. Barr-Whipple, *Family Group Sheets*.
501. Greer to Whipple, *2 Letters*.
502. Carl T. Whipple & Esther Mossman, Marriage License Register, 27 March 1907, Book I, District Court, Benton Co., Iowa: 217.
503. Jane Whipple to B. Whipple, *15 Letters*.
504. *Vinton Review*, Vinton, Iowa, 3 April 1907.
505. and 506. Jane Whipple to B. Whipple, *15 Letters*.
507. Catherine (Catlin) Mack to Blaine Whipple. Letters dated 28 March 1989 and 3 November 1995 at 201 8th Ave. N.E., Independence, Iowa 50644. In possession of Whipple (2004). (Hereafter C. Mack to Whipple, *2 Letters*).
508. Howard Lewis Catlin & Callie Catharine Whipple, Marriage License Register, 8 July 1908, Book I, District Court, Benton Co., Iowa: 329.
509. *Vinton Review*, Vinton, Iowa, 8 July 1908.
510. through 512. C. Mack to Whipple, *2 Letters*.
513. through 516. Jane Whipple to B. Whipple, *15 Letters*.

517. *Cedar Rapids Gazette*, Cedar Rapids, Iowa, date not provided.
518. Jane Whipple to B. Whipple, *15 Letters*.
519. and 520. R. Whipple to B. Whipple, *9 Letters*.
521. and 522. Jean (Whipple) Haight to Blaine Whipple. Letters dated 26 May 1989, 19 April & 20 Dec. 1995, and 29 May 1997 at 2760 Edgemont Ave., Waterloo, Iowa 50702, and letters dated 11 Dec. 2000 and 19 Dec. 2002 at 4301 Cimmaron Trail, Granbury, Texas 76049-5158. In possession of Whipple (2004). (Hereafter Haight to Whipple, *6 Letters*).
523. through 526. Bonnie (Britt) Bilderback to Blaine Whipple. Letter dated 11 Feb. 1996 at PO Box 357, 202 S. 5th St., Ava, Ill. 62907. In possession of Whipple (2004). (Hereafter Bilderback to Whipple, *Letter, 11 Feb. 1996*).
527. and 528. Jane Whipple to B. Whipple, *15 Letters*.
529. Greer to Whipple, *2 Letters*; and Haight to Whipple, *6 Letters*.
530. Greer to Whipple, *2 Letters*.
531. Gallaher to Whipple, *9 Letters*.
532. Jane Whipple to B.Whipple., *15 Letter.*
533. Gallaher to Whipple, *9 Letters*.
534. through 537. Jane Whipple to B. Whipple, *15 Letters*.
538. Department of the Interior, Bureau of Pensions document that was a part of James E. Whipple's application for a pension for service in the Spanish-American War; Pension Application No. 1407489. Question No. 5 asked: "Have you any children living? If so, please state their names and dates of their births." Answer: "One son, L. Blaine Whipple, born June 22, 1883." /s/ James E. Whipple. Dated 21 January 1913. Copy of document acquired by Blaine Whipple, 236 N.W. Sundown Way, Portland, Oreg. 97229-6575 30 May 1981 from the National Archives Trust Fund Board, Washington, D. C. 20408. In possession of Whipple 2004.; Date and place of marriage attested to by Lillian (LeFebre) Whipple, plaintiff in a petition in equity to be divorced from Blaine Whipple, defendant, filed in the District Court of Linn Co., Cedar Rapids, Iowa 9 Jan. 1926. Divorce No. 35081.; Divorce awarded to plaintiff Lillian Whipple; Blaine Whipple & Pearl J. Scott, Marriage License, 21 September 1927, Vol. 388, Record No.9-296: State of Nebraska, Dept. of Public Welfare, Bureau of Health, Division of Vital Statistics, Lincoln, Nebr.; and Blaine Whipple, Death Certificate Death No. 54-18847, Weakly Co., Tenn.
539. E. (Whipple) West to B. Whipple, *4 Letters*.
540. Blaine Whipple, comp., *Scott, A Name Worth Looking Into, a history-genealogy of the Scott Family of Québec Province, Canada and Minnesota and allied lines. The "Tanguay Dictionary" was the main source for the French Canadian information. Personal letters from the children of Ben and Nellie (Dolan) Scott were the main source of information for those lines. Copies at the Library of Congress, Minnesota Historical Society, and North Dakota Historical Society. The work has been updated by hand since publication. Sources of the updates are letters from various individuals involved who provide birth, marriage, death, and other pertinent information.* (Portland, Oreg.: Self published, 1981). (Hereafter B. Whipple, *Scott Genealogy*).
541. *McLeod County Chronicle*, Glencoe, Minn. 6 April 1998.
542. E. (Whipple) West to B. Whipple, *4 Letters*; and Baby (Ellen) Whipple, Death Certificate D No. 00722. File No. 33268-1909, Filed in August 1909, Dept. of Health, Bureau of Vital Statistics, Dept. 050 Org 2000, 2400 Troost, Ste. 1200, Kansas City, Mo.
543. Richard E. Whipple to Blaine Whipple. Letter dated 15 July 1998 at 4689 Lista Point, Eagen, Minn. 55122. In possession of Whipple (2004). The writer is a younger brother of the author. Richard Earl Whipple, Birth Certificate State File No. 6899. Registered No. 40, 18 Sept. 1933. Correction No. 44,835 dated 2 Sept. 1987 based on Baptismal Record. Surname originally given as Wipple, changed to Whipple, North Dakota Department of Health, Bismarck, N. Dak.

{ G 991 }

544. and 545. O'Donnell, *Eugene, Ind.*, 274-75.
546. through 548. Ibid., 213.
549. through 551. E. (Whipple) West to B. Whipple, *4 Letters*.
552. O'Donnell, *Eugene, Ind.*, 274-75.
553. Ibid., 206.
554. Ibid., 274-75.
555. E. (Whipple) West to B. Whipple, *4 Letters*.
556. O'Donnell, *Eugene, Ind.*, 274-75.
557. Mrs. Cora (Fultz) Pierson to Elaine Whipple West. Letter dated 15 November 1958 at 15649 Spaulding Ave., Markham, Ill. In possession of Blaine Whipple (2004). (Hereafter Pierson to Whipple, *Letter, 15 Nov. 1958*).
558. O'Donnell, *Eugene, Ind.*, 274-75.
559. Ibid., 206.
560. and 561. E. (Whipple) West to B. Whipple, *4 Letters*.
562. O'Donnell, *Eugene, Ind.*, 206 and E. (Whipple) West to B. Whipple, *4 Letters*.
563. Dimmock-Whipple, *Family Group Sheets*.
564. Pittman-Woods, *Family Group Sheet*.
565. Dimmock-Whipple, *Family Group Sheets*; and Pittman - Woods, *Family Group Sheet*.
566. Dimmock-Whipple, *Family Group Sheets*.
567. Pittman-Woods, *Family Group Sheet*.
568. through 572. Dimmock - Whipple, *Family Group Sheets*.
573. through 584. Roy Whipple to B. Whipple, *4 letters*.
585. and 586. Rumpf to Whipple, *3 letters*.
587. through 592. Roy Whipple to B. Whipple, *4 letters*.
593. through 598. Brown-Hall, *Family Group Sheet*.
599. and 600. *Register*, 105:66.
601. Westensee to Whipple, *Letters 1991 & 1992*, 395.
602. *Register*, 105:66.
603. Westensee to Whipple, *Letters 1991 & 1992*, 395.
604. through 608. *Register*, 105:66.
609. Henry A. Watkins entry, 1900 U.S. Census, Population Schedule, Albany City, Albany Co. N. Y., Vol. 4, Enumeration District 63, sheet 3, line 10, National Archives, Washington, D.C. (Hereafter Henry A. Watkins, *1900 US Census*).
610. Ethel Stanwood Bolton, comp., *Some Descendants of John Moore of Sudbury, Massachusetts* (1904). (Hereafter John Moore, *Sudbury, Mass.*).
611. and 612. Henry A. Watkins, *1900 US Census*.
613. Peters to Whipple, *Letter, 21 Feb. 1997*; and Leslie Lawrence Watkins, Death Certificate Thompkins Co., N. Y. Health Department.
614. through 624. Knowles to Whipple, *Letters 19 & 30 July 2000*.
625. H. Whipple to B. Whipple, *Letter, 04/20/1993*; and Knowles to Whipple, *Letters 19 & 30 July 2000*.
626. through 636. Knowles to Whipple, *Letters 19 & 30 July 2000*.
637. through 650. *Johnson and Whipple Family Genealogies* (Available at the Library of Congress, Call No. CS71, J7, 1963). (Hereafter Johnson/Whipple, *Fam. Genealogies*).
651. through 655. Crates to Whipple, *Letter, 11 Feb. 1991*.
656. and 657. Jenkins to Whipple, *E-mail 25 March & 30 May 2000*.
658. Maris to Whipple, *Letter, 11 April 1996*; and Knowles to Whipple, *Letters 19 & 30 July 2000*.
659. Maris to Whipple, *Letter, 11 April 1996*.
660. Ibid.; and Knowles to Whipple, *Letters 19 & 30 July 2000*.
661. and 662. Maris to Whipple, *Letter, 11 April 1996*; and Knowles to Whipple, *Letters 19*

& *30 July 2000*.
663. through 665. Knowles to Whipple, *Letters 19 & 30 July 2000*.
666. Erbland to Whipple, *Letters, Fam. Gp. Sheets*; and Knowles to Whipple, *Letters 19 & 30 July 2000*.
667. through 674. Knowles to Whipple, *Letters 19 & 30 July 2000*.
675. Erbland to Whipple, *Letters, Fam. Gp. Sheets*; and Knowles to Whipple, *Letters 19 & 30 July 2000*.
676. Erbland to Whipple, *Letters, Fam. Gp. Sheets*.
677. Ibid.; and Knowles to Whipple, *Letters 19 & 30 July 2000*.
678. Erbland to Whipple, *Letters, Fam. Gp. Sheets*; and Knowles to Whipple, *Letters 19 & 30 July 2000*.
679. Erbland to Whipple, *Letters, Fam. Gp. Sheets*.
680. Ibid.; and Knowles to Whipple, *Letters 19 & 30 July 2000*.
681. Erbland to Whipple, *Letters, Fam. Gp. Sheets*; and Knowles to Whipple, *Letters 19 & 30 July 2000*.
682. Erbland to Whipple, *Letters, Fam. Gp. Sheets*.
683. G. Whipple to B. Whipple, *Letter, 23 May 1991*.
684. and 685. H.Whipple to B. Whipple, *Letter, 04/20/1993*.
686. G. Whipple to B. Whipple, *Letter, 23 May 1991*.
687. H.Whipple to B. Whipple, *Letter, 04/20/1993*.
688. G. Whipple to B. Whipple, *Letter, 23 May 1991*.
689. H.Whipple to B. Whipple, *Letter, 04/20/1993*.
690. and 691. G. Whipple to B. Whipple, *Letter, 23 May 1991*.
692. and 693. Daley to Whipple, *8 letters*.
694. and 695. G. Whipple to B. Whipple, *Letter, 23 May 1991*.
696. and 697. Brandt to Whipple, *3 letters*.
698. Bills to Whipple, *Letter, Nov. 1995*.
699. Maris to Whipple, *Letter, 11 April 1996*; and Knowles to Whipple, *Letters 19 & 30 July 2000*.
700. through 702. Knowles to Whipple, *Letters 19 & 30 July 2000*.
703. Maris to Whipple, *Letter, 11 April 1996*; and Knowles to Whipple, *Letters 19 & 30 July 2000*.
704. through 718. Knowles to Whipple, *Letters 19 & 30 July 2000*.
719. Henry Whipple, 2:76-7; and Krueger to Whipple, *Letter, 7 Aug. 2000*.
720. Henry Whipple, 2:76; and Krueger to Whipple, *Letter, 7 Aug. 2000*.
721. through 725. Erbland to Whipple, *Letters, Fam. Gp. Sheets*.
726. through 729. Herrick-Whipple, *Family Group Sheets*.
730. through 732. J. Davis to Whipple, *Letter, 10 Feb. 1999*.
733. through 759. Reinhold to Whipple, *2 Letters*.
760. through 762. M.M. Whipple to Whipple, *6 Letters*.
763. through 764. Gallop to Whipple, *Letter 1 April 1996*.
765. and 768. M.M. Whipple to Whipple, *6 Letters*.
769. Padgett to Whipple, *Letter, 3 Dec. 1998 & 27 July 2000*; and Richard J. Bing, MD. to Blaine Whipple. Letter dated 20 Sept. 2002 at 99 N. El Molino Ave., Pasadena, Calif. 91101. In possession of Whipple (2004). (Hereafter J. Bing to Whipple, *Ltr,, 20 Sept. 2002*).
770. Padgett to Whipple, *Letter, 3 Dec. 1998 & 27 July 2000*.
771. Clark to Whipple, *Letter, 4 Jan. 1999*.
772. John W. Bing to Blaine Whipple. Letter dated 2 Nov. 2002 at 13 Perry Dr., Ewing, N. J. 08628. In possession of Whipple (2004). (Hereafter Bing to Whipple, *Letter 2 Nov. 02*).
773. Jordan to Whipple, *3 Letters*; and Padgett to Whipple, *Letter, 3 Dec. 1998 & 27 July 2000*.
774. Richard A. Hess to Blaine Whipple. E-mail Letters dated 20 and 22 March and 8 April 2002 at 8 M. St., Nantucket, Mass. 02554; e-mail NantucketCane@aol.com. In

775. possession of Whipple (2004). (Hereafter Hess to Whipple, *Letters, Mar. & Apr. 2002*).
and 776. Jordan to Whipple, *3 Letters*; and Padgett to Whipple, *Letter, 3 Dec. 1998 & 27 July 2000*.
777. through 781. Clark to Whipple, *Letter, 4 Jan. 1999*.
782. Ibid.; and Allen Whipple Clark to Blaine Whipple. Letter Dated 29 Sept. 2002 at 2525 Gregory St., Madison, Wisc. 53711. In possession of Whipple (2004). (Hereafter A. Clark to Whipple, *Letter, 29 Sept. 2002*).
783. and 784. Clark to Whipple, *Letter, 4 Jan. 1999*; and A. Clark to Whipple, *Letter, 29 Sept. 2002*.
785. and 786. A. Clark to Whipple, *Letter, 29 Sept. 2002*.
787. and 788. B. G. Holland, *9 letters*.
789. Holland to Whipple, *Letters*.
790. through 802. B. G. Holland, *9 letters*.
803. and 804. Powers to Whipple, *Letter 20 March 1996*.
805. J.F. Whipple to B. Whipple, *6 Letters*.
806. Henry Whipple, I:75.
807. through 810. J.F. Whipple to B. Whipple, *6 Letters*.
811. Henry Whipple, I:75; and J.F. Whipple to B. Whipple, *6 Letters*.
812. through 816. J.F. Whipple to B. Whipple, *6 Letters*.
817. Elizabeth (Whipple) Solano to Blaine Whipple. Letter dated 7 Oct. 1991 at PO Box 241, Avondale, Colo. 81022-0241. In possession of Whipple (2004). Provided Family Group Sheet and Pedigree Charts. (Hereafter Solano to Whipple, *Letter, 7 Oct. 1991*); and J. F. Whipple to B. Whipple, *6 Letters*.
818. and 819. Solano to Whipple, *Letter, 7 Oct. 1991*.
820. J.F. Whipple to B. Whipple, *6 Letters*.
821. Henry Whipple, I:75.
822. through 824. J.F. Whipple to B. Whipple, *6 Letters*.
825. through 828. Henry Whipple, I:97.
829. through 833. Kurapka to Whipple, *2 Letters*.
834. through 836. Henry Whipple, I:100.
837. through 841. Blackburn-Whipple, *Family Group Sheet*.
842. through 857. Henry Whipple, 2:90-91.
858. through 861. Sadler to Whipple, *Family Group Sheets*.
862. through 864. Brigham-Whipple, *Family Group Sheets*.
865. Ibid.; and Smith-Ward-Whipple, *Family Group Sheet*.
866. Author unable to find a town with this name, hence no county is named.
867. through 878. Smith-Ward-Whipple, *Family Group Sheet*.
879. Brigham-Whipple, *Family Group Sheets*.
880. Obitury of Mary Elizabeth (Smith) Redington, Miami, Okla. 3 June 1969, p. 3, col, 7 and 4 June page 3, col. 1. Name of newspaper not provided.
881. through 885. Smith-Ward-Whipple, *Family Group Sheet*.
886. through 895. Brigham-Whipple, *Family Group Sheets*.
896. Ibid.; Teague, *Family Record*; and 1920 U.S. Census, Population Schedule, San Mateo Co, Calif, Pescadero Precinct.
897. and 898. Brigham-Whipple, *Family Group Sheets*.
899. Calif, San Mateo Co., 1920, *U.S. Census*, SD, 7, ED, 82, Sh 2A, dw 23, fam. 23 (5 Jan.); and Teague, *Family Record*.
900. through 902. Brigham-Whipple, *Family Group Sheets*.
903. 1900 U.S. Census, Population Schedule, San Mateo County, Calif., Pescadero Twp. 5, SD 2, ED 43, (9 June).

904. Vital Records, *San Mateo Co, Calif.*, Death Certificate..
905. Ibid., Marriage Certificate..
906. Brigham-Whipple, *Family Group Sheets*.
907. and 908. Bowman-Miner, *Family Group Sheet*.
909. Author unable to find a town with this name, hence no county is named.
910. and 911. Randazzo to Whipple, *E-mail, 25 Oct. 01*.
912. through 915. R. Whipple to B. Whipple, *9 Letters*.
916. through 927. Tom Whipple, *Family Group Sheets*.
928. Green to Whipple, *5 letters*.
929. Author unable to find a town with this name, hence no county is named.
930. through 932. Green to Whipple, *5 letters*.
933. The Phillippines has had a long history of Moro insurgent movements dating to Spanish Rule. Resistance to colonization was especially strong among the Muslim population of Southwestern Mindanao and the Sulu Archipelago. With pride in the cultural heritage and a strong desire for independence, Moros fought Christian and foreign domination. Spanish control over the Moros was never complete, and the Muslim struggle carried over into the U. S. colonial era. The Moros earned a reputation as fierce fighters in combat against U. S. troops.
934. Walter J. Whipple to Blaine Whipple. Letters dated 7 February 1989, 10 July 1989, 18 May 1998 at P. O. Box 2644, Murphys, Calif. 95247. In possession of Whipple (2004). (Hereafter W. J. Whipple to B. Whipple, *3 letters*).
935. Green to Whipple, *5 letters*.
936. and 937. W.J Whipple to B. Whipple, *3 letters*.
938. through 944. Dudley Wentworth Stoddard to Blaine Whipple. Letters dated 20 April 1989, 18 March 1992, and 27 March 1992 at 340 E. 72nd St., New York, N. Y. 10021. In possession of Whipple (2004). (Hereafter Stoddard to Whipple, *3 letters*).
945. through 955. G.A. Whipple to Whipple, *Letter, December 1998*.
956. through 958. Zastrow-Whipple, *Family Group Sheet*.
959. through 967. H. Whipple to B. Whipple, *Letter, 04/20/1993*.
968. and 969. G. Whipple to Whipple, *2 Letters*.
970. Spitzer to Whipple, *Letter, 7 June 1998*; and HH Hildebrant to Whipple, *Letters, 2/1999; 7/2001*.
971. Hildebrant to Whipple, *Letters, 2/1999; 7/2001*.
972. Spitzer to Whipple, *Letter, 7 June 1998*; and HH Hildebrant to Whipple, *Letters, 2/1999; 7/2001*.
973. Hildebrant to Whipple, *Letters, 2/1999; 7/2001*.
974. Hildebrant to Whipple, *6 letters*.
975. Hal Hildebrant to Blaine Whipple. Letter dated 22 May 1998 at 905 Catalpa Way, Petaluma Calif. 94954. In Possession of Whipple (2004). (Hereafter H. Hildebrant to B. Whipple, *Letter, 22 May 1998*).
976. Hildebrant to Whipple, *6 letters*.
977. and 978. Whytlaw to Whipple, *3 Letters*.
979. through 981. The *Oregon* was built in 1881 in Scotland for speed and luxury and set several records in the Atlantic crossing – a big deal in those days. The builders saved money by building the hull of iron instead the much stronger steel which was the material of choice for vessels of this type. As a result the huge *Oregon* was so badly damaged when struck by a much smaller wooden schooner she sank in 130 feet of water before she could be towed into port. For a picture of the ship go to web page http://www.njscuba.net/sites/wreck_oregon.html.
982. through 987. *Register*, 113:296.

988. Ezra Stearns, *NH Genealogy*, 3:1162.
989. and 990. Henry Whipple, 2:109.
991. Ezra Stearns, *NH Genealogy*, 3:1162; and Henry Whipple, 2:109.
992. through 1011. Henry Whipple, 2:109, 110 and 111.
1012. Ezra Stearns, *NH Genealogy*, 3:1161.
1013. Henry Whipple, 2:114.
1014. through 1019. Ibid., 2:113.
1020. and 1021. Lothrop Withington-Katharyn Carlton Whipple Family Group Sheet, Supplied in 1990 by Nathan N. Withington, Sandwich Rd., Plymouth, Mass. 02360. This sheet contains his personal knowledge about his parents, siblings, and children. (Hereafter Withington-Whipple, *Family Group Sheet*).
1022. *Register*, 75:142.
1023. through 1026. Withington-Whipple, *Family Group Sheet*.
1027. Paul J. Whipple to Blaine Whipple. Letters dated 12 April and 25 April 1990 at Doten Rd., Plymouth, Mass. In possession of Whipple (2004). (Hereafter P. Whipple to B. Whipple, *2 Letters*).
1028. *Patriot Ledger*, Quincy, Mass., June 17, 1967.
1029. Henry Whipple, 2:119; and Miller - Whitley, *Family Group Sheets*.
1030. Vital Records, *Croydon, NH*, 263.
1031. Miller-Whitley, *Family Group Sheets*.
1032. and 1033. Henry Whipple, 2:120; and Miller-Whitley, *Family Group Sheets*.
1034. Miller-Whitley, *Family Group Sheets*.
1035. through 1038. Henry Whipple, 2:120; and Miller-Whitley, *Family Group Sheets*.
1039. Henry Whipple, 2:121; and Miller-Whitley, *Family Group Sheets*.
1040. Henry Whipple, 2:121.
1041. through 1055. Miller-Whitley, *Family Group Sheets*.
1056. through 1059. Klassy to Whipple, *5 Letters*.
1060. Shirley (Whipple) Liles to Blaine Whipple. Letters dated 11 Aug. and 23 Sept. 1993 at 4726 Windsong Park Dr., Collierville, Tenn. 38017-9330. In possession of Whipple (2004). (Hereafter Liles to Whipple, *2 Letters*).
1061. through 1070. Wilkin to Whipple, *3 Letters*.
1071. through 1074. Whipple to Whipple, *E-mail*.
1075. B. Williamson to B. Whipple, *3 Letters*.
1076. Author unable to find a town with this name, hence no county is named.
1077. through 1098. B. Williamson to B. Whipple, *3 Letters*.
1099. through 1104. J. Whipple to B. Whipple, *5 Letters*.
1105. Galen Whipple to Whipple, *Letter, 11 June 1998*; and Arnold to Whipple, *Letter 9 July 1998*.
1106. Galen Whipple to Whipple, *Letter, 11 June 1998*.
1107. Ibid.; and Arnold to Whipple, *Letter 9 July 1998*.
1108. and 1109. Arnold to Whipple, *Letter 9 July 1998*.
1110. through 1142. Vella to Whipple, *Ltrs, 8-22 & 9-1 2000*.
1143. through 1152. Haven-Jordan, *Family Group Sheets*.
1153. Author unable to find a town with this name, hence no county is named.
1154. through 1159. Haven-Jordan, *Family Group Sheets*.
1160. through 1162. Kahler to Whipple, *Letter, 18 Sept. 1991*.
1163. and 1164. Whitney-Hall, *Family Group Sheets*.
1165. through 1169. Ristau to Whipple, *2 Letters*.
1170. and 1171. Emery to Whipple, *2 Letters*.
1172. through 1186. Singer to Whipple, *2 letters*.
1187. through 1208. Deal-Putnam, *Family Group Sheet*.

TWELFTH GENERATION

5757. **Anne Montgomery**[12] **Getchell** (Arthur Vinton[11], Alice Leiby[10] **Coombs**, Joseph Jackson[9], Andrew[8], Ebenezer[7], Elisabeth[6] **Pratt**, Hannah[5] **Kennedy**, Elizabeth[4] **Annable**, Anne[3] **Whipple**, Matthew[2], Matthew[1])[1] was born in Boston, Mass. 14 September 1918 and married **Robert Emory Chaffee** in Boston 25 December 1941. Robert,[2] son of Emory Leon **Chaffee** and Marie Josephine **Kreutz**, was born in Belmont, Middlesex Co., Mass. 9 January 1918 and died 25 October 1974 in Wellesley Hills, Mass., at 56 years of age. Robert lived in Vienna in early childhood where he was placed in analysis with Anna Freud and was a student in the school run by her and Dorothy Tiffany Burlingham. He was graduated from Northeastern University and served in WWII as a commander in the U.S. Navy. He was a Deacon of the First Congregational Church of Wellesley Hills, a Past Master of Maugus Lodge of Masons, a member of the Institute of Electrical and Electronic Engineers, and a Director of the Parker Hill Medical Center. He was President of A.C. Getchell & Son Law Printers at the time of death.

Anne was graduated from Tufts Universary in 1940 (B.A. in history) and studied at Andover Newton Theological Seminary. She worked for the Canadian government during WWII in the Department of Munitions and Supplies. She later served on staff at Babson College, Rohm and Hass Chemical Co., and Temple Beth Elohim, all in Wellesley Hills. She was an incorporator of the Boston Mission Society (the social service branch of the United Church of Christ) and served on its Board as well as the Board of the New England School of Law. She was also a Deacon and member of the Church Council at the Wellesley Hills Congregational Church.

Anne Montgomery **Getchell** and Robert Emory **Chaffee** had the following children:

+ 6747 i. Elsa Getchell[13] **Chaffee** born 5 September 1943.

6748 ii. Donald Montgomery **Chaffee** born in Boston 3 August 1946 and married Margaret Elizabeth **Orvis** in East Greenwich, R.I. 15 August 1970. They were divorced in Northampton, Mass., 22 September 1971. Don earned a B.A. in Philosophy from Tufts University in 1968 and an M.A.T. from the U. of Mass. at Amherst in 1971. Following college he taught college-level history at the Norfolk and Walpole State Prisons and 4th and 5th grades in North Reading. After his father's death in 1974, he became President of the family publishing company until it was sold in 1976. Subsequently, he became a freelance writer, indexer, and computer consultant. He writes computer software manuals and his indexing assignments have included Jane Goodall's *The Chimpanzees of Gombe* and books published by Harvard University; Little, Brown & Co.; Houghton, Mifflin; Univ. Press of New England; Northeastern Press Univ. Press; Iowa State Univ. Press, and others. He is a Deacon at the Wellesley Hills Congregational Church, served on the Wellesley Hills Youth Commission and Wetlands Protection Committee, and as President of the Wellesley Hills Historical Society.

5759. **Addie Ruth**[12] **Owen** (Martha Anne[11] **Young**, Ruth Ann[10] **Cross**, William[9], Jesse[8], Stephen[7], Sarah[6] **Boardman**, Thomas[5], Elizabeth[4] **Perkins**, Elizabeth[3] **Whipple**, Matthew[2], Matthew[1])[3] was born in Clarksville, N.H. 17 October 1895 and died 24 October 1946 in Canaan, N.H., at 51 years of age. She married **Ray William French** in Canaan 14 January 1915. Ray,[4] son of Leroy Freeman **French** and Mattie Ruth **Fuller**, was born in Canaan 9 May 1892 and died 10 April 1964 in Stewartstown, N.H., at 71 years of age.

Addie Ruth **Owen** and Ray William **French** had the following child:
+   6749   i.   Owen Leroy[13] **French** born 27 November 1916.

5761. **Henry Richard**[12] **Ahrens Jr.** (Eunice[11] **Schenck**, Eunice Porter[10] **Wood**, Phebe Smith[9] **Whipple**, Stephen[8], Jonathan[7], Capt. Stephen[6], John[5], Matthew[4], Lt. John[3], Matthew[2], Matthew[1])[5] was born in New York, N.Y. 11 June 1907 and died 18 June 1967 in Appleton, Wisc., at 60 years of age. He married **Virginia Payne**. Virginia,[6] daughter of George Henry **Payne** and Mary Louise **Bruce**, was born 6 November 1909.

Henry Richard **Ahrens** Jr. and Virginia **Payne** had the following child:
     6750   i.   Richard William[13] **Ahrens** 7 born in New York, N.Y. 7 April 1932. He descends from both Matthew and John Whipple of Ipswich and is their ninth great grandson.

5762. **Proctor Patterson**[12] **Jones** (Ferne Catherine[11] **Patterson**, Proctor[10], Phebe Smith[9] **Whipple**, Stephen[8], Jonathan[7], Capt. Stephen[6], John[5], Matthew[4], Lt. John[3], Matthew[2], Matthew[1])[8] was born in Lakewood, Ohio 25 May 1916 and died 2 April 1999 in San Francisco, Calif., at 82 years of age.[9]

He married twice. (1) **Betty Weber** in Lakeland 15 August 1942. She was born in Cleveland, Cuyahoga Co., Ohio in 1915.[10] They were divorced in 1947. (2) **Martha Eloise Martin** in Zanesville, Ohio, 29 November 1947. She was born in Zanesville 6 July 1921.

Proctor studied drama and produced summer stock for a year before earning an undergraduate degree from Case Western Reserve in Cleveland, Ohio in 1937. He studied law at Harvard and Stanford and received his law degree from Case Western in 1948 and was admitted to the Ohio Bar. He moved to northern California after law school and was Secretary to Otto Preminger a major Hollywood director (*Exodus, Advise and Consent, The Cardinal,*etc.). He served in the U.S. Army during WWII in the European and Mediterranean theatres as a Special Services Officer with the rank of Captain. He learned to speak French in Algeria while serving with Air Force Intelligence. After the war he became active with the Young Republicans and unsuccessfully ran for Sheriff of San Mateo County, Calif., and served on numerous governmental boards in San Mateo, San Francisco, and Marin counties.

He began his professional career writing legal texts for publisher Bancroft-Whitney, worked as a professional photographer and author and founded the Proctor Jones Publishing Co. of San Francisco, publisher of fine arts books and mystery novels. He was honorary Counsul General of Tunisia from the 1970s until his death. He is author of *Idylls of France*, a book about the French countryside; *Classic Russian Idylls*, a book about the scenery of Russia; *At the Dawn of Glasnot: Soviet Portraits*, with an introduction by Armand Hammer; *Ransom of the Golden Bridge*; and *Napoleon: An Intimate Account of the Years of Supremacy 1800-1814*, with an introduction by Jean Tulard of Paris (1992). He was a member of the National Society of the Sons of the American Revolution.

Proctor Patterson **Jones** and Betty **Weber** had the following children:
- \+ 6751 i. Melinda[13] **Jones** born 25 May 1943.
- \+ 6752 ii. Greta Patterson **Jones** born 27 January 1946.

Proctor Patterson **Jones** and Martha Eloise **Martin** had the following children:
- \+ 6753 iii. John Beverly **Jones** born 29 January 1949.
- \+ 6754 iv. Martha **Jones** born 6 July 1950.
- 6755 v. Proctor Patterson **Jones** Jr. 11 born in Palo Alto, Santa Clara Co., Calif. 17 July 1952.
- 6756 vi. Jessica Haig **Jones**[12] was born in Palo Alto 11 September 1955.

5764. **Winthrop**[12] **Whipple** (Walter[11], Stephen Lovett[10], Stephen[9], Jonathan[8], Jonathan[7], Capt. Stephen[6], John[5], Matthew[4], Lt. John[3], Matthew[2], Matthew[1])[13] was born in 1904 and married **Simone LeMieux**.

{ G 999 }

Winthrop **Whipple** and Simone **LeMieux** had the following children:
    6757   i.   Donald[13] **Whipple**.[14]
    6758   ii.   Buzzy **Whipple**.[15]

5765. **Kenneth**[12] **Whipple** (Walter[11], Stephen Lovett[10], Stephen[9], Jonathan[8], Jonathan[7], Capt. Stephen[6], John[5], Matthew[4], Lt. John[3], Matthew[2], Matthew[1])[16] was born in Salem, Essex Co., Mass. 31 May 1906 and died 28 April 1989 in Lowell, Mass., at 82 years of age. He married **Margaret Ames** in Nashua, N.H. 27 March 1931. She was born in Brunswick, Maine 27 March 1906 and died 10 July 1987 in Marco Island, Fla., at 81 years of age.[17]

Kenneth **Whipple** and Margaret **Ames** had the following children:
    6759   i.   Kenneth[13] **Whipple** 18 born 27 September 1934.
    6760   ii.   Walter **Whipple** 19 born 1 September 1935.
+   6761   iii.   John Alan **Whipple** born 9 June 1940.

5766. **Martha**[12] **Whipple** (Walter[11], Stephen Lovett[10], Stephen[9], Jonathan[8], Jonathan[7], Capt. Stephen[6], John[5], Matthew[4], Lt. John[3], Matthew[2], Matthew[1])[20] was born in Nashua, N.H. 22 March 1915 and died there in 1995, at 80 years of age. She married **Albert Allen Davis** in Nashua 29 September 1934. Albert,[21] son of Fred **Davis** and Margaret **Coffey**, was born in Worcester, Worcester Co., Mass. 25 September 1911 and died 9 February 1973 in Nashua at 61 years of age. Martha jointly descends from brothers Matthew and John who settled in Ipswich, Mass. in 1638. She owns the original will of her 6th great grandfather, Matthew Whipple, (1664-1736) dated 26 July 1733 in Ipswich.

Martha **Whipple** and Albert Allen **Davis** had the following children:
+   6762   i.   Sally Ann[13] **Davis** born 14 February 1936.
    6763   ii.   Nancy Whipple **Davis**[22] born 12 May 1938 and married William W. Knight 16 February 1973.
+   6764   iii.   Susan Allen **Davis** born 3 November 1945.

5767. **Virginia Augusta**[12] **Taylor** (Augusta[11] **Whipple**, Stephen Lovett[10], Stephen[9], Jonathan[8], Jonathan[7], Capt. Stephen[6], John[5], Matthew[4], Lt. John[3], Matthew[2], Matthew[1])[23] was born in Salem, Essex Co., Mass. 6 August 1913 and died 21 July 1991 in Milwaukee, Wisc., at 77 years of age. She married **John Edward Pearson** in Lyme, Conn. 19 June 1937. He was born in Sodertilji, Sweden 1 December 1911.[24]

Virginia Augusta **Taylor** and John Edward **Pearson** had the following children:
+ 6765 i. Taylor Peter[13] **Pearson** born 27 February 1939.
+ 6766 ii. Stuart Robin **Pearson** born 13 July 1942.
+ 6767 iii. Kristen Augusta **Pearson** born 1 January 1946.

5768. **Carol Ashby**[12] **Taylor** (Augusta[11] **Whipple**, Stephen Lovett[10], Stephen[9], Jonathan[8], Jonathan[7], Capt. Stephen[6], John[5], Matthew[4], Lt. John[3], Matthew[2], Matthew[1])[25] was born in Brooklyn, N.Y. 14 January 1921 and married **Clinton Robert Carlisle** in Providence, R.I. 9 May 1943. Robert,[26] son of Frank Abbott **Carlisle** and Edith Pauline **MacGregor**, was born in Florida, Mass. 18 September 1920. Carol was a professional educator and was a member of state and national professional associations. She retired in June 1988 and began work as a Library Media Consultant. She descends from both Matthew and John Whipple of Ipswich.

Carol Ashby **Taylor** and Clinton Robert **Carlisle** had the following children:
6768 i. Susan Ashby[13] **Carlisle**[27] born in Providence 19 April 1947 and married Matthew **McCauley** in West Haven, Conn. 14 February 1986. Matthew,[28] son of Leon **McCauley** and Elfrieda (__), was born in Greenwich, Conn. 14 May 1956.
+ 6769 ii. Craig Robert **Carlisle** born 19 October 1949.
6770 iii. Scott Taylor **Carlisle**[29] born in Bangor, Maine 9 June 1952 and died 9 September 1978 in Worcester, Worcester Co., Mass. at 26 years of age. He married Priscilla **Bergman** in Simsbury, Conn., 29 January 1977. She is the daughter of Charles **Bergman** and Ilva (__).

5772. **Charles Lewis**[12] **Whipple II** (Charles Augustus[11], Charles Lewis[10], Stephen[9], Jonathan[8], Jonathan[7], Capt. Stephen[6], John[5], Matthew[4], Lt. John[3], Matthew[2], Matthew[1])[30] was born in Massachusetts 8 May 1914 and died 12 May 1991 in Northampton, Mass., at 77 years of age.[31] He married **Caroline Dalton** 16 March 1945. Caroline, daughter of Thomas **Dalton** and Elizabeth **Landon**, died 3 December 1967. Charles retired from the *Boston Globe* in 1979 after 43 years with the newspaper. He was its first Ombudsman. As editor of its editorial page, he advocated a halt to the U.S. bombing of North Vietnam and called for a negotiated end of the war in a series of six editorials during the spring of 1967. His editorial of 22 October 1973 urging Pres. Nixon to resign was the first published by a major American newspaper. He obtained an interview with Boston Red Sox baseball star Ted Williams in the late 1940s by telling the slugger he would give his right eye for an interview and then plucked out a glass eye he wore because of an injury. Following retirement he was invited by the Chinese government to edit the *China Daily*, an English language newspaper in Beijing (1979-82.) He also worked for Xinhua, the official Chinese News Agency.[32]

Charles Lewis **Whipple** II and Caroline **Dalton** had the following children:
+ 6771   i.   Charles Augustus[13] **Whipple** II born 2 September 1946.
+ 6772   ii. Jonathan Landon **Whipple** born 6 March 1949.

5777. **Jeanette R.**[12] **Whipple** (John Whitmore[11], Sidney[10], John Hitchings[9], John[8], Jonathan[7], Capt. Stephen[6], John[5], Matthew[4], Lt. John[3], Matthew[2], Matthew[1])[33] was born in Derry, N.H. 24 December 1907 and married **Edward Abbot Brown** in Raymond, N.H. 13 August 1927. Edward,[34] son of William **Brown** and Lavina **Woodward**, was born 10 April 1903 and died 22 December 1979 in Fitchburg, Worcerster Co., Mass., at 76 years of age. Buried in Forest Hill Cemetery.

Jeanette R. **Whipple** and Edward Abbot **Brown** had the following children:
6773   i.   Robert Edward[13] **Brown**[35] born in Derry 22 March 1928 and married Elenor **Zichelle**.
6774   ii. Jean Evelyn **Brown**[36] born 23 May 1930 and married Thomas **Glatiotis**.
6775   iii. Carleen Ruth **Brown**[37] born in Fitchburg 7 August 1933 and married Richard **Knoll**. He may have been Carleen's second husband.
+ 6776   iv. Marion H. **Brown** born 23 November 1934.

5778. **Ralph Kenneth**[12] **Dose** (Joanna Evans[11] **Keyes**, Charles Evans[10], George Everett[9], Mary Alden[8] **Gould**, Benjamin[7], Martha[6] **Gilbert**, Esther[5] **Perkins**, Serg. John[4], Elizabeth[3] **Whipple**, Matthew[2], Matthew[1])[38] was born in Kiefer, Okla. 14 July 1925 and died 7 September 1963 in Tulsa, Tulsa Co., Okla., at 38 years of age. He married **Helen Lucille Radman** in Tulsa 5 March 1948. Helen,[39] daughter of William Thompson **Redman** and Eva Josephine **Lafferty**, was born in Claremore, Okla. 12 July 1925. She also married **Hewitt Addington**. Ralph contracted polio at age 5 and the disease prevented his enlistment in the armed forces during WWII. The polio caused paralysis in his left leg and foot and he was operated on at age nine to enable him to walk without a brace. He studied architecture at Oklahoma Agricultural and Mechanical College at Stillwater. He was talented both musically and artistically. Kenneth worked for the Sinclair Oil Co. later as a Draftsman for Skelly Oil Co. for several years at the time of his death.

Ralph Kenneth **Dose** and Helen Lucille **Radman** had the following children:
+   6777   i.   Ralph Kenneth[13] **Dose** Jr. born 8 January 1948.
        6778   ii.   Dana Lynn **Dose**[40] born in Oklahoma City, Okla. 8 July 1950. He earned a B.S. degree from Oklahoma State University in 1974 and was Records Specialists with American Medical Systems at Minneapolis (2000). He officially changed his name to Travis Ryland **Derek**.

5779. **Dorothy Irene**[12] **Dose** (Joanna Evans[11] **Keyes**, Charles Evans[10], George Everett[9], Mary Alden[8] **Gould**, Benjamin[7], Martha[6] **Gilbert**, Esther[5] **Perkins**, Serg. John[4], Elizabeth[3] **Whipple**, Matthew[2], Matthew[1])[41] was born in Ponca City, Okla. 8 May 1928 and married **Edgar Walter Pralle** in Ponca City 10 July 1954. Edgar,[42] son of Walter Ernest **Pralle** and Valerie Louise Wilhelmine **Pennekamp**, was born in Enid, Garfield Co., Okla. 4 June 1925. He was graduated from high school in 1943 and then spent three years in the U.S. Navy as an Aviation Radioman and Aerial Gunner with a PBY squadron in North Africa and England. His crew was credited with sinking the last submarine in WWII off the coast of Brest, France. On its return flight to England, the plane was shot down near the Channel Islands. The crew received the Distinguished Flying Cross and Air Medal for sinking the U-Boat. He entered college after completing military service and earned a B.S. degree in Accounting and Finance from the U. of Oklahoma in 1950. Upon graduation he was employed by the Bank of Garber, Oklahoma a bank founded by his father in 1943. He moved up to Cashier and Vice President before succeeding his father as President in 1985

Dorothy was awarded a music scholarship at Oklahoma Agricultural and Mechanical College where she was graduated in 1950 with a Bachelor of Music Education degree and was an officer in Sigma Alpha Iota, the Honorary Music Society. She began her teaching career at Garber and later attended Oklahoma State University and the U. of Oklahoma and earned certification as elementary school principal and public school administrator. She was chosen as Oklahoma's Outstanding Elementary Principal in 1978. She spent 31 years in education, serves on the Board of Assistance of the Descendants of the Mayflower of Oklahoma, is Past President and Vice President of the Garber Athenian Club and a member of several professional organizations.

Dorothy Irene **Dose** and Edgar Walter **Pralle** had the following children:
        6779   i.   Steven Walter[13] **Pralle**[43] born in Enid 6 March 1958. He was a 4.0 student and High School Valedictorian at Garber High where he was active in music organizations. He earned awards for both piano and

trobone and played First Trombone in the All-State Band. He was graduated from Trinity University, San Antonio, Tex. in 1980 earning a B.S. with Honors as an accounting major. He attended law school at Southern Methodist University at Dallas while working for the Federal Reserve Bank. He joined Waste Management Co. in Oklahoma City as a Controller in 1986. After they transferred him to Tallahasse, he attended Florida State University working toward an MBA degree. He was transferred to Waste Management International assigned to Copenhagen Denmark in 1991 and became Special Projects Controller for the northern section of Europe.

6780 ii. Susan Carol **Pralle**[44] was born in Enid 19 December 1960 and married James Landon **Watson** in Dallas, Tex. 14 April 1994. James,[45] son of Donald Clark Watson and Marjorie Ellen Woods, was born in Dearborn, Mich. 30 July 1961. He was graduated from SMU magna cum laude in 1983 with a degree in Mechanical Engineering and is a Senior Engineer for Exxon Oil Co. in Baton Rouge, La. After graduating as valedictorian (4.0) from Garber High, Susan accepted a full scholarship to SMU in Dallas where she was graduated in 1983 with Bachelor of Business Administration degree in Real Estate Finance. While a student, she performed with the SMU Symphony and the Dallas Civic Symphony. She entered the world of work at Oklahoma City as Assistant Vice President of the Oklahoma Mortgage Co. After her marriage, she and her husband moved to Baton Rouge where she became a Mortgage Banker.

5780. **Dorothy Gene**[12] **Keyes** (George Everett[11], Charles Evans[10], George Everett[9], Mary Alden[8] **Gould**, Benjamin[7], Martha[6] **Gilbert**, Esther[5] **Perkins**, Serg. John[4], Elizabeth[3] **Whipple**, Matthew[2], Matthew[1])[46] was born in Sapulpa, Okla. 18 September 1920 and married twice. (1) **William Luther Murphy Jr.** in Topeka, Shawnee Co., Kans. 29 July 1939. William,[47] son of William Luther **Murphy** Sr. and Eliza **Jarvis**, was born in Topeka 11 January 1919 and died there 16 September 1956, at 37 years of age. (2) **Anthony Stanley Suidikas** in Wilson, Niagara Co., N.Y. 11 August 1942. Anthony,[48] son of Kazimir **Suidikas** and Rose Mary **Petruskas**, was born in Waukegan Lake, Ill. 2 May 1920. Both his parents were born in Lithuania.

Anthony was a paratrooper with the 82nd Airborn Division in WWII and with the 2nd Infantry Division in the Korean War. He was awarded 10 medals including two Purple Hearts and two Bronze Stars. He also served with NATO in Copenhagen, Denmark and with the Hawk Missile Forces in Germany. After retiring from the military, Anthony spent a year with the National Weather Service in the Artic, flying to the North Pole twice. He later had assignments at Winnemuka, Nev., Salt Lake City, and Lubbock, Tex. retiring in 1993 after 28 years of government service. He and Dorothy live in Lubbock. He dropped the first "i" in his surname.

Dorothy Gene **Keyes** and William Luther **Murphy** Jr. had the following child:
- +   6781   i.   Karen Sue[13] **Murphy** born 14 November 1940.

Dorothy Gene **Keyes** and Anthony Stanley **Suidikas** had the following children:
- +   6782   ii.   Gary Lee **Suidikas** born 3 October 1946.
- +   6783   iii.   Wayne Anthony **Suidikas** born 3 January 1948.
- +   6784   iv.   Georgia Kay **Suidikas** born 14 August 1949.
-      6785   v.   Dale Edward **Suidikas**[49] born in Fort Carson, Colo. 11 October 1950 and married Rita Lynn **Butler** in Lubbock 1 September 1994. She was born in Post, Garza Co., Tex. 27 June 1953.[50] Dale was in the U.S. Army and spent 24 months in Vietnam.
- +   6786   vi.   Gene Stanley **Suidikas** born 28 March 1952.
- +   6787   vii.   Cynthia Marie **Suidikas** born 29 November 1957.
-      6788   viii.   Glenn Alan **Suidikas**[51] born in Wildflecken, Germany 11 September 1962 and served 15 years in the U.S. Army. He was a helicopter and fixed wing mechanic on Kwajalein Island in the Pacific in 1998.

5782. Lawrence Gordon[12] **Bayles** (Eunice Britt[11] **Keyes**, Charles Evans[10], George Everett[9], Mary Alden[8] **Gould**, Benjamin[7], Martha[6] **Gilbert**, Esther[5] **Perkins**, Serg. John[4], Elizabeth[3] **Whipple**, Matthew[2], Matthew[1])[52] was born in Colby, Thomas Co., Kans. 31 August 1918 and died 10 November 1996 in Amarillo, Tex., at 78 years of age. He married **Martha Lue Neal** in Amarillo 24 March 1945. Martha,[53] daughter of Sidney Bruce **Neal** and Tyressa Frances **Webb**, was born in Alvord, Tex. 18 July 1925. Lawrence earned a degree in industrial engineering from Texas Technological College (now Texas Tech University) at Lubbock in 1944. After a period in the U.S. Navy he was employed at the Pantex Ordnance Plant in Amarillo.

Lawrence Gordon **Bayles** and Martha Lue **Neal** had the following children:
-      6789   i.   Ronald Melvin[13] **Bayles**[54] born in Amarillo 14 May 1947 and died 3 days later.
- +   6790   ii.   Kenneth Dale **Bayles** born 6 August 1948.
- +   6791   iii.   Shirley Ann **Bayles** born 13 July 1950.

{ G 1005 }

6792   iv.   Steven Jay **Bayles**[55] born in Amarillo 29 March 1960 and married twice. (1) Julie **Ashurst** in Amarillo 19 December 1981. She was born in Yuma, Ariz. 25 December 1964.[56] They were divorced in 1982. (2) Pamela Kaye **Prevost** in Alexandria, La. 25 July 1987. Pamela,[57] daughter of Dr. Hubert L. **Prevost** and Margaret (__), was born in Alexandria 30 December 1953. He married and divorced an unnamed woman between his marriages to Julie and Pamela. He earned a B.S. in Chemistry from West Texas State University, Canyon, Tex.

5783. **George Vincent**[12] **Bayles** (Eunice Britt[11] **Keyes**, Charles Evans[10], George Everett[9], Mary Alden[8] **Gould**, Benjamin[7], Martha[6] **Gilbert**, Esther[5] **Perkins**, Serg. John[4], Elizabeth[3] **Whipple**, Matthew[2], Matthew[1])[58] was born in Colby, Thomas Co., Kans. 7 March 1920 and died 15 June 1997 in Oklahoma City, Okla., at 77 years of age. He married **Glennis Virjeane Garrett** in Bethany, Okla. 30 May 1948. Virjeane,[59] daughter of Charles Walter **Garrett** and Zonabel **Neely**, was born in Anderson Chapel, Tex. 2 May 1930. George was an aerial gunner on B-25 medium bombers in the Army Air Corps during WWII. He served in the Pacific where one of his planes was shot down at Balikpapan in Borneo. After the war he became a Building Construction Manager and Estimator building many schools and commercial projects in Oklahoma City and surrounding area. Virjeane became a teacher of Speech and English at Bethany High.

George Vincent **Bayles** and Glennis Virjeane **Garrett** had the following children born in Oklahoma City:

6793   i.   Georgiana Dawn[13] **Bayles**[60] 21 March 1951 and died there in 1974, at 23 years of age. She married Randy **McDaniel** in Bethany 15 August 1970.
6794   ii.   Melanie Sue **Bayles**[61] 2 March 1953 and was graduated from Bethany Nazarene College (now Southern Nazarene University) in 1975 with a degree in Sociology. She became a Court Intake Counselor and lives in Bethany.
+   6795   iii.   Glennis Paige **Bayles** 9 August 1955.

5784. **John Junior**[12] **Bayles** (Eunice Britt[11] **Keyes**, Charles Evans[10], George Everett[9], Mary Alden[8] **Gould**, Benjamin[7], Martha[6] **Gilbert**, Esther[5] **Perkins**, Serg. John[4], Elizabeth[3] **Whipple**, Matthew[2], Matthew[1])[62] was born in Manhattan, Kans. 6 July 1922 and married **Penelope (Prescott) Adamson**, a widow, in Port Hueneme, Calif. 18 August

1946. Penelope,[63] daughter of Clarence Dean **Prescott** and Daphine Knopp **Parker**, was born in Greenville, N.H. 24 July 1922. She married (1) **Lt. John David Adamson**, a bomber pilot killed on a combat flight over Europe in the Spring of 1944. She was graduated from the U. of California at Santa Barbara in 1944 with a BA in Physical Education and became a Registered Physical Therapist in 1946. She worked with polio patients at Ventura Co. General Hospital until a vaccine was discovered and was then employed in an Orthopedic Outpatient Clinic.

John enlisted in the Navy as a Seaman in August 1942 and received a commission as Ensign, U.S. Naval Reserve in March 1944. He saw service in the Atlantic, Mediterranean, and Pacific. After the war he entered Texas Technological College at Lubbock and was graduated with Honors in June 1947 with a BS in Animal Science. He later attended graduate school at U.C. Davis and then went to work for the U.S. Navy at Port Hueneme as a Deep Ocean Diving and Salvage Developmental Engineer. He is a holder of seven patents and is author of numerous engineering technical documents and engineering trade journal articles. He retired from the U.S. Naval Reserve as a Lieutenant Commander and from the Naval Civil Engineering Laboratory, Port Hueneme, California. He was the first ordained Elder of the Congregation of the Orthodox Presbyterian denomination organized in Oxnard, California.

John Junior **Bayles** and Penelope (Prescott) **Adamson** had the following children:

+ 6796 i. Keri[13] **Bayles** born 14 October 1947.
+ 6797 ii. John Dean **Bayles** born 4 January 1949.
+ 6798 iii. Britt Clark **Bayles** born 9 January 1956.
+ 6799 iv. Meredith **Bayles** born 16 September 1961.

5785. **Ruth Alene**[12] **Bayles** (Eunice Britt[11] **Keyes**, Charles Evans[10], George Everett[9], Mary Alden[8] **Gould**, Benjamin[7], Martha[6] **Gilbert**, Esther[5] **Perkins**, Serg. John[4], Elizabeth[3] **Whipple**, Matthew[2], Matthew[1])[64] was born in Balmorhea, Tex. 27 November 1924 and married **Frank Boyd Burchard** there 11 September 1948. Frank,[65] son of Reeves Sinclair **Burchard** and Annie Belle **Hefner**, was born in Reeves Co., Tex. 13 October 1922. Frank claims descent from Pres. Zachary Taylor through his grandmother Ella Taylor. He was a pilot in WWII. Prior to retiring, he was simultaneously a cattle rancher, farmer, businessman, and an F.A.A. Air Traffic Controller. Ruth was a Registered Nurse and received her training at Lubbock Memorial Hospital.

Ruth Alene **Bayles** and Frank Boyd **Burchard** had the following children:
- \+ 6800 i. Janice Elizabeth[13] **Burchard** born 8 January 1950.
- \+ 6801 ii. Ray Alan **Burchard** born 22 December 1952.

5786. **Dilman Kar**[12] **Thomas** (Burt Byron[11], Ambrose[10], Dilla[9] **Beeman**, Daniel[8], Lydia[7] **Cogswell**, Samuel[6], Hannah[5] **Browne**, Judith[4] **Perkins**, Elizabeth[3] **Whipple**, Matthew[2], Matthew[1])[66] was born in Green Mt. Iowa 3 September 1888 and died 31 May 1941 in Clearwater, Fla., at 52 years of age. He married **Eva Bertha Bridge** 3 September 1908. Eva,[67] daughter of Charles Brant **Bridge** and Ella **Blanchard**, was born 9 December 1889 and died 21 August 1962 at 72 years of age.

Dilman Kar **Thomas** and Eva Bertha **Bridge** had the following children:
- 6802 i. Clifford Bridge[13] **Thomas**.[68]
- 6803 ii. Dilman Karr **Thomas**.[69]
- \+ 6804 iii. Ada Helen **Thomas** born 27 April 1917.

5787. **Eva Dillie**[12] **Thomas** (Burt Byron[11], Ambrose[10], Dilla[9] **Beeman**, Daniel[8], Lydia[7] **Cogswell**, Samuel[6], Hannah[5] **Browne**, Judith[4] **Perkins**, Elizabeth[3] **Whipple**, Matthew[2], Matthew[1])[70] was born in Canyon, Tex. 21 July 1909 and died 7 October 1991 in Greensboro, N. C., at 82 years of age. She married **Edward Ahmuty Driscoll** in New York, N.Y., 1 April 1930. He was born 14 October 1908 and died 18 June 1993 in Greensboro, N. C., at 84 years of age.

Eva Dillie **Thomas** and Edward Ahmuty **Driscoll** had the following children:
- \+ 6805 i. Vera Maky[13] **Driscoll**.
- 6806 ii. Carol Ela **Driscoll**.[71]
- 6807 iii. Judith Elaine **Driscoll**.[72]

5788. **Pres. John Calvin**[12] **Coolidge** (Col. John Calvin[11], Sarah Almeda[10] **Brewer**, Sally[9] **Brown**, Israel Putnam[8], Adam[7], Adam[6], Jacob[5], Judith[4] **Perkins**, Elizabeth[3] **Whipple**, Matthew[2], Matthew[1])[73] was born in Plymouth, Vt. 4 July 1872 and died 5 January 1933 in Northampton, Mass., at 60 years of age. He married **Grace Anna Goodhue** in Burlington, Chittenden Co., Vt. 4 October 1905. Grace,[74] daughter of Andrew Issachar **Goodhue** and Lemira **Barrett**, was born in Burlington 3 January 1879 and died 8 July 1957 in Northampton, at 78 years of age. President and Mrs. Coolidge were buried in Plymouth. Grace and Calvin were distant cousins. Their common ancestor was

John Calvin Coolidge, thirtieth President of The United States.

Matthew Whipple, Clothier, of Bocking, England. Grace descends through his youngest son, Elder John of Ipswich, Mass. while Calvin descends through his oldest son, Matthew, Jr. of Ipswich as well as through Elder John, making him a double descendant of Matthew Whipple, the Clothier.

He earned a B. A. from Amherst College in 1895, read law in the office of Messrs. Hammond & Field of Northampton, was admitted to the Bar 29 June 1897 and began practice in that city. He was elected to the Common Council and Vice President of the Northampton Savings Bank in 1898, served as City Solicitor 1899-1902, Chairman of the Republican County Committee of Hampshire County in 1904, defeated as candidate for Northampton Board of Education in 1905, elected to the State House of Representatives in 1906 (served two terms), served as Northampton Mayor 1910-11, elected to the State Senate in 1911 (served four terms and was Senate President 1914-15), elected Massachusetts Lieutenant Governor in 1915 (served three terms), elected Governor in 1919 (served two terms). His firmness and vigorous action as Governor at the time of the Boston Police Strike in the autumn of 1919 gave him a national reputation and he received a few votes for President at the 1920 Republican National Convention in Chicago. Senator Warren Harding won the nomination on the tenth ballot and Coolidge was nominated on the first ballot for Vice President. The Republican ticket easily won the election 2 November and he was inaugurated Vice President 4 March 1921. He won the office in his own right 4 November 1924 (382 electoral votes), defeating Democrat John W. Davis (136 votes) and Progressive Robert M. Lafollette (13 votes).

He was the 30th President of the United States, the second Vermonter and fifth native of New England to become President. Chester Allen Arthur (1881-85) was the other Vermonter. Both were elected Vice President and succeeded to the presidential office upon the death of the sitting President. The other New Englanders: John Adams (1987-1801), John Quincy Adams (1825-29), and Franklin Pierce (1853-57), a native of New Hampshire.

Coolidge, reserved, taciturn, parsimonious, was known as a Yankee of the Yankees. Self-respect, he said, depended on spending "less than you make." He was 33 before marrying because he was "not able to afford the extra expense" before then. He was more famous for his silences than for his speeches. His legislative creed was: "It is much more important to kill bad bills than to pass good ones." When he was nominated in 1924, the scandals of the Harding Cabinet were beginning to break and his dour, thrifty style was an enormous relief for his embarrassed party. Alice Longworth, Pres. Teddy Roosevelt's daughter, said the White House was distinctly improved under the influence of "Cautious Cal" and his unpretentiously attractive, intelligent wife. "The atmosphere," she said, "was as

KINSHIPS AMONG AMERICAN PRESIDENTS

Thomas PERKINS, d. 1588-92, of Hillmorton, Warwickshire, England
= Alice (KEBBLE?)

- Henry PERKINS = Elizabeth SAWBRIDGE
  - John PERKINS (1583-1654) of Ipswich, Mass.
    = Judith GATER
    - John PERKINS, Jr.
      = Elizabeth ——
      - Jacob PERKINS
        = Sarah WAINWRIGHT
        - Philippa PERKINS
          = Thomas EMERSON
          - Mary EMERSON
            = Stephen STORY
            - Philippa STORY
              = Ebenezer WOOD, Jr.
              - Hepzibah WOOD
                = Nathaniel FILLMORE
                - Nathaniel FILLMORE, Jr.
                  = Phoebe MILLARD
                  - **Millard FILLMORE**
                    1800-1874
                    13th U.S. President
                    =(1) Abigail POWERS
                    (2) Mrs. Caroline CARMICHAEL McIntosh
    - Jacob PERKINS
      = Elizabeth WHIPPLE
      - Judith PERKINS
        = Nathaniel BROWN
        - Jacob BROWN
          = Sarah BURNHAM
          - Adam BROWN
            = Esther PARKMAN
            - Adam BROWN, Jr.
              = Priscilla PUTNAM
              - Israel Putnam BROWN
                = Sally BRIGGS
                - Sally BROWN
                  = Israel C. BREWER
                  - Sarah Almeda BREWER
                    = Calvin Galusha COOLIDGE
                    - John Calvin COOLIDGE
                      = Victoria Josephine MOOR
                      - **(John) Calvin COOLIDGE (Jr.)**
                        1872-1933, 30th U.S. President
                        = Grace Anna GOODHUE
      - Jabez PERKINS
        = Hannah LATHROP
        - Hannah PERKINS
          = Joshua HUNTINGTON
          - Lydia HUNTINGTON
            = Ephraim BILL
            - Lydia BILL
              = Joseph HOWLAND
              - Susan HOWLAND
                = John ASPINWALL, Jr.
                - Mary Rebecca ASPINWALL
                  = Isaac ROOSEVELT
                  - James ROOSEVELT
                    = Sara DELANO
                    - **Franklin Delano ROOSEVELT**
                      1882-1945
                      32nd U.S. President
                      = (Anna) Eleanor ROOSEVELT
- Isaac PERKINS (bp. 1571), prob. The Isaac PERKINS, d. ante 1639, of Ipswich, Mass.
  = (2) Alice ——
  - Isaac PERKINS (bp. 1611/12), prob. The Isaac PERKINS (d. 1685) of Hampton, N.H.
    = Susanna ——
    - Rebecca PERKINS = John HUSSEY
      - John HUSSEY, Jr. = Ann INSKEEP
        - Margaret (1) = John = (2) Elizabeth
          RECORD / HUSSEY
          - Record HUSSEY
            = Miriam HARRY
            - Lydia HUSSEY
              = Jacob GRIFFITH
              - Amos GRIFFITH = Edith PRICE
                - Elizabeth Price GRIFFITH
                  = Joshua Vickers MILHOUS
                  - Franklin MILHOUS
                    = Almira Park BURDG
                    - Hannah MILHOUS
                      = Francis Anthony NIXON
                      - **Richard Milhous NIXON**
                        1913-1994
                        37th U.S. President
                        = Thelma Catherine (Pat) RYAN
          - Elizabeth HUSSEY
            = Daniel PRICE

Permission to use sketch given by Gary Boyd Roberts, New England Historic Genealogical Society, Boston.

different as a New England front parlor is from a back room in a speakeasy." To the public, Coolidge stood for traditional virtues: prudence, probity, common sense, understatement.

Not blessed with a great deal of stamina, he once joked that he kept fit by avoiding the big problems. The strain of office gradually wore him down and the death of his son Calvin from blood poisoning desolated him. In August 1927, on the fourth anniversary of his presidency, he issued the terse announcement: "I do not choose to run for President in 1928." He

{ G 1010 }

made his last public address as President 22 February 1929 at George Washington University in Washington, D.C. He attended Herbert Hoover's inauguration 4 March, and retired to Northampton. He contributed a daily column "Thinking Things Over with Calvin Coolidge" to the New York *Herald* and other newspapers 1930-31, and died of coronary thrombosis. Published works: *Have Faith in Massachusetts!* (1919), *The Price of Freedom: Speeches and Addresses* (1924), *Foundations of the Republic, Speeches and Addresses* (1926), and *The Autobiography of Calvin Coolidge* (1929).

Plymouth was the home of four generations of his Coolidge ancestors but the founder of the family in New England, John Coolidge, settled at Watertown, Mass. where he was made a freeman 25 May 1636. Calvin is the tenth generation from John as follows: Simeon,[1] Obadiah,[2] Obadiah,[3] Josiah,[4] Capt. John,[5] Calvin,[6] Galusha,[7] Calvin,[8] Col. John Calvin,[9] President Calvin.[10]

Pres. John Calvin **Coolidge** and Grace Anna **Goodhue** had the following children:
+ 6808 i. John[13] **Coolidge** born 7 September 1906.
  6809 ii. Calvin **Coolidge**[75] born in Northampton 13 April 1908 and died 7 July 1924 in Washington, D.C., at 16 years of age.

5793. **Frederick Eugene**[12] **Ellis** (Dr. Robert Hale[11], Frederick Orin[10], Mary Phillips[9] **Brown**, Aaron[8], John[7], John[6], Jacob[5], Judith[4] **Perkins**, Elizabeth[3] **Whipple**, Matthew[2], Matthew[1])[76] was born in Portland, Multnomah Co., Oreg. 26 August 1916 and married **Marilyn S. Segal** in Minneapolis, Minn. 1 August 1953. Marilyn,[77] daughter of Julius **Segal** and Sara L. (__), was born in Minneapolis 18 March 1926.

Frederick Eugene **Ellis** and Marilyn S. **Segal** had the following children:
6810 i. Jane Marilyn[13] **Ellis**[78] born in Chicago, Ill. 5 June 1953.
6811 ii. Frederick Eugene **Ellis** Jr.[79] born in Minneapolis 1 July 1954.
6812 iii. Anne Dwyn **Ellis**[80] born in Portland 18 July 1955.
6813 iv. Elizabeth Eloise **Ellis**[81] born in Minneapolis 25 December 1956.
6814 v. Miriam Day **Ellis**[82] born in Vancouver, B.C., Canada 20 December 1961.
6815 vi. Margaret Hale **Ellis**[83] born in Mt. Vernon, Wash. 1 February 1965.

5794. **Elizabeth Eleanor**[12] **Ellis** (Dr. Robert Hale[11], Frederick Orin[10], Mary Phillips[9] **Brown**, Aaron[8], John[7], John[6], Jacob[5], Judith[4] **Perkins**, Elizabeth[3] **Whipple**, Matthew[2], Matthew[1])[84] was born in Portland, Multnomah Co., Oreg. 8 November 1917 and married **Steward M. Jones** in Seattle, Wash. in 1944. She was an officer in the U.S. Navy WAVE Corps during WWII. Her husband, who was from Philadelphia, was also a U.S. Naval officer.

Elizabeth Eleanor **Ellis** and Steward M. **Jones** had the following children:
- 6816 i. Eleanor Elizabeth[13] **Jones**[85] born in Portland 5 February 1946.
- 6817 ii. Margery **Jones**[86] born in New York, N.Y. 20 November 1947.
- 6818 iii. Steward McReddie **Jones**[87] born in New York, N.Y. 25 March 1949.
- 6819 iv. Robert Randall **Jones**[88] born in Albuquerque, N. Mex. 12 September 1950.
- 6820 v. Richard Ellis **Jones**[89] born in Palo Alto, Santa Clara Co., Calif. 7 August 1954.
- 6821 vi. Carolyn Ruth **Jones**[90] born in Palo Alto 22 August 1960.

5795. **Robert E.**[12] **Wise** (Anna Hale[11] **Ellis**, Frederick Orin[10], Mary Phillips[9] **Brown**, Aaron[8], John[7], John[6], Jacob[5], Judith[4] **Perkins**, Elizabeth[3] **Whipple**, Matthew[2], Matthew[1])[91] was born in St. Albans, Vt. 26 December 1913 and died 5 March 1998 in Melrose, Mass., at 84 years of age. He married **Charlotte Cutts** in Boston, Mass. 17 August 1940. She was born in New York, N.Y. 26 December 1912.[92] Robert descends from both Matthew and John Whipple of Ipswich. His lineage runs from two of Matthew's children: John who married (3) Mary Stevens and Elizabeth who married Jacob Perkins. His descent from Elder John Whipple is through Mary who married Dea. Simon Stone.

Robert E. **Wise** and Charlotte **Cutts** had the following children:
- + 6822 i. Eugenia[13] **Wise** born 14 January 1942.
- + 6823 ii. Barbara **Wise** born 2 March 1944.
- + 6824 iii. John O. **Wise** born 17 November 1953.

5796. **Miriam**[12] **Wise** (Anna Hale[11] **Ellis**, Frederick Orin[10], Mary Phillips[9] **Brown**, Aaron[8], John[7], John[6], Jacob[5], Judith[4] **Perkins**, Elizabeth[3] **Whipple**, Matthew[2], Matthew[1])[93] was born 17 November 1916 and married **Byron W. Saunders**. He was born in June 1914 and died 4 January 1987 at 72 years of age.[94]

Miriam **Wise** and Byron W. **Saunders** had the following children:
- + 6825 i. William C.[13] **Saunders** born 18 March 1945.
- + 6826 ii. Martha **Saunders** born 10 May 1947.
- + 6827 iii. Carolyn **Saunders** born 5 June 1951.

5797. **William Oliver**[12] **Wise** Jr. (Anna Hale[11] **Ellis**, Frederick Orin[10], Mary Phillips[9] **Brown**, Aaron[8], John[7], John[6], Jacob[5], Judith[4] **Perkins**, Elizabeth[3] **Whipple**, Matthew[2], Matthew[1])[95] was born 24 July 1919 and married **Ruby Kent**. She was born 11 March 1923.[96]

William Oliver **Wise** Jr. and Ruby **Kent** had the following children:
- + 6828 i. William Oliver[13] **Wise** III born March 1954.
- 6829 ii. Cynthia Anne **Wise**[97] born 12 September 1954.

5799. **Rosamond**[12] **Leszkiewicz** (Miriam[11] **Ellis**, Frederick Orin[10], Mary Phillips[9] **Brown**, Aaron[8], John[7], John[6], Jacob[5], Judith[4] **Perkins**, Elizabeth[3] **Whipple**, Matthew[2], Matthew[1])[98] was born in 1922 and married **Robert Boyd Naylor** at Cherry Pt. USMCA, Havelock Co., N.C. 18 August 1944. Robert,[99] son of John E. **Naylor** and Florence **Cotton**, was born in Philadelphia, Penn. 4 November 1924 and died 23 February 1992 in Sun City West, Ariz., at 67 years of age.

Rosamond **Leszkiewicz** and Robert Boyd **Naylor** had the following children born in Weymouth, Norfolk Co., Mass.:
- 6830 i. Elizabeth Anne[13] **Naylor**[100] 25 February 1948.
- 6831 ii. Marjorie **Naylor**[101] 9 July 1949. She married Ray **Martin**[31] October 1981. Ray,[102] son of Richard Carl Martin and Cleo Fern Bonnell, was born in Los Angeles, Calif. 31 October 1942.

5801. **Wanda Ellis**[12] **Leszkiewicz** (Miriam[11] **Ellis**, Frederick Orin[10], Mary Phillips[9] **Brown**, Aaron[8], John[7], John[6], Jacob[5], Judith[4] **Perkins**, Elizabeth[3] **Whipple**, Matthew[2], Matthew[1])[103] was born in Braintree, Norfolk Co., Mass. 23 November 1924 and married **Warren Julian Loring** there 30 June 1951. Warren,[104] son of Julian Capen **Loring** and Olive Endicott **Jacobs**, was born 15 October 1921 and died 21 August 1984 in Barnstable, Barnstable Co., Mass., at 62 years of age.

Wanda Ellis **Leszkiewicz** and Warren Julian **Loring** had the following children:
- + 6832 i. Nancy Endicott[13] **Loring** born 7 June 1952.
- + 6833 ii. Randall Hale **Loring** born 29 May 1954.

+   6834   iii.   Susan Ellis **Loring** born 22 July 1958.

5803. **George Henry**[12] **Bragdon** (Ione[11] **Andrews**, Henry[10], Caleb[9], Molly[8] **Burnham**, Capt. Westley[7], Westley[6], Elizabeth[5] **Perkins**, Jacob[4], Elizabeth[3] **Whipple**, Matthew[2], Matthew[1])[105] was born in Beverly, Essex Co., Mass. in 1868 and died in October 1911 in Salem, Essex Co., Mass., at 43 years of age. He worked for the railroad and died in a train accident. Buried at Beverly, Mass. He married **Estella Martha Standley** in Wenham, Essex Co., Mass. 31 December 1893. Estella,[106] daughter of Edward F. **Standley** and Mary A. **Dodge,** was born in Wenham in 1873 and died there in 1912, at 39 years of age. Buried at Beverly.

George Henry **Bragdon** and Estella Martha **Standley** had the following children:

       6835   i.   Bernice[13] **Bragdon**[107] born in Beverly in 1896 and died in 1969 at 73 years of age. She married William **Carter.**
+   6836   ii.   Chester Stanley **Bragdon** born 1898.
+   6837   iii.   Henry **Bragdon** born 20 July 1899.
+   6838   iv.   William Edward **Bragdon** born 20 June 1902.
+   6839   v.   Hollis L. **Bragdon** born 10 April 1904.
+   6840   vi.   Sidney H. **Bragdon** born 19 August 1905.
+   6841   vii.   Frederick **Bragdon** born 21 May 1907.
+   6842   viii.   Esther Marjorie **Bragdon** born 14 July 1908.
+   6843   ix.   George Austin **Bragdon** born 19 April 1911.

5805. **Fannie Woodberry**[12] **Bragdon** (Ione[11] **Andrews**, Henry[10], Caleb[9], Molly[8] **Burnham**, Capt. Westley[7], Westley[6], Elizabeth[5] **Perkins**, Jacob[4], Elizabeth[3] **Whipple**, Matthew[2], Matthew[1])[108] was born in Essex, Essex Co., Mass. 28 December 1872 and died 8 July 1951 in Falmouth, Barnstable Co., Mass., at 78 years of age. She married **Otis Marvin Baker** in 1895. Otis,[109] son of Johial **Baker** and Celia M. **Doty**, was born in Falmouth 15 August 1870 and died 7 October 1952 in Beverly, Essex Co., Mass., at 82 years of age. Otis and Fanny are buried in the North Cemetery at Beverly.

Fannie Woodberry **Bragdon** and Otis Marvin **Baker** had the following children:

       6844   i.   Arthur Ellsworth[13] **Baker**[110] born in Beverly 30 August 1895 and died in 1918 in France, at 22 years of age. He was in WWI and is buried at the American Cemetery, Chateau Thierry, France.
+   6845   ii.   Lorin Marvin **Baker** born 8 January 1897.
+   6846   iii.   Clifford Doty **Baker** born 28 December 1900.

{ G 1014 }

+	6847	iv.	Roy Woodberry **Baker** born 25 January 1901.
+	6848	v.	Gordon Andrews **Baker** born 15 November 1904.
+	6849	vi.	Otis Clayton **Baker** born 21 March 1908.

5806. **Charles William[12] Bragdon** (Ione[11] **Andrews**, Henry[10], Caleb[9], Molly[8] **Burnham**, Capt. Westley[7], Westley[6], Elizabeth[5] **Perkins**, Jacob[4], Elizabeth[3] **Whipple**, Matthew[2], Matthew[1])[111] was born in Beverly, Essex Co., Mass. 11 January 1876 and died in 1963 at 87 years of age. He married **Annie Luetta Shordon**.

Charles William **Bragdon** and Annie Luetta **Shordon** had the following children:

	6850	i.	Deborah[13] **Bragdon**.[112]
	6851	ii.	Isabell **Bragdon**.[113]
	6852	iii.	Louis **Bragdon**.[114]

5812. **Emma Louise[12] Low** (Emma Louise[11] **Andrews**, Henry[10], Caleb[9], Molly[8] **Burnham**, Capt. Westley[7], Westley[6], Elizabeth[5] **Perkins**, Jacob[4], Elizabeth[3] **Whipple**, Matthew[2], Matthew[1])[115] was born in Essex, Essex Co., Mass. 7 April 1884 and died 4 June 1971 in Marblehead, Essex Co., Mass., at 87 years of age. She married **Frank Everett Raymond** in Essex 29 June 1910. Frank,[116] son of Benjamin F. **Raymond** and Lelia A. **Story**, was born in Essex 3 April 1882 and died in Salem, Essex Co., Mass.

Emma Louise **Low** and Frank Everett **Raymond** had the following children:

+	6853	i.	Frank Everett[13] **Raymond** born 11 January 1911.
+	6854	ii.	Roger Conant **Raymond** born 26 January 1913.
+	6855	iii.	Sumner **Raymond** born 8 March 1914.
+	6856	iv.	Lelia **Raymond** born 2 November 1916.
+	6857	v.	Alice **Raymond** born 11 October 1918.
+	6858	vi.	Pauline **Raymond** born 3 August 1920.
+	6859	vii.	Althine **Raymond** born 24 April 1924.

5816. **Ardelle[12] Low** (Emma Louise[11] **Andrews**, Henry[10], Caleb[9], Molly[8] **Burnham**, Capt. Westley[7], Westley[6], Elizabeth[5] **Perkins**, Jacob[4], Elizabeth[3] **Whipple**, Matthew[2], Matthew[1])[117] was born in Essex, Essex Co., Mass. 14 November 1899 and died 11 January 1978 in Ipswich, Essex Co., Mass., at 78 years of age. She married **Harold Alden Burnham** in Manchester, Essex Co., Mass. 31 August 1928. He was born in 1899.[118]

Ardelle **Low** and Harold Alden **Burnham** had the following children:

| + | 6860 | i. | Lois[13] **Burnham** born 28 July 1932. |

+ 6861 ii. Charles Alden **Burnham** born 13 July 1935.

5817. **Ceciline**[12] **Low** (Emma Louise[11] **Andrews**, Henry[10], Caleb[9], Molly[8] **Burnham**, Capt. Westley[7], Westley[6], Elizabeth[5] **Perkins**, Jacob[4], Elizabeth[3] **Whipple**, Matthew[2], Matthew[1])[119] was born in Essex, Essex Co., Mass. 20 December 1905 and married **Alfred W. Howes**. He died 10 October 1971.[120]

Ceciline **Low** and Alfred W. **Howes** had the following child:
+ 6862 i. Marsha Winslow[13] **Howes** born 16 June 1931.

5818. **Elston Brooks**[12] **Low** (Emma Louise[11] **Andrews**, Henry[10], Caleb[9], Molly[8] **Burnham**, Capt. Westley[7], Westley[6], Elizabeth[5] **Perkins**, Jacob[4], Elizabeth[3] **Whipple**, Matthew[2], Matthew[1])[121] was born in Essex, Essex Co., Mass. 8 December 1908 and married **Ruth Odell** in Salem, Essex Co., Mass. 25 August 1951. Ruth,[122] daughter of Raymond Hale **Odell** and Edna **Goodell**, was born in Salem 4 July 1918.

Elston Brooks **Low** and Ruth **Odell** had the following children:
+ 6863 i. Douglas Gilman[13] **Low** born 3 May 1952.
+ 6864 ii. Eunice **Low** born 7 October 1953.

5820. **Henry Foster**[12] **Andrews** (Henry Ward[11], Henry[10], Caleb[9], Molly[8] **Burnham**, Capt. Westley[7], Westley[6], Elizabeth[5] **Perkins**, Jacob[4], Elizabeth[3] **Whipple**, Matthew[2], Matthew[1])[123] was born in Essex, Essex Co., Mass. 27 December 1899 and died there 6 March 1979, at 79 years of age. Buried in Spring Street Cemetery. He married **Charlotte Martin** in Essex. He served as an Essex Selectman for 18 years, helped develop the Essex Shipbuilding Museum, served on the Shellfish Commission, and as a Director of the Camp Ann Savings Bank.

Henry Foster **Andrews** and Charlotte **Martin** had the following children:
6865 i. Helen[13] **Andrews**[124] married Frank **Storey**.
6866 ii. Virginia **Andrews**[125] married Charles **Mulchay**.
6867 iii. Walter **Andrews**[126] married Effie **Storey**.

5822. **Edna Frances**[12] **Andrews** (Frank Albert[11], Henry[10], Caleb[9], Molly[8] **Burnham**, Capt. Westley[7], Westley[6], Elizabeth[5] **Perkins**, Jacob[4], Elizabeth[3] **Whipple**, Matthew[2], Matthew[1])[127] was born in Essex, Essex Co., Mass. 10 February 1898 and died 6 July 1977 in Beverly, Essex Co., Mass., at 79 years of age. She married twice. (1) **Joseph Henry Gosbee** in Essex 19 May 1917. Joseph,[128] son of Henry David **Gosbee** and Flora

MacPherson, was born in Essex 21 January 1892 and died 5 October 1941 in Beverly, at 49 years of age. Both are buried in the North Beverly Cemetery. (2) **William Henry Crocker**.

Edna Frances **Andrews** and Joseph Henry **Gosbee** had the following child:
+   6868   i.   John Francis[13] **Gosbee** born 8 August 1919.

5823. **Viola Alberta**[12] **Andrews** (Frank Albert[11], Henry[10], Caleb[9], Molly[8] **Burnham**, Capt. Westley[7], Westley[6], Elizabeth[5] **Perkins**, Jacob[4], Elizabeth[3] **Whipple**, Matthew[2], Matthew[1])[129] was born in Essex, Essex Co., Mass. 14 February 1901 and married **Thomas William Entwistle Sr.** in Hopkinton, Middlesex Co., Mass. 24 October 1924. Thomas,[130] son of William **Entwistle** and Heilfrich (__), was born in Orangeburg, Rockland Co., N.Y. 8 January 1898 and died 9 April 1985 in Framingham, Middlesex Co., Mass., at 87 years of age. Buried at the Evergreen Cemetery, Woodville, Mass.

Viola Alberta **Andrews** and Thomas William **Entwistle** Sr. had the following children:
+   6869   i.   Jean Frances[13] **Entwistle** born 26 March 1930.
+   6870   ii.   Thomas William **Entwistle** Jr. born 11 January 1933.

5825. **Jean Dorothy**[12] **Andrews** (Frank Albert[11], Henry[10], Caleb[9], Molly[8] **Burnham**, Capt. Westley[7], Westley[6], Elizabeth[5] **Perkins**, Jacob[4], Elizabeth[3] **Whipple**, Matthew[2], Matthew[1])[131] was born in Essex, Essex Co., Mass. 7 August 1907 and died 7 June 1993 in Framingham, Middlesex Co., Mass., at 85 years of age. She married **Ralph Henry Whalen** who was born in Westborough, Worcester Co., Mass. 3 August 1901. Ralph,[132] son of Michael **Whalen** and Sara Elizabeth **Kane**, died 2 October 1968 in Hopkinton, Middlesex Co., Mass., at 67 years of age. Both are buried at Evergreen Cemetery, Woodville, Mass.

Jean Dorothy **Andrews** and Ralph Henry **Whalen** had the following child:
+   6871   i.   Ralph Henry[13] **Whalen** Jr. born 5 August 1930.

5826. **Frank Sydney**[12] **Andrews** (Frank Albert[11], Henry[10], Caleb[9], Molly[8] **Burnham**, Capt. Westley[7], Westley[6], Elizabeth[5] **Perkins**, Jacob[4], Elizabeth[3] **Whipple**, Matthew[2], Matthew[1])[133] was born in Essex, Essex Co., Mass. 18 May 1911 and married **Irvine Charlton Temple** in Nashua, N. H. 17 June 1931. Irvine,[134] daughter of Ellwood Irving **Temple** and Grace May **Charlton**, was born in Hartford, Conn. 9 March 1912.

Frank Sydney **Andrews** and Irvine Charlton **Temple** had the following children:
- \+ 6872 i. Sydney Byron[13] **Andrews** born 22 September 1932.
- \+ 6873 ii. Shirley Mae **Andrews** born 18 October 1934.
- \+ 6874 iii. Carole Joan **Andrews** born 8 September 1938.
- \+ 6875 iv. Betty Elaine **Andrews** born 1 February 1943.

5828. **Edward Francis**[12] **Mears Sr.** (David Edward[11], Sallie Maria[10] **Andrews**, Caleb[9], Molly[8] **Burnham**, Capt. Westley[7], Westley[6], Elizabeth[5] **Perkins**, Jacob[4], Elizabeth[3] **Whipple**, Matthew[2], Matthew[1])[135] was born in Essex, Essex Co., Mass. 9 October 1893 and died there in 1964, at 70 years of age. He married **Marjorie Almira Atwater** in Manchester, Essex Co., Mass. 20 May 1919. Marjorie,[136] daughter of Charles Alvarous **Atwater** and Sarah F. **Wright**, was born in Gloucester, Essex Co., Mass. 22 May 1895 and died 27 July 1983 in Peabody, Essex Co., Mass., at 88 years of age.

Edward Francis **Mears** Sr. and Marjorie Almira **Atwater** had the following children born in Essex:
- \+ 6876 i. Edward Francis[13] **Mears** Jr. 21 January 1920.
- 6877 ii. David Alonzo **Mears**[137] 26 September 1921 and married Mary **Ahern** in Brighton, Suffolk Co., Mass. 27 November 1943.

5831. **Leslie Francis**[12] **Andrews** (Robert Francis[11], Levi Smalley[10], Noah[9], John[8], Joanna[7] **Burnham**, Westley[6], Elizabeth[5] **Perkins**, Jacob[4], Elizabeth[3] **Whipple**, Matthew[2], Matthew[1])[138] was born in Rio de Janeiro, Brazil 13 March 1896 and died there 10 October 1975, at 79 years of age. He married **Alice Marcellino da Silva** who was born in Belem, State of Para, Brazil 19 October 1891. She died 12 May 1978 in Rio de Janeiro, at 86 years of age.[139]

Leslie Francis **Andrews** and Alice Marcellino da **Silva** had the following children:
- 6878 i. Robert[13] **Andrews**.[140]
- \+ 6879 ii. Frederick **Andrews**.
- \+ 6880 iii. Doris Alice **Andrews** born 27 September 1923.

5833. **Levi Charles Smalley**[12] **Leslie** (Florence[11] **Andrews**, Levi Smalley[10], Noah[9], John[8], Joanna[7] **Burnham**, Westley[6], Elizabeth[5] **Perkins**, Jacob[4], Elizabeth[3] **Whipple**, Matthew[2], Matthew[1])[141] was born in Rua Paissandu, Rio de Janeiro, Brazil 11 February 1892 and died 24 January 1949 in St. Louis, Independence Co., Mo., at 56 years of age. He married

Lucile Saunders Latta in Phillipsburg, N.J. 25 June 1912. She was born in New York, N.Y. 24 August 1892 and died 9 January 1964 in New York, at 71 years of age.[142]

Levi Charles Smalley **Leslie** and Lucile Saunders **Latta** had the following children:

    6881   i.   Levi Charles[13] **Leslie**[143] born in Sao Paulo, Brazil 25 December 1913 and died in 1981 in Philadelphia, Penn., at 67 years of age.

    6882   ii.   John Latta **Leslie**[144] born 12 December 1915 and died 17 March 1945 at 29 years of age. He married Elvira **Laine**.

+   6883   iii.   Alexander **Leslie** born 28 October 1917.

5834. **Herbert**[12] **Leslie** (Florence[11] **Andrews**, Levi Smalley[10], Noah[9], John[8], Joanna[7] **Burnham**, Westley[6], Elizabeth[5] **Perkins**, Jacob[4], Elizabeth[3] **Whipple**, Matthew[2], Matthew[1])[145] was born in Macacos, Rio de Janeiro, Brazil 25 November 1893 and died 9 June 1943 in Rio de Janeiro, at 49 years of age. He married twice. (1) **Jessica Sabolt**. (2) **Eileen Mary Nora Ashton** 1 June 1930. Eileen was born in 1904 and died 20 December 1997 at 93 years of age.[146]

Herbert **Leslie** and Jessica **Sabolt** had the following child:

    6884   i.   Jean Ann Sabolt[13] **Leslie**.[147]

Herbert **Leslie** and Eileen Mary Nora **Ashton** had the following children:

+   6885   ii.   Herbert Alexander **Leslie**.

+   6886   iii.   Noreen **Leslie** born in 1932.

5836. **Eleanor**[12] **Leslie** (Florence[11] **Andrews**, Levi Smalley[10], Noah[9], John[8], Joanna[7] **Burnham**, Westley[6], Elizabeth[5] **Perkins**, Jacob[4], Elizabeth[3] **Whipple**, Matthew[2], Matthew[1])[148] was born in Macacos, Rio de Janeiro, Brazil 6 February 1897 and died in 1985 at 88 years of age. She married **William Harrison Reem Irvin**. He was born in Altoona, Penn. in 1888 and died in 1959 in Rio de Janeiro, at 71 years of age.[149]

Eleanor **Leslie** and William Harrison Reem **Irvin** had the following child:

+   6887   i.   Florence Eleanor[13] **Irvin** born in 1919.

5843. **Margaret Ruth**[12] **Hents** (Lucinda Rivers[11] **Andrews**, Levi Smalley[10], Noah[9], John[8], Joanna[7] **Burnham**, Westley[6], Elizabeth[5] **Perkins**, Jacob[4], Elizabeth[3] **Whipple**, Matthew[2], Matthew[1])[150] was born 14 June

1898 and married **Frederic Speer Crocker** in Rio de Janeiro, Brazil 6 December 1919.

Margaret Ruth **Hents** and Frederic Speer **Crocker** had the following child:
+   6888   i.   Betty[13] **Crocker** born in 1929.

5847. **Margaret Alice[12] Andrews** (Dennis Rivers[11], Levi Smalley[10], Noah[9], John[8], Joanna[7] **Burnham**, Westley[6], Elizabeth[5] **Perkins**, Jacob[4], Elizabeth[3] **Whipple**, Matthew[2], Matthew[1])[151] was born in Ribeirao Preto, State of Sao Paulo, Brazil 7 June 1905 and died 8 September 1982 in Dallas, Tex., at 77 years of age. She married **Carlos Esselleur Seifert** in Rio de Janeiro, Brazil 7 June 1928. Carlos,[152] son of Karl **Seifert** and Maria **Palmer**, was born in Aguas, Calientes, Mexico 18 September 1896 and died 4 December 1952 in Rio de Janeiro, at 56 years of age.

Margaret Alice **Andrews** and Carlos Esselleur **Seifert** had the following children:
+   6889   i.   Margaret Louise[13] **Seifert** born 6 April 1929.
     6890   ii.   Barbara Kathleen **Seifert**[153] born in Rio de Janeiro 9 January 1932 and died there 25 August 1933, at 1 year of age.
+   6891   iii.   Patricia Mary **Seifert** born 20 January 1934.
+   6892   iv.   Charles Robert Grant Rivers **Seifert** born 14 September 1935.
+   6893   v.   Elizabeth Ann **Seifert** born 1 February 1937.
+   6894   vi.   William Palmer **Seifert** born 17 July 1938.

5849. **John Rivers[12] Andrews** (Dennis Rivers[11], Levi Smalley[10], Noah[9], John[8], Joanna[7] **Burnham**, Westley[6], Elizabeth[5] **Perkins**, Jacob[4], Elizabeth[3] **Whipple**, Matthew[2], Matthew[1])[154] was born in Juiz de Fora, Brazil 1910 and died there in March 1954, at 43 years of age. He married **Jenni Pucciarelli**.

John Rivers **Andrews** and Jenni **Pucciarelli** had the following child:
+   6895   i.   Dennis Rivers[13] **Andrews** born 29 April 1929.

5850. **Frances Archer[12] Strand** (Frances Archer[11] **McCandlish**, Randolph Walke[10], Eliza Whipple[9] **Putnam**, Douglas[8], Elizabeth[7] **Perkins**, Dr. Elisha[6], Dr. Joseph[5], Joseph[4], Elizabeth[3] **Whipple**, Matthew[2], Matthew[1])[155] was born in Evanston, Ill. 15 July 1950 and married **Mason Blake Caldwell III** in Kay Chapel at American University in Washington, D.C. 21 March 1970. Mason,[156] son of Mason Blake **Caldwell** Jr. and Jean Elizabeth **Moore**, was born in Portsmouth, Va. 9 February 1946.

Frances Archer **Strand** and Mason Blake **Caldwell** III had the following children:
- 6896 i. Mason Blake[13] **Caldwell** IV[157] born in Radford, Va. 20 May 1981.
- 6897 ii. Louisa Archer **Caldwell**[158] born in Norfolk, Va. 16 February 1985 and died there 5 September 1985, at less than 7 months of age.
- 6898 iii. Jessie Samantha **Caldwell**[159] born in Norfolk 17 February 1989.

5851. **Robert William**[12] **Strand** (Frances Archer[11] **McCandlish**, Randolph Walke[10], Eliza Whipple[9] **Putnam**, Douglas[8], Elizabeth[7] **Perkins**, Dr. Elisha[6], Dr. Joseph[5], Joseph[4], Elizabeth[3] **Whipple**, Matthew[2], Matthew[1])[160] was born in Evanston, Ill. 7 December 1951 and married **Elizabeth Ann Albrecht** in Richmond, Va. 28 August 1974. Elizabeth, daughter of Harold **Albrecht** and Ruth (__), was born 18 December 1952.

Robert William **Strand** and Elizabeth Ann **Albrecht** had the following children:
- 6899 i. Peter Albrecht[13] **Strand**[161] born in Fayettville, Washington Co., Ark. 23 October 1982.
- 6900 ii. Andrew Michael **Strand**[162] born in Denton, Tex. 24 February 1985.

5853. **Susan Holt**[12] **Strand** (Frances Archer[11] **McCandlish**, Randolph Walke[10], Eliza Whipple[9] **Putnam**, Douglas[8], Elizabeth[7] **Perkins**, Dr. Elisha[6], Dr. Joseph[5], Joseph[4], Elizabeth[3] **Whipple**, Matthew[2], Matthew[1])[163] was born in Evanston, Ill. 12 November 1956 and married **David Randolph Wilson** in Pottersville, N.J. 30 August 1984. David,[164] son of David **Wilson** and Margaret (__), was born in Pakistan 12 August 1954. They were divorced in Boston, Mass. in 2000.

Susan Holt **Strand** and David Randolph **Wilson** had the following children:
- 6901 i. Ross Patrick[13] **Wilson**[165] born in Kenshasa, Zaire 18 March 1984.
- 6902 ii. Kelly Robyn **Wilson**[166] born in Oxford, England 1 January 1987.

5855. **Anna Eleanor**[12] **Roosevelt** (Pres. Franklin Delano[11], James[10], Mary Rebecca[9] **Aspinwall**, Susan[8] **Howland**, Lydia[7] **Bill**, Lydia[6] **Huntington**, Hannah[5] **Perkins**, Jabez[4], Elizabeth[3] **Whipple**, Matthew[2], Matthew[1])[167] was born in New York, N.Y. 3 May 1906 and married three times. (1) **Curtis Bean Dall** in New York, N.Y. 5 June 1926. They were divorced before 1935. (2) **John Boettiger** in New York, N.Y. 18 January 1935. They were divorced in 1949. (3) **Dr. James A. Halsted** in Malibu, Calif. 11 November 1952.

Anna Eleanor **Roosevelt** and Curtis Bean **Dall** had the following children:
+   6903   i.   Anna[13] **Dall** born 25 March 1927.
+   6904   ii.   Curtis Roosevelt **Dall** born 19 April 1930.

Anna Eleanor **Roosevelt** and John **Boettiger** had the following child:
+   6905   iii.   John Roosevelt **Boettiger** born 30 March 1939.

5856. **Congressman James**[12] **Roosevelt** (Pres. Franklin Delano[11], James[10], Mary Rebecca[9] **Aspinwall**, Susan[8] **Howland**, Lydia[7] **Bill**, Lydia[6] **Huntington**, Hannah[5] **Perkins**, Jabez[4], Elizabeth[3] **Whipple**, Matthew[2], Matthew[1])[168] was born in New York, N.Y. 23 December 1907 and married four times. (1) **Betsey Cushing** in Brookline, Norfolk Co., Mass. 4 June 1930. She is the daughter of Dr. Harvey **Cushing**. They were divorced in 1940. (2) **Romelle Theresa Schneider** in Beverly Hills, Calif. 14 April 1941. She was born in 1916. They were divorced in 1955. (3) **Mrs. Gladys Irene Owens** in Los Angeles, Calif. 2 July 1956. She was born in 1917. They were divorced in 1969.[169] (4) **Mary Lena Winskill** in Hyde Park, N.Y. 3 October 1969. She was born in Heath, Franklin Co., Mass. 5 June 1939. James was educated at Groton and Harvard. He was a Colonel in the U.S. Marine Corps during World War II, a member of Congress (84th-89th congresses), and a U.S. Representative to the United Nations Economic and Social Council. He was also a teacher at the U. of California.

Congressman James **Roosevelt** and Betsey **Cushing** had the following children:
+   6906   i.   Sara Delano[13] **Roosevelt** born 13 March 1932.
+   6907   ii.   Kate **Roosevelt** born 16 February 1936.

Congressman James **Roosevelt** and Romelle Theresa **Schneider** had the following children:
     6908   iii.   James **Roosevelt** Jr.[170] born in Hollywood, Calif. 9 November 1945 and married Ann Martha **Conlon** in Cambridge, Mass. 15 June 1968. She is the daughter of Walter N. Conlon.[171]
     6909   iv.   Michael Anthony **Roosevelt**[172] born in Los Angeles 7 December 1946 and married Deborah Wilson **Horn** in Schenectady, N.Y. 21 August 1972. She is the daughter of F. Hubbard **Horn**.[173] Michael was educated at Harvard and Columbia Law School.

        6910   v.   Anna Eleanor **Roosevelt**[174] born in Santa Monica, Calif. 10 January 1948 and married Robert K. **Johnston.** She was educated at Stanford University.

Congressman James **Roosevelt** and Mrs. Gladys Irene **Owens** had the following child:
        6911   vi.   Hall Delano **Roosevelt** born June 1957. Adopted.

Congressman James **Roosevelt** had the following child:
        6912   vii.   Rebecca Mary **Roosevelt** born 1971.[175]

5858. **Elliott**[12] **Roosevelt** (Pres. Franklin Delano[11], James[10], Mary Rebecca[9] **Aspinwall**, Susan[8] **Howland**, Lydia[7] **Bill**, Lydia[6] **Huntington**, Hannah[5] **Perkins**, Jabez[4], Elizabeth[3] **Whipple**, Matthew[2], Matthew[1])[176] was born in New York, N.Y. 23 September 1910 and married five times. (1) **Elizabeth Browning Donnor** 16 January 1932. She is the daughter of William Henry **Donnor**.[177] They were divorced in 1933. (2) **Ruth Josephine Googins** Fort Worth, Tex. in Burlington, Iowa 22 July 1933.

They were divorced in 1944. (3) **Faye Margaret Emerson** in Grand Canyon, Colo. 3 December 1944. A Hollywood movie star, she was born in Elizabeth, La. 8 July 1917 and died 9 March 1983 in Hamden, Conn., at 65 years of age.[178] They were divorced in 1950. (4) **Minnewa Bell** in Miami Beach, Fla. 15 March 1951. She was born in 1911. They were divorced in 1960. (5) **Patricia Whithead** in Qualicum, B.C., Canada in November 1960.

Elliott **Roosevelt** and Patricia **Whithead** had the following child:
        6913   i.   Livingston Delano[13] **Roosevelt**. died in infancy.[179]

Elliott **Roosevelt** and Elizabeth Browning **Donnor** had the following child:
+   6914   ii.   William Donnor **Roosevelt** born 17 November 1932.

Elliott **Roosevelt** and Ruth Josephine **Googins** had the following children:
+   6915   iii.   Ruth Chandler **Roosevelt** born 9 May 1934.
+   6916   iv.   Elliott **Roosevelt** Jr. born 14 July 1936.
+   6917   v.   David Boynton **Roosevelt** born 3 January 1942.

5859. **Franklin Delano**[12] **Roosevelt Jr.** (Pres. Franklin Delano[11], James[10], Mary Rebecca[9] **Aspinwall**, Susan[8] **Howland**, Lydia[7] **Bill**, Lydia[6] **Huntington**, Hannah[5] **Perkins**, Jabez[4], Elizabeth[3] **Whipple**, Matthew[2], Matthew[1])[180] was born in Campobello Island, New Brunswick, Canada 17 August 1914 and died 17 August 1988 in Yonkers, N.Y., at 74 years of age.

He married five times. (1) **Ethel du Pont** in Wilmington, Del. 30 June 1937. Ethel,[181] daughter of Eugene **du Pont**, was born in Wilmington in 1915 and died 25 May 1965 in Grosse Pointe Farms, Mich., at 49 years of age. They were divorced in 1949. (2) **Suzanne Perrin** in New York, N. Y 31 August 1949. She is the daughter of Lee **Perrin**.[182] They were divorced in 1970. (3) **Mrs. Felicia Warburg Sarnoff** in New York, N.Y. 1 July 1970. (4) **Patricia Louise Oakes** in Dutchess Co., N.Y. 6 May 1977. She was born in Kingsville, Ohio 17 March 1951. (5) **Lynda Stevenson**. He was a Commander in the US Naval Reserve, served in the 81st-83rd Congresses as a Representative, was Under Secretary of Commerce (1962-65), and Chairman of the Equal Employment Opportunity Committee (1965-66).

Franklin Delano **Roosevelt** Jr. and Ethel du **Pont** had the following children:
- \+ 6918 i. Franklin Delano[13] **Roosevelt** III born 19 July 1939.
- \+ 6919 ii. Christopher du Pont **Roosevelt** born 21 December 1940.

Franklin Delano **Roosevelt** Jr. and Suzanne **Perrin** had the following child:
- 6920 iii. Nancy Suzanne **Roosevelt** born in New York, N.Y. 11 January 1952.[183]

5860. **John Aspinwall**[12] **Roosevelt** (Pres. Franklin Delano[11], James[10], Mary Rebecca[9] **Aspinwall**, Susan[8] **Howland**, Lydia[7] **Bill**, Lydia[6] **Huntington**, Hannah[5] **Perkins**, Jabez[4], Elizabeth[3] **Whipple**, Matthew[2], Matthew[1]) was born in Washington, D.C. 13 March 1916 and died 27 April 1981 in New York, N.Y., at 65 years of age. He married twice. (1) **Anne Lindsay Clark** in Nahant, Mass. 18 June 1938. Anne,[184] daughter of Franklin Haven **Clark** and Frances **Sturgis**, was born in Concord, Middlesex Co., Mass. 13 July 1916 and died 28 May 1973 in New York, N.Y., at 56 years of age. They were divorced in 1965. (2) **Irene E. Boyd** in New York, N.Y. 28 October 1965. Irene,[185] daughter of James Hallam **Boyd** and Mary Elizabeth **Watkins**, was born in New York State 8 March 1931. She also married **Benjamin Bandreth McAlpin III**.

John Aspinwall **Roosevelt** and Anne Lindsay **Clark** had the following children:
- \+ 6921 i. Haven Clark[13] **Roosevelt** born 5 June 1940.
- \+ 6922 ii. Anne Sturgis **Roosevelt** born 15 December 1942.
- 6923 iii. Sara Delano **Roosevelt**[186] born in Pasadena, Calif. December 1946 and died 12 August 1960 in Old Forge, Utica Co., N.Y., at 13 years of age. She was killed in a riding accident.
- 6924 iv. Joan Lindsay **Roosevelt** born in Poughkeepsie, N.Y. 25 August 1952.[187]

5861. **Hazel Georgia**[12] **Bradley** (Esther Myrtle[11] **Smith**, Julia Ann[10] **Stevens**, Melissa Esther[9] **Jones**, Mariah B.[8] **Ayers**, Lovica[7] **Stanton**, Lovica[6] **Gates**, Charity[5] **Perkins**, Jabez[4], Elizabeth[3] **Whipple**, Matthew[2], Matthew[1])[188] was born in Port Huron, Mich. 27 March 1896 and died 10 May 1973 in Belding, Mich., at 77 years of age. She was buried 12 May 1973 in Douglass Twp., Montcalm Co., Mich., Entrican Cemetery. She married twice. (1) **Frederick Melvin Holmes Sr.** in Windsor, Essex Co., Ontario, Canada 8 October 1912. Frederick,[189] son of Dixon J. **Holmes** and Ida D. **Strait**, was born in Greenville, Montcalm Co., Mich. 10 May 1884 and died there 12 November 1940, at 56 years of age. Buried at Forest Home Cemetery. They were divorced 10 December 1925. He married (2) **Anna Louise Tyson**. (2) **Melvin Delmar Dunn** in Port Huron 12 December 1925. Melvin,[190] son of William **Dunn** and Grace **Moneypenny**, was born 19 February 1895 and died 3 January 1964 at 68 years of age.

Hazel Georgia **Bradley** and Frederick Melvin **Holmes** Sr. had the following children:

    6925   i.   Blanche Vernice[13] **Holmes**[191] born in Port Huron, Mich. 2 August 1913 and died 16 March 1991 in Cadillac, Mich., at 77 years of age. Buried at Boon Cemetery. She married Ira C. **Dunn** in Port Huron in 1929. He was born 17 March 1913 and died 18 May 1960 at 47 years of age.[192]

    6926   ii.   Yvonne Lenore **Holmes**[193] born in Port Huron 28 October 1915 and died 18 October 1986 in Venice, Fla., at 70 years of age. She married twice. (1) Charles **Nettle** 19 August 1933. (2) Orlin Henry **Baker** in Wayne Co., Mich. 20 April 1968.

    6927   iii.   Ardas Myrtle **Holmes**[194] born in Port Huron 15 November 1917 and died 16 May 1995 in Cadillac, at 77 years of age. She married Walton A. **Schultz** in Port Huron 5 June 1937.

    6928   iv.   Betty Jane **Holmes**[195] born in Port Huron 15 June 1920 and married three times. (1) Earl **Thomas** in 1944. (2) Bernard **Davis** in 1945. They were divorced in 1946. (3) Burdell **Funk** 3 March 1977.

+   6929   v.   Frederick Melvin **Holmes** Jr. born 24 April 1924.

5876. **Joseph Harold**[12] **Huse** (Edwin Ralph[11], Luther Richards[10], Thomas[9], Robert[8], John[7], Elizabeth[6] **Hale**, Anna[5] **Short**, Sarah[4] **Whipple**, Lt. John[3], Matthew[2], Matthew[1])[196] was born in Indianapolis, Ind. 17 July 1899 and died 12 August 1973 in Hinsdale, Ill., at 74 years of age. He married **Thelma Lucille Brandes** in Indianapolis 30 April 1921. Thelma,[197] daughter of George James **Brandes** and Emma Blanche

{ G 1025 }

Milender, was born in Indianapolis 6 August 1901 and died 31 May 1976 in Hinsdale, at 74 years of age. Both were buried in Indianapolis.

Joseph Harold **Huse** and Thelma Lucille **Brandes** had the following child:
    6930 i. Nancy Carol[13] **Huse**[198] born in Chicago, Ill. 21 May 1928.

5882. **Paul Warren**[12] **Whipple** (John Godfrey[11], William Orland[10], William Ward[9], John[8], John[7], Capt. John[6], Hannah[5], John[4], Lt. John[3], Matthew[2], Matthew[1])[199] was born in Tonganoxie, Kans. 21 January 1915 and married **Irma Stark** in Silver Spring, Md. 20 November 1948. Irma,[200] daughter of Samuel **Stark** and Gertrude **Greenebaum**, was born in Brooklyn, N.Y. 18 May 1914 and died 3 February 1988 in Washington, D.C., at 73 years of age.

Paul Warren **Whipple** and Irma **Stark** had the following children:
    6931 i. Sara Elizabeth[13] **Whipple**[201] born 13 August 1952 and married Robert Charlton **Coles Jr**. in Annadale, Va, 18 April 1998.
    6932 ii. Laura Melanie **Whipple**[202] born in Washington, D.C. 15 May 1955.

5883. **Elizabeth Ann**[12] **Simson** (Helen Loveland[11] **Patch**, Robert Charles[10], William Johnson[9], John[8], Joseph[7], Hannah[6] **Whipple**, Hannah[5], John[4], Lt. John[3], Matthew[2], Matthew[1])[203] birth date unknown, married **Robert Carman Bills Jr**. Robert is the son of Robert Carman **Bills** Sr. and Rozalia **Schwilk**.[204]

Robert Carman **Bills** Jr. and Elizabeth Ann **Simson** had the following child:
    6933 i. John Patch[13] **Bills**.[205]

5884. **Jane Craven**[12] **McHarg** (Henry King[11], Henry King[10], Martha Whipple[9] **Patch**, Martha[8] **Safford**, Martha[7] **Whipple**, John[6], Capt. John[5], John[4], Lt. John[3], Matthew[2], Matthew[1])[206] was born in New York, N.Y. 10 March 1912 and married **Homer Morrison Byington, Jr.** 21 September 1932.

Jane Craven **McHarg** and Homer Morrison **Byington**, Jr. had the following child:
    6934 i. Homer Morrison[13] **Byington**, III.[207]

5888. **Shirley Anne**[12] **Whipple** (Raymond Arthur[11], Arthur Eli[10], John Henry[9], John[8], Lt. Edward[7], John[6], Capt. John[5], John[4], Lt. John[3], Matthew[2], Matthew[1])[208] was born in 1928 and married **George C. Adams** in 1957. George, son of George **Adams** and Elizabeth **Covel**, was born in 1928.

Shirley Anne **Whipple** and George C. **Adams** had the following children:

    6935   i.   Borden[13] **Adams**.[209]
    6936   ii. Glenn **Adams**.[210]

5894. **Cynthia Adele**[12] **Wanstall** (Theodore Laurence[11], Lura Amelia[10] **Whipple**, John Henry[9], John[8], Lt. Edward[7], John[6], Capt. John[5], John[4], Lt. John[3], Matthew[2], Matthew[1])[211] was born 20 September 1938 and married **Ralph Stone**.

Cynthia Adele **Wanstall** and Ralph **Stone** had the following children:

    6937   i.   Christopher[13] **Stone**[212] born 14 December 1965 and died of leukemia in 1975 at 9 years of age.
    6938   ii. Kimberly **Stone**.[213]

5896. **George Elmer**[12] **Wanstall** (Elmer[11], Lura Amelia[10] **Whipple**, John Henry[9], John[8], Lt. Edward[7], John[6], Capt. John[5], John[4], Lt. John[3], Matthew[2], Matthew[1])[214] was born in South Bend, Ind. 16 April 1941 and married **Caroline McMaster Savage** in Baltimore, Md. 17 August 1963. Caroline,[215] daughter of Dr. John Edward **Savage** and Louise **Townsend**, was born in Baltimore 24 February 1941.

George and Caroline were graduated from the U. of Michigan in 1963 following which he spent two years as an infantry Lieutenant in the Army. Upon release from active duty, he entered the insurance field and became a Regional Employee Benefits Manager for Lincoln National Life Insurance Company. During the period 1967-87, he was assigned to their offices in Norfolk, Va., Milwaukee, Wisc., and Minneapolis, Minn. He then became a Vice President at the home office in Fort Wayne, Ind., leaving in 1993 to become an Employee Benefits Consultant in Minneapolis.

George Elmer **Wanstall** and Caroline McMaster **Savage** had the following children:

    6939   i.   Andrew Thompson[13] **Wanstall**[216] born in Ft. Polk, La. 21 May 1965 and married Samantha Aquene **Lomasi** in Edina, Minn. 26 September 1998.
    6940   ii. Margaret Louise **Wanstall**[217] born in Milwaukee, Wisc. 1 October 1967.

5898. **Bruce Eric**[12] **Wanstall** (Elmer[11], Lura Amelia[10] **Whipple**, John Henry[9], John[8], Lt. Edward[7], John[6], Capt. John[5], John[4], Lt. John[3], Matthew[2], Matthew[1])[218] was born in Chicago, Cook Co., Ill. 18 February 1952 and married **Sally Sue Morris** 7 April 1978. She is the daughter of Hank **Morris** and Martha (__).[219]

Bruce Eric **Wanstall** and Sally Sue **Morris** had the following children:
- 6941 i. Aaron Foster[13] **Wanstall**[220] born in Ketchikan, Alaska 31 October 1978.
- 6942 ii. Shayne Eric **Wanstall**[221] born in Ketchikan 21 November 1981.
- 6943 iii. Levi Brandon **Wanstall**[222] born in Ketchikan 6 May 1987.

5899. **Robert Edward**[12] **Spence** (Laura Barker[11] **Wanstall**, Lura Amelia[10] **Whipple**, John Henry[9], John[8], Lt. Edward[7], John[6], Capt. John[5], John[4], Lt. John[3], Matthew[2], Matthew[1])[223] was born 5 June 1940 and married **Marilee Day Rosenberg** in Conway, N.H. 7 March 1964. She was born 6 June 1944.[224]

Robert Edward **Spence** and Marilee Day **Rosenberg** had the following children:
- 6944 i. Jon Edward[13] **Spence**[225] born 19 October 1965.
- 6945 ii. Scott David **Spence**.[226]

5900. **Donald Arthur**[12] **Spence** (Laura Barker[11] **Wanstall**, Lura Amelia[10] **Whipple**, John Henry[9], John[8], Lt. Edward[7], John[6], Capt. John[5], John[4], Lt. John[3], Matthew[2], Matthew[1]) was born 14 February 1943 and married **Sue Ellen Paiton** in Auburn, Maine 29 August 1964.

Donald Arthur **Spence** and Sue Ellen **Paiton** had the following children:
- 6946 i. Matthew[13] **Spence**.[227]
- 6947 ii. Jonathan **Spence**.[228]

5903. **Robert**[12] **Kelley** (Gertrude Louise[11] **Wanstall**, Lura Amelia[10] **Whipple**, John Henry[9], John[8], Lt. Edward[7], John[6], Capt. John[5], John[4], Lt. John[3], Matthew[2], Matthew[1])[229] was born 28 November 1941 and married twice. (1) **Janet (__)**. (2) **Rosemarie (__)**.

Robert **Kelley** and Rosemarie (__) had the following children:
- 6948 i. James[13] **Kelley**[230] born in 1967 and married Robyn (__).
- 6949 ii. Cheryl **Kelley**[231] born in 1967.
- 6950 iii. Lisa **Kelley**[232] born in 1970.
- 6951 iv. Robert **Kelley** Jr.[233] born in 1974 and married an unnamed person.

5904. **David**[12] **Kelley** (Gertrude Louise[11] **Wanstall**, Lura Amelia[10] **Whipple**, John Henry[9], John[8], Lt. Edward[7], John[6], Capt. John[5], John[4], Lt. John[3], Matthew[2], Matthew[1])[234] was born 2 August 1944 and died 29 September 1992, at 48 years of age. He married **Clorinda (__)**.

David **Kelley** and Clorinda (__) had the following children:
  6952 i. Christia[13] **Kelley**[235] born 10 September 1965.
  6953 ii. David **Kelley** Jr.[236] born in 1969.

5905. **Dianne**[12] **Kelley** (Gertrude Louise[11] **Wanstall**, Lura Amelia[10] **Whipple**, John Henry[9], John[8], Lt. Edward[7], John[6], Capt. John[5], John[4], Lt. John[3], Matthew[2], Matthew[1])[237] was born 11 November 1946 and married **Walter Carroll** 6 February 1965.

Dianne **Kelley** and Walter **Carroll** had the following children:
  6954 i. Wendy Marie[13] **Carroll**[238] born 11 December 1965 and married Jim **Brianna.**
  6955 ii. Bonnie **Carroll**[239] born in 1969 and married Thomas **Kelsey.**
  6956 iii. Darlene **Carroll**[240] born in 1973 and married Walter (__).

5906. **Madelaine**[12] **Kelley** (Gertrude Louise[11] **Wanstall**, Lura Amelia[10] **Whipple**, John Henry[9], John[8], Lt. Edward[7], John[6], Capt. John[5], John[4], Lt. John[3], Matthew[2], Matthew[1]) was born 11 November 1946 and married **Michael Ostrowski**.

Madelaine **Kelley** and Michael **Ostrowski** had the following children:
  6957 i. Michael[13] **Ostrowski**[241] born 6 December 1965 and married Kim (__).
  6958 ii. Kerrie Ann **Ostrowski**[242] born in 1969.
  6959 iii. Robert **Ostrowski**[243] born in 1970.

5907. **Patricia**[12] **Kelley** (Gertrude Louise[11] **Wanstall**, Lura Amelia[10] **Whipple**, John Henry[9], John[8], Lt. Edward[7], John[6], Capt. John[5], John[4], Lt. John[3], Matthew[2], Matthew[1])[244] was born 1 March 1953 and married **James Lemonosky**.

Patricia **Kelley** and James **Lemonosky** had the following children:
  6960 i. Kathy[13] **Lemonosky.**[245]
  6961 ii. Linda **Lemonosky**[246] married **George Kastranakis**.

5908. **Richard Ogborn**[12] **Whipple** (Richard Randolph[11], Guy Montrose[10], John Francis[9], Daniel[8], William[7], William[6], Capt. John[5], John[4], Lt. John[3], Matthew[2], Matthew[1])[247] was born in 1930 and married **Mary Patricia Young** 1951. She was born in 1930.[248]

Richard Ogborn **Whipple** and Mary Patricia **Young** had the following children:

    6962   i.   Miles R.[13] **Whipple**[249] born in 1956.
    6963   ii.   Graham **Whipple**[250] born in 1958 and died in 1960 at 2 years of age.
    6964   iii.   Derek J. J. **Whipple**[251] born in 1960.
    6965   iv.   Kelin X. **Whipple**[252] born in 1963.
    6966   v.   Galen C. **Whipple**[253] born in 1965.
    6967   vi.   Quincy R. **Whipple**[254] born in 1967.

5909. **Cornelia Jane**[12] **Whipple** (Richard Randolph[11], Guy Montrose[10], John Francis[9], Daniel[8], William[7], William[6], Capt. John[5], John[4], Lt. John[3], Matthew[2], Matthew[1])[255] was born in 1933 and married **F. Chandler Coddington Jr.** 1955. H was born in 1932.[256]

Cornelia Jane **Whipple** and F. Chandler **Coddington** Jr. had the following children:

    6968   i.   Gail E.[13] **Coddington**[257] born in 1957.
    6969   ii.   Linda G. **Coddington**[258] born in 1958.
    6970   iii.   Clara J. **Coddington**[259] born in 1962.

5912. **Bryan Randolph Rogers**[12] **Whipple** (Guy Montrose[11], Guy Montrose[10], John Francis[9], Daniel[8], William[7], William[6], Capt. John[5], John[4], Lt. John[3], Matthew[2], Matthew[1])[260] was born in Detroit, Mich. 1 March 1940 and married **Krista Ann Knudsen** in San Francisco, Calif. 28 October 1972. She is the daughter of Jan Augith **Knudsen** and Helen **Kumm**.[261] Bryan was graduated from the U. of Michigan in 1961 with a B.S.E. degree in Industrial Engineering and an M.B.A. in 1962. He has also taken postgraduate law training by correspondence. His work experience has been with railroads begining in 1962 as a Brakeman with the Southern Pacific Transportation Co. at Roseville and San Francisco rising to Senior Transportation Analyst. In 1973-74, he co-founded and managed the Freedom Train Project, Inc. which built the Rolling Museum Train for the 1975-76 Bicentennial Tour. He became a Vice President at PLM, Inc. a financial services firm specializing in railroad car leasing and repair, bulk transportations systems, etc. and has years of experience in the operating, marketing, and executive departments of Class I railroads. He is also a Consultant to railroads and rail-equipment leasing companies.

Bryan Randolph Rogers **Whipple** and Krista Ann **Knudsen** had the following children:

    6971   i.   Marisa Sarah[13] **Whipple**[262] born in San Francisco 11 June 1973.

　　　　6972　ii.　John Matthew **Whipple**[263] born in Berkeley, Calif. 3 June 1977.

5913. **William Stark**[12] **Whipple Jr.** (William S.[11], Herman M.[10], William Stark[9], John[8], Charles[7], Benjamin[6], Capt. John[5], John[4], Lt. John[3], Matthew[2], Matthew[1])[264] was born in Goffstown, N.H. 30 September 1945 and married **Kathryn Jean Starr** in Shawnee, Okla. 11 November 1967. Jean,[265] daughter of Jack **Starr** and Glendon Jean **Hebbe**, was born in Garden City, Kans. 11 October 1945. William retired as a Major from the U.S. Air Force in 1989.

William Stark **Whipple** Jr. and Kathryn Jean **Starr** had the following children:
　　　　6973　i.　William Stark[13] **Whipple** III[266] born at Maxwell AFB, Ala. 1 April 1970.
　　　　6974　ii.　Lisa Marie **Whipple**[267] born at Maxwell AFB 15 October 1971.
　　　　6975　iii.　Jennifer Lynn **Whipple**[268] born in Grand Junction, Colo. 6 November 1973. Adopted.

5914. **Gayle**[12] **Whipple** (Earle C.[11], George H.[10], Amos Woodbury[9], John[8], Charles[7], Benjamin[6], Capt. John[5], John[4], Lt. John[3], Matthew[2], Matthew[1])[269] was born in Goffstown, N.H. 15 June 1926 and married **Stephen Shost**.

Gayle **Whipple** and Stephen **Shost** had the following children:
　　　　6976　i.　Gregory[13] **Shost**[270] born in 1947 and married Carolyn **Kotarba** 1977. She is the daughter of Walter **Kotarba** and Mary (__).[271]
　　　　6977　ii.　Stephanie **Shost**[272] born in 1950 and married Larry **Jost** in 1981. He is the son of Dean **Jost** and Polly (__).[273]
　　　　6978　iii.　Duston **Shost**[274] born in 1955 and married Betty Ann **Rogers** in 1976. She is the daughter of Herbert **Rogers** and Yvonne (__).[275]
　　　　6979　iv.　Brandin **Shost**[276] born in 1958 and married Lise **Bofinger** 1983. She is the daughter of Paul **Bofinger** and Lenita (__).[277]

5915. **Janet**[12] **Whipple** (Earle C.[11], George H.[10], Amos Woodbury[9], John[8], Charles[7], Benjamin[6], Capt. John[5], John[4], Lt. John[3], Matthew[2], Matthew[1])[278] was born in Goffstown, N.H. 16 June 1930 and married **Deane Harris Morrison II** 3 March 1951. Deane,[279] son of Deane Harris **Morrison** and Isadora **Flanders**, was born in 1929 and died 25 February 1981, at 51 years of age.

Janet **Whipple** and Deane Harris **Morrison** II had the following children:
- 6980   i.   Deane Harris[13] **Morrison** III[280] born 7 June 1952.
- 6981   ii. David Earle **Morrison**[281] born 24 May 1954.
- 6982   iii. Gayle **Morrison**[282] born 25 March 1959.

5916. **Donald I.**[12] **Whipple** (Stanley I.[11], George H.[10], Amos Woodbury[9], John[8], Charles[7], Benjamin[6], Capt. John[5], John[4], Lt. John[3], Matthew[2], Matthew[1])[283] was born in Manchester, N.H. 29 December 1921 and married **Madlyn F. Moore** in Concord, Rockingham Co., N.H. 19 March 1945. Madlyn,[284] daughter of Ronald G. **Moore** and Kathleen F. **Rogers**, was born in Moncton, New Brunswick, Canada 17 February 1923. Donald attended public schools in Concord, joined the U.S. Navy in 1942, and was a commissioned Naval Aviator. He joined the Concord Electric Co. in 1950, retiring in 1986 as Assistant Vice President for Operations. He and Nancy lived in Concord in 1999.

Donald I. **Whipple** and Madlyn F. **Moore** had the following children:
- + 6983   i.   William Roger[13] **Whipple** born 5 June 1949.
-   6984   ii. James Irving **Whipple**[285] born in Concord 2 April 1952.

5917. **Richard Earle**[12] **Whipple** (Stanley I.[11], George H.[10], Amos Woodbury[9], John[8], Charles[7], Benjamin[6], Capt. John[5], John[4], Lt. John[3], Matthew[2], Matthew[1])[286] was born in Manchester, N.H. 18 July 1923 and married **Jane Eleanor Taylor** in Concord, Rockingham Co., N.H. 21 September 1947. She is the daughter of Linley H. **Taylor** and Bessie H. **Johnson**.[287]

Richard Earle **Whipple** and Jane Eleanor **Taylor** had the following children:
- 6985   i.   John[13] **Whipple**[288] born in Schenectady, N.Y. 4 February 1952.
- 6986   ii. Thomas **Whipple**[289] born in Laconia, N.H. 30 April 1955.
- 6987   iii. Richard Earle **Whipple** Jr.[290] born in Rochester, N.H. 16 December 1958. He was a Radioman in the U.S. Navy during WWII and earned an Electrical Engineering degree from the U. of N.H. He is retired.

5918. **Nancy**[12] **Litchfield** (Olive E.[11] **Whipple**, George H.[10], Amos Woodbury[9], John[8], Charles[7], Benjamin[6], Capt. John[5], John[4], Lt. John[3], Matthew[2], Matthew[1])[291] was born 20 July 1932 and married **Edward Chandler** 4 August 1950.

Nancy **Litchfield** and Edward **Chandler** had the following child:
- 6988   i.   Kathleen[13] **Chandler**[292] born 9 September 1952 and married twice: In December 1971 and 18 Aug. 1978. She was

divorced from both husbands. No information provided on their idenity.

5919. **Carol**[12] **Litchfield** (Olive E.[11] **Whipple**, George H.[10], Amos Woodbury[9], John[8], Charles[7], Benjamin[6], Capt. John[5], John[4], Lt. John[3], Matthew[2], Matthew[1])[293] was born 19 July 1934 and died 6 February 1985 at 50 years of age. She married **Charles Stenbeck** 8 October 1953.

Carol **Litchfield** and Charles **Stenbeck** had the following children:
- 6989 i. Frederick Randolph[13] **Stenbeck**[294] born 18 July 1954.
- 6990 ii. Lawrence **Stenbeck**[295] born 10 June 1956.

5920. **Thaddeus**[12] **Litchfield** (Olive E.[11] **Whipple**, George H.[10], Amos Woodbury[9], John[8], Charles[7], Benjamin[6], Capt. John[5], John[4], Lt. John[3], Matthew[2], Matthew[1])[296] was born 4 July 1935 and married **Helen Ann McCarthy** 25 April 1956. She was born 25 April 1936.[297]

Thaddeus **Litchfield** and Helen Ann **McCarthy** had the following children:
- 6991 i. Cheryl[13] **Litchfield**[298] born 14 July 1958 and married John C. **Senge**.
- 6992 ii. Valerie **Litchfield**[299] born 12 February 1960 and married Matthew **Salven**.
- 6993 iii. David **Litchfield**[300] born 14 May 1963.
- 6994 iv. Mary Beth **Litchfield**[301] born 15 April 1966.

5921. **Willard**[12] **Litchfield** (Olive E.[11] **Whipple**, George H.[10], Amos Woodbury[9], John[8], Charles[7], Benjamin[6], Capt. John[5], John[4], Lt. John[3], Matthew[2], Matthew[1])[302] was born 28 February 1941 and married **Marilyn Maxwell**.

Willard **Litchfield** and Marilyn **Maxwell** had the following children:
- 6995 i. Daniel[13] **Litchfield**[303] born 1 January 1973.
- 6996 ii. Matthas **Litchfield**[304] born 22 May 1976.

5923. **Lila Lee**[12] **Packard** (Merle Everett[11], Horace Sherman[10], Ebenezer James[9], Hosea[8], Dea. Zenas[7], Mary[6] **Perkins**, Dorothy[5] **Whipple**, Matthew[4], Lt. John[3], Matthew[2], Matthew[1])[305] was born 30 September 1924 and married twice. (1) **Harry George Woodworth Jr.** in Brown Co., Tex. 10 April 1943. Harry,[306] son of Harry George **Woodworth** and Agnes Frances **Samuelson**, was born in Brockton, Plymouth Co., Mass. 1 June 1924 and died 25 December 1944 in Europe, at 20 years of age. He was killed during the Battle of the Bulge in Europe in WWII. (2) **Tony Raymond Paparo** in Brockton 26 June 1965.

Lila Lee **Packard** and Harry George **Woodworth** Jr. had the following child born in Brockton:

    6997   i.   Harry George Joseph[13] **Woodworth**[307] 13 December 1943. Through his great great grandmother Almira D. Smith, wife of Norman G. Makepeace, Harry descends from Elder John Whipple of Ipswich and therefore has double descent from Matthew Whipple, Clothier of Bocking, England.

5925. **Elizabeth Rebecca**[12] **Whipple** (Lewis Grant[11], William Lewis[10], Heman[9], David[8], Eleazer[7], Eleazer[6], Nathan[5], Matthew[4], Lt. John[3], Matthew[2], Matthew[1]) birth date unknown, died in August 1991. She married **Leon Melvin Butler** in 1923.

Elizabeth Rebecca **Whipple** and Leon Melvin **Butler** had the following children:

    6998   i.   Leon Melvin[13] **Butler** Jr. died in February 1961.
    6999   ii.   Lt. Col. Charles Lewis **Butler** died in 1972 in Vietnam.
    7000   iii.   Jayne **Butler** born in Waterville, Maine in 1925.
    7001   iv.   Elizabeth Rebecca **Butler** born in Waterville in 1925.

5927. **Inez Eunice**[12] **Hamilton** (Jessie M.[11] **Washburn**, Lillian Jane[10] **Corson**, Jane[9] **Whipple**, John[8], Eleazer[7], Eleazer[6], Nathan[5], Matthew[4], Lt. John[3], Matthew[2], Matthew[1])[308] was born in Bingham, Maine 9 October 1909 and married twice. (1) **Winston Fayette Weller** in Boston, Mass. 19 December 1931. He was born in Chicago, Ill. 1 August 1906 and died 29 October 1938 in Westwood, Mass., at 32 years of age. (2) **Calvin Eugene Lair** 1 January 1941. He was born in Topeka, Shawnee Co., Kans. 29 July 1912 and died 27 May 1993 in Seattle, Wash., at 80 years of age.[309]

Inez Eunice **Hamilton** and Winston Fayette **Weller** had the following children:

  +   7002   i.   Nancy Jane[13] **Weller** born 26 September 1932.
  +   7003   ii.   Joanne **Weller** born 4 January 1935.

Inez Eunice **Hamilton** and Calvin Eugene **Lair** had the following child:

    7004   iii.   Mary Christina **Lair**[310] born in Salt Lake City, Utah 3 July 1941 and married **Geoffrey S. Ruskin.**

5929. **Julia Mabel**[12] **Smith** (Caroline May[11] **Campbell**, Lewis Cass[10], Lydia[9] **Averill**, Gideon[8], Bethia[7] **Whipple**, Zebulon[6], Samuel[5], Cyprian[4], Lt. John[3], Matthew[2], Matthew[1])[311] was born in Port Orchard, Wash. 21

July 1917 and married **Hubert Joseph Moller** 2 December 1944. Hubert,[312] son of Henry Christian **Moller** and Anna Rosaria **Kuhn**, was born in Gig Harbor, Wash. 20 April 1914.

Julia Mabel **Smith** and Hubert Joseph **Moller** had the following child:
- 7005 i. Nancy Ann[13] **Moller**[313] born in Tacoma, Pierce Co., Wash. 18 November 1946 and married Harold James **Ross Jr.** in Seattle, Wash. 8 November 1973. He was born in Seattle 7 January 1951.[314]

5930. **Lynn Ellen**[12] **Reighard** (William Madison[11], Ada[10] **Whipple**, George W.[9], John Russell[8], Zebulon[7], Zebulon[6], Samuel[5], Cyprian[4], Lt. John[3], Matthew[2], Matthew[1])[315] was born in Oakland, Calif. 5 December 1951 and married **Michael A. French** in Cupertino, Calif. 4 May 1974. He was born in Sacramento, Calif. 3 June 1949.[316]

Lynn Ellen **Reighard** and Michael A. **French** had the following children born in Kansas City, Mo:
- 7006 i. Jessica Ruth[13] **French**[317] 17 September 1979.
- 7007 ii. Kimberly Lynn **French**[318] 9 January 1982.

5931. **Joan Elise**[12] **Reighard** (William Madison[11], Ada[10] **Whipple**, George W.[9], John Russell[8], Zebulon[7], Zebulon[6], Samuel[5], Cyprian[4], Lt. John[3], Matthew[2], Matthew[1])[319] was born in Lodi, Calif. 5 March 1954 and married **David Andrew Cooper** in Palo Alto, Santa Clara Co., Calif. 12 May 1979. David,[320] son of William **Cooper** and Cynthia (__), was born in Pittsburgh, Penn. 2 January 1953.

Joan Elise **Reighard** and David Andrew **Cooper** had the following children born in Mountain View, Santa Clara, Co., Calif.:
- 7008 i. Michelle Ann[13] **Cooper**[321] 25 January 1981.
- 7009 ii. Katherine Faith **Cooper**[322] 1 January 1984.
- 7010 iii. Christopher William **Cooper**[323] 24 May 1986.

5932. **Eva Muryl**[12] **Shannon** (Maude Belle[11] **Kennison**, America Martha Jane[10] **Walker**, Calvin Augustus[9], Lydia[8] **Whipple**, Zebulon[7], Zebulon[6], Samuel[5], Cyprian[4], Lt. John[3], Matthew[2], Matthew[1])[324] was born in Clarksville, Butler Co., Iowa 28 July 1896 and died 8 October 1979 in Hampton, Franklin Co., Iowa, at 83 years of age. Buried Mt. Hope Cemetery, Waterloo, Iowa. She married **James Austin McCleary** in Sioux Falls, S. Dak. 4 October 1916.

Eva Muryl **Shannon** and James Austin **McCleary** had the following children:
+ 7011 i. Eileen Lucille[13] **McCleary** born 27 July 1920.
+ 7012 ii. James A. **McCleary** born 6 August 1929.

5947. **Ernin Emil**[12] **Frank** (Jessie May[11] **Thornton**, Clara May[10] **Walker**, Luther Martin[9], Lydia[8] **Whipple**, Zebulon[7], Zebulon[6], Samuel[5], Cyprian[4], Lt. John[3], Matthew[2], Matthew[1])[325] was born in Stanton, Stanton Co., Nebr. 16 January 1925 and married **Lenice Marie Koza** at St. Peter's Roman Catholic Church in Stanton 30 December 1944. Lenice,[326] daughter of Ben L. **Koza** and Marie J. **Seneca**, was born in Stanton 9 April 1925.

Ernin Emil **Frank** and Lenice Marie **Koza** had the following child born in Norfolk, Madison Co. Nebr.:
7013 i. Donald Ernin[13] **Frank** 24 April 1948.[327]

5948. **Clara Katherine**[12] **Frank** (Jessie May[11] **Thornton**, Clara May[10] **Walker**, Luther Martin[9], Lydia[8] **Whipple**, Zebulon[7], Zebulon[6], Samuel[5], Cyprian[4], Lt. John[3], Matthew[2], Matthew[1])[328] was born in Stanton, Stanton Co., Nebr. 14 September 1934 and married **Lloyd Frank Molacek** in Stanton 8 October 1953. Lloyd,[329] son of Joseph **Molacek** and Emma **Vacha**, was born in Howells, Nebr.

Clara Katherine **Frank** and Lloyd Frank **Molacek** had the following children born in Norfolk, Madison Co., Nebr.:
7014 i. Teresa Kay[13] **Molacek** in 1955.[330]
7015 ii. Cindy Jo **Molacek** 27 December 1956.[331]
7016 iii. Daniel Lloyd **Molacek** 24 May 1959.[332]
7017 iv. Patricia Ann **Molacek** 20 May 1960.[333]
7018 v. James Frank **Molacek** 23 June 1964.[334]

5949. **Doris Irene**[12] **Graham** (Goldie Helen[11] **Thornton**, Clara May[10] **Walker**, Luther Martin[9], Lydia[8] **Whipple**, Zebulon[7], Zebulon[6], Samuel[5], Cyprian[4], Lt. John[3], Matthew[2], Matthew[1])[335] was born in Louisville, Nebr. 26 December 1925 and married **Dayton Hennings**. Dayton,[336] son of Albert **Hennings** and Dora **Gauer**, was born in Hiawatha, Kans. 18 April 1923.

Doris Irene **Graham** and Dayton **Hennings** had the following children born in Omaha, Nebr.:
7019 i. Shirley Ann[13] **Hennings** 25 May 1949.[337]
7020 ii. Robert Charles **Hennings** 13 December 1951.[338]

7021 iii. Cathy Jo **Hennings** 12 April 1953.[339]
7022 iv. James Lee **Hennings** 4 January 1955.[340]

5950. **Betty Mae**[12] **Graham** (Goldie Helen[11] **Thornton**, Clara May[10] **Walker**, Luther Martin[9], Lydia[8] **Whipple**, Zebulon[7], Zebulon[6], Samuel[5], Cyprian[4], Lt. John[3], Matthew[2], Matthew[1])[341] was born in Louisville, Nebr. 7 September 1928 and married **Arnold Vogler** there 8 June 1947. He was born 15 January 1923.[342]

Betty Mae **Graham** and Arnold **Vogler** had the following child:
7023 i. Marvin[13] **Vogler** born 30 March 1951.[343]

5955. **Lewis Dale**[12] **Whipple** (Andrew Jackson[11], Andrew Bina[10], Andrew Jackson[9], Zebulon[8], Zebulon[7], Zebulon[6], Samuel[5], Cyprian[4], Lt. John[3], Matthew[2], Matthew[1])[344] was born in Conneaut, Ohio 4 August 1930 and married **Dorothy P. Cook** in Lewisville, Ark. 21 April 1950. Dorothy,[345] daughter of Loyce H. **Cook** and Oma **Hammontree**, was born in Plain Dealing, La. 3 November 1933. Lewis spent four years on active duty with the U.S. Air Force (1948-52). He was a part of the Army of Occupation in Japan, served at Celle Royal Air Force Station in Germany during the Berlin Airlift, and served during the Korean War. He joined the Caterpillar Tractor Co. after military service and retired to Louisiana after 30 years service, the last five years in Spokane, Wash. His retirement years are spent traveling, occasional consulting work for Caterpillar, and as Commander of the VFW Post.

Lewis Dale **Whipple** and Dorothy P. **Cook** had the following children:
+ 7024 i. Julia Ann[13] **Whipple** born 25 March 1955.
+ 7025 ii. Debra Ellen **Whipple** born 27 September 1956.

5956. **Graedon**[12] **Whipple** (Paul Darius[11], Andrew Bina[10], Andrew Jackson[9], Zebulon[8], Zebulon[7], Zebulon[6], Samuel[5], Cyprian[4], Lt. John[3], Matthew[2], Matthew[1])[346] birth date unknown, married **Ralph Hunt**.

Graedon **Whipple** and Ralph **Hunt** had the following children:
+ 7026 i. Judith Joy[13] **Hunt**.
+ 7027 ii. Diane Gay **Hunt**.
  7028 iii. Ralph Neal **Hunt**[347] married Virginia Sue **Long.**
+ 7029 iv. Mary Ann **Hunt**.

5957. **Sherman**[12] **Whipple** (Paul Darius[11], Andrew Bina[10], Andrew Jackson[9], Zebulon[8], Zebulon[7], Zebulon[6], Samuel[5], Cyprian[4], Lt. John[3], Matthew[2], Matthew[1])[348] birth date unknown, married twice. (1) **Jean Higley**. (2) **Kathleen Lavvorn**.

Sherman **Whipple** and Jean **Higley** had the following children:
    7030   i.   Richard Allen[13] **Whipple**.[349]
    7031   ii.   Duane Douglas **Whipple**.[350]

5958. **Phyllis Martha**[12] **Whipple** (Paul Darius[11], Andrew Bina[10], Andrew Jackson[9], Zebulon[8], Zebulon[7], Zebulon[6], Samuel[5], Cyprian[4], Lt. John[3], Matthew[2], Matthew[1])[351] birth date unknown, married **Paul Carnell**.

Phyllis Martha **Whipple** and Paul **Carnell** had the following children:
    7032   i.   Nancy Lou[13] **Carnell**.[352]
    7033   ii.   Cheryl Ann **Carnell**.[353]
    7034   iii.   Cara **Carnell**.[354]
    7035   iv.   Michael Paul **Carnell**.[355]
    7036   v.   Beth Irene **Carnell**.[356]

5959. **Paul Darius**[12] **Whipple Jr.** (Paul Darius[11], Andrew Bina[10], Andrew Jackson[9], Zebulon[8], Zebulon[7], Zebulon[6], Samuel[5], Cyprian[4], Lt. John[3], Matthew[2], Matthew[1])[357] was born in Conneaut, Ohio 17 March 1924 and married **Dorla Kathryn Olds**. Dorla,[358] daughter of Orin Kenneth **Olds** and Ethel Beatrice **Vosburgh**, was born in Sayre, Penn. 12 June 1928.

Paul Darius **Whipple** Jr. and Dorla Kathryn **Olds** had the following children:
+   7037   i.   Douglas Paul[13] **Whipple**.
    7038   ii.   Patti Lynn **Whipple**.[359]
    7039   iii.   David Lee **Whipple**[360] born in Boston, Mass. 4 May 1951.

5964. **Kenneth William Russel**[12] **Canaday** (Ida Adelle[11] **Whipple**, Russel Loring[10], Josiah Loring[9], Josiah Russell[8], Zebulon[7], Zebulon[6], Samuel[5], Cyprian[4], Lt. John[3], Matthew[2], Matthew[1])[361] was born in Kansas City, Jackson Co., Mo. 10 February 1909 and married twice. (1) **Dorothy Mary Engel**. She was born 29 July 1911.[362] (2) **June Elizabeth Jackson**. June,[363] daughter of Luther Richard **Jackson** and Potomac Alice "Lottie" **Petrie**, was born in Kansas City 2 February 1919 and died 23 April 2001 in Marble Falls, Tex., at 82 years of age.

Kenneth William Russel **Canaday** and Dorothy Mary **Engel** had the following children born in Kansas City:

    7040   i.   Barbara Kay[13] **Canaday**[364] 3 July 1936.

    7041   ii.   Sharon Rose **Canaday**[365] 16 March 1944.

    7042   iii.   Shirley Sue **Canaday**[366] 16 March 1944 and married George Thomas **Kinney.**

Kenneth William Russel **Canaday** and June Elizabeth **Jackson** had the following child born in Denver, Colo.:

    7043   iv.   April LaRoe **Canaday**[367] 13 September 1952 and married Peter William **Messerschmidt.** He was born in Copenhagen, Denmark 30 August 1960.[368]

5968. **Esther Laura**[12] **Reinhardt** (Stella Sybile[11] **Corwin**, Laura Marie[10] **Whipple**, Henry Frederick[9], Josiah Russell[8], Zebulon[7], Zebulon[6], Samuel[5], Cyprian[4], Lt. John[3], Matthew[2], Matthew[1])[369] was born in Cedar Falls, Black Hawk Co., Iowa 9 January 1925 and married **James Henry Newcomer** in Sadalia, Pettis Co., Mo. 29 July 1941. James,[370] son of Raymond **Newcomer** and Nettie **Logston**, was born in Waterloo, Black Hawk Co., Iowa 11 September 1920.

Esther Laura **Reinhardt** and James Henry **Newcomer** had the following children born in Cedar Falls:

    7044   i.   James Ralph[13] **Newcomer**[371] 20 October 1942. He married twice. (1) Sandra Lee **Sommer** in Preston, Minn. 26 June 1965. (2) Barbara Jo **Fennern** in Waterloo 9 June 1973.

    7045   ii.   Henry Lewis **Newcomer**[372] 15 October 1944 and married Mary Kay **Schneider** 26 October 1964.

    7046   iii.   Edward Dean **Newcomer**[373] 22 March 1947 and married Veronica Lee **Dean** 6 June 1965.

    7047   iv.   Carolyn Ruth **Newcomer**[374] 1 August 1948 and married James Glenn **Card** 19 December 1964.

5970. **Irma**[12] **Butterfield** (Glen[11], Caroline[10] **Cobb**, Julia[9] **Whipple**, William[8], Zebulon[7], Zebulon[6], Samuel[5], Cyprian[4], Lt. John[3], Matthew[2], Matthew[1])[375] was born in Venus, Nebr. 16 July 1916 and married twice. (1) **Milton A. Andrus** 30 June 1934. He was born 19 October 1914 and died 14 June 1960 at 45 years of age.[376] (2) **Hershal L. Halstead** 19 August 1961. They were living at Atkinson, Nebr. in 1969.

Irma **Butterfield** and Milton A. **Andrus** had the following children born in Atkinson:
- \+   7048   i.   Sharon Loree[13] **Andrus** 6 October 1935.
-      7049   ii.   Ronald Dean **Andrus**[377] 16 January 1938 and died there 15 November 1941, at 3 years of age.

5971. **Orma Jeanne**[12] **Butterfield** (Glen[11], Caroline[10] **Cobb**, Julia[9] **Whipple**, William[8], Zebulon[7], Zebulon[6], Samuel[5], Cyprian[4], Lt. John[3], Matthew[2], Matthew[1])[378] was born in Orchard, Nebr. 24 November 1929 and married **Leland C. Anderson** 1 May 1949.

Orma Jeanne **Butterfield** and Leland C. **Anderson** had the following children:
-      7050   i.   Glen[13] **Anderson** born in 1951.[379]
-      7051   ii.   Cathy Ann **Anderson** born in 1953.[380]
-      7052   iii.   Kevin **Anderson** born in 1957.[381]
-      7053   iv.   Bryan **Anderson** born in 1959.[382]
-      7054   v.   Heidi **Anderson** born in 1962.[383]

5975. **Richard Raybold**[12] **Whipple** (Harvey Abbott[11], Arthur[10], Zebulon[9], Henry[8], Joseph[7], Zebulon[6], Samuel[5], Cyprian[4], Lt. John[3], Matthew[2], Matthew[1])[384] was born 5 May 1924 and died 10 April 1987 at 62 years of age. He married **Sally deVeer** 16 June 1951.

Richard Raybold **Whipple** and Sally **deVeer** had the following children:
- \+   7055   i.   Cynthia Lee[13] **Whipple** born 5 July 1953.
- \+   7056   ii.   Richard Raybold **Whipple** Jr. born 8 May 1955.
- \+   7057   iii.   Robert deVeer **Whipple** born 26 August 1968.

5976. **Shirley Virginia**[12] **Whipple** (Harvey Abbott[11], Arthur[10], Zebulon[9], Henry[8], Joseph[7], Zebulon[6], Samuel[5], Cyprian[4], Lt. John[3], Matthew[2], Matthew[1])[385] was born in Providence, R.I. 9 April 1927 and married **Ralph Hinds** 2 April 1950.

Shirley Virginia **Whipple** and Ralph **Hinds** had the following children:
- \+   7058   i.   Ralph Winthrop[13] **Hinds** born 5 May 1951.
- \+   7059   ii.   Jeffrey Allan **Hinds** born 30 May 1952.
- \+   7060   iii.   Meredith Virginia **Hinds** born 10 March 1954.
-      7061   iv.   Kimberly Anita **Hinds**[386] born 20 December 1955 and married Kelly Gene **O'Brien** in Ripon, Wisc. 11 July 1977.
- \+   7062   v.   Pamela Marion **Hinds** born 12 November 1959.

5977. **Harvey Abbott**[12] **Whipple II** (Harvey Abbott[11], Arthur[10], Zebulon[9], Henry[8], Joseph[7], Zebulon[6], Samuel[5], Cyprian[4], Lt. John[3], Matthew[2], Matthew[1])[387] was born 5 July 1928 and married **Lesa Ann McNulty** in East Providence, R.I. 29 January 1955.

Harvey Abbott **Whipple** II and Lesa Ann **McNulty** had the following children:

- \+ 7063 i. Harvey Abbott[13] **Whipple** III born 24 August 1955.
- \+ 7064 ii. Lesa Ann **Whipple** born 2 December 1956.
- \+ 7065 iii. Sharon Mary **Whipple** born 26 December 1957.
- 7066 iv. David Braytonn **Whipple**[388] born in Providence 29 November 1958.
- \+ 7067 v. Kevin Karl **Whipple** born 2 July 1960.
- 7068 vi. Leslie Marion **Whipple** born in Providence 19 October 1961.
- \+ 7069 vii. Dorian Virginia **Whipple** born 12 March 1963.
- 7070 viii. Andred Raybold **Whipple**[389] born in Providence 13 May 1964.
- \+ 7071 ix. Nathan Waterman **Whipple** born 22 March 1967.

5978. **Kingsley Allan**[12] **Whipple** (Harvey Abbott[11], Arthur[10], Zebulon[9], Henry[8], Joseph[7], Zebulon[6], Samuel[5], Cyprian[4], Lt. John[3], Matthew[2], Matthew[1])[390] was born 20 February 1932 and married **Rose Marie Gregorie** 30 December 1961.

Kingsley Allan **Whipple** and Rose Marie **Gregorie** had the following children:

- \+ 7072 i. Marion Raybold[13] **Whipple** born 16 November 1962.
- 7073 ii. Kingsley Allan **Whipple** Jr.[391] born 16 January 1964.
- 7074 iii. Gregory Lawrence **Whipple**[392] born 1 May 1965 and married Kristine **Olson** in Kingston, R.I. 5 August 1989.

5979. **Christopher David**[12] **Whipple** (Harvey Abbott[11], Arthur[10], Zebulon[9], Henry[8], Joseph[7], Zebulon[6], Samuel[5], Cyprian[4], Lt. John[3], Matthew[2], Matthew[1])[393] was born 13 June 1968 and married **Lisa Dewether** 19 November 1988.

Christopher David **Whipple** and Lisa **Dewether** had the following children:

- 7075 i. Christopher David[13] **Whipple** Jr.[394]
- 7076 ii. Caroline Rose **Whipple**.[395]

5980. **Josephine Elizabeth**[12] **Spencer** (Hazel Susan[11] **Sanford**, Norman N.[10], Diantha[9] **Jones**, Oliver[8], Polly[7] **Whipple**, Zebulon[6], Samuel[5], Cyprian[4], Lt. John[3], Matthew[2], Matthew[1])[396] was born in Shelton, Mason Co., Wash. 17 October 1924 and died 4 March 1968 in Central Point,

{ G 1041 }

Oreg., at 43 years of age. She married **John Joseph Matthias** in Seattle, Wash. in 1942. He was born in Washburn, Bayfield Co., Wisc. 30 June 1920.[397]

Josephine Elizabeth **Spencer** and John Joseph **Matthias** had the following child:

    7077 i. Frances Charlotte[13] **Matthias**[398] born in San Bernardino, Calif. 2 July 1944 and married **John Floyd Mitchell** in Idaho 13 July 1964.

5985. **Grace Irene**[12] **Whipple** (Oran Porter[11], Joseph Walter[10], Jonathan Jones[9], Joseph[8], David[7], Samuel[6], Samuel[5], Cyprian[4], Lt. John[3], Matthew[2], Matthew[1])[399] was born in Ludlow, Pueblo Co., Colo. 5 May 1901 and died 18 July 1983 in Thousand Oaks, Ventura Co., Calif., at 82 years of age. She married **Ralph Albert Moore** in Argonia, Sumner Co., Kans. 5 October 1921. Ralph,[400] son of Jerome Fairbanks **Moore** and Agnes Armilla **Jesseph**, was born in Argonia 15 March 1897 and died 25 May 1966 in North Hollywood, Los Angeles Co., Calif., at 69 years of age. Ralph was a railroad Conductor. He served duing WWI with the 1st Co., 164th D.B. Battalion. Grace was a dressmaker and is buried in Glendale, Los Angeles Co., Calif.

Grace Irene **Whipple** and Ralph Albert **Moore** had the following children:

    7078 i. Wesley Wayne[13] **Moore**[401] born in Wichita, Sedgwick Co., Kans. 16 July 1922 and died 14 July 1943 in Sicily, Italy, at 20 years of age. A member of the U. S. Army during WWII, he was killed in the invasion of Sicily.
+ 7079 ii. Barbara Joanna **Moore** born 22 January 1928.

5995. **Grace**[12] **Whipple** (Henry Learned[11], Dr. Alfred Augustus[10], Henry Francisco[9], Joseph[8], David[7], Samuel[6], Samuel[5], Cyprian[4], Lt. John[3], Matthew[2], Matthew[1])[402] was born 20 August 1896 and died 29 October 1926 at 30 years of age. She married **Clement Casper Spencer**.

Grace **Whipple** and Clement Casper **Spencer** had the following children:

    7080 i. Charles Reed[13] **Spencer**[403] born in Quincy, Adams Co., Ill. 11 December 1918 and died 30 January 1944 during WWII in Italy, at 25 years of age.
    7081 ii. Richard Henry **Spencer**[404] born 27 June 1920.
    7082 iii. Stephen Lee **Spencer**[405] born 2 September 1922.

5996. **Arthur Paul**[12] **Whipple** (Merritt Pendell[11], Dr. Alfred Augustus[10], Henry Francisco[9], Joseph[8], David[7], Samuel[6], Samuel[5], Cyprian[4], Lt. John[3], Matthew[2], Matthew[1])[406] was born in Quincy, Adams Co., Ill. 17 July 1901 and died 27 November 1937 in Louisville, Ky., at 36 years of age. He married **Adele Mildred Miller** in Miami, Dade Co., Fla. 4 February 1928. Adele,[407] daughter of Charles **Miller** and Laura **Hardsaw**, was born in Princeton, Gibson Co., Ind. 12 November 1899 and died 20 March 1990 in Ponca City, Okla., at 90 years of age.

Arthur Paul **Whipple** and Adele Mildred **Miller** had the following children:

+ 7083 i. Arthur Paul[13] **Whipple** II born 11 December 1929.
+ 7084 ii. Nelson Frank Gordon **Whipple** born 2 December 1931.

5998. **Virginia Dallas**[12] **Whipple** (Merritt Pendell[11], Dr. Alfred Augustus[10], Henry Francisco[9], Joseph[8], David[7], Samuel[6], Samuel[5], Cyprian[4], Lt. John[3], Matthew[2], Matthew[1])[408] was born in Dallas, Tex. 25 June 1907 and died in 1989 at 82 years of age. She married twice. (1) **Wilfred Lee Brooke** in Rochester, Monroe Co., N.Y. 19 September 1927. Wilfred, son of Fred L. **Brooke** and Mina (__), was born in Oak Park Cook Co., Ill. abt 1904 and died there 1 November 1971, at 67 years of age. He was known as Bill and was the owner of the Fred L. Brooke Co., a colors, minerals, and solvents importer and broker to the paint varnish, lacquer, and printing ink industries. In later years he was a Vice President of Restaurant Management Corporation and a Sales Executive for VBrooke Inns, Inc. He was an Elder, Deacon, Sunday School Teacher, and Chair of the First Presbyterian Church of Oak Park. He was a graduate of Cornell University and was an Engineering Officer with the rank of Lieutenant during WWII (1942-45) aboard anti submarine patrol vessels on the Atlantic seaboard. (2) **John Boyd** in Oak Park 18 August 1979. He was born 13 May 1903.[409] Virginia was graduated from the U. of Rochester where she was a renowned both as a music school scholar and a student athlete and was a member of Theta Eta Sorority. A 57-year resident of Oak Park and Lombard, Ill., she was an active member of the First Presbyterian Church, The Erie Neighborhood House, First United Church, and the 19th Century Woman's Club.

Virginia Dallas **Whipple** and Wilfred Lee **Brooke** had the following children:
+ 7085 i. David Lee[13] **Brooke** born 18 March 1929.
+ 7086 ii. Wilfred Lee **Brooke** born 5 July 1930.
+ 7087 iii. John Almonte **Brooke** born 9 May 1934.

5999. **Ralph Alfred**[12] **Whipple** (Merritt Pendell[11], Dr. Alfred Augustus[10], Henry Francisco[9], Joseph[8], David[7], Samuel[6], Samuel[5], Cyprian[4], Lt. John[3], Matthew[2], Matthew[1])[410] was born in Rochester, Monroe Co., N.Y. 10 July 1909 and died there 3 May 1965, at 55 years of age. Some sources give the death date as 3 May 1974. He married **Jean Elizabeth Conner** after 1936. She was born in Rochester 5 July 1912.[411]

Ralph Alfred **Whipple** and Jean Elizabeth **Conner** had the following children:
+ 7088 i. Sharon Serene[13] **Whipple** born 27 September 1941.
+ 7089 ii. Stephanie **Whipple** born 1 October 1944.

6002. **Rev. Leroy Byron**[12] **Whipple** (William[11], Dr. Alfred Augustus[10], Henry Francisco[9], Joseph[8], David[7], Samuel[6], Samuel[5], Cyprian[4], Lt. John[3], Matthew[2], Matthew[1])[412] was born in Chicago, Ill. 8 January 1913 and died 4 November 1986 in St. Louis, Independence Co., Mo., at 73 years of age. He married **Eleanor Louise Barwick** in Springfield, Mass. 8 September 1940. She died 18 August 1999 in Colorado Springs, Colo. Byron earned a B.A. degree from Kearney State Teachers College, Kearney, Nebr. and a Bachelor of Divinity degree in 1940 from Andover Newton Theological Seminary, Newton Centre, Mass. He was ordained in June of that year at Hampden Association, Mass. He was Director of Christian Education and Youth Work at Walpole, Mass 1936-39; Associate Minister at Hope Congregational Church, Springfield, Mass. 1939-43; Minister at the First Congregational Church, Oskaloosa, Iowa, 1943-45; Minister at the Edwards Congregational Church, Northampton, Mass, 1945-54; and Minister at Maple Street Congregational Church, Danvers, Mass., 1954-63. His work with the Congregational Conference included Chair of the Essex South Committee on the Ministry, Chair of the State Committee on the Ministry, a member of the Committee on Institutional Ministers for the Massachusetts Council of Churches, and Chair of the State Board of Trustees. On

Rev. L. Byron and Eleanor Whipple. Photo courtesy of Elnette C. Whipple.

Sunday 13 October 1963, he was selected from among 100 candidates to become Senior Minister of the Brentwood Congregational United Church of Christ in St. Louis, Mo. He served in that capacity until 1981 and on 26 September 1982 he was made Pastor Emeritus and "The Whipple Fellowship Room" was dedicated in his honor. He was a member of the Mid County YMCA, the Brentwood Library, and the Rotary Club. He died of cancer at his home in Brentwood.[413] Both were buried in Hiram Memorial Park Cemetery in St. Louis.

Rev. Leroy Byron **Whipple** and Eleanor Louise **Barwick** had the following children:

    7090 i. Joanne Louise[13] **Whipple**[414] born in Springfield 9 July 1941 and was graduated from the U. of Connecticut School of Physical Therapy. She teaches in the Department of Physical Therapy at Regis University in Denver, lives in Arvada, Colo.

+   7091 ii. Joyce Ellen **Whipple** born 20 October 1943.

    7092 iii. John Miller **Whipple**[415] born in Northampton 25 September 1945 and married Joanne **Lockman.** He was graduated from Springfield College, Springfield, Mass. where he majored in physical education. He earned a Masters degree from Penn State and is a High School Principal in upstate New York (2000). His wife Joanne was married previously and has children Jim and Jennifer Lockman.

    7093 iv. James Byron **Whipple**[416] born in Northampton 8 January 1949 and died there 24 January 1949. He was born 2 months premature.

6003. **William**[12] **Whipple Jr.** (William[11], Dr. Alfred Augustus[10], Henry Francisco[9], Joseph[8], David[7], Samuel[6], Samuel[5], Cyprian[4], Lt. John[3], Matthew[2], Matthew[1])[417] was born in Chicago, Ill. 31 December 1916 and died 18 March 1977 in Marshall, Lyon Co., Minn., at 60 years of age. He married **Mary Elizabeth Moser** in Evanston, Ill. 24 August 1947.[418] Mary, a Journalism graduate from Northwestern University, began a writing career after her children were grown, concentrating on articles of interest to children and teenagers. Her articles have appeared in *Teens*, *Vision*, and *Catholic Miss*, all publications of church denominations. She has also been published in *Christian Home*. William received a B. A. from Kearney State College, Kearney, Nebr. and an M. A. and Ph.D. from Northwestern University, Evanston, Ill. He also attended Colorado State College at Ft. Collins, Colo. He began his teaching career at LaMar College, Beaumont, Tex. in 1955 and joined the faculty at Midwestern College, Wichita Falls, Tex. in 1960 as Chair of the Department of English. He was appointed Director of the Division of Humanities and Social Sciences in 1962. This Division included the Departments of English, Speech, Foreign Languages, Music and the Social Sciences (history, government, philosophy, and sociology). He became Chair of of the school of Humanities and Liberal Arts at Southwest State University in Marshall, Minn. in 1971. A veteran of WWII, he was a member of the American Assn. of University Professors and was published in professional journals. His poetry, short stories, criticism, and plays were published in literary magazines. He won the Creative Drama Award at Midwestern College. He died at his rural Marshall home. Services were held at the Rehkamp Funeral Home and burial was in the Marshall Cemetery.[419]

William **Whipple** Jr. and Mary Elizabeth **Moser** had the following children:

- + 7094 i. William[13] **Whipple** III born 30 August 1950.
- + 7095 ii. Stephen **Whipple** born 8 August 1952.
- + 7096 iii. Rand **Whipple** born 24 April 1955.
- + 7097 iv. Laurie **Whipple** born 10 August 1957.
-   7098 v. Gregory **Whipple**[420] born in Beaumont, Tex. 3 March 1958. He is married; no details provided. He was living in Dallas, Tex. in February 1989.

6004. **Alfreda Louise**[12] **Whipple** (William[11], Dr. Alfred Augustus[10], Henry Francisco[9], Joseph[8], David[7], Samuel[6], Samuel[5], Cyprian[4], Lt. John[3], Matthew[2], Matthew[1])[421] was born in Maywood, Cook Co., Ill 4 January 1918 and married **David Eugene Smith** in North Platte, Lincoln Co., Nebr. 22 August 1943. David,[422] son of Walter Edward **Smith** and Sada **Jordan**, was born 14 June 1916 and died 15 February 1996 in Gardner, Kans., at 79 years of age. He was a Lieutenant Colonel in the U.S. Air Force during WWII. Following the war he worked for the Union Pacific Railroad, retiring after 17 years. He then worked for the Social Security Administration for 12 years, retiring in 1978. The family moved to Olathe, Kans. in 1972 where he was President of the Olathe Historical Society and Chaplain of the National Assn. of Retired Employees. He also was a member of the First Baptist Church of Overland Park, Kans. and Nebraska Masonic Lodge No. 1. He died of cancer at the Meadowbrook Hospital in Gardner and was buried in the Leavenworth National Cemetery.

Alfreda Louise **Whipple** and David Eugene **Smith** had the following children:

- + 7099 i. Eugene Lee[13] **Smith** born 3 August 1945.

7100 ii. Byron Paul **Smith**[423] born in Long Beach, Calif. 26 October 1946 and married twice. (1) Nancy Ann **Boyles** in Overland Park 11 April 1969. Nancy,[424] daughter of Robert **Boyles** and Evelyn **Crews**, was born 18 August 1949. They were divorced in 1984. (2) Franci **Taylor** 2 July 1990. Franci,[425] daughter of S. A. **Taylor** and Madeline (__), was born 2 August 1947. They were divorced in 1995. Byron is a graduate of Omaha (Nebr.) University. He and Nancy adopted two Korean children: Kimberly, born 6 August, 1969, married Kenneth Edwards 27 June 1992 in Denver; Christian (Soon Duck), born 26 March 1971. Kimberly and Kenneth have twin sons, Justin and Tristin, and daughters Melanie and Olivia. Christian has a son Sheldon Sickles. Byron and family were living in Helena, Mont. in December 1997.

7101 iii. Beverly Ann **Smith**[426] born in North Platte, Lincoln Co., Nebr. 1 April 1949. Beverly, earned a B. A. degree from Ottawa University (Kans.) and an M. A. from Penn State. She was a member of the Peace Corps for three years and was teaching at Lansing Community College, Lansing, Mich. in 2000.

6005. **Marian Learned**[12] **Whipple** (William[11], Dr. Alfred Augustus[10], Henry Francisco[9], Joseph[8], David[7], Samuel[6], Samuel[5], Cyprian[4], Lt. John[3], Matthew[2], Matthew[1])[427] was born 25 April 1920 and married twice. (1) **Lester A. Saathoff** in North Platte, Lincoln Co., Nebr. 15 September 1940. He was born on a farm in Franklin Co., Nebr. 15 August 1916 and died of gangrene of the stomach 5 September 1949 in Kearney, Nebr., at 33 years of age.[428] (2) **Willie C. Christensen** in North Platte 29 February 1976. He was born in Norman, Nebr. 17 August 1908 and died of cancer 11 November 1986 in Nebraska, at 78 years of age.[429] Buried in Greenwood Cemetery, Sidney, Nebr.

Marian Learned **Whipple** and Lester A. **Saathoff** had the following children:
+ 7102 i. Hervy Andrew[13] **Saathoff** born 15 August 1941.
+ 7103 ii. Garret Wendell **Saathoff** born 27 September 1943.
+ 7104 iii. Arthur Kent **Saathoff** born 7 July 1947.
+ 7105 iv. Bonnie Jean **Saathoff** born 5 July 1948.
+ 7106 v. Leslie Sue **Saathoff** born 10 October 1949.

6007. **Elizabeth Olive**[12] **Whipple** (Burdette D.[11], James Spencer[10], Henry Francisco[9], Joseph[8], David[7], Samuel[6], Samuel[5], Cyprian[4], Lt.

John[3], Matthew[2], Matthew[1])[430] was born in Salamanca, Cattaraugus Co., N.Y 31 January 1909 and married **Thomas Hunt**.

Elizabeth Olive **Whipple** and Thomas **Hunt** had the following child:
    7107   i.   William Thomas[13] **Hunt**[431] born 10 June 1940.

6009. **Dean Sander**[12] **Whipple** (Dr. Willis Walton[11], James Spencer[10], Henry Francisco[9], Joseph[8], David[7], Samuel[6], Samuel[5], Cyprian[4], Lt. John[3], Matthew[2], Matthew[1])[432] was born in Salamanca, Cattaraugus Co., N.Y 10 June 1913 and died there 12 April 1968, at 54 years of age. He married **Marian Clements** 17 July 1940. She was born in Avon, N.Y.

Dean Sander **Whipple** and Marian **Clements** had the following children born in Salamanca:
+   7108   i.   Prof. Thomas Walton[13] **Whipple** 29 August 1942.
+   7109   ii.   Deanne Marie **Whipple** 13 December 1948.
    7110   iii.   Scott Allen **Whipple**[433] 5 October 1954.

6010. **Walton**[12] **Whipple** (Dr. Willis Walton[11], James Spencer[10], Henry Francisco[9], Joseph[8], David[7], Samuel[6], Samuel[5], Cyprian[4], Lt. John[3], Matthew[2], Matthew[1])[434] birth date unknown, married an unnamed person.

Walton **Whipple** had the following children:
    7111   i.   Randy[13] **Whipple**[435] born 31 August 1948.
    7112   ii.   Debbie **Whipple**[436] born 5 January 1954.

6011. **Rev. John Walton**[12] **Whipple** (Ara Leroy[11], Willis Walton[10], Henry Francisco[9], Joseph[8], David[7], Samuel[6], Samuel[5], Cyprian[4], Lt. John[3], Matthew[2], Matthew[1])[437] was born in Meadville, Penn. 21 August 1909 and married **Naomi Clemmer** 24 March 1934. Naomi is the daughter of William S. **Clemmer**.[438] John was graduated from the Missionary Training Institute, Nyack, N.Y. in 1933. He was Pastor of the Christian and Missionary Alliance Church at Olean, N.Y. After a year's training in Paris, John and the family were sent to French Indo-China where he did missionary work. Because of WWII they were back in the U.S. by the end of August 1942. They returned to southeast Asia in 1948 serving in Vietiane, Laos until May 1963 and retired in August 1963 in Glendale, California. In addition to the twins Ronald and Gail and daughter Isabelle, John and Naomi had twin sons born 10 April 1935 who died in infancy.

Rev. John Walton **Whipple** and Naomi **Clemmer** had the following children:

  7113 i. Ronald Gene[13] **Whipple**[439] born in Paris, France 18 April 1937 and married Mary Jean **Hoffman** of Philadelphia, Penn. in Zellwood, Fla, 29 January 1963.[440] She is the daughter of Rev. Wilbur Gerald **Hoffman**. Ronald teaches math and history and Mary Jean teaches organ and piano at the Du Bose Academy in Zellwood. Ronald was graduated from Stetson University in DeLand, Fla. with an A.B. degree in 1960.

+ 7114 ii. Gail Ann **Whipple** born 18 April 1937.

  7115 iii. Isabelle **Whipple**[441] born in Dalat, Vietnam 1 May 1941 and married Arthur **Dolder** in Glendale, Calif. 4 September 1965.

6018. **Eleanor**[12] **McGee** (Inez May[11] **Hobart**, Edwin Whipple[10], Sarah[9] **Whipple**, Samuel[8], David[7], Samuel[6], Samuel[5], Cyprian[4], Lt. John[3], Matthew[2], Matthew[1])[442] was born in Grass Lake, Mich. 13 July 1908[443] and married **Walter W. Hammond** in Angola, Ind. 3 May 1930. Walter,[444] son of Walter Wesley **Hammond** and Mabel Minerva **Griffith**, was born in New York, N.Y. 1 October 1904.

Eleanor **McGee** and Walter W. **Hammond** had the following children:

+ 7116 i. Walter Wesley[13] **Hammond** III born 12 April 1932.

+ 7117 ii. Ann Janet **Hammond** born 25 February 1935.

  7118 iii. Hobart Griffith **Hammond**[445] born in Ann Arbor, Mich. 2 January 1943 and married Susan Jane **Anderle** 6 August 1966. Susan,[446] daughter of William **Anderle** and Evelyn (__), earned a degree in Fine Arts from the U. of Oklahoma. Hobart earned a Business Administration degree from the U. of Oklahoma in 1967 and was a Second Lieutenant in the Armed Services in 1968.

6034. **Robert Hugh**[12] **Whipple** (Walter Henry[11], Watson H.[10], William[9], Samuel[8], David[7], Samuel[6], Samuel[5], Cyprian[4], Lt. John[3], Matthew[2], Matthew[1])[447] was born in Medina, Orleans Co., N.Y. 15 November 1923 and died 23 September 1991, at 67 years of age. Buried at Lynhaven Cemetery, Lyndonville, Orleans Co., N.Y. He married **Eleanor Bailey** in Islington, Norfolk Co., Mass. 12 September 1943. Eleanor,[448] daughter of Bernard Holbrook **Bailey** and Beatrice Eleanor **Phinney**, was born in Boston, Suffolk Co., Mass. 10 December 1923.

{ G 1049 }

Robert Hugh **Whipple** and Eleanor **Bailey** had the following children:
- + 7119 i. Marsha[13] **Whipple** born 17 July 1944.
- + 7120 ii. John Walter **Whipple** born 29 May 1947.
- + 7121 iii. Julia **Whipple** born 26 May 1952.
- + 7122 iv. Laura **Whipple** born 21 April 1955.

6035. **James Watson**[12] **Whipple** (Walter Henry[11], Watson H.[10], William[9], Samuel[8], David[7], Samuel[6], Samuel[5], Cyprian[4], Lt. John[3], Matthew[2], Matthew[1]) was born in Lyndonville, Orleans Co., N.Y. 27 July 1927 and married twice. (1) **Janet Marie Peters** in Lyndonville 10 January 1953. She was born in Medina, Orleans Co., N.Y. 26 February 1933 and died there 18 April 1963, at 30 years of age.[449] Buried at Lynhaven Cemetery, Lyndonville, N.Y. (2) **Carolyn Lee Kerr** in Middleport, Niagra Co., N.Y. 21 January 1965. Carolyn,[450] daughter of Ivan Fleming **Kerr** and Ruth Naomi **Lewis**, was born in Henderson, Ky. 18 September 1928. She married (1) **Edwin Francis**.

James Watson **Whipple** and Janet Marie **Peters** had the following children born in Medina:
- + 7123 i. James Robert[13] **Whipple** 9 January 1956.
- 7124 ii. William Gregory **Whipple**[451] 26 February 1957.
- 7125 iii. Catherine Janet **Whipple**[452] 2 July 1961.

James Watson **Whipple** and Carolyn Lee **Kerr** had the following child:
- + 7126 iv. Jeanne Carolyn **Whipple** born 20 December 1967.

6036. **David Doty**[12] **Whipple** (Hugh Scott[11], Francis Henry[10], William[9], Samuel[8], David[7], Samuel[6], Samuel[5], Cyprian[4], Lt. John[3], Matthew[2], Matthew[1])[453] was born in Akron, Ohio 26 December 1923 and married **Carolyn Terhune Decker** in Westfield, Union Co., N.J. 28 February 1953. She was born in Westfield 14 April 1927.[454] David is a retired Central Intelligence Agency officer and retired Executive Director of the Association of Former Intelligence Officers.

David Doty **Whipple** and Carolyn Terhune **Decker** had the following children:
- + 7127 i. Susan[13] **Whipple** born 15 January 1954.
- + 7128 ii. Marc Evan **Whipple** born 10 February 1956.
- + 7129 iii. Tim Decker **Whipple** born 1 August 1962.
- + 7130 iv. Scott Adams Montgomery **Whipple** was born 31 May 1964.

6037. **Scott Lloyd**[12] **Whipple** (Hugh Scott[11], Francis Henry[10], William[9], Samuel[8], David[7], Samuel[6], Samuel[5], Cyprian[4], Lt. John[3], Matthew[2], Matthew[1])[455] was born in Medina, Orleans Co., N.Y. 31 December 1925 and married **Barbara Jean Davis** in Newburyport 27 December 1952. She was born 2 September 1927.[456] Scott is an Executive Search Professional.

Scott Lloyd **Whipple** and Barbara Jean **Davis** had the following child:
- 7131 i. Scott Davis[13] **Whipple**[457] born in Stamford, Conn. 9 February 1967. Adopted.

6040. **John Michael**[12] **Scully** (Izobel[11] **Coulter**, Doris[10] **Whipple**, Edwin[9], Samuel[8], David[7], Samuel[6], Samuel[5], Cyprian[4], Lt. John[3], Matthew[2], Matthew[1])[458] was born in Concord, Contra Costa Co., Calif. 5 July 1960[459] and married **Patricia Molina** in Zephyr Cove, Nev., 9 February 1980. Patricia,[460] daughter of David **Molina** and Susan Lynn **Schultze**, was born in Tucson, Ariz. 29 June 1961.

John Michael **Scully** and Patricia **Molina** had the following children:
- 7132 i. Kimmarie Anne[13] **Scully**[461] born in Walnut Creek, Calif. 7 September 1980.
- 7133 ii. Susan Izobel **Scully**[462] born in Concord 24 May 1982.
- 7134 iii. Angela Linda **Scully**[463] born in Concord 23 July 1984.
- 7135 iv. Sophie Jean **Scully**[464] born in Corona, Calif. 30 July 1993.

6043. **Ruth Janis**[12] **Whipple** (Ralph Howard[11], Colby Favelle[10], Isaac[9], Hiram[8], David[7], Samuel[6], Samuel[5], Cyprian[4], Lt. John[3], Matthew[2], Matthew[1])[465] was born in Cleveland, Ohio 10 August 1913 and married **Simmons Smith** there 5 November 1938. He was born in Cleveland 10 October 1913.[466]

Ruth Janis **Whipple** and Simmons **Smith** had the following children:
- + 7136 i. Janis Marie[13] **Smith** born 27 September 1946.
- 7137 ii. Randall Simmons **Smith**[467] born in Rockford, Ill. 15 July 1949.

6044. **Genevieve Eynon**[12] **Whipple** (Ralph Howard[11], Colby Favelle[10], Isaac[9], Hiram[8], David[7], Samuel[6], Samuel[5], Cyprian[4], Lt. John[3], Matthew[2], Matthew[1])[468] was born in Cleveland, Cuyahoga Co., Ohio 23 June 1918 and married twice. (1) **Robert Sandals**. (2) **Arthur Lyman Jr.**

Genevieve Eynon **Whipple** and Robert **Sandals** had the following child:
- 7138 i. Douglas[13] **Sandals**[469] born 30 March 1943.

Genevieve Eynon **Whipple** and Arthur **Lyman** Jr had the following child:
+ 7139 ii. Cheryl **Lyman** born 28 November 1955.

6054. **Annie Mae**[12] **Ricker** (Annie Grace[11] **Hardy**, Lucy Ann[10] **Harriman**, Joel George[9], Lucy[8] **Ray**, Jonathan[7], Amos[6], Hannah[5] **Goodale**, Sarah[4] **Whipple**, Joseph[3], Matthew[2], Matthew[1])[470] was born in Clarksville, N.H. 26 January 1907 and married **Leon Allen** 22 December 1925.

Annie Mae **Ricker** and Leon **Allen** had the following children:
7140 i. Randolph Mayberry[13] **Allen**[471] born 22 December 1926.
7141 ii. Leona Mae **Allen**[472] born 6 July 1928 and died abt 1935.
7142 iii. Stanley Willard **Allen**[473] born 17 June 1929.
7143 iv. Winona Louise **Allen**[474] born 21 December 1931.

6055. **Arthur Walter**[12] **Ricker** (Annie Grace[11] **Hardy**, Lucy Ann[10] **Harriman**, Joel George[9], Lucy[8] **Ray**, Jonathan[7], Amos[6], Hannah[5] **Goodale**, Sarah[4] **Whipple**, Joseph[3], Matthew[2], Matthew[1])[475] was born in Clarksville, N.H. 12 April 1909 and died 26 October 1974, at 65 years of age. He married **Virginia Hope Carlton** 22 May 1942. She was born 22 December 1923.[476]

Arthur Walter **Ricker** and Virginia Hope **Carlton** had the following children:
7144 i. Rebecca Rose[13] **Ricker**[477] born 30 July 1943.
7145 ii. Velma Hope **Ricker**[478] born 6 March 1947.
7146 iii. Floyd **Ricker**[479] born 30 May 1948.
7147 iv. Florence Edna **Ricker**[480] born 24 June 1949.
7148 v. Josephine **Ricker**[481] born 23 August 1950.
7149 vi. Thomas **Ricker**[482] born 8 May 1956.
7150 vii. Arthur Walter **Ricker** Jr.[483] born 22 November 1957.

6056. **Freeman Otis**[12] **Ricker** (Annie Grace[11] **Hardy**, Lucy Ann[10] **Harriman**, Joel George[9], Lucy[8] **Ray**, Jonathan[7], Amos[6], Hannah[5] **Goodale**, Sarah[4] **Whipple**, Joseph[3], Matthew[2], Matthew[1])[484] was born in Clarksville, N.H. 10 February 1913 and married **Mattie Sweeney**.

Freeman Otis **Ricker** and Mattie **Sweeney** had the following children:
7151 i. Terry[13] **Ricker**.[485]
7152 ii. Timothy **Ricker**.[486]
7153 iii. Otis Freeman **Ricker**[487] born in Littleton, Grafton Co., N.H. 2 December 1936.
7154 iv. Burt **Ricker**.[488]
7155 v. Ronald **Ricker**.[489]

6059. **Lucy Ann**[12] **Ricker** (Annie Grace[11] **Hardy**, Lucy Ann[10] **Harriman**, Joel George[9], Lucy[8] **Ray**, Jonathan[7], Amos[6], Hannah[5] **Goodale**, Sarah[4] **Whipple**, Joseph[3], Matthew[2], Matthew[1])[490] was born in Clarksville, N.H. 28 July 1918 and married twice. (1) **William Edward Taylor**. He was born in Pittsburg, N.H. 25 June 1886 and died 17 April 1968 in Bryand Pond, Maine, at 81 years of age.[491] (2) **Burton Preston Cox**.

Lucy Ann **Ricker** and William Edward **Taylor** had the following children:

7156	i.	Asa Manley[13] **Taylor**[492] born in Woodstock, Maine 25 November 1940 and married Elsie **House**.
7157	ii.	William Edward **Taylor**[493] born in Bennington, Vt. 25 May 1943 and died 23 November 1969 in Bryand Pond, at 26 years of age.
7158	iii.	Etrulia Mertie **Taylor**[494] born in Woodstock, Maine 23 September 1946 and married Alpheus William **Brooks** in Mechanic Falls, Maine 22 November 1962.
7159	iv.	Waywood Eldwin **Taylor**[495] born in Woodstock 23 October 1950 and married three times. (1) Kathy (__) in 1974. (2) Bonnie (__) abt 1986. (3) Fay **Willison** abt 1989.

Lucy Ann **Ricker** and Burton Preston **Cox** had the following child:

7160	v.	Brenda Lee **Cox**[496] born in Bryand Pond 1 August 1956.

6075. **Mayland Earl**[12] **Harriman** (Charles Mayland[11], Daniel S.[10], Joel George[9], Lucy[8] **Ray**, Jonathan[7], Amos[6], Hannah[5] **Goodale**, Sarah[4] **Whipple**, Joseph[3], Matthew[2], Matthew[1])[497] was born in Warner, Merrimack Co., N.H. 1 November 1921 and married **Norma Leah Beeman** 1 January 1947. She was born in Essex, Mo. 15 February 1925.[498]

Mayland Earl **Harriman** and Norma Leah **Beeman** had the following children:

	7161	i.	Marilyn Evens[13] **Harriman**[499] born in New York, N.Y. 2 September 1949 and married three times. (1) Michael **Blanchard** in Port Arthur, Tex. 15 March 1968. He was born in New York, N.Y. 2 September 1949.500 (2) Clevan **Myers Jr.** 30 June 1972. (3) Clarence Haden **Cribbs Jr.** 12 April 1979.
+	7162	ii.	Jane Boyd **Harriman** born 8 November 1950.

6077. **Phyllis Jean**[12] **Davis** (Ruby Edna[11] **Harriman**, George Dearborn[10], Joel George[9], Lucy[8] **Ray**, Jonathan[7], Amos[6], Hannah[5] **Goodale**, Sarah[4] **Whipple**, Joseph[3], Matthew[2], Matthew[1])[501] was born in Lauramie

Township, Tippecanoe Co., Ind. 22 July 1930 and married **Don Robert Moore** in Rossville, Clinton Co., Ind. 10 June 1947. Don,[502] son of Henry Newton **Moore** and Mayme Ellen **Riggle,** was born in Madison Township, Carroll Co., Ind. 8 March 1926. He served in the U.S. Navy during WWII.

Phyllis has been active in genealogy for years serving on the Carroll Co. Historical Society Board of Directors since 1996 and as Curator for the same period. She was a guiding force in the expansion of the Society and started its Genealogy Department. Her memberships include: DAR, Wea Lea Chapter, White Co., Ind.; Colonial Dames XVII Century Post Quiatenon Chapter, Lafayette, Ind.; Piscataqua Pioneers, Ancient and Honorable Artillery Co.; Dames of Court of Honor; National Society, New England Women, Eunice Mather Chapter; Continental Society Daughters Indian Wars; Daughters of Colonial Wars; Delphi Business Women; Delphi American Legion Auxiliary, President for four years; and Delphi Veterans of Foreign Wars Auxiliary. Rebecca (Towne) Nurse, convicted of being a witch and hung during the Salem Witch hunt of 1692, was her great (8) grandmother.

Phyllis Jean **Davis** and Don Robert **Moore** had the following children:
- \+ 7163 i. Don Robert[13] **Moore** II born 13 October 1947.
- 7164 ii. Jackie Dean **Moore**[503] born 14 December 1948 and married Darlene **Scott** in Lafayette, Tippecanoe Co., Ind. 15 September 1974. He was born in Frankfort, Clinton Co., Ind. 1950.[504] They were divorced in Indianapolis, Ind. 5 November 1975. He served five-and-a-half years as an Army medic (4-1968-8-1973) including four-and-a-half years in Viet Nam. He was in an auto accident in February 1975 which caused memory loss.
- \+ 7165 iii. Gary Gene **Moore** born 18 January 1951.

6079. **Richard Lee**[12] **Davis** (Ruby Edna[11] **Harriman**, George Dearborn[10], Joel George[9], Lucy[8] **Ray**, Jonathan[7], Amos[6], Hannah[5] **Goodale**, Sarah[4] **Whipple**, Joseph[3], Matthew[2], Matthew[1])[505] was born in Frankfort, Clinton Co., Ind. 20 April 1935 and married **Wilma Jean Pattengale** in Delphi, Carroll Co., Ind. 16 May 1954. Wilma,[506] daughter of Orth **Pattengale** and Dorothy **Kaffman**, was born in Tippecanoe Co., Ind. 14 October 1936. Richard served in the Indiana National Guard for 10 years.

Richard Lee **Davis** and Wilma Jean Pattengale had the following children:
- \+ 7166 i. Richard Gene[13] **Davis** born 3 December 1954.
- \+ 7167 ii. Leetta Darlene **Davis** born 24 October 1957.

	7168	iii.	Michael Dean **Davis**[507] born in Lafayette, Tippecanoe Co., Ind. 18 September 1962 and married Dawn Delane **Hackerd** in Lafayette 31 December 1996.
	7169	iv.	Robert Lee **Davis**[508] born in Lafayette 10 February 1966.

6081. **Grace Elenore**[12] **Morgan** (Fredrick V.[11], Nehemiah[10], Samuel[9], Betsey[8] **Whipple**, Nehemiah[7], Benjamin[6], Francis[5], Jonathan[4], Joseph[3], Matthew[2], Matthew[1])[509] was born in Sweden, Maine 29 June 1884 and died 27 August 1947 in Line Ridge, Wisc., at 63 years of age. She married **Oscar Henry Duell**. Oscar,[510] son of Charles R. **Duell** and Welthea **Hayes**, was born 3 May 1871 and died 18 September 1940 in Line Ridge, at 69 years of age. They are buried in Bay Street Cemetery, Glens Falls, N.Y. Oscar was her second husband. No information provided on the first husband.

Grace Elenore **Morgan** and Oscar Henry **Duell** had the following children:

	7170	i.	Fred[13] **Duell**[511] born 21 May 1904 and died in September 1986 at 82 years of age.
+	7171	ii.	Earl Charles **Duell** born 29 December 1905.
+	7172	iii.	Dorothy **Duell** born 16 October 1908.
+	7173	iv.	Gladys Cora **Duell** born 19 June 1911.
	7174	v.	Robert O. **Duell**[512] born in Reedsburg, Wisc. 25 August 1914 and died 7 November 1986 in Orlando, Fla., at 72 years of age.
	7175	vi.	Cora Louise **Duell**[513] born in Line Ridge 17 November 1921 and died there 24 November 1921 at 7 days of age. Buried in Bay Street Cemetery, Glens Falls, N.Y.
	7176	vii.	Westina **Duell** born in Line Ridge 17 November 1923 and died 2 days after birth.

6089. **James Newton**[12] **Norton** (Charles Russel[11], Judge James Carmont[10], Harriet Whipple[9] **Carpenter**, Anner[8] **Whipple**, Nehemiah[7], Benjamin[6], Francis[5], Jonathan[4], Joseph[3], Matthew[2], Matthew[1])[514] was born in Marquette, McPherson Co., Kans. 8 March 1885 and married **Grace Lucille Gordon** in Wichita, Sedgwick Co., Kans. 21 January 1912. Grace,[515] daughter of Charles Barber **Gordon** and Emily **Cook**, was born in Arkansas City, Cowley Co., Kans. in June 1890 and died there in March 1967, at 76 years of age.

James Newton **Norton** and Grace Lucille **Gordon** had the following child:

+	7177	i.	Maurica B.[13] **Norton** born 19 December 1917.

6090. **Mary**[12] **Norton** (Charles Russel[11], Judge James Carmont[10], Harriet Whipple[9] **Carpenter,** Anner[8] **Whipple,** Nehemiah[7], Benjamin[6], Francis[5], Jonathan[4], Joseph[3], Matthew[2], Matthew[1])[516] was born in Marquette, McPherson Co., Kans. 28 November 1886 and died 5 November 1971 in Bakersfield, Calif., at 84 years of age. She married **Guy Hathaway Jaggard** in Puenta, Los Angeles Co., Calif. in August 1910. Guy,[517] son of Thomas **Jaggard** and Irene Frances **Coulter,** was born 23 July 1883 and died 21 November 1976 in Stockton, San Joaquin Co., Calif., at 93 years of age. Buried in Bakersfield.

Mary **Norton** and Guy Hathaway **Jaggard** had the following children:

	7178	i.	Guy Norton[13] **Jaggard**[518] born in Marquette 10 May 1911 and married Marie **Long** in Bakersfield 1 July 1938. Marie,[519] daughter of Ellis Russel **Long** and Minnie Belinda **Painter,** was born in Bakersfield 9 March 1913.
+	7179	ii.	Helen Margaret **Jaggard** born 14 September 1912.
+	7180	iii.	Ralph Warren **Jaggard** born 22 January 1914.
+	7181	iv.	Elizabeth Ann **Jaggard** born 9 February 1924.

6091. **Hugh Russell**[12] **Norton** (Charles Russel[11], Judge James Carmont[10], Harriet Whipple[9] **Carpenter,** Anner[8] **Whipple,** Nehemiah[7], Benjamin[6], Francis[5], Jonathan[4], Joseph[3], Matthew[2], Matthew[1])[520] was born in Marquette, McPherson Co., Kans. 14 December 1888 and died in 1924 in Los Angeles, Calif., at 35 years of age. He married **Albine Ruey Power** in Los Angeles in September 1914. She was born in Rayne, Acadia Co., La. 4 April 1894.[521]

Hugh Russell **Norton** and Albine Ruey **Power** had the following children:

| + | 7182 | i. | Phyllis Albine[13] **Norton** born 26 May 1915. |
| | 7183 | ii. | Marjorie Ann **Norton**[522] born in Monterey Park, Calif. 29 December 1922 and died in November 1991 in Pacific Palisades, Calif., at 68 years of age. She married Hugh Alexander **McKellar** in Los Angeles 28 May 1943. |

6093. **Walter Emmet**[12] **Norton** (Charles Russel[11], Judge James Carmont[10], Harriet Whipple[9] **Carpenter,** Anner[8] **Whipple,** Nehemiah[7], Benjamin[6], Francis[5], Jonathan[4], Joseph[3], Matthew[2], Matthew[1])[523] was born in Marquette, McPherson Co., Kans. 27 June 1893 and married **Ora Marie Schilling**.

Walter Emmet **Norton** and Ora Marie **Schilling** had the following child:

| + | 7184 | i. | Virginia Edith[13] **Norton** born 26 July 1914. |

6096. **John Dorwin**[12] **Franklin** (Angeline[11] **McKinley**, William Henry[10], Angeline[9] **Whipple**, Enoch[8], Nehemiah[7], Benjamin[6], Francis[5], Jonathan[4], Joseph[3], Matthew[2], Matthew[1])[524] was born in Williamsport, Warren Co., Ind. 22 September 1906 and died of heart failure 21 September 1967 in Cedar Rapids, Iowa, at 60 years of age. Buried in Belle Plaine, Benton Co., Iowa at Oak Hill Cemetery. He married **Marie Rosina Schultz** in Vinton, Benton Co., Iowa 25 December 1930. Marie,[525] daughter of Frank **Schultz** and Alma **Schumaker**, was born in Guttenburg, Iowa 28 June 1910 and died 27 May 1990 in Belle Plaine, at 79 years of age. John was an avid sports fan and won the 1947 contest to name the U. of Iowa Hawkeye football mascot. His winning name was "Herky the Hawk." The town of Belle Plaine named a park for him for his many contributions to the town's sports and athletic programs.

John Dorwin **Franklin** and Marie Rosina **Schultz** had the following children:
+ 7185 i. James Doyle[13] **Franklin** born 9 March 1931.
+ 7186 ii. Robert William **Franklin** born 4 February 1933.
+ 7187 iii. Shirley Jean **Franklin** born 18 December 1934.
+ 7188 iv. Donald Willard **Franklin** born 19 August 1938.
+ 7189 v. David Leonard **Franklin** born 21 May 1940.
+ 7190 vi. Virginia Kay **Franklin** born 18 July 1942.
+ 7191 vii. Thomas Arnold **Franklin** born 29 October 1944.
    7192 viii. Charles Roger **Franklin**[526] born in Belle Plaine 10 February 1949 and died there 21 September 1959, at 10 years of age. Buried in Oak Hill Cemetery.
    7193 ix. Richard Lawrence **Franklin**[527] born in Belle Plaine 10 February 1950.

6097. **Dorothy Marguerite**[12] **Franklin** (Angeline[11] **McKinley**, William Henry[10], Angeline[9] **Whipple**, Enoch[8], Nehemiah[7], Benjamin[6], Francis[5], Jonathan[4], Joseph[3], Matthew[2], Matthew[1])[528] was born in Williamsport, Warren Co., Ind. 19 November 1907 and died 13 May 1965 in El Paso, Tex., at 57 years of age. She married **Elmer Otis Woodford** in Cedar Falls, Black Hawk Co., Iowa, 20 August 1928. Elmer, son of John H. **Woodford** and Nola Adelaide **Nills**, was born in Table Grove, Ill. 3 June 1903 and died 1 December 1964 in Vinton, Benton Co., Iowa, at 61 years of age. Dorothy got the flu when visiting daughter Judy in El Paso and died there. Both are buried in Vinton's Evergreen Cemetery.

Dorothy Marguerite **Franklin** and Elmer Otis **Woodford** had the following children:
+ 7194 i. Nola Angeline[13] **Woodford** born 24 September 1933.

{ G 1057 }

+   7195   ii.   Joseph Franklin **Woodford** born 23 November 1936.
+   7196   iii.   Judith Ann **Woodford** born 5 May 1940.

6098. **Laura Charlotte**[12] **Franklin** (Angeline[11] **McKinley**, William Henry[10], Angeline[9] **Whipple**, Enoch[8], Nehemiah[7], Benjamin[6], Francis[5], Jonathan[4], Joseph[3], Matthew[2], Matthew[1])[529] was born in Williamsport, Warren Co., Ind. 29 May 1909 and died 26 November 1986 in Hartwick, Poweshiek Co., Iowa, at 77 years of age. She married **John Calvin Korns** in St. Ansgar, Mitchell Co., Iowa 10 March 1934. John,[530] son of Marvin Delno **Korns** and Verna **Rowland**, was born 14 December 1903 and died 1 July 1974 in Hartwick, at 70 years of age. Laura's uncle, Rev. Merton W. McKinley, Pastor of the St. Ansgar Methodist Church, performed their wedding ceremony. Laura and John began farming near Hardwick following their marriage. She recorded the McKinley family history and kept a descendant's book.

Laura Charlotte **Franklin** and John Calvin **Korns** had the following children:
+   7197   i.   William Franklin[13] **Korns** born 27 July 1935.
     7198   ii.   Kathryn June **Korns**[531] born in Grinnell, Powesheik Co., Iowa 9 June 1937.
+   7199   iii.   Dennis Dean **Korns** born 23 December 1945.
+   7200   iv.   Sharon Ann **Korns** born 26 October 1950.

6099. **Sylvia Fae**[12] **Franklin** (Angeline[11] **McKinley**, William Henry[10], Angeline[9] **Whipple**, Enoch[8], Nehemiah[7], Benjamin[6], Francis[5], Jonathan[4], Joseph[3], Matthew[2], Matthew[1])[532] was born in Vinton, Benton Co., Iowa 24 February 1912 and married **James Walter Knupp** there 11 September 1933. James,[533] son of Adam C. **Knupp** and Hanora **Malron**, was born 20 July 1911 and died 14 June 1998 in Fort Dodge, Iowa, at 86 years of age. Sylvia and James lived most of their married life in Fort Dodge where Jim retired from the insurance business.

Sylvia Fae **Franklin** and James Walter **Knupp** had the following children:
+   7201   i.   Marlene Jean[13] **Knupp** born 8 June 1933.
+   7202   ii.   Janis Elaine **Knupp** born 12 April 1936.
+   7203   iii.   John Franklin **Knupp** born 21 May 1938.
+   7204   iv.   Clyde Franklin **Knupp** born 7 January 1940.
+   7205   v.   Keith Franklin **Knupp** born 13 May 1946.

6102. **LaVon Elizabeth**[12] **McKinley** (James Hiram[11], William Henry[10], Angeline[9] **Whipple**, Enoch[8], Nehemiah[7], Benjamin[6], Francis[5], Jonathan[4], Joseph[3], Matthew[2], Matthew[1])[534] was born in Cedar Rapids, Iowa 12 March 1911 and died 3 July 1999 in Portland, Multnomah Co., Oreg., at 88 years of age. She married **Robert I. Schlarbaum** in Fairbanks, Buchanan Co., Iowa 28 March 1937. Bob,[535] son of Charles **Slocum** and Esty **Anderson**, was born in Knoxville, Iowa 7 November 1906 and died 1 July 1991 in King City, Washington Co., Oreg., at 84 years of age. Bob was adopted and raised by Elmer and Emma Schlarbaum. He moved his family to Portland in 1943 where he was a welder in the shipyards.

La Von and Bob were married by her uncle Rev. Merton McKinley in his home in Fairbanks, Iowa. This was Bob's second marriage. No details provided on his first wife. Bob and LaVon are buried in the Laurel Corridor, Riverview Abby Masusoleum, Portland.

Robert and LaVon, Sherwood, Oreg. Photo courtesy of LaVon Schlarbaum.

LaVon Elizabeth **McKinley** and Robert I. **Schlarbaum** had the following children:

    7206 i. Charles James[13] **Schlarbaum**[536] born in Vinton, Benton Co., Iowa 9 January 1938 and married twice. (1) Betty **McRay** 27 March 1963. (2) Marquean **Ayres** in Key Biscayne, Fla. 5 February 1979. Marquean,[537] daughter of Marques **Ayres** and Helen **Vott**, was born in Miami, Dade Co., Fla. 20 December 1929 and died there 5 April 1992, at 62 years of age. Buried in Key Biscane. Following his discharge from the U.S. Army where he served in Germany, Charles joined the Musicial Department of the Christiani Bros. Circus. He writes and arranges music and has been the Band Director for several circuses including 10 years with the Clyde Beatty Show. He has been inducted into the Circus Hall of Fame at Barabo, Wisc.

+ 7207 ii. Robert I. **Schlarbaum** Jr. born 1 September 1940.
+ 7208 iii. Carolyn Jeanette **Schlarbaum** born 13 July 1942.
+ 7209 iv. David Allen **Schlarbaum** born 10 November 1951.
+ 7210 v. Mary Ann Elizabeth **Schlarbaum** born 24 November 1953.

6107. **Nina Eileen**[12] **Franklin** (Janette[11] **McKinley**, William Henry[10], Angeline[9] **Whipple**, Enoch[8], Nehemiah[7], Benjamin[6], Francis[5], Jonathan[4], Joseph[3], Matthew[2], Matthew[1])[538] was born in Independence, Warren Co., Ind. 26 January 1906 and died 9 May 1985 in Portage, Porter Co., Ind., at 79 years of age.

She married **Joseph N. Nichalson** in Gary, Ind. 24 April 1942. Joseph,[539] son of Sam **Nichalson** and Sophia **Johnson**, was born in Chrisman, Ind. 11 January 1894 and died 22 April 1960 at 66 years of age. Nina and Joseph were in an auto accident that took his life and led to the development of rheumatoid arthritis for her. She eventually became an invalid and died of heart problems and other complications. Nina and Joseph are buried in McCool Cemetery, Portage.

Nina Eileen **Franklin** and Joseph N. **Nichalson** had the following child born in Gary:

    7211 i. Samuel Joseph[13] **Nicholson**[540] 11 April 1943 and married twice. (1) Sharon (__) 31 July 1982. (2) Kay **Straton** 26 June 1993.

6109. **Estella Eleanor**[12] **Franklin** (Janette[11] **McKinley**, William Henry[10], Angeline[9] **Whipple**, Enoch[8], Nehemiah[7], Benjamin[6], Francis[5], Jonathan[4], Joseph[3], Matthew[2], Matthew[1])[541] was born in Dayton, Ohio 7 January 1911 and died 7 August 1986 in Portage, Porter Co., Ind., at 75 years of age. She married **Dee L. Clemans** in Gary 26 December 1941. Dee,[542] son of Robert Newton **Clemans** and Bertha K. **Kirkendorfer**, was born 27 July 1911 and died 3 July 1975 in Portage, at 63 years of age. Estella and Dee are buried in Salem Cemetery, Fulton, Ind.

Estella Eleanor **Franklin** and Dee L. **Clemans** had the following children born in Fulton:

    7212 i. James David[13] **Clemans**[543] 9 October 1942.
    7213 ii. Jennie Mae **Clemans**[544] 9 March 1945 and married Donald **Rhoads** 4 September 1966.
    7214 iii. Bernie Louise **Clemans**[545] 30 June 1947 and died in infancy.

6110. **Frances Freda**[12] **Franklin** (Janette[11] **McKinley**, William Henry[10], Angeline[9] **Whipple**, Enoch[8], Nehemiah[7], Benjamin[6], Francis[5], Jonathan[4], Joseph[3], Matthew[2], Matthew[1])[546] was born in Wabash, Ind. 27 July 1912 and married **James Milton Horner** in Garyton, Ind. 29 June 1941. Gary-ton's name was later changed to Portage. James,[547] son of Milton **Horner** and Lizzie **Collier**, was born in Ft. Ritner, Ind. 26 February 1915.

Frances Freda **Franklin** and James Milton **Horner** had the following children:

+ 7215 i. Franklin Dee[13] **Horner** born 15 June 1944.
  7216 ii. (Infant) **Horner**[548] born 15 June 1944 and died at birth.
+ 7217 iii. Rita Janette **Horner** born 27 January 1949.

6111. **Naomi Ruth**[12] **Franklin** (Janette[11] **McKinley**, William Henry[10], Angeline[9] **Whipple**, Enoch[8], Nehemiah[7], Benjamin[6], Francis[5], Jonathan[4], Joseph[3], Matthew[2], Matthew[1])[549] was born in Pleasant Lake, Steuben Co., Ind. 9 July 1917 and married **George R. Hinshaw** in Portage, Porter Co., Ind. 1 July 1940. George,[550] son of James Elijah **Hinshaw** and Clari Alice **Claridge**, was born 8 October 1916.

Naomi Ruth **Franklin** and George R. **Hinshaw** had the following children:

7218 i. Ruth Ann[13] **Hinshaw**[551] born in Dayton, Ohio 6 August 1943 and married twice. (1) Tom **Reavis** 12 June 1965. (2) Les **Davis** 29 August 1988.
7219 ii. David Lee **Hinshaw**[552] born in Gary, Ind. 1 August 1946 and married Carol **Schwalenburg** 4 November 1972.
7220 iii. John Thomas **Hinshaw**[553] born in Oklahoma City, Okla. 31 July 1951 and married Ann **Chance** 9 October 1971.

6114. **Merton George**[12] **McKinley** (William Archibald[11], William Henry[10], Angeline[9] **Whipple**, Enoch[8], Nehemiah[7], Benjamin[6], Francis[5], Jonathan[4], Joseph[3], Matthew[2], Matthew[1])[554] was born in Vinton, Benton Co., Iowa 16 March 1916 and died 3 October 1977 in Iowa, at 61 years of age. Buried at Brandon, Iowa. He married **Eva DeMoss** in Littleton, Iowa 28 November 1940.

Merton George **McKinley** and Eva **DeMoss** had the following children:

7221 i. Alice Marie[13] **McKinley**[555] born in Urbana, Iowa 11 October 1943 and died 22 March 1944 in Iowa, at 5 months of age.
7222 ii. William Arch **McKinley**[556] born in Waterloo, Black Hawk Co., Iowa 25 February 1948 and married Teri **Freeburn** 5 July 1968.
7223 iii. Patricia Ann **McKinley**[557] born in Iowa 25 February 1949.
7224 iv. Lura Calista **McKinley**[558] born in Iowa 29 December 1953 and married Robert **Cook** 12 January 1974.

6117. **Clifford Hoffman**[12] **McKinley** (Grover Cleveland[11], William Henry[10], Angeline[9] **Whipple**, Enoch[8], Nehemiah[7], Benjamin[6], Francis[5], Jonathan[4], Joseph[3], Matthew[2], Matthew[1])[559] was born in Walker, Iowa 9 July 1917 and married **Lola Berneice LeVelle** in Waterloo, Black Hawk

Co., Iowa 2 August 1938. Lola,[560] daughter of Benjamin Franklin **LeVelle** and Mary Irene **Haymaker**, was born in Emmetsburg, Iowa 26 March 1916.

Clifford Hoffman **McKinley** and Lola Berneice **LeVelle** had the following children:
- + 7225 i. Gary Frederick[13] **McKinley** born 16 October 1939.
- + 7226 ii. Janet Faye **McKinley** born 23 June 1941.
- + 7227 iii. Cheryl Delilah **McKinley** born 5 December 1944.
- + 7228 iv. Michael Lee **McKinley** born 16 January 1946.
- + 7229 v. Tony Clifford **McKinley** born 17 September 1956.

6118. **Elizabeth Emily**[12] **McKinley** (Grover Cleveland[11], William Henry[10], Angeline[9] **Whipple**, Enoch[8], Nehemiah[7], Benjamin[6], Francis[5], Jonathan[4], Joseph[3], Matthew[2], Matthew[1])[561] was born in Brandon, Buchanan Co., Iowa 29 April 1920 and married **Roger Glenn Heiserman** in Independence, Buchanan Co., Iowa 25 June 1939. Roger,[562] son of Frank John **Heiserman** and Laura Mae **Cahill**, was born in Buchanan Co. 22 December 1917.

Elizabeth Emily **McKinley** and Roger Glenn **Heiserman** had the following child:
- + 7230 i. Karen Kaye[13] **Heiserman** born 11 February 1940.

6119. **Bernard Laverne**[12] **McKinley** (Grover Cleveland[11], William Henry[10], Angeline[9] **Whipple**, Enoch[8], Nehemiah[7], Benjamin[6], Francis[5], Jonathan[4], Joseph[3], Matthew[2], Matthew[1])[563] was born in Urbana, Iowa 23 November 1928 and married **Dorothy Ann Strong** in Ames, Iowa 11 June 1950. Dorothy,[564] daughter of Carl **Strong** and Emma **Porter**, was born 2 October 1931. Bernie was Mayor of Waterloo, Iowa from 1986 through 1991. He retired from the insurance business and he and Dorothy live in Waterloo (1998).

Bernard Laverne **McKinley** and Dorothy Ann **Strong** had the following children:
- + 7231 i. Bernard Laverne[13] **McKinley** born 16 July 1951.
- + 7232 ii. Daniel Grover **McKinley** born 20 October 1953.
- + 7233 iii. Kathleen Anne **McKinley** born 19 March 1955.
- + 7234 iv. Rebecca Sue **McKinley** born 24 February 1959.
- + 7235 v. Elizabeth Rose **McKinley** born 27 July 1962.

6120. **William Harry**[12] **McKinley** (John Carlysle[11], William Henry[10], Angeline[9] **Whipple**, Enoch[8], Nehemiah[7], Benjamin[6], Francis[5], Jonathan[4], Joseph[3], Matthew[2], Matthew[1])[565] was born in Benton Co., Iowa 15 August

1915 and died 10 November 1990 in Medford, Jackson Co., Oreg., at 75 years of age. Buried in Eastwood Cemetery. He married **Gladys Dos** in Waterloo, Black Hawk Co., Iowa 18 October 1936. Gladys,[566] daughter of Fred **Dos** and Anna **Edgeton**, was born in December 1919. William and Gladys moved to Vancouver, Wash. before 1943 and from there to Medford, Oreg. about 1949. He worked for the Otis Elevator Co. for 48 years.

William Harry **McKinley** and Gladys **Dos** had the following children:

    7236   i.   William Harold[13] **McKinley**[567] born in Waterloo 17 November 1937.

    7237   ii.   James Lee **McKinley**[568] born in Waterloo 18 November 1938 and married Sandra **Weist** 20 May 1956.

    7238   iii.   Carol Kay **McKinley**[569] was born in Waterloo 19 November 1939 and died 14 April 1971 in San Diego, Calif., at 31 years of age. She married Willis David **Jordon** 23 September 1959. They had three children. No information provided.

+   7239   iv.   Charles Dos **McKinley** born 15 July 1941.

    7240   v.   John Allen **McKinley**[570] born in Minneapolis, Minn. 22 April 1943.

    7241   vi.   Steven Arden **McKinley**[571] born in Medford 1 July 1950.

+   7242   vii.   Elizabeth Ann **McKinley** born 2 January 1952.

6122. **Dean Carlysle**[12] **McKinley** (John Carlysle[11], William Henry[10], Angeline[9] **Whipple**, Enoch[8], Nehemiah[7], Benjamin[6], Francis[5], Jonathan[4], Joseph[3], Matthew[2], Matthew[1])[572] was born in Garrison, Benton Co., Iowa 11 April 1920 and married **Marvel M. Peters** in Bellflower, Calif. 14 September 1944. Marvel,[573] daughter of Carl Christian **Peters** and Elsie **Schmiedel**, was born in Garrison 25 April 1921. Dean was raised on a farm near Vinton and served in the U.S. Marine Corps from 1941–46. Following WWII he became a chiropractor and practiced in El Paso, Texas for 40 years before retiring to Alto, N.Mex. in May 1989.

Dean Carlysle **McKinley** and Marvel M. **Peters** had the following children:

+   7243   i.   Mary Lynn[13] **McKinley** born 23 January 1946.

+   7244   ii.   Teri Dea **McKinley** born 16 December 1947.

6124. **Charles Russell**[12] **Shaffer** (Lura[11] **McKinley**, William Henry[10], Angeline[9] **Whipple**, Enoch[8], Nehemiah[7], Benjamin[6], Francis[5], Jonathan[4], Joseph[3], Matthew[2], Matthew[1])[574] was born in Hartford, Warren Co., Iowa 27 June 1920 and married **Norma Ellen Sloan** in Crescent City, Calif. 14 February 1943. Norma,[575] daughter of William **Sloan** and Edna **Bickner**, was born 9 August 1923.

Charles Russell **Shaffer** and Norma Ellen **Sloan** had the following children:

- 7245 i. Terry Russell[13] **Shaffer**[576] born in Crescent City 29 February 1944 and married Karen **Brown** 24 February 1968.
- 7246 ii. Marsha Eileen **Shaffer**[577] born in Waterloo, Black Hawk Co., Iowa 12 June 1947 and married Steven **Bowen** 27 January 1968.
- 7247 iii. Richard Burl **Shaffer**[578] born in Waterloo 4 October 1950 and married Lucille **Pereya** 4 October 1973.
- 7248 iv. Steven Arthur **Shaffer**[579] born in Phoenix, Ariz. 8 July 1953.

6125. Gail Carlysle[12] **Shaffer** (Lura[11] **McKinley**, William Henry[10], Angeline[9] **Whipple**, Enoch[8], Nehemiah[7], Benjamin[6], Francis[5], Jonathan[4], Joseph[3], Matthew[2], Matthew[1])[580] was born in Vinton, Benton Co., Iowa 2 August 1930 and married twice. (1) **Joan Strempke** in Independence, Buchanan Co., Iowa 25 November 1959. She is the daughter of Carl **Strempke** and Marcia **Sherman**.[581] They were divorced in June 1965. (2) **Betty June Swarts Boyer** 9 April 1965.

Gail Carlysle **Shaffer** and Joan **Strempke** had the following children:

- 7249 i. Christopher Gail[13] **Shaffer**[582] born in Olewein, Iowa 27 June 1960 and married Marcia Lynn **Sherman** 6 June 1982 in Perry, Iowa. They have 3 children; no details.
- 7250 ii. Bettina Arleen **Shaffer**[583] born in Olewein 1 October 1961 and married twice. (1) Kevin **Anderson** 22 June 1985. (2) Damien F. **Pincves** 30 July 1993.

6126. Donald Everett[12] **McKinley** (Edward Torrence[11], William Henry[10], Angeline[9] **Whipple**, Enoch[8], Nehemiah[7], Benjamin[6], Francis[5], Jonathan[4], Joseph[3], Matthew[2], Matthew[1])[584] was born in Brandon, Buchanan Co., Iowa 30 December 1914 and married **Ollie Marie Newkirk** in Fairbanks, Buchanan Co., Iowa 14 March 1937. Ollie,[585] daughter of Alvie **Newkirk** and Barbara **Berkley**, was born in Chenoa, Ill. 7 June 1914.

Donald Everett **McKinley** and Ollie Marie **Newkirk** had the following children born in Vinton, Benton Co., Iowa:

- 7251 i. Barbara Ann[13] **McKinley**[586] 4 July 1938 and married twice. (1) Earl **Boyles** 3 June 1958. They were divorced bef 1972. (2) Ernest **Riggle** 14 May 1972.
- 7252 ii. Mary Louise **McKinley**[587] 23 July 1939 and married Thomas E. **Bruce** 13 October 1971.
- 7253 iii. Mack **McKinley**[588] 4 January 1950 and died 26 June 1978 at 28 years of age. He married Deborah **Michael**.

7254 iv. Edward Dale **McKinley**[589] 25 July 1951 and married twice. (1) Vicki **Gunn** 26 August 1972. (2) Glenda **Donels** 16 September 1978.

7255 v. Donna Rae **McKinley**[590] 22 February 1954 and married Michael **Felker** 1 September 1973.

6127. **Marjorie Bernice**[12] **McKinley** (Edward Torrence[11], William Henry[10], Angeline[9] **Whipple**, Enoch[8], Nehemiah[7], Benjamin[6], Francis[5], Jonathan[4], Joseph[3], Matthew[2], Matthew[1])[591] was born in Brandon, Buchanan Co., Iowa 26 December 1916 and died there 14 January 1989, at 72 years of age. She married **Milo E. Stainbrook** in Brandon 8 August 1936. Milo,[592] son of Lloyd **Stainbrook** and Henryetta **Rouse**, was born 26 June 1915 and died 5 July 1967 in Brandon, at 52 years of age.

Marjorie Bernice **McKinley** and Milo E. **Stainbrook** had the following children born in Vinton, Benton Co., Iowa:

7256 i. Denny Edward[13] **Stainbrook**[593] 9 April 1939 and married Donna **Albough** 23 November 1956.

7257 ii. Jerry Lloyd **Stainbrook**[594] 17 March 1941 and died 16 December 1998 at 57 years of age. He married Leila **Mathews** 16 September 1960.

7258 iii. Sarah Ann Marie **Stainbrook**[595] 9 March 1948 and married **Thomas Thill** 16 August 1968.

7259 iv. Nancy Jo **Stainbrook**[596] 4 February 1950 and married Charles **Winters** 30 December 1974.

7260 v. Molly Sue **Stainbrook**[597] 24 June 1953 amd married twice. (1) Donald **Baker** 27 February 1982. (2) Larry **Hurs**.

6128. **Tracy Eugene**[12] **McKinley** (Edward Torrence[11], William Henry[10], Angeline[9] **Whipple**, Enoch[8], Nehemiah[7], Benjamin[6], Francis[5], Jonathan[4], Joseph[3], Matthew[2], Matthew[1])[598] was born in Brandon, Buchanan Co., Iowa 23 July 1918 and died of an anurism of the brain 23 March 1981 in Vinton, Benton Co., Iowa, at 62 years of age. He married **Dorothy Harriet Harmon** in Buchanan Co. 12 July 1948. Dorothy,[599] daughter of Lynn F. **Harmon** and Marvel **Brookman**, was born 11 April 1928. Tracy served in the Army during WWII and farmed near Brandon after the war.

Tracy Eugene **McKinley** and Dorothy Harriet **Harmon** had the following children:

7261 i. Gary Dale[13] **McKinley**[600] was born in Iowa City, Iowa 31 October 1946. He was adopted and married twice. (1)

Mary Kathleen **McLaughlin** 3 April 1968. (2) Pat **Bentley** 22 May 1982.

7262 ii. Eudena Rae **McKinley**[601] born in Oakland, Calif. 23 January 1949. She was adopted and married James E. **Sorenson** 12 July 1969.

7263 iii. Tracy Gene **McKinley**[602] born in Vinton 27 February 1951.

7264 iv. Timothy Lynn **McKinley**[603] born in Vinton 27 June 1957.

7265 v. Thomas Paige **McKinley**[604] born in Vinton 24 December 1959.

7266 vi. Mary Jean **McKinley**[605] born in Vinton 13 March 1961 and married **Jeffery Meyer** 10 October 1979.

7267 vii. Shelia Kay **McKinley**[606] born in Vinton 10 July 1962.

6129. **Robert Cecil**[12] **McKinley** (Edward Torrence[11], William Henry[10], Angeline[9] **Whipple**, Enoch[8], Nehemiah[7], Benjamin[6], Francis[5], Jonathan[4], Joseph[3], Matthew[2], Matthew[1])[607] was born in Brandon, Buchanan Co., Iowa 22 December 1919 and married **Yvonne Cleora Rice** in Waterloo, Black Hawk Co., Iowa 23 January 1944. Yvonne,[608] daughter of Jay M. **Rice** and Esther **Wolf**.

Robert Cecil **McKinley** and Yvonne Cleora **Rice** had the following child born in Iowa:

7268 i. Sharon Kaye[13] **McKinley**[609] 21 April 1946 and married twice. (1) Paul Allen **James** 5 June 1964. (2) Jerry **Seller**.

6130. **Ila Mae**[12] **McKinley** (Edward Torrence[11], William Henry[10], Angeline[9] **Whipple**, Enoch[8], Nehemiah[7], Benjamin[6], Francis[5], Jonathan[4], Joseph[3], Matthew[2], Matthew[1])[610] was born in Brandon, Buchanan Co., Iowa 4 July 1922 and married **Clarence LaVern Beyer** there 9 April 1944. Clarence,[611] son of Floyd **Beyer** and Velma **Andrews**, was born in Brandon 30 May 1923.

Ila Mae **McKinley** and Clarence LaVern **Beyer** had the following children:

7269 i. Linda Jo[13] **Beyer**[612] born in Urbana, Iowa 18 October 1945 and married Delbert **Berghoefer** 20 July 1969.

7270 ii. Allison Eugene **Beyer**[613] born in Vinton, Benton Co., Iowa 5 October 1946 and married Nancy **Bremer** 5 July 1970.

7271 iii. Patricia Kay **Beyer**[614] born in Vinton 28 July 1949 and married Gary **Janssen** 3 July 1971.

7272 iv. Mark LaVerne **Beyer**[615] born in Vinton 25 July 1952 and married three times. (1) Cinthia **Smith** 28 December 1970. (2) Valrie **Johnson** 16 September 1972. (3) Deborah **Rucker** 10 August 1993.

6131. **Belva Jean**[12] **McKinley** (Merton Wallace[11], William Henry[10], Angeline[9] **Whipple**, Enoch[8], Nehemiah[7], Benjamin[6], Francis[5], Jonathan[4], Joseph[3], Matthew[2], Matthew[1])[616] was born in Cedar Rapids, Linn Co., Iowa 4 December 1929 and married **Dean Duane Oldridge** in Chickaswa Co., Iowa, 9 May 1953.

Dean,[617] son of Ralph **Oldridge** and Opal **Franck**, was born in Buchanan Co., Iowa 10 January 1931 and died there 12 August 1977, Iowa, at 46 years of age.

Belva Jean **McKinley** and Dean Duane **Oldridge** had the following children:
+ 7273 i. Kenda Kay[13] **Oldridge** born 2 April 1958.
+ 7274 ii. Kamie Lea **Oldridge** born 14 November 1959.
+ 7275 iii. Kelly Lynn **Oldridge** born 20 June 1961.

6132. **Evelyn Lee**[12] **McKinley** (Merton Wallace[11], William Henry[10], Angeline[9] **Whipple**, Enoch[8], Nehemiah[7], Benjamin[6], Francis[5], Jonathan[4], Joseph[3], Matthew[2], Matthew[1])[618] was born in Osage, Mitchell Co., Iowa 2 January 1932 and married **John Willard Orr** in Omaha, Nebr. 7 June 1958. John,[619] son of Willard Johnston **Orr** and Sarah Lucille **Ely**, was born in Atkinson Co., Mo. 30 October 1923.

Much of the information on the first five generations of the McKinley family was provided by Evelyn, who in 1995 (second edition in 1996) compiled, edited, and self published *McKinley and Allied Families. Ancestors of Evelyn McKinley Orr.* During our volumnious correspondence, this compiler came to know Evelyn as a tenancious researcher who carefully recorded her sources. I am grateful that she was willing to share the results of her hard work. She and husband John live in Omaha (2000).

Evelyn Lee **McKinley** and John Willard **Orr** had the following children born in Omaha:
 7276 i. Tay Lynn[13] **Orr**[620] 17 March 1960.
+ 7277 ii. Tracey Ann **Orr** 24 May 1962.
+ 7278 iii. Terri Lu **Orr** 18 May 1964.

6133. **Doris Eileen**[12] **Wood** (Elizabeth[11] **McKinley**, William Henry[10], Angeline[9] **Whipple**, Enoch[8], Nehemiah[7], Benjamin[6], Francis[5], Jonathan[4], Joseph[3], Matthew[2], Matthew[1])[621] was born on a farm north of Brandon,

Buchanan Co., Iowa 26 February 1923. She married three times. (1) **Burl C. Smith** in Iowa. They were divorced in Iowa. (2) **Carl Gilchrist** in Vinton, Benton Co., Iowa 3 July 1947. (3) **Ben Hintze** in Rock Island, Ill. 15 September 1979. He died there 23 May 1989.[622]

Doris Eileen **Wood** and Carl **Gilchrist** had the following children:
+ 7279 i. Karla Kay[13] **Gilchrist** born 26 September 1950.
+ 7280 ii. Karan Ann **Gilchrist** born 18 July 1955.

6134. **Mardene Dot[12] Wood** (Elizabeth[11] **McKinley**, William Henry[10], Angeline[9] **Whipple**, Enoch[8], Nehemiah[7], Benjamin[6], Francis[5], Jonathan[4], Joseph[3], Matthew[2], Matthew[1])[623] was born in Vinton, Benton Co., Iowa 16 September 1924 and married three times. (1) **Dick Feiereisen** in Iowa City, Johnson Co., Iowa, 10 July 1947. They were divorced in Cedar Rapids, Iowa in February 1948. (2) **Melvin Hahn** in Cedar Rapids in 1966. They were divorced in Cedar Rapids in 1968. (3) **Don Roloff** in Cedar Rapids 10 October 1979. He died 23 September 1989.[624]

Mardene Dot **Wood** and Dick **Feiereisen** had the following child:
+ 7281 i. Carl Joe[13] **Feiereisen** born 7 January 1948.

6135. **Jack Edward[12] Wood** (Elizabeth[11] **McKinley**, William Henry[10], Angeline[9] **Whipple**, Enoch[8], Nehemiah[7], Benjamin[6], Francis[5], Jonathan[4], Joseph[3], Matthew[2], Matthew[1])[625] was born in Vinton, Benton Co., Iowa 22 February 1929 and died 16 June 1991 in Tucson, Ariz., at 62 years of age. He married twice. (1) **Bonnie Strong** in Cedar Rapids, Iowa 11 March 1950. They were divorced in 1963. (2) **Janice Lee** in 1974. They were divorced in 1978.

Jack Edward **Wood** and Bonnie **Strong** had the following children:
+ 7282 i. Kathy Jo[13] **Wood** born 10 October 1950.
+ 7283 ii. William Archer **Wood** born 19 January 1953.
  7284 iii. Bradley Scott **Wood**[626] born in Vinton 4 September 1958 and died 28 July 1962 in Waterloo, Black Hawk Co., Iowa, at 3 years of age.

6151. **Rev. Raymond Viles[12] Kearns** (Rev. Raymond Viles[11], Dr. Archibald Jackson[10], Eliza Roxana[9] **Whipple**, Enoch[8], Nehemiah[7], Benjamin[6], Francis[5], Jonathan[4], Joseph[3], Matthew[2], Matthew[1])[627] was born in Chicago, Cook Co., Ill. 6 September 1915 and was buried 10 May 1994 in Portland, Multnomah Co., Oreg. He married **Helen Bernice Reid** 7 September 1938. Helen,[628] daughter of Frank Archibald **Reid** and Ida **Schorer**, was born in Clyde, Kans. 12 October 1916.

Rev. Raymond Viles **Kearns** and Helen Bernice **Reid** had the following children:

  7285 i. Raymond John[13] **Kearns** [629] born 19 February 1940 and married an unnamed person 2 May 1982.
  7286 ii. Diane **Kearns**.[630]
  7287 iii. Betsy **Kearns**.[631]

6153. **Lt. Col. Archibald Gordon**[12] **Kearns** (Rev. Archibald Jackson[11], Dr. Archibald Jackson[10], Eliza Roxana[9] **Whipple**, Enoch[8], Nehemiah[7], Benjamin[6], Francis[5], Jonathan[4], Joseph[3], Matthew[2], Matthew[1])[632] was born in Alliance, Box Butte Co., Nebr. 16 August 1919 and married twice. (1) **Annette Blackburn** in Columbia, Richland Co., S.C. 19 July 1942. (2) **Geneen Mitchell** in Monument, Colo.

Lt. Col. Archibald Gordon **Kearns** and Annette **Blackburn** had the following children:

  7288 i. James Gordon[13] **Kearns**.[633]
  7289 ii. Anne Gibson **Kearns**.[634]
  7290 iii. David Blackburn **Kearns**.[635]
  7291 iv. Barbara **Kearns**.[636]
  7292 v. John Timothy **Kearns** [637] born 20 April 1953 and died 23 October 1998 in North Fort Myers, Fla., at 45 years of age.
  7293 vi. Catherine **Kearns**.[638]

6154. **Rev. Paul Searight**[12] **Kearns** (Rev. Archibald Jackson[11], Dr. Archibald Jackson[10], Eliza Roxana[9] **Whipple**, Enoch[8], Nehemiah[7], Benjamin[6], Francis[5], Jonathan[4], Joseph[3], Matthew[2], Matthew[1])[639] was born in Alliance, Box Butte Co., Nebr. 2 August 1921 and died 30 November 2003 in Costa Mesa, Calif., at 82 years of age. He married twice. (1) **Betty Joy Mauldin** in Houston, Tex. 19 October 1943. She was born in Fort Worth, Tex. 21 February 1925.[640] (2) **Ernestine Grissette-Shinto** in Fullerton, Orange Co., Calif. 23 November 1982.

Paul entered College in 1939 and was graduated four year later as a Phi Beta Kappa. In 1950 he was graduated from McCormick Seminary in Chicago and later earned a Doctor of Ministry degree from San Francisco Seminary. His first assignment was to a Presbyterian Church in Anadarko, a county seat town in south western Oklahoma. His goal had always to serve the church in the field of higher education and after three years at Anadarko, he became a Prebysterian University Pastor at what is now North Texas University and Texas' Women's University.

The family moved to San Francisco, Calif. in 1955 and Paul joined the staff of the Prebysterian Department of Campus Christian Life with

{ G 1069 }

responsibilities in 13 western states. Eight years later he was the Director of the University Christian Center near the American University in Beirut, Lebanon where he developed a strong interest in the history and culture and concerns of the Middle East. He returned to California in 1966 and began a 20-year career as Director of United Ministries in Higher Education in Southern California. His office was on the USC campus in Los Angeles where he also served part time as the designated Interim University Pastor on two occasions.

He died of prostate cancer and his cremains were interred in Harbor Lawn Memorial Park Cemetery in Costa Mesa. He was survived by his wife Ernestine, sons David, Philip and Lawrence, stepdaughter Billye Shinto-Littman; grandchildren Chris, James, Timothy, Anna, Emily, and Jackie; and brothers Gordon and Donald.

Rev. Paul Searight **Kearns** and Betty Joy **Mauldin** had the following children:
- 7294   i.   David Quin[13] **Kearns** [641] born in Corpus Christi, Nueces Co., Tex. 1 September 1944. He married twice. (1) Gaynelle **Groth**. (2) Nancy **Lee** in Hawaii.
- +   7295   ii.   Phillip Mauldin **Kearns** born 19 April 1947.
- +   7296   iii.   Lawrence Archibald **Kearns** born 5 May 1952.
- 7297   iv.   Paul Kimball **Kearns** [642] in Burlingame, San Mateo Co., Calif. 5 September 1955 and died 7 March 1975 in Santa Barbara, Calif., at 19 years of age.

6155. Rev. Robert Harry[12] **Kearns** (Rev. Archibald Jackson[11], Dr. Archibald Jackson[10], Eliza Roxana[9] **Whipple**, Enoch[8], Nehemiah[7], Benjamin[6], Francis[5], Jonathan[4], Joseph[3], Matthew[2], Matthew[1])[643] was born in Tekamah, Burt Co., Nebr. 27 December 1923 and died 20 July 2000 in Surprise, Ariz., at 76 years of age. He married **Elizabeth Stefanowicz** in Portland, Multnomah Co., Oreg. 19 May 1950.

Robert attended public schools in Missouri Valley, Iowa and Rocky Ford, Colo., graduating from high school at the latter. He attended Kansas Wesleyan University, Salina, Kans. and the U. of Colorado, Boulder before enlisting in the U.S. Navy in September 1942. He was a Naval Aviation Cadet and an Aerographer in the Navy Weather Service. Following discharge in 1946, he earned an undergraduate degree at Huron (S. Dak.) University and a Master of Divinity at McCormick Theological seminary, Chicago.

His 45-year service as a Minister began when he was ordained in the Presbyterian Church, USA in 1952 by the Presbytery of Huron. He was Pastor to congregations at Hamilton and Bathgate, N. Dak; Aberdeen and Boise, Idaho; and Durango, Colo. He served as an Interim Pastor during his semi-retirement years in Farmington, N.Mex, Canon City, Durango, Cortez, and the San Juan Larger parish, all in Colorado. He served as Chair for Presbytery and Synod in Idaho and Colorado and Moderator and Stated Clerk in Idaho and Colorado. He was a Director of the Spruce Haven Youth Camp in Durango and co-founder and Director of the Sunday Afternoon Ski Ministry at the Purgatory, Colo. resort area.

He died at home after a prolonged illness. Memorial services were held 29 July at Desert Palm Presbyterian Church in Sun City West, Ariz.

Rev. Robert Harry **Kearns** and Elizabeth **Stefanowicz** had the following children:

	7298	i.	Stephen Gary[13] **Kearns**[644] Stephen was living in San Francisco in July 2000.
+	7299	ii.	Rebecca Grace **Kearns.**
+	7300	iii.	Julia Elizabeth **Kearns.**

6156. **Donald Raymond[12] Kearns Ph.D.** (Rev. Archibald Jackson[11], Dr. Archibald Jackson[10], Eliza Roxana[9] **Whipple**, Enoch[8], Nehemiah[7], Benjamin[6], Francis[5], Jonathan[4], Joseph[3], Matthew[2], Matthew[1])[645] was born in Missouri Valley, Harrison Co., Iowa 27 June 1930 and married **Ruth Louise Balka** in Portland, Multnomah Co., Oreg. 13 January 1954.

Donald Raymond **Kearns** and Ruth Louise **Balka** had the following children:

| + | 7301 | i. | Elisabeth Louise[13] **Kearns.** |
| | 7302 | ii. | Jennifer Kathleen **Kearns** [646] married Jonathan Christopher **Heath** in Tempe, Maricopa Co, Ariz. 25 April 1992. |

6157. **William Perry[12] Whipple** (Milo Robert[11], William Perry[10], Cyrenius Thomas[9], Enoch[8], Nehemiah[7], Benjamin[6], Francis[5], Jonathan[4], Joseph[3], Matthew[2], Matthew[1])[647] was born in Cedar Rapids, Iowa 1 November 1913 and married **Gayle Schroeder** there 18 September 1937. Gayle,[648] daughter of William **Schroeder** and Emma **Schlesselman**, was born in Wellman, Iowa 23 January 1912 and died 10 November 1996 in Cedar Rapids at 84 years of age. Gayle had to drop out of Cedar Rapids Coe College in 1932 after her father died. It was the time of the "Great Depression" and there was no money for her to return for her senior year. She was, however, able to get a job at Peterson's Drug Store in Williamsburg where the family lived. Her evenings were spent piecing a quilt whose patterns came in weekly installments in the local newspaper, *The Gazette*. It included a block of each of the signs of the Zodiac. Embroidered around it were the traits attributed to that sign: Optimistic, generous, etc. Her desire to graduate from college never died and in the fall of

1935 she got a Saturday job at Killian's in Cedar Rapids and was allowed to enroll at half tuition because her brother Gilbert was also a student. Her tuition for the senior year was $75. She was graduated in 1936 three years behind her original class and was the only graduate to land a teaching job when she was hired to teach English at Arlington, Iowa.

After her marriage, she helped raise a family of two sons who both became teachers. She loved to read and persistently promoted libraires and recorded books for the blind. She read for the blind for 13 plus years and did all the reading for a student from Vinton who was completing a master's degree. Coe College established the "Gayle S. Whipple Browsing Area" at its library in the spring of 1997. It is a comfortable reading area with bookshelves displaying the library's newest arrivals. She died of ovarian cancer.

Bill was graduated from Cedar Rapids' Washington High School and Coe College. He was graduated from Coe cum laude with honors in Commerce and Finance and Speech and received the Courteney Award as the graduating letterman in a major sport with the highest grade point average and was elected to the Coe Athletic Hall of Fame. He was a member of the Sachem Senior Honor Mens' Society and was awarded "special distinction" in debate by Pi Kappa Delta, Honorary Speech Fraternity.

Upon his father's death in 1935, he took over the family insurance agency (Milo R. Whipple Agency), retiring in 1974 when he became an officer (Chairman in 1998) of the Hall-Perrine Foundation of Cedar Rapids. He is a past Vice Chair of the Board of American Federal Savings & Loan Assn. of Cedar Rapids and past Director of the following: Banks of Iowa, the Nissen Corporation, Mid-American Mutual Fund, American Insurance & Industrial Fund, Inter Ocean Reinsurance Co., Iowa State Association of Insurance Agents, and the Wick Foundation, Meth-Wick Manor.

He served 22 years on the Board of Trustees of Coe College including three years as Chair. He is also a Past President of the Board of Trustees of the Greater Metropolitan YMCA of Cedar Rapids (recipient of the John M. Ely Award for 12 years of service on the YMCA Board), Past Director of the Cedar Rapids Chamber of Commerce and recipient of its Community Recognition Award for significant contributions to the economic development and to the quality of life in the Cedar Rapids-Marion area, Chair of the Linn County Chapter of the American Red Cross, and Trustee of the Cedar Rapids Public Library. He is a member of the Pickwick Club, Elks Club, and Rotary. His hobbies include philately, signeviery, investments, sports, and Whipple family history.

At a Founders Day Convocation December 5, 2001, Bill was awarded Coe College's Founder Medal given to individuals of "rare and exceptional distinction" in their fields of work and to Coe. Medalists "exemplify in extraordinary degree the qualifies of a liberally educated person. Coe

President James Phifer said Bill represented "the best of our alumni, both in professional achievement and in commitment to the college." The December Convocation was only the third time in Coe's 150-year history that Founders' Medals have been awarded. Bill was recognized for his contributions to the college in 1996 when he was awarded an Honorary Degree at Commencement ceremonies. He and wife Gayle also established The William P. Whipple and Gayle Schroeder Whipple Endowed Chair in the Humanities at Coe.[649]

William Perry **Whipple** and Gayle **Schroeder** had the following children:
+   7303   i.   John William[13] **Whipple** born 5 July 1939.
+   7304   ii.   Robert Milo **Whipple** born 13 September 1943.

6160. **Mary Virginia**[12] **Tobin** (Virginia K.[11] **Whipple**, William Perry[10], Cyrenius Thomas[9], Enoch[8], Nehemiah[7], Benjamin[6], Francis[5], Jonathan[4], Joseph[3], Matthew[2], Matthew[1])[650] was born in Vinton, Benton Co., Iowa 11 November 1928 and died of pneumonia 27 May 1999 in Laguna Beach, Calif., at 70 years of age. Inurnment was at sea on 9 June. She married **Frederick Benning**. Her three children were living in Laguna Beach at the time of her death.

Mary Virginia **Tobin** and Frederick **Benning** had the following children:
    7305   i.   Michael[13] **Benning**.[651]
    7306   ii.   Magan **Benning**.[652]
    7307   iii.   Amanda **Benning**.[653]

6162. **Charles Stephan**[12] **Frederick** (Maude Maree[11] **Whipple**, Milo Enoch[10], Cyrenius Thomas[9], Enoch[8], Nehemiah[7], Benjamin[6], Francis[5], Jonathan[4], Joseph[3], Matthew[2], Matthew[1])[654] was born in Englewood, Arapahos Co., Colo. 21 September 1910 and died 17 March 1980 in Anacortes, Skagit Co., Wash., at 69 years of age. Buried at Fern Hill Cemetery. He married twice. (1) **Babe Naydine Brooks** in Deming, N. Mex. 6 May 1931. They were divorced in 1943. She married (2) **Elmo Elza Bartling**. and (3) **Frank Ziegler**. Naydine,[655] daughter of Carl Raymond **Brooks** and Jessie Maye **Brown**, was born in Armona, Kings Co, Calif. 29 August 1913. Charles married (2) **Barbara Anne Crawford**.

Charles Stephan **Frederick** and Babe Naydine **Brooks** had the following children:
+   7308   i.   Dawn Naydine[13] **Frederick** born 15 May 1936.
+   7309   ii.   Bruce Ellsworth **Frederick** born 2 February 1939.
+   7310   iii.   Colleen Charles-Ann **Frederick** born 22 August 1940.

6170. **James Dudley**[12] **Andrus** (Maude Maree[11] **Whipple**, Milo Enoch[10], Cyrenius Thomas[9], Enoch[8], Nehemiah[7], Benjamin[6], Francis[5], Jonathan[4], Joseph[3], Matthew[2], Matthew[1])[656] was born in Allegan, Allegan Co., Mich. 5 August 1929 and married **Della Meshkin** in Napoleon, Ohio 24 November 1950. Della,[657] daughter of John Peter **Meshkin** and Della Eleanor **Endriekus**, was born in Allegan Co. 12 February 1928.

James Dudley **Andrus** and Della **Meshkin** had the following children:
+   7311   i.   Vickie Lee[13] **Andrus** born 10 January 1952.
+   7312   ii.   James Albie **Andrus** born 19 August 1954.
+   7313   iii.   Daniel Clay **Andrus** born 14 August 1955.

6173. **Virginia**[12] **Whipple** (Carl Thornton[11], Selmon Thomas[10], Cyrenius Thomas[9], Enoch[8], Nehemiah[7], Benjamin[6], Francis[5], Jonathan[4], Joseph[3], Matthew[2], Matthew[1])[658] was born in Benton Co., Iowa and married twice. (1) **Joseph Mumbauer**. (2) **Marvin Holmes**. He died in 1962 in Shellsburg, Iowa.[659]

Virginia **Whipple** and Joseph **Mumbauer** had the following child:
     7314   i.   Patricia[13] **Mumbauer**[660] She had two children before being divorced from her husband. No details on names of children or husband provided.

Virginia **Whipple** and Marvin **Holmes** had the following children:
     7315   ii.   Michael **Holmes**.[661]
     7316   iii.   William **Holmes**.[662]
     7317   iv.   Shelley Rae **Holmes**[663] born in Benton Co. and married Michael Lyn **Lutz**. They were married in the Presbyterian Church in Vinton, Iowa with Michael's uncle, Clarence Lutz, conducting the ceremony. They have two sons; no details provided.

6174. **Frank**[12] **Whipple** (Carl Thornton[11], Selmon Thomas[10], Cyrenius Thomas[9], Enoch[8], Nehemiah[7], Benjamin[6], Francis[5], Jonathan[4], Joseph[3], Matthew[2], Matthew[1])[664] was born in Benton Co., Iowa in 1908 and was buried in Shellsburg, Iowa. He married twice. (1) **Mildred Dickson**. (2) **Alma Williams**.

Frank **Whipple** and Mildred **Dickson** had the following child:
     7318   i.   Jacqueline[13] **Whipple**[665] born in Benton Co. and married Gary **Crandell**.

Frank **Whipple** and Alma **Williams** had the following child:
  7319 ii. Frankie **Whipple**[666] born in Benton Co.

  6175. **George**[12] **Whipple** (Carl Thornton[11], Selmon Thomas[10], Cyrenius Thomas[9], Enoch[8], Nehemiah[7], Benjamin[6], Francis[5], Jonathan[4], Joseph[3], Matthew[2], Matthew[1])[667] was born in Benton Co., Iowa 30 March 1910 and died 22 February 1978 at 67 years of age. Buried at Evergreen Cemetery, Vinton. He married twice. (1) **Martha Rice**. (2) **Mardelle Robbins**.

George **Whipple** and Mardelle **Robbins** had the following children:
  7320 i. Dwayne[13] **Whipple**[668] is married and has two sons. No details provided.
  7321 ii. Thomas **Whipple**.[669]
  7322 iii. Edward **Whipple**[670] married Karen **Brown**.
  7323 iv. Donald **Whipple**.[671]
  7324 v. Carl Thornton **Whipple** II[672] married Ruthann **Miller**.

  6178. **Anna Catherine**[12] **Catlin** (Callie Catherine[11] **Whipple**, Selmon Thomas[10], Cyrenius Thomas[9], Enoch[8], Nehemiah[7], Benjamin[6], Francis[5], Jonathan[4], Joseph[3], Matthew[2], Matthew[1])[673] was born in Benton Co., Iowa 24 October 1913 and died 25 December 1997 in Independence, Buchanan Co., Iowa, at 84 years of age. Buried in Mt. Hope Cemetery. She married **Russell John Mack** in Jesup, Iowa 4 May 1941. Russell,[674] son of Samuel David **Mack** and Bertha Pearl **Grimm**, was born in Garrison, Benton Co., Iowa 19 April 1913 and died 8 June 2000 in Sargent Bluff, Iowa, at 87 years of age. Buried at Mt. Hope Cemetery, Independence, Iowa. He served with the U.S. Army in the Philippines during WWII. He was a road maintenance worker with the Iowa Department of Transportation before retiring in 1975 and a member of the First United Methodist Church in Jesup.

Anna Catherine **Catlin** and Russell John **Mack** had the following children:
+ 7325 i. Mary Catherine[13] **Mack** born 19 June 1950.
+ 7326 ii. Thomas Russell **Mack** born 22 May 1955.

  6179. **Elsie Laurel**[12] **Catlin** (Callie Catherine[11] **Whipple**, Selmon Thomas[10], Cyrenius Thomas[9], Enoch[8], Nehemiah[7], Benjamin[6], Francis[5], Jonathan[4], Joseph[3], Matthew[2], Matthew[1])[675] was born in Benton Co., Iowa 8 July 1916 and died 24 December 2002 in Connecticut, at 86 years of age. She married **Charles Louis Hovey** in Jesup, Iowa 27 December 1938. He was born 4 October 1915.[676]

Elsie Laurel **Catlin** and Charles Louis **Hovey** had the following children:
+ 7327 i. Kathleen Louise[13] **Hovey** born 21 October 1939.
+ 7328 ii. Marshall Lewis **Hovey** born 3 April 1944.

6180. **Ruby Aileen**[12] **Catlin** (Callie Catherine[11] **Whipple**, Selmon Thomas[10], Cyrenius Thomas[9], Enoch[8], Nehemiah[7], Benjamin[6], Francis[5], Jonathan[4], Joseph[3], Matthew[2], Matthew[1])[677] was born in Benton Co., Iowa 30 June 1920 and died 23 February 1998 in Jesup, Iowa, at 77 years of age. She married **John Edward Nesbit** in Jesup 12 December 1943. He was born in Black Hawk Co., Iowa 8 September 1921 and died 26 December 1980 in Waterloo, Black Hawk Co., Iowa, at 59 years of age.[678] Ruby, a homemaker, farmed with her husband in the Jesup area. She was a member of the Barclay Jolly Dozen and a 50-year member and past officer of the Barclay Presbyterian Church.

Ruby Aileen **Catlin** and John Edward **Nesbit** had the following children born in Waterloo:

7329 i. James Howard[13] **Nesbit**[679] 22 April 1947 and married Carol Ann Neilson **Condon** there 4 August 1984.
7330 ii. Timothy John **Nesbit**[680] 12 July 1960 and died in a dormitory fire at the U. of Northern Iowa 2 July 1980 in Cedar Falls, Iowa, at 19 years of age.

6181. **Anna Jeanette**[12] **Whipple** (William Walter[11], Selmon Thomas[10], Cyrenius Thomas[9], Enoch[8], Nehemiah[7], Benjamin[6], Francis[5], Jonathan[4], Joseph[3], Matthew[2], Matthew[1])[681] was born in Benton Co., Iowa 1 March 1913 and died 3 April 1997 in Vinton, Benton Co., at 84 years of age. She married **Leander Kalvig** in Nashua, Iowa. He was born 11 October 1912 and died 30 October 1988 at 76 years of age.[682] Both are buried in Section 18, Block 21, Lot 14, Maplewood Cemetery, Vinton. Jeanette was graduated from Vinton High School and taught Country School until her marriage. She and Lee owned and operated Lee's Grocery and Lee's Phillips 66 Service in Vinton. She retired from Cromer Distributing of Vinton.

Anna Jeanette **Whipple** and Leander **Kalvig** had the following children:
7331 i. Janet[13] **Kalvig**[683] born in Benton Co. 4 February 1941 and died there of injuries from a bicycle accident 14 May 1953, at 12 years of age. Buried in Section 18, Block 21, Lot 14, Maplewood Cemetery.
+ 7332 ii. Kay Ann **Kalvig** born 17 December 1941.

6184. **William Clarence**[12] **Whipple** (William Walter[11], Selmon Thomas[10], Cyrenius Thomas[9], Enoch[8], Nehemiah[7], Benjamin[6], Francis[5], Jonathan[4], Joseph[3], Matthew[2], Matthew[1])[684] was born in Vinton, Benton Co., Iowa 9 October 1919 and died 20 June 1998 in Cedar Rapids, Iowa, at 78 years of age.[685] He married **Frances Margaret Schoelerman** in Cedar Rapids 10 December 1939. Frances,[686] daughter of August **Schoelerman** and Ella **Struck**, was born in Keystone, Iowa 16 September 1918 and died there 30 July 2000, at 81 years of age. Frances was a member of St. John Luthern Church and the Keystone American Legion Auxiliary. She was a talented seamstress and did crafts and needlework. She also loved to cook and was a collector of recipes. William was graduated from Vinton High School and served in the Army Air Corps during WWII stationed in Florida and the Philippines. Following the war he was a home builder, restaurant and tavern owner, and auto salesman. He retired from a longtime position in truck and auto tire sales at Montgomery Ward's in Cedar Rapids. His funeral was held 23 June 1998 at St. John Lutheran Church in Keystone Rev. Bruce Kalwasser presiding. He was buried at the Keystone Cemetery with graveside military rites conducted by the Merkel-Bockholt American Legion Post 107 of Keystone. He was a member of the Post for many years.[687]

William Clarence **Whipple** and Frances Margaret **Schoelerman** had the following child:

+ 7333 i. Bruce A.[13] **Whipple** born 11 October 1942.

6185. **Richard Ellerman**[12] **Whipple** (Harrison Lincoln[11], Selmon Thomas[10], Cyrenius Thomas[9], Enoch[8], Nehemiah[7], Benjamin[6], Francis[5], Jonathan[4], Joseph[3], Matthew[2], Matthew[1])[688] was born in Vinton, Benton Co., Iowa 4 July 1928 and married twice. (1) **Rose Marie Thompson** in Vinton in June 1950. Rose is the daughter of Horace **Thompson** and Marjorie **Westinghouse**. They were divorced in Cedar Rapids, Iowa in April 1959. (2) **Ruth Bohner** in Dubuque, Iowa 14 May 1960. Ruth,[689] daughter of Fred **Bohner** and Harriett **Murphy**, was born in Des Moines, Iowa 30 August 1929. She married (1) **Douglas Surber** and they were divorced in Cedar Rapids 1 March 1959.

Following his graduation from the U. of Iowa in 1950 with a B. S. in Commerce, Richard sold industrial/construction equipment in Des Moines and in 1953 moved to Vinton where he was jointly involved in the insurance and petroleum distribution business. He joined the marketing staff of Collins Radio Co. in Cedar Rapids in 1959 retiring in 1974 as Director, Corporate Ofices, Rockwell International (Collins Division) headquartered in Washington, D.C.

He earned an MBA from James Madison University, Harrisonburg, Va., and began a second career in higher education. He is a Professor of Administration, Washington & Lee University, Lexington, Va.,Professor of Marketing, Roanoke College, and Professor of Accounting, Virginia Community College System (1998). In addition, he farmed from 1974-87 in Rockbridge County, Va. In July 1989 he became a Certified Consumer Arbitrator with the National Council of Better Business Bureau. In 1987 he was elected a National Director of the 35,000 member National Association of Clock/Watch Collectors and Tradesmen, an organization in which he remains very active and is recipient of its "Fellow" Award for Outstanding Service.

He has designated his step-children Douglas and Denise **Suber** as his legal heirs. Douglas was born 9 April 1950 and married Karen **Galyda** on 24 April 1976. They have sons Gregory, born 28 May 1978 and Phillip, born 21 March 1982. The family resides in Locust Grove, Va. (1999). Denise Marlene was born 3 August 1953 and married Donald R. **Pollock** 12 April 1980. Their children are Ryan Matthew Pollock, born 26 Aug. 1985 and Jessica Ruth Pollock, born 27 June 1989. The family lives in Roanoke, Va. (1999)

Richard Ellerman **Whipple** and Rose Marie **Thompson** had the following child:

+ 7334 i. Rick Stephen[13] **Whipple** born 16 March 1951.

6186. **Jean Earlene**[12] **Whipple** (Edward Clelland[11], Selmon Thomas[10], Cyrenius Thomas[9], Enoch[8], Nehemiah[7], Benjamin[6], Francis[5], Jonathan[4], Joseph[3], Matthew[2], Matthew[1])[690] was born in Waterloo, Black Hawk Co., Iowa 14 May 1925 and married twice. (1) **Robert Oman** in Waterloo 12 October 1947. They were divorced in December 1948. (2) **Robert Eugene Haight** in Waterloo 4 November 1956. Robert,[691] son of Lewis Cyrus **Haight** and Idelle Adelaide **Townley**, was born in David City, Nebr. 24 January 1931. He served in the U.S. Air Force, leaving with the rank of Captain. He was a Mechanical Engineer at Product Engineering Center, John Deere Waterloo Tractor Company for 40 years. He works as a Consultant to John Deere during retirement. Jean was was graduated from Gates Business College in Waterloo and worked for the Roth Packing Co. in Waterloo as an Executive Secretary to the Vice President of Finance. She was with the company full time for 15 years and filled in part-time after her children were born. Following Bob's retirement, the family moved to Granbury, Texas in 1998.

Jean Earlene **Whipple** and Robert Eugene **Haight** had the following children born in Waterloo:

+ 7335 i. Ronald Whipple[13] **Haight** 7 April 1958.
  7336 ii. James Robert **Haight**[692] 26 April 1960. He earned a degree with honors in Electronic Engineering Technology at

7337 iii. Laurie Jean **Haight**[693] 13 October 1962 and married twice. (1) James Bruce **Henry** in Fort Worth, Tex. 12 March 1988. They were divorced in Fort Worth in November 1991. (2) N. **Simpter** in Carson City, Nev., 18 October 1994. He was born in Woburn, Mass. 21 November 1946.[694] Barry's marriage to Laurie was his second. He has three children from his first marriage. He works as an independent Consultant to golfing equipment companies. Laurie, who earned a degree in Microbiology, was a golf professional at Ridglea County Club, Fort Worth for seven years. In 2001 she was Manager of an Old Navy store in North Richland Hills in the Fort Worth area.

6187. **Jack Clelland**[12] **Whipple** (Edward Clelland[11], Selmon Thomas[10], Cyrenius Thomas[9], Enoch[8], Nehemiah[7], Benjamin[6], Francis[5], Jonathan[4], Joseph[3], Matthew[2], Matthew[1])[695] was born in Waterloo, Black Hawk Co., Iowa 9 August 1927 and died 31 October 1989 in Clinton, Clinton Co., Iowa, at 62 years of age. Buried at Clinton Memorial Park. He married **Jane Kathryn Falb** in Elgin, Iowa 29 December 1950. Jane,[696] daughter of Walter C. **Falb** and Bernice M. **Phillips**, was born in Postville, Iowa 29 November 1928. Jack was in the Army (1945-47) and was a Professor of Accounting and Business at Clinton Community College.

Jack Clelland **Whipple** and Jane Kathryn **Falb** had the following children:
7338 i. Richard Clelland[13] **Whipple**[697] born in Postville, Iowa 31 July 1952 and died there the day after birth. Buried at Midwest Garden of Memories at Waterloo.
+ 7339 ii. Mark Clelland **Whipple** born 20 October 1954.
7340 iii. Lynne Ann **Whipple**[698] was born in Postville 30 May 1956 and married William Joseph **Hayden** in Clinton 29 November 1980. He was born 16 August 1953.[699] Lynne Ann earned both a B. A. and an M. A. in Instructional Design at the University of Iowa.

6189. **Robert Clarence**[12] **Britt** (Anna Bessie[11] **Whipple**, Selmon Thomas[10], Cyrenius Thomas[9], Enoch[8], Nehemiah[7], Benjamin[6], Francis[5], Jonathan[4], Joseph[3], Matthew[2], Matthew[1])[700] was born in Vinton, Benton Co., Iowa 6 October 1919 and married **Mary Ann Murphy** in Kahkoka, Clark Co., Mo. 7 November 1942.

Robert Clarence **Britt** and Mary Ann **Murphy** had the following children:
+ 7341 i. Rebecca Ann[13] **Britt** born 4 January 1947.
+ 7342 ii. Elizabeth Ellen **Britt** born 9 October 1951.
    7343 iii. Barbara Jone **Britt**[701] born 27 October 1955.

6190. **Patricia Ann**[12] **Britt** (Anna Bessie[11] **Whipple**, Selmon Thomas[10], Cyrenius Thomas[9], Enoch[8], Nehemiah[7], Benjamin[6], Francis[5], Jonathan[4], Joseph[3], Matthew[2], Matthew[1])[702] was born in Vinton, Benton Co., Iowa 13 October 1927 and married **Richard Francis Berger** in Bay Minnette, Ala. 29 December 1945. He was born 3 December 1925.[703]

Patricia Ann **Britt** and Richard Francis **Berger** had the following children:
+ 7344 i. Peggy Louise[13] **Berger** born 2 May 1949.
+ 7345 ii. Robert John **Berger** born 18 June 1954.

6191. **Donald Lewis**[12] **Britt** (Anna Bessie[11] **Whipple**, Selmon Thomas[10], Cyrenius Thomas[9], Enoch[8], Nehemiah[7], Benjamin[6], Francis[5], Jonathan[4], Joseph[3], Matthew[2], Matthew[1])[704] was born in Vinton, Benton Co., Iowa 21 May 1929 and married twice. (1) **Dorothy Fuerhelm Reinhart** in Vinton 22 April 1950. (2) **Lois Anderson**.

Donald Lewis **Britt** and Dorothy Fuerhelm **Reinhart** had the following children:
    7346 i. Francine Elaine[13] **Britt**[705] born in Waterloo, Black Hawk Co., Iowa 17 November 1952.
+ 7347 ii. Donald Lewis **Britt** Jr. born 21 October 1954.

Donald Lewis **Britt** and Lois **Anderson** had the following child:
    7348 iii. Susan Lenae **Britt**[706] born in Minneapolis, Minn. 20 October 1966 and married Dirk **Simmons**. They had two daughters. No details provided.

6192. **George Walter**[12] **Whipple** (Eugene Harold[11], Selmon Thomas[10], Cyrenius Thomas[9], Enoch[8], Nehemiah[7], Benjamin[6], Francis[5], Jonathan[4], Joseph[3], Matthew[2], Matthew[1])[707] was born in Des Moines, Iowa 23 February 1924 and married **Dorothy Pelissier**. She was born 3 April 1925.[708]

George Walter **Whipple** and Dorothy **Pelissier** had the following children:
+ 7349 i. Terry Rene[13] **Whipple** born 4 November 1943.
+ 7350 ii. Rita Gayle **Whipple** born 10 December 1947.
    7351 iii. Nicole Rene **Whipple**[709] born 26 June 1951.
    7352 iv. Nancy Leigh **Whipple**[710] born 16 November 1954.

6193. **Jacquelyn Ann**[12] **Whipple** (Eugene Harold[11], Selmon Thomas[10], Cyrenius Thomas[9], Enoch[8], Nehemiah[7], Benjamin[6], Francis[5], Jonathan[4], Joseph[3], Matthew[2], Matthew[1])[711] was born 31 January 1928 and married **Donald Bruce Morris**. He was born 24 September 1928.[712]

Jacquelyn Ann **Whipple** and Donald Bruce **Morris** had the following children:
+ 7353 i. Donald Eugene[13] **Morris** born 19 December 1945.
  7354 ii. Dennis Wayne **Morris**[713] born 21 November 1947.
  7355 iii. Patricia Ann **Morris**[714] born 25 July 1950 and married Eddie **Williamson** 1969.

6194. **Rosemary**[12] **Whipple** (Eugene Harold[11], Selmon Thomas[10], Cyrenius Thomas[9], Enoch[8], Nehemiah[7], Benjamin[6], Francis[5], Jonathan[4], Joseph[3], Matthew[2], Matthew[1])[715] was born 5 May 1936 and married **Robert F. Key**. He was born 30 December 1932.[716]

Rosemary **Whipple** and Robert F. **Key** had the following children:
  7356 i. Robert Drue[13] **Key**[717] born 12 September 1952.
  7357 ii. Michael Lee **Key**[718] born 6 February 1954.
  7358 iii. Kelly Marie **Key**[719] born 19 April 1963.

6195. **Carolyn Marie**[12] **Whipple** (Eugene Harold[11], Selmon Thomas[10], Cyrenius Thomas[9], Enoch[8], Nehemiah[7], Benjamin[6], Francis[5], Jonathan[4], Joseph[3], Matthew[2], Matthew[1])[720] was born 3 August 1945 and married **Richard Brumm**. He was born 1 February 1936.[721]

Carolyn Marie **Whipple** and Richard **Brumm** had the following children:
  7359 i. Jeffrey Allen[13] **Brumm**[722] born 22 September 1967. Adopted.
  7360 ii. Jennifer Rene **Brumm**[723] born 5 December 1969. Adopted.
  7361 iii. Justin **Brumm**[724] born 1 September 1982.

6196. **Colleen Lou**[12] **Gordon** (Martha Josephine Esther[11] **Whipple**, Selmon Thomas[10], Cyrenius Thomas[9], Enoch[8], Nehemiah[7], Benjamin[6], Francis[5], Jonathan[4], Joseph[3], Matthew[2], Matthew[1])[725] was born in Waterloo, Black Hawk Co., Iowa 24 February 1929 and married **William George Castner** in Vinton, Benton Co., Iowa 24 June 1951. William,[726] son of George Peter **Castner** and Mabel Minnie **Bruentrup**, was born in St. Paul, Minn. 13 October 1927.

Colleen Lou **Gordon** and William George **Castner** had the following children:
+ 7362 i. David Gordon[13] **Castner** born 8 September 1952.

{ G 1081 }

+ 7363 ii. Julie Jo **Castner** born 18 August 1954.
+ 7364 iii. Ann Louise **Castner** born 21 November 1955.

6197. **Jo Anne**[12] **Gordon** (Martha Josephine Esther[11] **Whipple**, Selmon Thomas[10], Cyrenius Thomas[9], Enoch[8], Nehemiah[7], Benjamin[6], Francis[5], Jonathan[4], Joseph[3], Matthew[2], Matthew[1])[727] was born in Hampton, Franklin Co., Iowa 27 March 1933 and married **Russell Robert Settlemyer** in Chillicothe, Livingston Co., Mo. 14 November 1955. Russell,[728] son of George Russell **Settlemyer** and Lorene Beulah **Proffitt**.

Jo Anne **Gordon** and Russell Robert **Settlemyer** had the following children:
+ 7365 i. Rebecca Sue[13] **Settlemyer** born 18 March 1956.
+ 7366 ii. Elizabeth Ellen **Settlemyer** born 5 September 1960.
+ 7367 iii. Anna Colleen **Settlemyer** born 21 September 1963.

6198. **Thomas Lee**[12] **Gallaher** (Clara Adalene[11] **Whipple**, Selmon Thomas[10], Cyrenius Thomas[9], Enoch[8], Nehemiah[7], Benjamin[6], Francis[5], Jonathan[4], Joseph[3], Matthew[2], Matthew[1])[729] was born in Vinton, Benton Co., Iowa 25 March 1933 and married **Martha Louise Haese** in Sault Ste. Marie, Chippewa Co., Mich., 7 July 1956. Louise,[730] daughter of Wayne Smith **Haese** and Martha Lee **Markgraf**, was born in San Antonio, Tex. 21 September 1936 and died at home of cancer 12 March 1997 in Muscatine, Iowa, at 60 years of age. Buried at Vinton's Evergreen Cemetery.

Tom spent two years in the U.S. Army stationed at Fort Chaffee, Ark., Sault Ste. Marie, Mich. and Edgewood, Md. He was graduated from Iowa State University at Ames in 1955 with a B.S. in Chemical Engineering and earned an MBA from St. Ambrose University, Davenport, Iowa in 1989. His career included positions with PPG in Corpus Christi, Tex., Chemplex Co. in Clinton, Iowa, and Grain Processing Corp. in Muscatine, Iowa. His work required him to travel to many parts of the world. At the time of his retirement in 1998 he was General Manager of GPC Equipment Co.

Thomas Lee **Gallaher** and Martha Louise **Haese** had the following children:
+ 7368 i. Anna Louise[13] **Gallaher** born 31 March 1961.
+ 7369 ii. Amy Lee **Gallaher** born 14 December 1964.

6199. **David Lyle**[12] **Gallaher** (Clara Adalene[11] **Whipple**, Selmon Thomas[10], Cyrenius Thomas[9], Enoch[8], Nehemiah[7], Benjamin[6], Francis[5], Jonathan[4], Joseph[3], Matthew[2], Matthew[1])[731] was born in Vinton, Benton Co., Iowa 25 May 1936 and married twice. (1) **Joan Diane Borne** in Nashua, Iowa 7 August 1958. Joan,[732] daughter of Harold O. **Borne** and Madelin **Belk**, was born in Omaha, Nebr. 19 March 1940. They were divorced in

Cerro Gordo Co., Iowa 12 January 1988. (2) **Kathleen (Hrubetz) Aanrud** in Joice, Worth Co., Iowa 27 May 1995. Kathleen,[733] daughter of Charles E. **Hrubetz** and Lucille J. **Knutson**, was born in Mason City, Iowa 9 March 1952. She married (1) **Merle Aanrud**. David earned a B. A. at the University of Northern Iowa at Cedar Falls Iowa and taught High School in Grand Junction, Aubudon, Estherville, and Clear Lake, Iowa. He did advanced degree work at the U. of Missouri and Drake University in Des Moines. He owned and managed a sport store in Mason City, Iowa and worked for Fleet Guard Filtration Manufacturing Co. in Lake Mills, Iowa.

David Lyle **Gallaher** and Joan Diane **Borne** had the following children:

   7370 i. Mark David[13] **Gallaher**[734] was born in Jefferson, Greene Co., Iowa 18 November 1959 and married twice. (1) Jennifer **Humestan** in Sioux Falls, S. Dak. 31 May 1985. They were divorced in Sioux Falls in 1991. (2) Sheila **(Grode) Keller** in Sioux Falls 30 July 1994. She is the daughter of Donald **Grode** and Eileen **Taylor.**[735] They were divorced in Sioux Falls in 1996.[736] Shelia also married (__) **Keller.**
+ 7371 ii. Todd Lyle **Gallaher** born 29 May 1963.
+ 7372 iii. Lori Diane **Gallaher** born 1 May 1969.

6200. Judith Ann[12] **Whipple** (Cyrenius Albert[11], Selmon Thomas[10], Cyrenius Thomas[9], Enoch[8], Nehemiah[7], Benjamin[6], Francis[5], Jonathan[4], Joseph[3], Matthew[2], Matthew[1])[737] was born in Waterloo, Black Hawk Co., Iowa 31 March 1939 and married **Richard Earl Shere** in Greenville, Montcalm Co., Mich. in 1955. He was born 12 May 1938.[738]

Judith Ann **Whipple** and Richard Earl **Shere** had the following children:

+ 7373 i. Renette Marie[13] **Shere** born 22 July 1956.
   7374 ii. De Ann Judith **Shere**[739] born 13 August 1958 and married Robert **Fortier.**
   7375 iii. Vicki Yvonne **Shere**[740] born 27 August 1963.
   7376 iv. Julie Dawn **Shere**[741] born 10 November 1964.
   7377 v. Rick Earl **Shere**[742] born 7 July 1966.

6201. Robert Mark[12] **Whipple** (Cyrenius Albert[11], Selmon Thomas[10], Cyrenius Thomas[9], Enoch[8], Nehemiah[7], Benjamin[6], Francis[5], Jonathan[4], Joseph[3], Matthew[2], Matthew[1])[743] was born in Waterloo, Black Hawk Co., Iowa 25 October 1948 and married **Carol Mary Nekola** in Traer, Iowa 5 September 1970. Carol,[744] daughter of Charles J. **Nekola** and Irene **Vokoun**, was born in Waterloo 23 June 1951.

Robert Mark **Whipple** and Carol Mary **Nekola** had the following children born in Waterloo:
>   7378   i.   Ryan Courtney[13] **Whipple**[745] 25 October 1975.
>   7379   ii.   Blair Rene **Whipple**[746] 6 February 1980.

6202. **Donald Wayne**[12] **Faris** (Nellie Jeanette[11] **Whipple**, Selmon Thomas[10], Cyrenius Thomas[9], Enoch[8], Nehemiah[7], Benjamin[6], Francis[5], Jonathan[4], Joseph[3], Matthew[2], Matthew[1])[747] was born in Vinton, Benton Co., Iowa 10 January 1933 and married **Mary Catherine Orthell** in Titonka, Iowa 11 June 1955. She was born in Titonka 15 December 1932.[748]

Donald Wayne **Faris** and Mary Catherine **Orthell** had the following children:
> + 7380   i.   Donald James[13] **Faris** born 25 August 1956.
>   7381   ii.   Mary Catherine **Faris**[749] born 17 February 1958.
>   7382   iii. Ann Elizabeth **Faris**[750] born 30 December 1959.
>   7383   iv.   John Thomas **Faris**[751] born 14 December 1961.
>   7384   v.   David Whipple **Faris**[752] born 30 November 1964.

6203. **James Russell**[12] **Faris** (Nellie Jeanette[11] **Whipple**, Selmon Thomas[10], Cyrenius Thomas[9], Enoch[8], Nehemiah[7], Benjamin[6], Francis[5], Jonathan[4], Joseph[3], Matthew[2], Matthew[1])[753] was born in Vinton, Benton Co., Iowa 17 October 1935 and died 16 June 1970 in Westminster, Orange Co., Calif., at 34 years of age. Buried at Westiminster Memorial Park. He married **Pat Lawson** in Madrid, Iowa 23 October 1960. She was born in Madrid 3 October 1935.[754]

James Russell **Faris** and Pat **Lawson** had the following children:
>   7385   i.   Susan Rae[13] **Faris**[755] born in Long Beach, Calif. 16 September 1966.
>   7386   ii.   Joel James **Faris**[756] born in Huntington Beach, Calif. 4 October 1968.

6204. **John Mark**[12] **Faris** (Nellie Jeanette[11] **Whipple**, Selmon Thomas[10], Cyrenius Thomas[9], Enoch[8], Nehemiah[7], Benjamin[6], Francis[5], Jonathan[4], Joseph[3], Matthew[2], Matthew[1])[757] was born in Belmond, Wright Co., Iowa 5 September 1947 and married **Janet Alice Klongerbo** in Clear Lake, Iowa 7 December 1968. She was born in Estherville, Iowa 19 October 1949.[758]

John Mark **Faris** and Janet Alice **Klongerbo** had the following children:
>   7387   i.   Michael John[13] **Faris**[759] born in Cedar Falls, Iowa 17 June 1969.
>   7388   ii.   Jennifer Anne **Faris** born in Fort Dodge, Iowa 25 March 1972.

6206. **Ellen Elaine**[12] **Whipple** (Lucien Blaine[11], James Ezekiel[10], Lucien Ransom[9], Enoch[8], Nehemiah[7], Benjamin[6], Francis[5], Jonathan[4], Joseph[3], Matthew[2], Matthew[1])[760] was born in Vinton, Benton Co., Iowa 6 August 1910 and married **Stephen Ely West** in Cedar Rapids, Iowa 14 December 1941. Stephen,[761] son of Charles Wesley **West** and Bessie Madge **Clingman**, was born in Denison, Crawford, Co., Iowa 20 August 1914 and died 26 January 1998 in Tucson, Pima Co., Ariz., at 83 years of age. The family lived on a farm at Buck Grove, Crawford Co., Iowa at the time of his birth.

Steve moved to Mt. Vernon, Linn Co., Iowa in 1916 and was graduated from High School there. He attended Iowa State University at Ames for two years before buying, from his grandfather's estate, the family farm located on the south outskirts of Mt. Vernon. It has been owned by a member of the West family for 124 years (2006). He was a member of the Linn County Farm Bureau, a Commissioner

Elaine (Whipple) West about 1943.

of the Linn County Soil District, the Linn County Board of Adjustment, the Cedar Valley Business Association, and the Linn-Jones Farm Service. He was an avid hunter and fisherman throughout the upper mid west, Canada, and Mexico. After he reached retirement age, he leased the farm on a share basis and he and Elaine wintered a year in Florida, a year in south Texas, 12 years in Guaymas and San Carlos, Sonara, Mexico, and in Tuc-

Stephen West High School graduation, Mt. Vernon. Photos courtesy of Elaine (Whipple) West.

{ G 1085 }

son for the last 12 years of his life where they owned a mobile home. He became an expert in the card game bridge while living in Tucson. During summer after retirement they vacationed 4 to 6 weeks around the upper midwest and Canada fishing and visiting friends.

Steve died of heart failure at the Tucson Medical Center Hospice after he had instructed his medical team not to keep him on life support. Following his death, two memorial services were held to celebrate his life.

Elaine Whipple at Ellis Park, Cedar Rapids, Iowa. She was a Park employee in the late 1930s.

The first was Saturday 31 January 1988 in the Recreation Hall at the Western Way Mobile Home Park on S. Kinney Way in Tucson, the second on 17 May in Mt. Vernon. He was cremated and his ashes scattered in a grove of trees on the family farm.

What Elaine remembers about her pre-teen years is that her father always brought her and brother

Steve West. Photos courtesy of Elaine (Whipple) West.

Steve and Elaine West farm. Photos courtesy of Elaine (Whipple) West.

First concrete barn and silo in Iowa on Steve and Elaine's farm.

Jimmy gifts when he returned after being away. Her fondest gift was a "a little China girl doll with black bobbed hair, round white face, and beautiful kimono." She thinks they were lucky to be kids before radio and TV because her Dad read wonderful stories to them. "I believe that is why I have such a vivid imagination. He painted pictures with words and we filled in the shapes and colors. Dad's love of books is one of his gifts

Steve West with lake trout.

through me to my daughters." She remembers they always had a car and he took them to rodeos, circuses, tent and Chautauqua shows, and to his work place. One car she remembers was an Apperson 8 Roadster. She also remembers living in Kansas City in the early 1920s when her father brought a crystal set radio home that you listened to through ear phones and manipulated a tiny wire to find a station. It was like a big spool with a square board on top and bottom with the spool wrapped with copper wires and the crystal mounted on top.

Elaine's remembrances of her mother in the early years was that she spoiled them, treating them like dolls with minds of their own. She was an excellent seamstress and made the children most of their clothes. She had curly short black hair, dark brown eyes, and tiny feet — size 3. Her family was great on hugging and kissing and she brought that trait to the Whipple family as well as a strong sense of right and wrong. Her mother was an outstanding cook and could satisfy the palates of an English grandmother, a French grandfather, a German stepfather, a "bohemian" second husband, and American kids. She was a happy homemaker who believed a home was a place to live in, not look at —

Susan (L) and Sandy with their uncle Blaine Whipple in the mid 1950s.

Four generations. Charles Wesley West with son Steve, mother Jane Margaret (Hayden) West, on her 100th birthday, and Sandy and Susan West. Jane lived to age 105. All photos courtesy of Elaine (Whipple) West.

{ G 1088 }

clean enough to be healthy but with a lived-in look. She died after a long debilitating illness weighing only 68 pounds.

Elaine has no real memory of her grandfather James E. Whipple but remembers her grandmother Ellen (Thompson) Whipple as a tall, stately, and soft spoken lady who lived with them in Vinton and helped care for her and Jimmy. She said older cousins described her grandmother's carriage, looks, and behaviour as "ladylike." She still has a 12-inch tall Flow blue pitcher (now a collectible) that belonged to her grandmother.

She remembers travelling with her folks during summer months in her preteen years as they put on dog and pony shows in small towns across Iowa. She also remembers the whole family went along when her father managed tent shows when they would spend a week at a time in small Kansas towns presenting plays such as *East Lynn, Girl of the Golden West, Face on the Baroom Floor,* etc. Jimmy sometimes played children roles in these productions.

After her mother's second marriage, the family lived on the west side of Cedar Rapids in a nice friendly neighborhood. Elaine says it was the first

West farm home on a snowy day in 2005.

Sandy, Steve, and Susan West.

Elaine and Susan West. Photos courtesy of Elaine (Whipple) West.

{ G 1089 }

Elaine Whipple, 1934.

Susan and Sandy West.

Sandy and Susan West, Christmas eve 1963.

Susan and Elaine West.

Susan West.

Sandy West. All photos courtesy of Elaine (Whipple) West.

time in years that she lived in the same house for more than a year. The home was near the Cedar river where she swam and boated in the summer and skated in the winter. She had a variety of jobs during the depression years of the 1930s: working at a dime store, a dress shop, an ice cream company, a manufacturing company, and an advertising company. She met her husband Steve on the Cedar Rapids Police Rifle Range. She was a member of the Cedar Rapids Amazons and Steve was a member of a rifle team that came to recruit the Amazons into the Illia Rifle Assn. She was also a member of a Harley Davidson Motorcycle Club.

Elaine, Steve, Susan, Sandy West and Keith M. Kent.

L to R Cousins Lee Allen Babbage, Andy Garland, Emily Jasperson and KC Babbage at Elaine West's 90th birthday party in Mt. Vernon. Photos courtesy of Elaine (Whipple) West.

{ G 1091 }

Elaine West getting ready for a Harley Davidson ride through the streets of Amana, Iowa on her 90th birthday.

Pat Drotzman, Bill and Blaine Whipple at Elaine West's 90th birthday party. All photos courtesy of David Blaine Jasperson.

Elaine's 90th birthday party at her Mt. Vernon, Iowa farm home in August 2000. L to R. Molly Schmidt, Blaine Whipple, Elaine West, Dave Jasperson, Susan West.

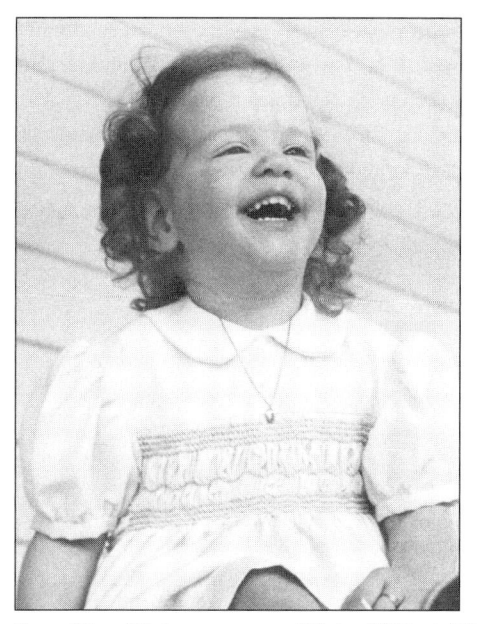

Ellen Elaine **Whipple** and Stephen Ely **West** had the following children:

7389 i. Susan Elaine[13] **West**[762] was born prematurely in Cedar Rapids 2 January 1946 and weighted 2 pounds 2 ounces. She remained in the hospital for four months before gaining sufficient weight to go home. She attended kindergarten in the country school built by her great great grandfather Wesley West on the north edge of their farm. West family members attended the school beginning in the 1860s. Following graduation from Mt. Vernon High School, she earned a degree in Library Science from the University of Northern Iowa at Cedar Falls. Her first job following college was with the Miles, Jackson Co., Iowa School District where she established a library for grades K through 12. After schools in the Miles district were consolidated, she entered the U. of Missouri where she earned a Masters Degree in Library Science. She later worked at the Kirkwood Community College Library in Cedar Rapids, the Cedar Rapids Public Library, and the Spencer, Clay Co., Iowa Library. In 1972 she spent nine weeks in Europe enrolled in a Social Science Seminar sponsored by the

Susan West. All photos courtesy of Elaine (Whipple) West.

Susan West, graduation, May 1968, U. of Northern Iowa, Cedar Falls, Iowa.

St. Petersburg, Fla. L.to R. Jerry Whipple, Linda Babbage, Jay Whipple, James Michael Whipple, Lee Babbage Jr., Sandy West holding Jon Garland and Susan West standing.

{ G 1093 }

U. of Northern Iowa. They studied at Oxford College in England and toured England, France, Germany—east and west—Austria, Italy, Poland, Hungray, and Russia. Following her father's triple by-pass heart surgery, she completed a nurse's aid course so she could be of help to him. She also worked in an Iowa nursing home. She is an avid Democrat and keeps abreast of local, state, and national issues and political leaders. She has a large library and music collection and is a sports fan.

   7390 ii. Sandra Lynn **West**[763] was born in Cedar Rapids 23 August 1949 and married twice. (1) Keith Matthew **Kent** in Madison, Dane Co., Wisc. 1 September 1970. Keith,[764] son of Amos **Kent** and Rosemary **Michalek**, was born in Richmond, Va. 20 January 1950. They were divorced in Tucson, Ariz. in 1991. (2) John Philip **Crandell** in Tucson 1 February 1997. John,[765] son of Ralph **Crandell** and Iyrl Lucille **Thorpe**, was born in Ann Arbor, Washtenaw Co., Mich. 3 July 1945. He married (1) Mary Sue **Hupp** in Tucson in 1965. They were divorced there in June 1988. After graduating from Mt. Vernon High School, Sandra attended Iowa State University for a year and earned an Associate Degree as a Lab Technician from Kirkwood Community College of Cedar Rapids. She moved to Madison, where she worked in an X-ray Lab and a Hospital before becoming a Veterinarian Technician and Manager of a Veterinary Clinic. She and her first husband moved to Tucson in the spring of 1986 where he worked as a Professional Photographer and she was an Instructor at the Pima Medical Institute and worked at an Animal Diagnostic Lab. Following their 1991 divorce, Sandy returned to college part time and was graduated with honors from the U. of Arizona in December 1997 and is now (2006) employed at Tucson Medical Center. Her hobbies are sewing and handicrafts.

Elaine, Sandy and Susan West and John Crandell at Steve's memorial service 17 May 1988 in Mt. Vernon.

John, Elaine, Sandy and Susan. Christmas 2001 in Tuscon, Ariz. Photos courtesy of Elaine (Whipple) West.

6207. **James Earl**[12] **Whipple** (Lucien Blaine[11], James Ezekiel[10], Lucien Ransom[9], Enoch[8], Nehemiah[7], Benjamin[6], Francis[5], Jonathan[4], Joseph[3], Matthew[2], Matthew[1])[766] was born in Vinton, Benton Co., Iowa 29 October 1911 and died 20 February 1983 in Pinellas, Fla., at 71 years of age. He was cremated. He married twice. (1) **Olive Maxine Hancock** in Rock Island, Ill. 10 November 1932. Olive,[767] daughter of Emmett **Hancock** and Elsie **Ware**, was born in Ottumwa, Iowa 1 October 1911 and died 11 April 1956 in Cedar Rapids, Iowa, at 44 years of age. Buried in Memorial Cemetery. (2) **Joyce Ann Reinet** in Cedar Rapids 1 June 1956. Joyce is the daughter of Clarence **Reinet** and Genevieve **Cline**.[768] Jimmy served 8 years, 3 months, and three weeks in the Naval Reserve including active duty from 7 December 1944 to 1 October 1945 and 5 June 1950 to 2 February 1952. He was a Pharmacist Mate Second Class. Before moving to Florida, he had a Culligan Bottled Water Route in Anamosa Iowa.

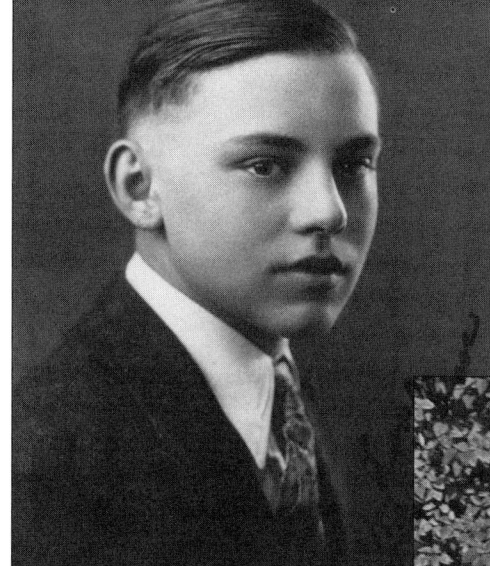

Jimmy Whipple High School graduation 1930, Cedar Rapids, Iowa.

Olive, Jimmy, and Nancy Lee Whipple. Photos courtesy of Elaine (Whipple) West.

{ G 1095 }

James Earl **Whipple** and Olive Maxine **Hancock** had the following child:
+   7391   i.   Nancy Lee[13] **Whipple** born 18 January 1935.

Nancy Lee Whipple.

Jimmy, Nancy Lee (center) and Olive Whipple.

Nancy Lee. All photos courtesy of Elaine (Whipple) West.

Nancy Lee, Jimmy, and Blaine Whipple with Elaine and Susan West at the West farm in 1946.

{ G 1096 }

James Earl **Whipple** and Joyce Ann **Reinet** had the following children:
+ 7392   ii.   James Michael **Whipple** born 9 October 1957.
+ 7393   iii. Jay Allen **Whipple** born 14 August 1959.
   7394   iv.   Jerry William **Whipple**[769] born in St. Petersburg, Fla. 7 Janury 1962.

Jimmy Whipple in front of Chas. H. Zastera Drug Store in Cedar Rapids. Charles was his step-father and Jimmy worked in the store after school and weekends. All photos courtesy of Elaine (Whipple) West.

Jerry Whipple, third grade 1970.

Front, Jerry: back L. to R. Jimmy and Jay Whipple.

{ G 1097 }

6208. **Patricia Ellen**[12] **Whipple** (Lucien Blaine[11], James Ezekiel[10], Lucien Ransom[9], Enoch[8], Nehemiah[7], Benjamin[6], Francis[5], Jonathan[4], Joseph[3], Matthew[2], Matthew[1])[770] was born in Des Moines, Iowa 1 February 1929 and the attending physician H.R. Peasley, M.D. "certified her eyes were treated as prescribed by law." Her parents were living at 1411 Locust. She died 3 October 2006 in Yankton, S. Dak. at 77 years of age. She married **Edwin LeRoy Drotzman** 18 June 1951. Eddie,[771] son of Edward **Drotzman** and Lucy **Lanke**, was born in Yankton 1 April 1926 and died 7 June 1964 in Sioux Falls, S. Dak., at 38 years of age. Both are buried in Sacred Heart Cemetery, Yankton.

Eddie was graduated from Yankton High School and joined the Marines where he saw service in the Pacific Theater during WWII. He was badly wounded at the Battle of Okinawa and spent a year in a Naval hospital in Memphis, Tenn. recuperating. Navy doctors were never able to remove all the shrapnel from his body and he had a steel plate in the forepart of his skull. After his release from the hospital he returned to Yankton were he worked as a carpenter and as a bartender. Upon his death from cancer, an autopsy showed his entire body was full of cancer believed to have been stimulated by the shell fragments that remained in his body.

Pat was graduated from High Schoool at Redfield, S. Dak. and moved to Yankton where she married and raised four boys. After the death of her husband in 1964 she worked in the Bookkeeping and Proof Department of First Dakota National Bank, retiring in June 1998 as an Assistant Vice President. She was a member of the Women of the Moose, the VFW Auxiliary, and the Interchange Club of Yankton.

Edward Drotzman and Patricia E. Whipple on their wedding day. Photo courtesy of Pat Drotzman.

Patricia Ellen **Whipple** and Edwin LeRoy **Drotzman** had the following children born in Yankton:
- 7395   i.   Michael James[13] **Drotzman** 6 August 1952.
- 7396   ii.   Larry Joseph **Drotzman** 2 September 1955.

      7397   iii.   Brian Scott **Drotzman**[772] 2 February 1958 and married Theresa Ann (Novak) **Schieffer** in Yankton 19 April 2000 in Yankton. Theresa,[773] daughter of Robert Joe **Novak** and Agnes Irene **Nehonsky**, was born in Tyndall, S. Dak. 19 April 1966. She married (1) Larry J. **Schieffer** in Tabor, S. Dak., 12 July 1986. They were divorced in South Dakota 11 August 1993. Brian spent several years in the U. S. Air Force and was stationed in several European locations. He is Head of Maintenance for a middle school in the Yankton School District.

      7398   iv.   Daniel Lee **Drotzman**[774] 18 November 1960. After graduating from Yankton High School, Dan spent an academic year at Montana State University at Bozeman, transferring to St. Cloud State University at St. Cloud, Minn. where he earned a B. A. in 1984. He was an active member of Delta Sigma Phi Fraternity and President of the Greek Council (Governing Board of all Campus Fraternal Organizations) at St. Cloud. He was also a Student Senator and Chief Justice of the Student Senate Judicial Council. Dan's work career began as an Employment Counselor in Minneapolis where he placed individuals in management positions with leading companies throughout the U.S. This was followed by a five-year stint with the BIC Corporation with assignments at Minneapolis, Houston, and Seattle. At the time

Dan Drotzman with his nephew Jason Drotzman, 13 May 2005, Yankton, S. Dak. Photo courtesy of Michael J. Drotzman.

Dan Drotzman. Photo courtesy of Michael J. Drotzman.

of his resignation, he was Sales Manager of the Commercial Products Division for the Western U.S. with an annual volume in excess of $30 million. He left BIC to become Membership Manager for the United States Chamber of Commerce as liaison between the Washington, D.C. office and Chamber organizations in Montana, Wyoming, South Dakota, Minnesota, Wisconsin, and Nebraska. He left this job to found Porcupine Productions, Inc., (a Minnesota corporation) the marketing and distribution arm of Lotto Greetings. In 2001, he became a Senior Recruiter for TPI, a Minneapolis Computer Consulting Firm with operations world wide.

6209. **Robert Blaine**[12] **Whipple** (Lucien Blaine[11], James Ezekiel[10], Lucien Ransom[9], Enoch[8], Nehemiah[7], Benjamin[6], Francis[5], Jonathan[4], Joseph[3], Matthew[2], Matthew[1])[775] was born in Martin, Bennett Co., S. Dak. 22 February 1930. He was born at 11:50 a.m. in a log cabin, the family home. He was baptized at Our Lady of Sacred Heart Church, Martin by Father Carroll. Sponsors were his uncle Arthur and aunt Clara Scott, brother and sister of his mother. He married **Ines Mae (Peterson) Steele** in Portland, Washington Co., Oreg. 6 August 1966 at the Cedar Hills Community Church. Ines, daughter of Owen Diamon **Peterson** and Josephine Berniece **Bartruff**, was born at Portland Sanitarium Hospital in Portland, Multnomah Co., Oreg. 24 September 1929.[776] Her parents lived at 1251 S.E. 20th, Portland. She married (1) **Harold Steele** in Portland 24 February 1951. They were married at 8 p.m. at the Valley Community United Prebysterian Church, 7850 SW Brentwood Ave., West Slope. Rev. H.A. Armstrong officiated. The bride, given away by her brother Wayne A. Peterson, wore a white satin dress with lace trim. Her three-quarter length veil was held by a white satin hat. She carried an orchid bouquet. Mrs. Robert O. Williams was Matron of Honor. Bridesmaids were Shirlee Spring, Pauline Pappas, and Carol Johnson. A church reception followed. Ines' grandfather Peter T. Peterson was born in Denmark in 1869 and died in Portland in 1940. The last family contact with Peterson family members still living in Denmark was after the end of WWII. The family was S. Uhler-Pedersen, Boghalder Alle 25 Stuen, Vanlose, Kobenhavn, Denmark. Ines' brother Norman visited the family while on leave from Army duty in Germany.

Robert Blaine **Whipple** and Ines Mae **Peterson** had the following child:
+ 7399 i. Blaine Scott[13] **Whipple** born 27 December 1968.

6210. **Nancy Jane**[12] **Whipple** (Lucien Blaine[11], James Ezekiel[10], Lucien Ransom[9], Enoch[8], Nehemiah[7], Benjamin[6], Francis[5], Jonathan[4], Joseph[3], Matthew[2], Matthew[1])777 was born at 10:35 p.m. at home in Ryder, Ward Co., N. Dak. 5 January 1932. Attending physician H. O. Graangaard, M.D. She died 26 December 1987 in Glencoe, McLeod Co., Minn., at 55 years of age. She married **Donald J. Jasperson** in Tracy, Lyon Co., Minn. 30 July 1950. Donald,[778] son of Harold George William **Jasperson** and Evelyn **Helgemo** (1910-2004.), was born in Tracy 11 November 1931. He married (2) **Barbara (Shipp) Bruns** in Glencoe 6 October 1990.

Obituary: Funeral services for Nancy J. Jasperson, 55, of Glencoe, Minn. were held December 29, 1987 at Christ Lutheran Church in Glencoe, with the Rev. Chester Hoversten officiating. Organist was Peggy Hatlestad. Music selections were "The Lord is My Shepherd," "The King is Coming," "Lead On, Oh King Eternal," and "Amazing Grace." Pallbearers were Maurice Stromswold, Ray Swanson, Rolland Olson, Paul Soule, Don McKee, and Robert Tibbets. The Glencoe Ambassadors served as Honorary Bearers. Internment in the Glencoe Cemetery.

Nancy Jane was baptized in Douglas, N. Dak. and confirmed in Bismarck, N.Dak. Her family lived in various communities before coming to Tracy, Minn. in 1946 where she graduated from high school.

She married Donald Jasperson at the Tracy Lutheran Church. They lived in Tracy, LeMars, Iowa, and Marshall and Appleton, Minn. before coming to Glencoe. She was active in her church as President of the ALCW and taught Sunday School in Marshall and was Superintendent of Sunday School in Appleton. She worked as a nurses' aid and held varied department store clerking jobs. As well as being a loving wife and mother, she was active in the Homemakers Club and she liked to fish, golf, play bridge, crochet, and do needle work. She died at the Glencoe Area Health Center following a lengthy battle with cancer.

Surviving are her husband, Donald, three daughters, and one son: Terri Ebert (husband Charles) of Luverne, Minn.; Donna Barney of Appleton; David Jasperson, (wife Jan) of Rochester, Minn.; and Molly Jasperson of Glencoe; five grandchildren, Katie, Sarah, and Amanda Ebert and Jeff and Leah Barney; mother, Pearl Whipple of Glencoe; brothers, Blaine

Whipple (wife Ines) of Portland, Ore. and Richard Whipple of Eagan, Minn.; two sisters, Patricia Drotzman of Yankton, S.Dak. and Mary Ann McPherson (husband Bill) of Littleton, Mass; mother-in-law Evelyn Hibbard (husband Jens) of Tracy; and half-sister Mrs. Elaine West (husband Stephen) of Mt. Vernon, Iowa; as well as nieces and nephews. She was preceded in death by her father. Visitation was held 28 December at Johnson-McBride Funeral Chapel in Glencoe.[779]

Nancy Jane **Whipple** and Donald J. **Jasperson** had the following children:
+   7400   i.   Terri Lynn[13] **Jasperson** born 11 October 1951.
+   7401   ii.   Donna Marie **Jasperson** born 10 May 1955.
+   7402   iii.   David Blaine **Jasperson** born 7 November 1959.
+   7403   iv.   Molly Jane **Jasperson** born 23 November 1966.

6212. **Mary Ann**[12] **Whipple** (Lucien Blaine[11], James Ezekiel[10], Lucien Ransom[9], Enoch[8], Nehemiah[7], Benjamin[6], Francis[5], Jonathan[4], Joseph[3], Matthew[2], Matthew[1])[780] was born at St. Alexius Hospital at 4:03 a..m. in Bismarck, Burleigh Co., N. Dak. 8 December 1937. She married **Billie Nathaniel McPherson** in Yankton, S. Dak. 21 August 1955. They were married in the first Methodist Church built when Yankton was Capitol of the Dakota Territory. Bill,[781] son of Nathaniel Leroy **McPherson** and Thelma Viola **Thornsberry**, was born in Waltonville, Ill. 2 February 1932. After four years in the U.S. Navy as an enlisted man, he earned both a Bachelor and Master of Science Degree in Poultry Science at the U. of Arkansas. He spent his entire working career in Poultry Research and Development in Ireland, Holland, and the U.S. He joined Cobb-Upjohn at Littleton, Mass. in 1967 as Head of Research and Development. This firm shipped millions of day-old chicks to breeding operations throughout the world. He also worked in Aquaculture and was Secretary of Aquagenetics, a subsidiary of Cobb-Upjohn. He retired in 1986 after 24 years and then joined the Poultry Research Department of Arbor Acres at Glastonbury, Conn., retiring from that job in 1994. Bill is the author of the *Cobb Broiler Management Guide,*, a text on poultry management first published in 1969. It has been translated into seven languages and is sold worldwide. He has authored or co-authored 17 scientific publications and is a sought-after speaker at Poultry Conferences in North and South America, Europe and India. He served three terms as President of the American Poultry Historical Society. He is also a collector of scales numbering approximately 200.

Mary Ann was graduated from High School at Yankton, S. Dak. and attended the U. of Arkansas at Fayetteville for two years. After marriage, the family lived in Ireland and Holland and upon return to the U.S. in

Pearl and Mary Ann Whipple, Bill McPherson, and Robert Whipple. Wedding 21 August 1955. Photo courtesy Mary Ann and Bill McPherson.

1967, she joined the U.S. Postal Service at Carlisle, Mass. where she retired in January 1998 after 23.5 years of service (7/1974-1/98). During that period she served three times as Officer-in-Charge of the Office. She is a member of the Old Concord Chapter of the Daughters of the American Revolution and has served the Chapter as Director, Chaplain, and Historian. Her avocation has been the theater and she has been a producer, actor, set dresser, stage manager, make-up technician, and costume designer for the Concord Players, the Littleton-Groton Theatre, and the Savoyard Light Opera Co. of Carlisle. She also collected vintage women's dresses, gowns, purses, compacts, and other odds and ends. Her collection was described as "extraordinary" by *The Sun* of Lowell, Mass in a front page article 20 March 2001. Her collection was on display at the Littleton Historical Society for three months beginning 10 April 2001.

The Whipple siblings. R to L: Dick, Mary Ann, Elaine, Pat, and Blaine. Yankton, S. Dak. 15 August 2004. Photo courtesy of Michael J. Drotzman.

In the early 1960s the family moved to Naas, Ireland where oldest daughter Billie June started school in a one-room school house with a pot bellied stove and outhouses. She got her knuckles rapped with a ruler the first day because she couldn't speak Gaelic. She carried her lunch to school in a paper bag. When they first arrived, the family lived in a bed and breakfast and Mary Ann and Melissa walked the country roads dur-

Mary Ann McPherson with her nephew Brian Drotzman, 14 May 2005, Sioux Falls, S. Dak. Photo courtesy of Michael J. Drotzman.

ing the day because they were expected to leave after breakfast. They ate their noon and evening meals at the Naas restaurant where dishes were washed in cold water with bar soap. As a result there was scum on everything they drank. They often found snails and earwigs in their salad.

They eventually found a row house with a small back yard to rent in the village of Clondolkin. Heat was supplied by fireplaces in the kitchen, dining, and living rooms. The fuel was peat which caused a fine dust to settle on the walls. While they had three bedrooms, they moved the girl's bed in their room heated by an electric heater they bought. They also bought a kerosene heater for the bathroom which was turned on about 30 minutes before bath time. Water was heated in a small water heater in the wall next to the fireplace which was its source of heat. The refrigerator, about the size of a microwave, was built into a wall in the kitchen. Milk was kept on the back steps and was always cold. They also had a wringer wash machine. All the kids in the neighborhood came to their house to play because Mary Ann was the only mother to allow them to play indoors out of the cold and rain.

By the time Billie June was ready for the third grade the family had moved to Hilversum, The Netherlands where she was enrolled in a private school and had a tutor to learn the Dutch language (Nederlance). She was a fast learner and became the family's interpreter. After a year and a half in the private school she transferred to an American Air Force School. Melissa started kindergarden in Hilversum. The family lived in two homes. The first was a "darling" thatched roof cottage at the edge of the woods and a short bike ride to the home of the Royal Princess. Their second home was a 3-story town house owned by a Director of the Heineken Brewery. The girls had a

L. to R. Billie June, Mary Ann, Bill, and Melissa McPherson, Volendam, The Netherlands, 1966. Photo courtesy of Mary Ann McPherson

balcony off their second floor bedroom. The family went to the Palace to give flowers to the Queen on her birthday. They returned to the U. S. in 1967 and settled in Littleton where both girls were graduated from High School.

Mary Ann **Whipple** and Billie Nathaniel **McPherson** had the following children:
+ 7404 i. Billie June[13] **McPherson** born 16 June 1956.
+ 7405 ii. Melissa Ann **McPherson** born 10 August 1959.

{ G 1105 }

6213. **Donna**[12] **Fultz** (Frank[11], Anna M.[10] **Whipple**, Lucien Ransom[9], Enoch[8], Nehemiah[7], Benjamin[6], Francis[5], Jonathan[4], Joseph[3], Matthew[2], Matthew[1])[782] birth date unknown, married **Nat Turner**.

Donna **Fultz** and Nat **Turner** had the following children:
    7406 i. Joan[13] **Turner**.[783]
    7407 ii. Joetta **Turner**.[784]
    7408 iii. Joyce **Turner**.[785]
    7409 iv. Judy **Turner**.[786]

6217. **Betty Lou**[12] **Holtz** (Suzie[11] **Fultz**, Anna M.[10] **Whipple**, Lucien Ransom[9], Enoch[8], Nehemiah[7], Benjamin[6], Francis[5], Jonathan[4], Joseph[3], Matthew[2], Matthew[1])[787] was born in 1921 and died 17 February 1980 at 59 years of age. She married **James Willett**.

Betty Lou **Holtz** and James **Willett** had the following children:
    7410 i. Jeff[13] **Willett**.[788]
    7411 ii. Jill **Willett**.[789]

6219. **Lee William**[12] **Watson** (Clara Belle[11] **Fultz**, Anna M.[10] **Whipple**, Lucien Ransom[9], Enoch[8], Nehemiah[7], Benjamin[6], Francis[5], Jonathan[4], Joseph[3], Matthew[2], Matthew[1])[790] was born 6 January 1913 and died 11 October 1976 at 63 years of age. He married **Velma Lorraine Knott** 25 December 1937. She was born 8 September 1920 and died 24 September 1978 at 58 years of age. [791]

Lee William **Watson** and Velma Lorraine **Knott** had the following children:
  + 7412 i. Donna Lee[13] **Watson** born 8 September 1938.
      7413 ii. Arthur Allen **Watson**[792] born 16 October 1940.
  + 7414 iii. Patricia Cynn **Watson** born 30 December 1946.
  + 7415 iv. Michael Harlan **Watson** born 22 September 1951.

6220. **Annabelle**[12] **Watson** (Clara Belle[11] **Fultz**, Anna M.[10] **Whipple**, Lucien Ransom[9], Enoch[8], Nehemiah[7], Benjamin[6], Francis[5], Jonathan[4], Joseph[3], Matthew[2], Matthew[1])[793] was born 14 October 1914 and married **Wilbur Albert Huckstadt** 9 December 1939.

Annabelle **Watson** and Wilbur Albert **Huckstadt** had the following child:
  + 7416 i. Donald Louis[13] **Huckstadt** born 13 December 1940.

6221. **Helen Virginia**[12] **Watson** (Clara Belle[11] **Fultz**, Anna M.[10] **Whipple**, Lucien Ransom[9], Enoch[8], Nehemiah[7], Benjamin[6], Francis[5], Jonathan[4],

Joseph[3], Matthew[2], Matthew[1])[794] was born 26 December 1919 and married **Clyde Louis Hendricks** 20 April 1941. He was born 2 March 1911.[795]

Helen Virginia **Watson** and Clyde Louis **Hendricks** had the following children:
- \+ 7417 i. Deanna Kay[13] **Hendricks** born 16 August 1945.
- \+ 7418 ii. Sandra Lee **Hendricks** born 13 May 1948.
- 7419 iii. Mary Jo **Hendricks**[796] born 28 November 1950.

6225. **Marianne**[12] **Pierson** (Cora[11] **Fultz**, Anna M.[10] **Whipple**, Lucien Ransom[9], Enoch[8], Nehemiah[7], Benjamin[6], Francis[5], Jonathan[4], Joseph[3], Matthew[2], Matthew[1])[797] birth date unknown, married **Robert Studdermann**.

Marianne **Pierson** and Robert **Studdermann** had the following children:
- \+ 7420 i. Richard[13] **Studdermann**.
- 7421 ii. Sherryl **Studdermann**[798] married Edwin Anderson **February** 1970.
- 7422 iii. Donald **Studdermann**.[799]
- 7423 iv. Randall Robert **Studdermann**.[800]

6228. **Vivian Ray**[12] **Sneary** (Ella Agnes[11] **Burgess**, Ellen[10] **Whipple**, Manley Nehemiah[9], Abraham[8], Nehemiah[7], Benjamin[6], Francis[5], Jonathan[4], Joseph[3], Matthew[2], Matthew[1])[801] was born in Arnett, Day Co., Okla. Territory 25 December 1904 and died 10 November 1994 in Salina, Saline Co., Kans., at 89 years of age. She married **Rollin D. Shields** in Canadian, Hemphill Co., Tex. 5 April 1925. He was born 23 August 1906 and died 10 September 1989 in Salina, at 83 years of age.[802] They were divorced (date not provided) and she moved to Colton, Calif. in 1944 where she worked for AT&T as a telephone operator until her retirement in 1966. She and Rollin were remarried in 1974 and they moved to Salina in 1976.

Vivian Ray **Sneary** and Rollin D. **Shields** had the following child:
- \+ 7424 i. Maurice Dean[13] **Shields** born 2 October 1925.

6229. **Veta Grace**[12] **Sneary** (Ella Agnes[11] **Burgess**, Ellen[10] **Whipple**, Manley Nehemiah[9], Abraham[8], Nehemiah[7], Benjamin[6], Francis[5], Jonathan[4], Joseph[3], Matthew[2], Matthew[1])[803] was born near Arnett in Ellis Co., Okla. 29 December 1907 and married **Chester Oren Woods** in Gage, Ellis Co., Okla. 28 October 1927. He was born near Arnett 21 December 1907 and is the son of Frederic Asa **Woods** and Annie May **Bondurant**.[804]

Veta Grace **Sneary** and Chester Oren **Woods** had the following children:
+ 7425 i. Jacquiline Genevieve[13] **Woods** born 27 July 1928.
+ 7426 ii. Josephine May **Woods** born 12 September 1931.
+ 7427 iii. Sonya Kay **Woods** born 24 September 1939.
+ 7428 iv. Wynola Carol **Woods** born 5 April 1941.
+ 7429 v. Chester Vance **Woods** born 3 November 1943.
+ 7430 vi. Conyetta Sue **Woods** born 4 February 1946.

6231. **Glenn William**[12] **Burgess** (William[11], Ellen[10] **Whipple**, Manley Nehemiah[9], Abraham[8], Nehemiah[7], Benjamin[6], Francis[5], Jonathan[4], Joseph[3], Matthew[2], Matthew[1])[805] was born in Kansas City, Jackson Co., Mo. 13 November 1910 and married **Thelma West** in Waterloo, Monroe Co., Ill. 3 June 1936. Thelma,[806] daughter of John **West** and Flo Ellen **Lightner**, was born in Chillicothe, Livingston Co., Mo. 15 April 1914.

Glenn William **Burgess** and Thelma **West** had the following children:
+ 7431 i. James Cercy[13] **Burgess** born 18 April 1947.
+ 7432 ii. Chapman Eugene **Burgess** born 20 July 1948.

6232. **Harold Wright**[12] **Burgess** (William[11], Ellen[10] **Whipple**, Manley Nehemiah[9], Abraham[8], Nehemiah[7], Benjamin[6], Francis[5], Jonathan[4], Joseph[3], Matthew[2], Matthew[1])[807] was born in Kansas City, Jackson Co., Mo. 6 June 1912 and died 26 September 1989 in Dubuque, Iowa, at 77 years of age. He married **Dorothy Weber** in Davenport, Iowa 11 December 1941. Dorothy,[808] daughter of Leo **Weber** and Mary **Schaal**, was born in Dubuque 10 October 1919 and died there 19 September 1989, at 69 years of age. Harold is buried in the Linwood Cemetery in Dubuque.

Harold Wright **Burgess** and Dorothy **Weber** had the following children:
+ 7433 i. Robert John[13] **Burgess** born 8 January 1944.
+ 7434 ii. William Charles **Burgess** born 25 July 1947.
+ 7435 iii. Steven James **Burgess** born 22 July 1952.

6233. **Marjorie Ellen**[12] **Burgess** (William[11], Ellen[10] **Whipple**, Manley Nehemiah[9], Abraham[8], Nehemiah[7], Benjamin[6], Francis[5], Jonathan[4], Joseph[3], Matthew[2], Matthew[1])[809] was born in Kansas City, Jackson Co., Mo. 18 November 1914 and married twice. (1) **Charles V. Champion** in Kansas City 3 July 1936. Charles,[810] son of Charles Virgil **Champion**, was born in Wisconsin 17 July 1912 and died 6 July 1967 in Pendelton, Umatilla Co. Oreg., at 54 years of age. (2) **Admiral Richard Mandelkorn** 10 January 1976.

Marjorie Ellen **Burgess** and Charles V. **Champion** had the following children:
- 7436 i. John Charles[13] **Champion**[811] born in Wilmington, Del. 11 October 1940 and died in a highway accident 13 July 1962 in California, at 21 years of age.
- 7437 ii. Jane Ellen **Champion**[812] born in Chillicothe, Livingston Co., Mo. 17 September 1944 and married Don **Cooney** in San Jose, Calif.
- 7438 iii. David Burgess **Champion**[813] born in Pendleton 21 January 1952 and married Jeanette **Ross**.

6234. **Dorothy Emma**[12] **Burgess** (William[11], Ellen[10] **Whipple**, Manley Nehemiah[9], Abraham[8], Nehemiah[7], Benjamin[6], Francis[5], Jonathan[4], Joseph[3], Matthew[2], Matthew[1])[814] was born in Chula, Livingston Co., Mo. 25 February 1917 and died 25 January 1989 in Kansas City, Jackson Co., Mo., at 71 years of age. She married **George Clement Hale** in Kansas City 3 January 1941. George,[815] son of George Grover **Hale** and Beulah Bessie **Leftwick**, was born in Kansas City 11 March 1916 and died there 5 January 1978, at 61 years of age. He worked the vaudeville circuit as a child through his teen years, performing with his parents.

Dorothy Emma **Burgess** and George Clement **Hale** had the following children born in Kansas City:
- 7439 i. Sharon Elizabeth[13] **Hale**[816] 18 October 1941 and married Peter **Reuter** there.
- 7440 ii. George Michael **Hale**[817] 13 June 1944 and married twice. (1) Marilyn **Maddox**. (2) Wanda (__).
- 7441 iii. Joseph Patrick **Hale**[818] 18 March 1946 and married Mary **Fugate**.
- + 7442 iv. Rosemary Cecile **Hale** 18 September 1948.
- 7443 v. Maureen Theresa **Hale**[819] 12 January 1950 and married Joel **Phillips**.
- + 7444 vi. Paul Christopher **Hale** was born 11 November 1952.
- 7445 vii. John Francis **Hale**[820] 15 July 1954 and married Colette **Weisner**.
- 7446 viii. Kathleen Marie **Hale**[821] 27 May 1957 and married Stanley **Stalnaker**.
- 7447 ix. Regina Ann **Hale**[822] 11 December 1960 and married Mitch **Ehrlich**.

6235. **Arthur Pershing**[12] **Burgess** (William[11], Ellen[10] **Whipple**, Manley Nehemiah[9], Abraham[8], Nehemiah[7], Benjamin[6], Francis[5], Jonathan[4], Joseph[3], Matthew[2], Matthew[1])[823] was born in Chula, Livingston Co., Mo. 12 May 1919 and married **Janney Vee Swan** in Kansas City, Jackson Co., Mo. 9 February 1944. Janney,[824] daughter of William Austin **Swan** and Jennie **(__)**, was born in Kansas City 5 November 1921.

Arthur Pershing **Burgess** and Janney Vee **Swan** had the following children:

    7448 i. Anne Louise[13] **Burgess**[825] born in Edmondton, Alberta, Canada 7 January 1945 and married Edward **Sanders** in Oswego, Labette Co., Kans.

    7449 ii. Susan Kay **Burgess**[826] was born in Kansas City, Kans. 14 August 1946 and married Charles **Seibel** in Oswego.

    7450 iii. Robin Lynn **Burgess**[827] born in Kansas City, Kans. 11 April 1951 and married Thomas **Lackey.**

    7451 iv. Jean Elaine **Burgess**[828] born in Oswego 11 February 1954 and married Mark **Olson.**

    7452 v. Gwen Ellen **Burgess**[829] born in Oswego 2 September 1955 and married Ankota **Sandal.**

6236. **Doris Fern**[12] **Burgess** (William[11], Ellen[10] **Whipple**, Manley Nehemiah[9], Abraham[8], Nehemiah[7], Benjamin[6], Francis[5], Jonathan[4], Joseph[3], Matthew[2], Matthew[1]) was born in Chula, Livingston Co., Mo. 21 February 1922 and married **Howard Wallace Worthington** in Kansas City, Jackson Co., Mo. 7 May 1944. Howard,[830] son of Leonard **Worthington** and Gladys **Harlan**, was born in Kansas City 1 March 1923 and died 1 October 1979 in St. Charles, Kane Co., Ill., at 56 years of age.

Doris Fern **Burgess** and Howard Wallace **Worthington** had the following children:

  + 7453 i. Janice Kay[13] **Worthington** born 22 November 1946.

    7454 ii. Richard Stephen **Worthington**[831] born in Oklahoma City, Okla. 20 September 1956.

  + 7455 iii. Julie Ann **Worthington** born 25 May 1961.

6237. **Helen Marie**[12] **Burgess** (William[11], Ellen[10] **Whipple**, Manley Nehemiah[9], Abraham[8], Nehemiah[7], Benjamin[6], Francis[5], Jonathan[4], Joseph[3], Matthew[2], Matthew[1])[832] was born in Chula, Livingston Co., Mo. 5 October 1924 and married twice. (1) **Emmett Eugene Adams** in Kansas City, Jackson Co., Mo. 12 April 1946. Emmett is the son of Emmett **Adams** and Frances **(__)**.[833] (2) **Verne K. Covell Sr.** in Kansas City 18 June 1960.

Helen Marie **Burgess** and Emmett Eugene **Adams** had the following child:
>   7456   i.   Samuel Eugene[13] **Adams**[834] born in Kansas City 3 October 1947 and married Lois **Cole** there 12 April 1970.

6238. **John Francis**[12] **Burgess** (William[11], Ellen[10] **Whipple**, Manley Nehemiah[9], Abraham[8], Nehemiah[7], Benjamin[6], Francis[5], Jonathan[4], Joseph[3], Matthew[2], Matthew[1])[835] was born in Chula, Livingston Co., Mo. 9 October 1929 and married **Shirley Roth** in Kansas City, Jackson Co., Mo. 29 October 1954. She was born 14 February 1932.[836]

John Francis **Burgess** and Shirley **Roth** had the following children born in Kansas City:
>   7457   i.   Barry John[13] **Burgess**[837] 17 August 1955 and married Deb (__).
> + 7458   ii.   Gary William **Burgess** 21 January 1957.
> + 7459   iii. Lauren Jean **Burgess** 20 September 1959.

6241. **Lavine**[12] **Van Dyke** (Carrie Emily[11] **Whipple**, Alphonso[10], Horatio[9], Nathan[8], Nehemiah[7], Benjamin[6], Francis[5], Jonathan[4], Joseph[3], Matthew[2], Matthew[1])[838] was born in Geneva, Ohio 3 January 1890 and died 28 March 1956 in Elyria, Ohio, at 66 years of age. She married **Otto F. Schowalter** in Madison, Ohio 1 September 1909. Otto,[839] son of Peter **Schowalter** and Maria **Eysmann**, was born in Donnellson, Iowa 24 March 1866 and died 3 June 1955 in Homestead, Fla., at 89 years of age.

Lavine **Van Dyke** and Otto F. **Schowalter** had the following children:
> + 7460   i.   Arthur Eastman[13] **Schowalter** born 30 July 1910.
> + 7461   ii.   Lawrence V. **Schowalter** born 13 September 1914.

6242. **Carroll Marcus**[12] **Van Dyke** (Carrie Emily[11] **Whipple**, Alphonso[10], Horatio[9], Nathan[8], Nehemiah[7], Benjamin[6], Francis[5], Jonathan[4], Joseph[3], Matthew[2], Matthew[1]) was born in Harper Fields, Ohio 21 May 1894 and died 27 July 1964 in Painesville, Ohio, at 70 years of age. He married **Martha Vernice Fuller** in Madison, Ohio 30 June 1921. Martha, daughter of William Emmet **Fuller** and Julietta **Lovett**, was born in Madison 24 January 1895. Carroll worked at Euclid Electric Company.

Carroll Marcus **Van Dyke** and Martha Vernice **Fuller** had the following children:
> + 7462   i.   Carroll Emmett[13] **Van Dyke** born 21 March 1922.
> + 7463   ii.   Lauretta **Van Dyke** born 31 July 1924.

	7464	iii.	Donald Dean **Van Dyke**[840] born in Painesville 14 May 1927 and married Beatrice **Davis** in Los Angeles, Calif. 23 December 1957. They were divorced in 1981.
+	7465	iv.	Clifford Fuller **Van Dyke** born 17 February 1934.

6243. **Ethel**[12] **Van Dyke** (Carrie Emily[11] **Whipple**, Alphonso[10], Horatio[9], Nathan[8], Nehemiah[7], Benjamin[6], Francis[5], Jonathan[4], Joseph[3], Matthew[2], Matthew[1])[841] was born in Madison, Ohio 24 September 1896 and died 1984 in Greenville, S.C., at 87 years of age. She married three times. (1) **Arthur Leipner** in Madison 5 January 1913. He was born in Cleveland, Ohio in 1894 and died there 13 June 1915, at 20 years of age.[842] (2) **Bert P. Lutz** abt 1925. (3) **Robert Slaker**.

Ethel **Van Dyke** and Arthur **Leipner** had the following child:

+	7466	i.	Beatrice[13] **Leipner** born 4 February 1914.

6245. **Stella Emma**[12] **Whipple** (Ira Orren[11], Alphonso[10], Horatio[9], Nathan[8], Nehemiah[7], Benjamin[6], Francis[5], Jonathan[4], Joseph[3], Matthew[2], Matthew[1])[843] was born 28 October 1898 and died 2 November 1977 at 79 years of age. She married **Ernest LaVern Greeley**. He was born 1 May 1896 and died 21 May 1981 at 85 years of age.[844]

Stella Emma **Whipple** and Ernest LaVern **Greeley** had the following children:

+	7467	i.	Eleanor Catherine[13] **Greeley** born 17 April 1924.
+	7468	ii.	Calvin Richard **Greeley** born 13 March 1925.
	7469	iii.	Winifred Joyce **Greeley**[845] born in Erie, Erie Co., Penn. 26 October 1932 and married Ronald **Bauer** in Cleveland, Ohio June 1953. They were divorced in Pittsburgh, Penn. in January 1960. Joyce studied at universities in California, Massachusetts, and Europe and eventually became a teacher of German at the secondary and college level. She is retired and lives in Fair Oaks, Calif. (1998).

6246. **Carl Wright**[12] **Whipple** (Ira Orren[11], Alphonso[10], Horatio[9], Nathan[8], Nehemiah[7], Benjamin[6], Francis[5], Jonathan[4], Joseph[3], Matthew[2], Matthew[1])[846] was born 21 May 1902 and died in 1968 at 66 years of age. He married **Alda Briggs** who was born 12 July 1906.[847]

Carl Wright **Whipple** and Alda **Briggs** had the following children:

+	7470	i.	Margaret May[13] **Whipple** born 8 March 1925.
+	7471	ii.	Carl James **Whipple** born 15 April 1927.

+	7472	iii.	Harold Vernon **Whipple** born 30 May 1928.
+	7473	iv.	Phyllis Jean **Whipple** born 28 August 1930.
+	7474	v.	Norman Lee **Whipple** born 4 June 1932.

6247. **Irene May**[12] **Whipple** (Ira Orren[11], Alphonso[10], Horatio[9], Nathan[8], Nehemiah[7], Benjamin[6], Francis[5], Jonathan[4], Joseph[3], Matthew[2], Matthew[1])[848] was born 10 March 1907 and married **Howard Ritter Good Sr.** He was born 11 March 1907.[849]

Irene May **Whipple** and Howard Ritter **Good** Sr. had the following children:

7475	i.	Shirley Jeanne[13] **Good**[850] born 7 December 1931.
7476	ii.	Howard Ritter **Good** Jr.[851] born 9 November 1936.

6248. **Lucy Freida**[12] **Whipple** (Ira Orren[11], Alphonso[10], Horatio[9], Nathan[8], Nehemiah[7], Benjamin[6], Francis[5], Jonathan[4], Joseph[3], Matthew[2], Matthew[1])[852] was born 28 August 1912 and died in February 1983 at 70 years of age. She married twice. (1) **Bruce Merle Miller**. He was born in 1912 and died in 1941 at 29 years of age.[853] (2) **Raymond Cromwell** who was born 2 November 1918. He married (2) **Maria Christina Salminen**.[854]

Lucy Freida **Whipple** and Raymond **Cromwell** had the following children:

7477	i.	Ronald James[13] **Cromwell**[855] born in Painesville, Ohio 15 December 1945 and died there abt June 1947, at 1 year of age.
7478	ii.	Connie Ray **Cromwell**[856] born in Painesville 1 March 1949 and married twice. The names of her husbands was not provided. She married second after the death of her first husband. She had a child with the first husband.
7479	iii.	Eric James **Cromwell**[857] born in Painesville 22 December 1951 and married Kathy **Urvas** who was born 22 December 1952.[858]

6249. **Joseph Albert**[12] **Whipple** (Eli Albert[11], Alphonso[10], Horatio[9], Nathan[8], Nehemiah[7], Benjamin[6], Francis[5], Jonathan[4], Joseph[3], Matthew[2], Matthew[1])[859] was born 7 August 1908 and died in 1977 at 68 years of age. He married **Grace Dean** 9 November 1929. She was born 8 June 1908 and died in 1946 at 38 years of age.

Joseph Albert **Whipple** and Grace **Dean** had the following children:

7480	i.	George Eli[13] **Whipple**[860] born 10 November 1930.
7481	ii.	Mary Ellen **Whipple**[861] born 11 January 1934.
7482	iii.	Iva Elizabeth **Whipple**[862] born 20 June 1935.

6250. **Oren Arthur**[12] **Whipple** (Eli Albert[11], Alphonso[10], Horatio[9], Nathan[8], Nehemiah[7], Benjamin[6], Francis[5], Jonathan[4], Joseph[3], Matthew[2], Matthew[1])[863] was born 24 July 1910 and died in 1979, at 68 years of age. He married **Marion Means** 26 January 1935. She was born 10 September 1915 and died in 1980, at 64 years of age.[864]

Oren Arthur **Whipple** and Marion **Means** had the following children:

    7483 i. Joan Lane[13] **Whipple**[865] born 25 January 1938 and married Don **Williams**.

    7484 ii. Janice Amy **Whipple**[866] born 3 March 1942 and married Don **Kendrick**.

6251. **Richard Eldsworth**[12] **Whipple** (Eli Albert[11], Alphonso[10], Horatio[9], Nathan[8], Nehemiah[7], Benjamin[6], Francis[5], Jonathan[4], Joseph[3], Matthew[2], Matthew[1])[867] was born 25 June 1912 and died 5 November 1986 at 74 years of age. He married **Mary Elizabeth Soden** 23 March 1944. She was born 25 March 1919.[868]

Richard Eldsworth **Whipple** and Mary Elizabeth **Soden** had the following children:

    7485 i. (Infant)[13] **Whipple**[869] stillborn born 30 November 1944.

    7486 ii. Jean Michele **Whipple**[870] born in Ashtabula Co., Ohio 3 June 1947 and married Lawrence **Lowery**.

    7487 iii. Lou Ann **Whipple**[871] born in Ashtabula Co. 29 June 1950 and married Douglas Lee **Montgomery** 22 January 1974.

6253. **Warren Harding**[12] **Whipple** (Eli Albert[11], Alphonso[10], Horatio[9], Nathan[8], Nehemiah[7], Benjamin[6], Francis[5], Jonathan[4], Joseph[3], Matthew[2], Matthew[1])[872] was born 31 October 1920 and married **Elizabeth Sue Britt Sears**. She died in January 1993.[873] Elizabeth married (1) (__) **Britt** and had a son Michael Britt, born 15 June 1946.

Warren Harding **Whipple** and Elizabeth Sue Britt **Sears** had the following child:

    7488 i. Richard Warren[13] **Whipple**[874] born 29 January 1952.

6255. **Florence Ilene**[12] **Whipple** (James Ford[11], Alphonso[10], Horatio[9], Nathan[8], Nehemiah[7], Benjamin[6], Francis[5], Jonathan[4], Joseph[3], Matthew[2], Matthew[1])[875] was born in Madison, Ohio 25 November 1906 and died 18 November 1988 in Nunan, Ga., at 81 years of age. She married **Arthur Fenlason** in Ripply, N.Y. 3 January 1931.

Florence Ilene **Whipple** and Arthur **Fenlason** had the following children:
- 7489 i. Lois Ann[13] **Fenlason**.[876]
- 7490 ii. Carolyn Louise **Fenlason**.[877]
- 7491 iii. James Leroy **Fenlason**[878] born in Madison 4 August 1934.[879]

6257. **Rollah Henry**[12] **Whipple** (James Ford[11], Alphonso[10], Horatio[9], Nathan[8], Nehemiah[7], Benjamin[6], Francis[5], Jonathan[4], Joseph[3], Matthew[2], Matthew[1])[880] was born in Madison, Ohio 20 September 1910 and died 22 November 1988 at 78 years of age. He married **Wilma Lela Rohrbaugh** in Ripply, N.Y. 18 November 1933.

Rollah Henry **Whipple** and Wilma Lela **Rohrbaugh** had the following children:
- 7492 i. Connie May[13] **Whipple**[881] born in Madison 20 September 1937 and married Robert **Nyman**.
- 7493 ii. James Leroy **Whipple**[882] born 26 March 1943 and married Jackie **Thompson**.

6258. **Dorothy Dorene**[12] **Whipple** (James Ford[11], Alphonso[10], Horatio[9], Nathan[8], Nehemiah[7], Benjamin[6], Francis[5], Jonathan[4], Joseph[3], Matthew[2], Matthew[1])[883] was born in Madison, Ohio 18 June 1912 and married **Paul Spelsmore** in Ripply, N.Y. 4 August 1942.

Dorothy Dorene **Whipple** and Paul **Spelsmore** had the following children:
- 7494 i. Sally[13] **Spelsmore**[884] born in Geneva, Ohio 2 June 1935 and married Robert **Marstellar** in California.
- 7495 ii. James **Spelsmore**[885] born 11 July 1947 and married Mary **Skidmore** in California.

6259. **Grace Geraldine**[12] **Whipple** (James Ford[11], Alphonso[10], Horatio[9], Nathan[8], Nehemiah[7], Benjamin[6], Francis[5], Jonathan[4], Joseph[3], Matthew[2], Matthew[1])[886] was born in Madison, Ohio 22 February 1914 and married **Elmer Bezdik** in Geneva, Ohio 23 November 1935.

Grace Geraldine **Whipple** and Elmer **Bezdik** had the following children:
- 7496 i. Greg[13] **Bezdik**.[887]
- 7497 ii. Janet Sue **Bezdik**[888] born in Geneva 12 March 1941 and married Al **Buber**.
- 7498 iii. Linda **Bezdik**[889] born in Geneva 27 March 1944 and married Richard **Veney**.
- 7499 iv. Donald **Bezdik**[890] born 14 February 1946 and married Dana **(__)**.

6260. **Elsie Madge**[12] **Whipple** (James Ford[11], Alphonso[10], Horatio[9], Nathan[8], Nehemiah[7], Benjamin[6], Francis[5], Jonathan[4], Joseph[3], Matthew[2], Matthew[1])[891] was born in Madison, Ohio 23 August 1916 and married **William Milo Wheeler** 4 August 1935.

Elsie Madge **Whipple** and William Milo **Wheeler** had the following children:
- 7500 i. Sherri Lee[13] **Wheeler**[892] born in Geneva, Ohio 7 August 1943.
- 7501 ii. Dorene Madge **Wheeler**[893] born in Geneva 27 October 1946.

6261. **Ray Wendell**[12] **Whipple** (James Ford[11], Alphonso[10], Horatio[9], Nathan[8], Nehemiah[7], Benjamin[6], Francis[5], Jonathan[4], Joseph[3], Matthew[2], Matthew[1])[894] was born in Madison, Ohio 12 September 1918 and married **Miriam Barton** 14 November 1942. Ray retired from the U.S. Airforce as a Lt. Colonel.

Ray Wendell **Whipple** and Miriam **Barton** had the following children:
- 7502 i. Rae Jean[13] **Whipple**[895] born in Geneva, Ohio 28 November 1943.
- 7503 ii. Randolph Barton **Whipple**[896] born in Colorado Springs, Colo. 21 January 1948.
- 7504 iii. Richard Ford **Whipple**[897] born in Omaha, Nebr. 10 August 1956.

6263. **Veda Louise**[12] **Greeley** (Roxey Alamanda[11] **Whipple**, Alphonso[10], Horatio[9], Nathan[8], Nehemiah[7], Benjamin[6], Francis[5], Jonathan[4], Joseph[3], Matthew[2], Matthew[1])[898] was born in Meadville, Penn. 14 June 1915 and married twice. (1) **Charles Joseph Claxon** 5 July 1937. Charles,[899] son of Reuben Harrison **Claxon** and Bernice **Davis**, was born in Taylorsville, Ill. 6 May 1914 and died 24 July 1986 in Lake Placid, Fla., at 72 years of age They were divorced in 1940. (2) **Bernard Lorraine Knapp** in Madison, Ohio 16 February 1951. Bernard,[900] son of Royal Ivan **Knapp** and Pearl Fern **Clemmer**, was born in Franklin, Penn. 2 August 1918 and died 30 March 1993 in Belair, Md., at 74 years of age.

Veda Louise **Greeley** and Charles Joseph **Claxon** had the following child:
- + 7505 i. Patricia Ann[13] **Claxon** born 2 August 1938.

Veda Louise **Greeley** and Bernard Lorraine **Knapp** had the following children:
- 7506 ii. Lorraine Lee **Knapp**[901] born in Painesville, Ohio 27 June 1953 and died there 25 December 1953 2 days shy of 6

months of age. Buried with her grandparents Roxey Whipple and LaVerne Greeley in the Greeley family plot at the Middle Ridge Cemetery in Madison.

7507 iii. Susan Louise **Knapp**[902] born in Painesville 27 June 1953.

6264. **Wallace Eugene**[12] **Whipple** (Nathan Wilson[11], Alphonso[10], Horatio[9], Nathan[8], Nehemiah[7], Benjamin[6], Francis[5], Jonathan[4], Joseph[3], Matthew[2], Matthew[1])[903] was born in Madison, Ohio 28 August 1914 and died of a heart attack at the San Bernardino Medical Center 3 August 1995 in San Bernardino, Calif., at 80 years of age. He married twice. (1) **June Strock** in Madison 17 October 1937. She was born in Madison 27 July 1919 and died there 24 July 1963, at 43 years of age.[904] (2) **Lorene Beall**. He lived in San Bernardino for 40 years where he was a member of the Optimists Club and Calvary Baptist Church. He was an auto mechanic for Mobile Oil Co. for 45 years.

Wallace Eugene **Whipple** and June **Strock** had the following child:
+ 7508 i. Kenneth Russell[13] **Whipple** born 20 October 1938.

6265. **Russell Elwood**[12] **Whipple** (Nathan Wilson[11], Alphonso[10], Horatio[9], Nathan[8], Nehemiah[7], Benjamin[6], Francis[5], Jonathan[4], Joseph[3], Matthew[2], Matthew[1])[905] was born in Lansing, Mich. 20 March 1916 and married twice. (1) **Rakel Evje** in Madison, Ohio, 3 August 1947. She was born in Olso, Norway 25 November 1909 and died 16 June 1993 in Fallbrook, Calif., at 83 years of age.[906] She was buried in the Riverside National Cemetery, Riverside, Calif. (2) **Faith-Constance Moser** in 1995.

Russell was raised in Ohio and received his higher education in Massachusetts. He earned a bachelor's degree in Social Science and Education at Springfield College (1940) and a master's degree in Public Relations at Boston University (1953). He lived in Oslo, Norway 1938-39 where he met his wife. He reads, writes, and speaks Norwegian. He enlisted in Marine Corps in 1941 and served in the first Marine Parachute Regiment. In later assignments on the Mainland and in Hawaii, he worked in information services, logistics, and industrial relations. He retired as a Major in 1963 at Camp Pendleton, Calif. and began a second career as a High School Teacher. After 14 years of teaching English and Speech at Fallbrook Union High School he retired and raises avocados and is active in the California Retired Teachers' Assn., Toastmasters International, Methodist Church, and The Military Order of World Wars.

Russell Elwood **Whipple** and Rakel **Evje** had the following children:
+ 7509 i. Ronald Elwood[13] **Whipple** born 26 October 1949.
+ 7510 ii. Mark Wilson **Whipple** born 26 September 1952.

6266. **Kenneth Elman**[12] **Whipple** (Nathan Wilson[11], Alphonso[10], Horatio[9], Nathan[8], Nehemiah[7], Benjamin[6], Francis[5], Jonathan[4], Joseph[3], Matthew[2], Matthew[1])[907] was born in Lansing, Mich. 4 January 1918 and married twice. (1) **Charlotte G. Crum** in Madison, Ohio, 12 October 1939. She was born in Cleveland, Ohio 20 June 1919 and died 7 November 1990 in Madison, at 71 years of age.[908] (2) **Donna McElwee**.

Kenneth Elman **Whipple** and Charlotte G. **Crum** had the following children:
+ 7511 i. Kristen D.[13] **Whipple** born 9 October 1942.
+ 7512 ii. Diana L. **Whipple** born 10 December 1946.

6267. **Sheldon Ray**[12] **Whipple** (Nathan Wilson[11], Alphonso[10], Horatio[9], Nathan[8], Nehemiah[7], Benjamin[6], Francis[5], Jonathan[4], Joseph[3], Matthew[2], Matthew[1])[909] was born in Painesville, Ohio 10 April 1926 and died 7 June 1982 in Madison, Ohio, at 56 years of age. He married **Joan Phyllis Nash** in Madison 12 October 1946. She was born in Painesville 11 December 1926.[910]

Sheldon Ray **Whipple** and Joan Phyllis **Nash** had the following children:
  7513 i. Susan Rae[13] **Whipple**[911] born in Loma Linda, Calif. 9 April 1949 and married Charles Martin **Jewett** in Madison 27 September 1987.
+ 7514 ii. Glen Kimball **Whipple** born 20 March 1952.
+ 7515 iii. Beth Eileen **Whipple** born 28 June 1955.
+ 7516 iv. Jon Wilson **Whipple** born 2 August 1956.
  7517 v. Paul Michael **Whipple**[912] born in Painesville 28 December 1962.
  7518 vi. Keith Lorin **Whipple**[913] born in Painesville 16 July 1964.

6268. **Roy Curwood**[12] **Whipple** (Nathan Wilson[11], Alphonso[10], Horatio[9], Nathan[8], Nehemiah[7], Benjamin[6], Francis[5], Jonathan[4], Joseph[3], Matthew[2], Matthew[1])[914] was born in Madison, Ohio 29 April 1928 and married **Winifred Jean Trisket** there 29 October 1946. She was born in Madison 22 October 1926.[915]

Roy C. Whipple at the grave of Laura Whipple at the Saybrook, Ohio cemetery.

Roy Curwood **Whipple** and Winifred Jean **Trisket** had the following children:
- \+ 7519 i. Cheryl Jean[13] **Whipple** born 21 February 1951.
- \+ 7520 ii. Debra Jean **Whipple** born 23 February 1954.
- \+ 7521 iii. David Roy **Whipple** born 20 July 1961.

6271. **R. Douglas**[12] **Whipple** (Royal Howard[11], Alphonso[10], Horatio[9], Nathan[8], Nehemiah[7], Benjamin[6], Francis[5], Jonathan[4], Joseph[3], Matthew[2], Matthew[1])[916] was born 27 September 1917 and died 15 December 1990 at 73 years of age. He married **Ruth I. Miller** who died 27 March 1990.[917]

R. Douglas **Whipple** and Ruth I. **Miller** had the following children:
- \+ 7522 i. Marla[13] **Whipple**.
- \+ 7523 ii. Dr. Robert **Whipple** born 3 May 1945.
- \+ 7524 iii. John **Whipple** born 8 August 1949.

6275. **Lillian Isabelle**[12] **Beddoes** (Jessie[11] **Brown**, Henry **Whipple**[10], Miranda[9] **Whipple**, Nathan[8], Nehemiah[7], Benjamin[6], Francis[5], Jonathan[4], Joseph[3], Matthew[2], Matthew[1])[918] was born in Harrison, Ill. 11 November 1896 and died 21 March 1970 in Milaca, Minn., at 73 years of age. She married twice. (1) **Arvid Linder** in Rockford, Winnebago Co. Ill.. He was born in Jonkoping, Sweden 28 November 1887[919] and died 17 November 1934 in Rockford. at 46 years of age married **Anna LaVon (__)**. (2) **Henry Brink** in Mitchell, S. Dak. in 1947.

Lillian Isabelle **Beddoes** and Arvid **Linder** had the following child:
- \+ 7525 i. Evelyn Isabell[13] **Linder** born 27 May 1914.

6284. **Frederick**[12] **Watkins** (Henry A.[11], Henry[10], Moses[9], Lois[8] **Mills**, Hepzibah[7] **Whipple**, Benjamin[6], Francis[5], Jonathan[4], Joseph[3], Matthew[2], Matthew[1])[920] was born in Potsdam, N.Y. 7 March 1894[921] and died 10 May 1943 in Brooklyn, N.Y., at 49 years of age.[922] He married **Alice Downer Briggs** 13 September 1930. Alice,[923] daughter of Walter A. **Briggs** and Alice Cary **Downer**, was born in Newark, Essex Co., N.J. 23 May 1901 and died 29 July 1984 in Medford, Burlington Co., N.J., at 83 years of age.[924] She married (2) **William Wehner**. Frederick and Alice were buried in Westfield, Union Co., N.J. Fairview Cemetery. Alice was a graduate of the New Jersey State Teachers College and was a First Grade School Teacher. She was a member of the DAR, No. 236881. Frederick was graduated from Cornell University with degrees in Mechanical and Electrical Engineering.

Frederick **Watkins** and Alice Downer **Briggs** had the following children:
- +   7526   i.   Carol Moore[13] **Watkins** born 16 October 1934.
- +   7527   ii.   William Moore **Watkins** born 28 June 1938.

6311. **Florence B.**[12] **Johnson** (Mary Lillian[11] **Whipple**, Ithamar Cyrus[10], Cyrus Avery[9], Ithamar[8], Rev. Benjamin[7], Benjamin[6], Francis[5], Jonathan[4], Joseph[3], Matthew[2], Matthew[1])[925] was born in Kansas City, Jackson Co., Mo. 4 January 1899 and died 22 September 1991 in Overland Park, Kans, at 92 years of age. She was buried in Mt. Moriah Cemetery, Kansas City, Mo. She married **Charles Myron Chandler** in Kansas City 25 November 1918. Charles,[926] son of Charles M. **Chandler** and Emma Estelle **Bullock**, was born in Cincinnati, Ohio 23 April 1892 and died 2 April 1963 in Grand Junction, Colo., at 70 years of age.

Florence B. **Johnson** and Charles Myron **Chandler** had the following children:
- +   7528   i.   Jane Elizabeth[13] **Chandler** born 25 August 1919.
-      7529   ii.   Barbara Ann **Chandler**[927] born in Kansas City 29 October 1921.
- +   7530   iii. George Myron **Chandler** born 23 February 1928.

6316. **Frederick Allan**[12] **Hart** (Fred J.[11], John P.[10], Florina H.[9] **Whipple**, Ithamar[8], Rev. Benjamin[7], Benjamin[6], Francis[5], Jonathan[4], Joseph[3], Matthew[2], Matthew[1])[928] was born in Auburn, Cayuga Co., N.Y. 18 January 1922 and died 11 August 1996 in Whittier, Los Angeles Co., Calif., at 74 years of age. Buried in Riverside National Cemetery, Riverside, Calif. He married **Juanita Bonnaire Francis** in Lynwood, Los Angeles Co., Calif. 5 June 1942. Juanita,[929] daughter of Garrett J. **Francis** and Emma May **Howell**, was born in Milford, Seward Co., Nebr. 17 April 1922.

Frederick Allan **Hart** and Juanita Bonnaire **Francis** had the following children:
- +   7531   i.   Julia Arlene[13] **Hart** born 9 March 1943.
- +   7532   ii.   Allan Lee **Hart** born 15 September 1946.
-      7533   iii. William Frederick **Hart**[930] born in Los Angeles, Calif. 11 January 1951.
- +   7534   iv.   Dale Francis **Hart** born 13 August 1953.

6318. **Wilma Mildred Martha**[12] **Morse** (Ella Maude[11] **Keeler**, Eliza Jane[10] **Whipple**, Daniel F.[9], Ithamar[8], Rev. Benjamin[7], Benjamin[6], Francis[5], Jonathan[4], Joseph[3], Matthew[2], Matthew[1])[931] was born in Erie Co., Penn. 22 May 1908 and died 18 November 1990 in Edinboro, Erie Co., at

82 years of age. She married **Owen Samuel Lewis** 28 March 1925. He was born in Crawford Co., Penn. 25 June 1905 and died 19 January 1970 in Erie, at 64 years of age. [932] Buried in Waterford Cemetery.

Wilma Mildred Martha **Morse** and Owen Samuel **Lewis** had the following children:

7535	i.	Charlotte[13] **Lewis**.[933]
7536	ii.	Loma Jean **Lewis**.[934]
7537	iii.	Lois **Lewis**.[935]
7538	iv.	Ila **Lewis**.[936]
7539	v.	Charles **Lewis**.[937]
7540	vi.	Paul **Lewis**.[938]
7541	vii.	Clarence **Lewis**.[939]

6321. **Leslie A.**[12] **Whipple** (Clayton J.[11], William Lemuel[10], Francis Jackson[9], Ithamar[8], Rev. Benjamin[7], Benjamin[6], Francis[5], Jonathan[4], Joseph[3], Matthew[2], Matthew[1])[940] was born in Winnepeg, Manitoba, Canada 2 April 1903 and died 18 August 1983 in Sarasota, Fla., at 80 years of age. He married three times. (1) **Marion Van Reipen Heath** in Philadelphia, Penn. 24 September 1927. She was born in Jersey City, N.J. 7 October 1903 and was the third generation to be born in the house purchased by her great grandfather following his wedding in 1845.[941] She died 11 November 1983 in Somerset, N.J., at 80 years of age. Both are buried in Mt. Hebron Cemetery Upper Montclair, N.J.

Marion attended The College of the City of Detroit (later Wayne State) and worked for McGraw Hill Publishers for 17 years. (2) **Bertrice Eileen McHugh** 3 July 1952. (3) **Florence Carr Kelly** in Verona, Essex Co., N.J. 29 August 1959. Following his mother's marriage to Lucius Cannon, Leslie assumed the Cannon surname. It is not known whether he was legally adopted but some of his descendants are known as Cannon, not Whipple.

Leslie A. **Whipple** and Marion Van Reipen **Heath** had the following children:

	7542	i.	Douglas Forrest[13] **Whipple**.
+	7543	ii.	Jean Carol **Cannon** born 9 January 1929.
+	7544	iii.	Douglas Forrest **Cannon** born 7 March 1931.

6332. **Mable Jeannette**[12] **Skelton** (Sylvia May[11] **Whipple**, Marcus Erastus[10], Francis Jackson[9], Ithamar[8], Rev. Benjamin[7], Benjamin[6], Francis[5], Jonathan[4], Joseph[3], Matthew[2], Matthew[1])[942] was born in Edinboro, Erie Co., Penn. 11 June 1922 and married **Harley Eisentrager** there 12

{ G 1121 }

June 1943. He was born 21 February 1917 and died 22 November 1982 in Kuna, Ada Co., Idaho, at 65 years of age.[943]

Mable Jeannette **Skelton** and Harley **Eisentrager** had the following children:
- \+ 7545 i. Paul Harley[13] **Eisentrager** born 20 March 1944.
- \+ 7546 ii. Daniel Lee **Eisentrager** Sr. born 10 April 1946.
- \+ 7547 iii. David Ray **Eisentrager** born 9 May 1949.
- \+ 7548 iv. Ruth Marie **Eisentrager** born 20 April 1954.
-   7549 v. Deborah Jean **Eisentrager**[944] born 1 August 1957.
- \+ 7550 vi. Joy Ann **Eisentrager** born 14 August 1960.

6333. **James John**[12] **Skelton** (Sylvia May[11] **Whipple**, Marcus Erastus[10], Francis Jackson[9], Ithamar[8], Rev. Benjamin[7], Benjamin[6], Francis[5], Jonathan[4], Joseph[3], Matthew[2], Matthew[1])[945] was born 2 February 1924 and married **Elena Mae Billings** in Edinboro, Erie Co., Penn. 13 February 1943. She was born 14 May 1924.

James John **Skelton** and Elena Mae **Billings** had the following children:
-   7551 i. Judy Mae[13] **Skelton**[946] born 21 February 1944.
- \+ 7552 ii. Donna Lee **Skelton** born 30 January 1945.
- \+ 7553 iii. Roberta Jean **Skelton** born 7 January 1949.
- \+ 7554 iv. Dennis James **Skelton** born 7 December 1952.
- \+ 7555 v. Terry Arden **Skelton** born 26 November 1955.
- \+ 7556 vi. Woodette Eileen **Skelton** born 7 December 1959.
- \+ 7557 vii. Cindy Lou **Skelton** born 22 June 1960.
-   7558 viii. Brian Eugene **Skelton**[947] born 2 October 1964 and died 10 October 1988 at 24 years of age.

6334. **Paul Mark**[12] **Skelton** (Sylvia May[11] **Whipple**, Marcus Erastus[10], Francis Jackson[9], Ithamar[8], Rev. Benjamin[7], Benjamin[6], Francis[5], Jonathan[4], Joseph[3], Matthew[2], Matthew[1])[948] was born 16 October 1926 and married twice. (1) **Mary Louise Whipple** 24 September 1949. No relationship has been found between Mary Louise and Paul Mark. She was born 12 April 1936.[949] (2) **Sylvia (___)**.

Paul Mark **Skelton** and Mary Louise **Whipple** had the following children:
- \+ 7559 i. Kathleen[13] **Skelton** born 8 July 1950.
-   7560 ii. Mark Todd **Skelton**[950] born 13 May 1954.
-   7561 iii. Timothy Paul **Skelton**[951] born 4 December 1955.
-   7562 iv. Kimberly Ann **Skelton**[952] born 10 July 1959 and married Kevin **Day**.
-   7563 v. Peter Matthew **Skelton**[953] born 6 October 1964.

6336. **Margaret Jane**[12] **Whipple** (Dr. Raymond Orson[11], Marcus Erastus[10], Francis Jackson[9], Ithamar[8], Rev. Benjamin[7], Benjamin[6], Francis[5], Jonathan[4], Joseph[3], Matthew[2], Matthew[1])[954] was born 5 November 1919 married twice. (1) James Ross **Wiley** in Lebanon, Penn. 17 June 1941. He was born 27 October 1918 and died 13 December 1965, at 47 years of age.[955] (2) **Harold George Yeagley** in Endwell, N.Y. 27 December 1983. He was born 25 January 1914 and died 17 May 1993 at 79 years of age. [956]

Margaret Jane **Whipple** and James Ross **Wiley** had the following children:
- + 7564 i. Ruth Ann[13] **Wiley** born 16 November 1943.
- + 7565 ii. Mary Elizabeth **Wiley** born 31 January 1946.
- + 7566 iii. Jeannette Louise **Wiley** born 19 September 1951.
- + 7567 iv. Nancy May **Wiley** born 22 January 1956.

6337. **Capt. Caryll Robbins**[12] **Whipple** (Carl Era[11], Marcus Erastus[10], Francis Jackson[9], Ithamar[8], Rev. Benjamin[7], Benjamin[6], Francis[5], Jonathan[4], Joseph[3], Matthew[2], Matthew[1])[957] was born in Altoona, Blair Co., Penn. 12 October 1927 and married **Jean Elizabeth Smith** in Warren, Penn. 14 July 1951. Jean,[958] daughter of William **Smith** and Esther M. **Anderson**, was born in Warren 7 October 1928. She is an accomplished musician, taught music in public schools in and around Washington, D.C., gave private piano lessons, and is a leader in church activities. Caryll was graduated from the U.S. Naval Academy in 1951 and earned a Ph.D. from Rensselaer Institute of Technology. An accomplished musician, he played trumpet in the Altoona Civic Symphony and bugle in the Naval Academy Bugle Corps. He retired from the Navy with the rank of Captain. He is a leader in his Methodist Church.

Capt. Caryll Robbins **Whipple** and Jean Elizabeth **Smith** had the following children:
- + 7568 i. Elizabeth Jean[13] **Whipple** born 12 March 1953.
- + 7569 ii. Laurie Ann **Whipple** born 8 May 1955.
-   7570 iii. Stephen Carl **Whipple**[959] born in Oxnard, Calif. 31 December 1957.
- + 7571 iv. Andrew Warren **Whipple** born 15 August 1963.
- + 7572 v. Daniel Marsh **Whipple** born 1 January 1969.

6338. **Nancy Louise**[12] **Whipple** (Carl Era[11], Marcus Erastus[10], Francis Jackson[9], Ithamar[8], Rev. Benjamin[7], Benjamin[6], Francis[5], Jonathan[4], Joseph[3], Matthew[2], Matthew[1])[960] was born in Altoona, Blair Co., Penn. 5 June 1931 and died in 1999, at 68 years of age. She married **Dr. John Francis Erbland** in Rochester, Monroe Co., N.Y. 2 February 1956. John,[961] son of Walter Joseph **Erbland** and Ada Mary **Hendricks**, was born in Fairport, Monroe Co., N.Y. 6 October 1930. John earned a Ph.D. from the U. of Rochester Strong Memorial Hospital in 1953 and was on the hospital staff until 1967 when he became a Research Scientist for Monsanto in Everett, Mass. In 1972 he moved his family to Evans, Ga. and enrolled in the School of Dentistry at the Medical College of Georgia. While studying for his D.MD. he taught biochemistry. Upon graduation he began a career of teaching and research in the Dental School, retiring 1 July 1996 as an Associate Professor. He was a member of the Lions Club in Massachusetts, Knights of Columbus, Third and Fourth degrees, in Georgia, active in Cub Scouts and Boy Scouts in New York, Massachusetts, and Georgia; Little League Baseball in Massachusetts and Georgia. He is one of two representatives from the Evans area on the Community Service Board for the mentally retarded, mental health, and substance abuse of East Central Georgia and is active in his church and Habitat for Humanity.

Nancy studied the piano and the flute as a youngster and played flute in the Altoona Civic Symphony and in the High School Orchestra and Bands. She attended Penn State before completing nurse's training at Strong Memorial Hospital School of Nursing. Her work experience includes Staff Nurse at Strong Memorial Hospital; Head Nurse and Supervisor at The Genesee Hospital in Rochester, N.Y., Supervisor at Hunt Memorial Hospital in Danvers, Mass. and at University Hospital in Augusta, Ga. She joined the staff of the Department of Veterans Affairs in Augusta and was certified in Psychiatric Nursing. She retired from the Veterans Administration 1 April 1995. She is a member of the American Nurses Assn., Warren Historical Society, Venango County Historical Society, Clarion County Historical Society, and the Crawford County Genealogical Societies, all in Pennsylvania; and the Augusta Genealogical Society of Augusta, Ga.

Nancy Louise **Whipple** and Dr. John Francis **Erbland** had the following children:

+ 7573 i. Joanna Louise[13] **Erbland** born 23 May 1957.
+ 7574 ii. Peter Jay **Erbland** born 26 June 1958.
+ 7575 iii. Mark David **Erbland** born 1 June 1962.
   7576 iv. Timothy John **Erbland**[962] born in Rochester, Monroe Co., N.Y. 9 July 1964.
   7577 v. Christopher Philip **Erbland**[963] born in Beverly, Essex Co., Mass. 8 July 1968.

6340. **Helen Marjorie**[12] **Yantis** (Bessie Belle[11] **Whipple**, Cephus Galusha[10], Samuel Elijah[9], Ithamar[8], Rev. Benjamin[7], Benjamin[6], Francis[5], Jonathan[4], Joseph[3], Matthew[2], Matthew[1])[964] was born in Niobrara, Knox Co. Nebr. 22 June 1891 and married **Emmet Vick**.[965]

Helen Marjorie **Yantis** and Emmet **Vick** had the following child:
    7578   i.   Helen Grey[13] **Vick**.[966]

6343. **Dr. Gordon Henry**[12] **Ira** (Florence Elsie[11] **Whipple**, Cephus Galusha[10], Samuel Elijah[9], Ithamar[8], Rev. Benjamin[7], Benjamin[6], Francis[5], Jonathan[4], Joseph[3], Matthew[2], Matthew[1])[967] was born in Lynch, Nebr. 7 March 1899 and died 31 July 1991 in Jacksonville, Fla., at 92 years of age. He married **Anis Agatha Tompkins** in Brooklyn, N.Y. 15 June 1928. She was born in Sheridan, Maine 2 April 1905.[968] Gordon attended Nebraska Weslyn University, Lincoln, Nebr. (1918-22), Stanford University (1923) and was graduated from the U. of Nebraska Medical School in 1928. He interned at the Long Island College Hospital in 1925 where he completed his Residency in Internal Medicine in 1927and 1928 and began his 60-year-long practice of Internal Medicine and Cardiology in Jacksonville, Fla. in 1928.

He was on the Staff of St. Lukes Hospital (Chief of General Medicine for 15 years), St. Vincent Hospital, Baptist Hospital, Methodist Hospital, and Daniel Memorial Hospital and was active in the Duval County Medical Society and Florida Medical Assn.; a member of the American Medical Assn., Southern Medical Assn., American Heart Assn., Florida, East Coast Medical Assn. and the American Diabetics Assn. He was a Trustee, Board Member, and Sunday School Teacher at the Riverside Park United Methodist Church, and an avid amateur golfer, winning tournaments in the senior division.

Dr. Gordon Henry **Ira** and Anis Agatha **Tompkins** had the following children:
+   7579   i.   Gordon Henry[13] **Ira** Jr. born 18 November 1929.
+   7580   ii.   Stewart Bentley **Ira** born 4 December 1931.
+   7581   iii.   Anis Louise **Ira** born 25 October 1936.

6344. **Naomi Grace**[12] **Ira** (Florence Elsie[11] **Whipple**, Cephus Galusha[10], Samuel Elijah[9], Ithamar[8], Rev. Benjamin[7], Benjamin[6], Francis[5], Jonathan[4], Joseph[3], Matthew[2], Matthew[1])[969] was born in Lynch, Nebr. 19 October 1900 and married **George Ryman Douglas** in Omaha, Nebr. 7 June 1925. He was born in Tepamah, Nebr. 16 January 1897. George,[970] son of George Washington **Douglas** and Feraby Ellen **Ryman**, died 24 April 1944 in Indianapolis, Ind., at 47 years of age. He is buried in Washington Park North Cemetery, Indianapolis. George attended (1918-22) Nebraska Weslyan where he earned a bachelors degree, working at the YMCA to help pay his way. His life's work was in life insurance and at his death at age 47 of a heart attack at home, he was Manager of Mutual Life of N.Y. He and Naomi were leaders of their Methodist College Group and he remained active in Methodist church activities until his death.

Naomi Grace **Ira** and George Ryman **Douglas** had the following children:
+   7582   i.   Mary Lou[13] **Douglas** born 30 April 1927.
+   7583   ii.   Jean Kathryn **Douglas** born 14 June 1930.
+   7584   iii.   Virginia Ellen **Douglas** born 22 September 1932.
+   7585   iv.   George Lynn **Douglas** born 27 November 1934.

6345. **Marshall Lofland**[12] **Whipple** (Charles Clifford[11], Cephus Galusha[10], Samuel Elijah[9], Ithamar[8], Rev. Benjamin[7], Benjamin[6], Francis[5], Jonathan[4], Joseph[3], Matthew[2], Matthew[1])[971] was born in Niobrara, Knox Co., Nebr. 15 July 1909 and married **Jeanne Phyllis Cline** in Tacoma, Pierce Co., Wash. 24 June 1939. Jeanne,[972] daughter of Frank Warren **Cline** and Nellie Irene **Craven**, was born in Topeka, Shawnee Co., Kans. 31 March 1918. Marshall is a retired paper salesman

Marshall L. and Jean Whipple. Photo courtesy of Marshall L. Whipple.

Marshall Lofland **Whipple** and Jeanne Phyllis **Cline** had the following children:
+   7586   i.   Laird Douglas[13] **Whipple** born 28 April 1942.
+   7587   ii.   Martha Sue **Whipple** born 18 August 1944.

6346. **Murray Douglas**[12] **Whipple** (Charles Clifford[11], Cephus Galusha[10], Samuel Elijah[9], Ithamar[8], Rev. Benjamin[7], Benjamin[6], Francis[5], Jonathan[4], Joseph[3], Matthew[2], Matthew[1])[973] was born in Niobrara, Knox Co., Nebr. 16 August 1912 and died 10 April 1969 in Puyallup, Wash., at 56 years of age. He married three times. (1) **Elsie Mae Walesby** 24 November 1934. She was born in Tacoma, Pierce Co., Wash. 10 April 1914.[974] (2) **Helen NaVella Remme** in September 1944. She was born in Ryder, Ward Co., N. Dak. 5 July 1920 and died 24 December 1961 in Tacoma, at 41 years of age.[975] (3) **Wilma Fausnacht**.

Murray Douglas **Whipple** and Elsie Mae **Walesby** had the following child:
+ 7588 i. Clifford Charles[13] **Whipple** born 20 January 1939.

Murray Douglas **Whipple** and Helen NaVella **Remme** had the following children:
    7589 ii. Timothy Douglas **Whipple**[976] born in Puyallup, 21 September 1945.
+ 7590 iii. Dennis Murray **Whipple** born 2 March 1948.
    7591 iv. Laurie Jane **Whipple**[977] born in Puyallup 9 April 1951 and married Frederic LeRoy **Faulkner** November 1980.[978] He was born 10 November 1943.[979]

6347. **Grey Gordon**[12] **Whipple** I (Charles Clifford[11], Cephus Galusha[10], Samuel Elijah[9], Ithamar[8], Rev. Benjamin[7], Benjamin[6], Francis[5], Jonathan[4], Joseph[3], Matthew[2], Matthew[1])[980] was born in Niobrara, Knox Co., Nebr. 18 May 1914 and died 10 June 1979 in Tacoma, Pierce Co., Wash. at 65 years of age.

He married **LoReta Clara Raymond** in Tacoma 27 November 1935. She was born 6 December 1913.[981]

Grey Gordon **Whipple** I and LoReta Clara **Raymond** had the following children:
+ 7592 i. Grey Gordon[13] **Whipple** II born 28 June 1937.
+ 7593 ii. Brandt Raymond **Whipple** born 15 December 1940.

6348. **Sherman Guy**[12] **Whipple** (Charles Clifford[11], Cephus Galusha[10], Samuel Elijah[9], Ithamar[8], Rev. Benjamin[7], Benjamin[6], Francis[5], Jonathan[4], Joseph[3], Matthew[2], Matthew[1])[982] was born in Niobrara, Knox Co., Nebr. 16 November 1919 and married **Annie Laurie Bailey** in San Mateo, San Mateo, Co., Calif. 20 December 1946. She was born 19 March 1923.[983]

Sherman Guy **Whipple** and Annie Laurie **Bailey** had the following children:
+ 7594 i. Chipps Sherman[13] **Whipple** born 28 March 1948.
+ 7595 ii. Russell Guy **Whipple** born 4 July 1949.
+ 7596 iii. Nan Celeste **Whipple** born 4 March 1952.
+ 7597 iv. Charles Ralph **Whipple** born 7 April 1956.

6349. **Lawrence Jerome**[12] **Whipple** (Charles Clifford[11], Cephus Galusha[10], Samuel Elijah[9], Ithamar[8], Rev. Benjamin[7], Benjamin[6], Francis[5], Jonathan[4], Joseph[3], Matthew[2], Matthew[1])[984] was born in Niobrara, Knox Co., Nebr. 19 March 1928 and married **Lucile Maureen McDiarmid** in Honolulu, Hawaii 22 February 1958. She was born in San Francisco, Calif. 18 February 1933.[985]

Lawrence Jerome **Whipple** and Lucile Maureen **McDiarmid** had the following children:
- \+   7598   i.   Scott Lawrence[13] **Whipple** born 17 May 1962.
-      7599   ii.   Thomas Peter **Whipple**[986] born in Honolulu 18 July 1966.

6350. **Helen Henley**[12] **Symons** (Mary Etta[11] **Bills**, George Dudley[10], Daniel F.[9], Elizabeth[8] **Whipple**, Rev. Benjamin[7], Benjamin[6], Francis[5], Jonathan[4], Joseph[3], Matthew[2], Matthew[1])[987] was born in Kansas City, Jackson Co., Mo. 29 June 1906. She married twice. (1) **Charles Ichamer Parrish** in Oak Park Cook Co., Ill. 29 December 1932. (2) **Glen Jones** in Anchorage, Alaska.

Helen Henley **Symons** and Charles Ichamer **Parrish** had the following child:
-      7600   i.   Robert[13] **Parrish**[988] born in River Forest, Ill. and married Bernice (__).

6351. **John Griffith**[12] **Symons** (Mary Etta[11] **Bills**, George Dudley[10], Daniel F.[9], Elizabeth[8] **Whipple**, Rev. Benjamin[7], Benjamin[6], Francis[5], Jonathan[4], Joseph[3], Matthew[2], Matthew[1])[989] was born in Kansas City, Jackson Co., Mo. 16 September 1911 and married twice. (1) **Edith Maude Rice** in Hinsdale, Ill. 16 October 1937. She died 22 March 1987.[990] (2) **Dorothy Grady** in Richland Center, Wisc. 26 June 1988.

John Griffith **Symons** and Edith Maude **Rice** had the following children:
-      7601   i.   John Griffith[13] **Symons** Jr. [991]
-      7602   ii.   Margaret Rice **Symons**.[992]

6352. **Sara Leigh**[12] **Symons** (Mary Etta[11] **Bills**, George Dudley[10], Daniel F.[9], Elizabeth[8] **Whipple**, Rev. Benjamin[7], Benjamin[6], Francis[5], Jonathan[4], Joseph[3], Matthew[2], Matthew[1])[993] was born in Evanston, Ill. 30 October 1917 and married **Robert Charles Brandt** in Oak Park, Cook Co., Ill. 21 June 1941. Robert,[994] son of Alfred Christian **Brandt** and Alice Charlotte **Wolff**, was born in Chicago, Ill. in 1917.

Sara Leigh **Symons** and Robert Charles **Brandt** had the following children:
- \+   7603   i.   Barbara Starr[13] **Brandt** born 1942.
- \+   7604   ii.   Barry Griffith **Brandt** born 16 September 1951.
- \+   7605   iii.   Julia Carol **Brandt** born 14 December 1954.

6353. **Robert Carman**[12] **Bills Jr.** (Robert Carman[11], Charles Brownell[10], Daniel F.[9], Elizabeth[8] **Whipple**, Rev. Benjamin[7], Benjamin[6], Francis[5],

Jonathan[4], Joseph[3], Matthew[2], Matthew[1])[995] birth date unknown, married **Elizabeth Ann Simson**. Liz is the daughter of Albert William **Simson** and Helen Loveland **Patch**.[996]

Robert Carmen **Bills** Jr. and Elizabeth Ann **Simson** had the following child:
  6933 i. John Patch[13] **Bills**.[997]

6354. **Colvin W.**[12] **Stidd** (Hepsey Leoline[11] **Whipple**, Cyrus Hanchett[10], Solomon[9], David[8], Rev. Benjamin[7], Benjamin[6], Francis[5], Jonathan[4], Joseph[3], Matthew[2], Matthew[1])[998] was born 3 March 1895 and died 18 October 1925 at 30 years of age. He married **Madeline Leighton** 30 November 1917.

Colvin W. **Stidd** and Madeline **Leighton** had the following child:
  7606 i. Beverley Leighton[13] **Stidd**.[999]

6355. **Gregory Wright**[12] **Stidd** (Hepsey Leoline[11] **Whipple**, Cyrus Hanchett[10], Solomon[9], David[8], Rev. Benjamin[7], Benjamin[6], Francis[5], Jonathan[4], Joseph[3], Matthew[2], Matthew[1])[1000] was born 26 November 1896 and died 17 February 1948 at 51 years of age. He married **Corrie Allison** in March 1920.

Gregory Wright **Stidd** and Corrie **Allison** had the following child:
  7607 i. Suzanne[13] **Stidd**[1001] born 20 November 1928.

6357. **Lorraine Lee**[12] **Stidd** (Hepsey Leoline[11] **Whipple**, Cyrus Hanchett[10], Solomon[9], David[8], Rev. Benjamin[7], Benjamin[6], Francis[5], Jonathan[4], Joseph[3], Matthew[2], Matthew[1])[1002] was born 31 May 1905 and married twice. (1) **Richard Vierich** 1 January 1920. (2) **Lawrence Foster** 2 December 1935.

Lorraine Lee **Stidd** and Richard **Vierich** had the following children:
  7608 i. Richard Wallace[13] **Vierich**[1003] born 28 September 1926.
  7609 ii. Sally Ann **Vierich**[1004] born 11 June 1928.

6359. **Jean Carlton**[12] **Whipple** (Carlton Gregory[11], Cyrus Hanchett[10], Solomon[9], David[8], Rev. Benjamin[7], Benjamin[6], Francis[5], Jonathan[4], Joseph[3], Matthew[2], Matthew[1])[1005] was born 5 May 1905 and died 17 November 1961 in San Fernando, Calif., at 56 years of age. She married twice. (1) **William Robert Ward** 21 December 1928. He was born 29 August 1906. They were divorced in October 1942.[1006] (2) **Don Fairnie** October 1949.

{ G 1129 }

Jean Carlton **Whipple** and William Robert **Ward** had the following children:

    7610   i.   Robert Carlton[13] **Ward**[1007] born in Chicago, Ill. 13 December 1929.

    7611   ii.   Nancy Lee **Ward**[1008] born in Fon Du Lac, Wisc. 16 October 1934.

6360. **Gregory Booth**[12] **Whipple** (Carlton Gregory[11], Cyrus Hanchett[10], Solomon[9], David[8], Rev. Benjamin[7], Benjamin[6], Francis[5], Jonathan[4], Joseph[3], Matthew[2], Matthew[1])[1009] was born 3 April 1908 and died 9 October 1973 in Los Angeles, Calif., at 65 years of age. He married **Virginia Fouch** in LaGrange, Cook Co., Ill. 6 January 1934. Virginia,[1010] daughter of Squire **Fouch** and Edna Amanda **Wright**, was born in LaGrange 31 October 1908 and died 29 March 1970 in Los Angeles, at 61 years of age.

Gregory Booth **Whipple** and Virginia **Fouch** had the following child:

+   7612   i.   Leslie Claire[13] **Whipple** born 26 December 1935.

6365. **Beatrice Eleanor**[12] **Scott** (Maude Luella[11] **Hoxie**, Lucina Jeanette[10] **Whipple**, Solomon[9], David[8], Rev. Benjamin[7], Benjamin[6], Francis[5], Jonathan[4], Joseph[3], Matthew[2], Matthew[1])[1011] was born 23 July 1906 and married **Arthur Erdman** January 1929.

Beatrice Eleanor **Scott** and Arthur **Erdman** had the following child:

    7613   i.   Louis Scott[13] **Erdman**[1012] born 19 September 1931.

6370. **Frederick Harold**[12] **Stuntz** (Minnie Margie[11] **Goodenow**, Arminda Rose[10] **Deriar**, Fannie[9] **Whipple**, Jonathan[8], Rev. Benjamin[7], Benjamin[6], Francis[5], Jonathan[4], Joseph[3], Matthew[2], Matthew[1])[1013] was born 14 December 1893 and died 15 February 1945, at 51 years of age. Buried in Lundy's Lane, Penn. Hope Cemetery. He married **Jennie Matthews**.

Frederick Harold **Stuntz** and Jennie **Matthews** had the following children:

    7614   i.   George[13] **Stuntz**[1014] born 5 March 1915.

    7615   ii.   Charles **Stuntz**[1015] born 27 January 1917.

6371. **Homer Ezra**[12] **Stuntz** (Minnie Margie[11] **Goodenow**, Arminda Rose[10] **Deriar**, Fannie[9] **Whipple**, Jonathan[8], Rev. Benjamin[7], Benjamin[6], Francis[5], Jonathan[4], Joseph[3], Matthew[2], Matthew[1])[1016] was born 5 August 1895 and died 28 August 1953 at 58 years of age. He married **Emeline Coburn**. She was born 15 September 1897.[1017]

Homer Ezra **Stuntz** and Emeline **Coburn** had the following children:
- 7616 i. Dorothea[13] **Stuntz**[1018] born 12 August 1917.
- 7617 ii. Carl **Stuntz**.[1019]
- 7618 iii. Merl **Stuntz**[1020] born 3 March 1923.

6372. **Gertrude**[12] **Stuntz** (Minnie Margie[11] **Goodenow**, Arminda Rose[10] **Deriar**, Fannie[9] **Whipple**, Jonathan[8], Rev. Benjamin[7], Benjamin[6], Francis[5], Jonathan[4], Joseph[3], Matthew[2], Matthew[1])[1021] was born in Elk Creek Township., Erie Co., Penn. 28 January 1900 and died 28 September 1995 in Fort Wayne, Allen Co., Ind., at 95 years of age. She married **Dr. Irwin Carl Krueger** in Girard, Erie Co. 19 September 1925. He was born in Erie, Erie Co. 14 July 1898 and died 14 March 1972 in Erie, at 73 years of age.[1022]

Gertrude **Stuntz** and Dr. Irwin Carl **Krueger** had the following children:
- + 7619 i. Irwin Carl[13] **Krueger** Jr. born 19 July 1928.
- 7620 ii. Charles Stuntz **Krueger**[1023] born 3 March 1930.

6373. **Paul Edmund**[12] **Stuntz** (Minnie Margie[11] **Goodenow**, Arminda Rose[10] **Deriar**, Fannie[9] **Whipple**, Jonathan[8], Rev. Benjamin[7], Benjamin[6], Francis[5], Jonathan[4], Joseph[3], Matthew[2], Matthew[1]) was born 17 May 1906 and died 4 September 1962, at 56 years of age. Buried in West Springfield, Penn. He married **Ruth Hall**.

Paul Edmund **Stuntz** and Ruth **Hall** had the following children:
- 7621 i. Robert[13] **Stuntz**[1024] born 9 April 1931.
- 7622 ii. Richard **Stuntz**[1025] born 18 October 1940.
- 7623 iii. Frederick **Stuntz**[1026] born 5 October 1942.
- 7624 iv. William **Stuntz**[1027] born 20 November 1948.

6380. **Freda Grant**[12] **Herrick** (Orlan Milo[11], Albert Eugene[10], Berthier H.[9], Melinda[8] **Whipple**, Moses[7], Capt. Thomas[6], Francis[5], Jonathan[4], Joseph[3], Matthew[2], Matthew[1])[1028] was born in Norwich, N. Y. 9 April 1904 and died there 5 June 1975, at 71 years of age. She married twice. (1) **(__) Karlson**. (2) **Arthur Horatio Potter**. Arthur,[1029] son of Walter F. **Potter** and Mabel Ellen **Stearns**, was born in Oxford, N.Y. 23 March 1906 and died 3 May 1982 in Ogdensburg, N.Y., at 76 years of age.

Freda Grant **Herrick** and (__) **Karlson** had the following children:
- 7625 i. Evelyn Marie[13] **Karlson**[1030] born 11 July 1921.
- 7626 ii. Orrest Claude **Karlson**[1031] born 16 December 1922.

{ G 1131 }

Freda Grant **Herrick** and Arthur Horatio **Potter** had the following children:
+ 7627 iii. Janet Yvonne **Potter** born 4 April 1933.
  7628 iv. James Walter **Potter**[1032] born 3 March 1936.
  7629 v. Sheila Ann **Potter**[1033] born in Leonardsville, N.Y. 2 October 1939.
  7630 vi. Burton David **Potter**[1034] born in Binghamton, N.Y. 3 February 1941.

6381. **Errol Bisbee**[12] **Olson** (Hazel Marie[11] **Bisbee**, George Ensign[10], Martha Melissa[9] **Herrick**, Melinda[8] **Whipple**, Moses[7], Capt. Thomas[6], Francis[5], Jonathan[4], Joseph[3], Matthew[2], Matthew[1])[1035] was born in Boone, Iowa 19 August 1918 and died July 1972 in Des Moines, Iowa, at 53 years of age. He married **Kay** (__). Kay was apparently his second wife and he adopted her children William and Michael.

Errol Bisbee **Olson** and Kay (__) had the following children:
  7631 i. Errolynn Marie[13] **Olson**.[1036]
  7632 ii. Jay **Olson**.[1037]

6382. **Joyce Marie**[12] **Olson** (Hazel Marie[11] **Bisbee**, George Ensign[10], Martha Melissa[9] **Herrick**, Melinda[8] **Whipple**, Moses[7], Capt. Thomas[6], Francis[5], Jonathan[4], Joseph[3], Matthew[2], Matthew[1])[1038] was born in Boone, Iowa 17 August 1920 and died 22 June 1953 in Rochester, Minn., at 32 years of age. She married **Joseph Bryant** abt 1939. He is the son of Andrew **Bryant** and Maza **Williams**.[1039] Joyce is buried at Westlawn Cemetery, Lehigh, Iowa.

Joyce Marie **Olson** and Joseph **Bryant** had the following children:
+ 7633 i. William Dee[13] **Bryant** born 25 December 1939.
+ 7634 ii. Jolene Marie **Bryant** born 11 December 1942.

6395. **Glenn Alonzo**[12] **Perkins** (Manson Burdell[11], Marissa Parmelia[10] **Dean**, Martha Putnam[9] **Whipple**, Duick[8], Charles[7], Francis[6], Francis[5], Jonathan[4], Joseph[3], Matthew[2], Matthew[1])[1040] was born in Sweeden Hill, Potter Co., Penn. 22 April 1884 and died 28 December 1946 at 62 years of age. He married **Carrie L. Graves** in Graves Corner, N.Y. 25 December 1904. Carrie, daughter of Roswell **Graves** and Phyrena **Hyde**, was born in Shongo Co., N.Y. 25 December 1888.

Glenn Alonzo **Perkins** and Carrie L. **Graves** had the following children:
+ 7635 i. Lois Irene[13] **Perkins** born 20 June 1911.
+ 7636 ii. Burdell **Perkins** born 31 March 1913.

        7637   iii.   Lena Adelaide **Perkins**[1041] born in Farmersville Station, N.Y. 25 March 1915 and married Chris **Pickering.** Chris was a major league baseball pitcher with the Baltimore Orioles and the New York Yankees.

\+   7638   iv.   Blanche Elizabeth **Perkins** born 11 October 1917.

        7639   v.   Glenn Alonzo **Perkins** Jr.[1042] born in Franklinville, N.Y. 13 December 1917 and died there in 1921, at 3 years of age.

\+   7640   vi.   Guy Andrew **Perkins** born 20 September 1921.

\+   7641   vii.   Marjorie Ruth **Perkins** born 12 February 1927.

6397. **Elsie Cecelia**[12] **Carr** (Edith May[11] **Whipple**, Martin Duick[10], Charles Jay[9], Duick[8], Charles[7], Francis[6], Francis[5], Jonathan[4], Joseph[3], Matthew[2], Matthew[1])[1043] was born in Elizabeth, N.J. 9 March 1906 and died 29 August 1967 in Cherry Hill, N.J. at 61 years of age. She married **Russell Knight** 28 July 1928. He was born in Newark, Licking Co., Ohio 8 September 1904 and died 19 October 1962 in Cherry Hill at 58 years of age.[1044]

Elsie Cecelia **Carr** and Russell **Knight** had the following children:

        7642   i.   Elsie Barbara[13] **Knight**[1045] born in Camden, N.J. 28 August 1929 and married William **Barbiers** 21 November 1953.

        7643   ii.   Joseph Russell **Knight**[1046] born 14 July 1939 and married Barbara **De Sasenic** 22 July 1967.

6398. **Ruth Genevieve**[12] **Carr** (Edith May[11] **Whipple**, Martin Duick[10], Charles Jay[9], Duick[8], Charles[7], Francis[6], Francis[5], Jonathan[4], Joseph[3], Matthew[2], Matthew[1])[1047] was born in Spartansburg, Penn. 4 June 1913 and died 30 April 1957 at 43 years of age. She married **Warren James Smith**. He was born 5 December 1910 and died 10 April 1976, at 65 years of age.[1048]

Ruth Genevieve **Carr** and Warren James **Smith** had the following children:

        7644   i.   Warren John[13] **Smith**[1049] born in Atlantic City, N.J. 17 November 1940 and married Alice **Hayden** 17 December 1960.

        7645   ii.   Richard Norris **Smith**[1050] born 19 June 1950.

6402. **Mildred Grace**[12] **Van Auken** (Barbara Grace[11] **Whipple**, Addison Willard[10], Charles Jay[9], Duick[8], Charles[7], Francis[6], Francis[5], Jonathan[4], Joseph[3], Matthew[2], Matthew[1])[1051] was born in Elmira, N.Y. 27 December 1912 and married **Frederick G. Fernquist** 16 April 1933. He was born 12 May 1911.[1052]

Mildred Grace **Van Auken** and Frederick G. **Fernquist** had the following children:

    7646   i.   James Frederick[13] **Fernquist**[1053] born in Elmira, N.Y. 13 June 1934 and married Sharon Elaine **Hewit** 19 July 1958.

    7647   ii.   Nancy Elaine **Fernquist**[1054] born 5 April 1936 and married Barry R. **Ward** 5 November 1955.

    7648   iii.   Richard Gene **Fernquist**[1055] born 28 August 1937 and married Carolyn **Lupton** 5 September 1959.

    7649   iv.   William Eric **Fernquist**[1056] born 24 August 1945 and married Patricia **Jones** 16 July 1966. She was born 25 December 1943.[1057]

6405. Malcolm Montieth[12] **Whipple Jr.** (Malcolm Monteith[11], Warner F.[10], Frank H.[9], Warner Wright[8], Levi[7], Francis[6], Francis[5], Jonathan[4], Joseph[3], Matthew[2], Matthew[1])[1058] was born in Bloomington, Ill. 9 July 1950 and married **Mary Dittmar** in LaSalle, Ill. 21 September 1974. Mary,[1059] daughter of Richard **Dittmar** and Irene **Zurinski**, was born in LaSalle 14 December 1951. Mary was graduated from Southern Illinois University at Carbondale and was employed as a writer for newspapers and radio stations and managed State Senator's Welsches' office for many years. Malcolm was graduated from the U. of Illinois' College of Communications in 1972 and was a sports broadcaster for several local radio stations for several years. He now farms all of the original Whipple farms in the Utica area. Because of changes in technology, he is able to farm the same land it took 10 men to farm 60 years ago.

Malcolm Montieth **Whipple** Jr. and Mary **Dittmar** had the following children:

    7650   i.   Christina Lynn[13] **Whipple**[1060] born in LaSalle 20 July 1975. She was graduated from Lake Forest College, Lake Forest, Ill. in 1997.

    7651   ii.   Ginny **Whipple**[1061] born in Peru, Ill. 2 September 1979. She was graduated from Loyola University in Chicago in 2002.

6406. William Warner[12] **Whipple** (Malcolm Monteith[11], Warner F.[10], Frank H.[9], Warner Wright[8], Levi[7], Francis[6], Francis[5], Jonathan[4], Joseph[3], Matthew[2], Matthew[1])[1062] was born in LaSalle, Ill. 15 January 1953 and married **Anne Kelly** in Addison, Ill. 26 May 1978. Anne,[1063] daughter of Jack **Kelly** and La Dean **Hansen**, was born in Addison 26 July 1954. Anne was graduated from the U. of Illinois in 1976 with a degree in Communications. William was graduated from the U. of Illinois in 1975 with a degree in Agricultural Economics. He earned an MBA at the U. of Hartford, Hartford, Conn., in 1982 and is a Senior Vice President, Agribusiness Group, and Executive Vice President of Harris Trust and Savings Bank, Chicago (1999).

William Warner **Whipple** and Anne **Kelly** had the following children:
- 7652 i. Robert William[13] **Whipple**[1064] born in Hartford, Conn. 24 March 1980. He was graduated from Pomona College in California in 2002 and began a banking career in San Francisco following graduation.
- 7653 ii. Kelly Anne **Whipple**[1065] born in Hartford, Conn. 24 May 1982.

6408. Gregory Baker[12] **Whipple** (Malcolm Monteith[11], Warner F.[10], Frank H.[9], Warner Wright[8], Levi[7], Francis[6], Francis[5], Jonathan[4], Joseph[3], Matthew[2], Matthew[1])[1066] was born in LaSalle, Ill. 11 August 1959 and married **Maria Jolanta Petelski** in Chicago, Ill. 11 October 1998. Yola,[1067] daughter of Eugene **Petelski**, was born in Poland. She is a practicing Architect and Engineer. Gregory earned a degree in Agricultural Economics from the U. of Illinois in 1981 and a MBA from the U. of Chicago in 1996. He has been President of the Irving Bank in Chicago since 1996. He and his wife Yola are developing row houses on Chicago's near west side into condominiums (1999).

Gregory Baker **Whipple** and Maria Jolanta **Petelski** had the following children born in Chicago:
- 7654 i. Ian Lucas[13] **Whipple** 4 May 2000.[1068]
- ii. Ashley Alexandra **Whipple** 14 February 2004.

6409. Beth Ann[12] **Whipple** (Malcolm Monteith[11], Warner F.[10], Frank H.[9], Warner Wright[8], Levi[7], Francis[6], Francis[5], Jonathan[4], Joseph[3], Matthew[2], Matthew[1])[1069] was born in LaSalle, Ill. 20 November 1961 and married **Michael Hahne** in Utica, Ill. 2 June 1990. Michael,[1070] son of William **Hahne** and Mary (__), was born in LaSalle 23 April 1964. Michael earned a degree in Physics from Northern Illinois University in 1990 and is a Physicist at the Argone National Laboratory at Lemont, Ill (1990). Beth was awarded a degree by Northern Illinois University at DeKalb in 1988 where she studied Business Systems and Analysis. She is a Human Resources Manager for Carus Chemical Corporation in Peru, Ill. (1999).

Beth Ann **Whipple** and Michael **Hahne** had the following children:
- 7655 i. Christopher Michael[13] **Hahne**[1071] born in Peru 16 April 1991.
- 7656 ii. Paige Ann **Hahne**[1072] born in Spring Valley, Ill. 19 July 1994.

6410. **Warner Michael**[12] **Whipple** (Warner William[11], Warner Ernest[10], Eugene Warner[9], Warner Wright[8], Levi[7], Francis[6], Francis[5], Jonathan[4], Joseph[3], Matthew[2], Matthew[1])[1073] was born in Duluth, Minn. 20 May 1945 and married **Elizabeth Harriette Palmer** 7 November 1966.

Warner Michael **Whipple** and Elizabeth Harriette **Palmer** had the following children:

    7657 i. Warner Richard[13] **Whipple**[1074] born 19 March 1969.
    7658 ii. Theodore Stuart **Whipple**[1075] born 6 April 1971.
    7659 iii. Caroline Phoebe **Whipple**[1076] born in 1974.
    7660 iv. Michelle **Whipple**.[1077]

6411. **Ruth Ann**[12] **Doyle** (Charlotte Louise[11] **Hopkins**, Laura Edna[10] **Whipple**, Eugene Warner[9], Warner Wright[8], Levi[7], Francis[6], Francis[5], Jonathan[4], Joseph[3], Matthew[2], Matthew[1])[1078] was born in Chicago, Cook Co., Ill. 10 May 1933 and married **James Lindell Gallop** there 19 August 1961. James,[1079] son of Charles **Gallop** and Maggie **Hartman**, was born in Mexico, Mo. 4 October 1932.

Ruth Ann **Doyle** and James Lindell **Gallop** had the following children:

+   7661 i. John Howard[13] **Gallop** born 14 May 1962.
+   7662 ii. Stuart James **Gallop** born 19 October 1963.
+   7663 iii. Thomas Luke **Gallop** born 7 July 1965.
+   7664 iv. David Andrew **Gallop** born 28 May 1969.

6412. **Thomas Luke**[12] **Doyle** (Charlotte Louise[11] **Hopkins**, Laura Edna[10] **Whipple**, Eugene Warner[9], Warner Wright[8], Levi[7], Francis[6], Francis[5], Jonathan[4], Joseph[3], Matthew[2], Matthew[1])[1080] was born in Chicago, Cook Co., Ill. 16 September 1936 and married **Claudette Wilt** there 14 February 1959. Claudette,[1081] daughter of Russell Hern **Wilt** and Doris **Tague**, was born in Chicago 16 December 1937.

Thomas Luke **Doyle** and Claudette **Wilt** had the following children:

    7665 i. Mark Thomas[13] **Doyle**[1082] born in Oak Park, Cook Co., Ill. 27 April 1964.
+   7666 ii. Douglas Lee **Doyle** born 14 December 1965.
    7667 iii. Nora Lynn **Doyle**[1083] born in Chicago Heights, Ill. 18 October 1974.

6413. **Robert**[12] **Jones** (Floyd Clendenen[11], Edith[10] **Clendenen**, Josephine[9] **Whipple**, Warner Wright[8], Levi[7], Francis[6], Francis[5], Jonathan[4], Joseph[3], Matthew[2], Matthew[1])[1084] was born in Los Angeles,

Co., Calif. and died there in 1957, at 29 years of age. He married **Mona (__)** in Los Angeles, Co.

Robert **Jones** and Mona (__) had the following child:
 7668 i. Ronald[13] **Jones**[1085] born in Los Angeles, Co. and married Nancy (__) in Los Angeles, Co.

6414. **Barbara**[12] **Bing** (Mary Allen[11] **Whipple**, Dr. Allen Oldfather[10], Rev. William Levi[9], Francis Rice[8], Levi[7], Francis[6], Francis[5], Jonathan[4], Joseph[3], Matthew[2], Matthew[1])[1086] birth date unknown, married **Rodney Arthur Storm** 25 December 1952.

Barbara **Bing** and Rodney Arthur **Storm** had the following child:
 7669 i. Jessica Tracy Marie[13] **Storm**[1087] born 1 September 1985.

6415. **John Whipple Ernst**[12] **Bing** (Mary Allen[11] **Whipple**, Dr. Allen Oldfather[10], Rev. William Levi[9], Francis Rice[8], Levi[7], Francis[6], Francis[5], Jonathan[4], Joseph[3], Matthew[2], Matthew[1])[1088] was born in New York, N.Y. 28 October 1939 and married twice. (1) **Janet Mueller** in Kabul, Afghanistan in 1965. They were divorced in 21 June 1984. (2) **Catherine Mercer** in Princeton, N.J. 23 May 1994.

John Whipple Ernst **Bing** and Janet **Mueller** had the following child:
 7670 i. Eric Whipple[13] **Bing**[1089] born in Estes Park, Colo. 22 October 1968.

6416. **Julianne Whipple**[12] **Bing** (Mary Allen[11] **Whipple**, Dr. Allen Oldfather[10], Rev. William Levi[9], Francis Rice[8], Levi[7], Francis[6], Francis[5], Jonathan[4], Joseph[3], Matthew[2], Matthew[1])[1090] was born in Baltimore, Md. 14 December 1943 and married **Geoffrey Dale Tasker**.

Julianne Whipple **Bing** and Geoffrey Dale **Tasker** had the following child:
 + 7671 i. Wendy Elizabeth[13] **Tasker** born 10 June 1965.

6418. **Foster Neales**[12] **Whipple** (Allen Oldfather[11], Dr. Allen Oldfather[10], Rev. William Levi[9], Francis Rice[8], Levi[7], Francis[6], Francis[5], Jonathan[4], Joseph[3], Matthew[2], Matthew[1])[1091] was born in Washington, D. C. 26 October 1944 and died of cancer in August 1978 at 33 years of age. She married twice. (1) **Richard E. Hess** in Knoxville, Tenn. 12 August 1967. Richard, son of Audrey Evans **Hess** and Betty **Roberts**, was born 25 November 1937.[1092] (2) **James Lee Snodgrass** 1973 or 1974.

James,[1093] son of James Robert **Snodgrass** and Charleen Ann **Smith**, was born in Shawnee, Okla. 7 February 1947.

Foster Neales **Whipple** and Richard E. **Hess** had the following child born in Knoxville:

    7672 i. Richard Allen[13] **Hess**[1094] 5 December 1969 and married Cindy Valrie **Prince** in George Town, Exuma Bahamas 27 May 1995.[1095] Cindy,[1096] daughter of Mikel **Prince** and Betty Jo (__), was born in Medina, Ohio 26 April 1969.

6437. **Bernard George**[12] **Holland** (Robert Edwin[11], Joseph Lester[10], Mary Henrietta[9] **Green**, Edwards Whipple[8], Stephen Whipple[7], Luci[6] **Whipple**, Edwards[5], Jonathan[4], Joseph[3], Matthew[2], Matthew[1])[1097] was born in Worcester, Worcester Co., Mass. 29 July 1948 and married **Mary Alice Westman** in Brunswick, Glynn Co., Ga. 23 August 1971. Mary,[1098] daughter of Harold Orrin **Westman** Sr. and Elizabeth **Ward**, was born in Juneau, Alaska 14 August 1950. Bernie was jointly adopted at an early age by his uncles Orace and Leslie Holland and raised by them and their wives. He entered the field of law enforcement after his discharge from military service. After retiring from law enforcement, he went to Alaska to work on the pipeline project. He is a Buddhist.

Bernard George **Holland** and Mary Alice **Westman** had the following children:

    7673 i. Joseph Edwin[13] **Holland**[1099] born in Juneau, Alaska 19 June 1973.
    7674 ii. Jason Allen **Holland**[1100] born in Juneau, Alaska 28 January 1978.
    7675 iii. Sang-Jin Choi **Holland**[1101] born in Seoul, Korea 12 September 1983. Adopted.

6438. **Edward Nichols**[12] **Powers** (Luva Marion[11] **Nichols**, Bertrand Fayette[10], Catherine[9] **Whipple**, Joel[8], Edmund Rice[7], Jonathan[6], Edwards[5], Jonathan[4], Joseph[3], Matthew[2], Matthew[1])[1102] was born in Springfield, Mass. 5 June 1923 and died 30 July 1976 in Palmer, Hampden Co., Mass., at 53 years of age. He married **Irene Booker** in Springfield 17 September 1946. Edward is buried in the Hillcrest Cemetery, Springfield.

Edward Nichols **Powers** and Irene **Booker** had the following children:

+   7676 i. Edward Michael[13] **Powers** born 22 June 1945.
+   7677 ii. June Marie **Powers** born 24 June 1946.

6439. **Shirley Luva**[12] **Powers** (Luva Marion[11] **Nichols**, Bertrand Fayette[10], Catherine[9] **Whipple**, Joel[8], Edmund Rice[7], Jonathan[6], Edwards[5], Jonathan[4], Joseph[3], Matthew[2], Matthew[1])[1103] was born in Springfield, Mass. 21 February 1925 and married **Richard Harvey Tucker** there 12 February 1949.

Shirley Luva **Powers** and Richard Harvey **Tucker** had the following children born in Springfield:

       7678   i.   Nancy Luva[13] **Tucker**[1104] 28 December 1950 and died there 11 May 1978, at 27 years of age. She married **Kevin Parker**.
+   7679   ii.   Patricia Ann **Tucker** 20 November 1953.
+   7680   iii.   Jacqueline Lee **Tucker** 22 August 1955.
+   7681   iv.   Susan **Tucker** 11 April 1958.
       7682   v.   Richard Charles **Tucker**[1105] 18 January 1961 and married Elizabeth Ann **Lozier** in Gloucester, Essex Co., Mass. 4 November 1995.

6440. **William Roy**[12] **Powers** (Luva Marion[11] **Nichols**, Bertrand Fayette[10], Catherine[9] **Whipple**, Joel[8], Edmund Rice[7], Jonathan[6], Edwards[5], Jonathan[4], Joseph[3], Matthew[2], Matthew[1])[1106] was born in Springfield, Mass. 19 February 1926 and married three times. (1) **Marion Keith** in Bangor, Maine, 27 December 1948. (2) **Hope Lincoln**. (3) **Paula (__)**. William and Paula were divorced in Charlotte, N.C. 6 October 1994.

William Roy **Powers** and Marion **Keith** had the following children:

+   7683   i.   Margaret[13] **Powers**.
+   7684   ii.   Frances **Powers** born 8 December 1949.
+   7685   iii.   Michael **Powers** born 15 November 1951.
+   7686   iv.   William Keith **Powers** born 13 October 1956.

6441. **Roy Clifford**[12] **Powers** (Luva Marion[11] **Nichols**, Bertrand Fayette[10], Catherine[9] **Whipple**, Joel[8], Edmund Rice[7], Jonathan[6], Edwards[5], Jonathan[4], Joseph[3], Matthew[2], Matthew[1])[1107] was born in Springfield, Mass. 29 September 1928 and married **Marilyn J. Wilhelmi** there 11 November 1947. Marilyn,[1108] daughter of Erwin F. **Wilhelmi** and Anna Selma **Hoessler**, was born in Holyoke, Mass. 27 March 1930.

Roy Clifford **Powers** and Marilyn J. **Wilhelmi** had the following children:

+   7687   i.   Kurt Roy[13] **Powers** born 29 December 1950.
+   7688   ii.   Mark Rodney **Powers** born 9 February 1955.

6442. **Robert Alfred**[12] **Powers** (Luva Marion[11] **Nichols**, Bertrand Fayette[10], Catherine[9] **Whipple**, Joel[8], Edmund Rice[7], Jonathan[6], Edwards[5], Jonathan[4], Joseph[3], Matthew[2], Matthew[1])[1109] was born in Springfield, Mass. 9 March 1932 and married **Barbara Luise Vestor** there 30 June 1956.

Robert Alfred **Powers** and Barbara Luise **Vestor** had the following children:
+ 7689 i. Brenda Luise[13] **Powers** born 14 October 1959.
+ 7690 ii. Rhoda Lee **Powers** born 27 December 1961.
+ 7691 iii. Robert Lewis **Powers** born 27 December 1961.

6445. **Jeremy Alfred**[12] **Whipple** (John Stevens[11], Herbert Foster[10], Simeon Foster[9], Simeon R.[8], Joel Green[7], Jonathan[6], Edwards[5], Jonathan[4], Joseph[3], Matthew[2], Matthew[1])[1110] was born in Marblehead, Essex Co., Mass. 13 August 1950 and married **Mamiko Iwasaki** in Tokyo, Japan 5 April 1978. Mamiko,[1111] daughter of Tsunejiro **Iwasaki** and Mitsuko **Suzuki**, was born in Tokyo 5 April 1951. She earned a Mus.M. degree from the New England Conservatory, Boston, in 1976 and is a professional organist. Jeremy earned an A.B. at Harvard in 1973. He is a Senior Editor of *Japan Echo* and related publications and a free-lance Japanese-to-English translator in Tokyo.

Jeremy Alfred **Whipple** and Mamiko **Iwasaki** had the following child:
7692 i. Steven Shinji[13] **Whipple**[1112] born in Tokyo 3 November 1981.

6448. **Elizabeth Faith**[12] **Whipple** (Emery Stevens[11], Herbert Foster[10], Simeon Foster[9], Simeon R.[8], Joel Green[7], Jonathan[6], Edwards[5], Jonathan[4], Joseph[3], Matthew[2], Matthew[1])[1113] was born in Honolulu, Hawaii 25 October 1959 and married twice. (1) **Glen K. Mussetter** in Idledale, Colo. 21 May 1977. They were divorced in Golden, Colo. 18 June 1980. (2) **Epimenio Albert Solano** in Avondale, Colo. 3 September 1983. Eppi,[1114] son of Luis B. **Solano** and Sinforosa **Sedillos**, was born in Las Vegas, N. Mex. 24 March 1950. He retired from the U.S. Air Force 1 Aug. 1991 and began a second career with the U.S. Postal Service at Pueblo, Colo. 7 Aug. 1993.

Elizabeth Faith **Whipple** and Epimenio Albert **Solano** had the following children:
7693 i. Elizabeth Ellen Gabrielle[13] **Solano**[1115] born in Honolulu 12 June 1986. Adopted.
7694 ii. Benjamin Michael Kalani **Solano**[1116] born in Honolulu 30 July 1986. Adopted.

7695 iii. Martin Alexander Pukahea **Solano**[1117] born in Honolulu 15 April 1991. Adopted 1 March 1993. He and Benjamin were born to the same mother.

6456. **Virginia Idelle**[12] **Kurapka** (Marian Idelle[11] **Beam**, Virginia Idelle[10] **Whipple**, Allen Lavier[9], Chandler[8], Samuel[7], John[6], Edwards[5], Jonathan[4], Joseph[3], Matthew[2], Matthew[1])[1118] was born in Baltimore, Md. 30 December 1959 and married **Brian Dennis Alan Keener** in McDonogh Md. 19 September 1992. Brian,[1119] son of Miles Herbert Lloyd **Keener** and Margaret Louise **Seifert**, was born in Miami, Dade Co., Fla. 19 July 1960 and died in August 1997, at 37 years of age. A graduate of Liverpool University, Brian was a teacher before his death. Virginia earned a B. A. from Washington College, Chestertown, Md. in 1982 and is a Foreign Service Officer with the U.S. Department of State.

Brian Dennis Alan **Keener** and Virginia Idelle **Kurapka** had the following children:
7696 i. Miles Christopher David[13] **Keener**[1120] born in Baltimore, Md. 28 May 1994.
7697 ii. Peter Alexander George **Keener**[1121] born in London, England 3 January 1997.

6462. **Elizabeth Dee**[12] **Whipple** (John Leonard[11], Leonard Langford[10], Samuel Dexter[9], Allen Benedict Chaffee[8], Samuel[7], John[6], Edwards[5], Jonathan[4], Joseph[3], Matthew[2], Matthew[1])[1122] was born in Moraga, Calif. 10 August 1970 and married **Mark Robert Moore** in Carefree, Ariz. 10 October 1998. He was born in Sydney, NSW, Australia 10 July 1970.[1123] Mark was the adopted child of Kenneth George Moore and Elaine Margret Goddard. Both parents were born in Sydney.

Elizabeth Dee **Whipple** and Mark Robert **Moore** had the following child:
7698 i. Rebecca Jane[13] **Moore**[1124] born in Gosford, NSW Australia 28 January 2000.

6472. **Leon Delbert**[12] **Sadler** (Lillian Alice[11] **Bess**, Lillian Belle[10] **Whipple**, Charles H.[9], Solomon[8], Russell[7], Solomon[6], Joseph[5], John[4], Joseph[3], Matthew[2], Matthew[1])[1125] was born in Angelica, N.Y. 10 November 1913 and died 29 May 1965 in Houston, Tex., at 51 years of age. He married **Grace Wilma Allen** in Genesse, Penn. 26 March 1938. She is the daughter of Edward **Allen** and Rosa **McCaslin**.[1126]

Leon Delbert **Sadler** and Grace Wilma **Allen** had the following children:
+ 7699 i. Leon Earl[13] **Sadler** born 8 August 1939.
+ 7700 ii. John Lee **Sadler** born 24 January 1954.

6473. **Lloyd Allen**[12] **Sadler** (Lillian Alice[11] **Bess**, Lillian Belle[10] **Whipple**, Charles H.[9], Solomon[8], Russell[7], Solomon[6], Joseph[5], John[4], Joseph[3], Matthew[2], Matthew[1])[1127] was born in New York State 5 April 1916 and married three times. (1) **Ernestine Washburn** in Wellsville, Allegany Co., N.Y. 14 March 1934. (2) **Doris Reynolds** in Hornell, N. Y. 15 March 1950. (3) **Ollie Mozell Nix** in 1975.[1128] She married (1) **Fredrick Henry Sadler** 11 October 1955. (See No. 6474.)

Lloyd Allen **Sadler** and Ernestine **Washburn** had the following children:
+ 7701 i. Shirley May[13] **Sadler** born 13 December 1936.
+ 7702 ii. Beverly Jean **Sadler** born 7 November 1937.
+ 7703 iii. Connie Ann **Sadler** born 30 September 1939.
+ 7704 iv. Judy Kay **Sadler** born 8 February 1941.

Lloyd Allen **Sadler** and Doris **Reynolds** had the following children:
  7705 v. Susan Marjorie **Sadler**[1129] born in Wellsville 29 April 1948 and married Lee **Peterman.** Adopted in 1955.
  7706 vi. Edward Curtis **Sadler**[1130] born in Wellsville 11 January 1950 and married Paula **Perry** abt 1970. Adopted in 1955.
+ 7707 vii. Lloyd Davis **Sadler** born 3 June 1955.
+ 7708 viii. Krista Lynn **Sadler** born 3 December 1956.

Lloyd Allen **Sadler** and Ollie Mozell **Nix** had the following child:
  7709 ix. Kerry Reagan **Sadler**[1131] born 1 October 1971. Adopted.

6474. **Fredrick Henry**[12] **Sadler** (Lillian Alice[11] **Bess**, Lillian Belle[10] **Whipple**, Charles H.[9], Solomon[8], Russell[7], Solomon[6], Joseph[5], John[4], Joseph[3], Matthew[2], Matthew[1])[1132] was born 26 April 1918 and died 23 December 1968 in Houston, Tex., at 50 years of age. He married **Ollie Mozell Nix** 11 October 1955.[1133] She married (2) **Lloyd Allen Sadler** 1975. (See No. 6473.)

Fredrick Henry **Sadler** and Ollie Mozell **Nix** had the following children:
+ 7710 i. Michael Glenn[13] **Sadler** born 2 December 1954.
+ 7711 ii. Frederick Lee **Sadler** born 19 February 1955.
+ 7712 iii. Deborah Gail **Sadler** born 4 February 1957.
  7713 iv. Cynthia Sue **Sadler**[1134] born 18 September 1958.
+ 7714 v. Sandra Lisa **Sadler** born 15 September 1961.

+ 7715 vi. Robert Dale **Sadler** born 14 June 1964.
  7716 vii. Richard John **Sadler**[1135] born 7 April 1966.

6475. **Everett Robert**[12] **Sadler** (Lillian Alice[11] **Bess**, Lillian Belle[10] **Whipple**, Charles H.[9], Solomon[8], Russell[7], Solomon[6], Joseph[5], John[4], Joseph[3], Matthew[2], Matthew[1])[1136] was born in Allen, N. Y. 23 November 1920 and married **Madeline Marie Restivo** 3 November 1945.

Everett Robert **Sadler** and Madeline Marie **Restivo** had the following children:
+ 7717 i. Barbara Ann[13] **Sadler** born 12 January 1948.
  7718 ii. Karen Lee **Sadler**[1137] born in St. Louis, Independence Co. Mo. 23 September 1949 and married David Brady **Cunningham** in Indianapolis, Ind. 2 May 1970.
  7719 iii. Mark Robert **Sadler**[1138] born in Indianapolis 24 October 1954 and died there 19 February 1991 at 36 years of age.
+ 7720 iv. Marsha Jean **Sadler** born 24 October 1954.
+ 7721 v. Craig Allen **Sadler** born 7 April 1959.
+ 7722 vi. Marilyn Kay **Sadler** born 15 March 1961.

6477. **Lillian Bessie**[12] **Sadler** (Lillian Alice[11] **Bess**, Lillian Belle[10] **Whipple**, Charles H.[9], Solomon[8], Russell[7], Solomon[6], Joseph[5], John[4], Joseph[3], Matthew[2], Matthew[1])[1139] was born 10 April 1925 and died 22 October 1998 in Longview, Tex. at 73 years of age. She married **John Lee Nix** 27 May 1951.[1140]

Lillian Bessie **Sadler** and John Lee **Nix** had the following children:
+ 7723 i. John Lee[13] **Nix** born 9 January 1953.
+ 7724 ii. Michael Lynn **Nix** born 29 November 1956.
+ 7725 iii. Randy Jay **Nix** born 27 June 1959.

6478. **Gladys Gertrude**[12] **Sadler** (Lillian Alice[11] **Bess**, Lillian Belle[10] **Whipple**, Charles H.[9], Solomon[8], Russell[7], Solomon[6], Joseph[5], John[4], Joseph[3], Matthew[2], Matthew[1])[1141] was born 15 August 1931 and married twice. (1) **Herbert Howard McIntyre** in Scio, N.Y. 11 October 1947. He is the son of Merle **McIntyre** and Nila **Clodges**.[1142] (2) **Oliver Andrew Pittfield** in Houston, Tex. 6 January 1954.

Gladys Gertrude **Sadler** and Herbert Howard **McIntyre** had the following children:
+ 7726 i. James Herbert[13] **McIntyre** born 11 January 1948.
+ 7727 ii. Gary Dwayne **McIntyre** born 26 January 1949.
+ 7728 iii. John Lee **McIntyre** born 17 February 1950.

+	7729	iv.	Carol Ann **McIntyre** born 13 April 1951.
	7730	v.	Gloria Jean **McIntyre**[1143] born 31 March 1952 and died 13 October 1968 in Houston, at 16 years of age.

6479. **Kenneth Paul**[12] **Sadler** (Lillian Alice[11] **Bess**, Lillian Belle[10] **Whipple**, Charles H.[9], Solomon[8], Russell[7], Solomon[6], Joseph[5], John[4], Joseph[3], Matthew[2], Matthew[1])[1144] was born in Wellsville, Allegany Co., N.Y. 7 August 1933 and died 13 February 1996 in Kilgore, Tex. at 62 years of age. He married **Thelma Gretchen Davenport** in Scio, N.Y. 3 July 1955. She[1145] was the daughter of Volney **Davenport** and Thelma **Stryker**.

Kenneth Paul **Sadler** and Thelma Gretchen **Davenport** had the following children:

+	7731	i.	Kenneth Paul[13] **Sadler** Jr. born 23 July 1956.
+	7732	ii.	Gretchen Elizabeth **Sadler** born 17 May 1958.
+	7733	iii.	Daniel Enos **Sadler** born 12 June 1959.
+	7734	iv.	Donald Leeman **Sadler** born 14 July 1960.
+	7735	v.	Rebecca Mae **Sadler** born 23 March 1962.
+	7736	vi.	Katherine Sue **Sadler** born 2 August 1963.

6481. **Eugene Richard**[12] **Sadler** (Lillian Alice[11] **Bess**, Lillian Belle[10] **Whipple**, Charles H.[9], Solomon[8], Russell[7], Solomon[6], Joseph[5], John[4], Joseph[3], Matthew[2], Matthew[1])[1146] was born 26 April 1938 and married **Ada Jane Dixon** in Wellsville, Allegany Co., N.Y. 4 July 1958. She is the daughter of Clyde **Dixon** and Mary (__).[1147]

Eugene Richard **Sadler** and Ada Jane **Dixon** had the following children:

+	7737	i.	Mary Jane[13] **Sadler** born 30 April 1960.
+	7738	ii.	Dianna Lynn **Sadler** born 25 August 1961.
	7739	iii.	Michael Eugene **Sadler**[1148] born 11 October 1963.
+	7740	iv.	Richard Lee **Sadler** born 8 December 1970.
	7741	v.	Sally Ann **Sadler**[1149] born 19 January 1974 and married Richard Wayne **Manuel** 8 April 1995.
	7742	vi.	Matthew Wayne **Sadler**[1150] born 16 October 1976.

6494. **Ray**[12] **Redington** (Mary Elizabeth[11] **Smith**, Ruby Sophronia[10] **Whipple**, William[9], Ira Martin[8], Elijah[7], Jeremiah[6], Joseph[5], John[4], Joseph[3], Matthew[2], Matthew[1])[1151] birth date unknown, and married twice. (1) **Violet Elizabeth Hoffman**. She married (2) **Joe Redington**. (2) **Doris (__)**.

Ray **Redington** and Violet Elizabeth **Hoffman** had the following children:
+ 7743 i. Tim[13] **Redington**.
+ 7744 ii. Tom **Redington**.

Ray **Redington** and Doris **(__)** had the following children:
+ 7745 iii. Wayne **Redington**.
+ 7746 iv. Linda **Redington**.

6495. **Joe**[12] **Redington** (Mary Elizabeth[11] **Smith**, Ruby Sophronia[10] **Whipple**, William[9], Ira Martin[8], Elijah[7], Jeremiah[6], Joseph[5], John[4], Joseph[3], Matthew[2], Matthew[1])[1152] was born in Oklahoma 1 February 1917 and died 24 June 1999 in Alaska, at 82 years of age. He married twice. (1) **Kathy Broadhead**. (2) **Violet Elizabeth Hoffman**. Violet married (1) **Ray Redington**. Vi provided the following details about Joe. Beginning with his youth he rode the rails as a migrant worker during the Depression and the Dust Bowl era. During WWII he was in the Army and served in Okinawa. He went to Alaska in 1948, purchasing his first dog sled as he crossed the border into Alaska where he worked for the U.S. Air Force salvaging downed airplanes by dog team and did commercial fishing. He survived dynamite explosions, crashed airplanes, foxes, and a myriad of other escapades. His most memorable accomplishment was the Iditarod Trail Sled Dog Race from Anchorage to Nome. He organized the first one in 1973 earning the title "Father of the Iditarod." He distinguished himself time after time finishing in the top five as late as 1988 at age 71. He was instrumental in the growth of long distance dog mushing from Europe to South Africa.

In celebration of the 1976 bicentennial, he organized the largest dog team ever assembled which pulled a tour bus filled with passengers up Knik Road. Joe took it as a personal challenge when people said mushing a dog team up Mt. McKinley couldn't be done. His team reached the summit. He was 62 at the time. He guided the first group of "Iditarod Challengers," dog mushing tourists from Knik to Nome in 1993. He organized "The Commemorative Serum Relay Race" to Nome in 1995 which began a successful immunization program for village children. His philosophy of life was "Anything the mind can conceive and believe, the mind can achieve." Violet Redington can be reached at huskydog@alaska.net.

Joe **Redington** and Kathy **Broadhead** had the following children:
+ 7747 i. Shiela[13] **Redington**.
+ 7748 ii. Joe **Redington** Jr.
+ 7749 iii. Raymie **Redington**.

{ G 1145 }

Joe **Redington** and Violet Elizabeth **Hoffman** had the following child:
    7750   iv.   Keith **Redington**.[1153]

    6497. **Richard H.**[12] **Sproat** Sr. (Mary Elizabeth[11] **Smith**, Ruby Sophronia[10] **Whipple**, William[9], Ira Martin[8], Elijah[7], Jeremiah[6], Joseph[5], John[4], Joseph[3], Matthew[2], Matthew[1])[1154] was born in Oklahoma Territory 12 June 1904 and died 29 January 2000 in Arkansas City, Cowley Co., Kans., at 95 years of age. Private burial in Parker Cemetery, Arkansas City. He married twice. (1) **Gertrude Esther Metzinger**. (2) **Lucille Blacksmith** in St. Joseph, Mo., 1945. Richard farmed in the Derby, Kans. area and worked for several construction companies. The family moved to Arkansas City in 1981. After his wife died in 1985, he returned to Wichita, Kans. but moved back to Arkansas City in 1997. He was a member of the Missionary Baptist Church. At the time of death his sons Raymond lived at Lawton, Okla., Richard, Jr., Marvin, Johnny, and Charles at St. Joseph, Mo. and daughters Colleen Van Dyke at Arkansas City, Patricia Tigner at Seattle, Wash., and Dorothy Young in Florida. He had 29 grandchildren, 40 great-grandchildren, and three great-great grandchildren.

Richard H. **Sproat** Sr. and Gertrude Esther **Metzinger** had the following children:
    7751   i.   Raymond[13] **Sproat**.[1155]
    7752   ii.   Richard **Sproat** Jr.[1156]
    7753   iii. Marvin **Sproat**.[1157]
    7754   iv.   Johnny **Sproat**.[1158]
    7755   v.   Charles **Sproat**.[1159]

Richard H. **Sproat** Sr and Lucille **Blacksmith** had the following children:
    7756   vi.   Colleen **Sproat**[1160] married (__) **Van Dyke**.
    7757   vii. Patricia **Sproat**[1161] married (__) **Tigner**.
    7758   viii. Dorothy **Sproat**[1162] married (__) **Young**.

    6498. **Edna Pearl**[12] **Sproat** (Mary Elizabeth[11] **Smith**, Ruby Sophronia[10] **Whipple**, William[9], Ira Martin[8], Elijah[7], Jeremiah[6], Joseph[5], John[4], Joseph[3], Matthew[2], Matthew[1])[1163] was born in Freeport, Kans. 29 July 1907 and died 10 April 2002 in Wichita, Sedgwick Co., Kans., at 94 years of age. She married **Jack Huey Trimmell** in Wolson Co., Kans. 25 September 1926.[1164] Jack,[1165] son of Charles **Trimmell** and Bertha **Cooper**, was born in Chitwood, Mo. 29 August 1906 and died 25 February 1971 in Wichita, at 64 years of age. Both are buried in Lakeview Cemetery, Wichita.

Edna Pearl **Sproat** and Jack Huey **Trimmell** had the following children:
- \+ 7759 i. Jack Reed[13] **Trimmell** born 15 August 1927.
- \+ 7760 ii. Harold Riley **Trimmell** born 8 October 1929.
- \+ 7761 iii. Dorothy Margaret **Trimmell** born 22 February 1932.
- \+ 7762 iv. Joseph Donald **Trimmell** born 12 July 1934.
- \+ 7763 v. Mary Lynn **Trimmell** born 25 May 1938.
- \+ 7764 vi. Younda Dee **Trimmell** born January 1941.
- \+ 7765 vii. Maurice Wayne **Trimmell** born 8 July 1943.
- \+ 7766 viii. Lillian Pearl **Trimmell** born 24 October 1948.
- \+ 7767 ix. Mercedes Jeanette **Trimmell** born 30 December 1950.

6499. **Mildred Elizabeth**[12] **Sproat** (Mary Elizabeth[11] **Smith**, Ruby Sophronia[10] **Whipple**, William[9], Ira Martin[8], Elijah[7], Jeremiah[6], Joseph[5], John[4], Joseph[3], Matthew[2], Matthew[1])[1166] was born in Buffalo, Mo. 25 March 1910 and married **Franklin Floyd Murphy** in Wichita, Sedgwick Co., Kans. 2 March 1930. Franklin,[1167] son of Chester **Murphy** and Lenora **Strasbaugh**, was born in Buff City, Kans. 24 February 1909 and died 28 February 2002 in Wichita, at 93 years of age. Buried at the White Chapel Cemetery, Wichita. Franklin retired from the Cardwell Manufacturing Co. where he was a Supervisor and sheet metal employee. At the time of his death sons Doyle lived in Puyallup, Wash., Darrell and John in Wichita, daughters Donna Ramsey at Richardson, Texas, Kathleen Whitlock at Hartford, Kansas, and Mary Hobson at Wichita. He had 17 grand children and 27 great-grandchildren.

Mildred Elizabeth **Sproat** and Franklin Floyd **Murphy** had the following children:
- \+ 7768 i. Doyle A.[13] **Murphy** born 5 December 1931.
- \+ 7769 ii. Donna Louise **Murphy** born 18 August 1933.
- \+ 7770 iii. Kathleen **Murphy** born 28 May 1935.
- \+ 7771 iv. Darrell Luther **Murphy** born 23 April 1940.
- \+ 7772 v. Mary Esther **Murphy** born 8 November 1942.
- \+ 7773 vi. John Harold **Murphy** born 3 January 1944.

6501. **Everett Leander (Sproat)**[12] **Richards** (Mary Elizabeth[11] **Smith**, Ruby Sophronia[10] **Whipple**, William[9], Ira Martin[8], Elijah[7], Jeremiah[6], Joseph[5], John[4], Joseph[3], Matthew[2], Matthew[1])[1168] was born in Dover, Kingfisher Co., Okla. 25 June 1915 and died 7 July 1996 in Liberal, Seward Co., Kansas, at 81 years of age. Buried in Hartville Cemetery, Hardesty, Texas Co., Oklahoma. He married **Alma Maxine Thurman**, daughter of William T. **Thurman**. Everett was adopted by Leander Washington Richards and Jane Matilda Burkdoll.

Everett Leander (Sproat) **Richards** and Alma Maxine **Thurman** had the following children:

- \+ 7774 i. Rodney Dean[13] **Richards**.
- \+ 7775 ii. Phyllis LaMoyne **Richards**.
- \+ 7776 iii. Deanna Kay **Richards**.
- \+ 7777 iv. Darrell Gene **Richards**.
- 7778 v. Everett Estel **Richards**[1169] born in Oklahoma 8 August 1938 and died here 9 January 1939, at 5 months of age.

6503. **Virgil Ray**[12] **Thompson** (Sara Jane[11] **Ward**, Ruby Sophronia[10] **Whipple**, William[9], Ira Martin[8], Elijah[7], Jeremiah[6], Joseph[5], John[4], Joseph[3], Matthew[2], Matthew[1])[1170] was born in Buffalo, Dallas Co., Mo. 2 February 1911 and died 3 August 1980 in Terre Haute, Vigo Co., Ind., at 69 years of age. He married four times. (1) **Blanche Mae Robertson** in Galesburg, Knox Co., Ill. 21 December 1930. She was born in Elida, N. Dak. 19 May 1911.[1171] (2) **Marjorie Evelyn Whitaker** in West Terre Haute 24 October 1942. She was born in Terre Haute 8 January 1920.[1172] (3) **Helen Bernice Reickard** in Kansas City, Jackson Co., Mo. in 1947. She was born in Rock Island, Ill. 19 July 1921.[1173] (4) **Marilyn Geneve Davis** 1956.

Virgil Ray **Thompson** and Blanche Mae **Robertson** had the following children:

- 7779 i. Mary Jane[13] **Thompson**[1174] born and died in 1932.
- 7780 ii. Alice Mae **Thompson**[1175] born in 1937 and died in 1959 at 22 years of age. She married Boyd Thomas **Drury** in 1957. He was born in 1930 and died in 1989 at 59 years of age.[1176]

Virgil Ray **Thompson** and Marilyn Geneve **Davis** had the following children:

- 7781 iii. Martha Rae **Thompson**[1177] born in 1958 and married (__) **Short**.
- 7782 iv. Gladys June **Thompson**[1178] born in 1959 and married (__) **Craft**.
- 7783 v. Brenda Lee **Thompson** born in 1960.[1179]

6504. **Dorothy Louise**[12] **Thompson** (Sara Jane[11] **Ward**, Ruby Sophronia[10] **Whipple**, William[9], Ira Martin[8], Elijah[7], Jeremiah[6], Joseph[5], John[4], Joseph[3], Matthew[2], Matthew[1])[1180] was born in 1913 and married **Frederick Earl Nolan**. He was born in 1908 and died in 1975 at 67 years of age.[1181]

Dorothy Louise **Thompson** and Frederick Earl **Nolan** had the following children:

    7784   i.   Sarah Ellen[13] **Nolan**[1182] born in 1932 and died in 1986 at 54 years of age. She married Harry Dean **Newell**.

    7785   ii.   Floyd Lawrence **Nolan**[1183] born in 1934 and married three times. (1) Charlotte Jean **Lonsdale**. (2) Millie **Johnson**. (3) Mary **(__)**.

    7786   iii.   Tommy Milton **Nolan**[1184] born in 1936 and married twice. (1) Tula Loretta **Fortson**. She married (2) Fredie Roy **Nolan**. (2) Betty Lou **Nelson**.

    7787   iv.   Frieda Deloris **Nolan** born in 1937.[1185]

    7788   v.   Fredie Roy **Nolan**[1186] was born in 1941 and married three times. (1) Tula Loretta **Fortson**. She married (1) Tommy Milton **Nolan**. (2) Rosemarie **Rae**. She was born in 1953.[1187] (3) Virginia Ruth **Smith**. She was born in 1944.[1188]

    7789   vi.   Ralph Kenneth **Nolan**.[1189]

6505. **Donald Louis**[12] **Thompson** (Sara Jane[11] **Ward**, Ruby Sophronia[10] **Whipple**, William[9], Ira Martin[8], Elijah[7], Jeremiah[6], Joseph[5], John[4], Joseph[3], Matthew[2], Matthew[1])[1190] was born in 1913 and died in 1974 at 61, years of age. He married twice. (1) **Mary Martha Armstrong**. She was born in 1916 and died in 1949 at 33 years of age.[1191] (2) **Dorothy Ruth Henderson**.

Donald Louis **Thompson** and Mary Martha **Armstrong** had the following children:

    7790   i.   Donald Louis[13] **Thompson** II[1192] born in 1937 and married twice. (1) Maxine Delores **Leonard**. (2) Betty Lou **Hooks**.

    7791   ii.   Marilyn Lucille **Thompson**[1193] born in 1938 and married James Earl **Colwell**. He was born in 1932.[1194]

    7792   iii.   Donna Jean **Thompson**[1195] born in 1940 and married Elman Woodrow **Bailey**. He was born in 1948.[1196]

    7793   iv.   Betty Jane **Thompson**[1197] born in 1941 and married twice. (1) Wayne Eugene **Jackson**. He was born in 1948.[1198] (2) Larry W. **Sargent**. He was born in 1934.[1199]

    7794   v.   Charles Leroy **Thompson**[1200] born in 1942 and married Sharon **(__)**.

Donald Louis **Thompson** and Dorothy Ruth **Henderson** had the following children:

    7795   vi.   Sharon Ruth **Thompson** born in 1952.[1201]

    7796   vii.   Glenda Kay **Thompson** born in 1954.[1202]

7797 viii. Michael **Thompson**[1203] born abt 1956 and married Mary Ann **Boatman.**

7798 ix. Debra Sue **Thompson**[1204] born in 1960 and married David Clayton **Higgins.**

6506. **Theodore**[12] **Thompson** (Sara Jane[11] **Ward**, Ruby Sophronia[10] **Whipple**, William[9], Ira Martin[8], Elijah[7], Jeremiah[6], Joseph[5], John[4], Joseph[3], Matthew[2], Matthew[1])[1205] was born in 1920 and died in 1945 at 25 years of age. He married **Mrs. Ruth M. Brooks** who was born in 1920.[1206]

Theodore **Thompson** and Mrs. Ruth M. **Brooks** had the following children:

7799 i. James Theodore[13] **Thompson**[1207] born in 1941 and married Charlene Kay **Haker** who was born in 1947.[1208]

7800 ii. Ronald Eugene **Thompson**[1209] born in 1942 and married Rosemary Ann **Bonezkowski** who was born in 1944.[1210]

6507. **Gladys Eileen**[12] **Thompson** (Sara Jane[11] **Ward**, Ruby Sophronia[10] **Whipple**, William[9], Ira Martin[8], Elijah[7], Jeremiah[6], Joseph[5], John[4], Joseph[3], Matthew[2], Matthew[1])[1211] was born in 1923 and married twice. (1) **Herbert Edward Ray** who was born in 1919.[1212] (2) **Theodore Edwin Moffett.**

Gladys Eileen **Thompson** and Herbert Edward **Ray** had the following children:

7801 i. Betty Lou[13] **Ray**[1213] born in 1943 and married Jeffry Richard **Hickman** who was born in 1943.[1214]

7802 ii. Connie Sue **Ray**[1215] born in 1947 and married twice. (1) Robert Michael **Menes** who was born in 1944.[1216] (2) Donald Ray **Craig** who was born in 1941.[1217]

6508. **Albert Leroy**[12] **Thompson** (Sara Jane[11] **Ward**, Ruby Sophronia[10] **Whipple**, William[9], Ira Martin[8], Elijah[7], Jeremiah[6], Joseph[5], John[4], Joseph[3], Matthew[2], Matthew[1])[1218] was born in 1930.[1219] He married twice. (1) **Beverly Joan Quinlan** who was born in 1930.[1220] (2) **Margaret Joan Willis** who was born in 1921.[1221]

Albert Leroy **Thompson** and Beverly Joan **Quinlan** had the following children:

7803 i. Albert Leroy[13] **Thompson** II[1222] born in 1949 and died in 1987 at 38 years of age. He married Annette Ethel **Fletcher** who was born in 1953.[1223]

7804 ii. Henry Edward **Thompson**[1224] born in 1950 and died the year of birth.

7805　iii.　Barbara Ann **Thompson**[1225] born in 1954 and married Michael Ray **Waltrip** who was born in 1949.[1226]

7806　iv.　Kenneth Otis **Thompson**[1227] married Lynn Marie **Lewis** who was born in 1954.[1228]

Albert Leroy **Thompson** and Margaret Joan **Willis** had the following children:

7807　v.　John Theodore **Thompson**[1229] born in 1960 and died in 1962 at 2 years of age.

7808　vi.　Theresa Eileen **Thompson**[1230] born in 1962 and married three times. (1) Jeffrey Lee **Wardlow** who was born in 1958.[1231] (2) Roger Dean **Powell** who was born in 1960.[1232] (3) Roger Danny **Simkins** who was born in 1960.[1233]

6509. **Robert Lee**[12] **Thompson** (Sara Jane[11] **Ward**, Ruby Sophronia[10] **Whipple**, William[9], Ira Martin[8], Elijah[7], Jeremiah[6], Joseph[5], John[4], Joseph[3], Matthew[2], Matthew[1])[1234] was born in 1939 and married **June Ann Smith**. She was born 28 August 1936 and died 2 June 1989 at 52 years of age.[1235]

Robert Lee **Thompson** and June Ann **Smith** had the following children:

7809　i.　Ruby Jane[13] **Thompson**[1236] born in 1961 and married Greggory Allen **Benskin** who was born 1963.[1237]

7810　ii.　Roberta June **Thompson**[1238] born in 1962 and married Dwaine David **Hubbel**l who was born in 1963.[1239]

+　7811　iii.　Walter Otis **Thompson** born in 1963.

6512. **Ruby Gertrude**[12] **Smith** (Cora A.[11] **Ward**, Ruby Sophronia[10] **Whipple**, William[9], Ira Martin[8], Elijah[7], Jeremiah[6], Joseph[5], John[4], Joseph[3], Matthew[2], Matthew[1])[1240] was born in 1918 and married twice. (1) **Edwin Wheeler Woosley**. He was born in 1908 and died in 1966, at 58 years of age.[1241] (2) **Wayne Thompson** who was born in 1906.[1242]

Ruby Gertrude **Smith** and Edwin Wheeler **Woosley** had the following children:

7812　i.　Alice June[13] **Woosley**[1243] born bef 1944 and married Lawrence Anthony **Gabel** who died in 1979.[1244]

7813　ii.　Mary Ann **Woosley**[1245] born in 1945 and married Roger Wayne **Hevland**.

6514. **Hazel Eileen**[12] **Smith** (Cora A.[11] **Ward**, Ruby Sophronia[10] **Whipple**, William[9], Ira Martin[8], Elijah[7], Jeremiah[6], Joseph[5], John[4], Joseph[3], Matthew[2], Matthew[1])[1246] was born in 1920 and married **William Leo McCulloch**.

{ G 1151 }

Hazel Eileen **Smith** and William Leo **McCulloch** had the following child:
  7814 i. Daniel Lee[13] **McCulloch**[1247] born in 1949 and married Mrs. Roberta **Wilburn** who was born 1948.[1248]

6515. **Samuel Alfred**[12] **Ward** (James Eugene[11], Ruby Sophronia[10] **Whipple**, William[9], Ira Martin[8], Elijah[7], Jeremiah[6], Joseph[5], John[4], Joseph[3], Matthew[2], Matthew[1])[1249] was born in Galesburg, Knox Co., Ill. 28 July 1922 and married three times. (1) **Virginia** (__). (2) **Julia** (__). (3) **Barbara** (__).

Samuel Alfred **Ward** had the following children:
  7815 i. David[13] **Ward**.[1250]
  7816 ii. James **Ward**.[1251]

6516. **Phyllis Marie**[12] **Ward** (James Eugene[11], Ruby Sophronia[10] **Whipple**, William[9], Ira Martin[8], Elijah[7], Jeremiah[6], Joseph[5], John[4], Joseph[3], Matthew[2], Matthew[1])[1252] was born in Galesburg, Knox Co., Ill. 18 February 1924 and married **David Neel**.

Phyllis Marie **Ward** and David **Neel** had the following children:
  7817 i. Diane[13] **Neel**[1253] married (__) **Wiedman**.
  7818 ii. Sandra **Neel**.[1254]
  7819 iii. Pam **Neel**.[1255]
  7820 iv. Susan **Neel**.[1256]

6517. **James Eugene**[12] **Ward II** (James Eugene[11], Ruby Sophronia[10] **Whipple**, William[9], Ira Martin[8], Elijah[7], Jeremiah[6], Joseph[5], John[4], Joseph[3], Matthew[2], Matthew[1])[1257] was born 4 November 1926.

James Eugene **Ward** II had the following children:
  7821 i. Wendy[13] **Ward**.[1258]
  7822 ii. Waverly **Ward**.[1259]

6518. **Merle Frederick**[12] **Ward** (James Eugene[11], Ruby Sophronia[10] **Whipple**, William[9], Ira Martin[8], Elijah[7], Jeremiah[6], Joseph[5], John[4], Joseph[3], Matthew[2], Matthew[1])[1260] was born in Earlsboro, Potawatomie Co., Okla. 13 October 1927 and married three times. (1) **Evelyn** (__). (2) **Linda** (__). (3) **Anita** (__) who died in 1986.[1261]

Merle Frederick **Ward** and Evelyn (__) had the following child:
  7823 i. James Eugene[13] **Ward** born in Houston, Tex. 1 December 1947.[1262]

6519. **Peggy Joyce**[12] **Ward** (James Eugene[11], Ruby Sophronia[10] **Whipple**, William[9], Ira Martin[8], Elijah[7], Jeremiah[6], Joseph[5], John[4], Joseph[3], Matthew[2], Matthew[1])[1263] was born in Mineola, Wood Co., Tex. 1 July 1931 and married **Duane Evert Vandenberg** in Houston, Tex., 10 November 1951. He is the son of Neilson **Vandenberg** and Pearl **Wayman**.[1264]

Peggy Joyce **Ward** and Duane Evert **Vandenberg** had the following children:
+ 7824 i. Linda Kay[13] **Vandenberg**.
+ 7825 ii. Rene Denise **Vandenberg** born 20 July 1953.
  7826 iii. David Duane **Vandenberg** born in Warrensburg, Johnson Co., Mo. 1 May 1959.[1265]
+ 7827 iv. James Neilson **Vandenberg** born 14 October 1960.

6520. **Allan Leonard**[12] **Teague** (William Thomas[11], Eunice Augusta[10] **Whipple**, William[9], Ira Martin[8], Elijah[7], Jeremiah[6], Joseph[5], John[4], Joseph[3], Matthew[2], Matthew[1])[1266] was born in Alameda, Calif. 30 October 1903 and died 29 December 1966 in Los Angeles, Calif., at 63 years of age. He married **Doris Hayes Claflin** in East Orange, Essex Co., N.J. 17 September 1929. Doris,[1267] daughter of Ward **Claflin** and Florence **Hayes**, was born in Brooklyn, N.Y. 24 July 1908 and died 20 September 1985 in Los Angeles, Calif., at 77 years of age. Allan was a Comptroller with Pacific Telephone.

Allan Leonard **Teague** and Doris Hayes **Claflin** had the following child:
+ 7828 i. Dianne[13] **Teague** born 25 January 1935.

6521. **Roland Bardo**[12] **Teague** (William Thomas[11], Eunice Augusta[10] **Whipple**, William[9], Ira Martin[8], Elijah[7], Jeremiah[6], Joseph[5], John[4], Joseph[3], Matthew[2], Matthew[1])[1268] was born in Oakland, Calif. 29 June 1907 and died in January 1980 in East Stroudsburg, Monroe Co., Penn., at 72 years of age. He married twice. (1) **Francese (__)** who died bef 1961.[1269] (2) **Margaret (__)** 26 May 1961. Roland was an Accountant for A.T. & T.

Roland Bardo **Teague** and Francese (__) had the following children:
+ 7829 i. Gail[13] **Teague** born 15 May 1938.
  7830 ii. Barbara **Teague**[1270] born 8 August 1941 and died in September 1988 at 47 years of age. She married Robert **Peterson** April 1962.
+ 7831 iii. John William **Teague** born 24 August 1942.

{ G 1153 }

6522. **Burton William**[12] **Teague** (William Thomas[11], Eunice Augusta[10] **Whipple**, William[9], Ira Martin[8], Elijah[7], Jeremiah[6], Joseph[5], John[4], Joseph[3], Matthew[2], Matthew[1])[1271] was born in Portland, Multnomah Co., Oreg. 12 October 1912 and died 6 February 1994, at 81 years of age. He married **Sarah Estes Reimer** in East Orange, Essex Co., N. J. 30 July 1938. Sarah,[1272] daughter of Arthur **Reimer** and Jennie **Estes**, was born 12 November 1912. Burton was an attorney with the Standard Oil Co. of N. J.

Burton William **Teague** and Sarah Estes **Reimer** had the following children:
- 7832 i. Barbara Estes[13] **Teague**[1273] born in Miami, Dade Co., Fla. 12 November 1942 and married Leendert **De Kruis** in Schiedam Suid-Holland 9 September 1981. He was born in Rotterdam, The Netherlands 26 August 1939.[1274]
- + 7833 ii. Gregory Bardo **Teague** born 14 November 1944.

6523. **Ethel Virginia**[12] **Teague** (Arthur[11], Eunice Augusta[10] **Whipple**, William[9], Ira Martin[8], Elijah[7], Jeremiah[6], Joseph[5], John[4], Joseph[3], Matthew[2], Matthew[1])[1275] was born in Pescadero, San Mateo Co., Calif. 24 April 1913 and died 26 August 1987 in Walnut Creek, Contra Costa Co., Calif., at 74 years of age. She married **John Paul Bonnell** 7 October 1933. He was born in Ft. Collins, Colo. 22 November 1908 and died 3 October 1977 in Sonora, Tuolomne Co., Calif., at 68 years of age.[1276] Both are buried in the Annapolis Cemetery, Annapolis, Tuolomne Co., Calif.

Ethel Virginia **Teague** and John Paul **Bonnell** had the following children:
- + 7834 i. Donald Paul[13] **Bonnell** born 13 February 1936.
- + 7835 ii. Jerry Richard **Bonnell** born 16 December 1939.

6524. **Elsie May**[12] **Teague** (Arthur[11], Eunice Augusta[10] **Whipple**, William[9], Ira Martin[8], Elijah[7], Jeremiah[6], Joseph[5], John[4], Joseph[3], Matthew[2], Matthew[1])[1277] was born in Pescadero, San Mateo Co., Calif. 18 May 1914 and died 22 May 1993 in Los Altos, Santa Clara Co., Calif., at 79 years of age. She married **Robert Martin Fincher** in San Francisco, Calif. 28 April 1933. Robert[1278] was the son of Robert **Fincher** and Matilda **Martin**, was born in Waxahachie, Tex. 2 September 1903 and died 11 July 1967 in Redwood City, San Mateo Co., Calif., at 63 years of age. Elsie and Robert are buried in the Alta Mesa Cemetery, Palo Alto, Calif.

Elsie May **Teague** and Robert Martin **Fincher** had the following children:
- + 7836 i. Doris Robin[13] **Fincher** born 2 April 1935.
- + 7837 ii. Susan Merle **Fincher** born 29 January 1939.

6525. **James Frederick**[12] **Teague** (Arthur[11], Eunice Augusta[10] **Whipple**, William[9], Ira Martin[8], Elijah[7], Jeremiah[6], Joseph[5], John[4], Joseph[3], Matthew[2], Matthew[1])[1279] was born in Pescadero, San Mateo Co., Calif. 13 January 1917 and died 29 December 1991 in Redwood City, San Mateo Co., Calif., at 74 years of age. He married **Lois Jeanne Hunt** in Reno, Nev. 14 February 1941. She is the daughter of Frederick **Hunt** and Alice **Hewitson**.[1280]

James Frederick **Teague** and Lois Jeanne **Hunt** had the following children:
- \+ 7838 i. Donna Jeanne[13] **Teague** born 15 September 1942.
- \+ 7839 ii. Sydney Elizabeth **Teague** born 7 January 1949.
- \+ 7840 iii. Deborah Anne **Teague** born 4 January 1956.

6527. **Janet Anne**[12] **Dearborn** (Eunice May[11] **Teague**, Eunice Augusta[10] **Whipple**, William[9], Ira Martin[8], Elijah[7], Jeremiah[6], Joseph[5], John[4], Joseph[3], Matthew[2], Matthew[1])[1281] was born in Palo Alto, Santa Clara Co., Calif. 23 January 1935 and married **Frederick Malkin Vogel** in Redwood City, San Mateo Co., Calif. 12 April 1958. He is the son of Peter **Vogel** and Anne **Malkin**.[1282]

Janet Anne **Dearborn** and Frederick Malkin **Vogel** had the following children:
- 7841 i. Sarah Anne[13] **Vogel**[1283] born in San Rafael, Marin Co., Calif. 13 February 1962 and married Keith Vincenz **Fischer** in Portola Valley, San Mateo Co., Calif. 27 May 1989. Keith,[1284] son of Hans **Fischer** and Adele **Vincenz**, was born in Frankfort, Germany 4 November 1962.
- \+ 7842 ii. David Frederick **Vogel** born 22 February 1964.

6528. **Lawrence Francis**[12] **Bowman** (Nancy[11] **Rice**, Ellen Boise[10] **Leland**, Alonzo[9], Jasper[8], Lydia[7] **Sherman**, Mary[6] **Whipple**, Lieut. James[5], Deacon James[4], Joseph[3], Matthew[2], Matthew[1])[1285] was born in Denver, Idaho 22 January 1895 and died 16 June 1973 in Vancouver, Clark Co., Wash., at 78 years of age. He married **Leora Pearl Grattan** in Grangeville, Idaho 20 August 1917. Leora,[1286] daughter of Ernest Franklin **Grattan** and Sophie Hannah **Davis**, was born in Sites, Idaho 23 January 1901 and died 10 December 1983 in Portland, Multnomah Co., Oreg., at 82 years of age.

Lawrence Francis **Bowman** and Leora Pearl **Grattan** had the following child:
- \+ 7843 i. Sandra Joanne[13] **Bowman** born 30 November 1934.

6529. **Grace**[12] **Treanor** (Mabel Frances[11] **Reynolds**, Helen[10] **Butterfield**, Elizabeth S.[9] **Reynolds**, Sarah W.R.[8] **Leland**, Thankful[7] **Sherman**, Mary[6] **Whipple**, Lieut. James[5], Deacon James[4], Joseph[3], Matthew[2], Matthew[1])[1287] was born in San Francisco, Calif. 5 May 1895 and died abt 1947 in Seattle, King Co., Wash. Buried in the Mt. Tamalpais Cemetery, San Rafael, Calif. under the name Grace Quiggle. She married **Charles Robert Corum**. Charles was born Lake Co., Calif. 24 July 1893 and died in June 1973 in Scottsdale, Ariz., at 79 years of age.[1288]

Grace **Treanor** and Charles Robert **Corum** had the following child:
+ 7844 i. Mabel Frances[13] **Corum** born 29 December 1915.

6534. **William Edmund**[12] **Whipple** (Francis John[11], Fancis Looby[10], Lysander Greenlief[9], Edmund[8], Perley[7], Lt. James[6], Lieut. James[5], Deacon James[4], Joseph[3], Matthew[2], Matthew[1])[1289] was born 16 March 1928 and married **Barbara Prudence Allan** in Sydney, NSW, Australia 10 May 1952. She was born in Australia 31 March 1933.[1290]

William Edmund **Whipple** and Barbara Prudence **Allan** had the following children born in Australia:
7845 i. Susan[13] **Whipple**.[1291]
7846 ii. Jenny **Whipple**.[1292]
7847 iii. Christine **Whipple**.[1293]
7848 iv. Allan **Whipple**.[1294]
7849 v. Robert **Whipple**.[1295]

6535. **Olwyn Dianne**[12] **Whipple** (Francis John[11], Fancis Looby[10], Lysander Greenlief[9], Edmund[8], Perley[7], Lt. James[6], Lieut. James[5], Deacon James[4], Joseph[3], Matthew[2], Matthew[1])[1296] was born 24 September 1931 and married **Edward William James Howes** in Sydney, NSW, Australia 30 April 1953. He was born in Australia 25 March 1928.[1297]

Olwyn Dianne **Whipple** and Edward William James **Howes** had the following child:
7850 i. Cathy Gai[13] **Howes**[1298] born in Australia 8 October 1954.

6536. **Jill Colleen**[12] **Whipple** (Leander Edmund[11], Fancis Looby[10], Lysander Greenlief[9], Edmund[8], Perley[7], Lt. James[6], Lieut. James[5], Deacon James[4], Joseph[3], Matthew[2], Matthew[1])[1299] was born in Orange, NSW, Australia 16 August 1929 and died there 30 May 1970. She married **James Andrew Auld** in Orange 14 July 1950. James,[1300] son of James **Auld** and Agnes **Smith**, was born 25 March 1926.

Jill Colleen **Whipple** and James Andrew **Auld** had the following children:
- + 7851 i. James Grant[13] **Auld** born 18 July 1955.
- 7852 ii. Bruce Edmund **Auld**[1301] born in Blayney NSW, Australia 14 March 1958 and died 27 September 1995 in Sydney, NSW, Australia, at 37 years of age. He was cremated and his ashes buried in Orange.
- + 7853 iii. Merin Joy **Auld** born 22 January 1962.

6537. **William Warwick**[12] **Whipple** (Leander Edmund[11], Fancis Looby[10], Lysander Greenlief[9], Edmund[8], Perley[7], Lt. James[6], Lieut. James[5], Deacon James[4], Joseph[3], Matthew[2], Matthew[1])[1302] was born in Orange, NSW, Australia 19 September 1932 and married **Yvonne Mary Skevington** there 26 January 1954. Yvonne,[1303] daughter of Herbert **Skevington** and Kathleen **Davis**, was born 24 March 1932.

William Warwick **Whipple** and Yvonne Mary **Skevington** had the following children:
- 7854 i. Robyn Jane[13] **Whipple**[1304] born in Orange 12 January 1956 and married Robert Wallace **Alderton** there 20 November 1982. He was born 4 August 1946.[1305]
- + 7855 ii. Darren John **Whipple** born 1 February 1962.

6538. **Dr. Reginald Thomas Milner**[12] **Whipple** (Reginald Joseph[11], Fancis Looby[10], Lysander Greenlief[9], Edmund[8], Perley[7], Lt. James[6], Lieut. James[5], Deacon James[4], Joseph[3], Matthew[2], Matthew[1])[1306] was born in Roseville, NSW, Australia 21 January 1931 and married **Patricia Anne Stanton** in Waverley, NSW, Australia 20 August 1965. Patricia,[1307] daughter of Richard Colin **Stanton** and Doris Eileen **Smith**, was born in Sydney, NSW, Australia 2 February 1936. Tom, a former Captain in the Australian Navy, is an Emeritus College Professor and is listed in *Who's Who in Australia*.

Dr. Reginald Thomas Milner **Whipple** and Patricia Anne **Stanton** had the following children born in Sydney:
- 7856 i. David Stanton Milner[13] **Whipple**[1308] 18 May 1971 and married Louise Collette **Bailey** in Leederville, Perth, Australia, 19 April 1997. He is an Electronics Engineer.
- 7857 ii. Penelope Anne Milner **Whipple**[1309] 8 October 1973 and is a Hospital Pharmacist (1999).

6539. **Rear Adm. Walter Jones**[12] **Whipple** (William[11], Lt. Col. Charles William[10], Maj. Gen. Amiel Weeks[9], David[8], David[7], James[6], Deacon Jacob[5], Deacon James[4], Joseph[3], Matthew[2], Matthew[1])[1310] was born in Cinclare, La. 22 March 1906 and married twice. (1) **Marian K. Leighton** in Mare Island Naval Shipyard, Calif. 11 June 1939. She was born in Lima, Ohio 20 June 1917 and died in 1992 at 75 years of age.[1311] (2) **Imogene Smith** 1 November 1993.[1312] Walter was appointed to the U.S. Naval Academy at Annapolis in 1922 and was graduated with the Class of 1926. His active duty included service as Executive Officer of the *USS Louisville*, Fleet Gunnery Officer under Adm. Wm. "Bull" Halsey in WWII, Captain of the *USS Nagato* in transit and at the Bikini Atoll Atomic Tests, Captain of the *USS Noble* and the *USS Mann*, and service at the Navy Ammunition Depot at Mare Island, Calif. Following his Navy retirement at Mare Island 30 June 1957, he was employed by Lockheed Missile & Space Co. and now (1998) lives at Murphys, Calif.

Rear Adm. Walter Jones **Whipple** and Marian K. **Leighton** had the following children:

- \+ 7858 i. Walter Leighton[13] **Whipple** born 23 June 1940.
- \+ 7859 ii. Roby Trent **Whipple** born 24 April 1946.
- 7860 iii. Margaret Randolph **Whipple**[1313] born in Bethesda, Md. 23 December 1952.

6540. **Brig. Gen. William**[12] **Whipple** (William[11], Lt. Col. Charles William[10], Maj. Gen. Amiel Weeks[9], David[8], David[7], James[6], Deacon Jacob[5], Deacon James[4], Joseph[3], Matthew[2], Matthew[1])[1314] was born in Cinclare, La. 4 February 1909 and married four times. (1) **Dixie Ancrum** in Quantico, Va. 30 March 1935. Dixie,[1315] daughter of Lt. Col. Calhoun **Ancrum**, was born in Germantown, Penn. 18 September 1911 and died 12 October 1955 in Orleans, France, at 44 years of age. Buried in Arlington, Va.. (2) **Renee Pauline Exiga** near Orleans, France 21 July 1956. Renee,[1316] daughter of Noel **Exiga** and Lea (__), was born in Marseilles, France 18 June 1923. They were divorced in Princeton, N.J. 9 May 1974. At the time of their marriage, Renee was the Director of a girl's school in France. After her marriage, she became a teacher in a private school in Princeton. (3) **Frances Edith (Gowans) Cheek** in Princeton 1 June 1974. At the time of their marriage Frances was a nationally known Psychotherapist. She was born in York Co., Ontario, Canada in December 1923 and died 20 April 1983 in Princeton, at 59 years of age.[1317] (4) **Alice Terry Goodloe** in Princeton 1 December 1984. Alice,[1318] daughter of Alfred Minor **Goodloe** and Edith **Jamison**, was born in Roanoke, Va. 30 January 1928. At the time of her marrige she was a Psychotherapist in New York City. After marriage, she earned a Ph.D. and became a prominent practitioner in the Princeton area.

After graduating from West Point in 1930, Bill spent three years at Oxford in England as a Rhodes Scholar. During World War II he headed the Logistical Planning Branch for the Normandy invasion in Gen. Dwight Eisenhower's headquarters in England. After the war, he was Secretary General in the U.S. Office of Military Government in Germany under Gen. Lucius Clay. Both before and after the war he was assigned to the U.S. Army Corps of Engineers developing water resource programs, notably in the Columbia river as the first District Commander of the Corps of Engineers (10/48-8/50) headquartered at Portland, Oreg. He retired with the rank of Brigadier General in 1960.

Upon retirement he became Chief Engineer to the New York World's Fair followed by a 14-year stint as head of the Water Resources Research Institute at Rutgers, University. That assignment was followed by 10 years with the New Jersey State Department of Environmental Protection. He left state employment in 1990 to become a principal of Greeley Polhemus, a consulting firm engaged in water resource planning and policy. He has written a number of books and published over 200 papers on water resource matters. After his final retirement, he continued to be active in professional activities on the national level. Beginning in 1996 his has been a major voice calling for water resource development to be coordinated with protection of the environment and for a program of national action to accomplish this goal. He is in excellent health and plays tennis year-round.

Brig. Gen. William **Whipple** and Dixie **Ancrum** had the following children:
+ 7861 i. Anne Calhoun[13] **Whipple** born 18 January 1936.
+ 7862 ii. William **Whipple** III was born 24 June 1938.
+ 7863 iii. Claire Randolph **Whipple** born 10 July 1947.

Brig. Gen. William **Whipple** and Renee Pauline **Exiga** had the following child:
+ 7864 iv. Philip Exiga **Whipple** born 27 July 1957.

6541. **Jane Randolph[12] Whipple** (William[11], Lt. Col. Charles William[10], Maj. Gen. Amiel Weeks[9], David[8], David[7], James[6], Deacon Jacob[5], Deacon James[4], Joseph[3], Matthew[2], Matthew[1])[1319] was born in Cinclare, La. 16 September 1910 and married **Arthur Donald Green** in Baton Rouge, La. 6 June 1935. Donald,[1320] son of Arthur L. **Green** and Christine A. **MacPherson**, was born in Dorchester, Mass. 24 October 1905 and died 26 April 1988 in Westfield, Union Co., N.J., at 82 years of age.

{ G 1159 }

Buried in Westfield, Fairview Cemetery. He earned a B. S. and M. S, from the Massachusetts Institute of Technology in 1926. His work included Head of the Development Division of Esso Research and Engineering Co.; JASCO of Germany where he helped invent Butyl rubber; Vice President of Enjay Company, an affiliate of Exxon. He retired in 1965.

Jane earned a Fine Arts degree in 1931 from Newcomb College of Tulane University where she was a member of the Phi Mu Sorority. She worked as an Administrator for non-profit organizations, including the Girl Scouts of USA, and is an artist. She is a member of the American Artist Professional League, the Westfield, N.J. Art Assn., President, then Director, and later Director of Publications of Federated Art Associations of New Jersey. She was a member of the Echo Lake Golf and Country Club and the Elizabeth and Cranford, N. J. Garden Clubs. She is a member of the National Society of DAR, Cranes Ford Chapter, the Colonial Dames of the XVII Century, and the Mayflower Society as a descendant of William Brewster. She has done extensive research on her maternal Randolph line and has traced her lineage back to the Emperor Charlemagne. Her first Randolph ancestor to arrive in North America was Henry, born in England in 1623 and emigrated to Virginia about 1642.

Jane Randolph **Whipple** and Arthur Donald **Green** had the following children:

	7865	i.	Janet Whipple[13] **Green**[1321] born in Elizabeth, N. J. 12 October 1936 and died 6 February 1942 in Summit, N. J, at 5 years of age. Buried in Fairview Cemetery, Westfield.
+	7866	ii.	Genevieve Randolph **Green** born 26 June 1939.
+	7867	iii.	Christine MacPherson **Green** born 29 September 1943.
+	7868	iv.	Virginia Whipple **Green** born 2 April 1946.

6542. **Genevieve Liddell**[12] **Whipple** (William[11], Lt. Col. Charles William[10], Maj. Gen. Amiel Weeks[9], David[8], David[7], James[6], Deacon Jacob[5], Deacon James[4], Joseph[3], Matthew[2], Matthew[1])[1322] was born in Cinclare, La. 29 September 1913 and died 24 January 1988 in Shreveport, La., at 74 years of age. She married **Robert Winfield Williams** in Baton Rouge, La. 19 June 1937. Robert,[1323] son of Winfield Scott **Williams** and Ida Louise **Jacobs**, was born in Ridgway, Penn. 23 September 1909 and died 17 July 1981 in Baton Rouge, La., at 71 years of age.

Genevieve Liddell **Whipple** and Robert Winfield **Williams** had the following children:

	7869	i.	John Winfield[13] **Williams**.[1324]
+	7870	ii.	Carolyn Randolph **Williams** born 17 March 1938.

           7871   iii.   Robert Stephen **Williams**[1325] born in Baton Rouge, La. 21 February 1941.
+   7872   iv.   Douglas Liddell **Williams** born 22 November 1946.

6544. **Sherburne**[12] **Whipple Jr.** (Sherburne[11], Lt. Col. Charles William[10], Maj. Gen. Amiel Weeks[9], David[8], David[7], James[6], Deacon Jacob[5], Deacon James[4], Joseph[3], Matthew[2], Matthew[1])[1326] birth date unknown, died in 1998. He married **Peg (__)**. Sherburne was graduated from West Point and was a Tank Commander during WWII.

Sherburne **Whipple** Jr. had the following children:
           7873   i.   Ben Grimes[13] **Whipple**.[1327]
           7874   ii.   Pegida **Whipple** died in 1998.[1328]

6546. **Sarah Bailey**[12] **Whipple** (Sherburne[11], Lt. Col. Charles William[10], Maj. Gen. Amiel Weeks[9], David[8], David[7], James[6], Deacon Jacob[5], Deacon James[4], Joseph[3], Matthew[2], Matthew[1])[1329] was born 13 October 1915 and died of ALS (Lou Gehrig's disease) 13 February 1980, at 64 years of age. She married **Col. Cornelis DeWitt Willcox Lang**. They were stationed on Oahu, Hawaii when Japan attacked Pearl Harbor 7 December 1941.

Sarah Bailey **Whipple** and Col. Cornelis DeWitt Willcox **Lang** had the following children:
           7875   i.   John Walton[13] **Lang**.[1330]
           7876   ii.   David Whipple **Lang**.[1331]
           7877   iii.   Edward Richards **Lang**.[1332]

6549. **Katherine C.**[12] **Collens** (Annette Bailey[11] **Whipple**, Lt. Col. Charles William[10], Maj. Gen. Amiel Weeks[9], David[8], David[7], James[6], Deacon Jacob[5], Deacon James[4], Joseph[3], Matthew[2], Matthew[1])[1333] was born in 1907 and died in 1992 at 85 years of age. She married **Jeremiah Hotchkiss Bartholomew Jr.**, son of Jeremiah H. **Bartholomew**.[1334]

Katharine C. **Collens** and Jeremiah H. **Bartholomew** Jr. had the following child:
+   7878   i.   Julia[13] **Bartholomew** born in 1937 and Linda, date unknown.

6558. **George Amiel**[12] **Whipple II** (Jack Van Horn[11], George Amiel[10], George Alonzo[9], David[8], David[7], James[6], Deacon Jacob[5], Deacon James[4], Joseph[3], Matthew[2], Matthew[1])[1335] was born 2 June 1929 and married **Hope Auchincloss** 11 June 1949 who was born 27 February 1919.[1336] George was an investment executive with the Paine-Webber in Rumson, N. J.

{ G 1161 }

George Amiel **Whipple** II and Hope **Auchincloss** had the following children:

 7879 i. Jack Van Horn[13] **Whipple** II[1337] born 3 March 1951.
 7880 ii. George Amiel **Whipple** III[1338] born 1 August 1952.
 7881 iii. Susan Auchincloss **Whipple**[1339] born 22 July 1953.

6562. **Arthur Harvey**[12] **Whipple** (David Ethen[11], Charles E.[10], David M.[9], Mathew A.[8], David[7], James[6], Deacon Jacob[5], Deacon James[4], Joseph[3], Matthew[2], Matthew[1])[1340] was born in Boise, Idaho 12 December 1910 and died 16 October 1986 in Hornbook, Calif., at 75 years of age. He married **Lavina Irene Nichols** in Reedsport, Douglas Co., Oreg. 9 June 1935. Lavina.[1341] daughter of George Edward **Nichols** and Mary J. **Cook**, was born in Elkton, Douglas Co., Oreg. 14 July 1917. Arthur and his brother Orval married Nichols sisters Lavina and Nora. (See No. 6563.

Arthur Harvey **Whipple** and Lavina Irene **Nichols** had the following children:

 7882 i. David A.[13] **Whipple**[1342] was born in Eugene, Lane Co., Oreg. 18 March 1936.
 7883 ii. Charles O. **Whipple**[1343] born in Sweet Home, Linn Co., Oreg. 9 January 1938.
 7884 iii. Irene E. **Whipple**[1344] born in Prineville, Oreg. 9 March 1951.

6563. **Orval Aaron**[12] **Whipple** (David Ethen[11], Charles E.[10], David M.[9], Mathew A.[8], David[7], James[6], Deacon Jacob[5], Deacon James[4], Joseph[3], Matthew[2], Matthew[1])[1345] was born in Boise, Idaho 6 July 1912 and died 1 October 1958 in Detroit, Marion Co., Oreg., at 46 years of age. Buried at Sweet Home, Oreg. He married **Nora Edvina Nichols** in Reedsport, Douglas Co., Oreg. 10 August 1935. Nora,[1346] daughter of George Edward **Nichols** and Mary J. **Cook**, was born in Winchester Bay, Douglas Co, Oreg. 16 August 1920. Orval and his brother Arthur married Nichols sisters, Nora and Lavina. (See No. 6562.)

Orval Aaron **Whipple** and Nora Edvina **Nichols** had the following children:

 + 7885 i. Dan Edward[13] **Whipple** born 9 June 1936.
  7886 ii. Orville Lee **Whipple**[1347] born in Lebanon, Linn Co., Oreg. 25 August 1937 and died 2 June 1983 in Blue River, Lane Co., Oreg., at 45 years of age. Buried at Sweet Home.
 + 7887 iii. Nellie Janette **Whipple** born 17 June 1939.
 + 7888 iv. Cora Bell **Whipple** born 26 February 1941.
 + 7889 v. Hellin Irene **Whipple** born 6 January 1944.
 + 7890 vi. Bob Aaron **Whipple** born 24 June 1947.

6569. George David[12] **Whipple** (Walter Ralph[11], William Isaac[10], Isaac Truax[9], James[8], James[7], James[6], Deacon Jacob[5], Deacon James[4], Joseph[3], Matthew[2], Matthew[1])[1348] was born in Webster City, Iowa 22 February 1937 and married **Carol Ann Jensen** there 13 October 1957. Carol,[1349] daughter of Howard Larain **Jensen** and Pauline Caroline **Hoover**, was born in Clinton, Clinton Co., Iowa 8 September 1936. George was raised in Webster City where he met Carol who moved there from Fon du Lac, Wisc. in 1953. The family moved to Conrad, Iowa in 1965 where George worked for the Chicago Northwestern Railroad. George and Carol share hobbies of fishing, gardening, traveling, lapidary, and repairing and refinishing antique furniture.

George David **Whipple** and Carol Ann **Jensen** had the following children:
- + 7891 i. Paula Kay[13] **Whipple** born 26 October 1961.
- + 7892 ii. Joel David **Whipple** born 28 May 1963.
- + 7893 iii. Todd Douglas **Whipple** born 24 January 1965.

6570. Burnette[12] **Creighton** (Minnie Grace[11] **Whipple**, Fred G.[10], Obed[9], Obed[8], Thomas[7], Col. Moses[6], Deacon Jacob[5], Deacon James[4], Joseph[3], Matthew[2], Matthew[1])[1350] was born in Glenburn, Calif. 16 June 1907 and married **Norma Mayo**. Norma,[1351] daughter of Norman **Mayo** and Minnie **Rice**, was born in San Louis Osbispo, Calif.

Burnette **Creighton** and Norma **Mayo** had the following children:
- 7894 i. John[13] **Creighton**[1352] Adopted.
- 7895 ii. Lynn **Creighton**[1353] born in Orange, Orange Co., Calif. 28 October 1944 and married William **Nilsen**. He was born in Brooklyn, N.Y.[1354]

6571. Evelyn Adelle[12] **Creighton** (Minnie Grace[11] **Whipple**, Fred G.[10], Obed[9], Obed[8], Thomas[7], Col. Moses[6], Deacon Jacob[5], Deacon James[4], Joseph[3], Matthew[2], Matthew[1])[1355] was born in Glenburn, Calif. 30 December 1911 and married **Raymond Scoggin** in Reno, Nev. 13 October 1931. Raymond was born in Miller, Mo. 15 October 1909 and died 13 October 1968 in Santa Cruz, Santa Cruz Co., Calif., at 58 years of age.[1356]

Evelyn Adelle **Creighton** and Raymond **Scoggin** had the following children:
- + 7896 i. Yvonne[13] **Scoggin** born 20 May 1934.
- + 7897 ii. John Henry **Scoggin** born 22 May 1935.

6572. **Virginia Lee**[12] **Whipple** (Harry Meryl[11], Fred G.[10], Obed[9], Obed[8], Thomas[7], Col. Moses[6], Deacon Jacob[5], Deacon James[4], Joseph[3], Matthew[2], Matthew[1])[1357] was born in Glenburn, Calif. 28 July 1920 and married **Newton Jacobsen** who was born in Winnipeg, Canada.[1358]

Virginia Lee **Whipple** and Newton **Jacobsen** had the following children:
- + 7898 i. Eric Newton[13] **Jacobsen** born 22 January 1947.
- + 7899 ii. Dennis Merle **Jacobsen** born 29 July 1949.
- + 7900 iii. Kristina Carol **Jacobsen** born 26 December 1953.

6573. **Sylvia Ruth**[12] **Hildebrant** (Lois Philena[11] **Whipple**, Fred G.[10], Obed[9], Obed[8], Thomas[7], Col. Moses[6], Deacon Jacob[5], Deacon James[4], Joseph[3], Matthew[2], Matthew[1])[1359] was born in Cedarville, Modoc Co., Calif. 29 March 1927 and married **Carl Henry Spitzer Jr.** in San Anselmo, Calif. 25 June 1949. Carl,[1360] son of Carl Henry **Spitzer** Sr. and Laura Blanch **Jones**, was born in San Francisco, Calif. 21 October 1923.

Sylvia Ruth **Hildebrant** and Carl Henry **Spitzer** Jr. had the following children:
- + 7901 i. Richard Carl[13] **Spitzer** born 24 April 1950.
- + 7902 ii. William Eric **Spitzer** born 1 May 1952.
- + 7903 iii. Raymond Lewis **Spitzer** born 1 May 1952.
- + 7904 iv. Ronald Walter **Spitzer** born 17 May 1955.
- + 7905 v. Evelyn Bernice **Spitzer** born 17 May 1957.
- + 7906 vi. Robert David **Spitzer** born 22 August 1961.

6574. **Harold Homer**[12] **Hildebrant** (Lois Philena[11] **Whipple**, Fred G.[10], Obed[9], Obed[8], Thomas[7], Col. Moses[6], Deacon Jacob[5], Deacon James[4], Joseph[3], Matthew[2], Matthew[1])[1361] was born in Kentfield, Calif. 13 October 1930 and married **Lura Marcene Wilson** in Ross, Calif. 30 January 1959. Lura,[1362] daughter of William Marcellus **Wilson** and Lura Eunice **Oliver**, was born in Canyon, Tex. 27 December 1925.

Harold Homer **Hildebrant** and Lura Marcene **Wilson** had the following children:
- 7907 i. Ronald William[13] **Hildebrant**[1363] born in San Francisco, Calif. 21 December 1959.
- + 7908 ii. Carl Wayne **Hildebrant** born 25 May 1961.
- + 7909 iii. Glenn Harold **Hildebrant** born 14 October 1963.
- 7910 iv. Diane Margaret **Hildebrant**[1364] born in San Francisco 24 September 1964 and married Jerold Wayne **Phillips** 7 May 1994. Jerry,[1365] son of Charles S. **Phillips** and Gwendolyn (__), was born in Petaluma, Calif. 22 February 1946.

6576. **Graeme Gardiner**[12] **Whytlaw** (Laura Alexander[11] **Gardiner**, Mary Powers[10] **Cooper**, Laurel[9] **Whipple**, David[8], Aaron[7], Col. Moses[6], Deacon Jacob[5], Deacon James[4], Joseph[3], Matthew[2], Matthew[1])[1366] was born in New York, N.Y. 13 January 1897 and died 15 February 1971 in Pocasset, Mass., at 74 years of age. Buried in Chatham, Mass. He married **Anna Krawl Suesbrich** in New York, N.Y. 9 October 1924. Anna,[1367] daughter of Gustave **Suesbrich** and Johanna **Krawl**, was born in Adams, Berkshire Co., Mass. 4 December 1894. Graeme's schooling was varied and included school attendance and tutoring at Glasgow, Scotland, Paris, France, Rome, Italy, Lausanne, Switzerland Frankfort, Germany St. Petersburg, Russia, Hale, England and New York City. He attended Harvard 1914/16 and again 1919/20. His military experience began in 1916 as an ambulance driver with the American Field Service attached to the 65th Division French Army in Argonne and Verdun. He was awarded the Croix De Guerre. In 1918 he joined the Royal Canadian Air Force as a Cadet in the Royal Flying Corps. His work experience began in 1920 as an apprentice with the Renfrew Mfg. Co. of Adams, Mass. and ended in 1962 as Manager, Application Research and Development, American Viscoe Corp. at Marcus Hook, Penn.

Graeme Gardiner **Whytlaw** and Anna Krawl **Suesbrich** had the following child:
+ 7911 i. Graeme Gardiner[13] **Whytlaw Jr.** born 3 August 1925.

6595. **Dr. G. Hoyt**[12] **Whipple** (Dr. George Hoyt[11], Dr. Ashley Cooper[10], Dr. Solomon M.[9], David[8], Aaron[7], Col. Moses[6], Deacon Jacob[5], Deacon James[4], Joseph[3], Matthew[2], Matthew[1])[1368] was born in San Francisco, Calif. abt 1917 and died 12 May 1999 in Gainesville, Fla., at 81 years of age.[1369] He married **Marta (__)**. Hoyt earned a bachelor of science degree from Wesleyan University in Middletown, Conn., attended Massachusetts Institute of Technology, and received a Ph.D. in Biophysics from the U. of Rochester. He was a Professor Emeritus of Radiological Health at the U. of Michigan's School of Public Health, a Consultant to the International Atomic Energy Commission, the World Health Organization, and the Commonwealth of Puerto Rico. He designed environmental surveys for nuclear power plants and lived in Gainesville the last four years of his life.

Dr. G. Hoyt **Whipple** and Marta (__) had the following children:
7912 i. Elizabeth[13] **Whipple**.[1370]
7913 ii. Dr. Margaret **Whipple**.[1371]
7914 iii. Andrew **Whipple**.[1372]

7915 iv. Dana **Whipple**.[1373]
7916 v. Matthew **Whipple**.[1374]

6601. **Lothrop**[12] **Withington Jr.** (Katharyn Carlton[11] **Whipple**, Sherman Leland[10], Dr. Solomon M.[9], David[8], Aaron[7], Col. Moses[6], Deacon Jacob[5], Deacon James[4], Joseph[3], Matthew[2], Matthew[1])[1375] was born 16 February 1917 and married twice. (1) **Lois Brewster**.[1376] They were divorced 8 March 1973. She is of Mayflower descent. (2) **Dorothy (Millican) Shed**. She is of Mayflower descent. When a candidate for President of the Harvard freshman class in March 1939, Lothrop, in an effort to gain name recognition, swallowed a live goldfish. This stunt received nationwide publicity and generated goldfish gulping contests in colleges across the country. The class voted not to have any officers. He was in the Army Air Corps from November 1940 through September 1945 and was one of the seven original helicopter pilots trained at the Sikorski Aircraft Factory in Connecticut. He later served on the Air Forces Board in Orlando, Fla. as Director of Rotary Wing Operational and Tactical Suitability Testing.

Lothrop **Withington** Jr. and Lois **Brewster** had the following children:
+ 7917 i. Lothrop[13] **Withington** III born 15 May 1942.
+ 7918 ii. Ellen **Withington** born 21 May 1943.
+ 7919 iii. Lydia Whipple **Withington** born 2 April 1947.
+ 7920 iv. Ellis Brewster **Withington** born 19 September 1953.

6603. **Marietta Louise**[12] **Withington** (Katharyn Carlton[11] **Whipple**, Sherman Leland[10], Dr. Solomon M.[9], David[8], Aaron[7], Col. Moses[6], Deacon Jacob[5], Deacon James[4], Joseph[3], Matthew[2], Matthew[1])[1377] was born in Brookline, Norfolk Co., Mass. 12 February 1920 and married **Spencer Hatch Brewster** there 23 May 1942. Spencer,[1378] son of Ellis W. **Brewster** and Ellen **Hatch**, was born in Plymouth, Mass. 28 October 1920. He was a helicopter pilot with the U.S. Air Corps during WWII (1942-45).

Marietta Louise **Withington** and Spencer Hatch **Brewster** had the following children:
+ 7921 i. Anne Withington[13] **Brewster** born 3 October 1943.
+ 7922 ii. Marietta **Brewster** born 16 June 1945.
+ 7923 iii. Spencer Hatch **Brewster** Jr. born 9 May 1947.
+ 7924 iv. Sarah **Brewster** born 23 January 1950.
+ 7925 v. Patience **Brewster** born 26 October 1952.
7926 vi. Katharyn **Brewster** born in Plymouth, Mass. 21 September 1957.

{ G 1166 }

6606. **Anne Platt**[12] **Withington** (Katharyn Carlton[11] **Whipple**, Sherman Leland[10], Dr. Solomon M.[9], David[8], Aaron[7], Col. Moses[6], Deacon Jacob[5], Deacon James[4], Joseph[3], Matthew[2], Matthew[1])[1379] was born in Brookline, Norfolk Co., Mass. 26 September 1926 and married **Benjamin B. Brewster** in Plymouth, Mass., 29 May 1948. Anne and Marietta married brothers Benjamin and Spencer Brewster.

Benjamin,[1380] son of Ellis W. **Brewster** and Ellen **Hatch**, was born in Plymouth 9 September 1925.

Anne Platt **Withington** and Benjamin B. **Brewster** had the following children:

+   7927   i.   Benjamin B.[13] **Brewster** Jr. born 24 June 1950.
+   7928   ii.   Penelope **Brewster** born 23 September 1952.
       7929   iii.   Abigail **Brewster**[1381] born in Plymouth 3 June 1955.
       7930   iv.   William Wrestling **Brewster**[1382] born in Plymouth 7 March 1965 and married Belinda Alexandra **Shobbrook** 12 September 1998. Belinda, daughter of Walter Vernon **Shobbrook** and Lena Mavis **Beaumont**, was born in Plymouth 13 February 1959.

6607. **Paul**[12] **Withington** (Katharyn Carlton[11] **Whipple**, Sherman Leland[10], Dr. Solomon M.[9], David[8], Aaron[7], Col. Moses[6], Deacon Jacob[5], Deacon James[4], Joseph[3], Matthew[2], Matthew[1])[1383] was born 7 November 1927 and married **Drusilla Greenwood**.

Paul **Withington** and Drusilla **Greenwood** had the following children:

       7931   i.   Mark Little[13] **Withington**[1384] married Susan Ellis **Parker**.
+   7932   ii.   Paul Tucker **Withington** born 10 June 1953.
       7933   iii.   David Neal **Withington**[1385] born in Plymouth, Mass. 10 February 1956.

6609. **Nathan Noyes**[12] **Withington** (Katharyn Carlton[11] **Whipple**, Sherman Leland[10], Dr. Solomon M.[9], David[8], Aaron[7], Col. Moses[6], Deacon Jacob[5], Deacon James[4], Joseph[3], Matthew[2], Matthew[1])[1386] was born in Plymouth, Mass. 29 June 1940 and married **June E. Hamilton** there 6 October 1962. June,[1387] daughter of Dr. Harold H. **Hamilton** and Marjorie **Lang**, was born in Plymouth 1 July 1940. Nathan is a Vice President and Financial Consultant with Shearson Lehman Hutton in Boston. He was owner of Boston's world famous Lock Ober Restaurant which has been a Boston mainstay since 1875.

Nathan Noyes **Withington** and June E. **Hamilton** had the following children:

    7934   i.   Nathan Noyes[13] **Withington** III born in Lubbock, Tex. 13 August 1964.[1388]

    7935   ii.   Heather Lee **Withington**[1389] born in Plymouth 18 July 1966.

    7936   iii.   Meghan Elizabeth **Withington**[1390] born in Plymouth 10 January 1979.

6610. **Sherman Leland**[12] **Whipple** III (Sherman Leland[11], Sherman Leland[10], Dr. Solomon M.[9], David[8], Aaron[7], Col. Moses[6], Deacon Jacob[5], Deacon James[4], Joseph[3], Matthew[2], Matthew[1])[1391] was born in Webster, Mass. 4 April 1920 and died 19 August 1971 in Cold Spring, N.Y., at 51 years of age. He married **Mettie Marie Barton** 10 June 1947.

Sherman Leland **Whipple** III and Mettie Marie **Barton** had the following children:

  +   7937   i.   Mettie Micheaux[13] **Whipple** born 17 July 1948.

  +   7938   ii.   Sherman Taylor **Whipple** born 31 May 1950.

  +   7939   iii.   Louise Barton **Whipple** born 13 April 1955.

6611. **Paul Jones**[12] **Whipple** (Sherman Leland[11], Sherman Leland[10], Dr. Solomon M.[9], David[8], Aaron[7], Col. Moses[6], Deacon Jacob[5], Deacon James[4], Joseph[3], Matthew[2], Matthew[1])[1392] was born in Plymouth, Mass. 15 August 1922 and married **Judith Tingley-Foor** 28 June 1947. She died 25 March 1988.[1393]

Paul Jones **Whipple** and Judith **Tingley-Foor** had the following children:

  +   7940   i.   Alan Morrison[13] **Whipple** born 28 August 1948.

  +   7941   ii.   Belinda **Whipple** born 26 January 1950.

  +   7942   iii.   Paul Hersey **Whipple** born 23 July 1952.

6612. **Margaret Louise**[12] **Whipple** (Sherman Leland[11], Sherman Leland[10], Dr. Solomon M.[9], David[8], Aaron[7], Col. Moses[6], Deacon Jacob[5], Deacon James[4], Joseph[3], Matthew[2], Matthew[1]) was born in Brookline, Norfolk Co., Mass. 22 October 1926 and married **Eduardo Adolfo Estrada** 21 June 1947. They were divorced in June 1968.

Margaret Louise **Whipple** and Eduardo Adolfo **Estrada** had the following children:

  +   7943   i.   Margarita Elisa[13] **Estrada** born 26 June 1948.

  +   7944   ii.   Olga Lucrecia **Estrada** born 17 August 1950.

  +   7945   iii.   Sandra Louise **Estrada** born 16 October 1951.

  +   7946   iv.   Carmen Patricia **Estrada** born 13 July 1953.

+	7947	v.	Suzanna Maria **Estrada** born 21 April 1956.
+	7948	vi.	Deborah Lily **Estrada** born 29 October 1958.
+	7949	vii.	Katherine Michelle **Estrada** born 13 March 1961.
	7950	viii.	Eduardo Roberto **Estrada**[1394] born in Guatemala City, Guatemala 25 January 1963.

6614. Joseph Drew[12] **Crowe** (Mabel Alice[11] **Drew**, Rubie Jane[10] **Whipple**, Barnabas Cooper[9], David[8], Aaron[7], Col. Moses[6], Deacon Jacob[5], Deacon James[4], Joseph[3], Matthew[2], Matthew[1])[1395] was born in Topsham, Sagadahoc Co., Maine 18 March 1915 and married **Julia Irene Stuart** in Kennebunk, York Co., Maine 12 September 1937.

Joseph Drew **Crowe** and Julia Irene **Stuart** had the following children:

	7951	i.	Ronald Alfred[13] **Crowe**[1396] born in West Buxton, Maine 14 May 1938.
	7952	ii.	Robert Allen **Crowe**[1397] born in West Buxton 21 October 1939.
	7953	iii.	Barbara Louise **Crowe**[1398] born in Bar Mills, Maine 25 July 1941.

6617. Richard Francis[12] **Quimby** (Isabel[11] **Drew**, Rubie Jane[10] **Whipple**, Barnabas Cooper[9], David[8], Aaron[7], Col. Moses[6], Deacon Jacob[5], Deacon James[4], Joseph[3], Matthew[2], Matthew[1])[1399] was born in Portland, Maine 2 May 1918 and married **Alberta (__)**.

Richard Francis **Quimby** and Alberta (__) had the following child:

| | 7954 | i. | Richard Francis[13] **Quimby Jr.**[1400] born in Portland in April 1942. |

6619. Ruth Anne[12] **Gordon** (Pauline Bryant[11] **Drew**, Rubie Jane[10] **Whipple**, Barnabas Cooper[9], David[8], Aaron[7], Col. Moses[6], Deacon Jacob[5], Deacon James[4], Joseph[3], Matthew[2], Matthew[1])[1401] was born in Portland, Maine 10 January 1928 and married **Sanford Cutler** there.

Ruth Anne **Gordon** and Sanford **Cutler** had the following children:

| | 7955 | i. | Charles Gordon[13] **Cutler**[1402] born 6 May 1951. |
| | 7956 | ii. | Drew Davidson **Cutler**[1403] born 11 April 1955. |

6628. George Aaron[12] **Whipple** (Perley Arthur[11], Aaron Mason[10], Barnabas Cooper[9], David[8], Aaron[7], Col. Moses[6], Deacon Jacob[5], Deacon James[4], Joseph[3], Matthew[2], Matthew[1])[1404] was born in Newport, Sullivan Co., N.H. 14 August 1935 and married **Hattie Emery Parker** 16 June 1957. George was living in Langdon, N.H. in 1985.

George Aaron **Whipple** and Hattie Emery **Parker** had the following child:

    7957   i.   Donna Lorraine[13] **Whipple**[1405] born 23 March 1961 and married John **Goodell**.

6629. Donald Edwin[12] **Whipple** (Perley Arthur[11], Aaron Mason[10], Barnabas Cooper[9], David[8], Aaron[7], Col. Moses[6], Deacon Jacob[5], Deacon James[4], Joseph[3], Matthew[2], Matthew[1])[1406] was born in Newport, Sullivan Co., N.H. 19 August 1938 and married **Irmgard Maria Kuhn** in Wurzburg, Germany 5 December 1959. Irmgard,[1407] daughter of Ludwig **Kuhn** and Ludwina **Schaeffer**, was born in Wurzburg 7 March 1942 and died of a brain tumor 1 May 1994 in Lebanon, N.H., at 52 years of age.

She was raised and educated in Germany. She and her husband lived in Arizona where they owned and operated a delicatessen in Prescott, Ariz. and in Nevada where she was a cashier at the Gold Coast Casino in Las Vegas. She lived the last 15 years in the Croydon-Newport area and was employed at the Sugar River Savings Bank in Newport at the time of death. She was survived by her husband, four daughters, mother, and brother Siegfried Kuhn. The latter two lived in Wurzburg. Donald was living in Prescott in 1985.

Donald Edwin **Whipple** and Irmgard Maria **Kuhn** had the following children:

  +   7958   i.   Susan Marie[13] **Whipple** born 9 July 1960.
  +   7959   ii.   Claudia Avis **Whipple** born 24 May 1961.
       7960   iii.   Patricia Ann **Whipple**[1408] born in Fitchburg, Worcester Co., Mass. 2 March 1963. She was living in Prescott in 1993.
  +   7961   iv.   Linda Lou **Whipple** born 7 May 1964.

6630. Martha Avis[12] **Whipple** (Perley Arthur[11], Aaron Mason[10], Barnabas Cooper[9], David[8], Aaron[7], Col. Moses[6], Deacon Jacob[5], Deacon James[4], Joseph[3], Matthew[2], Matthew[1])[1409] was born in Newport, Sullivan Co., N.H. 7 November 1953 and married **James Frederick Rice** in Croydon, N.H. 10 July 1971. He died 25 December 1990.

Martha Avis **Whipple** and James Frederick **Rice** had the following children born in Keene, N.Y.:

    7962   i.   Janet Lynn[13] **Rice**[1410] 15 April 1975 and died the day of birth.
    7963   ii.   Jessica Avis **Rice**[1411] 24 February 1978.
    7964   iii.   Heidi Lynn **Rice**[1412] 8 October 1979.
    7965   iv.   Daniel Perley **Rice**[1413] 6 May 1982.

6631. **Virginia May**[12] **Wright** (Veda May[11] **Whipple**, Aaron Mason[10], Barnabas Cooper[9], David[8], Aaron[7], Col. Moses[6], Deacon Jacob[5], Deacon James[4], Joseph[3], Matthew[2], Matthew[1])[1414] was born in Newport, Sullivan Co., N.H. 4 February 1925 and married twice. (1) **John Marshall Whitley** in San Antonio, Tex. 20 September 1946.[1415] He served in the Army in WWII in campaigns in Normandy, Northern France, Rhineland, and central Europe and was awarded the American Campaign Medal with four Bronze Stars and one Bronze Arrowhead, Purple Heart with Oak Leaf Clusters, Victory Ribbon, one Service Strip and three Overseas Service Bars He was wounded in the Normandy landings and was a part of the Berlin airlift and retired with the rank of sergeant after 37 years service. (2) **Alfred Winston Johnson** in Keene, N.H. 7 February 1964. Red,[1416] son of Oscar **Johnson** and Anna **Eriksson**, born in Brockton, Plymouth Co., Mass. 24 November 1916 and died 26 May 1993 in Keene, at 76 years of age. Virginia was graduated from Keene High School in 1943 and joined the Womens Army Corp where she attained the rate of corporal and was assigned duties at the Flight Surgeon's Office, AAF Military Training Center, San Antonio, Tex. She was living in Glendale, Ariz. in 1997.

Virginia May **Wright** and John Marshall **Whitley** had the following child:
+   7966   i.   Linda May[13] **Whitley** born 20 July 1947.

6633. **Everett Whipple**[12] **Wright** (Veda May[11] **Whipple**, Aaron Mason[10], Barnabas Cooper[9], David[8], Aaron[7], Col. Moses[6], Deacon Jacob[5], Deacon James[4], Joseph[3], Matthew[2], Matthew[1])[1417] was born in Keene, N.H. 17 February 1930 and married **Mary Alice Brannan** at an Air Force base near Bellview, Nebr. 25 January 1951. She was born in Iowa 30 March 1933.

Everett Whipple **Wright** and Mary Alice **Brannan** had the following children:
+   7967   i.   Carol Ann[13] **Wright** born 14 July 1951.
+   7968   ii.   Nancy Jo **Wright** born 6 September 1952.
+   7969   iii.   Joanne Ellen **Wright** born 7 September 1954.

6634. **Lawrence Blaine**[12] **Wright** (Veda May[11] **Whipple**, Aaron Mason[10], Barnabas Cooper[9], David[8], Aaron[7], Col. Moses[6], Deacon Jacob[5], Deacon James[4], Joseph[3], Matthew[2], Matthew[1])[1418] was born in Keene, N.H. 3 January 1932 and married **Margaret Martin** there 8 August 1953. Margaret,[1419] daughter of Alphonse **Martin** and Shirley **Coleman**, was born in Marlborough, N.H. 17 August 1934. He served with the Seabees in the U.S. Navy.

Lawrence Blaine **Wright** and Margaret **Martin** had the following children:
- \+   7970   i.   Christine May[13] **Wright** born 1 July 1954.
-      7971   ii.   Anthony Martin **Wright**[1420] born in Keene 4 October 1955 and married Margaret Hurt **Cody** there 20 October 1984. Anthony adopted Amy and Heather Wright. Amy was born 1 August 1974; Heather on 27 August 1976 in Keene.
- \+   7972   iii.   Patrick Drew **Wright** born 3 August 1957.
- \+   7973   iv.   Jon Andrae **Wright** born 1 December 1958.
-      7974   v.   Michelle Frances **Wright**[1421] born in Keene 14 January 1963.
-      7975   vi.   Nicole Margaret **Wright**[1422] born born in Keene 10 March 1970 and married Ernie **Smalley** there 26 June 1997.

6635. **Barbara Newton**[12] **Wright** (Veda May[11] **Whipple**, Aaron Mason[10], Barnabas Cooper[9], David[8], Aaron[7], Col. Moses[6], Deacon Jacob[5], Deacon James[4], Joseph[3], Matthew[2], Matthew[1])[1423] was born in Keene, N.H. 14 October 1933 and married twice. (1) **Robert Kevin Breen** there 21 June 1952. Robert,[1424] son of Leo **Breen** and Harriet **Duffy**, was born in Keene 12 May 1932 and died 5 April 1988 in Ashulot, N.H., at 55 years of age. He married **Pauline Pelkey** and Irmgard **Maier**. He served with the U. S. Army during the Korean conflict. Following the war he was employed at Minature Precision Ballbearing Co. (MPB) in Keene for 32 years and was a member of the Ashuelot Volunteer Fire Department. He was buried in the family lot at Evergreen Cemetery, Winchester, Cheshire Co. N.H. Veterans of Foreign Wars Post 3968 conducted graveside military services. (2) **Robert Lambert** in Troy, N.H. 16 March 1990.

Barbara Newton **Wright** and Robert Kevin **Breen** had the following children born in Keene:
- \+   7976   i.   Kevin Paul[13] **Breen** 29 July 1952.
- \+   7977   ii.   Kimberly Jane **Breen** 3 May 1956.
-      7978   iii.   Keith Robert **Breen**[1425] 21 July 1957 and died 25 July 1978 in Oklahoma City, Okla., at 21 years of age. He was a 1976 graduate of Keene High School and entered the U.S. Army in May 1978 and died shortly after completing basic training at Fort Still, Okla. Funeral arrangements were made by the O'Connor Funeral Home in Winchester.
- \+   7979   iv.   Karolee May **Breen** born 18 October 1958.
- \+   7980   v.   Kathleen Ann **Breen** born 18 October 1958.
-      7981   vi.   Kent Duffy **Breen**[1426] 27 March 1960 and married twice. (1) Karen **Kelley** in Winchester 28 May 1982. Karen is the daughter of Phillip **Kelley** and Barbara **Clark**.[1427] They were divorced in Keene in May 1985. (2) Marcia Ann

Richardson in Keene 31 August 1985. Marcia is the daughter of Alan **Richardson** and Karen **Almquist**.[1428] She married (1) (__) **Cobb** and had a son, Isaac John Cobb, born 7 January 1982 in Keene.

+   7982   vii.   Kelly Elizabeth **Breen** born 12 June 1963.

6636. **Charles Burgum**[12] **Wright** (Veda May[11] **Whipple**, Aaron Mason[10], Barnabas Cooper[9], David[8], Aaron[7], Col. Moses[6], Deacon Jacob[5], Deacon James[4], Joseph[3], Matthew[2], Matthew[1])[1429] was born in Keene, N.H. 16 October 1936 and married **Katherine Gail Cashman** in Templeton, Mass. 28 January 1957. Katherine,[1430] daughter of Chesley **Cashman** and Dorothy **Shattuck**, was born in Keene 11 March 1941.

Charles Burgum **Wright** and Katherine Gail **Cashman** had the following children:

        7983   i.   Susan[13] **Wright**[1431] born in Keene 17 May 1957 and married Thomas Scott **Rice** there 30 October 1993.
+   7984   ii.   Jaclyn **Wright** born 11 March 1959.
        7985   iii.   Lorri **Wright**[1432] born in Keene 11 March 1960.

6638. **Mary Lou**[12] **Jensen** (Ruth Mildred[11] **Whipple**, Edgar J.[10], Darwin[9], Harvey[8], Aaron[7], Col. Moses[6], Deacon Jacob[5], Deacon James[4], Joseph[3], Matthew[2], Matthew[1])[1433] was born in Cresco, Iowa 29 October 1932 and married **Donald Frederick Klassy** in LeRoy, Minn. 20 August 1955. Donald,[1434] son of Frank R. **Klassy** and Esther Ann **Lamon**, was born in LeRoy 27 April 1932. Mary Lou was a Junior High School teacher for 35.5 years, retiring in 1991. Among her favorite retirement activities are genealogy, collecting antiques, and gardening.

Mary Lou **Jensen** and Donald Frederick **Klassy** had the following child:
+   7986   i.   Paul Lamon[13] **Klassy** born 24 February 1961.

6639. **Shirley Yvonne**[12] **Whipple** (Raymond J.[11], Edgar J.[10], Darwin[9], Harvey[8], Aaron[7], Col. Moses[6], Deacon Jacob[5], Deacon James[4], Joseph[3], Matthew[2], Matthew[1])[1435] was born in Minnesota 20 September 1924 and married (__) **Liles**.

Shirley Yvonne **Whipple** and (__) **Liles** had the following children:
+   7987   i.   Gregory[13] **Liles** born 1947.
+   7988   ii.   Pamela **Liles** born 1949.
+   7989   iii.   Jeffrey **Liles** born 1951.
        7990   iv.   Scott **Liles** 1436 born in Orange Co., Calif. in 1960.

6640. **Robert Ray**[12] **Whipple** (Raymond J.[11], Edgar J.[10], Darwin[9], Harvey[8], Aaron[7], Col. Moses[6], Deacon Jacob[5], Deacon James[4], Joseph[3], Matthew[2], Matthew[1])[1437] was born in Minnesota 7 February 1929 and married twice. (1) **Nelora Townsend** November 1950. They were divorced in 1965. (2) **Joyce (__)** October 1983.

Robert Ray **Whipple** and Nelora **Townsend** had the following children:
+ 7991 i. Toby[13] **Whipple** born 18 March 1951.
 7992 ii. Richard **Whipple**[1438] born 7 March 1952 and died in February 1988 at 35 years of age. Buried in Orange Co., Calif.
+ 7993 iii. Jerry **Whipple** born 30 March 1953.
+ 7994 iv. Janielle **Whipple** born 4 April 1954.

6641. **Frank Addison**[12] **Brown** (William Joseph[11], Eva De Etta[10] **McMillin**, Elsie Elvira[9] **Whipple**, Tyler B.[8], Moses[7], Col. Moses[6], Deacon Jacob[5], Deacon James[4], Joseph[3], Matthew[2], Matthew[1])[1439] was born in Grand Forks, N. Dak. 19 May 1921 and died 5 September 1998 in Kirkland, Wash., at 77 years of age. He married **Mary Ellen Glass** in Grand Forks 15 July 1950. Mary,[1440] daughter of E. C. **Glass**, was born 29 July 1922.

Frank Addison **Brown** and Mary Ellen **Glass** had the following child:
+ 7995 i. Jeffrey Jonathan[13] **Brown** born 10 April 1951.

6642. **Elsie Ann**[12] **Brown** (William Joseph[11], Eva De Etta[10] **McMillin**, Elsie Elvira[9] **Whipple**, Tyler B.[8], Moses[7], Col. Moses[6], Deacon Jacob[5], Deacon James[4], Joseph[3], Matthew[2], Matthew[1])[1441] was born in Grand Forks, N. Dak. 31 March 1927 and married **Charles Robert Wilkin Jr.** in New York, N.Y. 13 February 1960. Charles,[1442] son of Charles Robert **Wilkin** Sr. and Dorothy Mae **Rumph**, born in Hope, Ark. 14 October 1931.

Elsie Ann **Brown** and Charles Robert **Wilkin** Jr. had the following children:
 7996 i. Eric Joseph[13] **Wilkin**[1443] born in Fort Worth, Tex. 3 September 1962. Adopted.
+ 7997 ii. Karen Elizabeth **Wilkin** born 5 September 1963.
 7998 iii. Rolf Brenden **Wilkin**[1444] born in Dallas, Tex. 30 December 1965 and married Kerry Anne **Pocius** in Fayetteville, Washington Co., Ark. 25 July 1995.
 7999 iv. Kurt Robert **Wilkin**[445] born in Dallas 7 December 1968 and married twice. (1) Julie Renee **Stewart.** (2) Lynne **Brooks** in Dallas, Tex. 29 August 1998.

{ G 1174 }

6643. **Barbara Jean**[12] **Brown** (William Joseph[11], Eva De Etta[10] McMillin, Elsie Elvira[9] Whipple, Tyler B.[8], Moses[7], Col. Moses[6], Deacon Jacob[5], Deacon James[4], Joseph[3], Matthew[2], Matthew[1])[1446] was born in Grand Forks, N. Dak. 15 March 1930 and married **John Robert Modisett** there 8 June 1953. John, son of John DeBoos **Modisett** and Marian (__), was born 10 December 1931.

Barbara Jean **Brown** and John Robert **Modisett** had the following children:
    8000 i. John DeBoos[13] **Modisett**[1447] born 25 January 1960. Adopted.
    8001 ii. Anne Brown **Modisett**[1448] born 31 March 1962. Adopted. She married Eric Christian **Punnett** in Winnetka, Ill. 14 July 1984.

6644. **Jocelyn Marie**[12] **Northfield** (Ivan Herbert[11], Jennie Viola[10] McMillin, Elsie Elvira[9] **Whipple**, Tyler B.[8], Moses[7], Col. Moses[6], Deacon Jacob[5], Deacon James[4], Joseph[3], Matthew[2], Matthew[1])[1449] was born in Duluth, Minn. 3 December 1922 and married **Robert I. Mather** in Atlanta, Ga. 12 February 1943.

Jocelyn Marie **Northfield** and Robert I. **Mather** had the following child:
    8002 i. Patricia Lynn[13] **Mather**[1450] born in Glen Ridge, Essex Co., N.J. 20 March 1950.

6652. **Katherine Elizabeth**[12] **Williamson** (Frances Elizabeth[11] **Whipple**, Howard Thompson[10], George Jacob[9], Harvey[8], Jacob[7], Col. Moses[6], Deacon Jacob[5], Deacon James[4], Joseph[3], Matthew[2], Matthew[1])[1451] was born 23 August 1948 and married **Robert Marion Pacholik** in Pelham Manor, N.Y. 14 June 1980. Kitty attended Duke University and the U. of California at Berkeley.

Katherine Elizabeth **Williamson** and Robert Marion **Pacholik** had the following children born in Sacramento, Calif.:
    8003 i. Thomas Williamson[13] **Pacholik**[1452] 17 October 1984.
    8004 ii. Julia Whipple **Pacholik**[1453] 15 August 1987.

6670. **Carolyn Case**[12] **Whipple** (James Blair[11], George Harvey[10], Fred Harvey[9], Harvey[8], Jacob[7], Col. Moses[6], Deacon Jacob[5], Deacon James[4], Joseph[3], Matthew[2], Matthew[1])[1454] was born in Denver, Colo. 2 November 1960 and married **Peter Sibner** in Wilmington, Vt. 17 September 1989. Peter is the son of Nat **Sibner** and Joan (__).

Carolyn Case **Whipple** and Peter **Sibner** had the following children born in Pittsfield, Berkshire Co., Mass.:

    8005 i.   Rebecca Blair[13] **Sibner**[1455] 8 August 1992.
    8006 ii.   Allison **Sibner**[1456] 2 June 1994.

6672. **Galen Charles**[12] **Whipple** (Charles Franklin[11], Louis Whiting[10], Charles Crary[9], Oliver[8], Jacob[7], Col. Moses[6], Deacon Jacob[5], Deacon James[4], Joseph[3], Matthew[2], Matthew[1])[1457] was born in Harvey, N. Dak. 10 May 1944 and married **Lynda DiAnn Larson** in Nielsville, Minn. 28 October 1967. Lynda,[1458] daughter of Emil **Larson** and Edna **Petske**, was born in Harvey 14 November 1944.

Galen Charles **Whipple** and Lynda DiAnn **Larson** had the following children:

 +   8007 i.   Paul Brian[13] **Whipple** born 28 November 1969.
       8008 ii.   John Thomas **Whipple**[1459] born in Dallas, Tex. 22 August 1972.
       8009 iii. Steven Gregory **Whipple**[1460] born in Plano, Tex. 5 June 1975.

6673. **Michael Henry**[12] **Arnold** (Irene Alice[11] **Whipple**, Louis Whiting[10], Charles Crary[9], Oliver[8], Jacob[7], Col. Moses[6], Deacon Jacob[5], Deacon James[4], Joseph[3], Matthew[2], Matthew[1])[1461] birth date unknown.

Michael Henry **Arnold** had the following children:

    8010 i.   Emily[13] **Arnold**.[1462]
    8011 ii.   Michael Christen **Arnold**.[1463]
    8012 iii. Jesse **Arnold**.[1464]

6682. **Addie Corinna**[12] **Emmons** (Alice Corinna[11] **Smith**, Charles Elbridge[10], Angeline[9] **Wenzel**, Mehitable[8] **Haven**, Abner[7], Jerusha[6] **Whipple**, Deacon Jacob[5], Deacon James[4], Joseph[3], Matthew[2], Matthew[1])[1465] was born 24 July 1881 and married **Jesse Crosby** 26 November 1908.

Addie Corinna **Emmons** and Jesse **Crosby** had the following child:

    8013 i.   George[13] **Crosby**[1466] born 21 May 1911.

6701. **Craig Alan**[12] **Jordan** (Gilbert Haven[11], Gilbert Haven[10], Imogene[9] **Haven**, Abner[8], Abner[7], Jerusha[6] **Whipple**, Deacon Jacob[5], Deacon James[4], Joseph[3], Matthew[2], Matthew[1])[1467] was born in San Diego, Calif. 13 August 1960 and married **Beth Anne Hall** in Upland, Calif. 11 June 1983. Beth,[1468] daughter of Oliver W. **Hall** and Dawn (__), was born 23 September 1966

Craig Alan **Jordan** and Beth Anne **Hall** had the following child:
    8014   i.   Joshua Timothy[13] **Jordan**[1469] born in Chino, Calif. 26 September 1983.

6709. **William Hazlett**[12] **Upson** II (John Wright[11], Marjory Alexander[10] **Wright**, Charles Baker[9], Susanna Whipple[8] **Baker**, Edward[7], Susannah[6] **Whipple**, Deacon Jacob[5], Deacon James[4], Joseph[3], Matthew[2], Matthew[1])[1470] was born in Peoria, Ill. 9 May 1955 and died 7 December 1987 in Middlebury, Vt., at 32 years of age. He married **Penny St. George** in April 1985.

William Hazlett **Upson** II and Penny St. **George** had the following child:
    8015   i.   Peggy Diane[13] **Upson**.[1471]

6710. **Cicely Ann**[12] **Whitney** (Wallace Lowell[11], Harry Erwin[10], Eli Harrison[9], William Flanagan[8], Moses[7], Jemima[6] **Whipple**, Deacon Jacob[5], Deacon James[4], Joseph[3], Matthew[2], Matthew[1])[1472] was born in Chico, Calif. 3 July 1943 and married **Richard Stafford**.

Cicely Ann **Whitney** and Richard **Stafford** had the following children:
    8016   i.   Rebecca Renee[13] **Stafford**[1473] born 3 September 1970.
    8017   ii.   Jon Richard **Stafford**[1474] born 27 March 1972 and married Dawn (__).
    8018   iii.   Aaron Keith **Stafford**[1475] born 3 August 1974.

6711. **Dale Craig**[12] **Whitney** (Wallace Lowell[11], Harry Erwin[10], Eli Harrison[9], William Flanagan[8], Moses[7], Jemima[6] **Whipple**, Deacon Jacob[5], Deacon James[4], Joseph[3], Matthew[2], Matthew[1])[1476] was born in Chico, Calif. 16 December 1945 and married **Norene May Shimer** in Yuba City, Calif. 19 December 1965. Norene,[1477] daughter of Clarence **Shimer** and Miriam **Myer**, was born in Merced, Calif. 27 February 1947.

Dale Craig **Whitney** and Norene May **Shimer** had the following children:
+   8019   i.   Kathryn Renee[13] **Whitney** born 4 December 1966.
+   8020   ii.   Cynthia Anne **Whitney** born 4 April 1969.
    8021   iii.   Tamara Lynne **Whitney**[1478] born in Yuba City 25 September 1970.

6712. **David Leroy**[12] **Whitney** (Wallace Lowell[11], Harry Erwin[10], Eli Harrison[9], William Flanagan[8], Moses[7], Jemima[6] **Whipple**, Deacon Jacob[5], Deacon James[4], Joseph[3], Matthew[2], Matthew[1])[1479] was born in Chico, Calif. 3 February 1949 and married **Miriam Haverstoch** She was born 13 July 1948.[1480]

David Leroy **Whitney** and Miriam **Haverstoch** had the following child:
    8022   i.   Lowell William[13] **Whitney**[1481] born 23 October 1972 and married Dana **Birkholz** 26 April 1997. She was born 10 November 1973.[1482]

6713. **Marjorie Jean**[12] **Hyatt** (Marion Burnett[11] **Fitch**, William Herbert[10], Henry H.[9], Lucretia Lavinia[8] **Hurd**, Nathan[7], Ruth[6] **Labree**, Ruth[5] **Putnam**, Ruth[4] **Whipple**, Joseph[3], Matthew[2], Matthew[1])[1483] was born 2 July 1923 and married **Charles Beal** 25 August 1948.

Marjorie Jean **Hyatt** and Charles **Beal** had the following children:
    8023   i.   Sally[13] **Beal**[1484] married (__) **Carter**.
    8024   ii.   Nancy **Beal**[1485] married (__) **Rodewall**.
    8025   iii.   Linda **Beal**[1486] married (__) **Camden**.

6714. **Barbara Patricia**[12] **Becker** (Gladys Eloise[11] **Fitch**, William Herbert[10], Henry H.[9], Lucretia Lavinia[8] **Hurd**, Nathan[7], Ruth[6] **Labree**, Ruth[5] **Putnam**, Ruth[4] **Whipple**, Joseph[3], Matthew[2], Matthew[1])[1487] was born in Chicago, Ill. 7 September 1932 and married twice. (1) **Gordon Ray Carlson** in Chicago 15 September 1951. Gordon,[1488] son of Gunnar **Carlson** and Hildagard **Malmquist**, was born in Grand Rapids, Mich. 23 March 1931 (2) Eric **Ristau** in Conyers, Ga., 20 May 1984. Eric, son of Frederick **Ristau** and Margaret **Karran**, was born in Grand Rapids 23 March 1931 and died 1 July 1998 in McDonough, Ga..

Barbara Patricia **Becker** and Gordon Ray **Carlson** had the following children:
+   8026   i.   Barbara Christine[13] **Carlson** was born 24 November 1952.
+   8027   ii.   Gregg Gordon **Carlson** born 8 January 1963.

6716. **Marguerite**[12] **Faust** (Helen[11] **Reed**, Ora J.[10], Sylvester P.[9], Lydia[8] **Hurd**, Nathan[7], Ruth[6] **Labree**, Ruth[5] **Putnam**, Ruth[4] **Whipple**, Joseph[3], Matthew[2], Matthew[1])[1489] was born in Lowell, Mass. 1 April 1931 and died 8 December 1995 in Bangor, Maine, at 64 years of age. She married **Theodore Prescott Emery Jr.** in Lowell 15 October 1950. Theodore,[1490] son of Theodore Prescott **Emery** and Florence Aurelia **Sawyer**, was born in Carmel, Maine 3 April 1928.

Marguerite **Faust** and Theodore Prescott **Emery** Jr. had the following children born in Bangor:
    8028   i.   Charles Richard[13] **Emery**[1491] 15 May 1953 and married Mary Beth **Coffin** in Presque Isle, Maine 18 July 1977. They were living in Murfreesboro, Tenn. in 1999.

        8029   ii.   Randall Keith **Emery**[1492] 23 April 1955 and married **Charlotte Miller** in Las Vegas, Clark Co., Nev. 31 December 1995. They were living in Kansas City, Mo. in 1999.

+   8030   iii.   Allan Reed **Emery** 31 March 1958.

+   8031   iv.   Theodore Prescott **Emery** III 8 December 1960.

6717. **Charles Allen**[12] **Faust** (Helen[11] **Reed**, Ora J.[10], Sylvester P.[9], Lydia[8] **Hurd**, Nathan[7], Ruth[6] **Labree**, Ruth[5] **Putnam**, Ruth[4] **Whipple**, Joseph[3], Matthew[2], Matthew[1])[1493] was born in Lowell, Mass. 15 November 1933 and married **Beverly Woods** in Schenectady, N.Y. 7 July 1962. Beverly,[1494] daughter of Robert **Woods** and Edith **Hardy**, was born 13 April 1937.

Charles Allen **Faust** and Beverly **Woods** had the following children:

        8032   i.   Elizabeth[13] **Faust**[1495] born 17 June 1965 and married David **Ellis** in Massachusetts 30 March 1996.

        8033   ii.   Charles **Faust**[1496] born in Schenectady 16 March 1969 and married Lisa **Keegan** in Greenville, S.C. 5 October 1996.

6718. **Nan Ellen**[12] **Bursek** (Janet Ruth[11] **Walthers**, Edward William[10], Sarah Martha[9] **Whitcomb**, Walter Scott[8], Roxelane[7] **Putnam**, Bailey[6], Timothy[5], Ruth[4] **Whipple**, Joseph[3], Matthew[2], Matthew[1])[1497] was born in Manitowoc, Wisc. 17 July 1957 and married **Paul J. Jagemann** there 21 April 1979. Paul,[1498] son of Paul **Jagemann** and Pauline **Gurchinoff**, was born in Manitowoc 8 January 1957.

Nan Ellen **Bursek** and Paul J. **Jagemann** had the following children:

        8034   i.   Erin Elizabeth[13] **Jagemann**[1499] born 18 April 1983.

        8035   ii.   Anthony Paul **Jagemann**[1500] born 13 March 1986.

6719. **Sue Ann**[12] **Bursek** (Janet Ruth[11] **Walthers**, Edward William[10], Sarah Martha[9] **Whitcomb**, Walter Scott[8], Roxelane[7] **Putnam**, Bailey[6], Timothy[5], Ruth[4] **Whipple**, Joseph[3], Matthew[2], Matthew[1])[1501] was born in Manitowoc, Wisc. 20 May 1960 and married **Thomas Sheldon Mielke** there 30 July 1983. Thomas,[1502] son of Sheldon **Mielke** and Mary **Birmingham**, was born in Atkinson, Wisc. 10 November 1960.

Sue Ann **Bursek** and Thomas Sheldon **Mielke** had the following child:

        8036   i.   Kathryn Regina[13] **Mielke**[1503] born 3 May 1987.

6722. **Virginia Stevens**[12] **Blankenhorn** (Virginia Coe[11] **Miller**, Georgianna Lucille[10] **Ammermann**, Anna Lydia[9] **Whitcomb**, Walter Scott[8], Roxelane[7] **Putnam**, Bailey[6], Timothy[5], Ruth[4] **Whipple**, Joseph[3],

Matthew[2], Matthew[1])[1504] was born in Pasadena, Calif. 25 May 1947 and married **Harold David Murphy** in Edinburgh, Scotland 19 June 1982. Harold,[1505] son of Edward **Murphy** and Florence **Harold**, was born in Tel Aviv, Israel 31 December 1952.

Virginia Stevens **Blankenhorn** and Harold David **Murphy** had the following child:
  8037 i. Charlotte Olivia Stevens[13] **Murphy**[1506] born in Portrush, Co. Antrim, Northern Ireland 11 January 1987.

  6724. **Stephen Howard**[12] **Singer** (Peggy Jean[11] **Miller**, Georgianna Lucille[10] **Ammermann**, Anna Lydia[9] **Whitcomb**, Walter Scott[8], Roxelane[7] **Putnam**, Bailey[6], Timothy[5], Ruth[4] **Whipple**, Joseph[3], Matthew[2], Matthew[1])[1507] was born in San Pedro, Calif. 10 January 1953 and married **Frances Sims** in Denver, Colo. 19 September 1987. Frances,[1508] daughter of Seymour **Sims** and Joan **Davis**, was born in Detroit, Mich. 19 July 1955. Both Stephen and Frances are geologists.

Stephen Howard **Singer** and Frances **Sims** had the following children born in Denver:
  8038 i. Scott Louis[13] **Singer**[1509] 18 July 1989.
  8039 ii. Sarah Christine **Singer**[1510] 11 August 1992.

  6725. **Andrew Porter**[12] **Singer** (Peggy Jean[11] **Miller**, Georgianna Lucille[10] **Ammermann**, Anna Lydia[9] **Whitcomb**, Walter Scott[8], Roxelane[7] **Putnam**, Bailey[6], Timothy[5], Ruth[4] **Whipple**, Joseph[3], Matthew[2], Matthew[1])[1511] was born in San Pedro, Calif. 25 January 1955 and married **Susan Elizabeth McNamara** in Santa Barbara, Calif. 20 July 1985. Susan, daughter of Dr. Thomas **McNamara** and Jean **Harrison**, was born in Oxnard, Calif. 27 November 1954.

Andrew Porter **Singer** and Susan Elizabeth **McNamara** had the following children born in Santa Cruz:
  8040 i. Patrick McNamara[13] **Singer**[1512] 8 February 1987.
  8041 ii. Gregory Harrison **Singer**[1513] 16 May 1989.
  8042 iii. David Whitcomb **Singer**[1514] 16 May 1989.

  6737. **Leland Glea**[12] **Sherburne Jr.** (Dorothy Mae[11] **Deal**, Koli Horace[10], Ettie Laura[9] **Coykendall**, Laura Emeline[8] **Putnam**, Hiram[7], Bailey[6], Timothy[5], Ruth[4] **Whipple**, Joseph[3], Matthew[2], Matthew[1])[1515] was born in Kalamazoo, Mich. 3 July 1939 and married **Beverly Jean Wright** in Roseland, Newton Co., Ind. 17 September 1960. Beverly, daughter of

Raymond Hugh **Wright** and Adelaide **Twyla**, was born in Marcellus, Cass Co., Mich. 16 January 1942.

Leland Glea **Sherburne** Jr. and Beverly Jean **Wright** had the following children:
+ 8043 i. Leland Glea[13] **Sherburne** III born 18 July 1961.
    8044 ii. Amy Jean **Sherburne**[1516] born in Kalamazoo 15 July 1969. Adopted.

6738. **James Lewis**[12] **Sherburne** (Dorothy Mae[11] **Deal**, Koli Horace[10], Ettie Laura[9] **Coykendall**, Laura Emeline[8] **Putnam**, Hiram[7], Bailey[6], Timothy[5], Ruth[4] **Whipple**, Joseph[3], Matthew[2], Matthew[1])[1517] was born in Kalamazoo, Mich. 16 October 1941 and married **Marilyn Darda** in Decatur, Van Buren Co., Mich. 31 December 1962. Marilyn,[1518] daughter of Charles Thomas **Darda** and Georgianna Edna **Louzon**, was born in Chicago, Ill. 18 September 1944.

James Lewis **Sherburne** and Marilyn **Darda** had the following children:
+ 8045 i. Jamie Lynn[13] **Sherburne** born 10 July 1963.
+ 8046 ii. Paula Jean **Sherburne** born 21 May 1964.
    8047 iii. James Lewis **Sherburne**[1519] born in Niles, Berrien Co., Mich. 21 June 1968.

6739. **Douglas Bernard**[12] **Sherburne** (Dorothy Mae[11] **Deal**, Koli Horace[10], Ettie Laura[9] **Coykendall**, Laura Emeline[8] **Putnam**, Hiram[7], Bailey[6], Timothy[5], Ruth[4] **Whipple**, Joseph[3], Matthew[2], Matthew[1])[1520] was born in Stockbridge, Mason Co., Mich. 30 November 1942 and married **Marianne Ketchum** in Lawton, Van Buren Co., Mich. 14 October 1961. She was born in Dallas, Tex. 23 December 1944.[1521]

Douglas Bernard **Sherburne** and Marianne **Ketchum** had the following children:
    8048 i. Lora Lynn[13] **Sherburne**[1522] born 3 March 1962 in Paw Paw, Mich. and died 24 June 1981 in Gobles, Van Buren Co., Mich. at 19 years of age.
    8049 ii. Steven Douglas **Sherburne**[1523] born 15 October 1963 in Paw Paw and married Judy Ann **Westcott** in Gobles 27 July 1985. She was born in Allegan, Allegan Co., Mich. 16 March 1965.[1524]
    8050 iii. Sarah Ann **Sherburne**[1525] born in Kalamazoo, Mich. 1 December 1975.

6741. **Alan Franklin**[12] **Smith** (Louise Elizabeth[11] **Deal**, Kirk James[10], Ettie Laura[9] **Coykendall**, Laura Emeline[8] **Putnam**, Hiram[7], Bailey[6], Timothy[5], Ruth[4] **Whipple**, Joseph[3], Matthew[2], Matthew[1])[1526] was born in Corpus Christi, Nueces Co., Tex. 26 January 1943 and married twice, (1) **Janet Sienkiewitz** in 1965. She was born in Muskegon, Muskegon Co., Mich. 22 February 1944. (2) **Vicky Law** 12 August 1978.

Alan Franklin **Smith** and Janet **Sienkiewitz** had the following children:
- 8051 i. Seren[13] **Smith**[1527] born in Lansing, Mich. in March 1971 and died the month of birth.
- 8052 ii. Jolyn **Smith**[1528] born in Charlotte, Eaton Co., Mich. 3 January 1972.
- 8053 iii. Nathan Alan **Smith**[1529] born in St. Johns, Clinton Co., Mich. 18 October 1973.

6742. **Kirk Wells**[12] **Smith** (Louise Elizabeth[11] **Deal**, Kirk James[10], Ettie Laura[9] **Coykendall**, Laura Emeline[8] **Putnam**, Hiram[7], Bailey[6], Timothy[5], Ruth[4] **Whipple**, Joseph[3], Matthew[2], Matthew[1])[1530] was born in Riverside, Calif. 17 September 1946 and married **Christel Fromm** in Ft. Campbell, Christian Co., Ky. 30 November 1966. He was born in Germany 30 September 1943.[1531]

Kirk Wells **Smith** and Christel **Fromm** had the following children:
- 8054 i. Donna Louise[13] **Smith**[1532] born in Ft. Campbell 24 February 1967 and married Grief **Lynch** in Dillon, Dillon Co., S.C., 22 July 1991.
- 8055 ii. Carmen **Smith**[1533] born in Ft. Bragg, Mendocino Co., Calif. 6 March 1972.

6744. **Sue Lynn**[12] **Smith** (Louise Elizabeth[11] **Deal**, Kirk James[10], Ettie Laura[9] **Coykendall**, Laura Emeline[8] **Putnam**, Hiram[7], Bailey[6], Timothy[5], Ruth[4] **Whipple**, Joseph[3], Matthew[2], Matthew[1])[1534] was born in Ovid, Clinton Co., Mich. 19 February 1951 and married **Gary Lee Sipkovsky** in St. Johns, Clinton Co., Mich., 14 July 1973. He was born in St. Johns 11 January 1951.[1535]

Sue Lynn **Smith** and Gary Lee **Sipkovsky** had the following children:
- 8056 i. Adrienne Lee[13] **Sipkovsky**[1536] born in Lansing, Mich. 16 May 1978.
- 8057 ii. Jessie Lynn **Sipkovsky**[1537] born in Lansing 1 July 1980.
- 8058 iii. Cory Franklin **Sipkovsky**[1538] born in Holt, Ingham Co., Mich. 10 February 1983.

6745. **Dwight David**[12] **Smith** (Louise Elizabeth[11] **Deal**, Kirk James[10], Ettie Laura[9] **Coykendall**, Laura Emeline[8] **Putnam**, Hiram[7], Bailey[6], Timothy[5], Ruth[4] **Whipple**, Joseph[3], Matthew[2], Matthew[1])[1539] was born in St. Johns, Clinton Co., Mich. 6 August 1952 and married **Mary Poisson** 15 December 1984. She was born in Detroit 22 February 1958.[1540]

Dwight David **Smith** and Mary **Poisson** had the following children:
  8059 i. Samantha Elizabeth[13] **Smith**[1541] born in Lansing, Mich. 29 November 1985.
  8060 ii. Hannah **Smith**[1542] born in Lansing 11 February 1989.
  8061 iii. Joshua **Smith**[1543] was born in Lansing 6 April 1993.

6746. **Franklin Wilbur**[12] **Smith** (Louise Elizabeth[11] **Deal**, Kirk James[10], Ettie Laura[9] **Coykendall**, Laura Emeline[8] **Putnam**, Hiram[7], Bailey[6], Timothy[5], Ruth[4] **Whipple**, Joseph[3], Matthew[2], Matthew[1])[1544] was born in St. Johns, Clinton Co., Mich. 17 February 1962. Buried under an oak tree north of St. Johns. He married twice. (1) **Claudia Rowe** in Lansing, Mich. 26 March 1984. (2) **Katherine Scott** in Lansing 1 October 1988. She was born in Lansing 23 February 1960.[1545]

Franklin Wilbur **Smith** and Katherine **Scott** had the following child:
  8062 i. Kaitlin Suzanne[13] **Smith**[1546] born in Lansing, 25 May 1994.

ENDNOTES, GENERATION TWELVE

1. and 2. Chaffee to Whipple, *2 Letters.*
3. and 4. Dodge to Whipple, *Letter, 6 April 1993.*
5. through 7. Ahrens to Whipple, *Letter, 25 May 1990.*
8. Jones to Whipple, *Letter 05/21/1991 & 01/16/1997.*
9. Obituary of Proctor Patterson Jones, *San Francisco Chronicle,* San Francisco, Calif. (8 April 1999).
10. through 12. Jones to Whipple, *Letter 05/21/1991 & 01/16/1997.*
13. P. T. Whipple, *3 Letters.*
14. through 19. J.A. Whipple, *2 Letters.*
20. through 22. Davis to Whipple, *Letter, 26 March 1989.*
23. and 24. Taylor P. Pearson to Blaine Whipple. Letter dated 6 March 1989 at 6531 Divine St., McLean, Va. 22101. In possession of Whipple (2004). Family group sheets and pedigree sheets provided. No sources other than personal knowledge cited. (Hereafter T. Pearson to Whipple, *Letter, 6 March 1989*).
25. through 29. Carlisle to Whipple, *Ltr, 20 March 1989.*
30. C.L. Whipple to Whipple, *Letter, 2 May 1989.*
31. Obituary of Charles L. Whipple, *Telegram & Gazette,* Worcester, Mass. (14 May 1991), A9.
32. *Telegram & Gazette,* Worcester, Mass., 14 May 1991, p. A9.
33. through 37. Kyle to Whipple, *2 Letters.*
38. through 48. Bayles to Whipple, *2 letters.*
49. and 50. Sudikas to Whipple, *Letter, 8 June 1998.*
51. through 65. Bayles to Whipple, *2 letters.*
66. through 72. Kelly to Whipple, *Letter, 17 May 1999.*
73. Burke's, *Presidential Families,* 463-74.
74. and 75. Ibid., 473.
76. through 98. Wise to Whipple, *3 Letters.*
99. through 102. Rosamond Naylor to Blaine Whipple. Letter dated 24 Nov. 1998 at 20623 Natchez Dr., Sun City West, Ariz. 85375. In possession of Whipple (2004). (Hereafter Naylor to Whipple, *Letter, 24 Nov. 1998*).
103. and 104. Wanda Ellis Leszkiewicz-Warren Julian Loring Family Group Sheet, supplied 16 Sept. 1998 by Wanda E. Loring, 164 Eileen St., Yarmouth, Mass. 02675-2009. In possession of Whipple (2004) No documentation provided. The information is from personal knowledge of her immediate family. (Hereafter Leszkiewicz-Loring, *Family Group Sheet*).
105. through 137. Storey to Whipple, *5 letters.*
138. through 154. Keener to Whipple, *Letters 30 May & 6 June 2000.*
155. through 166. Putnam-Whipple, *Family Group Sheet.*
167. through 177. Burke's, *Presidential Families,* 504.
178. through 187. Ibid., 505.
188. through 195. Workman to Whipple, *Letter, 26 April 1998.*
196. through 198. Huse to Whipple, *2 Letters.*
199. through 202. P. Whipple to B. Whipple, *Letter, 3 Jan. 1989.*
203. through 205. Bills to Whipple, *Letter, Nov. 1995.*
206. and 207. H. Byington to Whipple, *2 Letters.*
208. through 210. Adams to Whipple, *3 Letters.*
211. through 246. Wanstall to Whipple, *4 Letters.*
247. through 263. Bryan Whipple to B. Whipple, *3 letters.*
264. through 268. J. Whipple to Whipple, *Letter, 11 July 1989.*

{ G 1184 }

269. through 278. D. Whipple to B. Whipple, *Letter, 9 Feb. 1989.*
279. through 284. D. Whipple to B. Whipple, *Letter, 9 Feb. 1989* and H. Whipple to B. Whipple, *Letter 04/20/1993.*
285. H.Whipple to B. Whipple, *Letter, 04/20/1993.*
286. through 304. D. Whipple to B. Whipple, *Letter, 9 Feb. 1989.*
305. through 307. Woodworth to Whipple, *3 Letters.*
308. through 310. Dorian to Whipple, *Letter, 21 Aug. 2000.*
311. through 314. Ross to Whipple, *2 Letters.*
315. through 323. Reighard to Whipple, *2 Letters.*
324. Shannon-Kennison, *Family Group Sheet.*
325. through 327. Henry Whipple, 2:43.
328. through 340. Ibid., 2:44.
341. through 343. Ibid., 2:45.
344. and 345. L. Whipple to Whipple, *7 Letters.*
346. through 360. D.L. Whipple to Whipple, *Letter, 9 May 1994.*
361. through 368. Canaday to Whipple, *Various e-mail messages.*
369. through 374. Newcomer to Whipple, *Letter 14 April 1993.*
375. through 383. Henry Whipple, 2:36-7.
384. through 395. Joseph Whipple, *Family Bible.*
396. through 398. Matthais-Whipple, *Pedigree.*
399. through 401. Talmud-Whipple, *Family Group Sheets.*
402. through 405. E. Whipple to B. Whipple, *Various Letters.*
406. V. Whipple to B. Whipple, *Letter, 22 March 1989.*
407. Ibid.; and Thomas to Whipple, *Letter, 24 Jan. 2000.*
408. through 410.V. Whipple to B. Whipple, *Letter, 22 March 1989.*
411. Thomas to Whipple, *Letter, 24 Jan. 2000.*
412. through 418. E. Whipple to B. Whipple, *Various Letters.*
419. and 420. *Marshall Messenger*, Marshall, Minn., 25 April 1977.
421. through 426. Alfreda (Whipple) Smith to Blaine Whipple. Letters dated 16 Dec. 1988; 1 March 1989; 20 April 1993 at 1925 Mohawk Dr., Olathe, Kans. 66062. In possession of Whipple (2004). Enclosures included family group sheets, newspaper articles, and obituaries. (Hereafter A. Whipple to B. Whipple, *Various Letters*).
427. through 429. E. Whipple to B. Whipple, *Various Letters.*
430. Genealogy, *Western NY,* 262; and Thomas to Whipple, *Letter, 24 Jan. 2000.*
431. Thomas to Whipple, *Letter, 24 Jan. 2000.*
432. and 433. Thomas Walton Whipple-Elizabeth Ann Whiting Family Group Sheet, Supplied 18 April 1989 by Thomas W. Whipple, 2250 Par Lane, #1105, Willoughby Hills, Ohio 44094. In possession of Whipple (2004). Pedigree chart also provided. Source of early information from *The Genealogy and Family History of Western New York* by William R. Cutter, published in 1910. (Hereafter Whiting-Whipple, *Family Group Sheet*).
434. through 436. Thomas to Whipple, *Letter, 24 Jan. 2000.*
437. through 441. Burroughs, *Burroughs Ancestors.*
442. Henry Whipple, 2:30.
443. Ibid., 2:28.
444. through 446. Ibid., 2:30.
447. C. Whipple to B. Whipple, *3 Letters.*
448. through 452. Robert Hugh Whipple-Eleanor Bailey Family Group Sheet, supplied 7 Jan. 1997 by Eleanor (Bailey) Whipple, P. O. Box 280, Lyndonville, N. Y. 14098. In possession of Whipple (2004). These sheets represent the personal knowledge of the submitter. (Hereafter Bailey - Whipple, *Family Group Sheet*).

453. through 457. C. Whipple to B. Whipple, *3 Letters*.
458. Scully to Whipple, *E-Mail, 26 Mar. 2000*.
459. Henry Whipple, 2:32.
460. through 464. Scully to Whipple, *E-Mail, 26 Mar. 2000*.
465. through 469. Avery - Whipple, *Pedigree Chart*.
470. through 508. Moore to Whipple, *Letter 2 May 1994*.
509. through 513. Samuel Morgan I-Betsey Whipple Family Group Sheets.
514. through 523. Prescott to Whipple, *7 letters*.
524. Crawford to Whipple, *4 Letters*.
525. Orr to Whipple, *13 Letters*.
526. and 527. Crawford to Whipple, *4 Letters*.
528. Orr to Whipple, *13 Letters*.
529. Crawford to Whipple, *4 Letters*.
530. and 531. Orr to Whipple, *13 Letters*.
532. Crawford to Whipple, *4 Letters*.
533. Orr to Whipple, *13 Letters*.
534. through 537. Schlarbaum to Whipple, *Letter 7 March 1996*.
538. through 541. Orr to Whipple, *13 Letters*.
542. Horner to Whipple, *4 Letters*.
543. through 545. Orr to Whipple, *13 Letters*.
546. and 547. Horner to Whipple, *4 Letters*.
548. Orr to Whipple, *13 Letters*.
549. through 553. Horner to Whipple, *4 Letters*.
554. through 558. Orr to Whipple, *13 Letters*.
559. and 560. Clifford Hoffman McKinley to Blaine Whipple. Letters dated 30 Sept. 1989 and 17 Nov. 1995 at R.R. 2, Walker, Iowa 52352. In possession of Whipple (2004). Included family group sheets. (Hereafter C. McKinley to Whipple, *2 Letters*).
561. and 562. Elizabeth E. (McKinley) Heiserman to Blaine Whipple. Letters dated 16 June 1989 and 27 November 1995 at 825 Church St., Apt. 14, Jesup, Iowa 50648. In possession of Whipple (2004). Included family group sheets. (Hereafter Heiserman to Whipple, *2 Letters*).
563. and 564. Bernard Laverne McKinley to Blaine Whipple. Letter dated 22 Aug. 1994 at 28 Silver Lake, Waterloo, Iowa 50702. In possession of Whipple (2004). (Hereafter B. McKinley to Whipple, *Letter, 22 Aug. 1994*).
565. through 571. Orr to Whipple, *13 Letters*.
572. and 573. D. McKinley to Whipple, *5 Letters*.
574. through 615. Orr to Whipple, *13 Letters*.
616. and 617. Belva Jean (McKinley) Oldridge to Blaine Whipple. Letters dated 5 April 1993 and 17 Nov. 1995 at 2984 270th St., Winthrop, Iowa 50682. In possession of Whipple (2004). Included family group sheets. (Hereafter B. Oldridge to Whipple, *2 Letters*).
618. through 620. Orr to Whipple, *13 Letters*.
621. Hintze to Whipple, *Letter 28 Nov. 1995*.
622. Orr to Whipple, *13 Letters*.
623. through 626. Hintze to Whipple, *Letter 28 Nov. 1995*.
627. through 629. Kearns to Whipple, *Letter, 4 Aug. 1987*.
630. through 638. Kearns-Whipple, *Family Group Sheets*.
639. Ibid.; and P. Kearns obit, *L. A. Times*.
640. through 646. Kearns-Whipple, *Family Group Sheets*.
647. and 648. W.P. Whipple to B. Whipple, *3 Letters*.
649. *The Gazette*, Cedar Rapids, Iowa, 26 Nov. 2001, p. 5B.

650. through 653. E. (Whipple) West to B. Whipple, *4 Letters*.
654. Barr-Whipple, *Family Group Sheets*; and Ziegler to Whipple, *2 Letters*.
655. Ziegler to Whipple, *2 Letters*.
656. and 657. Barr-Whipple, *Family Group Sheets*.
658. through 672. Jane Whipple to B. Whipple, *15 Letters*.
673. through 674. C. Mack to Whipple, *2 Letters*.
675. Ibid.; and Colleen Castner to Blaine Whipple. letter dated 12 Jan. 2003 at 133 S.W. Normandy Rd., Apt. 7, Normandy Park, Wash. 98166. In possession of Whipple (2004). (Hereafter Castner to Whipple, *Letter, 12 Jan. 2003*).
676. through 680. C. Mack to Whipple, *2 Letters*.
681. Jane Whipple to B. Whipple, *15 Letters*; and Haight to Whipple, *6 Letters*.
682. and 683. Jane Whipple to B. Whipple, *15 Letters*.
684. William C. Whipple - Frances M. Schoelerman family group sheet, supplied October 1995 by William C. Whipple, 107 2nd Ave., Keystone, Iowa 52249. In possession of Whipple (2004). This sheet is personal to the family and cites no documentation. (Hereafter Whipple - Schoelerman, *Family Group Sheet*).
685. Obituary of William C. Whipple, *Cedar Rapids Gazette*, Cedar Rapids, Iowa (21 June 1998).
686. Whipple - Schoelerman, *Family Group Sheet*.
687. *Cedar Rapids Gazette*, Cedar Rapids, Iowa, 21 June 1998.
688. and 689. R. Whipple to B. Whipple, *9 Letters*.
690. through 694. Haight to Whipple, *6 Letters*.
695. through 699. Jane Whipple to B. Whipple, *15 Letters*.
700. Bilderback to Whipple, *Letter, 11 Feb. 1996*.
701. Jane Whipple to B. Whipple, *15 Letters*.
702. Bilderback to Whipple, *Letter, 11 Feb. 1996*.
703. Jane Whipple to B. Whipple, *15 Letters*.
704. through 706. Bilderback to Whipple, *Letter, 11 Feb. 1996*.
707. through 724. Jane Whipple to B. Whipple, *15 Letters*.
725. and 726. William George Castner-Colleen Lou Gordon Family Group Sheet, supplied 15 March 1994 by Colleen (Gordon) Castner, 133 SW Normandy Rd., Apt. 7, Normandy Park, Wash. 98166. In possession of Whipple (2004) This sheet represents personal knowledge citing no documentation. (Hereafter Castner - Gordon, *Family Group Sheet*).
727. Jo Anne (Gordon) Settlemyer to Blaine Whipple. Letter dated 27 May 1994 at 470 Nicklaus Dr. S.E., Rio Rancho, N. Mexico 87124. In possession of Whipple (2004). Included family group and pedigree sheets. (Hereafter Settlemyer to Whipple, *Letter, 27 May 1994*).
728. Greer to Whipple, *2 Letters*.
729. and 730. Thomas L. Gallaher to Blaine Whipple. Letters dated 2 Sept. 1993, 18 July, and 14 Aug. 2000, and 10 Dec. 2002 at 1106 Robin Rd., Muscatine, Iowa 52761. In possession of Whipple (2004. (Hereafter T. Gallaher to Whipple, *4 Letters*).
731. through 735. David Lyle Gallaher to Blaine Whipple. Letter dated 7 Dec. 1995 at 496 400th St., Joice, Iowa 50446. In possession of Whipple (2004). (Hereafter D. Gallaher to Whipple, *Letter, 7 Dec. 1995*).
736. T. Gallaher to Whipple, *4 Letters*.
737. through 742. Jane Whipple to B. Whipple, *15 Letters*.
743. through 746. Robert Mark Whipple-Carol Mary Nekola family group sheet, supplied October 1995 by Robert Mark Whipple, Rt. 1, Dysart, Iowa 52224. In possession of Whipple (2004). This sheet is for their immediate family and cites no documentation. (Hereafter Whipple - Nekola, *Family Group Sheet*).
747. through 759. Jane Whipple to B. Whipple, *15 Letters*.

760. through 764. E. (Whipple) West to B. Whipple, *4 Letters*.
765. John Philip Crandell, his home, Tuscon, Aria. with Blaine Whipple, February 1997 Notes in possession of Whipple (2004).
766. E. (Whipple) West to B. Whipple, *4 Letters*; and Birth announcement of James Earl Whipple, *Vinton Review*, Vinton, Iowa (1 Nov. 1911), "Born to Mr. and Mrs. Blaine Whipple Sunday Oct. 29, 1911, a son. This is the second child, the former being a daughter.
767. through 769 E. (Whipple) West to B. Whipple, *4 Letters*.
770. Patricia Ellen "Pat" (Whipple) Drotzman to Blaine Whipple. Letter dated 25 Aug. 1988 at 703 E. 18th, Yankton, S. Dak 57078. In possession of Whipple (2004). She is the author's sister. (Hereafter Drotzman to Whipple, *Letter, 25 Aug. 1988*); and Patricia Ellen Whipple, Birth certificate No. 077-22833, Registered No. 254, 1 Feb. 1929, Iowa State Department of Health, Des Moines, Iowa.
771. and 772 Drotzman to Whipple, *Letter, 25 Aug. 1988*.
773. Theresa Ann Drotzman to Blaine Whipple. 6 May 2000 at bdrotz@byelectric.com (701 E. 19th, Yankton, S. Dak. 57078). In possession of Whipple (2004). (Hereafter T. Drotzman to Whipple, *E-Mail 6 May 2000*).
774. Daniel Lee Drotzman to Blaine Whipple. Letter dated 2 Sept. 1998 at 5975 - 18 Wedgewood Lane, Plymouth, Minn. 55446. In possession of Whipple (2004). (Hereafter D.Drotzman to Whipple, *Letter, 2 Sept. 1998*).
775. Robert Blaine Whipple, Birth Certificate No. 344742, Registry Book 725, South Dakota State Board of Health, Division of Vital Statistics, Pierre, S. Dak.
776. Ines Mae Peterson, Birth Certificate State File No. 3187, Multnomah Co. Registrar's No. 3219, State Bureau of Vital Statistics, Salem, Oregon.
777. B. Whipple, *Scott Genealogy*; and Nancy Jane Whipple, Birth Certificate State File No. 12502, 3 February 1932, North Dakota Department of Health, Bismarck, N. Dak.
778. B. Whipple, *Scott Genealogy*, 48.
779. *McLeod County Chronicle*, Glencoe, Minn., 6 Jan. 1988.
780. Mary Ann (Whipple) McPherson to Blaine Whipple. Letter dated 26 March 1996 at 87 Goldsmith, Littleton, Mass. 01460. In possession of Whipple (2004.) She is the author's sister. (Hereafter McPherson to Whipple, *Letter, 26 March 1996*); and Mary Ann Whipple, Birth Certificate State File No. 1659, Registered No. 520, 8 January 1938, North Dakota Department of Health, Bismarck, N. Dak.
781. McPherson to Whipple, *Letter, 26 March 1996*.
782. through 800. E. (Whipple) West to B. Whipple, *4 Letters*.
801. Dimmock-Whipple, *Family Group Sheets*; and Pittman - Woods, *Family Group Sheet*.
802. Pittman-Woods, *Family Group Sheet*.
803. through 837. Dimmock - Whipple, *Family Group Sheets*.
838. through 844. Roy Whipple to B. Whipple, *4 letters*.
845. Winifred Joyce Greeley to Blaine Whipple. Letter dated 16 June 1998 at 8176 Toyon Ave., Fair Oaks, Calif. 95628. In possession of Whipple (2004). (Hereafter as W. Greeley to B. Whipple, *Letter, 16 June 1998*).
846. through 853. Roy Whipple to B. Whipple, *4 letters*.
854. Eleanor Greeley Treddenbarger to Blaine Whipple. letter dated 31 Aug. 1997 at 6901 Sutter Ave., Carmichael, Calif 95608. in possession of Whipple (2004). (Hereafter Treddenbarger to Whipple, *Letter, 31 Aug. 1997*).
855. through 857. Roy Whipple to B. Whipple, *4 letters*.
858. Treddenbarger to Whipple, *Letter, 31 Aug. 1997*.
859. through 897. Roy Whipple to B. Whipple, *4 letters*.
898. and 899. Rumpf to Whipple, *3 letters*.
900. through 902. Treddenbarger to Whipple, *Letter, 31 Aug. 1997*.

903. and 904. Roy Whipple to B. Whipple, *4 letters.*
905. and 906. R.E. Whipple to B. Whipple, *Letter, 21 June 1996.*
907. through 917. Roy Whipple to B. Whipple, *4 letters.*
918. and 919. Brown-Hall, *Family Group Sheet.*
920. Peters to Whipple, *Letter, 21 Feb. 1997.*
921. Frederick Watson, Birth Certificate New York Department of Health.
922. Frederick Watkins, Death Certificate City of New York Department of Health.
923. Peters to Whipple, *Letter, 21 Feb. 1997.*
924. Alice Downer Briggs, Birth certificate State of New Jersey.
925. Marge E. Chandler to Blaine Whipple. Letters dated 26 June 1990, 29 April 1991, 10 May and 23 May 1993, 22 June 1993 at 3905 Road 241, New Castle, Colo. 81647. In possession of Whipple (2004.) Family group sheets and pedigree sheet provided. (Hereafter Chandler to Whipple, *5 Letters*).
926. Johnson/Whipple, *Fam. Genealogies.*
927. Chandler to Whipple, *5 Letters.*
928. through 930. Crates to Whipple, *Letter, 11 Feb. 1991.*
931. through 939. Jenkins to Whipple, *E-mail 25 March & 30 May 2000.*
940. Maris to Whipple, *Letter, 11 April 1996*; and Knowles to Whipple, *Letters 19 & 30 July 2000.*
941. Maris to Whipple, *Letter, 11 April 1996.*
942. through 944. Erbland to Whipple, *Letters, Fam. Gp. Sheets.*
945. Ibid.; and Knowles to Whipple, *Letters 19 & 30 July 2000.*
946. through 953. Erbland to Whipple, *Letters, Fam. Gp. Sheets.*
954. Ibid.; and Knowles to Whipple, *Letters 19 & 30 July 2000.*
955. through 963. Erbland to Whipple, *Letters, Fam. Gp. Sheets.*
964. G. Whipple to B. Whipple, *Letter, 23 May 1991.*
965. and 966. H.Whipple to B. Whipple, *Letter, 04/20/1993.*
967. through 970. Daley to Whipple, *8 letters.*
971. and 972. Marshall Lofland Whipple to Blaine Whipple. Letters dated 1 Dec. 1988, 27 Feb. 1989 12 Dec. 1989, 22 Jan. 1990, and 18 Feb. 1994 at 13233 15th Ave. NE, Seattle, Wash. 98125. In Possession of Whipple (2004). His sources included a family Bible and he provided extensive family groups sheets. (Hereafter M. Whipple to B. Whipple, *5 letters*).
973. through 977. G. Whipple to B. Whipple, *Letter, 23 May 1991.*
978. H.Whipple to B. Whipple, *Letter, 04/20/1993.*
979. through 986. G. Whipple to B. Whipple, *Letter, 23 May 1991.*
987. through 994. Brandt to Whipple, *3 letters.*
995. through 997. Bills to Whipple, *Letter, Nov. 1995.*
998. through 1012. Knowles to Whipple, *Letters 19 & 30 July 2000.*
1013. through 1020. Henry Whipple, 2:77.
1021. Ibid., 2:77; and Krueger to Whipple, *Letter, 7 Aug. 2000.*
1022. Henry Whipple, 2:77; and Krueger to Whipple, *Letter, 7 Aug. 2000.*
1023. through 1027. Henry Whipple, 2:77.
1028. through 1034. Herrick - Whipple, *Family Group Sheets.*
1035. through 1039. J. Davis to Whipple, *Letter, 10 Feb. 1999.*
1040. through 1057. Reinhold to Whipple, *2 Letters.*
1058. through 1072. M.M. Whipple to Whipple, *6 Letters.*
1073. through 1076. Gallop to Whipple, *Letter 1 April 1996.*
1077. and 1078. M.M. Whipple to Whipple, *6 Letters.*
1079. through 1083. Gallop to Whipple, *Letter 1 April 1996.*
1084. and 1085. M.M. Whipple to Whipple, *6 Letters.*
1086. Padgett to Whipple, *Letter, 3 Dec. 1998 & 27 July 2000*; and Clark to Whipple, *Let-*

1087. Bing to Whipple, *Letter 2 Nov. 02.*
1088. Clark to Whipple, *Letter, 4 Jan. 1999.*
1089. Bing to Whipple, *Letter 2 Nov. 02.*
1090. Clark to Whipple, *Letter, 4 Jan. 1999.*
1091. Jordan to Whipple, *3 Letters*; and Padgett to Whipple, *Letter, 3 Dec. 1998 & 27 July 2000.*
1092. and 1093. Hess to Whipple, *Letters, Mar. & Apr. 2002.*
1094. Padgett to Whipple, *Letter, 3 Dec. 1998 & 27 July 2000.*
1095. and 1096. Hess to Whipple, *Letters, Mar. & Apr. 2002.*
1097. through 1101. B. G. Holland, *9 letters.*
1102. through 1109. Powers to Whipple, *Letter 20 March 1996.*
1110. through 1112. J.F. Whipple to B. Whipple, *6 Letters.*
1113. through 1117. Solano to Whipple, *Letter, 7 Oct. 1991.*
1118. through 1121. Kurapka to Whipple, *2 Letters*; and Keener to Whipple, *Letters 30 May & 6 June 2000.*
1122. through 1124. Blackburn - Whipple, *Family Group Sheet.*
1125. through 1150. Sadler to Whipple, *Family Group Sheets.*
1151. through 1163. Smith-Ward-Whipple, *Family Group Sheet.*
1164. Jack Huey Trimmelol & Edna Pearl Sproat, Marriage Record, 15 September 1926, Marriage Book O: 344, Wilson Co., Kans. Court House.
1165. through 1169. Smith-Ward-Whipple, *Family Group Sheet.*
1170. through 1284. Brigham - Whipple, *Family Group Sheets.*
1285. and 1286. Bowman - Miner, *Family Group Sheet.*
1287. and 1288. Randazzo to Whipple, *E-mail, 25 Oct. 01.*
1289. through 1309. Tom Whipple, *Family Group Sheets.*
1310. through 1313. W.J Whipple to B. Whipple, *3 letters.*
1314. through 1318. William Whipple, Jr to Blaine Whipple. Letter dated 20 April 1989 at 395 Mercer Rd., Princeton, N. J. 08540. In possession of Whipple (2004). (Hereafter Wm. Whipple to B. Whipple, *Letter, 20 April 1989*).
1319. through 1321. Green to Whipple, *5 letters.*
1322. and 1323. Douglas L. Williams to Blaine Whipple. Letter dated 20 Sept. 1989 at 7607 Creswell Rd., Shreveport, La. 71106. In possession of Whipple (2004.) Pedigree and family group sheets provided. (Hereafter Williams to Whipple, *Letter, 20 Sept. 1989*).
1324. Carolyn Williams Easton to Blaine Whipple. Letters dated 27 April 1990 and 15 April 1993 at 6516 Bannockburn Dr., Bethesda, Md. 20817. In possession of Whipple (2004.) Included pedigree and family group sheets. (Hereafter Easton to Whipple, *2 Letters*).
1325. Williams to Whipple, *Letter, 20 Sept. 1989.*
1326. through 1332. W.J Whipple to B. Whipple, *3 letters.*
1333. Ibid.; and Katherine Collens-Jeremiah H Bartholomew, Jr. Family Group Sheet, supplied 30 April 1993 by Julia (Bartholomew) Munn, 1423 Union St., Manchester, N. H 03104. In possession of Whipple (2004). This sheet cites no documentation and is based on personal knowledge of the submitter. (Hereafter Collens - Bartholomew, *Family Group Sheet*).
1334. Collens - Bartholomew, *Family Group Sheet.*
1335. through 1339. G.A. Whipple to Whipple, *Letter, December 1998.*
1340. through 1347. Zastrow - Whipple, *Family Group Sheet.*
1348. and 1349. G. Whipple to Whipple, *2 Letters.*
1350. through 1358. HH Hildebrant to Whipple, *Letters, 2/1999; 7/2001.*
1359. through 1363. Hildebrant to Whipple, *6 letters.*
1364. Ibid.; and HH Hildebrant to Whipple, *Letters, 2/1999; 7/2001.*

1365. HH Hildebrant to Whipple, *Letters, 2/1999; 7/2001*.
1366. and 1367. Whytlaw to Whipple, *3 Letters*.
1368. Henry Whipple, 2:114.
1369. through 1374. Obituary of G. Hoyt Whipple, *The Gainesville Sun*, Gainesville, Fla. (25 May 1999).
1375. and 1376. Lothrop Withington, Jr. to Blaine Whipple. Letter dated 13 Sept. 1998 at P.O. Box 1177, Manomet, Mass. 02345. In possession of Whipple (2004). (Hereafter Withington to Whipple, *Letter, 13 Sept. 1998*).
1377. and 1378. Spencer H. Brewster-Marietta Louise Withington Family Group Sheet, supplied February 1990 by Marietta Withington Brewster, Little Forge, Old Sandwich Rd., Plymouth, Mass. 02360 In possession of Whipple (2004). This sheet is her personal knowledge of herself, husband, and their children. (Hereafter S. Brewster-Withing, *Family Group Sheet*).
1379. through 1382. Benjamin B. Brewster-Anne Platt Withington Family Group Sheet, supplied February 1990 by Anne Platt Withington, 88 Warren Ave., Plymouth, Mass. 02360. In possession of Whipple (2004). This sheet list her personal knowledge of herself and husband and their children. (Hereafter Brewster-Withington, *Family Group Sheet*).
1383. through 1385. Paul Wittington to Blaine Whipple. Letter dated 15 Feb. 1990 at Sandwich Rd., Plymouth, Mass. 02360. In possession of Whipple (2004). (Hereafter P. Wittington, *Letter, 15 Feb. 1990*).
1386. through 1390. Withington-Whipple, *Family Group Sheet*.
1391. through 1394. P. Whipple to B. Whipple, *2 Letters*.
1395. Henry Whipple, 2:120.
1396. Miller - Whitley, *Family Group Sheets*; and Henry Whipple.
1397. through 1400. Henry Whipple, 2:120; and Miller - Whitley, *Family Group Sheets*.
1401. Miller - Whitley, *Family Group Sheets*; and Henry Whipple, *Whipple Descendents*.
1402. and 1403. Henry Whipple, 2:121; and Miller - Whitley, *Family Group Sheets*.
1404. through 1413. Miller - Whitley, *Family Group Sheets*.
1414. Ruth L. Nichior, comp., *Vital Statistics From the Town Records of Hampton Falls, NH Through 1899* (Hampton Falls, N. H.: Hampton Falls Free Library, 1976). (Hereafter Nichipor, *Hampton Falls Vital Records*).
1415. through 1421. Miller - Whitley, *Family Group Sheets*.
1422. Nichipor, *Hampton Falls Vital Records*.
1423. through 1432. Miller - Whitley, *Family Group Sheets*.
1433. and 1434. Klassy to Whipple, *5 Letters*.
1435. through 1438. Liles to Whipple, *2 Letters*.
1439. through 1450. Wilkin to Whipple, *3 Letters*.
1451. through 1454. B. Williamson to B. Whipple, *3 Letters*.
1454. through 1456. J. Whipple to B. Whipple, *5 Letters*.
1457. through 1460. Galen Whipple to Whipple, *Letter, 11 June 1998*.
1461. through 1464. Arnold to Whipple, *Letter 9 July 1998*.
1465. and 1466. Vella to Whipple, *Ltrs, 8-22 & 9-1 2000*.
1467. through 1469. Haven - Jordan, *Family Group Sheets*.
1470. through 1471. Kahler to Whipple, *Letter, 18 Sept. 1991*.
1472. through 1482. Whitney-Hall, *Family Group Sheets*.
1483. through 1488. Ristau to Whipple, *2 Letters*.
1489. through 1496. Emery to Whipple, *2 Letters*.
1497. through 1515. Singer to Whipple, *2 letters*.
1516. through 1546. Deal - Putnam, *Family Group Sheet*.

{ G 1191 }

THIRTEENTH GENERATION

6747. **Elsa Getchell**[13] **Chaffee** (Anne Montgomery[12] **Getchell**, Arthur Vinton[11], Alice Leiby[10] **Coombs**, Joseph Jackson[9], Andrew[8], Ebenezer[7], Elisabeth[6] **Pratt**, Hannah[5] **Kennedy**, Elizabeth[4] **Annable**, Anne[3] **Whipple**, Matthew[2], Matthew[1])[1] was born in Washington, D. C. 5 September 1943 and married **Daniel J. Distelhorst** in Wellesley Hills, Norfolk Co., Mass. 27 June 1970. He was born 7 October 1945.[2] Following graduation from Wheelock College, Boston, Mass. with a B. A. in 1965, Elsa taught in the Newton, Middlesex Co., Mass. school system and at the Kamehameha School in Honolulu, Oahu, Hawaii. She is the Director of Professional Programs, Lindaman Seminar Center, Division of Continuing Studies, Whitworth College at Spokane, Spokane Co., Wash. (1999).

Elsa Getchell **Chaffee** and Daniel J. **Distelhorst** had the following children:
    8063 i.   Jeffrey Scott[14] **Distelhorst**[3] born in Honolulu 21 December 1972.
    8064 ii.   Nathan **Distelhorst**[4] born in Spokane 28 March 1976.

6749. **Owen Leroy**[13] **French** (Addie Ruth[12] **Owen**, Martha Anne[11] **Young**, Ruth Ann[10] **Cross**, William[9], Jesse[8], Stephen[7], Sarah[6] **Boardman**, Thomas[5], Elizabeth[4] **Perkins**, Elizabeth[3] **Whipple**, Matthew[2], Matthew[1])[5] was born in Canaan, Essex Co.,Vt. 27 November 1916 and married **Hilda Estella Spencer** there 6 May 1939. Hilda,[6] daughter of Harry Delmore **Spencer** and Blanche Maude **House**, was born in Stewartstown, Coos Co., N.H. 30 November 1917 and died 15 July 1992 in Contoocook, Merrimac Co., N.H., at 74 years of age.

Owen Leroy **French** and Hilda Estella **Spencer** had the following child born in Laconia, Belknap Co., N. H.:
    8065 i.   Nancy Linda[14] **French**[7] 28 August 1943 and married **David Michael Dodge** in Portsmouth, Rockingham Co., N.H. 13 August 1966. She spent her freshman year at Middlebury College Vermont then transferred to the U. of New Hampshire, Durham, Strafford Co., where she was graduated in 1965 with a B. A. degree in Sociology. She then earned a Masters Degree in Library Science at Simmons College in Boston and later an M. A. in English from the U. of N.H. She worked as a College Librarian for several years including 18 years at the N.H. Vocational Technical College in Portsmouth and Stratham, both Rockingham Co. Her interest in family history-genealogy began in the mid 1970s and she has compiled three volumes of cemetery inscriptions from about 20 towns in the Colebrook, Coos Co.,

N.H. area (available from Higginson Books, Salem, Mass.). She does continuing research on families in the area and is known as "the cemetery lady."

6751. **Melinda**[13] **Jones** (Proctor Patterson[12], Ferne Catherine[11] **Patterson**, Proctor[10], Phebe Smith[9] **Whipple**, Stephen[8], Jonathan[7], Capt. Stephen[6], John[5], Matthew[4], Lt. John[3], Matthew[2], Matthew[1])[8] was born in Cleveland, Cuyahoga Co., Ohio 25 May 1943 and married **David Windisch**.

Melinda **Jones** and David **Windisch** had the following children:
+   8066   i.   Katherine Patterson[14] **Windisch** born 10 January 1963.
      8067   ii.   David Anthony **Windisch**[9] born in Miami, Dade Co., Fla. 31 May 1970.
      8068   iii.   Matthew Anthony **Windisch**[10] born in Miami 1 August 1971.

6752. **Greta Patterson**[13] **Jones** (Proctor Patterson[12], Ferne Catherine[11] **Patterson**, Proctor[10], Phebe Smith[9] **Whipple**, Stephen[8], Jonathan[7], Capt. Stephen[6], John[5], Matthew[4], Lt. John[3], Matthew[2], Matthew[1])[11] was born in Cleveland, Cuyahoga Co., Ohio 27 January 1946 and married **Michael Jones** in Winston-Salem, Forsyth Co., N.C. 2 June 1968.

Greta Patterson **Jones** and Michael **Jones** had the following child born in Wilson, Wilson Co., N. C.:
      8069   i.   Andrew Petree[14] **Jones**[12] 18 February 1976.

6753. **John Beverly**[13] **Jones** (Proctor Patterson[12], Ferne Catherine[11] **Patterson**, Proctor[10], Phebe Smith[9] **Whipple**, Stephen[8], Jonathan[7], Capt. Stephen[6], John[5], Matthew[4], Lt. John[3], Matthew[2], Matthew[1])[13] was born in Palo Alto, Santa Clara Co., Calif. 29 January 1949 and married **Roslyn Lewis** in Los Angeles, Los Angeles Co., Calif. 4 March 1984. She was born in Sydney, New South Wales, Australia 24 April 1953.[14]

John Beverly **Jones** and Roslyn **Lewis** had the following children born in Santa Monica, Los Angeles Co., Calif.:
      8070   i.   Austin Patterson[14] **Jones**[15] 28 August 1984.
      8071   ii.   Sydney Mara **Jones**[16] 16 April 1987.

6754. **Martha**[13] **Jones** (Proctor Patterson[12], Ferne Catherine[11] **Patterson**, Proctor[10], Phebe Smith[9] **Whipple**, Stephen[8], Jonathan[7], Capt. Stephen[6], John[5], Matthew[4], Lt. John[3], Matthew[2], Matthew[1])[17] was born in Palo Alto, Santa Clara Co., Calif. 6 July 1950 and married **Theodore A. Griffinger Jr.** in San Francisco, San Franciso Co., Calif. 3 July 1973.

Martha **Jones** and Theodore A. **Griffinger** Jr. had the following children:
> 8072 i. Whitney Armstrong[14] **Griffinger**[18] born in San Francisco 27 October 1977.
> 8073 ii. Elisabeth Patterson **Griffinger**[19] born in Berkeley, Alameda Co., Calif. 3 September 1979.

6761. **John Alan**[13] **Whipple** (Kenneth[12], Walter[11], Stephen Lovett[10], Stephen[9], Jonathan[8], Jonathan[7], Capt. Stephen[6], John[5], Matthew[4], Lt. John[3], Matthew[2], Matthew[1])[20] was born in Mt. Clemens, Macomb Co., Mich. 9 June 1940 and married **Linda Marie Spehar** there 29 August 1964. Linda,[21] daughter of Louis **Spehar** and Ann **Schroeder**, was born in Detroit, Wayne Co., Mich. 1 October 1941. They were divorced in July 1992.

John Alan **Whipple** and Linda Marie **Spehar** had the following children born in Warren, MaComb Co., Mich.:
> 8074 i. Keri Anne[14] **Whipple**[22] 7 December 1967.
> 8075 ii. Bradford Ames **Whipple**[23] 12 March 1970.

6762. **Sally Ann**[13] **Davis** (Martha[12] **Whipple**, Walter[11], Stephen Lovett[10], Stephen[9], Jonathan[8], Jonathan[7], Capt. Stephen[6], John[5], Matthew[4], Lt. John[3], Matthew[2], Matthew[1])[24] was born 14 February 1936 and married **John Adams** in Nashua, Hillsborough Co., N. H. 6 April 1957.

Sally Ann **Davis** and John **Adams** had the following children:
> + 8076 i. Laurie[14] **Adams** born 26 May 1958.
> 8077 ii. Lynne **Adams**[25] born 1 June 1960.
> 8078 iii. Julie J. **Adams**[26] born 5 June 1964.

6764. **Susan Allen**[13] **Davis** (Martha[12] **Whipple**, Walter[11], Stephen Lovett[10], Stephen[9], Jonathan[8], Jonathan[7], Capt. Stephen[6], John[5], Matthew[4], Lt. John[3], Matthew[2], Matthew[1])[27] was born 3 November 1945 and married **Gregory A. Hackney**.

Susan Allen **Davis** and Gregory A. **Hackney** had the following child:
> 8079 i. Stacey Allen[14] **Hackney**[28] born 25 September 1973.

6765. **Taylor Peter**[13] **Pearson** (Virginia Augusta[12] **Taylor**, Augusta[11] **Whipple**, Stephen Lovett[10], Stephen[9], Jonathan[8], Jonathan[7], Capt. Stephen[6], John[5], Matthew[4], Lt. John[3], Matthew[2], Matthew[1])[29] was born in Waterbury, New Haven Co., Conn. 27 February 1939 and married **Louise Goldsborough Patton** in Leesburg, Va. 1 July 1961. Louise,[30] daughter of Francis Landey **Patton** and Louise Dulin **Harrison**, was born in Washington, D.C. 23 September 1938.

Taylor Peter **Pearson** and Louise Goldsborough **Patton** had the following children:
+   8080   i.   Kristen Louise[14] **Pearson** born 25 June 1964.
    8081   ii.   Stephen Christopher **Pearson**[31] born at the U.S. Naval Hospital in Key West, Monroe Co., Fla. 22 October 1966 and married Wendy Nieske **Little** in Vienna, Fairfax Co., Va. 28 December 1996.[32]
+   8082   iii. David Scott **Pearson** born 8 April 1972.

6766. **Stuart Robin**[13] **Pearson** (Virginia Augusta[12] **Taylor**, Augusta[11] **Whipple**, Stephen Lovett[10], Stephen[9], Jonathan[8], Jonathan[7], Capt. Stephen[6], John[5], Matthew[4], Lt. John[3], Matthew[2], Matthew[1])[33] was born in Cleveland, Cuyahoga Co., Ohio 13 July 1942 and married **Lois Jane Bletcher** in Milwaukee, Milwaukee Co., Wisc. 19 August 1967. Lois,[34] daughter of Edgar George **Bletcher** and Jennie Florence **Murphy**, was born in Milwaukee 19 September 1946.

Stuart Robin **Pearson** and Lois Jane **Bletcher** had the following children:
    8083   i.   David Andrew[14] **Pearson**[35] born in Jacksonville, Pulaski Co., Ark. 12 November 1969.
    8084   ii.   Joy Anne **Pearson**[36] born in Abington, Penn. 16 August 1971 and married Darren Allen **Hartman** in Milwaukee 7 June 1997.

6767. **Kristen Augusta**[13] **Pearson** (Virginia Augusta[12] **Taylor**, Augusta[11] **Whipple**, Stephen Lovett[10], Stephen[9], Jonathan[8], Jonathan[7], Capt. Stephen[6], John[5], Matthew[4], Lt. John[3], Matthew[2], Matthew[1])[37] was born in Providence, Providence Co., R. I. 1 January 1946 and married **Neil Melvin Palash** in West Bend, Washington Co., Wisc. 17 June 1967. Neil,[38] son of Bernard **Palash** and Agatha (__), was born in Milwaukee, Milwaukee Co., Wisc. 28 June 1945.

Kristen Augusta **Pearson** and Neil Melvin **Palash** had the following children born in West Bend:
    8085   i.   Tamara Augusta[14] **Palash**[39] 11 February 1969 and married Robert **Powell** in Milwaukee 31 December 1994.
    8086   ii.   Rebecca Amanda **Palash**[40] 30 November 1971 and married Christopher **Barth** in Milwaukee 28 August 1993.

{ G 1195 }

6769. **Craig Robert**[13] **Carlisle** (Carol Ashby[12] **Taylor**, Augusta[11] **Whipple**, Stephen Lovett[10], Stephen[9], Jonathan[8], Jonathan[7], Capt. Stephen[6], John[5], Matthew[4], Lt. John[3], Matthew[2], Matthew[1])[41] was born in Milwaukee, Milwaukee Co., Wisc. 19 October 1949 and married **Margaret Mary McLaughlin** in South Windsor, Hartford Co., Conn. 26 May 1978. Margaret,[42] daughter of Bernard **McLaughlin** and Dorothy (__), was born in Hartford, Hartford Co., Conn. 9 May 1956.

Craig Robert **Carlisle** and Margaret Mary **McLaughlin** had the following children born in Hartford:
    8087   i.   Laura Cara[14] **Carlisle**[43] 24 August 1978.
    8088   ii. Erin Quinn **Carlisle**[44] 13 July 1981.
    8089   iii. Luke Taylor **Carlisle**[45] 21 March 1986.

6771. **Charles Augustus**[13] **Whipple II** (Charles Lewis[12], Charles Augustus[11], Charles Lewis[10], Stephen[9], Jonathan[8], Jonathan[7], Capt. Stephen[6], John[5], Matthew[4], Lt. John[3], Matthew[2], Matthew[1])[46] was born in Boston, Suffolk Co., Mass. 2 September 1946 and married twice. (1) **Kathleen Ann Brown**. (2) **Randi vonSteinwehr**.

Charles Augustus **Whipple** II and Kathleen Ann **Brown** had the following child born in Boston:
    8090   i.   Sarah Landon[14] **Whipple**[47] 21 June 1974.

Charles Augustus **Whipple** II and Randi **vonSteinwehr** had the following child born in Worcester, Worcester Co. Mass:
    8091   ii. Thomas Livingston **Whipple**[48] 11 July 1992.

6772. **Jonathan Landon**[13] **Whipple** (Charles Lewis[12], Charles Augustus[11], Charles Lewis[10], Stephen[9], Jonathan[8], Jonathan[7], Capt. Stephen[6], John[5], Matthew[4], Lt. John[3], Matthew[2], Matthew[1])[49] was born in Boston, Suffolk Co., Mass. 6 March 1949 and married **Margaret Agnew**.

Jonathan Landon **Whipple** and Margaret **Agnew** had the following child:
    8092   i.   Alison[14] **Whipple**[50] born in California.

6776. **Marion H.**[13] **Brown** (Jeanette R.[12] **Whipple**, John Whitmore[11], Sidney[10], John Hitchings[9], John[8], Jonathan[7], Capt. Stephen[6], John[5], Matthew[4], Lt. John[3], Matthew[2], Matthew[1])[51] was born in Fitchburg, Worcester Co., Mass. 23 November 1934 and married **Robert H. Kyle** there 26 February 1959. Robert,[52] son of Richard **Kyle** and Hazel **King**, was born in Charleston, Penobscot Co., Maine 12 March 1933.

Marion H. **Brown** and Robert H. **Kyle** had the following children:
+ 8093 i. Cindy Jean[14] **Kyle** born 14 May 1959.
    8094 ii. Roberta Louise **Kyle**[53] born in El Paso, El Paso Co., Tex. 15 February 1964.
    8095 iii. Mitchell Edward **Kyle**[54] born in Fort Dix, Burlington Co., N.J. 13 January 1966.

6777. **Ralph Kenneth**[13] **Dose Jr.** (Ralph Kenneth[12], Joanna Evans[11] **Keyes**, Charles Evans[10], George Everett[9], Mary Alden[8] **Gould**, Benjamin[7], Martha[6] **Gilbert**, Esther[5] **Perkins**, Serg. John[4], Elizabeth[3] **Whipple**, Matthew[2], Matthew[1])[55] was born in Tulsa, Tulsa Co., Okla. 8 January 1948 and married **Pamela Diane Roegels** there 7 August 1971. Pamela,[56] daughter of Sheldon G. **Roegels** and Ina Jane **Haywood**, was born in Tulsa 26 December 1950. Ken earned a B.A. in Sociology from the U. of Tulsa in 1971. He began work in the savings and loan industry and eventually joined the Bank of Oklahoma as Vice President and head of the Mortgage Banking Division.

Ralph Kenneth **Dose** Jr. and Pamela Diane **Roegels** had the following children born in Tulsa:
    8096 i. Cynthia Elise[14] **Dose**[57] 7 March 1977.
    8097 ii. Kendra Diane **Dose**[58] 10 October 1983.

6781. **Karen Sue**[13] **Murphy** (Dorothy Gene[12] **Keyes**, George Everett[11], Charles Evans[10], George Everett[9], Mary Alden[8] **Gould**, Benjamin[7], Martha[6] **Gilbert**, Esther[5] **Perkins**, Serg. John[4], Elizabeth[3] **Whipple**, Matthew[2], Matthew[1])[59] was born in Topeka, Shawnee Co., Kans. 14 November 1940 and married **Wayne Neal Sage** in Osage, Kans. in 1958. Wayne,[60] son of Carl C. **Sage** and Amelia M. **Job**, was born in Osage 15 November 1935. Karen was adopted by Anthony Suidikas in July 1945 and took his surname.

Karen Sue **Murphy** and Wayne Neal **Sage** had the following children:
+ 8098 i. Ricky Ray[14] **Sage** born 12 May 1959.
+ 8099 ii. Brenda Kay **Sage** born 21 November 1960.
+ 8100 iii. Brian Wayne **Sage** born 11 July 1964.
    8101 iv. Robert Russell **Sage**[61] born in Topeka 26 March 1970. He was graduated from Kansas State University, Manhattan.

6782. **Gary Lee**[13] **Suidikas** (Dorothy Gene[12] **Keyes**, George Everett[11], Charles Evans[10], George Everett[9], Mary Alden[8] **Gould**, Benjamin[7], Martha[6] **Gilbert**, Esther[5] **Perkins**, Serg. John[4], Elizabeth[3] **Whipple**, Matthew[2], Matthew[1])[62] was born in Fort Bragg, Cumberland Co., N.C. 3

October 1946 and married **Susan Marie Hedges** in Harrogate, England 28 June 1975. Susan,[63] daughter of Richard **Hedges** and Agnes A. **Reda**, was born in Baltimore, Baltimore City Co., Md. 13 October 1951. Gary served in the U.S. Army with tours of duty in Korea and Ethiopia.

Gary Lee **Suidikas** and Susan Marie **Hedges** had the following children born in Harrogate:
  8102 i. Jennifer Kay[14] **Suidikas**[64] 25 June 1976.
  8103 ii. Richard Anthony **Suidikas**[65] 4 April 1980.

6783. **Wayne Anthony**[13] **Suidikas** (Dorothy Gene[12] **Keyes**, George Everett[11], Charles Evans[10], George Everett[9], Mary Alden[8] **Gould**, Benjamin[7], Martha[6] **Gilbert**, Esther[5] **Perkins**, Serg. John[4], Elizabeth[3] **Whipple**, Matthew[2], Matthew[1])[66] was born in Fort Bragg, Cumberland Co., N.C. 3 January 1948 and married twice. (1) **Valerie Jean Bryant** in El Paso, El Paso Co., Tex. 8 January 1977. She was born 8 December 1958. They were divorced in 1980. (2) **Beatrice (Porras) Logan** in El Paso 25 March 1983. Beatrice, daughter of David Rodrigues **Porras** and Maria de Jesus **Castillo**, was born in Ysleta, El Paso Co., Tex. 4 February 1944.

Wayne Anthony **Suidikas** and Valerie Jean **Bryant** had the following child born in El Paso:
  8104 i. Christopher Wayne[14] **Suidikas**[67] 9 February 1978.

6784. **Georgia Kay**[13] **Suidikas** (Dorothy Gene[12] **Keyes**, George Everett[11], Charles Evans[10], George Everett[9], Mary Alden[8] **Gould**, Benjamin[7], Martha[6] **Gilbert**, Esther[5] **Perkins**, Serg. John[4], Elizabeth[3] **Whipple**, Matthew[2], Matthew[1])[68] was born in Fort Bragg, Cumberland Co., N.C. 14 August 1949 and married **Patrick Michael Keith** in El Paso, El Paso Co., Tex. 5 July 1969. Patrick,[69] son of Raleigh Rex **Keith** and Doris **Ketchersid**, was born in Roswell, Chaves Co., N. Mex. 28 January 1951. She earned a B. A. from the U. of Texas, Austin and is a school teacher. The family resides in El Paso.

Georgia Kay **Suidikas** and Patrick Michael **Keith** had the following children born in El Paso:
  8105 i. Trevor Michael[14] **Keith**[70] 18 September 1970.
  8106 ii. Kyle Wayne **Keith**[71] 28 June 1973.

6786. **Gene Stanley**[13] **Suidikas** (Dorothy Gene[12] **Keyes**, George Everett[11], Charles Evans[10], George Everett[9], Mary Alden[8] **Gould**, Benjamin[7], Martha[6] **Gilbert**, Esther[5] **Perkins**, Serg. John[4], Elizabeth[3] **Whip-**

ple, Matthew², Matthew¹)⁷² was born in San Francisco, San Francisco Co., Calif. 28 March 1952 and married **Barbara Jean Kent** in Fairfax, Fairfax City Area Co., Va. 13 October 1990. Barbara,⁷³ daughter of Charles Scott **Kent** and Ruth B. **Jines**, was born in Bloomington, Hennepin Co., Minn. 2 November 1956. Gene earned both a B. S. and a M. S. from Texas Tech University, Lubbock, with majors in Mathematics and Computers.

Gene Stanley **Suidikas** and Barbara Jean **Kent** had the following children born in Fairfax:
  8107 i. Erin Christine¹⁴ **Suidikas**⁷⁴ 8 November 1995.
  8108 ii. John Charles **Suidikas**⁷⁵ 8 November 1995.

6787. **Cynthia Marie**¹³ **Suidikas** (Dorothy Gene¹² **Keyes**, George Everett¹¹, Charles Evans¹⁰, George Everett⁹, Mary Alden⁸ **Gould**, Benjamin⁷, Martha⁶ **Gilbert**, Esther⁵ **Perkins**, Serg. John⁴, Elizabeth³ **Whipple**, Matthew², Matthew¹)⁷⁶ was born in Bremerhaven, Germany 29 November 1957 and married **William Ray Covey Jr.** in Juarez, Mexico 17 July 1974. William,⁷⁷ son of William Ray **Covey** and Peggy Ann **Bray**, was born in Rapid City, Pennington Co., S. Dak. 14 March 1957.

Cynthia Marie **Suidikas** and William Ray **Covey** Jr. had the following children:
  8109 i. Jeremy Michael¹⁴ **Covey**⁷⁸ born in Dallas, Dallas Co., Tex. 29 January 1976.
  8110 ii. Autumn Marie **Covey**⁷⁹ born in Lubbock, Lubbock Co., Tex. 20 November 1977.
  8111 iii. Heather Nichole **Covey**⁸⁰ born in El Paso, El Paso Co., Tex. 6 September 1986.
  8112 iv. Shelby Ann **Covey**⁸¹ born in El Paso 25 November 1991.

6790. **Kenneth Dale**¹³ **Bayles** (Lawrence Gordon¹², Eunice Britt¹¹ **Keyes**, Charles Evans¹⁰, George Everett⁹, Mary Alden⁸ **Gould**, Benjamin⁷, Martha⁶ **Gilbert**, Esther⁵ **Perkins**, Serg. John⁴, Elizabeth³ **Whipple**, Matthew², Matthew¹)⁸² was born in Amarillo, Potter Co., Tex. 6 August 1948 and married **Carole Jean Knowles** in Lubbock, Lubbock Co., Tex. 9 July 1971. Carole,⁸³ daughter of James Allan **Knowles** and Mary Ruth **Lang**, was born in Lubbock 26 January 1951. Kenneth earned a degree in Pharmacy at Southwestern Oklahoma State University at Weatherford, graduating Magna Cum Laude. He was President of his Honor Society and is listed in *Who's Who Among Students in American Universities and Colleges 1970-71*. He later studied at the Sunset School of Preaching, Lubbock, and became a Minister in the Church of Christ.

Kenneth Dale **Bayles** and Carole Jean **Knowles** had the following children:
- 8113 i. Aaron Lawrence[14] **Bayles**[84] born in Sharon, Mercer Co., Penn. 1 June 1977.
- 8114 ii. Benjamin Caleb **Bayles**[85] born in Amarillo, Potter Co., Tex. 1 September 1981.
- 8115 iii. Micah Nicole **Bayles**[86] born in Amarillo 15 August 1984.
- 8116 iv. Candace Elizabeth **Bayles**[87] born in Fort Worth, Tarrant Co., Tex. 20 April 1991.

6791. **Shirley Ann**[13] **Bayles** (Lawrence Gordon[12], Eunice Britt[11] **Keyes**, Charles Evans[10], George Everett[9], Mary Alden[8] **Gould**, Benjamin[7], Martha[6] **Gilbert**, Esther[5] **Perkins**, Serg. John[4], Elizabeth[3] **Whipple**, Matthew[2], Matthew[1])[88] was born in Amarillo, Potter Co., Tex. 13 July 1950 and married three times. (1) **Gary Wayne Smith** in Shamrock, Potter Co., Tex. 11 January 1972. They were divorced in 1974. (2) **Eddy Sisneros** in Albuquerque, Bernalillo Co., N. Mex. 18 June 1976. Eddy,[89] son of Edward **Sisneros** and Irene (_), was born in Albuquerque 9 April 1953. They were divorced in 1984. (3) **Russ Morrison** in Oklahoma City, Oklahoma Co., Okla. 30 December 1989.

Shirley Ann **Bayles** and Gary Wayne **Smith** had the following children:
- 8117 i. Gary Wayne[14] **Smith** Jr.[90] born 10 April 1973.
- 8118 ii. Jarrett Blaine **Smith**[91] born in Canyon, Randall Co., Tex. 10 April 1973. He was adopted by Eddie **Sisneros.**

Shirley Ann **Bayles** and Eddy **Sisneros** had the following child born in Albuquerque:
- 8119 iii. Brittney Ann **Sisneros**[92] 1 October 1978.

6795. **Glennis Paige**[13] **Bayles** (George Vincent[12], Eunice Britt[11] **Keyes**, Charles Evans[10], George Everett[9], Mary Alden[8] **Gould**, Benjamin[7], Martha[6] **Gilbert**, Esther[5] **Perkins**, Serg. John[4], Elizabeth[3] **Whipple**, Matthew[2], Matthew[1])[93] was born in Oklahoma City, Oklahoma Co., Okla. 9 August 1955 and married **Steven Ray Black** in Bethany, Oklahoma Co., Okla. 29 January 1983. Steven,[94] son of Robert Ray **Lemmons** and Mary Katherine **Minick**, was born in Oklahoma City 17 January 1958. Steve was adopted by Kenneth Ray Black after his mother's divorce from R. R. Lemons and marriage to Kenneth. He is the owner of Steve Black Construction Co. in Piedmont, Canadian Co., Okla. Glennis earned a B. A. degree in Sociology (1977) and an M. A. in Education (1987) from Bethany Nazarene College, Bethany. Her work experience began with the Oklahoma Department of Human Resources. In 1990 she began a teaching career in the Putnam City, Dewey Co., Okla. school system.

Glennis Paige **Bayles** and Steven Ray **Black** had the following children born in Oklahoma City:

    8120   i.   Jessica Ryan[14] **Black**[95] 2 August 1984.
    8121   ii. Steven Tanner **Black**[96] 27 April 1987.

6796. **Keri**[13] **Bayles** (John Junior[12], Eunice Britt[11] **Keyes**, Charles Evans[10], George Everett[9], Mary Alden[8] **Gould**, Benjamin[7], Martha[6] **Gilbert**, Esther[5] **Perkins**, Serg. John[4], Elizabeth[3] **Whipple**, Matthew[2], Matthew[1])[97] was born in Lubbock, Lubbock Co., Tex. 14 October 1947 and married **Thomas Lockwood Cordell** in Oxnard, Ventura Co., Calif. 20 May 1972. Thomas,[98] son of Edward Lawrence **Cordell** and Ida June **Lockwood**, was born in Riverside, Riverside Co., Calif. 24 January 1946. Tom was a Nuclear Reactor Operator in the U.S. Navy Submarine Service, retiring from the Naval Reserve as a Chief Petty Officer in 1991 after 24 years of service. He earned a degree in Architecture and Civil Engineering in 1986 from Texas Tech University, Lubbock, Lubbock Co. He was then employed as an Architect/Engineer by the Facilities Service Office in Kent, King Co., Wash. Keri earned a degree in History and Anthropology at the U. of California, Santa Barbara in 1971 and in Occupational Therapy at the U. of Pennsylvania, Philadelphia in 1972.

Keri **Bayles** and Thomas Lockwood **Cordell** had the following children born in Lubbock:

    8122   i.   Matthew Bayles[14] **Cordell**[99] 27 July 1974.
    8123   ii.   Krista **Cordell**[100] 17 January 1976.
    8124   iii. Kathleen **Cordell**[101] 26 January 1978.
    8125   iv. Chelsea **Cordell**[102] 20 October 1984.

6797. **John Dean**[13] **Bayles** (John Junior[12], Eunice Britt[11] **Keyes**, Charles Evans[10], George Everett[9], Mary Alden[8] **Gould**, Benjamin[7], Martha[6] **Gilbert**, Esther[5] **Perkins**, Serg. John[4], Elizabeth[3] **Whipple**, Matthew[2], Matthew[1])[103] was born in Lubbock, Lubbock Co., Tex. 4 January 1949 and marrried twice. (1) **Catherine Ann Mills** in Oxnard, Ventura Co., Calif. 21 June 1969. She is the daughter of Henry **Mills** and Mary (__).[104] They were divorced in 1976. (2) **Andrea Esther Krat** in Oceanside, San Diego Co., Calif. 6 May 1979. Andi,[105] daughter of Rubin Louis **Krat** and Caroline Shirley **Lerner**, was born in Hempstead, Long Island Co., N.Y. 12 January 1951. Dean earned a B. A. in Environmental Design from California State University, San Diego in 1972. He is a Construction Engineer specializing in design and fabrication of fine woodworking and furniture.

John Dean **Bayles** and Andrea Esther **Krat** had the following children born in San Diego, San Diego Co.:

    8126   i.   Ashley Elizabeth[14] **Bayles**[106] 8 June 1982.
    8127   ii.   Allison Robin **Bayles**[107] 10 December 1986.

6798. **Britt Clark**[13] **Bayles** (John Junior[12], Eunice Britt[11] **Keyes**, Charles Evans[10], George Everett[9], Mary Alden[8] **Gould**, Benjamin[7], Martha[6] **Gilbert**, Esther[5] **Perkins**, Serg. John[4], Elizabeth[3] **Whipple**, Matthew[2], Matthew[1])[108] was born in Oxnard, Ventura Co., Calif. 9 January 1956 and married **Betty Ann Fukutomi** there 21 June 1980. Betty,[109] daughter of Joe **Fukutomi** and Setsuko **Moroizumi**, was born in Oxnard 21 August 1956. Britt earned a Doctorate in Clinical Pharmacy in 1984 from the U. of California at San Francisco. He is a Lieutenant Commander in the Navy and has been stationed at Bethesda Naval Hospital, the U.S. Navy Hospital, Yokosukak Japan, and at San Diego. While living in Japan, Britt and Betty Ann adopted their two daughters, both at 5 days of age.

Britt Clark **Bayles** and Betty Ann **Fukutomi** adopted the following children:

    8128   i.   Britt Yuju[14] **Bayles**[110] born in Hiroshima, Japan 12 September 1988. Her birth name was **Johji Kondo** and the full name of the birth place is Minami-Ku, Hiroshima-Shi, Hiroshima-Ken, Honshu, Japan.
    8129   ii.   Micaela Erisa **Bayles**[111] born in Yamaguchi, Japan 5 June 1990. Her birth name is Hanako **Agari** and the complete name of her birth place is Hofu-shi, Yamaguchi-Ken, Honshu, Japan.

6799. **Meredith**[13] **Bayles** (John Junior[12], Eunice Britt[11] **Keyes**, Charles Evans[10], George Everett[9], Mary Alden[8] **Gould**, Benjamin[7], Martha[6] **Gilbert**, Esther[5] **Perkins**, Serg. John[4], Elizabeth[3] **Whipple**, Matthew[2], Matthew[1])[112] was born in Oxnard, Ventura Co., Calif. 16 September 1961 and married **Brian Loomis Sherman** in Las Vegas, Clark Co., Nev. 17 July 1983. Brian,[113] son of George Jack **Heil** and Susannah Louise **Loomis**, was born in Cleveland, Cuyahoga Co., Ohio 9 December 1956. He was adopted by William Herbert **Sherman**, his mother's second husband. He is a Registered Nurse. Merrry was awarded a B. S. in Speech and Hearing Therapy from U. of California, Santa Barbara in June 1983 and is a Church School Teacher.

Meredith **Bayles** and Brian Loomis **Sherman** had the following children born in California:
    8130   i.   Amber Joi[14] **Sherman**[114] in Santa Barbara, Santa Barbara Co., 15 May 1984.
    8131   ii.   Alyssa Brianne Loomis **Sherman**[115] in Santa Barbara 21 November 1985.
    8132   iii.   Amy Kerilyn **Sherman**[116] in Oxnard 26 January 1987.

6800. **Janice Elizabeth**[13] **Burchard** (Ruth Alene[12] **Bayles**, Eunice Britt[11] **Keyes**, Charles Evans[10], George Everett[9], Mary Alden[8] **Gould**, Benjamin[7], Martha[6] **Gilbert**, Esther[5] **Perkins**, Serg. John[4], Elizabeth[3] **Whipple**, Matthew[2], Matthew[1])[117] was born in Abilene, Taylor Co., Tex. 8 January 1950 and married **Paul John Lawrence** in Yukon, Canadian Co., Okla. 22 March 1975. Paul,[118] son of John Bryant **Lawrence** and Marie **Hicks**, was born in Ardmore, Okla. 10 June 1948. Paul earned a Ph.D. in Physics from the U. of Oklahoma, Norman, Cleveland Co., and is a College Professor at Tarleton State University, Stephenville, Erath Co., Tex. The family resides at Fort Worth, Tarrant Co., Tex. Janice was awarded a B. A from Southwestern Oklahoma University at Weatherford, Custer Co., and an M. A. from Central State University in Edmond, Oklahoma Co., Okla. She is a public school Special Education Teacher.

Janice Elizabeth **Burchard** and Paul John **Lawrence** had the following child born in Forth Worth:
    8133   i.   David Tarrant Buchard[14] **Lawrence**[119] 28 August 1989.

6801. **Ray Alan**[13] **Burchard** (Ruth Alene[12] **Bayles**, Eunice Britt[11] **Keyes**, Charles Evans[10], George Everett[9], Mary Alden[8] **Gould**, Benjamin[7], Martha[6] **Gilbert**, Esther[5] **Perkins**, Serg. John[4], Elizabeth[3] **Whipple**, Matthew[2], Matthew[1])[120] was born in Abilene, Taylor Co., Tex. 22 December 1952 and married **Floy Barbara Martinez** in Albuquerque, Bernalillo Co., N. Mex. 3 April 1982. Barbara,[121] daughter of Samuel Martin **Martinez** and Elena **Tejada**, was born in El Paso, El Paso Co., Tex. 8 May 1955. She is a Court Interpreter for Spanish and American sign language. Ray was graduated from Southwestern Oklahoma State University, Weatherford, Custer Co., and works in electronics at the Sandia Laboratory in Albuquerque.

Ray Alan **Burchard** and Floy Barbara **Martinez** had the following children born in Albuquerque:
    8134   i.   Deborah Denyse[14] **Burchard**[122] 12 February 1986.
    8135   ii.   Tamara Joi **Burchard**[123] 17 November 1988.

6804. **Ada Helen**[13] **Thomas** (Dilman Kar[12], Burt Byron[11], Ambrose[10], Dilla[9] **Beeman**, Daniel[8], Lydia[7] **Cogswell**, Samuel[6], Hannah[5] **Browne**, Judith[4] **Perkins**, Elizabeth[3] **Whipple**, Matthew[2], Matthew[1])[124] was born in Conrad, Grundy Co., Iowa 27 April 1917 and died 3 November 1995 in Austin, Travis Co., Tex., at 78 years of age. She married **Frank Warren Kelly Jr.** in Clearwater, Pinellas Co., Fla. 9 October 1938. Frank,[125] son of Frank Warren **Kelly** Sr. and Bertha **Doner**, died 24 September 1973 in Big Springs, Howard Co., Tex., at 55 years of age.

Ada Helen **Thomas** and Frank Warren **Kelly** Jr had the following child:
+   8136   i.   Daniel Robert[14] **Kelly**.

6805. **Vera Maky**[13] **Driscoll** (Eva Dillie[12] **Thomas**, Burt Byron[11], Ambrose[10], Dilla[9] **Beeman**, Daniel[8], Lydia[7] **Cogswell**, Samuel[6], Hannah[5] **Browne**, Judith[4] **Perkins**, Elizabeth[3] **Whipple**, Matthew[2], Matthew[1])[126] was born in Pittsfield, Berkshire Co., Mass. and married **Edgar Quaries Rooker** in Atlanta, Fulton Co., Ga.

Vera Maky **Driscoll** and Edgar Quaries **Rooker** had the following child:
     8137   i.   Martha Elaine[14] **Rooker**[127] married Jeffrey David **Jack**.

6808. **John**[13] **Coolidge** (Pres. John Calvin[12], Col. John Calvin[11], Sarah Almeda[10] **Brewer**, Sally[9] **Brown**, Israel Putnam[8], Adam[7], Adam[6], Jacob[5], Judith[4] **Perkins**, Elizabeth[3] **Whipple**, Matthew[2], Matthew[1])[128] was born in Northampton, Hampshire Co., Mass. 7 September 1906 and married **Florence Trumbull** in Plainfield, Windham Co., Conn. 23 September 1929. Florence,[129] daughter of Connecticut Gov. John H. **Trumbull**[130] and Maude **Usher**, was born in Plainfield 30 November 1904. He earned a B. A. at Amherst College, Amherst, Hampshire Co., and was an Executive, Director, and Trustee of various corporations. He was living in retirement at Farmington, Hartford Co., Conn. in 1975.

John **Coolidge** and Florence **Trumbull** had the following children:
+   8138   i.   Cynthia[14] **Coolidge** born 28 October 1933.
+   8139   ii.   Lydia **Coolidge** born 14 August 1939.

6822. **Eugenia**[13] **Wise** (Robert E.[12], Anna Hale[11] **Ellis**, Frederick Orin[10], Mary Phillips[9] **Brown**, Aaron[8], John[7], John[6], Jacob[5], Judith[4] **Perkins**, Elizabeth[3] **Whipple**, Matthew[2], Matthew[1])[131] was born in Beverly, Essex Co., Mass. 14 January 1942 and married **Orson S. Hathaway** in Melrose, Middlesex Co., Mass. 22 June 1963. Orson, son of Orson S. **Hathaway** Sr. and Dorothy **Dane**, was born in Manchester, Hillsborough

Co., N.H. 25 January 1941. They were divorced in Placentia, Orange Co., Calif. 2 February 1982.

Eugenia **Wise** and Orson S. **Hathaway** had the following children:
    8140   i.   Danforth O.[14] **Hathaway**[132] born in Vandenberg AFB, Santa Barbara, Santa Barbara Co., Calif. 23 December 1964.
+   8141   ii.   Paul D. **Hathaway** born 25 March 1970.

6823. **Barbara**[13] **Wise** (Robert E.[12], Anna Hale[11] **Ellis**, Frederick Orin[10], Mary Phillips[9] **Brown**, Aaron[8], John[7], John[6], Jacob[5], Judith[4] **Perkins**, Elizabeth[3] **Whipple**, Matthew[2], Matthew[1])[133] was born 2 March 1944 and married **John M. Lynch III** who was born 16 January 1945.[134]

Barbara **Wise** and John M. **Lynch** III L had the following children:
    8142   i.   Christina[14] **Lynch**[135] born 29 April 1972.
    8143   ii.   Michael F. **Lynch**[136] born 5 December 1974.
    8144   iii.   Matthew P. **Lynch**[137] born 8 March 1982.

6824. **John O.**[13] **Wise** (Robert E.[12], Anna Hale[11] **Ellis**, Frederick Orin[10], Mary Phillips[9] **Brown**, Aaron[8], John[7], John[6], Jacob[5], Judith[4] **Perkins**, Elizabeth[3] **Whipple**, Matthew[2], Matthew[1])[138] was born 17 November 1953 and married **Lisa Marson** who was born 28 June 1957.[139]

John O. **Wise** and Lisa **Marson** had the following children:
    8145   i.   Julia A.[14] **Wise**[140] born 3 November 1987.
    8146   ii.   Rachel G. **Wise**[141] born 29 November 1989.

6825. **William C.**[13] **Saunders** (Miriam[12] **Wise**, Anna Hale[11] **Ellis**, Frederick Orin[10], Mary Phillips[9] **Brown**, Aaron[8], John[7], John[6], Jacob[5], Judith[4] **Perkins**, Elizabeth[3] **Whipple**, Matthew[2], Matthew[1])[142] was born 18 March 1945 and married **Susan Thrasher**.

William C. **Saunders** and Susan **Thrasher** had the following children:
    8147   i.   Peter[14] **Saunders**[143] born 15 October 1977.
    8148   ii.   Brynn **Saunders**[144] born 26 September 1982.

6826. **Martha**[13] **Saunders** (Miriam[12] **Wise**, Anna Hale[11] **Ellis**, Frederick Orin[10], Mary Phillips[9] **Brown**, Aaron[8], John[7], John[6], Jacob[5], Judith[4] **Perkins**, Elizabeth[3] **Whipple**, Matthew[2], Matthew[1])[145] was born 10 May 1947 and married **Bahram Nabatian**.

Martha **Saunders** and Bahram **Nabatian** had the following children:
- 8149 i. Kaveh[14] **Nabatian**[146] born 16 June 1976.
- 8150 ii. Sohrob **Nabatian**[147] born 10 July 1980.
- 8151 iii. Shireen **Nabatian**[148] born 22 November 1982.

6827. **Carolyn**[13] **Saunders** (Miriam[12] **Wise**, Anna Hale[11] **Ellis**, Frederick Orin[10], Mary Phillips[9] **Brown**, Aaron[8], John[7], John[6], Jacob[5], Judith[4] **Perkins**, Elizabeth[3] **Whipple**, Matthew[2], Matthew[1])[149] was born 5 June 1951 and married **Robert Munger**.

Carolyn **Saunders** and Robert **Munger** had the following child:
- 8152 i. Loren[14] **Munger**[150] born 11 November 1988.

6828. **William Oliver**[13] **Wise** III (William Oliver[12], Anna Hale[11] **Ellis**, Frederick Orin[10], Mary Phillips[9] **Brown**, Aaron[8], John[7], John[6], Jacob[5], Judith[4] **Perkins**, Elizabeth[3] **Whipple**, Matthew[2], Matthew[1])[151] was born in March 1954 and married **Janis Miller**.

William Oliver **Wise** III and Janis **Miller** had the following children:
- 8153 i. Robert[14] **Wise**.[152]
- 8154 ii. Kent **Wise**.[153]
- 8155 iii. Sean **Wise**.[154]

6832. **Nancy Endicott**[13] **Loring** (Wanda Ellis[12] **Leszkiewicz**, Miriam[11] **Ellis**, Frederick Orin[10], Mary Phillips[9] **Brown**, Aaron[8], John[7], John[6], Jacob[5], Judith[4] **Perkins**, Elizabeth[3] **Whipple**, Matthew[2], Matthew[1])[155] was born in Weymouth, Norfolk Co., Mass. 7 June 1952 and married **James McNulty** in Windham, Cumberland Co., Maine 7 March 1983.

Nancy Endicott **Loring** and Christopher **Porter** had the following child:
- 8156 i. William Hale[14] **Loring**[156] born in Portland, Cumberland Co., Maine 16 July 1987.

6833. **Randall Hale**[13] **Loring** (Wanda Ellis[12] **Leszkiewicz**, Miriam[11] **Ellis**, Frederick Orin[10], Mary Phillips[9] **Brown**, Aaron[8], John[7], John[6], Jacob[5], Judith[4] **Perkins**, Elizabeth[3] **Whipple**, Matthew[2], Matthew[1])[157] was born in Concord, Middlesex Co., Mass. 29 May 1954 and married **Laure Ann Bentley** in Huntington, Suffolk Co., N.Y. 26 July 1980. Laure,[158] daughter of Hebert Howard **Bentley** and Joan Barbara **Kowalczyk**, was born 6 September 1955.

Randall Hale **Loring** and Laure Ann **Bentley** had the following children:
    8157   i.   Andrew Jacobs[14] **Loring**[159] born in Bangor, Penobscot Co., Maine 29 June 1987.
    8158   ii. Victoria Helen **Loring**[160] born in Bangor 11 May 1991.

6834. **Susan Ellis**[13] **Loring** (Wanda Ellis[12] **Leszkiewicz**, Miriam[11] **Ellis**, Frederick Orin[10], Mary Phillips[9] **Brown**, Aaron[8], John[7], John[6], Jacob[5], Judith[4] **Perkins**, Elizabeth[3] **Whipple**, Matthew[2], Matthew[1])[161] was born in Mineola, Long Island, N.Y. 22 July 1958 and married **Steven Carl Leunig** in Garden City, Nassau Co., N.Y. 12 March 1983. Steven,[162] son of Robert Charles **Leunig** and Blanche Mildred **Hassum**, was born in Mineola 31 January 1955.

Susan Ellis **Loring** and Steven Carl **Leunig** had the following children born in Mineola:
    8159   i.   Warren Robert[14] **Leunig**[163] 8 October 1986.
    8160   ii. Steven Ellis **Leunig**[164] 13 August 1988.

6836. **Chester Stanley**[13] **Bragdon** (George Henry[12], Ione[11] **Andrews**, Henry[10], Caleb[9], Molly[8] **Burnham**, Capt. Westley[7], Westley[6], Elizabeth[5] **Perkins**, Jacob[4], Elizabeth[3] **Whipple**, Matthew[2], Matthew[1])[165] was born in Beverly, Essex Co., Mass. in 1898 and died in October 1962 in Essex, Essex Co., Mass., at 64 years of age. He married **Evelyn Alberta Doyle** in Essex 1 July 1930. Evelyn,[166] daughter of John J. **Doyle** and Mary **Butler**, was born in Essex in 1902 and died there in 1966, at 64 years of age.

Chester Stanley **Bragdon** and Evelyn Alberta **Doyle** had the following children:
+   8161   i.   Helen[14] **Bragdon** born 28 March 1932.
+   8162   ii. Marylyn **Bragdon** born 17 August 1933.

6837. **Henry**[13] **Bragdon** (George Henry[12], Ione[11] **Andrews**, Henry[10], Caleb[9], Molly[8] **Burnham**, Capt. Westley[7], Westley[6], Elizabeth[5] **Perkins**, Jacob[4], Elizabeth[3] **Whipple**, Matthew[2], Matthew[1])[167] was born in Beverly, Essex Co., Mass. 20 July 1899 and died in February 1978 in Falmouth, Barnstable Co., Mass., at 78 years of age. He married **Bessie Robins**.

Henry **Bragdon** and Bessie **Robins** had the following child:
+   8163   i.   Hollis[14] **Bragdon** born 11 July 1925.

6838. **William Edward**[13] **Bragdon** (George Henry[12], Ione[11] **Andrews**, Henry[10], Caleb[9], Molly[8] **Burnham**, Capt. Westley[7], Westley[6], Elizabeth[5] **Perkins**, Jacob[4], Elizabeth[3] **Whipple**, Matthew[2], Matthew[1])[168] was born in Beverly, Essex Co., Mass. 20 June 1902 and died 23 January 1984 in Milford, Worcester Co., Mass., at 81 years of age. Buried in Edgell Grove Cemetery, Framingham, Middlesex Co., Mass. He married **Caroline Cardoza** in Falmouth, Barnstable Co., Mass. 7 February 1929. She was born 20 June 1907.[169]

William Edward **Bragdon** and Caroline **Cardoza** had the following children:
- 8164 i. Estelle Martha[14] **Bragdon**[170] born 27 March 1929 and married Jack Lester **Ours** who was born 17 July 1922 and died 19 August 1980 at 58 years of age.[171]
- + 8165 ii. Natalie Janet **Bragdon** born 28 August 1930.
- + 8166 iii. Edward Ernest **Bragdon** born 12 April 1941.

6839. **Hollis L.**[13] **Bragdon** (George Henry[12], Ione[11] **Andrews**, Henry[10], Caleb[9], Molly[8] **Burnham**, Capt. Westley[7], Westley[6], Elizabeth[5] **Perkins**, Jacob[4], Elizabeth[3] **Whipple**, Matthew[2], Matthew[1])[172] was born in Beverly, Essex Co., Mass. 10 April 1904 and died in November 1980 in W. Wareham, Plymouth Co., Mass., at 76 years of age. He married **Rhoda Smith**.

Hollis L. **Bragdon** and Rhoda **Smith** had the following child:
- 8167 i. Esther[14] **Bragdon**[173] married Stanley **Taylor**. They had five children; no details provided.

6840. **Sidney H.**[13] **Bragdon** (George Henry[12], Ione[11] **Andrews**, Henry[10], Caleb[9], Molly[8] **Burnham**, Capt. Westley[7], Westley[6], Elizabeth[5] **Perkins**, Jacob[4], Elizabeth[3] **Whipple**, Matthew[2], Matthew[1])[174] was born in Beverly, Essex Co., Mass. 19 August 1905 and died 12 August 1973 in Gloucester, Essex Co., Mass., at 67 years of age. He married **Sarah Burnham** in Essex, Essex Co., Mass. 4 December 1931. Sarah,[175] daughter of Moses **Burnham** and Susan **Goodhue**, was born in Essex 23 April 1907.

Sidney H. **Bragdon** and Sarah **Burnham** had the following children:
- 8168 i. Cynthia[14] **Bragdon**[176] born in Beverly 17 July 1937 and married Robert **Cameron.**
- + 8169 ii. George **Bragdon** born 14 August 1947.

6841. **Frederick**[13] **Bragdon** (George Henry[12], Ione[11] **Andrews**, Henry[10], Caleb[9], Molly[8] **Burnham**, Capt. Westley[7], Westley[6], Elizabeth[5] **Perkins**, Jacob[4], Elizabeth[3] **Whipple**, Matthew[2], Matthew[1])[177] was born in Beverly, Essex Co., Mass. 21 May 1907 and died 1 March 1993, at 85 years of age. He married **Anna Joseph Georgia**. They were divorced. There is a question as to Anna's surname. It is given both as Anna Joseph and Anna Joseph Georgia.

Frederick **Bragdon** and Anna Joseph **Georgia** had the following child:
+   8170   i.   Adelaide Martha[14] **Bragdon** born 1 April 1931.

6842. **Esther Marjorie**[13] **Bragdon** (George Henry[12], Ione[11] **Andrews**, Henry[10], Caleb[9], Molly[8] **Burnham**, Capt. Westley[7], Westley[6], Elizabeth[5] **Perkins**, Jacob[4], Elizabeth[3] **Whipple**, Matthew[2], Matthew[1])[178] was born in Beverly, Essex Co., Mass. 14 July 1908 and married twice. (1) **Gerald Francis Bowes** in Wareham, Plymouth Co., Mass. 17 June 1929. He was born in Sommerville, Middlesex Co., Mass. 5 July 1898 and died 7 July 1980 in Erie, Erie Co., Penn., at 82 years of age.[179] (2) **Herbert Hunziker** who died in 1986.[180] Esther was adopted at age 4 by Lawrence C. Baker.

Esther Marjorie **Bragdon** and Gerald Francis **Bowes** had the following children:
+   8171   i.   Gerald[14] **Bowes** born in 1930.
+   8172   ii.   Jean Clayton **Bowes** born 10 August 1931.
+   8173   iii.   Patricia **Bowes** born 1 October 1932.
+   8174   iv.   Robert **Bowes** born in 1935.

6843. **George Austin**[13] **Bragdon** (George Henry[12], Ione[11] **Andrews**, Henry[10], Caleb[9], Molly[8] **Burnham**, Capt. Westley[7], Westley[6], Elizabeth[5] **Perkins**, Jacob[4], Elizabeth[3] **Whipple**, Matthew[2], Matthew[1])[181] was born in Beverly, Essex Co., Mass. 19 April 1911 and died 31 January 1949 in Princeton, Worcester Co., Mass., at 37 years of age. Buried at Woodside Cemetery Westminister, Worcester Co. He married **Lillian Harriet Page** in Westminster 21 July 1934. Lillian,[182] daughter of Charles Elvin **Page** and Marie Sophia **Kremon**, was born in Westminster 1 April 1909.

George Austin **Bragdon** and Lillian Harriet **Page** had the following children:
     8175   i.   Mary Nickerson[14] **Bragdon**[183] born in Gardner, Worcester Co., Mass. 20 June 1935 and married Charles Robert **Pallman** in Middleton, Butler Co., Ohio 14 February 1957. Charles,[184] son of Charles **Pallman** and Ida **May,** was born in Middleton 24 September 1932.
+   8176   ii.   Roger Henry **Bragdon** born 10 November 1937.
+   8177   iii.   Jacqueline Maie **Bragdon** born 30 March 1950.

{ G 1209 }

6845. **Lorin Marvin**[13] **Baker** (Fannie Woodberry[12] **Bragdon**, Ione[11] **Andrews**, Henry[10], Caleb[9], Molly[8] **Burnham**, Capt. Westley[7], Westley[6], Elizabeth[5] **Perkins**, Jacob[4], Elizabeth[3] **Whipple**, Matthew[2], Matthew[1])[185] was born in Beverly, Essex Co., Mass. 8 January 1897 and married **Jenny Richardson**.

Lorin Marvin **Baker** and Jenny **Richardson** had the following child:
    8178   i.   Ruth[14] **Baker**.[186]

6846. **Clifford Doty**[13] **Baker** (Fannie Woodberry[12] **Bragdon**, Ione[11] **Andrews**, Henry[10], Caleb[9], Molly[8] **Burnham**, Capt. Westley[7], Westley[6], Elizabeth[5] **Perkins**, Jacob[4], Elizabeth[3] **Whipple**, Matthew[2], Matthew[1])[187] was born in Beverly, Essex Co., Mass. 28 December 1900 and died there 19 February 1984, at 83 years of age. Buried at Central Cemetery. He married **Helen Louise Teague** in Beverly 9 May 1925. Helen,[188] daughter of Albert Franklin **Teague** and Lena Sophia **Prentiss**, was born in Beverly 12 September 1902.

Clifford Doty **Baker** and Helen Louise **Teague** had the following children:
+   8179   i.   William Otis[14] **Baker** born 22 September 1926.
+   8180   ii.   Beverly **Baker** born 29 January 1928.

6847. **Roy Woodberry**[13] **Baker** (Fannie Woodberry[12] **Bragdon**, Ione[11] **Andrews**, Henry[10], Caleb[9], Molly[8] **Burnham**, Capt. Westley[7], Westley[6], Elizabeth[5] **Perkins**, Jacob[4], Elizabeth[3] **Whipple**, Matthew[2], Matthew[1])[189] was born in Beverly, Essex Co., Mass. 25 January 1901 and died 7 March 1961 in Antrim, Hillsborough Co., N. H., at 60 years of age. He married twice. (1) **Ruth Marion Baker** in Falmouth, Barnstable Co., Mass. 20 January 1924. They were divorced. Ruth,[190] daughter of Freeman **Baker** and Ethel **Walker**, was born in Falmouth 15 November 1904 and died there 6 October 1985, at 80 years of age. Buried at Darisville Cemetery. (2) **Edith Brooke** in 1946.

Roy Woodberry **Baker** and Ruth Marion **Baker** had the following children:
+   8181   i.   Joanne Marjorie[14] **Baker** born 22 December 1926.
+   8182   ii.   Philip Woodberry **Baker** born 17 March 1929.
    8183   iii.   Richard Davis **Baker**[191] born in Barnstable 10 August 1933 and married Susan **Simpson** in Falmouth. They were divorced.

6848. **Gordon Andrews**[13] **Baker** (Fannie Woodberry[12] **Bragdon**, Ione[11] **Andrews**, Henry[10], Caleb[9], Molly[8] **Burnham**, Capt. Westley[7], Westley[6], Elizabeth[5] **Perkins**, Jacob[4], Elizabeth[3] **Whipple**, Matthew[2], Matthew[1])[192] was born in Beverly, Essex Co., Mass. 15 November 1904 and died in 1981 in N. Beverly, at 76 years of age. He married **Gladys E. Bartlett** in Beverly 28 January 1928.

Gordon Andrews **Baker** and Gladys E. **Bartlett** had the following children:
+ 8184 i. Janis[14] **Baker**.
+ 8185 ii. Norman **Baker**.
    8186 iii. Robert **Baker**[193] born abt 1929 and died of spinal meningitis abt 1935.

6849. **Otis Clayton**[13] **Baker** (Fannie Woodberry[12] **Bragdon**, Ione[11] **Andrews**, Henry[10], Caleb[9], Molly[8] **Burnham**, Capt. Westley[7], Westley[6], Elizabeth[5] **Perkins**, Jacob[4], Elizabeth[3] **Whipple**, Matthew[2], Matthew[1])[194] was born in Beverly, Essex Co., Mass. 21 March 1908 and died 25 March 1988 in Zephyrhills, Pasco Co., Fla., at 80 years of age. He married twice. (1) **Audrey Robinson Glover** in Beverly. She was born in Beverly in 1914 and died in 1971 in Eastpaston,[195] Maine, at 57 years of age.[196] Buried at Falmouth, Barnstable Co., Mass. (2) **Emily Bunnell** in West Baldwin, Cumberland Co. Maine. Emily,[197] daughter of Fred J. **Bunnell** and Mable A. **Kimball**, was born in Westbrook, Cumberland Co., Maine 12 June 1906.

Otis Clayton **Baker** and Audrey Robinson **Glover** had the following children:
+ 8187 i. Louise[14] **Baker** born 16 February 1943.
    8188 ii. Dr. Arthur Willard **Baker**[198] born in Beverly 16 April 1944 and married Mary Helen **Barnett** in Falmouth 9 August 1969. Mary,[199] daughter of James Willis **Barnett** and Helen Elizabeth **Neilsen**, was born in Anchorage, Anchorage Borough, Alaska 20 January 1949.
+ 8189 iii. Patricia **Baker** born 12 June 1947.

6853. **Frank Everett**[13] **Raymond** (Emma Louise[12] **Low**, Emma Louise[11] **Andrews**, Henry[10], Caleb[9], Molly[8] **Burnham**, Capt. Westley[7], Westley[6], Elizabeth[5] **Perkins**, Jacob[4], Elizabeth[3] **Whipple**, Matthew[2], Matthew[1])[200] was born in Essex, Essex Co., Mass. 11 January 1911 and died 15 December 1974 in Salem, Essex Co., Mass., at 63 years of age. He married **Alice Mysliwy**.

Frank Everett **Raymond** and Alice **Mysliwy** had the following children:
+ 8190 i. Nancy[14] **Raymond**.
+ 8191 ii. Charles Everett **Raymond**.
+ 8192 iii. Alice Louise **Raymond** born 27 November 1934.
    8193 iv. Martha **Raymond**.[201]

{ G 1211 }

6854. **Roger Conant**[13] **Raymond** (Emma Louise[12] **Low**, Emma Louise[11] **Andrews**, Henry[10], Caleb[9], Molly[8] **Burnham**, Capt. Westley[7], Westley[6], Elizabeth[5] **Perkins**, Jacob[4], Elizabeth[3] **Whipple**, Matthew[2], Matthew[1])[202] was born in Essex, Essex Co., Mass. 26 January 1913 and married **Ida Elizabeth Chubb** in Kennebunk, York Co. Maine, 26 September 1939. Ida,[203] daughter of Elmer Thaxter **Chubb** and Bessie Lee **Edwards**, was born in Beverly, Essex Co., Mass. 29 September 1918.

Roger Conant **Raymond** and Ida Elizabeth **Chubb** had the following children:

+ 8194 i. Joanne Elizabeth[14] **Raymond** born 21 January 1942.
+ 8195 ii. Roger Conant **Raymond** born 20 September 1945.
+ 8196 iii. Susan Low **Raymond** born 9 December 1946.
+ 8197 iv. David Lee **Raymond** born 12 October 1948.
+ 8198 v. John Douglas **Raymond** born 29 October 1951.

6855. **Sumner**[13] **Raymond** (Emma Louise[12] **Low**, Emma Louise[11] **Andrews**, Henry[10], Caleb[9], Molly[8] **Burnham**, Capt. Westley[7], Westley[6], Elizabeth[5] **Perkins**, Jacob[4], Elizabeth[3] **Whipple**, Matthew[2], Matthew[1])[204] was born in Essex, Essex Co., Mass. 8 March 1914 and married **Mariam Billauer**.

Sumner **Raymond** and Mariam **Billauer** had the following children:

8199 i. Ruth Ann[14] **Raymond**.[205]
8200 ii. Barbara **Raymond**.[206]
8201 iii. Robert **Raymond**.[207]
8202 iv. Patricia **Raymond**.[208]
+ 8203 v. Linda **Raymond**.
8204 vi. James **Raymond**.[209]
8205 vii. Susan **Raymond**.[210]

6856. **Lelia**[13] **Raymond** (Emma Louise[12] **Low**, Emma Louise[11] **Andrews**, Henry[10], Caleb[9], Molly[8] **Burnham**, Capt. Westley[7], Westley[6], Elizabeth[5] **Perkins**, Jacob[4], Elizabeth[3] **Whipple**, Matthew[2], Matthew[1])[211] was born in Essex, Essex Co., Mass. 2 November 1916 and died 8 January 1979 in Boston, Suffolk Co., Mass., at 62 years of age. She married **Charles Ferguson**.

Lelia **Raymond** and Charles **Ferguson** had the following children:

8206 i. Ralph[14] **Ferguson**.[212]
8207 ii. Charles **Ferguson**.[213]
8208 iii. Barbara **Ferguson**.[214]
8209 iv. Martha **Ferguson**.[215]

6857. **Alice**[13] **Raymond** (Emma Louise[12] **Low**, Emma Louise[11] **Andrews**, Henry[10], Caleb[9], Molly[8] **Burnham**, Capt. Westley[7], Westley[6], Elizabeth[5] **Perkins**, Jacob[4], Elizabeth[3] **Whipple**, Matthew[2], Matthew[1])[216] was born in Essex, Essex Co., Mass. 11 October 1918 and died 27 April 1970 in Beverly, Essex Co., Mass., at 51 years of age. She married **Walter Abel Sr.**

Alice **Raymond** and Walter **Abel** Sr. had the following children:
    8210   i.   Walter[14] **Abel** Jr.[217]
    8211   ii.   Christopher **Abel**.[218]

6858. **Pauline**[13] **Raymond** (Emma Louise[12] **Low**, Emma Louise[11] **Andrews**, Henry[10], Caleb[9], Molly[8] **Burnham**, Capt. Westley[7], Westley[6], Elizabeth[5] **Perkins**, Jacob[4], Elizabeth[3] **Whipple**, Matthew[2], Matthew[1])[219] was born in Ipswich, Essex Co., Mass. 3 August 1920 and married **Paul Hurder**.

Pauline **Raymond** and Paul **Hurder** had the following child:
    8212   i.   Paul[14] **Hurder**.[220]

6859. **Althine**[13] **Raymond** (Emma Louise[12] **Low**, Emma Louise[11] **Andrews**, Henry[10], Caleb[9], Molly[8] **Burnham**, Capt. Westley[7], Westley[6], Elizabeth[5] **Perkins**, Jacob[4], Elizabeth[3] **Whipple**, Matthew[2], Matthew[1])[221] was born in Ipswich, Essex Co., Mass. 24 April 1924 and married **John Marsh**.

Althine **Raymond** and John **Marsh** had the following children:
    8213   i.   David[14] **Marsh**.[222]
    8214   ii.   Emily **Marsh**.[223]

6860. **Lois**[13] **Burnham** (Ardelle[12] **Low**, Emma Louise[11] **Andrews**, Henry[10], Caleb[9], Molly[8] **Burnham**, Capt. Westley[7], Westley[6], Elizabeth[5] **Perkins**, Jacob[4], Elizabeth[3] **Whipple**, Matthew[2], Matthew[1])[224] was born in Weymouth, Norfolk Co., Mass. 28 July 1932 and married twice. (1) **David Hastings** in Quincy, Norfolk Co., Mass. 13 June 1953. David,[225] son of Alfred **Hastings** and Helen **Fellores**, was born in Washington, D. C. 29 December 1927 and died 5 March 1976 in Stafford Springs, Tolland Co., Conn., at 48 years of age. (2) **Roger Reed Grimiwade**.

Lois **Burnham** and David **Hastings** had the following children born in Stafford Springs:
    8215   i.   Patricia[14] **Hastings**[226] 1 January 1958 and married David **Kritzman** there 12 April 1986.
    8216   ii.   Thomas Burnham **Hastings**s[227] 27 October 1959 and married Stephanie **Ratanski** in Brooklyn, N.Y. 31 May 1986.

{ G 1213 }

8217 iii. Steven David **Hastings**[228] 4 August 1963 and married Susan **Franco** in Canton, Norfolk Co., Mass., 19 March 1988.

6861. **Charles Alden**[13] **Burnham** (Ardelle[12] **Low**, Emma Louise[11] **Andrews**, Henry[10], Caleb[9], Molly[8] **Burnham**, Capt. Westley[7], Westley[6], Elizabeth[5] **Perkins**, Jacob[4], Elizabeth[3] **Whipple**, Matthew[2], Matthew[1])[229] was born in Quincy, Norfolk Co., Mass. 13 July 1935 and married **Marian Piraino** in Braintree, Norfolk Co., Mass. 28 July 1963. Marian, daughter of Thomas **Piraino** and Theodora (__), was born in Boston, Suffolk Co., Mass. 31 December 1939.

Charles Alden **Burnham** and Marian **Piraino** had the following children born in Essex, Essex Co., Mass.:

8218 i. Theodore Alden[14] **Burnham**[230] 21 March 1965.
8219 ii. Harold Anthony**Burnham**[231] 1 June 1967.
8220 iii. Deborah **Burnham**[232] 11 November 1968.

6862. **Marsha Winslow**[13] **Howes** (Ceciline[12] **Low**, Emma Louise[11] **Andrews**, Henry[10], Caleb[9], Molly[8] **Burnham**, Capt. Westley[7], Westley[6], Elizabeth[5] **Perkins**, Jacob[4], Elizabeth[3] **Whipple**, Matthew[2], Matthew[1])[233] was born 16 June 1931 and married **Davis Osman**.

Marsha Winslow **Howes** and Davis **Osman** had the following children:

8221 i. Catherine Howes[14] **Osman**[234] born 21 July 1956. She married and had a child but no information on husband or child was provided.
8222 ii. Keith Arman **Osman**[235] born 6 August 1960.
8223 iii. Lynn Francis **Osman**[236] born 19 September 1962.
8224 iv. Janice Lorraine **Osman**[237] born 7 May 1969.

6863. **Douglas Gilman**[13] **Low** (Elston Brooks[12], Emma Louise[11] **Andrews**, Henry[10], Caleb[9], Molly[8] **Burnham**, Capt. Westley[7], Westley[6], Elizabeth[5] **Perkins**, Jacob[4], Elizabeth[3] **Whipple**, Matthew[2], Matthew[1])[238] was born in Salem, Essex Co., Mass. 3 May 1952 and married **Barbara Louise Johnson** in Niantic, New London Co., Conn.

Douglas Gilman **Low** and Barbara Louise **Johnson** adopted the following child:

8225 i. Elizabeth[14] **Low**[239] born 3 January 1987.

6864. **Eunice**[13] **Low** (Elston Brooks[12], Emma Louise[11] **Andrews**, Henry[10], Caleb[9], Molly[8] **Burnham**, Capt. Westley[7], Westley[6], Elizabeth[5] **Perkins**, Jacob[4], Elizabeth[3] **Whipple**, Matthew[2], Matthew[1])[240] was born in Salem, Essex Co., Mass. 7 October 1953 and married **Richard Dock Sr.** in Kipnuk,[241] Ark. 26 August 1978.

Eunice **Low** and Richard **Dock** Sr. had the following children:
    8226   i.   Richard[14] **Dock** Jr.[424] born 18 October 1979.
    8227   ii.   Sheldon **Dock**.[243]

6868. **John Francis**[13] **Gosbee** (Edna Frances[12] **Andrews**, Frank Albert[11], Henry[10], Caleb[9], Molly[8] **Burnham**, Capt. Westley[7], Westley[6], Elizabeth[5] **Perkins**, Jacob[4], Elizabeth[3] **Whipple**, Matthew[2], Matthew[1])[244] was born in Danvers, Essex Co., Mass. 8 August 1919 and died there 17 July 1973, at 53 years of age. He married **Gloria Evelyn Fuller** in Beverly, Essex Co., Mass. 6 November 1943. Gloria,[245] daughter of Oscar Melvin **Fuller** and Constance Marie **Lunney**, died 12 November 1984 in Danvers, at 60 years of age. Both are buried in North Cemetery, Beverly.

John Francis **Gosbee** and Gloria Evelyn **Fuller** had the following children:
    8228   i.   Josette Marie[14] **Gosbee**[246] born in Beverly 22 February 1948.
    8229   ii.   John Joseph **Gosbee**[247] born in Beverly 10 August 1949 and married Lillian Frances **Stott** in Pleasant Hill, Contra Costa Co., Calif. 1 December 1996.
+   8230   iii. Adrienne Lee **Gosbee** born 29 January 1951.

6869. **Jean Frances**[13] **Entwistle** (Viola Alberta[12] **Andrews**, Frank Albert[11], Henry[10], Caleb[9], Molly[8] **Burnham**, Capt. Westley[7], Westley[6], Elizabeth[5] **Perkins**, Jacob[4], Elizabeth[3] **Whipple**, Matthew[2], Matthew[1])[248] was born in Milford, Worcester Co., Mass. 26 March 1930 and married **Kieran Michael Nolan** in Hopkinton, Middlesex Co., Mass. 4 October 1958. Kieran,[249] son of Michael Patrick **Nolan** and (__) **Dunne**, was born in Boston, Suffolk Co., Mass. 22 December 1928.

Jean Frances **Entwistle** and Kieran Michael **Nolan** had the following children:
    8231   i.   Michael Patrick[14] **Nolan**[250] born in Framingham, Middlesex Co., Mass. 13 July 1959.
+   8232   ii.   Thomas William **Nolan** born 3 September 1960.
+   8233   iii. James Kieran **Nolan** born 14 October 1961.
    8234   iv. Elizabeth Ann **Nolan**[251] born in Framingham 14 January 1964 and died 3 December 1996 in Woodbury, Gloucester Co., N.J., at 32 years of age. Buried in 1996 in Charlton, Saratoga Co., N.Y. She married Daniel **Kimble** in Phoenix, Maricopa Co., Ariz. 7 March 1988.

+ 8235 v. Joseph Francis **Nolan** born 12 February 1966.
8236 vi. Edward Raymond **Nolan**[252] born in Framingham 4 October 1967.

6870. **Thomas William**[13] **Entwistle** Jr. (Viola Alberta[12] **Andrews**, Frank Albert[11], Henry[10], Caleb[9], Molly[8] **Burnham**, Capt. Westley[7], Westley[6], Elizabeth[5] **Perkins**, Jacob[4], Elizabeth[3] **Whipple**, Matthew[2], Matthew[1])[253] was born 11 January 1933 and married twice. (1) **Diane Diaz**. They were divorced. (2) **Barbara Wailane**.

Thomas William **Entwistle** Jr. and Diane **Diaz** had the following children:
8237 i. Scott[14] **Entwistle**[254] born 11 July 1961.
8238 ii. Kristin **Entwistle**[255] born abt 1963.
8239 iii. Craig **Entwistle**[256] born abt 1965.
8240 iv. Erik **Entwistle**[257] born abt 1967.

6871. **Ralph Henry**[13] **Whalen** Jr. (Jean Dorothy[12] **Andrews**, Frank Albert[11], Henry[10], Caleb[9], Molly[8] **Burnham**, Capt. Westley[7], Westley[6], Elizabeth[5] **Perkins**, Jacob[4], Elizabeth[3] **Whipple**, Matthew[2], Matthew[1])[258] was born in Framingham, Middlesex Co., Mass. 5 August 1930 and died there 23 February 1994 at 63 years of age. Buried in Evergreen Cemetery, Woodville, Middlesex Co., Mass. He married **Gloria Manson-Stewart** in Natick, Middlesex Co., Mass. 27 October 1967. She was born in Lynn, Essex Co., Mass. 20 April 1926.[259]

Ralph Henry **Whalen** Jr. and Gloria **Manson-Stewart** had the following child born in Framington:
8241 i. Christopher Andrew[14] **Whalen**[260] 5 May 1969.

6872. **Sydney Byron**[13] **Andrews** (Frank Sydney[12], Frank Albert[11], Henry[10], Caleb[9], Molly[8] **Burnham**, Capt. Westley[7], Westley[6], Elizabeth[5] **Perkins**, Jacob[4], Elizabeth[3] **Whipple**, Matthew[2], Matthew[1])[261] was born in Framingham, Middlesex Co., Mass. 22 September 1932 and married twice. (1) **June Margaret Lang** in Westborough, Worcester Co., Mass. 14 July 1951. They were divorced. June,[262] daughter of Richard **Lang** and Agnes (__), was born in New Britain, Hartford Co., Conn. 24 May 1934. (2) **Doris Gates Inman** in Nashua, Hillsborough Co., N. H. 24 June 1960. They were divorced. Doris,[263] daughter of Clarence **Gates** and Lillian **Hansen**, was born in Westborough 9 February 1917 and died 22 January 1996 in Worcester, Worcester Co., Mass., at 78 years of age.

Sydney Byron **Andrews** and June Margaret **Lang** had the following children:
- + 8242 i. Robert Byron[14] **Andrews** born 19 June 1954.
- + 8243 ii. Wendy Lou **Andrews** born 27 August 1955.
- + 8244 iii. Thomas Mark **Andrews** born 15 September 1957.

Sydney Byron **Andrews** and Doris Gates **Inman** had the following child:
- + 8245 iv. Kathleen Louise **Andrews** born 16 November 1960.

6873. **Shirley Mae**[13] **Andrews** (Frank Sydney[12], Frank Albert[11], Henry[10], Caleb[9], Molly[8] **Burnham**, Capt. Westley[7], Westley[6], Elizabeth[5] **Perkins**, Jacob[4], Elizabeth[3] **Whipple**, Matthew[2], Matthew[1])[264] was born in Worcester, Worcester Co., Mass. 18 October 1934 and married **Donald Edwin Ware Jr.** in Westborough, Worcester Co., Mass. 26 September 1953. Donald, son of Donald Edwin **Ware** Sr. and Margaret Ethel **Trochelman**, was born in Chicago, Cook Co., Ill. 25 September 1934.

Shirley Mae **Andrews** and Donald Edwin **Ware** Jr. had the following children:
- + 8246 i. William Michael[14] **Ware** born 28 October 1954.
-   8247 ii. Linda Margaret **Ware**[265] born in Worcester 26 November 1956 and died there 22 June 1965, at 8 years of age. Buried at Pinegrove Cemetery, Westborough.
- + 8248 iii. Susan Elaine **Ware** born 10 April 1960.

6874. **Carole Joan**[13] **Andrews** (Frank Sydney[12], Frank Albert[11], Henry[10], Caleb[9], Molly[8] **Burnham**, Capt. Westley[7], Westley[6], Elizabeth[5] **Perkins**, Jacob[4], Elizabeth[3] **Whipple**, Matthew[2], Matthew[1])[266] was born in Worcester, Worcester Co., Mass. 8 September 1938 and married twice. (1) **Nelson Richard Nedde** in Wilmette, Lake Co., Ill. 6 September 1958. They were divorced. Nelson,[267] son of William **Nedde** Sr. and Eleanor (__), was born in Beaver Falls, Bever Co., Penn. 27 September 1936 and died 26 September 1990 in N. Attleboro, Bristol Co., Mass., at 53 years of age. (2) **Allen John Erler** in Northborough, Worcester Co., Mass. 13 February 1981. Allen, son of Frederick W. **Erler** and Mildred Louise **Meister**, was born in Lawrence, Essex Co. Mass. 10 June 1943.

Carole Joan **Andrews** and Nelson Richard **Nedde** had the following children:
-   8249 i. Deborah Lynn[14] **Ware**[268] born in Decatur, Macon Co., Ill. 15 February 1960.
- + 8250 ii. Ellen Marie **Ware** born 31 August 1961.

8251 iii. David Nelson **Ware**[269] born in Joilet, Cook Co., Ill. 5 September 1965 and married Yuhong **Zhang** in Durham, Strafford Co., N.H. in February 1995.

6875. **Betty Elaine**[13] **Andrews** (Frank Sydney[12], Frank Albert[11], Henry[10], Caleb[9], Molly[8] **Burnham**, Capt. Westley[7], Westley[6], Elizabeth[5] **Perkins**, Jacob[4], Elizabeth[3] **Whipple**, Matthew[2], Matthew[1])[270] was born in Worcester, Worcester Co., Mass. 1 February 1943 and married **James David Storey** in Pittsburgh, Allegheny Co., Penn. 18 March 1967. James,[271] son of William Ryan **Storey** and Maxine Anita **McCullough**, was born in Butler, Butler Co., Penn. 29 October 1939 and died 17 September 1992 in Lee Township, Allegan Co., Mich., at 52 years of age. Betty's husband James descends from Capt. John Whipple of Dorchester, Suffolk Co., Mass. and Providence, Providence Co., R.I.

Betty Elaine **Andrews** and James David **Storey** had the following children:

8252 i. Laura Elaine[14] **Storey**[272] born in Racine, Racine Co., Wisc. 6 October 1971.

8253 ii. David Ryan **Storey**[273] born in Milwaukee, Milwaukee Co., Wisc. 6 May 1973.

6876. **Edward Francis**[13] **Mears Jr.** (Edward Francis[12], David Edward[11], Sallie Maria[10] **Andrews**, Caleb[9], Molly[8] **Burnham**, Capt. Westley[7], Westley[6], Elizabeth[5] **Perkins**, Jacob[4], Elizabeth[3] **Whipple**, Matthew[2], Matthew[1])[274] was born in Essex, Essex Co., Mass. 21 January 1920 and married **Barbara Frances Handy** in Swampscott, Essex Co., Mass. 10 July 1941. Barbara,[275] daughter of Edward Freeman **Handy** and Adelaide Sophia **Lufkin**, was born in Lynn, Essex Co. 10 November 1920 and died 21 February 2000 in Kingston, Rockingham Co., N.H., at 79 years of age.

Edward Francis **Mears** Jr. and Barbara Frances **Handy** had the following children:

8254 i. David Edward[14] **Mears**[276] born in Lynn, Essex Co., Mass. 23 June 1943 and married Margaret Ann **Doyle** 7 May 1966.

+ 8255 ii. Linda Barbara **Mears** born 16 August 1945.

8256 iii. Elizabeth Ann **Mears**[277] born in Newburyport, Essex Co., Mass. 27 March 1958 and married Peter Harry **Tingley** in Amesbury, Essex Co., Mass. 22 August 1981.

6879. **Frederick**[13] **Andrews** (Leslie Francis[12], Robert Francis[11], Levi Smalley[10], Noah[9], John[8], Joanna[7] **Burnham**, Westley[6], Elizabeth[5]

Perkins, Jacob[4], Elizabeth[3] **Whipple**, Matthew[2], Matthew[1])[278] birth date unknown, married **Zilda Moura**.

Frederick **Andrews** and Zilda **Moura** had the following children:
  8257 i. Luis[14] **Andrews**.[279]
  8258 ii. Jorge **Andrews**.[280]
  8259 iii. May **Andrews**.[281]

6880. **Doris Alice**[13] **Andrews** (Leslie Francis[12], Robert Francis[11], Levi Smalley[10], Noah[9], John[8], Joanna[7] **Burnham**, Westley[6], Elizabeth[5] **Perkins**, Jacob[4], Elizabeth[3] **Whipple**, Matthew[2], Matthew[1])[282] was born in Rio de Janeiro, Brazil 27 September 1923 and married **Roberto Caracciolo** there 4 May 1946. Roberto,[283] son of Antonio **Caracciolo** and Florence **Raw**, was born in Rio de Janeiro in 1921.

Doris Alice **Andrews** and Roberto **Caracciolo** had the following children:
  8260 i. Regina Andrews[14] **Caracciolo**[284] born 25 April 1947.
  8261 ii. Eduardo Andrews **Caracciolo**[285] born 8 December 1949.

6883. **Alexander**[13] **Leslie** (Levi Charles Smalley[12], Florence[11] **Andrews**, Levi Smalley[10], Noah[9], John[8], Joanna[7] **Burnham**, Westley[6], Elizabeth[5] **Perkins**, Jacob[4], Elizabeth[3] **Whipple**, Matthew[2], Matthew[1])[286] was born in Philadelphia, Philadelphia City Co., Penn. 28 October 1917 and died 16 January 1978 in New York, N.Y., at 60 years of age. He married **Helen Elizabeth Stack** who was born in East Lansing, Ingham Co., Mich. 6 November 1920 and died 2 July 1982 in Torrington, Litchfield Co., Conn., at 61 years of age.[287]

Alexander **Leslie** and Helen Elizabeth **Stack** had the following children:
  8262 i. Sarah Dodge[14] **Leslie**[288] born 8 December 1952 and married Robert Louis **Welsch** 15 October 1988. He was born in St. Louis, Independence Co., Mo. 19 May 1950.
+ 8263 ii. Susan Andrews **Leslie** born 6 April 1956.

6885. **Herbert Alexander**[13] **Leslie** (Herbert[12], Florence[11] **Andrews**, Levi Smalley[10], Noah[9], John[8], Joanna[7] **Burnham**, Westley[6], Elizabeth[5] **Perkins**, Jacob[4], Elizabeth[3] **Whipple**, Matthew[2], Matthew[1])[289] birth date unknown, died in 1999. He married **Katherine Jean Sukola**.

Herbert Alexander **Leslie** and Katherine Jean **Sukola** had the following child:
  8264 i. Renee Zora[14] **Leslie**.[290]

6886. **Noreen**[13] **Leslie** (Herbert[12], Florence[11] **Andrews**, Levi Smalley[10], Noah[9], John[8], Joanna[7] **Burnham**, Westley[6], Elizabeth[5] **Perkins**, Jacob[4], Elizabeth[3] **Whipple**, Matthew[2], Matthew[1])[291] was born in England in 1932 and married **Thomas Vanderput** in 1954. He was born in 1925.

Noreen **Leslie** and Thomas **Vanderput** had the following children:
 8265 i. William[14] **Vanderput**[292] born 27 January 1959.
 8266 ii. Marina **Vanderput**[293] born 29 September 1960.

6887. **Florence Eleanor**[13] **Irvin** (Eleanor[12] **Leslie**, Florence[11] **Andrews**, Levi Smalley[10], Noah[9], John[8], Joanna[7] **Burnham**, Westley[6], Elizabeth[5] **Perkins**, Jacob[4], Elizabeth[3] **Whipple**, Matthew[2], Matthew[1])[294] was born in 1919 and died in 1997 at 78 years of age. She married **Losir Warneck de Carvalho Vianna**. He was born in 1919 and died in 1995 at 76 years of age.[295]

Florence Eleanor **Irvin** and Losir Warneck **de Carvalho Vianna** had the following children:
 + 8267 i. Silvia Maria Irvin **de Carvalho**[14] **Vianna** born 26 May 1944.
 + 8268 ii. Florence Ann **de Carvalho Vianna** born 31 March 1945.
 + 8269 iii. Paulo Irvin **de Carvalho Vianna** born 1 November 1949.
 + 8270 iv. Mary Eleanor Irvin **de Carvalho Vianna** born 9 June 1954.

6888. **Betty**[13] **Crocker** (Margaret Ruth[12] **Hents**, Lucinda Rivers[11] **Andrews**, Levi Smalley[10], Noah[9], John[8], Joanna[7] **Burnham**, Westley[6], Elizabeth[5] **Perkins**, Jacob[4], Elizabeth[3] **Whipple**, Matthew[2], Matthew[1])[296] was born in 1929 and married (__) **Crosby**.

Betty **Crocker** and (__) **Crosby** had the following children:
 8271 i. Elizabeth[14] **Crosby**[297] born abt 1944.
 8272 ii. Michael **Crosby**[298] born abt 1947.
 8273 iii. Denise **Crosby**[299] born abt 1957.

6889. **Margaret Louise**[13] **Seifert** (Margaret Alice[12] **Andrews**, Dennis Rivers[11], Levi Smalley[10], Noah[9], John[8], Joanna[7] **Burnham**, Westley[6], Elizabeth[5] **Perkins**, Jacob[4], Elizabeth[3] **Whipple**, Matthew[2], Matthew[1])[300] was born in Rio de Janeiro, Brazil 6 April 1929 and died 11 August 1997 in Gustard Wood, Wheathampstead, Herts Co., England, at 68 years of age. She married twice. (1) **Darwin Monaghen** in Rio de Janeiro in 1948. He was born in Ames, Story Co., Iowa abt 1924 and died abt 1988 in California.[301] (2) **Miles Herbert Lloyd Keener** in Dallas, Dallas Co., Tex. 30 July 1965. Miles,[302] son of Ulysses Grant **Keener** and Hazel Elizabeth **Mannington**, was born in Rio de Janeiro 10 October 1922.

Margaret Louise **Seifert** and Miles Herbert Lloyd **Keener** had the following children:

        8274   i.   Margaret Louise Cecilia[14] **Keener**[303] born in Dallas, Dallas Co., Tex. 24 July 1959.

+   8275   ii.   Brian Dennis Alan **Keener** born 19 July 1960.

+   8276   iii. Carlos Grant Patrick **Keener** born 9 January 1967.

6891. **Patricia Mary**[13] **Seifert** (Margaret Alice[12] **Andrews**, Dennis Rivers[11], Levi Smalley[10], Noah[9], John[8], Joanna[7] **Burnham**, Westley[6], Elizabeth[5] **Perkins**, Jacob[4], Elizabeth[3] **Whipple**, Matthew[2], Matthew[1])[304] was born in Barra Do Pirai, Estado do Rio de Janerio, Brazil 20 January 1934 and married **Mario Alberto Eberle Pettinelli** in Rio de Janeiro 27 December 1956. He was born in Caxias do Sul, Rio Grande do Sul, Brazil 9 May 1930 and died 23 December 1981 in Caxias do Sul, at 51 years of age.[305]

Patricia Mary **Seifert** and Mario Alberto Eberle **Pettinelli** had the following children born in Caxias do Sul:

        8277   i.   Cristina[14] **Pettinelli**[306] 5 November 1957.

        8278   ii.   Mario Caetano **Pettinelli**[307] 26 November 1959.

6892. **Charles Robert Grant Rivers**[13] **Seifert** (Margaret Alice[12] **Andrews**, Dennis Rivers[11], Levi Smalley[10], Noah[9], John[8], Joanna[7] **Burnham**, Westley[6], Elizabeth[5] **Perkins**, Jacob[4], Elizabeth[3] **Whipple**, Matthew[2], Matthew[1])[308] was born in Barra Do Pirai, Estado do Rio de Janerio, Brazil 14 September 1935 and married twice. (1) **Mary Jim Shannon** who was born in Paris, Lamar Co., Tex. 2 May 1942.[309] (2) **Rosemarie Cislaghi** who was born in Caxias do Sul, Rio Grande do Sul, Brazil 30 January 1963.[310]

Charles Robert Grant Rivers **Seifert** and Mary Jim **Shannon** had the following children:

        8279   i.   Nina Michelle[14] **Seifert**[311] born 22 February 1959.

        8280   ii.   Charles Robert **Seifert**[312] born 9 May 1960.

        8281   iii. Erika **Seifert**[313] born 17 November 1963.

6893. **Elizabeth Ann**[13] **Seifert** (Margaret Alice[12] **Andrews**, Dennis Rivers[11], Levi Smalley[10], Noah[9], John[8], Joanna[7] **Burnham**, Westley[6], Elizabeth[5] **Perkins**, Jacob[4], Elizabeth[3] **Whipple**, Matthew[2], Matthew[1])[314] was born in Barra Do Pirai, Estado do Rio de Janerio, Brazil 1 February 1937 and married **Morris Ward**.

Elizabeth Ann **Seifert** and Morris **Ward** had the following children:
    8282   i.   Victoria[14] **Ward**[315] born in 1961.
    8283   ii.   Mark **Ward**[316] born in July 1962.
    8284   iii.   Sandy **Ward**[317] born in 1969.
    8285   iv.   Renee **Ward**[318] born in 1970.

6894. **William Palmer**[13] **Seifert** (Margaret Alice[12] **Andrews**, Dennis Rivers[11], Levi Smalley[10], Noah[9], John[8], Joanna[7] **Burnham**, Westley[6], Elizabeth[5] **Perkins**, Jacob[4], Elizabeth[3] **Whipple**, Matthew[2], Matthew[1])[319] was born in Barra Do Pirai, Estado do Rio de Janerio, Brazil 17 July 1938 and married **Evelyn Gower** who was born in Dallas, Dallas Co., Tex. 10 November 1942.[320]

William Palmer **Seifert** and Evelyn **Gower** had the following children:
    8286   i.   Kerry[14] **Seifert**[321] born 11 February 1961 and died in 1991 at 30 years of age.
    8287   ii.   Lawrence **Seifert**[322] born in 1962.
    8288   iii.   Susan Penilope **Seifert**[323] born 8 September 1969 and married Samuel Osborne **Schlehuber** in Dallas, Tex. 19 April 1997.

6895. **Dennis Rivers**[13] **Andrews** (John Rivers[12], Dennis Rivers[11], Levi Smalley[10], Noah[9], John[8], Joanna[7] **Burnham**, Westley[6], Elizabeth[5] **Perkins**, Jacob[4], Elizabeth[3] **Whipple**, Matthew[2], Matthew[1])[324] was born 29 April 1929 and married **Vera (__)**.

Dennis Rivers **Andrews** and Vera (__) had the following children:
    8289   i.   Denise[14] **Andrews**.[325]
    8290   ii.   Daisy **Andrews**.[326]
    8291   iii.   Daniele **Andrews**.[327]

6903. **Anna**[13] **Dall** (Anna Eleanor[12] **Roosevelt**, Pres. Franklin Delano[11], James[10], Mary Rebecca[9] **Aspinwall**, Susan[8] **Howland**, Lydia[7] **Bill**, Lydia[6] **Huntington**, Hannah[5] **Perkins**, Jabez[4], Elizabeth[3] **Whipple**, Matthew[2], Matthew[1])[328] was born 25 March 1927 and was adopted by her stepfather John Boettiger. She married **Van H. Seagraves** in Phoenix, Maricopa Co., Ariz. in July 1948.

Anna **Dall** and Van H. **Seagraves** had the following children:
    8292   i.   David[14] **Seagraves**.[329]
    8293   ii.   Nicholas Delano **Seagraves** born in Portland, Multnomah Co., Oreg. in August 1949.[330]
    8294   iii.   Anna Eleanor **Seagraves** born 16 August 1955.[331]

6904. **Curtis Roosevelt**[13] **Dall** (Anna Eleanor[12] **Roosevelt**, Pres. Franklin Delano[11], James[10], Mary Rebecca[9] **Aspinwall**, Susan[8] **Howland**, Lydia[7] **Bill**, Lydia[6] **Huntington**, Hannah[5] **Perkins**, Jabez[4], Elizabeth[3] **Whipple**, Matthew[2], Matthew[1])[332] was born 19 April 1930 and married three times. (1) **Robin H. Edwards** in Santa Monica, Los Angeles Co., Calif. 23 May 1950. They were divorced bef 1955. (2) **Ruth W. Sublette** in March 1955. They were divorced bef 1961. (3) **Jeanette Schlottman** 2 May 1961. He was adopted by his stepfather John Boettiger and later assumed the name of Curtis Roosevelt. His daughter Juliana was christened as a Roosevelt.

Curtis Roosevelt **Dall** and Robin H. **Edwards** had the following child:
    8295   i.   Juliana[14] **Roosevelt** born in 1952.[333]

6905. **John Roosevelt**[13] **Boettiger** (Anna Eleanor[12] **Roosevelt**, Pres. Franklin Delano[11], James[10], Mary Rebecca[9] **Aspinwall**, Susan[8] **Howland**, Lydia[7] **Bill**, Lydia[6] **Huntington**, Hannah[5] **Perkins**, Jabez[4], Elizabeth[3] **Whipple**, Matthew[2], Matthew[1])[334] was born in Seattle, King Co., Wash. 30 March 1939 and married **Deborah Ann Bentley** in De Witt, Onondoga Co., N.Y. in August 1960. She was born in 1938.[335]

John Roosevelt **Boettiger** and Deborah Ann **Bentley** had the following children:
    8296   i.   Adam[14] **Boettiger**.[336]
    8297   ii.   Sara **Boettiger**.[337]
    8298   iii.   Joshua **Boettiger**.[338]

6906. **Sara Delano**[13] **Roosevelt** (Congressman James[12], Pres. Franklin Delano[11], James[10], Mary Rebecca[9] **Aspinwall**, Susan[8] **Howland**, Lydia[7] **Bill**, Lydia[6] **Huntington**, Hannah[5] **Perkins**, Jabez[4], Elizabeth[3] **Whipple**, Matthew[2], Matthew[1])[339] was born in Boston, Suffolk Co., Mass. 13 March 1932 and married twice. (1) **Anthony di Bonaventura** in New York, N.Y. 12 June 1953. He is the son of Fred **di Bonaventura**.[340] They were divorced in 1972. (2) **Ronald A. Wilford** in January 1973.

Sara Delano **Roosevelt** and Anthony **di Bonaventura** had the following children:
    8299   i.   Anthony Peter Christopher **di Bonaventura** born in Washington, D.C. 10 June 1954.[345]
    8300   ii.   Andrea Isabelle[14] **di Bonaventura**.[341] born 21 June 1956.
    8301   iii.   Peter John **di Bonaventura**.[343] born 25 November 1957.
    8302   iv.   Sarina Rosario **di Bonaventura**.[344] born 24 August 1959.
    8303   v.   Betsey Maria **di Bonaventura**.[342] born 22 May 1963.

6907. **Kate**[13] **Roosevelt** (Congressman James[12], Pres. Franklin Delano[11], James[10], Mary Rebecca[9] **Aspinwall**, Susan[8] **Howland**, Lydia[7] **Bill**, Lydia[6] **Huntington**, Hannah[5] **Perkins**, Jabez[4], Elizabeth[3] **Whipple**, Matthew[2], Matthew[1])[346] was born in New York, N.Y. 16 February 1936 and married **William Haddad** there 17 October 1959. He was born in Charlotte, Mecklenburg Co., N.C. 25 July 1928.[347]

Kate **Roosevelt** and William **Haddad** had the following children:
- 8304 i. Andrea Whitney[14] **Haddad**.[348]
- 8305 ii. Camilla Cushing **Haddad**.[349]
- 8306 iii. Laura Whitney **Haddad**.[350]

6914. **William Donnor**[13] **Roosevelt** (Elliott[12], Pres. Franklin Delano[11], James[10], Mary Rebecca[9] **Aspinwall**, Susan[8] **Howland**, Lydia[7] **Bill**, Lydia[6] **Huntington**, Hannah[5] **Perkins**, Jabez[4], Elizabeth[3] **Whipple**, Matthew[2], Matthew[1])[351] was born in New York, N.Y. 17 November 1932 and married **Karyl Kyle** in Denver, Denver Co., Colo. 14 June 1957. He was educated at Harvard.

William Donnor **Roosevelt** and Karyl **Kyle** had the following children:
- 8307 i. Dana Donnor[14] **Roosevelt**.[352]
- 8308 ii. (Son) **Roosevelt**.[353]
- 8309 iii. Christopher Kyle **Roosevelt** born in Meeker, Rio Blanco Co., Colo. 2 August 1959.[354]

6915. **Ruth Chandler**[13] **Roosevelt** (Elliott[12], Pres. Franklin Delano[11], James[10], Mary Rebecca[9] **Aspinwall**, Susan[8] **Howland**, Lydia[7] **Bill**, Lydia[6] **Huntington**, Hannah[5] **Perkins**, Jabez[4], Elizabeth[3] **Whipple**, Matthew[2], Matthew[1])[355] was born in Fort Worth, Tarrant Co., Tex. 9 May 1934 and married **Henry D. Lindsley III** there in April 1956. He is the son of Henry G. **Lindsley** Jr. [356]

Ruth Chandler **Roosevelt** and Henry D. **Lindsley** III had the following children:
- 8310 i. Chandler[14] **Lindsley**.[357]
- 8311 ii. Henry Hays **Lindsley**.[358]
- 8312 iii. Ruth Roosevelt **Lindsley**.[359]

6916. **Elliott**[13] **Roosevelt** Jr. (Elliott[12], Pres. Franklin Delano[11], James[10], Mary Rebecca[9] **Aspinwall**, Susan[8] **Howland**, Lydia[7] **Bill**, Lydia[6] **Huntington**, Hannah[5] **Perkins**, Jabez[4], Elizabeth[3] **Whipple**, Matthew[2],

Matthew¹)360 was born in Fort Worth, Tarrant Co., Tex. 14 July 1936 and married **Jo Anne McFadden** 24 January 1959.

Elliott **Roosevelt** Jr. and Jo Anne **McFadden** had the following children:
- 8313   i.   David Anthony¹⁴ **Roosevelt**.361
- 8314   ii. Elizabeth **Roosevelt**.362
- 8315   iii. Elliott **Roosevelt** III.363
- 8316   iv. Laura **Roosevelt**.364

6917. **David Boynton**¹³ **Roosevelt** (Elliott¹², Pres. Franklin Delano¹¹, James¹⁰, Mary Rebecca⁹ **Aspinwall**, Susan⁸ **Howland**, Lydia⁷ **Bill**, Lydia⁶ **Huntington**, Hannah⁵ **Perkins**, Jabez⁴, Elizabeth³ **Whipple**, Matthew², Matthew¹)365 was born in Fort Worth, Tarrant Co., Tex. 3 January 1942 and married **Michele Josephine Chopen** 28 April 1968. She is the daughter of Alexander P. **Chopen** and (__) **O'Connor**.366

David Boynton **Roosevelt** and Michele Josephine **Chopen** had the following children:
- 8317   i.   Nicholas¹⁴ **Roosevelt**.367
- 8318   ii. Matthew Chopen **Roosevelt** born in Glen Cove, Nassau Co., N.Y. 16 March 1972.368

6918. **Franklin Delano**¹³ **Roosevelt** III (Franklin Delano¹², Pres. Franklin Delano¹¹, James¹⁰, Mary Rebecca⁹ **Aspinwall**, Susan⁸ **Howland**, Lydia⁷ **Bill**, Lydia⁶ **Huntington**, Hannah⁵ **Perkins**, Jabez⁴, Elizabeth³ **Whipple**, Matthew², Matthew¹)369 was born in Wilmington, Newcastle Co., Del. 19 July 1939 and married **Grace Ramsey Goodyear** in Darin, Fairfield Co., Conn. 18 June 1962. Grace,370 daughter of Austin **Goodyear** and Louisa **Robbins**, was born in Montclair, Essex Co., N.J. in 1941.

Franklin Delano **Roosevelt** III and Grace Ramsey **Goodyear** had the following children:
- 8319   i.   Phoebe Louisa¹⁴ **Roosevelt**.371
- 8320   ii. Nicholas Martin **Roosevelt**.372
- 8321   iii. Amelia **Roosevelt**.373

6919. **Christopher du Pont**¹³ **Roosevelt** (Franklin Delano¹², Pres. Franklin Delano¹¹, James¹⁰, Mary Rebecca⁹ **Aspinwall**, Susan⁸ **Howland**, Lydia⁷ **Bill**, Lydia⁶ **Huntington**, Hannah⁵ **Perkins**, Jabez⁴, Elizabeth³ **Whipple**, Matthew², Matthew¹)374 was born in Philadelphia, Philadelphia City Co., Penn. 21 December 1940 and married **Rosalind Have-**

meyer in Concord, Rockingham Co., N.H. 12 June 1965. She is the daughter of Horace **Havemeyer** and (__) **Everdell**.[375]

Christopher du Pont **Roosevelt** and Rosalind **Havemeyer** had the following children:

    8322   i.   Emily[14] **Roosevelt**.[376]
    8323   ii. Kate **Roosevelt**.[377]
    8324   iii. Christopher Havemeyer **Roosevelt**.[378]

6921. **Haven Clark**[13] **Roosevelt** (John Aspinwall[12], Pres. Franklin Delano[11], James[10], Mary Rebecca[9] **Aspinwall**, Susan[8] **Howland**, Lydia[7] **Bill**, Lydia[6] **Huntington**, Hannah[5] **Perkins**, Jabez[4], Elizabeth[3] **Whipple**, Matthew[2], Matthew[1])[379] was born in Boston, Suffolk Co., Mass. 5 June 1940 and married **Hetty Archer Knowlton** in Beverly Farm, Essex Co., Mass. 26 November 1966. Hetty,[380] daughter of John Elliott **Knowlton**, was born in April 1938.

Haven Clark **Roosevelt** and Hetty Archer **Knowlton** had the following children:

    8325   i.   Sara Delano[14] **Roosevelt** born in 1968.[381]
    8326   ii. Wendy Clark **Roosevelt** born in 1970.[382]

6922. **Anne Sturgis**[13] **Roosevelt** (John Aspinwall[12], Pres. Franklin Delano[11], James[10], Mary Rebecca[9] **Aspinwall**, Susan[8] **Howland**, Lydia[7] **Bill**, Lydia[6] **Huntington**, Hannah[5] **Perkins**, Jabez[4], Elizabeth[3] **Whipple**, Matthew[2], Matthew[1])[383] was born in San Diego, San Diego Co., Calif. 15 December 1942 and married **Douglas Sigler Luke Jr.** in Hyde Park, Dutchess Co., N.Y. 20 June 1966. Douglas,[384] son of Douglas Sigler **Luke**, was born 1 October 1942.

Anne Sturgis **Roosevelt** and Douglas Sigler **Luke** Jr. had the following children:

    8327   i.   Haven Roosevelt[14] **Luke** born 14 January 1967.[385]
    8328   ii. David Russell **Luke** born 12 May 1969.[386]
    8329   iii. Lindsay Anne **Luke** born 27 December 1973.[387]

6929. **Frederick Melvin**[13] **Holmes Jr.** (Hazel Georgia[12] **Bradley**, Esther Myrtle[11] **Smith**, Julia Ann[10] **Stevens**, Melissa Esther[9] **Jones**, Mariah B.[8] **Ayers**, Lovica[7] **Stanton**, Lovica[6] **Gates**, Charity[5] **Perkins**, Jabez[4], Elizabeth[3] **Whipple**, Matthew[2], Matthew[1])[388] was born in Port Huron, St. Clair Co., Mich. 24 April 1924 and married **Frances May Hacker** in Stanton, Montcalm Co., Mich. 14 June 1946. Frances,[389] daughter of Frederick William **Hacker** and Cloe Opal **Burris**, was born in Entrican, Montcalm Co., Mich. 16 September 1927.

Frederick Melvin **Holmes** Jr. and Frances May **Hacker** had the following children:

    8330   i.   Thomas Gary[14] **Holmes**[390] born in Greenville, Montcalm Co., Mich. 14 November 1947 and married twice. (1) Karen Avon **Davis** in Greenville 30 August 1969. Karen,[391] daughter of Alan G. **Davis**, was born in Greenville in June 1947. They were divorced in 1978. (2) Cathy Jean **Rogers** in Las Vegas, Clark Co., Nev. 3 September 1980. Cathy,[392] daughter of Wilber Wilgus **Rogers** and Virginia June **Ells**, was born in Newburyport, Essex Co., Mass. 6 December 1954.

    8331   ii.   (Son) **Holmes**[393] born in Sheridan, Montcalm Co., Mich. 15 February 1950 and died the day of birth. Buried at Entrican Cemetery, Douglass Township.

    8332   iii.   Connie Lynn **Holmes**[394] born in Sheridan 8 November 1952 and married Jean-Paul **Bouchard** in Greenville 6 May 1972. They were divorced 26 May 1977.

+   8333   iv.   Marjean **Holmes** born 22 April 1958.

6983. William Roger[13] **Whipple** (Donald I.[12], Stanley I.[11], George H.[10], Amos Woodbury[9], John[8], Charles[7], Benjamin[6], Capt. John[5], John[4], Lt. John[3], Matthew[2], Matthew[1])[395] was born in Concord, Rockingham Co., N.H. 5 June 1949 and married **Nancy E. Daves** in San Francisco, San Francisco Co., Calif. 26 January 1974.

William Roger **Whipple** had the following children born in San Francisco:

    8334   i.   Joshua M.[14] **Whipple**[396] 22 November 1975.

    8335   ii.   Nathan J. **Whipple**[397] 22 July 1978.

7002. Nancy Jane[13] **Weller** (Inez Eunice[12] **Hamilton**, Jessie M.[11] **Washburn**, Lillian Jane[10] **Corson**, Jane[9] **Whipple**, John[8], Eleazer[7], Eleazer[6], Nathan[5], Matthew[4], Lt. John[3], Matthew[2], Matthew[1])[398] was born in Norridgewock, Somerset Co., Maine 26 September 1932 and married **Quarnig Levon Dorian** in New Hope, Bucks Co., Penn. 14 April 1962. He was born in Schwarmstedt, Germany 31 August 1922.[399]

Nancy Jane **Weller** and Quarnig Levon **Dorian** had the following children:

+   8336   i.   Winston Fayette[14] **Dorian** born 18 June 1964.

8337 ii. Anahid Celeste **Dorian**[400] born in New York, N.Y. 12 May 1966 and married Michael **Shurte Sr.** in Prescott, Yavapai Co., Ariz. 2 September 2000.
+ 8338 iii. Hamilton Haig **Dorian** born 24 September 1968.

7003. **Joanne**[13] **Weller** (Inez Eunice[12] **Hamilton**, Jessie M.[11] **Washburn**, Lillian Jane[10] **Corson**, Jane[9] **Whipple**, John[8], Eleazer[7], Eleazer[6], Nathan[5], Matthew[4], Lt. John[3], Matthew[2], Matthew[1])[401] was born in Boston, Suffolk Co., Mass. 4 January 1935 and married **Robert S. Mclandress** in Short Hills, Essex Co., N.J. 3 July 1958.[402] They were divorced in 1967.

Joanne **Weller** and Robert S. **Mclandress** had the following child:
  8339 i. John Kenneth[14] **Mclandress**[403] born in San Francisco, San Francisco Co., Calif. 15 December 1966.

7011. **Eileen Lucille**[13] **McCleary** (Eva Muryl[12] **Shannon**, Maude Belle[11] **Kennison**, America Martha Jane[10] **Walker**, Calvin Augustus[9], Lydia[8] **Whipple**, Zebulon[7], Zebulon[6], Samuel[5], Cyprian[4], Lt. John[3], Matthew[2], Matthew[1])[404] was born in Mitchell, Davison Co., S. Dak. 27 July 1920 and married twice. (1) **Glenn Leroy Hendricks** in Waterloo, Black Hawk Co., Iowa 9 December 1939. Glenn,[405] son of Martin Edgar **Hendricks** and Cycy Ben **Powers**, was born in Lorhville, Calhoun Co., Iowa 7 December 1918 and died 6 June 1998 in Des Moines, Polk Co., Iowa, at 79 years of age. They were divorced in Black Hawk Co. 8 August 1945. He married (2) **Irene Yazek**. She married (2) **Wilbur H. Yeutter** in Milford, Iowa 15 July 1951.

Eileen Lucille **McCleary** and Glenn Leroy **Hendricks** had the following child:
+ 8340 i. Kathie Joan[14] **Hendricks** born 12 August 1940.

7012. **James A.**[13] **McCleary** (Eva Muryl[12] **Shannon**, Maude Belle[11] **Kennison**, America Martha Jane[10] **Walker**, Calvin Augustus[9], Lydia[8] **Whipple**, Zebulon[7], Zebulon[6], Samuel[5], Cyprian[4], Lt. John[3], Matthew[2], Matthew[1])[406] was born in Sioux Falls, Minnehaha Co., S. Dak. 6 August 1929 and married **Lu Ann Wood** in Waterloo, Black Hawk Co., Iowa.

James A. **McCleary** and Lu Ann **Wood** had the following children:
  8341 i. Michael James[14] **McCleary**[407] born in Waterloo 20 November 1951.
  8342 ii. Patrick W. **McCleary**[408] born in Charles City, Floyd Co., Iowa 20 July 1956.

7024. **Julia Ann**[13] **Whipple** (Lewis Dale[12], Andrew Jackson[11], Andrew Bina[10], Andrew Jackson[9], Zebulon[8], Zebulon[7], Zebulon[6], Samuel[5], Cyprian[4], Lt. John[3], Matthew[2], Matthew[1])[409] was born in Columbus, Franklin Co., Ohio 25 March 1955 and married **Randall G. Nix** in Shreveport, Caddo Parish, La. 28 May 1971. Randall,[410] son of Devoy **Nix** and Lucille **Lee**, was born in Magnolia, Columbia Co., Ark. 8 December 1952.

Julia Ann **Whipple** and Randall G. **Nix** had the following children:
+   8343   i.   Craig Lewis[14] **Nix** born 27 December 1971.
+   8344   ii.   Michael Wayne **Nix** born 14 March 1975.

7025. **Debra Ellen**[13] **Whipple** (Lewis Dale[12], Andrew Jackson[11], Andrew Bina[10], Andrew Jackson[9], Zebulon[8], Zebulon[7], Zebulon[6], Samuel[5], Cyprian[4], Lt. John[3], Matthew[2], Matthew[1])[411] was born in Shreveport, Caddo Parish, La. 27 September 1956 and married twice. (1) **James Michael DiMarco** 23 October 1976. James,[412] son of Lucien **DiMarco** and Bernice **Naquin**, was born in New Orleans, Orleans Parish, La. 25 June 1953. They were divorced in St. Charles, Lafourche Parish, La. in 1988. (2) **Chris Michael Friloux** in Benton, Bossier Parish, La. 10 April 1990.

Debra Ellen **Whipple** and James Michael **DiMarco** had the following children:
+   8345   i.   Kelly Amber[14] **DiMarco** born 5 October 1977.
    8346   ii.   Cody Allen **DiMarco**[413] born in New Orleans 12 August 1980.

7026. **Judith Joy**[13] **Hunt** (Graedon[12] **Whipple**, Paul Darius[11], Andrew Bina[10], Andrew Jackson[9], Zebulon[8], Zebulon[7], Zebulon[6], Samuel[5], Cyprian[4], Lt. John[3], Matthew[2], Matthew[1])[414] birth date unknown, married twice. (1) **Larry David Miller**. (2) **Henry Bonebreake**.

Judith Joy **Hunt** and Larry David **Miller** had the following children:
    8347   i.   Wendy[14] **Miller**.[415]
    8348   ii.   Kevin **Miller**.[416]

7027. **Diane Gay**[13] **Hunt** (Graedon[12] **Whipple**, Paul Darius[11], Andrew Bina[10], Andrew Jackson[9], Zebulon[8], Zebulon[7], Zebulon[6], Samuel[5], Cyprian[4], Lt. John[3], Matthew[2], Matthew[1])[417] birth date unknown, married **Milton Donald Kaiser**.

Diane Gay **Hunt** and Milton Donald **Kaiser** had the following children:
    8349   i.   Andrew David[14] **Kaiser**.[418]
    8350   ii.   Jonathan **Kaiser**.[419]

7029. **Mary Ann**[13] **Hunt** (Graedon[12] **Whipple**, Paul Darius[11], Andrew Bina[10], Andrew Jackson[9], Zebulon[8], Zebulon[7], Zebulon[6], Samuel[5], Cyprian[4], Lt. John[3], Matthew[2], Matthew[1])[420] birth date unknown married twice. (1) **John Stone**. (2) **Donald R. Little**.

Mary Ann **Hunt** and John **Stone** had the following child:
    8351 i. Michael Adair[14] **Stone**.[421]

7037. **Douglas Paul**[13] **Whipple** (Paul Darius[12], Paul Darius[11], Andrew Bina[10], Andrew Jackson[9], Zebulon[8], Zebulon[7], Zebulon[6], Samuel[5], Cyprian[4], Lt. John[3], Matthew[2], Matthew[1])[422] birth date unknown married **Catherine Dipalma**.

Douglas Paul **Whipple** and Catherine **Dipalma** had the following children:
    8352 i. Meridith Catherine[14] **Whipple**.[423]
    8353 ii. Allyson Mary **Whipple**.[424]

7048. **Sharon Loree**[13] **Andrus** (Irma[12] **Butterfield**, Glen[11], Caroline[10] **Cobb**, Julia[9] **Whipple**, William[8], Zebulon[7], Zebulon[6], Samuel[5], Cyprian[4], Lt. John[3], Matthew[2], Matthew[1])[425] was born in Atkinson, Holt Co., Nebr. 6 October 1935 and married **Dean H. Prewitt** 8 September 1957.

Sharon Loree **Andrus** and Dean H. **Prewitt** had the following children:
    8354 i. Lori Ruth[14] **Prewitt** born 14 June 1958.[426]
    8355 ii. Jerry Dean **Prewitt** born 8 October 1959.[427]
    8356 iii. Steven Lee **Prewitt** born 8 December 1960 and died 2 May 1965 at 4 years of age.[428]
    8357 iv. Dallas James **Prewitt** born 12 May 1962.[429]
    8358 v. Tracy Louise **Prewitt** born 11 September 1963.[430]

7055. **Cynthia Lee**[13] **Whipple** (Richard Raybold[12], Harvey Abbott[11], Arthur[10], Zebulon[9], Henry[8], Joseph[7], Zebulon[6], Samuel[5], Cyprian[4], Lt. John[3], Matthew[2], Matthew[1])[431] was born in Providence, Providence Co., R.I 5 July 1953 and married **David Crimmin** in Glastonbury, Hartford Co., Conn. 18 June 1977.

Cynthia Lee **Whipple** and David **Crimmin** had the following children:
    8359 i. Matthew Royce[14] **Crimmin**[432] born 14 August 1981.
    8360 ii. Rebecca deVeer **Crimmin**[433] born 7 August 1984.
    8361 iii. Jedffrey Richard **Crimmin**[434] born 31 December 1987.

7056. **Richard Raybold**[13] **Whipple Jr** (Richard Raybold[12], Harvey Abbott[11], Arthur[10], Zebulon[9], Henry[8], Joseph[7], Zebulon[6], Samuel[5], Cyprian[4], Lt. John[3], Matthew[2], Matthew[1])[435] was born in Providence, Providence Co., R.I 8 May 1955 and married **Ellen Mosher** in Albany, Albany Co., N.Y. 2 June 1984.

Richard Raybold **Whipple** Jr. and Ellen **Mosher** had the following children:
    8362   i.   Christina Newel[14] **Whipple**[436] born 6 January 1987.
    8363   ii.   Lauren Alexandra **Whipple**[437] born 17 August 1988.

7057. **Robert deVeer**[13] **Whipple** (Richard Raybold[12], Harvey Abbott[11], Arthur[10], Zebulon[9], Henry[8], Joseph[7], Zebulon[6], Samuel[5], Cyprian[4], Lt. John[3], Matthew[2], Matthew[1])[438] was born 26 August 1968 and married **Cheryl Ann Protano** in Worcester, Worcester Co., Mass. 9 September 1984.

Robert deVeer **Whipple** and Cheryl Ann **Protano** had the following children:
    8364   i.   Alexandra Daniels[14] **Whipple**[439] born 4 June 1990.
    8365   ii.   Nathan Waterman **Whipple**[440] born in 1993.

7058. **Ralph Winthrop**[13] **Hinds** (Shirley Virginia[12] **Whipple**, Harvey Abbott[11], Arthur[10], Zebulon[9], Henry[8], Joseph[7], Zebulon[6], Samuel[5], Cyprian[4], Lt. John[3], Matthew[2], Matthew[1])[441] was born in Bangor, Penobscot Co., Maine 5 May 1951 and married twice. (1) **Debbie Hubbard** in Oconomewoc, Waukesha Co., Wisc. 30 December 1978. They were divorced in 1985. (2) **Pam Lynn Patterson** in Clarence, Erie Co., N.Y. 17 July 1987.

Ralph Winthrop **Hinds** and Debbie **Hubbard** had the following child:
    8366   i.   Winthrop Scott[14] **Hinds**[442] born 1 January 1980.

Ralph Winthrop **Hinds** and Pam Lynn **Patterson** had the following children:
    8367   ii.   Christine Elizabeth **Hinds**[443] born 11 May 1989.
    8368   iii.   Jacquelyn Paige **Hinds**[444] born 21 June 1991.

7059. **Jeffrey Allan**[13] **Hinds** (Shirley Virginia[12] **Whipple**, Harvey Abbott[11], Arthur[10], Zebulon[9], Henry[8], Joseph[7], Zebulon[6], Samuel[5], Cyprian[4], Lt. John[3], Matthew[2], Matthew[1])[445] was born in Bangor, Penobscot Co., Maine 30 May 1952 and married **Deborah Joy Syndal** in Port Angeles, Callam Co., Wash. 19 March 1977.

Jeffrey Allan **Hinds** and Deborah Joy **Syndal** had the following children:
    8369   i.   Emma Syndal[14] **Hinds**[446] born 18 August 1984.
    8370   ii.   Harrison Winthrop **Hinds**[447] born 22 January 1987.

7060. **Meredith Virginia**[13] **Hinds** (Shirley Virginia[12] **Whipple**, Harvey Abbott[11], Arthur[10], Zebulon[9], Henry[8], Joseph[7], Zebulon[6], Samuel[5], Cyprian[4], Lt. John[3], Matthew[2], Matthew[1])[448] was born in Rochester, Monroe Co., N.Y. 10 March 1954 and married twice. (1) **Keith Gerdman** in Oconomewoc, Waukesha Co., Wisc. 20 July 1974. They were divorced in 1979. (2) **Robert Sullivan** in Madison, Dane Co., Wisc. 24 June 1984.

Meredith Virginia **Hinds** and Robert **Sullivan** had the following children:
    8371 i. Padraig Ryan[14] **Sullivan**[449] born 4 December 1986.
    8372 ii. Delaney Michelle **Sullivan**[450] born 11 January 1990.

7062. **Pamela Marion**[13] **Hinds** (Shirley Virginia[12] **Whipple**, Harvey Abbott[11], Arthur[10], Zebulon[9], Henry[8], Joseph[7], Zebulon[6], Samuel[5], Cyprian[4], Lt. John[3], Matthew[2], Matthew[1])[451] was born in Rahway, Union Co., N.J. 12 November 1959 and married **Thomas Heinrich** in Oconomewoc, Waukesha Co., Wisc. 26 May 1984.

Pamela Marion **Hinds** and Thomas **Heinrich** had the following children:
    8373 i. Julia Marion[14] **Heinrich**[452] born 7 January 1989.
    8374 ii. Elizabeth Ann **Heinrich**[453] born 12 September 1990.

7063. **Harvey Abbott**[13] **Whipple III** (Harvey Abbott[12], Harvey Abbott[11], Arthur[10], Zebulon[9], Henry[8], Joseph[7], Zebulon[6], Samuel[5], Cyprian[4], Lt. John[3], Matthew[2], Matthew[1])[454] was born in Providence, Providence Co., R. I. 24 August 1955 and married **Kathleen Parker** in Brewster, Barnstable Co., Mass. 24 November 1990.

Harvey Abbott **Whipple** III and Kathleen **Parker** had the following children:
    8375 i. Matthew David[14] **Whipple**[455] born 24 March 1987.
    8376 ii. Alyssa Leslie **Whipple**[456] born 11 October 1990.

7064. **Lesa Ann**[13] **Whipple** (Harvey Abbott[12], Harvey Abbott[11], Arthur[10], Zebulon[9], Henry[8], Joseph[7], Zebulon[6], Samuel[5], Cyprian[4], Lt. John[3], Matthew[2], Matthew[1])[457] was born in Philadelphia, Philadelphia City Co., Penn. 2 December 1956 and married **Peter G. Nicholson** in Bristol, Bristol Co., R.I. 29 May 1982.

Lesa Ann **Whipple** and Peter G. **Nicholson** had the following children:
    8377 i. Peter Christopher[14] **Nicholson**[458] born 29 March 1985.
    8378 ii. Laura Abbott **Nicholson**[459] born 3 June 1988.

7065. **Sharon Mary**[13] **Whipple** (Harvey Abbott[12], Harvey Abbott[11], Arthur[10], Zebulon[9], Henry[8], Joseph[7], Zebulon[6], Samuel[5], Cyprian[4], Lt. John[3], Matthew[2], Matthew[1])[460] was born in Warwick, Kent Co., R.I. 26 December 1957 and married twice. (1) **Charles Robert Fish** in Warren, Bristol Co., R.I. 20 September 1980. They were divorced in 1985. (2) **Gary Michael Andres** in Brewster, Barnstable Co., Mass. 20 May 1994.

Sharon Mary **Whipple** and Charles Robert **Fish** had the following child:
 8379 i. Leha Mary[14] **Fish**[461] born 1 December 1985.

Sharon Mary **Whipple** and Gary Michael **Andres** had the following child:
 8380 ii. Elizabeth Mary **Andres**[462] born 7 September 1995.

7067. **Kevin Karl**[13] **Whipple** (Harvey Abbott[12], Harvey Abbott[11], Arthur[10], Zebulon[9], Henry[8], Joseph[7], Zebulon[6], Samuel[5], Cyprian[4], Lt. John[3], Matthew[2], Matthew[1])[463] was born in Providence, Providence Co., R.I. 2 July 1960 and married twice. (1) **Robin (__)** in Swansea, Bristol Co., Mass. in 1979. They were divorced in 1984. (2) **Debra Estrella** in Barrington, Bristol Co., R.I. 30 July 1988. Debra had a son, Jason Smith, born 17 April 1977.

Kevin Karl **Whipple** and Robin (__) had the following child:
 8381 i. Andrew Christian[14] **Whipple**[464] born 9 September 1979.

7069. **Dorian Virginia**[13] **Whipple** (Harvey Abbott[12], Harvey Abbott[11], Arthur[10], Zebulon[9], Henry[8], Joseph[7], Zebulon[6], Samuel[5], Cyprian[4], Lt. John[3], Matthew[2], Matthew[1])[465] was born in Providence, Providence Co., R.I. 12 March 1963 and married **William Anthony Robinson II** in Brewster, Barnstable Co., Mass. 6 October 1990. He is the son of William Anthony **Robinson** I.

Dorian Virginia **Whipple** and William Anthony **Robinson** II had the following children:
 8382 i. William Anthony[14] **Robinson** III[466] born 24 February 1992.
 8383 ii. Nicholas McNulty **Robinson**[467] born 30 June 1994.
 8384 iii. Megan Virginia **Robinson**[468] born 8 November 1998.

7071. **Nathan Waterman**[13] **Whipple** (Harvey Abbott[12], Harvey Abbott[11], Arthur[10], Zebulon[9], Henry[8], Joseph[7], Zebulon[6], Samuel[5], Cyprian[4], Lt. John[3], Matthew[2], Matthew[1])[469] was born in Providence, Providence Co., R.I. 22 March 1967 and married **Mara Goncalves** in Hyannis, Barnstable Co., Mass. 20 September 1991.

Nathan Waterman **Whipple** and Mara **Goncalves** had the following children:
- 8385 i. Victoria Sandra[14] **Whipple**[470] born 12 July 1993.
- 8386 ii. Michelle Elizabeth **Whipple**[471] born 10 October 1994.

7072. **Marion Raybold**[13] **Whipple** (Kingsley Allan[12], Harvey Abbott[11], Arthur[10], Zebulon[9], Henry[8], Joseph[7], Zebulon[6], Samuel[5], Cyprian[4], Lt. John[3], Matthew[2], Matthew[1])[472] was born 16 November 1962 and married **Gerald Andrew** in N. Kingston, Washington Co., R.I. 1 August 1992.

Marion Raybold **Whipple** and Gerald **Andrew** had the following child:
- 8387 i. Noah[14] **Andrew**.[473]

7079. **Barbara Joanna**[13] **Moore** (Grace Irene[12] **Whipple**, Oran Porter[11], Joseph Walter[10], Jonathan Jones[9], Joseph[8], David[7], Samuel[6], Samuel[5], Cyprian[4], Lt. John[3], Matthew[2], Matthew[1])[474] was born in Wichita, Sedgwick Co., Kans. 22 January 1928 and married **Douglas Norman MacDonald Sr.** in Los Angeles, Los Angeles Co., Calif. 24 April 1945. Douglas,[475] son of John Alexander **MacDonald** and Maude Lillian **Seavy**, was born in Chippewa, Ontario, Canada 29 September 1924. He has been a School Teacher and Principal and served in the Army Air Force during WWII. Barbara worked as an Office Manager.

Barbara Joanna **Moore** and Douglas Norman **MacDonald** Sr. had the following children:
- + 8388 i. Wesley John[14] **MacDonald** born 20 November 1946.
- 8389 ii. Douglas Norman **MacDonald** Jr.[476] born in Los Angeles 4 November 1948.

7083. **Arthur Paul**[13] **Whipple II** (Arthur Paul[12], Merritt Pendell[11], Dr. Alfred Augustus[10], Henry Francisco[9], Joseph[8], David[7], Samuel[6], Samuel[5], Cyprian[4], Lt. John[3], Matthew[2], Matthew[1])[477] was born in Rochester, Monroe Co., N.Y. 11 December 1929 and married **Joann Ruth DuBail** in St. Louis, Independence Co., Mo. 5 August 1954. She was born in St. Louis 23 or 25 September 1929.[478] Arthur was known as Chip and was living in Ponca City, Kay Co., Okla. in March 1989.

Arthur Paul **Whipple** II and Joann Ruth **DuBail** had the following children:
- + 8390 i. Arthur Paul[14] **Whipple** III born 17 September 1957.
- 8391 ii. Peter DuBail **Whipple**[479] born in Midland, Midland Co., Tex. 28 April 1959 and married twice. (1) Mary Catherine **Casey** 27 March 1982. She was born in Greenville, Greenville Co., S.C. 2 October 1960.[480] They were

divorced in 1989. (2) Joan Day **Blystone** 30 June 1996. She was born 10 January 1952.[481]

+ 8392 iii. Carol Miller **Whipple** born 27 December 1961.

7084. **Nelson Frank Gordon**[13] **Whipple** (Arthur Paul[12], Merritt Pendell[11], Dr. Alfred Augustus[10], Henry Francisco[9], Joseph[8], David[7], Samuel[6], Samuel[5], Cyprian[4], Lt. John[3], Matthew[2], Matthew[1])[482] was born in Rochester, Monroe Co., N.Y. 2 December 1931 and married three times. (1) **Mary Josephine Fradianni** in Hartford, Hartford Co., Conn. 24 October 1953. Mary,[483] daughter of Salvatore **Fradianni** and Carmela **Quatrale**, was born in Rocky Hill, Hartford Co., Conn. 2 October 1928. They were divorced 17 July 1967. (2) **Eve Guthrie Hartman** 11 July 1969. She was born in North Carolina 10 October 1943.[484] They were divorced 7 March 1988. (3) **Jean Barnes** in Charlotte, Mecklenburg Co., N.C. 14 August 1994. She was born in Charlotte 24 September 1933.

Nelson Frank Gordon **Whipple** and Mary Josephine **Fradianni** had the following children:

+ 8393 i. Karen Marie[14] **Whipple** born 3 September 1954.
  8394 ii. Sally Paula **Whipple**[485] born in New York, N.Y. 15 February 1959 and married William **Kelly** in Newington, Hartford Co., Conn. 12 February 1988. He was born 12 January 1959.[486]
  8395 iii. Nelson James **Whipple**[487] born in Concord, Rockingham Co. N. H. 9 February 1962 and married Jean **Keleher** in Chicago, Cook Co., Ill. 30 May 1991. She was born 13 February 1964.[488] They were divorced 24 September 1998.
+ 8396 iv. Dorcas Miller **Whipple** born 31 August 1964.

7085. **David Lee**[13] **Brooke** (Virginia Dallas[12] **Whipple**, Merritt Pendell[11], Dr. Alfred Augustus[10], Henry Francisco[9], Joseph[8], David[7], Samuel[6], Samuel[5], Cyprian[4], Lt. John[3], Matthew[2], Matthew[1])[489] was born in Rochester, Monroe Co., N.Y. 18 March 1929 and married twice. (1) **Meredith Hitchcock** in Oak Park Cook Co., Ill. 18 August 1957. Meredith is the daughter of Edward **Hitchcock** and Doris **Latimer**.[490] They were divorced in Oak Brook, Ill. 6 July 1972. (2) **Mary Lou Clark Bourne** in Rochester 20 January 1973. She was born in Rochester 22 February 1933.[491]

David Lee **Brooke** and Meredith **Hitchcock** had the following children:

+ 8397 i. Heather Loomis[14] **Brooke** born 20 June 1961.
+ 8398 ii. Frederick Lee **Brooke** II born 1 May 1963.

7086. **Wilfred Lee**[13] **Brooke** (Virginia Dallas[12] **Whipple**, Merritt Pendell[11], Dr. Alfred Augustus[10], Henry Francisco[9], Joseph[8], David[7], Samuel[6], Samuel[5], Cyprian[4], Lt. John[3], Matthew[2], Matthew[1])[492] was born in Rochester, Monroe Co., N.Y. 5 July 1930 and married **Mary Frances Domermuth** in Washington, D. C. 11 August 1951. She was born 27 October 1930.

Wilfred Lee **Brooke** and Mary Frances **Domermuth** had the following children:

    8399 i. Virginia Lucretia[14] **Brooke**[493] born in Massachusetts 16 March 1952 and married Michael A. **Ybarra** in New Braunfels,[494] Tex. 16 June 1985. He was born 20 May 1955.
+   8400 ii. Wilfred Lee **Brooke** III born 29 April 1953.
    8401 iii. Arthur Lee **Brooke**[495] born 22 May 1955 and married Katherine Marie **Kennedy** 26 August 1989.
+   8402 iv. Mina May **Brooke** born 24 January 1957.
+   8403 v. Charles Lee **Brooke** born 4 October 1958.

7087. **John Almonte**[13] **Brooke** (Virginia Dallas[12] **Whipple**, Merritt Pendell[11], Dr. Alfred Augustus[10], Henry Francisco[9], Joseph[8], David[7], Samuel[6], Samuel[5], Cyprian[4], Lt. John[3], Matthew[2], Matthew[1])[496] was born in Rochester, Monroe Co., N.Y. 9 May 1934 and married **Georgia Eisermann** in Oak Park Cook Co., Ill. 21 December 1958. She was born 1 December 1939.

John Almonte **Brooke** and Georgia **Eisermann** had the following children:

+   8404 i. Elizabeth Michelle[14] **Brooke** born 21 July 1961.
+   8405 ii. Cynthia Renee **Brooke** born 11 September 1962.
+   8406 iii. John Eisermann **Brooke** born 28 September 1966.
+   8407 iv. Katherine Blanchard **Brooke** born 7 May 1969.
    8408 v. Martha Suzanne **Brooke**[497] born 28 April 1972.

7088. **Sharon Serene**[13] **Whipple** (Ralph Alfred[12], Merritt Pendell[11], Dr. Alfred Augustus[10], Henry Francisco[9], Joseph[8], David[7], Samuel[6], Samuel[5], Cyprian[4], Lt. John[3], Matthew[2], Matthew[1])[498] was born in Germantown, Adams Co., Penn. 27 September 1941 and married **Lynn Selke** in Rochester, Monroe Co., N.Y. 13 July 1963. She was born 28 October 1939.[499]

Sharon Serene **Whipple** and Lynn **Selke** had the following children born in Rochester:

    8409 i. Andrew Lynn[14] **Selke**[500] 30 March 1967.
    8410 ii. Laura Serene **Selke**[501] 25 August 1971 and married Richard **Fisher** in Clearwater, Pinellas Co., Fla. 16 January 1999.

7089. **Stephanie**[13] **Whipple** (Ralph Alfred[12], Merritt Pendell[11], Dr. Alfred Augustus[10], Henry Francisco[9], Joseph[8], David[7], Samuel[6], Samuel[5], Cyprian[4], Lt. John[3], Matthew[2], Matthew[1])[502] was born in Rochester, Monroe Co., N.Y. 1 October 1944 and married **Clark Schuler** in Erie, Erie Co., Penn. 9 July 1966. He was born 20 August 1944.[503]

Stephanie **Whipple** and Clark **Schuler** had the following children:
+   8411   i.   Carrrie Lee[14] **Schuler** born 13 January 1969.
+   8412   ii.   Kimberly Marsh **Schuler** born 16 December 1970.

7091. **Joyce Ellen**[13] **Whipple** (Rev. Leroy Byron[12], William[11], Dr. Alfred Augustus[10], Henry Francisco[9], Joseph[8], David[7], Samuel[6], Samuel[5], Cyprian[4], Lt. John[3], Matthew[2], Matthew[1])[504] was born in Oskaloosa, Mahaska Co., Iowa 20 October 1943 and married **Charles Lester Pike**. She is a graduate of the U. of Massachusetts School of Nursing, Amherst, Hampshire Co. The family lives in Monument, El Paso Co., Colo. (2000)

Joyce Ellen **Whipple** and Charles Lester **Pike** had the following children:
+   8413   i.   Kimberly R.[14] **Pike** born 14 October 1967.
      8414   ii.   Heather **Pike**[505] born 27 January 1970 and was graduated from Fort Lewis College in Durango, La Plata Co., Colo. She spent two years in Uganda as a Missionary for World Harvest Mission and now teaches in Colorado Springs, El Paso Co., Colo. (2000)

7094. **William**[13] **Whipple III** (William[12], William[11], Dr. Alfred Augustus[10], Henry Francisco[9], Joseph[8], David[7], Samuel[6], Samuel[5], Cyprian[4], Lt. John[3], Matthew[2], Matthew[1])[506] was born in Kearney, Buffalo Co., Nebr. 30 August 1950 and married twice. (1) **Regina Goulware** 3 July 1972. She was born in Oklahoma City, Oklahoma Co., Okla. 2 August 1950. (2) **Linda Joyce Werner** 12 October 1985. She was born in Passaic, Passaic Co., N.J. 16 March 1961.[507] William adopted Linda's daughter Melrose Beth.

William **Whipple** III had the following child:
+   8415   i.   William[14] **Whipple** IV born 30 July 1973.

7095. **Stephen**[13] **Whipple** (William[12], William[11], Dr. Alfred Augustus[10], Henry Francisco[9], Joseph[8], David[7], Samuel[6], Samuel[5], Cyprian[4], Lt. John[3], Matthew[2], Matthew[1])[508] was born 8 August 1952 and married **Barbara (__)**. Stephen and Barbara adopted their first child, Brian, born 18 July 1972 in Rochester, Olmsted Co., Minn. The family was living in St. Cloud, Stearns Co., Minn. in February 1989.

Stephen **Whipple** and Barbara **(__)** had the following children born in Rochester:
  8416 i. Dennis[14] **Whipple**[509] 4 June 1975.
  8417 ii. Mark **Whipple**[510] 10 May 1978.
  8418 iii. Kevin **Whipple**[511] 1 April 1981.

7096. **Rand**[13] **Whipple** (William[12], William[11], Dr. Alfred Augustus[10], Henry Francisco[9], Joseph[8], David[7], Samuel[6], Samuel[5], Cyprian[4], Lt. John[3], Matthew[2], Matthew[1])[512] was born in Beaumont, Jefferson Co., Tex. 24 April 1955 and married **Betsy Dowd**.

Rand **Whipple** and Betsy **Dowd** had the following children born in Bloomsburg, Daupin Co., Penn.:
  8419 i. MacCambridge Dowd[14] **Whipple**[513] 21 March 1989.
  8420 ii. Walter **Whipple**[514] in September 1993.

7097. **Laurie**[13] **Whipple** (William[12], William[11], Dr. Alfred Augustus[10], Henry Francisco[9], Joseph[8], David[7], Samuel[6], Samuel[5], Cyprian[4], Lt. John[3], Matthew[2], Matthew[1])[515] was born in Bloomsburg, Daupin Co., Penn. 10 August 1957 and married **Robert Andred Sells** in Minneapolis, Hennepin Co., Minn. 6 September 1986.

Laurie **Whipple** and Robert Andred **Sells** had the following children born in Minneapolis:
  8421 i. Elizabeth Johanna[14] **Whipple**[516] 3 January 1989. Her surname is Whipple, not Sells.
  8422 ii. Andra Lee **Whipple**[517] 3 March 1992. Her surname is Whipple, not Sells.

7099. **Eugene Lee**[13] **Smith** (Alfreda Louise[12] **Whipple**, William[11], Dr. Alfred Augustus[10], Henry Francisco[9], Joseph[8], David[7], Samuel[6], Samuel[5], Cyprian[4], Lt. John[3], Matthew[2], Matthew[1])[518] was born in North Platte, Lincoln Co., Nebr. 3 August 1945 and married twice. (1) **Wanda Jane Millett** in Wahoo, Saunders Co., Nebr. 15 April 1966. She is the daughter of Walter **Millett** and Gladys **(__)**. They were divorced in 1977. (2) **Theresa Steinkamp** in Lake Oswego, Clackamas Co., Oreg. 29 September 1978. Theresa,[519] daughter of George **Steinkamp** and Elaine **Schmidt**, was born in Spokane, Spokane Co., Wash. 30 April 1956. Eugene and Wanda adopted a brother and sister in New York: Jose Lee, born 7 June 1969 and Ramona Wanda, born 13 January 1968. They also adopted Heather Jane, born 19 May 1972 in Anchorage, Anchorage Borough, Alaska. Eugene, a Civil Engineer, is a graduate of Omaha (Nebr.) University.

Eugene Lee **Smith** and Wanda Jane **Millett** had the following child born in Omaha:

 8423 i. Stacy Lee[14] **Smith**[520] 8 September 1967.

Eugene Lee **Smith** and Theresa **Steinkamp** had the following children:

 8424 ii. Joshua Lee Smith[521] born in Oakland, Alameda Co., Calif. 6 November 1980.

 8425 iii. Rachel Domenico **Smith**[522] born in Pueblo, Pueblo Co., Colo. 2 September 1985.

7102. **Hervy Andrew**[13] **Saathoff** (Marian Learned[12] **Whipple**, William[11], Dr. Alfred Augustus[10], Henry Francisco[9], Joseph[8], David[7], Samuel[6], Samuel[5], Cyprian[4], Lt. John[3], Matthew[2], Matthew[1])[523] was born in Kearney, Buffalo Co., Nebr. 15 August 1941 and married **Donna Mae Kovanda** in North Platte, Lincoln Co., Nebr. 15 November 1970.

Hervy Andrew **Saathoff** and Donna Mae **Kovanda** had the following children:

+ 8426 i. April Mae[14] **Saathoff** born 9 July 1971.
  8427 ii. Lea Ann **Saathoff**[524] born in North Platte 27 May 1973 and married Chad **Reece** in 1993.

7103. **Garret Wendell**[13] **Saathoff** (Marian Learned[12] **Whipple**, William[11], Dr. Alfred Augustus[10], Henry Francisco[9], Joseph[8], David[7], Samuel[6], Samuel[5], Cyprian[4], Lt. John[3], Matthew[2], Matthew[1])[525] was born in Kearney, Buffalo Co., Nebr. 27 September 1943 and married **Janet Ione Brown** in Murray, Salt Lake Co., Utah 1 November 1964.

Garret Wendell **Saathoff** had the following child:

 8428 i. Jonathan Wendel[14] **Saathoff**[526] born in Hahn Air Force Base, Germany 27 December 1975.

7104. **Arthur Kent**[13] **Saathoff** (Marian Learned[12] **Whipple**, William[11], Dr. Alfred Augustus[10], Henry Francisco[9], Joseph[8], David[7], Samuel[6], Samuel[5], Cyprian[4], Lt. John[3], Matthew[2], Matthew[1])[527] was born in Kearney, Buffalo Co., Nebr. 7 July 1947 and married **Mary Lou Sack** in North Platte, Lincoln Co., Nebr. 29 July 1970.

Arthur Kent **Saathoff** and Mary Lou **Sack** had the following children:

+ 8429 i. Michael Kent[14] **Saathoff** born 9 December 1972.
+ 8430 ii. Andi Marie **Saathoff** born 22 December 1974.

7105. **Bonnie Jean**[13] **Saathoff** (Marian Learned[12] **Whipple**, William[11], Dr. Alfred Augustus[10], Henry Francisco[9], Joseph[8], David[7], Samuel[6], Samuel[5], Cyprian[4], Lt. John[3], Matthew[2], Matthew[1])[528] was born in Kearney, Buffalo Co., Nebr. 5 July 1948 and married **Robert R. Smith Jr.** 8 October 1967.

Bonnie Jean **Saathoff** and Robert R. **Smith** Jr. had the following children:
+ 8431 i. Tami Jo[14] **Smith** born 10 January 1969.
  8432 ii. Robert Shawn **Smith**[529] born in North Platte, Lincoln Co., Nebr. 29 June 1972 and married Amy Jo **Sedlmajer** there 1 May 1999. She was born in Valentine, Cherry Co., Nebr. 20 June 1971.[530]

7106. **Leslie Sue**[13] **Saathoff** (Marian Learned[12] **Whipple**, William[11], Dr. Alfred Augustus[10], Henry Francisco[9], Joseph[8], David[7], Samuel[6], Samuel[5], Cyprian[4], Lt. John[3], Matthew[2], Matthew[1])[531] was born in North Platte, Lincoln Co., Nebr. 10 October 1949 and married **William Allen Burke** there 16 July 1971. He is the son of Keith **Burke** and Lenore **Allen**.

Leslie Sue Saathoff and William Allen Burke had the following children:
  8433 i. Jason Edward[14] **Burke**[532] born in Fort Riley, Geary Co., Kans. 26 September 1972 and married Apinya **Supap** in Seoul, South Korea, 28 November 1998.
  8434 ii. Keith **Burke**[533] born in North Platte 16 August 1975.

7108. **Prof. Thomas Walton**[13] **Whipple** (Dean Sander[12], Dr. Willis Walton[11], James Spencer[10], Henry Francisco[9], Joseph[8], David[7], Samuel[6], Samuel[5], Cyprian[4], Lt. John[3], Matthew[2], Matthew[1])[534] was born in Salamanca, Cattaraugus Co., N.Y 29 August 1942 and married **Elizabeth Ann Whiting** 4 June 1966. Elizabeth,[535] daughter of James Oliver **Whiting** and Lucretia Jean **Hill**, was born in Marietta, Washington Co., Ohio 14 June 1946. They were divorced in 1988.

Prof. Thomas Walton **Whipple** and Elizabeth Ann **Whiting** had the following children born in Toronto, York, Ontario, Canada:
  8435 i. Courtney Whiting[14] **Whipple**[536] 14 September 1974.
  8436 ii. Erin Whiting **Whipple**[537] 6 March 1976.

7109. **Deanne Marie**[13] **Whipple** (Dean Sander[12], Dr. Willis Walton[11], James Spencer[10], Henry Francisco[9], Joseph[8], David[7], Samuel[6], Samuel[5], Cyprian[4], Lt. John[3], Matthew[2], Matthew[1])[538] was born in Salamanca, Cattaraugus Co., N.Y 13 December 1948 and married twice. (1) **Donald Hauck** in Salamanca 22 April 1969. (2) **Patrick Mogon** in Salamanca 30 September 1978.

{ G 1240 }

Deanne Marie **Whipple** and Donald **Hauck** had the following children born in Salamanca:

  8437 i. Vicki Lynn[14] **Hauck**[539] 21 November 1971.
  8438 ii. Suzanne Marie **Hauck**[540] 29 April 1975.

7114. **Gail Ann**[13] **Whipple** (Rev. John Walton[12], Ara Leroy[11], Willis Walton[10], Henry Francisco[9], Joseph[8], David[7], Samuel[6], Samuel[5], Cyprian[4], Lt. John[3], Matthew[2], Matthew[1])[541] was born in Paris, France 18 April 1937 and married **Bowen Bruere Conser** in Fullerton, Orange Co., Calif. 9 November 1962.

Gail Ann **Whipple** and Bowen Bruere **Conser** had the following children born in Whittier, Los Angles Co., Calif.:

  8439 i. William[14] **Conser**[542] 3 October 1963.
  8440 ii. Cheryl Ann **Conser**[543] 25 August 1966.

7116. **Walter Wesley**[13] **Hammond III** (Eleanor[12] **McGee**, Inez May[11] **Hobart**, Edwin Whipple[10], Sarah[9] **Whipple**, Samuel[8], David[7], Samuel[6], Samuel[5], Cyprian[4], Lt. John[3], Matthew[2], Matthew[1])[544] was born in Baltimore, Baltimore City Co., Md. 12 April 1932 and married **Beatrice Eve Robertson** in 1955. He earned a degree in Public Administration from Michigan State University, East Lansing, Ingham Co.

Walter Wesley **Hammond** III and Beatrice Eve **Robertson** had the following children:

  8441 i. Douglas Hobart[14] **Hammond** born in Baltimore 1 March 1956.[545]
  8442 ii. Alison Anne **Hammond** born in Pittsburgh, Allegheny Co., Penn. 13 February 1958.[546]

7117. **Ann Janet**[13] **Hammond** (Eleanor[12] **McGee**, Inez May[11] **Hobart**, Edwin Whipple[10], Sarah[9] **Whipple**, Samuel[8], David[7], Samuel[6], Samuel[5], Cyprian[4], Lt. John[3], Matthew[2], Matthew[1])[547] was born in Danville, Montour Co., Penn. 25 February 1935 and married **Roger Glenn Kidston** 28 December 1956. Ann was graduated from the U. of Michigan, Ann Arbor, Washtenaw Co., in 1957 with a Degree in Speech Correction. Roger earned a law degree from the U. of Michigan Law School in 1956. The family was residing near Climax, Kalamazoo Co., Mich. in 1968 and Roger practiced law at Kalamazoo, Kalamazoo Co., Mich. He is a veteran of the U.S. Marine Corps.

Ann Janet **Hammond** and Roger Glenn **Kidston** had the following children:
- 8443 i. Cheryl Ann[14] **Kidston** born in Ann Arbor 14 December 1958.[548]
- 8444 ii. Cynthia Lynn **Kidston** born in Ann Arbor 11 September 1960.[549]
- 8445 iii. Kevin Scot **Kidston** born in Kalamazoo 5 November 1963.[550]

7119. **Marsha**[13] **Whipple** (Robert Hugh[12], Walter Henry[11], Watson H.[10], William[9], Samuel[8], David[7], Samuel[6], Samuel[5], Cyprian[4], Lt. John[3], Matthew[2], Matthew[1])[551] was born in Boston, Suffolk Co., Mass. 17 July 1944 and married **Ernst Jochen Nitzsche** in Schwabisch Hall, Germany 22 April 1973. Ernst,[552] son of Erwin Peter **Nitzsche** and Rosemarie **Buness**, was born in Berlin, Germany 24 January 1943.

Marsha **Whipple** and Ernst Jochen **Nitzsche** had the following children:
- 8446 i. Julia[55] **Nitzsche**[553] born in Fulda, Hessen, Germany 8 March 1976.
- 8447 ii. Jessica **Nitzsche**[554] born in Fulda, Hessen 26 November 1977.
- 8448 iii. Tobias **Nitzsche**[555] born in Lauterbach, Hessen, Germany 14 April 1980.

7120. **John Walter**[13] **Whipple** (Robert Hugh[12], Walter Henry[11], Watson H.[10], William[9], Samuel[8], David[7], Samuel[6], Samuel[5], Cyprian[4], Lt. John[3], Matthew[2], Matthew[1])[556] was born in Medina, Orleans Co., N.Y. 29 May 1947 and married **Brenda Jean Flynn** in Lyndonville, Orleans Co., N.Y. 21 August 1969 Brenda, daughter of Gordon Edward **Flynn** and Marian Janet **Allard**, was born in Medina 16 November 1948.[557]

John Walter **Whipple** and Brenda Jean **Flynn** had the following children:
- + 8449 i. Cassandra[14] **Whipple** born 30 May 1970.
- + 8450 ii. Thomas John **Whipple** born 6 April 1973.
- 8451 iii. Patrick Bailey **Whipple**[558] born in Rochester, Monroe Co., N.Y. 22 March 1976.

7121. **Julia**[13] **Whipple** (Robert Hugh[12], Walter Henry[11], Watson H.[10], William[9], Samuel[8], David[7], Samuel[6], Samuel[5], Cyprian[4], Lt. John[3], Matthew[2], Matthew[1])[559] was born in Medina, Orleans Co., N.Y. 26 May 1952 and married twice. (1) **Lynn Watts** in Lyndonville, Orleans Co., N.Y. 29 October 1970. Lynn,[560] son of Robert Laverne **Watts** and Crystal Virginia **Bayne**, was born 3 April 1952. (2) **James Bacon**.

Julia **Whipple** and Lynn **Watts** had the following children:
- \+ 8452 i. Michele Lynne[14] **Watts** born 9 March 1971.
- 8453 ii. James Robert **Watts**[561] born in Medina 25 April 1973.

7122. **Laura**[13] **Whipple** (Robert Hugh[12], Walter Henry[11], Watson H.[10], William[9], Samuel[8], David[7], Samuel[6], Samuel[5], Cyprian[4], Lt. John[3], Matthew[2], Matthew[1])[562] was born in Medina, Orleans Co., N.Y. 21 April 1955 and married **John Brian Belson** in Lyndonville, Orleans Co., N.Y. 26 January 1974. John,[563] son of Laverne Franklin **Belson** and Eleanor Genevieve **Batt**, was born in Brockport, Monroe Co., N.Y. 16 October 1953.

Laura **Whipple** and John Brian **Belson** had the following children born in Rochester, Monroe Co.:
- 8454 i. Adrienne[14] **Belson**[564] 13 April 1975.
- 8455 ii. Janet **Belson**[565] 24 July 1977.
- 8456 iii. Sarah **Belson**[566] 30 January 1979.

7123. **James Robert**[13] **Whipple** (James Watson[12], Walter Henry[11], Watson H.[10], William[9], Samuel[8], David[7], Samuel[6], Samuel[5], Cyprian[4], Lt. John[3], Matthew[2], Matthew[1])[567] was born in Medina, Orleans Co., N.Y. 9 January 1956 and married **Jeanne Steo** in Rochester, Monroe Co., N.Y. 8 October 1983. She was born in Rochester 29 September 1958.[568]

James Robert **Whipple** and Jeanne **Steo** had the following children: born in Rochester
- 8457 i. Matthew[14] **Whipple**[569] 21 December 1987.
- 8458 ii. Benjamin **Whipple**[570] 20 August 1989.

7126. **Jeanne Carolyn**[13] **Whipple** (James Watson[12], Walter Henry[11], Watson H.[10], William[9], Samuel[8], David[7], Samuel[6], Samuel[5], Cyprian[4], Lt. John[3], Matthew[2], Matthew[1])[571] was born in Medina, Orleans Co., N.Y. 20 December 1967 and married **Scott Goetze** in Lyndonville, Orleans Co., N.Y. 30 May 1987. He was born in Medina 26 July 1967.[572]

Jeanne Carolyn **Whipple** and Scott **Goetze** had the following children:
- 8459 i. Justin[14] **Goetze**[573] born in Las Vegas, Clark Co., Nev. 21 March 1990.
- 8460 ii. Thomas James **Goetze**[574] born in Tacoma, Pierce Co., Wash. 30 September 1994.

7127. **Susan**[13] **Whipple** (David Doty[12], Hugh Scott[11], Francis Henry[10], William[9], Samuel[8], David[7], Samuel[6], Samuel[5], Cyprian[4], Lt. John[3], Matthew[2], Matthew[1])[575] was born in Washington, D.C. 15 January 1954 and married **Christopher Kent Casselman** in Bon Lomond, Santa Cruz Co., Calif. 2 November 1975. Chris,[576] son of William Lucius **Casselman** and Barbara Jean **McKenzie**, was born in North Hollywood, Los Angeles Co., Calif. 16 January 1952. He is a Project Coordinator/Consultant with a computer company (1999). Susan is an Instructional Aide (1999).

Susan **Whipple** and Christopher Kent **Casselman** had the following children born in Santa Cruz, Santa Cruz Co. Calif.:
  8461 i. Alexander Glynn[14] **Casselman**[577] 13 January 1984.
  8462 ii. Katharine Gwenn **Casselman**[578] 26 July 1990.

7128. **Marc Evan**[13] **Whipple** (David Doty[12], Hugh Scott[11], Francis Henry[10], William[9], Samuel[8], David[7], Samuel[6], Samuel[5], Cyprian[4], Lt. John[3], Matthew[2], Matthew[1])[579] was born in Rangoon, Burma (now Myanmar) 10 February 1956 and married **Jeanne Stratford** in Midland Park, Bergen Co., N.J. 20 April 1980. Jeanne,[580] daughter of Eugene Francis **Stratford** and Helen Anne **Murphy**, was born in Rockville Centre, Nassau Co., N.Y. 8 December 1953. Marc is an Architect.

Marc Evan **Whipple** and Jeanne **Stratford** had the following children born in Los Angeles, Los Angeles Co., Calif.:
  8463 i. Tyler Stratford[14] **Whipple**[581] 9 May 1990.
  8464 ii. Max Doty **Whipple**[582] 21 August 1991.

7129. **Tim Decker**[13] **Whipple** (David Doty[12], Hugh Scott[11], Francis Henry[10], William[9], Samuel[8], David[7], Samuel[6], Samuel[5], Cyprian[4], Lt. John[3], Matthew[2], Matthew[1])[583] was born in Lubumbashi, Zaire 1 August 1962 and married **Anne Kearney Harvey** in Alexandria, Alexandria City Co., Va. 25 August 1995. Anne,[584] daughter of Albert Clyde **Harvey** and Nancy Glenn **Rutherford**, was born 4 July 1963. Tim is a Business Consultant (1999).

Tim Decker **Whipple** and Anne Kearney **Harvey** had the following child:
  8465 i. Tim Decker[14] **Whipple**[585] born in Prague, Czech Republic 25 June 1998.

7130. **Scott Adams Montgomery**[13] **Whipple** (David Doty[12], Hugh Scott[11], Francis Henry[10], William[9], Samuel[8], David[7], Samuel[6], Samuel[5], Cyprian[4], Lt. John[3], Matthew[2], Matthew[1])[586] was born in Falls Church,

Falls Church City Area Co., Va. 31 May 1964 and married **Philippa Jane Edwards** in Kew Gardens, Richmond, Surrey, England 25 July 1992. Philippa, born in Aldershot, Hampshire, England 7 May 1966, is the daughter of Judge John Braham Scott **Edwards** and Veronica M. **Dunbar**. Sam is a Broadcast Journalist and Philippa is a Barrister (1999).

Scott Adams Montgomery **Whipple** and Philippa Jane **Edwards** had the following child:
    8466   i.   William John Edwards[14] **Whipple**[587] born in London, England 5 September 1997.

7136. **Janis Marie**[13] **Smith** (Ruth Janis[12] **Whipple**, Ralph Howard[11], Colby Favelle[10], Isaac[9], Hiram[8], David[7], Samuel[6], Samuel[5], Cyprian[4], Lt. John[3], Matthew[2], Matthew[1])[588] was born in Cleveland, Cuyahoga Co., Ohio 27 September 1946 and married **Charles Feazel** 31 August 1968. He was born 30 April 1945.[589]

Janis Marie **Smith** and Charles **Feazel** had the following children:
    8467   i.   Christopher[14] **Feazel**[590] born in Bethesda, Montgomery Co., Md. 29 October 1971.
    8468   ii.   Kathlyn Ruth **Feazel**[591] born in Bartlesville, Washington Co., Okla. 16 May 1978.

7139. **Cheryl**[13] **Lyman** (Genevieve Eynon[12] **Whipple**, Ralph Howard[11], Colby Favelle[10], Isaac[9], Hiram[8], David[7], Samuel[6], Samuel[5], Cyprian[4], Lt. John[3], Matthew[2], Matthew[1])[592] was born 28 November 1955 and married **Ira Russell** who was born 28 August 1946.[593]

Cheryl **Lyman** and Ira **Russell** had the following child:
    8469   i.   Stara[14] **Russell**[594] born 7 April 1982.

7162. **Jane Boyd**[13] **Harriman** (Mayland Earl[12], Charles Mayland[11], Daniel S.[10], Joel George[9], Lucy[8] **Ray**, Jonathan[7], Amos[6], Hannah[5] **Goodale**, Sarah[4] **Whipple**, Joseph[3], Matthew[2], Matthew[1])[595] was born in Shreveport, Caddo Parish, La. 8 November 1950 and married **Stephen Gary Lockhart** in Port Arthur, Jefferson Co., Tex. 15 July 1967.

Jane Boyd **Harriman** and Stephen Gary **Lockhart** had the following child born in Port Arthur:
    8470   i.   Natalie Michelle[14] **Lockhart**[596] 20 April 1969.

7163. **Don Robert**[13] **Moore** II (Phyllis Jean[12] **Davis**, Ruby Edna[11] **Harriman**, George Dearborn[10], Joel George[9], Lucy[8] **Ray**, Jonathan[7], Amos[6], Hannah[5] **Goodale**, Sarah[4] **Whipple**, Joseph[3], Matthew[2], Matthew[1])[597] was born 13 October 1947 and married twice. (1) **Connie Lynn Christiansen** in Delphi, Carroll Co., Ind. 18 June 1966. She was born 16 October 1948.[598] (2) **Lois Ann Williams** in Carroll Co. 13 October 1990. Lois,[599] daughter of Ed **Williams** and Martha Lillian (__), was born in Cutler, Carroll Co. 11 April 1949.

Don Robert **Moore** II and Connie Lynn **Christiansen** had the following children:
- 8471 i. Robert Lee[14] **Moore**[600] born in Lafayette, Tippecanoe Co., Ind. 29 July 1967.
- 8472 ii. Darrell Dean **Moore**[601] born in Lafayette 27 November 1968.
- + 8473 iii. Crystal Renee **Moore** born 14 October 1972.

7165. **Gary Gene**[13] **Moore** (Phyllis Jean[12] **Davis**, Ruby Edna[11] **Harriman**, George Dearborn[10], Joel George[9], Lucy[8] **Ray**, Jonathan[7], Amos[6], Hannah[5] **Goodale**, Sarah[4] **Whipple**, Joseph[3], Matthew[2], Matthew[1])[602] was born 18 January 1951 and married **Debra Kay Hughes** in Flora, Carroll Co., Ind. 30 June 1973. Debra,[603] daughter of Marcus **Hughes** and Iris **Lane**, was born 14 July 1956. They were divorced in 1981. Debra Kay also married **Ron Osborn** and **Jeffery Perkins**. Gary served in the Army in Germany 1970-72.

Gary Gene **Moore** and Debra Kay **Hughes** had the following children:
- + 8474 i. Cody Lane[14] **Moore** born 8 March 1976.
- 8475 ii. Kinzie Dawn **Moore**[604] born in Lafayette, Tippecanoe Co., Ind. 26 September 1977.
- 8476 iii. Chase Jay **Moore**[605] born in Austin, Travis Co., Tex. 28 July 1979.

7166. **Richard Gene**[13] **Davis** (Richard Lee[12], Ruby Edna[11] **Harriman**, George Dearborn[10], Joel George[9], Lucy[8] **Ray**, Jonathan[7], Amos[6], Hannah[5] **Goodale**, Sarah[4] **Whipple**, Joseph[3], Matthew[2], Matthew[1])[606] was born in Lafayette, Tippecanoe Co., Ind. 3 December 1954 and married **Martha Jane Saubert** in Delphi, Carroll Co., Ind. 19 October 1975. She was born in Tippecanoe Co. 25 February 1957.[607]

Richard Gene **Davis** and Martha Jane **Saubert** had the following children born in Lafayette:
- + 8477 i. Hutch E.[14] **Davis** 14 January 1977.

8478 ii. Travis Levi **Davis**[608] 13 April 1979.
8479 iii. Casey Jo **Davis**[609] 21 May 1981.

7167. **Leetta Darlene**[13] **Davis** (Richard Lee[12], Ruby Edna[11] **Harriman**, George Dearborn[10], Joel George[9], Lucy[8] **Ray**, Jonathan[7], Amos[6], Hannah[5] **Goodale**, Sarah[4] **Whipple**, Joseph[3], Matthew[2], Matthew[1])[610] was born in Lafayette, Tippecanoe Co., Ind. 24 October 1957 and married twice. (1) **Rickey Lee Stapleton** in Delphi, Carroll Co., Ind. 14 February 1976. He was born in Tippecanoe Co. 16 August 1958.[611] (2) **Kenneth Ross Seiler** 30 March 1996. Kenneth,[612] son of Kenneth **Seiler** and Jessica **Oswalt**, was born in Tippecanoe Co. 4 March 1961.

Leetta Darlene **Davis** and Rickey Lee **Stapleton** had the following children:
8480 i. Rickey Lee[14] **Stapleton**[613] born in Tippecanoe Co. 23 August 1976.
8481 ii. Jesse Lee **Stapleton**[614] born in Lafayette 20 November 1980.

7171. **Earl Charles**[13] **Duell** (Grace Elenore[12] **Morgan**, Fredrick V.[11], Nehemiah[10], Samuel[9], Betsey[8] **Whipple**, Nehemiah[7], Benjamin[6], Francis[5], Jonathan[4], Joseph[3], Matthew[2], Matthew[1])[615] was born in Reedsburg, Sauk Co., Wisc. 29 December 1905 and died 7 February 1966 in Lime Ridge, Sauk Co., Wisc., at 60 years of age. He married **Emma Clara Bombard** in Lima, Pepin Co., Wisc. 15 July 1929. Emma,[616] daughter of William **Bombard** and Edith **Norton**, was born in Balltown, Maine 15 June 1910 and died 20 May 1960 in Lime Ridge, at 49 years of age. She also married **Clarence Jacobie**. Earl and Emma are buried in St. Alphonsus Cemetery, West Glens Falls, Warren Co., N.Y.

Earl Charles **Duell** and Emma Clara **Bombard** had the following children:
+ 8482 i. Joseph A.[14] **Duell** born 21 October 1930.
+ 8483 ii. Victoria **Duell** born 6 February 1936.
  8484 iii. Marion K. **Duell**[617] born in Lime Ridge 24 September 1938 and died there 30 March 1999, at 60 years of age. Buried in Pine View Cemetery, Queensbury, Warren Co., N.Y. She married William **Mellon** in Lake George, Warren Co., N.Y. 12 September 1959.

7172. **Dorothy**[13] **Duell** (Grace Elenore[12] **Morgan**, Fredrick V.[11], Nehemiah[10], Samuel[9], Betsey[8] **Whipple**, Nehemiah[7], Benjamin[6], Francis[5], Jonathan[4], Joseph[3], Matthew[2], Matthew[1])[618] was born in Reedsburg, Sauk Co., Wisc. 16 October 1908 and died there 13 September 1968, at 59 years of age. She married **Albert Fleming**.

Dorothy **Duell** and Albert **Fleming** had the following children born in Lime Ridge, Wisc:
> 8485 i. Albert Henry[14] **Fleming**[619] 1 October 1931.
> 8486 ii. Elenor **Fleming**[620] 11 August 1932.
> 8487 iii. George F. **Fleming**[621] 3 June 1937.
> 8488 iv. Robert Earl **Fleming**[622] 10 February 1944.

7173. **Gladys Cora**[13] **Duell** (Grace Elenore[12] **Morgan**, Fredrick V.[11], Nehemiah[10], Samuel[9], Betsey[8] **Whipple**, Nehemiah[7], Benjamin[6], Francis[5], Jonathan[4], Joseph[3], Matthew[2], Matthew[1])[623] was born in Reedsburg, Sauk Co., Wisc. 19 June 1911 and died 26 November 1986 in Dudley, Worcester Co., Mass., at 75 years of age. Buried in St. Alphonses Cemetery, West Glens Falls, Warren Co., N.Y. She married **Emmanuel Joseph Maille**.

Gladys Cora **Duell** and Emmanuel Joseph **Maille** had the following children born in Lime Ridge, Sauk Co., Wisc.:
> 8489 i. Earl Emmanuel[14] **Maille**[624] in 1928 and died there in 1998, at 70 years of age.
> 8490 ii. Doris Marie **Maille**[625] in 1929.
> 8491 iii. Edward Leo **Maille**[626] 10 June 1932.
> 8492 iv. William Wallace **Maille**[627] 21 June 1938.
> 8493 v. Sandra Augustine **Maille**[628] in 1942.
> 8494 vi. Harvey Thomas Reginald **Maille**[629] in 1945.

7177. **Maurica B.**[13] **Norton** (James Newton[12], Charles Russel[11], Judge James Carmont[10], Harriet Whipple[9] **Carpenter**, Anner[8] **Whipple**, Nehemiah[7], Benjamin[6], Francis[5], Jonathan[4], Joseph[3], Matthew[2], Matthew[1])[630] was born in Guthrie, Logan Co., Okla. 19 December 1917 and married **Zeb E. Baylis** in January 1937.

Maurica B. **Norton** and Zeb E. **Baylis** had the following children:
> 8495 i. James[14] **Baylis**.[631]
> 8496 ii. Betsy **Baylis**.[632]

7179. **Helen Margaret**[13] **Jaggard** (Mary[12] **Norton**, Charles Russel[11], Judge James Carmont[10], Harriet Whipple[9] **Carpenter**, Anner[8] **Whipple**, Nehemiah[7], Benjamin[6], Francis[5], Jonathan[4], Joseph[3], Matthew[2], Matthew[1])[633] was born in Emporia, Lyon Co., Kans. 14 September 1912 and died in April 1967 in Bakersfield, Kern Co., Calif., at 54 years of age. She married **Arthur Hufford** in Las Vegas, Clark Co., Nev. in May 1942.

Helen Margaret **Jaggard** and Arthur **Hufford** had the following child:
+   8497   i.   Mary Louise[14] **Hufford** born 24 August 1950.

7180. **Ralph Warren**[13] **Jaggard** (Mary[12] **Norton**, Charles Russel[11], Judge James Carmont[10], Harriet Whipple[9] **Carpenter**, Anner[8] **Whipple**, Nehemiah[7], Benjamin[6], Francis[5], Jonathan[4], Joseph[3], Matthew[2], Matthew[1])[634] was born in Colby, Thomas Co., Kans. 22 January 1914 and died 27 May 1986 in Sacramento, Sacramento Co., Calif., at 72 years of age. He married **Anna Mae Beard** in Las Vegas, Clark Co., Nev. 11 July 1937. She was born in Milano, Milam Co., Tex. 17 September 1909.[635]

Ralph Warren **Jaggard** and Anna Mae **Beard** had the following children:
+   8498   i.   Richard Allen[14] **Jaggard** born 1 October 1939.
      8499   ii. Ralph Warren **Jaggard** Jr[636] born in Modesto, Stanislaus Co., Calif. 21 July 1947 and married Sharon **Everstine** in Carmichael, Sacramento Co., Calif.

7181. **Elizabeth Ann**[13] **Jaggard** (Mary[12] **Norton**, Charles Russel[11], Judge James Carmont[10], Harriet Whipple[9] **Carpenter**, Anner[8] **Whipple**, Nehemiah[7], Benjamin[6], Francis[5], Jonathan[4], Joseph[3], Matthew[2], Matthew[1])[637] was born in Kingman, Kingman Co., Kans. 9 February 1924 and married **Richard Prescott** in Bakersfield, Kern Co., Calif. 26 December 1948. He died of brain cancer 30 April 1955.[638] Betty Ann earned a Bachelors Degree from Ills College (1947) and a Masters from the University of Pacific, Stockton, San Joaquin Co., Calif. (1965). She was an Engineering Instructor at San Joaquin Delta College in Stockton for 25 years. Her special genealogical interests are in the Carpenter, Norton, and Jaggard families. She does a great deal of volunteer work in her retirement and is a member of the Society of Genealogists in London.

Elizabeth Ann **Jaggard** and Richard **Prescott** had the following children:
+   8500   i.   Paul Richard[14] **Prescott** born 20 March 1953.
      8501   ii. Guy Henry **Prescott**[639] born in Stockton 20 March 1953 and married twice. (1) Janet **Green** in Stockton in May 1973. They were divorced abt 1983. (2) Jeanie **Slater** in Walnut Creek, Contra Costa Co., Calif. 12 March 1994.
+   8502   iii. Thomas Arnold **Prescott** born 7 June 1957.

7182. **Phyllis Albine**[13] **Norton** (Hugh Russell[12], Charles Russel[11], Judge James Carmont[10], Harriet Whipple[9] **Carpenter**, Anner[8] **Whipple**, Nehemiah[7], Benjamin[6], Francis[5], Jonathan[4], Joseph[3], Matthew[2], Matthew[1])[640] was born in Coalinga, Fresno Co., Calif. 26 May 1915 and married **Grant Burr Cooper** in Tiajuana, Mexico, 3 April 1935. Grant,[641] son of Louis Baxter **Cooper** and Johanna **Christensen**, was born in New York, N.Y. 1 April 1903 and died 3 May 1990 in Los Angeles, Los Angeles Co., Calif., at 87 years of age. He also married **Edna Claire Reynolds**.

Phyllis Albine **Norton** and Grant Burr **Cooper** had the following children:
- \+ 8503 i. Meredith Jane[14] **Cooper** born 17 July 1939.
- \+ 8504 ii. Grant Burr **Cooper** Jr. born 20 December 1941.
- 8505 iii. John Norton **Cooper**[642] born in Los Angeles 3 August 1946.

7184. **Virginia Edith**[13] **Norton** (Walter Emmet[12], Charles Russel[11], Judge James Carmont[10], Harriet Whipple[9] **Carpenter**, Anner[8] **Whipple**, Nehemiah[7], Benjamin[6], Francis[5], Jonathan[4], Joseph[3], Matthew[2], Matthew[1])[643] was born in Baldwin Park, Los Angeles Co., Calif. 26 July 1914 and married **Rupert Young** in Las Vegas, Clark Co., Nev. 14 December 1935. He was born in Greenville, Hunt Co., Tex. 16 November 1906 and died 19 May 1981 at 74 years of age.[644]

Virginia Edith **Norton** and Rupert **Young** had the following children:
- \+ 8506 i. Rupert Gordon[14] **Young** born 19 November 1936.
- \+ 8507 ii. Pamela **Young** born 20 March 1942.
- \+ 8508 iii. Michael Bernard **Young** born 21 October 1943.

7185. **James Doyle**[13] **Franklin** (John Dorwin[12], Angeline[11] **McKinley**, William Henry[10], Angeline[9] **Whipple**, Enoch[8], Nehemiah[7], Benjamin[6], Francis[5], Jonathan[4], Joseph[3], Matthew[2], Matthew[1])[645] was born in Dubuque, Dubuque Co., Iowa 9 March 1931 and died of a heart attack while attending a Convention of National School Boards in Houston, Harris Co., Texas 25 March 1977, at 46 years of age. He married **Mardell Reinberg** in Keystone, Benton Co., Iowa 11 February 1956. Mardell,[646] daughter of Herman **Reinberg** and Minnie **Sell**, was born 7 July 1937. She married (2) **Delbert Tinkey**.

James Doyle **Franklin** and Mardell **Reinberg** had the following children:
- \+ 8509 i. Cary John[14] **Franklin** born 26 November 1956.
- \+ 8510 ii. Cal James **Franklin** born 9 July 1958.
- \+ 8511 iii. Candace Marie **Franklin** born 6 September 1959.

7186. **Robert William**[13] **Franklin** (John Dorwin[12], Angeline[11] **McKinley**, William Henry[10], Angeline[9] **Whipple**, Enoch[8], Nehemiah[7], Benjamin[6], Francis[5], Jonathan[4], Joseph[3], Matthew[2], Matthew[1])[647] was born in Guttenburg, Clayton Co., Iowa 4 February 1933 and married **Barbara**

Wichmann in Cedar Rapids, Linn Co., Iowa 4 September 1959. Barbara,[648] daughter of Henry **Wichmann** and Mabel **Behrens**, was born 29 October 1937.

Robert William **Franklin** and Barbara **Wichmann** had the following children born in Cedar Rapids:
+ 8512 i. John Brian[14] **Franklin**[649] 18 April 1960 and married twice. (1) Lynn Lynnette **Carter** in Grandview, Jackson Co., Mo. 28 April 1984. Lynn is the daughter of Gary L. **Carter**.[650] (2) Julie Marie **McLarney** in Kansas City, Jackson Co., Mo. 21 May 1994.
+ 8513 ii. Daniel William **Franklin** 26 March 1961.
  8514 iii. Scott Robert **Franklin**[651] 26 May 1962.

7187. **Shirley Jean**[13] **Franklin** (John Dorwin[12], Angeline[11] **McKinley**, William Henry[10], Angeline[9] **Whipple**, Enoch[8], Nehemiah[7], Benjamin[6], Francis[5], Jonathan[4], Joseph[3], Matthew[2], Matthew[1])[652] was born in Vinton, Benton Co., Iowa 18 December 1934 and married **Robert John Crawford** in Belle Plaine, Benton Co., Iowa 28 February 1954. Robert,[653] son of Ralph E. **Crawford** and Edith **Lewis**, was born in Traer, Tama Co., Iowa 14 October 1930. Shirley is Board Secretary for the North Tama, Iowa School District. Over the years she has compiled extensive records and photographs of the McKinley family in a scrap-book. She says her Dad wanted to raise a football team of sons but she and her sister Virginia spoiled that dream. "But," she says, "he was my friend as well as Dad and always had an answer for my problems that made so much sense. I have always been proud of my McKinley relatives and how they viewed life and their good morals kept me on the straight and narrow when I was tempted in my younger years. So I believe example is so important to the younger generation."

Shirley J. (Franklin) Crawford. Photo courtesy of Shirley Crawford.

Shirley Jean **Franklin** and Robert John **Crawford** had the following children:
+ 8515 i. Linda Jean[14] **Crawford** born 13 September 1954.
+ 8516 ii. Penny Marie **Crawford** born 6 February 1956.
  8517 iii. James Kenan **Crawford**[654] born in Waterloo, Black Hawk Co., Iowa 18 August 1959 and married Nancy Agnes **Scott** in Cedar Rapids, Linn Co., Iowa 1 July 1995. She is the daughter of Harry Sidney **Scott** and Maggie Jane **Johnson**.[655]

7188. **Donald Willard**[13] **Franklin** (John Dorwin[12], Angeline[11] **McKinley**, William Henry[10], Angeline[9] **Whipple**, Enoch[8], Nehemiah[7], Benjamin[6], Francis[5], Jonathan[4], Joseph[3], Matthew[2], Matthew[1])[656] was born in Odebolt, Sac Co., Iowa 19 August 1938 and died 31 March 1997 in Silverton, Marion Co., Oreg., at 58 years of age. Buried in Woodland Cemetery, Des Moines, Polk Co., Iowa. He married **Cecelia Marian Brown** in Yuma, Yuma Co., Ariz. 8 June 1957. Cecelia,[657] daughter of Francis S. **Brown** and Phoebe Marna **Grimes**, was born in Des Moines 4 December 1940. They were divorced in 1980. She married (2) **Kenneth Hartsell** in Silverton in February 1980. Don was raised in Iowa, served in the U.S. Navy 1956-59, and moved to Oregon in 1962. He was awarded a degree in Education by Portland State University, Multnomah Co., in 1966. He taught Social Studies at Molalla, Clackamas Co., Oreg. Union High School his entire teaching career.

Donald Willard **Franklin** and Cecelia Marian **Brown** had the following children:
- + 8518 i. Elizabeth Marie[14] **Franklin** born 25 February 1959.
- 8519 ii. Cheryl Ann **Franklin**[658] born in Ames, Story Co., Iowa 8 September 1960 and died there 10 October at one month of age.
- 8520 iii. Matthew Carl **Franklin**[659] was born in Iowa City, Johnson Co., Iowa 9 November 1961 and married Jean **Martin** in Silverton 20 June 1984. She was born 8 March 1962.[660]
- + 8521 iv. Douglas John **Franklin** born 29 October 1965.

7189. **David Leonard**[13] **Franklin** (John Dorwin[12], Angeline[11] **McKinley**, William Henry[10], Angeline[9] **Whipple**, Enoch[8], Nehemiah[7], Benjamin[6], Francis[5], Jonathan[4], Joseph[3], Matthew[2], Matthew[1])[661] was born in Osceloa, Clarke Co., Iowa 21 May 1940 and married **Rita Johnson** in Keystone, Benton Co., Iowa 12 May 1961. Rita,[662] daughter of Charles Arthur **Johnson** Jr. and Dorothy **Bernstors**, was born in Keystone 24 February 1942.

David Leonard **Franklin** and Rita **Johnson** had the following children:
- + 8522 i. Kellie Jean[14] **Franklin** born 18 December 1961.
- 8523 ii. Todd Charles **Franklin**[663] born in Iowa City, Johnson Co., Iowa 11 December 1962 and married Patricia Courtney **Schneider** in Tampa, Hillsborough Co., Fla. 30 December 1995. Patricia,[664] daughter of William A. **Schneider** and Georgia K. **Langenecker**, was born 9 September 1968.

7190. **Virginia Kay**[13] **Franklin** (John Dorwin[12], Angeline[11] **McKinley**, William Henry[10], Angeline[9] **Whipple**, Enoch[8], Nehemiah[7], Benjamin[6], Francis[5], Jonathan[4], Joseph[3], Matthew[2], Matthew[1])[665] was born in Belle Plaine, Benton Co., Iowa 18 July 1942 and married **Richard Ray Engle** there 9 July 1960. Richard,[666] son of William **Engle** and Dora Helen **Prehn**, was born 11 November 1938. They were divorced 11 July 1985.

Virginia Kay **Franklin** and Richard Ray **Engle** had the following children:
- + 8524 i. Teresa Kay[14] **Engle** born 2 December 1960.
- + 8525 ii. Rodney Ray **Engle** born 18 November 1963.
- 8526 iii. Brett Richard **Engle**[667] born in Waterloo, Black Hawk Co., Iowa 29 August 1967.

7191. **Thomas Arnold**[13] **Franklin** (John Dorwin[12], Angeline[11] **McKinley**, William Henry[10], Angeline[9] **Whipple**, Enoch[8], Nehemiah[7], Benjamin[6], Francis[5], Jonathan[4], Joseph[3], Matthew[2], Matthew[1])[668] was born in Belle Plaine, Benton Co., Iowa 29 October 1944 and married **Pamela Kay Loeffler** in Brighton, Jefferson Co., Iowa 27 August 1967. Pamela,[669] daughter of Willard **Loeffler** and Ruth Elizabeth **Shuppy**, was born in Washington, Washington Co., Iowa 17 February 1947.

Thomas Arnold **Franklin** and Pamela Kay **Loeffler** had the following children:
- + 8527 i. Kimberly Jo[14] **Franklin** born 16 March 1968.
- 8528 ii. Tomi Jo **Franklin**[670] born in Cedar Rapids, Linn Co., Iowa 28 November 1972 and married Lonel Curtis **Kluver** in Portland, Multnomah Co., Oreg. 1 August 1998. He is the son of James **Kluver**.[671] Tomi was graduated from Oregon State University, Corvallis, Benton Co. in June 1995.

7194. **Nola Angeline**[13] **Woodford** (Dorothy Marguerite[12] **Franklin**, Angeline[11] **McKinley**, William Henry[10], Angeline[9] **Whipple**, Enoch[8], Nehemiah[7], Benjamin[6], Francis[5], Jonathan[4], Joseph[3], Matthew[2], Matthew[1])[672] was born in Vinton, Benton Co., Iowa 24 September 1933 and married **Merrill Johnson** 1 March 1953.

Nola Angeline **Woodford** and Merrill **Johnson** had the following child:
- + 8529 i. Merrilee Marguerite[14] **Johnson** born 2 February 1961.

7195. **Joseph Franklin**[13] **Woodford** (Dorothy Marguerite[12] **Franklin**, Angeline[11] **McKinley**, William Henry[10], Angeline[9] **Whipple**, Enoch[8], Nehemiah[7], Benjamin[6], Francis[5], Jonathan[4], Joseph[3], Matthew[2],

Matthew[1])[673] was born in Vinton, Benton Co., Iowa 23 November 1936 and married **Clarice Johnson** 21 March 1959.

Joseph Franklin **Woodford** and Clarice **Johnson** had the following children:

    8530   i.   Timothy Edmond[14] **Woodford**[674] born in Des Moines, Polk Co., Iowa 1 May 1961.
    8531   ii.   Blake Joseph **Woodford**[675] born 5 January 1965.
    8532   iii.   Lynn Elizabeth **Woodford**[676] born 15 August 1967.

7196. **Judith Ann**[13] **Woodford** (Dorothy Marguerite[12] **Franklin**, Angeline[11] **McKinley**, William Henry[10], Angeline[9] **Whipple**, Enoch[8], Nehemiah[7], Benjamin[6], Francis[5], Jonathan[4], Joseph[3], Matthew[2], Matthew[1])[677] was born in Vinton, Benton Co., Iowa 5 May 1940 and married twice. (1) **Jon M. Kueny** 20 August 1958. (2) **William Cadman** 26 November 1966.

Judith Ann **Woodford** and Jon M. **Kueny** had the following child:

+   8533   i.   Shane Woodford[14] **Kueny** born 27 February 1965.

Judith Ann **Woodford** and William **Cadman** had the following child:

    8534   ii.   Michelle Angela **Cadman**[678] born 23 March 1968 and married Michael John **Davis** in LaMirda, Los Angeles Co., Calif. 2 October 1993. He is the son of Mrs. Beth **Davis**.[679]

7197. **William Franklin**[13] **Korns** (Laura Charlotte[12] **Franklin**, Angeline[11] **McKinley**, William Henry[10], Angeline[9] **Whipple**, Enoch[8], Nehemiah[7], Benjamin[6], Francis[5], Jonathan[4], Joseph[3], Matthew[2], Matthew[1])[680] was born in Hartwick, Poweshiek Co., Iowa 27 July 1935 and married twice. (1) **Doris Ann Rhodes** 10 August 1958. Doris,[681] daughter of Charles Edward **Rhodes** and Doris Laurrene **Martin**, was born 10 August 1938. (2) **Janet Cronbaugh** 3 March 1973. William adopted Steve, Mark, and Darla Rinehart. No information on dates or places of birth or when the adoptions took place was provided. Darla **Rinehart** married Tim **Ingersol** on 11 January 1980.

William Franklin **Korns** and Doris Ann **Rhodes** had the following children:

+   8535   i.   Sherry Ann[14] **Korns** born 10 January 1959.
    8536   ii.   Janice Kay **Korns**[682] born in Rapid City, Pennington Co., S. Dak. 2 August 1960.
+   8537   iii.   Charles Eugene **Korns** born 8 August 1961.
    8538   iv.   Angela Sue **Korns**[683] born 15 November 1966.

7199. **Dennis Dean**[13] **Korns** (Laura Charlotte[12] **Franklin**, Angeline[11] **McKinley**, William Henry[10], Angeline[9] **Whipple**, Enoch[8], Nehemiah[7], Benjamin[6], Francis[5], Jonathan[4], Joseph[3], Matthew[2], Matthew[1])[684] was born in Grinnell, Poweshiek Co. Iowa 23 December 1945 and married **Linda K. Holtz** 16 October 1971. Linda,[685] daughter of Ralph N. **Holtz**, was born 25 October 1945.

Dennis Dean **Korns** and Linda K. **Holtz** had the following children:
    8539 i.   Blake Dean[14] **Korns**[686] born 18 July 1973.
    8540 ii.   Clay Dennis **Korns**[687] born 18 July 1973 and married Mary **Brouwer** in Pella, Marion Co. Iowa.
    8541 iii. Jason Anthony **Korns**[688] born in Amatitlan Guatemala 26 January 1981. Adopted 5 November 1985.

7200. **Sharon Ann**[13] **Korns** (Laura Charlotte[12] **Franklin**, Angeline[11] **McKinley**, William Henry[10], Angeline[9] **Whipple**, Enoch[8], Nehemiah[7], Benjamin[6], Francis[5], Jonathan[4], Joseph[3], Matthew[2], Matthew[1])[689] was born in Grinnell, Poweshiek Co. Iowa 26 October 1950 and married **John Delos McIntosh** 15 March 1980. John,[690] son of John B. **McIntosh**, was born 27 December 1945.

Sharon Ann **Korns** and John Delos **McIntosh** had the following child:
    8542 i.   Shawn Thomas[14] **McIntosh**[691] born 21 May 1971 and married Thuy Thi-Thanh **Tran** in Marion, Linn Co., Iowa 7 October 1995. Thuy is the daughter of Kim Binh **Tran** and Xe Thi **Trinh**.[692]

7201. **Marlene Jean**[13] **Knupp** (Sylvia Fae[12] **Franklin**, Angeline[11] **McKinley**, William Henry[10], Angeline[9] **Whipple**, Enoch[8], Nehemiah[7], Benjamin[6], Francis[5], Jonathan[4], Joseph[3], Matthew[2], Matthew[1])[693] was born in Vinton, Benton Co., Iowa 8 June 1933 and married twice. (1) **Norman Hand** in 1954. (2) **Gene Osborne**. Marlene taught country school 1930-31 and was a substitute teacher 1931-32 before marrying Norman her farmer husband. Their farming career began at the time of the drought and depression of the early 1930s and times were difficult. In the fall of 1936 when they had two children, one 3 years, one 6 months, he entered Iowa State University, Ames, Story Co. and was graudated in 1939 with a degree in Agronomy. In January 1940 he began a 2-year stint as Club Agent for Dallas Co., Iowa. The family moved to Fort Dodge, Webster Co., in 1942 where he became a Farm Manager for 20 plus years. Prior to his retirement he operated an Insurance Agency in Fort Dodge.

Marlene Jean **Knupp** and Norman **Hand** had the following children:
- \+   8543   i.   Lawrence[14] **Hand** born 3 November 1955.
-      8544   ii.   Jerry Dale **Hand** [694] born 31 May 1956 and married Leanna Carol **Field** in Fort Dodge 12 May 1979. She is the daughter of Dale T. **Field**.[695]
- \+   8545   iii.   Gary Lee **Hand** born 1 May 1958.
- \+   8546   iv.   Susan Nora **Hand** born 2 January 1960.
-      8547   v.   Thomas Allen **Hand** [696] born 16 September 1963 and died 27 November 1964 at 1 year of age.

7202. **Janis Elaine**[13] **Knupp** (Sylvia Fae[12] **Franklin**, Angeline[11] **McKinley**, William Henry[10], Angeline[9] **Whipple**, Enoch[8], Nehemiah[7], Benjamin[6], Francis[5], Jonathan[4], Joseph[3], Matthew[2], Matthew[1])[697] was born in Vinton, Benton Co., Iowa 12 April 1936 and married three times. (1) **William Greehey** in Las Vegas, Clark Co., Nev. 17 December 1953. (2) **Joe Fife**. (3) **Tom Geiser**.

Janis Elaine **Knupp** and William **Greehey** had the following children:
- \+   8548   i.   William Kim[14] **Greehey** born 16 July 1954.
-      8549   ii.   Sidney James **Greehey**[698] born in San Antonio, Bexar Co., Tex. 17 January 1956 and married Cheryl (__) in June 1982.
- \+   8550   iii.   Douglas Allen **Greehey** born 17 May 1960.

7203. **John Franklin**[13] **Knupp** (Sylvia Fae[12] **Franklin**, Angeline[11] **McKinley**, William Henry[10], Angeline[9] **Whipple**, Enoch[8], Nehemiah[7], Benjamin[6], Francis[5], Jonathan[4], Joseph[3], Matthew[2], Matthew[1])[699] was born in Ames, Story Co., Iowa 21 May 1938 and married twice. (1) **Jane Ellen Lautenschloger** in 1957. (2) **Loyce Rey Tisdale** 7 November 1996. Loyce is the daughter of Ray **Tisdale** and Evelyn **Calhoun**.[700] John was graduated from Iowa State University, Ames in 1960 with a degree in Forestry. He is employed as a Forest Manager for Conroe Post Co., Conroe, Montgomery Co., Tex. and has part ownership of a Mississippi corporation which raises timber.

John Franklin **Knupp** and Jane Ellen **Lautenschloger** had the following children:
- \+   8551   i.   Christine Fae[14] **Knupp** born 15 March 1958.
- \+   8552   ii.   Dianne Kay **Knupp** born 29 March 1959.
-      8553   iii.   Daniel Franklin **Knupp**[701] born in Ames 27 April 1960 and married Carole (__).
-      8554   iv.   Ann Marie **Knupp**[702] born in Lufkin, Angelina Co., Tex. 15 April 1971.

7204. **Clyde Franklin**[13] **Knupp** (Sylvia Fae[12] **Franklin**, Angeline[11] **McKinley**, William Henry[10], Angeline[9] **Whipple**, Enoch[8], Nehemiah[7], Benjamin[6], Francis[5], Jonathan[4], Joseph[3], Matthew[2], Matthew[1])[703] was born in Vinton, Benton Co., Iowa 7 January 1940 and married **Diane M. Messerly** in 1960. He was mayor of Fort Dodge, Webster Co., Iowa (1980-82) and also served as National President of the American Music Operator's Association. He and Diane own Amusematic, a company that places coin operated game machines, pool tables, juke boxes, etc., in various locations throughout Iowa.

Clyde Franklin **Knupp** and Diane M. **Messerly** had the following children:
+ 8555 i. Suzanne[14] **Knupp** born 1 January 1962.
  8556 ii. David Walter **Knupp**[704] born in January 1965.

7205. **Keith Franklin**[13] **Knupp** (Sylvia Fae[12] **Franklin**, Angeline[11] **McKinley**, William Henry[10], Angeline[9] **Whipple**, Enoch[8], Nehemiah[7], Benjamin[6], Francis[5], Jonathan[4], Joseph[3], Matthew[2], Matthew[1])[705] was born in Fort Dodge, Webster Co., Iowa 13 May 1946 and married three times. (1) **Peggy Smith** 11 December 1971. They were divorced 8 October 1981. (2) **Grace Syers** 23 October 1981. They were divorced before 26 June 1992. (3) **Sonja (__)** 26 June 1992.

Keith Franklin **Knupp** and Peggy **Smith** had the following children:
+ 8557 i. Anthony James[14] **Knupp** born 8 March 1972.
+ 8558 ii. Angela Marie **Knupp** born 1 July 1974.
  8559 iii. Amanda Lynn **Knupp**[706] born 12 March 1979.

7207. **Robert I.**[13] **Schlarbaum Jr.** (LaVon Elizabeth[12] **McKinley**, James Hiram[11], William Henry[10], Angeline[9] **Whipple**, Enoch[8], Nehemiah[7], Benjamin[6], Francis[5], Jonathan[4], Joseph[3], Matthew[2], Matthew[1])[707] was born in Vinton, Benton Co., Iowa 1 September 1940 and married **Betty Jo Ann Andrews** in Sherwood, Washington Co., Oreg. 29 October 1960. Betty,[708] daughter of Kenneth **Andrews** and Evelyn Millicent **Casteel**, was born 27 February 1942.

Robert I. **Schlarbaum** Jr. and Betty Jo Ann **Andrews** had the following children:
  8560 i. Gregory Robert[14] **Schlarbaum**[709] born in Newberg, Yamhill Co., Oreg. 8 October 1961 and died 14 April 1981 at 19 years of age.
+ 8561 ii. Roben Ileene **Schlarbaum** born 11 February 1963.

{ G 1257 }

7208. **Carolyn Jeanette**[13] **Schlarbaum** (LaVon Elizabeth[12] **McKinley**, James Hiram[11], William Henry[10], Angeline[9] **Whipple**, Enoch[8], Nehemiah[7], Benjamin[6], Francis[5], Jonathan[4], Joseph[3], Matthew[2], Matthew[1])[710] was born in Vinton, Benton Co., Iowa 13 July 1942 and married **Charles E. Taber Sr.** in San Francisco, San Francisco Co., Calif. 14 October 1961. Charles,[711] son of Willis Corbett **Taber** and Oda Mae **Simpson**, was born in Tyler Co., Mo. 9 January 1941. He is a Lieutenant with the Portland, Multnomah Co., Oreg. Fire Department.

Carolyn Jeanette **Schlarbaum** and Charles E. **Taber** Sr. had the following children:
+   8562   i.   Rebecca Pearl[14] **Taber** born 3 July 1962.
+   8563   ii.   Melinda Jeanette **Taber** born 4 December 1965.
     8564   iii.   Charles Edward **Taber** Jr.[712] born in Newberg, Yamhill Co., Oreg. 12 December 1967. Chuck is an avid fly fisherman and works for a computer company as a Technical Support Representative.

7209. **David Allen**[13] **Schlarbaum** (LaVon Elizabeth[12] **McKinley**, James Hiram[11], William Henry[10], Angeline[9] **Whipple**, Enoch[8], Nehemiah[7], Benjamin[6], Francis[5], Jonathan[4], Joseph[3], Matthew[2], Matthew[1])[713] was born 10 November 1951 and married **Christine Anne White** 7 March 1973. Christine,[714] daughter of George **White** and Lois **Robisen**, was born in Portland, Multnomah Co., Oreg. 4 February 1952. She was awarded a degree in Elementary Education from Eastern Oregon College at La Grande, Union Co. and is a Financial Aid Counselor at George Fox College in Newburg, Yamhill Co., Oregon. David earned a B. A. from Eastern Oregon College and an M. A. from Lewis & Clark College, Portland. His major was Elementary Education and after teaching two years in Prineville, Crook Co., Oreg., he began teaching at Mable Rose Elementary School in Newburg. His hobbies include skiing and white water rafting.

David Allen **Schlarbaum** and Christine Anne **White** had the following children:
     8565   i.   Brook Anne[14] **Schlarbaum**[715] born in Enterprise, Wallowa Co., Oreg. 6 December 1974.
     8566   ii.   Joshua David **Schlarbaum**[716] born in Newberg 23 June 1978.
     8567   iii.   Amanda Christine **Schlarbaum**[717] born in Newberg 2 May 1980.

7210. **Mary Ann Elizabeth**[13] **Schlarbaum** (LaVon Elizabeth[12] **McKinley**, James Hiram[11], William Henry[10], Angeline[9] **Whipple**, Enoch[8], Nehemiah[7],

Benjamin[6], Francis[5], Jonathan[4], Joseph[3], Matthew[2], Matthew[1])[718] was born 24 November 1953 and married twice. (1) **Douglas Edward Wilcox** in Sherwood, Washington Co., Oreg. 15 July 1972. Douglas,[719] son of Ralph **Wilcox** and Myrtle **Whealer**, was born in Portland, Multnomah Co., Oreg. 8 October 1947. (2) **Michael Willard Potter** in Tigard, Washington Co., Oreg. 23 September 1995. Michael,[720] son of Robert **Potter** and Lorraine **Johnson**, was born in Portland 8 September 1946.

Mary Ann Elizabeth **Schlarbaum** and Douglas Edward **Wilcox** had the following children born in Portland:

- 8568 i. Christopher Douglas[14] **Wilcox**[721] 1 July 1977 and died the day of birth.
- 8569 ii. Christa Elizabeth **Wilcox**[722] 7 November 1980.
- 8570 iii. Sarah Ann **Wilcox**[723] 31 July 1982 and died the day of birth.
- 8571 iv. Beathney Joy **Wilcox**[724] 11 June 1986.

7215. **Franklin Dee**[13] **Horner** (Frances Freda[12] **Franklin**, Janette[11] **McKinley**, William Henry[10], Angeline[9] **Whipple**, Enoch[8], Nehemiah[7], Benjamin[6], Francis[5], Jonathan[4], Joseph[3], Matthew[2], Matthew[1])[725] was born in Gary, Lake Co., Ind. 15 June 1944 and married **Kathy Shake** 24 August 1968.

Franklin Dee **Horner** and Kathy **Shake** had the following children:

- 8572 i. Ryan Gene H.[14] **Horner**[726] born in Cincinnati, Hamilton Co., Ohio 11 August 1971.
- 8573 ii. Jana Marie **Horner**[727] born in Orlando, Orange Co., Fla. 22 February 1976.

7217. **Rita Janette**[13] **Horner** (Frances Freda[12] **Franklin**, Janette[11] **McKinley**, William Henry[10], Angeline[9] **Whipple**, Enoch[8], Nehemiah[7], Benjamin[6], Francis[5], Jonathan[4], Joseph[3], Matthew[2], Matthew[1])[728] was born in Indianapolis, Marion Co., Ind. 27 January 1949 and married **John Allen Stuckey** 24 January 1970. He was born in Marion, Ind. 26 October 1948.[729] They were divorced in Indianapolis 12 September 1983. (2) **John Fox** 2 June 1984. He was born in North Vernon, Jennings Co., Ind. 25 December 1948. They were divorced in Indiana in 1995.

Rita Janette **Horner** and John Allen **Stuckey** had the following children:

- 8574 i. John Thomas[14] **Stuckey**[730] born in Marion 19 August 1970.
- 8575 ii. Eric James **Stuckey**[731] born in Wichita, Sedgwick Co., Kans. 13 March 1974.
- 8576 iii. Marc Joseph **Stuckey**[732] born in Wichita 10 August 1975.

{ G 1259 }

Rita Janette **Horner** and John **Fox** had the following child:

    8577   iv.   Angela Janette **Fox**[733] born in Indianapolis 20 March 1985.

7225. **Gary Frederick**[13] **McKinley** (Clifford Hoffman[12], Grover Cleveland[11], William Henry[10], Angeline[9] **Whipple**, Enoch[8], Nehemiah[7], Benjamin[6], Francis[5], Jonathan[4], Joseph[3], Matthew[2], Matthew[1])[734] was born in Walker, Linn Co., Iowa 16 October 1939 and married twice. (1) **Mary Jo Harriot** in Cedar Rapids, Linn Co., Iowa 15 October 1961. Mary,[735] daughter of Devo Joe **Harriot** and Mary **Kilbourne**, was born in Cedar Rapids 18 April 1943. They were divorced in 1981. (2) **Shelley Robins** in New York, N.Y. 26 August 1984. Shelley,[736] daughter of Alex **Robins** and Rose **Fox**, was born in Brooklyn, N.Y. 15 December 1950.

Gary Frederick **McKinley** and Mary Jo **Harriot** had the following children:

+   8578 i. Dawn Marie[14] **McKinley** born 9 July 1962.
    8579 ii. Gary Michael **McKinley**[737] born in Omaha, Douglas Co., Nebr. 27 February 1965.

Gary Frederick **McKinley** and Shelley **Robins** had the following child:

    8580 iii. Erica Montana **McKinley**[738] born in New York, N.Y. 30 April 1990.

7226. **Janet Faye**[13] **McKinley** (Clifford Hoffman[12], Grover Cleveland[11], William Henry[10], Angeline[9] Whipple, Enoch[8], Nehemiah[7], Benjamin[6], Francis[5], Jonathan[4], Joseph[3], Matthew[2], Matthew[1])[739] was born in Walker, Linn Co., Iowa 23 June 1941 and married twice. (1) **Keith LeRoy Dudley** in Vinton, Benton Co., Iowa 28 February 1960. Keith,[740] son of Carlton **Dudley** and Wilma Wavia **Wachel**, was born 22 May 1939. (2) **Dale Hilmer** in Walker 23 April 1988.

Janet Faye **McKinley** and Keith LeRoy **Dudley** had the following children:

+   8581 i. Timothy Scott[14] **Dudley** born 22 December 1960.
+   8582 ii. Todd LeRoy **Dudley** born 30 November 1962.
+   8583 iii. Rodney Mark **Dudley** born 3 April 1965.

7227. **Cheryl Delilah**[13] **McKinley** (Clifford Hoffman[12], Grover Cleveland[11], William Henry[10], Angeline[9] **Whipple**, Enoch[8], Nehemiah[7], Benjamin[6], Francis[5], Jonathan[4], Joseph[3], Matthew[2], Matthew[1])[741] was born in Vinton, Benton Co., Iowa 5 December 1944 and married **Daniel Frederick Elsbernd** in Linn Co., Iowa 7 August 1965. Daniel,[742] son of Herman H. **Elsbernd** and Erna M. (__), was born in Crosby, Divide Co., N. Dak. 17 December 1938.

{ G 1260 }

Cheryl Delilah **McKinley** and Daniel Frederick **Elsbernd** had the following children:
- + 8584 i. Shawn Daniel[14] **Elsbernd** born 29 March 1966.
- + 8585 ii. Kimberly Berniece **Elsbernd** born 18 January 1968.
- + 8586 iii. Jodi Ann **Elsbernd** born 9 December 1971.

7228. **Michael Lee**[13] **McKinley** (Clifford Hoffman[12], Grover Cleveland[11], William Henry[10], Angeline[9] **Whipple**, Enoch[8], Nehemiah[7], Benjamin[6], Francis[5], Jonathan[4], Joseph[3], Matthew[2], Matthew[1])[743] was born in Vinton, Benton Co., Iowa 16 January 1946 and married **Jeanne Irene Edgerly** in Iowa City, Johnson Co., Iowa 6 June 1968. Jeanne,[744] daughter of Edwin Floyd **Edgerly** and Audrey Mae **Phillips**, was born in Jacksonville, Duval Co., Fla.

Michael Lee **McKinley** and Jeanne Irene **Edgerly** had the following children:
- 8587 i. Ryan Clifford[14] **McKinley**[745] born in Fayetteville, Cumberland Co., N.C. 18 May 1972 and married Kristin **Austin** in Galena, Jo Daviess Co., Ill. 12 August 1995.
- 8588 ii. Christopher Michael **McKinley**[746] born in Fayetteville 15 November 1974.

7229. **Tony Clifford**[13] **McKinley** (Clifford Hoffman[12], Grover Cleveland[11], William Henry[10], Angeline[9] **Whipple**, Enoch[8], Nehemiah[7], Benjamin[6], Francis[5], Jonathan[4], Joseph[3], Matthew[2], Matthew[1])[747] was born in Vinton, Benton Co., Iowa 17 September 1956 and married **Manda Rae Shope** in Tama, Tama Co., Iowa 2 August 1980. Manda,[748] daughter of James Hubert **Shope** and Darlene Mae **Johnson**, was born in Charlton, Iowa 25 October 1957.

Tony Clifford **McKinley** and Manda Rae **Shope** had the following children born in Linn Co. Iowa:
- 8589 i. Clifford James[14] **McKinley**[749] 12 April 1983.
- 8590 ii. Cody Jon **McKinley**[750] 9 October 1984.
- 8591 iii. Margaret Ann **McKinley**[751] 2 December 1986.

7230. **Karen Kaye**[13] **Heiserman** (Elizabeth Emily[12] **McKinley**, Grover Cleveland[11], William Henry[10], Angeline[9] **Whipple**, Enoch[8], Nehemiah[7], Benjamin[6], Francis[5], Jonathan[4], Joseph[3], Matthew[2], Matthew[1])[752] was born in Independence, Buchanan Co., Iowa 11 February 1940 and married **Roger Ted Michael** in Walker, Linn Co., Iowa 14 October 1958. Roger,[753] son of Theodore John **Michael** and Agnes **Wilson**, was born in Walker 3 May 1939.

Karen Kaye **Heiserman** and Roger Ted **Michael** had the following children:
+ 8592 i. Lisa Marie[14] **Michael** born 19 August 1959.
+ 8593 ii. Bryan Roger **Michael** born 14 September 1961.
+ 8594 iii. Steven James **Michael** born 11 September 1965.
    8595 iv. John Andrew **Michael**[754] born in West Union, Iowa 11 December 1976.

7231. **Bernard Laverne**[13] **McKinley** (Bernard Laverne[12], Grover Cleveland[11], William Henry[10], Angeline[9] **Whipple**, Enoch[8], Nehemiah[7], Benjamin[6], Francis[5], Jonathan[4], Joseph[3], Matthew[2], Matthew[1])[755] was born in Vinton, Benton Co., Iowa 16 July 1951 and married **Susan Hughes** in Troy, Lincoln Co., Mich. 21 June 1981. Susan,[756] daughter of Clifford **Hughes** and Rose-Elizabeth **Walker**, was born in Detroit, Wayne Co., Mich. 10 September 1951.

Bernard Laverne **McKinley** and Susan **Hughes** had the following children:
    8596 i. Andrew[14] **McKinley**[757] born 10 December 1982.
    8597 ii. Lindsey **McKinley**[758] born 7 February 1986.
    8598 iii. Matthew **McKinley**[759] born 13 May 1989.

7232. **Daniel Grover**[13] **McKinley** (Bernard Laverne[12], Grover Cleveland[11], William Henry[10], Angeline[9] **Whipple**, Enoch[8], Nehemiah[7], Benjamin[6], Francis[5], Jonathan[4], Joseph[3], Matthew[2], Matthew[1])[760] was born in Vinton, Benton Co., Iowa 20 October 1953 and married **Sharon Willey** in Winona, Winona Co., Minn. 20 September 1980. Sharon,[761] daughter of Dwight **Willey** and Ruth (__), was born in Clarion, Wright Co., Iowa 19 September 1954.

Daniel Grover **McKinley** and Sharon **Willey** had the following children born in Winona:
    8599 i. Michele[14] **McKinley**[762] 16 May 1989.
    8600 ii. Casondra **McKinley**[763] 22 May 1992.

7233. **Kathleen Anne**[13] **McKinley** (Bernard Laverne[12], Grover Cleveland[11], William Henry[10], Angeline[9] **Whipple**, Enoch[8], Nehemiah[7], Benjamin[6], Francis[5], Jonathan[4], Joseph[3], Matthew[2], Matthew[1])[764] was born in Olewein, Fayette Co., Iowa 19 March 1955 and married twice. (1) **Stephen Wangemann** in Waterloo, Black Hawk Co. Iowa 24 May 1979. Stephen,[765] son of George **Wangemann** and Freida (__), was born in Sheboygan, Sheboygan Co., Wisc. in January 1948. (2) **Dave Merry** in Waterloo 22 December 1990. He was born 19 September 1949.

Kathleen Anne **McKinley** and Stephen **Wangemann** had the following child:
- 8601 i. Heidi[14] **Wangemann**[766] born in Bemidji, Beltramie Co., Minn. 28 September 1982.

7234. **Rebecca Sue**[13] **McKinley** (Bernard Laverne[12], Grover Cleveland[11], William Henry[10], Angeline[9] **Whipple**, Enoch[8], Nehemiah[7], Benjamin[6], Francis[5], Jonathan[4], Joseph[3], Matthew[2], Matthew[1])[767] was born in Iowa Falls, Hardin Co., Iowa 24 February 1959 and married **Philip Smith** 16 August 1980. Phil, son of Kenneth **Smith** and Carol **Belanze**, was born in Waterloo, Black Hawk Co., Iowa 9 January 1960.

Rebecca Sue **McKinley** and Philip **Smith** had the following children:
- 8602 i. Rachael[14] **Smith**[768] born in Marshalltown, Marshall Co., Iowa.
- 8603 ii. Caleb McKinley **Smith**[769] born in Dubuque, Dubuque Co., Iowa.
- 8604 iii. Kenneth **Smith**[770] born in South Bend, Saint Joseph Co., Ind. 12 May 1988.
- 8605 iv. Samuel **Smith**[771] born in South Bend 29 July 1991.

7235. **Elizabeth Rose**[13] **McKinley** (Bernard Laverne[12], Grover Cleveland[11], William Henry[10], Angeline[9] **Whipple**, Enoch[8], Nehemiah[7], Benjamin[6], Francis[5], Jonathan[4], Joseph[3], Matthew[2], Matthew[1])[772] was born in Cedar Falls, Black Hawk Co., Iowa 27 July 1962 and married **Scott Hottle** in Waterloo, Black Hawk Co., Iowa 8 June 1985. Scott,[773] son of Ray **Hottle** and Myrna **Nicol**, was born in Waterloo 17 August 1962.

Elizabeth Rose **McKinley** and Scott **Hottle** had the following children born in Waterloo:
- 8606 i. Molly[14] **Hottle**[774] 11 July 1988.
- 8607 ii. Jared **Hottle**[775] 25 March 1991.

7239. **Charles Dos**[13] **McKinley** (William Harry[12], John Carlysle[11], William Henry[10], Angeline[9] **Whipple**, Enoch[8], Nehemiah[7], Benjamin[6], Francis[5], Jonathan[4], Joseph[3], Matthew[2], Matthew[1])[776] was born in Davenport, Scott Co., Iowa 15 July 1941 and married **Sandra Lee Massi** in Reno, Washoe Co., Nev. 12 August 1962. Sandra,[777] daughter of Vera **Massi**, was born in Sacramento, Sacramento Co., Calif. 28 November 1942.

Charles Dos **McKinley** and Sandra Lee **Massi** had the following children:
    8608   i.   Shawn Marie[14] **McKinley**[778] born in Blackfoot,[779] Iowa 2 January 1963 and married Robert J. **Morris** in Kings Beach, Placer Co., Calif. 10 November 1990. Robert,[780] son of Wayne Sanford **Morris** and Mary Ann Emma **Krier**, was born in Sacramento 9 May 1965.
+   8609   ii.   Lance Lee **McKinley** born 1 September 1965.
+   8610   iii.   David Charles **McKinley** born 22 September 1966.

7242. **Elizabeth Ann**[13] **McKinley** (William Harry[12], John Carlysle[11], William Henry[10], Angeline[9] **Whipple**, Enoch[8], Nehemiah[7], Benjamin[6], Francis[5], Jonathan[4], Joseph[3], Matthew[2], Matthew[1])[781] was born in Medford, Jackson Co., Oreg. 2 January 1952 and married **Steven Leon Harmon**.[782] They were divorced 18 August 1980.

Elizabeth Ann **McKinley** had the following child:
    8611   i.   Analish Gladys[14] **McKinley**[783] born 12 May 1987.

7243. **Mary Lynn**[13] **McKinley** (Dean Carlysle[12], John Carlysle[11], William Henry[10], Angeline[9] **Whipple**, Enoch[8], Nehemiah[7], Benjamin[6], Francis[5], Jonathan[4], Joseph[3], Matthew[2], Matthew[1])[784] was born in San Diego, San Diego Co., Calif. 23 January 1946 and married **Kelly Rushing** there 9 October 1968. Kelly,[785] son of Vernon Holden **Rushing** and Willie K. **Huffstutle**, was born in Corpus Christi, Nueces Co., Tex. 3 May 1945.

Mary Lynn **McKinley** and Kelly **Rushing** had the following children:
+   8612   i.   Dean Holden[14] **Rushing** born 28 January 1973.
    8613   ii.   Davis **Rushing**[786] born in Houston, Harris Co., Tex. 6 June 1975.

7244. **Teri Dea**[13] **McKinley** (Dean Carlysle[12], John Carlysle[11], William Henry[10], Angeline[9] **Whipple**, Enoch[8], Nehemiah[7], Benjamin[6], Francis[5], Jonathan[4], Joseph[3], Matthew[2], Matthew[1])[787] was born 16 December 1947 and married twice. (1) **Donald Smith** in El Paso, El Paso Co., Tex. 20 June 1970. Donald,[788] son of David E. **Smith** and Thelma L. **Yeatherman**, was born in Ft. Worth, Tarrant Co., Tex. 16 January 1945. They were divorced in May 1993. (2) **Michael Zuffinetti** in Richardson, Dallas Co., Texas 29 November 1996. Michael,[789] son of Mario **Zuffinetti** and Wanda (__), was born in San Diego, San Diego Co., Calif. 16 November 1950.

Teri Dea **McKinley** and Donald **Smith** had the following children:
    8614   i.   Ryan Carlisle[14] **Smith**[790] born in El Paso 1 October 1974

and married Anne Marie **Plachetka** in Plano, Collin Co., Tex. 24 June 2000. Anne,[791] daughter of John **Plachetka** and Clare **Dauner,** was born in Kansas City, Jackson Co., Mo. 9 June 1977.

    8615   ii.   Blake E. **Smith**[792] born in El Paso 1 June 1978 and married Erin Danielle **McVay** in Austin, Travis Co., Tex. 2 August 2003. She is the daughter of Bruce **McVay** and Cheryl (__).[793]

    8616   iii.   Erinne **Smith**[794] born in Richardson 22 May 1980.

7273. **Kenda Kay**[13] **Oldridge** (Belva Jean[12] **McKinley**, Merton Wallace[11], William Henry[10], Angeline[9] **Whipple**, Enoch[8], Nehemiah[7], Benjamin[6], Francis[5], Jonathan[4], Joseph[3], Matthew[2], Matthew[1])[795] was born in Independence, Buchanan Co., Iowa 2 April 1958 and married **Gene Patrick Bagby** there 8 May 1982. Gene,[796] son of Joseph Charles **Bagby** and Mary Jean **Kane,** was born in Independence 25 August 1956.

Kenda Kay **Oldridge** and Gene Patrick **Bagby** had the following children born in Independence:

    8617   i.   Trevor Joseph[14] **Bagby**[797] 3 November 1982.
    8618   ii.   Amber Lea **Bagby**[798] 6 September 1983.

7274. **Kamie Lea**[13] **Oldridge** (Belva Jean[12] **McKinley**, Merton Wallace[11], William Henry[10], Angeline[9] **Whipple**, Enoch[8], Nehemiah[7], Benjamin[6], Francis[5], Jonathan[4], Joseph[3], Matthew[2], Matthew[1])[799] was born in Independence, Buchanan Co., Iowa 14 November 1959 and married twice. (1) **Marty James Becker** in Quasqueton, Buchanon Co., Iowa 3 February 1979. Marty,[800] son of James Robert **Becker** and Wilda June **Bantz**, was born in Independence 9 July 1957. They were divorced in Iowa in March 1988. (2) **Bruce Richard Creel** 14 November 1998.[801]

Kamie Lea **Oldridge** and Marty James **Becker** had the following child born in Independence:

    8619   i.   Joshua Dean[14] **Becker**[802] 13 January 1978.

7275. **Kelly Lynn**[13] **Oldridge** (Belva Jean[12] **McKinley**, Merton Wallace[11], William Henry[10], Angeline[9] **Whipple**, Enoch[8], Nehemiah[7], Benjamin[6], Francis[5], Jonathan[4], Joseph[3], Matthew[2], Matthew[1])[803] was born in Independence, Buchanan Co., Iowa 20 June 1961 and married **Robert Glenn Griswold** in Quasqueton, Buchanon Co., Iowa 16 July 1983. Robert,[804] son of Glenn Arthur **Griswold** and Harriet Martha **Kurtz**, was born in Independence 1 April 1961.

Kelly Lynn **Oldridge** and Robert Glenn **Griswold** had the following children:
- 8620 i. Bryce Robert[14] **Griswold**[805] born in Waterloo, Black Hawk Co., Iowa 27 August 1986.
- 8621 ii. Kelci Lynn **Griswold**[806] born in Waterloo 21 June 1988.

7277. **Tracey Ann**[13] **Orr** (Evelyn Lee[12] **McKinley**, Merton Wallace[11], William Henry[10], Angeline[9] **Whipple**, Enoch[8], Nehemiah[7], Benjamin[6], Francis[5], Jonathan[4], Joseph[3], Matthew[2], Matthew[1])[807] was born in Omaha, Douglas Co., Nebr. 24 May 1962 and married **David Duane Grimme** there 2 July 1982. David,[808] son of Duane **Grimme** and Carol **Hajek**, was born in Yankton, Yankton Co., S. Dak. 16 May 1961. He earned a degree in Chemistry at Chadron State College, Chadron, Dawes Co., Nebr. and a Masters degree in Business Administration from Tulane University, New Orleans, Orleans Parish, La. Tracey earned a Bachelor of Arts degree from Chadron State College. They live in West Monroe, Quachita Parish, La. (1999).

Tracey Ann **Orr** and David Duane **Grimme** had the following children:
- 8622 i. Benjamin David[14] **Grimme**[809] born in Rock Springs, Sweetwater Co., Wyo. 27 July 1985.
- 8623 ii. Sarah Marie **Grimme**[810] born in Rock Springs 8 September 1987.
- 8624 iii. Rachel Suzanne **Grimme**[811] born in Monroe, Quachita Parish, La. 27 September 1990.

7278. **Terri Lu**[13] **Orr** (Evelyn Lee[12] **McKinley**, Merton Wallace[11], William Henry[10], Angeline[9] **Whipple**, Enoch[8], Nehemiah[7], Benjamin[6], Francis[5], Jonathan[4], Joseph[3], Matthew[2], Matthew[1])[812] was born in Omaha, Douglas Co., Nebr. 18 May 1964 and married **Edward Lyle Rider Jr.** there 29 June 1989. Edward is son of Edward Lyle **Rider** Sr. and Barbara **Krupski**.[813] Terri was graduated from the U. of Nebraska, Omaha with a Bachelor of Arts degree and Edward earned a Bachelor of Arts Degree from Kearney State College (now the U. of Nebraska at Kearney, Buffalo Co.).

Terri Lu **Orr** and Edward Lyle **Rider** Jr. adopted the following child:
- 8625 i. Abigail Tay[14] **Rider**[814] born 19 March 1995. Adopted 17 April 1995.

7279. **Karla Kay**[13] **Gilchrist** (Doris Eileen[12] **Wood**, Elizabeth[11] **McKinley**, William Henry[10], Angeline[9] **Whipple**, Enoch[8], Nehemiah[7], Benjamin[6], Francis[5], Jonathan[4], Joseph[3], Matthew[2], Matthew[1])[815] was born in Vinton, Benton Co., Iowa 26 September 1950 and married twice. (1) **Randy Mann** in Muskogee, Muskogee Co., Okla. in February 1979. He was born 10 December 1951 and died in an auto accident 17 March 1981 at 29 years of age.[816] (2) **Seneca McIntosh** in Muskogee 15 July 1982. He was born 10 January 1952. They were divorced 20 May 1991.[817] Karla worked for the Veterans Administration in Iowa City, Johnson Co., for over 20 years before being transferred to Bridgeport, Harrison Co., W.Va. in January 1994. In October 1997 she became Chief of Personnel of the VA office in Dublin, Alameda Co., Calif.

Karla Kay **Gilchrist** and Randy **Mann** had the following child born in Muskogee:
  8626 i. Christopher Ryan[14] **Mann**[818] 17 October 1980. Adopted by Seneca McIntosh in 1984.

Karla Kay **Gilchrist** and Seneca **McIntosh** had the following child born in Iowa City:
  8627 ii. Noah **McIntosh**[819] 12 November 1983.

7280. **Karan Ann**[13] **Gilchrist** (Doris Eileen[12] **Wood**, Elizabeth[11] **McKinley**, William Henry[10], Angeline[9] **Whipple**, Enoch[8], Nehemiah[7], Benjamin[6], Francis[5], Jonathan[4], Joseph[3], Matthew[2], Matthew[1])[820] was born in Vinton, Benton Co., Iowa 18 July 1955 and married **Douglas Johnson** in Dubuque, Dubuque Co., Iowa 18 July 1981. Douglas,[821] son of Donald **Johnson** and Shirley (__), was born in East Moline, Rock Island Co., Ill. 18 October 1952.

Karan Ann **Gilchrist** and Douglas **Johnson** had the following children born in Dubuque:
  8628 i. Sarah Elizabeth[14] **Johnson**[822] 17 July 1982.
  8629 ii. Uriah Robert **Johnson**[823] 25 July 1984.
  8630 iii. Micah Carl **Johnson**[824] 26 March 1987.

7281. **Carl Joe**[13] **Feiereisen** (Mardene Dot[12] **Wood**, Elizabeth[11] **McKinley**, William Henry[10], Angeline[9] **Whipple**, Enoch[8], Nehemiah[7], Benjamin[6], Francis[5], Jonathan[4], Joseph[3], Matthew[2], Matthew[1])[825] was born in Cedar Rapids, Linn Co., Iowa 7 January 1948 and married twice. (1) **Sharon Piispannen** in Cedar Rapids 6 June 1970. They were divorced. She is the daughter of Roy **Piispannen** and Vera (__). (2) **Debbie Rock** in Butler, Butler Co., Penn. 24 August 1985. Carl retired as a Staff Sergeant from the U.S. Army after 20 years of service (1968-88). His duty included two missions in Viet Nam and three years in Germany.

Carl Joe **Feiereisen** and Sharon **Piispannen** had the following children:

    8631 i.   Tawnya[14] **Feiereisen**[826] born in Cedar Rapids 24 April 1972. Following graduation from St. Mary's College in San Antonio, Bexar Co., Tex. where she earned a B. A. degree majoring in Federal Justice, she joined the U.S. Army in 1995.

    8632 ii. John **Feiereisen**[827] born at Fort Hood, Bell Co., Tex. 6 May 1975.

7282. **Kathy Jo**[13] **Wood** (Jack Edward[12], Elizabeth[11] **McKinley**, William Henry[10], Angeline[9] **Whipple**, Enoch[8], Nehemiah[7], Benjamin[6], Francis[5], Jonathan[4], Joseph[3], Matthew[2], Matthew[1])[828] was born in Vinton, Benton Co., Iowa 10 October 1950 and married **Gary Miller** in Waterloo, Black Hawk Co., Iowa 13 May 1967. He was born in Summer, Bremer Co., Iowa 2 February 1944.[829]

Kathy Jo **Wood** and Gary **Miller** had the following children:

    8633 i.   Andrea[14] **Miller**[830] born in Waterloo 18 December 1967.

+ 8634 ii. Christopher **Miller** born 20 April 1972.

7283. **William Archer**[13] **Wood** (Jack Edward[12], Elizabeth[11] **McKinley**, William Henry[10], Angeline[9] **Whipple**, Enoch[8], Nehemiah[7], Benjamin[6], Francis[5], Jonathan[4], Joseph[3], Matthew[2], Matthew[1])[831] was born in Vinton, Benton Co., Iowa 19 January 1953 and died of a massive heart attack 17 February 1998, at 45 years of age. He married **Debra L. Geiger** in Vinton 20 January 1973. Debra,[832] daughter of Larry **Geiger** and Imogene (__), was born 4 September 1957. They were divorced in May 1981.

William Archer **Wood** and Debra L. **Geiger** had the following children born in Vinton:

    8635 i.   Brian Allen[14] **Wood**[833] 22 July 1973 and died 3 hours after birth.

    8636 ii. William Bean **Wood**[834] 14 March 1980.

7295. **Phillip Mauldin**[13] **Kearns** (Rev. Paul Searight[12], Rev. Archibald Jackson[11], Dr. Archibald Jackson[10], Eliza Roxana[9] **Whipple**, Enoch[8], Nehemiah[7], Benjamin[6], Francis[5], Jonathan[4], Joseph[3], Matthew[2], Matthew[1])[835] was born in Colorado Springs, El Paso Co., Colo. 19 April 1947 and married twice. (1) **Noel Juhl** in Port Angeles, Callam Co., Wash. She died in Santa Cruz, Santa Cruz Co., Calif.[836] (2) **Susanna R. Masters** in Easley, Pickens Co., S. C. 30 August 1991.

Phillip Mauldin **Kearns** and Noel **Juhl** had the following children:
- 8637   i.   Daniel[14] **Kearns**[837] born in 1973.
- 8638   ii. Christopher **Kearns**[838] born in 1975.
- 8639   iii. James **Kearns**[839] born in 1980.
- 8640   iv. Timothy **Kearns**[840] born in 1982.

7296. **Lawrence Archibald**[13] **Kearns** (Rev. Paul Searight[12], Rev. Archibald Jackson[11], Dr. Archibald Jackson[10], Eliza Roxana[9] **Whipple**, Enoch[8], Nehemiah[7], Benjamin[6], Francis[5], Jonathan[4], Joseph[3], Matthew[2], Matthew[1])[841] was born in Anadarko, Caddo Co., Okla. 5 May 1952 and married **Anne Larsen** in Santa Rosa, Sonoma Co., Calif. 28 October 1990.

Lawrence Archibald **Kearns** had the following children born in San Francisco, San Francisco Co., Calif.:
- 8641   i.   Anna Katherine[14] Carmack-**Kearns**[842] 5 September 1983. Her mother is Melinda **Carmack.**
- 8642   ii. Emily Elizabeth Pierce-**Kearns**[843] 28 March 1988. Her mother is Cheri **Pierce.**

7299. **Rebecca Grace**[13] **Kearns** (Rev. Robert Harry[12], Rev. Archibald Jackson[11], Dr. Archibald Jackson[10], Eliza Roxana[9] **Whipple**, Enoch[8], Nehemiah[7], Benjamin[6], Francis[5], Jonathan[4], Joseph[3], Matthew[2], Matthew[1])[844] birth date unknown, married **Dean Leffingwell**.

Rebecca Grace **Kearns** and Dean **Leffingwell** had the following children:
- 8643   i.   Tracy[14] **Leffingwell.**[845]
- 8644   ii. Emily **Leffingwell.**[846]

7300. **Julia Elizabeth**[13] **Kearns** (Rev. Robert Harry[12], Rev. Archibald Jackson[11], Dr. Archibald Jackson[10], Eliza Roxana[9] **Whipple**, Enoch[8], Nehemiah[7], Benjamin[6], Francis[5], Jonathan[4], Joseph[3], Matthew[2], Matthew[1])[847] birth date unknown, married **Kevin Eaklor**.

Julia Elizabeth **Kearns** and Kevin **Eaklor** had the following child:
- 8645   i.   Kristin[14] **Eaklor.**[848]

7301. **Elisabeth Louise**[13] **Kearns** (Donald Raymond[12], Rev. Archibald Jackson[11], Dr. Archibald Jackson[10], Eliza Roxana[9] **Whipple**, Enoch[8], Nehemiah[7], Benjamin[6], Francis[5], Jonathan[4], Joseph[3], Matthew[2], Matthew[1])[849] birth date unknown, married **Steven John Sampson** in Phoenix, Maricopa Co., Ariz. 15 October 1988.

Elisabeth Louise **Kearns** and Steven John **Sampson** had the following children:
>   8646   i.   Amber Louise[14] **Sampson**.[850]
>   8647   ii.   Monica Eileen **Sampson**.[851]

7303. **John William**[13] **Whipple** (William Perry[12], Milo Robert[11], William Perry[10], Cyrenius Thomas[9], Enoch[8], Nehemiah[7], Benjamin[6], Francis[5], Jonathan[4], Joseph[3], Matthew[2], Matthew[1])[852] was born in Cedar Rapids, Linn Co., Iowa 5 July 1939 and married **Betty Tsukano** in Molokai, Hawaii 10 July 1969. She was born there 14 February 1949.[853] John earned an undergraduate Degree at Monmouth College in Monmouth, Warren Co., Ill. and a Master's Degree at Rockford College, Rockford, Winnebago Co., Ill. An Elementary School Teacher, he has taught at Leaf River, Ogle Co., Ill., Kaunakakai, Molokai, Hawaii, and Cedar Rapids.

John William **Whipple** and Betty **Tsukano** had the following children:
>   8648   i.   Lori[14] **Whipple**[854] born in Honolulu, Hawaii 21 March 1967. Adopted in August 1969 at Molokai.
>   8649   ii.   Keith Katsumi **Whipple**[855] born in Honolulu 22 September 1970. Keith earned a Master's Degree in Teaching from Drake University, Des Moines, Polk Co., Iowa.

>   8650   iii.   William Perry **Whipple**[856] born in Cedar Rapids 29 October 1975. Bill began playing the piano at age 4 and at age 10 added the trombone to his musical accomplishments. While in middle school in Cedar Rapids, he won the prestigious Baldwin competition which includes a difficult theory test. His Cedar Rapids piano teachers, Bill and Pat Medley, recognized his "knack" for playing for his listeners and said he ranked among their top students. They taught him that the relationship between teacher and student should be more than just music. A three hour music lesson followed by lunch, a session in cooking, golf, and a walk in the garden was a normal day with the Medleys. While still in High School, he studied with Kenneth Amada (U. of Iowa, Iowa City, Johnson Co.) and Howard Aible, (U. of Northern Iowa, Cedar Falls, Black Hawk Co.). Though he plays jazz, he favors classical music with Haydn and Beethoven among his favorite composers. During his pre-college years he practiced piano four hours a day in summer and 2.5 hours daily during the school year. He has performed with Cedar Rapids Symphony, the Fort Dodge (Webster Co., Iowa) Symphony and the Waterloo / Cedar Falls Symphony and has given solo recitals in Arkansas, Iowa, Kansas, Massachusetts, Ohio, Wisconsin, and New York. His awards and honors include first prizes in the MTNA-Baldwin Junior Competition, levels DEF; IMTA-

state competitions; Clef Music Award (Cincinnati); and the Quad Cities Mozart Competition (Illinois). He performed at the 100th anniversary of Antonin Dvorak's sojourn in Spillville, Winneshiek Co., Iowa and at numerous festivals including the Tanglewood Institute in Lenox, Berkshire Co., Mass. He began his formal training at the U. of Cincinnati College Conservatory of Music as a scholarship student of William Black. He was the pianist for the CCM Wind Ensemble and the Symphony Band in Cincinnati. He received a Bachelor's Degree from the Manhattan School of Music in New York City in 1998, a Master's from the same institution in 2003. He also studied under of Donn-Alexandre Feder at the Manhattan School of Music.

7304. **Robert Milo**[13] **Whipple** (William Perry[12], Milo Robert[11], William Perry[10], Cyrenius Thomas[9], Enoch[8], Nehemiah[7], Benjamin[6], Francis[5], Jonathan[4], Joseph[3], Matthew[2], Matthew[1])[857] was born in Cedar Rapids, Linn Co., Iowa 13 September 1943 and married twice. (1) **Meredith Thomae** in Gladbrook, Tama Co., Iowa 20 March 1965. (2) **Sandra Engstrom** in Evanston, Cook Co., Ill. 24 August 1975. Robert earned an undergraduate degree (1965) Magna Cum Laude and Phi Beta Kappa at Coe College, Cedar Rapids, a Master's Degree from the U. of Iowa, Iowa City, Johnson Co. (1967), and a Doctorate from Northwestern University Evanston/Chicago (1972). His main interest was the development of math lab materials for students in grades 7-12. His Ph.D. dissertation was a comparison of laboratory approach vs. individual units approach for 8th grade geometry. He was Tutorial Professor in the Tutorial-Clinical Program in Education at Northwestern University, Chicago and taught at New Trier High School East, Winnetka, Cook Co., Ill. While at New Trier High he and Richard Rhoad and George Milauskas authored *Geometry For Enjoyment and Challenge* which became a standard high school text. It was published by McDouglas, Littell & Company, Evanston, Ill.

In his 30 plus years on the faculty at New Trier, he served as a Teacher of Mathematics and as an Adviser. When computers were first introduced for school use, he took the initiative to learn how to use them and then taught those skills to his colleagues and students. He developed computer programs for scoring sports competitions, helped plan management strategies for major sports events, and created the New Trier Athletic Department Web Page. He was designated a "Leader Teacher" which exemplifies the "core, soul, and conscience" of the school in March 1998.

Robert Milo **Whipple** and Meredith **Thomae** had the following child born in Cedar Rapids:

    8651   i.   Matthew Robert[14] **Whipple**[858] 24 April 1966 and was graudated from Northwestern University in 1988.

7308. **Dawn Naydine**[13] **Frederick** (Charles Stephan[12], Maude Maree[11] **Whipple**, Milo Enoch[10], Cyrenius Thomas[9], Enoch[8], Nehemiah[7], Benjamin[6], Francis[5], Jonathan[4], Joseph[3], Matthew[2], Matthew[1])[859] was born in Martinez, Contra Costa Co., Calif. 15 May 1936 and died 5 December 1956 in Bellingham, Whatcomb Co., Wash., at 20 years of age. She married **Frank Lyle Jackson** in Bellingham 15 January 1953. Frank,[860] son of Herbert **Jackson** and Helen (__), died 5 December 1956 in Bellingham. The entire family died in a fire at their home. All are buried at the Bayview Cemetery in Bellingham.

Dawn Naydine **Frederick** and Frank Lyle **Jackson** had the following children born and died in Bellingham:

    8652   i.   Lyle Shawn[14] **Jackson**[861] 3 August 1955 and died 5 December 1956, at 1 year of age.

    8653   ii.   Randy Scott **Jackson**[862] 23 July 1956 and died 5 December 1956, at less than 4 months of age.

7309. **Bruce Ellsworth**[13] **Frederick** (Charles Stephan[12], Maude Maree[11] **Whipple**, Milo Enoch[10], Cyrenius Thomas[9], Enoch[8], Nehemiah[7], Benjamin[6], Francis[5], Jonathan[4], Joseph[3], Matthew[2], Matthew[1])[863] was born in Holland, Ottawa Co., Mich. 2 February 1939 and married **Dorothy Ann Suhoversnik** in Enumclaw, King Co., Wash. 7 August 1971. Dorothy,[864] daughter of Louie **Suhoversnik** and Doris Irene **Mallery**, was born in Enumclaw 10 March 1950.

Bruce Ellsworth **Frederick** and Dorothy Ann **Suhoversnik** had the following children:

    8654   i.   Rebecca Louise[14] **Frederick**[865] born in Port Angeles, Clallam Co., Wash. 30 January 1976.

    8655   ii.   Heather Lee **Frederick**[866] born in Bremerton, Kitsap Co., Wash. 12 June 1979.

7310. **Colleen Charles-Ann**[13] **Frederick** (Charles Stephan[12], Maude Maree[11] **Whipple**, Milo Enoch[10], Cyrenius Thomas[9], Enoch[8], Nehemiah[7], Benjamin[6], Francis[5], Jonathan[4], Joseph[3], Matthew[2], Matthew[1])[867] was born in Martinez, Contra Costa Co., Calif. 22 August 1940 and married **Robert Eugene Little** in Friday Harbor, San Juan Co., Wash. 15 September 1956.

Robert, son of Ralph Elmer **Little** and Oma **Huntley**, was born in Bellingham, Whatcomb Co., Wash. 31 December 1934.

Colleen Charles-Ann **Frederick** and Robert Eugene **Little** had the following children:
+ 8656 i. Lisa Dawn[14] **Little** born 23 June 1961.
   8657 ii. Stacey Sue **Little**[868] born in Seattle, King Co., Wash. 4 April 1963 and married twice. (1) Steven Marc **Jorgensen** in Coulee City, Grant Co., Wash. 26 January 1983. They were divorced 31 January 1986. (2) Jerome **Bessett** in Soap Lake, Grant Co., Wash. 16 July 1988. Jerry,[869] son of Norman Henry **Bessett** and Barbara Ann **Griffith,** was born in Santa Maria, Santa Barbara Co., Calif. 14 August 1963.
   8658 iii. Rodney Evan **Little**[870] born in Bellevue, King Co., Wash. 19 October 1965 and married Cynthia Carol **Feezell** in Auburn, King Co., Wash. 17 December 1988. Cynthia,[871] daughter of Floyd A. **Feezell** and Evelyn **Skiles,** was born in Orange Co., Calif. 19 January 1965.

7311. **Vickie Lee**[13] **Andrus** (James Dudley[12], Maude Maree[11] **Whipple**, Milo Enoch[10], Cyrenius Thomas[9], Enoch[8], Nehemiah[7], Benjamin[6], Francis[5], Jonathan[4], Joseph[3], Matthew[2], Matthew[1])[872] was born in San Diego, San Diego Co., Calif. 10 January 1952 and married **Allman Avon Todd IV** in Allegan, Allegan Co., Mich. 22 September 1979. He is the son of Allman Avon **Todd** III and Lilian **(__)**.

Vickie Lee **Andrus** and Allman Avon **Todd** IV had the following children born in Kalamazoo, Kalamazoo Co., Mich:
   8659 i. Allman Avon[14] **Todd** V[873] 6 February 1982.
   8660 ii. Jonathan Andrew **Todd**[874] in July 1984.

7312. **James Albie**[13] **Andrus** (James Dudley[12], Maude Maree[11] **Whipple**, Milo Enoch[10], Cyrenius Thomas[9], Enoch[8], Nehemiah[7], Benjamin[6], Francis[5], Jonathan[4], Joseph[3], Matthew[2], Matthew[1])[875] was born in Allegan, Allegan Co., Mich. 19 August 1954 and married **Barbara Nietering** in Grand Haven, Ottawa Co., Mich. 18 May 1985. She is the daughter of George **Nietering** and Josie **(__)**.[876]

James Albie **Andrus** and Barbara **Nietering** had the following child born in Grand Haven:
   8661 i. Jessica Elizabeth[14] **Andrus**[877] 29 October 1987.

7313. **Daniel Clay**[13] **Andrus** (James Dudley[12], Maude Maree[11] **Whipple**, Milo Enoch[10], Cyrenius Thomas[9], Enoch[8], Nehemiah[7], Benjamin[6], Francis[5], Jonathan[4], Joseph[3], Matthew[2], Matthew[1])[878] was born in Allegan, Allegan Co., Mich. 14 August 1955 and married **Jerrolyn Martin** 10 December 1976. Jerrolyn,[879] daughter of John **Martin** and Lee **Gentry**, was born in Allegan.

Daniel Clay **Andrus** and Jerrolyn **Martin** had the following children born in Allegan:
    8662   i.   Ryan Christopher[14] **Andrus**[880] 29 May 1980.
    8663   ii. Shawn Patrick **Andrus**[881] 29 May 1980.

7325. **Mary Catherine**[13] **Mack** (Anna Catherine[12] **Catlin**, Callie Catherine[11] **Whipple**, Selmon Thomas[10], Cyrenius Thomas[9], Enoch[8], Nehemiah[7], Benjamin[6], Francis[5], Jonathan[4], Joseph[3], Matthew[2], Matthew[1])[882] was born in Independence, Buchanan Co., Iowa 19 June 1950 and married **James Lee Martin** there 10 June 1972. He was born in Sergeant Bluffs, Woodbury Co., Iowa 1 June 1947.[883]

Mary Catherine **Mack** and James Lee **Martin** had the following children born in Sioux City, Woodbury Co., Iowa:
    8664   i.   Owen David[14] **Martin**[884] in June 1977.
    8665   ii. Nicholas James **Martin**[885] 4 November 1980.
    8666   iii. Michael Thomas **Martin**[886] 8 May 1984.

7326. **Thomas Russell**[13] **Mack** (Anna Catherine[12] **Catlin**, Callie Catherine[11] **Whipple**, Selmon Thomas[10], Cyrenius Thomas[9], Enoch[8], Nehemiah[7], Benjamin[6], Francis[5], Jonathan[4], Joseph[3], Matthew[2], Matthew[1])[887] was born in Independence, Buchanan Co., Iowa 22 May 1955 and married **Grace Anna Augustine** 7 November 1981. She was born in Shelby, Toole Co., Mont. 21 February 1956.[888]

Thomas Russell **Mack** and Grace Anna **Augustine** had the following children:
    8667   i.   Christopher Elliot[14] **Mack**[889] born in Des Moines, Polk Co., Iowa 20 October 1982.
    8668   ii. Stephen Alexander **Mack**[890] born in Portland, Multnomah Co., Oreg. 1 April 1986.

7327. **Kathleen Louise**[13] **Hovey** (Elsie Laurel[12] **Catlin**, Callie Catherine[11] **Whipple**, Selmon Thomas[10], Cyrenius Thomas[9], Enoch[8], Nehemiah[7], Benjamin[6], Francis[5], Jonathan[4], Joseph[3], Matthew[2],

Matthew[1])[891] was born in St. Paul, Ramsey Co., Minn. 21 October 1939 and married **Robert Davidson** in West Springfield, Hampden Co., Mass. He was born in Ithaca, Tompkins Co., N.Y. 8 June 1938.[892]

Kathleen Louise **Hovey** and Robert **Davidson** had the following children born in West Hartford, Hartford Co., Conn.:
    8669   i.   Diane Marsha[14] **Davidson**[893] 30 May 1966.
    8670   ii. Suzanne Louise **Davidson**[894] 13 September 1968.

7328. **Marshall Lewis**[13] **Hovey** (Elsie Laurel[12] **Catlin**, Callie Catherine[11] **Whipple**, Selmon Thomas[10], Cyrenius Thomas[9], Enoch[8], Nehemiah[7], Benjamin[6], Francis[5], Jonathan[4], Joseph[3], Matthew[2], Matthew[1])[895] was born in Presque Isle, Aroostook Co., Maine 3 April 1944 and married **Sharon Morrison** 5 October 1963. She was born 14 April 1945.[896]

Marshall Lewis **Hovey** and Sharon **Morrison** had the following children:
    8671   i.   Robert Louis[14] **Hovey**[897] born in Yardley, Bucks Co., Penn. 7 November 1964.
    8672   ii. David Marshall **Hovey**[898] born in Avon, Hartford Co., Conn. 2 November 1966.
    8673   iii. Liane **Hovey**[899] born in Avon 20 February 1970.

7332. **Kay Ann**[13] **Kalvig** (Anna Jeanette[12] **Whipple**, William Walter[11], Selmon Thomas[10], Cyrenius Thomas[9], Enoch[8], Nehemiah[7], Benjamin[6], Francis[5], Jonathan[4], Joseph[3], Matthew[2], Matthew[1])[900] was born in Cedar Rapids, Linn Co., Iowa 17 December 1941 and married **Harold Arthur Heddinger** in Vinton, Benton Co., Iowa 11 January 1963. Harold,[901] son of Arthur James **Heddinger** and Ceva Mae **Blough**, was born in Iowa City, Johnson Co., Iowa 19 May 1936 and died of Acute Myeloid Leukemia in St. Luke's Hospital in Cedar Rapids 16 November 2004, at 68 years of age. Buried at Maplewood Cemetery, Vinton. Harold worked as an auto mechanic following his discharge from the Army in 1954 until March of 1967 when he became an assembler of printing equipment with Miehle-Goss-Dexter, the world's largest manufacturer of printing presses and graphic arts equipment. He retired from the firm 30 June 1996 after 29 years and 3 months of service. He was a member of the First United Methodist Church of Marion, Linn Co., Iowa and the International Assn. of Machinist and Aerospace Workers, AFL-CIO Harmony Lodge No. 831. After retirement he spent hours on the computer researching both his and Kay's genealogy and family history. He was buried with military honors provided by American Legion Post #298 of Marion.

Kay Ann **Kalvig** and Harold Arthur **Heddinger** had the following children:
+ 8674 i. Jeffery Lee[14] **Heddinger** born 29 August 1963.
   8675 ii. Bradley Jay **Heddinger**[902] born in Cedar Rapids 30 October 1964 and married Dianna Lynn **Hinman** there 8 August 1998. Dianna,[903] daughter of James Howard **Hinman** and Agnes Mae **Burke,** was born in Cedar Rapids 14 February 1964.

7333. **Bruce A.**[13] **Whipple** (William Clarence[12], William Walter[11], Selmon Thomas[10], Cyrenius Thomas[9], Enoch[8], Nehemiah[7], Benjamin[6], Francis[5], Jonathan[4], Joseph[3], Matthew[2], Matthew[1])[904] was born in Vinton, Benton Co., Iowa 11 October 1942 and married **Pat Walker** in Cedar Rapids, Linn Co., Iowa 30 July 1966. Bruce is a pharmacist at Hampton, Franklin Co., Iowa. (1998).

Bruce A. **Whipple** and Pat **Walker** had the following children:
   8676 i. Mark[14] **Whipple**[905] born 19 November 1967 and married Jackie **Morris.**
   8677 ii. Erin Marie **Whipple**[906] born 21 January 1978.

7334. **Rick Stephen**[13] **Whipple** (Richard Ellerman[12], Harrison Lincoln[11], Selmon Thomas[10], Cyrenius Thomas[9], Enoch[8], Nehemiah[7], Benjamin[6], Francis[5], Jonathan[4], Joseph[3], Matthew[2], Matthew[1])[907] was born in Des Moines, Polk Co., Iowa 16 March 1951 and married **Beth Hansen** in Clearwater Co., Idaho 16 April 1975. She was born in Vinton, Benton Co., Iowa 9 January 1953.[908]

Rick Stephen **Whipple** had the following children:
   8678 i. Samuel B.[14] **Whipple**[909] born in Caldwell, Canyon Co., Idaho 11 September 1981.
   8679 ii. Charles Richard **Whipple**[910] born in Caldwell 12 August 1984.
   8680 iii. Johanna Ruth Marie **Whipple**[911] born in McCall, Valley Co., Idaho 30 January 1988.

7335. **Ronald Whipple**[13] **Haight** (Jean Earlene[12] **Whipple,** Edward Clelland[11], Selmon Thomas[10], Cyrenius Thomas[9], Enoch[8], Nehemiah[7], Benjamin[6], Francis[5], Jonathan[4], Joseph[3], Matthew[2], Matthew[1])[912] was born in Waterloo, Black Hawk Co., Iowa 7 April 1958 and married **Andrea Dea Hoff** there 12 July 1986. Andrea,[913] daughter of Darrel **Hoff** and Ardith (__), was born in Vernon Co., Wisc. 25 March 1958. She has a degree in Art and Arts Management and a Teaching Certificate. Ron attended Iowa

State University, Ames, Story Co. and earned a B. S. from the U. of Northern Iowa, Cedar Falls, Black Hawk Co., with a major in Physics and a Masters in Business Administration. He also earned a Masters in Software Development from the U. of Iowa, Iowa City, Johnson Co. He works with software development in Austin, Travis Co., Texas in 2001.

Ronald Whipple **Haight** and Andrea Dea **Hoff** had the following children:
  8681 i. Sean Christopher[14] **Haight**[914] born in Waterloo 13 October 1988.
  8682 ii. Neil Edward **Haight**[915] born in Iowa City 28 November 1994.

7339. **Mark Clelland**[13] **Whipple** (Jack Clelland[12], Edward Clelland[11], Selmon Thomas[10], Cyrenius Thomas[9], Enoch[8], Nehemiah[7], Benjamin[6], Francis[5], Jonathan[4], Joseph[3], Matthew[2], Matthew[1])[916] was born in Sioux City, Woodbury Co., Iowa 20 October 1954 and died 29 February 1988 in Norfolk, Norfolk City Area Co., Va. at 33 years of age. Buried in Memorial Park, Clinton, Clinton Co., Iowa. He married **Christine Jo Bahnsen** in Clinton 19 June 1976. She was born 29 June 1955.[917] Mark's death at age 33 was attributed to family related heart disease. Its technical term is IHSS: idiopathic (an unknown disease) hypertrophic (thickening or excessive development of an organ) subaortic (below aorta) stenosis (narrowing). It is caused by a defect on chromosome 19 and is inherited. Autopsies of athletes who seem in excellent health often show this condition. Dr. Christine Steadman of Harvard Medical School began researching the condition in the early 1990s. Medication helps control symptoms.

Mark Clelland **Whipple** and Christine Jo **Bahnsen** had the following children:
  8683 i. Kimberly Frances[14] **Whipple**[918] born at the Walter Reed Army Medical Center in Washington, D.C. 5 August 1979.
  8684 ii. Matthew Clelland **Whipple**[919] born in Hampton, Hampton City Area Co., Va. 9 October 1984.
  8685 iii. Jessica Jane **Whipple**[920] born in Postville, Iowa 17 May 1987.

7341. **Rebecca Ann**[13] **Britt** (Robert Clarence[12], Anna Bessie[11] **Whipple**, Selmon Thomas[10], Cyrenius Thomas[9], Enoch[8], Nehemiah[7], Benjamin[6], Francis[5], Jonathan[4], Joseph[3], Matthew[2], Matthew[1])[921] was born 4 January 1947 and married **Tim Lange**.

Rebecca Ann **Britt** and Tim **Lange** had the following child:
  8686 i. Adam[14] **Lange**.[922]

7342. **Elizabeth Ellen**[13] **Britt** (Robert Clarence[12], Anna Bessie[11] **Whipple**, Selmon Thomas[10], Cyrenius Thomas[9], Enoch[8], Nehemiah[7], Benjamin[6], Francis[5], Jonathan[4], Joseph[3], Matthew[2], Matthew[1])[923] was born 9 October 1951 and married **Tom Cutsforth**.

Elizabeth Ellen **Britt** and Tom **Cutsforth** had the following children:
    8687 i. Britt[14] **Cutsforth**.[924]
    8688 ii. Sarah **Cutsforth**.[925]
    8689 iii. Thomas **Cutsforth**[926] born 24 June 1986.

7344. **Peggy Louise**[13] **Berger** (Patricia Ann[12] **Britt**, Anna Bessie[11] **Whipple**, Selmon Thomas[10], Cyrenius Thomas[9], Enoch[8], Nehemiah[7], Benjamin[6], Francis[5], Jonathan[4], Joseph[3], Matthew[2], Matthew[1])[927] was born 2 May 1949 and married **Larry Markey** 28 October 1967. They were divorced in October 1979.

Peggy Louise **Berger** and Larry **Markey** had the following children:
    8690 i. Barbara Jo[14] **Markey**[928] born 1 August 1968.
    8691 ii. Beth Janeen **Markey**[929] born 11 June 1970.
    8692 iii. Bernie Joseph **Markey**[930] born 10 February 1972.

7345. **Robert John**[13] **Berger** (Patricia Ann[12] **Britt**, Anna Bessie[11] **Whipple**, Selmon Thomas[10], Cyrenius Thomas[9], Enoch[8], Nehemiah[7], Benjamin[6], Francis[5], Jonathan[4], Joseph[3], Matthew[2], Matthew[1])[931] was born in Vinton, Benton Co., Iowa 18 June 1954 and died there 23 December 2003, at 49 years of age. He married three times. (1) **Ronda Rosalee Armstrong** in Vinton 26 October 1974. (2) **Diane Allar**. She had two sons by a previous marriage. No details provided. (3) **Cheryl Shaw** in Nashua, Chickasaw Co., Iowa 17 June 1993. They were married at the Little Brown Church. Bob was graduated from Vinton High School and worked as Director of Member Services for the Benton County REC for many years. He was a member of the Isaac Walton League and enjoyed hunting and fishing. He was also a golfer and served on the Board of the Town and Country Golf Club in Grundy Center, Grundy Co., Iowa. His services were at the Overton-Van Steenhuyse Funeral Home and he was buried in Evergreen Cemetery, both in Vinton. He died following a sudden illness.

Robert John **Berger** and Ronda Rosalee **Armstrong** had the following children:
    8693 i. Rachel Rosalee[14] **Berger**[932] born 15 December 1975.
    8694 ii. Resa Louise **Berger**[933] born 7 March 1979.

7347. **Donald Lewis**[13] **Britt** Jr. (Donald Lewis[12], Anna Bessie[11] **Whipple**, Selmon Thomas[10], Cyrenius Thomas[9], Enoch[8], Nehemiah[7], Benjamin[6], Francis[5], Jonathan[4], Joseph[3], Matthew[2], Matthew[1])[934] was born in Waterloo, Black Hawk Co., Iowa 21 October 1954 and married **Lynn (__)**.

Donald Lewis **Britt** Jr. and Lynn (__) had the following children:
- 8695 i. Angie[14] **Britt**.[935]
- 8696 ii. Guy **Britt**.[936]

7349. **Terry Rene**[13] **Whipple** (George Walter[12], Eugene Harold[11], Selmon Thomas[10], Cyrenius Thomas[9], Enoch[8], Nehemiah[7], Benjamin[6], Francis[5], Jonathan[4], Joseph[3], Matthew[2], Matthew[1])[937] was born 4 November 1943 and married twice. (1) **Sandra Wilson** in 1965. (2) **Ruth Newton** 1969.

Terry Rene **Whipple** and Sandra **Wilson** had the following children:
- 8697 i. Georgie[14] **Whipple**[938] born 27 August 1965.
- 8698 ii. Donette **Whipple**[939] born 20 February 1967.

Terry Rene **Whipple** and Ruth **Newton** had the following child:
- 8699 iii. Terry Rene **Whipple** Jr.[940] born 5 December 1970.

7350. **Rita Gayle**[13] **Whipple** (George Walter[12], Eugene Harold[11], Selmon Thomas[10], Cyrenius Thomas[9], Enoch[8], Nehemiah[7], Benjamin[6], Francis[5], Jonathan[4], Joseph[3], Matthew[2], Matthew[1])[941] was born 10 December 1947 and married **Ross Schuler** 2 January 1967.

Rita Gayle **Whipple** and Ross **Schuler** had the following children:
- 8700 i. Richard[14] **Schuler**[942] born 1 December 1967.
- 8701 ii. Robert Wayne **Schuler**[943] born 17 June 1970.
- 8702 iii. Ronald Wade **Schuler**[944] born 17 June 1970.

7353. **Donald Eugene**[13] **Morris** (Jacquelyn Ann[12] **Whipple**, Eugene Harold[11], Selmon Thomas[10], Cyrenius Thomas[9], Enoch[8], Nehemiah[7], Benjamin[6], Francis[5], Jonathan[4], Joseph[3], Matthew[2], Matthew[1])[945] was born 19 December 1945 and married **Rene Pinter** who was born 15 April 1946.[946]

Donald Eugene **Morris** and Rene **Pinter** had the following children:
- 8703 i. Christina Marie[14] **Morris**[947] born 14 August 1966.
- 8704 ii. Donald Lee **Morris**[948] born 3 September 1970.

7362. **David Gordon**[13] **Castner** (Colleen Lou[12] **Gordon**, Martha Josephine Esther[11] **Whipple**, Selmon Thomas[10], Cyrenius Thomas[9], Enoch[8], Nehemiah[7], Benjamin[6], Francis[5], Jonathan[4], Joseph[3], Matthew[2], Matthew[1])[949] was born in Webster City, Hamilton Co., Iowa 8 September 1952 and married **Beverly Jean Townsen** in Oregon City, Clackamas Co., Oreg. 7 January 1973. Beverly, daughter of Dwight **Townsen** and Jean **Slover**, was born in Denver, Denver Co., Colo. 1 April 1952.

David Gordon **Castner** and Beverly Jean **Townsen** had the following children born in Oakland, Alameda Co., Calif.:

  8705 i. Jeanne Marie[14] **Castner**[950] 16 May 1978.
  8706 ii. James David **Castner**[951] 2 April 1980.

7363. **Julie Jo**[13] **Castner** (Colleen Lou[12] **Gordon**, Martha Josephine Esther[11] **Whipple**, Selmon Thomas[10], Cyrenius Thomas[9], Enoch[8], Nehemiah[7], Benjamin[6], Francis[5], Jonathan[4], Joseph[3], Matthew[2], Matthew[1])[952] was born in Webster City, Hamilton Co., Iowa 18 August 1954 and married **Peter Paul Maloney** in Des Moines, King Co., Wash. 15 June 1974. Peter,[953] son of Thomas Paul **Maloney** and Theresa Bernadette **Warren**, was born in Salem, Essex Co., Mass. 21 October 1953.

Julie Jo **Castner** and Peter Paul **Maloney** had the following child born in Seattle, King Co., Wash.:

  8707 i. Sarah Castner[14] **Maloney**[954] 21 January 1991.

7364. **Ann Louise**[13] **Castner** (Colleen Lou[12] **Gordon**, Martha Josephine Esther[11] **Whipple**, Selmon Thomas[10], Cyrenius Thomas[9], Enoch[8], Nehemiah[7], Benjamin[6], Francis[5], Jonathan[4], Joseph[3], Matthew[2], Matthew[1])[955] was born in Webster City, Hamilton Co., Iowa 21 November 1955 and married **Frederick Steven Jestrab** in Des Moines, Polk Co., Iowa 17 December 1977. Frederick,[956] son of George August **Jestrab** and Phoebe **Hutcheson**, was born in Havre, Blaine Co., Mont. 21 September 1948.

Ann Louise **Castner** and Frederick Steven **Jestrab** had the following children:

  8708 i. Marek Castner[14] **Jestrab**[957] born in Seattle, King Co., Wash. 10 February 1985.
  8709 ii. Ross Castner **Jestrab**[958] born in Tucson, Pima Co., Ariz. 12 March 1992.

7365. **Rebecca Sue**[13] **Settlemyer** (Jo Anne[12] **Gordon**, Martha Josephine Esther[11] **Whipple**, Selmon Thomas[10], Cyrenius Thomas[9], Enoch[8], Nehemiah[7], Benjamin[6], Francis[5], Jonathan[4], Joseph[3], Matthew[2],

Matthew[1])[959] was born in Harlington, Cameron Co., Tex. 18 March 1956 and died of an aneurysm 22 May 2003 in Benson, Cochise Co., Ariz., at 47 years of age. She married **Joseph Leslie Greer** in Glendale, Maricopa Co., Ariz. 31 October 1980. Joseph, son of Carl John **Greer** and Josephine Clare **Hubbard**, was born in McNary, Apache Co., Ariz. 7 November 1950.

Rebecca Sue **Settlemyer** and Joseph Leslie **Greer** had the following children:

8710	i.	Jennifer Rebecca[14] **Greer**[960] born in Ogden, Weber Co., Utah 9 May 1984.
8711	ii.	David Blaine **Greer**[961] born in Ogden 21 May 1987.
8712	iii.	Thomas Joseph **Greer**[962] born in Tucson, Pima Co., Ariz. 9 September 1993.
8713	iv.	John Michael **Greer**[963] born in Tucson 3 December 1994.
8714	v.	Robert Matthew **Greer**[964] born in Tucson 23 August 1996.

7366. **Elizabeth Ellen**[13] **Settlemyer** (Jo Anne[12] **Gordon**, Martha Josephine Esther[11] **Whipple**, Selmon Thomas[10], Cyrenius Thomas[9], Enoch[8], Nehemiah[7], Benjamin[6], Francis[5], Jonathan[4], Joseph[3], Matthew[2], Matthew[1])[965] was born in Des Moines, Polk Co., Iowa 5 September 1960 and married **Joseph Hyrum Adams** in Phoenix, Maricopa Co., Ariz. 17 October 1982. He was born in Chicago, Cook Co., Ill. 7 August 1958.[966]

Elizabeth Ellen **Settlemyer** and Joseph Hyrum **Adams** had the following children:

8715	i.	Orion Joseph[14] **Adams**[967] born in Cottonwood, Yavapai Co., Ariz. 5 June 1983.
8716	ii.	Phillip Robert **Adams**[968] born in Phoenix 18 July 1984.

7367. **Anna Colleen**[13] **Settlemyer** (Jo Anne[12] **Gordon**, Martha Josephine Esther[11] **Whipple**, Selmon Thomas[10], Cyrenius Thomas[9], Enoch[8], Nehemiah[7], Benjamin[6], Francis[5], Jonathan[4], Joseph[3], Matthew[2], Matthew[1])[969] was born in Des Moines, Polk Co., Iowa 21 September 1963 and married three times. (1) **Daniel Cook** in San Diego, San Diego Co., Calif. 17 December 1983. Daniel,[970] son of Richard Eugene **Cook**, was born in Muncie, Delaware Co., Ind. 16 November 1953. (2) **Jay Worthen** in Albuquerque, Bernadillo Co., N. Mex. 6 November 1991. He was born in Wichita Falls, Wichita Co., Tex. 11 January 1958.[971] (3) **Patricio Ramone Sedillo** in Albuquerque 28 August 1993. He was born in Mountain Aire, Torrence Co., N. Mex. 9 April 1957.[972]

Anna Colleen **Settlemyer** and Daniel **Cook** had the following children born in San Diego:

      8717   i.   Kandice Jo[14] **Cook**[973] 26 June 1985.
      8718   ii.   Natalie Deanne **Cook**[974] 16 June 1986.
      8719 iii. Andrew Lee **Cook**[975] 16 April 1988.

7368. **Anna Louise**[13] **Gallaher** (Thomas Lee[12], Clara Adalene[11] **Whipple**, Selmon Thomas[10], Cyrenius Thomas[9], Enoch[8], Nehemiah[7], Benjamin[6], Francis[5], Jonathan[4], Joseph[3], Matthew[2], Matthew[1])[976] was born in Corpus Christi, Nueces Co., Tex. 31 March 1961 and married twice. (1) **Stephen Craig Bekel** in Bettendorf, Scott Co., Iowa 1 December 1984. Stephen,[977] son of Donald Lyle **Bekel** and Nancy **Teeter**, was born in Fairfield, Jefferson Co., Iowa 27 December 1963. They were divorced 31 December 1985. (2) **Gary Stephen McCleary** in Muscatine, Muscatine Co., Iowa 24 July 1992. Gary,[798] son of Jess Dennis **McCleary** and Gladys Mary **Lovell**, was born in Muscatine 1 February 1956. He married (1) **Margaret Louise Foss**. They were divorced in 1989. Anna Louise earned a B. A. Degree in Elementary Education from Iowa Wesleyan College at Mount Pleasant, Henry Co., in 1983.

Anna Louise **Gallaher** and Stephen Craig **Bekel** had the following child born in Muscatine:

      8720   i.   Benjamin Thomas[14] **Bekel**[979] 12 May 1985.

7369. **Amy Lee**[13] **Gallaher** (Thomas Lee[12], Clara Adalene[11] **Whipple**, Selmon Thomas[10], Cyrenius Thomas[9], Enoch[8], Nehemiah[7], Benjamin[6], Francis[5], Jonathan[4], Joseph[3], Matthew[2], Matthew[1])[980] was born in Corpus Christi, Nueces Co., Tex. 14 December 1964 and married **David William Scott** in Muscatine, Muscatine Co., Iowa 26 June 1993. David,[981] son of Donald Richard **Scott** and Jean Lorine **Brauns**, was born in Muscatine 9 March 1963. Amy earned a B, A. Degree in Special Studies at Marycrest College, Davenport, Scott Co., Iowa in 1988. She is a Counselor at Crossroads, a vocational facility for the handicapped. She and David farm west of Muscatine.

Amy Lee **Gallaher** and David William **Scott** had the following children born in Muscatine:

      8721   i.   Aaron Thomas[14] **Scott**[982] 27 January 2000.
      8722   ii.   Ean William **Scott**[983] 16 May 2002.

7371. **Todd Lyle**[13] **Gallaher** (David Lyle[12], Clara Adalene[11] **Whipple**, Selmon Thomas[10], Cyrenius Thomas[9], Enoch[8], Nehemiah[7], Benjamin[6], Francis[5], Jonathan[4], Joseph[3], Matthew[2], Matthew[1])[984] was born in Audubon, Audobon Co., Iowa 29 May 1963 and married **Deanna Marie Reis** in Nashua, Chickasaw Co., Iowa 20 May 1994. Deanna is the daughter of Kenneth **Ries** and Delores **Peterson**.[985] She was married previously and had sons Matt, born 15 June 1985 and Geoff, born 9 April 1988. No information on the first husband provided.

Todd Lyle **Gallaher** and Deanna Marie **Reis** had the following children born in Waterloo, Black Hawk Co., Iowa:
- 8723 i. Hannah Iliesh[14] **Gallaher**[986] 19 July 1995.
- 8724 ii. Alyssa Marie **Gallaher**[987] 24 March 1998.

7372. **Lori Diane**[13] **Gallaher** (David Lyle[12], Clara Adalene[11] **Whipple**, Selmon Thomas[10], Cyrenius Thomas[9], Enoch[8], Nehemiah[7], Benjamin[6], Francis[5], Jonathan[4], Joseph[3], Matthew[2], Matthew[1])[988] was born in Estherville, Emmett Co., Iowa 1 May 1969 and married **Bobby Ray Hasfjord** in Ventura, Cerro Gordo Co., Iowa 3 June 1990. Bobby, son of Merle T. **Hasfjord** and Edith **Gosling**, was born in Lancaster, Los Angeles Co., Calif. 21 October 1968.[989]

Lori Diane **Gallaher** and Bobby Ray **Hasfjord** had the following child born in Mason City, Cerro Gordo Co., Iowa:
- 8725 i. Austin Ray[14] **Hasfjord**[990] 21 July 1995.

7373. **Renette Marie**[13] **Shere** (Judith Ann[12] **Whipple**, Cyrenius Albert[11], Selmon Thomas[10], Cyrenius Thomas[9], Enoch[8], Nehemiah[7], Benjamin[6], Francis[5], Jonathan[4], Joseph[3], Matthew[2], Matthew[1])[991] was born 22 July 1956 and married **Neal Casabon**.

Renette Marie **Shere** and Neal **Casabon** had the following child:
- 8726 i. Nicole[14] **Casabon**.[992]

7380. **Donald James**[13] **Faris** (Donald Wayne[12], Nellie Jeanette[11] **Whipple**, Selmon Thomas[10], Cyrenius Thomas[9], Enoch[8], Nehemiah[7], Benjamin[6], Francis[5], Jonathan[4], Joseph[3], Matthew[2], Matthew[1])[993] was born in Belmond, Wright Co., Iowa 25 August 1956 and married **Holly (__)**.

Donald James **Faris** and Holly (__) had the following children:
- 8727 i. Jesse[14] **Faris**.[994]
- 8728 ii. Jami **Faris**.[995]

7391. **Nancy Lee¹³ Whipple** (James Earl¹², Lucien Blaine¹¹, James Ezekiel¹⁰, Lucien Ransom⁹, Enoch⁸, Nehemiah⁷, Benjamin⁶, Francis⁵, Jonathan⁴, Joseph³, Matthew², Matthew¹)⁹⁹⁶ was born in Cedar Rapids, Linn Co., Iowa 18 January 1935 and married three times. (1) **Gerald James Babbage** in Cedar Rapids 9 October 1954. He was born in Cedar Rapids 6 October 1935.⁹⁹⁷ They were divorced in St. Petersburg, Pinellas Co., Fla. in July 1963. He married (2)

Gerald James Babbage and Nancy Lee Whipple, Wedding photo, October 9, 1954, Cedar Rapids, Iowa.

Lee Allen Babbage, age 3.

L to R Linda (Babbage) Spruell, Blaine Whipple, Alycia D. Kelly, Nancy (Whipple) Nuce and Elaine West at the Vinton, Iowa Evergreen Cemetery in August 2000.

Lee Allen, 13, and Linda, 11, in St. Petersburg, Fla. Photos courtesy of Elaine (Whipple) West.

{ G 1284 }

Bonnie (__) in Cedar Rapids 9 December 1963. (2) **Harry Guy Garland** in St. Petersburg 23 October 1963. He was born in St. Petersburg.[998] They were divorced there 15 May 1969. (3) **John Bernard Nuce** in St. Petersburg 28 August 1969. John,[999] son of Bernard J. **Nuce** and Aletha Ann **Nagel**, was born in Anderson, Madison Co., Ind. 4 January 1939. They were divorced in St. Petersburg.

Nancy Lee **Whipple** and Gerald James **Babbage** had the following children:
+ 8729 i. Lee Allen[14] **Babbage** born 28 May 1955.
+ 8730 ii. Linda Ann **Babbage** born 31 January 1957.

Nancy Lee **Whipple** and Harry Guy **Garland** had the following children:
+ 8731 iii. Jon Robert **Garland** born 26 July 1964.
  8732 iv. Tina Marie **Garland**[1000] born in St. Petersburg 26 July 1969.

7392. **James Michael**[13] **Whipple** (James Earl[12], Lucien Blaine[11], James Ezekiel[10], Lucien Ransom[9], Enoch[8], Nehemiah[7], Benjamin[6], Francis[5], Jonathan[4], Joseph[3], Matthew[2], Matthew[1])[1001] was born in St. Petersburg, Pinellas Co., Fla. 9 October 1957 and married twice. (1) **Ann Darnell** in Florida in 1979. She was born in February 1961.[1002] They were divorced in Florida in 1984. (2) **Patty Anderson** in Florida 17 April 1986. She was born 22 January 1967.[1003]

James Michael Whipple St. Petersburg high school graduation.

James Michael **Whipple** and Ann **Darnell** had the following children born in St. Petersburg:
  8733 i. James Michael[14] **Whipple II**[1004] 8 October 1980.
  8734 ii. Kellie Lynn **Whipple**[1005] 2 October 1982.

James Michael **Whipple** and Patty **Anderson** had the following child born in St. Petersburg:
  8735 iii. Cory Ryan **Whipple**[1006] 27 October 1989.

James with James II and Kellie Lynn Whipple. Photos courtesy of Elaine (Whipple) West.

{ G 1285 }

7393. **Jay Allen**[13] **Whipple** (James Earl[12], Lucien Blaine[11], James Ezekiel[10], Lucien Ransom[9], Enoch[8], Nehemiah[7], Benjamin[6], Francis[5], Jonathan[4], Joseph[3], Matthew[2], Matthew[1])[1007] was born in St. Petersburg, Pinellas Co., Fla. 14 August 1959 and married **Lynne Ann Budd**. They are divorced.

Jay Allen Whipple St. Pertersburg high school graduation. Photo courtesy of Elaine (Whipple) West.

Nicole Elaine Whipple, 2005. Photo courtesy of Nicole Elaine Whipple.

Jay Allen **Whipple** and Lynne Ann **Budd** had the following child born in St. Petersburg:

    8736 i. Nicole Elaine[14] **Whipple**[1008] 12 July 1985.

7395. **Michael James**[13] **Drotzman** (Patricia Ellen[12] **Whipple**, Lucien Blaine[11], James Ezekiel[10], Lucien Ransom[9], Enoch[8], Nehemiah[7], Benjamin[6], Francis[5], Jonathan[4], Joseph[3], Matthew[2], Matthew[1])[1009] was born in Yankton, Yankton Co., S. Dak. 6 August 1952 and married **Ruth Ann Remund** in Appleton, Swift Co., Minn. 18 October 1978. Ruth,[1010] daughter of Lester Lyle **Remund** and Myrna Vynette **King**, was born in Graceville, Big Stone Co., Minn. 1 March 1960.

Michael James **Drotzman** and Ruth Ann **Remund** had the following children:

+   8737 i. Jessica Ashley[14] **Drotzman** born 27 October 1980.
    8738 ii. Jacob Lyle **Drotzman**[1011] born in Portsmouth, Portsmouth City Area Co., Va. 8 June 1983.
    8739 iii. Joseph Leroy **Drotzman**[1012] born in Portsmouth 8 June 1983.
    8740 iv. Jared Daniel **Drotzman**[1013] born in Parma, Cuyahoga Co., Ohio 2 November 1988.

7396. **Larry Joseph**[13] **Drotzman** (Patricia Ellen[12] **Whipple**, Lucien Blaine[11], James Ezekiel[10], Lucien Ransom[9], Enoch[8], Nehemiah[7], Benjamin[6], Francis[5], Jonathan[4], Joseph[3], Matthew[2], Matthew[1])[1014] was born in Yankton, Yankton Co., S. Dak. 2 September 1955 and died there of cancer 23 January 1995, at 39 years of age. Buried in Sacred Heart Cemetery. He married **Martha Irene Guerrero** in Las Vegas, Clark Co., Nev. 20 March 1982. Martha,[1015] daughter of Leoncio Francisco **Guerrero** and Delfa Clemencia **Rodriquez**, was born in Los Angeles, Los Angeles Co., Calif. 19 March 1957. Larry was graduated from Yankton High School and served for a short period in the U.S. Navy. He lived in Long Beach, Los Angeles Co., Calif. after his discharge where he became a refrigeration mechanic. The family moved to Sioux Falls, Minnehaha Co., S. Dak. before 1987 and later to Yankton where he was employed by the government working on the Yankton Missouri River Dam. After Larry's death, Martha moved the family to Trabuco Canyon, Orange Co., Calif. to be near her family.

Larry Joseph **Drotzman** and Martha Irene **Guerrero** had the following children born in Sioux Falls:
8741 i. Jason Ryan[14] **Drotzman**[1016] 17 February 1987.
8742 ii. Laura Ann **Drotzman**[1017] 28 May 1990.

7399. **Blaine Scott**[13] **Whipple** (Robert Blaine[12], Lucien Blaine[11], James Ezekiel[10], Lucien Ransom[9], Enoch[8], Nehemiah[7], Benjamin[6], Francis[5], Jonathan[4], Joseph[3], Matthew[2], Matthew[1])[1018] was born in Portland, Multnomah Co., Oreg. 27 December 1968 and married **Lorna Jo Zoerink** in Turner, Marion Co., Oreg. 14 August 1998. Lorna,[1019] daughter of Wayne **Zoerink** and Beverly Jean **Gerritson**, was born in Lakewood, Los Angeles Co., Calif. 1 December 1966. L. J. earned an Associate of Arts degree from Colorado Northwestern Community College at Rangely, Rio Blanco Co., Colo. in 1987. She attended on basketball and volleyball scholarships and was Captain of both teams. She was awarded a Bachelor of Science Degree from Colorado State University, Fort Collins, Larimer Co. in 1993 where she majored in Human Development and Family Studies. She has worked as an Education Assistant in Special Ed classes in Portland and for the Child Center (a day treatment center) in Eugene, Lane Co., Oreg. In the latter position she worked in schools and with families with children (ages 7-12) who have behavorial problems. She also worked for the Portland, Oreg. school system while simultaneously working for a Masters of Education Degree from Portland State University.

Scott was born at 12:24 p.m at Bess Kaiser Hospital in Portland and was 20 and 1/2 inches long and weighed 8 pounds 2 ounces. At age 4 he was 3' 2 1/2" and weighted 50 pounds; at 8 he was 4' 11 1/4" and 77 pounds;

at 12, 5' 5 3/4" and 131 pounds; at 18, 6'4" and 240 pounds. He earned varsity letters in football and wrestling at Sunset High School in Beaverton, Washington Co., Oreg.

He was graduated from Grinnell College, Grinnell, Poweshkiek Co., Iowa in June 1990 with a major in Economics and was both a Football (four years) and Basketball (three years) Letterman and Captain of both teams his senior year. He was awarded a Doctor of Jurisprudence Degree by the U. of Oregon Law School and inducted into the Order of the Coif in May 1998. He worked in the Trust Department of a major bank in Chicago, Cook Co., Ill. (1990-92) and as an Underwriter with Standard Insurance Co. of Portland (1993-95). He is trial lawyer and partner with the Portland law firm of Schwabe, Williamson, and Wyatt (2006).

Blaine Scott **Whipple** and Lorna Jo **Zoerink** had the following children born in Portland, Washington Co., Oreg.:

  8743 i. Spencer Blaine[14] **Whipple**[1020] 15 October 2001 at St. Vincent's Hospital at 10:42 p.m.; 6 pounds, 21 inches.

  8744 ii. Turner Collins **Whipple**[1021] 8 May 2004 at St. Vincent's Hospital at 1:24 a.m.; 7 pounds, 2 ounces, 18 inches.

7400. **Terri Lynn**[13] **Jasperson** (Nancy Jane[12] **Whipple**, Lucien Blaine[11], James Ezekiel[10], Lucien Ransom[9], Enoch[8], Nehemiah[7], Benjamin[6], Francis[5], Jonathan[4], Joseph[3], Matthew[2], Matthew[1])[1022] was born in Tracy, Lyon Co., Minn. 11 October 1951 and married **Charles Jacob Ebert** in Appleton, Swift Co., Minn. 20 September 1975. He was born in Clear Lake, Deuel Co., S. Dak. 26 January 1951 and died 14 June 2002 in Luverne, Rock Co., Minn., at 51 years of age. He was the son of Vance Leroy **Ebert** and Doris Helen **Warner**.[1023]

Obituary: Charles (Chuck) Jacob Ebert, age 51 of Luverne, Minn. passed away on Friday, June 14, 2002 at the Luverne Hospice Cottage. When Chuck was in grade school in Clear Lake, S. Dak. he moved with his family to Luverne where he graduated from High School in 1969. He continued his education at Minnesota's Winona State College (now University) and worked as a Marketing Manager at CWG-Tri State Insurance in Luverne. Over the years he continued with his insurance education and received the following titles and degrees: CPCU, CIC, ARM, AU, and ALCM.

Chuck was a member of Grace Lutheran Church in Luverne. He served as Past President of the Jaycees, Past President of the Luverne Toastmasters, Past Treasurer for the Music Boosters, Board Member for the Green Earth Players, and Scorekeeper for the High School Gymnastics Team. At the time of death he was Treasurer for Pheasants Forever. Above all, Chuck cherished the time he could spend with his family.

Chuck will be lovingly rememberd by his wife Terri of Luverne; his daughters Katie of Luverne, Sarah and Amanda of Marshall, Lyon Co., Minn.; his parents Vance and Doris Ebert of Luverne; his brothers Jim (Mary) of Bemidgi, Minn. and Paul (Dyan) of Elk River, Minn; his nieces Jessica (Ethan) Harvey of Little Falls, Minn. and Laurin Ebert of Elk River; his nephew Jake Ebert of Truman, Minn. His grandparents preceded him in death. Funeral services were 17 June at the Grace Luthern Church; burial in Maplewood Cemetery, Luverne. Donations to the First Farmers & Merchants Bank of Luverne for the Ebert Family Scholarship which will be awarded at the Pheasants Forever Banquet.[1024]

Terri attended grades two through eleven at Marshall, Lyon Co., Minn and was graduated from Appleton High School. She was also graduated from Alexandria, Douglas Co., Minn. Technical College (a 2-year course) and spent a year and a half at Moorhead State College in Moorhead, Clay Co., Minn. She worked in the Registrar's Office during the day and attended night classes. Following college she clerked for her parents at the Jasperson Department Store in Appleton and had an afternoon radio program on KBMO.

Terri and Chuck met while both were vacationing in Hawaii. After the family moved to Luverne, she joined the Rock County Sheriff's Department in August 1983 and is now the Dispatch Supervisor/Administrative Assistant to the Sheriff. The job includes managing the 911 System, suvervising/training dispatchers, giving drug tests to prisoners, transporting prisoners and mental patients to and from court/jail/prison. She trains Deputies on how to write reports, give drug tests, and how to use the fingerprint machine. She also works closely with the County Attorney and Family Services. She is President of the Communication Supervisors Organization for the Fifth Minnesota District.

Sarah, Amanda, and Terri Ebert at Jessica Drotzman and Eric Hammer's wedding, 14 May 2005, Sioux Falls, S. Dak. Photo courtesy of Michael J. Drotzman.

{ G 1289 }

She was a cast member of the musical "Oklahoma" in High School and began serious acting with the Luverne Readers Theater Productions where she has played leads in a number of productions. She also helped with makeup, costumes, and props and is a Board Member of the Green Earth Players. She taught Sunday School and Confirmation classes, served communion, and has been a reader in Luverne's Grace Lutheran Church.

Terri Lynn **Jasperson** and Charles Jacob **Ebert** had the following children:
- 8745   i.   Katherine Marie[14] **Ebert**[1025] born in Stevens Point, Portage Co., Wisc. 7 December 1977 and married Matthew A. **Mostad** in Luverne 27 November 2004.
- 8746   ii.   Sarah Elizabeth **Ebert**[1026] born in Fridley, Anoka Co., Minn. 17 September 1979.
- 8747   iii.   Amanda Louise **Ebert**[1027] born in Fridley 4 May 1981.

7401. **Donna Marie**[13] **Jasperson** (Nancy Jane[12] **Whipple**, Lucien Blaine[11], James Ezekiel[10], Lucien Ransom[9], Enoch[8], Nehemiah[7], Benjamin[6], Francis[5], Jonathan[4], Joseph[3], Matthew[2], Matthew[1])[1028] was born in Tracy, Lyon Co., Minn. 10 May 1955 and died 16 November 1989 in Appleton, Swift Co., Minn., at 34 years of age. Funeral services were held 19 November at Appleton's Zion Lutheran Church and internment was in the Appleton City Cemetery. She married **Gerald Dean Barney** in Appleton 22 July 1973. Gerald, son of Christian **Barney** and Hattie **Van Heurulan**, was born in Willmar, Kandiyohi Co., Minn. 11 March 1944. They were divorced in Appleton.

In 1982 at age 27, recently divorced, and raising two children, she was working as Legal Secretary in Appleton when she was diagnosed with a giant aneurysm on her brain stem. Four days after entering the hospital and after the doctors had tied off the aneurysm, she had a stroke which robbed her of her ability to walk and altered her memory (she couldn't remember the previous three years). She had limited use of her vocal chords because of a trachea tube and had to be fed by a stomach tube. In short, she had lost the ability to take care of herself and had to re-learn independent living skills.

She began a long recovery period which led to her acceptance at Courage Residence in Golden Valley, Hennepin Co., Minn. in September 1984. A Live-in Transitional Rehabilitation Facility where individuals 16 and older with disabilities learn independent living skills. When she first arrived she needed "hands-on" support but within a year had progressed to a point of needing little help. She made a successful transfer to using a walker as well as a wheel chair, learned to use her vocal chords, memory strategies, and how to cook. Her progress was such she was able to move into an apartment retrofitted for her disabilities in the fall of 1985. It was a long process but with grit and determination, she achieved a level of independence that allowed her to return to Appleton to help raise her two children.[1029]

Donna Marie **Jasperson** and Gerald Dean **Barney** had the following children born in Appleton:

    8748   i.   Jeffrey Dean[14] **Barney**[1030] 16 November 1975. Following graduation from Lac Qui Parle Valley High School at Appleton, he was graduated from the U. of Minnesota, Minneapolis where he attended with a golf scholarship. He spent the spring and summer months of 2002 and 2003 touring Europe.

    8749   ii.   Leah Marie **Barney**[1031] 5 February 1979. She was graduated from the University of Minnesota School of Pharmacy, Minneapolis with a Doctorate degree in 2004. While a student, she worked part time at a drug store in St. Paul, Ramsey Co., Minn. with her Grand Uncle Dick Whipple.

7402. **David Blaine**[13] **Jasperson** (Nancy Jane[12] Whipple, Lucien Blaine[11], James Ezekiel[10], Lucien Ransom[9], Enoch[8], Nehemiah[7], Benjamin[6], Francis[5], Jonathan[4], Joseph[3], Matthew[2], Matthew[1])[1032] was born in Marshall, Lyon Co., Minn. 7 November 1959 and married **Jan C. Knobbe** in Waukegan, Lake Co., Ill. 29 September 1984. Jan, daughter of Joseph William **Knobbe** and Jeanette Hildagaard **Caraver**, was born in Waukegan 2 September 1957.

Following graduation from High School in 1975, Jan attended Saint Teresa College in Winona, Winona Co., Minn. where she received a B.S. in Nursing in 1979. She was awarded an M.A. in Management and Health & Human Services from Saint Mary's University, Rochester, Olmsted Co., Minn. in 1996. She worked as the Neuro Staff Nurse at St. Mary's Hospital 1979-84; Assistant Head Nurse 1984-90; and Nurse Manager of the Neuro ICU beginning in 1990. She is also an Adjunct Faculty Member of Saint

Jan, Dave, and Emily Jasperson, Evergreen Cemetery, Vinton, Iowa, 2000. Photo courtesy of Blaine Whipple.

{ G 1291 }

Mary's University of Minnesota where she is a Systems Analyst, S&P-MICS Implementation Team. (2002).

Dave was graduated from the Appleton, Swift Co., Minn. High School (1978) where he was Quarterback of the Football Team, won the award as Outstanding Basketball Player as a senior, and the WCCO Young Achiever Award. He attended Concordia College in Moorhead, Clay Co., Minn. where he earned a B.A. in Business Administration & Communications (1982), and completed a course at Winona State University (1994) which led to a Parent Educator's Teaching License from the State of Minnesota. He was awarded an M.A. in Management from Saint Mary's University of Minnesota (1995). As a consequence of his thesis research, he developed the Father-Friendly Assessment Tool now used by managers and employees in the workplace. He later modified it so it can also be used as the Family-Friendly Assessment Tool.

Elaine West and Emily Jane at Elaine's 90th birthday, Mt. Vernon, Iowa.

He was Senior Credit Analyst with First Bank Systems, Inc., Rochester 1982-86; Executive Director of the Olmsted, Minn. County Historical Society 1986-90; Parent Educator with Parents are Important in Rochester (PAIIR), 1990-92; and from 1994 to present. He works in the Early Childhood Family Education Program in the Rochester School District with fathers, immigrants, incarcerated parents, non-English speaking parents, and first time parents (2005).

David Blaine **Jasperson** and Jan C. **Knobbe** had the following child born in Rochester:

  8750 i. Emily Jane[14] **Jasperson** 30 June 1992.[1033]

7403. **Molly Jane**[13] **Jasperson** (Nancy Jane[12] **Whipple**, Lucien Blaine[11], James Ezekiel[10], Lucien Ransom[9], Enoch[8], Nehemiah[7], Benjamin[6], Francis[5], Jonathan[4], Joseph[3], Matthew[2], Matthew[1])[1034] was born in Marshall, Lyon Co., Minn. 23 November 1966 and married **Kurt Roger Schmidt** at Christ Lutheran Church in Glencoe, McLeod Co., Minn. 8 May 1993. Kurt, son of Roger **Schmidt** and Marilyn **Wirtz**, was born in Glencoe 13 November 1967.[1035]

Kurt joined the army after graduating from Glencoe High School in June 1986 serving for two years. Upon discharge he attended Moorhead State University, Moorhead, Clay Co., Minn. for two years and then worked in the millwork department for Plato, McLeod Co., Minn. Millwork Co. In June of 1994 he completed a two year course in Mechanical Drafting at Rochester, Olmsted Co., Minn. Technical College and was hired to design and draw custom spiral staircases for Custom Iron in Zumbrota, Goodhue Co., Minn. He was employed by Nigon Woodworks in Rochester in 1997 where he designed kitchens, entertainment centers, and fireplace mantels and formed his own design and construction company in Stewartville, Goodhue Co. in 2005.

Stephanie and Luke, December 2003, Rochester, Minn.

Molly completed the first ten grades of school in Appleton, Swift Co., Minn., a small town in southwest Minnesota. The family moved to Glencoe in 1983 where she was graduated from High School in 1985. She completed her freshman year of college at Concordia College then transferred to Moorhead State University where she earned a Bachelor of Science Degree in Mass Communications in December 1991. Both colleges are located in Moorhead.

She took a year off between her sophomore and junior years to help care for her mother who was dying of breast cancer. During that year she also worked as a Secretary for Cargilll Corporation at Minnetonka, Hennepin Co., Minnesota, an easy drive from her Glencoe home. She worked directly for the Cargill family in the Waycross Division. She returned to college after her mother's death in December 1987.

She completed her Public Relations Internship at St. Luke's Hospital in Fargo, Cass Co., N. Dak. and worked in the Marketing Department for a custom cabinet manufacturer in Plato during the summer. Upon graduation she became the Public Relations Coordinator for the Southeastern Minnesota Private Industry Council, part of the Minnesota Department of Economic Security, in Rochester. In December 2000 she was hired as the Marketing and Communications Director for the Rochester Area Economic Development, Inc. where she is currently employed (2006).

Molly Jane **Jasperson** and Kurt Roger **Schmidt** had the following children born in Rochester:

    8751   i.   Stephanie Lynn[14] **Schmidt**[1036] 8 March 1996.
    8752   ii. Luke Anthony **Schmidt**[1037] 25 April 1998. Seven pounds 11 ounces, 18 1/4 inches long. Born at 3:21 p.m.

{ G 1293 }

7404. **Billie June**[13] **McPherson** (Mary Ann[12] **Whipple**, Lucien Blaine[11], James Ezekiel[10], Lucien Ransom[9], Enoch[8], Nehemiah[7], Benjamin[6], Francis[5], Jonathan[4], Joseph[3], Matthew[2], Matthew[1])[1038] was born in Russellville, Pope Co., Ark. 16 June 1956 and married **Robert Leon Mauro Jr.** in Westford, Middlesex Co., Mass. 28 August 1982. Bobby,[1039] son of Robert Leon **Mauro** and Toby K. **Krasiuk**, was born in Concord, Middlesex Co., Mass. 9 January 1956.

Bobby and Billie June Mauro. Photo courtesy of Billie June Mauro.

Jayme-Lee Mauro, Littleton, Mass. High School Graduation. Photo courtesy of Jayme-Lee Mauro.

Jayme and Greg Mauro. Photo courtesy of Billie June Mauro.

Billie June **McPherson** and Robert Leon **Mauro** Jr. had the following children born in Concord:

  8753 i. Jayme-Lee Jenkins[14] **Mauro**[1040] 16 April 1983. Weighed 7 lbs, 8 3/4 oz and was 21" long.

  8754 ii. Gregory Robert **Mauro**[1041] 19 February 1986. Weighed 8 lbs, 3 oz and was 22" long.

7405. **Melissa Ann**[13] **McPherson** (Mary Ann[12] **Whipple**, Lucien Blaine[11], James Ezekiel[10], Lucien Ransom[9], Enoch[8], Nehemiah[7], Benjamin[6], Francis[5], Jonathan[4], Joseph[3], Matthew[2], Matthew[1])[1042] was born in

Fayettville, Washington Co., Ark. 10 August 1959 and married **George Nicholas Giambanis** at St. Nicholas Greek Orthodox Church in Lexington, Middlesex Co., Mass. 30 August 1980. George,[1043] son of Nicholas John **Giambanis** and Mary **Mastoris**, was born in Piraeus, Greece 17 November 1959. Following graduation from High School Melissa was graduated from a 2-year culinary course at Johnson & Wales in Providence, Providence Co., R.I. She worked weekends at various cafes and restaurants and met her future husband at the school. Their son Nicholas enrolled in the school in the fall of 2002 following graduation from High School in Cherry Hill, Camden Co., N.J.

Nicholas Nathaniel Giambanis High School Graduation. Photo couresy of Nicholas Giambanis.

Amy Gambanis High School Graduation. Photo courtesy of Amy Giambanis.

Melissa Ann **McPherson** and George Nicholas **Giambanis** had the following children born in Marlton, Burlington Co., N.J.:

    8755   i.   Nicholas Nathaniel[14] **Giambanis**[1044] 7 June 1983.

    8756   ii.   Amy Nichole **Giambanis**[1045] 27 February 1985.

7412. **Donna Lee**[13] **Watson** (Lee William[12], Clara Belle[11] **Fultz**, Anna M.[10] **Whipple**, Lucien Ransom[9], Enoch[8], Nehemiah[7], Benjamin[6], Francis[5], Jonathan[4], Joseph[3], Matthew[2], Matthew[1])[1046] was born 8 September 1938 and died 27 September 1975 at 37 years of age. She married **Walter Henry Paluch** in December 1958.

Donna Lee **Watson** and Walter Henry **Paluch** had the following children:

    8757   i.   Karen Lynne[14] **Paluch**[1047] born 4 July 1959.
    8758   ii.   Mark Allen **Paluch**[1048] born 30 June 1961.
    8759   iii.   Marvin John **Paluch**[1049] born 20 June 1962.
    8760   iv.   Michael Dean **Paluch**[1050] born 11 June 1965.
    8761   v.   Danny E. **Paluch**[1051] born 30 November 1967.

7414. **Patricia Cynn**[13] **Watson** (Lee William[12], Clara Belle[11] **Fultz**, Anna M.[10] **Whipple**, Lucien Ransom[9], Enoch[8], Nehemiah[7], Benjamin[6], Francis[5], Jonathan[4], Joseph[3], Matthew[2], Matthew[1])[1052] was born 30 December 1946 and married **Steven Ellis Hawn** 2 September 1962. He was born 23 September 1942.[1053]

Patricia Cynn **Watson** and Steven Ellis **Hawn** had the following children:
    8762   i.   Marie Christine[14] **Hawn**[1054] born 27 November 1963.
    8763   ii. Nancy Lee **Hawn**[1055] born 5 October 1968.

7415. **Michael Harlan**[13] **Watson** (Lee William[12], Clara Belle[11] **Fultz**, Anna M.[10] **Whipple**, Lucien Ransom[9], Enoch[8], Nehemiah[7], Benjamin[6], Francis[5], Jonathan[4], Joseph[3], Matthew[2], Matthew[1])[1056] was born 22 September 1951 and married **Lourdes Geraldine Bernedette DeMassabielle**. She was born 22 February 1954.[1057]

Michael Harlan **Watson** and Lourdes Geraldine Bernedette **DeMassabielle** had the following children:
    8764   i.   Colleen Michelle[14] **Watson**[1058] born 9 August 1977.
    8765   ii. Lourdes Michelle **Watson**[1059] born 25 July 1978.

7416. **Donald Louis**[13] **Huckstadt** (Annabelle[12] **Watson**, Clara Belle[11] **Fultz**, Anna M.[10] **Whipple**, Lucien Ransom[9], Enoch[8], Nehemiah[7], Benjamin[6], Francis[5], Jonathan[4], Joseph[3], Matthew[2], Matthew[1])[1060] was born 13 December 1940 and married **Diane Mikota** 19 July 1969. She was born 15 September 1940.[1061]

Donald Louis **Huckstadt** and Diane **Mikota** had the following children:
    8766   i.   Valerie Jean[14] **Huckstadt**[1062] born 10 February 1970.
    8767   ii. Beverly Joan **Huckstadt**[1063] born 2 June 1973.

7417. **Deanna Kay**[13] **Hendricks** (Helen Virginia[12] **Watson**, Clara Belle[11] **Fultz**, Anna M.[10] **Whipple**, Lucien Ransom[9], Enoch[8], Nehemiah[7], Benjamin[6], Francis[5], Jonathan[4], Joseph[3], Matthew[2], Matthew[1])[1064] was born 16 August 1945 and married **John M. Jones** 4 August 1973. He was born 10 November 1944.[1065]

Deanna Kay **Hendricks** and John M. **Jones** had the following child:
    8768   i.   Aaron John[14] **Jones**[1066] born 1 June 1975.

7418. **Sandra Lee**[13] **Hendricks** (Helen Virginia[12] **Watson**, Clara Belle[11] **Fultz**, Anna M.[10] **Whipple**, Lucien Ransom[9], Enoch[8], Nehemiah[7], Benjamin[6], Francis[5], Jonathan[4], Joseph[3], Matthew[2], Matthew[1])[1067] was born 13 May 1948 and married **Gary Ralph Timmell** 10 September 1967. He was born 31 March 1945.[1068]

Sandra Lee **Hendricks** and Gary Ralph **Timmell** had the following children:
    8769   i.   Denise Lynn[14] **Timmell**[1069] born 19 July 1972.
    8770   ii.   David Kelly **Timmell**[1070] born 23 July 1976.

7420. **Richard**[13] **Studdermann** (Marianne[12] **Pierson**, Cora[11] **Fultz**, Anna M.[10] **Whipple**, Lucien Ransom[9], Enoch[8], Nehemiah[7], Benjamin[6], Francis[5], Jonathan[4], Joseph[3], Matthew[2], Matthew[1])[1071] birth date unknown, married **Gail Gruetzacher** in June 1968.

Richard **Studdermann** and Gail **Gruetzacher** had the following children:
    8771   i.   Brooke[14] **Studdermann**.[1072]
    8772   ii.   Courtney **Studdermann**.[1073]

7424. **Maurice Dean**[13] **Shields** (Vivian Ray[12] **Sneary**, Ella Agnes[11] **Burgess**, Ellen[10] **Whipple**, Manley Nehemiah[9], Abraham[8], Nehemiah[7], Benjamin[6], Francis[5], Jonathan[4], Joseph[3], Matthew[2], Matthew[1])[1074] was born in Arnett, Ellis Co., Okla. 2 October 1925 and married **Elizabeth Miller** in Woodward, Woodward Co., Okla. 24 September 1943. She was born in Gage, Ellis Co., Okla. 6 January 1924.[1075]

Maurice Dean **Shields** and Elizabeth **Miller** had the following children:
    8773   i.   Maurice Dean[14] **Shields** Jr.[1076] born in Shattuck, Ellis Co., Okla. 7 April 1944.
+   8774   ii.   Larry Rollin **Shields** born 2 August 1946.
+   8775   iii. Randy Steven **Shields** born 30 March 1950.

7425. **Jacquiline Genevieve**[13] **Woods** (Veta Grace[12] **Sneary**, Ella Agnes[11] **Burgess**, Ellen[10] **Whipple**, Manley Nehemiah[9], Abraham[8], Nehemiah[7], Benjamin[6], Francis[5], Jonathan[4], Joseph[3], Matthew[2], Matthew[1])[1077] was born in Ellis Co., Okla. 27 July 1928 and married **Loyd Edwin Wanger** in Gage, Ellis Co. 5 April 1947. Loyd,[1078] son of Benjamin Elvin **Wanger** and Edna **DeWeese**, was born in Woods Co., Okla. 8 August 1927.

Jacquiline Genevieve **Woods** and Loyd Edwin **Wanger** had the following children:
+   8776   i.   Sanzee Glee[14] **Wanger** born 15 February 1948.
+   8777   ii.   Ronald Loyd **Wanger** born 10 November 1950.

{ G 1297 }

+   8778   iii.   Marsha Nan **Wanger** born 14 April 1953.
+   8779   iv.   Rodney Ray **Wanger** born 8 January 1956.

7426. **Josephine May**[13] **Woods** (Veta Grace[12] **Sneary**, Ella Agnes[11] **Burgess**, Ellen[10] **Whipple**, Manley Nehemiah[9], Abraham[8], Nehemiah[7], Benjamin[6], Francis[5], Jonathan[4], Joseph[3], Matthew[2], Matthew[1])[1079] was born 12 September 1931 and married twice. (1) **Calvin Wyatt Sperry** in Gage, Ellis Co., Okla. 13 November 1949 or 1950. He died 12 May 1973 in Gage, at 46 years of age. Calvin,[1080] son of Ernest George **Sperry** and Martha LuVena **Burton**, was born in Lipscomb Co., Tex. in May 1926. (2) **Alvin Earnst** in Oklahoma City, Oklahoma Co., Okla. 7 August 1974.

Josephine May **Woods** and Calvin Wyatt **Sperry** had the following children:
+   8780   i.   Sharla Jo[14] **Sperry** born 29 February 1952.
+   8781   ii.   Sidney Kyle **Sperry** born 10 April 1956.
+   8782   iii.   Sabrina Sue **Sperry** born 5 January 1965.
     8783   iv.   Stuart Eldon **Sperry**[1081] born in Shattuck, Ellis Co., Okla. 24 April 1968 and married Stacie (__) in Oklahoma City 12 September 1999.

7427. **Sonya Kay**[13] **Woods** (Veta Grace[12] **Sneary**, Ella Agnes[11] **Burgess**, Ellen[10] **Whipple**, Manley Nehemiah[9], Abraham[8], Nehemiah[7], Benjamin[6], Francis[5], Jonathan[4], Joseph[3], Matthew[2], Matthew[1])[1082] was born in Shattuck, Ellis Co., Okla. 24 September 1939 and married **Jerl Eugene Hamilton** in Ellis Co. 16 June 1961. He is the son of John **Hamilton** and Bertha (__).

Sonya Kay **Woods** and Jerl Eugene **Hamilton** had the following children:
     8784   i.   Brent Lee[14] **Hamilton**[1083] born in Liberal, Seward Co., Kansas 8 July 1965 and married twice. (1) Jill (__). (2) Reagan (__).
     8785   ii.   Darcy Ann **Hamilton**[1084] born in Kansas 28 August 1967 and married twice. (1) Gilbert **Gonzales** in Colorado 20 July 1991. (2) Jeff **Smith**.

7428. **Wynola Carol**[13] **Woods** (Veta Grace[12] **Sneary**, Ella Agnes[11] **Burgess**, Ellen[10] **Whipple**, Manley Nehemiah[9], Abraham[8], Nehemiah[7], Benjamin[6], Francis[5], Jonathan[4], Joseph[3], Matthew[2], Matthew[1])[1085] was born in Shattuck, Ellis Co., Okla. 5 April 1941 and died 6 December 1994 in LaCrosse, Rush Co., Kans., at 53 years of age. She married **Jerry Earl Fields** in Gage, Ellis Co. 9 June 1962. Jerry,[1086] son of Harry **Fields** and Pauline (__), was born 7 September 1940.

Wynola Carol **Woods** and Jerry Earl **Fields** had the following children:
   8786   i.   Jeffery Earl[14] **Fields**[1087] born in Shattuck 25 December 1962.
   8787   ii. Michael Lynn **Fields**[1088] born in Liberal, Seward Co, Kans. 1 July 1969.

7429. **Chester Vance**[13] **Woods** (Veta Grace[12] **Sneary**, Ella Agnes[11] **Burgess**, Ellen[10] **Whipple**, Manley Nehemiah[9], Abraham[8], Nehemiah[7], Benjamin[6], Francis[5], Jonathan[4], Joseph[3], Matthew[2], Matthew[1])[1089] was born in Shattuck, Ellis Co., Okla. 3 November 1943 and married **Beverley Kay Fields** in Gage, Ellis Co. 9 August 1963. Beverley,[1090] daughter of Floyd **Fields** and Eula **Coffield**, was born 25 January 1945.

Chester Vance **Woods** and Beverley Kay **Fields** had the following children:
+ 8788   i.   Monte Shane[14] **Woods** born 16 March 1964.
+ 8789   ii.   Anthony Victor **Woods** born 23 July 1965.
+ 8790   iii. Matthew Brady **Woods** born 11 February 1969.
+ 8791   iv.   Corina Michelle **Woods** born 19 March 1974.

7430. **Conyetta Sue**[13] **Woods** (Veta Grace[12] **Sneary**, Ella Agnes[11] **Burgess**, Ellen[10] **Whipple**, Manley Nehemiah[9], Abraham[8], Nehemiah[7], Benjamin[6], Francis[5], Jonathan[4], Joseph[3], Matthew[2], Matthew[1])[1091] was born in Shattuck, Ellis Co., Okla. 4 February 1946 and married **William Lee Pittman** in Gage, Ellis Co. 23 January 1965. William,[1092] son of Arthur Ray **Pittman** and Mary Alice **Wisner**, was born in Mooreland, Woodward Co., Okla. 13 June 1946. Sue and Bill raise cattle on a 320 acre farm about 20 miles west of Muskogee, Muskogee Co., Okla. Bill also drives a school bus for the Haskell School System and Sue is a Secretary for a Farm Lending Institution in Broken Arrow (an eastern suburb of Tulsa). They both grew up on farms north and northwest of Gage (near the panhandle). Sue's parents, Chester and Grace, 93, still live on the family farm. (2001).

Conyetta Sue **Woods** and William Lee **Pittman** had the following children:
+ 8792   i.   Pamela Sue[14] **Pittman** born 14 August 1965.
+ 8793   ii.   Justin Arthur **Pittman** born 8 February 1972.
   8794   iii. Jill Brianna **Pittman**[1093] born in Buffalo, Harper Co., Okla. 7 September 1979. She is a junior at the U of Kansas in Lawrence, Douglas Co. (2001).

7431. **James Cercy**[13] **Burgess** (Glenn William[12], William[11], Ellen[10] **Whipple**, Manley Nehemiah[9], Abraham[8], Nehemiah[7], Benjamin[6], Francis[5], Jonathan[4], Joseph[3], Matthew[2], Matthew[1])[1094] was born in Springfield, Sangamon Co., Ill. 18 April 1947 and married **Debbie Triplett** there in December 1967.

James Cercy **Burgess** and Debbie **Triplett** had the following children born in Springfield:
    8795 i.   Tami Lynn[14] **Burgess**[1095] 10 October 1970.
    8796 ii.   James Cercy **Burgess** Jr.[1096] 9 August 1974.

7432. **Chapman Eugene**[13] **Burgess** (Glenn William[12], William[11], Ellen[10] **Whipple**, Manley Nehemiah[9], Abraham[8], Nehemiah[7], Benjamin[6], Francis[5], Jonathan[4], Joseph[3], Matthew[2], Matthew[1])[1097] was born in Springfield, Sangamon Co., Ill. 20 July 1948 and married **Betsy Cagle** in 1970.

Chapman Eugene **Burgess** and Betsy **Cagle** had the following children:
    8797 i.   Peter John[14] **Burgess**[1098] born 4 June 1971.
    8798 ii.   Angelica Venus **Burgess**[1099] born 3 September 1974.

7433. **Robert John**[13] **Burgess** (Harold Wright[12], William[11], Ellen[10] **Whipple**, Manley Nehemiah[9], Abraham[8], Nehemiah[7], Benjamin[6], Francis[5], Jonathan[4], Joseph[3], Matthew[2], Matthew[1])[1100] was born in Dubuque, Dubuque Co., Iowa 8 January 1944 and married **Donna Lee Fuller** in Chicago, Cook Co., Ill. 15 August 1970.

Robert John **Burgess** and Donna Lee **Fuller** had the following children:
    8799 i.   John Matthew[14] **Burgess**[1101] was born in Memphis, Shelby Co., Tenn. 20 October 1971.
    8800 ii.   Bryan **Burgess**[1102] born in Arlington Heights, Cook Co., Ill. 18 February 1973 and married Susan Leigh **Carpenter**.

7434. **William Charles**[13] **Burgess** (Harold Wright[12], William[11], Ellen[10] **Whipple**, Manley Nehemiah[9], Abraham[8], Nehemiah[7], Benjamin[6], Francis[5], Jonathan[4], Joseph[3], Matthew[2], Matthew[1])[1103] was born in Dubuque, Dubuque Co., Iowa 25 July 1947 and married **Karen Geisler** there 16 August 1969.

William Charles **Burgess** and Karen **Geisler** had the following children born in Dubuque:
    8801 i.   Bryan Joseph[14] **Burgess**[1104] 5 June 1977.
    8802 ii.   Amy Lynn **Burgess**[1105] 27 May 1978.
    8803 iii. Abby Marie **Burgess**[1106] 19 June 1980.

7435. **Steven James**[13] **Burgess** (Harold Wright[12], William[11], Ellen[10] **Whipple**, Manley Nehemiah[9], Abraham[8], Nehemiah[7], Benjamin[6], Francis[5], Jonathan[4], Joseph[3], Matthew[2], Matthew[1])[1107] was born in Dubuque, Dubuque Co., Iowa 22 July 1952 and married **Linda Brimeyer** there 25 June 1971.

Steven James **Burgess** and Linda **Brimeyer** had the following children born in Dubuque:

    8804   i.   Michael James[14] **Burgess**[1108] 12 November 1971.

    8805   ii.   Cynthia **Burgess**[1109] 26 February 1975.

7442. Rosemary Cecile[13] **Hale** (Dorothy Emma[12] **Burgess**, William[11], Ellen[10] **Whipple**, Manley Nehemiah[9], Abraham[8], Nehemiah[7], Benjamin[6], Francis[5], Jonathan[4], Joseph[3], Matthew[2], Matthew[1])[1110] was born in Kansas City, Jackson Co., Mo. 18 September 1948 and married **John Edward St. Angelo** there 25 January 1969. He was born in Providence, Providence Co., R.I 26 October 1946.[1111]

Rosemary Cecile **Hale** and John Edward **St. Angelo** had the following children:

    8806   i.   Monica Lynn[14] **St. Angelo**[1112] born in Providence 8 June 1969 and married Mark **Levandoski** in Kansas City in October 1997.

    8807   ii.   Nicholas John **St. Angelo**[1113] born in St. Paul, Ramsey Co., Minn. 3 July 1975.

    8808   iii. Carmelle Marie **St. Angelo**[1114] born in Whitefield, Lincoln Co., Maine 25 May 1978.

    8809   iv. Noelle Elaine **St. Angelo**[1115] born in Kansas City 13 December 1980.

7444. Paul Christopher[13] **Hale** (Dorothy Emma[12] **Burgess**, William[11], Ellen[10] **Whipple**, Manley Nehemiah[9], Abraham[8], Nehemiah[7], Benjamin[6], Francis[5], Jonathan[4], Joseph[3], Matthew[2], Matthew[1])[1116] was born in Kansas City, Jackson Co., Mo. 11 November 1952 and married **Sharon Anne Murphy** there 14 August 1971. She was born in Kansas City, Wyandotte Co., Kans. 20 November 1952.[1117]

Paul Christopher **Hale** and Sharon Anne **Murphy** had the following children:

+   8810   i.   Tiffany Marie[14] **Hale** born 11 October 1972.

    8811   ii.   Colleen Janel **Hale**[1118] born in Kansas City 7 June 1974 and married Martin Clell **Shelby** there. He was born in Osceola, St. Claire Co., Mo. 24 May 1970.[1119]

    8812   iii. Alexis Regina **Hale**[1120] born in Kansas City 28 March 1976.

    8813   iv. Jacob Edward **Hale**[1121] born in Kansas City 21 August 1977.

    8814   v.   Adam Michael **Hale**[1122] born in Kansas City 18 October 1978.

    8815   vi. Paul Conor **Hale**[1123] born in Kansas City 27 May 1981.

    8816   vii. Timothy Padraic **Hale**[1124] born in Kansas City 9 February 1983.

8817 viii. Micah Geordan **Hale**[1125] born in Kansas City 6 May 1985.
8818 ix. Madeline Corinne **Hale**[1126] born in Overland Park, Johnson Co., Kans. 17 December 1989.

7453. **Janice Kay**[13] **Worthington** (Doris Fern[12] **Burgess**, William[11], Ellen[10] **Whipple**, Manley Nehemiah[9], Abraham[8], Nehemiah[7], Benjamin[6], Francis[5], Jonathan[4], Joseph[3], Matthew[2], Matthew[1])[1127] was born in Stillwater, Payne Co., Okla. 22 November 1946 and married **Jimmie Anderson Rowe** in Modesto, Stanislaus Co., Calif. 31 December 1968. Jimmie,[1128] son of Jimmie Dale **Rowe** and Ida Jean **Scott**, was born in Ada, Pontotoc Co., Okla. 5 October 1948. They were divorced in Tulsa, Tulsa Co., Okla, 11 August 1983. He married (2) **Lynn Bartholomew** in Houston, Harris Co., Tex.

Janice Kay **Worthington** and Jimmie Anderson **Rowe** had the following children:
8819 i. Howard Anderson[14] **Rowe**[1129] born in Hoffman Estates, Cook Co., Ill. 22 October 1971.
8820 ii. Cody Chapman **Rowe**[1130] born in St. Charles, Kane Co., Ill. 18 October 1972.
8821 iii. Michael Lee Judson **Rowe**[1131] born 15 October 1981.

7455. **Julie Ann**[13] **Worthington** (Doris Fern[12] **Burgess**, William[11], Ellen[10] **Whipple**, Manley Nehemiah[9], Abraham[8], Nehemiah[7], Benjamin[6], Francis[5], Jonathan[4], Joseph[3], Matthew[2], Matthew[1])[1132] was born in Oklahoma City, Oklahoma Co., Okla. 25 May 1961 and married **John Gregory Westerman** in Troy, Lincoln Co., Mo. John, son of John **Westerman** and Dorothy **Zumwalt**, was born in Troy 5 August 1959.

Julie Ann **Worthington** and John Gregory **Westerman** had the following child born in Troy:
8822 i. John Howard[14] **Westerman**[1133] 5 November 1990.

7458. **Gary William**[13] **Burgess** (John Francis[12], William[11], Ellen[10] **Whipple**, Manley Nehemiah[9], Abraham[8], Nehemiah[7], Benjamin[6], Francis[5], Jonathan[4], Joseph[3], Matthew[2], Matthew[1])[1134] was born in Kansas City, Jackson Co., Mo. 21 January 1957 and married **Kara (__)** there.

Gary William **Burgess** and Kara (__) had the following children born in Kansas City:
8823 i. Kellen Kristine[14] **Burgess**[1135] 3 December 1987.
8824 ii. Cassie Marie **Burgess**[1136] 2 February 1989.

{ G 1302 }

7459. **Lauren Jean**[13] **Burgess** (John Francis[12], William[11], Ellen[10] **Whipple**, Manley Nehemiah[9], Abraham[8], Nehemiah[7], Benjamin[6], Francis[5], Jonathan[4], Joseph[3], Matthew[2], Matthew[1])[1137] was born in Kansas City, Jackson Co., Mo. 20 September 1959 and married **Mark Huff** in Columbia, Boone Co., Mo. in May 1991.

Lauren Jean **Burgess** and Mark **Huff** had the following children born in Ft. Myers, Lee Co., Fla.:
    8825   i.   Devin Christian[14] **Huff**[1138] 13 February 1993.
    8826   ii. Travis Forrest **Huff**.[1139]

7460. **Arthur Eastman**[13] **Schowalter** (Lavine[12] **Van Dyke**, Carrie Emily[11] **Whipple**, Alphonso[10], Horatio[9], Nathan[8], Nehemiah[7], Benjamin[6], Francis[5], Jonathan[4], Joseph[3], Matthew[2], Matthew[1])[1140] was born in Cleveland, Cuyahoga Co., Ohio 30 July 1910 and died 3 September 1981 in Elyria, Lorain Co., Ohio, at 71 years of age. He married **Alice Boter** in Holland, Ottawa Co., Mich. 20 June 1936. She was born there 19 April 1911.[1141]

Arthur Eastman **Schowalter** and Alice **Boter** had the following children:
    8827   i.   Sally[14] **Schowalter**[1142] born in Elyria 14 May 1940 and became Sara **Walters**. No explanation provided.
+ 8828   ii. Susan **Schowalter** born 14 May 1940.

7461. **Lawrence V.**[13] **Schowalter** (Lavine[12] **Van Dyke**, Carrie Emily[11] **Whipple**, Alphonso[10], Horatio[9], Nathan[8], Nehemiah[7], Benjamin[6], Francis[5], Jonathan[4], Joseph[3], Matthew[2], Matthew[1])[1143] was born in Cleveland, Cuyahoga Co., Ohio 13 September 1914 and died 4 August 1957 in St. Louis, Independence Co., Mo., at 42 years of age. He married **Roberta Temple** in Cleveland in 1939. She was born in Cleveland in May 1905 and died 25 July 1980, at 75 years of age.[1144] She married (2) **Lee Girardier** in 1963.

Lawrence V. **Schowalter** and Roberta **Temple** had the following children:
+ 8829   i.   Gale[14] **Schowalter** born 17 July 1942.
+ 8830   ii. Timothy Temple **Schowalter** born 1 November 1944.
+ 8831   iii. Eileen **Schowalter** born 23 June 1948.

7462. **Carroll Emmett**[13] **Van Dyke** (Carroll Marcus[12], Carrie Emily[11] **Whipple**, Alphonso[10], Horatio[9], Nathan[8], Nehemiah[7], Benjamin[6], Francis[5], Jonathan[4], Joseph[3], Matthew[2], Matthew[1])[1145] was born in Geneva, Ashtabula Co., Ohio 21 March 1922 and married four times. (1) **Letitia Spadea** in Ft. Lauderdale, Broward Co., Fla. in 1943. She was born in 1911. (2) **Maida Hitchcock** in 1960. (3) **Joanne Carter** in 1971. (4) **Joan Baker Smith** in 1980.

{ G 1303 }

Carroll Emmett **Van Dyke** and Letitia **Spadea** had the following children:

  8832 i. Carol[14] **Van Dyke**[1146] born in Ft. Lauderdale 31 May 1944.

  8833 ii. Linda **Van Dyke**[1147] born in Gainesville, Alachua Co., Fla. 31 March 1947.

  8834 iii. Gregory **Van Dyke**[1148] born in Gainesville 4 June 1949 on the day his father was graduated from the U. of Florida at Gainsville.

7463. **Lauretta**[13] **Van Dyke** (Carroll Marcus[12], Carrie Emily[11] **Whipple**, Alphonso[10], Horatio[9], Nathan[8], Nehemiah[7], Benjamin[6], Francis[5], Jonathan[4], Joseph[3], Matthew[2], Matthew[1])[1149] was born in Painesville, Lake Co., Ohio 31 July 1924 and married **Leland Robert Gerwin** in Madison, Lake Co., Ohio 15 September 1944. Leland,[1150] son of Herman Henry **Gerwin** and Pauline **Beeker**, was born in Gibsonburg, Sandusky Co., Ohio 30 July 1923.

Lauretta **Van Dyke** and Leland Robert **Gerwin** had the following children:

 + 8835 i. Christopher Lee[14] **Gerwin** born 25 December 1949.

 + 8836 ii. Steven Mark **Gerwin** born 25 November 1951.

 + 8837 iii. Robert Lee **Gerwin** born 11 September 1953.

  8838 iv. Paul David **Gerwin**[1151] born in Lakewood, Cuyahoga Co., Ohio 7 September 1955 and died 30 May 1995, at 39 years of age.

 + 8839 v. Charles Mathews **Gerwin** born 1 February 1958.

  8840 vi. Donald James **Gerwin**[1152] born in Royal Oak, Oakland Co., Mich. 10 November 1960 and married Karen **Leeper** in Southfield, Oakland Co., Mich. 25 June 1987. Karen,[1153] daughter of Richard **Leeper** and Theresa (__), was born in St. Clair Shores, St. Clair Co., Mich 26 December 1961. They were divorced in 1997.

  8841 vii. Timothy Lawrence **Gerwin**[1154] born in Royal Oak 10 April 1963.

  8842 viii. Jeffrey Lynn **Gerwin**[1155] born in Royal Oak 26 September 1966 and married Cinda **Rogers** in Seattle, King Co., Wash. 17 December 1990. She was born in Warsaw, Kosciusko Co., Ind. 23 January 1964.[1156]

7465. **Clifford Fuller**[13] **Van Dyke** (Carroll Marcus[12], Carrie Emily[11] **Whipple**, Alphonso[10], Horatio[9], Nathan[8], Nehemiah[7], Benjamin[6], Francis[5], Jonathan[4], Joseph[3], Matthew[2], Matthew[1])[1157] was born in Madison, Lake Co., Ohio 17 February 1934 and married **Joanne Veley** in Ashley,

Delaware Co., Ohio 23 December 1956. Joanne,[1158] daughter of James Walter **Veley** and Mary Helena **Sheets**, was born in Delaware 29 October 1934.

Clifford Fuller **Van Dyke** and Joanne **Veley** had the following children:
- 8843 i. Regina[14] **Van Dyke**[1159] born in Newark, Licking Co., Ohio 16 May 1959 and married David **Krueger** in Baltimore, Fairfield Co., Ohio.
- + 8844 ii. Laura **Van Dyke** born 16 May 1959.
- + 8845 iii. Brad Thomas **Van Dyke** born 8 February 1966.

7466. **Beatrice**[13] **Leipner** (Ethel[12] **Van Dyke**, Carrie Emily[11] **Whipple**, Alphonso[10], Horatio[9], Nathan[8], Nehemiah[7], Benjamin[6], Francis[5], Jonathan[4], Joseph[3], Matthew[2], Matthew[1])[1160] was born in Cleveland, Cuyahoga Co., Ohio 4 February 1914 and married **Leonard Turner** there 22 October 1936. He was born in Cleveland in 1910 and died in February 1993 in Greenville, Greenville Co., S.C., at 82 years of age.[1161]

Beatrice **Leipner** and Leonard **Turner** had the following child:
- + 8846 i. Allen[14] **Turner** born 20 December 1942.

7467. **Eleanor Catherine**[13] **Greeley** (Stella Emma[12] **Whipple**, Ira Orren[11], Alphonso[10], Horatio[9], Nathan[8], Nehemiah[7], Benjamin[6], Francis[5], Jonathan[4], Joseph[3], Matthew[2], Matthew[1])[1162] was born in Erie, Erie Co., Penn. 17 April 1924 and married **Wilbur LeRoy Treddenbarger** in Smith Center, Smith Co., Kans. 22 April 1946. He was born in Franklin, Franklin Co., Nebr. 19 August 1925. Wilbur was a U. S. Marine during WWII in the Pacific Theatre (Nov. 43-March 46) and was recalled to active duty during the Korean Conflict and was stationed at Camp LeJeune, N.C. and Ft. Monmouth, N.J. (July 1951-Nov. 1951). He was employed by Ohio Bell Telephone Co. in Painsville, Lake Co., Ohio (Oct. 1947-March 1956) and joined Pacific Bell Telephone Co. in Sacramento, Sacramento Co., Calif. in March 1956. He retired 1 April 1983.

Eleanor served in the U. S. Marine Corps Women's Reserve from 17 April 1944 to 3 April 1946 as an Aviation Machinist Mate at the El Toro Air Force Base, Santa Ana, Orange Co., Calif. She was a mechanic working on the F-4-U Corsair. Both before and after the war she was in banking working at the Cleveland Trust Bank in Cleveland, Cuyahoga Co. and Painesville, and the Ashbury Park Nat'l Bank and Trust Co., Ashbury Park, Monmouth Co., N.J. After her children were grown, she worked part time, first at Wells Fargo Bank in Carmichael, Sacramento Co., Calif. (1967-70) and then for *Carmichael Honda* (1970-79), retiring in 1979.

Eleanor Catherine **Greeley** and Wilbur LeRoy **Treddenbarger** had the following children:
- 8847 i. Debra Dianne[14] **Treddenbarger**[1163] born in Sacramento 14 May 1955 and married Thomas **DiMuccio** there 28 February 1975. Thomas,[1164] son of Nicholas **DiMuccio** and Peggy **Bryan,** was born in July 1954. Debra began work with the Chevron Corporation in February 1984. Her job requires her to travel world-wide.
- \+ 8848 ii. Rick Lee **Treddenbarger** born 29 September 1956.
- \+ 8849 iii. Sandra Kay **Treddenbarger** born 4 November 1960.

7468. Calvin Richard[13] **Greeley** (Stella Emma[12] **Whipple,** Ira Orren[11], Alphonso[10], Horatio[9], Nathan[8], Nehemiah[7], Benjamin[6], Francis[5], Jonathan[4], Joseph[3], Matthew[2], Matthew[1])[1165] was born in Erie, Erie Co., Penn. 13 March 1925 and married twice. (1) **Maria Christina Salminen** in Painesville, Lake Co., Ohio in July 1952. She was born in Painesville 1 June 1927.[1166] (2) **Kathryn Phelps** in Reno, Washoe Co., Nev. 31 March 1981. She was born 12 January 1933.[1167] Kathryn has children by a previous marriage. Maria married (2) **Raymond Cromwell**.

Calvin Richard **Greeley** and Maria Christina **Salminen** had the following child born in Painesville:
- 8850 i. Robert Michael[14] **Greeley**[1168] 28 April 1954 and married Patricia (__).

7470. Margaret May[13] **Whipple** (Carl Wright[12], Ira Orren[11], Alphonso[10], Horatio[9], Nathan[8], Nehemiah[7], Benjamin[6], Francis[5], Jonathan[4], Joseph[3], Matthew[2], Matthew[1])[1169] was born in Madison, Lake Co., Ohio 8 March 1925 and married **Elvis Leininger** in August 1946. He died in December 1993 in Ashtabula Co., Ohio.[1170]

Margaret May **Whipple** and Elvis **Leininger** had the following children:
- 8851 i. Linda[14] **Leininger**[1171] married Dick **Stewart**.
- 8852 ii. Kay **Leininger**[1172] married James **Williams**.
- 8853 iii. Jerry **Leininger**.[1173]
- 8854 iv. Doris **Leininger**.[1174]
- 8855 v. Timothy **Leininger**.[1175]

7471. Carl James[13] **Whipple** (Carl Wright[12], Ira Orren[11], Alphonso[10], Horatio[9], Nathan[8], Nehemiah[7], Benjamin[6], Francis[5], Jonathan[4], Joseph[3], Matthew[2], Matthew[1])[1176] was born in Madison, Lake Co., Ohio 15 April 1927 and married **Donna Maxine Cooper Ely** in Fort Wayne, Allen Co.,

Ind. 31 December 1953. She was born in Athens, Athens Co., Ohio 2 December 1926.

Carl James **Whipple** and Donna Maxine Cooper **Ely** had the following children:
- 8856 i. Michael Keith[14] **Whipple**[1177] born in Culver City, Los Angeles Co., Calif. 10 April 1949.
- 8857 ii. Bruce Walter **Whipple**[1178] born in Culver City 25 January 1951.
- 8858 iii. Laura Ann **Whipple**[1179] born in Geneva, Ashtabula Co., Ohio 22 November 1955.
- 8859 iv. Jeffrey James **Whipple**[1180] born in Painesville, Lake Co., Ohio 6 March 1960.

7472. **Harold Vernon**[13] **Whipple** (Carl Wright[12], Ira Orren[11], Alphonso[10], Horatio[9], Nathan[8], Nehemiah[7], Benjamin[6], Francis[5], Jonathan[4], Joseph[3], Matthew[2], Matthew[1])[1181] was born in Madison, Lake Co., Ohio 30 May 1928 and died in February 1989 in Painesville, Lake Co., Ohio, at 60 years of age. He married **Adeline Olmstead**.

Harold Vernon **Whipple** and Adeline **Olmstead** had the following children:
- 8860 i. Patricia[14] **Whipple**.[1182]
- 8861 ii. William **Whipple**.[1183]
- 8862 iii. Jonathan **Whipple**.[1184]

7473. **Phyllis Jean**[13] **Whipple** (Carl Wright[12], Ira Orren[11], Alphonso[10], Horatio[9], Nathan[8], Nehemiah[7], Benjamin[6], Francis[5], Jonathan[4], Joseph[3], Matthew[2], Matthew[1])[1185] was born in Painesville, Lake Co., Ohio 28 August 1930 and married **Harry Wilson Nash**.

Phyllis Jean **Whipple** and Harry Wilson **Nash** had the following children:
- 8863 i. David[14] **Nash**.[1186]
- 8864 ii. Dayl **Nash**.[1187]
- 8865 iii. Dennis **Nash**.[1188]
- 8866 iv. Douglas **Nash**.[1189]
- 8867 v. Darlene **Nash**.[1190]
- 8868 vi. Dudley **Nash**.[1191]

7474. **Norman Lee**[13] **Whipple** (Carl Wright[12], Ira Orren[11], Alphonso[10], Horatio[9], Nathan[8], Nehemiah[7], Benjamin[6], Francis[5], Jonathan[4], Joseph[3], Matthew[2], Matthew[1])[1192] was born in Painesville, Lake Co., Ohio 4 June 1932 and married **Ruth Ann Bender** in Madison, Lake Co., Ohio 1 January 1954.

Norman Lee **Whipple** and Ruth Ann **Bender** had the following children:

    8869   i.   Gloria Jean[14] **Whipple**.[1193]
    8870   ii.   Mark **Whipple**.[1194]
    8871   iii. Gail **Whipple**.[1195]

7505. **Patricia Ann**[13] **Claxon** (Veda Louise[12] **Greeley**, Roxey Alamanda[11] **Whipple**, Alphonso[10], Horatio[9], Nathan[8], Nehemiah[7], Benjamin[6], Francis[5], Jonathan[4], Joseph[3], Matthew[2], Matthew[1])[1196] was born 2 August 1938 and married twice. (1) **Thomas Murray Barge** in Austin, Travis Co., Tex. 10 December 1960. Thomas,[1197] son of Fred Anderson **Barge** and Ruth **Saxon**, was born in Austin 3 March 1938 and died 19 December 1990 in Austin, at 52 years of age. He took his own life. They were divorced 7 February 1978. (2) **Harold "Duke" Edward Rumpf**. Duke,[1198] son of Charles Clifford **Rumpf** and Anna Mae **Bartley**, was born in St. Mary's, Auglaize Co., Ohio 24 December 1922. Pat and Duke own and manage a "Mom and Pop" motel and restaurant in Johnson City, Blanco Co., Texas. Both were Real Estate Agents and met at a real estate seminar.

Patricia Ann **Claxon** and Thomas Murray **Barge** had the following children born in Austin:

    8872   i.   Mark Evan[14] **Barge**[1199] 29 July 1961 and married Tammy (__) in Kingsland, Kleberg Co., Tex. 23 November 1995. Mark was living in Kingsland in 1998 with a partner and her two children.
    8873   ii.   Lorie **Barge**[1200] 2 February 1964 and married Jeff **Brown** in Shelton, Mason Co., Wash. 9 November 1997. Lorie's birth name was Marjorie Lorraine Barge but she had it legally changed to Lorie Barge in 1980.

7508. **Kenneth Russell**[13] **Whipple** (Wallace Eugene[12], Nathan Wilson[11], Alphonso[10], Horatio[9], Nathan[8], Nehemiah[7], Benjamin[6], Francis[5], Jonathan[4], Joseph[3], Matthew[2], Matthew[1])[1201] was born 20 October 1938 and married **Donna Hughes** in California 24 March 1963. She was born 5 March 1943.[1202]

Kenneth Russell **Whipple** and Donna **Hughes** had the following child:
+   8874   i.   Ericka[14] **Whipple**.

7509. **Ronald Elwood**[13] **Whipple** (Russell Elwood[12], Nathan Wilson[11], Alphonso[10], Horatio[9], Nathan[8], Nehemiah[7], Benjamin[6], Francis[5], Jonathan[4], Joseph[3], Matthew[2], Matthew[1])[1203] was born in Chelsea, Suffolk

Co., Mass. 26 October 1949 and married **Muriel Enos** in Mt. Tamalpias Valley, Marin Co., Calif. 30 June 1973. She was born in Oakland, Alameda Co., Calif. 1 June 1953.[1204] Ronald and Muriel became members of the Hindu faith and are known as Kanda Alahan and Kamala Alahan.

Ronald Elwood **Whipple** and Muriel **Enos** had the following children:
  8875 i. Justin[14] **Whipple**[1205] born in Kealakekua, Hawaii Co., Hawaii 13 May 1974.
  8876 ii. Jeremy **Whipple**[1206] born in Fallbrook, San Diego Co., Calif. 1 February 1978.
  8877 iii. Kandiah Alahan **Whipple**[1207] born 27 June 1988.

7510. **Mark Wilson**[13] **Whipple** (Russell Elwood[12], Nathan Wilson[11], Alphonso[10], Horatio[9], Nathan[8], Nehemiah[7], Benjamin[6], Francis[5], Jonathan[4], Joseph[3], Matthew[2], Matthew[1])[1208] was born in Chelsea, Suffolk Co., Mass. 26 September 1952 and married **Lauren Dumble** in Fallbrook, San Diego Co., Calif. 14 January 1978. Lauren,[1209] daughter of Kenneth **Wade** and Barbara (Schwarzenberg) **Dumble**, was born in Hemet, Riverside Co., Calif. 6 January 1956. Mark and Lauren became members of the Hindu faith and he is known as Adi Alahan and she is known as Asha Alahan.

Mark Wilson **Whipple** and Lauren **Dumble** had the following children:
  8878 i. Vasuki Alahan[14] **Whipple**[1210] born in LaJolla, San Diego Co., Calif. 23 August 1979.
  8879 ii. Seyon Alahan **Whipple**[1211] born in Fallbrook 26 August 1982.
  8880 iii. Darshan Alahan **Whipple**[1212] born in Fallbrook 5 July 1988.

7511. **Kristen D.**[13] **Whipple** (Kenneth Elman[12], Nathan Wilson[11], Alphonso[10], Horatio[9], Nathan[8], Nehemiah[7], Benjamin[6], Francis[5], Jonathan[4], Joseph[3], Matthew[2], Matthew[1])[1213] was born in California 9 October 1942 and married **A. P. Giannini** in 1967. He was born in Bankok, Thailand in 1946.[1214]

Kristen D. **Whipple** and A. P. **Giannini** had the following children:
  8881 i. Aaron[14] **Giannini**[1215] born in San Rafael, Marin Co., Calif. in December 1970.
  8882 ii. Alisa **Giannini**[1216] born in Novato, Marin Co., Calif. In October 1972.

7512. **Diana L.**[13] **Whipple** (Kenneth Elman[12], Nathan Wilson[11], Alphonso[10], Horatio[9], Nathan[8], Nehemiah[7], Benjamin[6], Francis[5], Jonathan[4], Joseph[3], Matthew[2], Matthew[1])[1217] was born in Madison, Lake Co., Ohio 10 December 1946 and married **Arthur Shahan** there in 1964.

Diana L. **Whipple** and Arthur **Shahan** had the following children born in Madison:
- 8883   i.   Kenneth A.[14] **Shahan**[1218] 17 December 1964 and died there in July 1982, at 17 years of age.
- 8884   ii.   Daniel W. **Shahan**[1219] 23 October 1966.

7514. **Glen Kimball**[13] **Whipple** (Sheldon Ray[12], Nathan Wilson[11], Alphonso[10], Horatio[9], Nathan[8], Nehemiah[7], Benjamin[6], Francis[5], Jonathan[4], Joseph[3], Matthew[2], Matthew[1])[1220] was born in Painesville, Lake Co., Ohio 20 March 1952 and married **Carmen Dador Orio Sitay** in San Diego, San Diego Co., Calif. 5 December 1981. She was born in Basayan, Samar Island, Phillipines 30 June 1943.[1221]

Glen Kimball **Whipple** and Carmen Dador Orio **Sitay** had the following child:
- 8885   i.   Ryan Orio[14] **Whipple**[1222] born in National City, San Diego Co., Calif. 15 June 1988.

7515. **Beth Eileen**[13] **Whipple** (Sheldon Ray[12], Nathan Wilson[11], Alphonso[10], Horatio[9], Nathan[8], Nehemiah[7], Benjamin[6], Francis[5], Jonathan[4], Joseph[3], Matthew[2], Matthew[1])[1223] was born in Painesville, Lake Co., Ohio 28 June 1955 and married **Stanley Szczesniak** in Las Vegas, Clark Co., Nev. 2 December 1978. He was born in Cleveland, Cuyahoga Co., Ohio 12 November 1945.[1224]

Beth Eileen **Whipple** and Stanley **Szczesniak** had the following children:
- 8886   i.   Leah Marie[14] **Szczesniak**[1225] born in Cleveland 29 July 1980.
- 8887   ii.   Michelle Renee **Szczesniak**[1226] born in Cleveland 8 June 1982.
- 8888   iii.   Mary Angela **Szczesniak**[1227] born in Mayfield Heights, Cuyahoga Co., Ohio 21 January 1987.

7516. **Jon Wilson**[13] **Whipple** (Sheldon Ray[12], Nathan Wilson[11], Alphonso[10], Horatio[9], Nathan[8], Nehemiah[7], Benjamin[6], Francis[5], Jonathan[4], Joseph[3], Matthew[2], Matthew[1])[1228] was born in Painesville, Lake Co., Ohio 2 August 1956 and married **Linda Sue Miller** in Madison, Lake Co., Ohio 7 July 1979. She was born in Painesville 10 September 1955.

Jon Wilson **Whipple** and Linda Sue **Miller** had the following children born in Painesville:
    8889   i.   Jonathan Edward[14] **Whipple**[1229] 12 October 1981.
    8890   ii.   Christopher Michael **Whipple**[1230] 4 May 1984.
    8891   iii.   Nathaniel Wilson **Whipple** II[1231] 25 July 1985.

7519. **Cheryl Jean**[13] **Whipple** (Roy Curwood[12], Nathan Wilson[11], Alphonso[10], Horatio[9], Nathan[8], Nehemiah[7], Benjamin[6], Francis[5], Jonathan[4], Joseph[3], Matthew[2], Matthew[1])[1232] was born in Painesville, Lake Co., Ohio 21 February 1951 and married **Rodney James Fisher** in Madison, Lake Co., Ohio 12 September 1970. He was born in Wheeling, Ohio Co., W. Va. 14 April 1951.[1233]

Cheryl Jean **Whipple** and Rodney James **Fisher** had the following children born in Geneva, Ashtabula Co., Ohio:
    8892   i.   Laura LeAnn[14] **Fisher**[1234] 31 October 1974.
    8893   ii.   Ryan Jacob **Fisher**[1235] 28 February 1976.

7520. **Debra Jean**[13] **Whipple** (Roy Curwood[12], Nathan Wilson[11], Alphonso[10], Horatio[9], Nathan[8], Nehemiah[7], Benjamin[6], Francis[5], Jonathan[4], Joseph[3], Matthew[2], Matthew[1])[1236] was born in Painesville, Lake Co., Ohio 23 February 1954 and married **David Eugene Williamson** in Rock Falls, Whiteside Co., Ill. 16 December 1977. He was born in Sterling, Whiteside Co., Ill. 15 May 1948.[1237]

Debra Jean **Whipple** and David Eugene **Williamson** had the following children born in St. Petersburg, Pinella Co., Fla.:
    8894   i.   Kristopher Edward[14] **Williamson**[1238] 22 June 1978.
    8895   ii.   Kelli Dyan **Williamson**[1239] 29 January 1980.

7521. **David Roy**[13] **Whipple** (Roy Curwood[12], Nathan Wilson[11], Alphonso[10], Horatio[9], Nathan[8], Nehemiah[7], Benjamin[6], Francis[5], Jonathan[4], Joseph[3], Matthew[2], Matthew[1])[1240] was born in Painesville, Lake Co., Ohio 20 July 1961 and married twice. (1) **Barbara A. Wilberding** in Denver, Denver Co., Colo. 23 March 1983. She was born in Iowa 23 November 1960 and died 27 July 1990 in San Antonio, Bexar Co., Tex., at 29 years of age.[1241] (2) **Lisa Lauterstein Simon** 14 December 1991.

David Roy **Whipple** and Lisa Lauterstein **Simon** had the following child born in Riverside, Riverside Co., Calif:
    8896   i.   Joshua David[14] **Whipple**[1242] 10 March 1995.

7522. **Marla**[13] **Whipple** (R. Douglas[12], Royal Howard[11], Alphonso[10], Horatio[9], Nathan[8], Nehemiah[7], Benjamin[6], Francis[5], Jonathan[4], Joseph[3], Matthew[2], Matthew[1])[1243] birth date unknown, married **Dale Lambert**.

Marla **Whipple** and Dale **Lambert** had the following child:
    8897   i.   Heather[14] **Lambert**.[1244]

7523. **Dr. Robert**[13] **Whipple** (R. Douglas[12], Royal Howard[11], Alphonso[10], Horatio[9], Nathan[8], Nehemiah[7], Benjamin[6], Francis[5], Jonathan[4], Joseph[3], Matthew[2], Matthew[1])[1245] was born 3 May 1945.

Dr. Robert **Whipple** had the following children:
    8898   i.   Russell[14] **Whipple**[1246] born 18 August 1967.
    8899   ii.   Jeffrey **Whipple**[1247] born in November 1980.
    8900   iii. Christopher **Whipple**[1248] born 8 June 1983.

7524. **John**[13] **Whipple** (R. Douglas[12], Royal Howard[11], Alphonso[10], Horatio[9], Nathan[8], Nehemiah[7], Benjamin[6], Francis[5], Jonathan[4], Joseph[3], Matthew[2], Matthew[1])[1249] was born 8 August 1949.

John **Whipple** had the following children:
    8901   i.   Amy[14] **Whipple**.[1250]
    8902   ii.   Jessica **Whipple**.[1251]

7525. **Evelyn Isabell**[13] **Linder** (Lillian Isabelle[12] **Beddoes**, Jessie[11] **Brown**, Henry Whipple[10], Miranda[9] **Whipple**, Nathan[8], Nehemiah[7], Benjamin[6], Francis[5], Jonathan[4], Joseph[3], Matthew[2], Matthew[1])[1252] was born in Rockford, Winnebago Co., Ill. 27 May 1914 and died 10 October 1963 in Minneapolis, Hennepin Co., Minn., at 49 years of age. Buried in Union Cemetery, Mound, Hennepin Co., Minn. She married twice. (1) **Chester Arron Larson** in Rockford 26 March 1932. Chester,[1253] son of Aaron John **Larson** and Blanche E. **England**, was born in Havanna, Mason Co., Ill. 9 December 1909 and died 26 April 1978 in Spring Grove, Fillmore Co., Minn., at 68 years of age. Buried in Choice Cemetery, Preble Township, Mabel, Fillmore Co., Minn. They were divorced 11 May 1943. (2) **Martin Elof Shellstrom** in Rockford 5 June 1943. He is the son of John **Shellstrom** and Ellen **Seastone**. Chester married (2) **Frances Henderson**. (3) **Frieda Loffee** in Manitou Beach, Presque Isle Co., Mich. in 1952.

Evelyn Isabell **Linder** and Chester Arron **Larson** had the following children born in Rockford:

    8903   i.   John T.[14] **Larson**[1254] 19 April 1933 and married Mary Ann **Baas** in 1953.

    8904   ii.   Lillian I. **Larson**[1255] 3 November 1934 and married Lyle **Nestby**.

    8905   iii.   Chester A. **Larson**[1256] 9 July 1936 and married Dianne (__).

    8906   iv.   David A. **Larson**[1257] 30 July 1937 and married twice. (1) Linda **Clancy**. (2) Rebecca (__).

    8907   v.   Jeanette A. **Larson**[1258] 27 August 1939 and married Paul **Sayre**.

    8908   vi.   Gwendolyn A. **Larson**[1259] 10 October 1940 and married twice. (1) Victor **Zeman** in Stillwater, Washington Co., Minn. 9 September 1959. They were divorced in Hudson, St. Croix Co., Wisc. 21 September 1963. (2) Richard William **Sackrison** 24 October 1964. Richard,[1260] son of Richard **Sackrison** and Katherine **Phinney,** was born in Minneapolis 27 August 1937.

Evelyn Isabell **Linder** and Martin Elof **Shellstrom** had the following children:

    8909   vii.   Richard **Shellstrom**[1261] born in Sauk Rapids, Benton Co., Minn. 4 June 1944.

    8910   viii.   Kathleen **Shellstrom**[1262] born in Sauk Rapids 14 August 1945.

    8911   ix.   Judith **Shellstrom**[1263] born in Minneapolis 27 August 1948.

7526. **Carol Moore**[13] **Watkins** (Frederick[12], Henry A.[11], Henry[10], Moses[9], Lois[8] **Mills**, Hepzibah[7] **Whipple**, Benjamin[6], Francis[5], Jonathan[4], Joseph[3], Matthew[2], Matthew[1])[1264] was born in Brooklyn, N.Y. 16 October 1934[1265] and married **Harold Leslie Stead** in Ann Arbor, Washtenaw Co., Mich. 28 January 1961.[1266] Hal,[1267] son of Harold Leroy **Stead** and Isabel **Piper**, was born in Stubenville, Jefferson Co., Ohio 1 June 1930.[1268] He is a salesman and Professional Photographer. Carol was graduated from Cornell University, Ithaca, Warren Co., N.Y. in June 1956 where she was a member of the Alpha Xi Delta Sorority. She is a Histology Technician in a Hospital Pathology Lab. Her job is to slice tissue removed in surgery to make slides for the doctors to review.

Carol Moore **Watkins** and Harold Leslie **Stead** had the following children:

   +   8912   i.   Leslie Ann[14] **Stead** born 27 June 1963.

       8913   ii.   Sharon Lynn **Stead**[1269] born in Grosse Pointe Farms, Wayne Co., Mich. 17 December 1970.

7527. **William Moore**[13] **Watkins** (Frederick[12], Henry A.[11], Henry[10], Moses[9], Lois[8] **Mills**, Hepzibah[7] **Whipple**, Benjamin[6], Francis[5], Jonathan[4], Joseph[3], Matthew[2], Matthew[1])[1270] was born in Brooklyn, N.Y. 28 June 1938 and married **Virginia Mary Jaye** 11 December 1971. Virginia, daughter of Edward John **Jaye** and Ethel Erma **Schaufler**, was born in Long Branch, Monmouth Co., N.J. 19 July 1947. William is a Computer Consultant.

William Moore **Watkins** and Virginia Mary **Jaye** had the following children:
+ 8914 i. Allison Jaye[14] **Watkins** born 5 January 1973.
  8915 ii. Matthew Moore **Watkins**[1271] born in Summit, Union Co., N.J. 9 April 1976.

7528. **Jane Elizabeth**[13] **Chandler** (Florence B.[12] **Johnson**, Mary Lillian[11] **Whipple**, Ithamar Cyrus[10], Cyrus Avery[9], Ithamar[8], Rev. Benjamin[7], Benjamin[6], Francis[5], Jonathan[4], Joseph[3], Matthew[2], Matthew[1])[1272] was born in Kansas City, Jackson Co., Mo. 25 August 1919 and married **Marvin Bennett Cable** there 16 September 1945. Marvin,[1273] son of Charles Bennett **Cable** and Rosa Fern **Sleeth**, was born in Grenola, Elk Co., Kans. 30 January 1916. He was a Pilot of Troop Carriers (435th Troop Carrier Squadron) during WWII. Following the war he became an automobile dealer.

Jane Elizabeth **Chandler** and Marvin Bennett **Cable** had the following children:
  8916 i. Carl Bennett[14] **Cable**[1274] born 14 October 1946 and died the day of birth.
+ 8917 ii. Judith Ann **Cable** born 28 December 1947.
+ 8918 iii. Gail Elizabeth **Cable** born 15 April 1949.
+ 8919 iv. Janet Lynn **Cable** born 22 March 1952.
+ 8920 v. Karen Louise **Cable** born 6 August 1954.
  8921 vi. Dale Chandler **Cable**[1275] born in Arkansas City, Cowley Co., Kans. 13 October 1956.

7530. **George Myron**[13] **Chandler** (Florence B.[12] **Johnson**, Mary Lillian[11] **Whipple**, Ithamar Cyrus[10], Cyrus Avery[9], Ithamar[8], Rev. Benjamin[7], Benjamin[6], Francis[5], Jonathan[4], Joseph[3], Matthew[2], Matthew[1])[1276] was born in Kansas City, Jackson Co., Mo. 23 February 1928 and married **Marjorie Eleanor Sample** in New Castle, Garfield Co., Colo. 27 July 1952. Marjorie,[1277] daughter of Samuel John **Sample** and Elsie Knowles **Harris**, was born in New Castle 25 July 1926.

George Myron **Chandler** and Marjorie Eleanor **Sample** had the following children:
- + 8922 i. Susan Marlias[14] **Chandler** born 3 May 1953.
- + 8923 ii. Kathy Ruth **Chandler** born 24 July 1955.
-   8924 iii. Paul Dennis **Chandler**[1278] born in Glenwood Springs, Garfield Co., Colo. 30 September 1957 and died there 2 October 1957, at 3 days of age.
-   8925 iv. Elizabeth Elise **Chandler**[1279] born in New Castle 21 September 1958 and married Terry Sean **Porter** there 7 November 1992. Terry,[1280] son of Barton Frank **Porter** and Martha Ellen **Landcaster**, was born in New Castle 20 December 1955.

7531. **Julia Arlene**[13] **Hart** (Frederick Allan[12], Fred J.[11], John P.[10], Florina H.[9] **Whipple**, Ithamar[8], Rev. Benjamin[7], Benjamin[6], Francis[5], Jonathan[4], Joseph[3], Matthew[2], Matthew[1])[1281] was born in Los Angeles, Los Angeles Co., Calif. 9 March 1943 and married **Donald Robert Crates** in South Gate, Los Angeles Co., Calif. 6 January 1962. Donald,[1282] son of Earl Henry **Crates** and Jane Marie **Leonard**, was born in Brocton, Chautauqua Co., N.Y. 13 November 1938.

Julia Arlene **Hart** and Donald Robert **Crates** had the following children:
- + 8926 i. Marie Lynne[14] **Crates** born 18 August 1962.
- + 8927 ii. Robert Earl **Crates** born 1 March 1967.
-   8928 iii. Joseph Allan **Crates**[1283] born in Anaheim, Orange Co., Calif. 6 October 1975.

7532. **Allan Lee**[13] **Hart** (Frederick Allan[12], Fred J.[11], John P.[10], Florina H.[9] **Whipple**, Ithamar[8], Rev. Benjamin[7], Benjamin[6], Francis[5], Jonathan[4], Joseph[3], Matthew[2], Matthew[1])[1284] was born in Los Angeles, Los Angeles Co., Calif. 15 September 1946 and married **Janice Elaine Larson** in Las Vegas, Clark Co., Nev. 4 May 1968. She was born in Dubois, Clearfield Co., Penn. 3 November 1948.[1285]

Allan Lee **Hart** and Janice Elaine **Larson** had the following child:
- + 8929 i. Alicia Michele[14] **Hart** born 10 February 1969.

7534. **Dale Francis**[13] **Hart** (Frederick Allan[12], Fred J.[11], John P.[10], Florina H.[9] **Whipple**, Ithamar[8], Rev. Benjamin[7], Benjamin[6], Francis[5], Jonathan[4], Joseph[3], Matthew[2], Matthew[1])[1286] was born in Los Angeles, Los Angeles Co., Calif. 13 August 1953 and married three times. (1) **Karleen Elizabeth Stegmaier** in Norwalk, Los Angeles Co., Calif. 19 April

1975. Karleen,[1287] daughter of Norman **Stegmaier** and Rosalie Marie **Bell**, was born in Norwalk 2 December 1955. (2) **Vickie (__)**. (3) **Beth (__)**. She was born 27 February 1956.[1288]

Dale Francis **Hart** and Karleen Elizabeth **Stegmaier** had the following children:

        8930   i.   Diana Rochelle[14] **Hart**[1289] born in Anaheim, Orange Co., Calif. 21 May 1976.
        8931   ii.   Steven Nathaniel **Hart**[1290] born in Anaheim 14 July 1980.
        8932   iii. Daniel Frederick **Hart**[1291] born in Whittier, Los Angeles Co., Calif. 28 January 1982.

7543. **Jean Carol**[13] **Cannon** (Leslie A.[12] **Whipple**, Clayton J.[11], William Lemuel[10], Francis Jackson[9], Ithamar[8], Rev. Benjamin[7], Benjamin[6], Francis[5], Jonathan[4], Joseph[3], Matthew[2], Matthew[1])[1292] was born in Glen Ridge, Essex Co., N. J. 9 January 1929 and married three times. (1) **Bernard Charles Rogge** in Geneva, Ontario Co., N. Y. 11 August 1951. Bernard,[1293] son of Henry P. **Rogge** and Wanda Hermina **Oltmanns**, was born in Freeport, Nassau Co., N. Y. 28 August 1930. They were divorced in Lime Ridge, Sauk Co., Wisc. abt 1966. (2) **Robert Leslie Burton** in Upper Montclair, Essex Co., N. J. 14 August 1972. Robert, son of Leslie **Burton** and Grace (__), was born in Portsmouth, England 5 December 1936. They were divorced in Bloomfield, Essex Co., N. J. 30 May 1978. (3) **James Bowman Maris** in Summit, Union Co., N. J. 13 December 1986. James, son of James Bowman **Maris** and Ruth **Stanley**, was born in Newark, Essex Co., N. J. 21 November 1925.[1294]

Jean Carol **Cannon** and Bernard Charles **Rogge** had the following children:

+   8933   i.   Richard Charles[14] **Rogge** born 31 December 1952.
     8934   ii.   Diane Carol **Rogge**[1295] born in Waterloo, Seneca Co., N. Y. 15 November 1954 and died 8 August 1977 in Hudson, Columbia Co., N. Y., at 22 years of age. Buried in Glens Falls, Warren Co., N. Y.
+   8935   iii. Michael David Drew **Rogge** born 30 March 1957.
     8936   iv. Scott Douglas **Rogge**[1296] born in Lime Ridge 13 November 1965 and died 7 January 1970 in East Orange, Essex Co., N. J., at 4 years of age. Buried in Upper Montclair.

7544. **Douglas Forrest**[13] **Cannon** (Leslie A.[12] **Whipple**, Clayton J.[11], William Lemuel[10], Francis Jackson[9], Ithamar[8], Rev. Benjamin[7], Benjamin[6], Francis[5], Jonathan[4], Joseph[3], Matthew[2], Matthew[1])[1297] was born in Glen Ridge, Essex Co., N. J. 7 March 1931 and married **Helen Ison** in

Ohio 4 May 1963. Helen,[1298] daughter of Patrick Henry **Ison** and Victoria **May**, was born in Sandy Hook, Elliott Co., Ky. 31 July 1940.

Douglas Forrest **Cannon** and Helen **Ison** had the following children:
- 8937 i. Douglas Forrest[14] **Cannon** Jr.[1299] born in Summit, Union Co., N. J. 10 November 1965.
- 8938 ii. Bradley Jay **Cannon**[1300] born in Summit 19 January 1968 and married Patricia Elizabeth **Prochaska** in Annapolis, Ann Arundel Co., Md. 12 July 1997.

7545. **Paul Harley**[13] **Eisentrager** (Mable Jeannette[12] **Skelton**, Sylvia May[11] **Whipple**, Marcus Erastus[10], Francis Jackson[9], Ithamar[8], Rev. Benjamin[7], Benjamin[6], Francis[5], Jonathan[4], Joseph[3], Matthew[2], Matthew[1])[1301] was born 20 March 1944 and married **Dawn Susan Dyer** in Vacaville, Solano Co., Calif. 2 February 1967. She was born 25 July 1947.[1302]

Paul Harley **Eisentrager** and Dawn Susan **Dyer** had the following children:
- 8939 i. Paul Bradford[14] **Eisentrager**[1303] born 17 September 1971.
- 8940 ii. Mindy Elise **Eisentrager**[1304] born 10 March 1975.

7546. **Daniel Lee**[13] **Eisentrager Sr.** (Mable Jeannette[12] **Skelton**, Sylvia May[11] **Whipple**, Marcus Erastus[10], Francis Jackson[9], Ithamar[8], Rev. Benjamin[7], Benjamin[6], Francis[5], Jonathan[4], Joseph[3], Matthew[2], Matthew[1])[1305] was born 10 April 1946 and married twice. (1) **Sue Shope** 20 June 1967. She was born 11 January 1947. (2) **Carla Teresis Hystek** in Tahunga,[1306] Calif. 15 October 1977. She was born 15 October 1955.

Daniel Lee **Eisentrager** Sr. and Sue **Shope** had the following child:
- 8941 i. Christopher Blayn[14] **Eisentrager**[1307] born 9 October 1974.

Daniel Lee **Eisentrager** Sr. and Carla Teresis **Hystek** had the following children:
- 8942 ii. Candace Adrian **Eisentrager**[1308] born 29 April 1979.
- 8943 iii. Daniel Lee **Eisentrager** Jr.[1309] born 30 December 1980.

7547. **David Ray**[13] **Eisentrager** (Mable Jeannette[12] **Skelton**, Sylvia May[11] **Whipple**, Marcus Erastus[10], Francis Jackson[9], Ithamar[8], Rev. Benjamin[7], Benjamin[6], Francis[5], Jonathan[4], Joseph[3], Matthew[2], Matthew[1])[1310] was born 9 May 1949 and married **Faye Ann Newland** in Nampa, Canyon Co., Idaho 28 December 1971.

David Ray **Eisentrager** and Faye Ann **Newland** had the following children:

 8944 i. James David[14] **Eisentrager**[1311] born 17 March 1975.
 8945 ii. Michelle Faye **Eisentrager**[1312] born 15 January 1977.

7548. **Ruth Marie**[13] **Eisentrager** (Mable Jeannette[12] **Skelton**, Sylvia May[11] **Whipple**, Marcus Erastus[10], Francis Jackson[9], Ithamar[8], Rev. Benjamin[7], Benjamin[6], Francis[5], Jonathan[4], Joseph[3], Matthew[2], Matthew[1])[1313] was born 20 April 1954 and married **Wayne Eugene Durham** in Boise, Ada Co., Idaho 16 February 1974.

Ruth Marie **Eisentrager** and Wayne Eugene **Durham** had the following children:

 8946 i. Jennifer Michelle[14] **Durham**[1314] born 21 September 1974.
 8947 ii. Micah Joel **Durham**[1315] born 21 December 1980.
 8948 iii. Joella Marie **Durham**[1316] born 29 June 1984.
 8949 iv. Julianne Merrie **Durham**[1317] born 29 October 1985.

7550. **Joy Ann**[13] **Eisentrager** (Mable Jeannette[12] **Skelton**, Sylvia May[11] **Whipple**, Marcus Erastus[10], Francis Jackson[9], Ithamar[8], Rev. Benjamin[7], Benjamin[6], Francis[5], Jonathan[4], Joseph[3], Matthew[2], Matthew[1])[1318] was born 14 August 1960 and married **Roger Boyd Haney** in Portland, Multnomah Co., Oreg. 13 October 1984. He was born 25 January 1962.[1319]

Joy Ann **Eisentrager** and Roger Boyd **Haney** had the following children:

 8950 i. Joanna Joy[14] **Haney**[1320] born 27 September 1986.
 8951 ii. Benjamin David **Haney**[1321] born 20 June 1989.

7552. **Donna Lee**[13] **Skelton** (James John[12], Sylvia May[11] **Whipple**, Marcus Erastus[10], Francis Jackson[9], Ithamar[8], Rev. Benjamin[7], Benjamin[6], Francis[5], Jonathan[4], Joseph[3], Matthew[2], Matthew[1])[1322] was born 30 January 1945 and married twice. (1) **Thomas Woods** who was born 7 September 1943.[1323] (2) **Carl S. Smith** who was born 9 May 1936.[1324]

Donna Lee **Skelton** and Thomas **Woods** had the following children:

+ 8952 i. Vickie Lee[14] **Woods** born 18 January 1963.
 8953 ii. Richard James **Woods**[1325] born 23 November 1967 and married Lynn **Kusiak** 12 August 1995. She was born 30 July 1967.[1326]

7553. **Roberta Jean**[13] **Skelton** (James John[12], Sylvia May[11] **Whipple**, Marcus Erastus[10], Francis Jackson[9], Ithamar[8], Rev. Benjamin[7], Benjamin[6], Francis[5], Jonathan[4], Joseph[3], Matthew[2], Matthew[1])[1327] was born 7

January 1949 and married **Everett William Frick** in Edinboro, Erie Co., Penn. 11 May 1968. He was born 15 April 1942.[1328]

Roberta Jean **Skelton** and Everett William **Frick** had the following children:
- 8954 i. William James[14] **Frick**[1329] born 17 February 1974.
- 8955 ii. Kelly Jean **Frick**[1330] born 11 July 1976.

7554. **Dennis James**[13] **Skelton** (James John[12], Sylvia May[11] **Whipple**, Marcus Erastus[10], Francis Jackson[9], Ithamar[8], Rev. Benjamin[7], Benjamin[6], Francis[5], Jonathan[4], Joseph[3], Matthew[2], Matthew[1])[1331] was born 7 December 1952 and married twice. (1) **Mary McLallen**. (2) **Helen McLaughlin**. She was born 23 March 1961.[1332]

Dennis James **Skelton** and Mary **McLallen** had the following children:
- 8956 i. Dennis James[14] **Skelton** Jr.[1333] born 1 July 1976.
- 8957 ii. Devon Dawn **Skelton**[1334] born 6 May 1980.

Dennis James **Skelton** and Helen **McLaughlin** had the following children:
- 8958 iii. Daniel Patrick **Skelton**[1335] born 30 June 1989.
- 8959 iv. Ryan James **Skelton**[1336] born 18 December 1990.
- 8960 v. Jena Marie **Skelton**[1337] born 10 August 1993.

7555. **Terry Arden**[13] **Skelton** (James John[12], Sylvia May[11] **Whipple**, Marcus Erastus[10], Francis Jackson[9], Ithamar[8], Rev. Benjamin[7], Benjamin[6], Francis[5], Jonathan[4], Joseph[3], Matthew[2], Matthew[1])[1338] was born 26 November 1955 and married **Patricia Perri**. She was born 28 May 1959.[1339]

Terry Arden **Skelton** and Patricia **Perri** had the following children:
- 8961 i. Samantha Paige[14] **Skelton**[1340] born 30 January 1987.
- 8962 ii. Molly Kate **Skelton**[1341] born 24 July 1989.
- 8963 iii. Clay Beresford **Skelton**[1342] born 20 May 1994.

7556. **Woodette Eileen**[13] **Skelton** (James John[12], Sylvia May[11] **Whipple**, Marcus Erastus[10], Francis Jackson[9], Ithamar[8], Rev. Benjamin[7], Benjamin[6], Francis[5], Jonathan[4], Joseph[3], Matthew[2], Matthew[1])[1343] was born 7 December 1959 and married **Philip Sanders**.

Woodette Eileen **Skelton** and Philip **Sanders** had the following children:
- 8964 i. Jennifer[14] **Sanders**.[1344]
- 8965 ii. Dale James **Sanders**.[1345]

7557. **Cindy Lou**[13] **Skelton** (James John[12], Sylvia May[11] **Whipple**, Marcus Erastus[10], Francis Jackson[9], Ithamar[8], Rev. Benjamin[7], Benjamin[6], Francis[5], Jonathan[4], Joseph[3], Matthew[2], Matthew[1])[1346] was born 22 June 1960 and married **Karl F. Horvath Jr.** 23 May 1981. He was born 18 March 1960.[1347]

Cindy Lou **Skelton** and Karl F. **Horvath** Jr. had the following children:
- 8966 i. Alecia Mae[14] **Horvath**[1348] born 17 August 1984.
- 8967 ii. Jessica Lynn **Horvath**[1349] born 31 July 1987.

7559. **Kathleen**[13] **Skelton** (Paul Mark[12], Sylvia May[11] **Whipple**, Marcus Erastus[10], Francis Jackson[9], Ithamar[8], Rev. Benjamin[7], Benjamin[6], Francis[5], Jonathan[4], Joseph[3], Matthew[2], Matthew[1])[1350] was born 8 July 1950 and married **Larry Brown**.

Kathleen **Skelton** and Larry **Brown** had the following children:
- 8968 i. Jonathan[14] **Brown**[1351] born in Salmon, Lemhi Co., Idaho.
- 8969 ii. Heidi **Brown**[1352] born in Salmon.

7564. **Ruth Ann**[13] **Wiley** (Margaret Jane[12] **Whipple**, Dr. Raymond Orson[11], Marcus Erastus[10], Francis Jackson[9], Ithamar[8], Rev. Benjamin[7], Benjamin[6], Francis[5], Jonathan[4], Joseph[3], Matthew[2], Matthew[1])[1353] was born 16 November 1943 and married **Richard Leroy Smith** in Meyerstown, Lebanon Co., Penn. 7 September 1963. He was born 25 June 1943.[1354]

Ruth Ann **Wiley** and Richard Leroy **Smith** had the following children:
- + 8970 i. Richard James[14] **Smith** born 22 March 1967.
- + 8971 ii. Scott Gregory **Smith** born 16 October 1968.
- 8972 iii. Bradley Mark **Smith**[1355] born 15 July 1973 and married Deborah Leigh **Sheridan** in Philadelphia, Philadelphia City Co., Penn. 15 August 1998. She was born 28 March 1973.[1356]
- 8973 iv. Amy Beth **Smith**[1357] born 19 September 1976.

7565. **Mary Elizabeth**[13] **Wiley** (Margaret Jane[12] **Whipple**, Dr. Raymond Orson[11], Marcus Erastus[10], Francis Jackson[9], Ithamar[8], Rev. Benjamin[7], Benjamin[6], Francis[5], Jonathan[4], Joseph[3], Matthew[2], Matthew[1])[1358] was born 31 January 1946 and married **Boyd Hamilton Aebli** in Meyerstown, Lebanon Co., Penn. 29 August 1970. He was born 10 June 1943.[1359] They were divorced in 1990.

Mary Elizabeth **Wiley** and Boyd Hamilton **Aebli** had the following children:
- 8974 i. Kathryn Jane[14] **Aebli**[1360] born 11 January 1972.
- 8975 ii. Melanie Ann **Aebli**[1361] born 27 March 1974.

7566. **Jeannette Louise**[13] **Wiley** (Margaret Jane[12] **Whipple**, Dr. Raymond Orson[11], Marcus Erastus[10], Francis Jackson[9], Ithamar[8], Rev. Benjamin[7], Benjamin[6], Francis[5], Jonathan[4], Joseph[3], Matthew[2], Matthew[1])[1362] was born 19 September 1951 and married **Walter Zakrzewski** in Mansfield, Tioga Co., Penn. 22 December 1973. He was born 24 September 1952.[1363]

Jeannette Louise **Wiley** and Walter **Zakrzewski** had the following children:
- 8976 i. Carole Ann[14] **Zakrzewski**[1364] born 13 October 1978.
- 8977 ii. Lynda Marie **Zakrzewski**[1365] born 15 July 1984.
- 8978 iii. Jon Andrew **Zakrzewski**[1366] born 27 March 1987.

7567. **Nancy May**[13] **Wiley** (Margaret Jane[12] **Whipple**, Dr. Raymond Orson[11], Marcus Erastus[10], Francis Jackson[9], Ithamar[8], Rev. Benjamin[7], Benjamin[6], Francis[5], Jonathan[4], Joseph[3], Matthew[2], Matthew[1])[1367] was born 22 January 1956 and married **Arthur Otto Lyford** in Portland, Multnomah Co., Oreg. 13 June 1985. He was born 10 November 1954.[1368]

Nancy May **Wiley** and Arthur Otto **Lyford** had the following children:
- 8979 i. Jeffrey Ross[14] **Lyford**[1369] born 22 May 1986.
- 8980 ii. Molly May **Lyford**[1370] born 9 May 1988.

7568. **Elizabeth Jean**[13] **Whipple** (Capt. Caryll Robbins[12], Carl Era[11], Marcus Erastus[10], Francis Jackson[9], Ithamar[8], Rev. Benjamin[7], Benjamin[6], Francis[5], Jonathan[4], Joseph[3], Matthew[2], Matthew[1])[1371] was born in Rensselaer, Rensselaer Co., N.Y. 12 March 1953 and married **Robert Montgomery Brackbill II** 14 October 1978. He was born in Lancaster, Lancaster Co., Penn. 12 May 1957.[1372] Robert, a physician, practices in Reading, Berks Co., Penn. Elizabeth, educated at Western Maryland College, Westminster, and Thomas Jefferson University, Philadelphia, is a physician and homemaker and a member of the Covenant Church.

Elizabeth Jean **Whipple** and Robert Montgomery **Brackbill** II had the following children born in Reading:
- 8981 i. Andrew John[14] **Brackbill**[1373] 30 April 1980.
- 8982 ii. Emily Robbins **Brackbill**[1374] 16 November 1981.
- 8983 iii. Sarah Beth **Brackbill**[1375] 27 April 1984.
- 8984 iv. Rachel Anna **Brackbill**[1376] 30 May 1987.
- 8985 v. Robert Montgomery **Brackbill** III[1377] 15 September 1991.
- 8986 vi. Matthew Warren **Brackbill**[1378] 19 August 1993.
- 8987 vii. Ian Joseph **Brackbill**[1379] 10 November 1995.
- 8988 viii. Julia Elizabeth **Brackbill**[1380] 5 March 1998.

7569. **Laurie Ann**[13] **Whipple** (Capt. Caryll Robbins[12], Carl Era[11], Marcus Erastus[10], Francis Jackson[9], Ithamar[8], Rev. Benjamin[7], Benjamin[6], Francis[5], Jonathan[4], Joseph[3], Matthew[2], Matthew[1])[1381] was born in Madrid, Spain 8 May 1955 and married **Bruce Anthony DeMarco** 7 October 1978. He was born 7 January 1955.[1382] Laurie Ann earned a Bachelor's Degree from Penn State, University Park, Centre Co., Penn., a Master's Degree from the U. of Florida, Gainesville, and a Ph.D from the U. of Virginia, Chartlottesville, Charlottesville City Co.

Laurie Ann **Whipple** and Bruce Anthony **DeMarco** had the following children:
- 8989 i. Kellen Brian[14] **DeMarco**[1383] born 10 November 1983.
- 8990 ii. Caitlain Robbins **DeMarco**[1384] born 5 March 1987.
- 8991 iii. Chelsea Ann **DeMarco**[1385] born 4 January 1990.

7571. **Andrew Warren**[13] **Whipple** (Capt. Caryll Robbins[12], Carl Era[11], Marcus Erastus[10], Francis Jackson[9], Ithamar[8], Rev. Benjamin[7], Benjamin[6], Francis[5], Jonathan[4], Joseph[3], Matthew[2], Matthew[1])[1386] was born in Bethesda, Montgomery Co., Md. 15 August 1963 and married **Donna Katrina Daout** 4 June 1988. She was born 4 July 1963.[1387]

Andrew Warren **Whipple** and Donna Katrina **Daout** had the following children:
- 8992 i. Christina Marie[14] **Whipple**[1388] born 28 June 1995.
- 8993 ii. Spencer Robbins **Whipple**[1389] born 18 October 1996.

7572. **Daniel Marsh**[13] **Whipple** (Capt. Caryll Robbins[12], Carl Era[11], Marcus Erastus[10], Francis Jackson[9], Ithamar[8], Rev. Benjamin[7], Benjamin[6], Francis[5], Jonathan[4], Joseph[3], Matthew[2], Matthew[1])[1390] was born in Port Hueneme, Ventura Co., Calif. 1 January 1969 and married **Christina Marie Jessica Fanelli** in Smith Mountain Lake, Va. 4 September 1994. She was born 15 September 1971.[1391] He earned a Bachelor of Science Degree in Business Administration from Martha Washington College at Fredericksburg, Stafford Co., Va. and is a Community Service Supervisor for First Virginia Bank (1998).

Daniel Marsh **Whipple** and Christina Marie Jessica **Fanelli** had the following child born in Charlotte, Mecklenburg Co., N. C.:
- 8994 i. Joseph Michael[14] **Whipple**[1392] 11 October 1997.

7573. **Joanna Louise**[13] **Erbland** (Nancy Louise[12] **Whipple**, Carl Era[11], Marcus Erastus[10], Francis Jackson[9], Ithamar[8], Rev. Benjamin[7], Benjamin[6],

Francis[5], Jonathan[4], Joseph[3], Matthew[2], Matthew[1])[1393] was born in Rochester, Monroe Co., N.Y. 23 May 1957 and married **Lewis Anthony Caputa Jr.** in Augusta, Richmond Co., Ga. 30 May 1993. She attended Augusta College (now Augusta State University) at Augusta and Spring Hill College in Mobile, Mobile Co., Ala. before entering Emory University School of Nursing in Atlanta, Fulton Co., Ga. where she earned a Master's Degree in Psychiatric Nursing. Her work history includes Grady Memorial Hospital in Atlanta where she was a Clinical Nurse Specialist; Veterans Administration Hospital, Augusta; Emory University (Atlanta) Hospital, Transplant Team for Organ Transplants; Supervisor at a private Psychiatric Hospital in St. Augustine, Pinellas Co., Fla.; and Psychiatric Nurse Practioner for the Dept. of Public Health in Orange Park, Clay Co., Fla, She has held offices in the Organization of Dental Dames in Florida.

Joanna Louise **Erbland** and Lewis Anthony **Caputa** Jr. had the following child:

    8995   i.   Margaret Marian[14] **Caputa**[1394] born in Jacksonville, Duval Co., Fla. 28 November 1996.

7574. **Peter Jay**[13] **Erbland** (Nancy Louise[12] **Whipple**, Carl Era[11], Marcus Erastus[10], Francis Jackson[9], Ithamar[8], Rev. Benjamin[7], Benjamin[6], Francis[5], Jonathan[4], Joseph[3], Matthew[2], Matthew[1])[1395] was born in Rochester, Monroe Co., N.Y. 26 June 1958 and married **Diane Williams** in Evans, Columbia Co., Ga. 13 September 1980. Diane,[1396] daughter of Dr. Earl **Williams** and Kathy **Bolton**, was born in Gulfport, Harrison Co., Miss. 16 January 1958. Peter is an Aerospace Engineer. He attended Augusta College (now Augusta State University), Augusta, Richmond Co., Ga. and Georgia Tech, Atlanta, Fulton Co., where he received his Bachelors and Masters Degrees. He worked in Civil Service at Wright Patterson Air Force Base (in southwestern Ohio) in Aerospace Engineering until enrolling at Princeton University, Princeton, Mercer Co., N. J., where he earned a Masters Degree and Doctorate in Aeronautical Engineering. He was working in Aeronautical Sciences as a Technical Advisor in 2002.

Peter Jay **Erbland** and Diane **Williams** had the following children born in Dayton, Montgomery Co., Ohio:

    8996   i.   Andrew Garrett[14] **Erbland**[1397] 23 January 1988.
    8997   ii.   Daniel Thomas **Erbland**[1398] 16 September 1990.

7575. **Mark David**[13] **Erbland** (Nancy Louise[12] **Whipple**, Carl Era[11], Marcus Erastus[10], Francis Jackson[9], Ithamar[8], Rev. Benjamin[7], Benjamin[6], Francis[5], Jonathan[4], Joseph[3], Matthew[2], Matthew[1])[1399] was born in Rochester, Monroe Co., N.Y. 1 June 1962 and married twice. (1) **Nanci Collins** in Augusta, Richmond Co., Ga. in December 1987. (2) **Cathy Elizabeth Brown** in Augusta 23 December 1990. Cathy,[1400] daughter of Charles Clifton **Brown** and Mary Ruth **Gay**, was born 13 October 1968. Mark is a Pastor in a church in Clearwater, Aiken Co., S. C. and a Security Supervisor for Comcast Cable Co. He baptized his three daughters in 2002 with the Erbland grandparents in attendance.

Mark David **Erbland** and Cathy Elizabeth **Brown** had the following children born in Augusta:
    8998 i.   Courtney Elizabeth[14] **Erbland**[1401] 3 June 1993.
    8999 ii.   Casey Meredith **Erbland**[1402] 23 August 1995.
    9000 iii. Christina Nichole **Erbland**[1403] 20 November 1996.

7579. **Gordon Henry**[13] **Ira Jr.** (Dr. Gordon Henry[12], Florence Elsie[11] **Whipple**, Cephus Galusha[10], Samuel Elijah[9], Ithamar[8], Rev. Benjamin[7], Benjamin[6], Francis[5], Jonathan[4], Joseph[3], Matthew[2], Matthew[1])[1404] was born in Jacksonville, Duval Co., Fla. 18 November 1929 and married twice. (1) **Stephanie Diuguid** in Jacksonville 17 July 1954. Stephanie,[1405] daughter of Stephen **Diuguid** and Virginia Louise **Davis**, was born in Chicago, Cook Co., Ill. 31 May 1933. They were divorced in Jacksonville 13 January 1972. (2) **Joyce Malbon** in Kingsland, Camden Co., Ga. 30 March 1973. Joyce,[1406] daughter of Oscar Bernard **Malbon** and Arletta Virginia **West**, was born in Norfolk, Norfolk City Area Co., Va. 18 November 1944. Gordon, a Cardiologist, was Chief of Medicine at St. Lukes Hospital in Jacksonville for 25 years and established the Rescue Service Units in Duval County. The Hospital established a Lectureship in his name. Upon his retirement 31 May 1998, he was lauded for his research in cardiac care in emergency rescue situations. His research resulted in significant reduction in emergency care death rates.

Gordon Henry **Ira** Jr. and Stephanie **Diuguid** had the following children:
+   9001 i.   Stephen Reynolds[14] **Ira** born 27 August 1958.
    9002 ii.   Cynthia Tompkins **Ira**[1407] born in Durham, Durham Co., N.C. 15 August 1960.
    9003 iii. Gregory Thatcher **Ira**[1408] was born in Durham 12 May 1962 and married Elizabeth Louise **Clarkson** in Jacksonville. Elizabeth,[1409] daughter of Lawrence William **Clarkson** and Barbara **Stevenson**, was born in Palm Beach, Palm Beach Co., Fla. 25 July 1963. They were divorced in Jacksonville.
    9004 iv. Clifford Whipple **Ira**[1410] born in Jacksonville 30 January 1965.

7580. **Stewart Bentley**[13] **Ira** (Dr. Gordon Henry[12], Florence Elsie[11] **Whipple**, Cephus Galusha[10], Samuel Elijah[9], Ithamar[8], Rev. Benjamin[7], Benjamin[6], Francis[5], Jonathan[4], Joseph[3], Matthew[2], Matthew[1])[1411] was born in Jacksonville, Duval Co., Fla. 4 December 1931 and married **Elizabeth Anne Brown** there 1 May 1954. Elizabeth,[1412] daughter of George Charles **Brown** and Anne Winslow **Thiot**, was born in Jacksonville 12 October 1934.

Stewart Bentley **Ira** and Elizabeth Anne **Brown** had the following children:

    9005 i. Anis Winslow[14] **Ira**[1413] born in Jacksonville 31 August 1955 and married three times in Jacksonville. (1) Harry Lee **Collins III** 8 April 1978. They were divorced there in June 1983. (2) Edward Clayton **Jones Jr.** 23 December 1986. They were divorced there in June 1988. (3) Julian Bartow **Colbert III** 14 February 1992.

+ 9006 ii. Elizabeth Cecil **Ira** born 13 April 1958.
+ 9007 iii. Mary Stewart **Ira** born 3 April 1961.

7581. **Anis Louise**[13] **Ira** (Dr. Gordon Henry[12], Florence Elsie[11] **Whipple**, Cephus Galusha[10], Samuel Elijah[9], Ithamar[8], Rev. Benjamin[7], Benjamin[6], Francis[5], Jonathan[4], Joseph[3], Matthew[2], Matthew[1])[1414] was born in Jacksonville, Duval Co., Fla. 25 October 1936 and married **Barnwell Roy Daley Jr.** in Jacksonville 26 July 1958. Barney,[1415] son of Barnwell Roy **Daley** and Meta Margaret **Horne**, was born in Jacksonville 18 June 1934.

Anis Louise **Ira** and Barnwell Roy **Daley** Jr. had the following children:

+ 9008 i. Anis Margaret[14] **Daley** born 2 March 1960.
+ 9009 ii. Frances Cameron **Daley** born 4 July 1961.
+ 9010 iii. Susan Ira **Daley** born 9 May 1965.
+ 9011 iv. Anne Barnwell **Daley** born 15 April 1970.

7582. **Mary Lou**[13] **Douglas** (Naomi Grace[12] **Ira**, Florence Elsie[11] **Whipple**, Cephus Galusha[10], Samuel Elijah[9], Ithamar[8], Rev. Benjamin[7], Benjamin[6], Francis[5], Jonathan[4], Joseph[3], Matthew[2], Matthew[1])[1416] was born in Lynch, Boyd Co., Nebr. 30 April 1927 and married **Cecil Everett Evans** in Indianapolis, Marion Co., Ind. 24 November 1949. Cecil,[1417] son of William Henry **Evans** and Elizabeth **Casey**, was born in Kossuth, Washington Co., Ind. 8 January 1925. An Engineer, Cecil was educated at Purdue University, West Lafayette, Tippecanoe Co., Ind.

{ G 1325 }

Mary Lou **Douglas** and Cecil Everett **Evans** had the following children:
>   9012   i.   Gordon Casey[14] **Evans**[1418] born in Indianapolis 31 August 1950.
> + 9013   ii.   Karen Elizabeth **Evans** born 30 March 1953.
>   9014   iii. Sandra K. **Evans**[1419] born in Lafayette 21 August 1956.

7583. **Jean Kathryn**[13] **Douglas** (Naomi Grace[12] **Ira**, Florence Elsie[11] **Whipple**, Cephus Galusha[10], Samuel Elijah[9], Ithamar[8], Rev. Benjamin[7], Benjamin[6], Francis[5], Jonathan[4], Joseph[3], Matthew[2], Matthew[1])[1420] was born in St. Paul, Ramsey Co., Minn. 14 June 1930 and married **Chester Duane Allread** in Indianapolis, Marion Co., Ind. 15 June 1952.

Jean Kathryn **Douglas** and Chester Duane **Allread** had the following children:
> + 9015   i.   Rebecca Jean[14] **Allread** born 6 May 1956.
> + 9016   ii.   Jenifer Lynn **Allread** born 20 February 1959.
>   9017   iii. Stephen **Allread**[1421] born in Cincinnati, Hamilton Co., Ohio 8 July 1963 and married Lisa **Iker** in Milford, Claremont Co., Ohio 16 June 1991. No information provided on Stephen's first marriage. Lisa brought two children to his second marriage: Nicole and Matthew **Iker.**

7584. **Virginia Ellen**[13] **Douglas** (Naomi Grace[12] **Ira**, Florence Elsie[11] **Whipple**, Cephus Galusha[10], Samuel Elijah[9], Ithamar[8], Rev. Benjamin[7], Benjamin[6], Francis[5], Jonathan[4], Joseph[3], Matthew[2], Matthew[1])[1422] was born in St. Paul, Ramsey Co., Minn. 22 September 1932 and married twice. (1) **James H. Kirchhoffer.** (2) **Dr. Charles Ferris Sumner** in Orinda, Contra Costa Co., Calif. 9 February 1979. He was born in New Orleans, Orleans Parish, La. 4 December 1924.[1423] He also married **Frances Crillen**. Charles was a U.S Army Dentist now retired. He is licenced to practice law in California.

Virginia Ellen **Douglas** and James H. **Kirchhoffer** had the following children:
>   9018   i.   Lisa Ann[14] **Kirchhoffer**[1424] born in Cincinnati, Hamilton Co., Ohio 18 December 1958.
>   9019   ii.   Stephanie **Kirchhoffer**[1425] born 6 May 1961.
>   9020   iii. Ann Margaret **Kirchhoffer**[1426] born 11 August 1966 and married Mark **Wolz** in San Diego, San Diego Co., Calif. 15 September 1990.

7585. **George Lynn**[13] **Douglas** (Naomi Grace[12] **Ira**, Florence Elsie[11] **Whipple**, Cephus Galusha[10], Samuel Elijah[9], Ithamar[8], Rev. Benjamin[7], Benjamin[6], Francis[5], Jonathan[4], Joseph[3], Matthew[2], Matthew[1])[1427] was born in St. Paul, Ramsey Co., Minn. 27 November 1934 and married **Jeannette Louise Williams** in Indianapolis, Marion Co., Ind. 21 January 1957. Jeannette,[1428] daughter of Harry Lewis **Williams** and Mary Louise **Pierson**, was born in Battle Creek, Calhoun Co., Mich. 17 December 1935.

George Lynn **Douglas** and Jeannette Louise **Williams** had the following children:

+ 9021 i. Matthew Reyman[14] **Douglas** born 6 May 1958.
9022 ii. Andrew Lewis **Douglas**[1429] born in Indianapolis 29 April 1960 and married Lou Anne **Moore** in Lawrence Co., Ill. 31 October 1987.
9023 iii. Peter Bentley **Douglas**[1430] born in Indianapolis 17 April 1964 and married Patricia **Rogers** there 22 November 1988.
9024 iv. Mary Elizabeth Grace **Douglas**[1431] born in Indianapolis 11 June 1967.

7586. **Laird Douglas**[13] **Whipple** (Marshall Lofland[12], Charles Clifford[11], Cephus Galusha[10], Samuel Elijah[9], Ithamar[8], Rev. Benjamin[7], Benjamin[6], Francis[5], Jonathan[4], Joseph[3], Matthew[2], Matthew[1])[1432] was born in Tacoma, Pierce Co., Wash. 28 April 1942 and married **Dianne Enis Nelson** in Aberdeen, Chehalis Co., Wash. 21 March 1964. Dianne,[1433] daughter of Robert **Nelson** and Enis **Losli**, was born in Aberdeen 12 September 1942. Laird is a Food Specialist with the Del Monte Corporation.

Laird Douglas **Whipple** and Dianne Enis **Nelson** had the following children:

+ 9025 i. Kristin Sue[14] **Whipple** born 11 May 1968.
9026 ii. John Douglas **Whipple**[1434] born in Del Monte, Mindanao, Philippines 6 September 1969.
9027 iii. Paul Robert **Whipple**[1435] born in Manila, Philippines 22 December 1970.

7587. **Martha Sue**[13] **Whipple** (Marshall Lofland[12], Charles Clifford[11], Cephus Galusha[10], Samuel Elijah[9], Ithamar[8], Rev. Benjamin[7], Benjamin[6], Francis[5], Jonathan[4], Joseph[3], Matthew[2], Matthew[1])[1436] was born in Tacoma, Pierce Co., Wash. 18 August 1944 and married **Randolph Wayne McCormack** in Seattle, King Co., Wash. 8 February 1969. Randy,[1437] son of James **McCormack** and Magie Lee **Hamilton**, was born in Jacksonville, Duval Co., Fla. 2 November 1945.

{ G 1327 }

Martha Sue **Whipple** and Randolph Wayne **McCormack** had the following children:
- 9028 i. Robin Sue[14] **McCormack**[1438] born in Malmstrom AFB, Cascade, Cascade Co., Mont. 7 November 1971 and married Kevin MacFarland **Mills** in Edmonds, Snohomish Co., Wash. 30 December 1995.
- 9029 ii. Timothy James **McCormack**[1439] born in Vandenberg AFB, Santa Barbara, Santa Barbara Co., Calif. 8 October 1974.

7588. **Clifford Charles**[13] **Whipple** (Murray Douglas[12], Charles Clifford[11], Cephus Galusha[10], Samuel Elijah[9], Ithamar[8], Rev. Benjamin[7], Benjamin[6], Francis[5], Jonathan[4], Joseph[3], Matthew[2], Matthew[1])[1440] was born in Tacoma, Pierce Co., Wash. 20 January 1939 and married **Carole Ann Imus** 13 September 1963. They were divorced in September 1982.[1441]

Clifford Charles **Whipple** and Carole Ann **Imus** had the following children:
- 9030 i. Daniel Eugene[14] **Whipple**[1442] born in Seattle, King Co., Wash. 5 March 1968.
- 9031 ii. Patricia Lynn **Whipple**[1443] born in Renton, King Co., Wash. 6 February 1972.
- 9032 iii. Lance Alan **Whipple**[1444] born in Renton 27 August 1973.

7590. **Dennis Murray**[13] **Whipple** (Murray Douglas[12], Charles Clifford[11], Cephus Galusha[10], Samuel Elijah[9], Ithamar[8], Rev. Benjamin[7], Benjamin[6], Francis[5], Jonathan[4], Joseph[3], Matthew[2], Matthew[1])[1445] was born in Puyallup, Pierce Co., Wash. 2 March 1948 and married **Susan Arlene Hagar** in Tacoma, Pierce Co., Wash. 27 October 1973.[1446] She was born in Tacoma 14 February 1951.

Dennis Murray **Whipple** and Susan Arlene **Hagar** had the following children born in Puyallup:
- 9033 i. Brandon Douglas[14] **Whipple**[1447] 8 May 1977.
- 9034 ii. Emily Jane **Whipple**[1448] 9 April 1979.

7592. **Grey Gordon**[13] **Whipple II** (Grey Gordon[12], Charles Clifford[11], Cephus Galusha[10], Samuel Elijah[9], Ithamar[8], Rev. Benjamin[7], Benjamin[6], Francis[5], Jonathan[4], Joseph[3], Matthew[2], Matthew[1])[1449] was born in Tacoma, Pierce Co., Wash. 28 June 1937 and married **Lillian Anne Blaylock** in Salinas, Monterey Co., Calif. 13 July 1963. She was born in Salinas 6 October 1940.[1450] Lillian earned a Degree in Elementary Education from San Jose (Santa Clara Co.) State College in 1962 after having attended Hartnell Community College in Salinas (1960). She is a 1958 graduate of Salinas High School. A homemaker, her avocation is handweaving. She is certified as a Master Weaver by the Handweavers Guild of America and is known internationally for her fine handwoven silk garments and art pieces. She is active in the United Methodist Church where she sings in the choir and is in a hand-bell choir.

When he was 8, Grey's family moved from Tacoma to California where he completed his schooling: Burlingame San Mateo Co. High School (1955), Hartnell Community College (1957), and California State Polytechnic College in San Luis Obispo (San Luis Obispo Co.) in 1960 where he earned a Degree in Electrical Engineering. He spent three years as an officer in the U.S. Navy Civil Engineering Corps. and then joined Pacific Gas & Electric Company, retiring in 1995 after 34.5 years. In 1993 he co-authored a college textbook titled *Assembly Language: Byte-By-Byte, Programming in the IBM PC Environment*. He and Lillian have lived in Concord, San Diego Co., Calif. since 1977.

Grey Gordon **Whipple** II and Lillian Anne **Blaylock** had the following children:

- \+ 9035 i. Karen Denise[14] **Whipple** born 2 September 1966.
- 9036 ii. Brian Lee **Whipple**[1451] born in San Mateo, San Mateo, Co., Calif. 6 June 1969. Adopted.

7593. **Brandt Raymond**[13] **Whipple** (Grey Gordon[12], Charles Clifford[11], Cephus Galusha[10], Samuel Elijah[9], Ithamar[8], Rev. Benjamin[7], Benjamin[6], Francis[5], Jonathan[4], Joseph[3], Matthew[2], Matthew[1])[1452] was born in Tacoma, Pierce Co., Wash. 15 December 1940 and died 17 March 1978 in Yuba City, Sutter Co., Calif., at 37 years of age. He married twice. (1) **Dorothy Jean Thatcher** in San Leandro, Alameda Co., Calif. 17 May 1960. Dorothy,[1453] daughter of Robert Norman **Thatcher** and Marjory Frances **Park**, was born in Los Angeles, Los Angeles Co., Calif. 17 May 1940. They were divorced in Sutter Co., Calif. in 1975. (2) **Janet Lynn McLaughlin** 29 December 1975. She was born in Santa Monica, Los Angeles Co., Calif. 22 August 1945.[1454] Brandt was graduated from the U. of California at Berkeley, Alameda Co., in 1962. He was a High School teacher in Yuba City at the time of death.

Brandt Raymond **Whipple** and Dorothy Jean **Thatcher** had the following children:

- 9037 i. Robert Gordon[14] **Whipple**[1455] born in Berkeley, Calif. 5 March 1965 and married Margaret Susan **Thatcher** in Detroit, Wayne Co., Mich. 16 November 1991. She was born in Tucson, Pima Co., Ariz. 23 December 1959.[1456]

{ G 1329 }

		Margaret and Robert have two children by her former marriage: Emily Anne **Bates**, born 6 December 1981 at Rochester, Mich. and Lydia Kathrin **Bates**, born 2 Oct. 1986 at Lake Orion, Oakland Co., Mich.
9038	ii.	Jason John **Whipple**[1457] born in Yuba City 16 May 1968 and married Diana Kathleen **Sowin** in Marysville, Yuba Co., Calif. 27 December 1992. After graduating from Yuba City High School in 1986, Jason enlisted in the U.S. Marine Corps. After his discharge he entered San Jose State College, Santa Clara Co., Calif. and was awarded a Degree in Civil Engineering in 1997.

7594. **Chipps Sherman**[13] **Whipple** (Sherman Guy[12], Charles Clifford[11], Cephus Galusha[10], Samuel Elijah[9], Ithamar[8], Rev. Benjamin[7], Benjamin[6], Francis[5], Jonathan[4], Joseph[3], Matthew[2], Matthew[1])[1458] was born in San Mateo, San Mateo, Co., Calif. 28 March 1948 and married **Judy Kay Davis** in Seattle, King Co. Wash. 25 November 1972. She was born in Seattle 6 January 1949.[1459]

Chipps Sherman **Whipple** and Judy Kay **Davis** had the following children born in Bellevue, King Co., Wash.:

9039	i.	Sadie Ann[14] **Whipple**[1460] 9 February 1981.
9040	ii.	Bailey Kay **Whipple**[1461] 2 March 1983.

7595. **Russell Guy**[13] **Whipple** (Sherman Guy[12], Charles Clifford[11], Cephus Galusha[10], Samuel Elijah[9], Ithamar[8], Rev. Benjamin[7], Benjamin[6], Francis[5], Jonathan[4], Joseph[3], Matthew[2], Matthew[1])[1462] was born in San Carlos, San Mateo Co., Calif. 4 July 1949 and married twice. (1) **Pamela Anne Peck** in San Mateo, San Mateo, Co., Calif. 14 February 1969. She was born 16 July 1950. (2) **Kathleen Anne Casseday** in Reno, Washoe Co., Nev. 14 June 1985. She was born in Walla Walla, Walla Walla Co., Wash. 25 July 1953.[1463]

Russell Guy **Whipple** and Pamela Anne **Peck** had the following child born in Mineral Wells, Palo Pinto Co., Texas:

9041	i.	Jessie Sherman[14] **Whipple**[1464] 16 August 1969.

Russell Guy **Whipple** and Kathleen Anne **Casseday** had the following child born in Walla Walla:

9042	ii.	William Wayne **Whipple**[1465] 30 September 1989.

7596. **Nan Celeste**[13] **Whipple** (Sherman Guy[12], Charles Clifford[11], Cephus Galusha[10], Samuel Elijah[9], Ithamar[8], Rev. Benjamin[7], Benjamin[6], Francis[5], Jonathan[4], Joseph[3], Matthew[2], Matthew[1])[1466] was born in San Carlos, San Mateo Co., Calif. 4 March 1952 and married **Frederick Gordon Wilkinson** there in 1974. He was born in Detroit, Wayne Co., Mich. 5 March 1951 and died 29 August 1996 in Pioneer, Amador Co., Calif., at 45 years of age.[1467]

Nan Celeste **Whipple** and Frederick Gordon **Wilkinson** had the following children:

 9043 i. Adam Matthew[14] **Wilkinson**[1468] born in South Lake Tahoe, Placer Co., Calif. 12 March 1975 and married Amanda Belle **Van Vleck** in Pioneer 27 June 1998.

 9044 ii. Kelly Celeste **Wilkinson**[1469] born in Jackson, Amador Co. 19 September 1979.

7597. **Charles Ralph**[13] **Whipple** (Sherman Guy[12], Charles Clifford[11], Cephus Galusha[10], Samuel Elijah[9], Ithamar[8], Rev. Benjamin[7], Benjamin[6], Francis[5], Jonathan[4], Joseph[3], Matthew[2], Matthew[1])[1470] was born in San Carlos, San Mateo Co., Calif. 7 April 1956 and married **Charlotte Elizabeth Cowans** in Sunnyvale, Santa Clara Co., Calif. 10 September 1983. She was born in Oakland, Alameda Co., Calif. 19 February 1960.

Charles Ralph **Whipple** and Charlotte Elizabeth **Cowans** had the following children born in Redding, Shasta Co., Calif:

 9045 i. Kalie Jane[14] **Whipple**[1471] 4 June 1989.
 9046 ii. Russell Charles **Whipple**[1472] 30 July 1991.
 9047 iii. Wyatt William **Whipple**[1473] 12 April 1995.

7598. **Scott Lawrence**[13] **Whipple** (Lawrence Jerome[12], Charles Clifford[11], Cephus Galusha[10], Samuel Elijah[9], Ithamar[8], Rev. Benjamin[7], Benjamin[6], Francis[5], Jonathan[4], Joseph[3], Matthew[2], Matthew[1])[1474] was born in Honolulu, Oahu, Hawaii 17 May 1962 and married **Gail Atkinson**.

Scott Lawrence **Whipple** and Gail **Atkinson** had the following children born in Hawaii:

 9048 i. Ellis Ryan[14] **Whipple**[1475] 21 December 1994.
 9049 ii. Zachary Jordan **Whipple**[1476] 12 December 1996.

7603. **Barbara Starr**[13] **Brandt** (Sara Leigh[12] **Symons**, Mary Etta[11] **Bills**, George Dudley[10], Daniel F.[9], Elizabeth[8] **Whipple**, Rev. Benjamin[7], Benjamin[6], Francis[5], Jonathan[4], Joseph[3], Matthew[2], Matthew[1])[1477] was born in Aurora, Arapahoe Co., Colo. in 1942 and married **Richard Corwin Davis**.

Barbara Starr **Brandt** and Richard Corwin **Davis** had the following children:
- 9050 i. Shelia M.[14] **Davis**[1478] born 19 February 1971.
- 9051 ii. Jeffrey Garth **Davis**[1479] born 25 September 1976.
- 9052 iii. Rachelle Wendolyn **Davis**[1480] born 25 August 1979.

7604. **Barry Griffith**[13] **Brandt** (Sara Leigh[12] **Symons**, Mary Etta[11] **Bills**, George Dudley[10], Daniel F.[9], Elizabeth[8] **Whipple**, Rev. Benjamin[7], Benjamin[6], Francis[5], Jonathan[4], Joseph[3], Matthew[2], Matthew[1])[1481] was born in Park Ridge, Cook Co., Ill. 16 September 1951 and married **Rosina Miranda** 9 September 1978.

Barry Griffith **Brandt** and Rosina **Miranda** had the following children:
- 9053 i. Kathleen Danielle[14] **Brandt**[1482] born 19 December 1981.
- 9054 ii. Benjamin Joseph **Brandt**[1483] born 28 July 1986.

7605. **Julia Carol**[13] **Brandt** (Sara Leigh[12] **Symons**, Mary Etta[11] **Bills**, George Dudley[10], Daniel F.[9], Elizabeth[8] **Whipple**, Rev. Benjamin[7], Benjamin[6], Francis[5], Jonathan[4], Joseph[3], Matthew[2], Matthew[1])[1484] was born in Park Ridge, Cook Co., Ill. 14 December 1954 and married twice. (1) **Eric Anderson** 15 May 1982. (2) **Edmundo Tuevedo**.

Julia Carol **Brandt** and Edmundo **Tuevedo** had the following children:
- 9055 i. Sally Carmina[14] **Tuevedo**[1485] born 22 August 1995.
- 9056 ii. Edmundo Emiliando **Tuevedo**[1486] born 16 April 1996.

7612. **Leslie Claire**[13] **Whipple** (Gregory Booth[12], Carlton Gregory[11], Cyrus Hanchett[10], Solomon[9], David[8], Rev. Benjamin[7], Benjamin[6], Francis[5], Jonathan[4], Joseph[3], Matthew[2], Matthew[1])[1487] was born in Oak Park Cook Co., Ill. 26 December 1935 and married twice. (1) **Samuel Lewis** in Newton, Middlesex Co., Mass. 21 January 1956. Samuel,[1488] son of Harry **Lewis** and Jane **Reed**, was born in Meriden, Sullivan Co., N. H. 5 February 1930. They were divorced in Long Beach, Los Angeles Co., Calif. 7 March 1962. (2) **Harry Elmer Knowles Jr.** in Los Angeles, Los Angeles Co., Calif. 6 September 1969. Harry,[1489] son of Harry Elmer **Knowles** and Margaret Ethel **Amis**, was born in Tulsa, Tulsa Co., Okla. 23 March 1929.

Leslie Claire **Whipple** and Samuel **Lewis** had the following children:
+ 9057 i. Robin[14] **Lewis** born 5 December 1957.
   9058 ii. Wendy **Lewis**[1490] born in San Diego, San Diego Co., Calif. 1 July 1959 and married Michael **Mosley** in Rancho Santa Fe, Los Angeles Co., Calif. 30 May 1998.

7619. **Irwin Carl**[13] **Krueger Jr.** (Gertrude[12] **Stuntz**, Minnie Margie[11] **Goodenow**, Arminda Rose[10] **Deriar**, Fannie[9] **Whipple**, Jonathan[8], Rev. Benjamin[7], Benjamin[6], Francis[5], Jonathan[4], Joseph[3], Matthew[2], Matthew[1])[1491] was born in Erie, Erie Co., Penn. 19 July 1928 and married **Sophie Hedwig Werner** in Fort Wayne, Allen Co., Ind. 20 December 1958. She was born in Hackensack, Bergen Co., N. J. 11 January 1932.[1492]

Irwin Carl **Krueger** Jr. and Sophie Hedwig **Werner** had the following children:
   9059 i. Frederick Irwin[14] **Krueger**[1493] born 31 October 1959.
   9060 ii. Paul Gregory **Krueger**[1494] born in Fort Wayne 20 January 1962 and married Cheryl Denise **Baxter** in Indianapolis, Marion Co., Ind. 27 February 1999. She was born in Indianapolis 11 November 1969.[1495]
   9061 iii. Philip Jonathan **Krueger**[1496] born 11 July 1963.
   9062 iv. Heidi Elizabeth **Krueger**[1497] born 13 August 1965.
   9063 v. John Allen **Krueger**[1498] born 26 July 1967.
   9064 vi. Jason Charles **Krueger**[1499] born 8 May 1969.

7627. **Janet Yvonne**[13] **Potter** (Freda Grant[12] **Herrick**, Orlan Milo[11], Albert Eugene[10], Berthier H.[9], Melinda[8] **Whipple**, Moses[7], Capt. Thomas[6], Francis[5], Jonathan[4], Joseph[3], Matthew[2], Matthew[1])[1500] was born in Oxford, Orange Co., N.Y. 4 April 1933 and married **Wayne Douglas Williams** 15 July 1951.

Janet Yvonne **Potter** and Wayne Douglas **Williams** had the following children:
   9065 i. Wayne Douglas[14] **Williams** Jr.[1501] born in Oxford 14 April 1952.
+ 9066 ii. Karen Yvonne **Williams** born 21 December 1953.
   9067 iii. Marty Lee **Williams**[1502] born in Oxford 11 March 1955.
+ 9068 iv. Gregg Paul **Williams** born 1 December 1958.
   9069 v. Scott Allan **Williams**[1503] born in Cortland, Tompkins Co., N. Y. 19 August 1960 and married Diane S. (__).
+ 9070 vi. Donna Jean **Williams** born 12 April 1962.
+ 9071 vii. Sheli Ann **Williams** born 12 September 1966.

7633. **William Dee**[13] **Bryant** (Joyce Marie[12] **Olson**, Hazel Marie[11] **Bisbee**, George Ensign[10], Martha Melissa[9] **Herrick**, Melinda[8] **Whipple**, Moses[7], Capt. Thomas[6], Francis[5], Jonathan[4], Joseph[3], Matthew[2], Matthew[1])[1504] was born in Lehigh, Webster Co., Iowa 25 December 1939 and married **Dorothy Peterson** in S. Dak. abt 1959.

William Dee **Bryant** and Dorothy **Peterson** had the following children:

    9072 i. Cynthia[14] **Bryant**[1505] born in Fort Dodge, Webster Co., Iowa 14 January 1960.

    9073 ii. William Joseph **Bryant**[1506] born in Iowa City, Johnson Co., Iowa 11 October 1962 and married Kimberly (__) in Carmel, Monterey Co., Calif. 26 November 1994.

7634. **Jolene Marie**[13] **Bryant** (Joyce Marie[12] **Olson**, Hazel Marie[11] **Bisbee**, George Ensign[10], Martha Melissa[9] **Herrick**, Melinda[8] **Whipple**, Moses[7], Capt. Thomas[6], Francis[5], Jonathan[4], Joseph[3], Matthew[2], Matthew[1])[1507] was born in Lehigh, Webster Co., Iowa 11 December 1942 and married twice. (1) **Richard Alan Alper**. (2) **Steven Andrew Davis** in San Antonio, Bexar Co., Tex. 16 April 1979.

Jolene Marie **Bryant** and Steven Andrew **Davis** had the following children:

    9074 i. Bryant David[14] **Davis**[1508] born in San Francisco, San Francisco Co., Calif. 14 April 1981.

    9075 ii. Suzanne Joyce **Davis**[1509] born 1 September 1983.

7635. **Lois Irene**[13] **Perkins** (Glenn Alonzo[12], Manson Burdell[11], Marissa Parmelia[10] **Dean**, Martha Putnam[9] **Whipple**, Duick[8], Charles[7], Francis[6], Francis[5], Jonathan[4], Joseph[3], Matthew[2], Matthew[1])[1510] was born in Lyndon, Cattaraugus Co., N. Y. 20 June 1911 and married **Rev. Lavern Charles Reinhold** in Franklinville, Cattaraugus Co., N. Y. 17 October 1931. Lavern,[1511] son of Johann Edward **Reinhold** and Emilie Mathilde **Riemer**, was born in Saxonburg, Butler Co., Penn. 12 June 1905 and died 26 May 1980 in Rochester, Monroe Co., N.Y., at 74 years of age. Lavern was an ordained Minister of the Free Methodist church.

Lois Irene **Perkins** and Rev. Lavern Charles **Reinhold** had the following children:

  + 9076 i. Laverna Ann[14] **Reinhold** born 15 August 1932.
  + 9077 ii. Victor Eugene **Reinhold** born 8 September 1933.
  + 9078 iii. Faith Lee **Reinhold** born 3 February 1939.
  + 9079 iv. Edward John **Reinhold** born 5 May 1940.

7636. **Burdell**[13] **Perkins** (Glenn Alonzo[12], Manson Burdell[11], Marissa Parmelia[10] **Dean**, Martha Putnam[9] **Whipple**, Duick[8], Charles[7], Francis[6], Francis[5], Jonathan[4], Joseph[3], Matthew[2], Matthew[1])[1512] was born in Farmersville Station, Cattaraugus Co., N. Y. 31 March 1913 and married **Charlene Veth**.

Burdell **Perkins** and Charlene **Veth** had the following children:
- 9080 i. Glenn[14] **Perkins**.[1513]
- 9081 ii. Rinske **Perkins**.[1514]

7638. **Blanche Elizabeth**[13] **Perkins** (Glenn Alonzo[12], Manson Burdell[11], Marissa Parmelia[10] **Dean**, Martha Putnam[9] **Whipple**, Duick[8], Charles[7], Francis[6], Francis[5], Jonathan[4], Joseph[3], Matthew[2], Matthew[1])[1515] was born in Farmersville Station, Cattaraugus Co., N.Y. 11 October 1917 and married **Charles Oliver Causey**.

Blanche Elizabeth **Perkins** and Charles Oliver **Causey** had the following children:
- 9082 i. Charles Oliver[14] **Causey** Jr.[1516]
- 9083 ii. Grady **Causey**.[1517]
- 9084 iii. Lorenda **Causey**.[1518]
- 9085 iv. Kimberly **Causey**.[1519]

7640. **Guy Andrew**[13] **Perkins** (Glenn Alonzo[12], Manson Burdell[11], Marissa Parmelia[10] **Dean**, Martha Putnam[9] **Whipple**, Duick[8], Charles[7], Francis[6], Francis[5], Jonathan[4], Joseph[3], Matthew[2], Matthew[1])[1520] was born 20 September 1921 and married **Ilene Donaldson** who was born in Helena, Lewis and Clark Co., Mont.

Guy Andrew **Perkins** and Ilene **Donaldson** had the following child:
- 9086 i. Guy Andrew[14] **Perkins** Jr.[1521] born in Parma Center, Monroe Co., N. Y.

7641. **Marjorie Ruth**[13] **Perkins** (Glenn Alonzo[12], Manson Burdell[11], Marissa Parmelia[10] **Dean**, Martha Putnam[9] **Whipple**, Duick[8], Charles[7], Francis[6], Francis[5], Jonathan[4], Joseph[3], Matthew[2], Matthew[1])[1522] was born 12 February 1927 and died in 1982 in Reno, Washoe Co., Nev. at 55 years of age. She married **Hale Bennett**.

Marjorie Ruth **Perkins** and Hale **Bennett** had the following child:
- 9087 i. Lyndee[14] **Bennett**.[1523]

7661. **John Howard**[13] **Gallop** (Ruth Ann[12] **Doyle**, Charlotte Louise[11] **Hopkins**, Laura Edna[10] **Whipple**, Eugene Warner[9], Warner Wright[8], Levi[7], Francis[6], Francis[5], Jonathan[4], Joseph[3], Matthew[2], Matthew[1])[1524] was born in Oak Park Cook Co., Ill. 14 May 1962 and married **Jacqueline de Haas** in Austin, Travis Co., Tex. 20 June 1987. Jacqueline,[1525] daughter of George Duncan **de Haas** and Pierina **Anselome**, was born in Reno, Washoe Co., Nev. 17 October 1964.

John Howard **Gallop** and Jacqueline **de Haas** had the following children born in Austin:

    9088 i. Ariel Rachel[14] **Gallop**[1526] 7 September 1990.
    9089 ii. Marina Erin **Gallop**[1527] 28 February 1994.
    9090 iii. Max Christian **Gallop**[1528] 5 September 1997.

7662. **Stuart James**[13] **Gallop** (Ruth Ann[12] **Doyle**, Charlotte Louise[11] **Hopkins**, Laura Edna[10] **Whipple**, Eugene Warner[9], Warner Wright[8], Levi[7], Francis[6], Francis[5], Jonathan[4], Joseph[3], Matthew[2], Matthew[1])[1529] was born in Oak Park Cook Co., Ill. 19 October 1963 and married **Cynthia Brown** in Austin, Travis Co., Tex. 25 August 1990. Cynthia,[1530] daughter of Louis **Brown** and Bobbie Carol **Collins**, was born in Nurenburg, Germany 8 December 1966.

Stuart James **Gallop** and Cynthia **Brown** had the following children born in Toms River, Ocean Co., N. J.:

    9091 i. Kyle Elaine[14] **Gallop**[1531] 5 November 1993.
    9092 ii. Riley James **Gallop**[1532] 5 July 1997.

7663. **Thomas Luke**[13] **Gallop** (Ruth Ann[12] **Doyle**, Charlotte Louise[11] **Hopkins**, Laura Edna[10] **Whipple**, Eugene Warner[9], Warner Wright[8], Levi[7], Francis[6], Francis[5], Jonathan[4], Joseph[3], Matthew[2], Matthew[1])[1533] was born in Oak Park Cook Co., Ill. 7 July 1965 and married **Michelle Ann Hubner** in Wheaton, DuPage Co., Ill. 22 September 1990. Michelle,[1534] daughter of Thomas **Hubner** and Karen **Furlong**, was born 28 April 1966.

Thomas Luke **Gallop** and Michelle Ann **Hubner** had the following children:

    9093 i. Zachary Thomas[14] **Gallop**[1535] born in Elmhurst, DuPage Co., Ill. 16 January 1995.
    9094 ii. Lindsey Ann **Gallop**[1536] born in Toms River, Ocean Co., N. J. 18 March 1998.

7664. **David Andrew**[13] **Gallop** (Ruth Ann[12] **Doyle**, Charlotte Louise[11] **Hopkins**, Laura Edna[10] **Whipple**, Eugene Warner[9], Warner Wright[8], Levi[7], Francis[6], Francis[5], Jonathan[4], Joseph[3], Matthew[2], Matthew[1])[1537] was born in Oak Park Cook Co., Ill. 28 May 1969 and married **Susan Fox** in Wais,[1538] Mo. 2 July 1994. Susan,[1539] daughter of Thomas **Fox** and Jean **Engler**, was born 22 September 1965.

David Andrew **Gallop** and Susan **Fox** had the following child:
    9095   i.   Sydney Tyler[14] **Gallop**[1540] born 23 February 1997.

7666. **Douglas Lee**[13] **Doyle** (Thomas Luke[12], Charlotte Louise[11] **Hopkins**, Laura Edna[10] **Whipple**, Eugene Warner[9], Warner Wright[8], Levi[7], Francis[6], Francis[5], Jonathan[4], Joseph[3], Matthew[2], Matthew[1])[1541] was born in Evanston, Cook Co., Ill. 14 December 1965 and married **Maria Marcolini** in Chicago Heights, Cook Co., Ill. 1 July 1995. Maria,[1542] daughter of Vince **Marcolini** and Rose (__), was born in Chicago Heights 19 April 1968.

Douglas Lee **Doyle** had the following child born in Chicago Heights:
    9096   i.   Jessica Marie[14] **Doyle**[1543] 31 January 1990.

Douglas Lee **Doyle** and Maria **Marcolini** had the following child:
    9097   ii.   Melanie Rose **Doyle**[1544] born 30 June 1998.

7671. **Wendy Elizabeth**[13] **Tasker** (Julianne Whipple[12] **Bing**, Mary Allen[11] **Whipple**, Dr. Allen Oldfather[10], Rev. William Levi[9], Francis Rice[8], Levi[7], Francis[6], Francis[5], Jonathan[4], Joseph[3], Matthew[2], Matthew[1])[1545] was born 10 June 1965 and married **Paul Babb** 19 December 1987.

Wendy Elizabeth **Tasker** and Paul **Babb** had the following child born in Thousand Oaks, Ventura Co., Calif:
    9098   i.   Lilli Julianne[14] **Babb**[1546] 21 June 1994.

7676. **Edward Michael**[13] **Powers** (Edward Nichols[12], Luva Marion[11] **Nichols**, Bertrand Fayette[10], Catherine[9] **Whipple**, Joel[8], Edmund Rice[7], Jonathan[6], Edwards[5], Jonathan[4], Joseph[3], Matthew[2], Matthew[1])[1547] was born in Springfield, Hampden Co., Mass. 22 June 1945 and married twice. (1) **Joan DeAnglis** in New Hampshire 23 June 1968. (2) **Barbara Ann Pacheco** in New Hampshire 13 July 1985.

Edward Michael **Powers** and Joan **DeAnglis** had the following child:
    9099   i.   Stephanie Joan[14] **Powers**[1548] born 19 September 1969 and married Randy **Walsh** in New Hampshire 29 June 1996.

7677. **June Marie**[13] **Powers** (Edward Nichols[12], Luva Marion[11] **Nichols**, Bertrand Fayette[10], Catherine[9] **Whipple**, Joel[8], Edmund Rice[7], Jonathan[6], Edwards[5], Jonathan[4], Joseph[3], Matthew[2], Matthew[1])[1549] was born in Ludlow, Hampden Co., Mass. 24 June 1946 and died 30 June 1990 in Las Vegas, Clark Co., Nev., at 44 years of age. She married twice. (1) **Kenneth Broughear** in Chicopee Falls, Hampden Co., Mass. 10 September 1965. (2) **Gordon Baccus** in 1976. Buried as June Marie Powers.

June Marie **Powers** and Kenneth **Broughear** had the following child:
+   9100   i.   Dale[14] **Broughear** born 12 May 1970.

7679. **Patricia Ann**[13] **Tucker** (Shirley Luva[12] **Powers**, Luva Marion[11] **Nichols**, Bertrand Fayette[10], Catherine[9] **Whipple**, Joel[8], Edmund Rice[7], Jonathan[6], Edwards[5], Jonathan[4], Joseph[3], Matthew[2], Matthew[1])[1550] was born in Springfield, Hampden Co., Mass. 20 November 1953 and married **John Powers** in Chicopee, Hampden Co., Mass. 15 January 1972.

Patricia Ann **Tucker** and John **Powers** had the following children:
   9101   i.   John William[14] **Powers**[1551] born 19 October 1974.
   9102   ii.   Michael Patrick **Powers**[1552] born 1 March 1976.

7680. **Jacqueline Lee**[13] **Tucker** (Shirley Luva[12] **Powers**, Luva Marion[11] **Nichols**, Bertrand Fayette[10], Catherine[9] **Whipple**, Joel[8], Edmund Rice[7], Jonathan[6], Edwards[5], Jonathan[4], Joseph[3], Matthew[2], Matthew[1])[1553] was born in Springfield, Hampden Co., Mass. 22 August 1955 and married **Stephen Goldwaite** 2 June 1979.

Jacqueline Lee **Tucker** and Stephen **Goldwaite** had the following children born in Manchester, Hartford Co., Conn.:
   9103   i.   Sean Henry[14] **Goldwaite**[1554] 22 October 1984.
   9104   ii.   Daniel Stephen **Goldwaite**[1555] 20 October 1988.
   9105   iii.   Kevin Richard **Goldwaite**[1556] 17 October 1990.

7681. **Susan**[13] **Tucker** (Shirley Luva[12] **Powers**, Luva Marion[11] **Nichols**, Bertrand Fayette[10], Catherine[9] **Whipple**, Joel[8], Edmund Rice[7], Jonathan[6], Edwards[5], Jonathan[4], Joseph[3], Matthew[2], Matthew[1])[1557] was born in Springfield, Hampden Co., Mass. 11 April 1958 and married **James Mathews**.

Susan **Tucker** and James **Mathews** had the following children:
   9106   i.   Jason[14] **Mathews**[1558] born 13 April 1975.
   9107   ii.   Shannon **Mathews**[1559] born in 1978 and died 7 January 1981 at 2 years of age.

9108   iii.   Cynthia **Mathews**[1560] born in Springfield 15 May 1983.

7683. Margaret[13] **Powers** (William Roy[12], Luva Marion[11] **Nichols**, Bertrand Fayette[10], Catherine[9] **Whipple**, Joel[8], Edmund Rice[7], Jonathan[6], Edwards[5], Jonathan[4], Joseph[3], Matthew[2], Matthew[1])[1561] was born in Plainfield, Union Co., N. J. and married **William Lasure**.

Margaret **Powers** and William **Lasure** had the following child:
9109   i.   Keith[14] **Lasure**[1562] born in 1980 and died 10 December 1997 due to an automobile accident in Portland, Cumberland Co., Maine, at 17 years of age.

7684. Frances[13] **Powers** (William Roy[12], Luva Marion[11] **Nichols**, Bertrand Fayette[10], Catherine[9] **Whipple**, Joel[8], Edmund Rice[7], Jonathan[6], Edwards[5], Jonathan[4], Joseph[3], Matthew[2], Matthew[1])[1563] was born in Bangor, Penobscot Co., Maine 8 December 1949 and married **Harold Hudson**.

Frances **Powers** and Harold **Hudson** had the following children born in Bangor:
9110   i.   Heather[14] **Hudson**[1564] 23 May 1971 and died 23 November 1979 due to an automblie accident, at 8 years of age.
9111   ii.   Erica **Hudson**[1565] 21 August 1974.

7685. Michael[13] **Powers** (William Roy[12], Luva Marion[11] **Nichols**, Bertrand Fayette[10], Catherine[9] **Whipple**, Joel[8], Edmund Rice[7], Jonathan[6], Edwards[5], Jonathan[4], Joseph[3], Matthew[2], Matthew[1])[1566] was born 15 November 1951 and married **Delica Ann Swett** 20 February 1971.

Michael **Powers** and Delica Ann **Swett** had the following children:
9112   i.   Lucinda Joy[14] **Powers**[1567] born in Booth Town, Bay Harbor Co., Maine 14 October 1972.
9113   ii.   Joan Lynne **Powers**[1568] born in Homestead, Miami Dade Co., Fla. 26 September 1977.
9114   iii. Raymond Mathew **Powers**[1569] born at RAF Lakenheath, England 6 January 1989.

7686. William Keith[13] **Powers** (William Roy[12], Luva Marion[11] **Nichols**, Bertrand Fayette[10], Catherine[9] **Whipple**, Joel[8], Edmund Rice[7], Jonathan[6], Edwards[5], Jonathan[4], Joseph[3], Matthew[2], Matthew[1])[1570] was born in Plainfield, Union Co., N. J. 13 October 1956 and married **Mary Strickland** in Bangor, Penobscot Co., Maine 10 June 1978.

{ G 1339 }

William Keith **Powers** and Mary **Strickland** had the following children:
- 9115 i. David[14] **Powers**[1571] born 2 April 1980.
- 9116 ii. Heather **Powers**[1572] born in Bangor 5 May 1982.
- 9117 iii. Jessica **Powers**[1573] born in Phoenixville, Chester Co., Penn. 8 July 1986.

7687. **Kurt Roy**[13] **Powers** (Roy Clifford[12], Luva Marion[11] **Nichols**, Bertrand Fayette[10], Catherine[9] **Whipple**, Joel[8], Edmund Rice[7], Jonathan[6], Edwards[5], Jonathan[4], Joseph[3], Matthew[2], Matthew[1])[1574] was born in Springfield, Hampden Co., Mass. 29 December 1950 and married **Frances Marion Seed** in New Bedford, Bristol Co., Mass. 27 April 1973. Frances,[1575] daughter of Edward **Seed** and Marion **Jarvis**, was born in Acushnet, Bristol Co., Mass. 14 October 1952.

Kurt Roy **Powers** and Frances Marion **Seed** had the following children:
- 9118 i. Jonathan Kurt[14] **Powers**[1576] born in Dover Township., Tom's River, Ocean Co., N. J. 13 January 1976.
- 9119 ii. Erin Frances **Powers**[1577] born in Hackettstown, Warren Co., N.J. 4 February 1979.
- 9120 iii. Sara Marion **Powers**[1578] born in Hackettstown 7 May 1983.

7688. **Mark Rodney**[13] **Powers** (Roy Clifford[12], Luva Marion[11] **Nichols**, Bertrand Fayette[10], Catherine[9] **Whipple**, Joel[8], Edmund Rice[7], Jonathan[6], Edwards[5], Jonathan[4], Joseph[3], Matthew[2], Matthew[1])[1579] was born in Springfield, Hampden Co., Mass. 9 February 1955 and married twice. (1) **Amy Elizabeth Koetsch** in Springfield 15 September 1978. Amy,[1580] daughter of Raymond **Koetsch** and Patricia **Morgan**, was born in Springfield 14 August 1959. (2) **Kathleen Addison** in Springfield 2 August 1992. Kathleen,[1581] daughter of James **Addison** and Roberta **Manning**, was born in Springfield 13 September 1958.

Mark Rodney **Powers** and Amy Elizabeth **Koetsch** had the following children born in Springfield:
- 9121 i. Jodi Lynn[14] **Powers**[1582] 15 May 1981.
- 9122 ii. Karin Anne **Powers**[1583] 29 April 1983.

7689. **Brenda Luise**[13] **Powers** (Robert Alfred[12], Luva Marion[11] **Nichols**, Bertrand Fayette[10], Catherine[9] **Whipple**, Joel[8], Edmund Rice[7], Jonathan[6], Edwards[5], Jonathan[4], Joseph[3], Matthew[2], Matthew[1])[1584] was born in Springfield, Hampden Co., Mass. 14 October 1959 and married **Pierre Besette** in Hampden, Hampden Co., Mass. 1 August 1981.

Brenda Luise **Powers** and Pierre **Besette** had the following children:
    9123   i.   Jenifer Marie[14] **Besette**[1585] born 27 January 1987.
    9124   ii.   Michael Daniel **Besette**[1586] born at Griffis AFB, N.Y. 30 July 1987.

7690. **Rhoda Lee**[13] **Powers** (Robert Alfred[12], Luva Marion[11] **Nichols**, Bertrand Fayette[10], Catherine[9] **Whipple**, Joel[8], Edmund Rice[7], Jonathan[6], Edwards[5], Jonathan[4], Joseph[3], Matthew[2], Matthew[1])[1587] was born in Springfield, Hampden Co., Mass. 27 December 1961 and married **Nathan Crowell** in Ludlow, Hampden Co., Mass. 25 July 1987.

Rhoda Lee **Powers** and Nathan **Crowell** had the following children born in Springfield:
    9125   i.   Seth Clinton[14] **Crowell**[1588] 21 November 1992.
    9126   ii.   Emily Luva **Crowell**[1589] 13 September 1995.

7691. **Robert Lewis**[13] **Powers** (Robert Alfred[12], Luva Marion[11] **Nichols**, Bertrand Fayette[10], Catherine[9] **Whipple**, Joel[8], Edmund Rice[7], Jonathan[6], Edwards[5], Jonathan[4], Joseph[3], Matthew[2], Matthew[1])[1590] was born in Springfield, Hampden Co., Mass. 27 December 1961 and married **Karen Alves** in Hampden, Hampden Co., Mass. 1 July 1984.

Robert Lewis **Powers** and Karen **Alves** had the following children:
    9127   i.   Robert Michael[14] **Powers**[1591] born 12 February 1985.
    9128   ii.   Lori Elizabeth **Powers**[1592] born 31 October 1991.

7699. **Leon Earl**[13] **Sadler** (Leon Delbert[12], Lillian Alice[11] **Bess**, Lillian Belle[10] **Whipple**, Charles H.[9], Solomon[8], Russell[7], Solomon[6], Joseph[5], John[4], Joseph[3], Matthew[2], Matthew[1])[1593] was born in Wellsville, Allegany Co., N.Y. 8 August 1939 and married **Gloria Jean Reny** in Salamanca, Cattaraugus Co., N.Y 4 September 1958. She is the daughter of Harold **Reny** and Frances **Newell**.

Leon Earl **Sadler** and Gloria Jean **Reny** had the following children:
    +   9129   i.   Rock Lee[14] **Sadler** born 29 October 1959.
    +   9130   ii.   Cheryle Lorilee **Sadler** born 1 June 1963.
    +   9131   iii. James Norman **Sadler** born 15 August 1964.
    +   9132   iv.   Lee Michael **Sadler** born 18 August 1965.
    +   9133   v.   Melanie Frances **Sadler** born 7 April 1969.

7700. **John Lee**[13] **Sadler** (Leon Delbert[12], Lillian Alice[11] **Bess**, Lillian Belle[10] **Whipple**, Charles H.[9], Solomon[8], Russell[7], Solomon[6], Joseph[5], John[4], Joseph[3], Matthew[2], Matthew[1])[1594] was born in Oleans, Jefferson Co., N.Y. 24 January 1954.

John Lee **Sadler** had the following children:
    9134 i. (Baby)[14] **Sadler**[1595] born in 1982.
    9135 ii. (Baby) **Sadler**[1596] born in 1983.

7701. **Shirley May**[13] **Sadler** (Lloyd Allen[12], Lillian Alice[11] **Bess**, Lillian Belle[10] **Whipple**, Charles H.[9], Solomon[8], Russell[7], Solomon[6], Joseph[5], John[4], Joseph[3], Matthew[2], Matthew[1])[1597] was born in Wellsville, Allegany Co., N.Y. 13 December 1936 and married twice. (1) **Raymond Greene** in Friendship, Allegany Co., N.Y. 15 December 1956. (2) **Gerald Buddinger** in Friendship 14 June 1997.

Shirley May **Sadler** and Raymond **Greene** had the following children:
+   9136 i. Randall Raymond[14] **Greene** born 9 January 1959.
+   9137 ii. Michelle Louise **Greene** born 27 September 1974.

7702. **Beverly Jean**[13] **Sadler** (Lloyd Allen[12], Lillian Alice[11] **Bess**, Lillian Belle[10] **Whipple**, Charles H.[9], Solomon[8], Russell[7], Solomon[6], Joseph[5], John[4], Joseph[3], Matthew[2], Matthew[1])[1598] was born in Wellsville, Allegany Co., N.Y. 7 November 1937 and married **Wayne Oliver** in Wellsville abt 1955.

Beverly Jean **Sadler** and Wayne **Oliver** had the following children born in Bolivar, Allegany Co., N. Y.:
    9138 i. Steven[14] **Oliver**[1599] 18 January 1956.
    9139 ii. Kathy Ann **Oliver**[1600] 10 April 1958.

7703. **Connie Ann**[13] **Sadler** (Lloyd Allen[12], Lillian Alice[11] **Bess**, Lillian Belle[10] **Whipple**, Charles H.[9], Solomon[8], Russell[7], Solomon[6], Joseph[5], John[4], Joseph[3], Matthew[2], Matthew[1])[1601] was born in Wellsville, Allegany Co., N.Y. 30 September 1939 and married **Richard Wolfgang** in Wellsville abt 1955.

Connie Ann **Sadler** and Richard **Wolfgang** had the following children born in Cuba, Allegany Co., N. Y.:
    9140 i. Tammy Sue[14] **Wolfgang**[1602] 15 January 1956.
    9141 ii. Lori **Wolfgang**[1603] 4 July 1957.
    9142 iii. Michael **Wolfgang**[1604] in 1958.

7704. **Judy Kay**[13] **Sadler** (Lloyd Allen[12], Lillian Alice[11] **Bess**, Lillian Belle[10] **Whipple**, Charles H.[9], Solomon[8], Russell[7], Solomon[6], Joseph[5], John[4], Joseph[3], Matthew[2], Matthew[1])[1605] was born in Wellsville, Allegany Co., N.Y. 8 February 1941 and married **Frank Acker** 3 December 1960.

Judy Kay **Sadler** and Frank **Acker** had the following children born in Baytown, Harris Co., Texas:

    9143 i. Kevin[14] **Acker**[1606] 19 September 1962.
    9144 ii. Daniel Frank **Acker**[1607] 27 February 1970.

7707. **Lloyd Davis**[13] **Sadler** (Lloyd Allen[12], Lillian Alice[11] **Bess**, Lillian Belle[10] **Whipple**, Charles H.[9], Solomon[8], Russell[7], Solomon[6], Joseph[5], John[4], Joseph[3], Matthew[2], Matthew[1])[1608] was born in Wellsville, Allegany Co., N.Y. 3 June 1955 and married **Deborah Marie Mines** 17 March 1975. They were divorced in 1989.

Lloyd Davis **Sadler** and Deborah Marie **Mines** had the following children:

    9145 i. Priscilla Annette[14] **Sadler**[1609] married Joseph **Stevens** 4 November 1995.
+ 9146 ii. Charity Patricia **Sadler** born 18 September 1975.

7708. **Krista Lynn**[13] **Sadler** (Lloyd Allen[12], Lillian Alice[11] **Bess**, Lillian Belle[10] **Whipple**, Charles H.[9], Solomon[8], Russell[7], Solomon[6], Joseph[5], John[4], Joseph[3], Matthew[2], Matthew[1])[1610] was born in Wellsville, Allegany Co., N.Y. 3 December 1956 and married **Robert Carney** in 1975.

Krista Lynn **Sadler** and Robert **Carney** had the following children born in Webster, Harris Co., Texas:

    9147 i. Marcia Elaine[14] **Carney**[1611] 3 January 1978.
    9148 ii. Brian Patrick **Carney**[1612] 21 August 1982.
    9149 iii. Robert Allen **Carney**[1613] 10 January 1984.

7710. **Michael Glenn**[13] **Sadler** (Fredrick Henry[12], Lillian Alice[11] **Bess**, Lillian Belle[10] **Whipple**, Charles H.[9], Solomon[8], Russell[7], Solomon[6], Joseph[5], John[4], Joseph[3], Matthew[2], Matthew[1])[1614] was born in Houston, Harris Co., Tex. 2 December 1954 and married twice. (1) **Jo Lynn Broussard** in Kilgore, Gregg Co., Tex. in 1974. (2) **Annette Helen Gracia** in Denver, Denver Co., Colo. 19 January 1985.

Michael Glenn **Sadler** and Jo Lynn **Broussard** had the following children:

    9150 i. Michael Lynn[14] **Sadler**[1615] born in Overton, Rusk Co., Tex. 2 December 1974.

9151 ii. Christina Louise **Sadler**[1616] born in Kilgore 12 March 1976.
9152 iii. Kelli Jo **Sadler**[1617] born in Kilgore 30 September 1977.

Michael Glenn **Sadler** and Annette Helen **Gracia** had the following children born in Denver:
9153 iv. Veronica Ann **Sadler**[1618] 29 July 1987.
9154 v. Lauren Ashley **Sadler**[1619] 23 October 1993.

7711. **Frederick Lee**[13] **Sadler** (Fredrick Henry[12], Lillian Alice[11] **Bess**, Lillian Belle[10] **Whipple**, Charles H.[9], Solomon[8], Russell[7], Solomon[6], Joseph[5], John[4], Joseph[3], Matthew[2], Matthew[1])[1620] was born in Wellsville, Allegany Co., N.Y. 19 February 1955 and married four times. (1) **Nadine (__)** in Bethany, Oklahoma Co., Okla. in 1974. (2) **Sharon (__)** in 1983. (3) **Annette (__)** in Denver, Denver Co., Colo. in 1996. (4) **Esther Lampin** in Denver in 1998.

Frederick Lee **Sadler** and Nadine **(__)** had the following child:
9155 i. Candace[14] **Sadler**[1621] born in Oklahoma City, Oklahoma Co., Okla. abt 1975.

Frederick Lee **Sadler** and Sharon **(__)** had the following children born in Littleton, Apapahoe Co., Colo.:
9156 ii. Frederick **Sadler**[1622] abt 1984.
9157 iii. Michael **Sadler**[1623] abt 1985.

7712. **Deborah Gail**[13] **Sadler** (Fredrick Henry[12], Lillian Alice[11] **Bess**, Lillian Belle[10] **Whipple**, Charles H.[9], Solomon[8], Russell[7], Solomon[6], Joseph[5], John[4], Joseph[3], Matthew[2], Matthew[1])[1624] was born in Wellsville, Allegany Co., N.Y. 4 February 1957 and married **Gene Vickers** in 1979.

Deborah Gail **Sadler** and Gene **Vickers** had the following children:
9158 i. Jeffrey[14] **Vickers**.[1625]
9159 ii. Aaron **Vickers**.[1626]
9160 iii. Deborah **Vickers**[1627] born in 1981.

7714. **Sandra Lisa**[13] **Sadler** (Fredrick Henry[12], Lillian Alice[11] **Bess**, Lillian Belle[10] **Whipple**, Charles H.[9], Solomon[8], Russell[7], Solomon[6], Joseph[5], John[4], Joseph[3], Matthew[2], Matthew[1])[1628] was born in Wellsville, Allegany Co., N.Y. 15 September 1961 and married three times. (1) **(__) Reese**. (2) **(__) Chano**. (3) **Tommie Noble**. Sandra and Tommie Noble had three children, names not provided.

Sandra Lisa **Sadler** and (__) **Reese** had the following child:
    9161   i.   Wendy[14] **Reese**.[1629]

Sandra Lisa **Sadler** and (__) **Chano** had the following child:
    9162   ii.   Maria **Chano**.[1630]

7715. **Robert Dale**[13] **Sadler** (Fredrick Henry[12], Lillian Alice[11] **Bess**, Lillian Belle[10] **Whipple**, Charles H.[9], Solomon[8], Russell[7], Solomon[6], Joseph[5], John[4], Joseph[3], Matthew[2], Matthew[1])[1631] was born in Wellsville, Allegany Co., N.Y. 14 June 1964 and married **Shelly (__)**.

Robert Dale **Sadler** and Shelly (__) had the following children:
    9163   i.   Megan[14] **Sadler**.[1632]
    9164   ii.   Kayla **Sadler**.[1633]

7717. **Barbara Ann**[13] **Sadler** (Everett Robert[12], Lillian Alice[11] **Bess**, Lillian Belle[10] **Whipple**, Charles H.[9], Solomon[8], Russell[7], Solomon[6], Joseph[5], John[4], Joseph[3], Matthew[2], Matthew[1])[1634] was born in St. Louis, Independence Co., Mo. 12 January 1948 and married twice. (1) **Richard Elder** in Indianapolis, Marion Co., Ind. (2) **Stephen Lawrence Carr** in Indianapolis 8 April 1972.

Barbara Ann **Sadler** and Richard **Elder** had the following child:
    9165   i.   Kristie Marie[14] **Elder**[1635] born 11 April 1967.

Barbara Ann **Sadler** and Stephen Lawrence **Carr** had the following children:
    9166   ii.   Terrence Stephen **Carr**[1636] born 31 March 1968.
    9167   iii.   Chavela Marguerite **Carr**[1637] born 20 November 1969 and married Stanton **Rye** 19 September 1998.
    9168   iv.   Andrew Ryan **Carr**[1638] born 17 February 1973.

7720. **Marsha Jean**[13] **Sadler** (Everett Robert[12], Lillian Alice[11] **Bess**, Lillian Belle[10] **Whipple**, Charles H.[9], Solomon[8], Russell[7], Solomon[6], Joseph[5], John[4], Joseph[3], Matthew[2], Matthew[1])[1639] was born in Indianapolis, Marion Co., Ind. 24 October 1954 and married **Stephen Wayne Louden** there 14 February 1973.

Marsha Jean **Sadler** and Stephen Wayne **Louden** had the following children:
    9169   i.   Joshua Nathan[14] **Louden**[1640] born 4 March 1981.
    9170   ii.   Jacob Randall **Louden**[1641] born 23 January 1985.

7721. **Craig Allen**[13] **Sadler** (Everett Robert[12], Lillian Alice[11] **Bess**, Lillian Belle[10] **Whipple**, Charles H.[9], Solomon[8], Russell[7], Solomon[6], Joseph[5], John[4], Joseph[3], Matthew[2], Matthew[1])[1642] was born in Indianapolis, Marion Co., Ind. 7 April 1959 and married **Linda Kay Garwood** there 5 June 1982.

Craig Allen **Sadler** and Linda Kay **Garwood** had the following children born in St. Louis, Independence Co., Mo.:
    9171   i.   Christopher Allen[14] **Sadler**[1643] 9 April 1985.
    9172   ii. Laura M. **Sadler**[1644] 29 July 1988.

7722. **Marilyn Kay**[13] **Sadler** (Everett Robert[12], Lillian Alice[11] **Bess**, Lillian Belle[10] **Whipple**, Charles H.[9], Solomon[8], Russell[7], Solomon[6], Joseph[5], John[4], Joseph[3], Matthew[2], Matthew[1])[1645] was born in Indianapolis, Marion Co., Ind. 15 March 1961 and married **Stephen Murrell Biro Pinoara** there abt 1981.

Marilyn Kay **Sadler** and Stephen Murrell Biro **Pinoara** had the following child:
    9173   i.   Biro[14] **Pinoara**[1646] born abt 1982.

7723. **John Lee**[13] **Nix** (Lillian Bessie[12] **Sadler**, Lillian Alice[11] **Bess**, Lillian Belle[10] **Whipple**, Charles H.[9], Solomon[8], Russell[7], Solomon[6], Joseph[5], John[4], Joseph[3], Matthew[2], Matthew[1])[1647] was born 9 January 1953 and married **Carol Jo Flannery** 15 December 1976.

John Lee **Nix** and Carol Jo **Flannery** had the following children:
    9174   i.   Michon Danielle[14] **Nix**[1648] born 10 October 1980.
    9175   ii. Melissa Lynell **Nix**[1649] born 10 October 1980.

7724. **Michael Lynn**[13] **Nix** (Lillian Bessie[12] **Sadler**, Lillian Alice[11] **Bess**, Lillian Belle[10] **Whipple**, Charles H.[9], Solomon[8], Russell[7], Solomon[6], Joseph[5], John[4], Joseph[3], Matthew[2], Matthew[1])[1650] was born 29 November 1956 and married **Rebecca Sue Cobb** 3 June 1977.

Michael Lynn **Nix** and Rebecca Sue **Cobb** had the following children:
    9176   i.   Matthew Brandon[14] **Nix**[1651] born 15 June 1979.
    9177   ii. Michael Aaron **Nix**[1652] born 26 June 1987.

7725. **Randy Jay**[13] **Nix** (Lillian Bessie[12] **Sadler**, Lillian Alice[11] **Bess**, Lillian Belle[10] **Whipple**, Charles H.[9], Solomon[8], Russell[7], Solomon[6], Joseph[5], John[4], Joseph[3], Matthew[2], Matthew[1])[1653] was born 27 June 1959 and married **Venus Lynn Pryor** 18 February 1983.

Randy Jay **Nix** and Venus Lynn **Pryor** had the following child:
    9178   i.   Kimberlee Nicole[14] **Nix**[1654] born 26 October 1988.

7726. **James Herbert**[13] **McIntyre** (Gladys Gertrude[12] **Sadler**, Lillian Alice[11] **Bess**, Lillian Belle[10] **Whipple**, Charles H.[9], Solomon[8], Russell[7], Solomon[6], Joseph[5], John[4], Joseph[3], Matthew[2], Matthew[1])[1655] was born in Fillmore, Allegany Co., N.Y. 11 January 1948 and married **Debbie Marie Jordan** in Richmond, Fort Bend Co., Tex. 16 September 1972.

James Herbert McIntyre and Debbie Marie Jordan had the following children:
 +   9179   i.   Jennifer Deanne[14] **McIntyre** born 13 June 1971.
       9180   ii.   Jeanette Marie **McIntyre**[1656] born in Pasadena, Harris Co., Tex. 1 May 1973.

7727. **Gary Dwayne**[13] **McIntyre** (Gladys Gertrude[12] **Sadler**, Lillian Alice[11] **Bess**, Lillian Belle[10] **Whipple**, Charles H.[9], Solomon[8], Russell[7], Solomon[6], Joseph[5], John[4], Joseph[3], Matthew[2], Matthew[1])[1657] was born in Borger, Hutchinson Co., Tex. 26 January 1949 and married five times. (1) **Marilyn Carol Levia**. (2) **Marilyn (__)**. (3) **Lorie (__)**. (4) **Jessica (__)** 1986. (5) **Lorrie Francis** in 1992.

Gary Dwayne **McIntyre** and Marilyn Carol **Levia** had the following children:
 +   9181   i.   Carolyn Ann[14] **McIntyre** born 28 October 1971.
 +   9182   ii.   Kelly Joanne **McIntyre** born 3 October 1974.

Gary Dwayne **McIntyre** and Jessica **(__)** had the following child:
       9183   iii. Candace Jessica **McIntyre**[1658] born 23 April 1987.

Gary Dwayne **McIntyre** and Lorrie **Francis** had the following children:
       9184   iv.   Brittany Christine **McIntyre**[1659] born 4 August 1993.
       9185   v.   Victoria Sarah **McIntyre**[1660] born 4 August 1993.

7728. **John Lee**[13] **McIntyre** (Gladys Gertrude[12] **Sadler**, Lillian Alice[11] **Bess**, Lillian Belle[10] **Whipple**, Charles H.[9], Solomon[8], Russell[7], Solomon[6], Joseph[5], John[4], Joseph[3], Matthew[2], Matthew[1])[1661] was born in Wellsville, Allegany Co., N.Y. 17 February 1950 and married **Sandra Sue Lee** in Houston, Harris Co., Tex. 8 December 1969.

John Lee **McIntyre** and Sandra Sue **Lee** had the following children:
       9186   i.   Jamie Lynn[14] **McIntyre**[1662] born 25 October 1971.
 +   9187   ii.   Holly Johnnell **McIntyre** born 18 December 1975.

  9188 iii. John Thomas **McIntyre**[1663] born 21 April 1977 and married Grace Elizabeth **Ross** 19 September 1998.

7729. Carol Ann[13] **McIntyre** (Gladys Gertrude[12] **Sadler**, Lillian Alice[11] **Bess**, Lillian Belle[10] **Whipple**, Charles H.[9], Solomon[8], Russell[7], Solomon[6], Joseph[5], John[4], Joseph[3], Matthew[2], Matthew[1])[1664] was born in Borger, Hutchinson Co., Tex. 13 April 1951 and married three times. (1) **Derrick McVaney** in Houston, Harris Co., Tex. (2) **Robert William Scott** in 1966. (3) **Robert Ernest Butcher** in Houston 15 May 1971.

Carol Ann **McIntyre** and Robert William **Scott** had the following children:
+ 9189 i. Janet Lee[14] **Scott** born 2 August 1967.
  9190 ii. Robert Andrew **Scott**[1665] born 24 December 1968.

7731. Kenneth Paul[13] **Sadler Jr.** (Kenneth Paul[12], Lillian Alice[11] **Bess**, Lillian Belle[10] **Whipple**, Charles H.[9], Solomon[8], Russell[7], Solomon[6], Joseph[5], John[4], Joseph[3], Matthew[2], Matthew[1])[1666] was born in Wellsville, Allegany Co., N.Y. 23 July 1956 and married **Sherry Renee**.

Kenneth Paul **Sadler** Jr. and Sherry **Renee** had the following child:
  9193 i. Autumn Lynn **Sadler**[1667] born 18 September 1985.

7732. Gretchen Elizabeth[13] **Sadler** (Kenneth Paul[12], Lillian Alice[11] **Bess**, Lillian Belle[10] **Whipple**, Charles H.[9], Solomon[8], Russell[7], Solomon[6], Joseph[5], John[4], Joseph[3], Matthew[2], Matthew[1])[1668] was born in Wellsville, Allegany Co., N.Y. 17 May 1958 and married **Alan Stanley Brewer** in Belfast, Allegany Co., N.Y. 8 August 1975.

Gretchen Elizabeth **Sadler** and Alan Stanley **Brewer** had the following children:
+ 9194 i. Elizabeth Lynn[14] **Brewer** born 10 January 1976.
  9195 ii. Alan David **Brewer**[1669] born in Cuba, Allegany Co., N.Y. 27 January 1977.
  9196 iii. Lucas James **Brewer**[1670] born in Cuba 5 May 1979.

7733. Daniel Enos[13] **Sadler** (Kenneth Paul[12], Lillian Alice[11] **Bess**, Lillian Belle[10] **Whipple**, Charles H.[9], Solomon[8], Russell[7], Solomon[6], Joseph[5], John[4], Joseph[3], Matthew[2], Matthew[1])[1671] was born in Cuba, Allegany Co., N.Y. 12 June 1959 and married **Deborah Sanford** 28 August 1981.

Daniel Enos **Sadler** and Deborah **Sanford** had the following children:
  9197 i. Daniel Amos[14] **Sadler**[1672] born 14 December 1982.

9198 ii. Jessica Louise **Sadler**[1673] born 12 September 1986.

7734. **Donald Leeman**[13] **Sadler** (Kenneth Paul[12], Lillian Alice[11] **Bess**, Lillian Belle[10] **Whipple**, Charles H.[9], Solomon[8], Russell[7], Solomon[6], Joseph[5], John[4], Joseph[3], Matthew[2], Matthew[1])[1674] was born in Houston, Harris Co., Tex. 14 July 1960 and married **Sandra Marie Hand** in Belmont, Franklin Co., N.Y. 26 April 1980.

Donald Leeman **Sadler** and Sandra Marie **Hand** had the following children:
9199 i. Donald Joseph[14] **Sadler**[1675] born 15 September 1982.
9200 ii. Crystal Anne **Sadler**[1676] born 17 October 1983.
9201 iii. Holly Marie **Sadler**[1677] born 1 November 1985.

7735. **Rebecca Mae**[13] **Sadler** (Kenneth Paul[12], Lillian Alice[11] **Bess**, Lillian Belle[10] **Whipple**, Charles H.[9], Solomon[8], Russell[7], Solomon[6], Joseph[5], John[4], Joseph[3], Matthew[2], Matthew[1])[1678] was born in Houston, Harris Co., Tex. 23 March 1962 and married **Kermit Lee Veasey** 24 November 1984.

Rebecca Mae **Sadler** and Kermit Lee **Veasey** had the following children:
9202 i. Karen Loving[14] **Veasey**[1679] born 18 May 1988.
9203 ii. Michael Lee **Veasey**[1680] born 17 January 1992.
9204 iii. Brandon Scott **Veasey**[1681] born 10 February 1996.

7736. **Katherine Sue**[13] **Sadler** (Kenneth Paul[12], Lillian Alice[11] **Bess**, Lillian Belle[10] **Whipple**, Charles H.[9], Solomon[8], Russell[7], Solomon[6], Joseph[5], John[4], Joseph[3], Matthew[2], Matthew[1])[1682] was born 2 August 1963 and married **Ignacio Padron** 1 January 1981.

Katherine Sue **Sadler** had the following children:
9205 i. (Son)[14] **Sadler**[1683] born 15 April 1977.
9206 ii. Heather Mae **Sadler**[1684] born in Henderson, Rusk Co., Tex. 13 December 1980.

Katherine Sue **Sadler** and Ignacio **Padron** had the following child:
9207 iii. Martha Elena **Padron**[1685] born 4 December 1983.

Katherine Sue **Sadler** and Juan **Muniz** had the following child:
9208 iv. Juanita Marie **Sadler**[1686] born in Kilgore, Gregg Co., Tex. 20 December 1984.

7737. **Mary Jane**[13] **Sadler** (Eugene Richard[12], Lillian Alice[11] **Bess**, Lillian Belle[10] **Whipple**, Charles H.[9], Solomon[8], Russell[7], Solomon[6], Joseph[5], John[4], Joseph[3], Matthew[2], Matthew[1])[1687] was born 30 April 1960 and married **Roul R. Padron** 7 December 1981.

Mary Jane **Sadler** and Roul R. **Padron** had the following children born in Longview, Gregg Co., Tex.:

 9209 i. Sue Ann[14] **Padron**[1688] 8 September 1981.
 9210 ii. Maria Lynn **Padron**[1689] 21 December 1982.

7738. **Dianna Lynn**[13] **Sadler** (Eugene Richard[12], Lillian Alice[11] **Bess**, Lillian Belle[10] **Whipple**, Charles H.[9], Solomon[8], Russell[7], Solomon[6], Joseph[5], John[4], Joseph[3], Matthew[2], Matthew[1])[1690] was born in Houston, Harris Co., Tex. 25 August 1961 and married **James Haven** in Alexandria, Rapides Parish, La. 27 August 1979.

Dianna Lynn **Sadler** and James **Haven** had the following children born in Pineville, Rapides Parish, La.:

 9211 i. Kristy Ann[14] **Haven**[1691] 6 June 1980.
 9212 ii. James Keith **Haven**[1692] 15 September 1985.

7740. **Richard Lee**[13] **Sadler** (Eugene Richard[12], Lillian Alice[11] **Bess**, Lillian Belle[10] **Whipple**, Charles H.[9], Solomon[8], Russell[7], Solomon[6], Joseph[5], John[4], Joseph[3], Matthew[2], Matthew[1])[1693] was born 8 December 1970 and married **Juanita Marie Powell** in Alexandria, Rapides Parish, La. 9 December 1995. She was previously married to (__) **Manuel** and they had sons born in Pineville, Rapides Parish, La.: Richard Wayne **Manuel**, b. 17 Aug. 1984, and Clayton Eugene **Manuel**, b. 4 Dec. 1985.[1694]

Richard Lee **Sadler** and Juanita Marie **Powell** had the following child born in Pineville:

 9213 i. Michael Lee[14] **Sadler**[1695] 30 July 1996.

7743. **Tim**[13] **Redington** (Ray[12], Mary Elizabeth[11] **Smith**, Ruby Sophronia[10] **Whipple**, William[9], Ira Martin[8], Elijah[7], Jeremiah[6], Joseph[5], John[4], Joseph[3], Matthew[2], Matthew[1])[1696] birth date unknown, married **Kathleen Langholz**.

Tim **Redington** and Kathleen **Langholz** had the following children:

 + 9214 i. Laurie[14] **Redington**.
  9215 ii. Lisa **Redington**[1697] married Ed **Boots**.

7744. **Tom**[13] **Redington** (Ray[12], Mary Elizabeth[11] **Smith**, Ruby Sophronia[10] **Whipple**, William[9], Ira Martin[8], Elijah[7], Jeremiah[6], Joseph[5], John[4], Joseph[3], Matthew[2], Matthew[1])[1698] birth date unknown.

Tom **Redington** had the following children:
- 9216 i. Tommy Ray[14] **Redington**.[1699]
- 9217 ii. Karina **Redington**.[1700]
- 9218 iii. Billy **Redington**.[1701]

7745. **Wayne**[13] **Redington** (Ray[12], Mary Elizabeth[11] **Smith**, Ruby Sophronia[10] **Whipple**, William[9], Ira Martin[8], Elijah[7], Jeremiah[6], Joseph[5], John[4], Joseph[3], Matthew[2], Matthew[1])[1702] birth date unknown, married **Anne (__)**.

Wayne **Redington** and Anne (__) had the following children:
- 9219 i. Nicole[14] **Redington**.[1703]
- 9220 ii. Daniel **Redington**.[1704]

7746. **Linda**[13] **Redington** (Ray[12], Mary Elizabeth[11] **Smith**, Ruby Sophronia[10] **Whipple**, William[9], Ira Martin[8], Elijah[7], Jeremiah[6], Joseph[5], John[4], Joseph[3], Matthew[2], Matthew[1])[1705] birth date unknown. married **(__) Birch**.

Linda **Redington** and (__) **Birch** had the following children:
- 9221 i. William[14] **Birch**.[1706]
- 9222 ii. (Daughter) **Birch**.[1707]

7759. **Jack Reed**[13] **Trimmell** (Edna Pearl[12] **Sproat**, Mary Elizabeth[11] **Smith**, Ruby Sophronia[10] **Whipple**, William[9], Ira Martin[8], Elijah[7], Jeremiah[6], Joseph[5], John[4], Joseph[3], Matthew[2], Matthew[1])[1708] was born in Coyville, Wilson Co., Kans. 15 August 1927 and married **Rose Jean Barnes**. Rose,[1709] daughter of Winnie **Barnes** and Beulah **Howard**, was born in Oklahoma in 1934.

Jack Reed **Trimmell** and Rose Jean **Barnes** had the following children:
- + 9223 i. Robert Michael[14] **Trimmell**.
- + 9224 ii. Steven Riley **Trimmell**.
- + 9225 iii. Daryl Andrew **Trimmell** born 12 April 1951.
- + 9226 iv. Jack Gregory **Trimmell** Sr. born 19 February 1955.
- + 9227 v. Brian Lewis **Trimmell** born 9 August 1956.

7760. **Harold Riley**[13] **Trimmell** (Edna Pearl[12] **Sproat**, Mary Elizabeth[11] **Smith**, Ruby Sophronia[10] **Whipple**, William[9], Ira Martin[8], Elijah[7], Jeremiah[6], Joseph[5], John[4], Joseph[3], Matthew[2], Matthew[1])[1710] was born in Wichita, Sedgwick Co., Kans. 8 October 1929 and married **Dorothy Joan Furstenburg** there 19 November 1955. She was born 3 June 1933.[1711]

Harold Riley **Trimmell** and Dorothy Joan **Furstenburg** had the following children:

+ 9228 i. Wayne Alan[14] **Trimmell** born 23 October 1956.
9229 ii. Debra Joan **Trimmell**[1712] born in Little Falls, Morrison Co., Minn. 30 March 1958 and married Rick **Parkes** in Wichita 25 May 1978.
+ 9230 iii. Diane Janel **Trimmell** born 19 January 1960.
9231 iv. Rick James **Trimmell**[1713] born in Little Falls 1 March 1962.
+ 9232 v. Ronald Dean **Trimmell** born 19 June 1964.
9233 vi. Mike L. **Trimmell**[1714] born in Hutchinson, Reno Co., Kans. 17 April 1966.
9234 vii. Brad Gene **Trimmell**[1715] born in Wichita 26 March 1968 and died there 26 October 1978, at 10 years of age. Buried in Lakeview Cemetery, Wichita.

7761. **Dorothy Margaret**[13] **Trimmell** (Edna Pearl[12] **Sproat**, Mary Elizabeth[11] **Smith**, Ruby Sophronia[10] **Whipple**, William[9], Ira Martin[8], Elijah[7], Jeremiah[6], Joseph[5], John[4], Joseph[3], Matthew[2], Matthew[1])[1716] was born 22 February 1932 and died 28 May 1995 in Wichita, Sedgwick Co., Kans., at 63 years of age. She married **Harry Cheney** in Wichita. He was born 20 August 1925 and died in June 1976 in Wichita, at 50 years of age.[1717] Both are buried in the Lakeview Cemetery, Wichita.

Dorothy Margaret **Trimmell** and Harry **Cheney** had the following child:
+ 9235 i. D. H.[14] **Cheney** born in 1954.

7762. **Joseph Donald**[13] **Trimmell** (Edna Pearl[12] **Sproat**, Mary Elizabeth[11] **Smith**, Ruby Sophronia[10] **Whipple**, William[9], Ira Martin[8], Elijah[7], Jeremiah[6], Joseph[5], John[4], Joseph[3], Matthew[2], Matthew[1])[1718] was born in Wichita, Sedgwick Co., Kans. 12 July 1934 and married **Jennie Juanita Rosa** in Compton, Los Angeles Co., Calif. 23 June 1956. Jennie,[1719] daughter of Cecil **Rosa** and Delores **Gonzales**, was born in Compton 11 July 1937. Joe served in the U.S. Navy and retired from the Boeing Co.

Joseph Donald **Trimmell** and Jennie Juanita **Rosa** had the following children:

+ 9236 i. Joseph Leonard[14] **Trimmell** born 25 November 1956.
9237 ii. Jeanette Virginia **Trimmell**[1720] born in Compton 2 January 1958.
+ 9238 iii. Theresa Yvonne **Trimmell** born 1 November 1960.
+ 9239 iv. Jerome Anthony **Trimmell** born 21 November 1961.
9240 v. Cecil Donald **Trimmell**[1721] born in Compton 26 September 1963 and died 11 August 1966 in Seattle, King Co. Wash., at 2 years of age.

7763. **Mary Lynn**[13] **Trimmell** (Edna Pearl[12] **Sproat**, Mary Elizabeth[11] **Smith**, Ruby Sophronia[10] **Whipple**, William[9], Ira Martin[8], Elijah[7], Jeremiah[6], Joseph[5], John[4], Joseph[3], Matthew[2], Matthew[1])[1722] was born in Middletown, Wilson Co., Kans. 25 May 1938 and married **Carl Moore** in Wichita, Sedgwick Co., Kans. 11 June 1956. He was born 4 October 1934.[1723]

Mary Lynn **Trimmell** and Carl **Moore** had the following children:

9241 i. David[14] **Moore**[1724] born 11 January 1957.
+ 9242 ii. Debbie **Moore** born 15 August 1958.
9243 iii. Kathie **Moore**[1725] born 9 September 1962.
+ 9244 iv. Doug **Moore** born 3 June 1964.

7764. **Younda Dee**[13] **Trimmell** (Edna Pearl[12] **Sproat**, Mary Elizabeth[11] **Smith**, Ruby Sophronia[10] **Whipple**, William[9], Ira Martin[8], Elijah[7], Jeremiah[6], Joseph[5], John[4], Joseph[3], Matthew[2], Matthew[1])[1726] was born in January 1941 and married **John Edward Floyd**[1727] son of Charles **Floyd** and Willie **Brooks**.

Younda Dee **Trimmell** and John Edward **Floyd** had the following children:

+ 9245 i. Molly Jane[14] **Floyd** born 8 November 1959.
9246 ii. Cheri Christine **Floyd**[1728] born 8 January 1961.
9247 iii. Mark Charles **Floyd**[1729] born 27 February 1963.
9248 iv. Susan Carol **Floyd**[1730] born 29 December 1965.

7765. **Maurice Wayne**[13] **Trimmell** (Edna Pearl[12] **Sproat**, Mary Elizabeth[11] **Smith**, Ruby Sophronia[10] **Whipple**, William[9], Ira Martin[8], Elijah[7], Jeremiah[6], Joseph[5], John[4], Joseph[3], Matthew[2], Matthew[1])[1731] was born in Wichita, Sedgwick Co., Kans. 8 July 1943 and married twice. (1) **Luralynn M. (__)**. (2) **Rosie Virginia Beeghly** 8 June 1963. She was born 19 January 1941.[1732] They were divorced in 1988.

Maurice Wayne **Trimmell** and Rosie Virginia **Beeghly** had the following children:

        9249   i.   Jeanett Kristin[14] **Trimmell**[1733] born 15 April 1964.
+   9250   ii.   Darryl Wayne **Trimmell** born 25 June 1965.
+   9251   iii. William Edward **Trimmell** born 31 January 1969.

7766. **Lillian Pearl**[13] **Trimmell** (Edna Pearl[12] **Sproat**, Mary Elizabeth[11] **Smith**, Ruby Sophronia[10] **Whipple**, William[9], Ira Martin[8], Elijah[7], Jeremiah[6], Joseph[5], John[4], Joseph[3], Matthew[2], Matthew[1])[1734] was born 24 October 1948 and married **Robert Dunn**.

Lillian Pearl **Trimmell** and Robert **Dunn** had the following children:

        9252   i.   Eric Brockman[14] **Dunn**.[1735]
        9253   ii.   Lacie **Dunn**.[1736]
        9254   iii. Matthew Brockman **Dunn**[1737] born 2 August 1967 and died 11 August 1996 at 29 years of age.

7767. **Mercedes Jeanette**[13] **Trimmell** (Edna Pearl[12] **Sproat**, Mary Elizabeth[11] **Smith**, Ruby Sophronia[10] **Whipple**, William[9], Ira Martin[8], Elijah[7], Jeremiah[6], Joseph[5], John[4], Joseph[3], Matthew[2], Matthew[1])[1738] was born 30 December 1950 and married twice. (1) **(__) Schrimshaw**. (2) **(__) Smith**.

Mercedes Jeanette **Trimmell** and (__) **Schrimshaw** had the following child:

        9255   i.   Aaron[14] **Schrimshaw**.[1739]

Mercedes Jeanette **Trimmell** and (__) **Smith** had the following children:

        9256   ii.   Tricia **Smith**[1740] married Jake **Walker**.
        9257   iii. Linda **Smith**[1741] and married (__) **Kennedy**.
        9258   iv. Kristi **Smith**[1742] and married Damon **Baker**.

7768. **Doyle A.**[13] **Murphy** (Mildred Elizabeth[12] **Sproat**, Mary Elizabeth[11] **Smith**, Ruby Sophronia[10] **Whipple**, William[9], Ira Martin[8], Elijah[7], Jeremiah[6], Joseph[5], John[4], Joseph[3], Matthew[2], Matthew[1])[1743] was born in Wichita, Sedgwick Co., Kans. 5 December 1931 and married three times. (1) **Nancy Lou Lehto** in Wichita 21 September 1952. (2) **Terri McDowell** 28 February 1981. (3) **Edna (__)** abt 2000.

Doyle A. **Murphy** and Nancy Lou **Lehto** had the following child:
+   9259   i.   Michael[14] **Murphy** born 12 June 1953.

Doyle A. **Murphy** and Terri **McDowell** had the following children:
- 9260 ii. Shon Doyle **Murphy**[1744] born 29 May 1981.
- 9261 iii. Erin Kathleen **Murphy**[1745] born 8 January 1985.

7769. **Donna Louise**[13] **Murphy** (Mildred Elizabeth[12] **Sproat**, Mary Elizabeth[11] **Smith**, Ruby Sophronia[10] **Whipple**, William[9], Ira Martin[8], Elijah[7], Jeremiah[6], Joseph[5], John[4], Joseph[3], Matthew[2], Matthew[1])[1746] was born in Wichita, Sedgwick Co., Kans. 18 August 1933 and married **Dean Allen Ramsey** 2 August 1952. He was born 7 October 1932 and died 26 October 2001 in Dallas, Dallas Co., Tex., at 69 years of age.[1747]

Donna Louise **Murphy** and Dean Allen **Ramsey** had the following children:
- \+ 9262 i. Karla Denise[14] **Ramsey** born 19 July 1956.
- \+ 9263 ii. Carol Ann **Ramsey** born 3 December 1960.
- \+ 9264 iii. Karen Ruth **Ramsey** born 15 January 1965.

7770. **Kathleen**[13] **Murphy** (Mildred Elizabeth[12] **Sproat**, Mary Elizabeth[11] **Smith**, Ruby Sophronia[10] **Whipple**, William[9], Ira Martin[8], Elijah[7], Jeremiah[6], Joseph[5], John[4], Joseph[3], Matthew[2], Matthew[1])[1748] was born in Wichita, Sedgwick Co., Kans. 28 May 1935 and married twice. (1) **Carl Bennett** there 12 October 1952. (2) **Mearl Edvin Whillock** 30 June 1962. He was born 29 December 1935.[1749]

Kathleen **Murphy** and Carl **Bennett** had the following children:
- \+ 9265 i. Linda Kay[14] **Bennett** born 4 February 1955.
- 9266 ii. Sandra Lee **Bennett**[1750] born in Hays, Ellis Co., Kansas 12 August 1956 and died the day after birth.
- 9267 iii. Jeffrey Robert **Bennett**[1751] born 26 June 1959 and died 17 February 1977 in Wichita., at 17 years of age.

Kathleen **Murphy** and Mearl Edvin **Whillock** had the following child:
- \+ 9268 iv. Mearl Edvin **Whillock** II born 29 September 1962.

7771. **Darrell Luther**[13] **Murphy** (Mildred Elizabeth[12] **Sproat**, Mary Elizabeth[11] **Smith**, Ruby Sophronia[10] **Whipple**, William[9], Ira Martin[8], Elijah[7], Jeremiah[6], Joseph[5], John[4], Joseph[3], Matthew[2], Matthew[1])[1752] was born in Wichita, Sedgwick Co., Kans. 23 April 1940 and married **Linda Jane Walker** in Canton, Van Zandt Co., Miss. 31 January 1957. She was born 5 September 1940.[1753]

Darrell Luther **Murphy** and Linda Jane **Walker** had the following children:

- \+ 9269 i. Debra Ann[14] **Murphy** born 7 June 1958.
- 9270 ii. Darrell Luther **Murphy**[1754] born in Wichita 9 August 1962 and died 13 March 2000, at 37 years of age.
- \+ 9271 iii. James Franklin **Murphy** born 4 March 1964.

7772. **Mary Esther**[13] **Murphy** (Mildred Elizabeth[12] **Sproat**, Mary Elizabeth[11] **Smith**, Ruby Sophronia[10] **Whipple**, William[9], Ira Martin[8], Elijah[7], Jeremiah[6], Joseph[5], John[4], Joseph[3], Matthew[2], Matthew[1])[1755] was born in Wichita, Sedgwick Co., Kans. 8 November 1942 and married **Billy Raymond Hobson** there 13 August 1960. Billy,[1756] son of Billy Mac **Hobson** and Doris **Eskridge**, was born in Ackerman, Choctaw Co., Miss. 16 May 1942.

Mary Esther **Murphy** and Billy Raymond **Hobson** had the following children:

- \+ 9272 i. Mary Christine[14] **Hobson** born 15 July 1961.
- 9273 ii. Gregory Alan **Hobson**[1757] born 25 July 1962 and died the day of birth. Buried in Wichita Park Cemetery, Wichita.
- 9274 iii. Billy Emmett **Hobson**[1758] born in Wichita 12 July 1964 and married Kathy **Keller** in St. Louis, Independence Co., Mo. 3 October 1987. She was born 1 January 1967.[1759]
- 9275 iv. Robert Lee **Hobson**[1760] born in Wichita 4 January 1966.
- \+ 9276 v. Jeanne Sue **Hobson** born 27 October 1967.
- 9277 vi. Edward Comba **Hobson**[1761] born in June 1969.
- \+ 9278 vii. Mark Andrew **Hobson** born 19 March 1971.

7773. **John Harold**[13] **Murphy** (Mildred Elizabeth[12] **Sproat**, Mary Elizabeth[11] **Smith**, Ruby Sophronia[10] **Whipple**, William[9], Ira Martin[8], Elijah[7], Jeremiah[6], Joseph[5], John[4], Joseph[3], Matthew[2], Matthew[1])[1762] was born in Wichita, Sedgwick Co., Kans. 3 January 1944 and married **Linda Susan Peters** 16 June 1962. She was born 20 November 1945.[1763]

John Harold **Murphy** and Linda Susan **Peters** had the following children:

- \+ 9279 i. John Harold[14] **Murphy** II born 2 February 1964.
- \+ 9280 ii. Jeanette Arlene **Murphy** born 12 December 1964.

7774. **Rodney Dean**[13] **Richards** (Everett Leander (Sproat)[12], Mary Elizabeth[11] **Smith**, Ruby Sophronia[10] **Whipple**, William[9], Ira Martin[8], Elijah[7], Jeremiah[6], Joseph[5], John[4], Joseph[3], Matthew[2], Matthew[1])[1764] birth date unknown, married **Bernell Sue Briles**.

Rodney Dean **Richards** and Bernell Sue **Briles** had the following children:

        9281   i.   Leon Gene[14] **Richards**.[1765]
+   9282   ii.   Clellie Dean **Richards**.
+   9283   iii. Becky Lee **Richards**.

7775. **Phyllis LaMoyne**[13] **Richards** (Everett Leander (Sproat)[12], Mary Elizabeth[11] **Smith**, Ruby Sophronia[10] **Whipple**, William[9], Ira Martin[8], Elijah[7], Jeremiah[6], Joseph[5], John[4], Joseph[3], Matthew[2], Matthew[1])[1766] birth date unknown, married **James Carl Bohling**.

Phyllis LaMoyne **Richards** and James Carl **Bohling** had the following children:

+   9284   i.   Richard Carl[14] **Bohling**.
        9285   ii.   Robert Leo **Bohling**.[1767]
+   9286   iii. Lyndia Kay **Bohling**.
+   9287   iv. Leisha Rene **Bohling**.

7776. **Deanna Kay**[13] **Richards** (Everett Leander (Sproat)[12], Mary Elizabeth[11] **Smith**, Ruby Sophronia[10] **Whipple**, William[9], Ira Martin[8], Elijah[7], Jeremiah[6], Joseph[5], John[4], Joseph[3], Matthew[2], Matthew[1])[1768] birth date unknown, married **Thomas Ray Grice**.

Deanna Kay **Richards** and Thomas Ray **Grice** had the following children:

        9288   i.   Brenda Kay[14] **Grice**.[1769]
        9289   ii.   Gary Ray **Grice**[1770] and married Tammara **Douthit**.
        9290   iii. Priscilla Ann **Grice**.[1771]

7777. **Darrell Gene**[13] **Richards** (Everett Leander (Sproat)[12], Mary Elizabeth[11] **Smith**, Ruby Sophronia[10] **Whipple**, William[9], Ira Martin[8], Elijah[7], Jeremiah[6], Joseph[5], John[4], Joseph[3], Matthew[2], Matthew[1])[1772] birth date unknown, married **Treva Henry**.

Darrell Gene **Richards** and Treva **Henry** had the following children:

        9291   i.   Jason Wade[14] **Richards**.[1773]
        9292   ii.   Jared DeWayne **Richards**.[1774]

7747. **Shiela**[13] **Redington** (Joe[12], Mary Elizabeth[11] **Smith**, Ruby Sophronia[10] **Whipple**, William[9], Ira Martin[8], Elijah[7], Jeremiah[6], Joseph[5], John[4], Joseph[3], Matthew[2], Matthew[1])[1775] birth date unknown, married **Jerry Aomodt**.

Shiela **Redington** and Jerry **Aomodt** had the following children:
- 9293 i. James[14] **Aomodt**.[1776]
- 9294 ii. Jerry **Aomodt**.[1777]

7748. **Joe**[13] **Redington Jr.** (Joe[12], Mary Elizabeth[11] **Smith**, Ruby Sophronia[10] **Whipple**, William[9], Ira Martin[8], Elijah[7], Jeremiah[6], Joseph[5], John[4], Joseph[3], Matthew[2], Matthew[1])[1778] birth date unknown, married **Pam (__)**.

Joe **Redington** Jr. and Pam (__) had the following children:
- 9295 i. Joee Ray[14] **Redington**[1779] married Melanie (__).
- + 9296 ii. Heather **Redington**.

7749. **Raymie**[13] **Redington** (Joe[12], Mary Elizabeth[11] **Smith**, Ruby Sophronia[10] **Whipple**, William[9], Ira Martin[8], Elijah[7], Jeremiah[6], Joseph[5], John[4], Joseph[3], Matthew[2], Matthew[1])[1780] birth date unknown, married twice. (1) **Barbara (__)**. (2) **Kathy (__)**.

Raymie **Redington** and Barbara (__) had the following children:
- 9297 i. Ryan[14] **Redington**[1781] married Amanda (__).
- 9298 ii. Robert **Redington**.[1782]
- 9299 iii. Raymond Roy **Redington**[1783] married Julia **Flodin**.
- 9300 iv. Lisa Rae **Redington**.[1784]

Raymie **Redington** and Kathy (__) had the following child:
- 9301 v. Vernon **Redington**.[1785]

7811. **Walter Otis**[13] **Thompson** (Robert Lee[12], Sara Jane[11] **Ward**, Ruby Sophronia[10] **Whipple**, William[9], Ira Martin[8], Elijah[7], Jeremiah[6], Joseph[5], John[4], Joseph[3], Matthew[2], Matthew[1])[1786] was born in 1963 and married twice. (1) **Debra Marie Varble** who was born in 1962.[1787] (2) **Paula Annette Newport** who was born in 1966.[1788]

Walter Otis **Thompson** and Paula Annette **Newport** had the following children:
- 9302 i. Walter Otis[14] **Thompson** Jr.[1789]
- 9303 ii. Robert Edward Newport **Thompson**.[1790]

7824. **Linda Kay**[13] **Vandenberg** (Peggy Joyce[12] **Ward**, James Eugene[11], Ruby Sophronia[10] **Whipple**, William[9], Ira Martin[8], Elijah[7], Jeremiah[6], Joseph[5], John[4], Joseph[3], Matthew[2], Matthew[1])[1791] birth date unknown, married **David Newton White II** in Fayettville, Washington Co., Ark. 19 May 1974. David is the son of David Newton **White** and Wilma **Carr**.[1792]

Linda Kay **Vandenberg** and David Newton **White** II had the following children:
    9304 i. Emily Chase[14] **White** born in Hot Springs, Garland Co,. Ark. 27 March 1988.[1793]
    9305 ii. Matthew Cooper **White** born in Mesa, Mariposa Co., Ariz. 7 May 1991.[1794]

7825. **Rene Denise**[13] **Vandenberg** (Peggy Joyce[12] **Ward**, James Eugene[11], Ruby Sophronia[10] **Whipple**, William[9], Ira Martin[8], Elijah[7], Jeremiah[6], Joseph[5], John[4], Joseph[3], Matthew[2], Matthew[1])[1795] was born in Albany, Dougherty Co., Ga. 20 July 1953 and married twice. (1) **Leonard Higgs** 28 December 1970. (2) **Joe Fred Starr** in Fayettville, Washington Co., Ark. 6 August 1982.

Rene Denise **Vandenberg** and Joe Fred **Starr** had the following child:
    9306 i. John Gabriel[14] **Starr** born in Ft. Worth, Tarrent Co., Tex. 7 January 1991.[1796]

7827. **James Neilson**[13] **Vandenberg** (Peggy Joyce[12] **Ward**, James Eugene[11], Ruby Sophronia[10] **Whipple**, William[9], Ira Martin[8], Elijah[7], Jeremiah[6], Joseph[5], John[4], Joseph[3], Matthew[2], Matthew[1])[1797] was born in Warrensburg, Johnson Co., Mo. 14 October 1960 and married **Diane Schievelbein** in Sequin, Bexar Co., Tex. 31 August 1988.

James Neilson **Vandenberg** and Diane **Schievelbein** had the following child born in Little Rock, Pulaski Co., Ark.:
    9307 i. Matthew Killian[14] **Vandenberg** in August 1993.[1798]

7828. **Dianne**[13] **Teague** (Allan Leonard[12], William Thomas[11], Eunice Augusta[10] **Whipple**, William[9], Ira Martin[8], Elijah[7], Jeremiah[6], Joseph[5], John[4], Joseph[3], Matthew[2], Matthew[1])[1799] was born in Orange, Essex Co., N.J. 25 January 1935 and married **John Edwards Mundy** in Piedmont, Alameda Co., Calif. 4 April 1959. John is the son of Giles **Mundy** and Vera **Sells**.[1800]

Dianne **Teague** and John Edwards **Mundy** had the following children:
    9308 i. John Allan[14] **Mundy** born in Los Angeles, Los Angeles Co., Calif. 23 October 1962.[1801]
    9309 ii. Eric Justin **Mundy** born in Los Angeles 24 September 1969.[1802]

7829. **Gail**[13] **Teague** (Roland Bardo[12], William Thomas[11], Eunice Augusta[10] **Whipple**, William[9], Ira Martin[8], Elijah[7], Jeremiah[6], Joseph[5], John[4], Joseph[3], Matthew[2], Matthew[1])[1803] was born 15 May 1938 and married **Paul E. Hendrickson Jr.** 8 October 1961.

Gail **Teague** and Paul E. **Hendrickson** Jr. had the following children:
- 9310 i. Paul Dennis[14] **Hendrickson**.[1804]
- 9311 ii. Lorie **Hendrickson**[1805] born 4 April 1965 and married Douglas (__).
- 9312 iii. Bonnie **Hendrickson** born abt 1970.[1806]

7831. **John William**[13] **Teague** (Roland Bardo[12], William Thomas[11], Eunice Augusta[10] **Whipple**, William[9], Ira Martin[8], Elijah[7], Jeremiah[6], Joseph[5], John[4], Joseph[3], Matthew[2], Matthew[1])[1807] was born 24 August 1942 and married **Nancy Ann Nace** in River Edge, Bergen Co., N. J. 16 December 1962. Nancy,[1808] daughter of Arthur Elmer **Nace**, was born in River Edge.

John William **Teague** and Nancy Ann **Nace** had the following children:
- 9313 i. Francese Helen[14] **Teague** born 10 August 1963.[1809]
- 9314 ii. Tammy **Teague** born 12 September 1964.[1810]

7833. **Gregory Bardo**[13] **Teague** (Burton William[12], William Thomas[11], Eunice Augusta[10] **Whipple**, William[9], Ira Martin[8], Elijah[7], Jeremiah[6], Joseph[5], John[4], Joseph[3], Matthew[2], Matthew[1])[1811] was born in Baltimore, Baltimore City Co., Md. 14 November 1944 and married **Anna Carol Salter** in Cuttyhunk, Dukes Co., Mass. 16 June 1973. She was born in Morehead City, Carteret Co., N. C. 26 July 1946.[1812]

Gregory Bardo **Teague** and Anna Carol **Salter** had the following child:
- 9315 i. Corey Jason[14] **Teague** born in Boston, Suffolk Co., Mass. 6 July 1974.[1813]

7834. **Donald Paul**[13] **Bonnell** (Ethel Virginia[12] **Teague**, Arthur[11], Eunice Augusta[10] **Whipple**, William[9], Ira Martin[8], Elijah[7], Jeremiah[6], Joseph[5], John[4], Joseph[3], Matthew[2], Matthew[1])[1814] was born in Redwood City, San Mateo Co., Calif. 13 February 1936 and married twice. (1) **Katinka Martha Linda Rhodes** in Merced, Merced Co., Calif. 14 January 1955. She was born in Berkeley, Alameda Co., Calif. 9 January 1938.[1815] (2) **Mary Josephine Meisinger** in Palo Alto, Santa Clara Co., Calif. 17 November 1967. Mary,[1816] daughter of Thomas **Meisinger** and Florence **Fortman**, was born in Missoula, Missoula Co., Mont. 22 May 1939.

Donald Paul **Bonnell** and Katinka Martha Linda **Rhodes** had the following children:
- + 9316 i. Richard Paul[14] **Bonnell** born 7 July 1955.
- + 9317 ii. Robin Linda **Bonnell** born 26 June 1957.
- + 9318 iii. Erin Virginia **Bonnell** born 28 March 1959.

7835. **Jerry Richard**[13] **Bonnell** (Ethel Virginia[12] **Teague**, Arthur[11], Eunice Augusta[10] **Whipple**, William[9], Ira Martin[8], Elijah[7], Jeremiah[6], Joseph[5], John[4], Joseph[3], Matthew[2], Matthew[1])[1817] was born in Redwood City, San Mateo Co., Calif. 16 December 1939 and married **Dena Karen Wilkerson** in Los Altos, Santa Clara Co., Calif. 20 August 1965. Dena,[1818] daughter of Elmer Clyde **Wilkerson**, was born in San Francisco, San Francisco Co., Calif. 14 August 1945.

Jerry Richard **Bonnell** and Dena Karen **Wilkerson** had the following children born in Mountain View, Santa Clara, Co. Calif:
- 9319 i. Scott Lee[14] **Bonnell**[1819] 24 August 1970 and died there 27 October 1985, at 15 years of age.
- 9320 ii. Kristi Lynn **Bonnell** 9 January 1973.[1820]

7836. **Doris Robin**[13] **Fincher** (Elsie May[12] **Teague**, Arthur[11], Eunice Augusta[10] **Whipple**, William[9], Ira Martin[8], Elijah[7], Jeremiah[6], Joseph[5], John[4], Joseph[3], Matthew[2], Matthew[1])[1821] was born in Berkeley, Alameda Co., Calif. 2 April 1935 and married **Theodore David Isaac Toews**. Theodore,[1822] son of Benno **Toews**, was born in Alberta, Canada.

Doris Robin **Fincher** and Theodore David Isaac **Toews** had the following child:
- 9321 i. Lisa Robin[14] **Toews**[1823] born in Redwood City, San Mateo Co., Calif. 29 April 1963 and married Derek Lawrence **Steere** in Menlo Park, San Mateo Co., Calif. 6 August 1983.

7837. **Susan Merle**[13] **Fincher** (Elsie May[12] **Teague**, Arthur[11], Eunice Augusta[10] **Whipple**, William[9], Ira Martin[8], Elijah[7], Jeremiah[6], Joseph[5], John[4], Joseph[3], Matthew[2], Matthew[1])[1824] was born in Berkeley, Alameda Co., Calif. 29 January 1939 and married **Frederick Joseph Mitchell** in Redwood City, San Mateo Co., Calif. 14 May 1960. Frederick,[1825] son of Bryan **Mitchell** and Ruth **Dunagan**, was born in Des Moines, Polk Co., Iowa 1 June 1938.

Susan Merle **Fincher** and Frederick Joseph **Mitchell** had the following children:
- \+ 9322 i. Theodore Frederick[14] **Mitchell** born 24 November 1960.
- \+ 9323 ii. Tracey Ruth **Mitchell** born 24 July 1963.
- \+ 9324 iii. Dean Robert **Mitchell** born 15 October 1965.

7838. **Donna Jeanne**[13] **Teague** (James Frederick[12], Arthur[11], Eunice Augusta[10] **Whipple**, William[9], Ira Martin[8], Elijah[7], Jeremiah[6], Joseph[5], John[4], Joseph[3], Matthew[2], Matthew[1])[1826] was born in San Mateo, San Mateo, Co., Calif. 15 September 1942 and married **Danny Thomas Williamson** in Reno, Washoe Co., Nev. 17 April 1962. Danny is the son of John **Williamson**.[1827]

Donna Jeanne **Teague** and Danny Thomas **Williamson** had the following children:
- \+ 9325 i. James Teague[14] **Williamson** born 13 December 1962.
- 9326 ii. Richard Paul **Williamson**[1828] born in Redwood City, San Mateo Co., Calif. 22 June 1964 and married Elizabeth **Wachter** in Germany 12 November 1996.

7839. **Sydney Elizabeth**[13] **Teague** (James Frederick[12], Arthur[11], Eunice Augusta[10] **Whipple**, William[9], Ira Martin[8], Elijah[7], Jeremiah[6], Joseph[5], John[4], Joseph[3], Matthew[2], Matthew[1])[1829] was born in San Mateo, San Mateo, Co., Calif. 7 January 1949 and married **Raymond Lowell Whittle** in Reno, Washoe Co., Nev. abt 1969.

Sydney Elizabeth **Teague** and Raymond Lowell **Whittle** had the following child:
- 9327 i. Michael Brent[14] **Whittle**[1830] born in Redwood City, San Mateo Co., Calif. 31 December 1969 and married Lori **Philips** in Aptos, Santa Cruz Co., Calif. 5 October 1997.

7840. **Deborah Anne**[13] **Teague** (James Frederick[12], Arthur[11], Eunice Augusta[10] **Whipple**, William[9], Ira Martin[8], Elijah[7], Jeremiah[6], Joseph[5], John[4], Joseph[3], Matthew[2], Matthew[1])[1931] was born in Redwood City, San Mateo Co., Calif. 4 January 1956 and married twice. **Rorey Dean Virgin**. (2) **Gary Russell Barber**.

Deborah Anne **Teague** and Rorey Dean **Virgin** had the following child born in Vancouver, Clark Co., Wash.:
- 9328 i. Justin Dean[14] **Virgin** 21 August 1978.[1832]

Deborah Anne **Teague** and Gary Russell **Barber** had the following children born in Redwood City:

    9329   ii.   Gary Russell **Barber** Jr. 24 March 1986.[1833]

    9330   iii. Matthew Joseph **Barber** 15 January 1988.[1834]

7842. **David Frederick**[13] **Vogel** (Janet Anne[12] **Dearborn**, Eunice May[11] **Teague**, Eunice Augusta[10] **Whipple**, William[9], Ira Martin[8], Elijah[7], Jeremiah[6], Joseph[5], John[4], Joseph[3], Matthew[2], Matthew[1])[1835] was born in Mountain View, Santa Clara Co., Calif. 22 February 1964 and married **Victoria Lyn Winkler** in Hana, Maui, Hawaii 29 May 1997. Victoria,[1836] daughter of Richard **Winkler** and Susan **Benner**, was born in San Diego, San Diego Co., Calif. 21 April 1966.

David Frederick **Vogel** and Victoria Lyn **Winkler** had the following child:

    9331   i.   Kiley Evelyn[14] **Vogel** born in Santa Cruz, Santa Cruz Co., Calif. 3 November 1997.[1837]

7843. **Sandra Joanne**[13] **Bowman** (Lawrence Francis[12], Nancy[11] **Rice**, Ellen Boise[10] **Leland**, Alonzo[9], Jasper[8], Lydia[7] **Sherman**, Mary[6] **Whipple**, Lieut. James[5], Deacon James[4], Joseph[3], Matthew[2], Matthew[1])[1838] was born in Malheur Co., Oreg. 30 November 1934 and married **Rudy Bryan Miner** in Vancouver, Clark Co., Wash. 9 July 1954. Rudy,[1839] son of Henry Bryan **Miner** and Eva Beatrice **Sutterfield**, was born in Centerville, Reynolds Co., Mo. 1 June 1931.

Sandra Joanne **Bowman** and Rudy Bryan **Miner** had the following children:

+   9332   i.   Laurel Denise[14] **Miner** born 4 February 1955.

    9333   ii. David Bryan **Miner**[1840] born in Vancouver 24 January 1957 and married D'etta **Watts** in Florence, Lane Co., Oreg. 31 December 1983.

    9334   iii. Terry Lawrence **Miner**[1841] born in Duarte, Los Angeles Co., Calif. 1 March 1960.

    9335   iv. Patrick John **Miner**[1842] born in Duarte 28 February 1961 and died 22 September 1990 in Portland, Multnomah Co., Oreg., at 29 years of age.

7844. **Mabel Frances**[13] **Corum** (Grace[12] **Treanor**, Mabel Frances[11] **Reynolds**, Helen[10] **Butterfield**, Elizabeth S.[9] **Reynolds**, Sarah W.R.[8] **Leland**, Thankful[7] **Sherman**, Mary[6] **Whipple**, Lieut. James[5], Deacon James[4], Joseph[3], Matthew[2], Matthew[1])[1843] was born in San Francisco, San Francisco Co., Calif. 29 December 1915 and married **Joseph Francis Randazzo** in San Jose, Santa Clara Co., Calif. in February 1938. He was born in Omaha, Douglas Co., Nebr. 16 November 1910 and and died 9 February 1996 in San Jose, at 85 years of age. Buried in Gate of Heaven Cemetery, Los Altos, Santa Clara Co., Calif.[1844]

Mabel Frances **Corum** and Joseph Francis **Randazzo** had the following child:
+ 9336 i. Paula Joyce[14] **Randazzo** born 31 October 1942.

7851. **James Grant**[13] **Auld** (Jill Colleen[12] **Whipple**, Leander Edmund[11], Fancis Looby[10], Lysander Greenlief[9], Edmund[8], Perley[7], Lt. James[6], Lieut. James[5], Deacon James[4], Joseph[3], Matthew[2], Matthew[1])[1845] was born in Orange, New South Wales (NSW), Australia 18 July 1955 and married **Sandra Jane Scarvell** there 6 November 1976. Sandra,[1846] daughter of Edward Gordon **Scarvell** and Peggy May **Clemb**, was born in Australia 9 April 1954.

James Grant **Auld** and Sandra Jane **Scarvell** had the following children born in Orange:
9337 i. Trent Matthew[14] **Auld**[1847] 4 June 1979.
9338 ii. Kate Louise **Auld**[1848] 26 February 1981.

7853. **Merin Joy**[13] **Auld** (Jill Colleen[12] **Whipple**, Leander Edmund[11], Fancis Looby[10], Lysander Greenlief[9], Edmund[8], Perley[7], Lt. James[6], Lieut. James[5], Deacon James[4], Joseph[3], Matthew[2], Matthew[1])[1849] was born in Orange, New South Wales (NSW), Australia 22 January 1962 and married **Raymond Henry Cheal** there. He was born 27 March 1959.[1850]

Merin Joy **Auld** and Raymond Henry **Cheal** had the following children born in Gosford, NSW:
9339 i. Rowena Jill[14] **Cheal**[1851] 9 January 1984.
9340 ii. Jason Raymond **Cheal**[1852] 28 May 1988.
9341 iii. Stephen Henry **Cheal**[1853] 29 November 1992.

7855. **Darren John**[13] **Whipple** (William Warwick[12], Leander Edmund[11], Fancis Looby[10], Lysander Greenlief[9], Edmund[8], Perley[7], Lt. James[6], Lieut. James[5], Deacon James[4], Joseph[3], Matthew[2], Matthew[1])[1854] was born in Orange, New South Wales (NSW), Australia 1 February 1962 and married **Christine Margaret Mroz** there 4 February 1984. She was born 26 November 1957.[1855]

Darren John **Whipple** and Christine Margaret **Mroz** had the following children born in Australia:
9342 i. Ian Jozef[14] **Whipple**[1856] 29 May 1988.

9343 ii. Andrew John **Whipple**[1857] 21 December 1989.
9344 iii. Harrison James **Whipple**[1858] 24 November 1992.

7858. **Walter Leighton**[13] **Whipple** (Rear Adm. Walter Jones[12], William[11], Lt. Col. Charles William[10], Maj. Gen. Amiel Weeks[9], David[8], David[7], James[6], Deacon Jacob[5], Deacon James[4], Joseph[3], Matthew[2], Matthew[1])[1859] was born in Washington, D.C. 23 June 1940 and married **Jean Ewer** 11 September 1965. Jean,[1860] daughter of James G. **Ewer** and Ann **Tischhauser**, was born in San Antonio, Bexar Co., Tex. 10 May 1943.

Walter Leighton **Whipple** and Jean **Ewer** had the following children:
9345 i. Katharine Ann[14] **Whipple**[1861] born in Concord, Middlesex Co., Mass. 16 May 1972 and married (__) **Mulligan** in Santa Barbara, Santa Barbara Co., Calif.
9346 ii. Sarah Marie **Whipple**[1862] born in Ann Arbor, Washtenaw Co., Mich. 4 March 1974.

7859. **Roby Trent**[13] **Whipple** (Rear Adm. Walter Jones[12], William[11], Lt. Col. Charles William[10], Maj. Gen. Amiel Weeks[9], David[8], David[7], James[6], Deacon Jacob[5], Deacon James[4], Joseph[3], Matthew[2], Matthew[1])[1863] was born in Jamestown, Newport Co., R. I. 24 April 1946 and married **Edward Craibe** in Arnold, Calaveras Co., Calif.

Roby Trent **Whipple** and Edward **Craibe** had the following child:
+ 9347 i. Elizabeth Roby[14] **Craibe**.

7861. **Anne Calhoun**[13] **Whipple** (Brig. Gen. William[12], William[11], Lt. Col. Charles William[10], Maj. Gen. Amiel Weeks[9], David[8], David[7], James[6], Deacon Jacob[5], Deacon James[4], Joseph[3], Matthew[2], Matthew[1])[1864] was born in Princeton, Mercer Co., N. J. 18 January 1936 and married **Walter W. Anderson**.

Anne Calhoun **Whipple** and Walter W. **Anderson** had the following children:
9348 i. John Hart[14] **Anderson**[1865] married Beverly (__).
9349 ii. David Christian **Anderson**.[1866]

7862. **William**[13] **Whipple III** (Brig. Gen. William[12], William[11], Lt. Col. Charles William[10], Maj. Gen. Amiel Weeks[9], David[8], David[7], James[6], Deacon Jacob[5], Deacon James[4], Joseph[3], Matthew[2], Matthew[1])[1867] was born in Omaha, Douglas Co., Nebr. 24 June 1938 and married **Valerie Jane Smolka** in Wilmington, New Castle Co., Del. 23 July 1966.

Valerie,[1868] daughter of William **Smolka** and Anna (__), was born in Wilmington 9 June 1944. William is a graduate of both Princeton and Harvard Law School and was a member of the Finance Staff du DuPont Company until 1992 when he began the practice of law.

William **Whipple** III and Valerie Jane **Smolka** had the following children:

  9350   i.   Julie Anne[14] **Whipple**[1869] born in Wilmington 21 February 1968 and married Davis Handel **Jefferson** there 11 November 1995.

+ 9351   ii.   Lara Beth **Whipple** born 25 December 1969.

  9352   iii.   Jennifer Marie **Whipple**[1870] born in Sao Paulo, Brazil 13 August 1974.

7863. **Claire Randolph**[13] **Whipple** (Brig. Gen. William[12], William[11], Lt. Col. Charles William[10], Maj. Gen. Amiel Weeks[9], David[8], David[7], James[6], Deacon Jacob[5], Deacon James[4], Joseph[3], Matthew[2], Matthew[1])[1871] was born in Portland, Multnomah Co., Oreg. 10 July 1947 and married **Frank Joseph Steeh**.

Claire Randolph **Whipple** and Frank Joseph **Steeh** had the following children:

  9353   i.   Matthew[14] **Steeh**.[1872]
  9354   ii.   Diana **Steeh**.[1873]

7864. **Philip Exiga**[13] **Whipple** (Brig. Gen. William[12], William[11], Lt. Col. Charles William[10], Maj. Gen. Amiel Weeks[9], David[8], David[7], James[6], Deacon Jacob[5], Deacon James[4], Joseph[3], Matthew[2], Matthew[1])[1874] was born in Chinon, France 27 July 1957 and married **Jo Ann Tagliavia**.

Philip Exiga **Whipple** and Jo Ann **Tagliavia** had the following child:

  9355   i.   Jason[14] **Whipple**.[1875]

7866. **Genevieve Randolph**[13] **Green** (Jane Randolph[12] **Whipple**, William[11], Lt. Col. Charles William[10], Maj. Gen. Amiel Weeks[9], David[8], David[7], James[6], Deacon Jacob[5], Deacon James[4], Joseph[3], Matthew[2], Matthew[1])[1876] was born in Elizabeth, Union Co., N. J. 26 June 1939 and married twice. (1) **John Brodhead Freeman** in Westfield, Union Co., N. J. 16 March 1958. They were divorced in September 1968. (2) **Richard Malcolm Dunlop** in Westfield 27 June 1970.

Genevieve Randolph **Green** and John Brodhead **Freeman** had the following children:

   9356 i. Julia Randolph[14] **Freeman**[1877] married (__) **McMenamin**. They had two sons; no details provided.

+ 9357 ii. Christine Whipple **Freeman** born 17 February 1962.

7867. **Christine MacPherson**[13] **Green** (Jane Randolph[12] **Whipple**, William[11], Lt. Col. Charles William[10], Maj. Gen. Amiel Weeks[9], David[8], David[7], James[6], Deacon Jacob[5], Deacon James[4], Joseph[3], Matthew[2], Matthew[1])[1878] was born in Elizabeth, Union Co., N. J. 29 September 1943 and married **Harold Gordon Alderman** in Jacksonville Beach, Duval Co., Fla. 10 June 1966. He was born in Jacksonville 5 November 1935.[1879]

Christine MacPherson **Green** and Harold Gordon **Alderman** had the following children:

   9358 i. Derrick Widsith MacPherson[14] **Alderman**[1880] born in Santa Rosa, Sonoma Co., Calif. 31 August 1974.

   9359 ii. Jason Randolph Phillips **Alderman**[1881] born in Santa Rosa 19 July 1977.

7868. **Virginia Whipple**[13] **Green** (Jane Randolph[12] **Whipple**, William[11], Lt. Col. Charles William[10], Maj. Gen. Amiel Weeks[9], David[8], David[7], James[6], Deacon Jacob[5], Deacon James[4], Joseph[3], Matthew[2], Matthew[1])[1882] was born in Elizabeth, Union Co., N. J. 2 April 1946 and married four times. (1) **Lawrence Dunkle Hower III** in Westfield, Union Co., N. J. 11 September 1965. (2) **Raymond Barz** 16 July 1982. (3) **Conrad Vogel** in Solebury, Bucks Co., Penn. 10 August 1991. Conrad had daughters Lara and Mary Ann from a previous marriage. (4) **Russell Keith Branscom Jr.** 13 May 1995.

Virginia Whipple **Green** and Lawrence Dunkle **Hower** III had the following children:

+ 9360 i. Wendy Page[14] **Hower** born 20 July 1967.

   9361 ii. Nicholas James **Hower**[1883] born in Frankfurt, Germany 31 May 1970.

7870. **Carolyn Randolph**[13] **Williams** (Genevieve Liddell[12] **Whipple**, William[11], Lt. Col. Charles William[10], Maj. Gen. Amiel Weeks[9], David[8], David[7], James[6], Deacon Jacob[5], Deacon James[4], Joseph[3], Matthew[2], Matthew[1])[1884] was born in Baton Rouge, East Baton Rouge Parish, La. 17 March 1938 and married **Edward Easton IV** there 26 June 1959. Edward, son of Edward **Easton** and Emily deForest **Whitman**, was born in New York, N.Y. 8 July 1936.

{ G 1367 }

Carolyn Randolph **Williams** and Edward **Easton** IV had the following children born in Charlotte, Mecklenburg Co., N. C.:

  9362 i. Edward[14] **Easton** V[1885] 22 November 1965 and married Tammy Lynn **Yeyzeroff** 18 October 1992. She was born in Silver Spring, Montgomery Co., Md. 16 December 1966.[1886]

  9363 ii. William Whipple **Easton**[1887] 16 October 1969.

7872. Douglas Liddell[13] **Williams** (Genevieve Liddell[12] **Whipple**, William[11], Lt. Col. Charles William[10], Maj. Gen. Amiel Weeks[9], David[8], David[7], James[6], Deacon Jacob[5], Deacon James[4], Joseph[3], Matthew[2], Matthew[1])[1888] was born in Baton Rouge, East Baton Rouge Parish, La. 22 November 1946 and married **Kay Williams Nobile** in New Orleans, Orleans Parish, La. 27 December 1969. Kay,[1889] daughter of August A. **Nobile** Jr. and Carrie Lorgna **Williams**, was born in New Orleans 5 December 1948.

Douglas Liddell **Williams** and Kay Williams **Nobile** had the following children:

  9364 i. Bryan Liddell[14] **Williams**[1890] born in Alamogordo, Otero Co., N. Mex. 14 April 1971.

  9365 ii. Eric Matthew **Williams**[1891] born in Shreveport, Caddo Parish, La. 24 May 1978.

  9366 iii. Carrie Ellen **Williams**[1892] born in Shreveport 22 March 1981.

  9367 iv. Douglas Anthony **Williams**[1893] born in Shreveport 20 February 1985.

7878. Julia[13] **Bartholomew** (Katharine C.[12] **Collens**, Annette Bailey[11] **Whipple**, Lt. Col. Charles William[10], Maj. Gen. Amiel Weeks[9], David[8], David[7], James[6], Deacon Jacob[5], Deacon James[4], Joseph[3], Matthew[2], Matthew[1])[1894] was born in Hartford, Hartford Co., Conn. 26 August 1937 and married **Richard Condit Munn**.

Julia **Bartholomew** and Richard Condit **Munn** had the following children:

  9368 i. Katherine Tracy[14] **Munn**[1895] born in Oakland, Alameda Co., Calif. 2 October 1959.

  9369 ii. David Condit **Munn**[1896] born in Boston, Suffolk Co., Mass. 14 August 1961.

  9370 iii. Julia Lauren **Munn**[1897] born in Summit, Union Co., N. J. 18 July 1963 and married Alan Wadsworth **Hale** in Wellesley, Norfolk Co., Mass. 29 August 1992.

7885. **Dan Edward**[13] **Whipple** (Orval Aaron[12], David Ethen[11], Charles E.[10], David M.[9], Mathew A.[8], David[7], James[6], Deacon Jacob[5], Deacon James[4], Joseph[3], Matthew[2], Matthew[1])[1898] was born in Gardiner, Douglas Co., Oreg. 9 June 1936 and married twice. (1) **Cora Ann Zastrow** in Sweet Home, Linn Co., Oreg. 2 July 1966. Cora,[1899] daughter of Robert David **Zastrow** and Frieda Harriett **Fisher**, was born in Lebanon, Linn Co., Oreg. 12 February 1949. (2) **Barbara Jean Baker** in Portland, Multnomah Co., Oreg. 2 July 1993. Barbara,[1900] daughter of Paul James **Baker** and Elsie Bertha **Lussier**, was born in Eugene, Lane Co., Oreg. 16 May 1937.

Dan Edward **Whipple** and Cora Ann **Zastrow** had the following children born in Lebanon:

9371 i. Dawn Elaine[14] **Whipple**[1901] 21 May 1967 and married Kenneth Leland **Keffer** in Blue River, Lane Co., Oreg. 12 September 1992.

9372 ii. David Ethan **Whipple**[1902] 5 May 1968 and married Tammy Jo **Bainbridge** in Pendleton, Umatilla Co., Oreg. 1 July 1992.

7887. **Nellie Janette**[13] **Whipple** (Orval Aaron[12], David Ethen[11], Charles E.[10], David M.[9], Mathew A.[8], David[7], James[6], Deacon Jacob[5], Deacon James[4], Joseph[3], Matthew[2], Matthew[1])[1903] was born in Brownsville, Linn Co., Oreg. 17 June 1939 and married twice. (1) **Gus Donald Walker** in Sweet Home, Linn Co., Oreg. 12 August 1956. He was born in Brokenbonoren, McCurtain Co., Okla. 27 December 1937.[1904] (2) **Gerald Cummings** in Reno, Washoe Co., Nev. 24 March 1972. He was born in Hoquiam, Grays Harbor Co., Wash. 18 September 1936.

Nellie Janette **Whipple** and Gus Donald **Walker** had the following children:

9373 i. Carla Jean[14] **Walker**[1905] born in Sweet Home 5 June 1957.

9374 ii. Donny Gus **Walker**[1906] born in Lebanon, Linn Co., Oreg. 7 June 1958.

9375 iii. Kemberly Dawn **Walker**[1907] born in Albany, Linn Co., Oreg. 27 December 1960.

9376 iv. Robyn Jannette **Walker**[1908] born in Springfield, Lane Co., Oreg. 11 July 1963.

9377 v. Regina Ray **Walker**[1909] born in Eugene, Lane Co., Oreg. 10 April 1965.

Nellie Janette **Whipple** and Gerald **Cummings** had the following child born in Springfield:

9378 vi. Michel Sean **Cummings**[1910] 8 December 1967.

7888. **Cora Bell**[13] **Whipple** (Orval Aaron[12], David Ethen[11], Charles E.[10], David M.[9], Mathew A.[8], David[7], James[6], Deacon Jacob[5], Deacon James[4], Joseph[3], Matthew[2], Matthew[1])[1911] was born in Sweet Home, Linn Co., Oreg. 26 February 1941 and married **David S. Cook** there 11 April 1959.

Cora Bell **Whipple** and David S. **Cook** had the following children:
- 9379 i. David Silas[14] **Cook**[1912] born in Sweet Home 11 March 1960.
- 9380 ii. Glendena Marir **Cook**[1913] born in Salem, Marion Co., Oreg. 31 July 1961.
- 9381 iii. Danny Amos **Cook**[1914] born in Salem 31 July 1962.
- 9382 iv. Robert Allen **Cook**[1915] born in Denver, Denver Co., Colo. 16 July 1964.
- 9383 v. Debra Lee **Cook**[1916] born in Denver 17 October 1968.

7889. **Hellin Irene**[13] **Whipple** (Orval Aaron[12], David Ethen[11], Charles E.[10], David M.[9], Mathew A.[8], David[7], James[6], Deacon Jacob[5], Deacon James[4], Joseph[3], Matthew[2], Matthew[1])[1917] was born in Foster, Linn Co., Oreg. 6 January 1944 and married **Augest Mark** 30 July 1965.

Hellin Irene **Whipple** and Augest **Mark** had the following child born in Lebanon, Linn Co., Oreg.:
- 9384 i. Viola Edwina[14] **Mark**[1918] 1 January 1967 and married an unnamed person there 15 June 1986.

7890. **Bob Aaron**[13] **Whipple** (Orval Aaron[12], David Ethen[11], Charles E.[10], David M.[9], Mathew A.[8], David[7], James[6], Deacon Jacob[5], Deacon James[4], Joseph[3], Matthew[2], Matthew[1])[1919] was born in Sweet Home, Linn Co., Oreg. 24 June 1947 and married **Landy Sue Maroney** 11 April 1971. She was born in Denver, Denver Co., Colo. 29 March 1950.[1920]

Bob Aaron **Whipple** and Landy Sue **Maroney** had the following children born in Portland, Multnomah Co., Oreg.:
- 9385 i. Jennifer Jalene[14] **Whipple**[1921] 28 November 1970.
- 9386 ii. Pollyannas **Whipple**[1922] 5 February 1973.

7891. **Paula Kay**[13] **Whipple** (George David[12], Walter Ralph[11], William Isaac[10], Isaac Truax[9], James[8], James[7], James[6], Deacon Jacob[5], Deacon James[4], Joseph[3], Matthew[2], Matthew[1])[1923] was born in Webster City, Hamilton Co., Iowa 26 October 1961 and married **Randy Dale Wallace** in Marshalltown, Marshall Co., Iowa 5 June 1981. Randy,[1924] son of Richard Dale **Wallace** and Norma Kay **Zeisness**, was born in Marshalltown 18 January 1960.

Paula Kay **Whipple** and Randy Dale **Wallace** had the following children born in Marshalltown:
>   9387   i.   Adrian Lynn[14] **Wallace**[1925] 17 September 1985.
>   9388   ii. Grant Andrew **Wallace**[1926] 29 November 1987.

7892. **Joel David**[13] **Whipple** (George David[12], Walter Ralph[11], William Isaac[10], Isaac Truax[9], James[8], James[7], James[6], Deacon Jacob[5], Deacon James[4], Joseph[3], Matthew[2], Matthew[1])[1927] was born in Webster City, Hamilton Co., Iowa 28 May 1963 and married **Cindy LaRaye Arneson** in Las Vegas, Clark Co., Nev. 1 July 1989. Joel is in the construction business in Las Vegas.

Joel David **Whipple** and Cindy LaRaye **Arneson** had the following children:
>   9389   i.   Jaymason LaRaye[14] **Wallace**[1928] born 1 October 1989.
>   9390   ii. Garett David **Wallace**[1929] born 11 June 1991.

7893. **Todd Douglas**[13] **Whipple** (George David[12], Walter Ralph[11], William Isaac[10], Isaac Truax[9], James[8], James[7], James[6], Deacon Jacob[5], Deacon James[4], Joseph[3], Matthew[2], Matthew[1])[1930] was born in Webster City, Hamilton Co., Iowa 24 January 1965 and married **Mikel Michelle Thompson** in Marshalltown, Marshall Co., Iowa 15 August 1987. Mikel, daughter of David **Thompson** and Jewel **Huntington**, was born in Marshalltown 28 September 1966. Todd was graduated from Cornell College, Mt. Vernon, Linn Co., Iowa in 1987 and earned a graduate degree from Vanderbilt University, Nashville, Davidson Co., Tenn.

Todd Douglas **Whipple** and Mikel Michelle **Thompson** had the following child:
>   9391   i.   Kayla Jordan[14] **Whipple**[1931] born 22 January 1992.

7896. **Yvonne**[13] **Scoggin** (Evelyn Adelle[12] **Creighton**, Minnie Grace[11] **Whipple**, Fred G.[10], Obed[9], Obed[8], Thomas[7], Col. Moses[6], Deacon Jacob[5], Deacon James[4], Joseph[3], Matthew[2], Matthew[1])[1932] was born in Antioch, Contra Costa Co., Calif. 20 May 1934 and married **Anthony Joseph Mendivil** in Los Gatos, Santa Clara Co., Calif. 12 February 1955. Anthony,[1933] son of Joseph **Mendivil** and Grace (__), was born in Pittsburg, Contra Costa Co., Calif. 29 June 1929.

Yvonne **Scoggin** and Anthony Joseph **Mendivil** had the following children:
> + 9392   i.   Stephen Randolph[14] **Mendivil** born 19 July 1955.
> + 9393   ii. Gary Allen **Mendivil** born 4 December 1956.
> + 9394   iii. Yvette Adelle **Mendivil** born 2 May 1962.

9395 iv. Creighton Anthony **Mendivil**[1934] born in Englewood, Bergen Co., N. J. 8 June 1967.
+ 9396 v. Renee Adelle **Mendivil** born 25 October 1969.

7897. **John Henry**[13] **Scoggin** (Evelyn Adelle[12] **Creighton**, Minnie Grace[11] **Whipple**, Fred G.[10], Obed[9], Obed[8], Thomas[7], Col. Moses[6], Deacon Jacob[5], Deacon James[4], Joseph[3], Matthew[2], Matthew[1])[1935] was born in San Jose, Santa Clara Co., Calif. 22 May 1935 and married twice. (1) **Mary Zentimila** in Reno, Washoe Co., Nev. in February 1957. Mary,[1936] daughter of Michkael **Zentimilia** and Florence (__), was born in Monterey, Montgomery Co., Calif. (2) An unnamed person in Carson City, Carson City Co., Nev. 7 June 1997.

John Henry **Scoggin** and Mary **Zentimilia** had the following children born in Pacific Grove, Monterey Co., Calif.:
9397 i. Jacqueline Rene[14] **Scoggin**[1937] 13 February 1958.
9398 ii. Craig Brian **Scoggin**[1938] 23 April 1961.

7898. **Eric Newton**[13] **Jacobsen** (Virginia Lee[12] **Whipple**, Harry Meryl[11], Fred G.[10], Obed[9], Obed[8], Thomas[7], Col. Moses[6], Deacon Jacob[5], Deacon James[4], Joseph[3], Matthew[2], Matthew[1])[1939] was born in Piedmont, Alameda Co., Calif. 22 January 1947 and married **Joy White**. Joy,[1940] daughter of Curtis **White** and Marion (__), was born in Pocahontas, Randolph Co., Ark. 23 July 1946.

Eric Newton **Jacobsen** and Joy **White** had the following children:
9399 i. Lisa[14] **Jacobsen**[1941] born in Des Moines, King Co., Wash. 7 November 1975.
9400 ii. Chad **Jacobsen**[1942] born in Laguna Beach, Orange Co., Calif. 18 June 1987.

7899. **Dennis Merle**[13] **Jacobsen** (Virginia Lee[12] **Whipple**, Harry Meryl[11], Fred G.[10], Obed[9], Obed[8], Thomas[7], Col. Moses[6], Deacon Jacob[5], Deacon James[4], Joseph[3], Matthew[2], Matthew[1])[1943] was born in Piedmont, Alameda Co., Calif. 29 July 1949 and married **Sally Holland**. Sally,[1944] daughter of Byran **Holland** and Betty (__), was born in Berkeley, Alameda Co., Calif. 1 March 1951. They were divorced in 1984.

Dennis Merle **Jacobsen** and Sally **Holland** had the following child born in Fall River Mills, Shasta Co., Calif.:
9401 i. Lindsay[14] **Jacobsen**[1945] 29 December 1980.

7900. **Kristina Carol**[13] **Jacobsen** (Virginia Lee[12] **Whipple**, Harry Meryl[11], Fred G.[10], Obed[9], Obed[8], Thomas[7], Col. Moses[6], Deacon Jacob[5], Deacon James[4], Joseph[3], Matthew[2], Matthew[1])[1946] was born in Pleasant Hill, Contra Costa Co., Calif. 26 December 1953 and married **David Danford**. David,[1947] son of Kenneth **Danford** and Marion (__), was born in Mahnomen, Mahnomen Co., Minn. 2 March 1952.

Kristina Carol **Jacobsen** and David **Danford** had the following children born in Pleasant Hill:
    9402   i.   Ashley[14] **Danford**[1948] 22 July 1984.
    9403   ii.   Ian **Danford**[1949] 19 January 1989.

7901. **Richard Carl**[13] **Spitzer** (Sylvia Ruth[12] **Hildebrant**, Lois Philena[11] **Whipple**, Fred G.[10], Obed[9], Obed[8], Thomas[7], Col. Moses[6], Deacon Jacob[5], Deacon James[4], Joseph[3], Matthew[2], Matthew[1])[1950] was born in Berkeley, Alameda Co., Calif. 24 April 1950 and married **Sarma Velga Grasis** in Flagstaff, Conconino Co., Ariz. 30 May 1975. Sarma was born at the Geestacht Refugee Camp near Hamburg, Germany 13 September 1948.[1951] Her family is from Latvia and emigrated to the U. S. from Germany in 1953.

Richard Carl **Spitzer** and Sarma Velga **Grasis** had the following child born in Monument Valley, Utah:
    9404   i.   Arthur Richard[14] **Spitzer**[1952] 6 October 1975.

7902. **William Eric**[13] **Spitzer** (Sylvia Ruth[12] **Hildebrant**, Lois Philena[11] **Whipple**, Fred G.[10], Obed[9], Obed[8], Thomas[7], Col. Moses[6], Deacon Jacob[5], Deacon James[4], Joseph[3], Matthew[2], Matthew[1])[1953] was born in Hamilton Field AFB, Calif. 1 May 1952 and married **Fayanne Fife** in Miami, Dade Co., Fla. 5 January 1979. She was born in New York, N.Y. 5 November 1952.[1954]

William Eric **Spitzer** and Fayanne **Fife** had the following children:
    9405   i.   David William[14] **Spitzer**[1955] born in Walnut Creek, Contra Costa Co., Calif. 15 March 1983.
    9406   ii.   Steven Michael **Spitzer**[1956] born in Tucson, Pima Co., Ariz. 31 August 1986.

7903. **Raymond Lewis**[13] **Spitzer** (Sylvia Ruth[12] **Hildebrant**, Lois Philena[11] **Whipple**, Fred G.[10], Obed[9], Obed[8], Thomas[7], Col. Moses[6], Deacon Jacob[5], Deacon James[4], Joseph[3], Matthew[2], Matthew[1])[1957] was born in Hamilton Field AFB, Calif. 1 May 1952 and married **Susan Kay**

Myers in Tucson, Pima Co., Ariz. 7 July 1979. She was born in Valpraiso, Porter Co., Ind. 20 May 1950.[1958]

Raymond Lewis **Spitzer** and Susan Kay **Myers** had the following children:
- 9407 i. Rayetta Kay[14] **Spitzer**[1959] born 2 August 1985. Adopted 26 July 1989.
- 9408 ii. Shawn Charles **Spitzer**[1960] born 3 July 1986. Adopted 6 March 1989. Shawn and Rayetta are half siblings, born to the same mother.
- 9409 iii. Sarah Jane **Spitzer**[1961] born in Tucson 1 October 1988.

7904. **Ronald Walter**[13] **Spitzer** (Sylvia Ruth[12] **Hildebrant**, Lois Philena[11] **Whipple**, Fred G.[10], Obed[9], Obed[8], Thomas[7], Col. Moses[6], Deacon Jacob[5], Deacon James[4], Joseph[3], Matthew[2], Matthew[1])[1962] was born in Great Falls, Cascade Co., Mont. 17 May 1955 and married **Rebecca Joanne Cushman** in Flagstaff, Conconino Co., Ariz. 7 December 1985. She was born in Grand Rapids, Kent Co., Mich. 17 February 1960.[1963]

Ronald Walter **Spitzer** and Rebecca Joanne **Cushman** had the following children:
- 9410 i. Laura Doreen[14] **Spitzer**[1964] born in Grand Rapids 25 August 1988.
- 9411 ii. Bryce Andrew **Spitzer**[1965] born in Grand Rapids 23 December 1989.
- 9412 iii. Philip Austin **Spitzer**[1966] born in Grand Rapids 21 June 1992.
- 9413 iv. Paul Aron **Spitzer**[1967] born in Grand Rapids 20 April 1994.
- 9414 v. Lincoln Arie **Spitzer**[1968] born in Traverse City, Grand Traverse Co., Mich. 18 February 1997.

7905. **Evelyn Bernice**[13] **Spitzer** (Sylvia Ruth[12] **Hildebrant**, Lois Philena[11] **Whipple**, Fred G.[10], Obed[9], Obed[8], Thomas[7], Col. Moses[6], Deacon Jacob[5], Deacon James[4], Joseph[3], Matthew[2], Matthew[1])[1969] was born in Nogales, Santa Cruz Co., Ariz. 17 May 1957 and married **Eric Lee Abbott** in Parris Island, S.C. 2 April 1980. He was born in Peoria, Peoria Co., Ill. 6 September 1957. They were married a second time 7 June 1980 in Tuscon, Pima Co., Ariz. She teaches Science to seventh and eighth grade students in the Tuscon school system.

Evelyn Bernice **Spitzer** and Eric Lee **Abbott** had the following child born in Tucson:
- 9415 i. Kevin Justin[14] Abbott-**Spitzer**[1970] 3 March 1989.

7906. **Robert David**[13] **Spitzer** (Sylvia Ruth[12] **Hildebrant**, Lois Philena[11] **Whipple**, Fred G.[10], Obed[9], Obed[8], Thomas[7], Col. Moses[6], Deacon Jacob[5], Deacon James[4], Joseph[3], Matthew[2], Matthew[1])[1971] was born in Nogales, Santa Cruz Co., Ariz. 22 August 1961 and married **Marie Ann Bielefeld** in Tucson, Pima Co., Ariz. 17 August 1985. She was born in Cincinnati, Hamilton Co., Ohio 9 June 1961.[1972]

Robert David **Spitzer** and Marie Ann **Bielefeld** had the following child born in Tucson:
    9416   i.   David Jonathan[14] **Spitzer**[1973] 7 June 1990.

7908. **Carl Wayne**[13] **Hildebrant** (Harold Homer[12], Lois Philena[11] **Whipple**, Fred G.[10], Obed[9], Obed[8], Thomas[7], Col. Moses[6], Deacon Jacob[5], Deacon James[4], Joseph[3], Matthew[2], Matthew[1])[1974] was born in San Francisco, San Francisco Co., Calif. 25 May 1961 and married **Karen V. Puckett** in Petaluma, Sonoma Co., Calif. 19 July 1986. She was born in La Mesa, San Diego Co., Calif. 4 September 1965.[1975]

Carl Wayne **Hildebrant** and Karen V. **Puckett** had the following children born in Petaluma:
    9417   i.   Rebecca Alayne[14] **Hildebrant**[1976] 28 August 1993.
    9418   ii.   Daniel Ryan **Hildebrant**[1977] 6 September 1998.

7909. **Glenn Harold**[13] **Hildebrant** (Harold Homer[12], Lois Philena[11] **Whipple**, Fred G.[10], Obed[9], Obed[8], Thomas[7], Col. Moses[6], Deacon Jacob[5], Deacon James[4], Joseph[3], Matthew[2], Matthew[1])[1978] was born in San Francisco, San Francisco Co., Calif. 14 October 1963 and married **Melanie Kathleen Stamme** 30 July 1994. Melanie,[1979] daughter of Vernon C. **Stamme** and Joan (__), was born in Oakland, Alameda Co., Calif. 19 July 1962.

Glenn Harold **Hildebrant** and Melanie Kathleen **Stamme** had the following child born in Petaluma, Sonoma Co., Calif.:
    9419   i.   Angela Jeanette[14] **Hildebrant**[1980] 7 November 1997.

7911. **Graeme Gardiner**[13] **Whytlaw Jr.** (Graeme Gardiner[12], Laura Alexander[11] **Gardiner**, Mary Powers[10] **Cooper**, Laurel[9] **Whipple**, David[8], Aaron[7], Col. Moses[6], Deacon Jacob[5], Deacon James[4], Joseph[3], Matthew[2], Matthew[1])[1981] was born in Adams, Berkshire Co., Mass. 3 August 1925 and married **Marion Jeane Rice** in Altoona, Blair Co., Penn. 4 June 1949. Marion,[1982] daughter of Charles **Rice** and Margaret **Reighard**, was born in Altoona 5 May 1929. Graeme attended Williams College,

{ G 1375 }

Williamstown, Berkshire Co., Mass. in 1944, Stevens Institute of Technology in Hoboken, Chenango Co., N.Y. in 1945 and Princeton University, Princeton, Mercer Co., N.J., 1945-7 where he earned a B. S. in Mechanical Engineering. He began his working carrer in 1947 with the Bethlehem Steel Co. at Bethlehem, Clearfield Co., Penn. and retired as an Engineer with the Torrington Co. of Torrington, Litchfield Co., Conn. in 1986 at which time he moved to Cape Coral, Lee Co., Fla. As an avocation he was owner-producer of Triangle Playhouse in Torrington for a decade (1963-73).

Graeme Gardiner **Whytlaw** Jr. and Marion Jeane **Rice** had the following children:
- + 9420 i. Graeme Gardiner[14] **Whytlaw** III born 31 January 1950.
- + 9421 ii. Candace Terry **Whytlaw** born 25 April 1953.
- + 9422 iii. Debra Jeane **Whytlaw** born 19 August 1956.

7917. **Lothrop**[13] **Withington** III (Lothrop[12], Katharyn Carlton[11] **Whipple**, Sherman Leland[10], Dr. Solomon M.[9], David[8], Aaron[7], Col. Moses[6], Deacon Jacob[5], Deacon James[4], Joseph[3], Matthew[2], Matthew[1])[1983] was born 15 May 1942 and married twice. (1) **Bonnie Jean Lewis** 21 August 1971. She was born 6 September 1945.[1984] They were divorced in 1989. (2) **Marianne Gray** 1 July 1990. She was born 3 May 1955.[1985]

Lothrop **Withington** III and Bonnie Jean **Lewis** had the following children:
- 9423 i. Lothrop[14] **Withington** IV[1986] born 3 June 1975.
- 9424 ii. Ashley Elizabeth **Withington**[1987] born 6 April 1979.

7918. **Ellen**[13] **Withington** (Lothrop[12], Katharyn Carlton[11] **Whipple**, Sherman Leland[10], Dr. Solomon M.[9], David[8], Aaron[7], Col. Moses[6], Deacon Jacob[5], Deacon James[4], Joseph[3], Matthew[2], Matthew[1])[1988] was born 21 May 1943 and married **Peter Allen Dietrich** 9 July 1966. He was born 22 December 1941.[1989] They were divorced in 1979.

Ellen **Withington** and Peter Allen **Dietrich** had the following child:
- 9425 i. Peter Joshua[14] **Dietrich**[1990] born 10 February 1972.

7919. **Lydia Whipple**[13] **Withington** (Lothrop[12], Katharyn Carlton[11] **Whipple**, Sherman Leland[10], Dr. Solomon M.[9], David[8], Aaron[7], Col. Moses[6], Deacon Jacob[5], Deacon James[4], Joseph[3], Matthew[2], Matthew[1])[1991] was born 2 April 1947 and married **Evan Warren Holmes** 23 December 1967. He was born 23 August 1947.[1992]

Lydia Whipple **Withington** and Evan Warren **Holmes** had the following children:

    9426   i.   Brewster Warren[14] **Holmes**[1993] born 3 March 1972.
    9427   ii.   Zachary Tilden **Holmes**[1994] born 22 May 1975.
    9428   iii.   Bartlett Withington **Holmes**[1995] born 27 September 1978.

7920. **Ellis Brewster**[13] **Withington** (Lothrop[12], Katharyn Carlton[11] **Whipple**, Sherman Leland[10], Dr. Solomon M.[9], David[8], Aaron[7], Col. Moses[6], Deacon Jacob[5], Deacon James[4], Joseph[3], Matthew[2], Matthew[1])[1996] was born 19 September 1953 and married **Jennifer Carver Mahall** 19 June 1993. She was born 8 May 1968.[1997]

Ellis Brewster **Withington** and Jennifer Carver **Mahall** had the following child:

    9429   i.   Haley Elizabeth[14] **Withington**[1998] born 7 May 1997.

7921. **Anne Withington**[13] **Brewster** (Marietta Louise[12] **Withington**, Katharyn Carlton[11] **Whipple**, Sherman Leland[10], Dr. Solomon M.[9], David[8], Aaron[7], Col. Moses[6], Deacon Jacob[5], Deacon James[4], Joseph[3], Matthew[2], Matthew[1])[1999] was born in Valdosta, Lowndes Co., Ga. 3 October 1943 and married **George Keller** in Plymouth, Plymouth Co., Mass. 24 June 1961.

Anne Withington **Brewster** and George **Keller** had the following children:

    9430   i.   Jonathan B.[14] **Keller**[2000] born 19 January 1962.
    9431   ii.   Kimberly Anna **Keller**[2001] born 13 July 1963.

7922. **Marietta**[13] **Brewster** (Marietta Louise[12] **Withington**, Katharyn Carlton[11] **Whipple**, Sherman Leland[10], Dr. Solomon M.[9], David[8], Aaron[7], Col. Moses[6], Deacon Jacob[5], Deacon James[4], Joseph[3], Matthew[2], Matthew[1])[2002] was born in Champaign-Urbana, Champaign Co., Ill. 16 June 1945 and married **Javier Brockmann** in Plymouth, Plymouth Co., Mass. 16 March 1968.

Marietta **Brewster** and Javier **Brockmann** had the following children:

    9432   i.   Brewster[14] **Brockmann**[2003] born 21 July 1970.
    9433   ii.   Guillarmo **Brockmann**[2004] born 5 July 1972.
    9434   iii.   Tatiana **Brockmann**[2005] born 1 January 1978.

7923. **Spencer Hatch**[13] **Brewster Jr.** (Marietta Louise[12] **Withington**, Katharyn Carlton[11] **Whipple**, Sherman Leland[10], Dr. Solomon M.[9], David[8], Aaron[7], Col. Moses[6], Deacon Jacob[5], Deacon James[4], Joseph[3],

Matthew², Matthew¹)²⁰⁰⁶ was born in Plymouth, Plymouth Co., Mass. 9 May 1947 and married twice. (1) **Marilee Meyer** in July 1969. (2) **Lydia Weston** 28 November 1981.

Spencer Hatch **Brewster** Jr. and Marilee **Meyer** had the following children:
  9435 i. Forest¹⁴ **Brewster**²⁰⁰⁷ born 15 March 1970.
  9436 ii. Jebadiah **Brewster**²⁰⁰⁸ born 6 July 1971.

Spencer Hatch **Brewster** Jr. and Lydia **Weston** had the following child:
  9437 iii. Lydia **Brewster**²⁰⁰⁹ born 16 October 1982.

7924. **Sarah¹³ Brewster** (Marietta Louise¹² **Withington**, Katharyn Carlton¹¹ **Whipple**, Sherman Leland¹⁰, Dr. Solomon M.⁹, David⁸, Aaron⁷, Col. Moses⁶, Deacon Jacob⁵, Deacon James⁴, Joseph³, Matthew², Matthew¹)²⁰¹⁰ was born in Plymouth, Plymouth Co., Mass. 23 January 1950 and married **Bruce E. Tompkins** there 5 March 1977.

Sarah **Brewster** and Bruce E. **Tompkins** had the following child:
  9438 i. Emily¹⁴ **Tompkins**²⁰¹¹ born 26 April 1981.

7925. **Patience¹³ Brewster** (Marietta Louise¹² **Withington**, Katharyn Carlton¹¹ **Whipple**, Sherman Leland¹⁰, Dr. Solomon M.⁹, David⁸, Aaron⁷, Col. Moses⁶, Deacon Jacob⁵, Deacon James⁴, Joseph³, Matthew², Matthew¹)²⁰¹² was born in Plymouth, Plymouth Co., Mass. 26 October 1952 and married **Holland Chauncy Gregg III** there 18 June 1977.

Patience **Brewster** and Holland Chauncy **Gregg** III had the following children:
  9439 i. Holland Chauncy¹⁴ **Gregg** IV²⁰¹³ born 3 January 1978.
  9440 ii. Marietta **Gregg**²⁰¹⁴ born 12 February 1981.

7927. **Benjamin B.¹³ Brewster** Jr. (Anne Platt¹² **Withington**, Katharyn Carlton¹¹ **Whipple**, Sherman Leland¹⁰, Dr. Solomon M.⁹, David⁸, Aaron⁷, Col. Moses⁶, Deacon Jacob⁵, Deacon James⁴, Joseph³, Matthew², Matthew¹)²⁰¹⁵ was born in Plymouth, Plymouth Co., Mass. 24 June 1950 and married **Debra Lynn Ward** there 7 July 1984. Debra,²⁰¹⁶ daughter of Charlie Fletcher **Ward** and Betty Jane **Thompson**, was born in Mocksville, Davie Co., N.C. 26 April 1956.

Benjamin B. **Brewster** Jr. and Debra Lynn **Ward** had the following children born in Plymouth:
  9441 i. Hannah Ward¹⁴ **Brewster**²⁰¹⁷ 2 July 1985.

9442   ii.   Ellis Jane **Brewster**[2018] 24 September 1988.

7928. **Penelope**[13] **Brewster** (Anne Platt[12] **Withington**, Katharyn Carlton[11] **Whipple**, Sherman Leland[10], Dr. Solomon M.[9], David[8], Aaron[7], Col. Moses[6], Deacon Jacob[5], Deacon James[4], Joseph[3], Matthew[2], Matthew[1])[2019] was born in Plymouth, Plymouth Co., Mass. 23 September 1952 and married **Weston Keyes** there in 1979. Weston,[2020] son of Stanley Weston **Keyes** and Virginia May **Stevens**, was born in Newton, Middlesex Co., Mass. 7 September 1951.

Penelope **Brewster** and Weston **Keyes** had the following children born in York, York Co. Maine:
    9443   i.   Madagan[14] **Keyes**[2021] 20 April 1987.
    9444   ii.   Larkin **Keyes**[2022] 14 October 1989.

7932. **Paul Tucker**[13] **Withington** (Paul[12], Katharyn Carlton[11] **Whipple**, Sherman Leland[10], Dr. Solomon M.[9], David[8], Aaron[7], Col. Moses[6], Deacon Jacob[5], Deacon James[4], Joseph[3], Matthew[2], Matthew[1])[2023] was born in Plymouth, Plymouth Co., Mass. 10 June 1953. and married **Mary Cornelia Houbolt**.

Paul Tucker **Withington** and Mary Cornelia **Houbolt** had the following children:
    9445   i.   Lauren Cornelia[14] **Withington**[2024] born 28 May 1983.
    9446   ii.   Julianna Whitney **Withington**[2025] born 23 August 1989.

7937. **Mettie Micheaux**[13] **Whipple** (Sherman Leland[12], Sherman Leland[11], Sherman Leland[10], Dr. Solomon M.[9], David[8], Aaron[7], Col. Moses[6], Deacon Jacob[5], Deacon James[4], Joseph[3], Matthew[2], Matthew[1])[2026] was born in Boston, Suffolk Co., Mass. 17 July 1948 and married **Michael Schiro** 11 June 1977.

Mettie Micheaux **Whipple** and Michael **Schiro** had the following children born in Boston:
    9447   i.   Stephanie LeGrand[14] **Schiro**[2027] 2 January 1980.
    9448   ii.   Arthur Leland **Schiro**[2028] 23 June 1983.

7938. **Sherman Taylor**[13] **Whipple** (Sherman Leland[12], Sherman Leland[11], Sherman Leland[10], Dr. Solomon M.[9], David[8], Aaron[7], Col. Moses[6], Deacon Jacob[5], Deacon James[4], Joseph[3], Matthew[2], Matthew[1])[2029] was born in Nashville, Davidson Co., Tenn. 31 May 1950 and married **Kathlean Brown**.

Sherman Taylor **Whipple** and Kathlean **Brown** had the following children born in Weymouth, Norfolk Co., Mass.:

    9449   i.   Jessica Louise[14] **Whipple**[2030] 9 May 1977.

    9450   ii.   Matthew Sherman **Whipple**[2031] 3 September 1980.

7939. **Louise Barton**[13] **Whipple** (Sherman Leland[12], Sherman Leland[11], Sherman Leland[10], Dr. Solomon M.[9], David[8], Aaron[7], Col. Moses[6], Deacon Jacob[5], Deacon James[4], Joseph[3], Matthew[2], Matthew[1]) was born in Glen Cove, Nassau Co., N.Y. 13 April 1955 and married **John T. Gillock II** 14 May 1983.[2032] He also married **Ann Lebo**.

Louise Barton **Whipple** and John T. **Gillock** II had the following child born in Franklin, Simpson Co., Ky.:

    9451   i.   John T.[14] **Gillock III**[2033] 13 January 1988.

7940. **Alan Morrison**[13] **Whipple** (Paul Jones[12], Sherman Leland[11], Sherman Leland[10], Dr. Solomon M.[9], David[8], Aaron[7], Col. Moses[6], Deacon Jacob[5], Deacon James[4], Joseph[3], Matthew[2], Matthew[1])[2034] was born in Boston, Suffolk Co., Mass. 28 August 1948 and married **Sara Ellen Tallman** 30 October 1980.

Alan Morrison **Whipple** and Sara Ellen **Tallman** had the following children born in Plymouth, Plymouth Co., Mass.:

    9452   i.   Hanna Tallman[14] **Whipple**[2035] 28 December 1978.

    9453   ii.   Jacob Tallman **Whipple**[2036] 16 October 1985.

7941. **Belinda**[13] **Whipple** (Paul Jones[12], Sherman Leland[11], Sherman Leland[10], Dr. Solomon M.[9], David[8], Aaron[7], Col. Moses[6], Deacon Jacob[5], Deacon James[4], Joseph[3], Matthew[2], Matthew[1])[2037] was born in Boston, Suffolk Co., Mass. 26 January 1950 and married **David D. Worth** 15 June 1974.

Belinda **Whipple** and David D. **Worth** had the following children:

    9454   i.   Margaret Whipple[14] **Worth**[2038] born in Wendell, Franklin Co., Mass. 7 January 1977.

    9455   ii.   Moser William **Worth**[2039] born in Wareham, Plymouth Co., Mass. 19 October 1979.

    9456   iii.   Amos Tingley **Worth**[2040] born in Wareham 27 August 1981.

7942. **Paul Hersey**[13] **Whipple** (Paul Jones[12], Sherman Leland[11], Sherman Leland[10], Dr. Solomon M.[9], David[8], Aaron[7], Col. Moses[6], Deacon Jacob[5], Deacon James[4], Joseph[3], Matthew[2], Matthew[1])[2041] was born in

Boston, Suffolk Co., Mass. 23 July 1952 and married twice. (1) **Maryann Bonfiglio** 12 July 1975. (2) **Patricia Norton Cahalan** 14 February 1986.

Paul Hersey **Whipple** and Maryann **Bonfiglio** had the following children born in Plymouth, Mass.:

- 9457 i. Jason Tucker[14] **Whipple**[2042] 20 October 1976.
- 9458 ii. Nathan Alan **Whipple**[2043] 10 March 1978.
- 9459 iii. Colby Taylor **Whipple**[2044] 14 August 1980.

Paul Hersey **Whipple** and Patricia Norton **Cahalan** had the following child born in Boston:

- 9460 iv. Jillian Patricia **Whipple**[2045] 1 December 1988.

7943. **Margarita Elisa**[13] **Estrada** (Margaret Louise[12] **Whipple**, Sherman Leland[11], Sherman Leland[10], Dr. Solomon M.[9], David[8], Aaron[7], Col. Moses[6], Deacon Jacob[5], Deacon James[4], Joseph[3], Matthew[2], Matthew[1])[2046] was born in Boston, Suffolk Co., Mass. 26 June 1948 and married **Danilo Miron** in Guatemala City, Guatemala 3 December 1971.

Margarita Elisa **Estrada** and Danilo **Miron** had the following children born in Guatemala City:

- 9461 i. Luis Pedro[14] **Miron**[2047] 28 June 1973.
- 9462 ii. Alejandro **Miron**[2048] 12 July 1975.
- 9463 iii. Lisa Margarita **Miron**[2049] 20 February 1977.

7944. **Olga Lucrecia**[13] **Estrada** (Margaret Louise[12] **Whipple**, Sherman Leland[11], Sherman Leland[10], Dr. Solomon M.[9], David[8], Aaron[7], Col. Moses[6], Deacon Jacob[5], Deacon James[4], Joseph[3], Matthew[2], Matthew[1])[2050] was born in Guatemala City, Guatemala 17 August 1950 and married **Gustavo Giron** there in 1974.

Olga Lucrecia **Estrada** and Gustavo **Giron** had the following children born in Guatemala City:

- 9464 i. Gustavo[14] **Giron**[2051] 2 July 1975.
- 9465 ii. Diego **Giron**[2052] 3 October 1977.
- 9466 iii. Andres **Giron**[2053] 8 February 1981.
- 9467 iv. Maribelle **Giron**[2054] 15 October 1983.

7945. **Sandra Louise**[13] **Estrada** (Margaret Louise[12] **Whipple**, Sherman Leland[11], Sherman Leland[10], Dr. Solomon M.[9], David[8], Aaron[7], Col. Moses[6], Deacon Jacob[5], Deacon James[4], Joseph[3], Matthew[2],

Matthew[1])[2055] was born in Guatemala City, Guatemala 16 October 1951 and married **Guillermo Monroy** there 19 April 1974.

Sandra Louise **Estrada** and Guillermo **Monroy** had the following children:
- 9468 i. Guillermo[14] **Monroy**[2056] born in Guatemala City 27 January 1976.
- 9469 ii. Sandra Lucia **Monroy**[2057] born in Guatemala City 1 March 1980.
- 9470 iii. Christian **Monroy**[2058] born in Miami, Dade Co., Fla. 1 September 1987.

7946. **Carmen Patricia**[13] **Estrada** (Margaret Louise[12] **Whipple**, Sherman Leland[11], Sherman Leland[10], Dr. Solomon M.[9], David[8], Aaron[7], Col. Moses[6], Deacon Jacob[5], Deacon James[4], Joseph[3], Matthew[2], Matthew[1])[2059] was born in Guatemala City, Guatemala 13 July 1953 and married **Estuardo Bolanos** 12 November 1976.

Carmen Patricia **Estrada** and Estuardo **Bolanos** had the following children:
- 9471 i. Karla Maria[14] **Bolanos**[2060] born in Rochester, Monroe Co., N. Y. 25 February 1981.
- 9472 ii. Ana Gabriela **Bolanos**[2061] born in Guatemala City 8 October 1983.
- 9473 iii. Ana Sophia **Bolanos**[2062] born in Guatemala City 30 April 1985.

7947. **Suzanna Maria**[13] **Estrada** (Margaret Louise[12] **Whipple**, Sherman Leland[11], Sherman Leland[10], Dr. Solomon M.[9], David[8], Aaron[7], Col. Moses[6], Deacon Jacob[5], Deacon James[4], Joseph[3], Matthew[2], Matthew[1])[2063] was born in Guatemala City, Guatemala 21 April 1956 and married **Alberto Novella** 12 June 1978.

Suzanna Maria **Estrada** and Alberto **Novella** had the following children born in Guatemala City:
- 9474 i. Juan Pablo[14] **Novella**[2064] 10 May 1983.
- 9475 ii. Melani Marie **Novella**[2065] 22 January 1986.

7948. **Deborah Lily**[13] **Estrada** (Margaret Louise[12] **Whipple**, Sherman Leland[11], Sherman Leland[10], Dr. Solomon M.[9], David[8], Aaron[7], Col. Moses[6], Deacon Jacob[5], Deacon James[4], Joseph[3], Matthew[2], Matthew[1])[2066] was born in Guatemala City, Guatemala 29 October 1958 and married twice. (1) **Julio Lowenthan** December 1980. He died in August 1983 at 25 years of age.[2067] (2) **Carlos Escobar** 28 September 1986.

Deborah Lily **Estrada** and Carlos **Escobar** had the following children born in Miami, Dade Co. Fla.:

    9476   i.   Enrique[14] **Escobar**[2068] 5 August 1987.

    9477   ii.   Carolina **Escobar**[2069] 12 December 1998.

    9478   iii.   Monica **Escobar**[2070] 12 December 1998.

7949. **Katherine Michelle**[13] **Estrada** (Margaret Louise[12] **Whipple**, Sherman Leland[11], Sherman Leland[10], Dr. Solomon M.[9], David[8], Aaron[7], Col. Moses[6], Deacon Jacob[5], Deacon James[4], Joseph[3], Matthew[2], Matthew[1])[2071] was born in Guatemala City, Guatemala 13 March 1961 and married **Alvaro Wer** in Guatemala City 26 October 1984.

Katherine Michelle **Estrada** and Alvaro **Wer** had the following child born in Guatemala City:

    9479   i.   Alvaro[14] **Wer**[2072] 6 June 1988.

7958. **Susan Marie**[13] **Whipple** (Donald Edwin[12], Perley Arthur[11], Aaron Mason[10], Barnabas Cooper[9], David[8], Aaron[7], Col. Moses[6], Deacon Jacob[5], Deacon James[4], Joseph[3], Matthew[2], Matthew[1])[2073] was born in Wurzburg, Germany 9 July 1960 and married **Richard Paul Kimball** in Grantham, Sullivan Co., N.H. 30 September 1994. Richard is the son of Roger **Kimball** and Leona **Morrison**.[2074] Susan was living in Newport, Sullivan Co., N. H. in 1993.

Susan Marie **Whipple** and Richard Paul **Kimball** had the following children born in Prescott, Yavapai Co., Ariz.:

    9480   i.   Taysa Maria[14] **Kimball**[2075] 19 July 1980.

    9481   ii.   Adam Michael **Kimball**[2076] 13 January 1986.

7959. **Claudia Avis**[13] **Whipple** (Donald Edwin[12], Perley Arthur[11], Aaron Mason[10], Barnabas Cooper[9], David[8], Aaron[7], Col. Moses[6], Deacon Jacob[5], Deacon James[4], Joseph[3], Matthew[2], Matthew[1])[2077] was born in Wurzburg, Germany 24 May 1961 and married **Mitchell John Swenson** in Croydon, Sullivan Co., N. H., 6 June 1982. Mitchell is the son of Dean **Swenson** and Sheila **Lane**.[2078] Claudia was living in Grantham, Sullivan Co., N. H. in 1993.

Claudia Avis **Whipple** and Mitchell John **Swenson** had the following children born in Hanover, Grafton Co., N. H.:

    9482   i.   Nicholas Aaron[14] **Swenson**[2079] 31 August 1985.

    9483   ii.   Amanda Mae **Swenson**[2080] 20 January 1989.

7961. **Linda Lou**[13] **Whipple** (Donald Edwin[12], Perley Arthur[11], Aaron Mason[10], Barnabas Cooper[9], David[8], Aaron[7], Col. Moses[6], Deacon Jacob[5], Deacon James[4], Joseph[3], Matthew[2], Matthew[1])[2081] was born in Shirley, Middlesex Co., Mass. 7 May 1964 and married **(__) Richardson**. Linda was living in Las Vegas, Clark Co., Nev. in 1993.

Linda Lou **Whipple** had the following child born in Prescott, Yavapai Co., Ariz.:

    9484   i.   Edward Allan[14] **Whipple**[2082] 1 April 1986.

7966. **Linda May**[13] **Whitley** (Virginia May[12] **Wright**, Veda May[11] **Whipple**, Aaron Mason[10], Barnabas Cooper[9], David[8], Aaron[7], Col. Moses[6], Deacon Jacob[5], Deacon James[4], Joseph[3], Matthew[2], Matthew[1])[2083] was born in San Antonio, Bexar Co., Tex. 20 July 1947 and married **Kenneth Orean Miller Sr.** in Keene, Cheshire Co., N.H. 27 February 1965. Kenneth,[2084] son of Rufus **Miller** and Roberta **Kellogg**, was born in Keene 25 November 1944. Ken has been a Retail Department Store Manager or a District Manager with various retail companies on the east and west coasts since 1962. The family moved to Phoenix, Maricopa Co., Ariz. in November 1983.

Linda May **Whitley** and Kenneth Orean **Miller** Sr. had the following children born in Keene:

+   9485   i.   Kenneth Orean[14] **Miller** Jr. 15 June 1966.
    9486 ii. Colette May **Miller**[2085] 14 August 1969 and married George Andrew **Lavra** in Phoenix 27 March 1993. Andy,[2086] son of George **Lavra** and Rosa **La Spesa,** was born in San Diego, San Diego Co., Calif. 15 February 1960. He married (2) Katherine **Smith** in Phoenix 30 October 1982. Andy is a 1984 graduate of University Technical Institute (UTI) in Phoenix and is self employed (1999). Colette is the stepmother of Christopher **Lavra** born 17 Feb. 1983 and Anna Marie **Lavra**, born 10 May 1984. Both were born in Phoenix.
    9487 iii. Ryan Orean **Miller**[2087] 18 September 1973 and married Gail Marie **Lamphier** in Glendale, Maricopa Co., Ariz. 9 December 1995. Gail,[2088] daughter of Ernest **Lamphier** and Brooke **Ecker,** was born in Auburn, Cayuga Co., N.Y. 6 January 1971. She earned a Bachelor of Science Degree in Education in 1995 at Grand Canyon University, Phoenix. On 4 Feb. 1999, Ryan and Gail adopted Dylan Ray and Savanna Brooke **Wallace**, the son and daughter

of Gail's deceased sister, Lynn Ann **Wallace** (born 23 March 1969 in Auburn, N.Y., died 16 February 1997 in Phoenix). Dylan Ray was born 1 May 1992 and Savanna was born 11 November 1995. Both were born in Phoenix.

7967. **Carol Ann**[13] **Wright** (Everett Whipple[12], Veda May[11] **Whipple**, Aaron Mason[10], Barnabas Cooper[9], David[8], Aaron[7], Col. Moses[6], Deacon Jacob[5], Deacon James[4], Joseph[3], Matthew[2], Matthew[1])[2089] was born in Keene, Cheshire Co., N.H. 14 July 1951 and married twice. (1) **Ronald Lyle Prouty Sr.** 13 March 1970. They were divorced in 1983. (2) **Jerry Foster** 14 April 1990.

Carol Ann **Wright** and Ronald Lyle **Prouty** Sr. had the following children:

+ 9488 i. Ronald Lyle[14] **Prouty** Jr. born 15 March 1972.
+ 9489 ii. Kelly Jean **Prouty** born 2 October 1970.

7968. **Nancy Jo**[13] **Wright** (Everett Whipple[12], Veda May[11] **Whipple**, Aaron Mason[10], Barnabas Cooper[9], David[8], Aaron[7], Col. Moses[6], Deacon Jacob[5], Deacon James[4], Joseph[3], Matthew[2], Matthew[1])[2090] was born in Council Bluffs, Pottawattamie Co., Iowa 6 September 1952 and married **Thomas Hugh Ward** in Charlestown, Sullivan Co., N.H. 12 September 1970. Thomas,[2091] son of Ralph **Ward**, was born in Springfield, Windsor Co., Vt. 9 July 1950. He served in the U.S. Air Force from August 1973 to August 1983 and earned a B A in Managment from National Louis University in July 1999. Nancy Jo earned a B. A. in Finance from George Mason University, Fairfax, Fairfax City Area Co., Va.

Nancy Jo **Wright** and Thomas Hugh **Ward** had the following children:

+ 9490 i. Justine Elizabeth[14] **Ward** born 5 March 1971.
  9491 ii. Thaddeus Tyler Wright **Ward**[2092] born in Keene, Cheshire Co., N.H. 3 May 1973 and. was awarded an Associate Degree in Computer Electronics from Computer Learning Center, Alexandria, Alexandria City Co., Va. in July 1999.
  9492 iii. Hillary **Ward**[2093] stillborn in Louisiana 7 September 1977 and buried in Pineville, Rapides Parish, La.
  9493 iv. Ashlee Nichole **Ward**[2094] born in Norman, Cleveland Co., Okla. 27 January 1981. She was a student (1999) at James Madison University, Harrisonburg, Harrisonburg City Co., Va. working for a Bachelor's Degree.

{ G 1385 }

7969. **Joanne Ellen**[13] **Wright** (Everett Whipple[12], Veda May[11] **Whipple**, Aaron Mason[10], Barnabas Cooper[9], David[8], Aaron[7], Col. Moses[6], Deacon Jacob[5], Deacon James[4], Joseph[3], Matthew[2], Matthew[1])[2095] was born in Keene, Cheshire Co., N.H. 7 September 1954 and married **David Charles Vosburg** 24 May 1975. David,[2096] son of Charles **Vosburg**, was born in Bellows Falls, Windham Co., Vt. 23 January 1956. He is a building contractor (1999). Joanne is a graduate of the Keene Beauty Academy and is a self employed hairdresser (1999).

Joanne Ellen **Wright** and David Charles **Vosburg** had the following children:

  9494 i. Matthew David[14] **Vosburg**[2097] born in Springfield, Windsor Co., Vt. 2 March 1982.
  9495 ii. Dana Marie **Vosburg**[2098] born in Brattleboro, Windham Co., Vt. 1 November 1988.
  9496 iii. Ella **Vosburg**[2099] born in Brattleboro 5 October 1990.

7970. **Christine May**[13] **Wright** (Lawrence Blaine[12], Veda May[11] **Whipple**, Aaron Mason[10], Barnabas Cooper[9], David[8], Aaron[7], Col. Moses[6], Deacon Jacob[5], Deacon James[4], Joseph[3], Matthew[2], Matthew[1])[2100] was born in San Juan, Puerto Rico 1 July 1954 and married twice. (1) **David Buffum** in Keene, Cheshire Co., N.H. 14 July 1973. (2) **Charles Ronald Beauregard Jr.** in Keene 27 August 1977. Charles is the son of Charles Ronald **Beauregard** Sr.[2101]

Christine May **Wright** and Charles Ronald **Beauregard** Jr. had the following children born in Keene:

  9497 i. Charles Lawrence[14] **Beauregard**[2102] 21 May 1977.
  9498 ii. Andrew Luke **Beauregard**[2103] 9 August 1979.

7972. **Patrick Drew**[13] **Wright** (Lawrence Blaine[12], Veda May[11] **Whipple**, Aaron Mason[10], Barnabas Cooper[9], David[8], Aaron[7], Col. Moses[6], Deacon Jacob[5], Deacon James[4], Joseph[3], Matthew[2], Matthew[1])[2104] was born in Keene, Cheshire Co., N.H. 3 August 1957 and married **Kelly Daversa** in California 28 November 1981. She is the daughter of George **Daversa** and Ruth (___).[2105] At the time of their marriage, Patrick was in the U.S. Navy stationed at Coronado, San Diego Co., Calif.

Patrick Drew **Wright** and Kelly **Daversa** had the following children:

  9499 i. Nicole Marie[14] **Wright**[2106] born 26 January 1983.
  9500 ii. Daniel **Wright**.[2107]

{ G 1386 }

7973. **Jon Andrae**[13] **Wright** (Lawrence Blaine[12], Veda May[11] **Whipple**, Aaron Mason[10], Barnabas Cooper[9], David[8], Aaron[7], Col. Moses[6], Deacon Jacob[5], Deacon James[4], Joseph[3], Matthew[2], Matthew[1])[2108] was born in Keene, Cheshire Co., N.H. 1 December 1958 and married **Karen Mary Sullivan** there 4 September 1982. The daughter of Richard H. **Sullivan**, Karen is a 1981 graduate of the Cheshire Hospital School of Radiology Technology in Keene.[2109]

Jon Andrae **Wright** and Karen Mary **Sullivan** had the following children:
  9501 i. Nicolas Sullivan[14] **Wright**[2110] born 20 September 1985.
  9502 ii. Nathan **Wright**[2111] born 24 September 1987.
  9503 iii. Andrea **Wright**.[2112]

7976. **Kevin Paul**[13] **Breen** (Barbara Newton[12] **Wright**, Veda May[11] **Whipple**, Aaron Mason[10], Barnabas Cooper[9], David[8], Aaron[7], Col. Moses[6], Deacon Jacob[5], Deacon James[4], Joseph[3], Matthew[2], Matthew[1])[2113] was born in Keene, Cheshire Co., N.H. 29 July 1952 and married **Marcia Lee Fosdick** there 15 April 1972. Marcia,[2114] daughter of Theron **Fosdick** and Shirley **Sweeney**, was born in Oakland, Alameda Co., Calif. 14 September 1951.

Kevin Paul **Breen** and Marcia Lee **Fosdick** had the following children born in Keene:
  9504 i. Canaan Duffy[14] **Breen**[2115] 3 October 1972 and married Keri Ann **Ingemi** in Leomimster, Worcester Co., Mass. 14 June 1997.
  9505 ii. Trevor Arik **Breen**[2116] 14 August 1975.
  9506 iii. Kevin Marc **Breen**[2117] 1 October 1977.

7977. **Kimberly Jane**[13] **Breen** (Barbara Newton[12] **Wright**, Veda May[11] **Whipple**, Aaron Mason[10], Barnabas Cooper[9], David[8], Aaron[7], Col. Moses[6], Deacon Jacob[5], Deacon James[4], Joseph[3], Matthew[2], Matthew[1])[2118] was born in Keene, Cheshire Co., N.H. 3 May 1956 and married twice. (1) **William F. Dennis** in Keene 25 August 1973. William,[2119] son of Francis **Dennis** and Agnes **Lomanski**, was born in Keene 9 March 1954. They were divorced in Keene 9 February 1988. (2) **Gary Loveland** 15 July 1989. Kimberly and Gary were married in New Hampshire's White Mountains and she is a stepmother to Gary's children: Jeremy, born 28 July 1972, Selina, born 31 Dec. 1973, Jenny, born 28 Dec. 1983, and Shannon, born 11 April 1987. Selina married Wade Thomas on 6 May 1995 in East Swanzey, Cheshire Co., N.H. Kimberly is a Leadperson at The Miniature Precision Bearing Division of MPB Corporation in Keene (1999).

Kimberly Jane **Breen** and William F. **Dennis** had the following children:
- + 9507 i. Jason Oliver[14] **Dennis** born 2 February 1974.
- + 9508 ii. Jamie Olivia **Dennis** born 4 December 1978.

7979. **Karolee May**[13] **Breen** (Barbara Newton[12] **Wright**, Veda May[11] **Whipple**, Aaron Mason[10], Barnabas Cooper[9], David[8], Aaron[7], Col. Moses[6], Deacon Jacob[5], Deacon James[4], Joseph[3], Matthew[2], Matthew[1])[2120] was born in Keene, Cheshire Co., N.H. 18 October 1958 and married **Gary Hendrickson** there 22 October 1976. Gary,[2121] son of Ralph **Hendrickson** and Eleanor **Hiiua**, was born in Keene 29 October 1955.

Karolee May **Breen** and Gary **Hendrickson** had the following children:
- + 9509 i. Heidi Ann[14] **Hendrickson** born 26 February 1975.
- 9510 ii. Heath Andrew **Hendrickson**[2122] born in Keene 15 June 1976.
- + 9511 iii. Nathan Robert **Hendrickson** born 5 February 1979.

7980. **Kathleen Ann**[13] **Breen** (Barbara Newton[12] **Wright**, Veda May[11] **Whipple**, Aaron Mason[10], Barnabas Cooper[9], David[8], Aaron[7], Col. Moses[6], Deacon Jacob[5], Deacon James[4], Joseph[3], Matthew[2], Matthew[1])[2123] was born in Keene, Cheshire Co., N.H. 18 October 1958 and married twice. (1) **Gregory Wendell Orkins** in Keene 28 August 1975. He is the son of Gregory **Orkins** and Sandra **Boyd**.[2124] They were divorced in New Hampshire 22 September 1980. (2) **Carl Warren Curtis** in Keene 13 February 1982. Carl,[2125] son of Leland **Curtis** and Dorothy **Greenleaf**, was born in Keene 11 July 1939.

Kathleen Ann **Breen** and Carl Warren **Curtis** had the following children:
- 9512 i. Kyle Leland[14] **Curtis**[2126] born in Petersboro, Hillsborough Co., N.H. 7 April 1984.
- 9513 ii. Jacob Robert **Curtis**[2127] born in Petersboro 1 October 1988.

7982. **Kelly Elizabeth**[13] **Breen** (Barbara Newton[12] **Wright**, Veda May[11] **Whipple**, Aaron Mason[10], Barnabas Cooper[9], David[8], Aaron[7], Col. Moses[6], Deacon Jacob[5], Deacon James[4], Joseph[3], Matthew[2], Matthew[1])[2128] was born in Keene, Cheshire Co., N.H. 12 June 1963 and married **Claude Girard Gaudreau** in Northfield, Franklin Co., Mass. 30 June 1984. Claude,[2129] son of Raymond **Gaudreau** and Beatrice **Lavallee**, was born in Québec, Canada 4 September 1963.

Kelly Elizabeth **Breen** had the following child born in Keene:
- 9514 i. Erin Newton[14] **Breen**[2130] 22 November 1979.

Kelly Elizabeth **Breen** and Claude Girard **Gaudreau** had the following child born in Keene:

    9515   ii.   Joseph Raymone **Gaudreau**[2131] 12 July 1985.

7984. **Jaclyn**[13] **Wright** (Charles Burgum[12], Veda May[11] **Whipple**, Aaron Mason[10], Barnabas Cooper[9], David[8], Aaron[7], Col. Moses[6], Deacon Jacob[5], Deacon James[4], Joseph[3], Matthew[2], Matthew[1])[2132] was born in Keene, Cheshire Co., N.H. 11 March 1959 and married **Kevin D. Stone** in Marlborough, Cheshire Co., N.H. 5 February 1977. Kevin,[2133] son of Frank L. **Stone**, was born in Marlborough 20 February 1959. Jaclyn and **Richard B. Stromgren, Jr.** were domestic partners in 1997. Richard had children: Richard B., III, born 12 February 1985 and Christopher J., born 13 December 1986; both born in Keene.

Jaclyn **Wright** and Kevin D. **Stone** had the following children:
+   9516   i.   Jenie Beth[14] **Stone** born 1 August 1977.
+   9517   ii.   Kylene Rae **Stone** born 3 October 1978.
    9518   iii.   Jackson Lee **Stone**[2134] born in Keene 12 September 1980.

7986. **Paul Lamon**[13] **Klassy** (Mary Lou[12] **Jensen**, Ruth Mildred[11] **Whipple**, Edgar J.[10], Darwin[9], Harvey[8], Aaron[7], Col. Moses[6], Deacon Jacob[5], Deacon James[4], Joseph[3], Matthew[2], Matthew[1])[2135] was born in St. Louis Park, Hennepin Co., Minn. 24 February 1961 and married **Leslie Renee Johnson** in Hopkins, Hennepin Co., Minn. 3 September 1983. Leslie,[2136] daughter of Robert **Johnson** and Geraldine **Montgomery**, was born in Minneapolis, Hennepin Co., Minn. 24 September 1961.

Paul Lamon **Klassy** and Leslie Renee **Johnson** had the following children born in St. Louis Park:
    9519   i.   Kyle Joseph[14] **Klassy**[2137] 19 April 1987.
    9520   ii.   Matthew Robert **Klassy**[2138] 14 November 1988.
    9521   iii.   Jenna Elizabeth **Klassy**[2139] 26 April 1994.

7987. **Gregory**[13] **Liles** (Shirley Yvonne[12] **Whipple**, Raymond J.[11], Edgar J.[10], Darwin[9], Harvey[8], Aaron[7], Col. Moses[6], Deacon Jacob[5], Deacon James[4], Joseph[3], Matthew[2], Matthew[1])[2140] was born in Orange Co., Calif. in 1947.

Gregory **Liles** had the following children:
    9522   i.   Scott[14] **Liles**[2141] born in 1974.
    9523   ii.   Temsee **Liles**[2142] born in 1976.

7988. **Pamela**[13] **Liles** (Shirley Yvonne[12] **Whipple**, Raymond J.[11], Edgar J.[10], Darwin[9], Harvey[8], Aaron[7], Col. Moses[6], Deacon Jacob[5], Deacon James[4], Joseph[3], Matthew[2], Matthew[1])[2143] was born in Orange Co., Calif. in 1949.

Pamela **Liles** had the following children:
- 9524 i. Tamara[14] **Liles**[2144] born in 1974.
- 9525 ii. Trista **Liles**[2145] born in 1983.

7989. **Jeffrey**[13] **Liles** (Shirley Yvonne[12] **Whipple**, Raymond J.[11], Edgar J.[10], Darwin[9], Harvey[8], Aaron[7], Col. Moses[6], Deacon Jacob[5], Deacon James[4], Joseph[3], Matthew[2], Matthew[1])[2146] was born in Orange Co., Calif. in 1951.

Jeffrey **Liles** had the following children:
- 9526 i. Danielle[14] **Liles**[2147] born in 1974.
- 9527 ii. Nicholas **Liles**[2148] born in 1980.
- 9528 iii. Noah **Liles**[2149] born in 1981.

7991. **Toby**[13] **Whipple** (Robert Ray[12], Raymond J.[11], Edgar J.[10], Darwin[9], Harvey[8], Aaron[7], Col. Moses[6], Deacon Jacob[5], Deacon James[4], Joseph[3], Matthew[2], Matthew[1])[2150] was born 18 March 1951.

Toby **Whipple** had the following children:
- 9529 i. Rocky[14] **Whipple**[2151] born 11 June 1977.
- 9530 ii. Troy **Whipple**[2152] born 3 July 1979.
- 9531 iii. Terra **Whipple**[2153] born 2 December 1982.

7993. **Jerry**[13] **Whipple** (Robert Ray[12], Raymond J.[11], Edgar J.[10], Darwin[9], Harvey[8], Aaron[7], Col. Moses[6], Deacon Jacob[5], Deacon James[4], Joseph[3], Matthew[2], Matthew[1])[2154] was born 30 March 1953.

Jerry **Whipple** had the following child:
- 9532 i. Amanda[14] **Whipple**[2155] born 2 June 1990.

7994. **Janielle**[13] **Whipple** (Robert Ray[12], Raymond J.[11], Edgar J.[10], Darwin[9], Harvey[8], Aaron[7], Col. Moses[6], Deacon Jacob[5], Deacon James[4], Joseph[3], Matthew[2], Matthew[1])[2156] was born 4 April 1954.

Janielle **Whipple** had the following children:
- 9533 i. Tenile[14] **Whipple**[2157] born 24 August 1980.
- 9534 ii. Jenna **Whipple**[2158] born 4 February 1986.

7995. **Jeffrey Jonathan**[13] **Brown** (Frank Addison[12], William Joseph[11], Eva De Etta[10] **McMillin**, Elsie Elvira[9] **Whipple**, Tyler B.[8], Moses[7], Col. Moses[6], Deacon Jacob[5], Deacon James[4], Joseph[3], Matthew[2], Matthew[1])[2159] was born in Grand Forks, Grand Forks Co., N. Dak. 10 April 1951 and married twice. (1) **Deborah Maxine Nevin**. (2) **Leslie Joan Mathison** in Kirkland, King Co., Wash. 14 March 1992.

Jeffrey Jonathan **Brown** and Deborah Maxine **Nevin** had the following child:
    9535   i.   Jason Dieter[14] **Brown**[2160] born 25 July 1975.

Jeffrey Jonathan **Brown** and Leslie Joan **Mathison** had the following child:
    9536   ii.   Paul Thomas **Brown**[2161] born 27 July 1993.

7997. **Karen Elizabeth**[13] **Wilkin** (Elsie Ann[12] **Brown**, William Joseph[11], Eva De Etta[10] **McMillin**, Elsie Elvira[9] **Whipple**, Tyler B.[8], Moses[7], Col. Moses[6], Deacon Jacob[5], Deacon James[4], Joseph[3], Matthew[2], Matthew[1])[2162] was born in Dallas, Dallas Co., Tex. 5 September 1963 and married **John Winston Spencer** in Slidell, Saint Tammany Parish, La. 2 August 1986. John,[2163] son of Winston C. **Spencer** and Lynn Ann **North**, was born in Denver, Denver Co., Colo. 19 December 1959.

Karen Elizabeth **Wilkin** and John Winston **Spencer** had the following children born in Slidell:
    9537   i.   Evan Ruark[14] **Spencer**[2164] 11 March 1991.
    9538   ii.   Andrew Brenden **Spencer**[2165] 4 November 1993.
    9539   iii.   Daniel Wilkin **Spencer**[2166] 21 February 1998.

8007. **Paul Brian**[13] **Whipple** (Galen Charles[12], Charles Franklin[11], Louis Whiting[10], Charles Crary[9], Oliver[8], Jacob[7], Col. Moses[6], Deacon Jacob[5], Deacon James[4], Joseph[3], Matthew[2], Matthew[1])[2167] was born in Dallas, Dallas Co., Tex. 28 November 1969 and married **Julie Davis**. Julie,[2168] daughter of Lee **Davis** and Shirley **Knapp**, was born in Delta, Delta Co., Colo. 15 January 1971.

Paul Brian **Whipple** and Julie **Davis** had the following children born in Aurora, Colo.:
    9540   i.   Christopher Scott[14] **Whipple**[2169] 20 April 1995.
    9541   ii.   Rachel Cristene **Whipple**[2170] 21 April 1998.

8019. **Kathryn Renee**[13] **Whitney** (Dale Craig[12], Wallace Lowell[11], Harry Erwin[10], Eli Harrison[9], William Flanagan[8], Moses[7], Jemima[6] **Whipple**, Deacon Jacob[5], Deacon James[4], Joseph[3], Matthew[2], Matthew[1])[2171] was born in Yuba City, Sutter Co., Calif. 4 December 1966.

Kathryn Renee **Whitney** had the following children:

  9542 i. Whitney Brianne[14] **Ludwick**[2172] born in Yuba City 22 December 1987.

  9543 ii. Brandon Craig **Whitney**[2173] born in Yuba City 8 November 1989.

  9544 iii. Chelsey May **Whitney**[2174] born in Oroville, Butte Co., Calif. 25 February 1992.

  9545 iv. Jade Nicole **Whitney**[2175] born in Oroville 8 May 1996.

8020. **Cynthia Anne**[13] **Whitney** (Dale Craig[12], Wallace Lowell[11], Harry Erwin[10], Eli Harrison[9], William Flanagan[8], Moses[7], Jemima[6] **Whipple**, Deacon Jacob[5], Deacon James[4], Joseph[3], Matthew[2], Matthew[1])[2176] was born in Yuba City, Sutter Co., Calif. 4 April 1969 and married **Tadd Alan Pobst** in Lindsay, Tulare Co., Calif. 26 November 1994. Tadd,[2177] son of Thomas **Pobst** and Janice **Ark**, was born in Wabash, Wabash Co., Ind. 18 May 1965.

Cynthia Anne **Whitney** and Tadd Alan **Pobst** had the following children born in Bakersfield, Kern Co., Calif:

  9546 i. Jocelyn Taylor[14] **Pobst**[2178] 28 June 1996.

  9547 ii. Ethan McDaniel **Pobst**[2179] 22 June 1998.

8026. **Barbara Christine**[13] **Carlson** (Barbara Patricia[12] **Becker**, Gladys Eloise[11] **Fitch**, William Herbert[10], Henry H.[9], Lucretia Lavinia[8] **Hurd**, Nathan[7], Ruth[6] **Labree**, Ruth[5] **Putnam**, Ruth[4] **Whipple**, Joseph[3], Matthew[2], Matthew[1])[2180] was born in Chicago, Cook Co., Ill. 24 November 1952 and married **Jim Evans** in Dunwoody, DeKalb Co., Ga. 4 April 1977. Jim,[2181] son of Ralph Isaac **Evans** and Gillian Norton **Shubert**, was born in Ayer, Worcester Co., Mass. 5 March 1947.

Barbara Christine **Carlson** and Jim **Evans** had the following children born in Atlanta, Fulton Co., Ga.:

  9548 i. Anna Christine[14] **Evans**[2182] 26 September 1982.

  9549 ii. William Thomas **Evans**[2183] 26 September 1982.

8027. **Gregg Gordon**[13] **Carlson** (Barbara Patricia[12] **Becker**, Gladys Eloise[11] **Fitch**, William Herbert[10], Henry H.[9], Lucretia Lavinia[8] **Hurd**, Nathan[7], Ruth[6] **Labree**, Ruth[5] **Putnam**, Ruth[4] **Whipple**, Joseph[3],

Matthew², Matthew¹)²¹⁸⁴ was born in Atlanta, Fulton Co., Ga. 8 January 1963 and married **Emelda Helen Oliver** in Hapeville, Fulton Co., Ga. 26 April 1986. Cissy,²¹⁸⁵ daughter of James Thomas **Oliver** and Emelda Lou **Freiberger**, was born in East Point, Fulton Co. 16 June 1964.

Gregg Gordon **Carlson** and Emelda Helen **Oliver** had the following children born in East Point:
       9550   i.   Ashley Elizabeth¹⁴ **Carlson**²¹⁸⁶ 7 July 1989.
       9551   ii.   Matthew Gunnard **Carlson**²¹⁸⁷ 3 July 1992.

    8030. **Allan Reed**¹³ **Emery** (Marguerite¹² **Faust**, Helen¹¹ **Reed**, Ora J.¹⁰, Sylvester P.⁹, Lydia⁸ **Hurd**, Nathan⁷, Ruth⁶ **Labree**, Ruth⁵ **Putnam**, Ruth⁴ **Whipple**, Joseph³, Matthew², Matthew¹)²¹⁸⁸ was born in Farmington, Franklin Co., Maine 31 March 1958 and married twice. (1) **Alison Chakoumakos** in Farmington 8 January 1977. Alison,²¹⁸⁹ daughter of Charles **Chakoumakos** and Mary Alice **Golder**, was born 2 May 1958. She marrried (2) **Wetherbee Lanson**. (2) **Nancy Cyr** in Portland, Cumberland Co., Maine 4 July 1986. Nancy,²¹⁹⁰ daughter of Harold **Cyr** and Mary **Wentzell**, was born 14 June 1964. Allan and Nancy were living in Portland, Maine in 1999.

Allan Reed **Emery** and Alison **Chakoumakos** had the following child born in Farmington:
       9552   i.   Segue¹⁴ **Emery**²¹⁹¹ 26 May 1979.

Allan Reed **Emery** and Nancy **Cyr** had the following child born in Portland:
       9553   ii.   Faith Margeaux **Emery**²¹⁹² 25 November 1995.

    8031. **Theodore Prescott**¹³ **Emery III** (Marguerite¹² **Faust**, Helen¹¹ **Reed**, Ora J.¹⁰, Sylvester P.⁹, Lydia⁸ **Hurd**, Nathan⁷, Ruth⁶ **Labree**, Ruth⁵ **Putnam**, Ruth⁴ **Whipple**, Joseph³, Matthew², Matthew¹)²¹⁹³ was born in Farmington, Franklin Co., Maine 8 December 1960 and married **Jeanette Esquivel** there 19 March 1983. Jeanette, daughter of Paul **Esquivel** and Diane **Soule**, was born in Mt. Clemens, Macomb Co., Mich. Ted and Jeanette were living in Farmington in 1999.

Theodore Prescott **Emery** III and Jeanette **Esquivel** had the following children born in Farmington:
       9554   i.   Arion¹⁴ **Emery**²¹⁹⁴ 30 July 1983.
       9555   ii.   Lancaster John **Emery**²¹⁹⁵ 30 January 1991.

8043. **Leland Glea**[13] **Sherburne III** (Leland Glea[12], Dorothy Mae[11] **Deal**, Koli Horace[10], Ettie Laura[9] **Coykendall**, Laura Emeline[8] **Putnam**, Hiram[7], Bailey[6], Timothy[5], Ruth[4] **Whipple**, Joseph[3], Matthew[2], Matthew[1])[2196] was born in Paw Paw, Van Buren Co., Mich. 18 July 1961 and married **Darcy Kay Crosby** in Battle Creek, Calhoun Co., Mich. 5 September 1987. Darcy,[2197] daughter of Clarence Dale **Crosby** and Virginia **Angelo**, was born in Battle Creek 30 June 1955. She also married **Tolbert Rhea Criswell**.

Leland Glea **Sherburne** III and Darcy Kay **Crosby** had the following child born in Battle Creek:

    9556   i.   Bryan Anthony[14] **Sherburne**[2198] 13 March 1988.

8045. **Jamie Lynn**[13] **Sherburne** (James Lewis[12], Dorothy Mae[11] **Deal**, Koli Horace[10], Ettie Laura[9] **Coykendall**, Laura Emeline[8] **Putnam**, Hiram[7], Bailey[6], Timothy[5], Ruth[4] **Whipple**, Joseph[3], Matthew[2], Matthew[1])[2199] was born in Paw Paw, Van Buren Co., Mich. 10 July 1963 and married **James Dean Nave** in Murfreesboro, Rutherford Co., Tenn. 7 July 1990. He was born in Lapeer Co., Mich. 3 May 1965.[2200]

Jamie Lynn **Sherburne** and James Dean **Nave** had the following children:

    9557   i.   Jared Richard James[14] **Nave**[2201] born in Nashville, Davidson Co., Tenn. 7 April 1993.
    9558   ii.   Jacob Lewis **Nave**[2202] born in Murfreesboro 24 February 1997.

8046. **Paula Jean**[13] **Sherburne** (James Lewis[12], Dorothy Mae[11] **Deal**, Koli Horace[10], Ettie Laura[9] **Coykendall**, Laura Emeline[8] **Putnam**, Hiram[7], Bailey[6], Timothy[5], Ruth[4] **Whipple**, Joseph[3], Matthew[2], Matthew[1])[2203] was born in Paw Paw, Van Buren Co., Mich. 21 May 1964 and married **William Hank Mizell** in Murfreesboro, Rutherford Co., Tenn. 2 November 1984. He was born in Chicago, Cook Co., Ill. 19 February 1959.[2204]

Paula Jean **Sherburne** and William Hank **Mizell** had the following child born in Murfreesboro:

    9559   i.   Heather Dawn[14] **Mizell** 27 October 1987.[2205]

ENDNOTES, GENERATION THIRTEEN

1. through 4. Chaffee to Whipple, *2 Letters.*
5. through 7. Dodge to Whipple, *Letter, 6 April 1993.*
8. through 19. Jones to Whipple, *Letter 05/21/1991 & 01/16/1997.*
20. through 23. J.A. Whipple, *2 Letters.*
24. through 28. Davis to Whipple, *Letter, 26 March 1989.*
29. through 31. T. Pearson to Whipple, *Letter, 6 March 1989.*
32. Carlisle to Whipple, *Ltr, 20 March 1989.*
33. through 40. T. Pearson to Whipple, *Letter, 6 March 1989.*
41. through 45. Carlisle to Whipple, *Ltr, 20 March 1989.*
46. through 50. Charles Augustus Whipple to Blaine Whipple. Letter dated 11 Oct. 1995 at 16 Old Brook Station, Rd., P. O. Box 679, Princeton, Mass. 01541-0679. In possession of Whipple (2004). (Hereafter C.A. Whipple to Whipple, *Letter 11 Oct. 1995*).
51. through 54. Kyle to Whipple, *2 Letters.*
55. through 60. Bayles to Whipple, *2 letters.*
61. Sudikas to Whipple, *Letter, 8 June 1998.*
62. through 73. Bayles to Whipple, *2 letters.*
74. and 75. Sudikas to Whipple, *Letter, 8 June 1998.*
76. through 78. Bayles to Whipple, *2 letters.*
79. Sudikas to Whipple, *Letter, 8 June 1998.*
80. Bayles to Whipple, *2 letters.*
81. Sudikas to Whipple, *Letter, 8 June 1998.*
82. through 123. Bayles to Whipple, *2 letters.*
124. through 127. Kelly to Whipple, *Letter, 17 May 1999.*
128. and 129. Burke's, *Presidential Families,* 473.
130. Republican Governor, 1925-1931.
131. through 154. Wise to Whipple, *3 Letters.*
155. through 157. Leszkiewicz-Loring, *Family Group Sheet.*
158. Levi Whipple, Washington Co., Ohio Probate Records, Court House, Marietta, Ohio, Vol. 7, 179-181.
159. through 164. Leszkiewicz-Loring, *Family Group Sheet.*
165. through 194. Storey to Whipple, *5 letters.*
195. Author unable to find a town with this name, hence no county is named.
196. through 240. Storey to Whipple, *5 letters.*
241. Author unable to find a town with this name, hence no county is named.
242. through 277. Storey to Whipple, *5 letters.*
278. through 327. Keener to Whipple, *Letters 30 May & 6 June 2000.*
328. through 388. Burke's, *Presidential Families,* 504.
389. through 394. Workman to Whipple, *Letter, 26 April 1998.*
395. through 397. D. Whipple to B. Whipple, *Letter, 9 Feb. 1989.*
398. through 403. Dorian to Whipple, *Letter, 21 Aug. 2000.*
404. Shannon-Kennison, *Family Group Sheet.*
405. Glenn Leroy Hendricks-Eileen Lucille McCleery Family Group Sheet, supplied 2 July 1998 by Kathie Walsh, 218 Cape Way, Geneva, Ill. 60134. This sheets cites birth, marriage, and divorce records from Black Hawk Co., Iowa. (Hereafter Hendricks - McCleery, *Family Group Sheet*).
406. through 408. Shannon-Kennison, *Family Group Sheet.*
409. through 413. L. Whipple to Whipple, *7 Letters.*
414. through 424. D.L. Whipple to Whipple, *Letter, 9 May 1994.*

{ G 1395 }

425. through 430. Henry Whipple, 2:37.
431. through 473. Joseph Whipple, *Family Bible*.
474. through 476. Talmud-Whipple, *Family Group Sheets*.
477. through 478. V. Whipple to B. Whipple, *Letter, 22 March 1989*.
479. Ibid.; and Thomas to Whipple, *Letter, 24 Jan. 2000*.
480. V. Whipple to B. Whipple, *Letter, 22 March 1989*.
481. Thomas to Whipple, *Letter, 24 Jan. 2000*.
482. V. Whipple to B. Whipple, *Letter, 22 March 1989*; and Thomas to Whipple, *Letter, 24 Jan. 2000*.
483. V. Whipple to B. Whipple, *Letter, 22 March 1989*; and Thomas to Whipple, *Letter, 24 Jan. 2000*.
484. Thomas to Whipple, *Letter, 24 Jan. 2000*.
485. V. Whipple to B. Whipple, *Letter, 22 March 1989*; and Thomas to Whipple, *Letter, 24 Jan. 2000*.
486. Thomas to Whipple, *Letter, 24 Jan. 2000*.
487. V. Whipple to B. Whipple, *Letter, 22 March 1989*; and Thomas to Whipple, *Letter, 24 Jan. 2000*.
488. Thomas to Whipple, *Letter, 24 Jan. 2000*.
489. V. Whipple to B. Whipple, *Letter, 22 March 1989*; and David L. Brooke to Blaine Whipple. Letter dated 8 Dec. 1999 at 1325 7th St. S. #7A, Naples Fla. 34102-7355. In possession of Whipple (2004). (Hereafter D. Brooke to Whipple, *Letter, 8 Dec. 1999*).
490. and 491. D. Brooke to Whipple, *Letter, 8 Dec. 1999*.
492. and 493. V. Whipple to B. Whipple, *Letter, 22 March 1989*.
494. Author unable to find a town with this name, hence no county is named.
495. and 500. V. Whipple to B. Whipple, *Letter, 22 March 1989*.
501. Ibid.; and Thomas to Whipple, *Letter, 24 Jan. 2000*.
502. and 503. V. Whipple to B. Whipple, *Letter, 22 March 1989*.
504. through 517. E. Whipple to B. Whipple, *Various Letters*.
518. through 522. A. Whipple to B. Whipple, *Various Letters*.
523. through 533. E. Whipple to B. Whipple, *Various Letters*.
534. through 540. Whiting-Whipple, *Family Group Sheet*.
541. through 543. Burroughs, *Burroughs Ancestors*.
544. through 550. Henry Whipple, 2:30.
551. and 552. Bailey-Whipple, *Family Group Sheet*.
553. C. McKinley to Whipple, *2 Letters*.
554. through 571. Bailey-Whipple, *Family Group Sheet*.
572. through 587. C. Whipple to B. Whipple, *3 Letters*.
588. through 594. Avery - Whipple, *Pedigree Chart*.
595. through 614. Moore to Whipple, *Letter 2 May 1994*.
615. through 629. Samuel Morgan-Betsey Whipple, *Family Group Sheets*.
630. through 644. Prescott to Whipple, *7 letters*.
645. Orr to Whipple, *13 Letters*.
646. and 647. Crawford to Whipple, *4 Letters*.
648. Orr to Whipple, *13 Letters*.
649. Crawford to Whipple, *4 Letters*.
650. and 651. Orr to Whipple, *13 Letters*.
652. through 655. Crawford to Whipple, *4 Letters*.
656 through 660. Donald W. Franklin to Blaine Whipple. Letter dated 3 Feb. 1989 at 15974 S. Abiqua Rd., Silverton, Oreg. 97381. In possession of Whipple (2004). Includes family group sheets. (Hereafter D. Franklin To Whipple, *Letter 3 Feb. 1989*).

661. through 665. Crawford to Whipple, *4 Letters.*
666. Orr to Whipple, *13 Letters.*
667. Crawford to Whipple, *4 Letters.*
668. through 670. Thomas Arnold Franklin to Blaine Whipple. Letter dated 25 Nov. 1995 at 7035 SW 184th, Beaverton, Oreg. 97007. In possession of Whipple (2004). (Hereafter Franklin to Whipple, *Letter, 25 November 1995*).
671. and 672. Crawford to Whipple, *4 Letters.*
673. Orr to Whipple, *13 Letters.*
674. through 679. Crawford to Whipple, *4 Letters.*
680. Orr to Whipple, *13 Letters.*
681. Schlarbaum to Whipple, *Letter 7 March 1996.*
682. and 683. Crawford to Whipple, *4 Letters.*
684. Orr to Whipple, *13 Letters.*
685. Schlarbaum to Whipple, *Letter 7 March 1996.*
686. through 688. Crawford to Whipple, *4 Letters.*
689. Orr to Whipple, *13 Letters.*
690. Schlarbaum to Whipple, *Letter 7 March 1996.*
691. through 702. Crawford to Whipple, *4 Letters.*
703. Orr to Whipple, *13 Letters.*
704. Crawford to Whipple, *4 Letters.*
705. Orr to Whipple, *13 Letters.*
706. Crawford to Whipple, *4 Letters.*
707. through 724. Schlarbaum to Whipple, *Letter 7 March 1996.*
725. through 727 Horner to Whipple, *4 Letters.*
728. Orr to Whipple, *13 Letters.*
729. through 733. Horner to Whipple, *4 Letters.*
734. through 748. C. McKinley to Whipple, *2 Letters.*
749. through 751. Orr to Whipple, *13 Letters.*
752. through 753. Heiserman to Whipple, *2 Letters.*
754. through 775. B. McKinley to Whipple, *Letter, 22 Aug. 1994.*
776. through 778. Charles D. McKinley-Sandra Lee Massi Family Group Sheet, supplied 13 Feb. 2001 by Charles D. McKinley, 10286 Pleasant Grove School Rd., Elk Grove, Calif., 95624-9624. In possession of Whipple (2004). This sheet is based on personal family knowledge and cites no documentation (Hereafter McKinley-Massi, *Family Group Sheet*).
779. Author unable to find a town with this name, hence no county is named.
780. Charles D. McKinley-Sandra Lee Massi Family Group Sheet, supplied 13 Feb. 2001 by Charles D. McKinley, 10286 Pleasant Grove School Rd., Elk Grove, Calif., 95624-9624. In possession of Whipple (2004). This sheet is based on personal family knowledge and cites no documentation (Hereafter McKinley-Massi, *Family Group Sheet*).
781. through 783. Mrs. Elizabeth Ann (McKinley) Harmon to Blaine Whipple. Letter dated 22 Feb. 2001 at 5326 1/2 McLaughlin Dr., Central Point, Oreg. 97502-9446. In possession of Whipple (2004). (Hereafter Harmon to Whipple, *Letter, 22 Feb. 2001*).
784. through 794. D. McKinley to Whipple, *5 Letters.*
795. through 800. B. Oldridge to Whipple, *2 Letters.*
801. Orr to Whipple, *13 Letters.*
802. through 806. B. Oldridge to Whipple, *2 Letters.*
807. through 814. Orr to Whipple, *13 Letters.*
815. through 834. Hintze to Whipple, *Letter 28 Nov. 1995.*

835. through 851. Kearns-Whipple, *Family Group Sheets.*
852. through 858. W.P. Whipple to B. Whipple, *3 Letters.*
859. through 871. Ziegler to Whipple, *2 Letters.*
872. through 881. Barr-Whipple, *Family Group Sheets.*
882. through 899. C. Mack to Whipple, *2 Letters.*
900. through 903. Kay Ann Kalvig-Harold Arthur Heddinger Family Group Sheet, supplied 2 Sept. 2000 and e-mail message dated 12 Oct. 2000 and 18 April 2002 announcing the birth of Eric William Heddinger from Harold Arthur Heddinger [e-mail address HaroldHedd@aol.com], 3790 28th Ave., Marion, Iowa 52302-1489. In possession of Whipple (2004). This sheet is personal knowledge of the submitter's family. (Hereafter Kalvig - Heddinger, *Family Group Sheet*).
904. through 906. Whipple - Schoelerman, *Family Group Sheet.*
907. through 911. R. Whipple to B. Whipple, *9 Letters.*
912. through 914. Haight to Whipple, *6 Letters.*
915. through 920. Jane Whipple to B. Whipple, *15 Letters.*
921. Bilderback to Whipple, *Letter, 11 Feb. 1996.*
922. through 930. Jane Whipple to B. Whipple, *15 Letters.*
931. Ibid.; and Obituary of Robert John Berger, *Cedar Rapids Gazette,* Cedar Rapids, Iowa (25 Dec. 2003).
932. through 948. Jane Whipple to B. Whipple, *15 Letters.*
949. through 952. Castner-Gordon, *Family Group Sheet.*
953. Greer to Whipple, *2 Letters.*
954. and 955. Castner - Gordon, *Family Group Sheet.*
956. Greer to Whipple, *2 Letters.*
957. and 958. Castner - Gordon, *Family Group Sheet.*
959. through 964. Greer to Whipple, *2 Letters.*
965. through 968. Settlemyer to Whipple, *Letter, 27 May 1994.*
969. and 970. Greer to Whipple, *2 Letters.*
971. and 972. Settlemyer to Whipple, *Letter, 27 May 1994.*
973. and 974. Greer to Whipple, *2 Letters.*
975. Settlemyer to Whipple, *Letter, 27 May 1994.*
976. through 983. T. Gallaher to Whipple, *4 Letters.*
984. through 990. D.Gallaher to Whipple, *Letter, 7 Dec. 1995.*
991. through 995. Jane Whipple to B. Whipple, *15 Letters.*
996. through 1008. E. (Whipple) West to B. Whipple, *4 Letters.*
1009. Drotzman to Whipple, *Letter, 25 Aug. 1988.*
1010. through 1013. Jessica Drotzman to Blaine Whipple. Letter dated 30 Dec. 1996 at 622 W. 5th, Yankton, SD 57078. In possession of Whipple (2004). Family Group Sheets provided and sources included research at the County Court House in Yankton. (Hereafter J. Drotzman to Whipple, *Letter 30 Dec. 1996*).
1014. Drotzman to Whipple, *Letter, 25 Aug. 1988.*
1015. Delfa Clemencia Rodriquez Guerrero to Blaine Whipple. Letter dated 7 March 1995 at 11426 Allerton St., Whittier, Calif. 90606. In possession of Whipple (2004). (Hereafter Guerrero to Whipple, *Letter, 7 March 1995*).
1016. and 1017. Drotzman to Whipple, *Letter, 25 Aug. 1988.*
1018. Blaine Scott Whipple & Lorna Jo Zoerink, Marriage License, Local File No. 651005, 17 Aug. 1998, Lane County Oregon Court House, Eugene, Oreg.
1019. Lorna Jo Zoerink, Certificate of Live Birth District Certificate #7097-114661, 27 Dec. 1966, Register-Recorder/ County Court, County of Los Angeles, Los Angeles, Calif.

1020. Spencer Blaine Whipple, Certificate of Live Birth, Oregon Dept. of Human Services Health Division, Local File No. 005848, filed by Registrar Guadalupe V. Pilcher on. 22 Oct. 2001. Date of birth 15 Oct. 2001. On file at the office of the Washington County Registrar, Court House, Hillsboro, Oregon.

1021. Turner Collins Whipple, Certificate of Live Birth, Oregon Department of Human Services Health Division, Local File No. 010161 filed by Registrar Guadalupe V. Pilcher on 11 May 2004. Date of birth 8 May 2004. On file at the office of the Washington County Registrar, Court House, Hillsboro, Oregon.

1022. and 1023. Terry Lynn (Jasperson) Ebert to Blaine Whipple. Letter dated 26 April 1989 at 619 W. Main, Luverne, Minn. 56165. In possession of Whipple (2004.) She is a niece of the author.). (Hereafter Ebert to Whipple, *Letter, 26 April 1989*).

1024. through 1027. *Argus Leader*, Sioux Falls, S. Dak. 16 June 2002.

1028. B. Whipple, *Scott Genealogy*, 48.

1029. *McLeon County Chronicle*, Glencoe, Minn., p. 3, col. 1-3; includes her picture using a walker.

1030. and 1031. B. Whipple, *Scott Genealogy*, 48.

1032. and 1033. David Blaine Jasperson to Blaine Whipple. Letter dated 30 May 2004 at 445 17th St., SW, Rochester, Minn. 55902. In possession of Whipple (2004). (Hereafter Jasperson to Whipple, *Letter, 30 May 2004.)*

1034. B. Whipple, *Scott Genealogy.*, 49.

1035. Molly Jane (Jasperson) Schmidt to Blaine Whipple. E-mail dated 24 July 2000 at mollyschmidt@qwewt.net; (mail address 708 Bonner Ct., S. E., Stewartville, Minn. 55976.) In possession of Whipple (2004). (Hereafter Schmidt to Whipple, *E-mail 24 July 2000*).

1036. and 1037. B. Whipple, *Scott Genealogy*, 49.

1038. and 1039. McPherson to Whipple, *Letter, 26 March 1996.*

1040. and 1041. Billie June (McPherson) Mauro to Blaine Whipple. Letter dated 30 March 1989 at Robinwood Rd., Littleton, Mass. 01460. In possession of Whipple (2004). She is the author's niece. (Hereafter Mauro to Whipple, *Letter, 30 March 1989*).

1042. McPherson to Whipple, *Letter, 26 March 1996.*

1043. Melissa Ann (McPherson) Giambanis to Blaine Whipple. Letter dated 11 June 1993 at 1410 Autumn Lane, Cherry Hill, NJ 08003. In possession of Whipple (2004). She is the author's niece. (Hereafter Giambanis to Whipple, *Letter, 11 June 1993*).

1044. and 1045. B. Whipple, *Scott Genealogy*, 49.

1046. through 1073. E. (Whipple) West to B. Whipple, *4 Letters.*

1074. through 1090. Pittman-Woods, *Family Group Sheet.*

1091. Dimmock-Whipple, *Family Group Sheets.*

1092. Pittman-Woods, *Family Group Sheet.*

1093. through 1139. Dimmock-Whipple, *Family Group Sheets.*

1140. through 1160. Roy Whipple to B. Whipple, *4 letters.*

1161. through 1164. Eleanor Greeley Treddenbarger to Blaine Whipple. Letters dated 31 Aug. 1997 and 10 March 1998 at 6901 Sutter Ave., Carmichael, Calif. 95608. In possession of Whipple (2004). (Hereafter Eleanor Treddenbarger, *2 letters*).

1165. W. Greeley to B. Whipple, *Letter, 16 June 1998.*

1166. Treddenbarger to Whipple, *Letter, 31 Aug. 1997.*

1167. W. Greeley to B. Whipple, *Letter, 16 June 1998.*

1168. through 1195. Roy Whipple to B. Whipple, *4 letters.*

1196. through 1200. Rumpf to Whipple, *3 letters.*

1201. and 1202. Roy Whipple to B. Whipple, *4 letters.*

1203. through 1212. R.E. Whipple to B. Whipple, *Letter, 21 June 1996.*

1213. through 1250. Roy Whipple to B. Whipple, *4 letters*.
1251. through 1263. Brown-Hall, *Family Group Sheet*.
1264. Peters to Whipple, *Letter, 21 Feb. 1997*.
1265. Carol Moore Watkins, Baptismal entry, Church-In-The-Gardens, Forest Hills, NY.
1266. Harold Leslie Stead & Carol Moore Watkins, Marriage Return, 28 January 1961, Court House, Wayne Co., Mich.
1267. Peters to Whipple, *Letter, 21 Feb. 1997*.
1268. Harold Leslie Stead, Birth Certificate Ohio Department of Health, Columbus, Ohio.
1269. and 1270. Peters to Whipple, *Letter, 21 Feb. 1997*.
1271. Ibid., Based on an interview with his sister, Allison Jaye Watkins 15 Dec. 1995.
1272. through 1275. Cable to Whipple, *2 Letters*.
1276. through 1280. Chandler to Whipple, *5 Letters*.
1281. through 1291. Crates to Whipple, *Letter, 11 Feb. 1991*.
1292. through 1300. Maris to Whipple, *Letter, 11 April 1996*.
1301. through 1305. Erbland to Whipple, *Letters, Fam. Gp. Sheets*.
1306. Author unable to find a town with this name, hence no county is named.
1307. through 1403. Erbland to Whipple, *Letters, Fam. Gp. Sheets*.
1404. through 1425. Daley to Whipple, *8 letters*.
1426. Daniel F. Whipple obit, *Democratic Leader*, Cheyenne, Wyo.
1427. through 1431. Daley to Whipple, *8 letters*.
1432. through 1439. M. Whipple to B. Whipple, *5 letters*.
1440. G. Whipple to B. Whipple, *Letter, 23 May 1991*.
1441. H. Whipple to B. Whipple, *Letter, 04/20/1993*.
1442. through 1445. G. Whipple to B. Whipple, *Letter, 23 May 1991*.
1446. H. Whipple to B. Whipple, *Letter, 04/20/1993*.
1447. through 1476. G. Whipple to B. Whipple, *Letter, 23 May 1991*.
1477. through 1486. Brandt to Whipple, *3 letters*.
1487. through 1490. Knowles to Whipple, *Letters 19 & 30 July 2000*.
1491. Henry Whipple, 2:77; and Krueger to Whipple, *Letter, 7 Aug. 2000*.
1492. through 1499. Krueger to Whipple, *Letter, 7 Aug. 2000*.
1500. through 1503. Herrick-Whipple, *Family Group Sheets*.
1504. through 1509. J. Davis to Whipple, *Letter, 10 Feb. 1999*.
1510. through 1523. Reinhold to Whipple, *2 Letters*.
1524. through 1537. Gallop to Whipple, *Letter 1 April 1996*.
1538. Author unable to find a town with this name, hence no county is named.
1539. through 1544. Gallop to Whipple, *Letter 1 April 1996*.
1545. and 1546. Bing to Whipple, *Letter 2 Nov. 02*.
1547. through 1592. Powers to Whipple, *Letter 20 March 1996*.
1593. through 1695. Sadler to Whipple, *Family Group Sheets*.
1696. through 1785. Smith-Ward-Whipple, *Family Group Sheet*.
1786. through 1837. Brigham-Whipple, *Family Group Sheets*.
1838. through 1842. Bowman-Miner, *Family Group Sheet*.
1843. through 1844. Randazzo to Whipple, *E-mail 25 Oct. 01*.
1845. through 1858. Tom Whipple, *Family Group Sheets*.
1859. through 1862. Walter Leighton Whipple, Ph.D to Blaine Whipple. Undated letter at 770 Mariquita Dr., Santa Barbara, Calif. 93111-1410. In possession of Whipple (2004). (Hereafter W. Whipple to B. Whipple, *Undated Letter*).
1863. W.J Whipple to B. Whipple, *3 letters*.
1864. through 1866. Wm. Whipple to B. Whipple, *Letter, 20 April 1989*.

1867. through 1869. B. Whipple to B. Whipple, *Letter, 22 May 1998.*
1870. through 1875. Wm. Whipple to B. Whipple, *Letter, 20 April 1989.*
1876. and 1877. Green to Whipple, *5 letters.*
1878. and 1879. Christine M. (Green) Alderman to Blaine Whipple. Letter dated 9 May 1989 at 612 W. Cotati Ave., Cotati, Calif 94931. In possession of Whipple (2004). (Hereafter Alderman to Whipple, *Letter, 9 May 1989*).
1880. and 1881. Green to Whipple, *5 letters.*
1882. Virginia Green Branscom to Blaine Whipple. Letter dated 27 May 1998 at 2 Webster St., Nantucket Island, Mass. 02554. In possession of Whipple (2004). (Hereafter Branscom to Whipple, *Letter, 27 May 1998*).
1883. Green to Whipple, *5 letters.*
1884. through 1887. Easton to Whipple, *2 Letters.*
1888. through 1893. Williams to Whipple, *Letter, 20 Sept. 1989.*
1894. through 1897. Collens-Bartholomew, *Family Group Sheet.*
1898. through 1922. Zastrow-Whipple, *Family Group Sheet.*
1923. through 1931. G. Whipple to Whipple, *2 Letters.*
1932. through 1949. HH Hildebrant to Whipple, *Letters, 2/1999; 7/2001.*
1950. through 1965. Hildebrant to Whipple, *6 letters.*
1966. through 1968. Spitzer to Whipple, *Letter, 7 June 1998.*
1969. through 1975. Hildebrant to Whipple, *6 letters.*
1976. through 1980. HH Hildebrant to Whipple, *Letters, 2/1999; 7/2001.*
1981. and 1982. Whytlaw to Whipple, *3 Letters.*
1983. through 1998. Withington to Whipple, *Letter, 13 Sept. 1998.*
1999. through 2014. S. Brewster-Withington, *Family Group Sheet.*
2015. through 2022. Brewster-Withington, *Family Group Sheet.*
2023. through 2025. P. Wittington, *Letter, 15 Feb. 1990.*
2026. through 2072. P. Whipple to B. Whipple, *2 Letters.*
2073. through 2134. Miller-Whitley, *Family Group Sheets.*
2135. through 2139. Klassy to Whipple, *5 Letters.*
2140. through 2158. Liles to Whipple, *2 Letters.*
2159. through 2166. Wilkin to Whipple, *3 Letters.*
2167. through 2170. Galen Whipple to Whipple, *Letter, 11 June 1998.*
2171. through 2179. Whitney-Hall, *Family Group Sheets.*
2180. through 2187. Ristau to Whipple, *2 Letters.*
2188. through 2195. Emery to Whipple, *2 Letters.*
2196. through 2205. Deal-Putnam, *Family Group Sheet.*

FOURTEENTH GENERATION

8066. **Katherine Patterson**[14] **Windisch** (Melinda[13] **Jones**, Proctor Patterson[12], Ferne Catherine[11] **Patterson**, Proctor[10], Phebe Smith[9] **Whipple**, Stephen[8], Jonathan[7], Capt. Stephen[6], John[5], Matthew[4], Lt. John[3], Matthew[2], Matthew[1])[1] was born 10 January 1963 and married **Reyburn Ingle**.

Katherine Patterson **Windisch** and Reyburn **Ingle** had the following child:
    9560   i.   Cara Dawn[15] **Ingle**[2] born 20 October 1982.

8076. **Laurie**[14] **Adams** (Sally Ann[13] **Davis**, Martha[12] **Whipple**, Walter[11], Stephen Lovett[10], Stephen[9], Jonathan[8], Jonathan[7], Capt. Stephen[6], John[5], Matthew[4], Lt. John[3], Matthew[2], Matthew[1])[3] was born 26 May 1958 and married twice. (1) **William Shean** in Lexington, Middlesex Co., Mass. (2) **Charles Eugene Korns**. Charles,[4] son of William Franklin **Korns** and Doris Ann **Rhodes**, was born in Grinnell, Poweshiek Co., Iowa 8 August 1961. He married **Edwina Wright** 17 October 1981. Laurie and Charles are eleventh cousins. Their common ancestors are Matthew and Anne (Hawkins) Whipple.

Charles Eugene **Korns** and Laurie **Adams** had the following children:
    9561   i.   Calvin[15] **Korns**.[5]
    9562   ii.   Jenny Lee **Korns**[6] born 2 November 1993.

8080. **Kristen Louise**[14] **Pearson** (Taylor Peter[13], Virginia Augusta[12] **Taylor**, Augusta[11] **Whipple**, Stephen Lovett[10], Stephen[9], Jonathan[8], Jonathan[7], Capt. Stephen[6], John[5], Matthew[4], Lt. John[3], Matthew[2], Matthew[1])[7] was born at the U.S. Naval Hospital in Bethesda, Montgomery Co., Md. 25 June 1964 and married **John Joseph Markovich** in Falls Church, Falls Church City Area Co., Va. 21 May 1988. He was born in St. Louis, Independence Co., Mo. 29 January 1964.[8]

Kristen Louise **Pearson** and John Joseph **Markovich** had the following children:
    9563   i.   Kathryn Louise[15] **Markovich**[9] born in Ft. Knox, Hardin Co., Ky. 30 January 1991.
    9564   ii.   Rachel Elizabeth **Markovich**[10] born in Sulzbach, Germany 23 April 1994.
    9565   iii.   David John **Markovich**[11] born in Monterey, Montgomery Co., Calif. 11 August 1997.

8082. **David Scott**[14] **Pearson** (Taylor Peter[13], Virginia Augusta[12] **Taylor**, Augusta[11] **Whipple**, Stephen Lovett[10], Stephen[9], Jonathan[8], Jonathan[7], Capt. Stephen[6], John[5], Matthew[4], Lt. John[3], Matthew[2], Matthew[1])[12] was born at the U.S. Air Force hospital in Misawa, Japan 8 April 1972 and married **Christie Ann Munro** in Augusta, Richmond Co., Ga. 30 December 1995. She was born in Augusta.[13]

David Scott **Pearson** and Christie Ann **Munro** had the following child:
    9566 i. Sarah Elizabeth[15] **Pearson**[14] born in Heidelberg, Germany 2 March 1998.

8093. **Cindy Jean**[14] **Kyle** (Marion H.[13] **Brown**, Jeanette R.[12] **Whipple**, John Whitmore[11], Sidney[10], John Hitchings[9], John[8], Jonathan[7], Capt. Stephen[6], John[5], Matthew[4], Lt. John[3], Matthew[2], Matthew[1])[15] was born in Worcester, Worcester Co., Mass. 14 May 1959 and married **Robyn Frick** in Littleton, Grafton Co., N.H. 24 September 1983. Robyn,[16] son of Richard **Frick** and Sheryl **Daley**, was born in Tuscola, Douglas Co., Ill. 17 October 1958.

Cindy Jean **Kyle** and Robyn **Frick** adopted the following child:
    9567 i. Jessica Tianshing[15] **Frick**[17] born 10 August 1988.

8098. **Ricky Ray**[14] **Sage** (Karen Sue[13] **Murphy**, Dorothy Gene[12] **Keyes**, George Everett[11], Charles Evans[10], George Everett[9], Mary Alden[8] **Gould**, Benjamin[7], Martha[6] **Gilbert**, Esther[5] **Perkins**, Serg. John[4], Elizabeth[3] **Whipple**, Matthew[2], Matthew[1])[18] was born in Topeka, Shawnee Co., Kans. 12 May 1959 and married **Kelly Jo Ann Johnson** in Kansas City, Wyandotte Co., Kans. 2 March 1985. Kelly,[19] daughter of Robert Daniel **Johnson** and Mary Maddona **Russell**, was born in Omaha, Douglas Co., Nebr. 10 April 1962. They were divorced in 1997. Ricky was graduated from the Academy of Military Science, Knoxville, Knox Co., Tenn. in July 1985 with a B. S. in Business Administration and Business Accounting. He was also graduated from Washburn University at Topeka.

Ricky Ray **Sage** and Kelly Jo Ann **Johnson** had the following children:
    9568 i. Sarah Michele[15] **Sage**[20] born in Topeka 26 February 1987.
    9569 ii. Amy Catherine **Sage**[21] born in Wichita, Sedgwick Co., Kans. 17 December 1990.

8099. **Brenda Kay**[14] **Sage** (Karen Sue[13] **Murphy**, Dorothy Gene[12] **Keyes**, George Everett[11], Charles Evans[10], George Everett[9], Mary Alden[8] **Gould**, Benjamin[7], Martha[6] **Gilbert**, Esther[5] **Perkins**, Serg. John[4], Elizabeth[3] **Whipple**, Matthew[2], Matthew[1])[22] was born in Topeka, Shawnee Co., Kans. 21 November 1960 and married twice. (1) **Donald Albert Avery** in Topeka 9 October 1981. He was born in Clay Co., Kans. 1 May 1951.[23] (2) **Randy Becker** in Wabaunsee Co., Kans. in 1987.[24] His name was Randy McCoid before being adopted by a Rev. Becker. No further details provided.

Brenda Kay **Sage** and Randy **Becker** had the following child born in Topeka:
    9570 i.   Brandy Michele[15] **Becker**[25] 25 May 1979.

Brenda Kay **Sage** and Donald Albert **Avery** had the following children:
    9571 ii.   Nicole Marie **Avery**[26] born in Leavenworth, Leavenworth Co., Kans. 5 November 1982.
    9572 iii.   Andrew James **Avery**[27] born in Wamego, Pottawatomie Co., Kans. 22 May 1984.

8100. **Brian Wayne**[14] **Sage** (Karen Sue[13] **Murphy**, Dorothy Gene[12] **Keyes**, George Everett[11], Charles Evans[10], George Everett[9], Mary Alden[8] **Gould**, Benjamin[7], Martha[6] **Gilbert**, Esther[5] **Perkins**, Serg. John[4], Elizabeth[3] **Whipple**, Matthew[2], Matthew[1])[28] was born in Topeka, Shawnee Co., Kans. 11 July 1964 and married **Diana Espinosa (Mountjoy) Figueros** in Phoenix, Maricopa Co., Ariz. in 1990. Diana,[29] daughter of Anselmo **Figueroa** and Maria Irma **Espinosa**, was born in Nyssa, Malheur Co., Oreg. 6 September 1963. Brian was graduated from Emporia State University, Emporia, Lyon Co., Kans.

Brian Wayne **Sage** and Diana Espinosa **Mountjoy** had the following child born in Phoenix:
    9573 i.   Shaun Michael[15] **Sage**[30] 18 November 1990.

8136. **Daniel Robert**[14] **Kelly** (Ada Helen[13] **Thomas**, Dilman Kar[12], Burt Byron[11], Ambrose[10], Dilla[9] **Beeman**, Daniel[8], Lydia[7] **Cogswell**, Samuel[6], Hannah[5] **Browne**, Judith[4] **Perkins**, Elizabeth[3] **Whipple**, Matthew[2], Matthew[1])[31] was born in Germany and married **Susan Jane Andrews**.[32] She is the daughter of John **Andrews** and Barbara **Johnson**.

Daniel Robert **Kelly** and Susan Jane **Andrews** had the following child:
  +   9574 i.   Barbara Frances[15] **Kelly**.

8138. **Cynthia**[14] **Coolidge** (John[13], Pres. John Calvin[12], Col. John Calvin[11], Sarah Almeda[10] **Brewer**, Sally[9] **Brown**, Israel Putnam[8], Adam[7],

Adam[6], Jacob[5], Judith[4] **Perkins**, Elizabeth[3] **Whipple**, Matthew[2], Matthew[1])[33] was born in New Haven, New Haven Co., Conn. 28 October 1933 and married **S. Edward Jeter** in Farmington, Hartford Co., Conn. 26 September 1964. Edward,[34] son of Sherwood F. **Jeter** Jr. and Edwina **Pabst**, was born in Hartford, Hartford Co., Conn. 1 September 1937.

Cynthia **Coolidge** and S. Edward **Jeter** had the following child:
    9575   i.   Christopher Coolidge[15] **Jeter** born in Hartford 3 January 1967.[35]

8139. **Lydia**[14] **Coolidge** (John[13], Pres. John Calvin[12], Col. John Calvin[11], Sarah Almeda[10] **Brewer**, Sally[9] **Brown**, Israel Putnam[8], Adam[7], Adam[6], Jacob[5], Judith[4] **Perkins**, Elizabeth[3] **Whipple**, Matthew[2], Matthew[1])[36] was born in New Haven, New Haven Co., Conn. 14 August 1939 and married **Jeremy Whitman Sayles** in Farmington, Hartford Co., Conn. 17 June 1966. Jeremy,[37] son of Phil Whitman **Sayles** and Mildred **Jones**, was born in Schenectady, Schenectady Co., N.Y. 9 June 1937.

Lydia **Coolidge** and Jeremy Whitman **Sayles** had the following child born in Boston, Suffolk Co., Mass.:
    9576   i.   Jennifer Coolidge[15] **Sayles** 27 July 1970.[38]

8141. **Paul D.**[14] **Hathaway** (Eugenia[13] **Wise**, Robert E.[12], Anna Hale[11] **Ellis**, Frederick Orin[10], Mary Phillips[9] **Brown**, Aaron[8], John[7], John[6], Jacob[5], Judith[4] **Perkins**, Elizabeth[3] **Whipple**, Matthew[2], Matthew[1])[39] was born 25 March 1970 and married **Nancy E. Padilla** in California 13 January 1996. Nancy,[40] daughter of Ed **Padilla** and Cheryll **(__)**, was born in Hollywood, Los Angeles Co., Calif. 12 May 1974.

Paul D. **Hathaway** and Nancy E. **Padilla** had the following child born in Glendale, Maricopa Co., Ariz.:
    9577   i.   Logan D.[15] **Hathaway**[41] 19 March 1998.

8161. **Helen**[14] **Bragdon** (Chester Stanley[13], George Henry[12], Ione[11] **Andrews**, Henry[10], Caleb[9], Molly[8] **Burnham**, Capt. Westley[7], Westley[6], Elizabeth[5] **Perkins**, Jacob[4], Elizabeth[3] **Whipple**, Matthew[2], Matthew[1])[42] was born in Ipswich, Essex Co., Mass. 28 March 1932 and married twice. (1) **Samuel Stewart** in Portsmouth, Rockingham Co., N.H. in 1951. They were divorced in 1980. Samuel,[43] son of Neil **Stewart** and Mary **MacLeod**, was born in 1931. (2) **Gordon Ferris** in 1981. Marriage ended in divorce.

{ G 1405 }

Helen **Bragdon** and Samuel **Stewart** had the following children born in Ipswich:

    9578   i.   Samuel[15] **Stewart** Jr.[44] in 1956 and married Frances **Niksa** in Pittsfield, Berkshire Co., Mass. in 1982.

    9579   ii.   Randall **Stewart**[45] in 1960.

    9580   iii.   Pamela **Stewart**[46] in 1961.

8162. **Marylyn**[14] **Bragdon** (Chester Stanley[13], George Henry[12], Ione[11] **Andrews**, Henry[10], Caleb[9], Molly[8] **Burnham**, Capt. Westley[7], Westley[6], Elizabeth[5] **Perkins**, Jacob[4], Elizabeth[3] **Whipple**, Matthew[2], Matthew[1])[47] was born in Ipswich, Essex Co., Mass. 17 August 1933 and married **Edward Gear** in Essex, Essex Co., Mass. Marriage ended in divorce.

Marylyn **Bragdon** and Edward **Gear** had the following children:

    9581   i.   Thomas[15] **Gear**[48] born in 1958.

    9582   ii.   Edward **Gear** Jr.[49] born in 1961.

    9583   iii.   Nancy **Gear**[50] born in 1965.

    9584   iv.   Kenneth **Gear**[51] born in 1966.

8163. **Hollis**[14] **Bragdon** (Henry[13], George Henry[12], Ione[11] **Andrews**, Henry[10], Caleb[9], Molly[8] **Burnham**, Capt. Westley[7], Westley[6], Elizabeth[5] **Perkins**, Jacob[4], Elizabeth[3] **Whipple**, Matthew[2], Matthew[1])[52] was born 11 July 1925 and married **Delores (__)**.

Hollis **Bragdon** and Delores (__) had the following children:

    9585   i.   Gregg[15] **Bragdon**[53] married a woman whose given name is Kay and they had a son. No further details provided.

    9586   ii.   H. Joseph **Bragdon**.[54]

8165. **Natalie Janet**[14] **Bragdon** (William Edward[13], George Henry[12], Ione[11] **Andrews**, Henry[10], Caleb[9], Molly[8] **Burnham**, Capt. Westley[7], Westley[6], Elizabeth[5] **Perkins**, Jacob[4], Elizabeth[3] **Whipple**, Matthew[2], Matthew[1])[55] was born in Falmouth, Barnstable Co., Mass. 28 August 1930 and married **Chester John Molinari** in Milford, Worcester Co., Mass. 24 June 1956. Chester,[56] son of Chester **Molinari** and Rebecca **Linton**, was born in Milton, Norfolk Co., Mass. 24 April 1931.

Natalie Janet **Bragdon** and Chester John **Molinari** had the following children:

    9587   i.   Susan Lynn[15] **Molinari**[57] born in Brockton, Plymouth Co., Mass. 26 March 1958.

+   9588   ii.   Lisa Ann **Molinari** born 18 June 1960.

9589   iii.   Michelle Marie **Molinari**[58] born in Stoughton, Norfolk Co., Mass. 16 November 1964.

8166. **Edward Ernest**[14] **Bragdon** (William Edward[13], George Henry[12], Ione[11] **Andrews**, Henry[10], Caleb[9], Molly[8] **Burnham**, Capt. Westley[7], Westley[6], Elizabeth[5] **Perkins**, Jacob[4], Elizabeth[3] **Whipple**, Matthew[2], Matthew[1])[59] was born 12 April 1941 and married **Marie Carole Ghelli**.

Edward Ernest **Bragdon** and Marie Carole **Ghelli** had the following children:
+   9590   i.   Rose Ann[15] **Bragdon**.
    9591   ii.   Michael Carmen **Bragdon**[60] married Virginia **Long**.
    9592   iii. Lisa Ann **Bragdon**[61] born in 1968 and married Carl **Braun**.

8169. **George**[14] **Bragdon** (Sidney H.[13], George Henry[12], Ione[11] **Andrews**, Henry[10], Caleb[9], Molly[8] **Burnham**, Capt. Westley[7], Westley[6], Elizabeth[5] **Perkins**, Jacob[4], Elizabeth[3] **Whipple**, Matthew[2], Matthew[1])[62] was born in Ipswich, Essex Co., Mass. 14 August 1947 and married **Diane Preston** in Gloucester, Essex Co., Mass. 5 June 1971.

George **Bragdon** and Diane **Preston** had the following children born in Beverly, Essex Co., Mass.:
    9593   i.   Sarah[15] **Bragdon**[63] 7 September 1973.
    9594   ii.   Rachel **Bragdon**[64] 12 November 1975.

8170. **Adelaide Martha**[14] **Bragdon** (Frederick[13], George Henry[12], Ione[11] **Andrews**, Henry[10], Caleb[9], Molly[8] **Burnham**, Capt. Westley[7], Westley[6], Elizabeth[5] **Perkins**, Jacob[4], Elizabeth[3] **Whipple**, Matthew[2], Matthew[1])[65] was born 1 April 1931 and married **Walter Amos Jewett**.

Adelaide Martha **Bragdon** and Walter Amos **Jewett** had the following children:
+   9595   i.   Diane Leslie[15] **Jewett** born 5 July 1954.
+   9596   ii.   Catherine Ann **Jewett** born 22 April 1956.
+   9597   iii. Joanne Marie **Jewett** born 16 February 1959.
    9598   iv.   Charles Edward **Jewett**[66] born 2 February 1960.
+   9599   v.   Cynthia Irene **Jewett** born 14 April 1962.
    9600   vi.   William Walter **Jewett**[67] born 13 February 1967 and died 26 January 1972 at 4 years of age.

8171. **Gerald**[14] **Bowes** (Esther Marjorie[13] **Bragdon**, George Henry[12], Ione[11] **Andrews**, Henry[10], Caleb[9], Molly[8] **Burnham**, Capt. Westley[7], Westley[6], Elizabeth[5] **Perkins**, Jacob[4], Elizabeth[3] **Whipple**, Matthew[2], Matthew[1])[68] was born in Falmouth, Barnstable Co., Mass. in 1930 and married **Doris McManus** in Urbana, Champaign Co., Ill. in 1954.

Gerald **Bowes** and Doris **McManus** had the following children:
+   9601   i.   Gerald[15] **Bowes** born in 1956.
+   9602   ii.   Judith **Bowes** born abt 1960.

8172. **Jean Clayton**[14] **Bowes** (Esther Marjorie[13] **Bragdon**, George Henry[12], Ione[11] **Andrews**, Henry[10], Caleb[9], Molly[8] **Burnham**, Capt. Westley[7], Westley[6], Elizabeth[5] **Perkins**, Jacob[4], Elizabeth[3] **Whipple**, Matthew[2], Matthew[1])[69] was born in Falmouth, Barnstable Co., Mass. 10 August 1931 and married **Thomas Walter Nanius** in Newark, Essex Co., N.J. 9 October 1953. Thomas, son of Anthony Joseph **Nanius** and Anna Florence **Poska**, was born in Clinton Township, Penn. 11 August 1929.

Jean Clayton **Bowes** and Thomas Walter **Nanius** had the following children born in Irvington, Essex Co., N.J.:
   9603   i.   Gary Robert[15] **Nanius**[70] 21 September 1954 and died 24 December 1976 in Randolph, Morris Co., N.J., at 22 years of age.
+   9604   ii.   Craig Alan **Nanius** 18 January 1960.
   9605   iii.   Glen Thomas **Nanius**[71] 7 July 1962.

8173. **Patricia**[14] **Bowes** (Esther Marjorie[13] **Bragdon**, George Henry[12], Ione[11] **Andrews**, Henry[10], Caleb[9], Molly[8] **Burnham**, Capt. Westley[7], Westley[6], Elizabeth[5] **Perkins**, Jacob[4], Elizabeth[3] **Whipple**, Matthew[2], Matthew[1])[72] was born in Achusnet, Bristol Co., Mass. 1 October 1932 and married **Richard Prochaska** in Harlington, Cameron Co., Tex. 7 October 1955. Richard,[73] son of Charles **Prochaska** and Anna Helen **Solcany**, was born in Cleveland, Cuyahoga Co., Ohio 12 April 1932.

Patricia **Bowes** and Richard **Prochaska** had the following child:
   9606   i.   Lee[15] **Prochaska**[74] born in Valdosta AFB, Lowndes Co., Ga. 25 August 1956.

8174. **Robert**[14] **Bowes** (Esther Marjorie[13] **Bragdon**, George Henry[12], Ione[11] **Andrews**, Henry[10], Caleb[9], Molly[8] **Burnham**, Capt. Westley[7], Westley[6], Elizabeth[5] **Perkins**, Jacob[4], Elizabeth[3] **Whipple**, Matthew[2], Matthew[1])[75] was born in Falmouth, Barnstable Co., Mass. in 1935 and died in an auto accident in November 1986 in Conklin, Binghamton Co., N.Y., at 51 years of age. He married twice. (1) **Delores Kozlevker**. (2) **Claire (__)**.

Robert **Bowes** and Delores **Kozlevker** had the following children born in Conklin:

  9607 i. Robert[15] **Bowes**[76] abt 1960 and married Virginia (__).
  9608 ii. Kevin **Bowes**[77] abt 1962.
  9609 iii. Mark **Bowes**[78] abt 1966.
  9610 iv. Jill **Bowes**[79] abt 1968.

 8176. **Roger Henry**[14] **Bragdon** (George Austin[13], George Henry[12], Ione[11] **Andrews**, Henry[10], Caleb[9], Molly[8] **Burnham**, Capt. Westley[7], Westley[6], Elizabeth[5] **Perkins**, Jacob[4], Elizabeth[3] **Whipple**, Matthew[2], Matthew[1])[80] was born in Gardner, Worcester Co., Mass. 10 November 1937 and married **Celia Lenino** in Westminster, Worcester Co., Mass. Marriage ended in divorce. She is the daughter of Leo **Lenino** and Dorothy (__).

Roger Henry **Bragdon** and Celia **Lenino** had the following child born in Fitchburg, Worcester Co.:

  9611 i. Randall Allen[15] **Bragdon**[81] 28 July 1964.

 8177. **Jacqueline Maie**[14] **Bragdon** (George Austin[13], George Henry[12], Ione[11] **Andrews**, Henry[10], Caleb[9], Molly[8] **Burnham**, Capt. Westley[7], Westley[6], Elizabeth[5] **Perkins**, Jacob[4], Elizabeth[3] **Whipple**, Matthew[2], Matthew[1])[82] was born in Clinton, Worcester Co., Mass. 30 March 1950 and married **Michael Dennis Calcia** in Princeton, Worcester Co., Mass. 21 October 1967. Michael,[83] son of Albert Joseph **Calcia** and Josephine Marie **Serewicz**, was born in Clinton 16 February 1946.

Jacqueline Maie **Bragdon** and Michael Dennis **Calcia** had the following children:

  9612 i. Albert Michael[15] **Calcia**[84] born in Holden, Worcester Co., Mass. 18 July 1968 and died the day of birth. Buried at St. John's Cemetery, Clinton.
  9613 ii. Michele Lyn **Calcia**[85] born in Holden 19 August 1969.
  9614 iii. John Michael **Calcia**[86] born in Worcester, Worcester Co., Mass. 22 September 1972.
  9615 iv. Lisa Marie **Calcia**[87] born 31 December 1974.

{ G 1409 }

8179. **William Otis**[14] **Baker** (Clifford Doty[13], Fannie Woodberry[12] **Bragdon**, Ione[11] **Andrews**, Henry[10], Caleb[9], Molly[8] **Burnham**, Capt. Westley[7], Westley[6], Elizabeth[5] **Perkins**, Jacob[4], Elizabeth[3] **Whipple**, Matthew[2], Matthew[1])[88] was born in Beverly, Essex Co., Mass. 22 September 1926 and married **Ruth Holmes MacIntyre** in Manchester, Essex Co., Mass. 18 June 1949. Ruth,[89] daughter of Dr. William **MacIntyre** and Ann **Holmes**, was born 8 July 1922.

William Otis **Baker** and Ruth Holmes **MacIntyre** had the following children:

	9616	i.	Leigh[15] **Baker**[90] born in Danvers, Essex Co., Mass. 25 November 1950 and married Pasdal **Flannery** in Wenham, Essex Co., Mass. 22 June 1974.
+	9617	ii.	Bruce **Baker** born 6 May 1952.
+	9618	iii.	Christopher **Baker** born 16 December 1955.
+	9619	iv.	Douglas MacIntyre **Baker** born 20 February 1958.
+	9620	v.	Deborah **Baker** born 12 December 1960.

8180. **Beverly**[14] **Baker** (Clifford Doty[13], Fannie Woodberry[12] **Bragdon**, Ione[11] **Andrews**, Henry[10], Caleb[9], Molly[8] **Burnham**, Capt. Westley[7], Westley[6], Elizabeth[5] **Perkins**, Jacob[4], Elizabeth[3] **Whipple**, Matthew[2], Matthew[1])[91] was born in Beverly, Essex Co., Mass. 29 January 1928 and married **James Henry McElroy** there 17 April 1949. James,[92] son of James Henry **McElroy** and Beulah **Higgins**, was born in Beverly 11 January 1926 and died 17 December 1991 in Fryeburg, Oxford Co., Maine, at 65 years of age.

Beverly **Baker** and James Henry **McElroy** had the following children:

+	9621	i.	Stephen Baker[15] **McElroy** born 17 September 1950.
	9622	ii.	Edward James **McElroy** [93] born in Beverly 16 December 1951 and married twice. (1) Linda **Fitch** in Littleton, Grafton Co., N. H. 8 June 1974. Marriage ended in divorce in 1980. (2) Rebecca **Kent** 22 May 1982.
+	9623	iii.	Joan **McElroy** born 20 January 1954.

8181. **Joanne Marjorie**[14] **Baker** (Roy Woodberry[13], Fannie Woodberry[12] **Bragdon**, Ione[11] **Andrews**, Henry[10], Caleb[9], Molly[8] **Burnham**, Capt. Westley[7], Westley[6], Elizabeth[5] **Perkins**, Jacob[4], Elizabeth[3] **Whipple**, Matthew[2], Matthew[1])[94] was born in Hyannis, Barnstable Co., Mass. 22 December 1926 and married **Leo Sweeney** in Boston, Suffolk Co., Mass. 4 March 1948. Leo,[95] son of Walter **Sweeney** and Kathryn Mary **Connors**, was born in Salem, Essex Co., Mass. 10 May 1926.

Joanne Marjorie **Baker** and Leo **Sweeney** had the following children:
- \+   9624   i.   Cathleen Ruth[15] **Sweeney** born 4 January 1949.
- \+   9625   ii.   Sharon Anne **Sweeney** born 5 June 1951.
- \+   9626   iii.   Gail Margaret **Sweeney** born 15 November 1952.
- \+   9627   iv.   Laureen Ellen **Sweeney** born 31 March 1954.

8182. **Philip Woodberry[14] Baker** (Roy Woodberry[13], Fannie Woodberry[12] **Bragdon**, Ione[11] **Andrews**, Henry[10], Caleb[9], Molly[8] **Burnham**, Capt. Westley[7], Westley[6], Elizabeth[5] **Perkins**, Jacob[4], Elizabeth[3] **Whipple**, Matthew[2], Matthew[1])[96] was born in Barnstable, Barnstable Co., Mass. 17 March 1929 and married twice. (1) **Irene Nazer** in Antrim, Hillsborough Co., N. H. (2) **Harriet Abbott** in Topsfield, Essex Co., Mass. 27 December 1958. Harriet,[97] daughter of William C. **Abbott** and Frances **Rigdon**, was born in St. Paul, Ramsey Co., Minn. 14 November 1924.

Philip Woodberry **Baker** and Irene **Nazer** had the following children:
-      9628   i.   Ann Marie[15] **Baker**[98] born in Petersboro, Hillsborough Co., N. H. 24 July 1954 and married Edward **Ross** in Ann Arbor, Washtenaw Co., Mich. 27 December 1987.
- \+   9629   ii.   Philip Roy **Baker** born 3 May 1957.

Philip Woodberry **Baker** and Harriet **Abbott** had the following child born in Petersboro:
-      9630   iii.   Peter Brooke **Baker**[99] 28 August 1960.

8184. **Janis[14] Baker** (Gordon Andrews[13], Fannie Woodberry[12] **Bragdon**, Ione[11] **Andrews**, Henry[10], Caleb[9], Molly[8] **Burnham**, Capt. Westley[7], Westley[6], Elizabeth[5] **Perkins**, Jacob[4], Elizabeth[3] **Whipple**, Matthew[2], Matthew[1])[100] birth date unknown, married **Stephen Quattrocchi**.

Janis **Baker** and Stephen **Quattrocchi** had the following children:
-      9631   i.   Kimberly[15] **Quattrocchi**.[101]
-      9632   ii.   Jill **Quattrocchi**.[102]
-      9633   iii.   Amy **Quattrocchi**.[103]

8185. **Norman[14] Baker** (Gordon Andrews[13], Fannie Woodberry[12] **Bragdon**, Ione[11] **Andrews**, Henry[10], Caleb[9], Molly[8] **Burnham**, Capt. Westley[7], Westley[6], Elizabeth[5] **Perkins**, Jacob[4], Elizabeth[3] **Whipple**, Matthew[2], Matthew[1])[104] birth date unknown, married **Janice (__)**.

Norman **Baker** and Janice (_) had the following children:

    9634   i.   Laurie[15] **Baker**.[105]

    9635   ii.   Karen **Baker**.[106]

8187. **Louise**[14] **Baker** (Otis Clayton[13], Fannie Woodberry[12] **Bragdon**, Ione[11] **Andrews**, Henry[10], Caleb[9], Molly[8] **Burnham**, Capt. Westley[7], Westley[6], Elizabeth[5] **Perkins**, Jacob[4], Elizabeth[3] **Whipple**, Matthew[2], Matthew[1])[107] was born in Beverly, Essex Co., Mass. 16 February 1943 and married **Richard Powers** in Falmouth, Barnstable Co., Mass. in 1963. Marriage ended in divorce. Richard is the son of Richard **Powers**.

Louise **Baker** and Richard **Powers** had the following children:

    9636   i.   Kimberly[15] **Powers**[108] born 3 January 1966.

    9637   ii.   Karen **Powers**[109] born 2 May 1969.

8189. **Patricia**[14] **Baker** (Otis Clayton[13], Fannie Woodberry[12] **Bragdon**, Ione[11] **Andrews**, Henry[10], Caleb[9], Molly[8] **Burnham**, Capt. Westley[7], Westley[6], Elizabeth[5] **Perkins**, Jacob[4], Elizabeth[3] **Whipple**, Matthew[2], Matthew[1])[110] was born in Falmouth, Barnstable Co., Mass. 12 June 1947 and married twice. (1) **Theodore Robert Hoeckel II** in Falmouth. Theodore,[111] son of Theodore Robert **Hoeckel** and Dorothy (_), died in 1975. (2) **Gregory Reasoner** 11 May 1985.

Patricia **Baker** and Theodore Robert **Hoeckel** II had the following children:

    9638   i.   Heidi[15] **Hoeckel**[112] born 14 August 1969.

    9639   ii.   Theodore Robert **Hoeckel** III[113] born 1 March 1972.

8190. **Nancy**[14] **Raymond** (Frank Everett[13], Emma Louise[12] **Low**, Emma Louise[11] **Andrews**, Henry[10], Caleb[9], Molly[8] **Burnham**, Capt. Westley[7], Westley[6], Elizabeth[5] **Perkins**, Jacob[4], Elizabeth[3] **Whipple**, Matthew[2], Matthew[1])[114] birth date unknown, married **Frank Corral**.

Nancy **Raymond** and Frank **Corral** had the following children:

    9640   i.   Laurie Ann[15] **Corral**[115] born 5 April 1960 and married Eric Alan **Bell**. They had two children, no details provided.

    9641   ii.   Amy Louise **Corral**[116] born 16 March 1963.

    9642   iii. Bradley **Corral**[117] born 6 October 1965.

8191. **Charles Everett**[14] **Raymond** (Frank Everett[13], Emma Louise[12] **Low**, Emma Louise[11] **Andrews**, Henry[10], Caleb[9], Molly[8] **Burnham**, Capt. Westley[7], Westley[6], Elizabeth[5] **Perkins**, Jacob[4], Elizabeth[3] **Whip-**

ple, Matthew², Matthew¹)¹¹⁸ birth date unknown, was married but no information was provided on his wife.

Charles Everett **Raymond** had the following child:
+   9643   i.   Martha Jane¹⁵ **Raymond**.

8192. **Alice Louise**¹⁴ **Raymond** (Frank Everett¹³, Emma Louise¹² **Low**, Emma Louise¹¹ **Andrews**, Henry¹⁰, Caleb⁹, Molly⁸ **Burnham**, Capt. Westley⁷, Westley⁶, Elizabeth⁵ **Perkins**, Jacob⁴, Elizabeth³ **Whipple**, Matthew², Matthew¹)¹¹⁹ was born 27 November 1934 and married twice. (1) **Bernard Sidman**. (2) **Richard Murphy**.

Alice Louise **Raymond** and Bernard **Sidman** had the following children:
     9644   i.   Marcie Lee¹⁵ **Sidman**¹²⁰ born 24 April 1966.
     9645   ii.   Jon Eric **Sidman**¹²¹ born 10 November 1969.

8194. **Joanne Elizabeth**¹⁴ **Raymond** (Roger Conant¹³, Emma Louise¹² **Low**, Emma Louise¹¹ **Andrews**, Henry¹⁰, Caleb⁹, Molly⁸ **Burnham**, Capt. Westley⁷, Westley⁶, Elizabeth⁵ **Perkins**, Jacob⁴, Elizabeth³ **Whipple**, Matthew², Matthew¹)¹²² was born 21 January 1942 and married **Nicholas Mark Ferriter** in Charleston, Charleston Co., S.C. 10 June 1962. Nicholas,¹²³ son of Charles Arthur **Ferriter** and Patricia Ann **Flanigan**, was born in Portsmouth, Rockingham Co., N. H. 10 July 1940.

Joanne Elizabeth **Raymond** and Nicholas Mark **Ferriter** had the following children:
     9646   i.   Karin Louise¹⁵ **Ferriter**¹²⁴ born 18 September 1963.
     9647   ii.   Ann Margaret **Ferriter**¹²⁵ born 23 April 1965.
     9648   iii.   Jennifer Claire **Ferriter**¹²⁶ born 19 January 1968.
     9649   iv.   Mark Raymond **Ferriter**¹²⁷ born 10 August 1971.
     9650   v.   Sarah Rose **Ferriter**¹²⁸ born 16 April 1975.

8195. **Roger Conant**¹⁴ **Raymond** (Roger Conant¹³, Emma Louise¹² **Low**, Emma Louise¹¹ **Andrews**, Henry¹⁰, Caleb⁹, Molly⁸ **Burnham**, Capt. Westley⁷, Westley⁶, Elizabeth⁵ **Perkins**, Jacob⁴, Elizabeth³ **Whipple**, Matthew², Matthew¹)¹²⁹ was born 20 September 1945 and married **Martha Stiles** in Portsmouth, Rockingham Co., N.H. 14 March 1970. Martha,¹³⁰ daughter of Walter **Stiles** and Ellen **Johnson**, was born 1 November 1949.

{ G 1413 }

Roger Conant **Raymond** and Martha **Stiles** had the following children:

    9651   i.   Jay[15] **Raymond**[131] born 2 May 1972.
    9652   ii.   Leslie **Raymond**[132] born 8 November 1976.
    9653   iii.   Bruce **Raymond**[133] born 25 April 1980.

8196. **Susan Low**[14] **Raymond** (Roger Conant[13], Emma Louise[12] **Low**, Emma Louise[11] **Andrews**, Henry[10], Caleb[9], Molly[8] **Burnham**, Capt. Westley[7], Westley[6], Elizabeth[5] **Perkins**, Jacob[4], Elizabeth[3] **Whipple**, Matthew[2], Matthew[1])[134] was born 9 December 1946 and married **Nelson John Murray Jr.** in Kittery Point, York Co., Maine 25 August 1967. Nelson,[135] son of Nelson John **Murray** and Helen (__), was born 24 September 1942.

Susan Low **Raymond** and Nelson John **Murray** Jr. had the following children:

    9654   i.   Nelson John[15] **Murray**[136] born 17 February 1968.
    9655   ii.   Joseph Andrew **Murray**[137] born 2 February 1980.

8197. **David Lee**[14] **Raymond** (Roger Conant[13], Emma Louise[12] **Low**, Emma Louise[11] **Andrews**, Henry[10], Caleb[9], Molly[8] **Burnham**, Capt. Westley[7], Westley[6], Elizabeth[5] **Perkins**, Jacob[4], Elizabeth[3] **Whipple**, Matthew[2], Matthew[1])[138] was born 12 October 1948 and married **Martha Tobey**. Martha,[139] daughter of Ralph **Tobey** and Alice (__), was born 22 June 1950.

David Lee **Raymond** and Martha **Tobey** had the following children:

    9656   i.   Heather[15] **Raymond**[140] born 24 May 1975.
    9657   ii.   Elizabeth **Raymond**[141] born 3 September 1978.

8198. **John Douglas**[14] **Raymond** (Roger Conant[13], Emma Louise[12] **Low**, Emma Louise[11] **Andrews**, Henry[10], Caleb[9], Molly[8] **Burnham**, Capt. Westley[7], Westley[6], Elizabeth[5] **Perkins**, Jacob[4], Elizabeth[3] **Whipple**, Matthew[2], Matthew[1])[142] was born 29 October 1951 and married **Margaret White** who was born 19 September 1953.[143]

John Douglas **Raymond** and Margaret **White** had the following child:

    9658   i.   Adam[15] **Raymond**[144] born 10 August 1984.

8203. **Linda**[14] **Raymond** (Sumner[13], Emma Louise[12] **Low**, Emma Louise[11] **Andrews**, Henry[10], Caleb[9], Molly[8] **Burnham**, Capt. Westley[7], Westley[6], Elizabeth[5] **Perkins**, Jacob[4], Elizabeth[3] **Whipple**, Matthew[2], Matthew[1])[145] birth date unknown, married (__) **Siegel**.

Linda **Raymond** and (__) **Siegel** had the following child:

    9659   i.   (Son)[15] **Siegel**.[146]

8230. **Adrienne Lee**[14] **Gosbee** (John Francis[13], Edna Frances[12] **Andrews**, Frank Albert[11], Henry[10], Caleb[9], Molly[8] **Burnham**, Capt. Westley[7], Westley[6], Elizabeth[5] **Perkins**, Jacob[4], Elizabeth[3] **Whipple**, Matthew[2], Matthew[1])[147] was born in Beverly, Essex Co., Mass. 29 January 1951 and married **Joseph David Schier** there 31 May 1975. He was born in Lynn, Essex Co., Mass. 9 June 1946.[148]

Adrienne Lee **Gosbee** and Joseph David **Schier** had the following child:
+ 9660 i. David Joseph[15] **Schier** born 21 November 1979.

8232. **Thomas William**[14] **Nolan** (Jean Frances[13] **Entwistle**, Viola Alberta[12] **Andrews**, Frank Albert[11], Henry[10], Caleb[9], Molly[8] **Burnham**, Capt. Westley[7], Westley[6], Elizabeth[5] **Perkins**, Jacob[4], Elizabeth[3] **Whipple**, Matthew[2], Matthew[1])[149] was born in Framingham, Middlesex Co., Mass. 3 September 1960 and married **Kirsten Anderson** in South Glastonbury, Hartford Co., Conn. 21 September 1991. She is the daughter of Richard **Anderson** and Nancy (__).

Thomas William **Nolan** and Kirsten **Anderson** had the following children born in Hartford, Hartford Co., Conn.:
9661 i. Scott Thomas[15] **Nolan**[150] 15 June 1995.
9662 ii. James Michael **Nolan**[151] 1 January 1998.

8233. **James Kieran**[14] **Nolan** (Jean Frances[13] **Entwistle**, Viola Alberta[12] **Andrews**, Frank Albert[11], Henry[10], Caleb[9], Molly[8] **Burnham**, Capt. Westley[7], Westley[6], Elizabeth[5] **Perkins**, Jacob[4], Elizabeth[3] **Whipple**, Matthew[2], Matthew[1])[152] was born in Framingham, Middlesex Co., Mass. 14 October 1961 and married **Margaret Mahoney** in Ballston Lake, Saratoga Co., N.Y. 23 March 1991.

James Kieran **Nolan** and Margaret **Mahoney** had the following child:
9663 i. Kelly Ann[15] **Nolan**[153] born in Amsterdam, Schenectady Co., N.Y. 20 June 1992.

8235. **Joseph Francis**[14] **Nolan** (Jean Frances[13] **Entwistle**, Viola Alberta[12] **Andrews**, Frank Albert[11], Henry[10], Caleb[9], Molly[8] **Burnham**, Capt. Westley[7], Westley[6], Elizabeth[5] **Perkins**, Jacob[4], Elizabeth[3] **Whipple**, Matthew[2], Matthew[1])[154] was born in Framingham, Middlesex Co., Mass. 12 February 1966 and married **Johonna Weakley** in Ballston Lake, Saratoga Co., N.Y. 16 May 1992.

Joseph Francis **Nolan** and Johonna **Weakley** had the following children born in Niskayuna, Schenectady, Co., N. Y:
    9664 i. Casey Rian[15] **Nolan**[155] 25 March 1994.
    9665 ii. Carey Elizabeth **Nolan**[156] 25 July 1997.
    9666 iii. Cadey Jo **Nolan**[157] 14 September 1998.
    9667 iv. Carley Jean **Nolan**[158] 20 December 1999.

8242. **Robert Byron**[14] **Andrews** (Sydney Byron[13], Frank Sydney[12], Frank Albert[11], Henry[10], Caleb[9], Molly[8] **Burnham**, Capt. Westley[7], Westley[6], Elizabeth[5] **Perkins**, Jacob[4], Elizabeth[3] **Whipple**, Matthew[2], Matthew[1])[159] was born in Worcester, Worcester Co., Mass. 19 June 1954 and married **Jeanne Marie Hansen** in Chicago, Cook Co., Ill. 3 January 1976.

Robert Byron **Andrews** and Jeanne Marie **Hansen** had the following children born in Chicago, Ill.:
    9668 i. Christopher Robert[15] **Andrews**[160] 15 March 1979.
    9669 ii. Lauren Michelle **Andrews**[161] 29 August 1980.

8243. **Wendy Lou**[14] **Andrews** (Sydney Byron[13], Frank Sydney[12], Frank Albert[11], Henry[10], Caleb[9], Molly[8] **Burnham**, Capt. Westley[7], Westley[6], Elizabeth[5] **Perkins**, Jacob[4], Elizabeth[3] **Whipple**, Matthew[2], Matthew[1])[162] was born in Worcester, Worcester Co., Mass. 27 August 1955 and married twice. (1) **James Nelson Cyr** in West Brookfield, Worcester Co., Mass. 17 July 1976. (2) **Everett Peyrat**.

Wendy Lou **Andrews** and James Nelson **Cyr** had the following children born in Burlington, Chittendon Co., Vt.:
    9670 i. Sara June[15] **Cyr**[163] 21 July 1977.
    9671 ii. Jill Lee **Cyr**[164] 1 April 1981.
    9672 iii. Matthew James **Cyr**[165] 20 February 1983.

8244. **Thomas Mark**[14] **Andrews** (Sydney Byron[13], Frank Sydney[12], Frank Albert[11], Henry[10], Caleb[9], Molly[8] **Burnham**, Capt. Westley[7], Westley[6], Elizabeth[5] **Perkins**, Jacob[4], Elizabeth[3] **Whipple**, Matthew[2], Matthew[1])[166] was born in Worcester, Worcester Co., Mass. 15 September 1957 and married **Takae Kanai** in Tokyo, Japan 13 March 1984. Takae,[167] daughter of Yutaka **Kanai** and Keiko **Nishiwaki**, was born in Tokyo 16 October 1960.

Thomas Mark **Andrews** and Takae **Kanai** had the following children:
    9673 i. Rie Kanai[15] **Andrews**[168] born in Yokosuka, Japan 26 August 1985.

9674 ii. Motoyasu Kanai **Andrews**[169] born in Misawa, Japan 18 December 1986.

8245. **Kathleen Louise**[14] **Andrews** (Sydney Byron[13], Frank Sydney[12], Frank Albert[11], Henry[10], Caleb[9], Molly[8] **Burnham**, Capt. Westley[7], Westley[6], Elizabeth[5] **Perkins**, Jacob[4], Elizabeth[3] **Whipple**, Matthew[2], Matthew[1])[170] was born in Westborough, Worcester Co., Mass. 16 November 1960 and married twice. (1) **Theodore Martin Cioppa**. He was born in Torrington, Litchfield Co., Conn. 3 April 1963. (2) **David Lewis Rose** in Shrewsbury, Worcester Co., Mass. 24 September 1994. David,[171] son of David Ralph **Rose** and Maria Teresa **Viade**, was born in Beaver, Beaver Co., Penn. 12 September 1960.

Kathleen Louise **Andrews** and Theodore Martin **Cioppa** had the following child born in Worcester, Worcestor Co.,:

9675 i. Gillian Elizabeth[15] **Cioppa**[172] 17 April 1979.

Kathleen Louise **Andrews** and David Lewis **Rose** had the following children born in Worcester:

9676 ii. Joseph David **Rose**[173] 5 November 1994.
9677 iii. James William **Rose**[174] 2 September 1997.
9678 iv. Justin Benjamin **Rose**[175] 9 October 1998.

8246. **William Michael**[14] **Ware** (Shirley Mae[13] **Andrews**, Frank Sydney[12], Frank Albert[11], Henry[10], Caleb[9], Molly[8] **Burnham**, Capt. Westley[7], Westley[6], Elizabeth[5] **Perkins**, Jacob[4], Elizabeth[3] **Whipple**, Matthew[2], Matthew[1])[176] was born in Worcester, Worcester Co., Mass. 28 October 1954.

William Michael **Ware** and Laurie **Cummings** had the following child:

9679 i. Keith Guy[15] **Cummings-Ware**[177] born 19 July 1985.

8248. **Susan Elaine**[14] **Ware** (Shirley Mae[13] **Andrews**, Frank Sydney[12], Frank Albert[11], Henry[10], Caleb[9], Molly[8] **Burnham**, Capt. Westley[7], Westley[6], Elizabeth[5] **Perkins**, Jacob[4], Elizabeth[3] **Whipple**, Matthew[2], Matthew[1])[178] was born in Worcester, Worcester Co., Mass. 10 April 1960 and married three times. (1) **John Alden Clarke** in LaPorte, Harris Co., Tex. 28 February 1981. Marriage ended in divorce. John,[179] son of Gerald **Clarke** and Dorothy (__), was born in Alabama 22 March 1960. (2) **David E. Brown** in Pasadena, Houston Co., Tex. 4 August 1990. Marriage ended in divorce. He was born in Ohio. (3) **John Eric Brinley** in Friendswood, Galveston Co., Tex. 24 April 1999. John,[180] son of Elbert **Brinley** and Mildred **Gowen**, was born in Bonne Terre, Iron Co., Mo. 3 August 1956.

{ G 1417 }

Susan Elaine **Ware** and John Alden **Clarke** had the following children born in Bryan, Brazos Co, Tex.:
- 9680 i. Timothy Alden[15] **Clarke**[181] 7 July 1983.
- 9681 ii. Adam Keith **Clarke**[182] 29 October 1985.

8250. **Ellen Marie**[14] **Nedde** (Carole Joan[13] **Andrews**, Frank Sydney[12], Frank Albert[11], Henry[10], Caleb[9], Molly[8] **Burnham**, Capt. Westley[7], Westley[6], Elizabeth[5] **Perkins**, Jacob[4], Elizabeth[3] **Whipple**, Matthew[2], Matthew[1])[183] was born in Decatur, Macon Co., Ill. 31 August 1961 and married **William McKay Shipp** in Dranesville, Fairfax Co., Va. 16 June 1984. William,[184] son of Thomas **Shipp** and Winona Jacqueline **Shreve**, was born in Washington, D.C. 24 April 1960.

Ellen Marie **Nedde** and William McKay **Shipp** had the following children born in Washington:
- 9682 i. Nora Rose Nedde[15] **Shipp**[185] 12 November 1992.
- 9683 ii. Lillian Mae Nedde **Shipp**[186] 5 September 1995.

8255. **Linda Barbara**[14] **Mears** (Edward Francis[13], Edward Francis[12], David Edward[11], Sallie Maria[10] **Andrews**, Caleb[9], Molly[8] **Burnham**, Capt. Westley[7], Westley[6], Elizabeth[5] **Perkins**, Jacob[4], Elizabeth[3] **Whipple**, Matthew[2], Matthew[1])[187] was born in Lynn, Essex Co., Mass. 16 August 1945 and married **Rafe Henry Blood Sr.** in Seabrook, Rockingham Co., N. H. 23 January 1965. She was born in Westborough, Worcester Co., Mass. 11 January 1942.[188]

Linda Barbara **Mears** and Rafe Henry **Blood** Sr. had the following children:
- + 9684 i. Rafe Henry[15] **Blood** Jr. born 22 July 1965.
- 9685 ii. Tracey Lynn **Blood**[189] born in Newburyport, Essex Co., Mass. 26 September 1968 and married Todd Matthew **Bradsher** in Kensington, Rockingham Co. 4 May 1991. Todd,[190] son of Robert **Bradsher** and Doris **Fuller,** was born in Exeter, Rockingham Co. 20 December 1965.
- + 9686 iii. Christian Daniel **Blood** born 28 February 1971.

8263. **Susan Andrews**[14] **Leslie** (Alexander[13], Levi Charles Smalley[12], Florence[11] **Andrews**, Levi Smalley[10], Noah[9], John[8], Joanna[7] **Burnham**, Westley[6], Elizabeth[5] **Perkins**, Jacob[4], Elizabeth[3] **Whipple**, Matthew[2], Matthew[1])[191] was born 6 April 1956 and married **John Alexander Fraser III**.

Susan Andrews **Leslie** and John Alexander **Fraser** III had the following children:

  9687 i. John Alexander[15] **Fraser** IV.[192]
  9688 ii. Elizabeth **Fraser**.[193]
  9689 iii. William **Fraser**.[194]
  9690 iv. Simon **Fraser**.[195]

8267. **Silvia Maria Irvin de Carvalho**[14] **Vianna** (Florence Eleanor[13] **Irvin**, Eleanor[12] **Leslie**, Florence[11] **Andrews**, Levi Smalley[10], Noah[9], John[8], Joanna[7] **Burnham**, Westley[6], Elizabeth[5] **Perkins**, Jacob[4], Elizabeth[3] **Whipple**, Matthew[2], Matthew[1])[196] was born in Rio de Janeiro, Brazil 26 May 1944 and married **Joao Baptista Canto** there in 1967. He was born in Rio de Janeiro 11 August 1943.[197]

Silvia Maria Irvin de Carvalho **Vianna** and Joao Baptista **Canto** had the following children:
  9691 i. Antonio Carlos[15] **Canto**[198] born 17 November 1968.
  9692 ii. Joao Rodolfo **Canto**[199] born 4 May 1971.

8268. **Florence Ann de Carvalho**[14] **Vianna** (Florence Eleanor[13] **Irvin**, Eleanor[12] **Leslie**, Florence[11] **Andrews**, Levi Smalley[10], Noah[9], John[8], Joanna[7] **Burnham**, Westley[6], Elizabeth[5] **Perkins**, Jacob[4], Elizabeth[3] **Whipple**, Matthew[2], Matthew[1])[200] was born 31 March 1945 and married twice. (1) **Mario Signorinni.** (2) **Amaro Machado**.

Florence Ann **de Carvalho Vianna** and Mario **Signorinni** had the following child born in Rio de Janerio, Brazil:
  9693 i. Pedro[15] **Signorinni**[201] 20 October 1971.

Florence Ann **de Carvalho Vianna** and Amaro **Machado** had the following child:
  9694 ii. Maria Rita **Machado**[202] was born 10 May 1981.

8269. **Paulo Irvin de Carvalho**[14] **Vianna** (Florence Eleanor[13] **Irvin**, Eleanor[12] **Leslie**, Florence[11] **Andrews**, Levi Smalley[10], Noah[9], John[8], Joanna[7] **Burnham**, Westley[6], Elizabeth[5] **Perkins**, Jacob[4], Elizabeth[3] **Whipple**, Matthew[2], Matthew[1])[203] was born in Rio de Janeiro, Brazil 1 November 1949 and married **Maria Tereza Lysandro Albernaz**.

Paulo Irvin **de Carvalho Vianna** and Maria Tereza Lysandro **Albernaz** had the following children born in Rio:
>   9695   i.   Maria[15] **de Carvalho Vianna**[204] 3 October 1977.
>   9696   ii.   Francisco **de CarvalhoVianna**[205] 26 June 1978.

8270. **Mary Eleanor Irvin de Carvalho**[14] **Vianna** (Florence Eleanor[13] **Irvin**, Eleanor[12] **Leslie**, Florence[11] **Andrews**, Levi Smalley[10], Noah[9], John[8], Joanna[7] **Burnham**, Westley[6], Elizabeth[5] **Perkins**, Jacob[4], Elizabeth[3] **Whipple**, Matthew[2], Matthew[1])[206] was born 9 June 1954 and married **Joaquim Servera**.

Mary Eleanor Irvin **de Carvalho Vianna** and Joaquim **Servera** had the following children:
>   9697   i.   Christiana[15] **Servera**[207] born in Miami, Dade Co., Fla. 23 October 1978.
>   9698   ii.   Joao Paulo **Servera**[208] born in Rio de Janeiro, Brazil 25 February 1983.
>   9699   iii. Lucas **Servera**[209] born 12 July 1996.

8275. **Brian Dennis Alan**[14] **Keener** (Margaret Louise[13] **Seifert**, Margaret Alice[12] **Andrews**, Dennis Rivers[11], Levi Smalley[10], Noah[9], John[8], Joanna[7] **Burnham**, Westley[6], Elizabeth[5] **Perkins**, Jacob[4], Elizabeth[3] **Whipple**, Matthew[2], Matthew[1])[210] was born in Miami, Dade Co., Fla. 19 July 1960 and died in August 1997 at 37 years of age. He married **Virginia Idelle Kurapka** in McDonogh, Baltimore Co., Md. 19 September 1992. Virginia,[211] daughter of Peter James **Kurapka** IX and Marian Idelle **Beam**, was born in Baltimore, Baltimore City Co., Md. 30 December 1959. She earned a B. A from Washington College, Chestertown, Kent Co., Md. in 1982 and is (1999) a Foreign Service Officer with the U.S. Department of State. Brian, a graduate of Liverpool University in England, was a teacher before his death.

Brian Dennis Alan **Keener** and Virginia Idelle **Kurapka** had the following children:
>   7696   i.   Miles Christopher David[13] **Keener**[212] born in Baltimore 28 May 1994.
>   7697   ii.   Peter Alexander George **Keener**[213] born in London, England 3 January 1997.

8276. **Carlos Grant Patrick**[14] **Keener** (Margaret Louise[13] **Seifert**, Margaret Alice[12] **Andrews**, Dennis Rivers[11], Levi Smalley[10], Noah[9], John[8], Joanna[7] **Burnham**, Westley[6], Elizabeth[5] **Perkins**, Jacob[4], Elizabeth[3]

Whipple, Matthew[2], Matthew[1])[214] was born in Dallas, Dallas Co., Tex. 9 January 1967 and married **Patricia Jane Preiser** in Basking Ridge, Somerset Co., N.J. 2 October 1993. She is the daughter of Gidrey **Preiser** and Mary Jane **Dubois**.[215]

Carlos Grant Patrick **Keener** and Patricia Jane **Preiser** had the following child:
    9700   i.   Andrew Miles Grant[15] **Keener**[216] born in London, England 8 March 1998.

8333. **Marjean**[14] **Holmes** (Frederick Melvin[13], Hazel Georgia[12] **Bradley**, Esther Myrtle[11] **Smith**, Julia Ann[10] **Stevens**, Melissa Esther[9] **Jones**, Mariah B.[8] **Ayers**, Lovica[7] **Stanton**, Lovica[6] **Gates**, Charity[5] **Perkins**, Jabez[4], Elizabeth[3] **Whipple**, Matthew[2], Matthew[1])[217] was born in Belding, Ionia Co., Mich. 22 April 1958 and married **Steven George Workman** in Greenville, Montcalm Co., Mich. 14 March 1981. Steven, son of Kenneth Jay **Workman** and Delores Jean **Heether**, was born in Greenville 17 February 1958.

Marjean **Holmes** and Steven George **Workman** had the following children born in Manchester, Hillsborough Co., N. H.:
    9701   i.   Jacob Frederick[15] **Workman**[218] 30 January 1989.
    9702   ii.   Samuel Dixon **Workman**[219] 1 May 1991.

8336. **Winston Fayette**[14] **Dorian** (Nancy Jane[13] **Weller**, Inez Eunice[12] **Hamilton**, Jessie M.[11] **Washburn**, Lillian Jane[10] **Corson**, Jane[9] **Whipple**, John[8], Eleazer[7], Eleazer[6], Nathan[5], Matthew[4], Lt. John[3], Matthew[2], Matthew[1])[220] was born in New York, N.Y. 18 June 1964 and married **Constance Perigot** in Camp Pendleton, San Diego Co., Calif. 17 September 1989. She was born in California 20 December 1956.[221]

Winston Fayette **Dorian** and Constance **Perigot** had the following child:
    9703   i.   Winston Fayette[15] **Dorian** Jr.[222] born in Temecula, Riverside Co., Calif. 24 January 1991.

8338. **Hamilton Haig**[14] **Dorian** (Nancy Jane[13] **Weller**, Inez Eunice[12] **Hamilton**, Jessie M.[11] **Washburn**, Lillian Jane[10] **Corson**, Jane[9] **Whipple**, John[8], Eleazer[7], Eleazer[6], Nathan[5], Matthew[4], Lt. John[3], Matthew[2], Matthew[1])[223] was born 24 September 1968 and married **Shari Eyring** in Mesa, Mariposa Co., Ariz. 5 January 1991. She was born in Mesa 1 September 1970.[224]

Hamilton Haig **Dorian** and Shari **Eyring** had the following children born in Mesa:

    9704   i.   Rachel[15] **Dorian**[225] 12 July 1992.
    9705   ii.   Rebecca **Dorian**[226] 27 December 1993.
    9706   iii.   Sarah **Dorian**[227] 18 June 1997.
    9707   iv.   Hannah **Dorian**[228] 24 March 2000.

8340. **Kathie Joan**[14] **Hendricks** (Eileen Lucille[13] **McCleary**, Eva Muryl[12] **Shannon**, Maude Belle[11] **Kennison**, America Martha Jane[10] **Walker**, Calvin Augustus[9], Lydia[8] **Whipple**, Zebulon[7], Zebulon[6], Samuel[5], Cyprian[4], Lt. John[3], Matthew[2], Matthew[1])[229] was born in Waterloo, Black Hawk Co., Iowa 12 August 1940 and married **Edmond J. Walsh** in Hampton, Franklin Co., Iowa 26 June 1965. Edmond,[230] son of Edmond **Walsh** and Mary **Serach**, was born in Norristown, Montgomery Co., Penn. 13 September 1943 and died 24 May 1991 in Maywood, Cook Co., Ill., at 47 years of age. Buried in Garfield Cemetery, Campton Township, Kane Co. Ill.

Kathie Joan **Hendricks** and Edmond J. **Walsh** had the following children:

    9708   i.   Anne Shannon[15] **Walsh**[231] born in Arlington Heights, Cook Co., Ill. 27 November 1968 and married Matthew **Cesarone** in Geneva, Kane Co., Ill. 30 September 1995.
    9709   ii.   Megan Fitzgerald **Walsh**[232] born in Rockford, Winnebago Co., Ill. 23 January 1974.

8343. **Craig Lewis**[14] **Nix** (Julia Ann[13] **Whipple**, Lewis Dale[12], Andrew Jackson[11], Andrew Bina[10], Andrew Jackson[9], Zebulon[8], Zebulon[7], Zebulon[6], Samuel[5], Cyprian[4], Lt. John[3], Matthew[2], Matthew[1])[233] was born in Shreveport, Caddo Parish, La. 27 December 1971 and married **Traci Diane Dinkins** there 28 December 1991. Traci,[234] daughter of Marvin **Dinkins** and Dianne **Durr**, was born in Shreveport 27 September 1972.

Craig Lewis **Nix** and Traci Diane **Dinkins** had the following children:

    9710   i.   Spencer Blaine[15] **Nix**[235] born in Houston, Harris Co., Tex. 17 April 1993.
    9711   ii.   Blake Leighann **Nix**[236] born in Shreveport 18 December 1996.

8344. **Michael Wayne**[14] **Nix** (Julia Ann[13] **Whipple**, Lewis Dale[12], Andrew Jackson[11], Andrew Bina[10], Andrew Jackson[9], Zebulon[8], Zebulon[7], Zebulon[6], Samuel[5], Cyprian[4], Lt. John[3], Matthew[2], Matthew[1])[237] was born in Shreveport, Caddo Parish, La. 14 March 1975 and married

Angela Renee **Bullock** there 29 June 1996. Angela,[238] daughter of Richard **Bullock** and Joyce **Sanders**, was born at Camp LeJeune, Onslow Co., N.C. 20 November 1975.

Michael Wayne **Nix** and Angela Renee **Bullock** had the following children born in Shreveport:

   9712 i. Kaylee Michelle[15] **Nix**[239] 1 November 1995.
   9713 ii. Jared Michael **Nix**[240] 2 September 1997.

 8345. **Kelly Amber**[14] **DiMarco** (Debra Ellen[13] **Whipple**, Lewis Dale[12], Andrew Jackson[11], Andrew Bina[10], Andrew Jackson[9], Zebulon[8], Zebulon[7], Zebulon[6], Samuel[5], Cyprian[4], Lt. John[3], Matthew[2], Matthew[1])[241] was born in New Orleans, Orleans Parish, La. 5 October 1977.

Kelly Amber **DiMarco** and Charles **Hebert** had the following child:

   9714 i. Madison Nicole[15] **Hebert**[242] born in Metaire, Jefferson Parish, La. 8 October 1997.

 8388. **Wesley John**[14] **MacDonald** (Barbara Joanna[13] **Moore**, Grace Irene[12] **Whipple**, Oran Porter[11], Joseph Walter[10], Jonathan Jones[9], Joseph[8], David[7], Samuel[6], Samuel[5], Cyprian[4], Lt. John[3], Matthew[2], Matthew[1])[243] was born in Los Angeles, Los Angeles Co., Calif. 20 November 1946 and married **Miranda Jane Mitchell** there 19 October 1968. Miranda,[244] daughter of Allen Lawrence **Mitchell** and Marilyn Jane **Freeman**, was born in Woodland Hills, Los Angeles Co., Calif. 25 April 1948. She also married and divorced **Edward Michael Hannin**. Wesley is a Fire Inspector and served in the U.S. Navy in Vietnam.

Wesley John **MacDonald** and Miranda Jane **Mitchell** had the following children:

   9715 i. Murdoch Douglas[15] **MacDonald**[245] born in Santa Monica, Los Angeles Co., Calif. 1 November 1969 and married Heidi Lynn **McMahon** in Ojai, Ventura Co., Calif. 1 May 1999. Heidi,[246] daughter of Patrick **McMahon** and Kathleen (__), was born in Alexandria, Alexandria City Area Co., Va. 30 June 1973.
   9716 ii. Malai Kate **MacDonald**[247] born in Los Angeles 25 August 1972 and married Sonny Allan **Benavidez** in Ventura, Ventura Co., Calif. 11 September 1999. Sonny,[248] son of Jess Rodriquez **Benavidez** and Esther **Guzman**, was born 10 July 1970.

{ G 1423 }

9717 iii. Emily Susan **MacDonald**[249] was born in Chatsworth, Los Angeles Co., Calif. 1 January 1975 and married Alvaro **Casanova** in Las Vegas, Clark Co., Nev. 1 January 1996. Alvaro,[250] son of Antonio **Casanova** and Marguirita (__), was born in Muna, Mexico 10 October 1972.

9718 iv. Duncan George Alexander Donald **MacDonald**[251] was born in Ventura 12 March 1978.

9719 v. Fiona Maureen **MacDonald**[252] born in Ventura Co. 6 October 1979.

8390. **Arthur Paul**[14] **Whipple** III (Arthur Paul[13], Arthur Paul[12], Merritt Pendell[11], Dr. Alfred Augustus[10], Henry Francisco[9], Joseph[8], David[7], Samuel[6], Samuel[5], Cyprian[4], Lt. John[3], Matthew[2], Matthew[1])[253] was born in Billings, Yellowstone Co., Mont. 17 September 1957 and married **Elizabeth Milstead** in Stillwater, Payne Co., Okla. 9 March 1984. She was born in Ruston, Lincoln Parish, La. 20 September 1963.[254]

Arthur Paul **Whipple** III and Elizabeth **Milstead** had the following children:

9720 i. Duncan[15] **Whipple**[255] born in Cleveland, Cuyahoga Co., Ohio 13 May 1995.

9721 ii. Logan John **Whipple**[256] born in Columbus, Franklin Co., Ohio 17 December 1998. Adopted.

8392. **Carol Miller**[14] **Whipple** (Arthur Paul[13], Arthur Paul[12], Merritt Pendell[11], Dr. Alfred Augustus[10], Henry Francisco[9], Joseph[8], David[7], Samuel[6], Samuel[5], Cyprian[4], Lt. John[3], Matthew[2], Matthew[1])[257] was born in Billings, Yellowstone Co., Mont. 27 December 1961 and married **Karl A'Delbert Lynes** in Ponca City, Kay Co., Okla. 15 August 1981. He was born there 9 June 1961.[258]

Carol Miller **Whipple** and Karl A'Delbert **Lynes** had the following children:

9722 i. Jacob Matthew[15] **Lynes**[259] born in Stillwater, Payne Co., Okla. 10 March 1985.

9723 ii. Calah Christine **Lynes**[260] born in Tulsa, Tulsa Co., Okla. 10 March 1988.

8393. **Karen Marie**[14] **Whipple** (Nelson Frank Gordon[13], Arthur Paul[12], Merritt Pendell[11], Dr. Alfred Augustus[10], Henry Francisco[9], Joseph[8], David[7], Samuel[6], Samuel[5], Cyprian[4], Lt. John[3], Matthew[2], Matthew[1])[261] was born in Hartford, Hartford Co., Conn. 3 September 1954 and married **Harvey Arthur Thomas Jr.** in Newington, Hartford Co., Conn. 7 August 1976. Harvey,[262] son of Harvey Arthur **Thomas** and Ruth **Dunshee**, was born in Englewood, Bergen Co., N.J. 9 December 1951. Karen has done considerable genealogical research on her Whipple lineage and believes there is a possibility that her fifth great grandfather David Whipple may descend from David Whipple and Martha Reed, not from Samuel Whipple, Jr. and Mercy (__) as shown in this genealogy. If she is able to prove the alternative lineage, it means her line descends from Capt. John of Providence, not Matthew of Ipswich.

Karen Marie **Whipple** and Harvey Arthur **Thomas** Jr. had the following children:

  9724 i. Laura Carmela[15] **Thomas**[263] born in Summit, Union Co., N.J. 8 January 1980.

  9725 ii. Harvey Arthur **Thomas** III[264] born in Holland, Ottawa Co., Mich. 15 July 1990.

8396. **Dorcas Miller**[14] **Whipple** (Nelson Frank Gordon[13], Arthur Paul[12], Merritt Pendell[11], Dr. Alfred Augustus[10], Henry Francisco[9], Joseph[8], David[7], Samuel[6], Samuel[5], Cyprian[4], Lt. John[3], Matthew[2], Matthew[1])[265] was born in Concord, Rockingham Co., N.H. 31 August 1964 and married **Steven Gorski** in Hartford, Hartford Co., Conn. 11 July 1988. He was born there 6 July 1964.[266]

Dorcas Miller **Whipple** and Steven **Gorski** had the following children:

  9726 i. Samantha Nichole[15] **Gorski**[267] born in Hartford 11 October 1994.

  9727 ii. Marc Joseph **Gorski**[268] born 7 January 1998.

8397. **Heather Loomis**[14] **Brooke** (David Lee[13], Virginia Dallas[12] **Whipple**, Merritt Pendell[11], Dr. Alfred Augustus[10], Henry Francisco[9], Joseph[8], David[7], Samuel[6], Samuel[5], Cyprian[4], Lt. John[3], Matthew[2], Matthew[1])[269] was born in Hinsdale, Rock Island Co., Ill. 20 June 1961 and married **Terrance Buck** in Western Springs, Cook Co., Ill. 26 March 1988. Terrance,[270] son of Tonka Joe **Buck** and Verna Jeanette **Gillum**, was born in Forks, Clallam Co., Wash. 26 August 1964.

Heather Loomis **Brooke** and Terrance **Buck** had the following children:

  9728 i. Alexander Frederick[15] **Buck**[271] born in San Diego, San Diego Co., Calif. 27 November 1990.

  9729 ii. Samantha Elizabeth **Buck**[272] born in San Diego 26 August 1992.

  9730 iii. Nicholas Sebastian **Buck**[273] born in Oakland, Alameda Co., Calif. 10 August 1998.

8398. **Frederick Lee**[14] **Brooke** II (David Lee[13], Virginia Dallas[12] **Whipple**, Merritt Pendell[11], Dr. Alfred Augustus[10], Henry Francisco[9], Joseph[8], David[7], Samuel[6], Samuel[5], Cyprian[4], Lt. John[3], Matthew[2], Matthew[1])[274] was born in Hinsdale, Rock Island Co., Ill. 1 May 1963 and married **Maria Luisa Bonzanigo** in Lugano, Switzerland 31 August 1991. Maria,[275] daughter of Stefano **Bonzanigo** and Maura **Antognini**, was born in Zurich, Switzerland 27 September 1964 and was living in Bellinzona, Switzerland at the time of their marriage. The family lives in Basel, Switzerland where Fred is the franchised proprietor of the Inlingua Language School. (2000)

Frederick Lee **Brooke** II and Maria Luisa **Bonzanigo** had the following children born in Basel:

    9731 i.   Mark Edward Alexander[15] **Brooke**[276] 1 April 1995.
    9732 ii. Henry Stephen Frederick **Brooke**[277] 17 December 1996.
    9733 iii. Charles Michael Andrew **Brooke**[278] 5 April 1999.

8400. **Wilfred Lee**[14] **Brooke** III (Wilfred Lee[13], Virginia Dallas[12] **Whipple**, Merritt Pendell[11], Dr. Alfred Augustus[10], Henry Francisco[9], Joseph[8], David[7], Samuel[6], Samuel[5], Cyprian[4], Lt. John[3], Matthew[2], Matthew[1])[279] was born 29 April 1953 and married **Anita Marie Zibton** in Warrenville, DuPage Co., Ill. 3 July 1988. She was born 7 April 1953.

Wilfred Lee **Brooke** III and Anita Marie **Zibton** had the following children:

    9734 i.   Benjamin Michael[15] **Brooke**[280] born 16 October 1992.
    9735 ii. Zoe Aeriel Zibton **Brooke**[281] born 1 November 1994.

8402. **Mina May**[14] **Brooke** (Wilfred Lee[13], Virginia Dallas[12] **Whipple**, Merritt Pendell[11], Dr. Alfred Augustus[10], Henry Francisco[9], Joseph[8], David[7], Samuel[6], Samuel[5], Cyprian[4], Lt. John[3], Matthew[2], Matthew[1])[282] was born 24 January 1957 and married twice. (1) **James Earl Frantz** 23 May 1980. They were divorced 20 March 1981. (2) **Victor David Bernhardt** in Ft. Collins, Larimer Co., Colo. 13 November 1984. They were divorced in December 1988.

Mina May **Brooke** and Victor David **Bernhardt** had the following child born in Ft. Collins:

    9736 i.   Rachel Angela[15] **Bernhardt**[283] 28 February 1985.

8403. **Charles Lee**[14] **Brooke** (Wilfred Lee[13], Virginia Dallas[12] **Whipple**, Merritt Pendell[11], Dr. Alfred Augustus[10], Henry Francisco[9], Joseph[8], David[7], Samuel[6], Samuel[5], Cyprian[4], Lt. John[3], Matthew[2], Matthew[1])[284] was born 4 October 1958 and married **Candace Marie Knudson** 28 June 1991.

Charles Lee **Brooke** and Candace Marie **Knudson** had the following child:
>   9737   i.   Austin Lee[15] **Brooke**[285] born 13 May 1995.

8404. **Elizabeth Michelle**[14] **Brooke** (John Almonte[13], Virginia Dallas[12] **Whipple**, Merritt Pendell[11], Dr. Alfred Augustus[10], Henry Francisco[9], Joseph[8], David[7], Samuel[6], Samuel[5], Cyprian[4], Lt. John[3], Matthew[2], Matthew[1])[286] was born 21 July 1961 and married **Michael Francis** in Lake Forest, Lake Co., Ill. 11 August 1984. He was born 24 July 1961.

Elizabeth Michelle **Brooke** and Michael **Francis** had the following children:
>   9738   i.   Phoebe Michelle[15] **Francis**[287] born in Highland Park, Lake Co., Ill. 31 December 1988.
>   9739   ii.   Alexander Michael **Francis**[288] born 24 January 1991.
>   9740   iii. Kyle Benjamin **Francis**[289] born 21 September 1994.

8405. **Cynthia Renee**[14] **Brooke** (John Almonte[13], Virginia Dallas[12] **Whipple**, Merritt Pendell[11], Dr. Alfred Augustus[10], Henry Francisco[9], Joseph[8], David[7], Samuel[6], Samuel[5], Cyprian[4], Lt. John[3], Matthew[2], Matthew[1])[290] was born 11 September 1962 and married **James Kelly Kilduff** in Lake Forest, Lake Co., Ill. 9 April 1988. He was born 24 March 1960.

Cynthia Renee **Brooke** and James Kelly **Kilduff** had the following children:
>   9741   i.   Brooke Allison[15] **Kilduff**[291] born in Cincinnati, Hamilton Co., Ohio 27 January 1989.
>   9742   ii.   Grant Matthew **Kilduff**[292] born 17 March 1990.
>   9743   iii. Logan Michelle **Kilduff**[293] born 17 November 1991.
>   9744   iv.   Austin James **Kilduff**[294] born 28 May 1995.

8406. **John Eisermann**[14] **Brooke** (John Almonte[13], Virginia Dallas[12] **Whipple**, Merritt Pendell[11], Dr. Alfred Augustus[10], Henry Francisco[9], Joseph[8], David[7], Samuel[6], Samuel[5], Cyprian[4], Lt. John[3], Matthew[2], Matthew[1])[295] was born 28 September 1966 and married **Barbara Louise Dunne** 3 August 1991. She was born 27 September 1958.

John Eisermann **Brooke** and Barbara Louise **Dunne** had the following child:
>   9745   i.   Daniel Eisermann[15] **Brooke**[296] born 29 July 1994.

8407. **Katherine Blanchard**[14] **Brooke** (John Almonte[13], Virginia Dallas[12] **Whipple**, Merritt Pendell[11], Dr. Alfred Augustus[10], Henry Francisco[9], Joseph[8], David[7], Samuel[6], Samuel[5], Cyprian[4], Lt. John[3], Matthew[2], Matthew[1])[297] was born 7 May 1969 and married **Jeffrey Parker** 29 April 1995. He was born 11 January 1957.

{ G 1427 }

Katherine Blanchard **Brooke** and Jeffrey **Parker** had the following child:
    9746   i.   Chandler James[15] **Parker**[298] born 15 September 1998.

8411. **Carrie Lee**[14] **Schuler** (Stephanie[13] **Whipple**, Ralph Alfred[12], Merritt Pendell[11], Dr. Alfred Augustus[10], Henry Francisco[9], Joseph[8], David[7], Samuel[6], Samuel[5], Cyprian[4], Lt. John[3], Matthew[2], Matthew[1])[299] was born 13 January 1969 and married twice. (1) **Jeffery Miller** in Charlotte, Mecklenburg Co., N.C. 25 November 1989. (2) **Steven Charles Tisdale** 13 September 1997. He was born in Huntsville, Madison Co., Ala. 10 May 1966.[300]

Carrrie Lee **Schuler** and Jeffery **Miller** had the following child born in Charlotte:
    9747   i.   Rachel E.[15] **Miller**[301] 4 January 1992.

Carrrie Lee **Schuler** and Steven Charles **Tisdale** had the following children:
    9748   ii.   Bryant Alden **Tisdale**[302] born 17 June 1998.
    9749   iii.   Jacob Steven **Tisdale**[303] born 6 October 1999.

8412. **Kimberly Marsh**[14] **Schuler** (Stephanie[13] **Whipple**, Ralph Alfred[12], Merritt Pendell[11], Dr. Alfred Augustus[10], Henry Francisco[9], Joseph[8], David[7], Samuel[6], Samuel[5], Cyprian[4], Lt. John[3], Matthew[2], Matthew[1])[304] was born 16 December 1970 and married **John Van Oeffelen** in Sparta, Kent Co., Mich. 15 October 1994. He was born in Grand Rapids, Kent Co., Mich. 17 April 1969.[305]

Kimberly Marsh **Schuler** and John **Van Oeffelen** had the following children born in Grand Rapids:
    9750   i.   Jared M.[15] **Van Oeffelen**[306] 27 November 1996.
    9751   ii.   Taylor Kristine **Van Oeffelen**[307] 23 April 1998.

8413. **Kimberly R.**[14] **Pike** (Joyce Ellen[13] **Whipple**, Rev. Leroy Byron[12], William[11], Dr. Alfred Augustus[10], Henry Francisco[9], Joseph[8], David[7], Samuel[6], Samuel[5], Cyprian[4], Lt. John[3], Matthew[2], Matthew[1])[308] was born 14 October 1967 and married **Rev. Kevin Greene** in Wake Forest, Wake Co., N.C. She was graduated from Wake Forest College where she met and married Kevin. They were living in Richmond, Richmond Co., Va. in 2000.

Kimberly R. **Pike** and Rev. Kevin **Greene** had the following children:
    9752   i.   Emma Barwick[15] **Greene**[309] born 14 August 1996.
    9753   ii.   Coleman Pike **Greene**[310] born 27 March 1998.

8415. **William**[14] **Whipple IV** (William[13], William[12], William[11], Dr. Alfred Augustus[10], Henry Francisco[9], Joseph[8], David[7], Samuel[6], Samuel[5], Cyprian[4], Lt. John[3], Matthew[2], Matthew[1])[311] was born in Wichita Falls, Wichita Co., Tex. 30 July 1973 and married **Keranice Dhanraj** 18 July 1996.

William **Whipple** IV and Keranice **Dhanraj** had the following child:
    9754   i.   Kailyn[15] **Whipple**[312] born in Allentown, Lehigh Co., Penn. 12 January 1999.

8426. **April Mae**[14] **Saathoff** (Hervy Andrew[13], Marian Learned[12] **Whipple**, William[11], Dr. Alfred Augustus[10], Henry Francisco[9], Joseph[8], David[7], Samuel[6], Samuel[5], Cyprian[4], Lt. John[3], Matthew[2], Matthew[1])[313] was born in North Platte, Lincoln Co., Nebr. 9 July 1971 and married **Wilbur Allen Casper** in Hershey, Lincoln Co., Nebr. 9 October 1993. Wilbur,[314] son of Zenus Wilbur **Casper** and Amy Ellen **Thacker**, was born in Russell, Russell Co., Kans. 11 March 1968.

April Mae **Saathoff** had the following child born in North Platte:
    9755   i.   Andon Thomas[15] **Saathoff**[315] 30 April 1991. Adopted by Wilbur Casper on 30 May 1996; surname now Caspar.

8429. **Michael Kent**[14] **Saathoff** (Arthur Kent[13], Marian Learned[12] **Whipple**, William[11], Dr. Alfred Augustus[10], Henry Francisco[9], Joseph[8], David[7], Samuel[6], Samuel[5], Cyprian[4], Lt. John[3], Matthew[2], Matthew[1])[316] was born in Kearney, Buffalo Co., Nebr. 9 December 1972 and married **Kacey Edmonds**.

Michael Kent **Saathoff** and Kacey **Edmonds** had the following child born in North Platte, Lincoln Co., Nebr.:
    9756   i.   Micah Marklynn Edmonds[15] **Saathoff**[317] 4 July 1994.

8430. **Andi Marie**[14] **Saathoff** (Arthur Kent[13], Marian Learned[12] **Whipple**, William[11], Dr. Alfred Augustus[10], Henry Francisco[9], Joseph[8], David[7], Samuel[6], Samuel[5], Cyprian[4], Lt. John[3], Matthew[2], Matthew[1])[318] was born 22 December 1974 and married **Jeff Reinhard** in North Platte, Lincoln Co., Nebr. 23 April 1994.

Andi Marie **Saathoff** and Jeff **Reinhard** had the following children born in North Platte:
    9757   i.   Andrew Christopher[15] **Reinhard**[319] 24 March 1996.
    9758   ii. Aliana Jae **Reinhard**[320] 23 February 1998.

8431. **Tami Jo**[14] **Smith** (Bonnie Jean[13] **Saathoff**, Marian Learned[12] **Whipple**, William[11], Dr. Alfred Augustus[10], Henry Francisco[9], Joseph[8], David[7], Samuel[6], Samuel[5], Cyprian[4], Lt. John[3], Matthew[2], Matthew[1])[321] was born in North Platte, Lincoln Co., Nebr. 10 January 1969 and married **James Douglas Hoatson** there 23 September 1994.

Tami Jo **Smith** and James Douglas **Hoatson** had the following children born in North Platte:

    9759   i.   Hunter James[15] **Hoatson**[322] 12 July 1996.

    9760   ii.   Alexandria Jo **Hoatson**[323] 12 July 1996.

8449. **Cassandra**[14] **Whipple** (John Walter[13], Robert Hugh[12], Walter Henry[11], Watson H.[10], William[9], Samuel[8], David[7], Samuel[6], Samuel[5], Cyprian[4], Lt. John[3], Matthew[2], Matthew[1])[324] was born in Bremerton, Kitsap Co., Wash. 30 May 1970 and married **Alexander Clinton Sprague** in Lyndonville, Orleans Co., N.Y. 13 February 1993. Alexander,[325] son of Howard Whitman **Sprague** and Rhonda **Robbins**, was born in Syracuse, Onondaga Co., N.Y. 24 October 1967.

Cassandra **Whipple** and Alexander Clinton **Sprague** had the following children:

    9761   i.   Samuel Alexander[15] **Sprague**[326] born in Concord, Middlesex Co., Mass. 23 May 1994.

    9762   ii.   Ethan John **Sprague**[327] born in Boston, Suffolk Co., Mass. 18 August 1997.

8450. **Thomas John**[14] **Whipple** (John Walter[13], Robert Hugh[12], Walter Henry[11], Watson H.[10], William[9], Samuel[8], David[7], Samuel[6], Samuel[5], Cyprian[4], Lt. John[3], Matthew[2], Matthew[1])[328] was born in Rochester, Monroe Co., N.Y. 6 April 1973 and married **Katherine Ann Bischoff** in Colorado Springs, Colo. 16 May 1997. Katherine,[329] daughter of Ervin Charles **Bischoff** and Paula Eudema **Willis**, was born in Lawrenceburg, Dearborn Co., Ind. 29 May 1976.

Thomas John **Whipple** and Katherine Ann **Bischoff** had the following child born in Fayetteville, Cumberland Co., N.C.

    9763   i.   Sean Patrick[15] **Whipple**[330] 30 December 1997.

8452. **Michele Lynne**[14] **Watts** (Julia[13] **Whipple**, Robert Hugh[12], Walter Henry[11], Watson H.[10], William[9], Samuel[8], David[7], Samuel[6], Samuel[5], Cyprian[4], Lt. John[3], Matthew[2], Matthew[1])[331] was born in Medina, Orleans Co., N.Y. 9 March 1971 and married **Eric Todd Harling** in Lyndonville, Orleans Co., N.Y. 14 August 1993. Eric,[332] son of Leon Chester **Harling** and Sandra Jean **Harris**, was born in Lockport, Niagara Co., N.Y. 17 July 1971.

Michele Lynne **Watts** and Eric Todd **Harling** had the following children born in Medina:
    9764   i.   Alexandra Laurenne[15] **Harling**[333] 7 November 1995.
    9765   ii.   Jessica Paige **Harling**[334] 18 June 1998.

8473. **Crystal Renee**[14] **Moore** (Don Robert[13], Phyllis Jean[12] **Davis**, Ruby Edna[11] **Harriman**, George Dearborn[10], Joel George[9], Lucy[8] **Ray**, Jonathan[7], Amos[6], Hannah[5] **Goodale**, Sarah[4] **Whipple**, Joseph[3], Matthew[2], Matthew[1])[335] was born in Lafayette, Tippecanoe Co., Ind. 14 October 1972 and married **Johnny Ray Hitch** in Radnor, Carroll Co., Ind. 14 October 1989. Johnny,[336] son of Richard **Hitch** and Jackie **Payne**, was born in Lafayette 3 October 1971.

Crystal Renee **Moore** and Johnny Ray **Hitch** had the following children born in Lafayette:
    9766   i.   Johnny Ray[15] **Hitch** Jr.[337] 7 March 1990.
    9767   ii.   Thorn Lee **Hitch**[338] 28 January 1993.

8474. **Cody Lane**[14] **Moore** (Gary Gene[13], Phyllis Jean[12] **Davis**, Ruby Edna[11] **Harriman**, George Dearborn[10], Joel George[9], Lucy[8] **Ray**, Jonathan[7], Amos[6], Hannah[5] **Goodale**, Sarah[4] **Whipple**, Joseph[3], Matthew[2], Matthew[1])[339] was born in Lafayette, Tippecanoe Co., Ind. 8 March 1976 and married **Angela Jean Bingaman** 10 February 1996. She is the daughter of John **Bingaman** and Charlotte (__).

Cody Lane **Moore** and Angela Jean **Bingaman** had the following child:
    9768   i.   Ashton Laine[15] **Moore**[340] born 16 July 1996.

8477. **Hutch E.**[14] **Davis** (Richard Gene[13], Richard Lee[12], Ruby Edna[11] **Harriman**, George Dearborn[10], Joel George[9], Lucy[8] **Ray**, Jonathan[7], Amos[6], Hannah[5] **Goodale**, Sarah[4] **Whipple**, Joseph[3], Matthew[2], Matthew[1])[341] was born in Lafayette, Tippecanoe Co., Ind. 14 January 1977 and married **Elizabeth E. Bledsoe**.

Hutch E. **Davis** and Elizabeth E. **Bledsoe** had the following children:
    9769   i.   Devan[15] **Davis**.[342]
    9770   ii.   Nathan **Davis**.[343]

8482. **Joseph A.**[14] **Duell** (Earl Charles[13], Grace Elenore[12] **Morgan**, Fredrick V.[11], Nehemiah[10], Samuel[9], Betsey[8] **Whipple**, Nehemiah[7], Benjamin[6], Francis[5], Jonathan[4], Joseph[3], Matthew[2], Matthew[1])[344] was born in Lime Ridge, Sauk Co., Wisc. 21 October 1930 and married **Mary Elizabeth Seymour** in Lake George, Warren Co., N.Y. 27 December 1957. Mary,[345] daughter of James **Seymour** and Mildred **McCoffreg**, was born in West Cambridge, Middlesex Co., Mass. 2 November 1934 and died 25 August 1998 in Passaic, Passiac Co., N.J., at 63 years of age. Buried in St. Mary's Cemetery, Malone, Franklin Co., N.Y.

Joseph A. **Duell** and Mary Elizabeth **Seymour** had the following children:

    9771   i.   Mark David[15] **Duell**[346] born in El Paso, El Paso Co., Tex. 16 September 1958 and married Lanelle **Warrick** in Seattle, King Co., Wash. in 1997.

    9772   ii.   Michele Annette **Duell**[347] born in El Paso 20 July 1959.

    9773   iii.   Maureen Elizabeth **Duell**[348] born in Abilene, Taylor Co., Tex. 18 August 1962.

+   9774   iv.   Melanie Katheleen **Duell** born 3 October 1964.

8483. **Victoria**[14] **Duell** (Earl Charles[13], Grace Elenore[12] **Morgan**, Fredrick V.[11], Nehemiah[10], Samuel[9], Betsey[8] **Whipple**, Nehemiah[7], Benjamin[6], Francis[5], Jonathan[4], Joseph[3], Matthew[2], Matthew[1])[349] was born in Lime Ridge, Sauk Co., Wisc. 6 February 1936 and married twice. (1) **John O'Hara** in Lime Ridge 19 February 1955. (2) **Ray King** in Lime Ridge 28 February 1975.

Victoria **Duell** and John **O'Hara** had the following children:

+   9775   i.   Michael[15] **O'Hara** born 23 February 1956.
+   9776   ii.   Philip **O'Hara** born 29 may 1959.

8497. **Mary Louise**[14] **Hufford** (Helen Margaret[13] **Jaggard**, Mary[12] **Norton**, Charles Russel[11], Judge James Carmont[10], Harriet Whipple[9] **Carpenter**, Anner[8] **Whipple**, Nehemiah[7], Benjamin[6], Francis[5], Jonathan[4], Joseph[3], Matthew[2], Matthew[1])[350] was born in Bakersfield, Kern Co., Calif. 24 August 1950 and married **Gordon Graham** in Silver Spring, Morris Co., Md. 22 October 1977. He was born in Chatanooga, Hamilton Co., Tenn. 31 October 1950.[351]

Mary Louise **Hufford** and Gordon **Graham** had the following children:

    9777   i.   Nicholas Hathaway[15] **Graham**[352] born in Tacoma Park, Prince Georges Co., Md. 26 July 1981.

    9778   ii.   Haley Elizabeth **Graham**[353] born in Tacoma Park 9 December 1982.

9779 iii. Samantha Marie **Graham**[354] born in Virginia Beach, Norfolk Co., Va. 3 June 1987.

9780 iv. Benjamin Holloway **Graham**[355] born in Virginia Beach 10 November 1988.

8498. **Richard Allen**[14] **Jaggard** (Ralph Warren[13], Mary[12] **Norton**, Charles Russel[11], Judge James Carmont[10], Harriet Whipple[9] **Carpenter**, Anner[8] **Whipple**, Nehemiah[7], Benjamin[6], Francis[5], Jonathan[4], Joseph[3], Matthew[2], Matthew[1])[356] was born in Petaluma, Sonoma Co., Calif. 1 October 1939 and married twice. (1) **Susanne Garland** in Carmichael, Sacramento Co., Calif. Susanne,[357] daughter of Edgar S. **Garland** and Sybl (__), was born in Carmichael 14 August 1941. (2) **Diane Schaber**.

Richard Allen **Jaggard** and Susanne **Garland** had the following children:
9781 i. Cindy Ann[15] **Jaggard**[358] born in Modesto, Stanislaus Co., Calif. 13 September 1961.
9782 ii. Melisa Robin **Jaggard**[359] born in Modesto, 30 March 1963.
9783 iii. Richard Edgar **Jaggard**[360] born in Roseville, Placer Co., Calif. 21 September 1965.

8500. **Paul Richard**[14] **Prescott** (Elizabeth Ann[13] **Jaggard**, Mary[12] **Norton**, Charles Russel[11], Judge James Carmont[10], Harriet Whipple[9] **Carpenter**, Anner[8] **Whipple**, Nehemiah[7], Benjamin[6], Francis[5], Jonathan[4], Joseph[3], Matthew[2], Matthew[1])[361] was born in Stockton, San Joaquin Co., Calif. 20 March 1953 and married **Roberta Ann Lewis** there 28 July 1979. Roberta,[362] daughter of Jack **Lewis** and Harriett Ruth **Merritt**, was born in Stockton 29 December 1949.

Paul Richard **Prescott** and Roberta Ann **Lewis** had the following children born in Turlock, Stanislaus Co., Calif.:
9784 i. James Richard[15] **Prescott**[363] 17 February 1984.
9785 ii. Edward Lewis **Prescott**[364] 19 July 1988.

8502. **Thomas Arnold**[14] **Prescott** (Elizabeth Ann[13] **Jaggard**, Mary[12] **Norton**, Charles Russel[11], Judge James Carmont[10], Harriet Whipple[9] **Carpenter**, Anner[8] **Whipple**, Nehemiah[7], Benjamin[6], Francis[5], Jonathan[4], Joseph[3], Matthew[2], Matthew[1])[365] was born in Stockton, San Joaquin Co., Calif. 7 June 1957 and married **Roselyne Dagand** in Anncey, Haute Savoie, France 28 December 1984. She was born in Anncey 18 July 1957.

{ G 1433 }

Thomas Arnold **Prescott** and Roselyne **Dagand** had the following children:
>   9786   i.   Graham William[15] **Prescott**[366] born in Anchorage, Anchorage Borough, Alaska 29 May 1988.
>   9787   ii. Gabriella Geneviene **Prescott**[367] born in Bogota, Columbia 24 October 1992.

8503. **Meredith Jane**[14] **Cooper** (Phyllis Albine[13] **Norton**, Hugh Russell[12], Charles Russel[11], Judge James Carmont[10], Harriet Whipple[9] **Carpenter**, Anner[8] **Whipple**, Nehemiah[7], Benjamin[6], Francis[5], Jonathan[4], Joseph[3], Matthew[2], Matthew[1])[368] was born in Los Angeles, Los Angeles Co., Calif. 17 July 1939 and married **Robert Knox Worrell Jr.** there 6 October 1961. Robert,[369] son of Robert Knox **Worrell** and Doris **Lakenan**, was born in San Diego, San Diego Co., Calif. 21 April 1932.

Meredith Jane **Cooper** and Robert Knox **Worrell** Jr. had the following children born in Los Angles:
> + 9788   i.   Ann Elizabeth[15] **Worrell** 29 June 1962.
>   9789   ii.   Robert Knox **Worrell** III[370] 19 October 1963.
>   9790   iii. Scott Cooper **Worrell**[371] 17 August 1966.

8504. **Grant Burr**[14] **Cooper Jr.** (Phyllis Albine[13] **Norton**, Hugh Russell[12], Charles Russel[11], Judge James Carmont[10], Harriet Whipple[9] **Carpenter**, Anner[8] **Whipple**, Nehemiah[7], Benjamin[6], Francis[5], Jonathan[4], Joseph[3], Matthew[2], Matthew[1])[372] was born in Los Angeles, Los Angeles Co., Calif. 20 December 1941 and married **Kathleen Maureen Skeehan** there 23 March 1968. Kathleen,[373] daughter of John Knight **Skeehan** and Bette **Moya**, was born in Sewickley, Allegheny Co., Penn. 14 February 1943.

Grant Burr **Cooper** Jr. and Kathleen Maureen **Skeehan** had the following children born in Newport Beach, Orange Co., Calif.:
>   9791   i.   Grant Burr Casey[15] **Cooper**[374] 31 July 1973.
>   9792   ii. Christian Norton **Cooper**[375] 5 August 1976.

8506. **Rupert Gordon**[14] **Young** (Virginia Edith[13] **Norton**, Walter Emmet[12], Charles Russel[11], Judge James Carmont[10], Harriet Whipple[9] **Carpenter**, Anner[8] **Whipple**, Nehemiah[7], Benjamin[6], Francis[5], Jonathan[4], Joseph[3], Matthew[2], Matthew[1])[376] was born in Covina, Los Angeles Co., Calif. 19 November 1936 and married **Marsha Jean Gillis** in California 11 July 1958. She was born in Los Angeles, Los Angeles Co., Calif. 28 November 1939.[377]

Rupert Gordon **Young** and Marsha Jean **Gillis** had the following children:
- + 9793 i. Jeffery[15] **Young** born 2 May 1962.
- + 9794 ii. Janiene **Young** born 8 April 1963.
- + 9795 iii. Joan **Young** born 8 April 1963.

8507. **Pamela**[14] **Young** (Virginia Edith[13] **Norton**, Walter Emmet[12], Charles Russel[11], Judge James Carmont[10], Harriet Whipple[9] **Carpenter**, Anner[8] **Whipple**, Nehemiah[7], Benjamin[6], Francis[5], Jonathan[4], Joseph[3], Matthew[2], Matthew[1])[378] was born in Covina, Los Angeles Co., Calif. 20 March 1942 and married **Fred Overstreet** 24 July 1965. He was born in Los Angeles, Los Angeles Co., Calif. 2 July 1942.[379]

Pamela **Young** and Fred **Overstreet** had the following children:
- + 9796 i. Christine[15] **Overstreet** born 18 August 1967.
- 9797 ii. Cory **Overstreet**[380] born in Covina 24 May 1970.

8508. **Michael Bernard**[14] **Young** (Virginia Edith[13] **Norton**, Walter Emmet[12], Charles Russel[11], Judge James Carmont[10], Harriet Whipple[9] **Carpenter**, Anner[8] **Whipple**, Nehemiah[7], Benjamin[6], Francis[5], Jonathan[4], Joseph[3], Matthew[2], Matthew[1])[381] was born in Covina, Los Angeles Co., Calif. 21 October 1943 and married **Nicki Burroughs** 14 February 1965. He was born in Oakland, Alameda Co., Calif. 4 January 1948.[382]

Michael Bernard **Young** and Nicki **Burroughs** had the following children:
- 9798 i. Morgan[15] **Young**[383] born in Covina 26 March 1968.
- 9799 ii. Eric **Young**[384] born in Carlsbad, San Diego Co., Calif. 1 June 1969.
- + 9800 iii. Holly **Young** born 11 September 1970.

8509. **Cary John**[14] **Franklin** (James Doyle[13], John Dorwin[12], Angeline[11] **McKinley**, William Henry[10], Angeline[9] **Whipple**, Enoch[8], Nehemiah[7], Benjamin[6], Francis[5], Jonathan[4], Joseph[3], Matthew[2], Matthew[1])[385] was born in Cedar Rapids, Linn Co., Iowa 26 November 1956 and married twice. (1) married **Lynn Marie Grotenhuls** in St. Paul, Ramsey Co., Minn. 14 August 1982. (2) **Kristin Makholm** 19 December 1992.

Cary John **Franklin** and Kristin **Makholm** had the following child:
- 9801 i. Lila Johanna[15] **Franklin**[386] born 7 December 1996.

8510. **Cal James**[14] **Franklin** (James Doyle[13], John Dorwin[12], Angeline[11] **McKinley**, William Henry[10], Angeline[9] **Whipple**, Enoch[8], Nehemiah[7], Benjamin[6], Francis[5], Jonathan[4], Joseph[3], Matthew[2], Matthew[1])[387] was born in Cedar Rapids, Linn Co., Iowa 9 July 1958 and married **Kimberle Jo Deason** 5 September 1992. She is the daughter of Dr. Keith **Deason**.[388]

Cal James **Franklin** and Kimberle Jo **Deason** had the following children:
- 9802 i. Sydney Jo[15] **Franklin**.[389]
- 9803 ii. Kelley Leigh **Franklin**[390] born 17 June 1997.
- 9804 iii. James O. **Franklin**[391] born 23 October 1998.

8511. **Candace Marie**[14] **Franklin** (James Doyle[13], John Dorwin[12], Angeline[11] **McKinley**, William Henry[10], Angeline[9] **Whipple**, Enoch[8], Nehemiah[7], Benjamin[6], Francis[5], Jonathan[4], Joseph[3], Matthew[2], Matthew[1])[392] was born in Cedar Rapids, Linn Co., Iowa 6 September 1959 and married **G. Thomas Ahern** in San Francisco, San Francisco Co., Calif. 5 March 1988. Thomas,[393] son of Edward James **Ahern** and Barbara **McKee**, was born 9 April 1958.

Candace Marie **Franklin** and G. Thomas **Ahern** had the following children:
- 9805 i. Kelsey Marie[15] **Ahern**.[394]
- 9806 ii. Ryan Thomas **Ahern**[395] born 19 July 1992.
- 9807 iii. Tess Candace **Ahern**[396] born 26 June 1995.

8513. **Daniel William**[14] **Franklin** (Robert William[13], John Dorwin[12], Angeline[11] **McKinley**, William Henry[10], Angeline[9] **Whipple**, Enoch[8], Nehemiah[7], Benjamin[6], Francis[5], Jonathan[4], Joseph[3], Matthew[2], Matthew[1])[397] was born in Cedar Rapids, Linn Co., Iowa 26 March 1961 and married **Susan Marie Miller** there 12 September 1987. Susan,[398] daughter of Lawrence Gary **Miller** and Jane Ann **Hantelmann**, was born in Dubuque, Dubuque Co., Iowa 26 June 1966.

Daniel William **Franklin** and Susan Marie **Miller** had the following twins born in Cedar Rapids on different days. Cassie was born just before midnight on the 22nd while Joshua was born just after midnight on the 23rd.:
- 9808 i. Cassie Marie[15] **Franklin**[399] 22 February 1988.
- 9809 ii. Joshua John **Franklin**[400] 23 February 1988.

8515. **Linda Jean**[14] **Crawford** (Shirley Jean[13] **Franklin**, John Dorwin[12], Angeline[11] **McKinley**, William Henry[10], Angeline[9] **Whipple**, Enoch[8], Nehemiah[7], Benjamin[6], Francis[5], Jonathan[4], Joseph[3], Matthew[2], Matthew[1])[401] was born in Waterloo, Black Hawk Co., Iowa 13 September 1954 and married **Nathaniel Ware Bryant** in Traer, Tama Co., Iowa 27 October 1973. Nathaniel,[402] son of Charles Brate **Bryant** and Elizabeth Ann **Callow**, was born 12 August 1949.

Linda Jean **Crawford** and Nathaniel Ware **Bryant** had the following children born in Milwaukee, Milwaukee Co., Wisc:

    9810   i.   Cadence Elizabeth[15] **Bryant**[403] 23 September 1974 and married Thomas Perri **Stamm** 23 July 1993. He is the son of Robert E. **Stamm Jr.** [404]

    9811   ii.   Caleb Eli **Bryant**[405] 7 October 1976.

8516. **Penny Marie**[14] **Crawford** (Shirley Jean[13] **Franklin**, John Dorwin[12], Angeline[11] **McKinley**, William Henry[10], Angeline[9] **Whipple**, Enoch[8], Nehemiah[7], Benjamin[6], Francis[5], Jonathan[4], Joseph[3], Matthew[2], Matthew[1])[406] was born in Waterloo, Black Hawk Co., Iowa 6 February 1956 and married **David Lee Benter** in Traer, Tama Co., Iowa 24 June 1978. David,[407] son of Martin **Benter** and Connie Thomas **Pilcher**, was born 24 January 1957.

Penny Marie **Crawford** and David Lee **Benter** had the following children born in Cedar Rapids, Linn Co., Iowa:

    9812   i.   Aaron Lee[15] **Benter**[408] 1 November 1978.

    9813   ii.   Shea Adam Robert **Benter**[409] 25 June 1985.

8518. **Elizabeth Marie**[14] **Franklin** (Donald Willard[13], John Dorwin[12], Angeline[11] **McKinley**, William Henry[10], Angeline[9] **Whipple**, Enoch[8], Nehemiah[7], Benjamin[6], Francis[5], Jonathan[4], Joseph[3], Matthew[2], Matthew[1])[410] was born in San Diego, San Diego Co., Calif. 25 February 1959 and married **Michael Carr** in Missouri 5 April 1980. She served in the U.S. Army 1980-84 and is a Secretary in a law office.

Elizabeth Marie **Franklin** and Michael **Carr** had the following children born in Cape Girardeau, Cape Girardeau Co., Mo.:

    9814   i.   Damien[15] **Carr**[411] 5 May 1986.

    9815   ii.   Courtney Leigh **Carr**[412] 9 May 1989.

8521. **Douglas John**[14] **Franklin** (Donald Willard[13], John Dorwin[12], Angeline[11] **McKinley**, William Henry[10], Angeline[9] **Whipple**, Enoch[8], Nehemiah[7], Benjamin[6], Francis[5], Jonathan[4], Joseph[3], Matthew[2], Matthew[1])[413] was born in Portland, Multnomah Co., Oreg. 29 October 1965 and married twice. (1) **Merriann Ellis** in Cannon Beach, Clatsop Co., Oreg. 1 July 1985. She was born 29 June 1965.[414] (2) **Jacqueline Lynette Irwin** in Astoria, Clatsop Co., Oreg. 1 May 1992. Jacqueline is the daughter of Jack **Irwin**.[415]

Douglas John **Franklin** and Merriann **Ellis** had the following children born in Seaside, Clatsop Co. Oreg.:

    9816   i.   John Scott[15] **Franklin**[416] 16 March 1986.

    9817   ii.   Ashley Marie **Franklin**[417] 9 May 1989.

8522. **Kellie Jean**[14] **Franklin** (David Leonard[13], John Dorwin[12], Angeline[11] **McKinley**, William Henry[10], Angeline[9] **Whipple**, Enoch[8], Nehemiah[7], Benjamin[6], Francis[5], Jonathan[4], Joseph[3], Matthew[2], Matthew[1])[418] was born in Iowa City, Johnson Co., Iowa 18 December 1961 and married three times. (1) **Steven Edward Thacker** in Independence, Jackson Co., Mo. 8 August 1987. He is the son of Charles **Thacker** and Lupe (__). (2) **Bradley David Sievers** in Keystone, Benton Co., Iowa 27 November 1993. Bradley is the son of Eelf **Sievers** and Janice **Junge**.[419] (3) **Derrick Frank Patterson** in Traer, Tama Co., Iowa 20 June 1998.

Kellie Jean **Franklin** and Steven Edward **Thacker** had the following children:

    9818   i.   Cody David[15] **Thacker**[420] born in Wichita, Sedgwick Co., Kans. 18 August 1988.

    9819   ii.   Matthew Charles **Thacker**[421] born 3 June 1991.

8524. **Teresa Kay**[14] **Engle** (Virginia Kay[13] **Franklin**, John Dorwin[12], Angeline[11] **McKinley**, William Henry[10], Angeline[9] **Whipple**, Enoch[8], Nehemiah[7], Benjamin[6], Francis[5], Jonathan[4], Joseph[3], Matthew[2], Matthew[1])[422] was born in Waterloo, Black Hawk Co., Iowa 2 December 1960 and married **Troy Allen Meester** in Traer, Tama Co., Iowa 11 October 1986. He is the son of Al **Meester**.[423]

Teresa Kay **Engle** and Troy Allen **Meester** had the following children:

    9820   i.   Tiffany Kay[15] **Meester**[424] born in Colorado Springs, El Paso Co., Colo. 26 October 1988.

    9821   ii.   Taylor Ann **Meester**[425] born 21 January 1991.

8525. **Rodney Ray**[14] **Engle** (Virginia Kay[13] **Franklin**, John Dorwin[12], Angeline[11] **McKinley**, William Henry[10], Angeline[9] **Whipple**, Enoch[8], Nehemiah[7], Benjamin[6], Francis[5], Jonathan[4], Joseph[3], Matthew[2], Matthew[1])[426] was born in Waterloo, Black Hawk Co., Iowa 18 November 1963 and married **Suzanne Tugman** in Colorado.

Rodney Ray **Engle** and Suzanne **Tugman** had the following children:

    9822   i.   Savannah Rae[15] **Engle**[427] born 7 April 1992.

    9823   ii.   Ellie Rae **Engle**[428] born 4 March 1994.

    9824   iii.   Colton Thomas **Engle**[429] born 29 August 1997.

8527. **Kimberly Jo**[14] **Franklin** (Thomas Arnold[13], John Dorwin[12], Angeline[11] **McKinley**, William Henry[10], Angeline[9] **Whipple**, Enoch[8], Nehemiah[7], Benjamin[6], Francis[5], Jonathan[4], Joseph[3], Matthew[2], Matthew[1])[430] was born in Cedar Falls, Black Hawk Co., Iowa 16 March 1968 and married **Braden Hartwick Barrett** 4 August 1990. He is the son of Gene **Barrett** and Maxine **Hartwick**.[431]

Kimberly Jo **Franklin** and Braden Hartwick **Barrett** had the following child:
    9825   i.   Tyler Franklin[15] **Barrett**[432] born 21 March 1995.

8529. **Merrilee Marguerite**[14] **Johnson** (Nola Angeline[13] **Woodford**, Dorothy Marguerite[12] **Franklin**, Angeline[11] **McKinley**, William Henry[10], Angeline[9] **Whipple**, Enoch[8], Nehemiah[7], Benjamin[6], Francis[5], Jonathan[4], Joseph[3], Matthew[2], Matthew[1])[433] was born in Pasadena, Los Angeles Co., Calif. 2 February 1961 and married **Michael Stephen Copelan** in Shundon,[434] Calif. 10 June 1995.

Merrilee Marguerite **Johnson** and Michael Stephen **Copelan** had the following child:
    9826   i.   Ryan Michael[15] **Copelan**[435] born 29 November 1996.

8533. **Shane Woodford**[14] **Kueny** (Judith Ann[13] **Woodford**, Dorothy Marguerite[12] **Franklin**, Angeline[11] **McKinley**, William Henry[10], Angeline[9] **Whipple**, Enoch[8], Nehemiah[7], Benjamin[6], Francis[5], Jonathan[4], Joseph[3], Matthew[2], Matthew[1])[436] was born 27 February 1965 and married **Laua Evon Sissou**, daughter of John W. **Sissou**, 5 January 1991.[437]

Shane Woodford **Kueny** and Laura Evon **Sissou** had the following children:
    9827   i.   Kattlin Mary Anne[15] **Kueny**[438] born 2 July 1992.
    9828   ii. Henry Shane **Kueny**.[439]

8535. **Sherry Ann**[14] **Korns** (William Franklin[13], Laura Charlotte[12] **Franklin**, Angeline[11] **McKinley**, William Henry[10], Angeline[9] **Whipple**, Enoch[8], Nehemiah[7], Benjamin[6], Francis[5], Jonathan[4], Joseph[3], Matthew[2], Matthew[1])[440] was born in Rapid City, Pennington Co., S. Dak. 10 January 1959 and married (__) **Johnson**.

Sherry Ann **Korns** and (__) **Johnson** had the following child:
    9829   i.   Amanda Jo[15] **Johnson**[441] born 25 September 1996.

8537. **Charles Eugene**[14] **Korns** (William Franklin[13], Laura Charlotte[12] **Franklin**, Angeline[11] **McKinley**, William Henry[10], Angeline[9] **Whipple**, Enoch[8], Nehemiah[7], Benjamin[6], Francis[5], Jonathan[4], Joseph[3], Matthew[2], Matthew[1])[442] was born in Grinnell, Poweshiek Co., Iowa 8 August 1961 and married twice. (1) **Edwina Wright** 17 October 1981. (2) **Laurie Adams**. Laurie,[443] daughter of John **Adams** and Sally Ann **Davis**, was born 26 May 1958. She also married **William Shean** in Lexington, Middlesex Co., Mass. Laurie and Charles Eugene are eleventh cousins. Their common ancestors are Matthew and Anne (Hawkins) Whipple.

Charles Eugene **Korns** and Laurie **Adams** had the following children:
    9561   i.   Calvin[15] **Korns**.[444]
    9562   ii.   Jenny Lee **Korns**[445] born 2 November 1993.

Charles Eugene **Korns** and Edwina **Wright** had the following child:
    9830   iii.   Blaine Kupka **Korns**[446] born 1 May 1987.

8543. **Lawrence**[14] **Hand** (Marlene Jean[13] **Knupp**, Sylvia Fae[12] **Franklin**, Angeline[11] **McKinley**, William Henry[10], Angeline[9] **Whipple**, Enoch[8], Nehemiah[7], Benjamin[6], Francis[5], Jonathan[4], Joseph[3], Matthew[2], Matthew[1])[447] was born 3 November 1955 and died 12 May 1988 in Honduras, at 32 years of age. He married twice. (1) **Bobbi Jean Wingerson** 27 March 1976. She is the daughter of Robert **Wingerson** and Bea (__).[448] (2) **Della Hicks** in 1983. Larry was killed in a truck accident in the mountains of Honduras while in the U.S. Army. He was attached to a Heavy Equipment Engineering Group building a road through the mountains. He was buried in Fort Dodge, Webster Co., Iowa with full military honors.

Lawrence **Hand** and Bobbi Jean **Wingerson** had the following children:
    9831   i.   Patti[15] **Hand**[449] born 26 April 1977.
    9832   ii.   Rachel **Hand**.[450]

8545. **Gary Lee**[14] **Hand** (Marlene Jean[13] **Knupp**, Sylvia Fae[12] **Franklin**, Angeline[11] **McKinley**, William Henry[10], Angeline[9] **Whipple**, Enoch[8], Nehemiah[7], Benjamin[6], Francis[5], Jonathan[4], Joseph[3], Matthew[2], Matthew[1])[451] was born 1 May 1958 and married twice. (1) **Mary Jo Kirby** 5 February 1977. They were divorced in 1983. (2) **Jeanne** (__) in November 1983.

Gary Lee **Hand** and Mary Jo **Kirby** had the following children:
    9833   i.   Addie Jo[15] **Hand**[452] born 14 July 1977.
    9834   ii.   Lynn Marie **Hand**[453] born 3 April 1981.

8546. **Susan Nora**[14] **Hand** (Marlene Jean[13] **Knupp**, Sylvia Fae[12] **Franklin**, Angeline[11] **McKinley**, William Henry[10], Angeline[9] **Whipple**, Enoch[8], Nehemiah[7], Benjamin[6], Francis[5], Jonathan[4], Joseph[3], Matthew[2], Matthew[1])[454] was born 2 January 1960 and married **Garry O'Dell** in Olivet, Eaton Co., Mich. 24 December 1978.

Susan Nora **Hand** and Garry **O'Dell** had the following children:
    9835   i.   Rebecca Lynn[15] **O'Dell**[455] born 20 May 1982.
    9836   ii.   Isaac Lee **O'Dell**[456] born 3 March 1984.

8548. **William Kim**[14] **Greehey** (Janis Elaine[13] **Knupp**, Sylvia Fae[12] **Franklin**, Angeline[11] **McKinley**, William Henry[10], Angeline[9] **Whipple**, Enoch[8], Nehemiah[7], Benjamin[6], Francis[5], Jonathan[4], Joseph[3], Matthew[2], Matthew[1])[457] was born in Fort Dodge, Webster Co., Iowa 16 July 1954 and married twice. (1) **Jane (__)** in Dallas, Tex. 5 May 1980. (2) **Sharon Elizabeth Fleeman** in British West Indies 7 August 1992. She is the daughter of William Wayne **Fleeman**.[458]

William Kim **Greehey** and Jane (__) had the following child:
    9837   i.   William Christopher[15] **Greehey**[459] born 24 September 1982.

8550. **Douglas Allen**[14] **Greehey** (Janis Elaine[13] **Knupp**, Sylvia Fae[12] **Franklin**, Angeline[11] **McKinley**, William Henry[10], Angeline[9] **Whipple**, Enoch[8], Nehemiah[7], Benjamin[6], Francis[5], Jonathan[4], Joseph[3], Matthew[2], Matthew[1])[460] was born in San Antonio, Bexar Co., Tex. 17 May 1960 and married twice. (1) **Sharon (__)**. They were divorced in 1983. (2) **Margaret Ann Brooks** 4 August 1990. Margaret,[461] daughter of Benjamin Franklin **Brooks** and Rosemary **King**, was born 23 November 1966.

Douglas Allen **Greehey** and Margaret Ann **Brooks** had the following child:
    9838   i.   Mary Elizabeth[15] **Greehey**[462] born 6 February 1991.

8551. **Christine Fae**[14] **Knupp** (John Franklin[13], Sylvia Fae[12] **Franklin**, Angeline[11] **McKinley**, William Henry[10], Angeline[9] **Whipple**, Enoch[8], Nehemiah[7], Benjamin[6], Francis[5], Jonathan[4], Joseph[3], Matthew[2], Matthew[1])[463] was born in Fort Dodge, Webster Co., Iowa 15 March 1958 and married **Steven Seversen** in Humboldt, Humboldt Co., Iowa 28 December 1979.

Christine Fae **Knupp** and Steven **Seversen** had the following children:
- 9839 i. Ryan[15] **Seversen**.[464] Adopted.
- 9840 ii. Kathryn **Seversen**[465] born 27 March 1981.
- 9841 iii. Michael Jacob **Seversen**[466] born 3 November 1982.

8552. **Dianne Kay**[14] **Knupp** (John Franklin[13], Sylvia Fae[12] **Franklin**, Angeline[11] **McKinley**, William Henry[10], Angeline[9] **Whipple**, Enoch[8], Nehemiah[7], Benjamin[6], Francis[5], Jonathan[4], Joseph[3], Matthew[2], Matthew[1])[467] was born in Ames, Story Co., Iowa 29 March 1959 and married **Scott Empringham**.

Dianne Kay **Knupp** and Scott **Empringham** had the following child:
- 9842 i. Loren Elizabeth[15] **Empringham**.[468]

8555. **Suzanne**[14] **Knupp** (Clyde Franklin[13], Sylvia Fae[12] **Franklin**, Angeline[11] **McKinley**, William Henry[10], Angeline[9] **Whipple**, Enoch[8], Nehemiah[7], Benjamin[6], Francis[5], Jonathan[4], Joseph[3], Matthew[2], Matthew[1])[469] was born in Garrison, Benton Co., Iowa 1 January 1962 and married **Don Sawyer** 20 October 1983.

Suzanne **Knupp** and Don **Sawyer** had the following children:
- 9843 i. Jennifer[15] **Sawyer**.[470]
- 9844 ii. Ryan Charles **Sawyer**[471] born 25 August 1991.

8557. **Anthony James**[14] **Knupp** (Keith Franklin[13], Sylvia Fae[12] **Franklin**, Angeline[11] **McKinley**, William Henry[10], Angeline[9] **Whipple**, Enoch[8], Nehemiah[7], Benjamin[6], Francis[5], Jonathan[4], Joseph[3], Matthew[2], Matthew[1])[472] was born in Fort Dodge, Webster Co., Iowa 8 March 1972.

Anthony James **Knupp** had the following child:
- 9845 i. Austin James[15] **Knupp**.[473]

8558. **Angela Marie**[14] **Knupp** (Keith Franklin[13], Sylvia Fae[12] **Franklin**, Angeline[11] **McKinley**, William Henry[10], Angeline[9] **Whipple**, Enoch[8], Nehemiah[7], Benjamin[6], Francis[5], Jonathan[4], Joseph[3], Matthew[2], Matthew[1])[474] was born in Fort Dodge, Webster Co., Iowa 1 July 1974 and married **Kendall Kihega** 9 April 1994.

Angela Marie **Knupp** and Kendall **Kihega** had the following child:
- 9846 i. Sierra[15] **Kihega**[475] born 16 October 1997.

8561. **Roben Ileene**[14] Schlarbaum (Robert I.[13], LaVon Elizabeth[12] McKinley, James Hiram[11], William Henry[10], Angeline[9] Whipple, Enoch[8], Nehemiah[7], Benjamin[6], Francis[5], Jonathan[4], Joseph[3], Matthew[2], Matthew[1])[476] was born in Portland, Multnomah Co., Oreg. 11 February 1963 and married twice. (1) **Michael Duane Gross** 20 December 1980. Michael,[477] son of LeRoy **Gross** and Yvonne **Bear**, was born in Vancouver, Clark Co., Wash. 16 April 1959. (2) **David Wayne Huggens** in Tualatin, Washington Co., Oreg. 21 August 1993. David,[478] son of Lindsay Jean **Huggens** and Gloria Lane **Moll**, was born in Mobile, Mobile Co., Ala. 2 October 1964.

Roben Ileene **Schlarbaum** and Michael Duane **Gross** had the following child born in Portland:
    9847   i.   Joshua Michael[15] **Gross**[479] 5 October 1981.

Roben Ileene **Schlarbaum** and David Wayne **Huggens** had the following child born in Mobile :
    9848   ii.   Sierra Christene **Huggens**[480] 22 March 1994.

8562. **Rebecca Pearl**[14] **Taber** (Carolyn Jeanette[13] **Schlarbaum**, LaVon Elizabeth[12] **McKinley**, James Hiram[11], William Henry[10], Angeline[9] **Whipple**, Enoch[8], Nehemiah[7], Benjamin[6], Francis[5], Jonathan[4], Joseph[3], Matthew[2], Matthew[1])[481] was born 3 July 1962 and married twice. (1) **Ronald Raymond Douglas** in Sherwood, Washington Co., Oreg. 6 June 1987. He was born in Corpus Christi, Nueces Co., Tex. 15 July 1958.[482] (2) **Richard Lee Vessey** 29 August 1994. Richard,[483] son of Donald **Vessey**, and Betty **Gougat**, was born in Portland, Multnomah Co., Oreg. 23 August 1952. Rebecca earned a B. A. in Business Economics from George Fox College, Newburg, Yamhill Co., Oreg. Both Rebecca and Richard are mail carriers in Portland, Multnomah Co., Oreg.

Rebecca Pearl **Taber** and Richard Lee **Vessey** had the following child born in Portland:
    9849   i.   Cole Richard[15] **Vessey**[484] 5 October 1994.

8563. **Melinda Jeanette**[14] **Taber** (Carolyn Jeanette[13] **Schlarbaum**, LaVon Elizabeth[12] **McKinley**, James Hiram[11], William Henry[10], Angeline[9] **Whipple**, Enoch[8], Nehemiah[7], Benjamin[6], Francis[5], Jonathan[4], Joseph[3], Matthew[2], Matthew[1])[485] was born in Newberg, Yamhill Co., Oreg. 4 December 1965 and married **Gerald Michael Babcock** there 31 July 1993. Gerald,[486] son of James Douglas **Babcock** and Lourdes Emily **Rodriquez**, was born in San Francisco, San Francisco Co., Calif. 17 July

{ G 1443 }

1966. Melinda works in Customer Service for a computer company and Gerald is a Mail Carrier in Tigard, Washington Co., Oreg.

Melinda Jeanette **Taber** and Gerald Michael **Babcock** had the following children born in Portland, Multnomah Co., Oreg.:
- 9850   i.   Austin Michael[15] **Babcock**[487] 3 January 1996.
- 9851   ii.   Zachary Charles **Babcock**[488] 6 March 1997.

8578. **Dawn Marie**[14] **McKinley** (Gary Frederick[13], Clifford Hoffman[12], Grover Cleveland[11], William Henry[10], Angeline[9] **Whipple**, Enoch[8], Nehemiah[7], Benjamin[6], Francis[5], Jonathan[4], Joseph[3], Matthew[2], Matthew[1])[489] was born in New York, N.Y. 9 July 1962 and married **Paul Southwick** in New Jersey 11 April 1987.

Dawn Marie **McKinley** and Paul **Southwick** had the following child:
- 9852   i.   Zachary Paul[15] **Southwick**[490] born 3 October 1990.

8581. **Timothy Scott**[14] **Dudley** (Janet Faye[13] **McKinley**, Clifford Hoffman[12], Grover Cleveland[11], William Henry[10], Angeline[9] **Whipple**, Enoch[8], Nehemiah[7], Benjamin[6], Francis[5], Jonathan[4], Joseph[3], Matthew[2], Matthew[1])[491] was born in Benton Co., Iowa 22 December 1960 and married **Christina Crowley** in Linn Co., Iowa 1 May 1982. They were divorced in 1989.

Timothy Scott **Dudley** and Christina **Crowley** had the following children born in Linn Co.:
- 9853   i.   Joseph Scott[15] **Dudley**[492] 13 September 1982.
- 9854   ii.   Jacob Timothy **Dudley**[493] 16 April 1984.
- 9855   iii.   Luke John **Dudley**[494] 19 January 1986.
- 9856   iv.   Jeremy William **Dudley**[495] 5 September 1988.

8582. **Todd LeRoy**[14] **Dudley** (Janet Faye[13] **McKinley**, Clifford Hoffman[12], Grover Cleveland[11], William Henry[10], Angeline[9] **Whipple**, Enoch[8], Nehemiah[7], Benjamin[6], Francis[5], Jonathan[4], Joseph[3], Matthew[2], Matthew[1])[496] was born in Benton Co., Iowa 30 November 1962 and married **Michelle McAtee** 8 April 1989.

Todd LeRoy **Dudley** and Michelle **McAtee** had the following children:
- 9857   i.   Nicole Lynne[15] **Dudley**[497] born 19 August 1993.
- 9858   ii.   Natalie Logan **Dudley**[498] born 31 October 1996.

8583. **Rodney Mark**[14] **Dudley** (Janet Faye[13] **McKinley**, Clifford Hoffman[12], Grover Cleveland[11], William Henry[10], Angeline[9] **Whipple**, Enoch[8], Nehemiah[7], Benjamin[6], Francis[5], Jonathan[4], Joseph[3], Matthew[2], Matthew[1])[499] was born in Black Hawk Co., Iowa 3 April 1965 and married **Sandra Bries** 21 September 1991.

Rodney Mark **Dudley** and Sandra **Bries** had the following children:
    9859   i.   Heather Renee[15] **Dudley**[500] born 15 July 1992.
    9860   ii.   Haley Jo **Dudley**[501] born 16 June 1995.

8584. **Shawn Daniel**[14] **Elsbernd** (Cheryl Delilah[13] **McKinley**, Clifford Hoffman[12], Grover Cleveland[11], William Henry[10], Angeline[9] **Whipple**, Enoch[8], Nehemiah[7], Benjamin[6], Francis[5], Jonathan[4], Joseph[3], Matthew[2], Matthew[1])[502] was born in Linn Co., Iowa 29 March 1966 and married **Karen Marie Showers** in Ottumwa, Wapello Co., Iowa 4 November 1989. Karen,[503] daughter of Leonard LeRoy **Showers** and Kathryn Ann **Fitzgerald**, was born in Pella, Marion Co., Iowa 1 December 1967.

Shawn Daniel **Elsbernd** and Karen Marie **Showers** had the following children born in Waterloo, Black Hawk, Iowa:
    9861   i.   Courtney Dawn[15] **Elsbernd**[504] 28 November 1991.
    9862   ii.   Cory Jacob **Elsbernd**[505] 4 August 1993.

8585. **Kimberly Berniece**[14] **Elsbernd** (Cheryl Delilah[13] **McKinley**, Clifford Hoffman[12], Grover Cleveland[11], William Henry[10], Angeline[9] **Whipple**, Enoch[8], Nehemiah[7], Benjamin[6], Francis[5], Jonathan[4], Joseph[3], Matthew[2], Matthew[1])[506] was born in Linn Co., Iowa 18 January 1968 and married **Gregory Allen Heckart** in Ottumwa, Wapello Co., Iowa 2 June 1990. Gregory,[507] son of Gary Craig **Heckart** and Barbara Kay **Huber**, was born in Ottumwa 5 January 1967.

Kimberly Berniece **Elsbernd** and Gregory Allen **Heckart** had the following children born in Mason City, Cerro Gordo Co., Iowa:
    9863   i.   Danielle Mildred[15] **Heckart**[508] 1 April 1993.
    9864   ii.   Gary Walter **Heckart**[509] 27 February 1995.

8586. **Jodi Ann**[14] **Elsbernd** (Cheryl Delilah[13] **McKinley**, Clifford Hoffman[12], Grover Cleveland[11], William Henry[10], Angeline[9] **Whipple**, Enoch[8], Nehemiah[7], Benjamin[6], Francis[5], Jonathan[4], Joseph[3], Matthew[2], Matthew[1])[510] was born in Linn Co., Iowa 9 December 1971 and married **Rodney Lynn Wooten** in Ames, Story Co., Iowa 23 July 1994. Rodney,[511] son of Harry Wayne **Wooten** and Linda Irene **McMillien**, was born 15 April 1972.

Jodi Ann **Elsbernd** and Rodney Lynn **Wooten** had the following child born in St. Louis Park, Hennepin Co., Minn.:

    9865   i.   Benjamin John[15] **Wooten**[512] 7 February 1997.

8592. **Lisa Marie**[14] **Michael** (Karen Kaye[13] **Heiserman**, Elizabeth Emily[12] **McKinley**, Grover Cleveland[11], William Henry[10], Angeline[9] **Whipple**, Enoch[8], Nehemiah[7], Benjamin[6], Francis[5], Jonathan[4], Joseph[3], Matthew[2], Matthew[1])[513] was born in Olewein, Fayette Co., Iowa 19 August 1959 and married **Scott Jacobsen** in West Union, Fayette Co., Iowa 25 October 1983. Scott,[514] son of Robert Dwayne **Jacobsen** and Darlene **Drewes**, was born in West Union 30 June 1962.

Lisa Marie **Michael** had the following child born in West Union:

    9866   i.   Jeremy John[15] **Michael**[515] 25 July 1980.

Lisa Marie **Michael** and Scott **Jacobsen** had the following children born in West Union:

    9867   ii.   Niccki Mae **Jacobsen**[516] 25 May 1985.
    9868   iii.   Jodi Lynn **Jacobsen**[517] 20 August 1988.

8593. **Bryan Roger**[14] **Michael** (Karen Kaye[13] **Heiserman**, Elizabeth Emily[12] **McKinley**, Grover Cleveland[11], William Henry[10], Angeline[9] **Whipple**, Enoch[8], Nehemiah[7], Benjamin[6], Francis[5], Jonathan[4], Joseph[3], Matthew[2], Matthew[1])[518] was born in Olewein, Fayette Co., Iowa 14 September 1961 and married **Sandy Heying** in West Union, Fayette Co., Iowa 28 May 1983. Sandy,[519] daughter of Dennis **Heying** and Marian **Bodensteiner**, was born in New Hampton, Franklin Co., Iowa 6 July 1963.

Bryan Roger **Michael** and Sandy **Heying** had the following children:

    9869   i.   Chelsey Rae[15] **Michael**[520] born in Kansas City, Jackson Co., Mo. 27 June 1991.
    9870   ii.   Hannah Rose **Michael**[521] born in Overland Park, Johnson Co., Kans. 30 January 1995.

8594. **Steven James**[14] **Michael** (Karen Kaye[13] **Heiserman**, Elizabeth Emily[12] **McKinley**, Grover Cleveland[11], William Henry[10], Angeline[9] **Whipple**, Enoch[8], Nehemiah[7], Benjamin[6], Francis[5], Jonathan[4], Joseph[3], Matthew[2], Matthew[1])[522] was born in Waterloo, Black Hawk Co., Iowa 11 September 1965 and married **Dianne Ford** in Olewein, Fayette Co., Iowa 13 September 1986. Dianne,[523] daughter of Paul **Ford** and Germaine **Doyle**, was born in West Union, Fayette Co., Iowa 11 March 1962.

Steven James **Michael** and Dianne **Ford** had the following children born in Waterloo:

  9871 i. Katie Marie[15] **Michael**[524] 21 November 1987.
  9872 ii. Logan James **Michael**[525] 21 September 1990.

8609. **Lance Lee**[14] **McKinley** (Charles Dos[13], William Harry[12], John Carlysle[11], William Henry[10], Angeline[9] **Whipple**, Enoch[8], Nehemiah[7], Benjamin[6], Francis[5], Jonathan[4], Joseph[3], Matthew[2], Matthew[1])[526] was born in Vallejo, Solano Co., Calif. 1 September 1965 and married **Stephanie Elisabeth (DiIullo) Kaempfer** in Sacramento, Sacramento Co., Calif. 7 December 1985. Stephanie,[527] daughter of Steven **DiIullo** and Mary **Foran**, was born in Sacramento 12 January 1964. She was adopted by (__) Kaempfer, her mother's second husband.

Lance Lee **McKinley** and Stephanie Elisabeth (DiIullo) **Kaempfer** had the following children born in Sacramento:

  9873 i. Christopher Lee[15] **McKinley**[528] 23 April 1986 and died there 8 August 1986 at less than 4 months of age. Buried at St. Marys Cemetery.
  9874 ii. Mikael Christopher **McKinley**[529] 27 July 1987.
  9875 iii. Spencer Charles **McKinley**[530] 9 August 1989.

8610. **David Charles**[14] **McKinley** (Charles Dos[13], William Harry[12], John Carlysle[11], William Henry[10], Angeline[9] **Whipple**, Enoch[8], Nehemiah[7], Benjamin[6], Francis[5], Jonathan[4], Joseph[3], Matthew[2], Matthew[1])[531] was born in Honolulu, Oahu, Hawaii 22 September 1966.

David Charles **McKinley** and Tammy Reachelle **Chapman** had the following child born in Sacramento, Sacramento Co., Calif:

  9876 i. Zachary David[15] **McKinley**[532] 27 May 1993.

8612. **Dean Holden**[14] **Rushing** (Mary Lynn[13] **McKinley**, Dean Carlysle[12], John Carlysle[11], William Henry[10], Angeline[9] **Whipple**, Enoch[8], Nehemiah[7], Benjamin[6], Francis[5], Jonathan[4], Joseph[3], Matthew[2], Matthew[1])[533] was born in Houston, Harris Co., Tex. 28 January 1973 and married **Erica Nicole Dobson** there 24 October 1998. Erica,[534] daughter of William Van **Dobson** and Marie Jeanette **Wilson**, was born in Houston 15 March 1972.

Dean Holden **Rushing** and Erica Nicole **Dobson** had the following children:
  9877 i. Holden Andrew[15] **Rushing**[535] born in Houston 8 May 2002.
  9878 ii. Alexandria Nicole **Rushing**[536] born in Austin, Travis Co., Tex. 15 November 2002.

8634. **Christopher**[14] **Miller** (Kathy Jo[13] **Wood**, Jack Edward[12], Elizabeth[11] **McKinley**, William Henry[10], Angeline[9] **Whipple**, Enoch[8], Nehemiah[7], Benjamin[6], Francis[5], Jonathan[4], Joseph[3], Matthew[2], Matthew[1])[537] was born in Valpraiso, Porter Co., Ind. 20 April 1972 and married **Rebecca Garfield** 6 May 1995.

Christopher **Miller** and Rebecca **Garfield** had the following child:
  9879 i. Colin Rhea[15] **Miller**[538] born in Pt. Royal, Beaufort Co., S.C. 17 November 1995.

8656. **Lisa Dawn**[14] **Little** (Colleen Charles-Ann[13] **Frederick**, Charles Stephan[12], Maude Maree[11] **Whipple**, Milo Enoch[10], Cyrenius Thomas[9], Enoch[8], Nehemiah[7], Benjamin[6], Francis[5], Jonathan[4], Joseph[3], Matthew[2], Matthew[1])[539] was born in Bellevue, King Co., Wash. 23 June 1961 and married **Steven Charles McConnell** in Anacortes, Skagit Co., Wash. 6 June 1981. Steven,[540] son of Charles Vernon **McConnell** and Alice **Hoover**, was born in White Salmon, Klictitat Co., Wash. 18 August 1958.

Lisa Dawn **Little** and Steven Charles **McConnell** had the following child born in Anacortes:
  9880 i. Sharayah Nicole[15] **McConnell**[541] 2 December 1988.

8674. **Jeffery Lee**[14] **Heddinger** (Kay Ann[13] **Kalvig**, Anna Jeanette[12] **Whipple**, William Walter[11], Selmon Thomas[10], Cyrenius Thomas[9], Enoch[8], Nehemiah[7], Benjamin[6], Francis[5], Jonathan[4], Joseph[3], Matthew[2], Matthew[1])[542] was born in Cedar Rapids, Linn Co., Iowa 29 August 1963 and married **Laurie Jean Buelow** in Camanche, Clinton Co., Iowa, 15 August 1987. Laurie,[543] daughter of Earl George **Buelow** and June Faye **Weber**, was born in Clinton, Clinton Co., Iowa 4 February 1965.

Jeffery Lee **Heddinger** and Laurie Jean **Buelow** had the following children:
  9881 i. Leah Terese[15] **Heddinger**[544] born in Rocky Mount, Nash Co., N. C. 11 November 1994.
  9882 ii. Eric William **Heddinger**[545] born in Burnsville, Dakota Co., Minn. 10 October 2000.

8729. **Lee Allen**[14] **Babbage** (Nancy Lee[13] **Whipple**, James Earl[12], Lucien Blaine[11], James Ezekiel[10], Lucien Ransom[9], Enoch[8], Nehemiah[7], Benjamin[6], Francis[5], Jonathan[4], Joseph[3], Matthew[2], Matthew[1])[546] was born in Cedar Rapids, Linn Co., Iowa 28 May 1955 and married twice. (1) **Bonnie Wilson** in St. Petersburg, Pinellas Co., Fla. 19 October 1982. They were divorced in Florida. Bonnie's marriage to Lee was her second. She had a son with her first husband. (2) **Margaret Ann Googe** in Hammland,[547] La. 10 June 1989. Maggie,[548] daughter of Middleton William **Googe** and Sarah Ava **Whitfield**, was born in Ocala, Marion Co., Fla. 30 September 1957. She married (1) **(__) Ferrell**. They had sons Keith, born 26 April 1976, and Kevin, born 8 April 1978, in Gainesville, Alachua Co., Fla. No information provided on first husband.

KC, Maggie, Lee Allen Sr., and Lee Allen Jr Babbage.

Lee Allen **Babbage** and Margaret Ann **Googe** had the following children:

    9883 i. Lee Allen[15] **Babbage** Jr.[549] born in Daytona Beach, Volusia Co., Fla. 12 June 1987.

    9884 ii. KC **Babbage** born in Tampa, Hillsborough Co., Fla. 17 June 1990.[550]

KC Babbage. Photos courtesy of KC Babbage.

{ G 1449 }

8730. **Linda Ann**[14] **Babbage** (Nancy Lee[13] **Whipple**, James Earl[12], Lucien Blaine[11], James Ezekiel[10], Lucien Ransom[9], Enoch[8], Nehemiah[7], Benjamin[6], Francis[5], Jonathan[4], Joseph[3], Matthew[2], Matthew[1])[551] was born in Cedar Rapids, Linn Co., Iowa 31 January 1957 and married four times. (1) **Robin Lee Spruell** in St. Petersburg, Pinellas Co., Fla. 3 November 1973. He was born in St. Petersburg 12 January 1958. They were divorced in St. Petersburg 3 December 1975. (2) **Gilbert Loren Kelly** in Whitney, Hill Co., Tex. 26 October 1978. Gilbert, son of Gilbert Loren **Kelly** and Margaret Ann (__), was born in San Bernardino, San Bernardino Co., Calif. 18 February 1958. (3) **Harry Leman**. (4) Re-married **Robin Lee Spruell**.

Lee and Linda Babbage. Photo courtesy of Elaine (Whipple) West.

Linda Ann **Babbage** and Robin Lee **Spruell** had the following child born in St. Petersburg:

9885   i.   Adam Lee[15] **Spruell**[552] 10 June 1974 and married at the War Veterans' Memorial Park, 9600 Bay Pines Blvd. Monique (__) in St. Petersburg 26 October 2001.

Linda Ann **Babbage** and Gilbert Loren **Kelly** had the following children:

9886   ii.   Alycia Dawn **Kelly**[553] born in Whitney 4 March 1980.
9887   iii.   Gilbert Lavern **Kelly**[554] born in Houston, Harris Co., Tex. 10 January 1982.

8731. **Jon Robert**[14] **Garland** (Nancy Lee[13] **Whipple**, James Earl[12], Lucien Blaine[11], James Ezekiel[10], Lucien Ransom[9], Enoch[8], Nehemiah[7], Benjamin[6], Francis[5], Jonathan[4], Joseph[3], Matthew[2], Matthew[1])[555] was born in St. Petersburg, Pinellas Co., Fla. 26 July 1964 and married twice. (1) **Kimberly Ellain Guth** in St. Petersburg 22 February 1987. Kimberly,[556] daughter of Linda L. **Goddard**, was born in St. Petersburg 28 June 1966 and died there 17 July 2000, at 34 years of age. They were divorced in

Jon Robert Garland, High School Graduation, 1982. Photo courtesy of Jon Garland.

{ G 1450 }

Florida in May 1989. (2) **Linda Leilannie Elgin** in St. Petersburg 19 March 1997.[557] She married (1) **James Fox**.

Jon Robert **Garland** and Kimberly Ellain **Guth** had the following child born in St. Petersburg:
    9888   i.   Andrew E.[15] **Garland**[558] 12 July 1987.

Jon Robert **Garland** had the following child born in St. Petersburg:
    9889   ii.   Jon Robert **Garland II**[559] 22 April 1989. Jon's mother was Claudett **Wright**. His parents were domestic partners.

Andy Garland, High School graduation, St. Petersburg, Fla. 2005. Photo courtesy of Elaine (Whipple) West.

Jon Robert **Garland** and Linda Leilannie **Elgin** had the following child born in St. Petersburg:
    9890   iii.   Sean D. **Garland**[560] 15 April 1998.

8737. **Jessica Ashley**[14] **Drotzman** (Michael James[13], Patricia Ellen[12] **Whipple**, Lucien Blaine[11], James Ezekiel[10], Lucien Ransom[9], Enoch[8], Nehemiah[7], Benjamin[6], Francis[5], Jonathan[4], Joseph[3], Matthew[2], Matthew[1])[561] was born in Bad Constatt, Germany 27 October 1980.

Jessica Ashley **Drotzman** and Eric **Hammer** had the following child born in Sioux Falls, Minnehaha Co., S. Dak.:
    9891   i.   Logan Michael[15] **Hammer**[562] 23 February 2004 at 4:42 p.m. and weighed 9 pounds 6 ounces; 21 inches long.

Jessica and Eric's wedding day, May 14, 2005 Sioux Falls, SD. Photo courtesy of Michael J. Drotzman.

{ G 1451 }

Joe Drotzman, Mike Drotzman, Eric Hammer, Ruth Drotzman and Jake Drotzman standing. Jared Drotzman, Jessica Drotzman, and Logan Hammer seated. 14 May 2005. Photo courtesy of Michael J. Drotzman.

8774. **Larry Rollin**[14] **Shields** (Maurice Dean[13], Vivian Ray[12] **Sneary**, Ella Agnes[11] **Burgess**, Ellen[10] **Whipple**, Manley Nehemiah[9], Abraham[8], Nehemiah[7], Benjamin[6], Francis[5], Jonathan[4], Joseph[3], Matthew[2], Matthew[1])[563] was born in Alva, Woods Co., Okla. 2 August 1946 and died 11 July 1974 in Salina, Saline Co., Kans., at 27 years of age. He married **Cheri Lynn Phillips** in Kansas City, Jackson Co., Mo. 14 January 1967. She was born in Chillicothe, Livingston Co., Mo. 23 November 1946.[564]

Larry Rollin **Shields** and Cheri Lynn **Phillips** had the following child:
+ 9892 i. Loreli Renee[15] **Shields** born 5 August 1967.

8775. **Randy Steven**[14] **Shields** (Maurice Dean[13], Vivian Ray[12] **Sneary**, Ella Agnes[11] **Burgess**, Ellen[10] **Whipple**, Manley Nehemiah[9], Abraham[8], Nehemiah[7], Benjamin[6], Francis[5], Jonathan[4], Joseph[3], Matthew[2], Matthew[1])[565] was born in Wichita, Sedgwick Co., Kans. 30 March 1950 and married **Jocelyn Fern Claassen** in Whitewater, Butler Co., Kans. 29 May 1971. She was born in Newton, Harvey Co., Kans. 17 April 1951.[566]

{ G 1452 }

Randy Steven **Shields** and Jocelyn Fern **Claassen** adopted the following child born in Wichita:
> 9893   i.   Taylor Dean[15] **Shields**[567] 16 July 1987.

8776. **Sanzee Glee**[14] **Wanger** (Jacquiline Genevieve[13] **Woods**, Veta Grace[12] **Sneary**, Ella Agnes[11] **Burgess**, Ellen[10] **Whipple**, Manley Nehemiah[9], Abraham[8], Nehemiah[7], Benjamin[6], Francis[5], Jonathan[4], Joseph[3], Matthew[2], Matthew[1])[568] was born in Shattuck, Ellis Co., Okla. 15 February 1948 and married twice. (1) **Harry Lee Pittman** in Fargo, Ellis Co., Okla. 21 February 1970. Harry,[569] son of Harry Leander **Pittman** and Julia **Hayes**, was born in Shattuck 24 August 1949. (2) **Grady Robinson Suthers** in Fargo 26 May 1995. He was born in Shattuck 16 June 1946.[570]

Sanzee Glee **Wanger** and Harry Lee **Pittman** had the following children:
> +   9894   i.   Eric Loyd[15] **Pittman** born 3 May 1971.
> +   9895   ii.   Zaneta Zoe **Pittman** born 12 June 1975.
>   9896   iii.   Jarrod Heath **Pittman**[571] born in Chula Vista, San Diego Co., Calif. 12 April 1980.
>   9897   iv.   Damara Grace **Pittman**[572] born in Chula Vista 4 May 1982.

8777. **Ronald Loyd**[14] **Wanger** (Jacquiline Genevieve[13] **Woods**, Veta Grace[12] **Sneary**, Ella Agnes[11] **Burgess**, Ellen[10] **Whipple**, Manley Nehemiah[9], Abraham[8], Nehemiah[7], Benjamin[6], Francis[5], Jonathan[4], Joseph[3], Matthew[2], Matthew[1])[573] was born in Shattuck, Ellis Co., Okla. 10 November 1950 and married **Susan Elaine Dunne** in Churdan, Greene Co., Iowa, 26 April 1975.

Ronald Loyd **Wanger** and Susan Elaine **Dunne** had the following children:
> 9898   i.   Stephanie Kay[15] **Wanger**[574] born in Ft. Dodge, Webster Co., Iowa 4 March 1976.
> 9899   ii.   Jason Orin **Wanger**[575] born in Sioux City, Woodbury Co., Iowa in May 1980 and died shortly after birth.
> 9900   iii.   Veronica Sue **Wanger**[576] born in Sioux City 25 April 1981 and married Patrick **Gunderson** in Yacolt, Clark Co., Wash. 19 June 1999.
> 9901   iv.   Emory Ronald **Wanger**[577] born in Sioux City 27 January 1984.

8778. **Marsha Nan**[14] **Wanger** (Jacquiline Genevieve[13] **Woods**, Veta Grace[12] **Sneary**, Ella Agnes[11] **Burgess**, Ellen[10] **Whipple**, Manley Nehemiah[9], Abraham[8], Nehemiah[7], Benjamin[6], Francis[5], Jonathan[4], Joseph[3], Matthew[2], Matthew[1])[578] was born in Shattuck, Ellis Co., Okla.

14 April 1953 and married **John Robert Miller** in Fargo, Ellis Co., Okla. 5 February 1977. He was born 26 August 1950.[579]

Marsha Nan **Wanger** and John Robert **Miller** had the following children:
- 9902 i. Meredith Jacquiline[15] **Miller**[580] born in Watertown, Codington Co., S. Dak. 25 March 1979.
- 9903 ii. Brittany Danielle **Miller**[581] born in Manchester, Delaware Co., Iowa 14 November 1982.

8779. **Rodney Ray**[14] **Wanger** (Jacquiline Genevieve[13] **Woods**, Veta Grace[12] **Sneary**, Ella Agnes[11] **Burgess**, Ellen[10] **Whipple**, Manley Nehemiah[9], Abraham[8], Nehemiah[7], Benjamin[6], Francis[5], Jonathan[4], Joseph[3], Matthew[2], Matthew[1])[582] was born in Shattuck, Ellis Co., Okla. 8 January 1956 and married three times. (1) **Alice Ilene Wadsworth** in Fargo, Ellis Co., Okla. 27 December 1975. She was born in Ellensburg, Kittitas Co., Wash. 4 December 1957.[583] (2) **Kimberly Ann (Keith) Roark** in Canadian, Hemphill Co., Tex. 30 November 1984. She was born in Oklahoma City, Oklahoma Co., Okla. 23 March 1956.[584] (3) **Ann Carol (Houston) Jenkins** in Stillwater, Payne Co., Okla. 3 May 1997. She was born in Enid, Garfield Co., Okla. 17 August 1951.[585]

Rodney Ray **Wanger** and Alice Ilene **Wadsworth** had the following children born in Shattuck:
- 9904 i. Heath Laramie[15] **Wanger**[586] 25 August 1976 and married Crystal Leigh **Neely** in Lake Tahoe, Douglas Co., Nev. 6 July 2000. Crystal,[587] daughter of Shade Allen **Neely** and Sara Lynn **Baird**, was born in Corpus Christi, Nueces Co., Tex. 1 August 1977.
- 9905 ii. Lacey Dawn **Wanger**[588] 3 October 1979.

Rodney Ray **Wanger** and Kimberly Ann Keith **Roark** had the following child born in Woodward, Woodward, Co., Okla.:
- 9906 iii. Seth Bradley **Wanger**[589] 25 November 1988.

8780. **Sharla Jo**[14] **Sperry** (Josephine May[13] **Woods**, Veta Grace[12] **Sneary**, Ella Agnes[11] **Burgess**, Ellen[10] **Whipple**, Manley Nehemiah[9], Abraham[8], Nehemiah[7], Benjamin[6], Francis[5], Jonathan[4], Joseph[3], Matthew[2], Matthew[1])[590] was born in Shattuck, Ellis Co., Okla. 29 February 1952 and married **Thomas Irvin Drake** in Gage, Ellis Co., Okla. 22 May 1971. Thomas,[591] son of Irvin **Drake** and Betty **Cresswell**, was born 17 January 1952.

Sharla Jo **Sperry** and Thomas Irvin **Drake** had the following children:
+ 9907 i. Jennifer Jo[15] **Drake** born 21 November 1974.
    9908 ii. Debra Dawn **Drake**[592] born in Stillwater, Payne Co., Okla. 8 June 1977 and married Gary Ronald **Young** 16 December 1995. He was born 21 November 1974.[593]

8781. **Sidney Kyle**[14] **Sperry** (Josephine May[13] **Woods**, Veta Grace[12] **Sneary**, Ella Agnes[11] **Burgess**, Ellen[10] **Whipple**, Manley Nehemiah[9], Abraham[8], Nehemiah[7], Benjamin[6], Francis[5], Jonathan[4], Joseph[3], Matthew[2], Matthew[1])[594] was born in Shattuck, Ellis Co., Okla. 10 April 1956 and married twice. (1) **Brenda Gail Schabacher** in Cherokee, Alfalfa Co., Okla. 28 July 1978. She is the daughter of Duane Lee **Schabacher** and Verna Ruth **Farabee**.[595] (2) **Lisa Dianne Allen** in Abilene, Dickinson Co., Kans. 6 May 1989. Lisa,[596] daughter of Carroll Edmond **Allen** and Darlene Mae **Kuhlmann**, was born in Boulder, Boulder Co., Colo. 6 December 1961. She married (1) **Michael Leland Chase**. They had Adam Michael born 13 June 1983 and Kari LeAnne born 21 October 1985 in Cherokee.

Sidney Kyle **Sperry** and Brenda Gail **Schabacher** had the following children:
    9909 i. Reed Calvin[15] **Sperry**[597] born in Hastings, Adams Co., Nebr. 2 January 1980.
    9910 ii. Tyler Cale **Sperry**[598] born in Cherokee 14 August 1983.

Sidney Kyle **Sperry** and Lisa Dianne **Allen** had the following children:
    9911 iii. Trenton Wyatt **Sperry**[599] born in Edmond, Oklahoma Co., Okla. 25 December 1989.
    9912 iv. Ryan Andrew **Sperry**[600] born in Tulsa, Tulsa Co., Okla. 14 June 1991.

8782. **Sabrina Sue**[14] **Sperry** (Josephine May[13] **Woods**, Veta Grace[12] **Sneary**, Ella Agnes[11] **Burgess**, Ellen[10] **Whipple**, Manley Nehemiah[9], Abraham[8], Nehemiah[7], Benjamin[6], Francis[5], Jonathan[4], Joseph[3], Matthew[2], Matthew[1])[601] was born in Shattuck, Ellis Co., Okla. 5 January 1965 and married **Jay Harding** in Cherokee, Alfalfa Co., Okla. 8 June 1985. Jay,[602] son of Harry Louis **Harding** and Emma Jo **Chapple**, was born in Plattsburgh, Clinton Co., N.Y. 25 January 1961.

Sabrina Sue **Sperry** and Jay **Harding** had the following children:
    9913 i. Joshua John[15] **Harding**[603] born in Oklahoma Co., Okla. 2 May 1987.
    9914 ii. John Zachary **Harding**[604] born in Oklahoma Co. in August 1988.

{ G 1455 }

9915 iii. Anna Elizabeth **Harding**[605] born in Oklahoma Co. 5 January 1993.
9916 iv. Kathryn Lee **Harding**[606] born in Midwest City, Oklahoma Co. 4 August 1994.
9917 v. J. Calvin **Harding**[607] born in Clackamas, Clackamas Co, Oreg. 7 April 1999.

8788. **Monte Shane**[14] **Woods** (Chester Vance[13], Veta Grace[12] **Sneary**, Ella Agnes[11] **Burgess**, Ellen[10] **Whipple**, Manley Nehemiah[9], Abraham[8], Nehemiah[7], Benjamin[6], Francis[5], Jonathan[4], Joseph[3], Matthew[2], Matthew[1])[608] was born in Shattuck, Ellis Co., Okla. 16 March 1964 and married **Kristi Dawn Terrel** in Follett, Lipscomb Co., Tex.

Monte Shane **Woods** and Kristi Dawn **Terrel** had the following children in Shattuck:
9918 i. Tanner Shane[15] **Woods**[609] 28 October 1987.
9919 ii. Shelbi Lane **Woods**[610] 19 September 1990.
9920 iii. Dakota Blane **Woods**[611] 31 May 1995.

8789. **Anthony Victor**[14] **Woods** (Chester Vance[13], Veta Grace[12] **Sneary**, Ella Agnes[11] **Burgess**, Ellen[10] **Whipple**, Manley Nehemiah[9], Abraham[8], Nehemiah[7], Benjamin[6], Francis[5], Jonathan[4], Joseph[3], Matthew[2], Matthew[1])[612] was born in Shattuck, Ellis Co., Okla. 23 July 1965 and married twice. (1) **Darlene Nichole Shain** in Las Vegas, Clark Co., Nev. 16 December 1990. She was born in Pratt, Pratt Co., Kans. 16 November 1968.[613] (2) **Terri Lea Jones** in Salpulpa, Creek Co., Okla. 31 October 1998. She was born in Pyor, Mayes Co., Okla. 18 October 1967.[614] Before marrying Anthony, Terri had a son Baylor Allan born 22 April 1995 in Tulsa, Tulsa Co., Okla.

Anthony Victor **Woods** and Terri Lea **Jones** had the following child:
9921 i. Banner Vance[15] **Woods**[615] born in Tulsa, 30 July 1999.

8790. **Matthew Brady**[14] **Woods** (Chester Vance[13], Veta Grace[12] **Sneary**, Ella Agnes[11] **Burgess**, Ellen[10] **Whipple**, Manley Nehemiah[9], Abraham[8], Nehemiah[7], Benjamin[6], Francis[5], Jonathan[4], Joseph[3], Matthew[2], Matthew[1])[616] was born in Cortez, Montezuma Co., Colo. 11 February 1969 and married twice. (1) **Judy (__)** in Stillwater, Payne Co., Okla. 25 May 1990. She was born in Nowata, Nowata Co., Okla. 28 September 1963.[617] (2) **Amy Michelle Nance** in Grand Blanc, Genesse Co., Mich. 5 August 2000. She was born in Pontiac, Oakland Co., Mich. 3 November 1973.[618]

Matthew Brady **Woods** and Judy **(_)** had the following children born in Cushing, Payne Co., Okla.:

  9922 i. Lindsay Brooke[15] **Woods**[619] 11 March 1991.

  9923 ii. Courtney Braden **Woods**[620] 30 September 1994.

8791. **Corina Michelle**[14] **Woods** (Chester Vance[13], Veta Grace[12] **Sneary**, Ella Agnes[11] **Burgess**, Ellen[10] **Whipple**, Manley Nehemiah[9], Abraham[8], Nehemiah[7], Benjamin[6], Francis[5], Jonathan[4], Joseph[3], Matthew[2], Matthew[1])[621] was born in Shattuck, Ellis Co., Okla. 19 March 1974.

Corina Michelle **Woods** had the following children born in Shattuck:

  9924 i. Narsissis Devonty[15] **Woods**[622] 15 September 1994.

  9925 ii. Demetriana **Woods**.[623]

8792. **Pamela Sue**[14] **Pittman** (Conyetta Sue[13] **Woods**, Veta Grace[12] **Sneary**, Ella Agnes[11] **Burgess**, Ellen[10] **Whipple**, Manley Nehemiah[9], Abraham[8], Nehemiah[7], Benjamin[6], Francis[5], Jonathan[4], Joseph[3], Matthew[2], Matthew[1])[624] was born in Mooreland, Woodward Co., Okla. 14 August 1965 and married **Kenneth John Glennie** there 4 June 1983. Kenneth,[625] son of John **Glennie** and Beverly **Keith**, was born in Woodward 22 September 1962.

Pamela Sue **Pittman** and Kenneth John **Glennie** had the following children:

  9926 i. Myka Deone[15] **Glennie**[626] born in Amarillo, Potter Co., Tex. 20 May 1990.

  9927 ii. Joseph Tyler **Glennie**[627] born in Austin, Travis Co., Tex. 18 August 1993.

8793. **Justin Arthur**[14] **Pittman** (Conyetta Sue[13] **Woods**, Veta Grace[12] **Sneary**, Ella Agnes[11] **Burgess**, Ellen[10] **Whipple**, Manley Nehemiah[9], Abraham[8], Nehemiah[7], Benjamin[6], Francis[5], Jonathan[4], Joseph[3], Matthew[2], Matthew[1])[628] was born in Bartlesville, Washington Co., Okla. 8 February 1972 and married **Jana Catherine Rodman** in Tulsa, Tulsa Co., Okla. 4 September 1993. Jana,[629] daughter of Fred **Rodman** and Elna **Sehested**, was born in Oklahoma City, Oklahoma Co., Okla. 10 February 1971.

Justin Arthur **Pittman** and Jana Catherine **Rodman** had the following child born in Tulsa:

  9928 i. Audrey Faith[15] **Pittman**[630] 7 August 2000.

8810. **Tiffany Marie**[14] **Hale** (Paul Christopher[13], Dorothy Emma[12] **Burgess**, William[11], Ellen[10] **Whipple**, Manley Nehemiah[9], Abraham[8], Nehemiah[7], Benjamin[6], Francis[5], Jonathan[4], Joseph[3], Matthew[2], Matthew[1])[631] was born in Kansas City, Jackson Co., Mo. 11 October 1972 and married **David Jonathan Noel** there 6 August 1994. He was born in Kansas City 6 June 1973.[632]

Tiffany Marie **Hale** and David Jonathan **Noel** had the following child born in Snellville,[633] Ga.:
    9929 i.   Joshua David[15] **Noel**[634] 2 June 1997.

8828. **Susan**[14] **Schowalter** (Arthur Eastman[13], Lavine[12] **Van Dyke**, Carrie Emily[11] **Whipple**, Alphonso[10], Horatio[9], Nathan[8], Nehemiah[7], Benjamin[6], Francis[5], Jonathan[4], Joseph[3], Matthew[2], Matthew[1])[635] was born in Elyria, Lorain Co., Ohio 14 May 1940 and married **(__) Ruffing**.

Susan **Schowalter** and (__) **Ruffing** had the following children:
    9930 i.   Rodney[15] **Ruffing**[636] born 17 April 1965.
    9931 ii. Sara **Ruffing**[637] born 9 April 1972. Adopted.

8829. **Gale**[14] **Schowalter** (Lawrence V.[13], Lavine[12] **Van Dyke**, Carrie Emily[11] **Whipple**, Alphonso[10], Horatio[9], Nathan[8], Nehemiah[7], Benjamin[6], Francis[5], Jonathan[4], Joseph[3], Matthew[2], Matthew[1])[638] was born in Cleveland, Cuyahoga Co., Ohio 17 July 1942 and married **Judy Coleman** in Bethany, Howard Co., Md. 28 August 1969. She was born 16 October 1947.[639]

Gale **Schowalter** and Judy **Coleman** had the following children:
    9932 i.   Donnie[15] **Schowalter**[640] born 14 December 1972.
    9933 ii. Jody **Schowalter**[641] born 16 May 1979.
    9934 iii. David **Schowalter**[642] born 5 August 1982.

8830. **Timothy Temple**[14] **Schowalter** (Lawrence V.[13], Lavine[12] **Van Dyke**, Carrie Emily[11] **Whipple**, Alphonso[10], Horatio[9], Nathan[8], Nehemiah[7], Benjamin[6], Francis[5], Jonathan[4], Joseph[3], Matthew[2], Matthew[1])[643] was born in Cleveland, Cuyahoga Co., Ohio 1 November 1944 and married **Judy Ami Shull** in Carrollton, Carroll Co., Md. 12 September 1967. She was born in Carlisle, Cumberland Co., Penn. 20 November 1944.[644]

Timothy Temple **Schowalter** and Judy Ami **Shull** had the following children born in Denver, Denver Co., Colo.
    9935 i.   Katherine Elise[15] **Schowalter**[645] 27 October 1971.

   9936 ii. Marie Lynn **Schowalter**[646] 22 August 1973.

8831. **Eileen**[14] **Schowalter** (Lawrence V.[13], Lavine[12] **Van Dyke**, Carrie Emily[11] **Whipple**, Alphonso[10], Horatio[9], Nathan[8], Nehemiah[7], Benjamin[6], Francis[5], Jonathan[4], Joseph[3], Matthew[2], Matthew[1])[647] was born in Cleveland, Cuyahoga Co., Ohio 23 June 1948 and married **Larry Forestal** in Boulder, Boulder Co., Colo. 19 June 1971. They were divorced abt 1988.

Eileen **Schowalter** and Larry **Forestal** had the following children:
   9937 i. Sean[15] **Forestal**[648] born 14 June 1976.
   9938 ii. Colin **Forestal**[649] born 20 February 1978.

8835. **Christopher Lee**[14] **Gerwin** (Lauretta[13] **Van Dyke**, Carroll Marcus[12], Carrie Emily[11] **Whipple**, Alphonso[10], Horatio[9], Nathan[8], Nehemiah[7], Benjamin[6], Francis[5], Jonathan[4], Joseph[3], Matthew[2], Matthew[1])[650] was born in East Cleveland, Cuyahoga Co., Ohio 25 December 1949 and married twice. (1) **Christine Joyce** in Royal Oak, Oakland Co., Mich. 28 December 1968. They were divorced in 1971. (2) **Rene Kuraoka** in Honolulu, Oahu, Hawaii 13 April 1984.

Christopher Lee **Gerwin** and Christine **Joyce** had the following child born in Royal Oak:
   9939 i. Mona[15] **Gerwin**[651] 2 August 1969.

Christopher Lee **Gerwin** and Rene **Kuraoka** had the following children born in Redondo Beach, Los Angeles Co., Calif.:
   9940 ii. Cole A. **Gerwin**[652] 28 September 1986.
   9941 iii. Chelsea Lee **Gerwin**[653] 14 August 1991.

8836. **Steven Mark**[14] **Gerwin** (Lauretta[13] **Van Dyke**, Carroll Marcus[12], Carrie Emily[11] **Whipple**, Alphonso[10], Horatio[9], Nathan[8], Nehemiah[7], Benjamin[6], Francis[5], Jonathan[4], Joseph[3], Matthew[2], Matthew[1])[654] was born in Brooklyn, Cuyahoga Co., Ohio 25 November 1951 and married **Kathleen Susan Finken** in Ann Arbor, Washtenaw Co., Mich. 16 June 1973. Kathleen, daughter of Warren **Finken** and Mary **Cannon**, was born in Dayton, Montgomery Co., Ohio 12 May 1951.

Steven Mark **Gerwin** and Kathleen Susan **Finken** had the following children born in Southfield, Mich.:
   9942 i. Eric Justin[15] **Gerwin**[655] 3 April 1978.
   9943 ii. Daniel Jay **Gerwin**[656] 15 October 1981.
   9944 iii. Meganne Marie **Gerwin**[657] 12 April 1985.

8837. **Robert Lee**[14] **Gerwin** (Lauretta[13] **Van Dyke**, Carroll Marcus[12], Carrie Emily[11] **Whipple**, Alphonso[10], Horatio[9], Nathan[8], Nehemiah[7], Benjamin[6], Francis[5], Jonathan[4], Joseph[3], Matthew[2], Matthew[1])[658] was born in Lakewood, Cuyahoga Co., Ohio 11 September 1953 and married **Pamela Hargreaves** in Royal Oak, Oakland Co., Mich. 16 October 1976. Pamela,[659] daughter of Ronald **Hargreaves** and Marilyn **Roberts**, was born in Royal Oak 6 May 1956.

Robert Lee **Gerwin** and Pamela **Hargreaves** had the following children:
    9945 i. Michael Robert[15] **Gerwin**[660] born in Royal Oak 30 July 1979.
    9946 ii. Matthew Brian **Gerwin**[661] born 24 March 1981.

8839. **Charles Mathews**[14] **Gerwin** (Lauretta[13] **Van Dyke**, Carroll Marcus[12], Carrie Emily[11] **Whipple**, Alphonso[10], Horatio[9], Nathan[8], Nehemiah[7], Benjamin[6], Francis[5], Jonathan[4], Joseph[3], Matthew[2], Matthew[1])[662] was born in Lakewood, Cuyahoga Co., Ohio 1 February 1958 and married **Kathy Marie Spazea** in Royal Oak, Oakland Co., Mich. 5 April 1982. Kathy,[663] daughter of Joseph **Spazea** and Olga **(__)**, was born in Royal Oak 4 March 1961.

Charles Mathews **Gerwin** and Kathy Marie **Spazea** had the following children born in Detroit, Wayne Co., Mich.:
    9947 i. Lindsey Marie[15] **Gerwin**[664] 26 March 1987.
    9948 ii. Lisa Rene **Gerwin**[665] 26 March 1987.

8844. **Laura**[14] **Van Dyke** (Clifford Fuller[13], Carroll Marcus[12], Carrie Emily[11] **Whipple**, Alphonso[10], Horatio[9], Nathan[8], Nehemiah[7], Benjamin[6], Francis[5], Jonathan[4], Joseph[3], Matthew[2], Matthew[1])[666] was born in Newark, Licking Co., Ohio 16 May 1959 and married **Thomas Landis** in Baltimore, Fairfield Co., Ohio 11 August 1979. Thomas,[667] son of Thomas **Landis**, was born in Baltimore 27 November 1957. Thomas, with his parents and two brothers and their spouses, farm 2,000 acres in Ohio.

Laura **Van Dyke** and Thomas **Landis** had the following children:
    9949 i. Leslie Ann[15] **Landis**[668] born in Newark 5 September 1980.
    9950 ii. Charles Arnold **Landis**[669] born in Lancaster, Fairfield Co., Ohio 15 February 1982.
    9951 iii. Betsey Jo **Landis**[670] born in Lancaster 23 June 1983.
    9952 iv. Holly Rose **Landis**[671] born in Lancaster 11 May 1986.

8845. **Brad Thomas**[14] **Van Dyke** (Clifford Fuller[13], Carroll Marcus[12], Carrie Emily[11] **Whipple**, Alphonso[10], Horatio[9], Nathan[8], Nehemiah[7],

Benjamin[6], Francis[5], Jonathan[4], Joseph[3], Matthew[2], Matthew[1])[672] was born in Newark, Licking Co., Ohio 8 February 1966 and married **Junee Lutz** in Baltimore, Fairfield Co., Ohio 22 November 1991. She was born 5 June 1955.[673]

Brad Thomas **Van Dyke** and Junee **Lutz** had the following child:
    9953   i.   Courtney[15] **Van Dyke**[674] born 12 October 1992.

8846. **Allen**[14] **Turner** (Beatrice[13] **Leipner**, Ethel[12] **Van Dyke**, Carrie Emily[11] **Whipple**, Alphonso[10], Horatio[9], Nathan[8], Nehemiah[7], Benjamin[6], Francis[5], Jonathan[4], Joseph[3], Matthew[2], Matthew[1])[675] was born in Cleveland, Cuyahoga Co., Ohio 20 December 1942 and married **Evelyn Kellett** in Greenville, S.C.

Allen **Turner** and Evelyn **Kellett** had the following children born in Greenville:
    9954   i.   Kelly Ann[15] **Turner**[676] 19 October 1973.
    9955   ii.   James Andrew **Turner**[677] 26 March 1977.

8848. **Rick Lee**[14] **Treddenbarger** (Eleanor Catherine[13] **Greeley**, Stella Emma[12] **Whipple**, Ira Orren[11], Alphonso[10], Horatio[9], Nathan[8], Nehemiah[7], Benjamin[6], Francis[5], Jonathan[4], Joseph[3], Matthew[2], Matthew[1])[678] was born in Sacramento, Sacramento Co., Calif. 29 September 1956 and married **Valerie Tanler** in Carmichael, Sacramento Co., Calif. 1 February 1975. Valerie,[679] daughter of George Wayne **Tanler** and Doris **Cramer**, was born 24 June 1957.

Rick Lee **Treddenbarger** and Valerie **Tanler** had the following child born in Sacramento:
    9956   i.   Rebecca Lynnette[15] **Treddenbarger**[680] 24 December 1976 and married Samuel David **Richards** in Folsom, Sacramento Co., Calif. 19 October 1996. Samuel,[681] son of Joseph **Richards** and Anne **Hale**, was born 18 August 1976.

8849. **Sandra Kay**[14] **Treddenbarger** (Eleanor Catherine[13] **Greeley**, Stella Emma[12] **Whipple**, Ira Orren[11], Alphonso[10], Horatio[9], Nathan[8], Nehemiah[7], Benjamin[6], Francis[5], Jonathan[4], Joseph[3], Matthew[2], Matthew[1])[682] was born in Sacramento, Sacramento Co., Calif. 4 November 1960 and married **Patrick Michael Smith** in Lake Tahoe, Placer Co., Calif. 3 December 1988. He was born 8 April 1971.[683]

Sandra Kay **Treddenbarger** and Patrick Michael **Smith** had the following child born in Sacramento:

    9957   i.   Michelle Nichole[15] **Smith**[684] 29 November 1990.

8874. **Ericka**[14] **Whipple** (Kenneth Russell[13], Wallace Eugene[12], Nathan Wilson[11], Alphonso[10], Horatio[9], Nathan[8], Nehemiah[7], Benjamin[6], Francis[5], Jonathan[4], Joseph[3], Matthew[2], Matthew[1])[685] was born in San Francisco, San Francisco Co., Calif. and married **Michael Skaggs** in 1982.

Ericka **Whipple** and Michael **Skaggs** had the following children born in Guernville, Sonoma Co., Calif.:

    9958   i.   Stacey[15] **Skaggs**[686] 23 July 1983.
    9959   ii.   Michael **Skaggs** Jr.[687] 23 February 1985.

8912. **Leslie Ann**[14] Stead (Carol Moore[13] Watkins, Frederick[12], Henry A.[11], Henry[10], Moses[9], Lois[8] Mills, Hepzibah[7] Whipple, Benjamin[6], Francis[5], Jonathan[4], Joseph[3], Matthew[2], Matthew[1])[688] was born in Grosse Pointe Farms, Wayne Co., Mich. 27 June 1963[689] and married **Charles Michael Peters** there 22 June 1985.[690] Mike,[691] son of Roger Verne **Peters** and Carole Martha **Mathews**, was born in El Paso, El Paso Co., Tex. 21 March 1962. He was graduated from the College of Engineering, U. of Michigan at Ann Arbor, Washtenaw Co., in May 1984 and is a Computer Engineer. Leslie was graduated from the U. of Michigan School of Education at Ann Arbor in May 1985 and is a member of the DAR, No. 733599.

Leslie Ann **Stead** and Charles Michael **Peters** had the following children:

    9960   i.   Jonathan Roger[15] **Peters**[692] was born at Maricopa Medical Center in Phoenix, Maricopa Co., Ariz. 17 September 1994 and weighed 9 pounds 1.5 ounces at birth and was 21 inches long. He was placed for adoption with Leslie and Mike Peters at birth and the adoption was finalized 15 Aug. 1995 at the Maricopa Co. Juvenille Court, Durango Facility, Phoenix. He was baptized at the Dove of the Desert United Methodist Church. The adoption placement papers are in possession of the Peters.

    9961   ii.   Matthew Harold **Peters**[693] was born at Good Samaritan Medical Center in Phoenix 1 April 1995 and weighed 6 pounds 13.8 ounces at birth. He was 20 1/4 inches long. He was baptized at Dove of the Desert United Methodist Church.

    9962   iii.   Emily Carolyn **Peters**[694] born in Glendale, Maricopa Co., Ariz. 6 October 1997.

8914. Allison Jaye[14] **Watkins** (William Moore[13], Frederick[12], Henry A.[11], Henry[10], Moses[9], Lois[8] **Mills**, Hepzibah[7] **Whipple**, Benjamin[6], Francis[5], Jonathan[4], Joseph[3], Matthew[2], Matthew[1])[695] was born in Plainfield, Union Co., N.J. 5 January 1973 and married **John Dunham** in Las Vegas, Clark Co., Nev. 18 October 1997. He was born in Toledo, Lucas Co., Ohio 11 February 1973.[696]

Allison Jaye **Watkins** and John **Dunham** had the following child born in Lansing, Ingham Co., Mich.:
    9963   i.   Tylar Jaye[15] **Dunham**[697] 7 July 1998.

8917. Judith Ann[14] **Cable** (Jane Elizabeth[13] **Chandler**, Florence B.[12] **Johnson**, Mary Lillian[11] **Whipple**, Ithamar Cyrus[10], Cyrus Avery[9], Ithamar[8], Rev. Benjamin[7], Benjamin[6], Francis[5], Jonathan[4], Joseph[3], Matthew[2], Matthew[1])[698] was born in Kansas City, Jackson Co., Mo. 28 December 1947 and married **Myrl William Kelly** 3 June 1967. Myrl,[699] son of Earl **Kelly** and Irene **Coram**, was born in Chautauqua, Co., Kans. 14 November 1944.

Judith Ann **Cable** and Myrl William **Kelly** had the following children born in Wichita, Sedgwick, Co, Kans.:
+   9964   i.   Elizabeth Jane[15] **Kelly** 21 July 1971.
    9965   ii.   Alex William **Kelly**[700] 16 May 1973.
    9966   iii.   Drew Michael **Kelly**[701] 27 March 1976.
    9967   iv.   Rachel Diane **Kelly**[702] 28 June 1978.

8918. Gail Elizabeth[14] **Cable** (Jane Elizabeth[13] **Chandler**, Florence B.[12] **Johnson**, Mary Lillian[11] **Whipple**, Ithamar Cyrus[10], Cyrus Avery[9], Ithamar[8], Rev. Benjamin[7], Benjamin[6], Francis[5], Jonathan[4], Joseph[3], Matthew[2], Matthew[1])[703] was born in Kansas City, Jackson Co., Mo. 15 April 1949 and married **Donald R. Nevin** in Lawrence, Douglas Co., Kans. 20 December 1970. Donald,[704] son of Laverne **Nevin** and Ruth **Chapman**, was born in Herington, Dickinson Co., Kans. 13 June 1948

Gail Elizabeth **Cable** and Donald R. **Nevin** had the following children:
    9968   i.   Emily Jane[15] **Nevin**[705] born in Spokane, Spokane Co., Wash. 28 March 1977.
    9969   ii.   Andrew Colin **Nevin**[706] born in Missoula, Missoula Co., Mont. 31 May 1980.

8919. **Janet Lynn**[14] **Cable** (Jane Elizabeth[13] **Chandler**, Florence B.[12] **Johnson**, Mary Lillian[11] **Whipple**, Ithamar Cyrus[10], Cyrus Avery[9], Ithamar[8], Rev. Benjamin[7], Benjamin[6], Francis[5], Jonathan[4], Joseph[3], Matthew[2], Matthew[1])[707] was born in Arkansas City, Cowley Co., Kans. 22 March 1952 and married **Timothy P. Ells** in Hingham, Plymouth Co., Mass, 3 March 1982. Timothy,[708] son of John **Ells** and Natalie **Rupinsky**, was born in Hingham 13 June 1956.

Janet Lynn **Cable** and Timothy P. **Ells** had the following children born in Hingham:

    9970   i.   David Andrew[15] **Ells**[709] 29 June 1984.
    9971   ii.   Katherine Liane **Ells**[710] 22 April 1986.
    9972   iii.   Laura Jane **Ells**[711] 4 April 1989.

8920. **Karen Louise**[14] **Cable** (Jane Elizabeth[13] **Chandler**, Florence B.[12] **Johnson**, Mary Lillian[11] **Whipple**, Ithamar Cyrus[10], Cyrus Avery[9], Ithamar[8], Rev. Benjamin[7], Benjamin[6], Francis[5], Jonathan[4], Joseph[3], Matthew[2], Matthew[1])[712] was born in Arkansas City, Cowley Co., Kans. 6 August 1954 and married **Daniel J. Toughey** in Kansas City, Jackson Co., Mo. 31 August 1986. Daniel,[713] son of Thomas James **Toughey** and Jane **Leary**, was born 28 June 1956.

Karen Louise **Cable** and Daniel J. **Toughey** had the following children born in Overland Park, Johnson Co., Kans.:

    9973   i.   Erin Jane[15] **Toughey**[714] 6 July 1988.
    9974   ii.   Patrick Daniel **Toughey**[715] 12 September 1990.

8922. **Susan Marlias**[14] **Chandler** (George Myron[13], Florence B.[12] **Johnson**, Mary Lillian[11] **Whipple**, Ithamar Cyrus[10], Cyrus Avery[9], Ithamar[8], Rev. Benjamin[7], Benjamin[6], Francis[5], Jonathan[4], Joseph[3], Matthew[2], Matthew[1])[716] was born in Glenwood Springs, Garfield Co., Colo. 3 May 1953 and married **Alan Dale Dean Reed** in New Castle, Garfield Co., Colo. 6 January 1979. Alan,[717] son of Dale Dean **Reed** and Wilma Jean **Higby**, was born in Enid, Garfield Co., Okla. 29 September 1954.

Susan Marlias **Chandler** and Alan Dale Dean **Reed** had the following children born in Montrose Co., Colo.:

    9975   i.   Marlise Erin[15] **Reed**[718] 27 April 1980.
    9976   ii.   Charles Alan **Reed**[719] 23 September 1982.

8923. **Kathy Ruth**[14] **Chandler** (George Myron[13], Florence B.[12] **Johnson**, Mary Lillian[11] **Whipple**, Ithamar Cyrus[10], Cyrus Avery[9], Ithamar[8],

Rev. Benjamin[7], Benjamin[6], Francis[5], Jonathan[4], Joseph[3], Matthew[2], Matthew[1])[720] was born in Glenwood Springs, Garfield Co., Colo. 24 July 1955 and married **George Stephen Henry** in New Castle, Garfield Co., Colo. 6 August 1977. George,[721] son of David Edward **Henry** and Elin Grace **Gustafson**, was born in Albuquerque, Bernalillo Co., N. Mex. 16 July 1953. Kathy is a Community College Administrator.

Kathy Ruth **Chandler** and George Stephen **Henry** had the following children born in Glenwood Springs:
- 9977 i. Zachary Andrew[15] **Henry**[722] 13 August 1987.
- 9978 ii. Hilary Elise **Henry**[723] 5 October 1989.

8926. Marie Lynne[14] **Crates** (Julia Arlene[13] **Hart**, Frederick Allan[12], Fred J.[11], John P.[10], Florina H.[9] **Whipple**, Ithamar[8], Rev. Benjamin[7], Benjamin[6], Francis[5], Jonathan[4], Joseph[3], Matthew[2], Matthew[1])[724] was born in South Gate, Los Angeles Co., Calif. 18 August 1962 and married twice. (1) **Steven Jeffrey Campbell** in Norwalk, Los Angeles Co., Calif. 4 April 1981. He was born in Norwalk 8 October 1962.[725] They were divorced in 1988. (2) **Daniel Ray Burks** in Big Bear, San Bernardina Co., Calif. 25 January 1992. He was born 30 June 1958.[726]

Marie Lynne **Crates** and Daniel Ray **Burks** had the following children born in Anaheim, Orange Co., Calif.:
- 9979 i. Rachelle[15] **Burks**[727] 31 May 1981.
- 9980 ii. Shadow **Burks**[728] 26 September 1990.

8927. Robert Earl[14] **Crates** (Julia Arlene[13] **Hart**, Frederick Allan[12], Fred J.[11], John P.[10], Florina H.[9] **Whipple**, Ithamar[8], Rev. Benjamin[7], Benjamin[6], Francis[5], Jonathan[4], Joseph[3], Matthew[2], Matthew[1])[729] was born in Anaheim, Orange Co., Calif. 1 March 1967 and married **Dana Michail Hebert** in Reno, Nev. 30 June 1990. She was born 18 November 1970.[730]

Robert Earl **Crates** and Dana Michail **Hebert** had the following children:
- 9981 i. Hannah Elizabeth[15] **Crates**[731] born in Portland, Multnomah Co., Oreg. 25 February 1991.
- 9982 ii. Zachary Nolan **Crates**[732] born in Portland 14 November 1993.
- 9983 iii. Shelby Lynn **Crates**[733] born in Redmond, DesChutes Co, Oreg. 4 September 1996.

8929. Alicia Michele[14] **Hart** (Allan Lee[13], Frederick Allan[12], Fred J.[11], John P.[10], Florina H.[9] **Whipple**, Ithamar[8], Rev. Benjamin[7], Benjamin[6], Francis[5], Jonathan[4], Joseph[3], Matthew[2], Matthew[1])[734] was born in Huntington Beach, Orange Co., Calif. 10 February 1969 and married **Gordon Gossman** in Banning, San Bernardino Co., Calif. 14 July 1991. He was born 22 August 1962.

Alicia Michele **Hart** and Gordon **Gossman** had the following children:
    9984   i.   Andrew Allan[15] **Gossman**[735] born 6 February 1993.
    9985   ii.   Jonathan **Gossman**[736] born 31 March 1995.

8933. **Richard Charles**[14] **Rogge** (Jean Carol[13] **Cannon**, Leslie A.[12] **Whipple**, Clayton J.[11], William Lemuel[10], Francis Jackson[9], Ithamar[8], Rev. Benjamin[7], Benjamin[6], Francis[5], Jonathan[4], Joseph[3], Matthew[2], Matthew[1])[737] was born in Bad Kreuznach, Germany 31 December 1952 and married **Patricia O'Neill** in Lake George, Warren Co., N.Y. 8 September 1974. Patricia,[738] daughter of Andrew **O'Neill** and Marilyn **Entermann**, was born in Teaneck, Bergen Co., N.J. 26 June 1954.

Richard Charles **Rogge** and Patricia **O'Neill** had the following children born in Lime Ridge, Sauk Co., Wisc.:
    9986   i.   Dustin Charles[15] **Rogge**[739] 19 August 1978.
    9987   ii.   Sean Henry **Rogge**[740] 16 February 1985.

8935. **Michael David Drew**[14] **Rogge** (Jean Carol[13] **Cannon**, Leslie A.[12] **Whipple**, Clayton J.[11], William Lemuel[10], Francis Jackson[9], Ithamar[8], Rev. Benjamin[7], Benjamin[6], Francis[5], Jonathan[4], Joseph[3], Matthew[2], Matthew[1])[741] was born in New Brunswick, Middlesex Co., N.J. 30 March 1957 and married **Marianne Elizabeth Lemery** in Lime Ridge, Sauk Co., Wisc. 8 September 1984. Marianne,[742] daughter of Charles Edward **Lemery** and Eleanor Mary **Olsen**, was born in Lime Ridge 5 April 1961.

Michael David Drew **Rogge** and Marianne Elizabeth **Lemery** had the following children born in Lime Ridge:
    9988   i.   Michael David[15] **Rogge**[743] 16 October 1985.
    9989   ii.   Heather Diane **Rogge**[744] 2 January 1987.

8952. **Vickie Lee**[14] **Woods** (Donna Lee[13] **Skelton**, James John[12], Sylvia May[11] **Whipple**, Marcus Erastus[10], Francis Jackson[9], Ithamar[8], Rev. Benjamin[7], Benjamin[6], Francis[5], Jonathan[4], Joseph[3], Matthew[2], Matthew[1])[745] was born 18 January 1963 and married **Fred Dzara** 7 February 1987.

Vickie Lee **Woods** and Fred **Dzara** had the following children:
    9990   i.   Quenton Elliott[15] **Dzara**[746] born 23 August 1987.
    9991   ii.   Faith Alene **Dzara**[747] born 9 December 1989.

8970. **Richard James**[14] **Smith** (Ruth Ann[13] **Wiley**, Margaret Jane[12] **Whipple**, Dr. Raymond Orson[11], Marcus Erastus[10], Francis Jackson[9], Ithamar[8], Rev. Benjamin[7], Benjamin[6], Francis[5], Jonathan[4], Joseph[3], Matthew[2], Matthew[1])[748] was born 22 March 1967 and married **Jessica Shannon** in New Bedford, Bristol Co., Mass. 20 March 1994. She was born 29 June 1970.[749]

Richard James **Smith** and Jessica **Shannon** had the following children:
- 9992 i. Victoria Shannon[15] **Smith**[750] born 7 October 1994.
- 9993 ii. Abigail Lynn **Smith**[751] born 21 February 1997.

8971. **Scott Gregory**[14] **Smith** (Ruth Ann[13] **Wiley**, Margaret Jane[12] **Whipple**, Dr. Raymond Orson[11], Marcus Erastus[10], Francis Jackson[9], Ithamar[8], Rev. Benjamin[7], Benjamin[6], Francis[5], Jonathan[4], Joseph[3], Matthew[2], Matthew[1])[752] was born 16 October 1968 and married **Stacy Marie Martin** in Oswego, Oswego Co., N.Y. 11 August 1990. She was born 8 September 1970.[753] They were divorced in 1998.

Scott Gregory **Smith** and Stacy Marie **Martin** had the following child:
- 9994 i. Jesse Royer[15] **Smith**[754] born 3 October 1993.

9001. **Stephen Reynolds**[14] **Ira** (Gordon Henry[13], Dr. Gordon Henry[12], Florence Elsie[11] **Whipple**, Cephus Galusha[10], Samuel Elijah[9], Ithamar[8], Rev. Benjamin[7], Benjamin[6], Francis[5], Jonathan[4], Joseph[3], Matthew[2], Matthew[1])[755] was born in Charleston, Charleston Co., S.C. 27 August 1958 and married **Martha Helen Mead** in Jacksonville, Duval Co., Fla. 13 June 1983. Martha,[756] daughter of Joseph William **Mead** Jr. and Eleanor Elizabeth **King**, was born in Jacksonville 28 May 1958.

Stephen Reynolds **Ira** and Martha Helen **Mead** had the following children:
- 9995 i. Christine Virginia[15] **Ira**[757] born in Memphis, Shelby Co., Tenn. 1 January 1989.
- 9996 ii. Stephanie Marie **Ira**[758] born in Chatanooga, Hamilton Co., Tenn. 14 November 1994.

9006. **Elizabeth Cecil**[14] **Ira** (Stewart Bentley[13], Dr. Gordon Henry[12], Florence Elsie[11] **Whipple**, Cephus Galusha[10], Samuel Elijah[9], Ithamar[8], Rev. Benjamin[7], Benjamin[6], Francis[5], Jonathan[4], Joseph[3], Matthew[2], Matthew[1])[759] was born in Jacksonville, Duval Co., Fla. 13 April 1958 and married **Patrick Murphy Williams III** there 12 March 1983. Patrick,[760] son of Patrick Murphy **Williams** II and Dorothy Anne **Skinner**, was born in North Wilkesboro, Wilkes Co., N.C. 30 June 1954.

Elizabeth Cecil **Ira** and Patrick Murphy **Williams** III had the following children born in Jacksonville:
- 9997 i. James Cameron[15] **Williams**[761] 7 January 1987.
- 9998 ii. Elizabeth Winslow **Williams**[762] 22 February 1989.

9007. **Mary Stewart**[14] **Ira** (Stewart Bentley[13], Dr. Gordon Henry[12], Florence Elsie[11] **Whipple**, Cephus Galusha[10], Samuel Elijah[9], Ithamar[8], Rev. Benjamin[7], Benjamin[6], Francis[5], Jonathan[4], Joseph[3], Matthew[2], Matthew[1])[763] was born in Jacksonville, Duval Co., Fla. 3 April 1961 and married **Robert Henry Farnell II** there 19 April 1986. Robert,[764] son of Norris **Farnell** Jr. and Sarah Annette **Thomson**, was born in Jacksonville 5 February 1960.

Mary Stewart **Ira** and Robert Henry **Farnell** II had the following children born in Jacksonville:
- 9999 i. Anne Bentley[15] **Farnell**[765] 1 May 1988.
- 10000 ii. Robert Henry **Farnell** III[766] 23 October 1990.
- 10001 iii. Vann Elizabeth **Farnell**[767] 14 December 1993.

9008. **Anis Margaret**[14] **Daley** (Anis Louise[13] **Ira**, Dr. Gordon Henry[12], Florence Elsie[11] **Whipple**, Cephus Galusha[10], Samuel Elijah[9], Ithamar[8], Rev. Benjamin[7], Benjamin[6], Francis[5], Jonathan[4], Joseph[3], Matthew[2], Matthew[1])[768] was born in Jacksonville, Duval Co., Fla. 2 March 1960 and married **John Sims Rhyne Jr.** there 23 April 1983. Sims,[769] son of John Sims **Rhyne** and Doris **Jones**, was born in LaFayette, Walker Co., Ga. 19 November 1959.

Anis Margaret **Daley** and John Sims **Rhyne** Jr. had the following children born in Jacksonville:
- 10002 i. John Sims[15] **Rhyne** III[770] 12 March 1986.
- 10003 ii. Anne Clayton **Rhyne**[771] 7 August 1988.
- 10004 iii. Gordon Thomas **Rhyne**[772] 20 February 1992.

9009. **Frances Cameron**[14] **Daley** (Anis Louise[13] **Ira**, Dr. Gordon Henry[12], Florence Elsie[11] **Whipple**, Cephus Galusha[10], Samuel Elijah[9], Ithamar[8], Rev. Benjamin[7], Benjamin[6], Francis[5], Jonathan[4], Joseph[3], Matthew[2], Matthew[1])[773] was born in Jacksonville, Duval Co., Fla. 4 July 1961 and married twice. (1) **Charles William Perry Jr.** in Jacksonville 14 September 1985. Charles,[774] son of Charles William **Perry** and Mildred **Tarpley**, was born in Mobile, Mobile Co., Ala. 16 February 1951. They were divorced in Birmingham, Talladaga Co., Ala. 17 September 1992. (2)

{ G 1468 }

Aubrey Derrill Crowe in Birmingham 13 November 1993. Aubrey,[775] son of Aubrey Glen **Crowe** and Minnie Lee **Williford**, was born in Orion,[776] Ala. 29 November 1936.

Frances Cameron **Daley** and Charles William **Perry** Jr. had the following children born in Birmingham:
  10005 i. Cameron Tarpley[15] **Perry**[777] 13 October 1987.
  10006 ii. Charles William **Perry** III[778] 31 August 1989.

Frances Cameron **Daley** and Aubrey Derrill **Crowe** had the following children born in Birmingham:
  10007 iii. Carson Derrill Barnwell **Crowe**[779] 25 October 1995.
  10008 iv. Cullen Lofland Whipple **Crowe**[780] 12 March 1997.

9010. **Susan Ira**[14] **Daley** (Anis Louise[13] **Ira**, Dr. Gordon Henry[12], Florence Elsie[11] **Whipple**, Cephus Galusha[10], Samuel Elijah[9], Ithamar[8], Rev. Benjamin[7], Benjamin[6], Francis[5], Jonathan[4], Joseph[3], Matthew[2], Matthew[1])[781] was born in Jacksonville, Duval Co., Fla. 9 May 1965 and married **William Martin Hamner** there 21 July 1990. William,[782] son of William Ray **Hamner** and Janice **Kyzer**, was born in Tuscaloosa, Tuscaloosa Co., Ala. 13 August 1962.

Susan Ira **Daley** and William Martin **Hamner** had the following children:
  10009 i. Mary Annis[15] **Hamner**[783] born in Tuscaloosa 25 July 1992.
  10010 ii. Rachel Margaret **Hamner**[784] born in Tuscaloosa 28 February 1995.
  10011 iii. William Martin **Hamner** Jr.[785] born in Atlanta, Fulton Co., Ga. 25 July 1996.

9011. **Anne Barnwell**[14] **Daley** (Anis Louise[13] **Ira**, Dr. Gordon Henry[12], Florence Elsie[11] **Whipple**, Cephus Galusha[10], Samuel Elijah[9], Ithamar[8], Rev. Benjamin[7], Benjamin[6], Francis[5], Jonathan[4], Joseph[3], Matthew[2], Matthew[1])[786] was born in Jacksonville, Duval Co., Fla. 15 April 1970 and married **Curry Gary Pajcic** there 18 November 1995. Curry,[787] son of Gary Curtis **Pajcic** and Susan Ann **Winch**, was born in Tallahassee, Leon Co., Fla. 20 June 1969.

Anne Barnwell **Daley** and Curry Gary **Pajcic** had the following child born in Jacksonville:
  10012 i. Daley Anne[15] **Pajcic**[788] 14 June 1998.

9013. **Karen Elizabeth**[14] **Evans** (Mary Lou[13] **Douglas**, Naomi Grace[12] **Ira**, Florence Elsie[11] **Whipple**, Cephus Galusha[10], Samuel Elijah[9], Ithamar[8], Rev. Benjamin[7], Benjamin[6], Francis[5], Jonathan[4], Joseph[3], Matthew[2], Matthew[1])[789] was born in Lafayette, Tippecanoe Co., Ind. 30 March 1953 and married **Charles Michael Horn** in Indianapolis, Marion Co., Ind. 2 October 1981. Charles,[790] son of Donald E. **Horn** and Roberta Lu **Wise**, was born in Winchester, Randolph Co., Ind. 27 May 1954.

Karen Elizabeth **Evans** and Charles Michael **Horn** had the following children born in Indianapolis:
    10013 i.   Whitney Elizabeth[15] **Horn**[791] 30 April 1983.
    10014 ii.   Evan Michael **Horn**[792] 1 May 1985.

9015. **Rebecca Jean**[14] **Allread** (Jean Kathryn[13] **Douglas**, Naomi Grace[12] **Ira**, Florence Elsie[11] **Whipple**, Cephus Galusha[10], Samuel Elijah[9], Ithamar[8], Rev. Benjamin[7], Benjamin[6], Francis[5], Jonathan[4], Joseph[3], Matthew[2], Matthew[1])[793] was born in Laurel, Prince Georges County, Md. 6 May 1956 and married **Timothy Herrlinger** in Mariemont,[794] Okla. 31 July 1976. Timothy,[795] son of Rev. John **Herrlinger** and Doris (__), was born in Ohio 22 August 1957.

Rebecca Jean **Allread** and Timothy **Herrlinger** had the following child born in Oceanside, San Diego Co., Calif:
    10015 i.   Kr   n[15] **Herrlinger**[796] 22 October 1986.

9016. **Jenifer Lynn**[14] **Allread** (Jean Kathryn[13] **Douglas**, Naomi Grace[12] **Ira**, Florence Elsie[11] **Whipple**, Cephus Galusha[10], Samuel Elijah[9], Ithamar[8], Rev. Benjamin[7], Benjamin[6], Francis[5], Jonathan[4], Joseph[3], Matthew[2], Matthew[1])[797] was born in Cincinnati, Hamilton Co., Ohio 20 February 1959 and married **John Allen Spencer** there 17 January 1981. John,[798] son of John **Spencer** and Dorothy (__), was born in Cleveland, Cuyahoga Co., Ohio 24 December 1958. Both Jenifer and John were graduated from Miami University of Ohio at Oxford, Butler Co. She earned a degree in Education and his degree was in Business Administration.

Jenifer Lynn **Allread** and John Allen **Spencer** had the following children:
    10016 i.   John Haven[15] **Spencer**[799] born in Charlotte, Mecklenburg Co., N.C. 22 August 1984.
    10017 ii.   Jean Kathryn **Spencer**[800] born in Ft. Collins, Larimer Co., Colo. 28 January 1988.

9021. **Matthew Reyman**[14] **Douglas** (George Lynn[13], Naomi Grace[12] **Ira**, Florence Elsie[11] **Whipple**, Cephus Galusha[10], Samuel Elijah[9], Ithamar[8], Rev. Benjamin[7], Benjamin[6], Francis[5], Jonathan[4], Joseph[3], Matthew[2], Matthew[1])[801] was born in Indianapolis, Marion Co., Ind. 6 May 1958 and married **Nancy Sokolsky** in Richmond, Richmond Co., Va. 8 September 1984. Nancy, daughter of Stuart **Sokolsky** and Marilyn **Davis**, was born 29 June 1958.

Matthew Reyman **Douglas** and Nancy **Sokolsky** had the following children born in Indianapolis:

    10018   i.   Lauren Davis[15] **Douglas**[802] 5 January 1986.
    10019   ii.   Stuart William **Douglas**[803] 31 March 1990.

9025. **Kristin Sue**[14] **Whipple** (Laird Douglas[13], Marshall Lofland[12], Charles Clifford[11], Cephus Galusha[10], Samuel Elijah[9], Ithamar[8], Rev. Benjamin[7], Benjamin[6], Francis[5], Jonathan[4], Joseph[3], Matthew[2], Matthew[1])[804] was born in Del Monte, Mindanao, Philippines 11 May 1968 and married **Bryan Hilton Dale** in Walnut Creek, Contra Costa Co., Calif. 25 June 1995. He was born 8 May 1967.[805]

Kristin Sue **Whipple** and Bryan Hilton **Dale** had the following child born in Denver, Denver Co., Colo.:

    10020   i.   Tyler Robert[15] **Dale**[806] 8 February 1998.

9035. **Karen Denise**[14] **Whipple** (Grey Gordon[13], Grey Gordon[12], Charles Clifford[11], Cephus Galusha[10], Samuel Elijah[9], Ithamar[8], Rev. Benjamin[7], Benjamin[6], Francis[5], Jonathan[4], Joseph[3], Matthew[2], Matthew[1])[807] was born in Daly City, San Mateo Co., Calif. 2 September 1966. Adopted. She married **Mark Shants Orozco** in Walnut Creek, Contra Costa Co., Calif. 16 May 1987. He was born in Berkeley, Alameda Co., Calif. 7 November 1960. They were divorced 6 November 1995.

Karen Denise **Whipple** and Mark Shants **Orozco** had the following child born in Concord, Contra Costa Co., Calif.:

    10021   i.   Brian Shants[15] **Orozco**[808] 14 November 1987.

9057. **Robin**[14] **Lewis** (Leslie Claire[13] Whipple, Gregory Booth[12], Carlton Gregory[11], Cyrus Hanchett[10], Solomon[9], David[8], Rev. Benjamin[7], Benjamin[6], Francis[5], Jonathan[4], Joseph[3], Matthew[2], Matthew[1])[809] was born in Providence, Providence Co., R.I 5 December 1957 and married twice. (1) **Edward Remigio** in Honolulu, Oahu, Hawaii 21 December 1979. They were divorced in Honolulu 8 March 1981. (2) **Robert Todd**

Calaway in Beaumont, Jefferson Co., Tex. in November 1984. Robert,[810] son of Vincent **Calaway** and Patricia **Muirhead**, was born in Beaumont 31 May 1965 and died 7 March 1999 in Twenty-Nine Palms, San Bernardino Co., Calif., at 33 years of age.

Robin **Lewis** and Edward **Remigio** had the following child born in Honolulu:
    10022 i.   Jasmin Leilani[15] **Remigio**[811] 6 December 1980.

Robin **Lewis** and Robert Todd **Calaway** had the following children:
    10023 ii.   Jeramiah Vincent Gregory **Calaway**[812] born in Gretna, Jefferson Parish, La. 9 November 1985.
    10024 iii. Jade **Calaway**[813] born in Brunswick, Glynn Co., Ga. 9 September 1988.

    9066. Karen Yvonne[14] **Williams** (Janet Yvonne[13] **Potter**, Freda Grant[12] **Herrick**, Orlan Milo[11], Albert Eugene[10], Berthier H.[9], Melinda[8] **Whipple**, Moses[7], Capt. Thomas[6], Francis[5], Jonathan[4], Joseph[3], Matthew[2], Matthew[1])[814] was born in Oxford, Orange Co., N.Y. 21 December 1953 and married **Roger Conant**.

Karen Yvonne **Williams** and Roger **Conant** had the following children:
    10025 i.   Amie Lynn[15] **Conant**[815] born 9 February 1979.
    10026 ii.   Amanda Lee **Conant**[816] born 23 July 1981.
    10027 iii. Andrew Lane **Conant**[817] born 2 April 1986.
    10028 iv. Anne Leslie **Conant**[818] born 8 May 1989.

    9068. Gregg Paul[14] **Williams** (Janet Yvonne[13] **Potter**, Freda Grant[12] **Herrick**, Orlan Milo[11], Albert Eugene[10], Berthier H.[9], Melinda[8] **Whipple**, Moses[7], Capt. Thomas[6], Francis[5], Jonathan[4], Joseph[3], Matthew[2], Matthew[1])[819] was born 1 December 1958 and married **Anne M. Coloton**.

Gregg Paul **Williams** and Anne M. **Coloton** had the following children:
    10029 i.   Bryan Joseph[15] **Williams**[820] born 21 April 1989.
    10030 ii.   Kelly Lynn **Williams**[821] born 10 November 1993.

    9070. Donna Jean[14] **Williams** (Janet Yvonne[13] **Potter**, Freda Grant[12] **Herrick**, Orlan Milo[11], Albert Eugene[10], Berthier H.[9], Melinda[8] **Whipple**, Moses[7], Capt. Thomas[6], Francis[5], Jonathan[4], Joseph[3], Matthew[2], Matthew[1])[822] was born 12 April 1962 and married **Gary W. Friot**.

Donna Jean **Williams** and Gary W. **Friot** had the following children:
- 10031 i. Rebecca Anne[15] **Friot**[823] born 17 August 1985.
- 10032 ii. Suzanna Marie **Friot**[824] born 2 October 1990.
- 10033 iii. Alicia Jean **Friot**[825] born 10 March 1992.

9071. **Sheli Ann**[14] **Williams** (Janet Yvonne[13] **Potter**, Freda Grant[12] **Herrick**, Orlan Milo[11], Albert Eugene[10], Berthier H.[9], Melinda[8] **Whipple**, Moses[7], Capt. Thomas[6], Francis[5], Jonathan[4], Joseph[3], Matthew[2], Matthew[1])[826] was born in Massena, St. Lawrence Co., N.Y. 12 September 1966 and married **Alonzo Wayne Ellison**.

Sheli Ann **Williams** and Alonzo Wayne **Ellison** had the following children:
- 10034 i. Alonzo Jordan[15] **Ellison**[827] born 1 February 1987.
- 10035 ii. Benjamin Douglas **Ellison**[828] born 30 May 1989.

9076. **Laverna Ann**[14] **Reinhold** (Lois Irene[13] **Perkins**, Glenn Alonzo[12], Manson Burdell[11], Marissa Parmelia[10] **Dean**, Martha Putnam[9] **Whipple**, Duick[8], Charles[7], Francis[6], Francis[5], Jonathan[4], Joseph[3], Matthew[2], Matthew[1])[829] was born in Parma Center, Monroe Co., N.Y. 15 August 1932 and married **Donald George Phillips** in North Chili, Monroe Co., N.Y. He was born in Niagara Falls, Niagara Co., N.Y. 13 September 1931.[830]

Laverna Ann **Reinhold** and Donald George **Phillips** had the following children:
- 10036 i. Keith Allen[15] **Phillips**[831] was born in Rochester, Monroe Co., N.Y. 25 May 1956.
- + 10037 ii. Kathy Ann **Phillips** born 18 March 1958.

9077. **Victor Eugene**[14] **Reinhold** (Lois Irene[13] **Perkins**, Glenn Alonzo[12], Manson Burdell[11], Marissa Parmelia[10] **Dean**, Martha Putnam[9] **Whipple**, Duick[8], Charles[7], Francis[6], Francis[5], Jonathan[4], Joseph[3], Matthew[2], Matthew[1])[832] was born in Orelan, Jefferson Co., N.Y. 8 September 1933 and married twice. (1) **Mary Lorraine Kunkle** in Blairsville, Indiana Co., Penn. 18 August 1957. (2) **Eunice Michaels**. She was born in Jamestown, Chautauqua Co., N.Y. 24 May 1961.[833]

Victor Eugene **Reinhold** and Mary Lorraine **Kunkle** had the following children:
- + 10038 i. Victor Eugene[15] **Reinhold** born 4 April 1958.
- 10039 ii. Lavern **Reinhold**[834] born in Rochester, Monroe Co., N.Y. 22 August 1960.

Victor Eugene **Reinhold** and Eunice **Michaels** had the following child born in Hamburg, Greene Co., N.Y.:

    10040 iii.   Joshua **Reinhold**[835] 7 June 1994.

9078. **Faith Lee**[14] **Reinhold** (Lois Irene[13] **Perkins**, Glenn Alonzo[12], Manson Burdell[11], Marissa Parmelia[10] **Dean**, Martha Putnam[9] **Whipple**, Duick[8], Charles[7], Francis[6], Francis[5], Jonathan[4], Joseph[3], Matthew[2], Matthew[1])[836] was born 3 February 1939 and married **John Cronin**.

Faith Lee **Reinhold** and John **Cronin** had the following children:
    10041 i.   Chris[15] **Cronin**[837] born in Reno, Washoe Co., Nev. 2 August 1961.
    10042 ii.   Lavern **Cronin**[838] born in Rochester, Monroe Co., N.Y. 18 July 1962.

9079. **Edward John**[14] **Reinhold** (Lois Irene[13] **Perkins**, Glenn Alonzo[12], Manson Burdell[11], Marissa Parmelia[10] **Dean**, Martha Putnam[9] **Whipple**, Duick[8], Charles[7], Francis[6], Francis[5], Jonathan[4], Joseph[3], Matthew[2], Matthew[1])[839] was born 5 May 1940 and married **Dona Marie Berle** in Rochester, Monroe Co., N.Y. 10 May 1963. Dona,[840] daughter of Donald J. **Berle** and Marie Elaine **Carle**, was born in Churchville, Monroe Co., N.Y. 17 February 1942. She earned degrees as a Registered Nurse, Bachelor of Science, and Master of Science. John earned the Bachelor of Arts degree from Roberts Wesleyan College, Rochester, Master of Science and Doctor of Philosophy degrees from American Institute, Birmingham, Talladage Co., Alabama and Doctor of Divinity degree from International School of Theology, Fontana, San Bernadino Co., California. He is Founder and Chief Executive Officer of Christian Care Ministry & Medi-Share Program operating in 50 states and 55 foreign nations. They are headquartered in Melbourne, Brevard Co., Fla. (1998). He was formerly Vice President of two insurance companies and a Marketing Director of Eastman Kodak Co. in Rochester, Monroe Co., N.Y.

Edward John **Reinhold** and Dona Marie **Berle** had the following children:
  + 10043 i.   Eric John[15] **Reinhold** born 28 October 1964.
  + 10044 ii.   Baron Vaughn **Reinhold** born 27 October 1966.
    10045 iii.   Kerstin Berle **Reinhold**[841] born in Fort Worth, Tarrant Co., Tex. 12 August 1969.
    10046 iv.   Edward John **Reinhold** III[842] born in Miami, Dade Co., Fla. 27 April 1978.

9100. **Dale**[14] **Broughear** (June Marie[13] Powers, Edward Nichols[12], Luva Marion[11] Nichols, Bertrand Fayette[10], Catherine[9] Whipple, Joel[8], Edmund Rice[7], Jonathan[6], Edwards[5], Jonathan[4], Joseph[3], Matthew[2], Matthew[1])[843] was born 12 May 1970.

Dale **Broughear** and Diane **Dibble** had the following children born in Las Vegas, Clark Co., Nev.:
    10047 i.   Jeffrey[15] **Dibble**[844] 3 October 1991.
    10048 ii.   Jessica **Dibble**[845] in December 1996.

9129. **Rock Lee**[14] **Sadler** (Leon Earl[13], Leon Delbert[12], Lillian Alice[11] **Bess**, Lillian Belle[10] **Whipple**, Charles H.[9], Solomon[8], Russell[7], Solomon[6], Joseph[5], John[4], Joseph[3], Matthew[2], Matthew[1])[846] was born in Augusta, Kennebec Co., Maine 29 October 1959 and had the following child:
    10049 i.   Renee Louise[15] **Sadler**[847] born 27 September 1992.

9130. **Cheryle Lorilee**[14] **Sadler** (Leon Earl[13], Leon Delbert[12], Lillian Alice[11] **Bess**, Lillian Belle[10] **Whipple**, Charles H.[9], Solomon[8], Russell[7], Solomon[6], Joseph[5], John[4], Joseph[3], Matthew[2], Matthew[1])[848] was born in Gardiner, Kennebec Co., Maine 1 June 1963 and married **Raymond Robert Goodsell** in Friendship, Allegany Co., N.Y. 12 June 1982. Raymond is the son of Robert **Goodsell** and Barbara **Wallace**.[849]

Cheryle Lorilee **Sadler** and Raymond Robert **Goodsell** had the following children:
    10050 i.   Adam James[15] **Goodsell**[850] born 14 June 1982.
    10051 ii.   Kelly Elizabeth **Goodsell**[851] born 2 November 1983.

9131. **James Norman**[14] **Sadler** (Leon Earl[13], Leon Delbert[12], Lillian Alice[11] **Bess**, Lillian Belle[10] **Whipple**, Charles H.[9], Solomon[8], Russell[7], Solomon[6], Joseph[5], John[4], Joseph[3], Matthew[2], Matthew[1])[852] was born in Wellsville, Allegany Co., N.Y. 15 August 1964 and married **Joni Estelle Shelly** in Friendship, Allegany Co., N.Y. 20 October 1984. Joni is the daughter of Robert **Shelly** and Joyce **Clark**.[853]

James Norman **Sadler** and Joni Estelle **Shelly** had the following children:
    10052 i.   Lydia Joyce[15] **Sadler**[854] born 13 August 1985.
    10053 ii.   Samuel Mason **Sadler**[855] born 18 January 1987.

9132. **Lee Michael**[14] **Sadler** (Leon Earl[13], Leon Delbert[12], Lillian Alice[11] **Bess**, Lillian Belle[10] **Whipple**, Charles H.[9], Solomon[8], Russell[7], Solomon[6], Joseph[5], John[4], Joseph[3], Matthew[2], Matthew[1])[856] was born in

Wellsville, Allegany Co., N.Y. 18 August 1965 and married **Heidi Lynn Baldwin** in Friendship, Allegany Co., N.Y. 25 May 1991. Heidi is the daughter of John **Baldwin** and Theresa **Ayers**.[857]

Lee Michael **Sadler** and Heidi Lynn **Baldwin** had the following children:
    10054 i.   Lee Mitchell[15] **Sadler**[858] born 25 November 1992.
    10055 ii.   Kyle Wesley **Sadler**[859] born 7 December 1994.

9133. **Melanie Frances**[14] **Sadler** (Leon Earl[13], Leon Delbert[12], Lillian Alice[11] **Bess**, Lillian Belle[10] **Whipple**, Charles H.[9], Solomon[8], Russell[7], Solomon[6], Joseph[5], John[4], Joseph[3], Matthew[2], Matthew[1])[860] was born in Wellsville, Allegany Co., N.Y. 7 April 1969 and married **Eric Charles Avery** in Friendship, Allegany Co., N.Y. 18 June 1988. Eric is the son of Kenneth **Avery** and Mildred **Lee**.[861]

Melanie Frances **Sadler** and Eric Charles **Avery** had the following children:
    10056 i.   Amanda Lynn[15] **Avery**[862] born 7 July 1988.
    10057 ii.   April Dawn **Avery**[863] born 23 August 1989.
    10058 iii. Deric Charles **Avery**[864] born 15 March 1991.
    10059 iv. Joshua David **Avery**[865] born 9 September 1994.

9136. **Randall Raymond**[14] **Greene** (Shirley May[13] **Sadler**, Lloyd Allen[12], Lillian Alice[11] **Bess**, Lillian Belle[10] **Whipple**, Charles H.[9], Solomon[8], Russell[7], Solomon[6], Joseph[5], John[4], Joseph[3], Matthew[2], Matthew[1])[866] was born 9 January 1959 and married **Anna Mae (__)** in Florida, abt 1988.

Randall Raymond **Greene** and Anna Mae (__) had the following children:
    10060 i.   Joshua[15] **Greene**[867] born 15 July 1989.
    10061 ii.   Joel **Greene**[868] born 25 July 1992.

9137. **Michelle Louise**[14] **Greene** (Shirley May[13] **Sadler**, Lloyd Allen[12], Lillian Alice[11] **Bess**, Lillian Belle[10] **Whipple**, Charles H.[9], Solomon[8], Russell[7], Solomon[6], Joseph[5], John[4], Joseph[3], Matthew[2], Matthew[1])[869] was born in Cuba, Allegany Co., N.Y. 27 September 1974 and married **Frank Raymond** in Florida in December 1991.

Michelle Louise **Greene** and Frank **Raymond** had the following children born in Florida:
    10062 i.   Frank[15] **Raymond**[870] 27 July 1992.
    10063 ii.   Matthew **Raymond**[871] 5 February 1996.
    10064 iii. Amanda Ann **Raymond**[872] 28 July 1998.

9146. **Charity Patricia**[14] **Sadler** (Lloyd Davis[13], Lloyd Allen[12], Lillian Alice[11] **Bess**, Lillian Belle[10] **Whipple**, Charles H.[9], Solomon[8], Russell[7], Solomon[6], Joseph[5], John[4], Joseph[3], Matthew[2], Matthew[1])[873] was born 18 September 1975 and had the following child:

    10065   i.   Skylar Grant[15] **Sadler**[874] born in Webster, Harris Co., Tex. 22 November 1996.

9179. **Jennifer Deanne**[14] **McIntyre** (James Herbert[13], Gladys Gertrude[12] **Sadler**, Lillian Alice[11] **Bess**, Lillian Belle[10] **Whipple**, Charles H.[9], Solomon[8], Russell[7], Solomon[6], Joseph[5], John[4], Joseph[3], Matthew[2], Matthew[1])[875] was born in Houston, Harris Co., Tex. 13 June 1971 and married **Sonny Britton** in Anahuac, Chambers Co., Tex.

Jennifer Deanne **McIntyre** and Sonny **Britton** had the following child:

    10066   i.   Chelsea[15] **Britton**.[876]

9181. **Carolyn Ann**[14] **McIntyre** (Gary Dwayne[13], Gladys Gertrude[12] **Sadler**, Lillian Alice[11] **Bess**, Lillian Belle[10] **Whipple**, Charles H.[9], Solomon[8], Russell[7], Solomon[6], Joseph[5], John[4], Joseph[3], Matthew[2], Matthew[1])[877] was born in Pasadena, Harris Co., Tex. 28 October 1971 and married **Douglas E. Biddy** in Houston, Harris Co., Tex. 3 January 1998.

Carolyn Ann **McIntyre** had the following child:

    10067   i.   Wendi Nicole[15] **McIntyre**[878] born 20 January 1990.

9182. **Kelly Joanne**[14] **McIntyre** (Gary Dwayne[13], Gladys Gertrude[12] **Sadler**, Lillian Alice[11] **Bess**, Lillian Belle[10] **Whipple**, Charles H.[9], Solomon[8], Russell[7], Solomon[6], Joseph[5], John[4], Joseph[3], Matthew[2], Matthew[1])[879] was born 3 October 1974 and had the following child:

    10068   i.   Christopher Rei[15] **McIntyre**[880] born in Olean, Jefferson Co., N.Y. 11 June 1998.

9187. **Holly Johnnell**[14] **McIntyre** (John Lee[13], Gladys Gertrude[12] **Sadler**, Lillian Alice[11] **Bess**, Lillian Belle[10] **Whipple**, Charles H.[9], Solomon[8], Russell[7], Solomon[6], Joseph[5], John[4], Joseph[3], Matthew[2], Matthew[1])[881] was born 18 December 1975.

Holly Johnnell **McIntyre** and David **Allen** had the following child:

    10069   i.   Jacob Charles[15] **Allen**[882] born in Clear Lake City, Harris Co., Tex. 31 October 1998.

9189. **Janet Lee**[14] **Scott** (Carol Ann[13] **McIntyre**, Gladys Gertrude[12] **Sadler**, Lillian Alice[11] **Bess**, Lillian Belle[10] **Whipple**, Charles H.[9], Solomon[8], Russell[7], Solomon[6], Joseph[5], John[4], Joseph[3], Matthew[2], Matthew[1])[883] was born in Pasadena, Harris Co., Tex. 2 August 1967.

Janet Lee **Scott** and Gregory Lee **Farris** had the following children:
    10070 i.   Daniel Aaron[15] **Farris**[884] born 25 October 1989.
    10071 ii. Brittney Lee **Farris**[885] born 23 October 1993.

9194. **Elizabeth Lynn**[14] **Brewer** (Gretchen Elizabeth[13] **Sadler**, Kenneth Paul[12], Lillian Alice[11] **Bess**, Lillian Belle[10] **Whipple**, Charles H.[9], Solomon[8], Russell[7], Solomon[6], Joseph[5], John[4], Joseph[3], Matthew[2], Matthew[1])[886] was born in Cuba, Allegany Co., N.Y. 10 January 1976.

Elizabeth Lynn **Brewer** and Jason **Ciazzia** had the following child born in Wellsville, Allegany Co., N.Y.:
    10072 i.   Christopher Alan[15] **Brewer**[887] 5 October 1993.

Elizabeth Lynn **Brewer** and Clayton **Hulin** had the following children born in Wellsville:
    10073 ii. Alexander David **Hulin**[888] 10 August 1994.
    10074 iii. Amelia Elizabeth **Hulin**[889] 6 November 1998.

9214. **Laurie**[14] **Redington** (Tim[13], Ray[12], Mary Elizabeth[11] **Smith**, Ruby Sophronia[10] **Whipple**, William[9], Ira Martin[8], Elijah[7], Jeremiah[6], Joseph[5], John[4], Joseph[3], Matthew[2], Matthew[1])[890] birth date unknown, had the following children:
    10075 i.   Justin[15] **Redington**.[891]
    10076 ii. Wyatt **Redington**.[892]

9223. **Robert Michael**[14] **Trimmell** (Jack Reed[13], Edna Pearl[12] **Sproat**, Mary Elizabeth[11] **Smith**, Ruby Sophronia[10] **Whipple**, William[9], Ira Martin[8], Elijah[7], Jeremiah[6], Joseph[5], John[4], Joseph[3], Matthew[2], Matthew[1])[893] birth date unknown, had the following children:
    10077 i.   Jerry Lee[15] **Trimmell**.[894]
    10078 ii. Lacy Rene **Trimmell**.[895]

9224. **Steven Riley**[14] **Trimmell** (Jack Reed[13], Edna Pearl[12] **Sproat**, Mary Elizabeth[11] **Smith**, Ruby Sophronia[10] **Whipple**, William[9], Ira Martin[8], Elijah[7], Jeremiah[6], Joseph[5], John[4], Joseph[3], Matthew[2], Matthew[1])[896] birth date unknown, married **April Jean**.

Steven Riley **Trimmell** and April **Jean** had the following children:
- 10079 i. Jason Thomas[15] **Trimmell**.[897]
- 10080 ii. Andrew Louis **Trimmell**.[898]
- 10081 iii. Steven Joseph **Trimmell**[899]
- 10082 iv. Tammy **Trimmell**[900] born 20 April 1977 and married (__) **Arnold.**

9225. **Daryl Andrew**[14] **Trimmell** (Jack Reed[13], Edna Pearl[12] **Sproat**, Mary Elizabeth[11] **Smith**, Ruby Sophronia[10] **Whipple**, William[9], Ira Martin[8], Elijah[7], Jeremiah[6], Joseph[5], John[4], Joseph[3], Matthew[2], Matthew[1])[901] was born 12 April 1951 and died in July 1982 in Wichita, Sedgwick Co., Kans., at 31 years of age. He served in the Vietnam War.

Daryl Andrew **Trimmell** had the following children:
- 10083 i. Jennie[15] **Trimmell**[902] born in Upper Darby, Delaware Co., Penn.
- 10084 ii. Aimee **Trimmell**.[903]

9226. **Jack Gregory**[14] **Trimmell Sr**. (Jack Reed[13], Edna Pearl[12] **Sproat**, Mary Elizabeth[11] **Smith**, Ruby Sophronia[10] **Whipple**, William[9], Ira Martin[8], Elijah[7], Jeremiah[6], Joseph[5], John[4], Joseph[3], Matthew[2], Matthew[1])[904] was born 19 February 1955 and married **Rebecca Sue Shellabarger** in Wichita, Sedgwick Co., Kans. 19 September 1975. Rebecca,[905] daughter of Carl **Shellabarger** and Myrtle **Busch**, was born in Shirley, Van Buren Co., Ark. 8 January 1958.

Jack Gregory **Trimmell** Sr and Rebecca Sue **Shellabarger** had the following children born in Wichita:
- \+ 10085 i. Candy Ann[15] **Trimmell** 29 October 1975.
- 10086 ii. Holly Marie **Trimmell**[906] 16 April 1980.
- 10087 iii. Jack Gregory **Trimmell**[907] 5 October 1982.
- 10088 iv. Terence Nicholas **Trimmell**[908] 21 July 1987.
- 10089 v. Dawn Noel **Trimmell**[909] 26 November 1994.
- 10090 vi. Nicholas Reed **Trimmell**[910] 7 December 1999.

9227. **Brian Lewis**[14] **Trimmell** (Jack Reed[13], Edna Pearl[12] **Sproat**, Mary Elizabeth[11] **Smith**, Ruby Sophronia[10] **Whipple**, William[9], Ira Martin[8], Elijah[7], Jeremiah[6], Joseph[5], John[4], Joseph[3], Matthew[2], Matthew[1])[911] was born in Wichita, Sedgwick Co., Kans. 9 August 1956 and married **Tamala Sue Penny** there 29 December 1975. She was born 13 May 1958.[912]

Brian Lewis **Trimmell** and Tamala Sue **Penny** had the following children born in Wichita:
    10091 i. Chris James[15] **Trimmell**[913] 29 October 1976.
    10092 ii. Michael Lewis **Trimmell**[914] 5 February 1979.
    10093 iii. Aimee Michelle **Trimmell**[915] 6 October 1981.

9228. **Wayne Alan**[14] **Trimmell** (Harold Riley[13], Edna Pearl[12] **Sproat**, Mary Elizabeth[11] **Smith**, Ruby Sophronia[10] **Whipple**, William[9], Ira Martin[8], Elijah[7], Jeremiah[6], Joseph[5], John[4], Joseph[3], Matthew[2], Matthew[1])[916] was born in Wichita, Sedgwick Co., Kans. 23 October 1956 and married twice. (1) **Alicia Lindscott** there 10 December 1983. (2) **Catherine Ann Hindle** 22 May 1992. She was born 4 January 1953.[917]

Wayne Alan **Trimmell** and Alicia **Lindscott** had the following children:
    10094 i. Robert Johnson[15] **Trimmell**[918] born 12 March 1982.
    10095 ii. Jessica **Trimmell**[919] born 3 June 1984.
    10096 iii. Wayne **Trimmell**[920] born 5 June 1985.

9230. **Diane Janel**[14] **Trimmell** (Harold Riley[13], Edna Pearl[12] **Sproat**, Mary Elizabeth[11] **Smith**, Ruby Sophronia[10] **Whipple**, William[9], Ira Martin[8], Elijah[7], Jeremiah[6], Joseph[5], John[4], Joseph[3], Matthew[2], Matthew[1])[921] was born in Little Falls, Morrison Co., Minn. 19 January 1960 and married **Larry Eugene Loveall**.

Diane Janel **Trimmell** and Larry Eugene **Loveall** had the following child:
    + 10097 i. Shawn[15] **Loveall**.

9232. **Ronald Dean**[14] **Trimmell** (Harold Riley[13], Edna Pearl[12] **Sproat**, Mary Elizabeth[11] **Smith**, Ruby Sophronia[10] **Whipple**, William[9], Ira Martin[8], Elijah[7], Jeremiah[6], Joseph[5], John[4], Joseph[3], Matthew[2], Matthew[1])[922] was born in Little Falls, Morrison Co., Minn. 19 June 1964 and married twice. (1) **Michelle (__)**. (2) **Dawna (__)**.

Ronald Dean **Trimmell** and Michelle (__) had the following child:
    10098 i. Rachel[15] **Trimmell**[923] born in 1987.

Ronald Dean **Trimmell** and Dawna (__) had the following child:
    10099 ii. Randy **Trimmell**[924] born in 1992.

9235. **D. H.**[14] **Cheney** (Dorothy Margaret[13] **Trimmell**, Edna Pearl[12] **Sproat**, Mary Elizabeth[11] **Smith**, Ruby Sophronia[10] **Whipple**, William[9], Ira Martin[8], Elijah[7], Jeremiah[6], Joseph[5], John[4], Joseph[3], Matthew[2], Matthew[1])[925] was born in Wichita, Sedgwick Co., Kans in 1954 and married **Candice Cozad**.

D. H. **Cheney** and Candice **Cozad** had the following children:
    10100 i.   Ryan James[15] **Cheney**[926] born in 1980.
    10101 ii.   Lindsay Susan **Cheney**[927] born in 1982.

9236. **Joseph Leonard**[14] **Trimmell** (Joseph Donald[13], Edna Pearl[12] **Sproat**, Mary Elizabeth[11] **Smith**, Ruby Sophronia[10] **Whipple**, William[9], Ira Martin[8], Elijah[7], Jeremiah[6], Joseph[5], John[4], Joseph[3], Matthew[2], Matthew[1])[928] was born in Lynnwood, Los Angeles Co., Calif. 25 November 1956 and married twice. (1) **Cynthia Mary Bosar** in Wichita, Sedgwick Co., Kans. 13 May 1976. (2) **Kelly Louise Klugh** in Honolulu, Oahu, Hawaii 7 January 1995.

Joseph Leonard **Trimmell** and Cynthia Mary **Bosar** had the following children:
+   10102 i.   Michael Leonard Anthony[15] **Trimmell** born 10 March 1976.
    10103 ii.   Derrick Anthony Joseph **Trimmell**[929] born in Heidleburg, Germany 26 October 1978 and married Rachel **Montano** in Marysville, Yuba Co., Calif. 20 November 1999.
    10104 iii. Sarah Marie Elizabeth **Trimmell**[930] born 18 April 1983.

9238. **Theresa Yvonne**[14] **Trimmell** (Joseph Donald[13], Edna Pearl[12] **Sproat**, Mary Elizabeth[11] **Smith**, Ruby Sophronia[10] **Whipple**, William[9], Ira Martin[8], Elijah[7], Jeremiah[6], Joseph[5], John[4], Joseph[3], Matthew[2], Matthew[1])[931] was born in Las Vegas, Clark Co., Nev. 1 November 1960 and married twice. (1) **Danny Birmingham** bef 1980. (2) **Jim Brooks** bef 1983.

Theresa Yvonne **Trimmell** and Danny **Birmingham** had the following child:
+   10105 i.   Catherine Virginia Rosa[15] **Trimmell** born in 1980.

Theresa Yvonne **Trimmell** and Jim **Brooks** had the following child:
    10106 ii.   Cory Lee **Brooks**[932] born in 1983.

9239. **Jerome Anthony**[14] **Trimmell** (Joseph Donald[13], Edna Pearl[12] **Sproat**, Mary Elizabeth[11] **Smith**, Ruby Sophronia[10] **Whipple**, William[9], Ira Martin[8], Elijah[7], Jeremiah[6], Joseph[5], John[4], Joseph[3], Matthew[2],

Matthew[1])[933] was born in Compton, Los Angeles Co., Calif. 21 November 1961 and married **Cindy Hays** in Wichita, Sedgwick Co., Kans. 5 August 1993.

Jerome Anthony **Trimmell** and Cindy **Hays** had the following children:
    10107 i.   Isaac Taylor[15] **Trimmell**[934] born 5 August 1993.
    10108 ii.   Dillon Garrett **Trimmell**[935] born 1 September 1999.

9242. **Debbie**[14] **Moore** (Mary Lynn[13] **Trimmell**, Edna Pearl[12] **Sproat**, Mary Elizabeth[11] **Smith**, Ruby Sophronia[10] **Whipple**, William[9], Ira Martin[8], Elijah[7], Jeremiah[6], Joseph[5], John[4], Joseph[3], Matthew[2], Matthew[1])[936] was born 15 August 1958 and married **Bob Hill**.
Debbie **Moore** and Bob **Hill** had the following children:
    10109 i.   Ami[15] **Hill**.[937]
    10110 ii.   Andrew **Hill**.[938]

9244. **Doug**[14] **Moore** (Mary Lynn[13] **Trimmell**, Edna Pearl[12] **Sproat**, Mary Elizabeth[11] **Smith**, Ruby Sophronia[10] **Whipple**, William[9], Ira Martin[8], Elijah[7], Jeremiah[6], Joseph[5], John[4], Joseph[3], Matthew[2], Matthew[1])[939] was born 3 June 1964 and married **Marci (__)**.

Doug **Moore** and Marci (__) had the following children:
    10111 i.   Ashli[15] **Moore**.[940]
    10112 ii.   Cody **Moore**.[941]
    10113 iii. Briana **Moore**.[942]

9245. **Molly Jane**[14] **Floyd** (Younda Dee[13] **Trimmell**, Edna Pearl[12] **Sproat**, Mary Elizabeth[11] **Smith**, Ruby Sophronia[10] **Whipple**, William[9], Ira Martin[8], Elijah[7], Jeremiah[6], Joseph[5], John[4], Joseph[3], Matthew[2], Matthew[1])[943] was born in Wichita, Sedgwick Co., Kans. 8 November 1959 and married **John Jefferson Johnson**. John,[944] son of William **Johnson** and Janyce **Crews**, was born 2 March 1961.

Molly Jane **Floyd** and John Jefferson **Johnson** had the following children:
    10114 i.   Lori Elizabeth[15] **Johnson**[945] born 10 September 1984.
    10115 ii.   Sara Nichole **Johnson**[946] born 1 February 1988.
    10116 iii. Julie Kathleen **Johnson**[947] born 17 September 1991.

9250. **Darryl Wayne**[14] **Trimmell** (Maurice Wayne[13], Edna Pearl[12] **Sproat**, Mary Elizabeth[11] **Smith**, Ruby Sophronia[10] **Whipple**, William[9], Ira Martin[8], Elijah[7], Jeremiah[6], Joseph[5], John[4], Joseph[3], Matthew[2], Matthew[1])[948] was born 25 June 1965 and married **Vanessa (__)**.

Darryl Wayne **Trimmell** and Vanessa **(__)** had the following children:
    10117   i.   Noah[15] **Trimmell**[949] born 17 March 1997.
    10118   ii. Abram **Trimmell**[950] born 18 May 1998.

9251. **William Edward**[14] **Trimmell** (Maurice Wayne[13], Edna Pearl[12] **Sproat**, Mary Elizabeth[11] **Smith**, Ruby Sophronia[10] **Whipple**, William[9], Ira Martin[8], Elijah[7], Jeremiah[6], Joseph[5], John[4], Joseph[3], Matthew[2], Matthew[1])[951] was born in San Francisco Co., Calif. 31 January 1969 and married **Shawna Lynell Gorham**. Shawna is the daughter of Glenn **Gorham** and Wilma **(__)**.[952]

William Edward **Trimmell** and Shawna Lynell **Gorham** had the following children born in Wichita, Sedgwick Co., Kans.:
    10119   i.   William Luc-David[15] **Trimmell**[953] 26 April 2000.
    10120   ii. Mychaella Faythe Maree **Trimmell**[954] 3 November 2001.

9259. **Michael**[14] **Murphy** (Doyle A.[13], Mildred Elizabeth[12] **Sproat**, Mary Elizabeth[11] **Smith**, Ruby Sophronia[10] **Whipple**, William[9], Ira Martin[8], Elijah[7], Jeremiah[6], Joseph[5], John[4], Joseph[3], Matthew[2], Matthew[1])[955] was born in Wichita, Sedgwick Co., Kans. 12 June 1953 and married **Debra Dehnert** 24 April 1976.

Michael **Murphy** and Debra **Dehnert** had the following children:
    10121   i.   Spencer James[15] **Murphy**[956] born 15 August 1995.
    10122   ii. Dylan Jeffry **Murphy**[957] born 12 February 1999.

9262. **Karla Denise**[14] **Ramsey** (Donna Louise[13] **Murphy**, Mildred Elizabeth[12] **Sproat**, Mary Elizabeth[11] **Smith**, Ruby Sophronia[10] **Whipple**, William[9], Ira Martin[8], Elijah[7], Jeremiah[6], Joseph[5], John[4], Joseph[3], Matthew[2], Matthew[1])[958] was born in Jackson, Hinds Co., Miss. 19 July 1956 and married **Robert L. McLain** 14 April 1979. He was born 15 December 1947.[959]

Karla Denise **Ramsey** and Robert L. **McLain** had the following child born in Dallas, Dallas Co., Tex.:
    10123   i.   Stefani[15] **McLain**[960] 4 May 1981.

9263. **Carol Ann**[14] **Ramsey** (Donna Louise[13] **Murphy**, Mildred Elizabeth[12] **Sproat**, Mary Elizabeth[11] **Smith**, Ruby Sophronia[10] **Whipple**, William[9], Ira Martin[8], Elijah[7], Jeremiah[6], Joseph[5], John[4], Joseph[3], Matthew[2], Matthew[1])[961] was born in Jackson, Hinds Co., Miss. 3 December 1960 and married **Donald Kirk** 7 June 1980.

Carol Ann **Ramsey** and Donald **Kirk** had the following children born in Dallas, Tex.:
    10124   i.   Kaitlin Janelle[15] **Kirk**[962] 14 February 1990.
    10125   ii.   Kacey Madison **Kirk**[963] 9 March 1995.

9264. **Karen Ruth**[14] **Ramsey** (Donna Louise[13] **Murphy**, Mildred Elizabeth[12] **Sproat**, Mary Elizabeth[11] **Smith**, Ruby Sophronia[10] **Whipple**, William[9], Ira Martin[8], Elijah[7], Jeremiah[6], Joseph[5], John[4], Joseph[3], Matthew[2], Matthew[1])[964] was born in Jackson, Hinds Co., Miss. 15 January 1965 and married **Russell Dean Stewart**. He was born 17 November 1957.[965]

Karen Ruth **Ramsey** and Russell Dean **Stewart** had the following children:
    10126   i.   Jessica Marie[15] **Stewart**[966] born in Garland, Dallas Co., Tex. 13 October 1982.
    10127   ii.   Justin Dean Alexander **Stewart**[967] born 19 September 1986.

9265. **Linda Kay**[14] **Bennett** (Kathleen[13] **Murphy**, Mildred Elizabeth[12] **Sproat**, Mary Elizabeth[11] **Smith**, Ruby Sophronia[10] **Whipple**, William[9], Ira Martin[8], Elijah[7], Jeremiah[6], Joseph[5], John[4], Joseph[3], Matthew[2], Matthew[1])[968] was born in Wichita, Sedgwick Co., Kans. 4 February 1955 and married **Jon Whitworth** there 8 February 1974.

Linda Kay **Bennett** and Jon **Whitworth** had the following child born in Wichita:
    10128   i.   Sean Bleu[15] **Whitworth**[969] 3 September 1978.

9268. **Mearl Edvin**[14] **Whillock II** (Kathleen[13] **Murphy**, Mildred Elizabeth[12] **Sproat**, Mary Elizabeth[11] **Smith**, Ruby Sophronia[10] **Whipple**, William[9], Ira Martin[8], Elijah[7], Jeremiah[6], Joseph[5], John[4], Joseph[3], Matthew[2], Matthew[1])[970] was born in Wichita, Sedgwick Co., Kans. 29 September 1962 and married three times. (1) **Rhonda Sue Irwin** 26 September 1981. (2) **Glenda Wade** 1 February 1986. (3) **Sue Wellbrock** 19 January 1990.

Mearl Edvin **Whillock** II and Glenda **Wade** had the following child born in Wichita:
    10129   i.   Derrick Robert[15] **Whillock**[971] 17 December 1986.

9269. **Debra Ann**[14] **Murphy** (Darrell Luther[13], Mildred Elizabeth[12] **Sproat**, Mary Elizabeth[11] **Smith**, Ruby Sophronia[10] **Whipple**, William[9], Ira Martin[8], Elijah[7], Jeremiah[6], Joseph[5], John[4], Joseph[3], Matthew[2], Matthew[1]) was born in Wichita, Sedgwick Co., Kans. 7 June 1958 and died there 15 February 1992, at 33 years of age. She married **Gordon MacPhail** in Wichita 25 March 1978. He was born in Wichita 6 April 1957.[972]

Debra Ann **Murphy** and Gordon **MacPhail** had the following child born in Wichita:
    10130   i.   Christopher Lee[15] **MacPhail**[973] 31 May 1984.

9271. **James Franklin**[14] **Murphy** (Darrell Luther[13], Mildred Elizabeth[12] **Sproat**, Mary Elizabeth[11] **Smith**, Ruby Sophronia[10] **Whipple**, William[9], Ira Martin[8], Elijah[7], Jeremiah[6], Joseph[5], John[4], Joseph[3], Matthew[2], Matthew[1])[974] was born in Wichita, Sedgwick Co., Kans. 4 March 1964 and married **Michelle Orman** 5 October 1986. She was born 12 April 1967.[975]

James Franklin **Murphy** and Michelle **Orman** had the following children:
    10131   i.   Heather Dawn[15] **Murphy**[976] born 20 October 1986.
    10132   ii.   Dana Renee **Murphy**[977] born 26 April 1990.

9272. **Mary Christine**[14] **Hobson** (Mary Esther[13] **Murphy**, Mildred Elizabeth[12] **Sproat**, Mary Elizabeth[11] **Smith**, Ruby Sophronia[10] **Whipple**, William[9], Ira Martin[8], Elijah[7], Jeremiah[6], Joseph[5], John[4], Joseph[3], Matthew[2], Matthew[1])[978] was born in Wichita, Sedgwick Co., Kans. 15 July 1961 and married twice. (1) **Robin Joel South** in Wichita 9 October 1981. Robin,[979] son of Frederick **South** and Carolyn **Lutschg**, was born in Kansas 4 May 1960. They were divorced in Estherville, Emmett Co., Iowa 2 October 1989. (2) **James T. Earnest Turpin** in Bullhead City, Mohave Co., Ariz. 26 November 1992. James,[980] son of Paul **Turpin** and Nancy **Leek**, was born in Sacramento, Sacramento Co., Calif. 1 May 1962. He adopted Holly Elizabeth and Jessica Lynn South.

Mary Christine **Hobson** and Robin Joel **South** had the following children:
    10133   i.   Robin Joel[15] **South** Jr.[981] born in Wichita 16 February 1982.
+   10134   ii.   Holly Elizabeth **South** born 11 December 1984.
    10135   iii.   Jessica Lynn **South**[982] born in Ft. Hood, Bell Co., Tex. 4 May 1987.

9276. **Jeanne Sue**[14] **Hobson** (Mary Esther[13] **Murphy**, Mildred Elizabeth[12] **Sproat**, Mary Elizabeth[11] **Smith**, Ruby Sophronia[10] **Whipple**, William[9], Ira Martin[8], Elijah[7], Jeremiah[6], Joseph[5], John[4], Joseph[3], Matthew[2], Matthew[1])[983] was born in Wichita, Sedgwick Co., Kans. 27 October 1967 and married **Terry Scott** in Chattanooga, Hamilton Co., Tenn. 31 December 1994. He was born in Indianapolis, Marion Co., Ind. 1 June 1953.[984]

Jeanne Sue **Hobson** and Terry **Scott** had the following children:
    10136 i.   Brian Joshua[15] **Scott**[985] born 19 July 1996.
    10137 ii.   Alena Joy **Scott**[986] born 9 September 1998.

9278. **Mark Andrew**[14] **Hobson** (Mary Esther[13] **Murphy**, Mildred Elizabeth[12] **Sproat**, Mary Elizabeth[11] **Smith**, Ruby Sophronia[10] **Whipple**, William[9], Ira Martin[8], Elijah[7], Jeremiah[6], Joseph[5], John[4], Joseph[3], Matthew[2], Matthew[1])[987] was born 19 March 1971 and had the following child born in Wichita, Sedgwick Co., Kans.:
    10138 i.   Timothy Nicolas[15] **Hobson**[988] 4 April 2000 and died the day of birth. Buried in Kennsington Cemetery, Wichita.

9279. **John Harold**[14] **Murphy II** (John Harold[13], Mildred Elizabeth[12] **Sproat**, Mary Elizabeth[11] **Smith**, Ruby Sophronia[10] **Whipple**, William[9], Ira Martin[8], Elijah[7], Jeremiah[6], Joseph[5], John[4], Joseph[3], Matthew[2], Matthew[1])[989] was born in Wichita, Sedgwick Co., Kans. 2 February 1964 and married **Laura (__)**.

John Harold **Murphy** II and Laura (_) had the following children:
    10139 i.   John Herold[15] **Murphy** III[990] born 20 March 1993.
    10140 ii.   Melanie Ann **Murphy**[991] born 9 June 1994.

9280. **Jeanette Arlene**[14] **Murphy** (John Harold[13], Mildred Elizabeth[12] **Sproat**, Mary Elizabeth[11] **Smith**, Ruby Sophronia[10] **Whipple**, William[9], Ira Martin[8], Elijah[7], Jeremiah[6], Joseph[5], John[4], Joseph[3], Matthew[2], Matthew[1])[992] was born in Wichita, Sedgwick Co., Kans. 12 December 1964 and married twice. (1) **Michael Dewayne Patterson** 7 April 1984. (2) **Christopher Schild** abt 1988.

Jeanette Arlene **Murphy** and Michael Dewayne **Patterson** had the following child:
    10141 i.   Blake Dewayne[15] **Patterson**[993] born 15 October 1984.

Jeanette Arlene **Murphy** and Christopher **Schild** had the following children:
    10142 ii.   Calvin Justin **Schild**[994] born 27 July 1989.
    10143 iii. Clinton Jordan **Schild**[995] born 1 October 1991.

9282. **Clellie Dean**[14] **Richards** (Rodney Dean[13], Everett Leander (Sproat)[12], Mary Elizabeth[11] **Smith**, Ruby Sophronia[10] **Whipple**, William[9], Ira Martin[8], Elijah[7], Jeremiah[6], Joseph[5], John[4], Joseph[3], Matthew[2], Matthew[1])[996] birth date unknown, married **Ginger Lee**.

Clellie Dean **Richards** and Ginger **Lee** had the following children:
    10144 i.   Caleb Ray[15] **Richards**.[997]
    10145 ii.   Karla Rene **Richards**.[998]
    10146 iii. Clancy Lee **Richards**.[999]

9283. **Becky Lee**[14] **Richards** (Rodney Dean[13], Everett Leander (Sproat)[12], Mary Elizabeth[11] **Smith**, Ruby Sophronia[10] **Whipple**, William[9], Ira Martin[8], Elijah[7], Jeremiah[6], Joseph[5], John[4], Joseph[3], Matthew[2], Matthew[1])[1000] birth date unknown, married **Terry Lee Gilbert**.

Becky Lee **Richards** and Terry Lee **Gilbert** had the following children:
    10147 i.   Melyssa Lee Ann[15] **Gilbert**.[1001]
    10148 ii.   Krystal Lanae **Gilbert**.[1002]

9284. **Richard Carl**[14] **Bohling** (Phyllis LaMoyne[13] **Richards**, Everett Leander (Sproat)[12], Mary Elizabeth[11] **Smith**, Ruby Sophronia[10] **Whipple**, William[9], Ira Martin[8], Elijah[7], Jeremiah[6], Joseph[5], John[4], Joseph[3], Matthew[2], Matthew[1])[1003] birth date unknown, married **Annette Robertson**.

Richard Carl **Bohling** and Annette **Robertson** had the following child:
    10149 i.   James Denver Carl[15] **Bohling**.[1004]

9286. **Lyndia Kay**[14] **Bohling** (Phyllis LaMoyne[13] **Richards**, Everett Leander (Sproat)[12], Mary Elizabeth[11] **Smith**, Ruby Sophronia[10] **Whipple**, William[9], Ira Martin[8], Elijah[7], Jeremiah[6], Joseph[5], John[4], Joseph[3], Matthew[2], Matthew[1])[1005] birth date unknown, married **William Kent Latta**.

Lyndia Kay **Bohling** and William Kent **Latta** had the following children:
    10150 i.   Tyler Remington[15] **Latta**.[1006]
    10151 ii.   Riley Hugh **Latta**.[1007]
    10152 iii. Shelby Kay **Latta**.[1008]

9287. **Leisha Rene**[14] **Bohling** (Phyllis LaMoyne[13] **Richards**, Everett Leander (Sproat)[12], Mary Elizabeth[11] **Smith**, Ruby Sophronia[10] **Whipple**, William[9], Ira Martin[8], Elijah[7], Jeremiah[6], Joseph[5], John[4], Joseph[3], Matthew[2], Matthew[1])[1009] birth date unknown, married **Todd Burden**.

Leisha Rene **Bohling** and Todd **Burden** had the following child:
    10153 i.   Kara Danae[15] **Burden**.[1010]

9296. **Heather**[14] **Redington** (Joe[13], Joe[12], Mary Elizabeth[11] **Smith**, Ruby Sophronia[10] **Whipple**, William[9], Ira Martin[8], Elijah[7], Jeremiah[6], Joseph[5], John[4], Joseph[3], Matthew[2], Matthew[1])[1011] birth date unknown, married **David Lee**.

Heather **Redington** and David **Lee** had the following child:
    10154 i.   Robert[15] **Lee**.[1012]

9316. **Richard Paul**[14] **Bonnell** (Donald Paul[13], Ethel Virginia[12] **Teague**, Arthur[11], Eunice Augusta[10] **Whipple**, William[9], Ira Martin[8], Elijah[7], Jeremiah[6], Joseph[5], John[4], Joseph[3], Matthew[2], Matthew[1])[1013] was born in San Mateo, San Mateo, Co., Calif. 7 July 1955 and married three times. (1) **Susan K. Hoagland** 17 May 1974. (2) **Pamela Colvin**. (3) **Sandra Kelly Ferreira** in Dublin, Alameda Co., Calif. 19 December 1987.

Richard Paul **Bonnell** and Susan K. **Hoagland** had the following children:
    10155 i.   Shane[15] **Bonnell**[1014] born in Orange, Orange Co., Calif. 14 October 1974.
    10156 ii.   Jason Lee **Bonnell** born in California 12 September 1975.[1015]

Richard Paul **Bonnell** and Sandra Kelly **Ferreira** had the following child:
    10157 iii.   Henry Joseph **Bonnell** born in Walnut Creek, Contra Costa Co., Calif. 22 September 1988.[1016]

9317. **Robin Linda**[14] **Bonnell** (Donald Paul[13], Ethel Virginia[12] **Teague**, Arthur[11], Eunice Augusta[10] **Whipple**, William[9], Ira Martin[8], Elijah[7], Jeremiah[6], Joseph[5], John[4], Joseph[3], Matthew[2], Matthew[1])[1017] was born in Walnut Creek, Contra Costa Co., Calif. 26 June 1957 and married **Joey Alverson** 10 June 1979.

Robin Linda **Bonnell** and Joey **Alverson** had the following children:
    10158 i.   Sonny James[15] **Alverson** born 13 November 1978.[1018]
    10159 ii.   Robert Lee William **Alverson**[1019] born in Sacramento, Sacramento Co., Calif. 16 February 1980 and died there 7 January 1984, at 3 years of age.
    10160 iii.   Daniel Ryan **Alverson** born in Sacramento 12 December 1983.[1020]

9318. **Erin Virginia**[14] **Bonnell** (Donald Paul[13], Ethel Virginia[12] **Teague**, Arthur[11], Eunice Augusta[10] **Whipple**, William[9], Ira Martin[8], Elijah[7], Jeremiah[6], Joseph[5], John[4], Joseph[3], Matthew[2], Matthew[1])[1021] was born in Oakland, Alameda Co., Calif. 28 March 1959 and married **James Leroy Selvage II** in Houston, Harris Co., Tex. 29 April 1983. James,[1022] son of James Leroy **Selvage** and Judy **Calvin**, was born in Greenville, Clearfield Co., Penn. 24 October 1958.

Erin Virginia **Bonnell** and James Leroy **Selvage** II had the following child born in Castro Valley, Alameda Co., Calif.:
  10161 i. James Leroy[15] **Selvage** III 13 January 1988.[1023]

9322. **Theodore Frederick**[14] **Mitchell** (Susan Merle[13] **Fincher**, Elsie May[12] **Teague**, Arthur[11], Eunice Augusta[10] **Whipple**, William[9], Ira Martin[8], Elijah[7], Jeremiah[6], Joseph[5], John[4], Joseph[3], Matthew[2], Matthew[1])[1024] was born in Redwood City, San Mateo Co., Calif. 24 November 1960 and married **Julie Muller** in San Francisco, San Francisco Co., Calif. 23 January 1988. Julie,[1025] daughter of Steven **Muller** and Margie **Hellman**, was born in Philadelphia, Philadelphia City Co., Penn. 2 May 1957.

Theodore Frederick **Mitchell** and Julie **Muller** had the following children born in San Francisco:
  10162 i. Matthew McLean[15] **Mitchell** 30 March 1993.[1026]
  10163 ii. Anne **Mitchell** 21 April 1995.[1027]

9323. **Tracey Ruth**[14] **Mitchell** (Susan Merle[13] **Fincher**, Elsie May[12] **Teague**, Arthur[11], Eunice Augusta[10] **Whipple**, William[9], Ira Martin[8], Elijah[7], Jeremiah[6], Joseph[5], John[4], Joseph[3], Matthew[2], Matthew[1])[1028] was born in Redwood City, San Mateo Co., Calif. 24 July 1963 and married **James William Ardwan Jr.** there 17 June 1989. He is the son of James William **Ardwan**.[1029]

Tracey Ruth **Mitchell** and James William **Ardwan** Jr. had the following child born in Redwood City:
  10164 i. Morganne Elizabeth[15] **Ardwan** 11 July 1997.[1030]

9324. **Dean Robert**[14] **Mitchell** (Susan Merle[13] **Fincher**, Elsie May[12] **Teague**, Arthur[11], Eunice Augusta[10] **Whipple**, William[9], Ira Martin[8], Elijah[7], Jeremiah[6], Joseph[5], John[4], Joseph[3], Matthew[2], Matthew[1])[1031] was born in Redwood City, San Mateo Co., Calif. 15 October 1965 and married **Sue (__)**.

Dean Robert **Mitchell** and Sue (__) had the following child:
  10165 i. Hunter Frederick[15] **Mitchell** born 5 April 1996.[1032]

{ G 1489 }

9325. **James Teague**[14] **Williamson** (Donna Jeanne[13] **Teague**, James Frederick[12], Arthur[11], Eunice Augusta[10] **Whipple**, William[9], Ira Martin[8], Elijah[7], Jeremiah[6], Joseph[5], John[4], Joseph[3], Matthew[2], Matthew[1])[1033] was born in San Mateo, San Mateo, Co., Calif. 13 December 1962 and married **Yvonne Marie Flores** in Redwood City, San Mateo Co., Calif. 27 June 1987. She is the daughter of Carlo **Flores** and Ruth **Smith**.[1034]

James Teague **Williamson** and Yvonne Marie **Flores** had the following children:
  10166 i. Eric James[15] **Williamson** born in Redwood City 9 June 1991.[1035]
  10167 ii. David Michael **Williamson** born 12 September 1996.[1036]

9332. **Laurel Denise**[14] **Miner** (Sandra Joanne[13] **Bowman**, Lawrence Francis[12], Nancy[11] **Rice**, Ellen Boise[10] **Leland**, Alonzo[9], Jasper[8], Lydia[7] **Sherman**, Mary[6] **Whipple**, Lieut. James[5], Deacon James[4], Joseph[3], Matthew[2], Matthew[1])[1037] was born 4 February 1955 and married twice. (1) **James Hays** in Medford, Jackson Co., Oreg., 21 June 1976. (2) **Patrick Hansen** in Ashland, Jackson Co., Oreg. 25 August 1985.

Laurel Denise **Miner** and James **Hays** had the following children:
  10168 i. Surya James Ellington[15] **Hays**[1038] born in Portland, Multnomah Co., Oreg. 28 August 1977.
  10169 ii. Ariel Rose Amethyst **Hays**[1039] born in Ashland 11 February 1979.

Laurel Denise **Miner** and Patrick **Hansen** had the following child born in Ashland:
  10170 iii. Chloe Lee **Hansen**[1040] 26 July 1985.

9336. **Paula Joyce**[14] **Randazzo** (Mabel Frances[13] **Corum**, Grace[12] **Treanor**, Mabel Frances[11] **Reynolds**, Helen[10] **Butterfield**, Elizabeth S.[9] **Reynolds**, Sarah W.R.[8] **Leland**, Thankful[7] **Sherman**, Mary[6] **Whipple**, Lieut. James[5], Deacon James[4], Joseph[3], Matthew[2], Matthew[1])[1041] was born in Los Angeles, Los Angeles Co., Calif. 31 October 1942 and married twice. (1) **Stephen Philip Zoccoli** in Santa Clara, Santa Clara Co., Calif. 23 January 1965. Stephen,[1042] son of Filppo **Zoccoli** and Emanuela **Cupani**, was born in New Brighton, Beaver Co., Penn. 26 March 1926. They were divorced in 1974. (2) **William P. Lewicki** in Lake Tahoe, Placer Co., Calif. 16 May 1998.

Paula Joyce **Randazzo** and Stephen Philip **Zoccoli** had the following children:
- \+ 10171 i. Philip Anthony[15] **Zoccoli** born 31 March 1966.
- \+ 10172 ii. Michael Stephen **Zoccoli** born 21 November 1967.

9347. **Elizabeth Roby**[14] **Craibe** (Roby Trent[13] **Whipple**, Rear Adm. Walter Jones[12], William[11], Lt. Col. Charles William[10], Maj. Gen. Amiel Weeks[9], David[8], David[7], James[6], Deacon Jacob[5], Deacon James[4], Joseph[3], Matthew[2], Matthew[1])[1043] birth date unknown, married **Lee Williamson** in Arnold, Calaveras Co., Calif.

Elizabeth Roby **Craibe** and Lee **Williamson** had the following child:
- 10173 i. Thomas Michael[15] **Williamson**.[1044]

9351. **Lara Beth**[14] **Whipple** (William[13], Brig. Gen. William[12], William[11], Lt. Col. Charles William[10], Maj. Gen. Amiel Weeks[9], David[8], David[7], James[6], Deacon Jacob[5], Deacon James[4], Joseph[3], Matthew[2], Matthew[1])[1045] was born in Wilmington, New Castle Co., Del. 25 December 1969 and married **James Wiest** there 18 June 1993. They were divorced in Wilmington in March 1995.

Lara Beth **Whipple** and James **Wiest** had the following child born in Wilmington:
- 10174 i. James Robert[15] **Wiest**[1046] 9 January 1994.

9357. **Christine Whipple**[14] **Freeman** (Genevieve Randolph[13] **Green**, Jane Randolph[12] **Whipple**, William[11], Lt. Col. Charles William[10], Maj. Gen. Amiel Weeks[9], David[8], David[7], James[6], Deacon Jacob[5], Deacon James[4], Joseph[3], Matthew[2], Matthew[1])[1047] was born in Summit, Union Co., N. J. 17 February 1962 and married twice. (1) **Richard Lee Hebner**. (2) **Walter D. Mack** in Penfield, Monroe Co., N.Y. 14 August 1983.[1048]

Christine Whipple **Freeman** and Walter D. **Mack** had the following children born in Rochester, Monroe Co., N. Y.:
- 10175 i. Kimberly Marie[15] **Mack**[1049] 7 August 1986.
- 10176 ii. Genevieve Randolph **Mack**[1050] 20 September 1988.

9360. **Wendy Page**[14] **Hower** (Virginia Whipple[13] **Green**, Jane Randolph[12] **Whipple**, William[11], Lt. Col. Charles William[10], Maj. Gen. Amiel Weeks[9], David[8], David[7], James[6], Deacon Jacob[5], Deacon James[4],

Joseph[3], Matthew[2], Matthew[1])[1051] was born in Ozark, Dale Co., Ala. 20 July 1967 and married **Troy Matthew Livingston** in South Thomaston, Knox Co., Maine 25 June 1994.

Wendy Page **Hower** and Troy Matthew **Livingston** had the following child born in Fairbanks, Fairbanks North Star Borough, Alaska:
    10177 i.   Dylan Todd[15] **Livingston**[1052] 25 April 1997.

9392. **Stephen Randolph**[14] **Mendivil** (Yvonne[13] **Scoggin**, Evelyn Adelle[12] **Creighton**, Minnie Grace[11] **Whipple**, Fred G.[10], Obed[9], Obed[8], Thomas[7], Col. Moses[6], Deacon Jacob[5], Deacon James[4], Joseph[3], Matthew[2], Matthew[1])[1053] was born in San Jose, Santa Clara Co., Calif. 19 July 1955 and married **Linda Kendree** in Los Gatos, Santa Clara Co., Calif. 29 May 1981. Linda,[1054] daughter of Al **Kendree** and Barbara (__), was born in San Mateo, San Mateo, Co., Calif. 4 March 1957.

Stephen Randolph **Mendivil** and Linda **Kendree** had the following children born in Los Gatos:
    10178 i.   Courtney Lynn[15] **Mendivil**[1055] 2 January 1983.
    10179 ii.   Carrie Anne **Mendivil**[1056] 29 July 1984.
    10180 iii. Anna Danielle **Mendivil**[1057] 30 October 1989.

9393. **Gary Allen**[14] **Mendivil** (Yvonne[13] **Scoggin**, Evelyn Adelle[12] **Creighton**, Minnie Grace[11] **Whipple**, Fred G.[10], Obed[9], Obed[8], Thomas[7], Col. Moses[6], Deacon Jacob[5], Deacon James[4], Joseph[3], Matthew[2], Matthew[1])[1058] was born in Castro Valley, Alameda Co., Calif. 4 December 1956 and married **Laurel Gale** in Seattle, King Co., Wash. 5 August 1983. Laurel,[1059] daughter of Jack **Gale** and Arlys (__), was born 6 December 1959.

Gary Allen **Mendivil** and Laurel **Gale** had the following children born in Juneau, Juneau Borough, Alaska:
    10181 i.   Ryan Scott[15] **Mendivil**[1060] 2 October 1990.
    10182 ii.   Davis Craig **Mendivil**[1061] 21 November 1993.

9394. **Yvette Adelle**[14] **Mendivil** (Yvonne[13] **Scoggin**, Evelyn Adelle[12] **Creighton**, Minnie Grace[11] **Whipple**, Fred G.[10], Obed[9], Obed[8], Thomas[7], Col. Moses[6], Deacon Jacob[5], Deacon James[4], Joseph[3], Matthew[2], Matthew[1])[1062] was born in Englewood, Bergen Co., N.J. 2 May 1962 and married **Scott Herbert** in Los Gatos, Santa Clara Co., Calif. 12 May 1990. Scott,[1063] son of William **Herbert** and Thelma (__), was born in San Jose, Santa Clara Co., Calif. 10 September 1963.

Yvette Adelle **Mendivil** and Scott **Herbert** had the following children:

 10183 i. Brandon Scott[15] **Herbert**[1064] born in Sacramento, Sacramento Co., Calif. 5 November 1992.

 10184 ii. Nicolan Anthony **Herbert**[1065] born in Pleasanton, Alameda Co., Calif. 16 May 1997.

9396. **Renee Adelle**[14] **Mendivil** (Yvonne[13] **Scoggin**, Evelyn Adelle[12] **Creighton**, Minnie Grace[11] **Whipple**, Fred G.[10], Obed[9], Obed[8], Thomas[7], Col. Moses[6], Deacon Jacob[5], Deacon James[4], Joseph[3], Matthew[2], Matthew[1])[1066] was born in Pittsburg, Conta Costa Co., Calif. 25 October 1969 and married **Paul Croisetiere** in Los Gatos, Santa Clara Co., Calif. 21 May 1989. Paul,[1067] son of Paul **Croisetiere** and Susan (__), was born 13 November 1958.

Renee Adelle **Mendivil** and Paul **Croisetiere** had the following children born in San Jose, Santa Clara Co., Calif.:

 10185 i. Tyler Austin[15] **Croisetiere**[1068] 21 April 1992.

 10186 ii. Emily Rachael **Croisetiere**[1069] 18 October 1993.

9420. **Graeme Gardiner**[14] **Whytlaw III** (Graeme Gardiner[13], Graeme Gardiner[12], Laura Alexander[11] **Gardiner**, Mary Powers[10] **Cooper**, Laurel[9] **Whipple**, David[8], Aaron[7], Col. Moses[6], Deacon Jacob[5], Deacon James[4], Joseph[3], Matthew[2], Matthew[1])[1070] was born 31 January 1950 and married **Susan Danker** 7 September 1974.

Graeme Gardiner **Whytlaw** III and Susan **Danker** had the following children:

 10187 i. Graeme Gardiner[15] **Whytlaw** IV[1071] born in Torrington, Litchfield Co., Conn.

 10188 ii. Amanda Grace **Whytlaw**[1072] born in Torrington 4 June 1978.

 10189 iii. Jessica Elizabeth **Whytlaw**[1073] born in Torrington 23 December 1979.

 10190 iv. Ryan Alexander Gardiner **Whytlaw**[1074] born in Torrington 17 February 1982.

 10191 v. Katherine Marie **Whytlaw**[1075] born in Ashbury Park, Monmouth Co., N.J. 12 August 1985.

9421. **Candace Terry**[14] **Whytlaw** (Graeme Gardiner[13], Graeme Gardiner[12], Laura Alexander[11] **Gardiner**, Mary Powers[10] **Cooper**, Laurel[9] **Whipple**, David[8], Aaron[7], Col. Moses[6], Deacon Jacob[5], Deacon James[4], Joseph[3], Matthew[2], Matthew[1])[1076] was born 25 April 1953 and married twice. (1) **Akira Tanaka** 28 December 1974. (2) **Jonathan Chase** 3 July 1988.

Candace Terry **Whytlaw** and Akira **Tanaka** had the following child born in Takehara, Japan.
      10192   i.   Keoko[15] **Tanaka**[1077] 28 June 1981.

    9422. **Debra Jeane**[14] **Whytlaw** (Graeme Gardiner[13], Graeme Gardiner[12], Laura Alexander[11] **Gardiner**, Mary Powers[10] **Cooper**, Laurel[9] **Whipple**, David[8], Aaron[7], Col. Moses[6], Deacon Jacob[5], Deacon James[4], Joseph[3], Matthew[2], Matthew[1])[1078] was born 19 August 1956 and married **Charles Goller** 21 July 1984.

Debra Jeane **Whytlaw** and Charles **Goller** had the following child born in Portland, Cumberland Co., Maine:
      10193   i.   Taylor Maxwell[15] **Goller**[1079] 10 September 1987.

    9485. **Kenneth Orean**[14] **Miller Jr.** (Linda May[13] **Whitley**, Virginia May[12] **Wright**, Veda May[11] **Whipple**, Aaron Mason[10], Barnabas Cooper[9], David[8], Aaron[7], Col. Moses[6], Deacon Jacob[5], Deacon James[4], Joseph[3], Matthew[2], Matthew[1])[1080] was born in Keene, Cheshire Co., N.H. 15 June 1966 and married twice. (1) **Shannon Gale Houle** in Keene 4 April 1987. Shannon,[1081] daughter of Terrence **Houle** and Gale **Laordno**, was born in Phoenix, Maricopa Co., Ariz. 30 November 1967. (2) **Angela Lynn Rouleau** in Phoenix 15 December 1989. Angela,[1082] daughter of Ronald **Rouleau** and Virginia **Clapp**, was born in Keene 12 May 1967. She was graduated from Apollo College in Phoenix on 7 May 1993 with a degree as a Medical Assistant. Kenny served in the U.S. Coast Guard as a Fireman 1987-88. He was stationed in Boston, Suffolk Co., Mass. He was graduated from the Arizona Police Academy in May 1995 and joined the Avondale, Maricopa Co., Ariz. Police Department in 1996.

Kenneth Orean **Miller** Jr. and Shannon Gale **Houle** had the following child born in Phoenix:
      10194   i.   Robert Alan[15] **Miller**[1083] 3 March 1988.

Kenneth Orean **Miller** Jr. and Angela Lynn **Rouleau** had the following children born in Phoenix:
      10195   ii.   Dana Joseph **Miller**[1084] 24 November 1989.
      10196   iii. Lauren Yvonne **Miller**[1085] 7 November 1994.

    9488. **Ronald Lyle**[14] **Prouty Jr.** (Carol Ann[13] **Wright**, Everett Whipple[12], Veda May[11] **Whipple**, Aaron Mason[10], Barnabas Cooper[9], David[8], Aaron[7], Col. Moses[6], Deacon Jacob[5], Deacon James[4], Joseph[3], Matthew[2], Matthew[1])[1086] was born 15 March 1972 and married **Jody (__)**.

Ronald Lyle **Prouty** Jr. and Jody (__) had the following children:
- 10197 i. Mikala Stephenie[15] **Prouty**[1087] born 30 June 1992.
- 10198 ii. Anthony Michael **Prouty**[1088] born 11 February 1994.

9489. **Kelly Jean**[14] **Prouty** (Carol Ann[13] **Wright**, Everett Whipple[12], Veda May[11] **Whipple**, Aaron Mason[10], Barnabas Cooper[9], David[8], Aaron[7], Col. Moses[6], Deacon Jacob[5], Deacon James[4], Joseph[3], Matthew[2], Matthew[1])[1089] was born 2 October 1970 and married **James Robarge**.

Kelly Jean **Prouty** and James **Robarge** had the following children:
- 10199 i. Gabriel[15] **Robarge**[1090] born 5 November 1989.
- 10200 ii. Ciera Marie **Robarge**[1091] born 19 August 1993.

9490. **Justine Elizabeth**[14] **Ward** (Nancy Jo[13] **Wright**, Everett Whipple[12], Veda May[11] **Whipple**, Aaron Mason[10], Barnabas Cooper[9], David[8], Aaron[7], Col. Moses[6], Deacon Jacob[5], Deacon James[4], Joseph[3], Matthew[2], Matthew[1])[1092] was born in Keene, Cheshire Co., N.H. 5 March 1971 and married **Bradley Wegner** in Louise Co., Va. 9 September 1998.[1093] He earned a degree in Economics from the U. of Virginia, Charlottesville, Charlottesville City Co. in May 1987 and a MBA from the U. of North Carolina at Chapel Hill, Orange Co., in 1991. Justine was awarded a B. A. in Psychology with high honors by the U. of Virginia in May 1996.

Justine Elizabeth **Ward** and Bradley **Wegner** had the following child born in Reston, Fairfax Co., Va.:
- 10201 i. Delia Mae[15] **Wegner**[1094] 29 March 1999.

9507. **Jason Oliver**[14] **Dennis** (Kimberly Jane[13] **Breen**, Barbara Newton[12] **Wright**, Veda May[11] **Whipple**, Aaron Mason[10], Barnabas Cooper[9], David[8], Aaron[7], Col. Moses[6], Deacon Jacob[5], Deacon James[4], Joseph[3], Matthew[2], Matthew[1])[1095] was born in Keene, Cheshire Co., N.H. 2 February 1974 and married **Amy Wilson** in Marlborough, Cheshire Co., N.H. 12 October 1996.

Jason Oliver **Dennis** and Amy **Wilson** had the following children:
- 10202 i. Paige Caitlyn[15] **Dennis**[1096] born 19 February 1996.
- 10203 ii. Chloe Morgan **Dennis**[1097] born 11 September 1998.

9508. **Jamie Olivia**[14] **Dennis** (Kimberly Jane[13] **Breen**, Barbara Newton[12] **Wright**, Veda May[11] **Whipple**, Aaron Mason[10], Barnabas Cooper[9], David[8], Aaron[7], Col. Moses[6], Deacon Jacob[5], Deacon James[4], Joseph[3],

Matthew², Matthew¹)¹⁰⁹⁸ was born in Keene, Cheshire Co., N.H. 4 December 1978 and married **Richie Castine** in West Swanzey, Cheshire Co., N.H. 24 April 1999.

Jamie Olivia **Dennis** and Richie **Castine** had the following child:
    10204 i.   Eric Michael¹⁵ **Castine**¹⁰⁹⁹ born 24 February 1996.

9509. **Heidi Ann¹⁴ Hendrickson** (Karolee May¹³ **Breen**, Barbara Newton¹² **Wright**, Veda May¹¹ **Whipple**, Aaron Mason¹⁰, Barnabas Cooper⁹, David⁸, Aaron⁷, Col. Moses⁶, Deacon Jacob⁵, Deacon James⁴, Joseph³, Matthew², Matthew¹)¹¹⁰⁰ was born in Keene, Cheshire Co., N.H. 26 February 1975 and married **Henry Wilson** 6 June 1997.

Heidi Ann **Hendrickson** and Henry **Wilson** had the following children:
    10205 i.   Robert Andrew Henrickson¹⁵ **Wilson**¹¹⁰¹ born in Keene 19 March 1995.
    10206 ii.   Remington Henry Hendrickson **Wilson**¹¹⁰² born in Keene 11 January 1997.
    10207 iii. Ranger Wayne Hendrickson **Wilson**¹¹⁰³ born in Petersboro, Hillsborough Co., N.H. 17 August 1998.

9511. **Nathan Robert¹⁴ Hendrickson** (Karolee May¹³ **Breen**, Barbara Newton¹² **Wright**, Veda May¹¹ **Whipple**, Aaron Mason¹⁰, Barnabas Cooper⁹, David⁸, Aaron⁷, Col. Moses⁶, Deacon Jacob⁵, Deacon James⁴, Joseph³, Matthew², Matthew¹)¹¹⁰⁴ was born in Keene, Cheshire Co., N.H. 5 February 1979 and married **Betty Angela Castor** 25 December 1997.

Nathan Robert **Hendrickson** and Betty Angela **Castor** had the following children:
    10208 i.   Yanna Lynn¹⁵ **Hendrickson**¹¹⁰⁵ born in Keene 29 December 1996.
    10209 ii.   Raven Sierra **Hendrickson**¹¹⁰⁶ born 3 December 1998.

9516. **Jenie Beth¹⁴ Stone** (Jaclyn¹³ **Wright**, Charles Burgum¹², Veda May¹¹ **Whipple**, Aaron Mason¹⁰, Barnabas Cooper⁹, David⁸, Aaron⁷, Col. Moses⁶, Deacon Jacob⁵, Deacon James⁴, Joseph³, Matthew², Matthew¹)¹¹⁰⁷ was born in Keene, Cheshire Co., N.H. 1 August 1977.

Jenie Beth **Stone** and Greg **Hale** had the following child born in Keene:
    10210 i.   Coty C. Michael¹⁵ **Hale**¹¹⁰⁸ 24 June 1998.

9517. **Kylene Rae**[14] *Stone (Jaclyn*[13] ***Wright**, Charles Burgum*[12]*, Veda May*[11] ***Whipple**, Aaron Mason*[10]*, Barnabas Cooper*[9]*, David*[8]*, Aaron*[7]*, Col. Moses*[6]*, Deacon Jacob*[5]*, Deacon James*[4]*, Joseph*[3]*, Matthew*[2]*, Matthew*[1]*)*[1109] was born in Keene, Cheshire Co., N.H. 3 October 1978 and married **Canaan Miller** in East Swanzey, Cheshire Co., N. H. 13 January 1997.

Kylene Rae **Stone** and Canaan **Miller** had the following child:
    10211   i.   Caelyn Autumn[15] **Miller**[1110] born in Oak Grove, Christian Co., Ky. 24 September 1997.

ENDNOTES, GENERATION FOURTEEN

1. and 2. Jones to Whipple, *Letter 05/21/1991 & 01/16/1997*.
3. Davis to Whipple, *Letter, 26 March 1989*.
4. Schlarbaum to Whipple, *Letter 7 March 1996*.
5. and 6. Crawford to Whipple, *4 Letters*.
7. and 8. T. Pearson to Whipple, *Letter, 6 March 1989*.
9. through 11. Carlisle to Whipple, *Ltr, 20 March 1989*.
12. T. Pearson to Whipple, *Letter, 6 March 1989*.
13. and 14. Carlisle to Whipple, *Ltr, 20 March 1989*.
15. through 17. Kyle to Whipple, *2 Letters*.
18. through 30. Bayles to Whipple, *2 letters*.
31. and 32. Kelly to Whipple, *Letter, 17 May 1999*.
33. through 38. Burke's, *Presidential Families*, 473.
39. Wise to Whipple, *3 Letters*; and Eugenia Wise Hathaway to Blaine Whipple. Letter dated 11 Jan. 1999 at 2007 Hock Ave., Placentia, CA 92870. In posession of Whipple (2005). (Hereafter cited as Hathaway to Whipple, *Letter, 11 Jan. 1999*).
40. and 41. Hathaway to Whipple, *Letter, 11 Jan. 1999*.
42. through 190. Storey to Whipple, *5 letters*.
191. through 209. Keener to Whipple, *Letters 30 May & 6 June 2000*.
210. through 213. Kurapka to Whipple, *2 Letters*; and Keener to Whipple, *Letters 30 May & 6 June 2000*.
214. through 216. Keener to Whipple, *Letters 30 May & 6 June 2000*.
217. through 219. Workman to Whipple, *Letter, 26 April 1998*.
220. through 228. Dorian to Whipple, *Letter, 21 Aug. 2000*.
229. Hendricks - McCleery, *Family Group Sheet*.
230. through 232. Shannon - Kennison, *Family Group Sheet*.
233. through 242. L. Whipple to Whipple, *7 Letters*.
243. through 252. Talmud - Whipple, *Family Group Sheets*.
253. and 254. V. Whipple to B. Whipple, *Letter, 22 March 1989*.
255. and 256. Thomas to Whipple, *Letter, 24 Jan. 2000*.
257. through 260. V. Whipple to B. Whipple, *Letter, 22 March 1989*.
261. through 264. Thomas to Whipple, *Letter, 24 Jan. 2000*.
265. V. Whipple to B. Whipple, *Letter, 22 March 1989*.
266. through 268. Thomas to Whipple, *Letter, 24 Jan. 2000*.
269. V. Whipple to B. Whipple, *Letter, 22 March 1989*; and D. Brooke to Whipple, *Letter, 8 Dec. 1999*.
270. through 273. D. Brooke to Whipple, *Letter, 8 Dec. 1999*.
274. V. Whipple to B. Whipple, *Letter, 22 March 1989*; and D. Brooke to Whipple, *Letter, 8 Dec. 1999*.
275. through 278. D. Brooke to Whipple, *Letter, 8 Dec. 1999*.
279. V. Whipple to B. Whipple, *Letter, 22 March 1989*.
280. and 281. D. Brooke to Whipple, *Letter, 8 Dec. 1999*.
282. through 284. V. Whipple to B. Whipple, *Letter, 22 March 1989*.
285. D. Brooke to Whipple, *Letter, 8 Dec. 1999*.
286. and 287. V. Whipple to B. Whipple, *Letter, 22 March 1989*.
288. and 289. D. Brooke to Whipple, *Letter, 8 Dec. 1999*.
290. and 291. V. Whipple to B. Whipple, *Letter, 22 March 1989*.
292. through 294. D. Brooke to Whipple, *Letter, 8 Dec. 1999*.
295. V. Whipple to B. Whipple, *Letter, 22 March 1989*; and D. Brooke to Whipple, *Let-*

296.   *ter, 8 Dec. 1999.*
296.   D. Brooke to Whipple, *Letter, 8 Dec. 1999.*
297.   V. Whipple to B. Whipple, *Letter, 22 March 1989*; and D. Brooke to Whipple, *Letter, 8 Dec. 1999.*
298.   D. Brooke to Whipple, *Letter, 8 Dec. 1999.*
299.   V. Whipple to B. Whipple, *Letter, 22 March 1989*; and Thomas to Whipple, *Letter, 24 Jan. 2000.*
300.   through 303. Thomas to Whipple, *Letter, 24 Jan. 2000.*
304.   V. Whipple to B. Whipple, *Letter, 22 March 1989*; and Thomas to Whipple, *Letter, 24 Jan. 2000.*
305.   through 307. Thomas to Whipple, *Letter, 24 Jan. 2000.*
308.   through 323. E. Whipple to B. Whipple, *Various Letters.*
324.   through 334. Bailey - Whipple, *Family Group Sheet.*
335.   through 343. Moore to Whipple, *Letter 2 May 1994.*
344.   through 349. Samuel Morgan I-Betsey Whipple *Family Group Sheets.*
350.   through 384. Prescott to Whipple, *7 letters.*
385.   through 391. Crawford to Whipple, *4 Letters.*
392.   and 393. Orr to Whipple, *13 Letters.*
394.   through 396. Crawford to Whipple, *4 Letters.*
397.   through 400. Orr to Whipple, *13 Letters.*
401.   through 409. Crawford to Whipple, *4 Letters.*
410.   and 411. D. Franklin To Whipple, *Letter 3 Feb. 1989.*
412.   Crawford to Whipple, *4 Letters.*
413.   and 414. D. Franklin To Whipple, *Letter 3 Feb. 1989.*
415.   Crawford to Whipple, *4 Letters.*
416.   D. Franklin To Whipple, *Letter 3 Feb. 1989.*
417.   through 422. Crawford to Whipple, *4 Letters.*
423.   Orr to Whipple, *13 Letters.*
424.   through 429. Crawford to Whipple, *4 Letters.*
430.   through 432. Franklin to Whipple, *Letter, 25 November 1995.*
433.   Crawford to Whipple, *4 Letters.*
434.   Author unable to find a town with this name, hence no county is named.
435.   through 441. Crawford to Whipple, *4 Letters.*
442.   Schlarbaum to Whipple, *Letter 7 March 1996.*
443.   Davis to Whipple, *Letter, 26 March 1989.*
444.   and 445. Crawford to Whipple, *4 Letters.*
446.   Schlarbaum to Whipple, *Letter 7 March 1996.*
447.   through 475. Crawford to Whipple, *4 Letters.*
476.   through 487. Schlarbaum to Whipple, *Letter 7 March 1996.*
488.   Crawford to Whipple, *4 Letters.*
489.   through 512. C. McKinley to Whipple, *2 Letters.*
513.   through 525. Heiserman to Whipple, *2 Letters.*
526.   through 532. McKinley-Massi, *Family Group Sheet.*
533.   through 536. D. McKinley to Whipple, *5 Letters.*
537.   and 538. Hintze to Whipple, *Letter 28 Nov. 1995.*
539.   through 541. Ziegler to Whipple, *2 Letters.*
542.   through 545. Kalvig - Heddinger, *Family Group Sheet.*
546.   E. (Whipple) West to B. Whipple, *4 Letters.*
547.   Author unable to find a town with this name, hence no county is named.
548.   E. (Whipple) West to B. Whipple, *4 Letters.*

{ G 1499 }

549. and 550. Interview, Margaret (Maggie) Babbage, 2441 8th Ave. S.W., Cedar Rapids, Iowa 52404, with Blaine Whipple, 30 July 2000 Transcript in possession of Whipple (2005). (Hereafter cited as Maggie Babbage, *Interview*).
551. through 555. E. (Whipple) West to B. Whipple, *4 Letters*.
556. Andrew E. Garland to Blaine Whipple. Letter dated 8 Feb. 2001 at 921 65th St. S., St. Petersburg, FL 33707. In possession of Whipple (2005). (Hereafter cited as Garland to Whipple, *8 Feb.2001*).
557. through 560. E. (Whipple) West to B. Whipple, *4 Letters*.
561. J. Drotzman to Whiple, *Letter 30 Dec. 1996*.
562. Dortzman to Whipple, *E-mail, 2/ 26 /04*.
563. through 630. Pittman - Woods, *Family Group Sheet*.
631. and 632. Dimmock - Whipple, *Family Group Sheets*.
633. Author unable to find a town with this name, hence no county is named.
634. Dimmock - Whipple, *Family Group Sheets*.
635. through 677. Roy Whipple to B. Whipple, *4 letters*.
678. through 684. Eleanor Treddenbarger, *2 letters*.
685. through 687. Roy Whipple to B. Whipple, *4 letters*.
688. Peters to Whipple, *Letter, 21 Feb. 1997*.
689. Leslie Ann Stead, Birth certificate. Birth record from Cottage Hospital, Grosse Pointe Farms, MI, Court House, Wayne Co, MI. (Hereafter cited as Leslie Ann Stead, *Birth Certificate*).
690. Charles Michael Peters & Leslie Ann Stead, Marriage Return, Court House, Wayne Co, MI. (Hereafter cited as Stead-Peters, *Marriage Record*).
691. through 694. Peters to Whipple, *Letter, 21 Feb. 1997*.
695. through 697. Ibid., Based on an interview with Allison Watkins 15 Dec. 1995.
698. through 715. Cable to Whipple, *2 Letters*.
716. through 723. Chandler to Whipple, *5 Letters*.
724. through 736. Crates to Whipple, *Letter, 11 Feb. 1991*.
737. through 744. Maris to Whipple, *Letter, 11 April 1996*.
745. through 754. Erbland to Whipple, *Letters, Family Group Sheets*.
755. through 775. Daley to Whipple, *8 letters*.
776. Author unable to find a town with this name, hence no county is named.
777. through 793. Daley to Whipple, *8 letters*.
794. Author unable to find a town with this name, hence no county is named.
795. through 803. Daley to Whipple, *8 letters*.
804. through 806. M. Whipple to B. Whipple, *5 letters*.
807. and 808. G. Whipple to B. Whipple, *Letter, 23 May 1991*.
809. through 813. Knowles to Whipple, *Letters 19 & 30 July 2000*.
814. through 828. Herrick - Whipple, *Family Group Sheets*.
829. through 842. Reinhold to Whipple, *2 Letters*.
843. through 845. Powers to Whipple, *Letter 20 March 1996*.
846. through 889. Sadler to Whipple, *Family Group Sheets*.
890. through 1012. Smith-Ward-Whipple, *Family Group Sheet*.
1013. through 1036. Brigham - Whipple, *Family Group Sheets*.
1037. through 1040. Bowman - Miner, *Family Group Sheet*.
1041. and 1042. Randazzo to Whipple, *E-mail, 25 Oct. 01*.
1043. and 1044. W.J Whipple to B. Whipple, *3 letters*.
1045. Wm. Whipple to B. Whipple, *Letter, 20 April 1989*.
1046. B. Whipple to B. Whipple, *Letter, 22 May 1998*.
1047. through 1050. Genevieve G. Dunlop to Blaine Whipple. Letter dated 2 Sept. 1998

at 928 W. Gilbert Rd., Palatine, IL 60067-5904. In possession of Whipple (2005.) Family Group Sheet of immediate family provided. (Hereafter cited as Dunlop to Whipple, *Letter, 2 Sept. 1998*).
1051. and 1052. Branscom to Whipple, *Letter, 27 May 1998*.
1053. through 1079. H.H. Hildebrant to Whipple, *Letters, 2/1999; 7/2001*.
1080. through 1110. Miller - Whitley, *Family Group Sheets*.

FIFTEENTH GENERATION

9574. **Barbara Frances**[15] **Kelly** (Daniel Robert[14], Ada Helen[13] **Thomas**, Dilman Kar[12], Burt Byron[11], Ambrose[10], Dilla[9] **Beeman**, Daniel[8], Lydia[7] **Cogswell**, Samuel[6], Hannah[5] **Browne**, Judith[4] **Perkins**, Elizabeth[3] **Whipple**, Matthew[2], Matthew[1])[1] was born in Melbourne, Brevard Co., Fla. and married **Paul Marton Thompson**. He is the son of Paul Millard **Thompson** and Elizabeth **Suzanne**.

Barbara Frances **Kelly** and Paul Marton **Thompson** had the following children:
    10212   i.   Katlin Danielle[16] **Kelly-Thompson**.[2]
    10213   ii.   Stryker Andrews **Kelly-Thompson**.[3]

9588. **Lisa Ann**[15] **Molinari** (Natalie Janet[14] **Bragdon**, William Edward[13], George Henry[12], Ione[11] **Andrews**, Henry[10], Caleb[9], Molly[8] **Burnham**, Capt. Westley[7], Westley[6], Elizabeth[5] **Perkins**, Jacob[4], Elizabeth[3] **Whipple**, Matthew[2], Matthew[1])[4] was born in Brockton, Plymouth Co., Mass. 18 June 1960 and married **James Joseph Mickel** there 1 October 1983. James, son of Edward **Mickel** and Elsie **Blanchard**, was born in Boston, Suffolk Co., Mass. 7 December 1951.

Lisa Ann **Molinari** and James Joseph **Mickel** had the following child born in Stoughton, Norfolk Co., Mass.:
    10214   i.   Jennifer Marie[16] **Mickel** 19 February 1984.[5]

9590. **Rose Ann**[15] **Bragdon** (Edward Ernest[14], William Edward[13], George Henry[12], Ione[11] **Andrews**, Henry[10], Caleb[9], Molly[8] **Burnham**, Capt. Westley[7], Westley[6], Elizabeth[5] **Perkins**, Jacob[4], Elizabeth[3] **Whipple**, Matthew[2], Matthew[1])[6] birth date unknown, married **Stephen Glennon**.

Rose Ann **Bragdon** and Stephen **Glennon** had the following child:
    10215   i.   Brandon Edward[16] **Glennon**[7] born in 1986.

9595. **Diane Leslie**[15] **Jewett** (Adelaide Martha[14] **Bragdon**, Frederick[13], George Henry[12], Ione[11] **Andrews**, Henry[10], Caleb[9], Molly[8] **Burnham**, Capt. Westley[7], Westley[6], Elizabeth[5] **Perkins**, Jacob[4], Elizabeth[3] **Whipple**, Matthew[2], Matthew[1])[8] was born 5 July 1954 and married **Robert Gentile**.

Diane Leslie **Jewett** and Robert **Gentile** had the following children:
    10216   i.   Victoria Lynn[16] **Gentile**[9] born 29 January 1975.
    10217   ii.   Kevin Paul **Gentile**[10] born 23 December 1978.

9596. **Catherine Ann**[15] **Jewett** (Adelaide Martha[14] **Bragdon**, Frederick[13], George Henry[12], Ione[11] **Andrews**, Henry[10], Caleb[9], Molly[8] **Burnham**, Capt. Westley[7], Westley[6], Elizabeth[5] **Perkins**, Jacob[4], Elizabeth[3] **Whipple**, Matthew[2], Matthew[1])[11] was born 22 April 1956 and married **Stephen Bland**.

Catherine Ann **Jewett** and Stephen **Bland** had the following children:
    10218   i.   Justin Edward[16] **Bland**[12] born 8 August 1980.
    10219   ii.   Wendy Melissa **Bland**[13] born 17 March 1982.

9597. **Joanne Marie**[15] **Jewett** (Adelaide Martha[14] **Bragdon**, Frederick[13], George Henry[12], Ione[11] **Andrews**, Henry[10], Caleb[9], Molly[8] **Burnham**, Capt. Westley[7], Westley[6], Elizabeth[5] **Perkins**, Jacob[4], Elizabeth[3] **Whipple**, Matthew[2], Matthew[1])[14] was born 16 February 1959 and married **Phillip Neely**.

Joanne Marie **Jewett** and Phillip **Neely** had the following children:
    10220   i.   Jennifer Marie[16] **Neely**[15] born 23 July 1978.
    10221   ii.   Elizabeth Marie **Neely**[16] born 4 March 1980.

9599. **Cynthia Irene**[15] **Jewett** (Adelaide Martha[14] **Bragdon**, Frederick[13], George Henry[12], Ione[11] **Andrews**, Henry[10], Caleb[9], Molly[8] **Burnham**, Capt. Westley[7], Westley[6], Elizabeth[5] **Perkins**, Jacob[4], Elizabeth[3] **Whipple**, Matthew[2], Matthew[1])[17] was born 14 April 1962 and married **Stephen Grundy**.

Cynthia Irene **Jewett** and Stephen **Grundy** had the following children:
    10222   i.   Joshua Stephen[16] **Grundy**[18] born 12 December 1982.
    10223   ii.   Jessica Cynthia **Grundy**[19] born 23 April 1984.

9601. **Gerald**[15] **Bowes** (Gerald[14], Esther Marjorie[13] **Bragdon**, George Henry[12], Ione[11] **Andrews**, Henry[10], Caleb[9], Molly[8] **Burnham**, Capt. Westley[7], Westley[6], Elizabeth[5] **Perkins**, Jacob[4], Elizabeth[3] **Whipple**, Matthew[2], Matthew[1])[20] was born in Urbana, Champaign Co., Ill. in 1956 and married twice. (1) **Diane (__)**. (2) An unnamed person in San Diego, San Diego Co., Calif. in 1984.

Gerald **Bowes** and Diane (__) had the following child:
    10224   i.   Jason[16] **Bowes**[21] born abt 1984.

9602. **Judith**[15] **Bowes** (Gerald[14], Esther Marjorie[13] **Bragdon**, George Henry[12], Ione[11] **Andrews**, Henry[10], Caleb[9], Molly[8] **Burnham**, Capt. Westley[7], Westley[6], Elizabeth[5] **Perkins**, Jacob[4], Elizabeth[3] **Whipple**, Matthew[2], Matthew[1])[22] was born abt 1960 and married **William Rockwood**.

Judith **Bowes** and William **Rockwood** had the following child:
  10225 i.   Kevin[16] **Rockwood**[23] born abt 1986.

9604. **Craig Alan**[15] **Nanius** (Jean Clayton[14] **Bowes**, Esther Marjorie[13] **Bragdon**, George Henry[12], Ione[11] **Andrews**, Henry[10], Caleb[9], Molly[8] **Burnham**, Capt. Westley[7], Westley[6], Elizabeth[5] **Perkins**, Jacob[4], Elizabeth[3] **Whipple**, Matthew[2], Matthew[1])[24] was born in Irvington, Essex Co., N.J. 18 January 1960 and married **Elenoa Bainimarama** in the Fiji Islands 9 February 1983. Elenoa,[25] daughter of Manasa **Bainimarama** and Mereani **Daunakamakama**, was born in the Fiji Islands 4 December 1961.

Craig Alan **Nanius** and Elenoa **Bainimarama** had the following children:
  10226 i.   Robert Manasa[16] **Nanius**[26] born in the Fiji Islands 16 March 1985.
  10227 ii. Brenda Jean **Nanius**[27] born in Killeen, Bell Co., Tex. 6 September 1986.

9617. **Bruce**[15] **Baker** (William Otis[14], Clifford Doty[13], Fannie Woodberry[12] **Bragdon**, Ione[11] **Andrews**, Henry[10], Caleb[9], Molly[8] **Burnham**, Capt. Westley[7], Westley[6], Elizabeth[5] **Perkins**, Jacob[4], Elizabeth[3] **Whipple**, Matthew[2], Matthew[1])[28] was born in Wenham, Essex Co., Mass. 6 May 1952 and married twice. (1) **Anne Butcher** in Shreveport, Caddo Parish, La. 7 August 1976. Marriage ended in divorce. (2) **Kimberly Korcuba** in Bermuda 12 June 1987. Kimberly, daughter of James C. **Korcuba** and Priscilla S. (__), was born in Baltimore, Baltimore City Co., Md. 20 November 1965.

Bruce **Baker** and Kimberly **Korcuba** had the following child born in Portland, Cumberland Co., Maine:
  10228 i.   Nathan James[16] **Baker**[29] 22 January 1989.

9618. **Christopher**[15] **Baker** (William Otis[14], Clifford Doty[13], Fannie Woodberry[12] **Bragdon**, Ione[11] **Andrews**, Henry[10], Caleb[9], Molly[8] **Burnham**, Capt. Westley[7], Westley[6], Elizabeth[5] **Perkins**, Jacob[4], Elizabeth[3] **Whipple**, Matthew[2], Matthew[1])[30] was born in Wenham, Essex Co., Mass. 16 December 1955 and married **Robin Cohen** in Kingston, Rockingham Co., N.H. 30 August 1981. Robin,[31] daughter of Harold F. **Cohen** and Rhoda **Markson**, was born in Boston, Suffolk Co., Mass. 20 1956.

Christopher **Baker** and Robin **Cohen** had the following children:
> 10229   i.   Meredith Anne[16] **Baker**[32] born 28 December 1986.
> 10230   ii.   Jessica **Baker**[33] born 1 June 1989.

9619. **Douglas MacIntyre**[15] **Baker** (William Otis[14], Clifford Doty[13], Fannie Woodberry[12] **Bragdon**, Ione[11] **Andrews**, Henry[10], Caleb[9], Molly[8] **Burnham**, Capt. Westley[7], Westley[6], Elizabeth[5] **Perkins**, Jacob[4], Elizabeth[3] **Whipple**, Matthew[2], Matthew[1])[34] was born in Beverly, Essex Co., Mass. 20 February 1958 and married **Joan Mary Burke** in Hamilton, Essex Co., Mass. 20 June 1987. Joan,[35] daughter of Joseph Barnard **Burke** Jr. and Elaine Marie **MacDonald**, was born in Virginia Beach, Norfolk Co., Va. 11 October 1962.

Douglas MacIntyre **Baker** and Joan Mary **Burke** had the following children:
> 10231   i.   Victoria Vail[16] **Baker**[36] born in Boston, Suffolk Co., Mass. 2 March 1989.
> 10232   ii.   Dyland Albert Teague **Baker**[r37] born in Sudbury, Ontario, Canada 19 September 1991.

9620. **Deborah**[15] **Baker** (William Otis[14], Clifford Doty[13], Fannie Woodberry[12] **Bragdon**, Ione[11] **Andrews**, Henry[10], Caleb[9], Molly[8] **Burnham**, Capt. Westley[7], Westley[6], Elizabeth[5] **Perkins**, Jacob[4], Elizabeth[3] **Whipple**, Matthew[2], Matthew[1])[38] was born in Beverly, Essex Co., Mass. 12 December 1960 and married **James Black** in Wenham, Essex Co., Mass. 17 September 1983. He was born in Salem, Essex Co., Mass. 1 March 1958.[39]

Deborah **Baker** and James **Black** had the following children born in Salem:
> 10233   i.   Harrison MacIntyre[16] **Black**[40] 14 December 1990.
> 10234   ii.   Andrew Porter **Black**[41] 26 March 1992.

9621. **Stephen Baker**[15] **McElroy** (Beverly[14] **Baker**, Clifford Doty[13], Fannie Woodberry[12] **Bragdon**, Ione[11] **Andrews**, Henry[10], Caleb[9], Molly[8] **Burnham**, Capt. Westley[7], Westley[6], Elizabeth[5] **Perkins**, Jacob[4], Elizabeth[3] **Whipple**, Matthew[2], Matthew[1])[42] was born in Beverly, Essex Co., Mass. 17 September 1950 and married **Susan Reppart Hickox** in Littleton, Grafton Co., N.H. 18 January 1975. She was born in South Carolina.[43]

Stephen Baker **McElroy** and Susan Reppart **Hickox** had the following children born in Westborough, Worcester Co., Mass.:
> 10235   i.   Julia Delaney[16] **McElroy**[44] 4 February 1976.
> 10236   ii.   Sean Alexander **McElroy**[45] 9 August 1977.

9623. **Joan**[15] **McElroy** (Beverly[14] **Baker**, Clifford Doty[13], Fannie Woodberry[12] **Bragdon**, Ione[11] **Andrews**, Henry[10], Caleb[9], Molly[8] **Burnham**, Capt. Westley[7], Westley[6], Elizabeth[5] **Perkins**, Jacob[4], Elizabeth[3] **Whipple**, Matthew[2], Matthew[1])[46] was born in Abington, Plymouth Co., Mass. 20 January 1954 and married **Steven Sweeney** in Littleton, Grafton Co., N.H. 1 September 1973.

Joan **McElroy** and Steven **Sweeney** had the following children:
- 10237 i. Christine[16] **Sweeney**[47] born 21 March 1975.
- 10238 ii. Aaron John **Sweeney**[48] born 8 March 1977.

9624. **Cathleen Ruth**[15] **Sweeney** (Joanne Marjorie[14] **Baker**, Roy Woodberry[13], Fannie Woodberry[12] **Bragdon**, Ione[11] **Andrews**, Henry[10], Caleb[9], Molly[8] **Burnham**, Capt. Westley[7], Westley[6], Elizabeth[5] **Perkins**, Jacob[4], Elizabeth[3] **Whipple**, Matthew[2], Matthew[1])[49] was born in Petersboro, Hillsborough Co., N.H. 4 January 1949 and married **Frank Edward Hilton II** in Weymouth, Norfolk Co., Mass. 23 January 1971. Frank,[50] son of Frank Edward **Hilton** and Mary **Gardner**, was born in Weymouth 8 May 1946.

Cathleen Ruth **Sweeney** and Frank Edward **Hilton** II had the following children:
- 10239 i. Frank Edward[16] **Hilton** III[51] born in Weymouth 2 September 1972.
- 10240 ii. Debra Gail **Hilton**[52] 3 November 1974.
- 10241 iii. Michael Patrick **Hilton**[53] born in Brighton, Norfolk Co., Mass. 24 June 1977.
- 10242 iv. Richard Barrett **Hilton**[54] born in Boston, Suffolk Co., Mass. 22 September 1980.

9625. **Sharon Anne**[15] **Sweeney** (Joanne Marjorie[14] **Baker**, Roy Woodberry[13], Fannie Woodberry[12] **Bragdon**, Ione[11] **Andrews**, Henry[10], Caleb[9], Molly[8] **Burnham**, Capt. Westley[7], Westley[6], Elizabeth[5] **Perkins**, Jacob[4], Elizabeth[3] **Whipple**, Matthew[2], Matthew[1])[55] was born in Petersboro, Hillsborough Co., N.H. 5 June 1951 and married twice. (1) **Kevin Hynes**. (2) **John Cordella** in Lawrence, Essex Co. Mass. 17 April 1983. John,[56] son of David Paul **Cordella** and Dorothy **Quinn**, was born in Hartford, Hartford Co., Conn. 9 October 1959.

Sharon Anne **Sweeney** and Kevin **Hynes** had the following child born in Weymouth, Norfolk Co., Mass.:
- 10243 i. Kerry Lyne[16] **Hynes**[57] 11 November 1971.

Sharon Anne **Sweeney** and John **Cordella** had the following children:
>   10244   ii.   Joanne Allyson **Cordella**[58] born 6 January 1985.
>
>   10245   iii. Sarah Jane **Cordella**[59] born 10 November 1986.

9626. **Gail Margaret**[15] **Sweeney** (Joanne Marjorie[14] **Baker**, Roy Woodberry[13], Fannie Woodberry[12] **Bragdon**, Ione[11] **Andrews**, Henry[10], Caleb[9], Molly[8] **Burnham**, Capt. Westley[7], Westley[6], Elizabeth[5] **Perkins**, Jacob[4], Elizabeth[3] **Whipple**, Matthew[2], Matthew[1])[60] was born in Concord, Rockingham Co., N.H. 15 November 1952 and married **James Robert Mason** in Weymouth, Norfolk Co., Mass. 23 November 1974. James,[61] son of James **Mason** and Katherine Tribble **Elrode**, was born in Newport, Newport Co., R.I. 21 November 1950.

Gail Margaret **Sweeney** and James Robert **Mason** had the following children:
>   10246   i.   Jenille Renee[16] **Mason**[62] born in Monterey, Montgomery Co., Calif. 20 January 1977.
>
>   10247   ii.   Kristina Nicole **Mason**[63] born in Virginia Beach, Norfolk Co., Va. 11 May 1983.

9627. **Laureen Ellen**[15] **Sweeney** (Joanne Marjorie[14] **Baker**, Roy Woodberry[13], Fannie Woodberry[12] **Bragdon**, Ione[11] **Andrews**, Henry[10], Caleb[9], Molly[8] **Burnham**, Capt. Westley[7], Westley[6], Elizabeth[5] **Perkins**, Jacob[4], Elizabeth[3] **Whipple**, Matthew[2], Matthew[1])[64] was born in Portland, Cumberland Co., Maine 31 March 1954 and married **Bruce Guy Palmer** in Manti, Sampete Co., Utah 10 October 1974. Bruce,[65] son of Kent Brimhall **Palmer** and Susie Isabell **Dewitt**, was born in Farmington, San Juan Co., N.M. 3 April 1953.

Laureen Ellen **Sweeney** and Bruce Guy **Palmer** had the following children:
>   10248   i.   Leo Kent[16] **Palmer**[66] born in Weymouth, Norfolk Co., Mass. 12 June 1977.
>
>   10249   ii.   Gordon Ronald **Palmer**[67] born in Mesa, Mariposa Co., Ariz. 17 October 1978.
>
>   10250   iii. Margaret Ruth **Palmer**[68] born in Snowflake, Navajo Co., Ariz. 10 April 1980.
>
>   10251   iv.   Mandi Jo **Palmer**[69] was born in Snowflake 11 January 1983.

9629. **Philip Roy**[15] **Baker** (Philip Woodberry[14], Roy Woodberry[13], Fannie Woodberry[12] **Bragdon**, Ione[11] **Andrews**, Henry[10], Caleb[9], Molly[8] **Burnham**, Capt. Westley[7], Westley[6], Elizabeth[5] **Perkins**, Jacob[4], Elizabeth[3] **Whipple**, Matthew[2], Matthew[1])[70] was born in Petersboro, Hillsborough Co., N.H. 3 May 1957 and married **Tamsin Bisel** in Antrim, Hillsborough Co., N.H. 27 June 1981.

Philip Roy **Baker** and Tamsin **Bisel** had the following child:
    10252   i.   Stephanie[16] **Baker**[71] born 2 September 1986.

    9643. Martha Jane[15] **Raymond** (Charles Everett[14], Frank Everett[13], Emma Louise[12] **Low**, Emma Louise[11] **Andrews**, Henry[10], Caleb[9], Molly[8] **Burnham**, Capt. Westley[7], Westley[6], Elizabeth[5] **Perkins**, Jacob[4], Elizabeth[3] **Whipple**, Matthew[2], Matthew[1])[72] birth date unknown, married **Bruce Paskowski**.

Martha Jane **Raymond** and Bruce **Paskowski** had the following child:
    10253   i.   Heidi[16] **Paskowski**[73] born 8 March 1972.

    9660. David Joseph[15] **Schier** (Adrienne Lee[14] **Gosbee**, John Francis[13], Edna Frances[12] **Andrews**, Frank Albert[11], Henry[10], Caleb[9], Molly[8] **Burnham**, Capt. Westley[7], Westley[6], Elizabeth[5] **Perkins**, Jacob[4], Elizabeth[3] **Whipple**, Matthew[2], Matthew[1])[74] was born in Beverly, Essex Co., Mass. 21 November 1979 and married **Lisa Marie Carey**. Lisa,[75] daughter of John **Carey** and Sharon (**__**), was born in Pennsylvania 3 December 1982.

David Joseph **Schier** and Lisa Marie **Carey** had the following child born in Melbourne, Brevard Co., Fla.:
    10254   i.   Isiah David[16] **Schier**[76] 6 March 2001.

    9684. Rafe Henry[15] **Blood** Jr. (Linda Barbara[14] **Mears**, Edward Francis[13], Edward Francis[12], David Edward[11], Sallie Maria[10] **Andrews**, Caleb[9], Molly[8] **Burnham**, Capt. Westley[7], Westley[6], Elizabeth[5] **Perkins**, Jacob[4], Elizabeth[3] **Whipple**, Matthew[2], Matthew[1])[77] was born in Newburyport, Essex Co., Mass. 22 July 1965 and married **Michele Lynn Parker** in Kensington, Rockingham Co., N.H. 10 October 1987. Michele,[78] daughter of Paul Truman **Parker** and Joanne **Borkevist**, was born in Exeter, Rockingham Co., N.H. 23 September 1966.

Rafe Henry **Blood** Jr. and Michele Lynn **Parker** had the following children born in Portsmouth, Rockingham Co., N.H.:
    10255   i.   Jessica Emily[16] **Blood**[79] 20 September 1989.
    10256   ii.   Rafe Parker **Blood**[80] 28 July 1992.
    10257   iii.   Benjamin Stephen **Blood**[81] 23 November 1998.

9686. **Christian Daniel**[15] **Blood** (Linda Barbara[14] **Mears**, Edward Francis[13], Edward Francis[12], David Edward[11], Sallie Maria[10] **Andrews**, Caleb[9], Molly[8] **Burnham**, Capt. Westley[7], Westley[6], Elizabeth[5] **Perkins**, Jacob[4], Elizabeth[3] **Whipple**, Matthew[2], Matthew[1])[82] was born in Newburyport, Essex Co., Mass. 28 February 1971 and married **Carol Ann LaPlante**. Carol,[83] daughter of Arthur Joseph **LaPlante** and Mary **Adams**, was born in Dover, Strafford Co., N.H. 21 December 1962.

Christian Daniel **Blood** and Carol Ann **LaPlante** had the following children born in Exeter, Rockingham Co., N.H.:
    10258 i.   Emily Rose[16] **Blood**[84] 20 April 1997.
    10259 ii.   Lucas Arthur **Blood**[85] 27 January 2000.

9774. **Melanie Katheleen**[15] **Duell** (Joseph A.[14], Earl Charles[13], Grace Elenore[12] **Morgan**, Fredrick V.[11], Nehemiah[10], Samuel[9], Betsey[8] **Whipple**, Nehemiah[7], Benjamin[6], Francis[5], Jonathan[4], Joseph[3], Matthew[2], Matthew[1])[86] was born in Abilene, Taylor Co., Tex. 3 October 1964 and married **Mohamed Benmerrchouce** in Troy, N.Y. 17 September 1990.[87]

Melanie Katheleen **Duell** and Mohamed **Benmerrchouce** had the following children:
    10260 i.   Alexandra[16] **Benmerrchouce**[88] born in Albany, Albany Co., N.Y. 29 April 1989.
    10261 ii.   Leila **Benmerrchouce**[89] born in Albany 2 December 1991.
    10262 iii. Kevin **Benmerrchouce**[90] born in Lime Ridge, Sauk Co., Wisc. 27 October 1993.

9775. **Michael**[15] **O'Hara** (Victoria[14] **Duell**, Earl Charles[13], Grace Elenore[12] **Morgan**, Fredrick V.[11], Nehemiah[10], Samuel[9], Betsey[8] **Whipple**, Nehemiah[7], Benjamin[6], Francis[5], Jonathan[4], Joseph[3], Matthew[2], Matthew[1])[91] was born in Lime Ridge, Sauk Co., Wisc. 23 February 1956 and died 3 June 2000 in Balltown, Maine, at 44 years of age. He married **Linda Coughlin** in Balltown 11 June 1983. She was born 14 August 1957 and died 29 November 2000 in Balltown, at 43 years of age.[92] Both are buried at Morningside Cemetery Hartford, Washington Co., N.Y.

Michael **O'Hara** and Linda **Coughlin** had the following child born in Balltown:
    10263 i.   John[16] **O'Hara** 28 January 1986.[93]

9776. **Philip**[15] **O'Hara** (Victoria[14] **Duell**, Earl Charles[13], Grace Elenore[12] **Morgan**, Fredrick V.[11], Nehemiah[10], Samuel[9], Betsey[8] **Whipple**, Nehemiah[7], Benjamin[6], Francis[5], Jonathan[4], Joseph[3], Matthew[2], Matthew[1])[94] was born in Lime Ridge, Sauk Co., Wisc. 29 May 1959 and married **Sue Bonhot** in Balltown, Maine 15 October 1988. She was born in St. Mary, Pleasants Co., W. Va. 11 June 1963. They were divorced in 1990.

Philip **O'Hara** and Sue **Bonhot** had the following child born in Lime Ridge:
    10264 i.   Brian[16] **O'Hara**[95] in 1990.

9788. **Ann Elizabeth**[15] **Worrell** (Meredith Jane[14] **Cooper**, Phyllis Albine[13] **Norton**, Hugh Russell[12], Charles Russel[11], Judge James Carmont[10], Harriet Whipple[9] **Carpenter**, Anner[8] **Whipple**, Nehemiah[7], Benjamin[6], Francis[5], Jonathan[4], Joseph[3], Matthew[2], Matthew[1])[96] was born 29 June 1962 and married **Steven Rex Layton**.

Ann Elizabeth **Worrell** and Steven Rex **Layton** had the following children born in Newport Beach, Orange Co., Calif.:
    10265 i.   Elizabeth Anne[16] **Layton**[97] 20 April 1988.
    10266 ii.   Amy Katherine **Layton**[98] 23 November 1989.

9793. **Jeffery**[15] **Young** (Rupert Gordon[14], Virginia Edith[13] **Norton**, Walter Emmet[12], Charles Russel[11], Judge James Carmont[10], Harriet Whipple[9] **Carpenter**, Anner[8] **Whipple**, Nehemiah[7], Benjamin[6], Francis[5], Jonathan[4], Joseph[3], Matthew[2], Matthew[1])[99] was born in Hemet, Riverside Co., Calif. 2 May 1962 and married **Kathy Jensen** in Solvang, Santa Barbara Co., Calif. 22 June 1985. She was born 23 January 1961.[100]

Jeffery **Young** and Kathy **Jensen** had the following child:
    10267 i.   Ashley[16] **Young**[101] born 24 August 1990.

9794. **Janiene**[15] **Young** (Rupert Gordon[14], Virginia Edith[13] **Norton**, Walter Emmet[12], Charles Russel[11], Judge James Carmont[10], Harriet Whipple[9] **Carpenter**, Anner[8] **Whipple**, Nehemiah[7], Benjamin[6], Francis[5], Jonathan[4], Joseph[3], Matthew[2], Matthew[1])[102] was born in Hemet, Riverside Co., Calif. 8 April 1963 and married **Brian Borror** in Solvang, Santa Barbara Co., Calif. in September 1981. He was born in Visalia, Calif. 1958.[103]

Janiene **Young** and Brian **Borror** had the following children born in Solvang:
    10268 i.   Jeniffer[16] **Borror**[104] in 1986.
    10269 ii.   Scott **Borror**[105] in 1990.

9795. **Joan**[15] **Young** (Rupert Gordon[14], Virginia Edith[13] **Norton**, Walter Emmet[12], Charles Russel[11], Judge James Carmont[10], Harriet Whipple[9] **Carpenter**, Anner[8] **Whipple**, Nehemiah[7], Benjamin[6], Francis[5], Jonathan[4], Joseph[3], Matthew[2], Matthew[1])[106] was born in Hemet, Riverside Co., Calif. 8 April 1963 and married **Todd Bimat** in Solvang, Santa Barbara Co., Calif. 19 May 1984. He was born in Tarlier,[107] Calif. 20 July 1961.[108]

Joan **Young** and Todd **Bimat** had the following child born in Solvang:
    10270   i.   Trent[16] **Bimat**[109] 1 May 1989.

9796. **Christine**[15] **Overstreet** (Pamela[14] **Young**, Virginia Edith[13] **Norton**, Walter Emmet[12], Charles Russel[11], Judge James Carmont[10], Harriet Whipple[9] **Carpenter**, Anner[8] **Whipple**, Nehemiah[7], Benjamin[6], Francis[5], Jonathan[4], Joseph[3], Matthew[2], Matthew[1])[110] was born in Covina, Los Angeles Co., Calif. 18 August 1967 and married twice. (1) **Jerry Estrada** in San Gabriel, Orange Co., Calif. 11 January 1992. He was born 22 December 1965.[111] (2) **Mathew Hood Woodin**.

Christine **Overstreet** and Jerry **Estrada** had the following child born in Los Angeles, Los Angeles Co., Calif.:
    10271   i.   Olivia Victoria[16] **Estrada**[112] 1 May 1992.

Christine **Overstreet** and Mathew Hood **Woodin** had the following child born in Arcadia, Los Angeles Co., Calif.:
    10272   ii.   Braden Hood **Woodin**[113] 11 March 1997.

9800. **Holly**[15] **Young** (Michael Bernard[14], Virginia Edith[13] **Norton**, Walter Emmet[12], Charles Russel[11], Judge James Carmont[10], Harriet Whipple[9] **Carpenter**, Anner[8] **Whipple**, Nehemiah[7], Benjamin[6], Francis[5], Jonathan[4], Joseph[3], Matthew[2], Matthew[1])[114] was born in Carlsbad, San Diego Co., Calif. 11 September 1970 and married **Robert Apadaco**.

Holly **Young** and Robert **Apadaco** had the following child born in Carlsbad:
    10273   i.   Michael[16] **Apadaco**[115] 30 August 1989.

9892. **Loreli Renee**[15] **Shields** (Larry Rollin[14], Maurice Dean[13], Vivian Ray[12] **Sneary**, Ella Agnes[11] **Burgess**, Ellen[10] **Whipple**, Manley Nehemiah[9], Abraham[8], Nehemiah[7], Benjamin[6], Francis[5], Jonathan[4], Joseph[3], Matthew[2], Matthew[1])[116] was born in Salina, Saline Co., Kans. 5 August 1967 and married twice. (1) **Shawn Erickson** in Salina 16 June 1992. He was born there 8 August 1971.[117] (2) **Keith Downey** in St. Mary's, Pottawatomie Co., Kans. 11 November 1995. He was born 17 July 1970.[118]

Loreli Renee **Shields** and Shawn **Erickson** had the following child born in Salina:

  10274 i. Kortnei Ryan[16] **Erickson**[119] 29 June 1991.

Loreli Renee **Shields** and Keith **Downey** had the following child born in Topeka, Shawnee Co., Kans.:

  10275 ii. Joshua Keith **Downey**[120] 17 July 1996.

9894. **Eric Loyd**[15] **Pittman** (Sanzee Glee[14] **Wanger**, Jacquiline Genevieve[13] **Woods**, Veta Grace[12] **Sneary**, Ella Agnes[11] **Burgess**, Ellen[10] **Whipple**, Manley Nehemiah[9], Abraham[8], Nehemiah[7], Benjamin[6], Francis[5], Jonathan[4], Joseph[3], Matthew[2], Matthew[1])[121] was born 3 May 1971 and married four times. (1) **Kelly Sylvester** in Woodward, Woodward Co., Okla. 31 December 1989. (2) **Tonya Schmidt**. (3) **Kay (__)**. (4) **Kasey (__)**.

Eric Loyd **Pittman** and Kelly **Sylvester** had the following children born in Shattuck, Ellis Co., Okla.:

  10276 i. Stetson Dakota[16] **Pittman**[122] 9 April 1991.
  10277 ii. Eric Loyd **Pittman** Jr.[123] 26 March 1993.

Eric Loyd **Pittman** and Tonya **Schmidt** had the following child born in Custer City, Custer Co., Okla.:

  10278 iii. Skylar Dawn **Pittman**[124] 4 February 1996.

9895. **Zaneta Zoe**[15] **Pittman** (Sanzee Glee[14] **Wanger**, Jacquiline Genevieve[13] **Woods**, Veta Grace[12] **Sneary**, Ella Agnes[11] **Burgess**, Ellen[10] **Whipple**, Manley Nehemiah[9], Abraham[8], Nehemiah[7], Benjamin[6], Francis[5], Jonathan[4], Joseph[3], Matthew[2], Matthew[1])[125] was born in Corpus Christi, Nueces Co., Tex. 12 June 1975 and married **Paul Lamb** in Fargo, Ellis Co., Okla. 12 August 1995. He was born 5 August 1972.[126]

Zaneta Zoe **Pittman** and Paul **Lamb** had the following child born in Shattuck, Ellis Co., Okla.:

  10279 i. Alexis Danae[16] **Lamb**[127] 19 July 1998.

9907. **Jennifer Jo**[15] **Drake** (Sharla Jo[14] **Sperry**, Josephine May[13] **Woods**, Veta Grace[12] **Sneary**, Ella Agnes[11] **Burgess**, Ellen[10] **Whipple**, Manley Nehemiah[9], Abraham[8], Nehemiah[7], Benjamin[6], Francis[5], Jonathan[4], Joseph[3], Matthew[2], Matthew[1])[128] was born in Stillwater, Payne Co., Okla. 21 November 1974 and married **Billy David Young** in Gage, Ellis Co., Okla. 1 July 1995. Billy,[129] son of David **Young** and Polly (__), was born in Alva, Woods Co., Okla. 12 December 1973.

Jennifer Jo **Drake** and Billy David **Young** had the following children born in Norman, Cleveland Co., Okla.:
  10280 i. Kurstyn Jo[16] **Young**[130] 18 June 1999.
  10281 ii. Ashlyn Brooke **Young**[131] 22 August 2000.

9964. **Elizabeth Jane**[15] **Kelly** (Judith Ann[14] **Cable**, Jane Elizabeth[13] **Chandler**, Florence B.[12] **Johnson**, Mary Lillian[11] **Whipple**, Ithamar Cyrus[10], Cyrus Avery[9], Ithamar[8], Rev. Benjamin[7], Benjamin[6], Francis[5], Jonathan[4], Joseph[3], Matthew[2], Matthew[1])[132] was born in Wichita, Sedgwick Co., Kans. 21 July 1971 and married **Brian Richards** there 24 July 1993.

Elizabeth Jane **Kelly** and Brian **Richards** had the following child born in Wichita:
  10282 i. Micah John[16] **Richards**[133] 29 January 1998.

10037. **Kathy Ann**[15] **Phillips** (Laverna Ann[14] **Reinhold**, Lois Irene[13] **Perkins**, Glenn Alonzo[12], Manson Burdell[11], Marissa Parmelia[10] **Dean**, Martha Putnam[9] **Whipple**, Duick[8], Charles[7], Francis[6], Francis[5], Jonathan[4], Joseph[3], Matthew[2], Matthew[1])[134] was born in Lockport, Niagara Co., N.Y. 18 March 1958 and died in 1981 in Mt. Dora, Lake Co., Fla., at 23 years of age.

Kathy Ann **Phillips** had the following children:
  10283 i. Jason[16] **Meadows**.[135]
  10284 ii. Carrie **Meadows**.[136]

10038. **Victor Eugene**[15] **Reinhold** (Victor Eugene[14], Lois Irene[13] **Perkins**, Glenn Alonzo[12], Manson Burdell[11], Marissa Parmelia[10] **Dean**, Martha Putnam[9] **Whipple**, Duick[8], Charles[7], Francis[6], Francis[5], Jonathan[4], Joseph[3], Matthew[2], Matthew[1])[137] was born in Jacksonville, Onslow Co., N.C. 4 April 1958 and married **Dian Ruth Rosenbaum**. She was born 9 April 1962.[138]

Victor Eugene **Reinhold** and Dian Ruth **Rosenbaum** had the following children:
  10285 i. Robert Mathew[16] **Reinhold**[139] born 9 April 1991.
  10286 ii. Eric Andrew **Reinhold**[140] born 26 December 1992.

10043. **Eric John**[15] **Reinhold** (Edward John[14], Lois Irene[13] **Perkins**, Glenn Alonzo[12], Manson Burdell[11], Marissa Parmelia[10] **Dean**, Martha Putnam[9] **Whipple**, Duick[8], Charles[7], Francis[6], Francis[5], Jonathan[4], Joseph[3],

Matthew[2], Matthew[1])[141] was born in Dearborn, Wayne Co., Mich. 28 October 1964 and married **Kimberly Mitts** in Miami, Dade Co., Fla. 4 June 1988. She is the daughter of Richard **Mitts** and Linda **McFarlane**.[142]

Eric John **Reinhold** and Kimberly **Mitts** had the following children:
   10287 i. Kayln Marie[16] **Reinhold**[143] born in Anapolis, Ann Ariendel Co., Md. 28 September 1992.
   10288 ii. Kara **Reinhold**[144] born in Mt. Dora, Lake Co., Fla. 28 May 1995.
   10289 iii. Kyler David **Reinhold**[145] born in Mt. Dora 27 April 1998.

 10044. **Baron Vaughn**[15] **Reinhold** (Edward John[14], Lois Irene[13] **Perkins**, Glenn Alonzo[12], Manson Burdell[11], Marissa Parmelia[10] **Dean**, Martha Putnam[9] **Whipple**, Duick[8], Charles[7], Francis[6], Francis[5], Jonathan[4], Joseph[3], Matthew[2], Matthew[1])[146] was born in Rochester, Monroe Co., N.Y. 27 October 1966 and married **Jamie Barcus** in Stockton, San Joaquin Co., Calif. She is the daughter of James **Barcus** and Sue (__).[147] Baron was graduated from the U.S. Naval Academy, Class of 1990.

Baron Vaughn **Reinhold** and Jamie **Barcus** had the following child born in Mt. Dora, Lake Co., Fla.:
   10290 i. Meghan[16] **Reinhold**[148] 17 September 1997.

 10085. **Candy Ann**[15] **Trimmell** (Jack Gregory[14], Jack Reed[13], Edna Pearl[12] **Sproat**, Mary Elizabeth[11] **Smith**, Ruby Sophronia[10] **Whipple**, William[9], Ira Martin[8], Elijah[7], Jeremiah[6], Joseph[5], John[4], Joseph[3], Matthew[2], Matthew[1])[149] was born in Wichita, Sedgwick Co., Kans. 29 October 1975 and married **Shawn Michael Wilson**.

Candy Ann **Trimmell** and Shawn Michael **Wilson** had the following children:
   10291 i. Tyler Dale[16] **Wilson**[150] born 1 August 1993.
   10292 ii. Cassie Renee **Wilson**[151] born 29 October 1995.
   10293 iii. Blake Gregory **Wilson**[152] born 28 September 1996.

 10097. **Shawn**[15] **Loveall** (Diane Janel[14] **Trimmell**, Harold Riley[13], Edna Pearl[12] **Sproat**, Mary Elizabeth[11] **Smith**, Ruby Sophronia[10] **Whipple**, William[9], Ira Martin[8], Elijah[7], Jeremiah[6], Joseph[5], John[4], Joseph[3], Matthew[2], Matthew[1])[153] birth date unknown, married **Christina (__)**.

Shawn **Loveall** and Christina (__) had the following child:
   10294 i. Page[16] **Loveall**[154] born 5 August 1999.

10102. **Michael Leonard Anthony**[15] **Trimmell** (Joseph Leonard[14], Joseph Donald[13], Edna Pearl[12] **Sproat**, Mary Elizabeth[11] **Smith**, Ruby Sophronia[10] **Whipple**, William[9], Ira Martin[8], Elijah[7], Jeremiah[6], Joseph[5], John[4], Joseph[3], Matthew[2], Matthew[1])[155] was born in Wichita, Sedgwick Co., Kans. 10 March 1976 and married **Roberta Panther** in Cherokee, Swain Co., N. C. 15 January 1998.

Michael Leonard Anthony **Trimmell** and Roberta **Panther** had the following child:

    10295   i.   Rebekah Shaeleigh[16] **Trimmell**[156] born 8 March 2000.

10105. **Catherine Virginia Rosa**[15] **Trimmell** (Theresa Yvonne[14], Joseph Donald[13], Edna Pearl[12] **Sproat**, Mary Elizabeth[11] **Smith**, Ruby Sophronia[10] **Whipple**, William[9], Ira Martin[8], Elijah[7], Jeremiah[6], Joseph[5], John[4], Joseph[3], Matthew[2], Matthew[1])[157] was born in 1980. It appears she was adopted by Danny Birmingham, her mother's husband.

Catherine Virginia Rosa **Trimmell** had the following child:

    10296   i.   Christian Dianne[16] **Trimmell**[158] born 1 April 1999.

10134. **Holly Elizabeth**[15] **South** (Mary Christine[14] **Hobson**, Mary Esther[13] **Murphy**, Mildred Elizabeth[12] **Sproat**, Mary Elizabeth[11] Smith, Ruby Sophronia[10] Whipple, William[9], Ira Martin[8], Elijah[7], Jeremiah[6], Joseph[5], John[4], Joseph[3], Matthew[2], Matthew[1])[159] was born in Wahiawa, Oahu, Hawaii 11 December 1984 and had the following child born in Temple, Bell Co., Tex.:

    10297   i.   Kaylee Elizabeth **Scott**[16] 22 November 2001.[160]

10171. **Philip Anthony**[15] **Zoccoli** (Paula Joyce[14] **Randazzo**, Mabel Frances[13] **Corum**, Grace[12] **Treanor**, Mabel Frances[11] **Reynolds**, Helen[10] **Butterfield**, Elizabeth S.[9] **Reynolds**, Sarah W.R.[8] **Leland**, Thankful[7] **Sherman**, Mary[6] **Whipple**, Lieut. James[5], Deacon James[4], Joseph[3], Matthew[2], Matthew[1])[161] was born in San Jose, Santa Clara Co., Calif. 31 March 1966 and married twice. (1) **Pamela Lenee Riboni** in San Jose in November 1992. (2) **Valerie Diggs Barreda** Tracy, San Joaquin Co., Calif. 4 July 1998. She is the daughter of Glynbruce James **Barreda** and Julia Anita **Dalcin**.

Philip Anthony **Zoccoli** and Pamela Lenee **Riboni** had the following child born in Morgan Hill, Santa Clara Co., Calif.:

    10298   i.   Nicholas Stephen[16] **Zoccoli**[162] 10 September 1993.

{ G 1515 }

Philip Anthony **Zoccoli** and Valerie Diggs **Barreda** had the following child born in Tracy:

    10299 ii.   Lucas **Zoccoli**[163] 19 May 2000.

    10172. **Michael Stephen**[15] **Zoccoli** (Paula Joyce[14] **Randazzo**, Mabel Frances[13] **Corum**, Grace[12] **Treanor**, Mabel Frances[11] **Reynolds**, Helen[10] **Butterfield**, Elizabeth S.[9] **Reynolds**, Sarah W.R.[8] **Leland**, Thankful[7] **Sherman**, Mary[6] **Whipple**, Lieut. James[5], Deacon James[4], Joseph[3], Matthew[2], Matthew[1])[164] was born in San Jose, Santa Clara Co., Calif. 21 November 1967 and married **Alisa Daun Johnson** 1 June 1991. Alisa,[165] daughter of Brent Tew **Johnson** and Shauna Lin **Manwhring**, was born in February 1966.

Michael Stephen **Zoccoli** and Alisa Daun **Johnson** had the following children born Tracy, San Joaquin Co., Calif.:

    10300 i.   Tyler Anthony[16] **Zoccoli**[166] 22 February 1995.
    10301 ii.   Joseph Michael **Zoccoli**[167] 7 May 1997.
    10302 iii. Stephen Blake **Zoccoli**[168] 12 May 1999.

ENDNOTES, GENERATION FIFTEEN

1. through 3. Kelly to Whipple, *Letter, 17 May 1999*.
4. through 80. Storey to Whipple, *5 letters*.
81. Stoddard to Whipple, *3 letters*.
82. through 85. Storey to Whipple, *5 letters*.
86. through 95. Samuel Morgan I - Betsey Whipple, *Family Group Sheets*.
96. through 106. Prescott to Whipple, *7 letters*.
107. Author unable to find a town with this name, hence no county is named.
108. through 115. Prescott to Whipple, *7 letters*.
116. through 131. Pittman - Woods, *Family Group Sheet*.
132. and 133. Cable to Whipple, *2 Letters*.
134. through 148. Reinhold to Whipple, *2 Letters*.
149. through 160. Smith-Ward-Whipple, *Family Group Sheet*.
161. through 168. Randazzo to Whipple, *E-mail, 25 Oct. 01*.

GENEALOGY APPENDIX

TABLE OF CONTENTS

APPENDIX G-1
John Hawkins Family of Bocking, Essex Co., England	1520

APPENDIX G-2
Descendants of Francis Dane 1615-1697	1525
Descendants of Edmund Faulkner	1530
Abigail (Dane) Faulkner 1652-1729/30	1538
Photograph	1540
Extended Dane Family Accused of Witchcraft in 1692	1544
Indictment of Abigail (Dane) Faulkner	1548
Abigail (Dane) Faulkner Verdict and Death Sentence	1551
Reversal of Attainder of Abigail Faulkner and Others	1558
Dane Family Endnotes	1561
Faulkner Family Endnotes	1563
Abigail (Dane) Faulkner Endnotes	1565

APPENDIX G-3
Thomas Crosby abt 1510 to Hepzibah (Crosby) Whipple 1797	1569
Illustration of All Saints Church abt 1250, Home Upon Spaulding Moor	1570

APPENDIX G-4
George West abt. 1720 to Susan Elaine and Sandra Lynn West 1946-	1596
Jacob Clingman 1734 to Susan Elaine and Sandra Lynn West 1946-	1601
Napoleon LeFebre to Susan Elaine and Sandra Lynn West 1946-	1603
Conrad Ruhl abt 1840 to Susan Elaine and Sandra Lynn West 1946-	1605

APPENDIX G-5
Jean Scott abt 1700 to Pearl Julia Scott 1988-	1610
Scott Photographs	1615-17
Fort Chambly, Quebec Province, Canada	1627
Francis Hamel abt 1600 to Pearl Julia Scott 1988-	1629

Marcia Trudeau abt 1590 to Flevia Trudeau 1821	1637
Dominque Monty abt 1680 to Marie Monty	1645
Roger Dolan abt 1810 to Ellen "Nellie" Dolan 1884-	1648
Patrick Darmody abt 1821 to Julia Darmody 1862-1899	1652
Why Kerian Dolan and Patrick Darmody Left the Emerald Isle	1655

APPENDIX G-6

Joseph Drotzman 1861 to Jared Daniel Drotzman 1988	1677
Drotzman Photographs	1678-90
Lester Lyle Remund 1917 to Jared Daniel Droztman 1988	1691
Otis King to Jared Daniel Drotzman 1988	1693
Jose Dela' Luzcoverrero (Guerrero) to Laura Ann Drotzman 1990	1695
Jose Rodriquez abt 1867 to Laura Ann Drotzman 1990	1698

APPENDIX G-7

Peder Madsen abt 1838 to Ines Mae Peterson 1929-	1700
Peterson Photographs	1701-02; 1704-06; 1711
Henry Abraham Frye 1836-1890 to Agnes Faye Frye 1876-1962	1721
Friederich L. Bartruff 1826-1902 to Josephine B. Bartruff 1901-1995	1725
Bartruff photographs	1728-29
John Steele 1882 to BreAnna Jo Steele 1990-	1770
Steele Photographs	1717-78
Karl Wilhelm Matzke abt 1845 to Lena Matzke 1902-1981	1780
Lyder Martinson abt 1910 to BreAnna Jo Steele 1990	1787
John Pape 1828 to BreAnna Jo Steele 1990-	1788
Jan Petrus Zoerink abt 1840 to Lorna Jo Zoerink 1966	1802
Zoerink Photographs	1807-08

APPENDIX G-8

Harold G. W. Jasperson 1908-1944 to Emily Jane Jasperson 1992-	1820
Jasperson Photographs	1821-28; 1830-32

APPENDIX G-9

Mace R. McPherson to Melissa Ann McPherson 1959-	1834
McPherson Photographs	1835, 1837-39
Robert Thornborough-Thornsberry to Melissa Ann McPherson 1959-	1839
Alfonso Mauro to Gregory Robert Mauro 1986-	1845
Dimitrios Gambanis to Amy Nichole Giambanis 1985-	1846
Dimitrios Mastoris 1850 to Amy Nichole Giambanis 1885-	1848

APPENDIX G-10

Whipple Vital Records	1850

APPENDIX G-1

JOHN HAWKINS FAMILY OF
BOCKING, ESSEX COUNTY, ENGLAND

(Hawkins lineage of Anne Hawkins, Generation 2, No. 6, wife of Matthew Whipple.)

FIRST GENERATION

1. **John**[1] **Hawkins**,[1] son of John Hawkins of Braintree, Essex Co., England was born in Essex Co. about 1570 and died there in 1619 at 49 years of age. He married twice. (1) Unnamed. (2) **Mary Levitt** 21 February 1603/04 in Essex Co. She died 3 May 1635 in Bocking, Essex Co., at 54 years of age.[2] His title was Gentleman. He was the oldest son and heir, a Trustee for the poor and is believed to have lived in a fine mansion in Great Square in Braintree. A tablet identifying his tomb is in the north chancel wall of St. Michael the Archangel Church which dates from 1199. Unfortunately the Church Register only dates from 1660. The will is found in Commissary Court of London Wills, Essex and Hertfordshire Division, Essex Reference Office, Chelmsford. Reference D/AWB 43/133.

John **Hawkins** and an unnamed first wife had the following children:

    2.   i.   Eleanor[2] **Hawkins**[3] baptized in Bocking 6 March 1595 and was buried there in 1609.

+   3.   i.   John **Hawkins** III.

    4.   iii.   Francis **Hawkins**.

    5.   iv.   Mary **Hawkins**[4] born abt 1590 and married Matthew **Wright** 8 November 1610.

John **Hawkins** and Mary **Levitt** had the following children:

+   6.   v.   Anne **Hawkins** born abt 1604.

    7.   vi.   Sarah **Hawkins** born abt 1605 and married William **Coppin** 26 September 1622.[5]

SECOND GENERATION

3. John[2] **Hawkins** III. (John[1])[6] was born in Essex County, England and died 8 September 1633 in Bocking, Essex County. He married Sara **Wood** probably in Bocking about 1615. Sara, daughter of George **Wood** and Margaret (__), was born, probably in Bocking,[7] where her father was a

Clothier. His will, dated 17 December 1636–37, proved 2 March 1636/37, identifies Sara as his daughter and as "widow, late the wife of John Hawkins gentleman deceased." He left Sara 200 pounds "which her said husband did owe unto me at the time of his death."

John Hawkins III was a member of the Grocers' Company and an Alderman of the City of London in 1626. The Grocers' Company was founded in 1345 from the Fraternity of St. Anthony which was under the protection of the Abbot of Bury St. Edmunds. Among his properties were messuages and tenements in Tolleshunt, Bushes, Salcott, Wigborough, and Verley, the messuage where the family lived in Braintree, and two little tenements adjoining the Braintree churchyard. The Braintree messauge and two tenements were left to wife Sara, "so long as she remained a widow," and to son Abraham. Bequeaths in his will, written 3 September 1633 and proved 18 October 1633: Eldest son John, messuages and lands in Barking and other parishes; son Robert, messuages and tenements in Old Newton, Suffolk; daughter Sara, £600 each at age 18 and 21; daughter Margaret, £500 each at age 18 and 21; daughter Mary, messuages, etc. in Bradwell next the sea; daughter Judith, messuages, etc. in Finchfield, Essex; brother-in-law John Kent, 100 marks for his care and pains to be taken as one of the executors; to my loving friend Mr. Collins of Braintree, 40 shillings to buy him a ring and four pounds per annum during his ministry there; my mother, Mary Hawkins, widow, £16 a year, etc. (This would be Mary Levitt, his step-mother.) My friend William Lingwood, £20; my sister Kent and my sister Edes, 30 shillings apiece to make them rings; my brother Francis Hawkins, my sister Archer, and my sister Whipple, 40 shillings apiece as remembrances from me. (Sister Whipple is Anne Hawkins, wife of Matthew Whipple.) My cousin Tomson, my aunt Woodward, and my aunt Goodaye, 10 shillings apiece; loving friends and neighbors Adrian Mott and Joseph Loomys were also mentioned. Loomys was one of the witnesses.

An inquisition[9] taken at Braintree 16 April 1643 by the Court of Wards disclosed that "long before his death, John was seized in his demesne as of fee (inter alia) of a capital messuage in Braintree, in his own tenure or occupation held of Robert the Earl of Warwick (a leader of the national Puritan movement), as of his Manor of Braintree by fealty and rent, and of two cottages there in the occupation of Robert Woodward and Jeremie Gray; also of Drakes Croft, formerly Broom Croft, in Braintree, held of Katherine Lady Wentworth, as of her Manor of Coldham Hall in Wethersfield; also of six acres of land in the occupation of Martin Skinner, lately purchased of Isaac Skinner, son of the said Martin and Anne, his wife; also three rods, parcel of Braintreefield with the messuage built thereon, and of other buildings purchased of Richard Green and Richard Bedwell, and held of the Manor of Black Notley; also of two parcels called Copfield, and two parcels of land called Crossfield, all in Bocking, and held of Roger Wentworth as of his Manor of Bocking; also of two other parcels of land called Swallow Lovells in Bocking, now or late in the occupation of John Curtis and purchased of Henry Edes and John Edes, Clerk; and of a messuage in Bocking called Pirles or Brocks, purchased of the said John Curtis, the said Swallow Lovells and Pirles are held of Roger Wentworth, Esquire, as of his Manor of Bocking Hall by fealty, suit at court and yearly rent." His will dated 3 September last before this inquisition is quoted as far as concerns his lands. The said John Hawkins, the elder, also held lands in many other parts of Essex, also in the Isle of Ely, county of Cambridge, and in the county of Suffolk. John Hawkins, aged 17 on 30 January last past, is his son and next heir.

John's will confirms that Anne (Hawkins) Whipple also had a brother Francis and another sister who married an Archer unless her sister Mary, husband of Matthew Wright, was widowed and remarried a man named Archer between 8 November 1610 (marriage date to Wright) and 3 September 1633, the date of John's will. John's father-in-law, George Wood, died a little over three years after John. John Kent, also a Bocking Clothier and executor of John's estate, was also the executor of George Wood's estate. He was a son-in-law to Wood and husband to one of Sara (Wood) Hawkins' sisters. Another of Sara's sisters married a Jeremy Edes. A Henry and John Edes are mentioned in John Hawkins' Court of Wards inquisition.

John **Hawkins** III and Sara **Wood** had the following children:

- 8. i. John³ **Hawkins** probably 30 January 1617.
- 9. ii. Abraham **Hawkins** bef 1633.
- 10. iii. Frances **Hawkins** bef 1633. She married Sir John **Dawes** in Essex County. They had sons Robert, John, and William and daughter Elizabeth who married Peter Fisher, D.D. The Dawes estate went to Sir Robert, the eldest son, who, along with his brother John, died without issue so the estate eventually passed to youngest son Sir William Dawes, D. D. He was born 12 September 1671 at Lyons and married Frances Darcy, a sister and co-heir of Sir Robert Darcy of Great Bracksted, Baronet. Upon William's death the estate went to his son Sir Darcy Dawes and a daughter, wife of Sir William Milner of Yorkshire, Baronet.[10]
- 11. iv. Sara **Hawkins**[11] bef 1633 and died abt 1640. She married Sir Stephen **White** bef 1640 and in that year he established a charity of "six pounds thirteen shillings and four-pence yearly out of a farm in Black and White Notley for the giving, upon All-Saints day, unto six poor women of Brain-

tree, of honest and good behavior, and frequenters of the Church and divine service there; to each a gown of good cloth ready made of the value of 14s and to each of the said women, four 2-penny loaves of wheaten-bread upon the first Sunday of every month in the year, after Sermon in the afternoon, and to the upper Church-warden, one shilling and four-pence." This charity is "to be the love and affection" which he bore to his "late wife and to the parishioners of this town, for the sake of her and her friends."

12.	v.	Margaret **Hawkins**[12] bef 1633.
13.	vi.	Mary **Hawkins**[13] bef 1633.
14.	vii.	Judith **Hawkins**[14] bef 1633.
15.	viii.	Robert **Hawkins** Esq bef. September 1633.

6. **Anne**[2] **Hawkins** (John[1])[15] was born in Bocking, Essex Co., England abt 1604 and died abt 1643 in Ipswich, Essex Co., Mass. She married **Matthew Whipple** in Bocking 7 May 1622.

(See Generation 2, No. 6 for a continuation of the Hawkins lineage.)

HAWKINS FAMILY ENDNOTES

1. W.F. Quinn, *A History of Braintree and Bocking*, (Lavenham, Suffolk, England: Lavenham Press Limited, 1981. (Hereafter Quinn); May Cunningham and Stephen A. Warner, *Braintree and Bocking, a Pictorial Account of Two Essex Townships*, (Arnold Fairbairns Printers). (Hereafter Cunnington;) and Mary Lovering Holman and George R. Marvin, M.A., editors, *Abstracts of English Records Gathered Principally in Devonshire and Essex in a Search for the Ancestry of Roger Dearing c 1624-1676 and Matthew Whipple c 1560-1618*, (Boston, 150 copies privately published, 1928) 518. (Hereafter Holman & Marvin.)
2. Holman & Marvin 518.
3. *History of Bocking*, Manuscript Rawlinson Essex 5, p. 32, Bodleian Library, Oxford England. [The Bodleian Library at Oxford University was the first public library in Europe and is the second largest in England. It opened 8 Nov. 1602 to replace the Oxford library destroyed in the 1550s and is entitled to receive a free copy of every new book published in England. It contains approximately six million books and over 144,000 manuscripts, including many rare items in both categories. Its collections in English history, early printing, Shakespeare, and biblical and Arabic material are especially notable. (Hereafter *Bocking*, Rawlinson.)
4. Ibid. and Holman & Marvin 518.
5. *Bocking*, Rawlinson.
6. Cunnington, 16-20; Rev. Philip Morant, *The History and Antiquities of the County of Essex*, 2 volumes published between 1763 and 1768. (Hereafter Morant); and Holman & Marvin.
7. *Register* 41:253.
8. Nicholas Ives is the husband of Johane Whipple, daughter of Elder Matthew and sister of Matthew Whipple, Jr.

9. Inquisition: The act of inquiring; investigation.
10. The Court of Wards and Liveries replaced a looser system of administering the King's feudal dues and was established by Statutes passed in 1540 (32 Henry VIII c.46) and 1542 (33 Henry VIII c. 22). When a Tenant-in-Chief (holding land directly from the Crown) died, and his or her land reverted to the Crown until the heir paid a sum of money (a relief) and was then able to take possession (Livery or Seisin) of the lands. However, if the heir was under age (under 21 for a male heir and under 14 for an heiress) [John's male heir, John, Jr. was 17] the Wardship of the heir, custody of their lands and the right to arrange their marriage passed to the Monarch, until the heir came of age. The Wardship and marriage was usually kept in Crown hands, but was sold, sometimes to the next of kin, often simply to the highest bidder. The Court was a financial institution, responsible for collecting these feudal revenues. However, it also had to cope with the practical and legal consequences arising from Wardship and Livery. When feudal tenures were abolished by the Long Parliament in 1645, the Court also came to an end. The abolition of the Court was confirmed by Charles II in 1660 (12 Charles II c.24).

    When a Tenant-in-Chief died, the inquisition post mortem was taken, usually in response to a writ of diem clausit extrtemum or mandamus issued out of Chancery and was taken before the County Escheator who returned his findings to Chancery. Another copy went to the Court of Wards and Liveries. The Court's local representative, the Feodary, had to attend every inquisition to prevent fraud, and in time he conducted his own survey of the lands, which usually gave a higher value than did the jury.

    People wishing to buy a Wardship, or to lease some of the lands put in a petition to the Master of Wards and if the petition was granted, an indenture was drawn up between the Court and the petitioner; a Fine (sum of money) for the Wardship was agreed, and the grantor's name, the Fine, and the terms of its payment were entered on a schedule. The revenue raised through Wardship had and the leasing of lands had to be accounted for. These accounts, submitted to the Court, were of the medieval and early modern 'charge and discharge' type: i.e. revenue receipts are followed by payments made out of those receipts.

    When an heir came of age, he passed out of Wardship but could not enter upon his inheritance until, like heirs of full age, he sued out his Livery. This process was complicated and eventually resulted in a warrant being issued for the Livery to pass under the Great Seal. The Court had its own jurisdiction and a Ward could only sue or be sued in this Court. Wardship often led to litigation, primarily through the illegal retention sale, or leasing of a Ward's land or through their 'waste'. References for readers interesting in seeking information on the disposition of John's property include H. E. Bell, An Introduction to the History and Records of the Court of Wards and Liveries (Cambridge, 1953) and J. Hurstfield, The Queen's Wards (London, 1958).

    Hawkins, a man of wealth, left a relatively young family. His son and heir John was only 17 daughters Sara and Margaret were apparently younger. The Robert Woodward occupying one of the cottages in Braintree was probably a cousin and son of his aunt Woodward.
11. Morant 387, 397.
12. Ibid 398.
13. and 14. Thomas F. Waters, 1:466-67.
15. *Parish Registers,* Bocking, St. Mary's Church. Salt Lake City: Family History Library, Film #1471886, Item 12, 1588-1639. Baptisms, 1561-1605; burials, 1558-1628, marriages, 1593-1639. Original records at the Essex Record Office, Chelmsford England. A second register with baptisms from 1606-1654 is missing. A third register, Item 13 on the film includes baptisms from 1655-68 and marriages and burials from 1655-70.

APPENDIX G-2

DESCENDANTS OF FRANCIS DANE 1615–1697

(Dane lineage of Abigail Lamson, Gerneration 5 No. 204, wife of Francis Whipple.)

FIRST GENERATION

1. **Rev. Francis**[1] **Dane** (John[A] Dane)[1] great (8) grandfather of the author, was baptized 20 November 1615 in Bishop's-Storfford, England and died 17 February 1696/97 in Andover, Essex Co., Massachusetts. He married three times. (1) **Elizabeth Ingalls** in Andover.[2] Elizabeth, daughter of Edmund **Ingalls**, died there 9 June 1667. (2) **Mary Thomas** in Andover 21 September 1667. Mary, daughter of William **Thomas** and Agnes **Chandler**, was born abt 1629 and died there 18 February 1688/89.[3] (3) **Hannah (Chandler) Abbot** in Andover in 1690. Hannah, daughter of William **Chandler** and Agnes **Bayford**, died in Andover, 2 June 1711.[4] She married (1) **George Abbot** in Roxbury 12 December 1646.[5]

Rev. Francis **Dane** and Elizabeth **Ingalls** had the following children born in Andover:

+	2.	i.	Elizabeth[2] **Dane** born abt 1741.
+	3.	ii.	Nathaniel **Dane** born abt 1645.
	4.	iii.	Hannah **Dane**[6] married Capt. William **Goodhue**.
	5.	iv.	Phebe **Dane**[7] and married Joseph **Robinson** there 30 May 1671.
+	6.	v.	Abigail **Dane** born 13 October 1652.
+	7.	vi.	Francis **Dane** born 8 December 1656.

SECOND GENERATION

2. **Elizabeth**[2]**Dane** (Rev. Francis[1], John[A] Dane)[8] was born in Andover, Essex Co. Mass. abt 1641 and died there 15 April 1722, at 81 years of age. She married **Stephen Johnson** there 5 November 1661. He died in Andover 30 November 1690, at 50 years of age.[9] Elizabeth was accused of and confessed to being a Witch during the Salem trials of 1692.

Elizabeth **Dane** and Stephen **Johnson** had the following children born in Andover:

	8.	i.	Elizabeth[3] **Johnson**[10] born and died 4 February 1667.

{ G 1525 }

+	9	ii.	Francis **Johnson** 15 March 1666.
	10.	iii.	Ann **Johnson**[11] 25 February 1668 and died there 26 June 1699 at 1 year of age.
	11.	iv	Elizabeth **Johnson** about 1670. She confessed to being a witch.
	12.	v.	Stephen **Johnson**[12] 4 February 1672.
	13.	vi.	Mary **Johnson**[13] 21 March 1673 and died there 22 March 1673 at 2 days of age.
	14.	vii.	Abigail **Johnson**[14] 22 May 1675.
	15.	viii.	Benjamin **Johnson**[15] 12 August 1677.
	16.	ix.	Joseph **Johnson**[16] 12 August 1677.
	17.	x.	Stephen **Johnson**[17] 7 December 1679.
	18.	xi	Abigail **Johnson**[18] 16 March 1681-82.

3. **Nathaniel**[2] **Dane** (Rev.Francis[1], John[A] Dane)[19] was born in Andover, Essex Co. Mass. abt 1645 and died there 14 April 1725, at 80 years of age. He married **Deliverance Hasseltine** there 12 December 1672. She was born abt 1654 and died in Andover 15 June 1735.[20]

Nathaniel **Dane** and Deliverance **Hasseltine** had the following children, probably born in Andover:

19.	i.	Nathaniel[3] **Dane**[21] 18 June 1674 and died there 16 October 1674, at 4 months of age.
20.	ii.	Nathaniel **Dane**[22] 1 December 1675.
21.	iii.	Francis **Dane**[23] 1 October 1678 and died there 3 November 1679 at 1 year of age.
22.	iv.	Hannah **Dane** in 1680 and married Samuel **Osgood** in 1702.
23.	v.	Francis **Dane**.[24]
24.	vi.	Daniel **Dane**[25] 26 March 1684.
25.	vii.	Mary **Dane**[26] in 1688 and married Andrew **Allen**.
26.	viii.	Deliverance **Dane**[27] in 1694 and married Joseph **Foster**.
27.	ix.	Abigail **Dane**[28] 27 December 1698.

6. **Abigail**[2] **Dane** (Rev. Francis[1], John[A] Dane)[29] was born in Andover, Essex Co., Mass. 13 October 1652 and died there 5 February 1729/30, at 77 years of age. She married **Francis Faulkner** there 12 October 1675. Francis, son of Edmund **Faulkner** and Dorothy **Robinson**, was born in Andover abt 1651 and died there 19 September 1732, at 78 years of age.[30] Abigail was accused and convicted of Witchcraft during the 1692 Salem trials.

{ G 1526 }

Abigail **Dane** and Francis **Faulkner** had the following children born in Andover:

    28.   i.   Elizabeth[3] **Faulkner**[31] 4 July 1676 and died there 17 August 1678, at 2 years of age.

    29.   ii.   Elizabeth **Faulkner**[32] 7 December 1678 and married there (____) **Butterick**.

    30.   iii.   Dorothy **Faulkner**[33] 10 or 15 February 1680 and married there Samuel **Nurse** 25 November 1798. She was 12 when charged with being a witch and spent 30 days in jail before being released on bail.

+   31.   iv.   Abigail **Faulkner** 12 August 1683. She was 10 when charged with being a witch and spent 30 days in jail before being released on bail.

    32.   v.   Frances **Faulkner**[34] 29 April 1684 and died there 7 January 1735/36, at 50 years of age. She married Corp. Daniel **Faulkner** there 12 or 13 May 1724.

+   33.   vi.   Edmund **Faulkner** 2 April 1688 and married Elizabeth **Marston** there 19 February 1715.

+   34.   vii.   Paul **Faulkner** after 1689 and died there 9 January 1751. He married Sarah **Lamson** there 17 October 1714.

+   35.   viii.   Ammi Ruhamah **Faulkner** 20 March 1693 and died 4 August 1756 in Acton, Middlesex Co., Mass., at 63 years of age. He married Hannah **Ingalls** in Andover 7 June 1726.

7. **Francis**[2] **Dane** (Rev. Francis[1], John[A] Dane)[35] was born 8 December 1656 in Andover, Essex Co., Mass. and died 8 November 1738. He married **Hannah Poor** 16 November 1681.

Francis **Dane** and Hannah **Poor** had the following children:

    36.   i.   Francis[3] **Dane**[36] born before 1683 and apparently died young.

    37.   ii.   Francis **Dane**[37] born 22 April 1683 and died 22 September 1683, at 6 months of age.

    38.   iii.   Abiel **Dane**[38] born 17 September 1686 and died 22 September 1686 at 5 days of age.

    39.   iv.   Hannah **Dane**[39] born in 1687 and died in 1708, at 21 years of age.

    40.   v.   Francis **Dane**[40] born 19 August 1690.

+   41.   vi.   John **Dane** born 18 September 1692.

    42.   vii.   Joseph **Dane**[41] born 5 April 1696.

    43.   viii.   Daniel **Dane**[42] born 24 April 1698.

    44.   ix.   Mary **Dane**[43]

THIRD GENERATION

9. **Francis**[3] **Johnson** (Elizabeth[2] Dane, Rev. Francis[1], John[A] Dane)[44] born 15 March 1666 in Andover, Essex Co., Mass. and died in 1739. He married **Sarah Hawkes** there 11 February 1693.

Francis **Johnson** and Sarah **Hawkes** had the following children born in Andover:

45.	i.	Sarah[4] **Johnson**[45] 30 October 1693.
46.	ii.	Francis **Johnson**[46] 28 February 1695/96.
47.	ii.	William **Johnson**[47] in 1708.
48.	iii.	(Daughter) **Johnson**[48] 21 June 1712.
49.	iv.	Susannah **Johnson**.[49]

22. **Hannah**[3] **Dane** (Nathaniel[2], Rev. Francis[1], John[A] Dane)[50] was born in 1680 in Andover, Essex Co., Mass. and married twice. (1) **Samuel Osgood** there in 1702. Samuel, son of John **Osgood** and Mary **Clements**, was born 10 March 1665 in Andover and died there 22 April 1717.[51] (2) **James Pearson** 5 November 1724.

Hannah **Dane** and Samuel **Osgood** had the following child born in Andover:

509.	i.	Samuel[4] **Osgood**[52] in 1702 and died before July 1748. He married Hannah **Osgood** 9 November 1727.

31. **Abigail**[3] **Faulkner** (Abigail[2] Dane, Rev. Francis[1], John[A] Dane)[53] was born 12 August 1683 in Andover, Essex Co., Mass. and died 26 December 1746, at 63 years of age. She married **Thomas Lamson** there 6 April or 4 June 1708. Thomas, son of John **Lamson** and Martha **Perkins**,[54] was born in Ipswich 3 January 1682 and died there in July 1767, at 85 years of age. He married two more times in Ipswich. (2) **Sarah Rindge** 18 June 1747. (3) **Ruth Bowls** 25 March 1758. Thomas' will signed with his mark 12 August 1765 with a codicil in February 1767 was proved 27 July 1767. He mentions his wife Ruth and children (1) **Abigail**, wife of **Francis Whipple**, Esq., of Westborough, Mass., (2) **Martha**, wife of **Abraham Knowlton** of Shrewsbury, Mass., (3) **Sarah**, wife of **Aaron Forbush**, (4) **Elizabeth**, wife of **Jacob Fisk** of Hardwick, Worcester Co., Mass., Thomas, deceased. The inventory dated 24 August 1767 valued the estate at £174 18 8.[55]

Abigail **Faulkner** and Thomas **Lamson** had the following children:

50.	i.	Paul[4] **Lamson**[56] died before 1743.
51.	ii.	Sarah **Lamson**[57] married Aaron **Forbush** 11 November 1747.

{ G 1528 }

+	52.	iii.	Abigail **Lamson** born 15 February 1708.
	53.	iv.	Thomas **Lamson**[58] born in Ipswich, Essex Co., Mass. 8 April 1710 and died there 31 August 1751, at 41 years of age. He married Mary **Adams** in Ipswich 11 August 1732.
+	54.	v.	Martha **Lamson** born about 1713.
+	55.	vi.	Elizabeth **Lamson** born in 1724.

33. **Edmund**[3] **Faulkner** (Abigail[2]Dane, Rev.Francis[1], John[A] Dane)[59] was born 2 April 1688 in Andover, Essex Co., Mass. and married **Elizabeth Marston** there 19 February 1719. Elizabeth died there 23 May 1728.[60]

Edmund **Faulkner** and Elizabeth **Marston** had the following children born in Andover:

	56.	i.	Elizabeth[4] **Faulkner**[61] 2 June 1715 and died there 20 June 1715, at 18 days of age.
	57.	ii.	John **Faulkner**[62] 9 September 1718.
	58.	iii.	(Child) **Faulkner**[63] 1 January 1725.

34. **Paul**[3] **Faulkner** (Abigail[2] Dane, Rev.Francis[1], John[A] Dane)[64] was born abt 1689 in Andover, Essex Co., Mass. and died there 9 January 1751. He married twice. (1) **Sarah Lamson** 17 October 1714 in Ipswich, Essex Co., Mass.[65] (2) **Hannah Sheffeld** 3 January 1723/24 in Andover.

Paul **Faulkner** and Sarah **Lamson** had the following children born in Andover:

	59.	i.	Sarah[4] **Faulkner**[66] 2 December 1715 and married Gideon **Stiles** there 30 November 1736.
	60.	ii.	Paul **Faulkner**.[67]

Paul **Faulkner** and Hannah **Sheffeld** had the following children born in Andover:

	61.	iii.	Samuel[4] **Faulkner**[68] 8 October 1724 and died there 8 August 1737, at 12 years of age.
	62.	iv	Dorathy **Faulkner**[69] 30 January 1726.
	63.	v.	Elizabeth **Faulkner**[70] 27 March 1728.
	64.	vi.	Nathaniel **Faulkner**[71] 13 April 1729 and died there 18 July 1737, at 8 years of age.
	65.	vii.	Edmond **Faulkner**[72] 24 June 1730 and died there 10 November 1736, at 6 years of age.
	66.	viii.	(Child) **Faulkner**[73] 27 June 1734.
	67.	ix.	Benjamin **Faulkner**[74] 6 May 1736 and died there 10 November 1736, at 6 months of age.

{ G 1529 }

68. x. Paul **Faulkner**[75] 30 June 1737.
69. xi. Hannah **Faulkner**.[76]

35. **Ammi**[3] **Ruhamah Faulkner** (Abigail[2]Dane, Rev. Francis[1], John[A] Dane)[77] was born 20 March 1693 in Andover, Essex Co., Mass. and died 4 August 1756 in Acton, Middlesex Co., Mass., at 63 years of age. He married **Hannah Ingalls** in Andover 7 June 1726.

Ammi Ruhamah **Faulkner** and Hannah **Ingalls** had the following children born in Andover:

70. i. Hannah **Faulkner**[78] 12 March 1727.
71. ii. Francis **Faulkner**[79] 16 September 1728.
72. iii. James **Faulkner**[80] 23 October 1730.

41. **John**[3] **Dane** (Francis[2], Rev.Francis[1], John[A] Dane)[81] was born 18 September 1692 in Andover, Essex Co., Mass. and married **Sarah Chandler** there.

John **Dane** and Sarah **Chandler** had the following child born in Andover:

73. i. Sarah **Dane**.[82]

DESCENDANTS OF EDMUND FAULKNER

(Faulkner lineage of Abigail Lamson, Generation 5, No. 204, wife of Francis Whipple.)

FIRST GENERATION

1. **Edmund**[1] **Faulkner**,[1] great (8) grandfather of the author, was born, probably, in King's Clear, Southampton Co., England and died 18 January 1686/87 in Andover, Essex Co., Mass. He married **Dorothy (__) Robinson** in Salem, Essex Co. Mass. 4 February 1647. She was born in England[2] and died 2 December 1688[3] in Andover.[4] A widow when she married Edmund, her maiden name is unknown. That she and Faulkner were married in Salem suggests that she and her son Joseph were from there. There were several Robinsons in early Salem and Joseph was a popular name among them but the name of her first husband is unknown. There is no record that her son Joseph was born in Salem. Edmund's birthplace is presumed to be King's Clear because his brother Francis, who

{ G 1530 }

bequeathed him £200 in his will dated 1 September 1662, listed his residence as King's Clear. He also identified Edmund as a resident of New England. The many bequeaths included in the will indicates Francis was quite wealthy. The name was spelled Fawconer and Fawkener in England. The article "Positive Pedigrees and Authorized Arms" by Wm. S. Appleton in the July 1894 *Register* says Edmond Fawkener of Andover, Mass. from King's County Cleere, Hampshire was eligible to wear the family Arms which were Sable, three Falcons Argent, beaked, legged and belled Or. G. Andrews Moriarty, Jr., Chair of the Committee on Heraldry for the New England Historic Genealogical Society, identified the Arms as: Sable three Falcons silver beaked legged and belled gold. The Crest was identified as A wheat-sheaf gold banded silver. Edmund, along with John Woodbridge, Andover's first Minister, purchased the Indian land known as Cochichewick from Sagamore Cutshemache of the Naumkeag Tribe for £6 and a red coat. It was then named Andover. He and Simon Bradstreet were the only two early settlers called "Mister." He served as Selectman, Town Clerk 1674-77, and in 1662 received the first Andover license for a vintner and innholder.

Edmund[1] **Faulkner** and Dorothy (__) **Robinson** had the following children born in Andover:

+ 2. i. Mary[2] **Faulkne**r.
+ 3. ii. Francis **Faulkne**r abt 1651.
+ 4. iii. John **Faulkne**r in 1654.
+ 5. iv. Hannah **Faulkne**r in 1658.

SECOND GENERATION

2. Mary[2] Faulkner (Edmund[1])[5] was born in Andover, Essex Co., Mass., birthdate unknown and married **Joseph Marble** there 30 May 1671.[6]

Mary **Faulkner** and Joseph **Marble** had the following child born in Andover:
6. i. Dorothy[3] **Marble**[7] died abt 1673.

3. Francis[2] Faulkner (Edmund[1])[8] was born in Andover, Essex Co., Mass. abt 1651 and died there 19 September 1732, at 78 years of age. He married **Abigail Dane** there 12 October 1675. Abigail, daughter of Rev. Francis **Dane** and Elizabeth **Ingalls** was born in Andover 13 October 1652[9] and died 5 February 1729/30, at 77 years of age.[10] She was convicted of being a witch in the Salem witch trials of 1692. Read her story below.

{ G 1531 }

Francis **Faulkner** and Abigail **Dane** had the following children born in Andover:

+ 7. i. Paul[3] **Faulkner**.
  8. ii. Elizabeth **Faulkner**[11] 4 July 1676 and died there 17 August 1678, at 2 years of age.
  9. iii. Elizabeth **Faulkner**[12] 7 December 1678.
  10. iv Dorothy **Faulkner**[13] 10 or 15 February 1680 and married Samuel **Nurse** of Danvers, Essex Co., Mass. in Andover 25 Nov. 1708. She was charged, at age 12, with being a witch in 1692 and spent 30 days in the Salem jail until bail was posted.
+ 11. v. Abigail **Faulkner** 12 August 1683.
  12. vi. Frances **Faulkner**[14] 29 April 1686 and died there 7 January 1735/36, at 49 years of age. She married Daniel **Faulkner** there 12 May 1724. Daniel, son of John **Faulkner** and Sarah **Abbott,** was born 29 April 1686. They were first cousins.
+ 13. vii Edmund **Faulkner** 2 April 1688.
+ 14. viii. Amni Ruhamah **Faulkner** 20 March 1693.

4. John[2] **Faulkner** (Edmund[1])[15] was born in Andover, Essex Co., Mass. in 1654 and died there in 1706, at 52 years of age. He married **Sarah Abbott** who died in 1723.[16]

John **Faulkner** and Sarah **Abbott** had the following children born in Andover:

  15. i. Sarah[3] **Faulkner**[17] died there 1 September 1689.
+ 16. ii. Hannah **Faulkner**.
  17. iii. Daniel **Faulkner**[18] 29 April 1686 and married Frances **Faulkner** there 12 May 1724. Frances[19] daughter of Francis **Faulkner** and Abigail **Dane**, was born in Andover 29 April 1686 and died there 7 January 1735/36, at 49 years of age. Frances and Daniel were first cousins.

5. Hannah[2] **Faulkner** (Edmund[1])[20] was born in Andover, Essex Co., Mass. in 1658 and died there 22 February 1697/98, at 39 years of age.[21] She married **Capt. Pascoe Chubb** there 24 May 1689.[22] He died there 22 February 1697/98.[23] Hannah and Pascoe were murdered by Indians during their attack on Andover.

Hannah **Faulkner** and Capt. Pascoe **Chubb** had the following child born in Andover:

  18 i. Hannah[3] **Chubb**[24] and married John **Abbott,** son of Thomas **Abbott.** After her parents were killed by the Indians, Hannah was raised by her uncle Francis Faulkner.

{ G 1532 }

THIRD GENERATION

7. **Paul**[3] **Faulkner** (Francis[2], Edmund[1])[25] was born in Andover, Essex Co., Mass. and died there 9 January 1751. He married twice. (1) **Sarah Lamson** in Ipswich, Essex Co., Mass. 17 October 1714. Sarah,[26] daughter of John **Lamson** and Martha **Perkins,** was born in Ipswich in 1683 and died in 1715 at 32 years of age. In addition to Sarah, they had a son Paul, date and place of birth unknown. (2) **Hannah Sheffeld** in Andover 3 January 1723/24.[27]

Paul **Faulkner** and Sarah **Lamson** had the following child:
+ 19 i. Sarah[4] **Faulkner** born 2 December 1715.

Paul **Faulkner** and Hannah **Sheffeld** had the following children born in Andover:
- 20. ii. Samuel **Faulkner**[28] 8 October 1724 and died there 8 August 1737, at 12 years of age.
- 21. iii. Dorathy **Faulkner**[29] 30 January 1725/26.
- 22. iv. Elizabeth **Faulkner**[30] 27 March 1728.
- 23. v. Nathaniel **Faulkner**[31] 13 April 1729 and died there 18 July 1737, at 8 years of age.
- 24. vi. Edmond **Faulkner**[32] 24 June 1730 and died there 10 November 1736, at 6 years of age.
- 25. vii. (Child) **Faulkner**[33] 27 June 1734.
- 26. viii. Benjamin **Faulkner**[34] 6 May 1736 and died there 10 November 1736, at 6 months of age.
- 27. ix. Paul **Faulkner**[35] 30 June 1737.
- 28. x. Hannah **Faulkner**[36] 11 March 1738/39.

11. **Abigail**[3] **Faulkner** (Francis[2], Edmund[1])[37] was born in Andover, Essex Co., Mass. 12 August 1683 and died 26 December 1746 in Ipswich, Essex Co., Mass., at 63 years of age. She married **Thomas Lamson** in Andover 6 April 1708. (Date of intent to marry 31 March 1707/08.) Thomas,[38] son of John **Lamson** and Martha **Perkins**,[39] was born in Ipswich 3 January 1682 and died there in July 1767, at 85 years of age. He married (2) **Sarah Rindge** in Ipswich 18 June 1747.[40] (Date of intent to marry.) (3) **Ruth Bowls** in Ipswich 25 March 1758. (Date of intent to marry.) Thomas, a yeoman, also dealt in real estate, buying and selling about a dozen times between 1713 and 1755. One of his purchases was from James Whipple who on 15 July 1730 sold him for £1,100 his "new dwelling house, barn, outhousing, orchard, and about 70 acres of upland meadow and meadow ground . . . his homestead on about 20 acres . . . about two

{ G 1533 }

acres of pine swamp . . . a piece of land on the northeasterly side of Black Brook . . . and about seven acres that bounds southerly upon Mr. Saltonstall's heir's farm."[41] Thomas' will was signed with his mark 12 August 1765 with a codicil in February 1767 and proved 27 July 1767. He mentions his wife Ruth and children (1) Abigail, wife of Francis Whipple, Esq. of Westborough; (2) Martha, wife of Abraham Knowlton of Shrewsbury; (3) Sarah, wife of Aaron Forbush; (4) Elizabeth, wife of Jacob Fisk of Hardwick; (5) Thomas deceased. The inventory dated 24 August 1767 valued the estate at 174 pounds 18 shillings 8 pence.[42]

Abigail **Faulkner** and Thomas **Lamson** had the following children born in Ipswich:

  29. i. Paul[4] **Lamson**[43] 6 March 1714-15 and died bef 1743.
  30. ii. Sarah **Lamson**[44] baptized 20 Aug. 1721 and married Aaron **Forbush** of Hardwick, Worcester Co., Mass. 11 November 1747. (Date of intent to marry). She joined The Hamilton Church 7 June 1741.
+ 31. iii. Abigail **Lamson** 15 February 1708.
  32. iv. Thomas **Lamson**[45] 8 April 1710 and died there 31 August 1751, at 41 years of age.[46] He married Mary **Adams** in Ipswich 11 August 1732. (Date of intent to marry.) Mary,[47] daughter of Nathaniel **Adams** Jr. and Abigail **Kimball**, was born in Ipswich. She married (2) Robert **Potter** in Ipswich 1 October 1760. (Date of intent to marry.) Thomas was a "husbandman" of Ipswich who joined the church in Hamilton 18 February 1727. On 8 July 1747, he purchased for £250 (bills of New Tenor) the "full one half part with one half of the buildings thereon standing" of his father's homestead (which his father had bought from James Whipple 15 July 1730), one-half of his upland and meadow, one-half of his salt marsh and thatch ground, one-half of his "quick stock and husbandry utensils," and one-half of his "common right in the thick wood (Eighth) of Ipswich." Apparently they were going to jointly farm the land. He died intestate and his widow Mary was appointed administratrix of his estate which was valued at £289, 15 shillings. The estate was divided from the state of his father's and his portion was further divided with one-half to his oldest son Thomas and the other half to the widow and his other six children. When dividing the buildings, Thomas received "the westerly end of Dwelling house to the middle of the chimney right up and down . . . and six foot and nine inches of the westerly end of the cellar

under the easterly end of said house, and half the corn house, to the middle beam right up and down ... also a garden spot containing about eight rods on the southerly side of the highway aforesaid of the dwelling house ... and half the well, and to have liberty to pass round the house as his occasion may be. He was also allowed "a convenient way through the land of the widow and heirs aforesaid." The proposed division was accepted by the Superior Court at Salem 24 October 1759.[48]

+ 33. v. Martha **Lamson** abt 1713.
+ 34. vi. Elizabeth **Lamson**[49] in 1724.

13. **Edmund**[3] Faulkner (Francis[2], Edmund[1])[50] was born in Andover, Essex Co., Mass. 2 April 1688 and married twice. (1) **Elizabeth Marston** in Andover 19 February 1714/15[51] who died there 23 May 1728.[52] (2) **Dorcas Buxton**. Edmund is also identified as Edmond in some vital records.

Edmund **Faulkner** and Elizabeth **Marston** had the following children born in Andover:

35. i. Elizabeth[4] **Faulkner** 2 June 1715[53] and died there 20 June 1715, at 18 days of age.[54]
36. ii. John **Faulkner** 9 September 1718.[55]
37. iii. (Child) **Faulkner**.[56] The child was unnamed and may have died at birth.

14. **Ammi Ruhamah**[3] Faulkner (Francis[2], Edmund[1])[57] was born in Andover, Essex Co., Mass. 20 March 1693 and died abt 1757. He married **Hannah Ingalls** in 1726. Ammi Ruhamah means "My people have obtained mercy." It's from the Old Testament, Book of Hosea, Chapter 2, Verse 1: "Say he unto your brethren Ammi; and to your sisters Ruhamah." Ammi is "My people." Ruhamah is "that hath obtained mercy." The name is based on the fact his mother Abigail was pardoned by Massachusetts Gov. Phipps on her conviction for witchcraft.

Ammi Ruhamah **Faulkner** and Hannah **Ingalls** had the following children born in Andover:

38. i. Hannah[4] **Faulkner** 12 March 1726/27.[58]
39. ii. Francis **Faulkner** 16 September 1728.[59]
40. iii. James **Faulkner** 25 October 1730.[60]

16. **Hannah**[3] Faulkner (John[2], Edmund[1])[61] was born in Andover, Essex Co., Mass., birth date unknown, and died 27 December 1759. She married **James Howe** 8 January 1722/23. James,[62] son of John **Howe** and Hannah

{ G 1535 }

(__), was born in Ipswich, Essex Co. and died 22 December 1771 at 76 years of age.

Hannah **Faulkner** and James **Howe** had the following child:

+   41   i.   James[4] **Howe** born 27 October 1723.

FOURTH GENERATION

19. **Sarah**[4] **Faulkner** (Paul[3], Francis[2], Edmund[1])[63] was born in Andover, Essex Co., Mass. 2 December 1715 and married **Gideon Stiles** there 30 November 1736. He was born in Boxford, Essex Co., Mass. 26 February 1711.[64]

Sarah **Faulkner** and Gideon **Stiles** had the following children born in Boxford:

     34.   i.   David[5] **Stiles** 2 April 1738.[65] He and his brother Jesse were baptized on the same day. It is possible they were twins.
     35.   ii.   Jesse **Stiles** 2 April 1738.[66]
     36.   iii.   Sarah **Stiles** 12 August 1744.[67]

31. **Abigail**[4] **Lamson** (Abigail[3] Faulkner, Francis[2] Edmund[1])[68] was born in Ipswich, Essex Co., Mass. 15 February 1708 and died 22 December 1799 in New Braintree, Worcester Co., Mass., at 91 years of age. She married **Francis Whipple** in in the Third Parish of Ipswich, known as the Hamlet Parish. Rev. Samuel Wigglesworth performed the ceremony 11 May 1726. (Intent to marry was also recorded.) Francis,[69] son of Jonathan **Whipple** and Frances **Edwards,** was baptized in Ipswich 4 November 1705 by Rev. Wigglesworth and died 2 July 1787 in New Braintree, at 82 years of age. Francis and Abigail joined the Evangelical Congregational Church of Westborough, Worcester Co., Mass. by letter 6 January 1734. Abigail's brother Francis visited Westborough in February 1744 and her husband Francis took him to meet Rev. Parkman who noted in his diary of 13 February that "religious affairs more steadily managed at Ipswich than in past."[70] Abigail was probably buried in same New Braintree's Cemetery as Francis but no stone marks her grave. Abigail Lamson and Francis Whipple had the following 11 children. See Generation No. 5, Number 204 for a list of these children.

33. **Martha**[4] **Lamson** (Abigail[3] Faulkner, Francis[2], Edmund[1])[71] was born in Ipswich, Essex Co., Mass. abt 1713 and married **Abraham Knowlton** of Shrewsbury, Worcester Co., Mass. in January 1734. (Date of intent to marry.) Abraham,[72] son of Thomas **Knowlton** and Margery **Carter,** was born in Marlborough, Middlesex Co., Mass. 30 April 1703 and died 3

November 1768 at 65 years of age. Martha joined the Hamilton church 20 May 1733.

Martha **Lamson** and Abraham **Knowlton** had the following children:

+ 37. i. Paul[5] **Knowlton** born 17 April 1736.
   38. ii. Silas **Knowlton** born 9 September 1737.[73]
   39. iii. Abraham **Knowlton** born 19 September 1742[74] and died young.
   40. iv. Robert **Knowlton** born 18 March 1744[75] and died young.
   41. v. Sarah **Knowlton**[76] born 24 January 1746 and married David **Drury** in 1765.
   42. vi. Martha **Knowlton**[77] born 24 January 1748 and married Thomas **Drury** in 1769.
   43. vii. Abraham **Knowlton**[78] born 25 November 1750 and married Lydia **Batchelder**.

34. **Elizabeth**[4] **Lamson** (Abigail[3] Faulkner, Francis[2], Edmund[1]) was baptized in Ipswich, Essex Co., Mass., 12 January 1723/24 and married **Jacob Fisk** 3 November 1743.[79] (Date of intent to marry.) Jacob,[80] son of Ebenezer **Fisk** and Eliz. **Fuller,** was born in Wenham, Essex Co., Mass. 26 December 1721.

Elizabeth **Lamson** and Jacob **Fisk** had the following children:

   44. i. Elizabeth[5] **Fisk**[81] born 14 March 1745 and married David **Allen**.
   45. ii. Jonathan **Fisk**[82] born 17 May 1747 and died 22 May 1747 in Wenham, at 5 days of age.
   46. iii. Abigail **Fisk** born 17 August 1750.[83]
   47. iv. Sara **Fisk** born 28 December 1752.[84]
   48. v. (Daughter) **Fisk** born 24 September 1758.[85]

41. **James**[4] **Howe** (Hannah[3] Faulkner, John[2], Edmund[1])[86] was born in Haverhill, Essex Co., Mass., 27 October 1723 and died 14 January 1806 at 82 years of age. He married **Jemima Farnum** 6 February 1752. She was born in Andover, Essex Co., Mass. 21 March 1730.[87]

James **Howe** and Jemima **Farnum** had the following child:

+ 49. i. David[5] **Howe** baptized in Ipswich, Essex Co., Mass. 12 January 1723/24

{ G 1537 }

ABIGAIL (DANE) FAULKNER
MY (BAINE WHIPPLE) FAVORITE ANCESTRESS[1]

Almost everyone in 1692 the educated and the unlearned believed in a material (visible) world and a spiritual (invisible) world. Heaven with its Angels was a reality as was Hell and its Devils. People believed inhabitants of the invisible world could intrude on the visible world. Consequently, every accident, every sudden or unusual illness of man or beast, every inexplicable or menacing circumstance of any sort was apt to raise the cry of witchcraft.

Abigail (Dane) Faulkner was my great (7) grandmother. She was born in Andover in 1652 and died there in 1730.[2] If Andover had had a newspaper in 1692, the following would have been the lead story in the issue of August 12:

PROMINENT ANDOVER WOMAN CHARGED WITH WITCHCRAFT

Abigail Faulkner, Sr., of Andover was indicted August 11, for the "detestable crime of witchcraft." The wife of Lieut. Francis Faulkner, she is one of the most prominent women in the township. The Grand Jury indicted her twice for practicing "sorceries wickedly, maliciously, and feloniously." Indictment No. 1 charges her with bewitching Martha Sprague, 16, of Boxford; Indictment No. 2 with bewitching Sarah Phelps, 9, of Andover. The indictments were handed down in the name of our Sovereign Lord King William and our Lady Queen Anne. Edmund Faulker, her father-in-law, is one of the founders of the Township and one of the few original Proprietors dignified with the title of Mr.[3] Rev. Francis Dane, her father, has been Andover's senior Minister since 1648.[4] Her trial date is set for September 17 in Salem. She will appear before the special Court of Oyer and Terminer (hear and determine), Magistrates John Hathorne, Jonathan Corwin, and John Higginson presiding.[5] A guilty verdict would mean a sentence of death by hanging. Mrs. Faulkner, mother of five, is pregnant. She is an Andover native.[6]

In February of 1692 a small group of girls in Salem Village ranging in age from 9 to 17 began acting strange and bizarre. They had fits, uttered foolish and nonsensical speeches, made odd gestures, and contorted

{ G 1538 }

themselves into grotesque postures. Their actions were reminiscent of the bewitched children in Rev. Cotton Mathers *Memorable Providences Relating to Witchcraft and Possessions,* published in Boston in 1689. Mather was a Minister of the Second Church in Boston (North Church).[7]

Dr. Griggs of Salem village examined the girls and finding no physical cause for their afflictions concluded they were bewitched. Rev. Samuel Parris of Salem Village, whose 9-year-old daughter was among the group, conferred with clergy and elders from half a dozen surrounding towns. After meeting privately with the girls and applying the therapy of prayer with discouraging results, the ministers decided the girls must name their tormentors so the witches could be brought to justice.[8]

All that remained was to discover who they were. A dog was fed a cake of rye meal, made with the children's urine and baked in the ashes. After the dog had eaten, the "afflicted" children went into fits and convulsions and claimed to see into the invisible world "ruled by the Devil and inhabited by specters and ghosts." This new-found spectral sight made it possible for the girls to see who was causing their afflictions. Spectral evidence could now be used to name witches and wizards.

The witchcraft hunt divides into two major phases: Salem Village and Andover. More were accused and arrested in Andover than in Salem Village. The Salem phase began March 1, the Andover phase July 15. Among the leaders of the afflicted circle in Andover were Martha Sprague and Sarah Phelps. While appearing harmless and innocent in the real world, the witch had a specter in the invisible world which inflicted excruciating pain by pinching, pricking, and tormenting. The authorities conducting the witch trials deemed irrelevant and frivolous testimony based on the fact other people, including themselves, could not see what the girls saw. In 1692, it was believed the girl's spectral power was the means God provided to detect witches.

Place yourself in the Salem Courtroom August 11, 1692. You are Abigail Faulkner, 40, about two months pregnant, have five children and a sick husband at home. Your father-in-law is a founder of the Township where your father has been minister for 34 years. You have lived in Andover all your life and no one has ever known you to be other than a God-fearing woman. Today you are being examined by three Magistrates of the Commonwealth, charged with the most heinous crime known to man. Two girls you don't know claim you have bewitched them. You have to answer, and answer alone as the law does not allow you representation.

Three afflicted girls from Salem, all strangers to you, are part of the examination. What they do, how they act, will determine if you are convicted. This is the darkest time of your life—more frightening than the Indian attack on Andover May 5, 1689 when your sister-in-law Hannah, her husband Capt. Pascoe Chubb, and three others were killed, two houses and barn and the cattle in them burned, and the Meeting House set afire.

The hearing begin with Magistrate Hathorne reading the charge: "You are apprehended for witchcraft." "I know nothing of it," you say while looking around the room. At your glance the afflicted fall to the floor in fits. Hathorne: "Do you not see?" "Yes, but it is the Devil does it in my shape." Mary Walcott: "I was first tormented last night but have seen Faulkner's specter for two months." "Ann Putnam: "Faulkner pulled me off my horse last night but I saw her before." Mary Warren: "I saw Faulkner with other witches but was not hurt by her till lately." Following their testimony the girls again fall into fits. Your touch ends their contortion. Hawthorne: "For the credit of your town, confess the truth." Your niece, Elizabeth Johnson, 22, (No. 11 under Descendants of Rev. Francis Dane) was charged a day earlier and confessed, saying she was carried to a witch meeting at the village on a pole and that you were there. She is sitting with the afflicted and urges you to confess.

Mary Ann (Whipple) McPherson and Blaine Whipple airborn in May 2003. Great (7) grandchildren of Abigail (Dane) Faulkner convicted of being a witch in a 1692 trial in Salem Mass.

What do you do? The witch hunts are in their sixth month. Scores have been arrested. Six have been hanged: two others died in prison. A pattern has developed. Those who confess are spared. Those who maintain their innocence are condemned and hanged. Among the hanged is Elizabeth, wife of your first cousin James Howe, Jr. She refused to confess.[9] It is an agonizing decision. Life is precious, your family needs you. What do you do?

Things don't go well as the examination progresses. Nine-year-old

Sarah Phelps went into fits, claiming you as the cause. Idly, you pick up a cloth from the table and squeeze it. The girls immediately fall into fits claiming Daniel Eames and Capt. Floyd were on the cloth as it lay on the table. You remind the Magistrates you looked at some of the girls earlier in Andover and they were not afflicted, but Hathorne rules it inadmissible, "You only began afflicting yesterday. You used to conjure (practice magic or legerdemain) with a sieve," he charges. "That's not so. You are repeating an old story proved untrue long ago." You can think of nothing else to say except "I'm sorry the girls are afflicted." Sorry isn't enough because you didn't shed a tear when saying it. Finally, you know what you must do. You are not a witch. God would not require you to plead guilty when you are not. Your plea is not guilty. The examination is over. No decision is made.

By the time of the second examination August 30, your first cousin Martha Carrier and four others who refused to confess have been condemned and hanged. Your widowed sister Elizabeth Johnson, (see No. 2 under descendants of Rev. Francis Dane) mother of your niece Elizabeth, was charged and confessed the previous day, implicating you.

You begin the second hearing as you ended the first—denying the charge. Known for their bullying and absurd leading questions, the Magistrates were relentless in getting the answers they wanted. You finally admit to looking at the girls with an "evil eye" and to pinching your hands together. "But if the Devil took advantage of that, it was the Devil, not me that afflicted the girls." You are found guilty on September 17. The verdict still exists on a document in the Massachusetts State Archives: "The Jury find Abigail Faulkner, wife of Francis Faulkner of Andover, guilty of the felony of witchcraft committed on the body of Martha Sprague also on the body of Sarah Phelps. SENTENCE OF DEATH PLACED ON ABIGAIL FAULKNER[10] Because she was pregnant, she was reprieved until after the birth of her child.

Reading about the 1692 witchcraft trials is mind boggling. The reader has no point of reference, no understanding of how Judges conducted the trials or on what basis juries returned guilty verdicts. It seems absurd that a person could be accused, let alone tried for the crime of witchcraft. But in 1692 existence of the Devil, who was a fallen Angel (Ephesians 6:12), was accepted by everyone.

Cotton Mather, one of the colony's leading ministers, believed New England was originally the Devil's territory, that the Devil was irritated that a people of God settled there, and was fighting for converts in Salem, Andover, and other New England towns to prevent Christianity from winning the New World.[11] He believed the testimony of the witch accusers and told the people of Massachusetts there were thousands of Devils among them (Mark 5:15). He said they were led by a Prince called Beelzebub whose Angels were soldiers like "vast regiments of cruel and bloody French dragoons overrunning a pillaged neighborhood."[12]

Mather did much to convince the people to believe in Devils. He said the only person who could doubt the existence of the Devil is one who is under his influence. He preached the end of the world was near and that God was allowing the Devil to plague the world until the Second Coming. He said the Devil knew the end was near so he recruited new followers and set them loose to attack Christians. "The devils swarm about us like the frogs of Egypt," he said.[13] Even those who were skeptical came to believe what Mather and many other ministers were preaching and came to accept that their own wives, children, parents, and siblings were Devils.

Spectral evidence wasn't accepted by everyone, but is was by Mather and he recommended the speedy and vigorous prosecution "of such as have rendered themselves obnoxious; according to the best directions given in the laws of God and the wholesome statutes of the English nation for the detection of witchcraft. We must make just as much use of all advice from the invisible world as God sends. It permits spirits from the unseen regions to visit us with surprising informations, we are to inquire what cause there is for such things.[14] To do less was to allow the Devil "get so far into our faith, we come at length to believe his lies."[15]

"Rules for the finding out of witches" included: 1) If any man or woman be notoriously defamed for a witch this yields a strong suspicion. 2) Testimony from a fellow-witch or magician is a fit presumption to cause a straight examination. 3) If death, or at least some mischief follow cursing and banning, the person should be examined, though not necessarily convicted. 4) If mischief follows enmity, quarreling, or threatening, it is a great presumption of witchcraft. 5) The son or daughter, man-servant or maid-servant, familiar friend, near neighbor, or old companion of a known and convicted witch is open to suspicion of witchcraft for witchcraft is an art learned and conveyed from man to man. 6) The party suspected has the Devil's mark; for when the devil covenants with them he always leaves his mark so he knows them for his own—a mark that can't be explained in nature. 7) If the suspect is unconstant or contrary when examined it suggests a guilty conscience stops the freedom of utterance.[16]

Jurors were instructed on what evidence could convict. 1) The free and voluntary confession by the accused supported by witnesses or further inquiry. 2) Two good and honest witnesses testifying they had personal knowledge that either the accused made a league with the Devil or did some known practice of witchcraft "is a pregnant proof of a league formerly made between them." 3) Proof that the suspect entertained a familiar spirit, and had conference with it in the likeness of some visible creatures.

{ G 1542 }

4) If the witnesses affirm upon oath the suspect did something which infers a covenant made—used enhancements, divined things before they come to pass, raised tempests, raised the form of a dead man to appear.[17]

Bernard of Batcomb's *Guide to Grand Jurymen*[18] elaborated on evidence to convict. 1) The witches mark on the baser sort of witches is insensitive, and will not bleed. Some are like a teat; some but a blewish spot; some a red one; and some sunken flesh. But the witches do sometimes cover them. 2) By the witches words. As when they have been heard calling on, speaking to, or talking of their familiars; when heard telling of hurt they have done to man or beast; when heard threatening of such hurt; when heard relating their transportations. 3) By the witches deeds. As when they have been seen with their spirits, or seen secretly feeding their imps. Or, when their pictures, puppets, and their hellish compositions are found. 4) By the witches ecstasies;[19] with the delight whereof witches are so taken, they hardly conceal the same. 5) By fellow witches confessing their own witchcraft and bearing witness against others with sufficient proof—they have seen them with their spirits, have received spirits from them, have seen them use witchery-tricks to do harm, can show the mark upon them, have attended meetings together. 6) By the witches own confession of giving their souls to the Devil.[20]

Records of the jury deliberations aren't available but it seems clear Abigail's conviction was based on the spectral evidence of Mary Walcott, Ann Putnam, and Mary Warren of Salem Village, Martha Sprague of Boxford, and Sarah Phelps of Andover. Warren also testified she saw Abigail with other witches. The jury must have given credence to the evidence of Abigail's sister and niece, both named Elizabeth Johnson, who confessed to the charge of witchcraft and said Abigail was one of them. The fact her first cousin Martha Carrier and Elizabeth Howe, wife of her first cousin James Howe, Jr., were both convicted and hanged must have weighed heavily with the jury.

Abigail was made of stern stuff. On December 3, after 78 days in Salem prison, she petitioned Governor William Phipps for a pardon, pointing out the evidence against her was spectral and that after she was condemned, the confessors who implicated her admitted they wronged her and that their testimony was false.[21]

The petition worked. She was released from prison a few days later. But Abigail was not through. Determined to clear her name, she wrote the Massachusetts Legislature in 1703 noting she was accused by the afflicted who "pretended to see me by their sprectral sight (not with their bodily eyes) and that I afflicted them, . . . these being all that gave in any evidence against me upon oath, yet the jury (upon only their testimony) brought me in guilty, and the sentence of death was passed upon me." She

{ G 1543 }

said that despite Gov. Phipps pardon, the official record still showed her a "malefactor convict . . . of the most heinous crimes that mankind can supposed to be guilty of, which besides its utter ruining and defacing my reputation, will certainly expose myself to imminent danger by new accusations, which will thereby be the more readily believed, will remain as a perpetual brand of infamy upon my family."

On July 20, 1703, the House of Representatives ordered a Bill be drafted to disallow spectral evidence stating "no specter evidence may hereafter be accounted valid, or sufficient to take away the life, or good name, of any person or persons within this Province, and that the infamy, and reproach, cast on the names and posterity of the said accused and condemned persons may in some measure be rolled away."[22] Thus the attainder (forfeiture of property and loss of civil rights of a person sentenced to death) of Abigail Faulkner and others was reversed.

One task remained. People imprisoned in those days were responsible for paying the jailer for all costs associated with their incarceration. Abigail and others petitioned the Legislature to be reimbursed and in 1712 she received £20 as partial payment of her costs. Abigail (Dane) Faulkner displayed courage and fortitude far beyond the norm for the time. I'm proud to call her my ancestress.

* * *

EXTENDED DANE FAMILY MEMBERS ACCUSED OF WITCHCRAFT IN 1692:

CHARGED	NAME, AGE, TOWN	FAMILY BRANCH
Apr. 21	Nehemiah Abbot, Jr. 29, Topsfield. The only person to be released following a preliminary hearing.	Howe family
May 18	Dr. Roger Toothaker, 58, Billerica. **Died in prison** June 16.	Allen family
May 28	Martha (Allen) Carrier, 38, Andover. Imprisoned. Condemned Aug. 5. **Hanged** Aug 19.	Allen family

{ G 1544 }

May 28	Margaret Toothaker, 9, Billerica. Imprisoned.	Allen family
May 28	Mary (Allen) Toothaker, 47, Billerica. Imprisoned. Found not guilty Feb. 1, 1693.	Allen family
May 28	Elizabeth (Jackson) Howe, 53, Topsfield. Imprisoned. **Hanged** July 19.	Howe family
July 21	Andrew Carrier, 15, Andover. Imprisoned. Released on bail mid October.	Allen family
July 21	Richard Carrier, 18, Andover. Imprisoned. Released on bail mid October.	Allen family
July 22	Martha (Toothaker) Emerson, 24, Haverhill. Imprisoned. Cleared Jan. 12, 1693.	Allen family
Aug. 10	Elizabeth Johnson, 22, Andover. **Granddaughter.** Imprisoned 6 months. **Condemned** Jan. 12, 1693. Reprieved. Released February 1693.	Dane family
Aug. 10	Sarah Carrier, 7, Andover. Imprisoned. Released on bail Oct. 6.	Allen family
Aug. 10	Thomas Carrier, Jr., 10. Andover. Imprisoned. Released on bail Oct. 6.	Allen family

Aug. 11	Abigail (Dane) Faulkner 40, Andover. **Daughter.** Imprisoned. **Condemned** Sept. 17. Reprieved for pregnancy. Released about Dec. 8.	Dane family
Aug. 24	Sarah Bridges, 17, Andover. Imprisoned 6 weeks. Released on bail about Oct. 6. Found not guilty Jan. 12, 1693.	Howe family
Aug. 25	John Jackson, Sr. 50, Rowley. Imprisoned.	Howe family
Aug. 25	John Jackson, Jr. 22, Rowley. Imprisoned.	Howe family
Aug. 29	Abigail Johnson, 10, Andover. **Granddaughter.** Imprisoned 5 weeks. Released on bail Oct. 6.	Dane family
Aug. 29	Elizabeth (Dane) Johnson, 51, Andover. **Daughter.** Imprisoned 5 months. Found not guilty Jan. 7, 1693.	Dane family
Aug. 30	Stephen Johnson, 13, Andover. **Grandson.** Imprisoned 5 weeks. Released on bail Oct. 6.	Dane family
Sept. 7	Deliverance Dane, 37, Andover. **Daughter-in-law.** Imprisoned 13 weeks. Released about Dec. 8.	Dane family

Sept. 7	Rebecca (Aslet) Johnson, 40, Andover. Imprisoned 13 weeks. Released on bail about Dec. 8. Case dismissed Jan. 7, 1693.	Dane family
Sept. 7	Rebecca Johnson, Jr. 17, Andover. Imprisoned 13 weeks. Released on bail about Dec. 8.	Dane family
Sept. 7	Male slave of Nathaniel, son of Rev. Dane. Imprisoned 8 weeks.	Dane family
Sept. 7	Abigail Faulkner, Jr., 9, Andover. **Granddaughter.** Imprisoned 1 month. Released on bail Oct. 6. Cleared by proclamation May 1693.	Dane family
Sept. 7	Dorothy Faulkner, 12, Andover. **Granddaughter.** Imprisoned 1 month. Released on bail Oct. 6. Cleared by proclamation May 1693.	Dane family
Sept. 7	John Saide, Jr. 13, Andover. Imprisoned.	Dane family

Elizabeth (widow of Stephen) Johnson was the oldest daughter of Francis and Elizabeth (Ingalls) Dane. Her daughter, Elizabeth, Jr., was the first member of the immediate Dane family to be accused (Aug. 10). Before the month was out, Elizabeth, Sr. and her other two children were charged. Including the Faulkners, this meant two daughters and five grandchildren were accused and thrown into prison. Elizabeth Johnson's brother-in-law Timothy was the husband of Rebecca Aslet and father of Rebecca Johnson, Jr. John Saide, Jr. was related by marriage through Elizabeth's sister-in-law, Susannah Johnson, Jr.

James Howe was Dane's brother-in-law by his wife Elizabeth Dane.

{ G 1547 }

Their son, James Howe, Jr., married Elizabeth Jackson, thereby creating the Jackson relationship. Nehemiah Abbot, Jr. was the son of Mary Howe and Nehemiah Abbot, Sr.; Sarah Bridges was the daughter of Sarah Howe and John Bridges, making them grandchildren of Elizabeth and great nephew and niece of Rev. Dane.

Progenitors of the Allen family were Andrew Allen and Faith Ingalls, sister of Rev. Dane's first wife, Elizabeth (died in 1676). Allen, born in England in 1616, was an original Andover proprietor. Their daughter Mary married Dr. Roger Toothaker; their daughter Martha married Thomas Carrier. Martha Carrier, niece of Rev. Dane's wife, was accused May 28, the first from Andover. She was jailed in Salem and put in chains.[1] Her sons Richard, 18, and Andrew, 15, were arrested July 22 and refused to confess or accuse their mother until they were tied neck to feet. This produced a confession and an acknowledgement that their mother was a witch.[2] She was condemned August 5 and her two youngest, Thomas, Jr. 10, Sarah, 7, and her niece, Elizabeth Johnson, Jr., 22, were arrested August 10. The two children were coerced into naming their mother as a witch.[3] Abusing her children was a tactic to induce her to confess. She never did. The four children were forced to watch their mother's execution on Aug. 19. They must have wondered if they would be next.[4]

LEGAL ACTIONS FILED

INDICTMENT NO. 1 AGAINST ABIGAIL FAULKNER:

The jurors for our Sovereign Lord and Lady King and Queen do present that Abigail Faulkner, wife of Francis Faulkner of Andover, in the county of Essex aforesaid husband, on or about the beginning of August in the year aforesaid and divers other days and times as well before as after certain detestable arts called witchcraft and sorceries wickedly maliciously and feloniously hath used, practices, and exercises at end in the town of Boxford in the county of Essex aforesaid in and upon the said Martha Sprague the day and year aforesaid and divers other days and times both before and after was and is tortured, afflicted, consumed, pined, waster, and tormented, and also for sundry other acts of witchcraft by the said Abigail Faulkner committed and one before and since that time—against the peace of our Sovereign Lord and Lady, the King and Queen, their crown and dignity and the form of the statute in that case made and provided.

The language in indictment No. 2 was similar. "... practiced and exercised at and in the town of Andover in the county of Essex in, upon, and against one Sarah Phelps, daughter of Samuel Phelps of Andover, husbandman, by which said wicked acts the said Sarah Phelps the day and year aforesaid and divers other days and times both before and after, was and is tortured, afflicted, consumed, pined, wasted, and tormented, and also for sundry other acts of witchcraft by the said Abigail Faulkner committed and done before and since that time . . ."

TRANSCRIPT OF ABIGAIL FAULKNER'S EXAMINATION.

August 11, 1692. Mr. Hathorne, Mr. Corwin, & Capt. Higginson present. When she was brought into the room the afflicted persons fell down. Mr. HA: You are here, apprehended for witch-craft. Answer: I know nothing of it. With the cast of her eye, Mary Walcott & the rest afflicted, Mary Warren and others fell down. It was said to her, do you not see. She said yes but it is the Devil does it in my shape. Mary Walcott said she had seen her two months a good while ago but was not hurt by her till last night. Ann Putnam said she had seen said Faulkner but was not hurt by her till last night & then she pulled me off my horse. Mary Warren said she had seen her in company with other witches but was not hurt by her till lately.

Mary Warren & others of the afflicted were struck down into fits & helped out of their fits by a touch of Abigail Faulkner's hand. she was urged to confess the truth for the credit of her town. Her cousin [niece] Eliz. Johnson urged her with that. But she refused to do it saying God would not require her to confess that she was not guilty of. Phelp's daughter complained her afflicting her, but she denied that she had anything to do with witchcraft. She said Faulkner had a cloth in her hand, that when she squeezed in her hand the afflicted fell into grievous fits, as was observed. The afflicted said Daniel Eames and Capt. Floyd was upon that cloth when it was upon the table.

She said she was sorry they were afflicted but she was told & it was observed she did not shed a tear. Mary Warren was pulled under the table & was helped out of her fit by a touch of said Faulkner. She said she had looked on some of these afflicted when they came to Andover & hurt them not. But she was told it was before she had began to afflict them. She was told that it was reported she used to conjure with a seiv (sic). But she said it was not so, that story was cleared up.

SECOND EXAMINATION BEFORE JOHN HATHORNE.

August 30, 1692. Before magistrate John Hathorne. Abigail Faulkner, before their Majesty's Justices at first denied witchcraft as she had done before. But afterward she owned that she was angry at what folk said when her cousin [niece] Eliz. Johnson was taken up and folk laugh & said her sister Johnson would come out next & she did look with an evil eye on the afflicted persons & did consent that they should be afflicted because they were the cause of bringing her kindred out. And she did wish them ill & her spirit being raised she did pinch her hands together & she knew not but that the devil might take that advantage but it was the devil, not she that afflicted them. This she said she did at Capt. Chandler's garrison the night after Eliz. Johnson had been examined before Capt. Bradstreet in the day. Attest: Simon Willard.

DEPOSITIONS AGAINST ABIGAIL FAULKNER SEPT. 17.

Rose Foster v. Abigail Faulkner. The deposition of Rose Foster who testifieth & saith I have been most grievously afflicted and tormented by Abigail Faulkner of Andover. Also I have seen Abigail Faulkner or her appearance most grievously afflict and torment Martha Sprague, Sarah Phelps, and Hannah Bigsbe since the beginning of August and I verily believe that Abigail Faulkner is a witch and that she has often afflicted me and the aforesaid persons by acts of witchcrafts.

Mary Walcott v. Abigail Faulkner. The deposition of Mary Walcott who testifieth and saith that about the 9th August 1692 I was most dreadfully afflicted by a woman that told me her name was Abigail Faulkner. But on the 11th of August, being the day of the examination of Abigail Faulkner, she did most dreadfully afflict me during the time of her examination. I saw Abigail Faulkner or her appearance most grievously afflict and torment Sarah Phelps and Ann Putnam and I verily believe in my heart that Abigail Faulkner is a witch and that she has often afflicted me and the aforesaid persons by acts of witchcraft.

Martha Sprague v. Abigail Faulkner. The deposition of Martha Sprague who testifieth and saith that I have been most grievously afflicted and tormented by Abigail Faulkner of Andover since the beginning of August 1692, also I saw Abigail Faulkner or her appearance most grievously torment and afflict Hannah Bigsbe and Rose Foster, and Sarah Phelps. And I verily believe in my heart that Abigail Faulkner is a witch & that she has often afflicted me and several others by acts of witchcraft.

Mary Warren v. Abigail Faulkner. The deposition of Marry Warren who testifieth and saith that Abigail Faulkner of Andover did most grievously afflict and torment me on 11th August 1692 during the time of her examination for if she did but look upon me she would strike me down or almost choke me. Also on the day of her examination I saw Abigail Faulkner or her appearance most grievously afflict and torment Mary Walcott, Ann Putnam, and Sarah Phelps and I verily believe that Abigail Faulkner is a witch and that she has often afflicted me and several others by acts of witchcraft.

Sarah Phelps v. Abigail Faulkner. The deposition of Sarah Phelps who testifieth and saith that about the beginning of August 1692 I was most grievously afflicted and tormented by Abigail Faulkner or her appearance. But most dreadfully she did torment me on 11 August, being the day of her examination. For if she did but look upon me she would strike me down or almost choke me. Also since the beginning of August I have seen Abigail Faulkner or her appearance most grievously afflict and torment Mary Walcott, Ann Putnam, and Martha Sprague and I verily believe in my heart that Abigail Faulkner is a witch and that she has very often afflicted me and the aforesaid persons by acts of witchcraft.

Ann Putnam v. Abigail Faulkner. The deposition of Ann Putnam who testifieth and saith that about the 9th of August 1692 I was afflicted by a woman which told me her name was Faulkner. But on the 11th of August, being the day of the examination of Abigail Faulkner, she did most dreadfully torment me during the time of her examination. Also on the day of her examination I saw Abigail Faulkner or her appearance most grievously afflict and torment Mary Walcott and Sarah Phelps. And I believe that Abigail Faulkner is a witch and that she has often afflicted me and several others by acts of witchcraft.

VERDICT AND DEATH SENTENCE V. ABIGAIL FAULKNER

September 1692. At a Court of Oyer and Terminer holden at Salem by adjournment September 1692. Abigail Faulkner of Andover, indicted and arraigned for the crime of felony by witchcraft committed on the bodies of Martha Sprague. Evidence being called and sworn in open court. Matter of fact committed the jury.

The jury find Abigail Faulkner, wife of Francis Faulkner of Andover, guilty of the felony of witchcraft committed on the body of Martha Sprague, also on the body of Sarah Phelps.

CONFESSIONS OF DOROTHY FAULKNER, ABIGAIL FAULKNER, JR. SEPTEMBER 16, 1692.

Dorothy Faulkner and Abigail Faulkner, children to Abigail Faulkner of Andover, now in prison, confessed before the honored magistrates upon their examination here in Salem on the 16 day of this instant September 1692 that their mother appeared and made them witches; and also Martha Tyler, Johanna Tyler, and Sarah Wilson and Joseph Draper all acknowledge that they were lead into that dreadful sin of witchcraft by her means, the aforesaid Abigail Faulkner.

The above named persons each & every one of them did affirm before the Grand Inquest that the above written evidence are truth.

RECOGNIZANCE FOR DOROTHY FAULKNER AND ABIGAIL FAULKNER, JR., OCT. 6, 1692.

Know all men by these presents that I John Osgood, Sr. of Andover in the county of Essex in New England, and Nathaniel Dane, Sr. of the same town & county aforesaid, husbandmen, are holden and firmly bound jointly and severally to their Majesties King William & Queen Mary of England & Scotland, France, & Ireland, King & Queen, defenders of the faith, in the full & just sum of five hundred pounds sterling for the true & just payment of which said sum of five hundred pounds to their Majesties King William & Queen Mary we do bind our heirs, executors, administrators, and assigns firmly & by these presents dated in Salem the sixth day of October in the year of our Lord one thousand six hundred & ninety two and in the fourth year of the reign of our Majesties King William and Queen Mary, King and Queen of England, Scotland, France, & Ireland, defenders of the faith.

The condition of this obligation is such that whereas the above named John Osgood, Sr. & Nathaniel Dane, Sr., husbandmen, both of the town of Andover in the county of Essex in New England have taken into their care and custody the bodies of Dorothy Faulkner, aged about ten years, and Abigail Faulkner, aged about eight years, who was both committed to their Majesties jail in Salem in the county of Essex in New England for having used, practiced, & committed divers acts of witchcraft upon the bodies of sundry persons who themselves also have confessed the same. If that the aforesaid John Osgood, Sr. & Nathaniel Dane, Sr. aforsaid husbandmen shall well & truly keep the aforesaid Dorothy Faulkner & Abigail Faulkner & them secure until they shall recieve order from George Corwin Sheriff of the county of Essex to deliver the aforesaid Dorothy Faulkner & Abigail Faulkner unto William Downton, now keeper of their Majesties jail in Salem, or to any other whom the aforesaid George Corwin shall appoint, that then they shall forthwith deliver the same Dorothy Faulkner & Abigail Faulkner according to his order. And if the above found do perform the above mentioned articles & shall pay unto George Corwin the Sheriff aforesaid, the forfieture of said bond for their Majestie's use in case of default, then this obligation shall be void & of no effect or otherwise to stand in full force & virtue. In witness hereof we have set our hands & seals this six day of October in the year of our Lord one thousand six hundred ninety & two and in the fourth year of their majestie's reign.

The above was signed by John Osgood and Nathaniel Dane and witnessed by Joshua Conant, Elizur Keysar, and Joseph Phippen, Jr.

PETITION OF ABIGAIL FAULKNER, DEC. 3, 1692.

The humble petition of Abigail Faulkner unto his Excellency Sir William Phipps, Knight and Governor of their Majesties dominions in America, humbly sheweth:

That your poor and humble petitioner, having been this four months in Salem prison and condemned to die, having had no other evidence against me but the specter evidences and the confessors which confessors have lately since I was condemned owed to myself and others and do still own that they wronged me and what they had said against me was false; and that they would not that I should have been put to death for a thousand worlds, for they never should have enjoyed themselves again in this world; which undoubtedly I should have been put to death had it not pleased the Lord I had been with child. Thanks be to the Lord, I know myself altogether innocent & ignorant of the crime of witchcraft which is laid to my charge. As will appear at the great day of judgment (may it please your excellency) my husband about five years ago was taken with fits which did very much impair his memory and understanding but with the blessing of the Lord upon my endeavors did recover of them again but now through grief and sorrow they are returned to him again as bad as ever they were. I having six children and having little or nothing to subsist on, being in a manner without a head to do any thing for myself or them, and being closely confined can see no other ways but we shall all perish. Therefore may it please your Excellency, your poor humble petitioner do humbly beg and implore of your Excellency to take it into your pious and judicious consideration that some speedy course may be taken with me for my releasement that I and my children perish not through means of my close confinement here which undoubtedly we shall if the Lord does not mightily prevent and your poor petitioner shall forever pray for your health and happiness in this life and eternal felicity in the world to come, so prays.

Your poor afflicted humble servant, petitioner Abigail Faulkner. From Salem prison December 3d: 1693.

MEMORANDUM

That on the thirteenth day of January 1692 in the fourth year of the reign of our Soverign Lord & Lady William & Mary, the grace of God of England &c, King & Queen defenders of the faith &c. Personally appeared before William Stoughton, Esq., Chief Justice of their Majesty's Province of the Massachusetts Bay in New England Francis Faulkner, husbandman, and Joseph Marble, mason, both of Andover in the county of Essex, and acknowledged themselves to be jointly & severally indebted unto our said Sovereign Lord & Lady & the survivor of them their heirs & successors in the sum of one hundred pounds to be levied on their or either of their lands and tenements, goods, & chattels for the use of our said Sovereign Lord & Lady, the King & Queen or survivor of them, on condition that Dorothy Faulkner and Abigail Faulkner, having stood committed for suspicion of witchcraft, shall make their personal appearance before the Justices of our said Sovereign Lord & Lady, the King & Queen, at the next Court of Assizes and general jail delivery to be holden for the county of Essex, then & there to answer to all such matters & things as shall in their Majesty's behalf be alleged against them and to do and receive that which by the said court shall be then & there enjoined them & thence not to depart without license. Attest: Jonathan Elatson, Clerk.

PETITION OF FRANCIS FAULKNER, ET. AL.

March 2, 1702. To his Excellency, the Governor, and Council, and Representatives now in General Court assembled at Boston:

The petition of several of the inhabitants of Andover, Salem Village, & Topsfield humbly sheweth:

That whereas in the year 1692 some of your petitioners and the near relations of others of them, viz: Rebecca Nurse, Mary Estey, Abigail Faulkner, Mary Parker, of Andover, John Procter & Elizabeth his wife; Elizabeth Howe, Samuel Wardwell & Sarah his wife, were accused of witchcraft by certain possessed persons, and thereupon were apprehended and imprisoned, and at a Court held at Salem were condemned upon the evidence of the aforesaid possessed persons; and sentence of death hath been executed on them (except Abigail Faulkner, Elizabeth Procter, & Sarah Wardwell) of whose innocency those that knew them are well satisfied. And whereas the invalidity of the aforesaid evidence and the great wrong which (through errors & mistakes in those trials) was then done, hath since plainly appeared which we doubt not but this honored Court is sensible of. Your petitioners being dissatisfied and grieved, that (besides what the aforesaid condemned persons have suffered in their persons and estates) their names are exposed to infamy and reproach, while their trial & condemnation stands upon public record. We therefore humbly pray this Honored Court, that something may be publicly done to take off infamy from the names and memory of those who have suffered as aforesaid, that none of their surviving relations, nor their posterity, may suffer reproach upon that account. And your petitioners shall ever pray &c.

Dated March 2d 1702/03 Signed:

Francis Faulkner	Phebe Robinson
Abigail Faulkner	Samuel Wardwell
Sarah Wardwell	John Tarbel
John Parker	John Nurse
Joseph Parker	Peter Cloyse, Sr.
Nathaniel Dane	Isaac Estey, Jr.
Francis Dane	Sarah Gill
Mary Howe	Rebecca Preston
Abigail Howe	Thorndick Procter
Isaac Estey	Benjamin Procter
Samuel Nurse	

In the House of Representatives March 18th 1702. Read & sent up.

PETITION OF ABIGAIL FAULKNER, SR.

June, 1703. To the Honorable the Great and General Court of the Province of the Massachusetts Bay assembled at Boston.

The petition of Abigail, the wife of Francis Faulkner of Andover in the county of Essex, humbly sheweth that whereas in the year 1692 when many were accused & imprisoned at Salem as witches and some executed, myself was accused by the afflicted who pretended to see me by their spectral sight (not with their bodily eyes) and that I afflicted them upon whose accusations (and theirs only) I was examined, imprisoned, and brought to trial, these being all that gave in any evidence against me upon oath. Yet the jury (upon only their testimony) brought me in guilty, & the sentence of death was passed upon me. But it pleased God to put it into the heart of his Excellency, Sir William Phipps, to grant me a reprieve and at length a pardon, the sufficiency of the proof being in said pardon

{ G 1555 }

expressed as the inducement to the granting thereof so that through the great goodness of God I am yet preserved.

The pardon having so far had its effect as that I am as yet suffered [to] live but this only as a malefactor convict upon record of the most heinous crimes that mankind can be supposed to be guilty of, which besides it utter ruining and defacing my reputation, will certainly expose myself to imminent danger by new accusations, which will thereby be the more readily believed will remain as a perpetual brand of infamy upon my family. And I knowing my own innocency as to all such crimes (as will at the last fully appear) and being so defamed in my reputation and my life exposed besides the odium cast upon my posterity.

Do humbly pray that this high honorable Court will please to take my case into serious consideration and order the defacing of the record against me so that I and mine may be freed from the evil consequences thereof.

Any your petitioner, as in duty bound, shall ever pray.

Boston June 13, 1703. The Court ordered the reading of her trial. Reverse of Case # 113 & #114. Messrs. Sprague, Seabury, Savage.

RESPONSE OF THE GENERAL COURT

In the House of Representatives, July 20th, 1703.

In answer to the petitions of Abigail Faulkner, and sundry of the inhabitants of Andover, in the behalf of sundry persons in and late of said town & elsewhere, who in the year 1692 were indicted, accused, and condemned, & many of them executed for the crime of felony by witchcraft. And whereas it is conceived by many worthy and pious persons that the evidence given against many of the said condemned persons was weak and insufficient as to taking away the lives of sundry so condemned &ca. Wherefore it is though meet and it is hereby ordered that a Bill be drawn up for preventing the like procedure for the future, and that no spectral evidence may hereafter be accounted valid, or sufficient to take away the life, or good name of any person or persons within this Province, and that the infamy and reproach cast on the names and posterity of the said accused and condemned persons may in some measure be rolled away. Sent up for concurrence. James Converse, Speaker.

(Reverse). Order for bringing in a bill to reverse the Attainder (forfeiture of property and loss of civil rights of a person sentenced to death or utlawed) of Abigail Faulkner &ca of witchcraft.

That a Bill be brought in to acquit Mary (sic) Faulkner and the other present petitioners severally of the penalties to which they are liable upon the said convictions and judgments in the said Courts and estate them in their just credit and reputation as if no such judgment had been had.

In Council. July 21, 1703. Agreed to.

PETITION OF PHILLIP ENGLISH, ET. AL.

To his Excellency the Governor, and the Honorable Council and General Assembly for the Province of the Massachusetts Bay in New England convened at Boston May 25th 1709, the humble address and motion of several of the inhabitants of the said Province some of which had their near relations, either parents or others, who suffered death in the dark and doleful times that past over this Province in the year 1692 under the supposition and in that gloomy day by some (thought proved) of being guilty of witchcraft which we have all the reason in the world to hope and believe they were innocent of, and others of that either ourselves or some of our relations have been imprisoned, impaired, and blasted in our reputations and estates by reason of the same. It's not our intent, neither do we reflect on the judges or jurors concerned in those sorrowful trials whom we hope [and believe] did that which they though was right in that hour of darkness. But that which we move and pray for is that you would please to pass some suitable Acts in your wisdom you may think meet and proper that shall (so far as may be) restore the reputations to the posterity of the suffers and remunerate them as to what they have been damnified in their estates thereby. We do not without remorse and grief recount these sorrowful things. But we humbly conceive that we are bound in conscience and duty to God and to ourselves, relatives, and posterity, and country. Humbly to make this motion, praying God to direct you in this and all your weighty consultations.

We subscribe your sorrowful and distressed suppliants.

Phillip English	John Tarbell	Isaac Estey
Isack Estey, Sr.	John Parker	Joseph Esty
Benjamin Procter	Joseph Parker	Samuel Nurse
John Procter	John Johnson	Benj. Nurse
Thorndick Procter	**Francis Faulkner**	John Preston
George Jacobs	Samuel Nurse, Jr.	

ACCOUNT OF ABIGAIL FAULKNER, SR.

Sept. 13, 1710. To the Honorable Committee sitting in Salem. An account of the suffering of Abigail Faulkner of Andover and of 2 of her children for supposed witchcraft, and of the damage she sustained thereby in the year 1692.

1. I suffered imprisonment four months and my children were in prison about a month. And upon my trial I was condemned upon such evidence as is now generally thought to be insufficient as may be seen in the court records of my trial. I humbly pray that the Attainder may be taken off, and that my name that has been wronged may be restored.

2. I was at the whole charge of providing for myself and my children during the time of our imprisonment.

3. Money paid the Sheriff, Keeper, King's Attorney [&c] for prison fees, court charges, & for bonds, and for my reprieve & pardon, £10.

4. My expenses in providing for myself & children while we were in prison: time and expenses in journey and attending the courts were considerable, which I leave to the Honorable Committee & the General Court to allow me what may be thought reasonable, which will be to my satisfaction & if it be but [£10]. Signed Abigail Faulkner.

REVERSAL OF ATTAINDER — OCTOBER 17, 1711

Province of Massachusetts Bay. An Act to reverse the Attainders of George Burroughs and others for witchcraft.

Forasmuch as in the year of our Lord one thousand six hundred ninety two, several towns within this Province were infested with a horrible witchcraft or possession of devils. And at a special Court of Oyer and Terminer holden at Salem in the county of Essex in the same year, 1692: George Burroughs of Wells, John Procter, George Jacobs, John Willard, Giles Corey, and [ ] his wife, Rebecca Nurse, and Sarah Good, all of Salem aforesaid; Elizabeth Howe of Ipswich; Mary Eastey, Sarah Wild, and Abigail Hobbs, all of Topsfield; Samuel Wardwell, Mary Parker, Martha Carrier, **Abigail Faulkner,** Anne Foster, Rebecca Eames, Mary Post, and Mary Lacey, all of Andover; Mary Bradbury of Salisbury; and Dorcas Hoar of Beverly, were severally indicted and convicted and attainted of witchcraft and some of them put to death, other lying still under the like sentence of the said Court, and liable to have the same executed upon them.

The influence and energy of the evil spirits so great at that time acting in and upon those who were the principal accusers and witnesses proceeding so far as to cause a prosecution to be had of persons of known and good reputation, which caused a great dissatisfaction and a stop to be put thereunto until their majesty's pleasure should be known therein. And upon a representation thereof accordingly made of her late majesty Queen Mary, the second of blessed memory, by her royal letter given at her Court at Whitehall the fifteenth of April 1693, was graciously pleased to approve the care and circumspection therein; and to will and require that in all proceedings against persons accused for witchcraft, or being possessed by the devil, the greatest moderation and all due circumspection be used, so far as the same may be without impediment to the ordinary course of justice.

And some of the principal accusers and witnesses in those dark and severe prosecutions have since discovered themselves to be persons of profligate and vicious conversation.

Upon the humble petitions and suit of several of the said persons and of the children of others of them whose parents were executed, be it declared and enacted by his Excellency the Governor, Council and Representatives in the General Court assembled and by the authority of the same, that the several convictions, judgments, and attainders against the said George Burroughs, John Procter, George Jacob, John Willard, Giles Corey and [ ] Corey, Rebecca Nurse, Sarah Good, Elizabeth Howe, Mary Easty, Sarah W[ild], Abigail Hobbs, Samuel Wardwell, Mary Parker, Martha Carrier, **Abigail Faulkner,** Anne Foster, Rebecca Eames, Mary Post, Mary Lacey, Mary Bradbury, and Dorcas [Hoar], and every of them be and hereby are reversed, made and declared to be null and void to all intents, constructions, and purposes whatsoever, as if no such convictions, judgments, or attainders had ever [been] had or given. And that no penalties or forfeitures of goods or chattels be by the said judgments and attainders or either of them had or incurred.

Any law, usage, or custom to the contrary notwithstanding. And that no sheriff, constable, jailer, or other officer shall be liable to any prosecution in the law for anything they then legally and in the execution of their respective offices.

Made and passed by the Great and General Court or Assembly of her Majesty's Province of the Massachusetts Bay in New England held at Boston the 17th day of October 1711.

GOVERNOR DUDLEY'S ORDER FOR PAYMENT

By his Excellency the Governor. Whereas the General Assembly in their last Session accepted the report of their Committee appointed to consider of the damages sustained by sundry persons prosecuted for witchcraft in the year 1692, Viz't

	£	s.	d.		£	s.	d.
Elizabeth Howe	12	0	0	John Procter & wife	150	0	0
George Jacobs	79	0	0	Sarah Wild	14	0	0
Mary Eastey	20	0	0	Mary Bradbury	20	0	0
Mary Parker	8	0	0	**Abigail Faulkner**	20	0	0
Geo. Burroughs	50	0	0	Abigail Hobbs	10	0	0

Giles Corey & wife				21	0	0
Anne Foster	6	10	0			
Rebecca Nurse	25	0	0	Rebeccah Eames	10	0	0
John Willard	20	0	0	Dorcas Hoar	21	17	0
Sarah Good	30	0	0	Mary Post	8	14	0
Martha Carrier	7	6	0	Mary Lacey	8	10	0
Samuel Wardwell & wife				36	15	0

The whole amounting unto five hundred seventy eight pounds and twelve shillings.

I do by & with the advice and consent of her Majesty's Council, hereby order you to pay the above sum of five hundred seventy eight pounds & twelve shillings to Stephen Sewall, Esq., who together with the gentlemen of the Committee that estimated and reported the said damages are desired & directed to distribute the same in proportion as above to such of the said persons as are living, and to those that legally represent them that are dead according to the law directs & for which this shall be your warrant.

Given under my hand at Boston the 17 day of December 1711. Signed J. Dudley.

LETTER OF THIRTY-FOUR VICTIMS AND RELATIVES

December 1711. Whereas we the subscribers are informed that his Excellency the Governor, Honorable Council, and General Assembly of this Province have been pleased to hear our supplication and answer our prayer in passing an Act in favor of us respecting our reputations and estates, which we humbly and gratefully acknowledge.

And inasmuch as it would be chargeable and trouble-some for all or many of us to go to Boston on this affair; Wherefore we have and do authorize and request our trusty friend, the worshipful Stephen Sewall, Esq., to procure us a copy of the said Act, and to do what may be further proper and necessary for the reception of what is allowed us and to take and receive the same for us and to transact any other thing referring to the premises on our behalf that may be requisite or convenient.

Essex. December 1711

James Eames in behalf of his mother Rebecca Eames.
Samuel Preston on behalf his wife Sarah Preston.
Samuel Osgood on behalf his mother Mary Osgood.
John Parker & Joseph Parker sons of Mary Parker, deceased.
Charles Burrough, eldest son.
John Johnson in behalf of his mother Rebecca Johnson & his sister.

Francis Johnson on behalf of his mother, brother, & sister Elizabeth.
Joseph Emerson on behalf of wife Martha Emerson of Haverhill.
George Jacob on behalf of his father who suffered.
John Moulton on behalf of his wife Elizabeth, the daughter of Giles Corey who suffered.
Robert Pease on behalf of his wife Annies King on behalf of her mother.
Thorndick Procter on behalf of his father John Procter who suffered.
Benjamin Procter, son of the abovesaid.

John Barker	Lawrence Lacy
Abigail Faulkner	John Marston
Abraham Foster	Thomas Carrier
Nathaniel Dane	Joseph Wilson
Samuel Wardwell	Mary Post
John Wright	Dorcas Hoar
Ebenezer Barker	Willem Town
Samuel Nurse	Jacob Esty
Edward Bishop	John Frie

DANE FAMILY ENDNOTES

1. *Register.* 2:387, 3:66, 8:148, 85:84.
2. *Ibid.*, 2:337 and *The Essex Antiquarian, A Monthly Magazine Devoted to the Biography and Genealogy, History, and Antiquities of Essex County, Massachusetts.* Vol. 5, Nos. 10-12, Oct.-Dec. 1901, 192. (Hereafter *Essex Antiquarian.*)
3. *Register*, 8:148.
4. *Ibid.*, 2:387, 3:66, 8:148 and 85:84.
5. The Chandlers emigrated to the American colonies in 1637. Hannah's first husband, George Abbot, left her his whole estate and named her sole executrix. She was to dispose of the same among their children and his oldest son John was to have a double portion. They had seven children, all born in Andover. His estate was valued at £487, 12, 5. *Essex Co. Probate Records,* File No. 43.
6. *Register.*, 8:148.
7. *Ibid.* 3:66, 8:148
8. *Register*, 8:148 and *Early Vital Records of the Commonwealth of Massachusetts to the Year 1850 on CD Rom.* Wheat Ridge, CO: Search and Research Publishing Corporation, 1997. Andover marriages 202, deaths 479. (Hereafter *Essex Co., MA, Vital Records.*)
9. *Essex Antiquarian*, same as note 2 and *Essex Co., MA. Vital Records*, Andover deaths 482.
10. *Essex Co., MA, Vital Records*, Andover deaths 479.
11. *Ibid.*, Andover births 225, deaths 478.
12. *Ibid.*, births 232.
13. *Ibid.*, births 299, deaths 481.

14. through 16. *Ibid.*, births 225.
17. *Ibid.*, births 232.
18. *Ibid.*, births.
19. *Register*, 3:66, 8:148.
20. through 22. *Ibid.*, 8:148.
23. *Ibid.*, 2:387, 8:148.
24. through 28. *Ibid*, 8:148.
29. *Ibid.* and *Essex Co., MA. Vital Records,* Andover deaths 433.
30. Helen Abbots, "The Faulkner Family of Andover," Andover Historical Society, Andover, Mass. (Hereafter Abbots) *Essex Co., MA, Vital Records*, Andover births 143, deaths 433.
31. Abbots, *Essex Co., MA, Vital Records,* Andover births 143, deaths 433.
32. *Ibid.* Abbots and Andover births and Ammi Ruhammah-Hannah Ingalls *Family Group Sheets,* supplied in May 1990 by Mildred K. Meyer, 5557 Mapleridge Dr., Cincinnati, Ohio. Cites *Vital Records* of Andover and Acton. Mass. (Hereafter Faulkner-Ingalls *Family Group Sheets.*)
33. Abbots, *Essex Co., MA. Vital Records,* Andover births 143, marriages 122.
34. Abbots, *Essex Co., MA, Vital Records,* Andover births 143, marriages 270, deaths 433, Faulkner-Ingalls, *Family Group Sheet.*
35. *Register*, 8:148.
36. through 38. *Ibid.*, 2:379, 8:148.
39. through 43. *Ibid.*, 8:148.
44. *Essex Co., MA, Vital Records,* Andover births 227, marriage 199, and *Essex Antiquarian,* Vol. 5, Nos. 10-12, Oct.-Dec. 1901, 192.
45. *Essex Co., MA, Vital Records,* Andover births 231.
46. *Ibid.*, births.
47. *Ibid.*, 232.
48. *Ibid.*, 233.
49. *Ibid.*, 232.
50. *Register*, 8:148, 13:120.
51. *Ibid.*, 13:118-120, 107:156.
52. *Ibid.* 13:120.
53. William J. Lamson, comp., *Descendants of William Lamson of Ipswich, Mass. 1634 - 1917.* New York: Tobias A. Wright, 1917. 32-38. (Hereafter Lamson *Family Genealogy.*); Abbots, *Essex Co., MA, Vital Records.* Andover births 142, marriages 122; Ipswich marriages 270.
54. George A. Perkins, M.D., comp., *The Family of John Perkins of Ipswich, Massachusetts.* Salem: Printed for the author by the Salem Press Publishing and Printing Co., 1889. Complete in Three Parts: Part I. Quartermaster John Perkins. Part II. Deacon Thomas Perkins. Part III. Sergeant Jacob Perkins, 11-14. (Hereafter *The Family of John Perkins of Ipswich, Mass.*)
55. *Lamson Family Genealogy*, 32-38, *Essex Co., MA, Vital Records,* Ipswich marriages 151 and 271, deaths 613.
56. *Lamson Family Genealogy*, 37.
57. *Ibid.*, 37-38.
58. *Ibid.*, 37, 57-60 and *Essex Co., MA, Vital Records,* Ipswich deaths 612.
59. Abbots, *Essex Co., MA, Vital Records,* Andover births 143, marriages 270.
60. Abbots, *Essex Co., MA, Vital Records,* Andover deaths 433.
61. *Essex Co., MA, Vital Records,* Andover births and deaths 143.
62. and 63. *Ibid.*, Andover births 143.
64. Abbots, *Essex Co., MA, Vital Records.* Andover marriages 270, deaths 434.
65. *Lamson Family Genealogy,* 25 and *Essex Co., MA, Vital Records.* Andover marriages 123, deaths 434.

66. *Essex Co., MA, Vital Records.* Andover marriages 123,
67. Date and place of birth unknown.
68. *Essex Co., MA, Vital Records.* Andover births 144, deaths 434.
69. *Ibid.*, births 142.
70. *Ibid.*, births 143.
71. *Ibid.*, births 144, deaths 434.
72. *Ibid.*, births 143, deaths 433.
73. *Ibid.*, births 144.
74. *Ibid.*, births 142, deaths 433.
75. *Ibid.*, births 144.
76. *Ibid.*, births 143.
77. Abbots, *Essex Co., MA, Vital Records,* Andover births 142, and Ammi Ruhammah-Hannah Ingalls *Family Group Sheets.*
78. through 80. *Essex Co., MA, Vital Records,* Andover births 143.
81. *Register,* 8:148.
82. *Ibid.*, 2:379.

FAULKNER FAMILY ENDNOTES

1. Abbots, *Register,* 2:378; 3:65; 39:70-71; 45:187-8; 82:153, Essex Co., MA, *Vital Records,* Andover deaths, 433.
2. Abbots. Andover was incorporated as a town May 6, 1646 and was named for the town in Hants county, England, which had been the home of many of its settlers. A Committee was appointed by the General Court on June 1, 1652 to lay out the bounds between Andover and Cambridge, and the same day the Court granted that five or six hundred acres laid out by Rowley, without their line near Andover town, should belong to Andover. On April 7, 1855 a part of Andover was established as North Andover.
3. *Register,* 2:377 gives the date of death as 14 Feb. 1667.
4. Essex Co., MA, *Vital Records,* Andover deaths, 434.
5. Abbots.
6. *Register,* 3:66.
7. *Ibid.*, 2:377.
8. Abbots, Essex Co., MA, *Vital Records,* Andover marriages, 122; deaths, 436.
9. *Register,* 8:148.
10. Essex Co., MA, *Vital Records,* Andover deaths, 433.
11. Abbots, Essex Co., MA, *Vital Records,* Andover births 143, deaths 433.
12. Abbots, Andover births 143.
13. *Ibid.*, and Andover marriages 122.
14. Abbots, *Vital Records.* births 143, marriages 270, deaths 433.
15. through 17. Abbots.
18. *Register,* 2:379.
19. Abbots.
20. *Ibid.*; and Essex Co., MA, *Vital Records,* Andover births 143, marriages 270, deaths 433.
21. Abbots, *Vital Records,* Andover marriages 122, and *Register,* 2:380.
22. *Register,* 2:380.
23. Essex Co., MA, *Vital Records,* Andover marriages 122.
24. *Register,* 2:380.

{ G 1563 }

25. Abbots.
26. *Ibid.* and Essex Co., MA, *Vital Records*, Andover marriages 132, deaths 434.
27. Lamson, *Family Genealogy*, 25 and Essex Co., MA, *Vital Records*, Andover marriages, 123; Andover deaths, 434.
28. *Lamson Family Genealogy*, 25.
29. Essex Co., MA, *Vital Records*, Andover births 144, deaths, 434.
30. Ibid., Andover births 142.
31. Ibid., Andover births 143.
32. Ibid., Andover births 144, deaths, 434.
33. Ibid., Andover births 143, deaths 433.
34. Ibid., Andover births 144.
35. Ibid., Andover births 142, deaths 433.
36. Ibid., Andover births 144.
37. Ibid., Andover births 143.
38. Lamson, *Family Genealogy*, 32-8; Abbots, Essex Co., MA, *Vital Records*, Andover births, 142; Andover marriages, 122; Ipswich marriages, 270.
39. Lamson, *Family Genealogy*, 32-8; and Essex Co., MA, *Vital Records*, Ipswich marriages, 151 and 271; deaths, 613.
40. *The Family of John Perkins of Ipswich, Mass.*
41. Lamson, *Family Genealogy*, 32-83.
42 James Whipple was the younger brother of Jonathan Whipple who son Francis married Thomas' second daughter, Abigail in Ipswich in May 1726.
43. *Lamson Family Genealogy*, 32-38.
44. Lamson, *Family Genealogy*, 37.
45. Ibid., 37-38.
46. Ibid., 37, 57, Essex Co., MA, *Vital Records*, Ipswich deaths 612.
47. Essex Co., MA, *Vital Records*, Ipswich deaths 612.
48. Lamson, *Family Genealogy*, 57, 59.
49. Beginning 4 Feb. 1737, Massachusetts issued a new series of notes called New Tenor money that was legislated to have three times the value of equivalent denomination from earlier emissions. Inflation soon devalued the New Tenor money.
50. *Lamson Descendants*, 37, 57.
51. Abbots, Essex Co., MA, *Vital Records*, Andover births 143, marriages 270.
52. Abbots.
53. Essex Co., MA, *Vital Records*, Andover deaths 433.
54. Ibid., Andover births, 143.
55. Ibid., Andover deaths, 143. Edmond and Elizabeth had another child named Elizabeth who died in Andover. Her birth was not reported in the birth vital statistics.
56. Ibid., Andover births 143.
57. Ibid., Andover births 143.
58. Abbots, Essex Co., MA, *Vital Records*, Andover births 142.
59. Essex Co., MA, *Vital Records*, Andover births 143.
60. Ibid., Andover births 143.
61. Ibid., Andover births, 143.
62. and 63. *Register*, 112:142.
64. Essex Co., MA, *Vital Records*, Andover marriages 123.
65. and 66. *Ibid.*, Boxford births 94.
67. Ibid., 95.
68. Ibid., 96.
69. Lamson, *Family Genealogy*, 32-8; and Death notice for Abigail Whipple, *Massachu-*

{ G 1564 }

setts *Spy/Worcester Gazette*, Worcester, Mass. (22 Jan. 1800, Vol. XXVIII), p. 3.
70. Essex Co., MA, *Vital Records*, Ipswich births 391, marriages 453; *Early Vital Records of Worcester Co., Mass. to About 1850*, (Wheat Ridge, Colo.: Search & Research Publishing Corporation, 1999), New Braintree deaths 160; and Henry Whipple 1:53.
71. *Parkman Family Papers,* Rev. Ebenezer Parkman, *Diary*, 14 June 1764 - 13 July 1771. American Antiquarian Society, Worcester, Mass., 91.
72. through 79. Lamson, *Family Genealogy*, 37.
80. Essex Co., MA, *Vital Records*, Ipswich births 270.
81. through 86. Lamson, *Family Genealogy*, 38.
87. and 88. *Register*, 112:143.

ABIGAIL (DANE) FAULKNER ENDNOTES

1. This article first appeared in *Heritage Quest Magazine*, Issue #77, September/October 1993 under Blaine Whipple's byline.
2. Andover is 25 miles north of Boston and originally included the present towns of Andover, North Andover, and that part of Lawrence south of the Merrimack river. It was called Cochichawick by the Indians and was part of the territory of the Naumkeag and within the domain of the Massachusetts tribe. The Sagamore was Cushamache who lived near Dorchester, Mass. The Andover of today represents the southern part of the original 17th century Andover Township. North Andover represents the northern part.
3. In 1644 the General Court granted ownership of the Township to 23 proprietors. A church was formed Oct. 24, 1645 with John Woodbridge as pastor. In 1646, Faulkner, eighth great grandfather of the author, and Rev. Woodbridge, acting on behalf of the proprietors, paid Sagamore Cutshaamache £6 and a red coat for the land within the Township. Roger, the Indian, and his company were given liberty to take alewives in the river for their own consumption so long as they did spoil any or steal corn or fruit belonging to the English. Roger was also granted permission to use the four acres he then cultivated. Most Indians were living north of the Merrimack river and Andover was considered the frontier. Sarah Loring Bailey, *Historical Sketches of Andover, Massachusetts*. Boston: Houghton, Mifflin & Co., 1880, 11. Edmond Faulkner, who married Dorothy Robinson 4 Feb. 1648, died 18 Jan. 1687. Dorothy died in 1668.
4. Francis Dane became Minister when Rev. Woodbridge returned to England. Born in Essex Co., England, he was 33 at the time and had no formal education for the ministry. He served 49 years until his death at age 82. Unlike most towns which had two ministers, Dane was Andover's only minister until 1682 when Rev. Thomas Barnard of Hadley, Hampshire Co., Mass. was appointed assistant. Dane is an eighth great grandfather of the author. He died in Andover 17 February 1696/97. His wife, Elizabeth Ingalls, was a daughter of Edmund Ingalls, born in England in 1598.
5. The Oyer and Terminer Court was an archaic form of an old English judicial system. Some felt creating this Court without the vote of the people was illegal as precedence limited its power to civil cases. The Magistrates had no formal legal training. Puritans had a low opinion of lawyers and did not permit the professional practice of law in the Colony, consequently those accused had no counsel. Nor did the Judges acknowledge that fine old English concept of innocent until proved guilty. The "W" was added to Hathorne's name by Nathaniel, great great grandson of the Magistrate and

notable American author from 1830 to 1852.

6. Two of Abigail's daughters, 12-year-old Dorothy and 9-year-old Abigail, Jr. were accused in the infamous Andover Touch Test on September 7. Both were imprisoned for a month, being released on bail in Oct. 7 and cleared by proclamation in May 1693. Abigail Faulkner, Jr., who married Thomas Lamson of Ipswich 6 April 1708 is the author's great (6) grandmother.

7. Cotton Mather was the first of Increase Mather's nine children and grandson of Rev. Richard Mather, first teacher of the Dorchester, Mass. Church. Richard (1596-1660), born in Lowton near Liverpool, England was suspended from his ministry at Toxeth Park Chapel in 1635 because of his Puritan leanings. He immigrated to Massachusetts that year and was with the Dorchester Church from its founding in August 1636 until his death. He helped shape New England's Congregational way, collaborating in preparing the Psalms in meter for the *Bay Psalm Book* and wrote the original draft of the Cambridge Platform in 1648. He was one of the men responsible for the "Half Way Covenant" and advocated the plan against fierce opposition by those who insisted on the necessity of personal conversion.

8. A few townspeople distrusted the diagnosis since the girls used their "illness" to rebel against every restriction placed on them by adult society. These people believed the girls were doing what every young person would if they dared and suggested a good whipping might solve the problem. But the suggestion outraged most people. With the Devil in command, the poor girls had no choice. Contempt of discipline was a common symptom of demoniac possession. These "afflicted children," everyone called them children regardless of their age, needed the prayers of the parish, not its derision. To the believers, it was plain the Devil was at work in Salem Village and equally plain had commissioned witches there. Marion L. Starkey, *The Devil in Massachusetts*. New York: Time Incorporated, 1949.

9. Elizabeth (Jackson) Howe was 13 years older than Abigail. In 1692 her husband had been without sight for about seven years and Elizabeth had assumed the full burden of caring for him and managing the farm. A complaint was filed against her 28 May for afflicting Mary Walcott, Abigail Williams, Mercy Lewis, and Ann Putnam, Jr. She was arrested May 31 and refused to confess, saying "If it was the last moment I was to live, God knows I am innocent of anything of this nature." She was tried 30 June and despite many depositions supporting her character and Christian behavior, she was condemned 2 July and hung 19 July. Enders A. Robinson, *Salem Witchcraft and Hathorne's House of Seven Gables*. Bowie, MD: Heritage Books, Inc., 1992, 286.

10. Of Abigail's examination, Sarah Loring Bailey wrote: Her conduct in the Courts was worthy of her position, free alike from credulous weakness on the one hand and scornful defiance on the other. Either from her own good sense, or upheld by the wise counsels of her father (who never yielded to the delusion), she showed the greatest discretion, paying due deference to the Court, yet never losing her firmness and dignity. That she was not to be intimidated by superstitious terrors, the examiners knew, did not argue with her about 'peace and judgment to come' but they urged her to confess 'for the credit of her town.' This seems almost to have a spice of malice and meanness in it, for to hint even that the fair name of the town was to suffer from the family of the Minister was not to help him who had recently been involved in difficulties with his parishioners. Bailey further believes Abigail acted under instructions of her father who saw that only concession of some points could save her, and could advise it conscientiously since neither he or any one else at the time could know with certainty that the Devil was not concerned in these "extraordinary manifestations." Bailey, 216, 224.

11. Mather's prayer for New England: "And now, O thou Hope of New-England, and

{ G 1566 }

the Saviour thereof in the time of trouble. Do thou look mercifully down upon us, & rescue us, out of the trouble which at this time does threaten to swallow us up. Let Satan be shortly bruised under our feet, and let the covenanted vassals of Satan, which have traitorously brought him in upon us, be gloriously conquered, by the powerful and gracious presence in the midst of us. Abhor us not, O God, but cleanse us, but heal us, but save us, for the sake of thy Glory, enwrapped in our salvations. By thy Spirit, lift up a standard against our infernal adversaries, let us quickly find these making of us glad, according to the days wherein we have been afflicted. Accept of us all our endeavors to glorify thee, in the fires that are upon us; and among the rest, let these my poor and weak essays, composed with what years, what cares, what prayers, thou only knowest, not want the acceptance of the Lord." *Ibid.*, 33.

12. Cotton Mather, *Cotton Mather on Witchcraft: Thee Wonders of the Invisible World*. New York: Dorest Press, 1999, 39. First published at Boston in October 1692.
13. *Ibid.*, 38.
14. *Ibid.*, 24-25.
15. *Ibid.*, 24.
16. *Ibid.*, 27-30.
17. *Ibid.*, 29-30.
18. Bernard of Batcomb—Other than in Mather's book, the author has been unable to find any references to this person or publication.
19. Ecstasies—The trance, frenzy, or rapture associated with mystic or prophetic exaltation.
20. Cotton Mather, 32-32.
21. Massachusetts Archives, *Witchcraft*. Boston, Mass., 1656-1750. Vol. 135, 103.
22. *Ibid.*, 10.

ENDNOTES — EXTENDED DANE FAMILY

For further information on the Salem Witchcraft Trials, see Generation No. 4, Ruth Whipple, No. 79.

See Generation 5, No. 204, Francis Whipple, for a continuation of the Dane and Faulkner lineages through the Whipple family.

1. Martha Carrier was born about 1654 in Andover and married Thomas Carrier, about 20 years her senior, in 1674. They lived in Billerica and moved to Andover about 1686. She was arrested May 31 and taken to Salem Village for examination. Hathorne asked the Salem girls who afflicted them. "Goody Carrier," responded Susannah Sheldon. "She bites me, pinches me, & tells me she would cut my throat, if I did not sign her book." Ann Putnam, Jr. complained of a pin stuck in her. Mary Warren cried out that she was pricked. Hathorne to Martha: "You see. You look upon them & they fall down." Martha: "It is false. The Devil is a liar. I looked upon none since I came into the room but you." The examination concluded as follows: "The tortures of the afflicted were so great that there was no enduring of it, so that she was ordered away & to be bound hand & foot with all expedition; the afflicted in the meanwhile almost killed, to the great trouble of all the spectators, magistrates, & others. Note, as soon as she was well bound, they all had strange & sudden ease. Mary Walcott told the magistrates that this woman told her that she had been a witch these 40 years."

    Samuel Preston, Jr., a witness against Martha, testified that two years previously he had differences with Martha and soon after "lost a cow in a strange manner, being cast upon her back with her heels up in firm ground when she was very lusty, it being in June." Phoebe Chandler, 11, testified, "The last Sabbath day I went to meeting, & Richard Carrier, son of Martha Carrier, looked very earnestly upon me, & immediately my hand began to pain me greatly, & I had a strange burning at my stomach, & then was struck deaf that I could not hear any of the prayer, nor the singing, till the two or three last words of the singing." John Rogers, about 50, testified that seven years ago, in a dispute with Martha, "she gave forth several threatening words as she often used to do and in a short time this deponent had two large lusty sows that were lost." W. Elliot Woodward, *Records of Salem Witchcraft, Copied from the Original Documents*, 2 vols. (Roxbury, MA, 1864). Vol. 2,. 56-57, 61-66.

Mary Lacey, Jr. was examined July 21. She confessed and then joined the afflicted circle. Her spectral sight allowed her to testify as follows: "Goody Carrier came to us in her spirit, sometimes in the likeness of a cat, sometimes in the likeness of a bird." Hathorne wanted to know if the cat sucked. "I cannot tell but believe they do suck her body." Hathorne: "Did you hear the 77 witches names called over?" Mary answered affirmatively and said "Goody Carrier told me the Devil said to her she should be a **Queen in Hell.**" Hathorne: "Who was to be King?" Mary: "The minister, Mr. Burroughs, a pretty little man, and he has come to us sometimes in his spirit in the shape of a cat & I think sometimes in his proper shape." "Examinations," *Witchcraft Collection,* Essex Institute.

Cotton Mather would later write of Martha Carrier, "This rapant hag was the person of whom the confessions of the witches, and of her own children among the rest, agreed that the Devil has promised her that she should be Queen of Hell." Cotton Mather, *The Wonders of the Invisible World.* Boston, 1692. (Reprinted with additions, 1862). 159.

Martha's uncle, Francis Dane, defended her. He reported she had been the victim of malicious gossip. By this time, Dane was suspect. In addition to Martha, Dane's niece Mary (Allen) Toothaker, nephew-in-law Dr. Roger Toothaker, and niece-in-law Elizabeth (Jackson) Howe had all been accused and arrested. Martha Carrier and Elizabeth Howe were hanged the same day. Under the circumstances, it was a brave act for Rev. Dane to speak out for the Queen of Hell.

2. Cotton Mather was present at the examination of Richard and Andrew Carrier July 22. Despite his preliminary instructions to the boys, they refused to confess. Magistrate Hathorne, not used to fortitude in teenagers, ordered them carried to another chamber where their feet and hands were bound. After awhile, Richard was returned to Hathorne's presence and questioned intensively before finally confessing. "Examinations," *Witchcraft Collections,* Essex Institute. Salem, 1692.

   On July 23, John Proctor who was in the Salem jail wrote that Richard and Andrew would not confess until tied "neck and heels, till blood was ready to come out of their noses, and it is creditably believed and reported this was the occasion of making them confess what they never did by reason. They said one had been a witch a month, and another five weeks, and that their mother had made them so." Upham, vol. 2. 311.

3. Judge Hathorne and the other examiners asked Sarah how long she had been a witch. "Ever since I was six years old," she responded. Hathorne, "You said you saw a cat once. What did that say to you?" "It said it would tear me to pieces, if I would not set my hand to the book." Hathorne asked if she functioned as a witch in body or spirit. "In spirit. My mother carried me thither to afflict." "How did your mother carry you while she was in prison?" "She came like a black cat." "How did you know that it was your mother?" "The cat told me so, that she was my mother." Upham, vol. 2. 209-10.

4. For complete details of the inter-relationships of the families related to Rev. Francis Dane, see Enders A. Robinson, *Salem Witchcraft and Hawthorne's House of Seven Gables,* Bowie, MD: Heritage Books, Inc. 1992. 273-300.

THOMAS CROSBY ABT 1510 TO HEPZIBAH CROSBY 1797

(Crosby lineage of Hepzibah Crosby, Generation 6, No. 492, wife of Benjamin Whipple.)

FIRST GENERATION

1. **Thomas**[1] **Crosby**[1] was born in York Co., England abt 1510 and was buried 16 March 1558/59 in Holme Upon Spalding Moor, York Co. He married **Mrs. Jannett Bell** in York Co. abt 1542. She was born in England and died there abt 1569. She married (1) **John Bell**. She and her sons John and Thomas Bell were appointed residuary legatees and executors of John's will dated 7 August 1537 and proved 3 October 1537.[2] After Thomas Crosby's death, she moved from the Hamlet of Bursea in the Parish of Holme Upon Spalding Moor to the adjoining Manor of Gribthorpe in the Parish of Bubwith. This Parish included nine Manors: Bubwith, Menthorpe, Breighton, Gunby, Willitoft, Harlthorpe, Faggathorpe, Gribthrope, and Spaldington, several of which had Chapels under the Bubwith Parish Church. Bubwith's ancient Church is on the east bank of the river Derwent.

In her will of 5 November 1568 she directed that she be buried in the churchyard at Bubwith and made bequeaths to Crosby sons Miles, Anthony, Ralph, and Nicholas as well as naming them executors. John Bell III, grandson, Katheren Myllington, and the poor of Bubwith Parish also received bequeaths. Miles Crosby was given the lease and good will of her farmhold and one quarter wheat, "wishing him to be good to his other brethern," Nicholas, "one chest which was his fathers and my best brass pot, willing that he shall give to Anthony his brother v s," and one-half of the Close at Harlthorpe called the Whyn Close,[3] Ralph, one yearling "whye" (heifer; young cow). Anthony and Ralph were given the other half of of the Harlthorpe Close "during the term of the lease." The rest of her goods were also left to the four sons.[4]

Holme Upon Spalding Moor in York County is an extensive Parish about 22 miles southeast of the city of York and lies in a flat plain bounded on the east by a range of hills called the Wolds. It's Church, which the author visited in 1998, dates to 1250. The town is bounded on the north by the Parishes of Seaton Ross, Everingham, Harswell, and Shipton, on the east by the Parishes of Market Weighton, North Cliff

All Saints Church, Home Upon Spaulding Moor, about 1250.

(formerly part of Sancton), South Cliff (formerly part of North Cave), and Hotham, on the south by the modern Parishes of Bishopsoil and Wallingfen (formerly parts of Eastrington), and on the west by the Parishes of Spaldington, Gribthorpe, and Forrathorpe (formerly Townships and Chapelries of the Parish of Bubwith).

The first reference to Thomas Crosby in York is on a Muster-Roll of 30 Henry VIII (1538) where he is identified as an archer with a bow living at Shipton, a Parish adjoining Holme Upon Spaulding Moor. The Miles and William Crosby on the same Roll may be his father and brother. Thomas' name also appears on the Yorkshire Lay Subsidy 303-322 with an Assessment of 12 pence on goods valued at £6 in 36 Henry VIII (1538).

Thomas **Crosby** and Mrs. Jannett **Bell** had the following children all born in York County:

+ 2 i. Miles[2] **Crosby** abt 1543.
+ 3 ii. Anthony **Crosby** abt 1545.
   4 iii. Ralph **Crosby**[5] abt 1547 and died unmarried in 1570 in Bubwith at 23 years of age. He was identified as a yeoman in his will dated 25 April 1570. Brothers Miles, Anthony, and Nicholas received bequeaths and were named executors. The will was proved 9 July 1570.[6]
   5 iv. Nicholas **Crosby**[7] abt 1550.

{ G 1570 }

SECOND GENERATION

2. **Miles**[2] **Crosby** (Thomas[1])[8] was born in York Co, England abt 1543 and died in 1573 in Gribthorpe in Bubwith, York Co., at 30 years of age. He married **Alison (__)** in York Co. Miles was identified as a husbandman in his will dated 6 January 1573/74. He left the lease of his farmhold to Alison and his child. His brother Nicholas was left "my raiment" (clothing). Residue of goods "to wife Alison and daughter Ann, they to be executors; and if my wife have another child, said child to share with them."[9]

Miles Crosby and Alison (__) had the following child born in Gribthorpe:
    6   i.   Anne **Crosby**.[10]

3. **Anthony**[2] **Crosby** (Thomas[1])[11] was born in Holme Upon Spalding Moor, York Co, England abt 1545 and died there in 1599, at 54 years of age. He married **Alison (__)** there abt 1570. She may have been a Blansherd as a John Blansherd was witness to Anthony's will.[12] Also, Alison was a beneficiary of the will of John Blancharde of Bubwith dated 20 October 1571 where she is identified as Alison Crosbie.[13] As a youth, Anthony moved with his mother from Holme Upon Spalding Moor to the adjoining Township or Manor, Gribthorpe in the parish of Bubwith, where she leased a farm. She also leased Whyn Close in the adjoining Manor of Harlthorpe. She left the Gribthorpe farm to her son Miles and the Whyn Close to Anthony where he probably settled. On 7 April 1580 Anthony was a witness to the will of Robert Riche, the elder, of Lathorne in Angleton, a Parish adjacent to Harlthorpe on the north. He also witnessed the will of Robarte Essingwood of Harethorp on 24 January 1590/91.[14] He was a yeoman and in 1592 purchased, by Fine, a 100-acre farm in Holme Upon Spalding Moor.[15] He also acquired a Close called Leonard Scayles in Wheldrake, a parish about eight miles northwest of Holm, where he was residing at the time of his death. His original will is preserved in the Probate Registry at York. He directed that his body be buried in the Church or churchyard of Wheldrake and made the following bequeaths: to wife Alison, my Close in Wheldrake called Leonard Scayles and two of my best kyne (cows); to son Thomas "all and singular my lands whatsoever lying and being in Holme in Spaldingmore, one yoke of my best oxen which he will chose and my base wayne (low wagon) with yokes and teams to serve four oxen, my young black mare, my bridle, and my saddle." To his grandchildren, children of George Westobye of Wheldrake, Luke, William, John, Thomas, and Richard, £10 each at age 21 or when bound apprentices "to some good trade or occupation." He gave his servant Richard Jackson 20 pence "so he be diligent and trustie to his service

this year following, otherwise to surcease" (end his employment). Isabell Stevenson, his maid servant, was given 20 pence and the poor people of Wheldrake 10 shillings. "The rest of my goods and cattle unbequeathed to Alison and Thomas, they discharging my debts and funeral expenses." He also made them executors. The will was probated 7 March 1599-1600.

Anthony **Crosby** and Alison (__) had the following children:

+ 7 i. Ellen[3] **Crosby** born abt 1571.
+ 8 ii. Thomas **Crosby** born abt 1575.

THIRD GENERATION

7. **Ellen**[3] **Crosby** (Anthony[2], Thomas[1])[16] was born in Holme Upon Spalding Moor, York Co, England abt 1571 and married **George Westobie** abt 1586.

Ellen **Crosby** and George **Westobie** had the following children born in Wheldrake, York Co.:

9 i. Luke[4] **Westobie**.[17]
10 ii. William **Westobie**.[18]
11 iii. John **Westobie**.[19]
12 iv. Thomas **Westobie**.[20]
13 v. Richard **Westobie**.[21]

8. **Thomas**[3] **Crosby** (Anthony[2], Thomas[1])[22] was born in Bubwith, York Co., England abt 1575 and died 6 May 1661 in Rowley, Essex Co. Mass., at 85 years of age. He married **Jane Sotheron** in Holme Upon Spalding Moor, York Co. 19 October 1600. Jane,[23] daughter of William **Sotheron** and Constance **Lambert**, was christened there 4 March 1582 and died in 1662 in Rowley. The earliest known English record to mention Thomas identifies him as executor of his father's will in 1599. By that will he inherited half of his father's goods and the 100-acre freehold farm on Holme Upon Spaulding Moor. After taking up residence on the farm, he married Jane. Based on taxes paid, Jane's father was the wealthiest resident of the parish. Thomas Crosby and William Millington, Sotheron's sons-in-law, ranked next in wealth. Only 19 of the over 150 households in Holme Upon Spalding Moor paid taxes.[24]

Thomas followed his son Simon, who arrived in New England the spring of 1635. Thomas arrived, probably, in the fall of 1638 with Rev. Ezekiel Rogers, making him about 65 years old when he left England. He may be the only member of Rogers' original company not to settle at

Rowley. He never made application for admission as a freeman, held public offices, or took part in public affairs. The first New England record to mention him is dated 16 April 1640 when he accepted five lots of 60 acres in Cambridge, Middlesex Co. Mass. as security for a loan to Stephen Daye. Daye was the operator of the first printing press set up in the English colonies.

According to the *Jewett Family of America Year Book of 1911*, "Reverend Joseph Glover brought the first printing press to the colonies. Glover contracted with Stephen Daye at Cambridge 7 June 1638, to go to New England at Glover's expense in the *John of London* and to be foreman of the press. Glover died on the voyage, and Daye set up the press at Newtowne, now Cambridge Mass. This press is often referred to as having been brought over for Harvard College, but as Harvard College did not exist until 1639, and as the printing press did not go there it was evidently never intended for Harvard. Thomas Crosby had an interest in the printing press and remained at Newtowne with Daye. Whether the interest was acquired after the death of Glover, or was an original one, is not known."

Thomas probably resided with his daughter-in-law Rachel and her sons after his son Simon died. When Rachel remarried and moved to Braintree, Norfolk Co., Mass. Thomas bought the Cary Lathum homestead in Cambridge in July 1645 and lived there until moving to Rowley where he was living by October 1649 when he was identified in a sale of property in Cambridge as being from "Rowley, County Essex." As a Rowley Proprietor, he received various grants of land[25] and bought John Haseltine's homestead on 20 April 1656. It consisted of a dwelling house, barn, orchard, home lot, planting lot, meadows, gates in the commons or ox pasture and about 22 acres of upland and meadow.[26]

After his father, William (4th generation) died, Dr. Anthony (5th generation) Crosby moved with his grandparents to New England. In a joint deed of gift signed 12 February 1658/59 by the mark and seal of both Thomas and Jane at Rowley, Anthony "our well beloved grandchild of the same town" was left all & every part of our whole estate . . . whether houses or land, in old England and in New England, bills, bonds, rents, and arrears, with all debts and demands that are anyways due unto us or unto either of us, from any person or persons whatsoever, in New England or Old England . . . giving and granting our full power to ask, demand, receive, and recover, by all lawful ways & means, of all and every person or persons, as fully and amply every way as we ourselves might have done before we signed and sealed this our deed of gift." It reserved "sufficient maintenance for ourselves during our natural life" from Anthony or "20 pounds per annum to be paid to us while we live together and to the survivor of us, at our choice."[27]

Thomas **Crosby** and Jane **Sotheron** had the following children born in Holme Upon Spalding Moor:

	14	i.	Anthony[4] **Crosby**[28] abt 1602 and died there in June 1632, at 29 years of age.
+	15	ii.	Thomas **Crosby** abt 1604.
+	16	iii.	William **Crosby** abt 1606.
+	17	iv.	Simon **Crosby** abt 1608.

FOURTH GENERATION

15. Thomas[4] **Crosby** (Thomas[3], Anthony[2], Thomas[1])[29] was born in Holme Upon Spalding Moor, York Co, England abt 1604 and died there 28 December 1658, at 54 years of age. He married **Prudence (__)** there abt 1633. Thomas was remembered with bequeaths from his grandparents William and Constance Sotheron. On a Subsidy of 16 Charles I (1640), Thomas and his uncle John Sotheron each paid 37s 4d on goods valued at £7. Of the 15 persons taxed in Holme Upon Spaulding Moor, they were the wealthiest with estates valued at more than double anyone else.[30] He remained in England and all of his children were daughters so his line ended. Daughters Jane and Katherine married into families of the Armorial landed gentry. His will was signed 25 November 1658 and he died 28 December. However, the will was not proved until 19 April 1669, a decade later. Daughter Prudence Bower was given "the messuage, tenement, or house wherein I now dwell with all houses, buildings, stables, barns, orchards, gardens, Closes, lands, profits, commodities, herediatments, and appurtenances, and two Closes called Pigh Hills, two Closes called Sadler Closes, and the Close called Chantry Close." If Prudence had no heirs, the property was to go to her sister Jane Belt. Jane, wife of Jasper Belt of Pocklington, York Co., was given "all the rest and residue of my lands, tenements, and hereditaments whatsoever, as well in my own occupation as in the occupation of any other person or persons whatsoever." Loving wife Prudence was left £40 annually during her natural life "in full satisfaction of her dower or thirds forth of my estate, real and personal" and all the "household goods belonging to the dwelling house, and one cow which she will chose." His nephews Thomas, Symon, and Joseph, sons of his deceased younger brother Simon, were given £10 each; grandchildren Robert Belt "my gray filly," Sarah Belt, £10, and Thomasin Bower, £10. His son-in-law Jasper Belt was made sole executor.

Thomas **Crosby** and Prudence (__) had the following children born in Holme Upon Spalding Moor:
+   18   i.   Jane[5] **Crosby** abt 1634.
+   19   ii.   Prudence **Crosby** abt 1636.
      20   iii.   Katherine **Crosby**[31] was interred there 2 May 1640.

16. **William**[4] **Crosby** (Thomas[3], Anthony[2], Thomas[1])[32] was born in Holme Upon Spalding Moor, York Co, England abt 1606 and died there abt 1640. He married **Anne Wright** in Seaton, York Co. She died 22 June 1636 in Holme Upon Spalding Moor.[33]

William **Crosby** and Anne **Wright** had the following children:
      21   ii.   Thomas **Crosby**[34] baptized in Seaton 18 December 1633 and died there 2 days later.
+   22   i.   Dr. Anthony **Crosby** baptized 5 October 1635.

17. **Simon**[4] **Crosby** (Thomas[3], Anthony[2], Thomas[1])[35] was born in Holme Upon Spalding Moor, York Co., England abt 1608 and died in September 1639 in Cambridge Middlesex Co., Mass., at 31 years of age.

He married **Anne Brigham** in Holme Upon Spalding Moor 21 April 1634. Anne,[36] daughter of Thomas **Brigham** and Isabel **Watson**, was born in Holme Upon Spalding Moor abt 1606 and died 11 October 1675 in Braintree, Norfolk Co., Mass., at 69 years of age. She married (2) Rev. **William Tompson** in Braintree bef October 1645. Ann was the administrator of her father's estate in March 1632/33 and was bequeathed five shillings in her mother's will dated 8 June 1674. She apparently received her share of her parents' estate when she married Simon.[37]

Anne didn't settle Simon's estate until six years after his death. In 1645, then married to Rev. Tompson, she petitioned the General Court for power to have it inventoried, administered, and distributed, pledging that the children would receive their "portions according as they were agreed by the Reverend Mr. Shepard & Elders & Deacons of Cambridge . . . or as the Court shall think meet." The Court required her to post "good security to pay the children's portions" and she agreed (on the 21 of the 7th month) with the Elders and Deacons of the Cambridge Church that her sons would receive the following: "Thomas, the eldest, 70 li, Simon 50 li, Joseph 50 li to be paid at age 20."[38] If Thomas attended Harvard and the cost was "to heavy for the parents to bear" 20 li of his portion was to be used "for his learning." Rev. Tompson, gave "leave to Anne to dispose of £30 of her estate as she herself pleaseth."[39] Joseph Jewett of Rowley was engaged as agent to dispose of the various parcels of land.[40] Rev. Cotton Mather characterized Rev. Tompson as a "very powerful and successful preacher" and Tompson collaborated with Rev. Richard Mather in the publication of several books. Tompson was afflicted with melancholia the last seven years of his life and Richard Mather said, "He fell into the bath of the Devil, a black melancholy, which for divers years almost wholly disabled him for the exercise of his ministry . . . but the pastors and the faithful of the churches in the neighborhood kept resisting the Devil in his cruel assaults upon Mr. Tompson by continually drawing near to God with ardent supplications on his behalf: and by praying always, without fainting, without ceasing, they saw the Devil at length flee from him, and God himself draw unto him, with unutterable joy. The end of that man was peace."[41] Anne final years as a widow were difficult financially because of her husband's long period of derangement.

The first known reference to Simon in England identifies him as a legatee of William Sotheron, his grandfather. The grandfather's will, dated 2 December 1616, includes a bequeath of 10 shilling for Simon. He was bequeathed 13 pounds, six shilling, eight pence by his grandmother Constance Sotheron in her will dated 14 November 1622.[42] He and his father Thomas borrowed £400 by mortgaging five messuages in Holme Upon Spaulding Moor on 17 September 1632. They transferred the mortgage to Sir Marmaduke Langdale and Richard Meadley on 24 March 1633/34. The deed from the Crosby's to Langdale and Meadley with Thomas' and Simon's signatures is still preserved at Holme. About a year later Simon left for New England.

As the first Crosby in New England, he has always been identified as "Simon Crosby the Emigrant." Along with Anne and 8-week-old son Thomas, he left London 18 April 1635 on the *Susan and Ellen* and arrived in Boston in July. A manuscript in the Public Record offices in London includes the three Crosbys on the list of its passengers. They presented Certificates from their local Minister and Justice of the Peace attesting that "they are no subsedy men; & are comfortable to ye orders & discipline of the Church of England." According to the Proprietors' records of Cambridge, he bought a homestead with house and three acres from William Spencer and several other parcels from other sellers who were leaving to establish a new settlement in Connecticut. He took the freeman's oath 3 March 1635/36 and thus qualified for full citizenship rights.[43] He was elected Selectman 7 November 1636 and again 1637 and was Constable and Surveyor of Highway in 1637. He only lived in New England for four years, dying in September 1638 at age 30. His estate was appraised at 444 pounds 4 shillings 4 pence, large for a man of his age at that time. The estate was not settled until 1645.

Simon **Crosby** and Anne **Brigham** had the following children:
+   23   i.   Thomas[5] **Crosby**.
+   24   ii.   Simon **Crosby** born August 1637.
     25   iii. Joseph **Crosby**[44] born in Cambridge, Mass. in February 1638/39 and died 26 November 1695 in Braintree, at 56 years of age. He was raised by his mother and stepfather Rev. William Tompson. He was a Trooper under Capt. Thomas Prentice and quartermaster under Thomas Swift in King Philip's War, 1675-77.[45] He took the freeman's oath 30 May 1690 and served the citizens of Braintree in many capacities: Selectman, Constable, and as a member of the Convention to form a Provisional Government following Gov. Andros' removal.[46]

FIFTH GENERATION

18. **Jane**[5] **Crosby** (Thomas[4], Thomas[3], Anthony[2], Thomas[1])[47] was born in Holme Upon Spalding Moor, York Co., England abt 1634 and died 20 May 1703 in Pocklington, York Co., England, at 68 years of age. She married **Jasper Belt** in Holme Upon Spalding Moor 11 January 1654/55.

Jane **Crosby** and Jasper **Belt** had the following children born in Pocklington:
     26   i.   Robert[6] **Belt**[48] abt 1657 and died 25 March 1690 in Bossall, York Co., England, at 32 years of age. He married an unnamed person and left unknown descendants. All of his uncles died without issue so he became sole heir of the Bossall estates of his grandfather Sir Robert Belt.
     27   ii.   Sarah **Belt**[49] abt 1659 and married her cousin William **Bower** Jr. of Bridlington, York Co. He was the son of William **Bower** and Prudence **Crosby**.

19. **Prudence**[5] **Crosby** (Thomas[4], Thomas[3], Anthony[2], Thomas[1])[50] was born in Holme Upon Spalding Moor, York Co, England abt 1636 and married **William Bower** of Bridlington, York Co. 7 June 1655.

Prudence **Crosby** and William **Bower** had the following children:
     28   i.   Thomasin[6] **Bower**.[51]
     29   ii.   William **Bower** Jr. married Sarah **Belt**. Sarah,[52] daughter of Jasper **Belt** and Jane **Crosby**, was born in Pocklington, Co. York abt 1659. William and Sarah were cousins.

{ G 1577 }

22. Dr. **Anthony**[5] **Crosby** (William[4], Thomas[3], Anthony[2], Thomas[1])[53] was baptized in Holme Upon Spalding Moor, York Co, England 5 October 1635 and was buried 16 January 1672/73 in Rowley, Essex Co., Mass. He married **Prudence Wade** in Rowley 28 December 1659.[54] Prudence, daughter of Jonathan **Wade** and Susanna (__),[55] was born in Ipswich, Essex Co., Mass. abt 1638 and died 1 September 1711 in Watertown, Middlesex Co., Mass., at 73 years of age. She married (2) Rev. **Seaborn Cotton** 9 July 1673 and (3) Lt. **John Hammond** in 1689. The earliest mention of Anthony in New England was in 1651 when he was 16 and the town of Rowley paid him and John Trumble "for going with hogs to the neck."[56] He studied medicine and practiced in Rowley and the surrounding towns. When he returned to England abt 1662 to attend to his inheritance, he appointed Robert Lord, Sr. of Ipswich his attorney to complete a property exchange with John Pickard of Rowley. In the exchange, Anthony gave up the 37-acre Manning farm in Rowley for 700 acres of village land, upland and meadow, and 20 bushels of wheat.[57] He was back in Rowley by 6 May 1663 when he acknowledged some deeds at Salem before William Hathorne, Assistant.[58] His age is confirmed in a deposition on 27 March 1660 as "about 23" and on 28 November 1671 as "aged about 35 years."[59] He died intestate and his estate was inventoried with a net value of 380 pounds 3 shillings 3 pence.[60]

Dr. Anthony **Crosby** and Prudence **Wade** had the following children born in Rowley:

+ 30 i. Thomas[6] **Crosby** 4 March 1660/61.
  31 ii. Jonathan **Crosby**[61] 26 January 1663/64[62] and was buried there 27 May 1664 at almost 4 months of age
  32 iii. Jonathan **Crosby**[63] 28 October 1665[64] and moved to York, York Co., Maine.
  33 iv. Nathaniel **Crosby**[65] 5 February 1666/67[66] and died young.
  34 v. Nathaniel **Crosby**[67] 27 September 1668[68] and died there 7 March 1699/1700, at 31 years of age. He married Elizabeth **Bennett** in Rowley 13 December 1693.

23. **Thomas**[5] **Crosby** (Simon[4], Thomas[3], Anthony[2], Thomas[1])[69] was baptized in Holme Upon Spalding Moor, York Co, England, 26 February 1634/35 and died 13 June 1702 in Boston, Suffolk Co., Mass., at 67 years of age. He married **Sarah (__)** in Cambridge, Middlesex Co., Mass. abt 1662. Sarah married (2) John **Miller** of Yarmouth, Barnstable Co., Mass. as his second wife abt 1704.

Thomas was graduated from Harvard College in 1653 and began preaching in Eastham, Barnstable Co., Mass. in 1655. Although never ordained or settled as pastor, he continued as the Minister until 1670. Later he became a merchant at Harwich, Barnstable Co. He died while on a business trip to Boston. His estate was inventoried at 1,091 pounds, 16 shillings. Deducting debts of 717 pounds 16 shillings, his heirs divided 374 pounds among themselves.[70] His descendants lived on Cape Cod for many years and about 1780 some of them settled at Yarmouth, Nova Scotia.

Thomas **Crosby** and Sarah (__) had the following children born in Eastham:

35	i.	Thomas[6] **Crosby**[71] 7 April 1663.
36	ii.	Simon **Crosby**[72] 5 July 1665.
37	iii.	Sarah **Crosby**[73] 24 March 1666/67 and died 20 March 1705/06 at 38 years of age. She married Silas **Sears** of Yarmouth abt 1693.
38	iv.	Joseph **Crosby**[74] 27 January 1668/69.
39	v.	(Baby) **Crosby**[75] 27 January 1668/69. This baby, sex unknown, a twin of Joseph, died at birth.
40	vi.	John **Crosby**[76] 4 December 1670 and was buried there 11 February 1670/71.
41	vii.	William **Crosby**[77] in March 1672/73.
42	viii.	Ebenezer **Crosby**[78] 28 March 1675.
43	ix.	Anne **Crosby**[79] 14 April 1678 and married William **Luse**.
44	x.	Mercy **Crosby**[80] 14 April 1678.
45	xi.	Increase **Crosby**[81] 14 April 1678 and died young.
46	xii.	Eleazer **Crosby**[82] 31 March 1680.

24. Simon[5] **Crosby** (Simon[4], Thomas[3], Anthony[2], Thomas[1])[83] was born in Cambridge, Middlesex Co., Mass. in August 1637 and died 22 January 1725/26 in Billerica, Middlesex Co., Mass., at 88 years of age. He married **Rachel Bracket** in Braintree, Norfolk Co., Mass. 15 July 1659. Rachel,[84] daughter of Dea. Richard **Bracket** and Alice (__), was born in Boston, Suffolk Co., Mass. 3 November 1639 and died aft 1726 in Billerica. Simon was two when his father died and he was raised by his mother and grandfather, **Thomas Crosby** in Newtowne, now Cambridge, until 1645 when his mother married Rev. **William Tompson** and moved to Braintree where Tompson was the Minister. Simon and Rachel remained in Braintree for approximately a year before moving with their daughter Rachel to Billerica. Billerica takes its name from Billericay, Essex Co., England, home of some of Billerica's earliest settlers. Page references from Rev. Henry Hazen's book on the history, including a genealogical register, of Billerica[85] will be in parentheses from here forward. The Crosbys were in Billerica by 1660 and lived on the north side of Bare Hill (25) where he built a log home and cleared some of his 3.5 acres to plant crops. Over the next 15 years he received several grants of land from the town, gradually expanding his farm operation [76-9]. He was appointed to the Committee to Lay Out Land on 9 December 1663 and gradually took on greater public responsibilities. He was appointed Constable on 28 January 1664 (again in 1677-78), Deputy to the General Court in 1690, '91, '97, and '98. He served 28 years as Selectman from 1671-'99 and again in 1701. Over the years he also served as Surveyor of Highways, on a Committee to run a line between Billerica and Chelmsford, on the Committee for gratuities on land, on the Grand Jury, as Commissioner for County Rates, on the Committee to examine the town accounts, Tithingman, Assessor, and Surveyor of Fences and Highways [80-81, 85].

He was first granted a license to keep "a house of public entertainment" on 27 November 1672 and from then on up to 1693 he was referred to in the public records as "landlord." Heretofore, he was known as "Mister." The license was issued annually at a cost of £20. Typical license terms: he could sell wine, beer, ale, cider, rum, brandy, and other liquors but could not allow playing at cards, dice, tables, bowls, billiards, nine pins, or any other unlawful game; no person other than a member of his family could be on the premises after dark on Saturday, on the Sabbath, or other times of God's public worship, and no one was to be "tipling or drinking" after 9 p.m. Any stranger who remained in excess of 48 hours was to be reported to a Selectman or the Constable. He could not sell wine or liquor to Indians or Negroes. He was not to buy "or take to pawn" any stolen goods "nor willingly or knowingly harbor in his house or barn or stable . . . any rogues, vagabonds, thieves, sturdy beggars, or masterless men or women, or other notorious offenders whatsoever." He was not to serve people of "idle conversation and given to tipling." He was to keep a "true assize & measure in his pots, bread, and otherwise in uttering of wine, beer, ale, cider, rum, brandy, or other liquors and . . . sell by sealed measure . . . maintain good order and rule . . . [offer] at least two beds for entertainment of strangers & travellers." [82-4].

He signed his will 7 June 1717 and named sons Thomas and Josiah as executors. His wife, all his children, and some grandchildren were included. To Rachel: the whole use & improvement of my dwelling house and all the rooms therein, and all the utensils & bedding to be at her disposal during her natural life . . . and the use of three gardens and the yard, & the house belonging to the yard and out of the orchard what fruit & cider may be needful, & a sufficiency to provide a maid or a nurse, according to her necessity, and the use of a horse to carry her to meeting, or when she hath occasion to ride forth, and her choice of two cows to be constantly provided for winter & summers and six sheep to be kept & maintained by my executors so long as they shall see reason to keep sheep for themselves, and if they keep no sheep I order that they provide for their mother annually 12 pounds of merchantable wool. I, give unto my loving wife, what swine I have to be at her dispose, and grant her liberty for the future to raise what may be for her use; and a continual supply of corn & meal and malt & firewood for her comfortable subsistence at all times, and further I do order my executors to pay unto my dear wife six pounds in money annually during her natural life.

To: **Eldest son Simon:** I have alaready given him his double portion in my estate in full by a deed of gift of lands & meadows.

To: The rest of my sons, each 80 pounds, to my daughters, each 60 pounds, accounting what each of them have had as part of their portions. **Thomas** has received of me in our way of trade 20 pounds. **Joseph** has received in land and help about building 20 pounds. **Josiah** has received in part of his portion in land 30 pounds. **Nathan** has received in part of his portion 20 pounds in land and meadow.

Daughter **Rachel, wife of Ephraim Kidder,** has received 50 pounds in the sale of that land I sold unto my son-in-law Ephraim and 10 pounds besides which she is to receive. Daughter **Hannah, wife of Samuel Danforth,** has received 16 pounds. Daughter **Mary, wife of John Blanchard,** has received 15 pounds in his purchase and 15 pounds in household stuff, in part of her portion 30 pounds. Daughter **Sarah, wife of William Rawson** of Braintree, has received in part of her portion 58 pounds in household stuff, cattle, and money. To **grandson John Crosby** 15 pounds and to **granddaughter Rachel Danforth** 10 pounds. His estate was appraised 18 March 1724/25 at 761 pounds for 377 acres of land and buildings and 8 pounds 13 shillings for personal property [85-8]. He was buried in the Old South Burying-ground about a mile from the town center of Billerica. [85-9.]

Simon **Crosby** and Rachel **Bracket** had the following children born in Braintree:

	47	i.	Rachel[6] **Crosby**[86] 20 August 1660 and married Ephraim **Kidder** 6 January 1685. Alive in June 1717.
+	48	ii.	Simon **Crosby** in 1663.
	49	iii.	Thomas **Crosby**[87] 10 March 1665. Alive in June 1717.
+	50	iv.	Joseph **Crosby** born 5 July 1669.
	51	v.	Hannah **Crosby**[88] 30 March 1672 and died 3 October 1752 in Billerica, at 80 years of age. She married twice. (1) Samuel **Danforth** in Billerica 8 January 1694/95. Samuel,[89] son of Jonathan **Danforth**, was born in Billerica 5 February 1665/66 and died there 19 April 1742, at 76 years of age. (2) Enoch **Kidder** in Billerica 4 June 1743. Enoch,[90] son of James **Kidder** and Anna **Moore**, was born

{ G 1581 }

			16 September 1664 and died 1 December 1752 in Billerica, at 88 years of age. He married (1) Mary **Haywood** in Billerica.
+	52	vi.	Nathan **Crosby** 9 February 1674/75.
	53	vii.	Josiah **Crosby**[91] 11 November 1677. Alive in June 1717.
	54	viii.	Mary **Crosby**[92] 23 November 1680. Alive in June 1717.
	55	ix.	Sarah **Crosby**[93] 27 July 1684 and married William **Rawson** in Massachusetts 16 October 1706. Alive in June 1717.

SIXTH GENERATION

30. **Thomas**[6] **Crosby** (Dr. Anthony[5], William[4], Thomas[3], Anthony[2], Thomas[1])[94] was born in Rowley, Essex Co., Mass. 4 March 1660/61 and married **Deborah (__)** there abt 1686. He was a school teacher in Hampton, Rockingham Co., N.H. for several years.

Thomas **Crosby** and Deborah (__) had the following children born in Hampton:

	56	i.	Hannah[7] **Crosby**[95] 27 December 1687.
	57	ii.	Abigail **Crosby**[96] 2 June 1689.
	58	iii.	Prudence **Crosby**[97] 8 March 1691/92.
	59	iv.	Jonathan **Crosby**[98] 8 May 1694 and died young.
	60	v.	Mehatabel **Crosby**[99] 5 January 1695/96.
	61	vi.	Elizabeth **Crosby**[100] 26 April 1699.
	62	vii.	Jonathan **Crosby**[101] 24 January 1700/01.
	63	viii.	Samuel **Crosby**[102] 22 November 1703.

48. **Simon**[6] **Crosby** (Simon[5], Simon[4], Thomas[3], Anthony[2], Thomas[1])[103] was born in Braintree, Norfolk Co., Mass. in 1663 and married twice. (1) **Hannah (__)** in Billerica, Middlesex Co., Mass. who died there 6 May 1702. (2) **Abigail Whittaker** in Billerica 16 March 1702/03. Abigail was the daughter of John **Whittaker** and died 31 March 1755 in Billerica.[104] She married (1) **John Parker** in Billerica 13 December 1696. They had a son John, born 14 May 1698 in Billerica.

Simon **Crosby** and Hannah (__) had the following children born in Billerica:

+	64	i.	Lt. Simon[7] **Crosby** 23 August 1689.
	65		Abigail **Crosby**[105] 6 January 1691.
	66	iii.	John **Crosby**[106] 11 April 1694 and died there 6 January 1695/96, at 1 year of age.
	67	iv.	John **Crosby**[107] 18 April 1696.

	68	v.	Samuel **Crosby**[108] 4 October 1698 and married Dorothy **Brown** there 9 December 1729. Samuel lived in Shrewsbury, Worcester Co., Mass.
	69	vi.	Hannah **Crosby**[109] 12 June 1700.
	70	vii.	Mary **Crosby**[110] 1 May 1702.
+	71	viii.	James **Crosby** 29 May 1704.
	72	ix.	Phineas **Crosby**[111] 26 November 1705.
+	73	x.	Solomon **Crosby** 8 April 1708.
	74	xi.	Nathaniel **Crosby**[112] 3 December 1710 and died there 28 May 1711, at 5 months of age.
	75	xii.	Rachel **Crosby**[113] 7 June 1712.
	76	xiii.	Benjamin **Crosby**[114] 16 December 1715.

50. **Joseph**[6] **Crosby** (Simon[5], Simon[4], Thomas[3], Anthony[2], Thomas[1])[115] was born in Billerica, Middlesex Co. Mass. 5 July 1669 and died there abt 1736. He married **Sarah French** there 6 May 1691. Sarah,[116] daughter of Lt. William **French** and Mary **Lothrop**, was born in Billerica 29 October 1671 and died there probably between 8 July 1727 when she released some dower in land[117] and 29 December 1727 when Joseph deeds land to their daughter Hannah Watts. She did not sign the deed.[118]

A review of Middlesex Co. deeds shows Joseph dealt extensively in real estate from 1707 to 1728. He was named Constable in 1695/96 and in 1712 was granted a place to build a pew in the Meeting House. Nine years after the death of his wife, he petitioned the Court at Cambridge to have his children care for him. The petition, dated 31 August 1736: The petitioner is aged 68 years or upward, and has for some time past been unable to support himself by business of any sort. That he has five sons now living, viz: David of Shrewsbury, Joseph of Worcester, both of the county of Worcester; William and Thomas, both of the town of Billerica, and Robert of Northtown, all living in the county of Middlesex: has also six daughters now living, viz: Sarah, the wife of Ephraim Abbot of Andover, in the county of Essex; Rachel, the wife of Thomas Wyman of Billerica; Mary, the wife of Eleazer Ellis of Dedham; Prudence, the wife of Jeremiah Fisher of Needham, both in the county of Suffolk; Deborah, the wife of Peter Russell of Andover, and Hannah, the wife of (__) Watts of Boston, to and amongst whom to set them well forth in the world the petitioner has distributed his lands and estate to the value of several thousand of pounds as he accounts, not reserving to himself anything competent for his subsistence, nor being able to do it by his own work and labor; and therefore praying this Court would take the premises into their consideration and to direct that the petitioner may be maintained and relieved by his respective children or their husbands (being of sufficient ability), as the Province Law therein directs and that they may be respectively assessed thereto as the Court in their great wisdom shall see meet, and in order thereto that they be properly cited to appear before this Court to answer the premises, etc. How the petition was resolved is unknown. He may have moved to Worcester to live with the family of his eldest son Joseph as a death record of a Joseph Crosby there corresponded to the age he would have been. It is apparent he had died before 23 December 1737 because his name did not appear with those of his brothers who on that date petitioned for a distribution of their father's estate.

Joseph **Crosby** and Sarah **French** had the following children born in Billerica:

+	77	i.	Joseph[7] **Crosby** 2 September 1692.
+	78	ii.	Sarah **Crosby** 12 June 1694.
+	79	iii.	Rachel **Crosby** 18 April 1695.
+	80	iv.	William **Crosby** 13 February 1697/8.
+	81	v.	Mary **Crosby** 12 January 1699/00.
+	82	vi.	Thomas **Crosby** 12 October 1701.
+	83	vii.	David **Crosby** 27 March 1703.
+	84	viii.	Prudence **Crosby** 11 May 1705.
+	85	ix.	Hannah **Crosby** 9 March 1706/07.
+	86	x.	Deborah **Crosby** 13 July 1709.
	87	xi.	Robert **Crosby**[119] 20 July 1711 and was living in Northtown in August of 1736 according to a reference in a Court record. Townsend was called Northtown at one time and the northern end of Billerica was also called the North town.
	88	xii.	Peletiah **Crosby**[120] 5 November 1713 and is believed to have died young.

52. **Nathan**[6] **Crosby** (Simon[5], Simon[4], Thomas[3], Anthony[2], Thomas[1])[121] was born in Braintree, Norfolk Co., Mass. 9 February 1674/75 and died 11 April 1749 in Billerica, Middlesex Co. Mass., at 74 years of age. He married **Sarah Shed** in Billerica 28 September 1706.

Nathan **Crosby** and Sarah **Shed** had the following children born in Billerica:

	89	i.	Sarah[7] **Crosby**[122] 22 December 1706.
	90	ii.	Nathan **Crosby**[123] 5 April 1708 and married twice. (1) Hannah **Martin** of Chelmsford, Middlesex Co. Mass. there 4 June 1735. (2) Ann **Tarbell**, the widow of Samuel **Parker**, there 14 July 1757.
+	91	iii.	Rachel **Crosby** 30 March 1710.

{ G 1584 }

+	92	iv.	Dorothy **Crosby** 9 April 1712.
	93	v.	Catherine **Crosby**[124] 18 February 1713/14.
+	94	vi.	Oliver **Crosby** 21 January 1716/17.
+	95	vii.	Mary **Crosby** 17 May 1722.

SEVENTH GENERATION

64. **Lt. Simon**[7] **Crosby** (Simon[6], Simon[5], Simon[4], Thomas[3], Anthony[2], Thomas[1])[125] was born in Billerica, Middlesex Co., Mass. 23 August 1689 and died there 2 February 1771, at 81 years of age. He married twice. (1) **Rachel Kettle** there 18 July 1711. (2) **Abigail Kidder** there 9 June 1714. Abigail,[126] daughter of Enoch **Kidder** and Mary **Haywood**, was born in Billerica 6 December 1694 and died there 7 November 1748, at 53 years of age.

Lt. Simon **Crosby** and Abigail **Kidder** had the following children born in Billerica:

+	96	i.	Lt. Francis[8] **Crosby** 25 October 1715.
	97	ii.	Abigail **Crosby**[127] 5 June 1717 and married Samuel **Winship** of Lexington, Middlesex Co., Mass. there in 1748.
	98	iii.	Samuel **Crosby**[128] 20 May 1719 and died there 9 July 1745, at 26 years of age.
	99	iv.	John **Crosby**[129] 19 April 1721 and died there 6 November 1743, at 22 years of age.
	100	v.	Mary **Crosby**[130] 3 October 1722 and married Ebenezer **Richardson** there 4 October 1764.
	101	vi.	Stephen **Crosby**[131] 27 February 1723/24 and died there 8 July 1734, at 10 years of age.
	102	vii.	Ephraim **Crosby**[132] 27 November 1725 and died there 29 August 1728, at 2 years of age.
	103	viii.	Elizabeth **Crosby**[133] 24 October 1727 and died there 4 July 1734, at 6 years of age.
	104	ix.	Hannah **Crosby**[134] 2 April 1730.
	105	x.	Ephraim **Crosby**[135] 13 October 1731.
	106	xi	Persis **Crosby**[136] 9 August 1733.
	107	xii.	Elizabeth **Crosby**[137] 10 February 1737/38 and married Adam (__).

71. **James**[7] **Crosby** (Simon[6], Simon[5], Simon[4], Thomas[3], Anthony[2], Thomas[1])[138] was born in Billerica, Middlesex Co., Mass. 29 May 1704 and married **Sarah (__)** there 1 February 1727-28.

{ G 1585 }

James **Crosby** and Sarah (__) had the following children born in Billerica:
+ 108 i. James[8] **Crosby** 5 October 1728.
+ 109 ii. Sampson **Crosby** 21 October 1731.

73. **Solomon**[7] **Crosby** (Simon[6], Simon[5], Simon[4], Thomas[3], Anthony[2], Thomas[1])[139] was born in Billerica, Middlesex Co. Mass. 8 April 1708 and died there bef July 1746. He married **Cathrine** (__) there. Cathrine signed a bond as his widow on 28 July 1746.

Solomon **Crosby** and Cathrine (__) had the following children born in Billerica:
110 i. Solomon[8] **Crosby**[140] 14 May 1740.
111 ii. Simon **Crosby**[141] 14 September 1741.
112 iii. John **Crosby**[142] 7 August 1744.

77. **Joseph**[7] **Crosby** (Joseph[6], Simon[5], Simon[4], Thomas[3], Anthony[2], Thomas[1])[143] was born in Billerica, Middlesex Co., Mass. 2 September 1692 and married Hannah (__) in Worcester, Worcester Co., Mass. where he was living bef 1719. Administration of his estate was granted in Worcester in 1744 and guardians appointed there for his children Joseph and Catherine in 1746.

Joseph **Crosby** and Hannah (__) had the following Children born Worcester:
113. i. Sarah **Crosby**[144] 5 May 1719.
114 ii. Joseph **Crosby**[145] 16 August 1731.
115 iii. Catherine **Crosby**[146] 6 November 1733.

78. **Sarah**[7] **Crosby** (Joseph[6], Simon[5], Simon[4], Thomas[3], Anthony[2], Thomas[1])[147] was born in Billerica, Middlesex Co., Mass. 12 June 1694 and married twice. (1) **Thomas Hunt** there. Thomas,[148] son of Samuel **Hunt** and Mary (__), died 16 September 1709 in Billerica. (2) **Ephraim Abbott** in Andover, Essex Co, Mass. 11 January 1715/16. Ephraim,[149] son of John **Abbott** and Sarah **Barker**, was born in Andover 15 August 1682 and died there 8 June 1748, at 65 years of age.

Sarah **Crosby** and Thomas **Hunt** had the following child born in Billerica:
116 i. Sarah[8] **Hunt**[150] 20 November 1709.

Sarah **Crosby** and Ephraim **Abbott** had the following children born in Andover:
117 ii. Sarah **Abbott**[151] 25 January 1715/16.

118	iii.	Ephraim **Abbott**[152] 22 July 1718.	
119	iv.	Mary **Abbott**[153] baptized 10 July 1720.	
120	v.	Joshua **Abbott**[154] 25 September 1722.	
121	vi.	Daniel **Abbott**[155] 3 September 1724.	
122	vii.	Elizabeth **Abbott**[156] 3 September 1724.	
123	viii.	Josiah **Abbott**[157] 26 September 1728.	
124	ix.	Ebenezer **Abbott**[158] 20 February 1731.	
125	x.	Peter **Abbott**[159] 8 May 1734.	
126	xi.	Martha **Abbott**[160] 13 July 1737.	

79. **Rachel**[7] **Crosby** (Joseph[6], Simon[5], Simon[4], Thomas[3], Anthony[2], Thomas[1])[161] was born in Billerica, Middlesex Co., Mass. 18 April 1695 and died 18 January 1757, at 61 years of age. She married twice. (1) **Samuel Stearns** in Billerica bef 1719. Samuel,[162] son of John **Stearns** and Elizabeth **Bigelow**, was born in Billerica 8 January 1693 and died there bef 1730. (2) **Thomas Wyman**. Thomas,[163] son of William **Wyman** and Prudence **Putnam**, was born 23 August 1687 and died 21 January 1760 at 72 years of age.

Rachel **Crosby** and Samuel **Stearns** had the following children born in Billerica:

127	i.	Benjamin[8] **Stearns**.[164]
128	ii.	Rachel **Stearns**[165] 6 June 1720 and married Nathan **Hutchinson.**
129	iii.	Elizabeth **Stearns**[166] 3 April 1722 and married Capt. Jonathan **Wilson** of Bedford, Middlesex Co., Mass. there. He was killed 19 April 1775 during the battle of Lexington and Concord.[167]
130	iv.	Prudence **Stearns**[168] 30 March 1724 and married John **Needham** there 21 January 1742.
131	v.	Samuel **Stearns**[169] 1 June 1726.
132	vi.	Mary **Stearns**[170] 1 July 1728.

Rachel **Crosby** and Thomas **Wyman** had the following children born in Billerica:

133	vii.	Thomas **Wyman**[171] 4 March 1730/31.
134	viii.	Lucy **Wyman**[172] 23 August 1733.
135	ix.	Sybil **Wyman**[173] 29 August 1735.
136	x.	Simon **Wyman**[174] in 1739.

80. **William**[7] **Crosby** (Joseph[6], Simon[5], Simon[4], Thomas[3], Anthony[2], Thomas[1])[175] was born in Billerica, Middlesex Co., Mass. 13 February 1697/98 and died there 1 January 1754, at 55 years of age. He married **Han-**

{ G 1587 }

nah Ross** there bef 1721. Hannah,[176] daughter of Thomas **Ross** and Sarah (__), was born in Billerica 13 May 1702 and died there 4 November 1756, at 54 years of age. William served as Surveyor of Highways in 1730 and 1731 and was appointed to run the line between Bedford and Billerica in 1737. He was a Tithingman in 1752. He accumulated a goodly amount of land before his death and was referred to as "Mr." His will, dated 31 December 1753, left the following bequeaths:

To my **well beloved wife Hannah** the east half of my dwelling house reserving liberty to my other heirs and executors room in the kitchen for baking and brewing and going to the well for water and reserving the cellar under the east room for the use of my other heirs in the other end of the house; three good cows to be brought up to her yard; my best mare; conveniancy in the barn; to be kept summer and winter out of my estate; liberty to keep two hogs, and 30 bushels of Indian corn and 10 bushels of rye yearly; three bushels of malt and six barrels of cider and the barrels to put the cider in; all the household stuff within doors that she stands in need of; **my Negro woman Jenney and her young child** to be at her disposal, the child if it should live to be given by my wife to any of my daughters which she shall think proper; a privilege in the gardens and what sauce is needful yearly; one bushel of salt to be brought to her yearly; sufficient fire wood and pine brought to her door ready cut; 90 weight of good beef and 200 weight of good pork to be laid up for her yearly; liberty in the barn and to the well to pass and repass at all times which it is needful for her; six sheep to be kept for her and she to have the benefit and privilege of the wool yearly; 20 pounds of flax from the swinge. **To my three well beloved son Jesseniah, Hezekiah, and Seth** all my real estate in lands situate and lying in Billerica and Bedford and all my buildings excepting what I have willed to my wife and when my wife has done, the same to return to my three sons; all my utensils out doors, all my stock of creatures, and all my moveable estate to be equally divided between them; and **my Negro man Robin** to be at their disposal. Jesseniah shall not come in for any more of my estate than his equal part above mentioned, for I have already given him by a deed of sale as much as I think is his part or proportion for his double portion and it shall come into the apprisement with any other estate and that to be took out of his part or proportion.

To **my well beloved son William** all my lands in Townsend lying in two lots containing about 125 acres and my will is that Jesseniah, Hezekiah, and Seth shall go up and clear and help him build, and give him stock, and make him equal to one of them as near as it can be esteemed by reasonable men.

To **my grandchildren Hannah, Millesent, Robert, and Prudence,** children of my daughter Hannah Cuttler, deceased, the sum of 26 pounds

13 shillings and 4 pence to be paid equally to them as they arrive to lawful age, which sum with what I have already done for their mother in her life time shall be their full part and portion of my estate.

To **my beloved daughter Martha Danforth** the sum of 32 pounds three shillings to be paid before the end of five years which together with what I have already done for her shall be her full portion out of my estate. To **my well beloved daughter Sarah Swan,** the sum of 34 pounds one shilling and four pence to be paid before the end of five years which with what I have already done for her shall be her full part or portion out of my estate.

To **my well beloved three youngest daughters, Rebecca, Rhoda, and Mary** the sum of 66 pounds 13 shillings 4 pence to each to be paid as they arrive to age or marriage if sooner, which sum shall be their full portion out of my estate. It is also my will that my three daughters shall have room and liberty to live in my dwelling house so long as they live unmarried, they to pay or provide for their board when they work for themselves. It is my will that William shall have liberty of living and room in my house so long as he lives unmarried, he to provide for himself after he comes to age or when he goes to work on his place.

My executors to be Jesseniah and Hezekiah and they shall have all my money, bonds, notes, and to pay all my just debts.[177]

William **Crosby** and Hannah **Ross** had the following children born in Billerica:

137	i.	Hannah[8] **Crosby**[178] 6 January 1721/22. Married (__) **Cutler**.
138	ii.	William **Crosby**[179] 27 August 1723 and died in infancy.
139	iii.	Martha **Crosby**[180] 12 January 1724/25. Married (__) **Danforth**.
140	iv.	Prudence **Crosby**[181] 28 November 1726 and died young.
141	v.	Jessaniah **Crosby**[182] 7 October 1728. Alive after January 1754.
142	vi.	Sarah **Crosby**[183] 27 June 1730 and died 2 April 1756 at 25 years of age. She married Timothy **Swan** of Cambridge, Middlesex Co., Mass. 24 September 1748. Timothy,[184] son of John **Swan** and Elizabeth (__), was born 3 August 1720 and died 19 October 1780 at 60 years of age.
143	vii.	Peletiah **Crosby**[185] 10 March 1731/32 and died 15 days later.
144	viii.	Hezekiah **Crosby**[186] 31 January 1732/33. Alive after January 1754.
145	ix.	Seth **Crosby**[187] 8 August 1734. Alive after January 1754.
146	x.	Rebecca **Crosby**[188] 21 July 1738. Alive after January 1754.
147	xi.	William **Crosby**[189] 4 January 1739 and was living in 1753 when his father executed his will.
148	xii.	Rhoda **Crosby**[190] 30 November 1740. Alive after January 1754.
149	xiii	Mary **Crosby**[191] 26 April 1742. Alive after January 1754.

{ G 1589 }

81. **Mary**[7] **Crosby** (Joseph[6], Simon[5], Simon[4], Thomas[3], Anthony[2], Thomas[1])[192]. was born in Billerica, Middlesex Co., Mass. 12 January 1699/00 and married **Eleazer Ellis** in Dedham, Norfolk Co., Mass., 5 June 1718.

Mary **Crosby** and Eleazer **Ellis** had the following children born in Dedham, Norfolk, Co., Mass.:

150	i.	Mary[8] **Ellis**.[193]
151	ii.	Mehitable **Ellis**.[194]
152	iii.	Timothy **Ellis**.[195]
153	iv.	Hannah **Ellis**.[196]
154	v.	Eleazer **Ellis**.[197]
155	vi.	Rachel **Ellis**.[198]
156	vii.	Eleazer **Ellis**.[199]
157	viii.	William **Ellis**.[200]

82. **Thomas**[7] **Crosby** (Joseph[6], Simon[5], Simon[4], Thomas[3], Anthony[2], Thomas[1])[201] was born in Billerica, Middlesex Co., Mass. 12 October 1701 and died there 7 December 1745, at 44 years of age. He married twice. (1) **Anna Parker** in Chelmsford, Middlesex Co., Mass., 24 June 1724. (Date of intent to marry.) Anna was born in Billerica 3 April 1692 and died there 20 September 1729, at 37 years of age.[202] (2) **Susanna Brown** in Billerica bef March 1730/31.

Thomas **Crosby** and Anna **Parker** had the following children born in Billerica:

158	i.	Thomas[8] **Crosby**[203] 13 December 1724.
159	ii.	Anna **Crosby**[204] 18 April 1727.
160	iii.	Jacob **Crosby**[205] 19 September 1729.

Thomas **Crosby** and Suanna **Brown** had the following children born in Billerica:

161	iv.	Susanna **Crosby**[206] 2 March 1730/31.
162	v.	Sarah **Crosby**[207] 10 February 1732/33.
163	vi.	Samuel **Crosby**[208] 21 December 1734.
164	vii.	Elizabeth **Crosby**[209] 9 December 1736.
165	viii.	William **Crosby**[210] 17 August 1740 and died 13 September 1740, at less than 1 month of age.

83. **David**[7] **Crosby** (Joseph[6], Simon[5], Simon[4], Thomas[3], Anthony[2], Thomas[1])[211] was born in Billerica, Middlesex Co., Mass. 27 March 1703 and died in Shrewsbury, Worcester Co., Mass. He married **Sarah Foster** in Billerica bef 1727. Sarah,[212] daughter of Thomas **Foster** and Hepzibah

{ G 1590 }

(__), was born in Billerica 30 June 1709. The Crobsy's were living in Shrewsbury by August 1738 where David was a shoemaker. David's brother Joseph was an early settler in Worcester and was in the leather business there in 1740.

David **Crosby** and Sarah **Foster** had the following children:

    166   i.   Hannah[8] **Crosby**[213] who married Adonijah **Rice** in Westborough, Worcester Co., Mass., 3 July 1751. Adonijah was the son of Charles **Rice**.

+   167   ii.   Hepzibah **Crosby** born 17 October 1727.

    168   iii. David **Crosby**[214] born in Shrewsbury, Worcester Co., Mass. 5 June 1729.

    169   iv. Sarah **Crosby**[215] born in Shrewsbury 5 May 1731 and married Robert **Cook** in Westborough, 6 February 1749.[216] Robert was the son of Cornelius **Cook**. Rev. Ebenezer Parkman of Westborough recorded in his diary of 31 January 1749 that the neighborhood was full of talk about Robert Cook and Sarah, "two young things who propose marriage." His entry on the first of February noted he "warmly inveighed against the liberty allowed to young people." On the 16th, he went to Shrewsbury to see Sarah's mother who had not given her consent to the marriage. She said she had only given Robert Cook "leave to court her daughter." She was less upset after her new son-in-law asked her pardon "as to anything he had offended her in." Parkman was back in Shrewsbury on 14 March to talk to Sarah's father about the conduct of the newlyweds. He said "their conduct was a concern of the Westborough church for many months" and they were "under the frowns of our church."[217]

EIGHTH GENERATION

167. **Hepzibah**[8] **Crosby** (David[7], Joseph[6], Simon[5], Simon[4], Thomas[3], Anthony[2], Thomas[1])[218] was born in Shrewsbury, Worcester Co., Mass. 17 October 1727 and died 16 May 1797 in Whipple Hollow, Rutland Co, Vt. at 69 years of age. She married **Benjamin Whipple** in Westborough, Worcester Co., Mass. 7 August 1749. He was born in Ipswich, Essex Co., Mass. 23 April 1727.[219]

(See Generation 6, No. 492, Benjamin Whipple, for a continuation of the lineage through the Whipple family.)

{ G 1591 }

ENDNOTES

1. Eleanor Davis Crosby, *Simon Crosby The Emigrant: His English Ancestry, and Some of his American Descendants.* Boston: Press of Geo. H. Ellis Co, 1914, 9-12 (hereafter Simon Crosby, *Descendants*). Eleanor Davis Crosby credited J. Gardner Bartlett for most of the research for her book. Simon, grandson of Thomas, was the first Crosby to come to New England. Eleanor begins the Crosby lineage with John, born about 1440, and his son Miles, born about 1483. While admitting that "a great deal of uncertainty surrounds the absolute connection of the first two generations," she believed that the "preponderance of probability" supported the links she set forth. This genealogy does not include John and Miles. It begins the lineage with Thomas Crosby and his wife Jannett Bell. Readers interested in the first two generations are referred to pages 1-8 in Eleanor's book. This author began his search for the Crosby family on a visit to York and Holme Upon Spaulding Moor in 1998.
2. Prerogative and Exchequer of York Wills, vol. 2, fol. 252 (Hereafter P. and E. York Wills.)
3. Close – a hut, a cottage; a small house. An enclosed place, especially a small field or piece of land surrounded by a wall, hedge, or fence of any kind held as private property.
4. P. and E. York Wills, vol. 18, fol. 49.
5. Simon Crosby, *Descendants* 12.
6. P. and E. York Wills, vol. 19, fol. 178.
7. Simon Crosby, *Descendants* 12.
8. *Ibid.* 9, 12.
9. P. and E. York Wills, vol. 19, fol. 613.
10. Simon Crosby, *Descendants* 12.
11. Ibid., 12-16.
12. Ibid., 15-16.
13. P. and E. York Wills, vol. 19, fol. 450.
14. *Ibid.*, vol. 21, fol. 446, and vol. 24, fol. 547.
15. For over five centuries land in England was conveyed by "Fine," a process where the grantee (plaintiff) brought a friendly lawsuit against the grantor (deforciant) for the premises to be conveyed. The deforciant acknowledged the right of the plaintiff to the premises for a consideration and the record of the suit was enrolled in Court Archives called "Fleet of Fines," the Fine being the Court fees. The document whereby Anthony acquired his property reads as follows: Final Concord made in the Queens Court at Hartford Castle on the morrow of All Saints, 34 Elizabeth (2 Nov. 1592) between Anthony Crosby, plaintiff, and Thomas Lambert and his wife Jane, Francis Lambert, Philip Lambert, John Lambert, and George Lambert, deforciants, of one messuage, one toft (ruined building), one garden, 60 acres of arable land, 30 acres of meadow, 10 acres of pasture, and Commons Right in pasture for all beasts, with all appurtenances, in Holme in Spaldyngmore, of which by Plea of Covenant the said Thomas, Jane, Francis, Philip, John, and George recognize the aforesaid premises to be the right of said Anthony, and they remise, quit claim, and warrant for themselves and their heirs to the said Anthony and his heirs against themselves and their heirs forever. For which acknowledgment, quit claim, warranty, etc. the said Anthony gave the said Thomas, Jane, Francis, Philip, John, and George 40 pounds sterling. Fleet of Fines, Yorkshire, Michaelmas term, part 1, 34 and 35 Elizabeth (1592).
16. Simon Crosby, *Descendants* 12, 15.
17. through 21. *Ibid.*, 15.
22. *Ibid.*, 12, 15.
23. *Ibid.*, 20. This source cites the Parish Register at Holme for her baptism and Essex

Institute Records, Salem, Mass. for her death.
24. See Lay Subsidy, Holme Beacon, East Riding of Yorkshire, 7 James I (1609), East Riding of Yorkshire, 204-401.
25. "Book of Possessions" for Rowley is organized by the different types of land grants — house-lots, uplands, meadows, and marshes. Thomas received one acre in the Third Division of fresh marsh, two acres in the Second Division of upland, and two acres in the Third Division of salt marsh. "Focus on Rowley," *Great Migration Newsletter*, October-December 2001, Vol. 10, No. 4. Boston: New England Historic Genealogical Society, 30.
26. Rowley Town Records, printed volume, 26, pages 31, 33, and 46 and Ipswich Court Deeds at Salem, vol. 2, fol. 124.
27. Ipswich Deeds at Salem, vol. 2, fol. 116.
28. Simon Crosby, *Descendants* 20, 29.
29. *Ibid.*, 20, 29, 32.
30. Lay Subsidy, Yorkshire, 205-463.
31. Simon Crosby, *Descendants* 32.
32. *Ibid.*, 20, 32-33.
33. and 34. *Ibid.*, 33.
35. *Ibid.*, 43-65.
36. *Ibid.*, 56-7.
37. P. and E. York Wills, vol. 42, fol. 281. Her Cambridge property is found on pages 60 and 91 of the *Proprietors Records*.
38. li is another symbol for £.
39. Mass. State Archives, vol. 15B, 181-82.
40. Details of those transactions are in Middlesex Co. Deeds, vol 1, fol. 35, 44, 163; vol. 2, fol. 50; vol. 3, fol. 368.
41. Richard Mather, *Magnalia Christi Americana*, vol. 1, 438.
42. P. and E. York Wills, vol. 35, fol. 492, and vol. 37, fol. 252.
43. Records of Mass. Colony, vol. 1:153
44. Simon Crosby, *Decendants* 58-59.
45. Bodge, George M., *Soldiers in King Philip's War*. Boston, privately published, 1891. Republished, Genealogical Publishing Co., Baltimore: 1976, 83, 94, 364.
46. *Records of Massachusetts Colony*, vol. 36, fol. 104; *Records of Braintree*, pages 11, 12, 17-19, 22, 24, 25-7, 30 in the printed volume. After William and Mary of Orange became King and Queen of England in Feb. 1689, Gov. Andros was jailed by rebellious colonists in Boston and was returned to England to stand trial.
47. through 50. Simon Crosby, *Descendants* 32.
51. *Ibid.*, 30.
52. *Ibid*, 32.
53. *Ibid.*, 32-35.
54. *Early Vital Records of the Commonwealth of Massachusetts to the Year 1850 on CD-ROM* (Wheat Ridge, CO: Search & Research Publishing Corporation, 1997), Rowley marriages, 277. (Hereafter Essex Co., MA, *Vital Records*).
55. Simon Crosby, *Descendants* 35.
56. Rowley Town Records, printed volume, 73.
57. Ipswich Deeds at Salem, vol. 2, fol. 64, 64, 119.
58. Ipswich Deeds at Salem, vol. 2, fol. 151-52.
59. Essex Co. Court Files, September 1660 and Suffolk Co. Court Files, No. 162102.
60. Essex Co. Probate Records, File No. 6589.
61. Simon Crosby, *Descendants* 35.
62. Essex Co., MA, *Vital Records*, Rowley births 57.

{ G 1593 }

63. Simon Crosby, *Descendants*, 35.
64. Essex Co., MA, *Vital Records*, Rowley births 57.
65. Simon Crosby, *Descendants*, 35.
66. Essex Co., MA, *Vital Records*, Rowley births 57.
67. Simon Crosby, *Descendants* 35.
68. Essex Co., MA, *Vital Records*, Rowley births 57.
69. and 70. Simon Crosby, *Descendants* 58.
71. Eleanor Davis Crosby, *Simon Crosby The Emigrant: His English Ancestry, and Some of his American Descendants,* Press of Geo. H. Ellis Co., Boston, 1914. 58. (Hereafter *Simon Crosby Descendants*).
72. thru 82. *Ibid.*
83. *Ibid.*, 66-91 and Rev. Henry A. Hazen, comp., *A History of Billerica, Massachuetts, With A Genealogical Register,* A. Williams and Co., Boston, 1883. 27. (Hereafter *Billerica Genealogical Register*).
84. *Ibid.*, and *Simon Crosby Descendants*, 66.
85. *Simon Crosby The Emigrant* and *Billerica Genealogical Register*.
86. and 87. *Billerica Genealogical Register*, 27.
88. *Billerica Genealogical Register*, 27, 36
89. *Billerica Genealogical Register*, 36.
90. *Billerica Genealogical Register*, 81-82.
91 thru 93. *Billerica Genealogical Register*.
94. *Simon Crosby Descendants*, 35.
95. thru 102. *Ibid.*
103. *Billerica Genealogical Register*, 27.
104. *Ibid.*, 27, 104.
105. thru 114. *Billerica Genealogical Register*, 27.
115. *Simon Crosby Descendants*, 92 and *Billerica Genealogical Register*, 27.
116. Ibid.
117. Middlesex Co., Mass. Deeds, 26:529.
118. Middlesex Co., Mass. Deeds, 30:9.
119. and 120. *Simon Crosby Descendants*, 94.
121. *Billerica Genealogical Register*, 28, 130.
122. thru 124. *Billerica Genealogical Register*, 28.
125. *Ibid.*, 26-27.
126. *Ibid.*, 28, 82.
127. thru 137. *Billerica Genealogical Register*, 28.
138. *Billerica Genealogical Register*, 27-28.
139 *Ibid.*
140. *Billerica Genealogical Register*, 28.
141. *Ibid.*, 28-29.
142. *Ibid.*, 28.
143. thru 146. *Simon Crosby Descendants*, 92.
147 thru 160. *Ibid.*
161. thru 163. *Ibid.*, 93.
164. thru 170. *Simon Crosby Descendants*, 93 and *Billerica Genealogical Register.* 140.
171. *Billerica Genealogical Register*, 93 and *Billerica Genealogical Register.* 167.
172. *Ibid* and *Billerica Genealogical Register.* 141, 167.
173. *Ibid.*, and *Billerica Genealogical Register*, 167.
174. *Ibid.*
175. *Simon Crosby Descendants*, 93 and *Billerica Genealogical Register.* 28.

176. and 177. Commonwealth of Massachusetts, Middlesex *Registry of Probate*. Entrd. Lib. 26, p. 237.
178. thru 180. *Simon Crosby Descendants*, 102 and *Billerica Genealogical Register*. 28.
181. *Ibid.*, 103 and *Billerica Genealogical Register.* 28.
182. *Ibid.*, and *Billerica Genealogical Register*. 28-29.
183. *Ibid.*, and *Billerica Genealogical Register*, 28.
184. *Simon Crosby Descendant*s, 103.
185. *Ibid.*, and *Billerica Genealogical Register*, 28.
186. *Simon Crosby Descendants*, 103 and *Billerica Genealogical Register,* 28. Massachusetts Archives, 97:163; Commonwealth of Massachusetts, Middlesex Co., *Registry of Probate*, 128:374.
187. *Simon Crosby Descendants,* 103 and *Billerica Genealogical Register*, 28, 30, 70.
188. thru 191. *Ibib.*, and *Billerica Genealogical Register*, 28.
192 thru 200. *Simon Crosby Descendants*, 93.
201 and 202. *Ibid.* and *Billerica Genealogical Register,* 28.
203. and 204. *Ibid.*
205. *Simon Crosby Descendants*, 93 and *Billerica Genealogical Register*, 28, 30.
206. thru 210. *Ibid.* and *Billerica Genealogical Register*, 28.
211. *Simon Crosby Descendants*, 93 and *Billerica Genealogical Register*, 28. Francis G. Walett., *The Diary of Ebenezer Parkman 1703 1782*, American Antiquarian Society, Worcester, Mass., 1974. 50, 72, 82, 91, 128, 155, 233. (Hereafter *Parkman Diary*).
212. *Simon Crosby Descendants*, 93 and *Billerica Genealogical Register*, 54.
213. *Parkman Diary*, 240.
214. *Billerica Genealogical Register*, 28.
215. and 216. *Ibid.*, and *Parkman Diary*, 190 91, 233.
217. *Ibid.*
218. Henry Burdett Whipple., *Matthew Whipple of Bocking, England & Descendants*, Vol. 1, 1965, Vol. 2, 1969, High Point, NC, 1:55; 2:64. *Vermont Vital Statistics to 1876*, Family History Library film #065930273, Salt Lake City, Utah. *Billerica Genealogical Register*, 28.
219. Franklin P. Rice, *Vital Records of Westborough, Mass. To The End of The Year 1849*, Worcester, Mass., 1903. Birth, 105, marriages, 218. Search & Research Publishing Corporation, 1997, *Early Vital Records of the Commonwealth of Massachusetts to the Year 1850 on CD ROM*, Wheat Ridge, CO., 1979. Ipswich births, 391. *Vermont Vital Statistics to 1876*.

APPENDIX G-4

GEORGE WEST CA 1720 TO
SUSAN ELAINE AND SANDRA LYNN WEST 1946–

*(West lineage of Susan Elaine and Sandra Lynn West.
See Generation 12., No. 6206, Ellen Elaine Whipple West.)*

FIRST GENERATION

1. **George**[1] **West**,[1] son of Thomas **West**, birth date unknown.

George **West** had the following child:
+   2   i.   Elijah[2] **West**.

SECOND GENERATION

2. **Elijah**[2] **West** (George[1])[1] birth date unknown. Elijah died abt 1788 in Delaware. He married **Mary Williams** abt 1755. Elijah was an English sailor until about age 30 when he left the sea to settle in either Kentucky or the Carolinas. He and Mary had a daughter and four sons.

Elijah **West** and Mary **Williams** had the following child:
+   3   i.   Eli[3] **West** born abt 1781.

THIRD GENERATION

3. **Eli**[3] **West** (Elijah[2], George[1])[2] was born in Delaware abt 1781 and died in 1852 in Miami Co., Indiana, at 71 years of age. He married **Sarah (Guffin) Row** in Brachen Co., Kentucky 4 January 1805. Sarah,[3] daughter of George **Guffin** and Mary **Lang**, was born in Virginia 23 October 1780 and died 5 October 1867 in Fayette Co., Ohio, at 86 years of age. The family probably descends from the eighteenth century McGuffin family of Newbry in Northern Ireland. Three sons and one daughter migrated to America in the early 1700s and are the progenitors of most Guffins in America.[4] Eli was lame and taught school near Lexington, Fayette Co., Kentucky. The family moved to Adams County, Ohio about 1810 and six

years later to Fayette County Ohio where other members of Eli's family lived. They eventually moved to Indiana. They had three daughters and four sons.

Eli **West** and Sarah (Guffin) **Row** had the following child:
+   4   i.   Wesley[4] **West** born 10 October 1808.

FOURTH GENERATION

4. **Wesley[4] West** (Eli[3], Elijah[2], George[1])[5] was born in Lexington, Fayette Co., Kentucky 10 October 1808 and died 13 May 1894 in Mt. Vernon, Linn Co., Iowa, at 85 years of age. He married **Polly Ann McKay** in Ohio, 14 November 1835. Polly,[6] daughter of Isaac **McKay** and Sallie **Pavey**, was born in Fayette Co., Ohio 11 September 1821 and died 3 October 1913 in Mt. Vernon, at 92 years of age. She was one of 10 children. The Pavey family originated in Normandy and the first Paveys to settle in the American colonies moved to New Hampshire the last decade of the 1600s.[7] The McKay family originated in Scotland and in 1854, Wesley, with two of his brothers and others interested in following the frontier, went to Iowa to determine the benefits of a move there. Wesley and Polly owned two "forest farms" in Ohio. Eleven of their 13 children were born there and three died there. Polly wanted her children to be educated and was not keen to move to "the wilds of Iowa" until Wesley convinced her that educational opportunities were available at the newly founded "college on the hill" (Cornell College) in Mount Vernon. He purchased 90 acres at the edge of town and the family moved in 1859. At least 90 of their descendants have attended Cornell College. The family has funded two scholarships and Merle West, a grandson of Wesley and Polly, gave a million dollars to the college in 1976 for a science building named the Merle S. West Science Center and $2.7 million to a West Scholarship Fund. In addition, he gave a million dollars to the Klamath Falls, Oregon hospital renamed the Eva Scott West Hospital for his mother. Two daughters were born after the move to Iowa. Wesley prospered in Iowa and by the time of his death in 1894 was able to give each of their surviving 10 children a farm or money of equal value.

Wesley **West** and Polly Ann **McKay** had the following child:
+   5   i.   Ely[5] **West** born 29 June 1854.

FIFTH GENERATION

5. Ely[5] **West** (Wesley[4], Eli[3], Elijah[2], George[1])[8] was born in Fayette Co., Ohio 29 June 1854 and died 19 December 1936 in Mt. Vernon, Linn Co., Iowa, at 82 years of age. He married **Jane Margaret Hayden** 2 March 1876. Jane,[9] daughter of Nathaniel **Hayden** and Mariah **Pierce**, was born in Princeton, Scott Co., Iowa 5 May 1855 and died 21 August 1960 in Mt. Vernon, at 105 years of age. She was the youngest of seven children. Her parents moved the family to Iowa from Ohio in 1854. Jane's life went from birth in a log cabin in 1855 to the wonders of the modern age in 1960. She lived during the terms of 19 presidents: James Buchanan, Abraham Lincoln, Andrew Johnson, Ulysses S. Grant, Rutherford B. Hayes, James A. Garfield, Chester A. Arthur, Grover Cleveland, Benjamin Harrison, William McKinley, Theodore Roosevelt, William H. Taft, Woodrow Wilson, Warren G. Harding, Calvin Coolidge, Herbert C. Hoover, Franklin D. Roosevelt, Harry S Truman, and Dwight D. Eisenhower. Ely, tenth born and sixth son, was five when the family moved to Iowa. After his marriage to Jane he worked for his father until buying land northwest of Mechanicsville, Jones Co., Iowa where they built a home and farmed until 1882 when they returned to Mount Vernon and purchased 220 acres two miles south of town adjacent to the military road that ran from Dubuque to Iowa City. In 1896 they built a new house on the foundation of the original house. The new house burned to the ground four years later so they built another on the same foundation. They moved into Mt. Vernon in 1911.

Ely **West** and Jane Margaret **Hayden** had the following child:
+   6   i.   Charles Wesley[6] **West** was born 7 February 1877.

SIXTH GENERATION

6. Charles Wesley[6] **West** (Ely[5], Wesley[4], Eli[3], Elijah[2], George[1])[10] was born in Mt. Vernon, Linn Co., Iowa 7 February 1877 and died 6 March 1965 in Marshalltown, Marshall Co., Iowa, at 88 years of age. He married **Bessie Madge Clingman** in David City, Butler Co., Nebraska 1 January 1908. Bessie,[11] daughter of Stephen **Clingman** and Anne Elizabeth **Myers**, was born in Cedarville, Stephenson Co., Illinois 7 February 1877 and died 27 March 1959 in Eldora, Hardin Co., Iowa, at 82 years of age. Bessie was a school teacher and a clerk in an attorney office in Pierre, Hughes Co., South Dakota when she met her future husband. Bessie wrote a history of the Clingman family containing anecdotes of many individuals. It is in possession of Elaine (Whipple) West in 2005. Charles, the oldest of seven children, attended Cedar Valley school, just as his parents had and his children and a granddaughter would. The school was on land owned by his father and when the school finally closed the land reverted to Wesley's heirs. Following this basic education he was graduated from a business college in Cedar Rapids, Linn Co., Iowa in the early 1900s and moved to Pierre, where he joined the West Land Company, a real estate brokerage firm owned by his uncle Elijah West. The firm sold farm land and city property. Two of their three children were born in Pierre before they moved back to Iowa where they farmed near Buck Grove, Crawford Co. They later moved to Wesley's home farm near Mount Vernon where Charles helped form the Linn County Farm Bureau and the Linn County Co-op in Cedar Rapids. He worked for the Co-op until sometime in the 1930s when they moved to Eldora where he was still managing the Farm Bureau Oil Co. in his 80s until he suffered a stroke in the late 1950s.

Charles Wesley **West** and Bessie Madge **Clingman** had the following **children:**

	7	i.	Lucille[7] **West**.[12] Died in Marshalltown, Marshall Co., Iowa in March 2004.
	8	ii.	Richard **West**.[13]
+	9	iii.	Wesley C. **West** born 17 September 1910.
+	10	iv.	Stephen Ely **West** born 20 August 1914.

SEVENTH GENERATION

9. **Wesley C**.[7] **West** (Charles Wesley[6], Ely[5], Wesley[4], Eli[3], Elijah[2], George[1])[14] was born in Pierre, S. Dak. 17 September 1910 and died 8 February 2000 in Madison, Dane Co., Wisconsin, at 89 years of age. He married **Kathryn Stassi** in 1959. Wesley grew up on the family farm near Mt. Vernon, Linn Co. Iowa and was graduated from Cornell College (Mt. Vernon) in 1935. He worked at the Des Moines, Polk Co., Iowa *Register* before serving in the U.S. Navy 1942-45. Following military service he ran a soft water service and self-service laundry in Beloit, Rock Co., Wisconsin, selling both in 1949 when he moved to Madison and started the Town and Country Furniture Store with two associates. They started the Ethan Allen Carriage House in 1969 and sold both stores upon retirement. Wesley served two terms as President of the Wisconsin Retail Furniture Assn., and one term as a Director of the National Home Furnishing Assn. Following retirement, he and Kathryn wintered in Florida. He was

a charter member of the Beloit Optimist Club, a member of the West Madison Optimist Club, and served a term as Governor of the Wisconsin District. He was a volunteer Consultant of SCORE in Madison and in Florida, a member of the Blackhawk Country Club, on the board of Directors of the YMCA 1977-83, and St. Dunstan's Episcopal Church in Madison and St. Martin's Episcopal Church in Florida. His memorial service was 15 February at St. Dunstan's.

Wesley C. **West** and Kathryn **Stassi** had the following children:

11	i.	Charles[8] Westly **West** III.[15] He married Susan (__). The family was living in Lakewood, Jefferson Co., Colorado in 2005.
12	ii.	Mary **West**.[16] She was living in Scottsdale, Maricopa Co., Arizona in 2005.
13	iii.	Sarah **West**.[17] She married Jerry **Kerkman**. They were divorced and she was living in Mequon, Ozaukee Co., Wisconsin in 2005.
14	iv.	Karen **West**.[18] Living in Madison, Dane Co., Wisconsin in 2005.

10. **Stephen Ely**[7] **West** (Charles Wesley[6], Ely[5], Wesley[4], Eli[3], Elijah[2], George[1])[19] was born in Denison, Crawford Co., Iowa 20 August 1914 and died 26 January 1998 in Tucson, Pima Co. Arizona, at 83 years of age. The family lived on a farm at Buck Grove, Crawford Co. at the time of his birth. He married **Ellen Elaine Whipple** in Cedar Rapids, Linn Co. Iowa, 14 December 1941. Elaine,[20] daughter of Lucien Blaine **Whipple** and Lillian Neva **LeFebre**, was born 6 August 1910 in Vinton, Benton Co., Iowa and was living on the West farm in Mt. Vernon, Iowa in 2006 with her daughter Susan.

Stephen Ely **West** and Ellen Elaine **Whipple** had the following children born in Cedar Rapids:

15	i.	Susan Elaine[8] **West**[21] 2 January 1946.
16	ii.	Sandra Lynn **West**[22] 23 August 1949.

(See Generation 12, No. 6206, Ellen Elaine Whipple West for a continuation of the West lineage.)

{ G 1600 }

JACOB CLINGMAN 1734 TO SUSAN ELAINE AND SANDRA LYNN WEST 1946–

(Clingman lineage of Susan Elaine and Sandra Lynn West, See Generation 12, No. 6206, Elaine Whipple West.)

FIRST GENERATION

1. **Jacob[1] Clingman** birth date unknown, had the following child:
+   2   i.   John Michael[2] **Clingman** born in October 1734.

SECOND GENERATION

2. **John Michael[2] Clingman** (Jacob[1])[1] was born in Germany in October 1734 and died 26 January 1816 in Ohio, at 81 years of age. He married **Anne Elizabeth Miller** in Pennsylvania 15 April 1756. She was born in Germany 19 February 1730.[2]

John Michael **Clingman** and Anne Elizabeth **Miller** had the following child:
+   3   i.   John[3] **Clingman** born 9 February 1774.

THIRD GENERATION

3. **John[3] Clingman** (John Michael[2], Jacob[1])[3] was born in Pennsylvania 9 February 1774 and died 23 May 1854 in Ohio, at 80 years of age. He married **Mary Ashton Briggs**.

John **Clingman** and Mary Ashton **Briggs** had the following child:
+   4   i.   Abner Briggs[4] **Clingman** born 13 July 1797.

FOURTH GENERATION

4. **Abner Briggs[4] Clingman** (John[3], John Michael[2], Jacob[1])[4] was born in Northumberland, Northumberland Co., Pennsylvania 13 July 1797 and died abt 1895 in Oregon. Abner's formal schooling ended after three months and he taught himself after that. He had a knack for mathematics and mastered the art of surveying and eventually became Scioto Co., Ohio Surveyor. His interest in education led him to co-found with John Addams the first library

(72 books, no fiction) in Cedarville, Stephenson Co., Illinois. Abner was quite old when he moved to Oregon and is buried in the Pine Grove Cemetery six miles west of Halsey, Linn Co. He married **Sarah Woolever** 16 May 1822.

Abner Briggs **Clingman** and Sarah **Woolever** had the following child:
+   5   i.   Stephen[5] **Clingman** born 9 August 1845.

FIFTH GENERATION

5. **Stephen[5] Clingman** (Abner Briggs[4], John[3], John Michael[2], Jacob[1])[5] was born in Cedarville, Stephenson Co, Illinois 9 August 1845 and died 1 August 1932 in David City, Butler Co., Nebraska, at 86 years of age. He married **Anne Elizabeth Myers** 24 September 1874. Anne,[6] daughter of David **Myers** and Anne **Hatton**, was born in Dalton, Wayne Co., Ohio in 1848 and died 12 February 1934 in David City, at 85 years of age. Stephen was graduated from Cornell College at Mt Vernon, Linn Co., Iowa and from the U. of Iowa at Iowa City, Johnson Co. with a law degree. He met his future wife Anne while a student at Cornell College. The newly weds farmed for a while near Cedarville and then moved to David City where Stephen became a prominent member of the community. He served on the School and Library Boards, the City Council, and as County Judge.

Stephen **Clingman** and Anne Elizabeth **Myers** had the following child:
+   6   i.   Bessie Madge[6] **Clingman** born 7 February 1877.

SIXTH GENERATION

6. **Bessie Madge[6] Clingman** (Stephen[5], Abner Briggs[4], John[3], John Michael[2], Jacob[1])[7] was born in Cedarville, Stephenson Co., Illinois 7 February 1877 and died 27 March 1959 in Eldora, Hardin Co., Iowa, at 82 years of age. She married **Charles Wesley West** in David City, Butler Co., Nebraska 1 January 1908. Charles,[8] son of Ely **West** and Jane Margaret **Hayden**, was born in Mt. Vernon, Linn Co., Iowa 7 February 1877 and died 6 March 1965 in Marshalltown, Marshall Co., Iowa, at 88 years of age. Charles, the oldest of seven children, attended Cedar Valley school near Mt. Vernon, just as his parents had and his children and a granddaughter would. The school was on land owned by his father and when the school finally closed the land reverted to Wesley's heirs. Following this basic education he was graduated from a business college in Cedar Rapids, Linn Co., Iowa in the early 1900s and moved to Pierre, Hughes Co., South Dakota where he

joined the West Land Company, a real estate brokerage firm owned by his uncle Elijah West. The firm sold farm land and city property. Two of their three children were born in Pierre before they moved back to Iowa where they farmed near Buck Grove Crawford Co., Iowa. They later moved to Wesley's home farm near Mount Vernon where Charles helped form the Linn county Farm Bureau and the Linn county Co-op in Cedar Rapids. He worked for the Co-op until sometime in the 1930s when they moved to Eldora, Harden county, Iowa where he was still managing the Farm Bureau Oil Co. in his 80s until he suffered a stroke in the late 1950s. Bessie was a school teacher and a clerk in an attorney office in Pierre when she met her future husband. Bessie wrote a history of the Clingman family containing anecdotes of many individuals. It is in possession of Elaine (Whipple) West in 2006.

Bessie Madge **Clingman** and Charles Wesley **West** had the following children:

    7   i.   Lucille[7] **West**.[9]
    8   ii.   Richard **West**.[10]
+   9   iii.   Wesley C. **West** born 17 September 1910. See numbers 9., 11., 12., 13., and 14. in the West family above.
+   10   iv.   Stephen Ely **West** born 20 August 1914. See numbers 10., 15., and 16. in the West Family above.

(See Generation No. 12, Ellen Elaine Whipple West for a continuation of the Clingman lineage.)

NAPOLIAN LEFEBRE TO SUSAN ELAINE AND SANDRA LYNN WEST 1946–

(LeFebre lineage of Susan Elaine and Sandra Lynn West. See Generation 12, No. 6026, Elaine Whipple West.)

FIRST GENERATION

1. **Napolian**[1] **LeFebre**[1] birth date unknown, was French-Canadian and it is believed his wife was a Flatfoot Indian.

Napolian **LeFebre** had the following child:
+   2   i.   Henry[2] **LeFebre**.

{ G 1603 }

SECOND GENERATION

2. **Henry**[2] **LeFebre** (Napolian[1])[2] was born in Canada and married **Helen Margarite Ruhl**. Helen,[3] daughter of Conrad **Ruhl** and Helen **Forest**, was born in Chicago, Cook Co. Illinois. They were divorced. Helen married (2) **Gustav E. Kloss**.

Henry **LeFebre** and Helen Margarite **Ruhl** had the following children:

+ 3   i.   Lillian Neva[3] **LeFebre** born 20 November 1888.
   4   ii. Raymond **LeFebre**[4] born in Chicago, Ill..

THIRD GENERATION

3. **Lillian Neva**[3] **LeFebre** (Henry[2], Napolian[1])[5] was born in Chicago, Cook Co. Illinois 20 November 1888 and died 30 April 1941 in Cedar Rapids, Linn Co., Iowa, at 52 years of age. She and her second husband Charles Harold **Zastera** are buried in Cedar Rapid's Oak Hill Cemetery. She married twice. (1) **Lucien Blaine Whipple** in Beattie Marshall Co., Kansas 18 December 1908. Blaine,[6] son of James Ezekiel **Whipple** and Malissa "Ellen" **Thompson**, was born in Eugene, Vermillion Co., Indiana 22 June 1883 and died 27 August 1954 in Dresden, Weakley Co., Tennessee, at 71 years of age. He married (2) **Pearl Julia Scott** in Albion, Boone Co., Nebraska 21 September 1927. Blaine's death certificate was altered by Court Order on 22 September 1954, File C-26755, to correct his birth year to be 1883, not 1885 as originally shown. He and Pearl are buried in Vinton, Benton Co., Iowa, Evergreen Cemetery (Lot 23, Block L). Lillian and Blaine were divorced in Cedar Rapids 16 March 1926. She married (2) **Charles Harold Zastera** in Vinton in July 1928. Charles was born in Cedar Rapids 23 September 1889 and died 30 June 1964 in Cedar Rapids, at 74 years of age.[7]

Lillian attended a convent school for part of her early education and after her mother divorced Henry and married Gustav E. Kloss, the family lived in Mexico for five years (most of her teen years) where her stepfather was an Electrical Engineer for a large silver mine. Their community had one other American family and a large population of Chinese. Lillian taught English to the Chinese children. By the time of her marriage to Blaine she was working in the costume department and Blaine was a producer and an actor in traveling tent shows. They were married by a Justice of the Peace at the Court House in Beattie. Charles Harold Zastera owned a drug store in Cedar Rapids.

{ G 1604 }

Lillian Neva **LeFebre** and Lucien Blaine **Whipple** had the following children:
- 5   i.   Helen[4] **Whipple**[8] born prematurely at St. Lukes Hospital in Kansas City, Jackson Co., Missouri 20 August 1909 and died the day of birth.
- +   6   ii.   Ellen Elaine **Whipple** born 6 August 1910.
- +   7   iii.   James Earl **Whipple** born 29 October 1911.

(See Generation 12, No. 6206 Ellen Elaine Whipple West and No. 6207, James Earl Whipple for a continuation of the LeFebre lineage.)

CONRAD RUHL CA 1840 TO SUSAN ELAINE AND SANDRA LYNN WEST 1946–

(Ruhl lineage of Susan Elaine and Sandra Lynn West, See Generation 12, No. 6206, Ellen Elaine Whipple West.)

FIRST GENERATION

1. **Conrad**[1] **Ruhl** birth date unknown, married **Helen Forest** in Chicago, Cook, Co., Illinois. Helen, daughter of John **Forest** and Margarite **Richie**, was born in Paisley, Scotland abt 1845 and died in Chicago where she is buried in Rose Hill Cemetery. Conrad was a fireman at the time of the Great Chicago fire in October 1871 that killed 250, left 90,000 homeless, and destroyed about 4 square miles of the central city. He was fired for disobeying orders of his Captain to enter a burning building whose three story interior had been completely engulfed in flames.[1]

Conrad **Ruhl** and Helen **Forest** had the following children:
- +   2   i.   Helen Margarite[2] **Ruhl**.
- +   3   ii.   Mary Catherine **Ruhl**.
-     4   iii.   Christian May **Ruhl**, birthdate unknown, died in Detroit, Wayne Co., Michigan. He married twice. (1) Edna (__) who died abt 1918. (2) an unnamed woman with three children. No details provided.[2]

SECOND GENERATION

2. **Helen Margarite**[2] **Ruhl** (Conrad[1]) birth date unknown, was born in Chicago, Cook Co., Illinois and married twice. (1) **Henry LeFebre**, son of Napolian **LeFebre**, was born in Canada, date unknown. (2) **Gustav E. Kloss**. Gustav was born in Germany abt 1870 and died 23 May 1937 in Chicago at 66 years of age. He is buried in Rose Hill Cemetery. Gus' parents migrated to the Chicago area when he was a youngster. After completing high school he worked on the family dairy. He became an engineer and worked in Mexico as a silver mine supervisor and later, in Atlanta, Fulton Co., Georgia., Los Angeles, Calif., and Kansas City, Jackson Co., Missouri. He was affiliated with the Franklin Ice Cream Co. in the latter location and had an interest in dried milk operations in Missouri and Kansas with Blaine Whipple, husband of his step-daughter Lillian. He was President of the National Association of Practical Refrigeration Engineers in 1923. At the time of his death he was affiliated with the Henry Bauers Chemical Co. in Chicago.[3]

Helen Margarite **Ruhl** and Henry **LeFebre** had the following children:
+   5   i.   Lillian Neva[3] **LeFebre** born 20 November 1888.
     6   ii.   Raymond **LeFebre** born in Chicago, Illinois.[4]

Helen Margarite **Ruhl** and Gustav E. **Kloss** had the following child:
     7   iii.   Lorin **Kloss**[5] born 15 December 1908. His art teacher at McKinley high school in Cedar Rapids, Linn Co., Iowa was the famed artist Grant Wood. Lorin later attended the Art Institute of Chicago and became head of the Art Department of Chicago's Fish Furniture Co.[6]

3. **Mary Catherine**[2] **Ruhl** (Conrad[1])[7] birth date unknown, married **Julius May** who died 28 April 1937 in Long Beach, Los Angeles Co., California and is buried at Grand View Cemetery in Glendale, Los Angeles Co., California. His family owned a hotel near Lincoln Park in Chicago. He worked for the telephone company in Chicago until his retirement when he moved to Los Angeles. The mother of Gloria Swanson, the famous Hollywood movie star, was part of the May family. Alice May and Lillian LeFebre used to take dancing lessons with Gloria when they were youngsters.[8]

Mary Catherine **Ruhl** and Julius **May** had the following children:
     8   i.   Alice[3] **May**.[9]
     9   ii.   Robert **May**.[10]

THIRD GENERATION

5. **Lillian Neva**[3] **LeFebre** (Helen Margarite[2] Ruhl, Conrad[1])[11] was born in Chicago, Cook Co., Illinois 20 November 1888 and died 30 April 1941 in Cedar Rapids, Linn Co., Iowa at 52 years of age. She married twice. (1) **Lucien Blaine Whipple** in Beattie, Marshall Co., Kans., 18 December 1908. Blaine, son of James Ezekiel **Whipple** and Malissa "Ellen" **Thompson**, was born in Eugene, Vermillion Co., Indiana 22 June 1883 and died in Dresden, Weakley Co., Tennessee 27 August 1954 at 71 years of age. He is buried in the Evergreen Cemetery in Vinton, Benton Co., Iowa. They were divorced in Cedar Rapids, Linn Co., Iowa 16 March 1926. He married (2) **Pearl Julia Scott** in Albion, Boone Co., Nebraska 21 September 1927. Lillian married (2) **Charles Harold Zastera** in Vinton, Iowa in July 1928. Charles was born in Cedar Rapids 23 September 1889 and died there 30 June 1964 at 74 years of age. Lillian and Charles are buried in Oak Hill Cemetery, Cedar Rapids.[12]

Lillian Neva **LeFebre** and Lucien Blaine **Whipple** had the following children:

	10	i.	Helen[4] **Whipple**[13] born in Kansas City, Jackson Co., Mo. 20 August 1909 and died the day of birth. She was born prematurely at St. Lukes Hospital. The medical attendant was Dr. H.F. Mather.[14]
+	11	ii.	Ellen Elaine **Whipple** born in Cedar Rapids 6 August 1910.[15]
+	12	iii.	James Earl **Whipple** born in Cedar Rapids 29 October 1911.[16]

(See Generation 12, No. 6206, Ellen Elaine Whipple West and No. 6207, James Earl Whipple for a continuation of the Ruhl lineage.)

WEST FAMILY ENDNOTES

1. through 6. Ellen Elaine (Whipple) West to Blaine Whipple. Letters dated 12 Dec. 1982, 17 Oct. 1983, 2 Aug. 2000, and 11 June 2003 at 497 Hwy 1, Mt. Vernon, Iowa 52314. In possession of Whipple (2006.) Elaine West is a sister of the author. She has been researching the Whipple and West families for close to 50 years and her sources are multiple and varied. (Hereafter Elaine Whipple West.)
7. See Charles C. Pavey, *The Pavey Family of Ohio*, privately published in two manuscript volumes (copy at the Allen County Public Library, Fort Wayne, Ind.) for the early history of the family.
8. Ellen Whipple West.
9. R. L. Guffin, *The Guffin Family in America*. Tuscaloosa, Ala.: Biography Press, 1975.
10. through 22. Ellen Whipple West.

CLINGMAN FAMILY ENDNOTES

1. through 10. Ellen Elaine (Whipple) West to Blaine Whipple. Letters dated 12 Dec. 1982, 17 Oct. 1983, 2 Aug. 2000, and 11 June 2003 at 497 Hwy 1, Mt. Vernon, Iowa 52314. In possession of Whipple (2005.) Elaine West is a sister of the author. She has been researching the Whipple and West families for close to 50 years and her sources are multiple and varied. (Hereafter Elaine Whipple West.)

LEFEBRE FAMILY ENDNOTES

1. through 5. Ellen Elaine (Whipple) West to Blaine Whipple. Letters dated 12 Dec. 1982, 17 Oct. 1983, 2 Aug. 2000, and 11 June 2003 at 497 Hwy 1, Mt. Vernon, IA 52314. In possession of Whipple (2005.) Elaine West is a sister of the author. She has been researching the Whipple and West families for close to 50 years and her sources are multiple and varied.. (Hereafter Elaine Whipple West.)
6. Department of the Interior, Bureau of Pensions document that was a part of James W. Whipple's application for a pension for service in the Spanish-American War; Pension Application No. 1407489. Question No. 5 asked: "Have you any children living? If so, please state their names and dates of their births." Answer: "One son, L. Blaine Whipple, born June 22, 1883." /s/ James E. Whipple. Dated 21 January 1913. Copy of document acquired by Blaine Whipple 30 May 1981 from the National Archives Trust Fund Board, Washington, D. C. 20408. Date and place of marriage attested to by Lillian (LeFebre) Whipple, plaintiff in a petition in equity to be divorced from Blaine Whipple, defendant, filed in the District Court of Linn Co., Cedar Rapids, Iowa 9 Jan. 1926. Divorce No. 35081. Blaine Whipple & Pearl J. Scott, Marriage License, 21 September 1927, Vol. 388, Record No.9-296: State of Nebraska, Dept. of Public Welfare, Bureau of Health, Division of Vital Statistics, Lincoln, Nebr. and Blaine Whipple, Death Certificate Death No. 54-18847, Weakly Co., Tenn.
7. Elaine Whipple West.
8. Ibid.; and Baby (Ellen) Whipple, Death Certificate D No. 00722. File No. 33268-1909, Filed in August 1909, Dept. of Health, Bureau of Vital Statistics, Dept. 050 Org 2000,,2400 Troost, Ste. 1200, Kansas City, Mo.

RUHL FAMILY ENDNOTES

1. through 13. Ellen Elaine (Whipple) West to Blaine Whipple. Letters dated 12 Dec. 1982, 17 Oct. 1983, 2 Aug. 2000, and 11 June 2003 at 497 Hwy 1., Mt. Vernon, Iowa 52314. In possession of Whipple at 236 NW Sundown Way, Portland, Oreg. 97229. (2005) Elaine West is a sister of the author. She has been researching the Whipple, West, LeFebre, Ruhl, and Clingman families for 50 years and her sources are multiple and varied. (Hereafter Elaine Whipple West.)
14. *Ibid.* and Baby (Ellen) Whipple, Death Certificate D No. 00722. File No. 33268-1909, Filed in August 1909, Dept. of Health, Bureau of Vital Statistics, Dept. 050 Org

2000,,2400 Troost, Ste. 1200, Kansas City, Mo.
15. and 16. Elaine Whipple West.

APPENDIX G-5

JEAN SCOTT CA 1700
TO PEARL JULIA SCOTT 1905-1988

(Scott lineage of Pearl Julia Scott, Generation 11, No. 9253, wife of L. Blaine Whipple.)

FIRST GENERATION

1. **Jean**[1] **Scott**[1] was born in Sligo, Ireland in the late 1600s and married **Marie Cracheten** there. She was born in Sligo.[2]

Jean **Scott** and Marie **Cracheten** had the following child:
+   2   i.   Andrew[2] **Scott** born abt 1713.

SECOND GENERATION

2. **Andrew**[2] **Scott** (Jean[1])[3] was born in Sligo, Ireland, abt 1713 and died 9 July 1812 in Chambly, Québec, Canada, at 99 years of age. He married twice. (1) **Charlotte (Serre) Barthelot** in Chambly 23 May 1779. Charlotte,[4] daughter and eleventh child of Andre **Serre** (maybe Cere) and Marie Anne **Boilard,** was born in Cote St. Laurent, Québec Province, 26 May 1726. She married (1) **Michel Barthelot.** (Serre, Charlotte, Ve Michel Barthelot. Ve is the abbreviation for Veuve, which is widow.)[5] Berthelot is the more common way of spelling the name and there is a street in Québec City named Berthelot. Andre and Charlotte lived together for a number of years before their marriage was solemnized by the Catholic Church. The record of their marriage performed by Father Mennard is as follows:

"The twenty-third May, 1779, I, the undersigned pastor of St. Joseph de Chambly, heard the confession and gave communion to the man named Andre Scot of Irish nationality, native of Slagai (Sligo), son of Jean Scot and of Marie Cracheten, his father and mother of the said Parish of Slagai in Ireland and Charlotte Serre dit St. Jean [see endnote 17 in the Hamel family for definition of dit], widow of first nuptials with Michel Barthelot of the Parish of Montreal, and on the same day, by a specific and special directive from Monsieur Montgolfier, Vicar General of the Diocese of Québec, without publication of any bann, I received the

{ G 1610 }

mutual consent of marriage of the said Andre Scot and of the said Charlotte Serre dit St. Jean, presently living in the Seigneury (see endnote 11 in the Hamel family for definition of Seigneury) of M. de Labruaire, Parish of Longueuil, and gave them the nuptial blessing following the rite prescribed by our holy mother the church in the presence of Francois Petrimoulx, Captain of the Militia, Jean Pairaut, and Charles Genest, residents of this Parish, who all signed with us, the spouses having declared themselves unable to sign, and in view of the fact, before their marriage, the said spouses had children together, of whom three are still living, namely Andre (age 20), Joseph, and Charlotte, whom they have acknowledged and do acknowledge in the present company and in the presence of the said witnesses as being their own children and their legitimate heirs in the future. At Chambly the day, month, and year stated. Signed Francois Petrimoulx, Jean Pairaut, Charles Genest, Mennard, Priest."[6]

(2) Lucie Truchon (also Lucie Truchon dit Leveille) in Longueuil, Québec Province 10 May 1790. Andre was described as husband of Lucie Leveille at his death. Lucie[7] was the daughter of Joseph **Truchon** and Marie **Denoyon**. Both her parents were dead when she married Andre. The 6 May 1790 Marriage Contract to Lucie stated Andre lived in the Seiniory of Montarville and was the widower of deceased Charlotte Serre. Advising him on the Contract were his son Andre and friends Francois Treant and Joseph Lacombe. The bride was identified as Lucie Truchon de Leveille and defunct Marie Denoyon. She was advised by her sisters Marie Catherine Truchon and Marie Louise Truchon, and her brother-in-law Jean de Thiriagne. The Contract provided that the "future married couple" would openly disclose all their personal property, house and land, and any acquired after the marriage and to treat it like "the customs of Paris, followed in the Province of Québec," i.e. as community property except property and revenue valued at 350 pounds sterling and two coppers or shillings, old rate of exchange brought to the union by Lucie. They agreed that any debt at the time of the marriage was the responsibility of the one who incurred it. The Contract described Andre as an "elderly man" with "weakness" and he agreed to bestow and reward his future wife "for labors and for her full attentions during their life" all of his property, then valued at 900 pounds sterling, old rate of exchange, after his death. The Contract was read aloud and signed in the Notary's Chambers (Maitre S. Racicot, Notary) at Poncherville Borough, Montreal "in front of witnesses who signed and the future couple and others appearing who did not know to sign." Andre and Lucie each signed with an X. Notary Racicot and Joseph Lacombe signed as witnesses. Andre and Lucie were married 22 years. He was buried 10 July 1812, age 99, at Chambly.[8]

{ G 1611 }

Andrew **Scott** and Charlotte **Serre** had the following children:

+ 3 i. Andre[3] **Scott** born abt 1759.
    4 ii. Joseph **Scott**[9] born in Longueuil, Québec Province, Canada. Living in Chambly, Québec in 1786.
    5 iii. Charlotte **Scott**[10] born in Longueuil.

THIRD GENERATION

3. **Andre**[3] **Scott** (Andrew[2], Jean[1])[11] was born in Longueuil, Québec Province, Canada abt 1759 and was buried 25 September 1839 in Chambly, Québec. He married **Marie Ursule Trahan** in Chambly 26 April 1786.[12] Andre and Marie entered into a "wedding treaty and agreement" (Marriage Contract) 22 April 1786 in the presence of his parents, Andre Sr. and Charlotte Sere of Longueiul Parish, his brother Joseph, and friends Mr. Baptiste Papinau and Mr. Nicolas Patinaut. Marie was identified as the daughter of Francois **Trahan** and Marie Ursule **Godreau** of Chambly. In addition to her parents, she was represented by her cousin Mr. Francois Ainsi and Mr. Jean-Marie Vincelet, a friend. The wedding was to take place as soon as "one party will request the other." The agreement provided that debts incurred before the marriage would be the sole obligation of the one incurring the debt and that all property acquired after the marriage will be community property. Andre agreed to give Marie 300 pounds sterling or shillings and 20 copper coin, old rate exchange as a marriage settlement. The survivor of the marriage was to receive a "preference share" of 150 shillings and 20 coppers, old rate of exchange, and "linen, wearing apparels and furnished bed ... before the transition of the community part." The preference share was to be available for the survivor to bring to a future wedding. The contract was entered into at Chambly at the Notary Chambers of J. B. Grise. The contracting couple and most of the witnesses signed with an X. The St. Joseph de Chambly Church records identify Andre "as a day laborer of this Parish" at the time of his death.[13]

Andre **Scott** and Marie Ursule **Trahan** had the following children born in Chambly, Québec, Canada:

+ 6 i. Andre[4] **Scott**.
    7 ii. Charles **Scott**[14] in 1812 and died 15 January 1815 in Chambly at 2 years of age.

FOURTH GENERATION

6. **Andre**[4] **Scott** (Andre[3], Andrew[2], Jean[1])[15] was born in Chambly, Québec, Canada and married **Sophie Demers** in Québec Province, 5 October 1812. Sophie[16] was the daughter of Joseph **Demers** and Marie **Larreau.**

Andre **Scott** and Sophie **Demers** had the following children: born in Chambly:

   8   i.   Andre[5] **Scott**[17] baptized 3 August 1813 in St. Joseph de Chambly Catholic church and died there 27 January 1814.

+ 9   ii. Joseph **Scott** in 1815.

FIFTH GENERATION

9. **Joseph**[5] **Scott** (Andre[4], Andre[3], Andrew[2], Jean[1])[18] was born in Chambly, Québec, Canada in 1815, maybe 1821 according to the Certificate of Death which stated he was 51 at time of death. The death record also confirmed his place of birth and his parent's place of birth as being Canada. He died 17 May 1872 of dysentery in Corcoran, Hennepin Co., Minnesota, at 56 years of age. He married **Philomene (Florin) Trudeau** in Chambly 12 January 1841. Flevia,[19] daughter of Toussaint **Trudeau** and Marie **Monty**, was born in Chambly in 1821 and died 15 October 1906 in Corcoran, at 85 years of age. She is buried at Corcoran's Ste Jesnne de Chantal Cemetery. She married (2) Prisque **Noel**. (3) Joseph **Menard**, both in Hennepin Co., Minnesota. The Scott family emigrated to Illinois by 1850 (daughter Elizabeth was born in Illinois in 1850) and then to Minnesota near Minneapolis. It is not known where or how long the family lived in Illinois but they were among the first settlers to arrive in Corcoran, Minnesota in 1855. Corcoran is in the northwestern part of Hennepin County bounded on the north by Hassan, on the east by Maple Grove, on the south by Medina, and on the west by Greenwood, all in Hennepin County. By section lines, it is 12 miles west of Minneapolis and five miles north. Benjamin Punder, the first settler, also arrived in 1855 as did R.B. Corcoran and on 11 May 1858, at a meeting in Corcoran's house, the town was organized and by common consent took his name. The area was entirely agricultural with no village or large settlement and no thoroughfare other than the State and town roads. The timber was gradually cut and comfortable farm houses replaced settler's cabins. In 1895 the population of a little over 1,000 lived on nearly 200 farms. There were nine school districts, two post offices, Corcoran and Dupont, two

{ G 1613 }

stores, and four churches: St. Thomas Catholic Church, St. John's French Catholic Church, German Evangelical Assn., and Lutheran.[20] In 1855 the family included Joseph, 40, Flevia, 35, Joseph, Jr, 13, Didas, 11, Sedaly, 9, Matilda, 8, and Elizabeth, 5; all born in Canada except Elizabeth. Joseph acquired a 120-acre farm in Section 29 and began his farming career. The land was heavily timbered with maple, oak, elm, and linden. Interspersed among the timber were low lands of natural meadow. The topsoil was heavy, black loam and produced grain, Indian corn, potatoes, hay, small fruits, and vegetables. The farm was valued at $960 in 1869 and included 25 improved, 55 unimproved, and 40 woodland acres. Personal property was valued at $421 and livestock at $366. The livestock included two horses, four milk cows, two other cattle, four sheep, and three swine. Their machinery was valued at $85. The value of their farm production that year was estimated as $430: 16 pounds of wool, 150 pounds of butter, 900 pounds of maple sugar, seven gallons of molasses, 10 tons of hay, 150 bushels of spring wheat, 200 bushels of oats, 100 bushels of Indian corn, and one bushel of peas and beans. They sold $20 worth of forest products and slaughtered farm animals worth $40. According to the 1870 U.S. Minnesota census, Joseph, Joseph, Jr., and Didace had become U.S. citizens but Flevia had not. Joseph and Flevia were recorded as "unable to read or write." Didace worked as a farm hand for his father and at the time of Joseph's death of dysentry 17 May 1872, the farm passed to him. Joseph, Jr. had previously acquired and was farming the adjacent 120 acres. The census of 1880 and 1900 show that Flevia was living with Didace and his family.

Joseph **Scott** and Philomene (Florin) **Trudeau** had the following children:

+	10	i.	Joseph[6] **Scott Jr.** born in January 1842.
+	11	ii.	Didace (Didas) **Scott** born 27 November 1844.
	12	iii.	Sedaly **Scott**[21] born in Chambly in 1846 and died 13 March 1891 at 44 years of age. She married Joseph **Gardner**.
	13	iv.	Matilda **Scott**[22] born in Chambly in 1847 and married Louis **LaPray** in February 1867.
	14	v.	Elizabeth **Scott**[23] born in Illinois in 1850 and married Alfred **Gervais** 16 December 1867.
	15	vi.	Mary **Scott**[24] born in Corcoran in 1859 and married (__) **Pomerlian** in 1877.
	16	vii.	Emma **Scott**[25] born in Corcoran in 1860 and died 24 December 1939 at 79 years of age. She married Peter **Audette** 18 October 1874.

SIXTH GENERATION

10. **Joseph**[6] **Scott Jr.** (Joseph[5], Andre[4], Andre[3], Andrew[2], Jean[1])[26] was born in Chambly, Québec, Canada in January 1842 and died 26 January 1925 in Corcoran, Hennepin Co., Minnesota, at 83 years of age. The place of death may have been Osseo, Hennepin Co., Minnesota. He married **Celina Gervais** in Corcoran 11 November 1867. Celina,[27] daughter of Louis Pierre **Gervais** and Mary **Trembley**, was born in Champlain, Clinton, Co., N.Y. in August 1849 and died 20 October 1925 in Corcoran, at 76 years of age.

Joseph Scott Jr. and Celina Gervais had the following children born in Corcoran:

	17	i.	Mary Agnes[7] **Scott**[28] in 1868.
	18	ii.	Henry **Scott**[29] in January 1871.
	19	iii.	Frank **Scott**[30] in 1872.
	20	iv.	Mary Virginia **Scott**[31] 10 Mach 1874.
	21	v.	Leo **Scott**[32] in 1876.
	22	vi.	Emma **Scott**[33] in September 1878.
	23	vii.	Rosa **Scott**[34] in November 1880.
	24	viii.	Obeline **Scott**[35] in January 1883.
+	25	ix.	Joseph Alfred **Scott** in December 1884.
	26	x.	Louis D. **Scott**[36] in July 1886.
	27	xi.	Emile A. **Scott**[37] in December 1888.
	28	xii.	Joseph Alfred **Scott**[38] in May 1891.

11. **Didace (Didas)**[6] **Scott** (Joseph[5], Andre[4], Andre[3], Andrew[2], Jean[1])[39] was born in Québec Province, Canada 27 November 1844 and died 27 April 1929 in Corcoran, Hennepin Co., Minnesota, at 84 years 5 months, 14 days of age.[40] He married **Angeline Hamel** in Dayton, Hennepin Co., Minnesota 23 November 1868 at St. John the Baptist Church. Pierre Hamel and Anaise Hamel were witnesses and

Didas Scott with sons Louis and Amos, Corcoran, Minn.

Father Maurer presided. Angeline,[41] daughter of Lange Charles **Hamel** and Eugenie **Moffett**, was born in St. Eloi, Québec, Canada 18 March 1852 and died 2 May 1915 of cancer of the rectum in Corcoran, at 63 years of age. Didace began farming at Corcoran in 1855 and was remembered by contemporaries as a successful farmer, a gregarious, friendly fellow, quick to tell a story, and a good neighbor. French was his native tongue and he did not speak English and could not read or write. In 1873, at 28 and with a wife and three children to support, he had to cope with the financial panic of that year as well as with a severe blizzard. While

Didas and Angeline (Hamel) Scott.

still reeling from those two setbacks, he was faced with the grasshopper plagues of 1874 and 1876. He, Angeline, and his mother Flevia are buried in the French Corcoran Cemetery (Ste. Jesnne de Chantal). A large tombstone marks their grave.

The author and his uncle Leonard Scott of Minneapolis visited the Cemetery in 1971 and while standing at the Scott grave were approached by a gentleman in his 80s who wanted to know if we knew Didace. When we explained our relationship, he volunteered that he had known Didace well, that he was a fine

Angeline (Hamel) Scott with son Louis and an unnamed daughter.

{ G 1616 }

friend and neighbor, and held in high regard in the Corcoran community. He gave directions to the old Scott homestead and the farmers living there gave the author large photographs of Didace and Angeline which had been stored in the farm house attic for years.

Didas and Angeline (Hamel) Scott farm home near Concoran, Hennepin Co., Minn. 1971

Didace (Didas) **Scott** and Angeline **Hamel** had the following children born in Corcoran:

29   i.   Hector[7] **Scott**[42] 14 November 1869 and died 1 July 1938 in Hamel, Hennepin Co., Minn., at 68 years of age. Buried in St. Anne Cemetery, Hamel. He married Eugenia **Marcoux**. They had eight children.

30   ii.   Angeline (Evangeline) **Scott**[43] 3 July 1871 (baptized 13 Aug. 1871 at St. John the Baptist Church, Dayton, Minn.). Joseph Hamel and Mathilde Trudeau were Godparents Angeline died in 1917 at 45 years of age. She married (__) **Boucher**.

31   iii.   Virginia **Scott**[44] 21 February 1873 (baptized 30 March 1873 at St. John the Baptist Church). Toussaint Trudeau and Hermine Scott Audette were Godparents. Virginia died 10 January 1925 in Delano, Wright Co., Minn., at 51 years of age. She married Napoleon Bonaparte **Hamel** in Minneapolis, Hennepin Co., Minnesota 25 August 1897. She worked in Minneapolis in the 1890s and met her future husband there. He was called Nap by the family. He was from St. Ephrem, Québec and descended from the original Hamel settlers of Québec as was Virginia's mother. After their marriage they moved to Delano where they owned and operated a restaurant and bakery for many years.

32   iv.   Phillip **Scott**[45] 14 November 1874 (baptized 8 Dec. 1874 at St. John the Baptist Chruch). Jean Baptiste Trudeau and Adele Hamel were Godparents. Phillip died of cancer 5

{ G 1617 }

	33	v.	April 1950 in Corcoran at 75 years of age. He married Lillian **Bouchard** in Minnesota. Lillian was born in 1884 and died in 1948 in Minnesota, at 64 years of age.[46] Both are buried in the French Corcoran Cemetery.
	33	v.	William **Scott**[47] 1 October 1876 and left home as a young man. It is believed he eventually married and lived in California.
+	34	vi.	Adele **Scott** 20 September 1878.
+	35	vii.	John **Scott** 25 August 1880.
+	36	viii.	Benoni **Scott** 25 September 1882.
	37	ix.	Theodore **Scott**[48] 8 February 1884 and died 9 April 1945 at 61 years of age.
	38	x.	Amos **Scott**[49] 11 November 1885 and died in 1958 at 72 years of age. Buried in St. Anne Cemetery, Hamel.
+	39	xi.	Elise **Scott** in August 1888.
	40	xii.	Louis **Scott**[50] 8 February 1890.

SEVENTH GENERATION

25. Joseph Alfred[7] Scott (Joseph[6], Joseph[5], Andre[4], Andre[3], Andrew[2], Jean[1])[51] was born in Osseo, Hennepin Co., Minnesota in December 1884. He changed his name to Fred Joseph Scott.

Joseph Alfred **Scott** had the following child:

	41	i.	Naomi[8] **Scott**.[52]

34. **Adele**[7] **Scott** (Didace (Didas)[6], Joseph[5], Andre[4], Andre[3], Andrew[2], Jean[1])[53] was born in Corcoran, Hennepin Co., Minnesota 20 September 1878 (baptized 22 Sept. 1878 at St. John the Baptist Church, Dayton, Hennepin Co., Minnesota). Pierre Audett and Celina Gervais were Godparents. Adele died of cancer in June 1939 at 60 years of age. She married **Tuffel Michaud**.

Adele **Scott** and Tuffel **Michaud** had the following children:

	42	i.	Adeline[8] **Michaud** born in Hennepin Co. 7 September 1900 and married (__) **Howe**.[54]
+	43	ii.	Edward Joseph **Michaud** born 8 March 1902.
	44	iii.	Mabel **Michaud** born in Hennepin Co. in June 1904 and died in 1986 at 82 years of age. She married (__) **Burnham**.[55]

35. **John**[7] **Scott** (Didace (Didas)[6], Joseph[5], Andre[4], Andre[3], Andrew[2], Jean[1])[56] was born in Corcoran, Hennepin Co., Minnesota 25 August 1880

and died 11 September 1963 in Hamel, Hennepin Co., Minnesota, at 83 years of age. He married **Mary Pouliot**. Both are buried in Hamel's St. Anne Catholic Cemetery. They had four children.

John **Scott** and Mary **Pouliot** had the following child:
    45   i.   Donald[8] **Scott**.[57]

36. **Benoni**[7] **Scott** (Didace (Didas)[6], Joseph[5], Andre[4], Andre[3], Andrew[2], Jean[1])[58] was born in Corcoran, Hennepin Co., Minnesota 25 September 1882 and died 8 January 1935 in Minot, Ward Co., North Dakota, at 52 years of age. He married **Ellen "Nellie" Dolan** in Hamel, Hennepin, Co., Minnesota 25 June 1903. Nellie,[59] daughter of Thomas **Dolan** and Julia **Darmody**, was born in Maple Grove, Hennepin Co., Minnesota 27 August 1884 and died 2 June 1953 in Underwood, McLean Co., North Dakota, at 68 years of age.[60] She was born on a farm near Maple Grove, the eldest of seven children and named Ellen after her grandmother Ellen Darmody but was always called Nellie. Her mother died in childbirth 34 days before Nellie's 15th birthday and the role of care-giver to the other children fell to her. Her formal schooling also ended. She was 5' 4" with smiling blue eyes, a light complexion, and black hair usually worn up-swept from the face, short at the sides, and pug at the back. She was 20 when her first child was born, 41 when the fourteenth and last was born and was the major family influence in the lives of her 12 surviving children. Four of her sons served during WWII, amassing a total of 17 years in uniform. About half their time was overseas in such hot spots as London during the fire bombing, North Africa, Italy, France, Germany, and on convoy duty in the North Atlantic.

    She was a renowned cook and baker and the family always had several extra at Sunday dinner. She was everybody's "good neighbor," always available to help families in time of sickness. She served as a midwife and prepared the dead for burial when the family lived in Douglas, Ward Co. North Dakota. She baked bread for the Douglas Hotel during WWI, did the washing for farm worker transits, as well as washing for some of the townspeople. Water for washing was hauled from the neighbor's well and heated on the cook stove. The family had a cistern which was filled with snow in the winter and rain in the spring and summer. She had her share of pain and suffered terribly from gallstone attacks most of her adult life. She also had diabetes, a thyroid problem, and glaucoma, eventually loosing the sight of one eye. She died of an apparent heart attack early in the morning. Her funeral was held in Minneapolis and she was buried in Block 9, Lot 22, Grave 3, St. Anne Catholic Cemetery in Hamel with all of her children in attendance at her graveside. Ben, the eighth of 12 chil-

Nellie Scott with 12 of her surviving children in Underwood, N. Dak. July 1937. Row 1 L to R. Bob, Nellie, Alice. Row 2 L to R. Clara, Edwidge, Pearl, Babe. Row 3 L to R. Arthur, Don, Jack, Bill, Gordon, Leonard. Photos courtesy of Blaine Whipple.

dren, was born on the family farm at Corcoran and worked there during his youth. It is believed his schooling ended after the sixth grade. He left farm work to become a clerk in his uncle Hector's General Store in Hamel. He was 5' 6", broad shouldered, and deep chested. He weighed approximately 160 pounds, had grey eyes, reddish hair, and a rudy complexion. He

Nellie Scott with her seven sons in Underwood, N. Dak. in July 1937. L to R. Don, Arthur, Jack, Bill, Bob, Gordon, and Leonard.

walked with a limp most of his adult life because a broken leg was improperly set. He left clerking to join the Soo Railroad Line which ran through Hamel starting as a laborer and worked his way up to section boss. He was transferred from Hamel to Logan in 1910, later to Drake McHenry Co., and finally to Douglas, Ward Co., all in North Dakota. He earned the respect of his crew of Armenians because he worked harder than any of them. While small, he had tremendous strength and could

10 of the 12 Scott children. L to R. Alice Johnson, Babe Ronning, Clara Gunderson, Edwidge Bjorlie, Pearl Whipple. Back Row. Gordon, Leonard, Bill, Don, and Arthur Scott.

carry a railroad tie single-handedly and drive spikes with the best of them. An accomplished shot with rifle, shotgun, and revolver, he supplemented the family larder with geese, pheasant, prairie chicken, and rabbit. His oldest son Leonard often wondered why the kids didn't all become jumpy since they ate so many jackrabbits and prairie chicken. In the summer he and some of his sons made beer in the cellar and he had a still in the bunk house in Douglas where the section laborers lived. Unlike the average per-

Pearl and Leonard Scott, Hamel Minn., 1906.

son of today, Ben never owned an automobile, never owned his own home, or had a bank account. He died of stomach cancer at age 52 after a seven-week stay in Minot's Mercy Hospital during which time he suffered intense pain. He is buried in Block 9, Lot 28, St. Anne Catholic Cemetery, Hamel.

Benoni **Scott** and Ellen "Nellie" **Dolan** had the following children:

- \+ 46 i. Leonard Joseph[8] **Scott** born 16 August 1904.
- \+ 47 ii. Pearl Julia **Scott** born 29 August 1905.
- \+ 48 iii. John Milton **Scott** born 25 November 1906.
- \+ 49 iv. Edwidge Elise **Scott** born 31 March 1908.
-     50 v. Lydia **Scott**[61] born in Hamel 19 January 1910 (baptised 13 Feb. 1910 as Mary Scott by Father Combettes at St. Anne Church, Hamel). Her sponsors were William and Mary Dolan. The church has no death record for her so she probably died and was buried in either Logan (town no longer exists) or Drake, McHenry Co., North Dakota.
- \+ 51 vi. Arthur E. **Scott** born 10 January 1912.
- \+ 52 vii. William W. **Scott** born 23 January 1913.
- \+ 53 viii. Clara Angeline **Scott** born 8 January 1915.
- \+ 54 ix. Margaret **Scott** born 10 July 1917.
- \+ 55 x. Gordon Lawrence **Scott** born 13 October 1918.
- \+ 56 xi. Donald **Scott** born 6 February 1920.
-     57 xii. Alice Irene **Scott**[62] born in Douglas 20 November 1922 and died there 3 days later of bronchial pneumonia.
- \+ 58 xiii. Alice Irene **Scott** born 29 November 1923.
- \+ 59 xiv. Robert Dale **Scott** born 1 November 1925.

39. **Elise**[7] **Scott** (Didace (Didas)[6], Joseph[5], Andre[4], Andre[3], Andrew[2], Jean[1])[63] was born in Corcoran, Hennepin Co., Minnesota in August 1888 and died 14 January 1982 in Mountain View, Santa Clara Co., California, at 93 years of age. She married **John Clayton** in Saskatoon, Saskatchean, Canada. A brief obituary of Elise was printed in the *Minneapolis Star* 19 January 1982.

Elise **Scott** and John **Clayton** had the following children:

- \+ 60 i. Elise[8] **Clayton**.
- \+ 61 ii. Mary Lou **Clayton**.
- \+ 62 iii. John Scott **Clayton** born 9 December 1915.
- \+ 63 iv. Richard Lawrence **Clayton** born 13 April 1918.

{ G 1622 }

EIGHTH GENERATION

43. **Edward Joseph**[8] **Michaud** (Adele[7] Scott, Didace (Didas)[6], Joseph[5], Andre[4], Andre[3], Andrew[2], Jean[1])[64] was born in Hennepin Co., Minnesota 8 March 1902.

Edward Joseph **Michaud** had the following child:
    64   i.   Claire[9] **Michaud** born in Hennepin Co., Minnesota.[65]

46. **Leonard Joseph**[8] **Scott** (Benoni,[7] Didace (Didas)[6], Joseph[5], Andre[4], Andre[3], Andrew[2], Jean[1])[66] was born in Hamel, Hennepin Co., Minnesota 16 August 1904 and died 22 August 1989 in Minneapolis, Hennepin Co., Minnesota, at 85 years of age. He married **Irene Mary McCarthy** in Minneapolis 9 October 1937. Irene,[67] daughter of Edward **McCarthy** and Mary **Doran**, was born in Swift City, Fairfield Township, Benton Co., Minnesota 21 December 1908 and died 11 June 1999 in Minneapolis, at 90 years of age.

Leonard Joseph **Scott** and Irene Mary **McCarthy** had the following children:
    65   i.   Dr. Donald **Scott** born 11 October 1942.[68]
    66   ii.   Mary Kathleen **Scott** born 26 November 1943.[69]
    67   iii.   Patricia Ann **Scott** 31 January 1947.[70]
    68   iv.   Janet Elizabeth **Scott**.[71]

47. **Pearl Julia**[8] **Scott** (Benoni[7,] Didace (Didas)[6], Joseph[5], Andre[4], Andre[3], Andrew[2], Jean[1])[72] was born in Hamel. Hennepin Co., Minnesota 29 August 1905 and died 1 April 1988 in Glencoe, McLeod Co., Minnesota, at 82 years of age. She married **Lucien Blaine Whipple** in Albion, Boone Co., Nebraska 21 September 1927. Blaine,[73] son of James Ezekiel **Whipple** and Malissa "Ellen" **Thompson**, was born in Eugene, Vermillion Co., Indiana 22 June 1883 and died 27 August 1954 in Dresden, Weakley Co., Tennessee, at 71 years of age.

Pearl Julia **Scott** and Blaine **Whipple** had the following children:
    69   i.   Patricia Ellen **Whipple** born 1 February 1929.[74]
    70   ii   Robert Blaine **Whipple** born 22 February 1930.[75]
    71   iii.   Nancy Jane **Whipple** born 5 January 1932.[76]
    72   iv.   Richard Earl **Whipple** born 12 September 1933.[77]
    73   v.   Mary Ann **Whipple** born 8 December 1937.[78]

48. **John Milton**[8] **Scott** (Benoni[7,] Didace (Didas)[6], Joseph[5], Andre[4], Andre[3], Andrew[2], Jean[1])[79] was born in Hamel, Hennepin Co., Minnesota 25 November 1906 and died 26 September 1955 in Butte, Silver Bow Co.,

Montana, at 48 years of age. He married **Merle M. Minow** in Bowbells, Burke Co., North Dakota 26 March 1928. Merle,[80] daughter of Herman **Minow** and Katherine M. **Korst**, was born 24 November 1909 in Flaxton, Burke Co. and died 19 June 1995 in Butte, at 85 years of age.

John Milton **Scott** and Merle M. **Minow** had the following children:

    74   i.   Dwayne Joseph **Scott** born 30 March 1928.[81]
    75   ii.   June **Scott** born 26 October 1930.[82]
    76   iii.   Marlene Dawn **Scott** born 27 February 1937.[83]
    77   iv.   Darryl John **Scott** born 24 November 1938.[84]
    78   v.   William R. **Scott** born 7 February 1945.[85]
    79   vi.   Thomas E. **Scott** born 22 June 1948.[86]

49. **Edwidge Elise**[8] **Scott** (Benoni[7], Didace (Didas)[6], Joseph[5], Andre[4], Andre[3], Andrew[2], Jean[1])[87] was born in Hamel, Hennepin Co., Minnesota 31 March 1908 and died 11 February 2004 in Costa Mesa, Orange Co., California, at 95 years of age. She married **Carl Sidney Bjorlie** in Douglas, Ward Co., North Dakota 20 August 1930. Sid,[88] son of Sven J. **Bjorlie** and Karen **Johnson**, was born in Pekin, Nelson Co., North Dakota 20 May 1903 and died 29 October 1978 in Minot, Ward Co., North Dakota, at 75 years of age.

Tuts **Scott** and Sid **Bjorlie** had the following children:

    80   i.   Phyllis Irene **Bjorlie** born 5 September 1931.[89]
    81   ii.   Clarice Mae **Bjorlie** born 4 March 1933.[90]

51. **Arthur E.**[8] **Scott** (Benoni[7], Didace (Didas)[6], Joseph[5], Andre[4], Andre[3], Andrew[2], Jean[1])[91] was born 10 January 1912 in Drake, McHenry Co., North Dakota and died 9 November 1993 in Underwood, Mclean Co., North Dakota, at 81 years of age. He married **Josephine Ulrich** 9 November 1943 in Endres Community, Mclean Co., North Dakota. Jo,[92] daughter of Frank J. **Ulrich** and Helen **Meier**, was born 26 May 1914 in Endres Community and died 1 April 2005 in Bismarck, Burleigh Co., North Dakota, at 90 years of age. Both are buried in Underwood.

Arthur E. **Scott** and Jo **Ulrich** had the following children:

    82   i.   Shelia Ann **Scott** born 8 August 1944.[93]
    83   ii.   Patrick Michael **Scott** born 5 May 1948.[94]
    84   iii.   Timothy Robert **Scott** born 27 October 1950.[95]
    85   iv.   Mary Jo **Scott** born 23 May 1953.[96]
    86   v.   James Francis **Scott** born 30 December 1954.[97]

52. **William W.**[8] **Scott** (Benoni[7,] Didace (Didas)[6], Joseph[5], Andre[4], Andre[3], Andrew[2], Jean[1])[98] was born 23 January 1913 in Drake, McHenry Co., North Dakota and died 17 July 2003 in Kansas City, Jackson Co., Missouri, at 90 years of age. He married **Ruth E. Smith** 3 January 1946 in Minneapolis, Hennepin Co., Minnesota. Ruth,[99] daughter of Clifford I. **Smith** and Bessi **Aebrank**, was born 7 October 1916 in Mason City, Cerro Gordo Co., Iowa and died 23 November 1988, at 72 year of age.

Bill **Scott** and Ruth **Smith** had the following child:
    87   i.   Julie Ann **Scott**.[100]

53. **Clara Angeline**[8] **Scott** (Benoni[7,] Didace (Didas)[6], Joseph[5], Andre[4], Andre[3], Andrew[2], Jean[1])[101] was born 8 January 1915 in Drake, McHenry Co., North Dakota and died 9 September 2001 in Underwood, Mclean Co., North Dakota, at 86 years of age. She married **Gunder O. Gunderson** 15 June 1940 in Underwood. Gunder,[102] son of Thor **Gunderson** and Inger **Riskedahl** was born in Bowdon, Wells Co., North Dakota 1 October 1912 and died 11 March 1989 in Bismarck, Burleigh Co., North Dakota, at 76 years of age. Both are buried in Turtle Lake, Mclean Co., North Dakota.

Clara Angeline **Scott** and Gunder O. **Gunderson** had the following children:
    88   i.   Thomas James **Gunderson** born 27 December 1940.[103]
    89   ii.   Michael Jerome **Gunderson** born 17 April 1943.[104]
    90   iii.   Robert Lee **Gunderson** born 13 August 1946.[105]

54. **Margaret**[8] **Scott** (Benoni[7,] Didace (Didas)[6], Joseph[5], Andre[4], Andre[3], Andrew[2], Jean[1])[106] was born 10 July 1917 in Drake, McHenry Co., North Dakota and died 27 August 1977 of cancer in Bismarck, Burleigh Co., North Dakota, at 60 years of age. She married **Rudolph H. Ronning** 5 September 1942 in Santa Anna, Orange Co., California. Rudy[107] was born in Ryder, Ward County, North Dakota 14 January 1916 and died 5 November 1965 in Fargo, Cass County, North Dakota, at 49 years of age.

Babe **Scott** and Rudy **Ronning** had the following children:
    91   i.   Carole Marie **Ronning** born 25 November 1947.[108]
    92   ii.   Constance Scott **Ronning** 15 August 1953.[109]

55. **Gordon Lawrence**[8] **Scott** (Benoni[7,] Didace (Didas)[6], Joseph[5], Andre[4], Andre[3], Andrew[2], Jean[1])[110] was born 13 October 1918 in Douglas, Ward Co., North Dakota and died in 1995 in Mesa, Maricopa Co., Arizona at 77 years of age. Buried in Underwood Mclean Co., North Dakota. He married **Catherine R. Baldner** 16 April 1941 in Washington, D. C.

Kay,[III] daughter of Charles Henry **Baldner** and Marion **Reed**, was born 29 April 1916 in Garrison, Mclean Co., North Dakota. Living in 2006.

Gordon Lawrence **Scott** and Kay **Baldner** had the following children:
- 93   i.   Laurel Kay **Scott** born 11 October 1942.[112]
- 94   ii.   David Charles **Scott** born 22 July 1950.[113]

56. **Donald**[8] **Scott** (Benoni[7,] Didace (Didas)[6], Joseph[5], Andre[4], Andre[3], Andrew[2], Jean[1])[114] was born 6 February 1920 in Douglas, Ward Co., North Dakota and died 26 March 2004 in Underwood, Mclean Co., North Dakota, at 84 years of age. He married **Florence S. Eisenmann** 6 August 1946 in Underwood. Flossie,[115] daughter of Frank **Eisenmann** and Elizabeth **Stadick**, was born 25 February 1925 in Underwood and died there. Both are buried in Underwood.

Don **Scott** and Flossie **Eisenmann** had the following children:
- 95   i.   Tracy J. **Scott** born 10 May 1947.[116]
- 96   ii.   Phyllis A. **Scott** born 10 October 1948.[117]
- 97   iii.   Jacqueline **Scott** born 5 January 1952.[118]
- 98   iv.   Charles K. **Scott** born 12 May 1955.[119]

58. **Alice Irene**[8] **Scott** (Benoni[7,] Didace (Didas)[6], Joseph[5], Andre[4], Andre[3], Andrew[2], Jean[1])[120] was born 29 November 1923 in Douglas, Ward Co., North Dakota (living in 2006) and married **Burnell B. Johnson** 22 May 1944 in Sioux Falls. Minnehaha Co., South Dakota. Burnell,[121] son of Heddor **Johnson** and Eva **Monroe**, was born 18 July 1923 in Bismarck, Burleigh Co., North Dakota. (Living in 2006.)

Alice **Scott** and Burnell **Johnson** had the following children:
- 99   i.   Terry Jerome **Johnson** born 23 February 1945.[122]
- 100   ii.   Barbara Jo **Johnson** born 30 November 1948.[123]
- 101   iii.   Gregory A. **Johnson** born 11 August 1952.[124]
- 102   iv.   Jeffry Lynn **Johnson** born 31 May 1954.[125]
- 103   v   Jay Dolan **Johnson** was born 21 October 1961.[126]

59. **Robert Dale**[8] **Scott** (Benoni[7,] Didace (Didas)[6], Joseph[5], Andre[4], Andre[3], Andrew[2], Jean[1])[127] was born 1 November 1925 in Douglas, Ward Co., North Dakota and died 21 August 1965 in Minot, Ward Co., North Dakota, at 39 years of age. Buried in Underwood, Mclean Co. North Dakota. He married **Leona C. Fetzer** in Underwood 5 September 1952. Leona,[128] daughter of Benjamin **Fetzer** and Emilia **Buechler**, was born 16 April 1929 in Max, Mclean Co., North Dakota.

Bob **Scott** and Leona **Fetzer** had the following children:
    104   i.   Robert Lee **Scott** born 8 February 1953.[129]
    105   ii.   Brenda Lee **Scott** born 4 September 1956.[130]

(See Generation 11, No. 9253, Pearl Julia Scott, wife of L. Blaine Whipple, for a continuation of the Scott lineage.)

FORT CHAMBLY, QUÉBEC PROVINCE, CANADA

Chambly in Québec Province of Canada was home of Fort Chambly and the Scott families before they moved to the United States. It is about 50 miles northeast of Montreal. The Fort was built in 1665 below the rapids of the Richelieu river and the area was governed by Three Rivers until 1690 when it came under the jurisdiction of Montreal. Its territory was immense and throughout the years various Parishes were carved from it. Made of wood, the Fort was 144 feet square with 15 foot high palisades. It housed a shed, barracks, a chapel, and the commander's quarters. After 1670 it doubled as a trading post, became an important center for the fur trade, and by 1681 17 families numbering 81 individuals settled around it. It was rebuilt of stone and completed in September 1711.

The Americans captured the Fort in 1775 and abandoned it in June 1776. British General John Burgoyne assembled his Army of 7,000 at the Fort prior to his invasion of the American colonies in June 1777. His Army was defeated at Saratoga, N. Y. in October, a battle generally considered the turning point of the American Revolutionary War. French patriots from Boucherville, Longueuil, and Chambly attempted a minor rebellion against the British in 1837-38. Included among the active patriots were Pierre, Joseph, and Michel Trudeau. Troops were gradually withdrawn beginning in 1847 and the Fort abandoned in 1854. It was transferred to the Government of Canada in 1856 which eventually designated it a National Park and restored the Fort.

Emigration of French-Canadians to the United States increased from about 1840—when the Scott and Hamel families left—to the beginning of the twentieth century. By the middle of the nineteenth century, other than Montreal and Québec, the the Province was agricultural and nine out of ten French-Canadians lived in this rural environment. The family farm was the basic unit of production and oriented toward self sufficiency. Wheat was the major cash crop and the success or failure of its harvest largely determined the prosperity of artisans, mechanics, and small businessmen employed in villages where mills were located. Peas and potatoes were major items in the diet.

{ G 1627 }

However, the farmer was not an efficient cultivator and productivity was low. He tilled the soil, planted, and harvested according to age-old custom and stubbornly resisted change. He did not use manure or any other fertilizer, kept turning the same topsoil with a shallow plow, sowed unclean and unimproved seed, allowed weeds to grow everywhere, and knew little about crop rotation. Wheat was planted in the same fields yearly until signs of declining productivity forced the farmer to move to the fallow areas. The farms were also infested with insects and suffered the injurious effects of blight.

As one observer wrote, "deprived for 90 years of all means of improvement, devoid of professional teaching, agriculture in Québec could only end by a degeneration into a deplorable routine."

An equally important basic problem was the lack of education. By 1838 when the Diocese of Québec only had 178 Catholic schools few could read and write. This educational backwardness among a peasant society perpetuated their strong conservatism and resistance to change, even when change was to their benefit. When in 1849 the Québec Parliament studied the relationship between education and agricultural improvement, it determined without education, agriculture would not improve. Unfortunately, it took many decades before education at the primary grade level would be required. As is evident in both the Scott and Hamel families, when signatures were required on records, the priest and/or the Notary who wrote the document found it necessary to add the phrase *"ils n'ont su ssigne,"* meaning they could not write – not even their names.

Simultaneously, land became scarce and increasingly expensive and in the years after 1820, the scarcity of money became even more acute. Under the *seigneury system* (see endnote 11 in the Hamel family for a definition), absentee landowners did not pay their taxes and ignored their responsibilities toward the construction of roads, bridges, and drains, and authorities seldom repaired roads that were in deplorable condition much of the year. With farms unable to support a growing population and with little capital to purchase tillable land, a crisis developed in the Province. The solution: emigrate.

In the years before the Civil War, French-Canadians in substantial numbers settled in the upper midwest. The Illinois French population increased from nearly 8,000 in 1851 to about 20,000 in 1859. The French population around Detroit may have been larger. Wisconsin and Minnesota attracted a large number. The Scott's spent about a year in Illinois before settling permanently in Minnesota. The Hamel's original destination was Minnesota It was in Minnesota the families joined forces and founded the American branch of the family tree.

FRANCOIS HAMEL ABT 1600 TO PEARL J. SCOTT 1905-1988

(Hamel lineage of Pearl Julia Scott, Generation No. 11, No. 9253, wife of L. Blaine Whipple.)

FIRST GENERATION

1. **Francois**[1] **Hamel**[1] was born in Avremesnil, Normandie, France and died there after 3 September 1689.[2] He married an unnamed person there. The first known Hamel is Wautier the First who lived about 1200. He and his descendants were Seigneurs, a Lord and Master in a system of feudal relations. The earliest known of what became the Québec Hamel families lived at Saint-Aubin, Avremesnil (Seine-Inferieure), a small village on the Saane river about 10 miles southwest of Dieppe in the Rouen Diocese in the old Province of Normandie in the north of France). Many documents concerning the family in Avremesnil survive. The *Hotel Dieu Register of the Sick* indicates Francois suffered from an infirmity in 1689.[3] He was the father of at least four children with son Francois, a farmer at Avremesnil, the likely heir to the family goods. Jean and Charles settled in Nouvelle, France before emigrating to New France.

Francois **Hamel** had the following children:

- + 2 i. Charles[2] **Hamel** born abt 1624.
- + 3 ii. Jean **Hamel** born abt 1634.
-   4 iii. Francois **Hamel**[4] born in Avremesnil, Normandie, France and remained there where he farmed in the Parish of Saint-Aubin de Avremesnil.
-   5 iv. Anne **Hamel**[5] born in Avremesnil and died bef 14 May 1671 in France, at approximately 31 years of age. She married Jacques **Jullien** 3 June 1663. Anne and her husband were members of the "bourgeois" from the Canton of Bacqueville, Dieppe, Dept. of the Seine-Inferieure. The last known communication involving family members is dated 14 May 1671 in the form of an Agreement between Francois and Jacques. Francois was living in Avremesnil and was acting for his brothers Charles and Jean of Québec in the settlement of the inheritance of their deceased sister.[6]

{ G 1629 }

SECOND GENERATION

2. **Charles**[2] **Hamel** (Francois[1])[7] was born in Avremesnil, Normandie, France abt 1624 and died aft 7 September 1711 in Sainte-Foy Québec, Canada, at approximately 87 years of age. He married twice. (1) **Judith Auvray** in Avremesnil abt 1651. She was born in Normandy. (2) **Catherine Lemaistre** in Sainte-Jacques, Dieppe, France 19 June 1656. She was born in France abt 1633 and was 23 at the time of marriage. A copy of the Marriage Contract exists in Dieppe.[8] Charles received his first grant of land (60 arpents[9] (partially wooded) in New France along Sainte-Michel road in Sainte-Foy from Rev. Father Jerome Lallement, S.J.[10] in 1662 and added to his holdings another 50 arpents on 24 February 1663. He built, near the King's Road leading to Cap-Rouge, a 44 by 20 foot log house with fireplace, double foyer, and a shingle roof. It was divided lengthwise into three rooms; the end room had three wardrobes. His grants are found on the Government Survey Map of 1685, p. 42. On 25 November 1676, Charles bought a house and small acreage from Mr. Noel Pinguet for his son Charles and lent his son Jean £260 of the "City of Tours" secured by a promissory note. The money was repaid 24 June 1684. He was appointed Expert Appraiser in Sainte-Foy 6 September 1711 when he was well into his 80s. According to the census of 1666 and 1681, he had four head of cattle. His land was in the Seigneury[11] of Sillery which today would be in the suburb of Sainte-Foy. In March of 1677, Charles and Catherine took in Francois Fouquees, age seven-and-a-half, "to help as a domestic servant" in return for "food and lodging." The Bond containing the details of the "adoption" required them to care for Francois as their own child for nine years and to give him "Christian instructions for the good of his soul."

Charles **Hamel** and Judith **Auvray** had the following child:
+   6   i.   Jean[3] **Hamel** born in 1652.

Charles **Hamel** and Catherine **Lemaistre** had the following child:
     7   ii.   Charles **Hamel**[12] born in Québec, Canada in 1659 and died in 1728 in Sainte-Foy Québec, at 69 years of age. He married Angelique **Levasseur** in Sainte-Foy abt 1682. Angelique,[13] daughter of Jean **Levasseur** and Marguerite **Richard**, was baptized in Québec 9 June 1661 and was buried 14 May 1740 in Sainte-Foy. Charles attended the Jesuit College and was a regular chorister on the coast Sainte-Michel all his life. He farmed in Ancienne-Lorette. His marriage contract with Angelique is dated 13 January 1682. They had eight sons and six daughters.

3. **Jean**[2] **Hamel** (Francois[1])[14] was born in Avremesnil, Normandie, France abt 1634 and died 11 October 1674 in Sainte-Foy Québec, Canada, at 40 years of age. He married **Marie Auvray** in Avremesnil abt 1656. She was born in France in 1638 and died in 1716 in Sainte-Foy, at 78 years of age. She married (2) **Rene Pelletier** in Québec Province in 1679.[15] Sisters Marie and Judith Auvray married brothers Jean and Charles Hamel. Judith died before the families moved to Québec in New France. It is believed Jean in the summer of 1656 accompanied by Marie and Charles' 4-year-old son Jean. Before marrying the Auvray sisters, both made sure the women would agree to move to New France. They must have arrived in the fall because Jean signed a lease the day after Christmas 1656 agreeing to work the land of Jean Gloria. Under terms of the lease he could not cut and sell wood but could cut firewood for his own use from "behind the house and nowhere else."

Seven years later on 21 October 1663, he purchased for five Sols (currency equal to 1/20th of a Livre[16]) land on the Sainte-Michel road in Sainte-Foy from Nicholas Gaudry dit[17] Bourbonniere. Payment was due annually on All Saints Day. On 12 February 1664 he acquired additional land from Antoine Duhamel dit Marette Purchase. That winter he built a 30 by 18 foot house and a 60 by 20 foot barn and stable on the farm. After Duhamel's death 20 October 1665, Jean purchased his land from the estate for 500 Livres in gold Pistoles.[18] His farm bordered the MacKay property and the Belmont Cemetery on the west and was identified as Number 111, 112, 113. After his death at age 40 he was buried in Québec Cemetery. The inventory of his estate showed he owned 35 arpents (approximately 30 acres) of tillable land and 16.5 arpents (approximately 14 acres) in preparation; 1 horse, 2 oxen trained for ploughing, 7 cows, 10 pigs, and 12 hens; some wheat, barley, pease, and hay. Four days after his funeral 13 October 1674, Marie gave birth to Francois, their sixth child. On 11 December 1697 she contracted to marry **Rene Pelletier**, a carpenter.[19] Pelletier raised the children as his own, improved the land left to Marie, and after Marie's death sold the family farm to his stepsons for 3,000 Livres. Marie's estate was inventoried in May 1717.[20]

Approximately 1,600 descendants of Jean and Charles Hamel attended a reunion 18 and 19 July 1981 at Sainte-Foy near Québec. They came from all over North America, France, Arabia, and Japan to walk where their earliest New World ancestors had settled. A plaque commemorating the 325th anniversary of the brothers arrival in New France was unveiled.

Jean **Hamel** and Marie **Auvray** had the following children born in Sainte-Foy Québec, Canada:

+ 8 i. Jean Francois³ **Hamel** 24 July 1661.
  9 ii. Pierre **Hamel**[21] in 1664 and died there in 1722, at 58 years of age. He married Felicite **Levasseur** in Québec Province in 1688. She was the daughter of Pierre **Levasseur** and Jeanne **de Chanverlange**. The marriage contract was signed 17 October 1688.[22]
  10 iii. Marie-Anne **Hamel**[23] in 1664 and died in 1731 at 67 years of age. She married Jean Caille dit le **Picard** in 1683. Jean, a carpenter, moved to Québec from the Ile de France. They had 13 children and lived in Québec and in Saint-Augustin.
  11 iv. Charlotte **Hamel**[24] In 1669 and died in infancy.
  12 v. Ignace-Germain **Hamel**[25] in 1672 and died in 1732 at 60 years of age. The family's first priest, he was ordained 6 June 1696 and served as a Canon in the Cathedral of Québec.
  13 vi. Francois **Hamel**[26] In 1674 and married Marguerite **Lemay** in 1721. They lived in Sainte-Croix-de-Lotbiniere. Many of the Hamels from the Bois-Francs region of Québec are descended from their sons Antoine and Alexis.

THIRD GENERATION

6. **Jean**³ **Hamel** (Charles², Francois¹)[27] was born in Avremesnil, Normandie, France in 1652 and died abt 1709. He married **Christine-Charlotte Gaudry** abt 1677. She was the daughter of Nicolas **Gaudry** and Agnes **Morin**.[28] Jean was 4 when he arrived in New France. He acquired land in Champigny (see Ordinance Survey Map of 1685) which he sold to Louis Moreau in April 1688. He moved to Sainte-Croix of Lotbiniere in 1681 where he became guardian of the farm of Lord Rene-Louis Chartier, King's Counselor and Civil and Criminal Prosecutor for the Provost of Québec with the rank of Lieutenant General. In November 1684, Lord Chartier gave him a large plot of land on the St. Lawrence river lying between the lands of Jean Beaudet and Jacques Gauthier. The latter was the father-in-law of his son Charles Joseph. In December 1695 and February 1698, the Ursuline Sisters[29] gave Jean large grants from their holdings at Platon Sainte-Croix.[30]

Jean **Hamel** and Christine-Charlotte **Gaudry** had the following children born in Sainte-Croix, Québec:

+ 14 i. Charles-Joseph⁴ **Hamel**.

{ G 1632 }

15	ii.	Elizabeth-Ursule **Hamel** [31] and married Francois **Gauthier**. Francois,[32] son of Jacques **Gauthier** and Elizabeth-Ursule **de Nevers**, was born in Québec Province.
16	iii.	Marie-Catherine **Hamel**[33] and married Joseph **Gauthier** in Sainte-Croix. Joseph,[34] son of Jacques **Gauthier** and Elizabeth-Ursule **de Nevers**, was born in Québec Province.

8. **Jean Francois**[3] **Hamel** (Jean[2], Francois[1])[35] was born in St. Foy, Québec, Canada 24 July 1661 and died in September 1733 in Lorette, Québec, Canada, at 72 years of age. He married **Anne Felicite LaVasseur** abt April 1685. Anne,[36] daughter of Jean **LaLevasseur** and Marguerite **Richard**, was baptized in Québec 23 April 1667 and was buried 25 September 1748 in l'Ancienne-Lorette, Québec Province. Jean-Francois and Anne's marriage contract is dated 23 April 1685. They had six sons and seven daughters and settled in Champigny at Lorette. On 5 January 1701 their home burned down and three sons and two daughters, all under 8, perished. They were buried 8 January at Sainte-Foy. Descendants of the family occupied the ancestral homestead until the beginning of the 20th century.[37]

Jean Francois **Hamel** and Anne Felicite **LaVasseur** had the following child:

+	17	i.	Jean[4] **Hamel** born 11 September 1702.

FOURTH GENERATION

14. **Charles-Joseph**[4] **Hamel** (Jean[3], Charles[2], Francois[1])[38] was baptized in Sainte-Michel of Sillery, Québec Province, Canada, 11 August 1679 and married **Marie-Angelique Gauthier** in Sainte-Croix, Québec 27 June 1701. Marie-Angelique,[39] daughter of Jacques **Gauthier** and Elizabeth-Ursule **de Nevers**, was born in Québec Province. Charles-Joseph and his sisters Elizabeth-Ursule and Marie-Catherine married children of Jacques and Elisabeth-Ursule Gauthier. Charles-Joseph and Angelique had 10 children.

Charles-Joseph **Hamel** and Marie-Angelique **Gauthier** had the following child:

18	i.	Jean[5] **Hamel** [40] born in Sainte-Croix, Québec abt 1710 and married twice. (1) Angelique **Baury** in Sainte Sulpice, Québec 20 February 1730. (2) Catherine **Vegeart** in Vercheres, Québec 3 October 1735.

17. **Jean**[4] **Hamel** (Jean Francois[3], Jean[2], Francois[1])[41] born 11 September 1702 and married **Marie Anne Constantin**.[42]

{ G 1633 }

Jean **Hamel** and Marie Anne **Constantin** had the following child:
+ 19 i. Louis Antoine[5] **Hamel** born 10 December 1730.

FIFTH GENERATION

19. **Louis Antoine**[5] **Hamel** (Jean[4], Jean Francois[3], Jean[2], Francois[1])[43] was born 10 December 1730 and married **Madeleine Sedliot** in 1764.[44]

Louis Antoine **Hamel** and Madeleine **Sedliot** had the following child:
+ 20 i. Joseph Valentin[6] **Hamel**.

SIXTH GENERATION

20. **Joseph Valentin**[6] **Hamel** (Louis Antoine[5], Jean[4], Jean Francois[3], Jean[2], Francois[1])[45] birth date unknown, married **Marie Louise Fontaine** in 1764.[46]

Joseph Valentin **Hamel** and Marie Louise **Fontaine** had the following child:
+ 21 i. Lange Charles[7] **Hamel** born 21 June 1812.

SEVENTH GENERATION

21. **Lange Charles**[7] **Hamel** (Joseph Valentin[6], Louis Antoine[5], Jean[4], Jean Francois[3], Jean[2], Francois[1])[47] was born in L'Isle-Verte, Québec Province, Canada 21 June 1812 and died 26 August 1887 in Hamel, Hennepin Co., Minnesota of Bright Disease (kidney disease), at 75 years of age; buried at St. Anne Cemetery, Hamel. He married **Eugenie Moffett** in L'Isle-Verte 24 January 1837. Eugenie[48] daughter of Gabriel **Moffett**, was born in Canada 29 July 1822 and died 6 April 1874 in Hamel, at 51 years of age.[49] Lange arrived in Minnesota in early 1855 at age 43 from his home in St. Eloi Parish, Québec, Province, acquired land and built a log cabin so his family could join him. They arrived in the fall of 1856: wife Eugenie, 34, children Marguerite-Eugenie, 12, Lange Jr., 10, William, 7, Narcesse, 6, Angelina, 4, and Anaise, 3. Seventeen-year-old Joseph was attending school in Québec City and followed a year later. Five more children were born in Minnesota. Lange wore a large, black, bushy beard, had deep-set piercing eyes, large ears, and was bald except for hair just above his ears. The Sioux Indian uprising in 1862 caused Lange to take his family to Minneapolis, Hennepin Co. for safety. As more people moved into the area, a

church with cemetery was built on the edge of the Hamel farm. In 1887, the Minneapolis and Pacific Railroad, later known as the Soo Line, expanded into the western part of the state and a depot was built on son William's land and was named "Hamel Station." It operated until 1963.[50]

Lange Charles **Hamel** and Eugenie **Moffett** had the following children:

  22 i. Anaise[8] **Hamel**[51] baptized in Saint-Eloi, Québec Province 19 August 1853 and died in September 1944. She married Joseph **Hamel**. They had three children.

  23 ii. Joseph Octave **Hamel**[52] born in L 'Isle-Verte, Québec Province 18 January 1839 and died unmarried 12 November 1904 at 65 years of age.

  24 iii. Marie Severine **Hamel**[53] born in Canada 24 January 1841 and died in infancy.

  25 iv. Lange **Hamel**[54] born in Canada 18 July 1842 and died in infancy.

  26 v. Marguerite Eugenie **Hamel**[55] born in L 'Isle-Verte 1 July 1844 and died in 1917 at 73 years of age. She married Romain **Pouliot** in Minnesota in 1857. They had 14 children.

  27 vi. Lang Charles **Hamel** Jr.[56] was born in L 'Isle-Verte 15 February 1846 and died in 1892 at 46 years of age. He married Mary **Marcoux** in Minneapolis in 1873. They had four children.

  28 vii. William **Hamel**[57] born in L 'Isle-Verte 18 March 1849 and died 6 October 1919 at 70 years of age. He married Cordelia **Christian** in Minnesota 7 September 1874. They had 11 children; one died in infancy.

  29 viii. Nelson **Hamel**[58] was born in Canada in 1850 and died 10 June 1918 at 67 years of age. He married Celina **LaBelle** in Minneapolis in November 1867. They had nine children.

+ 30 ix. Angelina **Hamel** born 18 March 1852.

  31 x. Euphemia **Hamel**[59] born in Hamel 18 May 1857 and died 17 October 1943 at 86 years of age.[60] She married twice. (1) Fabian **Michaud**. (2) Napoleon **Campbell**.

  32 xi. Adele **Hamel**[61] born in Minnesota and married Pierre **Marcoux**. They had 12 children.

  33 xii. Francis **Hamel**[62] born in Hamel in April 1860 and married Josephine **Laurent** in Minneapolis. They had one child.

  34 xiii. Mary **Hamel**[63] born in Hamel in 1866 and died in 1899 at 33 years of age.[64] She married David **Carufel** in Minnesota. They had eight children.

  35 xiv. Eugene **Hamel**[65] born in Hamel in September 1869 and died in infancy.

EIGHTH GENERATION

30. **Angelina**[8] **Hamel** (Lange Charles[7], Joseph Valentin[6], Louis Antoine[5], Jean[4], Jean Francois[3], Jean[2], Francois[1])[66] was born in St. Eloi, Québec, Canada 18 March 1852 and died 2 May 1915 in Corcoran, Hennepin Co., Minnesota, at 63 years of age of cancer of the rectum. She married **Didace (Didas) Scott** in Dayton, Hennepin Co., Minnesota 23 November 1868. Didace,[67] son of Joseph **Scott** and Philomene (Florin) **Trudeau**, was born in Québec Province, Canada 27 November 1844 and died 27 April 1929 in Corcoran of apoplexy, at 84 years, 5 months, 14 days of age.[68] They had 12 children.

Angela **Hamel** and Didace **Scott** had the following child born in Corcoran:
+ 36 i.   Benoni[9] **Scott** 25 September 1882.

NINTH GENERATION

36. **Benoni**[9] **Scott** (Angela[8], Lange Charles[7], Joseph Valentin[6], Louis Antoine[5], Jean[4], Jean Francois[3], Jean[2], Francois[1])[69] was born in Corcoran, Hennepin Co., Minnesota 25 September 1882 and died 8 January 1935 of stomach cancer in Minot, Ward Co., North Dakota, at 52 years of age. He married **Ellen "Nellie" Dolan** in Hamel, Hennepin Co., Minnesota 25 June 1903. Nellie, daughter of Thomas **Dolan** and Julia **Darmody**, was born in Maple Grove, Hennepin Co., Minnesota and died 2 June 1953 in Underwood, McLean Co., North Dakota, at 68 years of age. They had 12 children.

Benoni **Scott** and Nellie **Dolan** had the following child born in Hamel:
+   i.   37.   Pearl Julia **Scott** born 29 August 1905 and died 1 April 1988 in Glencoe, McLeod Co., Minnesota, at 82 years of age.

(See Generation 11, No. 9253, Pearl Julia Scott, wife of L. Blaine Whipple for a continuation of the Hamel lineage.)

MACIA (MATHIAS) TRUDEAU CA 1590 TO FLEVIA TRUDEAU 1906

(Trudeau lineage of Pearl Julia Scott, Generation 11, No. 9253, wife of L. Blaine Whipple.)

FIRST GENERATION

1. **Macia (Mathias)**[1] **Trudeau**[1] was born in Marsilac in Poitou, France and died in France. He married twice: (1) **Francoise Nau** or **Nelle** in St. Marguerite de la Rochelle, France 3 November 1611.[2] (2) **Anne Martin** in St. Marguerite 4 February 1630. She married (1) **Francois Girard**.

Macia (Mathias) **Trudeau** and Francoise Nau ou **Nelle** had the following children born in St. Marguerite de la Rochelle:

+ 2 ii. Francois[2] **Trudeau**.
  3 ii. Marie **Trudeau**[3] baptized 27 September 1612.
  4 iii. Michelle **Trudeau**[4] baptized 21 October 1616.
  5 iv. Etienne **Trudeau**[5] baptized 14 July 1615.
  6 v.   Marguerite **Trudeau**[6] baptized 21 October 1617.
  7 vi. Jeanne **Trudeau**[7] baptized 23 October 1619.

SECOND GENERATION

2. **Francois**[2] **Trudeau** (Macia (Mathias)[1])[8] was baptized in St. Marguerite de la Rochelle France, 4 October 1613 and died in 1649 in Notre-Dame-de-Cogne, City of La Rochelle, France. He married **Catherine Matinier** in France. She was born in France and was buried 27 March 1670 in Notre-Dame de la Rochelle, France.[9] Three sons, Jean, Etienne, and Mathias, survived her. Francois was a master mason and lived in the Parish of Notre Dame, the street of the same name at 1 'Echelle de la Couronne (the ladder of the crown) where he died. He was buried 1 December 1649. Catherine was living in the family home at the time of her death.

Francois **Trudeau** and Catherine **Matinier** had the following children born in St. Marguerite de la Rochelle, France:

  8 i.   Antoine[3] **Trudeau**[10] baptized 16 March 1635.
  9 ii. Toussaint **Trudeau**[11] baptized 29 September 1636.

{ G 1637 }

	10	iii.	Jean **Trudeau**[12] and married Anne **Caillaud** in France in January 1660. He was a Master Architect and lived at Montmerle, a country area of Bresse, in 1670.
	11	iv.	Martial **Trudeau**[13] baptized 17 February 1647 and married Marie **Fau**. He was a Master Mason and Stone Cutter and was living in Paris, St. Honore street, Parish of St. Germain 1 Auxerrois in 1670.
+	12	v.	Etienne **Trudeau** born 4 June 1641.
	13	vi.	Francois **Trudeau**[14] 2 March 1645.
	14	vii.	Pierre **Trudeau**[15] In March 1650 and was buried 22 May 1652 in Notre-Dame-de-Cogne, City of La Rochelle, France.

THIRD GENERATION

12. **Etienne**[3] **Trudeau** (Francois[2], Macia (Mathias)[1])[16] was born in Notre-Dame-de-Cogne, City of La Rochelle, France 4 June 1641 (baptized in St. Marguerite de la Rochelle 15 September 1641) and died in July 1712 in Montreal, Québec Canada, at 71 years of age. He married **Adrienne Barbier** in Montreal 10 January 1667. Adrienne,[17] daughter of Gilbert M. **Barbier** and Catherine **La Vau**, was born in Montreal 20 August 1652 and died aft 19 December 1717 in Québec Province, at approximately 65 years of age. She spent four years with the Hospitaliers (Sisters) and then entered the Hotel-Dieu (Hospital), intending to become a member of the Institute. But her parents arranged for her marriage with Etienne and they raised 13 sons and one daughter. She was still alive 19 December 1717 when she partitioned her property among her children before retiring to the home of her son Jean-Baptiste, until her death. No death certificate has been found.

Etienne is the common ancestor of all the Trudeau families of Canada and the U.S.A. Flevie Trudeau who married Joseph Scott 12 January 1841 in Chambly, Québec is his great great grand daughter and he is the author's great (6) grandfather. He is also the great (6) grandfather of Pierre-Elliot Trudeau, former prime minister of Canada. Pierre was born 18 October 1919 in Montreal, was elected to the House of Commons in 1965, served as Minister of Justice and Attorney General 1967-68 and succeeded Lester Pearson as Prime Minister and Liberal Party Leader in 1968 serving until 1979 and again from 1980-84.[18] Etienne was a Master Carpenter by age 18 and already noted for his fine work. He signed a contract 8 June 1659 "to do five years of military service" and sailed for New France 2 July aboard the *Saint Andre*, a ship of 300 tons. Upon arrival in

Ville-Marie, the original name for Montreal, he was assigned to work for the Sulpicians.[19] His first major skirmish with the Indians occurred 6 May 1662 when he and two others were attacked by a band of Iroquois. They were able to hold their own until rescued by a force from Sainte-Marie. On 1 February 1663 he was attached to the sixth squad of the 20-squad defense force organized to defend Montreal. Each squad was comprised of seven men. His squad was commanded by corporal Gilbert Barbier, his future father-in-law.

Upon the expiration of his contract as a mercenary soldier, Etienne was granted land at Montreal 10 January 1665 and received an apprentice license as a Stonemason 15 January 1673 and with Master Masons Michel Vouvier and Mathurin Collin built many of the houses in "primitive" Montreal.

He was granted "three arpents (a unit of measurement equaling 0.85 acres) of river frontage by twenty deep" at Longueuil on 12 March 1675. In 1684 he was living in Boucherville, Québec where his children were baptised in the church on the south shore. He acquired additional land on 23 August 1688 from the clergy of the Hotel-Dieu of Montreal. He and Adrienne spent their final years on their farm at Longueuil which was managed by their son Charles and his wife Madeleine Loisel. In return for being named heir to the farm and its livestock (4 oxen, 6 cows, 2 horses, 4 pigs, 6 ewes 24 chicken), Charles and Madeleine agreed to take care of his parents.[20]

Etienne **Trudeau** and Adrienne **Barbier** had the following children:

+ 15   i.   Etienne[4] **Trudeau**.
  16   ii. Francois **Trudeau**[21] baptized in Montreal 21 December 1673. He was in Louisana in 1706.
+ 17   iii. Pierre **Trudeau** born 24 September 1669.
  18   iv. Marie **Trudeau**[22] Born in Montreal 27 January 1672 and married Jean **Arnaud** there 27 November 1690. Jean,[23] son of Bertrand **Arnaud** and Marguerite **de Munsay**, was Magistrate to the Parliament of Bordeaux. They had three sons and three daughters.
  19   v.   Toussaint **Trudeau**[24] born in Montreal 19 January 1676 and died 12 February 1753 in Lorgue Pointe, Québec Province, at 77 years of age. He married twice. (1) Barbe **Goyau** in Longueuil, Québec Province 23 November 1705. Barbe[25] was the daughter of Guillaume **Goyau** and Helene **Benoit**. (2) Michel **Dubuc**. Before his marriage Toussaint hired out for a trip to Lake Erie. He and Barbe had a son and a daughter.[26]

{ G 1639 }

20	vi.	Nicolas **Trudeau**[27] born in Montreal 20 February 1678 and died there unmarried 20 June 1699, at 21 years of age.
21	vii.	Jean-Baptiste **Trudeau** [28] born in Montreal 11 April 1680 and died 26 June 1754 in Terrebonne, Québec Province, at 74 years of age. He married Marie-Madeleine **Parant** in Montreal 1 September 1715. Marie-Madeleine,[29] daughter of Joseph **Parant** and Marie-Madeleine **Maret**, was born in 1692 and died in 1735, at 43 years of age.[30] He went to Detroit by way of Lake Erie in 1701. Jean-Baptiste and Marie-Madeleine had five sons and five daughters.
22	viii.	Joseph **Trudeau**[31] born in Montreal 19 July 1682 and died there 3 May 1745, at 62 years of age. He married Genevieve **Lamarre-Belisle** in Pointe-aux-Trembles de Montrea 18 January 1718. Genevieve[32] was the daughter of Henry **Belisle** and Catherine **de Mosny**. Joseph and Genevieve had three sons and four daughters.
+ 23	ix.	Charles **Trudeau** born 25 March 1684.
24	x.	Laurent **Trudeau**[33] born in Longueuil, Québec Province 7 March 1686 and died 2 April 1730 in Montreal, at 44 years of age. He married Marie-Anne **Billeron** in Montreal 25 September 1719. She[34] was the daughter of Pierre **Billeron** and Marie-Marthe **Forcier**. They had four sons and four daughters.
25	xi.	Louis **Trudeau**[35] born in Longueuil 7 December 1687 and was baptized in Boucherville, Québec Province the day of birth. He married twice. (1) Marie-Charlotte **Aubuchon** in Pointe-aux-Trembles de Montrea 30 November 1715. The daughter of Jacques **Aubuchon** and Marie-Ursule **Etienne**, Marie-Charlotte died in childbirth along with their son 11 February 1718 in Québec.[36] (2) Marie-Josephe **Roy** in Montreal 31 May 1719. She was the daughter of Pierre **Roy** and Catherine **Ducharme**.[37] Louis was a Master Carpenter. He and Marie had three sons and five daughters.
+ 26	xii.	Bertrand **Trudeau** born 7 August 1689.
27	xiii.	Augustin **Trudeau**[38] born in Montreal 23 September 1691 and died 18 November 1709 in Longueuil, at 18 years of age.
28	xiv.	Jacques-Antoine **Trudeau**[39] born in Longueuil 15 November 1694 and baptized in Boucherville two days later.

{ G 1640 }

FOURTH GENERATION

15. **Etienne**[4] **Trudeau** (Etienne[3], Francois[2], Macia (Mathias)[1])[40] was baptized in Montreal 14 November 1667 and married **Marie Bleau** in Adhemar, Québec Province, Canada, 23 November 1699. Marie,[41] daughter of Francois **Bleau** and Elisabeth **Benoit**, was born in 1679 and died in 1749 in Canada, at 70 years of age. Her surname is given as Blot in Tanguay. They had three sons and three daughters, only two of whom are listed here.

Etienne **Trudeau** and Marie **Bleau** had the following children:
    29   i.   Etienne[5] **Trudeau**[42] married Agnes **Gariepy**.
    30   ii.   Marie **Trudeau**[43] born 6 October 1705.

17. **Pierre**[4] **Trudeau** (Etienne[3], Francois[2], Macia (Mathias)[1])[44] was born in Montreal, Canada 24 September 1669 and died abt 1740. He married **Charlotte Menard** in Longue-Pointe, Québec Province 19 November 1698. At 19, Pierre signed on with Nicolas Perrot for a trip to the Maskoutin Indians of the Nadoussin region. Four years later (8 April 1692), he signed a contract to go to the Outaouais.[45] By the time of his wedding, he had accummulated a stake in the fur trade. Pierre and Charlotte had eight sons and eight daughters. Pierre's descendants have taken the surnames of Barbier, Tredo, Trudo, Trutaut, Treteau, Truto, and Waterhole.

Pierre **Trudeau** and Charlotte **Menard** had the following children:
  +   31   i.   Pierre Joseph[5] **Trudeau** born 12 November 1699.
        32   ii.   Marie Josette **Trudeau**[46] born 1 March 1701.
        33   iii.   Marie Catherine **Trudeau**[47] born 3 April 1702.
        34   iv.   Charlotte **Trudeau**[48] born 24 July 1703.
        35   v.   Pierre **Trudeau**[49] born 16 December 1704.

23. **Charles**[4] **Trudeau** (Etienne[3], Francois[2], Macia (Mathias)[1])[50] was born in Longueuil, Québec Province, Canada 25 March 1684 (baptized in Boucherville the next day) and died in Longueuil 21 March 1742, at 57 years of age. He married **Marie-Madeleine Loisel** in Pointe-aux-Trembles de Montrea 17 November 1710. Marie-Madeleine[51] daughter of Joseph **Loisel** and Jeanne **Langlois**, was born in Pointe-aux-Trembles de Montrea 22 March 1694. They had five sons and seven daughters.

Charles **Trudeau** and Marie-Madeleine **Loisel** had the following child:
  +   36   i.   Toussaint[5] **Trudeau** born in 1727.

26. **Bertrand**[4] **Trudeau** (Etienne[3], Francois[2], Macia (Mathias)[1])[52] was born in Longueuil, Québec Province 7 August 1689 and married **Marie-Anne Gervais** in Montreal, Canada 30 June 1716. Marie-Anne was the daughter of Charles **Gervais** and Marie **Boyer**.[53] Bertrand was a Blacksmith. They had five sons and seven daughters.

Bertrand **Trudeau** and Marie-Anne **Gervais** had the following child:
    37   i.   Amable[5] **Trudeau**.[54]

FIFTH GENERATION

31. **Pierre Joseph**[5] **Trudeau** (Pierre[4], Etienne[3], Francois[2], Macia (Mathias)[1])[55] was born 12 November 1699 and married **Marie-Joseph Boudreau** in Longue-Pointe, Québec Province 6 June 1735.

Pierre Joseph **Trudeau** and Marie-Joseph **Boudreau** had the following child:
+   38   i.   Jean-Louis[6] **Trudeau**.

36. **Toussaint**[5] **Trudeau** (Charles[4], Etienne[3], Francois[2], Macia (Mathias)[1])[56] was born in 1727 and married **Genevieve Patenaude**,[57] daughter of Etienne **Patenaude** and Marie Angelique **Lamarre**.

Toussaint **Trudeau** and Genevieve **Patenaude** had the following children:
    39   i.   Genevieve[6] **Trudeau**[58] married Joseph **Benoit**, son of Joseph **Benoit** and Josephte (__), in Longueuil, Québec Province 7 April 1777.[59]
    40   ii.   Louise **Trudeau**[60] married Joseph **Hebert**, son of Francois **Hebert** and Marguerite **Brideur**, in Longueuil 21 January 1782.[61]
    41   iii.   Marie **Trudeau**[62] married Augustin **Brodeur**, son of Augustin **Brodeur** and Josephte **Charron** in Longueuil 18 Octobr 1785.[63]
    42   iv.   Charlotte **Trudeau**[64] married Joseph **Joly**, son of Michel **Joly** and Josephte **Sansoucy**, in Longueuil 4 February 1788.[65]
    43   v.   Elizabeth **Trudeau**[66] married Thomas **McLaud**, son of Pierre **McLaud** and Marie (__), in Chambly, Québec 10 February 1800.[67]
    44   vi.   Archange **Trudeau**[68] married Amable **Brunelle**, son of Joseph **Brunelle** and Charlotte **Lussier**, in Chambly 7 February 1803.[69]
+   45   vii.   Toussaint **Trudeau**.

SIXTH GENERATION

38. **Jean-Louis**[6] **Trudeau** (Pierre Joseph[5], Pierre[4], Etienne[3], Francois[2], Macia (Mathias)[1])[70] birth date unknown, married **Marie Larcheveque** in Longue-Pointe, Québec Province 1 August 1768.

Jean-Louis **Trudeau** and Marie **Larcheveque** had the following child:
+   46   i.   Louis[7] **Trudeau**.

45. **Toussaint**[6] **Trudeau** (Toussaint[5], Charles[4], Etienne[3], Francois[2], Macia (Mathias)[1])[71] was born in Québec Province and married **Marie Monty**, daughter of Joseph Antoine **Monty** and Marie-Catherine **Piedalu**, in Chambly, Québec 16 November 1801.[72]

Toussaint **Trudeau** and Marie **Monty** had the following children:
     47   i.   Narcisse[7] **Trudeau**[73] married Domithilde **Marcil**, daughter of Antoine **Marcil** and Julie **Frenchette**, in Chambly, Québec 1 February 1842.
+   48   ii.   Philomene (Florin) **Trudeau** born in 1821.

SEVENTH GENERATION

46. **Louis**[7] **Trudeau** (Jean-Louis[6], Pierre Joseph[5], Pierre[4], Etienne[3], Francois[2], Macia (Mathias)[1])[74] birth date unknown, married **Marguerite Gagne** in St-Philippe de Laprairie, Québec Province, Canada, 11 July 1808.

Louis **Trudeau** and Marguerite **Gagne** had the following child:
+   49   i.   Louis[8] **Trudeau**.

48. **Philomene (Florin)**[7] **Trudeau** (Toussaint[6], Toussaint[5], Charles[4], Etienne[3], Francois[2], Macia (Mathias)[1])[75] was born in Chambly, Québec, Canada in 1821 and died 15 October 1906 in Corcoran, Hennepin Co., Minnesota, at 85 years of age. She married three times. (1) **Joseph Scott** in Chambly 12 January 1841. Joseph, son of Andre **Scott** and Sophie **Demers,** was born in Chambly in 1815 or 1821 (his Certificate of Death stated he was 51 at time of death which equates to a birth year of 1821) and died 17 May 1872 of dysentery in Corcoran. Both are buried at Ste Jesnne de Chantal Cemetery, Corcoran. (2) Prisque **Noel**. (3) Joseph **Menard,** both in Hennepin County. "Flevia" and Joseph had two sons and four daughters.

{ G 1643 }

Flevia **Trudeau** and Joseph **Scott** had the following child born in Corcoran:
+   50   i.   Didace[8] (Didas) **Scott** 27 November 1844.

EIGHTH GENERATION

49. **Louis**[8] **Trudeau** (Louis[7], Jean-Louis[6], Pierre Joseph[5], Pierre[4], Etienne[3], Francois[2], Macia (Mathias[1])[76] birth date unknown, married **Louise Dupuis** in St-Philippe de Laprairie, Québec Province, Canada 19 November 1838.

Louis **Trudeau** and Louise **Dupuis** had the following children:
    57   i.   Joseph[9] **Trudeau**[77] married Malvina **Cardinal** in St-Constant de Laprairie 19 October 1874.
    58   ii.   Charles-Emile **Trudeau**.[78]

50. **Didace (Didas)**[8] **Scott** (Philomene (Florin)[7], Toussaint[6], Toussaint[5], Charles[4], Etienne[3], Francois[2], Macia (Mathias)[1]) was born in Québec Providence, Canada 27 November 1844 and died 27 April 1929 in Corcoran, Hennepin Co., Minnesota, at 84 years 5 months 14 days of age. He married **Angeline Hamel** in Dayton, Hennepin Co., Minnesota 23 November 1868 at St. John The Baptist Church. Angeline, daughter of Lange Charles **Hamel** and Eugenie **Moffett**, was born in St. Elois, Québec Province 18 March 1852 and died 2 May 1915 of cancer of the rectum in Corcoran, at 63 years of age. They had eight son and four daughters.

Didace **Scott** and Angeline **Hamel** had the following child born in Corcoran:
+   59   i.   Benoni[9] **Scott** 25 September 1882.

NINTH GENERATION

59. **Benoni**[9] **Scott** (Didace (Didas)[8] **Scott** (Philomene (Florin)[7], Toussaint[6], Toussaint[5], Charles[4], Etienne[3], Francois[2], Macia (Mathias)[1]) was born in Corcoran, Hennepin Co., Minnesota 25 September 1882 and died 8 January 1935 in Minot, Ward Co., North Dakota of stomach cancer, at 52 years of age. He married **Ellen "Nellie" Dolan** in Hamel, Hennepin, Co., Minnesota 25 June 1903. Nellie, daughter of Thomas **Dolan** and Julia **Darmody**, was born in Maple Grove, Hennepin Co., Minnesota 27 August 1884 and died 2 June 1953 in Underwood Mclean Co., North Dakota at 68 years of age. They had seven sons and seven daughters.

Ben **Scott** and Nellie **Dolan** had the following child born in Hamel:
+ 60 i. Pearl Julia **Scott** 29 August 1905.

(See Generation 11, No. 9253, Pearl J. Scott, wife of L. Blaine Whipple for a continuation of the Trudeau lineage.)

DOMINIQUE MONTY ABT 1680 TO MARIE MONTY ABT 1780

(Monty lineage of Pearl Julia Scott, Generation 11, No. 9253, wife of L. Blaine Whipple.)

FIRST GENERATION

1. **Dominique**[1] **Monty**[1] was born in France and married **Jeanne Benoist** abt 1700.

Dominique **Monty** and **Jeanne Benoist** had the following child:
+ 2 i. Jean[2] **Monty**.

SECOND GENERATION

2. **Jean**[2] **Monty** (Dominique[1])[2] birth date unknown, married **Marie Marthe Poyer** in Chambly, Québec, Canada 27 February 1729. Marie,[3] daughter of Jacques **Poyer** and Marguerite **Dubois**, was born 20 August 1710. She married (2) **Philippe Meunier** in Québec Province 17 February 1760.

Jean **Monty** and Marie Marthe **Poyer** had the following children born in Chambly:

    3 i. Marguerite[3] **Monty**[4] and married Jean-Baptiste Clement **Racine** there 9 February 1750.
+ 4 ii. Amable **Monty**.
    5 iii. Genevieve **Monty**[5] and married Pierre **Binet** there 27 January 1756.
    6 iv. Francois **Monty**[6] and married Marie-Joseph **Bergevin** in Québec Province 21 January 1760.

{ G 1645 }

	7	v.	Gaspard **Monty**[7] and married Marie-Therese **Desnoyers** there 19 May 1760.
	8	vi.	Marie-Angelique **Monty**[8] in 1742 and married twice. (1) Louis **Courtin** there 23 May 1761. (2) Jean-Baptiste **Mauray** in Montreal, Canada 4 February 1782.
+	9	vii.	Claude **Monty.**
	10	viii.	Clement **Monty**[9] and married Louise **Boileau** there 27 February 1764.
	11	ix.	Genevieve-Amable **Monty**[10] 28 January 1746.
+	12	x.	Joseph Antoine **Monty** 20 March 1747.
	13	xi.	Marie **Monty**[11] and married Joseph **Bolleau** there 14 February 1763.
	14	xii.	Marie-Francoise **Monty**[12] 16 September 1748 and died there 22 October 1748, 1 month and 6 days of age.

THIRD GENERATION

4. **Amable**[3] Monty (Jean[2], Dominique[1])[13] was born in Chambly, Québec, Canada and married twice. (1) **Marie-Anne Lebert** in Laprairie, Québec Province, Canada 4 November 1754. Marie-Anne,[14] daughter of Jacques **Lebert**, was born in Québec Province in 1737. (2) **Angelique Letourneau** in Québec Province 4 July 1757.

Amable **Monty** and Angelique **Letourneau** had the following children born in Laprairie:
15	i.	Marie-Angelique[4] **Monty**[15] 10 February 1758.
16	ii.	Amable **Monty**[16] 6 January 1759.

9. **Claude**[3] Monty (Jean[2], Dominique[1])[17] was born in Chambly, Québec, Canada and married **Marie-Anne Boyer** there.

Claude **Monty** and Marie-Anne **Boyer** had the following child born in Chambly:
17	i.	Claude[4] **Monty**[18] 7 June 1760.

12. **Joseph Antoine**[3] Monty (Jean[2], Dominique[1])[19] was born in Chambly, Québec, Canada 20 March 1747 and died there in 1829, at 82 years of age. He married **Marie-Catherine Piedalu** in Chambly 1 October 1770. Marie-Catherine,[20] daughter of Julien-Betrand **Piedalu** and Felicite **Bourassa**, was born in Laprairie, Québec Province 11 September 1751.

{ G 1646 }

Joseph Antoine **Monty** and Marie-Catherine **Piedalu** had the following child:
+   18   i.   Marie[4] **Monty.**

FOURTH GENERATION

18. **Marie**[4] **Monty** (Joseph Antoine[3], Jean[2], Dominique[1])[21] birth date unknown, married **Toussaint Trudeau** in Chambly, Québec, Canada 16 November 1801. Toussaint,[22] son of Toussaint **Trudeau** and Genevieve **Patenaude**, was born in Québec Province.

Marie **Monty** and Toussaint **Trudeau** had the following children:
   19   i.   Narcisse[5] **Trudeau**[23] married Domithilde **Marcil** in Chambly 1 February 1842. She was the daughter of Antoine **Marcil** and Julie **Frechette**.
+ 20   ii. Philomene (Florin) **Trudeau** born in 1821.

FIFTH GENERATION

20. **Philomene (Florin)**[5] **Trudeau** (Marie[4] Monty, Joseph Antoine[3], Jean[2], Dominique[1])[24] was born in Chambly, Québec, Canada in 1821 and died 15 October 1906 in Corcoran, Hennepin Co., Minnesota, at 85 years of age. She married three times. (1) **Joseph Scott** in Chambly 12 January 1841. Joseph, son of Andre **Scott** and Sophie **Demers** was born in Chambly in 1815 or 1821 (his Certificate of Death stated he was 51 at time of death which supports the 1821 date) and died 17 May 1872 of dysentery in Corcoran, at 56 years of age.[25] Both are buried at Ste Jesnne de Chantal Cemetery, Corcoran. (2) **Prisque Noel** (3) **Joseph Menard**, both in Hennepin county. Flevia and Joseph had two sons and five daughters.

Philomene **Trudeau** and Joseph **Scott** had the following child born in Québec Province:
+ 21   i.. Didace[6] (Didas) **Scott** 27 November 1844.

SIXTH GENERATION

21. **Didace (Didas)**[6] **Scott** (Philomene (Florin)[5] Trudeau (Marie[4] Monty, Joseph Antoine[3], Jean[2], Dominique[1]) was born in Québec Province, Canada 27 November 1844 and died 27 April 1929 in Corcoran, Hennepin Co., Minnesota, at 84 years 5 months 14 days of age. He married **Angeline Hamel** in Dayton, Hennepin Co., Minnesota 23 November

1868 at St. John the Baptist Church. Angeline, daughter of Lange Charles **Hamel** and Eugenie **Moffett**, was born in St. Eloi, Québec Province 18 March 1852 and died 2 May 1915 in Corcoran, at 63 years of age. They had eight sons and four daughters.

Didace **Scott** and Angeline **Hamel** had the following child born in Corcoran:

+ 22 i. Benoni[7] **Scott** 25 September 1882

22. **Benoni**[7] **Scott** (Didace (Didas)[6] Scott (Philomene (Florin)[5] Trudeau (Marie[4] Monty, Joseph Antoine[3], Jean[2], Dominique[1]) was born in Corcoran, Hennepin Co., Minnesota 22 September 1882 and died 8 January 1935 in Minot, Ward Co., North Dakota, at 52 years of age. He married **Ellen "Nellie" Dolan** in Hamel, Hennepin Co., Minnesota 25 June 1903. Nellie, daughter of Thomas **Dolan** and Julia **Darmody**, was born in Maple Grove, Hennepin Co., Minnesota 27 August 1884 and died 2 June 1953 in Underwood, Mclean Co., North Dakota, at 68 years of age. They had seven sons and seven daughters.

Benoni **Scott** and Nellie **Dolan** had the following child born in Hamel:

+ 23 i. Pearl[8] Julia **Scott** 29 August 1905.

(See Generation 11, No. 9253, Pearl Julia Scott, wife of L. Blaine Whipple for a continuation Monty lineage.)

ROGER DOLAN CA ABT 1810
TO ELLEN "NELLIE" DOLAN 1848-1953

(Dolan lineage of Pearl Julia Scott, Generation 11, No. 9253, wife of L. Blaine Whipple.)

FIRST GENERATION

1. **Roger**[1] **Dolan**[1] was born in Ireland and had the following child:

+ 2 i. Kerian (Keran)[2] **Dolan** born between 1826-1829.

SECOND GENERATION

2. **Kerian (Keran)[2] Dolan** (Roger[1])[2] was born in County Cork, Ireland probably in 1826 and died 18 September 1907 in Minneapolis, Hennepin Co., Minnesota, at 81 years of age. He married **Margaret Rourke** abt 1858. She was born 3 December 1839 in either New York state or Rhode Island[3] and died 6 February 1898 in Minnesota, at 58 years of age. Kerian left Ireland for the U.S. from Liverpool, England on the *De Witt Clinton* arriving at the Port of New York 15 October 1849.[4] The ship manifest of passengers identified him as a 23-year-old farmer. John Dolan, 26, who may be his brother, was listed on the second line below Kieran. If the manifest is correct, Kieran's birth year is 1826. Emigration was a lifesaver for the man or woman able to afford passage to the U.S. or Canada. The London *Times* "gloated over the Irish exodus, and gleefully announced that in a short time a Celt would be as rare in Ireland as a red Indian on the shores of Manhattan." Of the million Irish who emigrated between 1849-54, only 20 percent sailed directly from Ireland; 75 percent left from Liverpool.[5]

According to his obituary, Kieran died at St. Mary's Hospital in Minneapolis.[6] He had been a resident of Minnesota for more than 40 years and was the father of 14 children, 10 of whom survived him. The author has only been able to identify 11 of the 14. His wife died 10 years previously. The funeral was to take place at the home of his son Thomas at 1514 6th St. N., Minneapolis with internment at St. Anne's Cemetery in Hamel, Hennepin Co. Minnesota. His age was given as 78. If correct, his birth year was 1829. He and Margaret are buried in Block 4, Lot 11, Grave 2 and 5 (Margaret in 5).

When the Dolans left New York is unknown but it was before 1865 since son John was born in Michigan abt 1864. If the information in his obituary is correct, the family was in Minnesota by 1866. On 1 August 1872, a Kerian Dolan was granted a 160-acre homestead in Minnesota by the United States government. It's legal description was "the west half of the southeast quarter and the east half of the southwest quarter of Section 17 in Township 103 of Range 25 in the District of Lands subject to sale at Jackson, Minnesota" according to the official plat of the survey of said land returned to the General Land Office by the Surveyor General.[7] Ulysses S. Grant was President.

The family lived in Walnut Lake Township, Faribault Co. before moving to Plymouth Township in Hennepin Co. Both the 1875 state census and their daughter Mary's birth certificate place them in Walnut Lake. According to the 1895 state census, they moved to Hennepin Co. abt 1876. Plymouth is in the center of the county. The western half of the county

{ G 1649 }

was heavily timbered and the eastern portion was mixed prairie meadow and brush land. Antoine LeCount, Plymouth's first settler, had arrived about 23 years earlier.

Kerian (Keran) **Dolan** and Margaret **Rourke** had the following children:

+ 3	i.	Thomas[3] **Dolan** born abt 1860.
4	ii.	Catherine **Dolan**[8] born in New York State abt 1861.
5	iii.	Keran **Dolan**[9] born in New York State abt 1863.
6	iv.	John **Dolan**[10] born in Michigan abt 1864. He is buried in Block 4, Lot 11, Grave 6 St. Anne Cemetery, Hamel, Minn.
7	v.	Margaret **Dolan**[11] born in Minnesota abt 1869.
8	vi.	Mary E. **Dolan**[12] born in Walnut Lake Twp. Faribault Co., Minnesota 13 October 1874.
9	vii.	Elizabeth **Dolan**[13] born in Minnesota 31 October 1876 (baptized 26 November by Father Ladriere). Patrick Davery and Bridget Johnson were her Godparents.[14]
10	viii.	Anna **Dolan**[15] born in Minnesota 22 December 1878 (baptized 30 December by Father Ladriere). Patrick Darmody and Helen Davery were were Godparents.[16] She died 14 February 1879 in Minnesota, at 1 month 23 days of age[17] and was buried 16 February 1879 in St. Patrick Cemetery, Maple Grove, Hennepin Co., Minnesota.
11	ix.	Bernard **Dolan**[18] born in Osseo, Hennepin Co., Minnesota 19 April 1880 (baptized by Father Ladriere). John Davery and Mary Ryan were Godparents.[19] Bernard died in Maple Grove. He married Winifred (__). Bernard and Winifred are buried in St. Patrick Catholic Cemetery.
12	x.	Sarah **Dolan**[20] born in Minnesota abt 1883.
13	xi.	William **Dolan**[21] born in Minnesota abt 1886.

THIRD GENERATION

3. **Thomas**[3] **Dolan** (Kerian (Keran)[2], Roger[1])[22] was born in New York State abt 1860 and died 15 June 1944 in Minneapolis, Hennepin Co., Minnesota, at 82 years of age.[23] He married twice. (1) **Julia Darmody** in Minnesota 19 November 1883 at St. Vincent de Paul Church in Osseo, Hennepin Co., Minnesota. Witnesses were Philip and Margaret Darmody, siblings of the bride. Father Payette performed the ceremony. Julia,[24] daughter of Patrick **Darmody** and Ellen **Peters**, was born in Minnesota 25 February 1862 and died 24 July 1899 in Maple Grove, Hennepin Co., Minnesota, at 37 years of age. She and an unnamed child died in child-

{ G 1650 }

birth. (2) **Barbara Sweigert** in Minnesota. She was born in 1872 and died 13 July 1947 in Minneapolis, at 75 years of age.[25] Buried at St. Patricks Cemetery, Maple Grove, Minnesota.

Tom's New York native town and county are unknown. One grandson believes it was a "Shanty town" near Utica in Oneida Co. When he and Julia were married in in 1883 he began farming in Maple Grove. Their marriage license disclosed that he could not write as he signed the document with an X. When Julia died during childbirth in 1899, their oldest daughter Nellie, 15, became the caretaker of the younger children. Tom eventually gave up farming and moved to Minneapolis where he operated a saloon for a few years before joining city government working for the street department.

Thomas **Dolan** and Julia **Darmody** had the following children born in Maple Grove:

+ 14 i. Ellen "Nellie"[4] **Dolan** 27 August 1884.
   15 ii. Margaret **Dolan**[26] in February 1887 and died in 1951 in Minneapolis, at 64 years of age. She married Arthur E. **Frick** in Minnesota. Both are buried in St. Patrick Catholic Cemetery in Maple Grove.
   16 iii. Mary **Dolan**[27] in May 1890 and died in Bowbells, Burke Co., North Dakota. She married Richard **Frick**. He was married twice.
   17 iv. Patrick W. **Dolan**[28] in December 1892 and died 8 August 1981 in Flint, Genesse Co., Michigan, at 88 years of age. He married twice. (1) Clara **Frick**. No details on marriage (2) other than they had been married 52 years at the time of his death.
   18 v. Thomas E. **Dolan**[29] 25 February 1895 and died 6 May 1948 in Spokane, Spokane Co., Washington, at 53 years of age. He married Martha Imelda **Nunn** who was born 15 April 1895 and died 1 March 1968 in Spokane, at 72 years of age.[30] Both are buried in Holy Cross Cemetery.
   19 vi. Martha Agnes **Dolan**[31] in June 1897 and married Ed **Hurley**.
   20 vii. (Infant) **Dolan**[32] 24 July 1899. Died during childbirth.

FOURTH GENERATION

14. **Ellen "Nellie"**[4] **Dolan** (Thomas[3], Kerian (Keran)[2], Roger[1])[33] was born in Maple Grove, Hennepin Co., Minnesota 27 August 1884 and died 2 June 1953 in Underwood, McLean Co., North Dakota, at 68 years of age. She married **Benoni Scott** in Hamel, Hennepin Co., Minnesota 25

{ G 1651 }

June 1903. Benoni, son of Didace **Scott** and Angeline **Hamel**, was born 25 September 1882 in Corcoran, Hennepin Co., Minnesota and died 8 January 1935 in Minot, Ward Co., North Dakota, at 52 years of age. They had seven sons and seven daughters.

Nellie **Dolan** and Ben **Scott** had the following child born in Hamel:
+   21   i.   Pearl Julia[5] **Scott** 29 August 1905.

(See Generation 11, No. 9253, Pearl Julia Scott, wife of L. Blaine Whipple for a continuation of the Dolan lineage.)

PATRICK DARMODY, ABT 1821 TO JULIA DARMODY, 1862-1899

(Darmody lineage of Pearl Julia Scott, Generation 11, No. 9253, wife of L. Blaine Whipple.)

FIRST GENERATION

1. **Patrick**[1] **Darmody**[1] was born in County Tipperary, Ireland about 1821 and died 5 February 1879 in Maple Grove, Hennepin Co., Minnesota, at 57 years of age. He married **Ellen Peters** abt 1855. She was born in County Tipperary, Ireland and died in Maple Grove.[2] The 1870 census identifies her birthplace as Ireland, no locale given. She was living on the original Darmody farm in Maple Grove according to the 1885 census with sons Michael, 29, Philip, 20, and daughter Margaret, 27. Patrick and Helen are buried at St. Patrick Cemetery, Maple Grove. His large tombstone has no date of birth but identifies his birth place as County Tipperary, Ireland.

Patrick arrived in New York 20 May 1850 from Waterford, Ireland on the Bark *Alert*. His age was listed as 17 on the passenger manifest.[3] If he was 17, his birth year is 1833. The tombstone may have been placed at a time later than his death as it gives his death date as 5 December 1880 and his age as 55. The records at St. Vincent de Paul Catholic Church in Osseo, Hennepin Co., Minnesota state his death occurred 5 December 1879, age 58. If the church records are correct, his birth year was 1821. The 1870 federal census supports the earlier date. It listed his age as 50 and shows the family lived on a 120-acre farm in Maple Grove Township. The 1870 federal census states

{ G 1652 }

that Ellen was 45, Michael, 14, Margaret, 12, Ellen, 11, Julia, 7, Philip, 5. The 1885 Minnesota state census tracts with the children ages but adds five years to Ellen. The census states all the children were born in Minnesota so Patrick and Ellen must have been in the state by 1856.

In 1869 their farm was valued at $1,200 and comprised 20 improved acres, 20 unimproved acres, and 80 acres of woodland. They had two horses, four milk cows, three other cattle, five swine, and one sheep with a total value of $415. They sold forest products worth $30, slaughtered animals worth $145, and raised other farm products worth $598. They raised 200 bushels of spring wheat, 30 bushels of Indian corn, 150 bushels of oats, 4 bushels of peas and beans, 60 bushels of Irish potatoes, 11 ton of hay, and 300 pounds of butter.

The census reports spell the family name Darmody. Patrick's tombstone spells it Dormody. Older stones are Darmody, newer ones Dormody. The marriage license issued to Julia and Tom Dolan spells it Darmody.

Patrick **Darmody** and Ellen **Peters** had the following children:

	2	i.	Michael[2] **Darmody**[4] born in Minnesota abt 1856.
	3	ii.	Margaret **Darmody**[5] born in Minnesota abt 1858.
	4	iii.	Ellen **Darmody**[6] born in Minnesota abt 1859.
+	5	iv.	Julia **Darmody** born 25 February 1862.
	6	v.	Philip **Darmody**[7] 26 March 1865 (baptized 27 March by Father Genis).[8] Michael and Margaret Kelliner were Godparents.
	7	vi.	Bridget **Darmody**[9] in Maple Grove in 1867 (baptized 1 May 1867 by Father Nicolas).[10] John Mullin and Mary Gleason Godparents.

SECOND GENERATION

5. **Julia**[2] **Darmody** (Patrick[1])[11] was born in Minnesota 25 February 1862 and died in childbirth along with the baby 24 July 1899 in Maple Grove, Hennepin Co., Minnesota, at 37 years of age.

She married **Thomas Dolan** in Minnesota 19 November 1883 at St. Vincent de Paul Church in Osseo, Hennepin Co., Minnesota. Witnesses were Philip and Margaret Darmody, siblings of Julia. Father Payette performed the ceremony.[12] Tom, son of Kerian (Keran) **Dolan** and Margaret **Rourke**, was born in New York State abt 1860 and died 15 June 1944 in Minneapolis, Hennepin Co., Minnesota, at 82 years of age. He married (2) Barbara **Sweigert** in Minnesota. Tom began farming in Maple Grove in 1883. Their marriage license shows he could not write as he signed the document with an X. He eventually

{ G 1653 }

gave up farming and moved to Minneapolis where he operated a saloon for a few years before joining city government working for the street department.

Julia Darmody and Thomas **Dolan** had the following children born in Maple Grove:

+ 8 i. Ellen "Nellie"[3] **Dolan** 27 August 1884.

9 ii. Margaret **Dolan**[13] in February in 1887 and died in 1951 in Minneapolis, at 64 years of age. She married Arthur E. **Frick** in Minnesota. Both are buried in St. Patrick Catholic Cemetery, Maple Grove.

10 iii. Mary **Dolan**[14] in May 1890 and died in Bowbells, Burke Co., North Dakota. She married Richard **Frick**.

11 iv. Patrick W. **Dolan**[15] in December 1892 and died 8 August 1981 in Flint, Genesse Co., Michigan, at 88 years of age. He married twice. (1) Clara **Frick**. The only thing known about (2) is they were married 52 years at the time of his death.

12 v. Thomas E. **Dolan**[16] 25 February 1895 and died 6 May 1948 in Spokane, Spokane Co., Washington, at 53 years of age. He married Martha Imelda **Nunn** who was born 15 April 1895 and died 1 March 1968 in Spokane, at 72 years of age.[17] Both are buried in Holy Cross Cemetery.

13 vi. Martha Agnes **Dolan**[18] in June 1897 and married Ed **Hurley**.

14 vii. (Infant) **Dolan**[19] 24 July 1899 and died during childbirth.

THIRD GENERATION

8. **Ellen "Nellie"**[3] **Dolan** (Julia[2] Darmody, Patrick[1])[20] was born in Maple Grove, Hennepin Co., Minnesota 27 August 1884 and died 2 June 1953 in Underwood, McLean Co., N. Dak., at 68 years of age. She married **Benoni Scott** in Hamel, Hennepin Co., Minnesota 25 June 1903. Ben, son of Didace (Didas) **Scott** and Angela **Hamel**, was born in Corcoran, Hennepin Co., Minnesota 25 September 1882 and died 8 January 1935 in Minot, Ward Co., North Dakota, at 52 years of age.[21] They had seven sons and seven daughters. Nellie was named Ellen after her mother's sister of the same name. Ellen was three years older than Julia.

Nellie **Dolan** and Ben **Scott** had the following child born in Hamel:

+ 15 i. Pearl Julia[4] **Scott** 29 August 1904.

(See Generation 11, No. 9253, Pearl Julia Scott, wife of L. Blaine Whipple for a continuation of the Darmody lineage.)

WHY KERIAN DOLAN AND PATRICK DARMODY LEFT THE EMERALD ISLE[1]

The year 2006 is the 159th anniversary of "Black '47," the worst year of the famine in Ireland. Today's Irish descendant is so far removed from basic knowledge of his forebearers that many ascribe romantic notions to their life. Nothing could be farther from the truth. About a million came to the United States between 1845-1850 in a sad march away from famine and fever. They marched onto the shores of "the best poor man's country on earth" and up the streets of New York where they believed "every day is like Christmas for the meat."

I have three sets of Irish ancestors. Andrew Scott, my great (4) was born in Sligo circa 1713, migrated to Québec Province, Canada sometime before 1759 where he lived a successful life with two wives, raised three children and died at age 99.

Kieran Dolan, my great (2) grandfather arrived in New York 15 October 1849 on the *De Witt Clinton* from Liverpool, England. Various sources suggest he was born between 1826-1831 in County Cork. He lived in New York and Michigan before settling in Minnesota circa 1864 where he and his wife Margaret Rourke farmed and raised 14 children. Margaret died at 58, Kieran at 81.

Patrick Darmody my great (2) grandfather left County Tipperary as a teen-ager, sailing on the bark *Alert*. He arrived in New York City 2 May 1850 and was farming in Hennepin County, Minnesota 10 years later. His birth date is unknown but was probably about 1825. He married Helen, also born in County Tipperary, and they raised six children in Maple Grove, Minnesota. He died 8 December 1880 of brain fever. None of these men would have been able to achieve their level of success had they remained in Ireland. And their life span would have been shorter.

The main parade of Irish immigrants began to form in September 1845 when farmers sniffed "a dampish putrid" odor coming from the fields. Before the month ended, the potato stalks were "black as your shoe and burned to the clay." In five years, during what Benjamin Disraeli called "the single root that changed the history of the world," Ireland lost one quarter of her population: a million and a half dead and a million gone to America.

IRELAND LACKED INDUSTRY

At the time of the great potato famine, Ireland wasn't industrialized and its few industries were moribund. Agricultural employment did not exist. Farms were too small to require hired labor – over 93 percent were smaller than 30 acres; 45 percent had less than five acres. Three-quarters of the laborers had no regular employment, working only when potatoes were being planted, cultivated, and harvested. In 1835, there were 2,385,000 jobless, because no work was available. Without a patch of land to grow potatoes, a family starved.

In 1843 a Royal Commission (known as the Devon Commission after its chairman the Earl of Devon) was appointed to document conditions in Ireland. It visited every part of Ireland, heard 1,100 witnesses, and its three volume report concluded that the possession of a piece of land was literally the difference between life and death; that the principal cause of Irish misery was the relationship between landlord and tenant.

Two conditions denied the tenant incentive and security: (1) when his lease expired or was terminated, improvements he made became the landlord's without compensation and (2) he was a tenant "at will" with no security because a landlord could evict whenever he chose. When evicted, families wandered about begging, crowding the already swarming lanes and slums of towns, or lived in ditches by the roadside until, wasted by disease and hardship, "they die in a little time."

The Irish, according to the Commission, suffered more than people in any other country in Europe. "In many districts their only food is the potato, their only beverage, water; their cabins are seldom a protection against the weather; a bed or blanket is a rare luxury; and their pigs and manure heap constitute their only property."

Housing conditions were beyond words. The census of 1841 graded houses into four classes: the fourth and lowest class consisted of windowless mud cabins of a single room. Nearly half of the rural population lived in the lowest class. In parts of Ireland more than three-fifths of the houses were one-room cabins. Furniture was a luxury. In 1837 the approximately 9,000 inhabitants of Tullahobagly, County Donegal, had 10 beds, 93 chairs, and 243 stools. Pigs slept with their owners, manure heaps were outside entry doors, sometimes even inside. The evicted and unemployed put roofs over ditches, burrowed into banks, or lived in bog holes.

FAMILIES SURVIVED ON HALF-ACRE PLOTS

Most leases had clauses prohibiting land subdivision but were seldom enforced. Land was divided and subdivided and split into smaller and still smaller fragments until families were surviving on plots as small as half an acre. As the population increased, parents let their children occupy a portion of their holdings rather than turn them out to starve. The children in turn did the same for their children and in a comparatively short time up to 10 families were settled on land which could provide for only one.

In West Ireland, subdivision was aggravated by a system of joint tenancy known as "rundale" whereby the land was rented in common and divided so that each tenant received a portion of the good, bad, and medium quality land the farm contained. For example, in Liscananawn, County Mayo, 167 acres of three qualities was divided into 330 portions – each of 110 persons had three portions. This desperate competition led to enormous rents.

Day laborers, too poor to rent land, eked out an existence by conacre. Conacre was a contract, not a lease, to use a portion of land to grow one crop. No landlord-tenant relationship was created. The plots were small. A quarter-acre was more common than half an acre in Tipperary. The land owner prepared the soil for planting and the contractor provided the seed, planted it, cultivated and harvested it. Rent was high: £10 to £14 an acre for good ground £6 for poor.

This system of small plots, high rents, and frantic competition for land coupled with the dense population subsisting at the lowest level, created the Irish dependence on the potato. When the crop was good, the potato generated great quantities of food produced at a minor cost. An acre-and-a-half would provide a family of five or six with food for 12 months. To grow the same amount of grain required four to six times as much acreage and some knowledge of tilling. Planting potatoes only require a spade.

The potato was food for people, cattle, pigs, and fowl. It was nourishing and simple to cook. Yet it was a dangerous crop because it did not keep and could not be stored from one season to another. The nearly 2.5 million laborers with no regular employment lived on starvation rations in the summer when the old crop was eaten and the new not yet harvested. June, July, and August were called the "meal months" because meal had to be eaten. The laborers bought meal on credit at exhorbitant prices from the scourge of the Irish village, the dreaded Gombeen man.

In Ireland's backward areas cooking food other than the potato had become a lost art. In Kerry, Donegal, the country west of the Shannon river, and part of West Cork, the population lived so exclu-sively on the potato that no trade in any other food existed. Bread was scarcely seen and ovens were unknown. There was no means of distributing home-grown food and no knowledge of how to use it. Economic necessity compelled the small farmer to sell what he grew. Wheat, oats, and barley were not regarded as food – they were grown to pay the rent, the first necessity of life in Ireland. It would be a desperate man who ate up his rent because failure to pay meant eviction and death by slow starvation.

Potatoes were suited to the moist soil of Ireland. Trenches were dug, beds made, the potato sets laid on the ground, and earthed up again. The trenches provided drainage so crops could be grown in wet ground, the spade made it possible to plant on hillsides where a plough could not be used. As the population increased, potatoes were grown in bogs and up mountains, where no other crops would have been possible.

POTATOES, NOT MONEY, DETERMINED VALUE OF LABOR

The potato, not money, was the basic factor to determine the value of labor. Farmers and landlords gave their laborers a cabin and a piece of potato ground, or permitted them to put up a conacre. Wages were not paid in money but were credited against rent at a rate varying from four to eight pence a day. The laborer's real reward was the patch of potato ground.

The laborer only dealt with money when he sold a pig for a few shillings and used the money to buy clothing for the family. The poorest laborers could not afford a pig and were so unfamiliar with money, they did not recognize coins and notes. This did not mean money was not prized. It was prized in the extreme. Money meant ability to purchase land, and land was life itself in Ireland. However wretched a family, if they had a little money they would hoard it to pay land rent rather than improve their living conditions.

The census of 1851 reported 24 potato crop failure between 1728 and 1839, including complete failures in 1740, 1800, and 1839. Thus its unreliability as a crop was an accepted fact and the possibility of another failure caused no particular alarm. In early July 1845, the crop looked good until the hot, dry weather gave way to three weeks of low temperature and a succession of chilling rains and some fog. In early August, England's Isle of Wright reported disease in the potato crop. This was the first recorded evidence that "blight" had crossed the Atlantic.[2]

Britain's leading horticultural publication, *The Gardeners' Chronicle and Horticultural Gazette,* reported in mid-September that "the potato Murrain has unequivocally declared in Ireland. The crops about Dublin are suddenly perishing." By mid-October, disastrous reports poured in from all sections of the country. As digging progressed, the news grew steadily worse. When first dug, many potatoes were sound but within a few days had become a stinking mass of corruption.

The consequences of a potato failure are not immediate and the first effect is plenty, not scarcity, because people dispose of their potatoes before they become useless. Famine begins five or six months after a failure. By then, every scrap of food, every partially-diseased potato, everything edible was consumed. This meant the government had until April or May to prepare to feed the people.

FAMINE—AN OPPORTUNITY TO PROFIT

By spring 1846, people in many districts had begun to starve and local relief commissioners had formed committees to raise money to buy food for resale to the distressed. An Irish Board of Works was formed to create employment in public works and fever hospitals were authorized. Similar efforts during previous periods of famine had not been successful. History was to be repeated.

Laissez faire, a theory that individuals should pursue their own interests with as little interference from government as possible was, almost without exception, the belief held by the politicians and high government officials responsible for Ireland. The loss was to be made good by the operation of private enterprise using the normal channels of commerce – in short, famine was an opportunity for profit.

Charles Edward Treyelyan, head of the all-powerful Department of Treasury and watchdog of the nation's money-bags, was in charge of the various famine relief programs. He believed the food shortage "would be aggravated in a fearful degree" if traders confined "themselves to what in ordinary circumstances might be considered fair profits." When the Marquess of Sligo complained in October that the Commissariat Officer at Westport was refusing to sell food to people who were starving because they couldn't pay the trader's exorbitant prices, he was told "we must bear in mind if an article is scarce a smaller quantity must be made to last for a longer time, and that high price is the only criterion by which consumption can be economized." Treyelyan regretted the "evil" of an insufficient food supply but believed providing more would be "a crying injustice to the rest of the country."

Government officials and relief committee members treated the destitute with impatience and contempt. Sympathy and kindness were not on the agenda in December 1845. English newspapers pictured the Irish, not as helpless famine victims, but as cunning and bloodthirsty desperadoes. *Punch* published cartoons week after week depicting the Irishman as a filthy, brutal creature, an assassin and a murderer, begging for money – under a pretense of buying food – to spend on weapons. Ireland was a disturbing thought and it was a comfort to be able to believe its people were not starving or, if some of them were, the depravity of the Irish was such that they deserved to starve.

Because many ate seed stock to fend off starvation, about one-third less acreage was planted in 1846. With their naturally optimistic temperament that plenty follows scarcity, Irish hopes were high. Weather was warm during May and June and the plants grew strong. However, by the middle of July, disease was more prevalent in the early crop than in 1845. By

August 3, it was apparent the crop was a total failure.

Reports from Cork to Dublin said the crop was a "waste of putrefying vegetation." One report said 32 miles of potato fields "in full bloom" became "scorched black" overnight. Disaster was universal. The September 2, 1846 London *Times* described it as "total annihilation." By the end of autumn, all berries, edible roots, and cabbage leaves had been eaten. The blighted fields had been combed over and over until nothing edible remained.

The fungus *phytophthora infestans* caused the blight but scientists and farmers were ignorant of the cause so there was no understanding of its nature or any idea of how to treat it. It was 15 years before blight was acknowledged to be the work of a fungus and nearly 40 years before a spray was developed. Though it remains as a serious plant pestilence, complete destruction of a crop no longer takes place because threatened crops are now sprayed with copper compounds.

M. J. Berkeley of Northamptonshire, England, whose studies on fungi had been published in *English Flora* in 1836, observed minute fungi on blighted parts of leaves and tubers in the summer of 1845. In January 1846, in an article in the *Journal of the Horticultural Society of London*, he described the fungus as a parasite and claimed it caused blight. The general belief was that "wet putrefaction" and "dropsy" caused blight. With little evidence to support his theory, it was almost universally rejected and wasn't accepted until well into the 20th century. By a stroke of poetic justice, much of the final research was carried out at the Albert Agricultural College, Glasnevin, Dublin.

BITTER COLD WINTER

The winter of 1846-47 was the most severe in living memory. Snow fell early in November; frost was continuous. Icy gales, with a force unknown since the famous great wind of 1839 produced snow, hail, and sleet. Roads were impassable and transport was brought to a stand still. To the people, it seemed that nature had joined Ireland's enemies. Normally, the prevailing wind is a west wind, and though the approach of winter is usually heralded by a gale blowing up out of the Atlantic, it is mild in spite of its force. But this autumn the wind came from Russia and was icy. All of Europe was gripped in bitter cold and by the middle of December the Thames was a mass of floating ice.

One of the compensations of the 19th century Irish peasant's life was warmth. A supply of peat was almost universal and a peat fire burned night and day, some as long as a century. The family spent the cold, wet days of winter indoors, and though dressed in rags, they endured little hardship. Not this winter. The 1846 crop failure forced the ill-clad peasant in rain, snow, and icy gales to labor on public works so he could feed his family. More often than not, he was already starving.

The people understood little of what was happening and became bewildered. Irish was spoken in rural districts; English was barely understood and not at all in the west. No attempt was made to explain the catastrophe. The first to succumb were the poorest of all, the squatters who had put up huts of sods in a bog, or on the seashore where they harvested seaweed for potato manure. Their small crop of potatoes had always been their only means of existence and when it was lost, they abandoned their hovels and descended on the towns in droves.

Five thousand beggars roamed the streets of Cork. Oranmore in Galway had "hundreds of poor creatures wandering about." Thurles in Tipperary reported large numbers of half-starving people pouring in from the surrounding country. They slept in ditches and in doorways, begged, and were driven away. People died at a rate of 100 a week in Cork in December.

William Forster, a minister in Norwich, England and a respected member of the Quaker community, his son W. E., and others went to Ireland to investigate the extent of the famine. They reported "destitution and suffering far exceeding that which had been at first supposed." Children were "like skeletons, their features sharpened with hunger and their limbs wasted, so that there was little left but bones, their hands and arms, in particular, being much emaciated, and the happy expression of infancy gone from their faces, leaving the anxious look of premature old age."

Forster offered a donation to start a soup kitchen every place he visited. With the exception of Castlerea the offer was gratefully accepted. The Catholic priest at Castlerea declined because acceptance would bring the poor from the surrounding country into the town, "by which they would be overwhelmed." In January 1847 at Bundorragha in Galway, Forster said all sheep and cows were gone, all poultry killed, only one pig left, and no dogs. His son after visiting Clifden County Galway, said men and women were "more like famished dogs than fellow creatures." He decried reports in English newspapers that Irish starvation was exaggerated.

As the winter continued with unrelenting severity, frantic appeals for food poured into the government offices at Whitehall from all over Ireland. Money was useless in Limerick because there was no food to buy. Cork's Nicholas Cummins, Justice of the Peace, wrote that "unless something is immediately done the people must die." The Relief Inspector at Sligo wrote he was unable to adequately describe the desperate circumstances there. The Commissariat Office at Burtonport, County Donegal, wrote that "the distress of the wretched people is heart-rending; something ought to be done (as) there is absolutely nothing in the place for food." A Colonel Jones wrote that the people had reached a state of panic because of the lack of food.

February was the worst month of the terrible winter. Heavy snow falls and fierce gales made roads impassable. Carts could not be used. Horses sank in drifts and had to be dug out. Families without food or fuel took to their beds. Many died believing it was the will of God.

SOUP KITCHENS OPENED IN 1847

Two new government programs were begun early in 1847. (1) Soup kitchens, a favorite English philanthropic activity, were established throughout the country. The goal: feed the laborer so he could work his plot of ground or work for a farmer and produce food for the next harvest and earn enough to support his family. (2) Distressed persons were classified as paupers, placed under the Irish Poor Law[3] and given "outdoor" relief paid for by local taxes. Previously, only workhouse inmates were eligible for relief and the capacity of the workhouses determined who could be fed. By the end of January 31,000 pints of soup were distributed daily to about a tenth of the destitute population in West Cork. Crowds waited for hours at distribution centers, sometimes all night, and savage struggles took place when distribution began.

By early February private enterprise was finally functioning with supplies of Indian corn and Indian meal beginning to arrive from North America. Two-hundred-fifty ships carrying 50,000 tons of foodstuffs were in Cork harbor February 26. But it was to late. Destitution and disorganization had gone too far; high prices and lack of money put the long-expected food out of reach of the starving laborer. Ireland was ruined.

IRISH "BLACK FEVER"

Fever is a natural consequence of famine. The government was warned in the autumn of 1846 to expect an epidemic. It arrived at the end of March in the form of *typhus* and relapsing fever, filling the Irish with terror. Rickettsia, the microscopic organisms that cause typhoid, attack the small blood vessels, especially those of the skin and brain. With blood circulation impeded, the patient becomes all but unrecognizable as the face swells, and the skin becomes a dark, congested hue (giving typhus its Irish name of *black fever*). Temperature rises; in severe cases limbs twitch violently; patients rave in delirium, throwing themselves about, and as the fever becomes so intense some jump out of windows or into a river in search of cooling relief. Additional symptoms include vomiting, agonizing sores develop, sometimes gangrene causing the loss of fingers, toes, and feet. The odor from the typhus patient is almost intolerable. A medical officer of the Tralee jail where typhus was rampant wrote, "when the door was opened he was forcibly driven back by the smell."

Relapsing fever is transmitted by a louse which has swallowed blood containing the micro-organisms of the disease. Once infected, progress is rapid. High fever and vomiting begin within a few hours and continue for days. A crisis with profuse sweating follows, succeeded by extreme exhaustion. If the patient survives, the symptoms can be repeated three or four times before the fever leaves. It is often accompanied by jaundice. Observers in Cork in 1847 described victim's skin as "all gaunt, yellow, hideous."

OUTBREAKS OF DYSENTERY, DROPSY, AND SCURVY

Dysentery was also rampant. Bacillary dysentery, known as the *bloody flux* is caused by a group of bacilli conveyed in contaminated food and the excrement of infected humans and flies. The bacilli are swallowed with infected food or inhaled from excrement and multiply in the stomach and bowels. Inflamation, ulcers, and finally gangrene follow, with intense pain, diarrhea, violent straining, and the passing of clots of blood. It was easy to tell who had the disease by the clots of blood on the ground around their cabins.

Another appalling condition, now infectious, was *famine dropsy*.[4] William Bennett of the Society of Friends described it in March 1847 as "that horrid disease – the results of long continued famine and low living—in which the limbs and body swell most frightfully and finally burst." Scurvy, previously unknown because the potato provided the necessary vitamin C, was prevalent. Scurvy is painful and revolting. Gums become spongy, teeth fall out, joints are enlarged causing acute suffering. Boood vessels burst under the skin, especially on the legs. In its advanced state, legs turn black up to the middle of the thigh. The Irish called scurvy black leg.

By the spring of 1847 starvation had so reduced the people that Sidney Godolphin Osborne, later one of Florence Nightingale's helpers in the Crimea, wrote that "the skin had a peculiar appearance, rough and dry like parchment and hung in folds; eyes had sunk into the head, shoulder bones were so high the neck seemed to have sunk into the chest; faces were so wasted (they) looked like a skull; and there was an extraordinary pallor such as (he) had never seen before. The starving children were skeletons, many too far gone to walk… many had lost their voices." He never heard a child cry or moan from pain or shed a tear or a cry. Two, three, or four in a bed "lie and died, if suffering ever silent, unmoved."

IRISH WORKHOUSES

In March 1847, the Central Board of Health sent doctors to inspect and report on conditions of the workhouses of Cork, Bandon, Bantry, and Lurgan. They reported conditions in the Cork workhouse as "utterly wretched and deplorable, (with) a death taking place every hour." The workhouse was overcrowded, lacked ventilation, the drains were deficient, and the stench almost insupportable, even in cold weather. Bandon was without order and completely chaotic. One-hundred-and-two boys slept in 24 beds in a ward 25 by 30 feet, in some cases six to a bed; 700 slept and ate in the hall. There were 45 beds in the convalescent ward for 125 fever patients. The drains were "revolting" and "disgusting stench lasts all day."

The wards in the Bantry workhouse were clean and orderly, but "language would fail to give an adequate idea of (the) state of its fever hospital," the inspecting doctor said. "It was appalling, awful, heart sickening." He "did not think it possible to exist in a civilized and Christian community." Fever patients were "lying naked on straw, the living and the dead together. The doctor was ill and no one had been near the hospital for two days. There was no medicine, no drink, no fire; wretched beings were crying out, 'water, water' but there was no one to give it to them; the sole attendant was one pauper nurse, utterly unfit."

Conditions in Lurgan were equally horrible. The dead were buried four yards from the fever hospital and the hospital well was in the center of the burial ground. The Master had died, the Matron was ill; two of the doctors were down with typhus; everything had fallen into confusion; and the Board of Guardians did not seem to know anything except that the workhouse was overcrowded.

Deaths in the workhouses and in hospitals were only part of the total. Doctors who worked in Dublin through the epidemic wrote that vast numbers of poor remained at home and never thought of applying for hospital care. Many deaths were unrecorded because the horror of fever even conquered the bond of family affection. Parents deserted their children; children their parents. Neighbors, usually kind and generous, would not enter a cabin where fever was known to exist, and in lonely districts fever-stricken persons died without anyone coming near them, their bodies left to rot. Families buried relatives in fields and on hillsides, intending "to get church rites for the bones in better times." In Clifden, corpses were burned, in other districts they were buried under the cabin floor. In Leitrim, many were buried in ditches, unknown to anyone. The total of those who died during the fever epidemics and of famine diseases will never be known, but probably about 10 times more died of disease than of starvation.

THEY FLEE TO NORTH AMERICAN AND GREAT BRITIAN

Before the potato failure, to leave Ireland was regarded as the most terrible of all fates and transportation was the most dreaded of sentences.[5] But after the autumn and winter of 1846-47, terrified and desperate, they began to flee a land which seemed accursed. They crossed the ocean to Canada and the United States or the Irish Sea to Britain. About a million and a quarter went to North America; an even larger number to Great Britain, landing at Liverpool, Glasgow, and the ports of south Wales. Fever went with them and the path to a new life became a path of horror.

The vast majority who left in 1846 went to Canada despite their belief justice and opportunity would be denied them under the Union Jack. Some considered Canada an Ireland with more room. They believed the U. S. offered greater opportunity, a belief reinforced by the 1839 report of Lord Durham, Canadian High Commissioner and Governor General, who contrasted the two sides of the border as follows: "On the American side all is bustle and activity; on the British side, with the exception of a few favored spots, all seems waste and desolation. The ancient City of Montreal which is naturally the commercial capital of Canada, will not bear the least comparison with Buffalo, which is the creation of yesterday."

To offset the attractions of the U.S., the British made passage to Canada cheaper and gave free passage into the interior of those who declared their intentions of settling in Canada. The desire to populate Canada was not the only reason Britain encouraged Irish emigration. It wanted to prevent migration into England. In 1827, 18 years before the famine, a Parliamentary committee proposed low fares to their North American colonies so the mother country wouldn't be deluged "with poverty and wretchedness and equalize the state of the English and Irish peasantry." But cheaper passage didn't work. After reaching Canada, many walked across the border into the U.S.

The first immigrant ship arrived at Québec April 24, 1846. From early August until the ice closed the St. Lawrence river, an unprecedented number reached Québec. The 1847 flight, for the first time in history, began in the winter. Despite it being the most sever winter in living memory, about 30,000 landed in the U. S. An officer of the Society of Friends described emigrants boarding ships as "joyful at their escape, as from a doomed land." A landlord at Tervoe was begged by his tenants for assistance to emigrate as "the greatest blessing he could bestow."

Three-quarters of emigrants crossing the Atlantic sailed from Liverpool; 95 percent were Irish. As no passenger could board his vessel until the cargo had been loaded, the emigrant had to spend at least one, generally two or three nights, in the low Irish lodging houses of Liverpool. The squalor and filth of the houses was notorious and thousands who had escaped typhus infection in Ireland were infected before leaving Liverpool.

"COFFIN SHIPS"

More than 85,000 sailed directly from Irish ports: Sligo, Dublin, Baltimore, Ballina, Westport, Tralee, and Killala. Fewer left from Waterford because access to Liverpool was easier. Their wild desire to get out combined with utter ignorance of the sea and of geography, caused many to book ships that were overcrowded and which sailed without adequate provisions. Some were called "coffin ships."

A typical example of a coffin ship was the 330 ton barque *Elizabeth and Sarah* built in 1762. It sailed from Killala, County Mayo, in July 1847, arriving at Québec in September. The officer at Killala certified 212 passengers; she carried 276. She should have carried 12,532 gallons of water but only had 8,700 gallons in leaky casks. The law required seven pounds of provisions be given weekly to each passenger. No distribution was ever made. She had 36 berths, four for the crew, 32 shared by 276 passengers who otherwise slept on the deck. No sanitary convenience of any kind was provided and the state of the vessel was "horrible and disgusting beyond the power of language to describe." During the eight-week crossing, passengers starved and were tortured by thirst. 'Forty-two died. The ship broke down and was towed into the St. Lawrence by a steamer.

FEW EMIGRANTS HAD TECHNICAL SKILLS

Few Irish brought technical skills to their new home. They were not carpenters, butchers, green grocers, glaziers, masons, or tailors. For most, their knowledge was limited to the spade-culture of a patch of potatoes. They had to assimilate into American life as best they could. The majority drifted into unskilled, irregular, badly-paid work, cleaning yards and stables, unloading vehicles and ships, and pushing carts. The mass of under-paid casual labor produced the notorious Irish slums of the east coast of the United States. With rare exception, they were the most unfortunate and poorest of the immigrants. They took longer to be accepted, longer to become genuinely assimilated, and waited longer for the opportunities offered by the United States.

However, emigrants who left after the failure of 1848 were of a class Ireland could ill afford to lose. To deter immigration of the helpless and diseased, fares to Canada were raised so the small ruined farmer had to stay home. Farmers of substance, well provided for the journey, left for the U.S. Landlords offered to defer their rent for a year if they stayed. There

{ G 1666 }

were few takers.

Half of all Irish immigrants to the U.S. before, during, and after the famine disembarked at New York, a city of 630,000, half immigrants. Boston was the second most popular port. For mostly a rural people who had no cities until the Danes invaded, the Irish looked upon New York as "heaven's front parlor" and soon brought it a larger Irish population than Dublin. Their first view of New York was heavily wooded Staten Island and the spiral of Trinity Episcopal Church. Horse-drawn street cars moved up Fifth Avenue to 34th Street where "the sticks" began. Harlem was a country town. Right off, the immigrant was in for three disappointments. First, the streets weren't paved with gold. Second, they weren't paved at all. Third, he would be expected to pave them.

THE IRISH QUARTER

Upon arrival, the immigrant went straight to the Irish quarter, called "Irish town," "Paddy town," or "The Irish Channel," where he associated exclusively with his fellow-countrymen and had no contact with American culture or American ideas. His countrymen surrounded him in such numbers that his glimpses of American manners, morals, and religion were few and faint, wrote an American journalist. It was a hideous life and the way to forget was to drink. Whiskey dulled physical pain, disappointment, and bereavement. Birthdays, weddings, christenings, and national and political festivals were celebrated with whiskey. The words "Irishman" and "drunkard" became synonymous. A drunken, fighting, law-breaking man was the Irish image. Both united and isolated by clannishness, they were soon exploited by the political bosses. The vote of the naturalized Irishman was as good as the vote of any New England Yankee and his vote was bought with a glass of whiskey and jobs and favors handed out at political headquarters.

But the newcomers demonstrated incredible generosity and filial love by saving to bring brothers, sisters, aunts, uncles, and parents over to join them. In Ireland they were great hoarders of small coins, hiding coppers in thatched roofs or burying them in a field. Over here, their frugality became a banking legend. In the 15 years after the famine the Irish sent home $65 million in "Letters from America," as remittances were called. New York's Emigrant Industrial bank, founded in 1851 to protect the savings of Irish laborers, remitted $30 million to Ireland in its first three decades. "Such a beautiful story of unforgotten affection is unmatched in the world records of human attachment," said Robert Murray, an unsentimental Scot who was chief officer of the Provincial Bank on the receiving end in Ireland.

T. N. Redington, Under Secretary for Ireland and a Galway landlord, pronounced the famine over at the end of 1849. There were about a million destitute in the workhouses and on relief at the time. If you were Kerian Dolan and Patrick Darmody, do you think you would have stayed in Ireland?

SCOTT FAMILY ENDNOTES

1. through 4. Veronique Gassette to Blaine Whipple. Letters dated 1 & 12 Aug. 1985; 5 Nov. 1985; 4, 16 & 26 Jan. 1986; 25 Aug. 1986; 9 Nov. 1986 at 21 Heath St., S. Burlington, VT 05401. In possession of Whipple at 236 NW Sundown Way, Portland, OR 97229-6575 (1999). Her sources included the "Tanguay Dictionary;" "Dictionnaire Genealogique Des Familles Du Québec," Jette, 1983; "Supplement to Tanguay" by Leboeuf; "Repertoire of Marriages for Chambly;" "Repertoire of Marriages for Pontbriand;" Church Register for St. Joseph de Chambly; personal research at the Archives Nationales Du Québec Montreal). (Hereafter cited as Gassette to Whipple).
5. Printed Repertoire of Marriages for Chambly.
6. Gasette to Whipple. From a microfilm of the parish register of St. Joseph de Chambly, copy made at the Public Archives of Québec at the National Archives of Québec, 100 Notre Dame St., East, Montreal.
7. Gassette to Whipple.
8. through 12. The author has a copy of the contract, written in French, and an inventory of Lucie's property, which included three corsets., Marriages, Andre Scott & Lucie Truchon, Archives Nationales Du Québec Montreal. 6 May 1790.
13. through 15. Marriages, Andre Scott & Marie Ursule Trahant, Archives Nationales Du Québec Montreal. 22 April 1786, The contract is written in French. The author has a copy. For further information on the Canadian Scott and allied families, see Chambly entries on film #543-828 at the Family History Library, Salt Lake City, Utah; also Rev. Cyprien Tanguay, *Dictionnaire Genealogiques Des Familles Canadiennes*, a standard French-Canadian genealogical reference in seven volumes of over 600 pages each. Originally published in the nineteenth century.
16. Blaine Whipple, comp., *Scott, A Name Worth Looking Into, a history-genealogy of the Scott Family of Québec Province, Canada and Minnesota and allied lines*. The *"Tanguay Dictionary"* was the main source for the French Canadian information. Personal letters from the children of Ben and Nellie (Dolan) was the main source of information for those lines. Copies available at the Library of Congress, Minnesota Historical Society, and North Dakota Historical Society. The work has been updated by hand since publication. Sources of the updates are letters from various individuals involved who provide birth, marriage, death, and other pertinent information. (Portland, Oreg: Self published, 1981), 185 (hereafter cited as B. Whipple, *Scott Genealogy*).
17. Gassette to Whipple, *8 Letters*.
18. *Scott Genealogy*; and Joseph Scott, Death Certificate Death Record 1872, page 4, line 5, filed 4 Jan. 1873, State of Minnesota, County of Hennepin, Town of Corcoran, Minneapolis, Minn. (hereafter cited as Joseph Scott, *Death Certificate*).
19. *Scott Genealogy*.
20. R.J. Baldwin, "Corcoran," *History of Minneapolis and Hennepin County Minnesota*,

Vol. II, Munsell Publishing Co., New York and Chicago, 1895, 1341-2.
21. through 27. *Scott Genealogy*.
28. Naomi McGarry to Blaine Whipple. Letters dated 24 July 1981; 25 Sept. 1981; 28 Jan. 1982 at 3989 Wisconsin Ave. N., Minneapolis, MN 55427. In possession of Whipple at 236 NW Sundown Way, Portland, OR 97229-6575 (2004). Naomi McGarry has done extensive genealogical research on the family of her grandfather Joseph Scott, Jr. and his ancestors.).
29. through 38. *Scott Genealogy*.
39. Ibid. and Didace Scott, Death Certificate Reg. District No. 2892, No. l in Registration book, 169, filed 13 June 1929, Section of Vital Statistics Registration of the Minnesota Dept. of Health, Minneapolis, Minn. His date and names of parents are confirmed on his death record and was provided by his son Phillip.
40. Didace died at home of apoplexy at 1:30 p.m. His son Philip provided the information for his Certificate of Death. State of Minnesota Division of Vital Statistics, File 5/13, 1929, Chas. Stiehler, Registrar, Registration Book 169.
41. *Scott Genealogy*; and Angela (Hamel) Scott, Death Certificate Registration Book No. 29, filed 26 May 1915, Section of Vital Statistics Registration of the Minnesota Dept. of Health, Minneapolis, Minn. According to the death certificate, Angeline died at home. Information for the death certificate was provided by her sister Marguerite (Hamel) Pouliot. State of Minnesota Division of Vital Statistics, Registration Book 29.
42. through 57. Scott *Genealogy*.
58. Ibid.; and Benoni Scott, Death Certificate State File No. 5153; Registered No. 10, 8 Feb. 1935, Department of Health, State of North Dakota, 600 E. Boulevard Ave. Dept. 301, Bismarck, ND 58505-0200.
59. Scott *Genealogy*.
60. In a 1952 letter to the author, who was in the U. S. Navy during the Korean War, Nellie, his grandmother, closed with what she termed "a gift to me," an old Irish verse, that brought her solace during trying times:
May the road rise up to meet you,
May the wind be always at your back,
May the sunshine warm your faces,
And the rain fall softly upon your fields.
But until we meet again, may God forever
hold you in the palm of his hands.
61. and 62. Scott *Genealogy*.
63. Suzanne (LaGrandeur) Clayton to Blaine Whipple. Letter dated 4 Jan. 1993 at 28 Callingham Rd., Pittsford, NY 14534. In possession of Whipple at 236 NW Sundown Way, Portland, OR 97229-6575 (2004).
64. through 130. Scott *Genealogy*.

FORT CHAMBLY ENDNOTES

1. A relative of the author, Brig. General William Whipple was one of the American negotiators of the surrender of Gen. Burgoyne's Army following the Battle of Saratoga. He also signed the Declaration of Independence for New Hampshire.
2. The author visited Chambly, the St. Joseph de Chambly Church, and the Fort in the summer of 2003.
3. Joseph E. Lemire, "The Emigration from Québec," *Je Me Souviens*. Woonsocket, RI: A

{ G 1669 }

Publication of the American-French Genealogical Society, vol. 25, No. 2, Autumn 2002. 37.
4. Lemire 41.

HAMEL FAMILY ENDNOTES

1. Brother Jean-Ernest (Adrien Hamel, compiler), *Genealogie de la Famille Hamel 1656-1950*, Maison Provinciale Freres Maristes, Iberville, Province of Québec, Canada,. (Hereafter *Hamel Genealogy.*) The Hamel Genealogy lists over 10,000 descendants of Jean and Charles Hamel.
2. Hamel means hamlet or small village. It comes from the Saxon word "ham" borrowed from the Hebrew meaning small group of people. The name has been known in France for at least seven centuries and today the small French town of Hamel (about 500 inhabitants) is in the Department of the Somme, between Corbie and Amiens.
3. *Hotel Dieu Register of the Sick* 3 Sept. 1689.
4. Hamel *Genealogy* 17.
5. *Ibid.*, 17.
6. Thomas J. Laforest, *Our French Canadian Ancestors,* Vol. 5. Palm Harbor, Fla.: LISI Press, 1987, 82. (Hereafter *French Canadians.*)
7. *Ibid.*, 12-15.
8. *Ibid.*
9. Arpen—a former French unit of area equal to 0.85 acre.
10. S. J.—Society of Jesus, Jesuits.
11. Seigneury—a landed estate held in Canada by feudal tenure until 1854.
12. *French, Canadians* 12-15.
13. *French, Canadians* 8:171.
14. Hamel, *Genealogy* 9-12.
15. Blaine Whipple, comp., *Scott, A Name Worth Looking Into, a History-Genealogy of the Scott Family of Québec Province, Canada and Minnesota and Allied Lines.* The "Tanguay Dictionary" was the main source for the French Canadian information. Personal letters from the children of Ben and Nellie (Dolan) Scott were the main source of information for those lines. Copies available at the Library of Congress, Minnesota Historical Society, and North Dakota Historical Society. The work has been updated by hand since publication. Sources of the updates are letters from various individuals involved who provide birth, marriage, death, and other pertinent information. Portland, OR: Self published, 1981, 189. (Hereafter *Scott Genealogy*).
16. Livre—a French money of account, afterwards a silver coin equal to 20 sous until 1794. Sous—a French coin of low value later used to designate the five-centine piece; the smallest amount of money.
17. Dit—a dit name was an extension to an existing name and became a part of the original basic name. The custom of having *dit* names began with nobles and kings and was used to establish positive identity. Use of *dit* names came into common usage in France in the late 1500. Families of 14, 16, and 18 children were not uncommon and produced unreasonable numbers of duplicate names. It created a problem of proper identification for authorities. Judges, police chiefs, priests, and others in authority had to know definitely whom they were dealing with so the use of *dit* names came into common usage. The assigned *dit* name usually represented an attribute of the person. Romain Becquet, a huge man, was given the *dit* name of La Montagne (the moun-

tain man) and became Romain Becquet dit Lamontagne. When the number of children decreased, *dit* names were no longer needed.
18. Pistole—Any of several gold coins used in various European counties until the late 19th century.
19. *Marriage Contract 11 Nov. 1697, Registry Duquet.*
20. Hamel *Genealogy.*
21. *French, Canadians.*
22. *French, Canadians* 8:172-3.
23. French, *Canadians* 5:85.
24. through 26. *Ibid.*, 5:85.
27. Hamel, *Genealogy.*
28. *Dictionnaire Tanguay* (Premier dictionnaire francophone d'amerique, il a ete publie a partir de 1891. 8 volumes il couvre des origines jusqu'en 1800), 1:256. (Hereafter Tanguay, *Dictionary*).
29. Ursuline Sisters—the first order of religious women to serve in North America. They arrived in Québec, Canada in 1639. Founded by Angela Merici in Italy, they were committed not only to prayer but also to action where there was a need. At the time of their formation, only the rich had the luxury of education so the Ursuline Sisters took teaching as their special mission. Today there are about 2,700 Ursuline sisters in North America serving from Alaska to Tabasco, Mexico and from Maine to California. They lead retreats, assist in prisons, teach at every level from elementary school to college. They are also artists and musicians.
30. Hamel *Genealogy.*
31. French, *Canadians.*
32. through 34. *Ibid.*, 11:67.
35. *Scott Genealogy* 189.
36. French, *Canadians* 8:172.
37. French *Canadian* 5:84-85.
38. Hamel, *Genealogy.*
39. French, *Canadians* 11:67.
40. Hamel, *Genealogy.*
41. through 46. *Scott Genealogy* 188.
47. *Ibid.* and Lange Hamel, Death Certificate Death Record 1887, page 56, line 1, filed 11 Jan. 1888, State of Minnesota, County of Hennepin, Town of Medina, St. Paul, Minn.
48. *Scott Genealogy*, 124; and Eugenie (Moffett) Hamel, Death Certificate Death Record of 1874, page 47, line 5, filed 12 Jan. 1875, State of Minnesota, County of Hennepin, Town of Medina, Minneapolis, Minn.
49. Eugenie's Certificate of Death states that she arrived in Minnesota in August 1856, was born in Canada, and died of apoplexy (stroke).
50. Hennepin Co. Certificate of Death Record; certified by the Director of Licensing in Death Record 1887, p. 56, l. 1.
51. Hamel, *Genealogy* 119.
52. *Ibid.* 118.
53. *Scott Genealogy* 124.
54. *Ibid.*
55. Hamel, *Genealogy* 118.
56. through 58. *Ibid.*
59. *Scott Genealogy* 124.
60. Hamel, *Genealogy* 119.
61. *Scott Genealogy* 124.

{ G 1671 }

62. *Ibid.* 119.
63. *Scott Genealogy.*
64. Hamel, *Genealogy* 119.
65. *Scott Genealogy.*
66. *Ibid.*; and Angela (Hamel) Scott, Death Certificatae Registration Book No. 29, filed 26 May 1915, Section of Vital Statistics Registration of the Minnesota Dept. of Health, Minneapolis, Minn. Her death certificate confirms her date of birth and the names of her parents.
67. *Ibid.*; and Didace Scott, Death Certificate Reg. District No. 2892, No. 1 in Registration Book, 169, filed 13 June 1929, Section of Vital Statistics Registration of the Minnesota Dept. of Health, Minneapolis, Minn.
68. His date and names of parents are confirmed on his death record provided by his son Phillip.
69. *Ibid.* and Benoni Scott, Death Certificate State File No. 5153, Registered No. 10, 8 Feb. 1935, Department of Health, State of North Dakota, 600E Boulevard Ave. Dept. 301, Bismarck, N. Dak. 58505-0200.

TRUDEAU FAMILY ENDNOTES

1. P. Archange Godbout, O.F.M. Fondateur, (Premier President et membre emerite de la Societe Genealogique Canadienne-francaise, *Les Passagers Du Saint-Andre La Recrue de 1659*, Publication No. 5 (Montreal: Publications de la Societe Genealogique Canadienne-Francaise, 1964), 131-2. (Hereafter Saint-Andre, *Voyage to Canada*).
2. Blaine Whipple, comp., *Scott, A Name Worth Looking Into, a history-genealogy of the Scott Family of Québec Province, Canada and Minnesota and allied lines. The "Tanguay Dictionary"* was the main source for the French Canadian information. Personal letters from the children of Ben and Nellie (Dolan) was the main source of information for those lines. Copies available at the Library of Congress, Minnesota Historical Society, and North Dakota Historical Society. The work has been updated by hand since publication. Sources of the updates are letters from various individuals involved who provided birth, marriage, death, and other pertinent information. (Portland, OR: Self published, 1981). (Hereafter Scott *Genealogy*).
3. through 15. Saint-Andre, *Voyage to Canada*, 132.
16. *Ibid.*, 132-3; and *Dictionnaire Tanguay* (Premier dictionnaire francophone d'amerique, il a ete publie a partir de 1891. 8 volumes il couvre des origines jusqu'en 1800), 1:575-6. (Hereafter Tanguay, *Dictionary*).
17. Saint-Andre, *Voyage to Canada*, 132-3; and Tanguay, *Dictionary*, 1:24.
18. See the following for biographies on Prime Minister Pierre Trudeau: T. Butson, *Pierre Trudeau* (1986); Richard Gwyn, *The Northern Magus* (1980); G. Radwanski, *Trudeau* (1978).
19. Sulpician – one of an order of priests established in France in 1642 to educate men for the ministry. Soon afterwards it was introduced in Canada and into the United States in 1791.
20. Thomas J. LaForest *Our French Canadian Ancestors*, vol. 1 Palm Harbor, Fla.: LISI Press, 1993, 239-48. (Hereafter French, *Canadians*.)
21. Thomas J. LaForest., *Our French Canadian Ancestors* (Palm Harbor, FL: LISI Press, 1993), 242.; and Tanguay, *Dictionary*, 1:575.
22. Saint-Andre, *Voyage to Canada*, 133; French, *Canadians*, 242; and Tanguay, *Dictionary*, 1:575.

23. Saint-Andre, *Voyage to Canada*, 132.
24. French, *Canadians*, 242; and Tanguay, *Dictionary*, 1:575.
25. French, *Canadians*, 242.
26. Records of Notary Antoine Adhemar of Montreal.
27. Saint-Andre, *Voyage to Canada*, 133; French, *Canadians*, 242; and Tanguay, *Dictionary*, 1:575.
28. Saint-Andre, *Voyage to Canada*, 133; and Tanguay, *Dictionary*, 1:575.
29. Saint-Andre, *Voyage to Canada*, 133; and French, *Canadians*, 242.
30. For further information about Jean-Baptiste, who was a Blacksmith, see the records of Notaries Antoine Adhemar and Hodiesne. The archives of both Notaries are in the Court House in Montreal.
31. Saint-Andre, *Voyage to Canada*, 133; French, *Canadians*, 242; and Tanguay, *Dictionary*, 1:575.
32. Saint-Andre, *Voyage to Canada*, 133; and French, *Canadians*, 242.
33. Saint-Andre, *Voyage to Canada*, 133; French, *Canadians*, 243; and Tanguay, *Dictionary*, 1:575.
34. Saint-Andre, *Voyage to Canada*, 133; and French, *Canadians*, 243.
35. and 36. Saint-Andre, *Voyage to Canada*, 133.
37. *Ibid.*, 133; and French, *Canadians*, 243.
38. Saint-Andre, *Voyage to Canada*, 133; and French, *Canadians*, 243.
39. Saint-Andre, *Voyage to Canada*, 133; French, *Canadians*, 243; and Tanguay, *Dictionary*, 1:575.
40. Saint-Andre, *Voyage to Canada*, 132-3; French, *Canadians*, 241; and Tanguay, *Dictionary*, 1:575.
41. Saint-Andre, *Voyage to Canada*, 132-3; and French, *Canadians*, 241.
42. Tanguay, *Dictionary*, 1:576. The marriage contract, made by Antaine at Adhemar, is dated 22 November 1699 in Montreal.
43. *Ibid.*, 1:576.
44. Saint-Andre, *Voyage to Canada*, 133; Tanguay, *Dictionary*, 1:575; and French, *Canadians*, 242. Their wedding date is also given as 10 November.
45. The service contracts are in the records of Notary Antoine Adhemar in Montreal.
46. Tanguay, *Dictionary*, 1:576.
47. through 49. *Ibid.*, 1:576.
50. Saint-Andre, *Voyage to Canada*, 132-3; French, *Canadians*, 242-3; and Tanguay, *Dictionary*, 1:575.
51. French, *Canadians*, 242-3; and Tanguay, *Dictionary*, 1:396.
52. Saint-Andre, *Voyage to Canada*, 133; French, *Canadians*, 243; and Tanguay, *Dictionary*, 1:575.
53. Saint-Andre, *Voyage to Canada*, 133; and French, *Canadians*, 243.
54. Saint-Andre, *Voyage to Canada*, 133.
55. Brother Adrien Hamel to Blaine Whipple. Letter dated 14 Aug. 1984 at Freres Maristes, Iverville, P.Q., Canada J2X 4J3. In possession of Whipple (2005). (Hereafter Hamel to Whipple, *Letter, 14 Aug. 1984*); and Tanguay, *Dictionary*, 1:576.
56. Scott *Genealogy*.
57. through 69. *Ibid.*, 185.
70. Hamel to Whipple, *Letter, 14 Aug. 1984*.
71. through 73. Scott *Genealogy*.
74. Hamel to Whipple, *Letter, 14 Aug. 1984*.
75. Scott *Genealogy*.
76. through 78. Hamel to Whipple, *Letter, 14 Aug. 1984*.

MONTY FAMILY ENDNOTES

1. Blaine Whipple, comp., *Scott, A Name Worth Looking Into*, a history-genealogy of the Scott Family of Québec Province, Canada and Minnesota and allied lines. The "Tanguay Dictionary" was the main source for the French Canadian information. Personal letters from the children of Ben and Nellie (Dolan) was the main source of information for those lines. Copies available at the Library of Congress, Minnesota Historical Society, and North Dakota Historical Society. The work has been updated by hand since publication. Sources of the updates are letters from various individuals involved who provided birth, marriage, death, and other pertinent information. (Portland, OR: Self published, 1981). (Hereafter Scott *Genealogy*).
2. *Dictionnaire Tanguay* (Premier dictionnaire francophone d'amerique, il a ete publie a partir de 1891. 8 volumes il couvre des origines jusqu'en 1800), 6:78. (Hereafter Tanguay, *Dictionary*).
3. *Ibid.*, 6:78, 439.
4. through 18. *Ibid.*, 6:78.
19. Scott *Genealogy*; and Tanguay, *Dictionary*, 6:78.
20. Tanguay, *Dictionary*, 6:78, 354.
21. through 24. Scott *Genealogy*.
25. *Ibid.*; and Joseph Scott, Death Certificate Death Record 1872, page 4, line 5, filed 4 Jan. 1873, State of Minnesota, County of Hennepin, Town of Corcoran, Minneapolis, Minn.

DOLAN FAMILY ENDNOTES

1. Blaine Whipple, comp., *Scott, A Name Worth Looking Into*, a history-genealogy of the Scott Family of Québec Province, Canada and Minnesota and allied lines. The "Tanguay Dictionary" was the main source for the French Canadian information. Personal letters from the children of Ben and Nellie (Dolan) was the main source of information for those lines. Copies available at the Library of Congress, Minnesota Historical Society, and North Dakota Historical Society. The work has been updated by hand since publication. Sources of the updates are letters from various individuals involved who provided birth, marriage, death, and other pertinent information. (Portland, OR: Self published, 1981), 138. (Hereafter Scott *Genealogy*);
2. Scott *Genealogy*.
3. Scott *Genealogy*. Some U.S. census reports give Margaret's birth state as New York, other as Rhode Island.
4. Kerian Dolan entry; SS De Witt Clinton Passenger Manifest, 15 Oct. 1849, p. 1, line 1; *Passenger Lists of Vessels arriving at New York, 15 Oct. 1849*; Micropublication M237, roll 84; National Archives. Washington, D. C.
5. Brian Mitchell, *Pocket Guide to Irish Genealogy*. Baltimore, Md.: Clearfield Co., 1991, 6.
6. Obituary of Kerian Dolan, *Minneapolis Journal*, Minneapolis, Minn. (18 Sept. 1907), p. 16. col. 2.
7. United States of America to Kerian Dolan, Sale of Land, Homestead Certificate No. 1675, Application 2050 (it may be 2450 or 2950), 160-acre homestead, Vol. 245: 372. Bureau of Land Management - Eastern states, 7450 Boston Blvd., Springfield, Va. 22153.
8. through 11. Scott *Genealogy*.

12. and 13. *Ibid.*, 138.
14. Elizabeth Dolan, Baptismal entry, 26 November 1876, "Registers of St. Vincent de Paul Catholic Church, Osseo, Minn." Page 34.
15. Scott *Genealogy*.
16. Anna Dolan, Baptismal entry, 30 Dec. 1878, "Register of St. Vincent de Paul Catholic Church, Osseo, Minn." Page 69.
17. *Church Registers* St. Vincent de Paul Catholic Church, Osseo, Minn., 12.
18. Scott *Genealogy*.
19. Bernard Dolan, Baptismal entry, 6 May 1880, "Register of St. Vincent de Paul Catholic Church, Osseo, Minn." Page 84.
20. and 21. Scott *Genealogy*.
22. Ibid.; and St. Vincent de Paul Catholic Church, *Church Registers*, Osseo, Minn.
23. The author and his brother and sisters met Thomas at his home in Minneapolis in the spring of 1943. They were traveling by train from Watford City, North Dakota to Viroqua, Wisconsin with a stopover in Minneapolis. He was frail, had difficulty walking, and seemed interested in finally meeting his five great grandchildren who ranged in age from 5 to to 14. He died about a month later.
24. through 29. Scott Genealogy.
30. through 33. *Ibid.*, 136.

DARMODY FAMILY ENDNOTES

1. Blaine Whipple, comp., *Scott, A Name Worth Looking Into, a history-genealogy of the Scott Family of Québec Province, Canada and Minnesota and allied lines. The "Tanguay Dictionary"* was the main source for the French Canadian information. Personal letters from the children of Ben and Nellie (Dolan) was the main source of information for those lines. Copies available at the Library of Congress, Minnesota Historical Society, and North Dakota Historical Society. The work has been updated by hand since publication. Sources of the updates are letters from various individuals involved who provided birth, marriage, death, and other pertinent information. (Portland, OR: Self published, 1981), 141. (Hereafter Scott *Genealogy*);
2. Scott *Genealogy*, 141. The possibility of the surname Davery is suggested by the fact that Patrick Darmody and Helen Davery were godparents of Anna Dolan, daughter of Kerian Dolan and Margaret Rourke.
3. *Alert* passenger manifest 20 May 1850 p. 2, l. 28. Micro publication M237 roll 88. National Archives, Washington. D.C.
4. through 7. Scott *Genealogy* 141.
8. Philip Darmody, Baptismal entry, 27 March 1865, "Registers of St. Vincent de Paul Catholic Church, Osseo, Minn.," Page 163.
9. Scott *Genealogy*, 141.
10. Bridget Darmody, Baptismal entry, 1 May 1867, "Registers of St. Vincent de Paul Catholic Church, Osseo, Minn.," Page 166.
11. Scott *Genealogy*.
12. *Ibid.*; and St. Vincent de Paul Catholic Church., *Church Registers*, Osseo, Minn.*Marriage Record*.
13. through 16. Scott *Genealogy*.

{ G 1675 }

17. through 20. Scott *Genealogy* 136.
21. *Ibid*.; and Benoni Scott, Death Certificate State File No. 5153; Registered No. 10, 8 Feb. 1935, Department of Health, State of North Dakota, 600 E. Boulevard Ave. Dept. 301, Bismarck, ND 58505-0200.

WHY KERIAN DOLAN AND PATRICK DARMODY LEFT THE EMERAL ISLE ENDNOTES

1. An article similar to this written by the author, was published under the title "Why They Left the Emerald Isle," in *Heritage Quest The Genealogy Magazine*, Issue 72, November/December 1997. Heritage Quest, 593 West 100 North, PO Box 329, Bountiful, Utah 84011-0329.
2. England received a report in 1844 that a previously unknown disease had attacked the potato crop in North America.
3. The Irish Poor Law was passed in 1838 and was to be funded by a tax on Irish property. Its author, George Nicholls, said its purpose was two-fold: mitigating the suffering of the Irish poor and prevent them from coming to England in search of a living.
4. "Famine dropsy" has no connection with the condition normally termed dropsy. It is produced by starvation in its last stages and is medically known as hunger edema.
5. A "sentence of transportation" was to be transported out of Ireland for committing a crime. By 1848, teenagers were courting transportation as a means to escape the country. One youth, asked if he knew what transportation meant, said even if he had chains on his legs he would have something to eat; anything was better than starving and sleeping out at night

APPENDIX G-6

JOSEPH DROTZMAN 1861 TO JARED DANIEL DROTZMAN 1988-

(Drotzman lineage of Edwin Leoy Drotzman, Generation 12, No. 6208, husband of Patricia Ellen Whipple.)

FIRST GENERATION

1. **Joseph**[1] **Drotzman**[1] was born 6 August 1861 and died 16 December 1935 in Yankton, Yankton Co., South Dakota, at 74 years of age. He married Julia (__) who was born 13 August 1871 and died 14 October 1953 in Yankton, at 82 years of age.[2]

Joseph Drotzman and **Julia (__)** had the following children born in Yankton:

	2	i.	Hattie[2] **Drotzman**.[3]
	3	ii.	Dovie **Drotzman**.[4]
	4	iii.	Edna **Drotzman**.[5]
	5	iv.	William **Drotzman**.[6]
+	6	v.	Edward **Drotzman** 18 August 1898.

SECOND GENERATION

6. **Edward**[2] **Drotzman** (Joseph[1])[7] was born in Yankton, Yankton Co., South Dakota 18 August 1898 and died there 16 December 1952, at 54 years of age. He married **Lucy Lanke** there 11 July 1921. Lucy was born in Prairie Du Chien, Crawford Co., Wisconsin 16 February 1900 and died 26 August 1973 in Yankton, at 73 years of age.[8]

Edward **Drotzman** and Lucy **Lanke** had the following children born in Yankton:

	7	i.	Geraldine[3] **Drotzman**[9] 20 June 1922 and died 10 June 1971 in Sommerset, Saint Croix Co., Wisconsin, at 48 years of age. She married Paul **Jahnke** in Yankton 13 September 1961. Paul was born in 1907 and died in 1975 in Osceloa, Polk Co., Wisconsin, at 68 years of age.[10] Both are buried at Farmington West, Jefferson Co., Wisconsin.
+	8	ii.	Lorraine **Drotzman** 7 June 1924.

{ G 1677 }

+ 9 iii. Edwin LeRoy **Drotzman** 1 April 1926.
+ 10 iv. Rodney **Drotzman** 3 November 1927.

THIRD GENERATION

8. **Lorraine**[3] **Drotzman** (Edward[2], Joseph[1])[11] was born in Yankton, Yankton Co., South Dakota 7 June 1924 and died 16 April 1992 in Pomona, Los Angeles Co., California, at 67 years of age. She married **Kenneth Modereger** in Yankton 12 July 1947. Kenneth was born in Yankton 1 December 1924.[12]

Lorraine **Drotzman** and Kenneth **Modereger** had the following children born in Yankton:

11 i. Edward Joseph[4] **Modereger**[13] 27 March 1949.
12 ii. Robert Allen **Modereger**[14] 23 March 1951.
13 iii. William M. **Modereger**[15] 12 June 1954.
14 iv. Mary Louise **Modereger**[16] 31 December 1957.

9. **Edwin LeRoy**[3] **Drotzman** (Edward[2], Joseph[1])[17] was born in Yankton, Yankton Co., South Dakota 1 April 1926 and died 7 June 1964 in Sioux Falls, South Dakota, at 38 years of age. Buried in Sacred Heart Cemetery, Yankton. He married **Patricia Ellen Whipple** in Yankton 18 June 1951. Pat was born in Des Moines, Polk Co., Iowa 1 February 1929. Following graduation from Yankton High School, Eddie joined the Marines and received his recruit training at Camp Pendleton near San Diego, California. During training it was drummed into the recruits how fiendish the Japanese were. They were told about the Bataan death march, the kamikaze pilots crashing into our ships, that the Japanese would never surrender. Following training he was assigned to the 6th Marine Division and shipped to the Pacific Theater

Eddie as a newly recruited 19-year-old Marine in 1945.

Pat, High School graduation, Redfield, S. Dak. high school, 1946.

where he was wounded during the Battle of Okinawa which was the largest amphibious invasion of the Pacific campaign and the last major campaign and bloodiest battle of the Pacific War. The importance of Okinawa, largest of the Ryukyu island chain, is that it is only 375 miles from the Japanese home island of Kyushu. Capturing it would lead to the invasion of the Japanese mainland.

Evidence that The United States intended to win the battle is the 300 warships, 1,139 other ships involved and that 60,000 military personnel (two Marine and two Army Divisions) landed at Hagushi Bay April 1, 1945, the first day of the battle. Of these numbers, 34 allied ships and craft of all types were sunk, mostly by kamikazes, 368 ships and craft damaged, 763 Navy aircraft lost, 5,000 Navy and almost 8,000 Marine and Army dead, and 36,000 wounded. Combat stress also caused large numbers of psychiatric casualties and there were more than 26,000 non-battle casualties during this 82-day campaign. The cost of this battle played a major role in the decision to use the atomic bomb against Japan just six weeks later. Projecting the casualties at Okinawa indicated one million deaths for the planned invasion of Japan and American leaders agreed they could not sacrifice so many lives.

Pat. 15 August 2004.

April 1 began and ended with the heaviest concentration of naval gunfire ever to support an amphibious landing. Ten battleships, 9 cruisers, 23 destroyers and destroyer escorts and 117 rocket gunboats fired 3,800 tons of shells on Okinawa during the first 24 hours. During this "storm of steel," 16,000 troops of the 7th and 96th Infantry Divisions of the XXIV Corps and the 1st and 6th Marine Divisions of the III Amphibious Corps landed on the beaches in the first hour.

Leading the powerful Japanese 32nd Army were three men from the Samurai elite. General Mitsuru Ushijima was the main Commander, Lieutenant General Isamu Cho was Chief-of-Staff, and Colonel Hiromichi Yahara was the Chief Planning Officer. They planned a war of attrition based on a defensive strategy rather than an all-out attack and built a system of defense, especially in the southern portion of the island where their 100,000 soldiers could put the attacking forces and naval armada at risk. Ushijima turned Okinawa into an ocean fortress by digging elaborate networks of tunnels connected to strategically located artillery. He stored enough water and essential supplies to last an extended period. His plan was to lure the invaders inland by allowing unopposed landing and then overpower them. This was in marked contrast to previous battles of fighting the enemy landing on their beaches and wasting soldiers, resources and time. They also had The Divine Wind, the suicide force of hundreds *kamikaze* bombers and naval vessels. Despite the heroism of the suicide pilots, the *kamikaze* missions failed.

The Allied battle strategy included four phases: 1) advance to the eastern coast, April 1-4. 2) clear the northern part of the island, April 4-18. 3) occupy the outlying islands, April 10 - June 26. 4) the main battle against 32nd Army which began April 6 and ended June 21. Only mild opposition was encountered during phases 1-3 but phase 4 was extremely difficult because the Japanese were well entrenched and Allied naval shelling did not penetrate their tunneled fortifications.

Hundreds of kamikaze aircraft called *kikusui* - *"floating chrysanthemum"* for the Imperial symbol of Japan - began attacking the allied fleet April 6. By the end of the campaign 1,465 *kamikaze* flights had sunk 30 American ships and damaged 164 others. The battleship *Yamato*, the largest warship

Pat with her grandchildren. L to R: Jared Drotzman, Jessica Hammer with great grandson Logan, Laura, Jason and Jacob Drotzman at Yankton 15 August 2005. Photo courtesy of Michael J. Drotzman

{ G 1680 }

ever built, accompanied by the light cruiser *Yahagi* and eight destroyers left for Okinawa April 6 with no protective air-power. American carrier-based bombers were launched at 10 a.m. April 7 and for the next two hours the Japanese force was under constant attack. *Yamato* was hit by 12 bombs and seven torpedoes before blowing up and sinking. *Yahagi* was hit by bombs and went dead in the water. The destroyer *Hamakaze* was sunk with a bomb and torpedo hit. Three destroyers were so badly damaged they had to be scuttled. Four other destroyers could not return to Japan. Only 23 officers and 246 enlisted men of the *Yamato's* crew of 2,747 survived. The cruiser lost 446 and the destroyers 720 men. American losses were 10 planes and 12 men. This was the last Japanese naval action of the war.

The death of their Commander-in-Chief, President Franklin D. Roosevelt, was announced on April 12 and by April 19, soldiers and marines were in a fierce battle along the fortified outer ring of the Shuri Line. The Shuri defenses were deeply dug into the limestone cliffs and included artillery of various calibers. American losses grew as soldiers and marines assaulted defensive points on the line with the deceptive names of Sugar Loaf, Chocolate Drop, Conical Hill, Strawberry Hill, and Sugar Hill. But the troops rejoiced when the May 8 news announced the surrender of Nazi Germany.

Eddie was pulled from the front lines May 12 after 41 days of fighting for medical treatment due to battle fatigue. By then monsoon rains had turned contested slopes and roads into a morass which impacted both the tactical and medical situations. Troops were mired in mud and flooded roads inhibited evacuation of wounded to the rear. They lived on fields sodden by rain, part garbage dump and part graveyard.

By May 23, the Allied forces had put so much pressure on the Shuri Line that the Japanese fell back to the Kiykamu Peninsula, their final defensive position, leaving rear guard troops to slow the American advance. Private Drotzman, 19, was severely wounded May 27 by shell fragments in his head, arms, and legs and was awarded the Purple Heart Medal for wounds received in action. He was transferred to the United States June 28 and assigned to the U. S. Naval Hospital at Memphis, Tennessee to recuperate. Navy doctors were never able to remove all the shrapnel from his body and they placed a steel plate in the forepart of his skull. After almost a year at the hospital, he was discharged 24 May 1946, age 20, and returned to Yankton. An autopsy following his death 18 years later showed his body was full of cancer believed to have been stimulated by the shell fragments that remained in his body.

The 82-day battle for Okinawa was the worst fighting of the Pacific war, surpassing the brutal combats of Tarawa, Peleliu, and Iwo Jima. By the time all organized fighting ceased June 21, more than 107,000 Japanese soldiers were killed; 23,764 were sealed in caves or buried by the Japanese; 10,755 were captured or surrendered; and there were at least 42,000 and maybe as many as 142,000 civilian casualties. Suicide was the choice of many during the final days. Rather than surrender, which meant disgrace for both the men and their families, many Japanese soldiers held grenades against their stomachs. Generals Ushijima and Cho committed ceremonial *hara kiri* (suicide) on the last day. General Yahara escaped to Tokyo.

Okinawa made Japan a defeated and demoralized nation. The Imperial Army was destroyed, the Navy crippled, and all vital supply lines eliminated. After Hiroshima and Nagasaki, Emperor Hirohito accepted unconditional surrender and the war ended on August 15, 1945.

Edwin LeRoy **Drotzman** and Patricia Ellen **Whipple** had the following children born in Yankton:

+   15   i.   Michael James[4] **Drotzman**[6] August 1952.
+   16   ii.   Larry Joseph **Drotzman**[2] September 1955.
      17   iii.   Brian Scott **Drotzman**[18] 2 February 1958 and married Theresa Ann **Novak** there 19 April 2000 Theresa,[19] daughter of Robert Joe **Novak** and Agnes Irene **Nehonsky,** was born in Tyndall, Bon Homme Co., South Dakota 19 April 1966. She married (1) Larry J. **Schieffer** in Tabor,

Jason and Laura Drotzman with their uncle Brian Drotzman, 14 May 2005, Sioux Falls, SD. Photo courtesy of Michael J. Drotzman.

Bon Homme Co. 12 July 1986. They were divorced 11 August 1993. Alicia **Schieffer,** her daughter, lives with Brian and Theresa.

18 iv. Daniel Lee **Drotzman**[20] 18 November 1960. After graduating from Yankton High School, Dan spent an academic year at Montana State University at Bozeman, Gallatin Co. transferring to St. Cloud State University at St. Cloud, Stearns Co., Minnesota where he earned a BA in 1984. He was an active member of Delta Sigma Phi Fraternity and President of the Greek Council (Governing Board of all campus fraternal organizations). He was also a student Senator and Chief Justice of the Student Senate Judicial Council. Dan's work career began as an Employment Counselor in Minneapolis where he placed individuals in management positions with leading companies throughout the U.S. This was followed by a five-year stint with the BIC Corporation with assignments at Minneapolis, Hennepin Co., Minnesota, Houston, Harris Co., Texas, and Seattle, King Co., Washington. At the time of his resignation, he was Sales Manager of the Commercial Products Division for the Western U.S. with an annual volume in excess of $30 million. Following BIC he was Membership Manager for the United States Chamber of Commerce as liaison between the Washington, D.C. office and Chamber organizations in Montana, Wyoming, South Dakota, Minnesota, Wisconsin, and Nebraska. He left this job to found Porcupine Productions, Inc., (a Minnesota corporation) the marketing and distribution arm of Lotto Greetings. In 2001, he became a senior recruiter for TPI, a Minneapolis computer consulting firm with operations world wide.

Brian Drotzman, November 1972. Photo courtesy of Blaine Whipple.

Brian in Yankton 2004. Photo courtesy of Michael J. Drotzman.

Dan Drotzman, November 1972. Photo courtesy of Blaine Whipple.

{ G 1683 }

10. **Rodney**[3] **Drotzman** (Edward[2], Joseph[1])[21] was born in Yankton, Yankton Co., South Dakota 3 November 1927 and died 14 January 1981 in Sioux Falls, Minnehaha Co., South Dakota, at 53 years of age. Buried in Yankton. He married **Betty Ann Gobel** in Yankton 19 October 1954. She was born 18 September 1933.[22]

Rodney **Drotzman** and Betty Ann **Gobel** had the following children born in Yankton:
- + 19 i. James Kenneth[4] **Drotzman**[25] July 1955.
- + 20 ii. Kay Ann **Drotzman**[13] November 1956.
- + 21 iii. Karen **Drotzman**[29] December 1957.

FOURTH GENERATION

15. **Michael James**[4] **Drotzman** (Edwin LeRoy[3], Edward[2], Joseph[1])[23] was born in Yankton, Yankton Co., South Dakota 6 August 1952 and married **Ruth Ann Remund** in Appleton, Swift Co., Minnesota 18 October 1978. Ruth,[24] daughter of Lester Lyle **Remund** and Myrna Vynette **King**, was born in Graceville, Big Stone Co., Minnesota 1 March 1960. Mike joined the inactive Naval reserve in Sioux Falls, Minnehaha Co., South Dakota in March 1970 and was graduated from Yankton High School in May. By August he was at Boot Camp at the Naval Training Center in San Diego, California. Following Boot Camp he completed a Data Processing course at the San Diego Service School Command and then was assigned to the *USS Oriskany* CVA 34, an attack aircraft carrier, at its home port of Alameda, California. Between May 1971 and May 1974, the ship was on patrol in the western Pacific. In May 1974 Mike

Mike and Ruth Drotzman at Jessica Drotzman and Eric Hammer's wedding, Sioux Falls, 14 May 2005. Photo courtesy of Michael J. Drotzman.

joined the fleet Combat Training Center Atlantic in Dam Neck, Virginia. He was assigned to the Tactical Support Center Training. From there he was assigned to Commander Patrol Wing 5 in Brunswick, Maine then to more training in Key West Florida. This was followed by duty aboard the first super aircraft carrier in the world, the *USS Forrestal* CV 59 and the *USS John F. Kennedy* CV 67, an all-purpose, multi-mission aircraft carrier. He completed a Mediterranean cruise with the *Forrestal* and a North Atlantic cruise with the *Kennedy*. The *Forrestal*, launched 11 December 1954 was decommissioned 11 September 1993. It displaced 78,200 tons, was 1,063 feet long, had a speed of 30 knots, carried 85 aircraft and had a crew of 2,700 and an air wing of 2,480. The *Kennedy* was commissioned 7 September 1968 at 82,000 tons, 1,052 feet in length, 30+ knots, 85 aircraft, a crew of 3,117 and an air wing of 2,480. It is the only conventionally powered carrier in the Atlantic fleet and is equipped with the most advanced command, control, communica-

Mike Drotzman with grandson Logan Hammer, 14 August 2005. Photos courtesy of Michael J. Drotzman

Jake Drotzman 14 August 2004.

{ G 1685 }

tions, and information systems in the Navy. It's homeport is Mayport, Florida. After marrying Ruth in November 1978, they moved to Stuttgart West Germany in July 1979 where he was assigned to HQ United States European Command. Daughter Jessica was born in Bad Constatt, West Germany 27 October 1980. After three years in West Germany, he was assigned to the Naval Training Command, Instructor Training School in Norfolk, Virginia in August 1982 and then became a ASWOC instructor at the Fleet Combat Training Center in Dam Neck. Twins Jacob and Joseph were born in Portsmouth, Virginia 8 June 1982. He was back aboard the *Kennedy* from September 1985 to March 1987 and participated in its Mediterranean cruise. His final assignment was with the Navy Finance Center in Cleveland, Ohio from January 1988 until his retirement in August 1990 with the rank of

Jared Drotzman with Nephew Logan Hammer 14 August 2004.

Jared. Photos courtesy of Michael J. Drotzman.

Joseph Leroy Drotzman, Yankton High School Senior.

Jacob Lyle Drotzman, Yankton High School Senior.

Data Processing Senior Chief. Son Jared was born in Parma, Ohio 2 November 1988. He was awarded the following decorations, medals, badges, citations, and campaign ribbons: Navy achievement Medal, Joint Service Commendation Medal, 3 Meritorious Unit Commendations, 5 Good Conduct Awards, National Defense Service Medal, 2 Vietnam Service Medals, 2 Navy and Marine Corps Overseas Service Ribbons, 2 Sea Service Deployment Ribbons, and the Vietnam Campaign Service Medal.

Michael James **Drotzman** and Ruth Ann **Remund** had the following children:

+ 22 i. Jessica Ashley[5] **Drotzman**[25] 27 October 1980.
  23 ii. Jacob Lyle **Drotzman**[26] born in Portsmouth, Portsmouth City Area Co., Virginia 8 June 1983.
  24 iii. Joseph Leroy **Drotzman**[27] born in Portsmouth 8 June 1983.
  25 iv. Jared Daniel **Drotzman**[28] born in Parma, Cuyahoga Co. Ohio 2 November 1988.

16. **Larry Joseph**[4] **Drotzman** (Edwin LeRoy[3], Edward[2], Joseph[1])[29] was born in Yankton, Yankton Co., South Dakota 2 September 1955 and died there of cancer 23 January 1995, at 39 years of age. Buried in Sacred Heart Cemetery. He married **Martha Irene Guerrero** in Las Vegas, Clark Co., Nevada 20 March 1982. Martha,[30] daughter of Leoncio Francisco **Guerrero** and Delfa Clemencia **Rodriquez**, was born in Los Angeles, Los Angeles Co., California 19 March 1957. Larry was graduated from Yankton High School and served for a short period in the U.S. Navy. He lived in Long Beach, Los Angeles Co., after his discharge where he became a refrigeration mechanic. The family moved to Sioux Falls, Minnehaha Co., South Dakota before 1987 and later to Yankton where he was employed by the government working on the Yankton Missouri river dam. After Larry's death, Martha, Jason, and Laura moved to Trubaco Canyon, Orange Co., California to be near her family.

Larry Drotzman. Photo courtesy of Blaine Whipple.

Martha Drotzman, 14 August 2005, Yankton, SD. Photo courtesy of Michael J. Drotzman.

{ G 1687 }

Jason's high school graduation, June 2005.

Jason Ryan and Laura Ann Drotzman.

Cousins Jason and Jared Drotzman. Photos courtesy of Jared Drotzman.

Larry Joseph **Drotzman** and Martha Irene **Guerrero** had the following children born in Sioux Falls:

  26 i. Jason Ryan[5] **Drotzman**[31] 17 February 1987.

  27 ii. Laura Ann **Drotzman**[32] 28 May 1990.

Laura Drotzman.

{ G 1688 }

Jason and Laura Drotzman with their grandmother Pat Drotzman. Sioux Falls, SD., 14 May 2005. Photos courtesy of Michael J. Drotzman.

19. **James Kenneth**[4] **Drotzman** (Rodney[3], Edward[2], Joseph[1])[33] was born in O'Neill, Holt Co., Nebraska 25 July 1955 and married **Diane Pearson** in Yankton, Yankton Co., South Dakota in June 1974.

James Kenneth **Drotzman** and Diane **Pearson** had the following children born in Yankton:

 28 i. Joshua[5] **Drotzman**[34] 6 January 1977.
 29 ii. Cody **Drotzman**[35] 24 February 1981.

20. **Kay Ann**[4] **Drotzman** (Rodney[3], Edward[2], Joseph[1])[36] was born in Yankton, Yankton Co., South Dakota 13 November 1956 and married **Stephen Pokorney** in Gayville, Yankton Co., South Dakota 31 December 1992.

Kay Ann **Drotzman** and Stephen **Pokorney** had the following children born in Yankton:

 30 i. Dillon James[5] **Pokorney**[37] 31 March 1994.
 31 ii. Rachael Elizabeth **Pokorney**[38] 1 July 1996.

21. **Karen**[4] **Drotzman** (Rodney[3], Edward[2], Joseph[1])[39] was born in Yankton, Yankton Co., South Dakota 29 December 1957 and married **Daniel (__)** 12 February 1992.

{ G 1689 }

Karen **Drotzman** and Daniel (__) had the following child:

32   i.   Jennifer[5] (__)[40] born in Idaho 12 August 1977.

FIFTH GENERATION

22. **Jesssica**[5] **Ashley Drotzman** (Michael James[4], Edwin LeRoy[3], Edward[2], Joseph[1])[41] was born in Bad Constaff, Germany 27 October 1980 and married **Eric Donald Hammer** 14 May 2005 in Yankton, Yankton Co., S. Dakota. Eric, son of Jeffrey **Hammer** and Mona **Gossen** was born 31 January 1980 in Marshall, Lyon Co., Minn.

Jessica Ashley **Drotzman** and Eric Donald **Hammer** had the following child born in Sioux Falls, Minnehaha Co., South Dakota:

Jessica and Logan Hammer, 14 August 2004, Yankton, SD. Photo courtesy of Michael J. Drotzman.

33   i.   Logan Michael **Hammer** 23 February 2004.

(See Generation 12, No. 6208, Patricia Ellen Whipple, wife of Edwin LeRoy Drotzman, to review 16 generations of the Whipple line.)

DROTZMAN FAMILY ENDNOTES

1. through 16. Jessica Drotzman to Blaine Whipple. Letter dated 30 Dec. 1996 at 622 W. 5th, Yankton, SD 57078. In possession of Whipple (2005). Family Group Sheets provided and sources included research at the County Court House in Yankton. (Hereafter J. Drotzman to Whiple, *Letter 30 Dec. 1996).*
17. Pat (Whipple) Drotzman to Blaine Whipple. Letter dated 25 Aug. 1988 at 703 E. 18th, Yankton, SD 57078. In possession of Whipple (2005.) She is the author's sister.). (Hereafter Drotzman to Whipple, *Letter, 25 Aug. 1988).*
18. Drotzman to Whipple, *Letter, 25 Aug. 1988.*
19. Theresa Ann Drotzman to Blaine Whipple 6 May 2000 at bdrotz@byelectric.com (701 E. 19th, Yankton, S. Dak. 57078). In possession of Whipple (2005).
20. Daniel Lee Drotzman to Blaine Whipple. Letter dated 2 Sept. 1998 at 5975 - 18 Wedgewood Lane, Plymouth, Minn. 55446. In possession of Whipple (2005).
21. J. Drotzman to Whiple, *Letter 30 Dec. 1996.*
22. Ibid.
23. Drotzman to Whipple, *Letter, 25 Aug. 1988.*

24. through 28. J. Drotzman to Whiple, *Letter 30 Dec. 1996.*
29. Drotzman to Whipple, *Letter, 25 Aug. 1988.*
30. Delfa Clemencia Rodriquez Guerrero to Blaine Whipple. Letter dated 7 March 1995 at 11426 Allerton St., Whittier, Los Angeles Co., Calif. 90606. In possession of Whipple (2005).
31. Drotzman to Whipple, *Letter, 25 Aug. 1988.*
32. Ibid.
33. through 41. J. Drotzman to Whiple, *Letter 30 Dec. 1996.*

LESTER LYLE REMUND 1917 TO JARED DANIEL DROTZMAN 1988

(Remund lineage of Jared Daniel Drotzman. See Generation 13, No. , 8740 son of Ruth Ann Remund)

FIRST GENERATION

1. **Lester Lyle**[1] **Remund,**[1] son of Edward **Remund** and Emma **Janke,** was born in Wilmont, Roberts Co., South Dakota 23 July 1917 and died 8 September 1982 in Appleton, Swift Co., Minn., at 65 years of age. Buried in Wilmont. He married **Myrna Vynette King** in Wilmont 23 September 1941. Myrna,[2] daughter of Otis **King** and Irene Elizabeth **Babb,** was born in there 5 December 1920.

Lester Lyle **Remund** and Myrna Vynette **King** had the following children:
   2   i.   Marlo Allen[2] **Remund**[3] born in Graceville, Big Stone Co., Minnesota 21 October 1944 and married Loralie **Thora** in North St. Paul, Ramsey Co., Minnesota 26 October 1974.
   3   ii. June Elaine **Remund**[4] born in Browns Valley, Traverse Co., Minnesota 16 June 1952 and married Daryl **Vindersler** in Appleton, 6 March 1976.
   4   iii. Russell Edward **Remund**[5] born in Browns Valley 22 April 1955.
+ 5   iv. Ruth Ann **Remund** born 1 March 1960.

SECOND GENERATION

5. **Ruth Ann**[2] **Remund** (Lester Lyle[1])[6] was born in Graceville, Big Stone Co., Minnesota 1 March 1960 and married **Michael James Drotzman** in Appleton, Minnesota 18 October 1978. Michael,[7] son of Edwin

{ G 1691 }

LeRoy **Drotzman** and Patricia Ellen **Whipple,** was born in Yankton, Yankton Co., South Dakota 6 Autust 1952.

Ruth Ann **Remund** and Michael James **Drotzman** had the following children:
+ 6 i. Jessica Ashley[3] **Drotzman** born in Bad Constatt, Germany 27 October 1980.
   7 ii. Jacob Lyle **Drotzman**[8] born in Portsmouth, Virgina 8 June 1983.
   8 iii. Joseph Leroy **Drotzman**[9] born in Portsmouth, 8 June 1983.
   9 iv. Jared Daniel **Drotzman**[10] born in Parma, Ohio 2 November 1988. He completed his junior year at Yankton High School, in 2006.

THIRD GENERATION

6. **Jessica Ashley**[4] **Drotzman** (Ruth Ann[3] Remund, Myrna Vynette[2] King, Otis[1]) was born in Bad Constatt, German 27 October 1980 and married **Eric Donald Hammer.** Eric, son of Jeffrey **Hammer,** was born in Yankton, Yankton Co., South Dakota 20 May 2005.

Jessica Ashley **Drotzman** and Eric Donald **Hammer** had the following child born in Sioux Falls, Minnehaha Co., South Dakota:
   10 i. Logan Michael **Hammer**[1] 23 February 2004.

(See Generation 13, No. 7395, Ruth Ann Remund for a continuation of the Whipple lineage.)

REMUND FAMILY ENDNOTES

1. Jessica Drotzman to Blaine Whipple. Letter dated 30 Dec. 1996 at 622 W. 5th, Yankton, S. Dak. 57078. In possession of Whipple (2005). Family Group Sheets provided and sources included research at the County Court House in Yankton.
2. Ibid.
3. Ibid.
4. Ibid.
5. Ibid.
6. Ibid.
7. Pat (Whipple) Drotzman to Blaine Whipple. Letter dated 25 Aug. 1988 at 703 E. 18th, Yankton, SD 57078. In possession of Whipple (2005). She is the author's sister.

8. Ibid.
9. Ibid.
10. Ibid.
11. Ibid.

OTIS KING TO JARED DANIEL DROTZMAN 1988-

(King lineage to Ruth Ann Remund, Generation 13, No. 7395, wife of Michael James Drotzman.)

FIRST GENERATION

1. **Otis**[1] **King** birth date unknown married **Irene Elizabeth Babb** in Sisseton, Roberts Co., South Dakota 14 February 1920. Irene,[1] daughter of John **Babb** and Miriam **Bostwick**, was born in Wilmont, Roberts Co., South Dakota 29 January 1901.

Otis **King** and Irene Elizabeth **Babb** had the following children born in Wilmont:

+ 2 i.   Myrna Vynette[2] **King** 5 December 1920.
  3 ii. Merton Otis **King**[2] 21 August 1922 and died there 22 September 1939, at 17 years of age.
  4 iii. Wendell Forrest **King**[3] 22 September 1924 and died 5 January 1944 in Davenport, Scott Co., Iowa, at 19 years of age.
  5 iv. Donna Jeanne **King**[4] 26 August 1926 and married twice. (1) Floyd **Stoll** in Webster, Day Co., South Dakoata 3 September 1946. (2) John **Deville** 28 October 1982.
  6 v.   Alta Beth **King**[5] 7 October 1928 and married Elmer **McNish** in Topeka, Shawnee Co., Kans., 9 June 1952.
  7 vi. Leslie Lynn **King**[6] 6 August 1930 and married Armina **Kelley** in Topeka, Shawnee Co., Kans., 2 November 1962.[7]
  8 vii. Shirley Ruth **King**[8] 19 June 1933 and married twice. (1) Loren **Arwood** in Huron, Beadle Co., South Dakota 2 May 1952. (2) Orville **Thompson** 19 June 1961.
  9 viii. Beverly Susan **King**[9] 27 October 1935 and died there 3 June 1966, at 30 years of age.
  10 ix. Roger Leigh **King** 4 July 1938 and married Gayle **Christensen** there 4 September 1960.

{ G 1693 }

11		x.	Barbara Jeanette **King**[10] 28 September 1940 and married James **Madison** there 28 May 1960.
12		xi.	Franklin David **King**[11] 21 December 1944 and married Cecilia **Pottyebaum** in Orient, Hand Co., South Dakota 8 May 1965.

SECOND GENERATION

2. **Myrna Vynette**[2] **King** (Otis[1])[12] was born in Wilmont, Roberts Co., South Dakota 5 December 1920 and married **Lester Lyle Remund** there 23 September 1941. Lester,[13] son of Edward **Remund** and Emma **Janke,** was born in Wilmont 23 July 1917 and died 8 September 1982 in Appleton, Swift Co., Minnesota, at 65 years of age. He is buried in Wilmont.

Myrna Vynette **King** and Lester Lyle **Remund** had the following children:

	13	i.	Marlo Allen[3] **Remund**[14] born in Graceville, Big Stone Co., Minnesota 21 October 1944 and married Loralie **Thora** in North St. Paul, Ramsey Co., Minnesota 26 October 1974.
	14	ii.	June Elaine **Remund**[15] born in Browns Valley, Traverse Co., Minnesota 16 June 1952 and married Daryl **Vindersler** in Appleton 6 March 1976.
	15	iii.	Russell Edward **Remund**[16] born in Browns Valley 22 April 1955.
+	16	iv.	Ruth Ann **Remund** born 1 March 1960.

THIRD GENERATION

16. **Ruth Ann**[3] **Remund** (Myrna Vynette[2] King, Otis[1])[17] see No. 5 p. 1665

FOURTH GENERATION

17. **Jessica Ashley**[4] **Drotzman** (Ruth Ann[3] Remund, Myrna Vynette[2] King, Otis[1])[18] see No. 6 p. 1666

(See Generation 13, No. 7395, Michael Drotzman, son of Patricia Ellen (Whipple), Drotzman to review 16 generations of the Whipple lineage.

KING FAMILY ENDNOTES

1. Jessica Drotzman to Blaine Whipple. Letter dated 30 Dec. 1996 at 622 W. 5th, Yankton, S. Dak. 57078. In possession of Whipple at 236 NW Sundown Way, Portland, OR 97229-6575 (2004). Family group sheets provided and sources included research at the county court house in Yankton, S. Dak.
2. through 18.
19. Pat (Whipple) Drotzman to Blaine Whipple. Letter dated 25 Aug. 1988 at 703 E. 18th, Yankton, S. Daj. 57078. In possession of Whipple at 236 NW Sundown Way, Portland, OR 97229-6575 (2004). She is the author's sister.
20. J. Drotzman to Whiple, *Letter 30 Dec. 1996.*
21. through 23. Ibid.
24. Birth Announcement received by Blaine Whipple.

JOSE DELA' LUZCOVERRERO TO LAURA ANN DROTZMAN 1990-

(Guerrero lineage of Laura Ann Drotzman. See Generation 13, No. 7396, Larry Joe Drotzman, her father.)

FIRST GENERATION

1. **Dr. Jose DeLa**[1] **LuzCoverrero**[1] birth date unknown, married **Julina Orozco** in Nicaragua where she was born.[2]

Dr. Jose DeLa **LuzCoverrero** and Julina **Orozco** had the following child:
+   2   i.   Miguel Lucio[2] **Guerrero** was born abt 1875.

SECOND GENERATION

2. **Miguel Lucio**[2] **Guerrero** (Dr. Jose DeLa[1] LuzCoverrero)[3] was born in Leon, Dept. De Leon, Nicaraqua abt 1875 and Miguel died in March 1964 at 88 years of age. He married **Esther Sampson Osorio** in Leon abt 1900. Esther,[4] daughter of Dudley **Sampson,** was born in Leon abt 1875 and died 4 April 1959 at 83 years of age. Miguel was a cattle rancher.

{ G 1695 }

Miguel Lucio **Guerrero** and Esther Sampson **Osorio** had the following children born in Leon:

3   i.   Emma Esther[3] **Guerrero**[5] in 1901 and died in child birth as did her baby boy in 1931 in Nicaragua, at 30 years of age. She married Pedro **Alvarado** in Nicaragua in 1931.

4   ii.   Miquel **Guerrero**[6] in 1903 and died in 1982 in Nicaragua, at 79 years of age. He married three times. (1) Juana **Alvarado** in 1922. (2) Victoria (__) death date unknown. (3) Erlinda (__) who died in child birth.

5   iii.   Rufino **Guerrero**[7] in 1904 and married Maria **Robleto** in Nicaragua in 1925. He was living in Venezula in 1995.

6   iv.   Susanna Guadaupe **Guerrero**[8] in 1906 and died there 1906 9 months after birth from a fall.

7   v.   Ramiro **Guerrero**[9] in 1908 and married Estella **Delgado** in 1934. He had five children and was living in Danney, California in 1995.

8   vi.   Douglas **Guerrero**[10] in 1911 and married Aide **Castellon** in 1939. He was a practicing pharmacist in Manaqua in 1995.

9   vii.   Susanna **Guerrero**[11] in 1917 and married Dr. Eduardo Narvaez **Lopez** in 1936. He died in 1955.

+ 10   viii.   Leoncio Francisco **Guerrero** 19 August 1919.

11   ix.   Dennis **Guerrero**[12] in 1921 and married Rapaella (__) in 1944. They had four children and were living in Lake Tahoe, Calif. in 1995.

12   x.   Julia **Guerrero**[13] in 1923 and married Pablo **Moltalvan** in 1940. She had five children and was living in Miami, Dade Co., Florida in 1995.

13   xi.   Esther **Guerrero**[14] in 1925 and married Julian **Bendania** in 1949. She had four children and was living in Miami in 1995.

THIRD GENERATION

10. **Leoncio Francisco**[3] **Guerrero** (Miguel Lucio[2], Dr. Jose DeLa[1] LuzCoverrero)[15] was born in Leon, Dept. De Leon, Nicaraqua 19 August 1919 and married **Delfa Clemencia Rodriquez** in Los Angeles, Los Angeles Co., California 14 February 1946. Delfa,[16] daughter of Jose **Rodriquez** and Delfa Clemencia **Cabezas**, was born in Manaqua, Nicaraqua 26 March 1924.

Leoncio Francisco **Guerrero** and Delfa Clemencia **Rodriquez** had the following children born in Los Angeles:

    14   i.   Sylvia S.[4] **Guerrero**[17] 19 November 1947 and married Ray C. **Boone** Jr. in Temple City, Los Angeles Co., California 1 July 1967.

    15   ii.   Esther Emma **Guerrero**[18] 12 August 1949 and married Michael Leigh **Jones** in Whittier, Los Angeles Co., California 30 August 1975.

    16   iii.   Leoncio Francisco **Guerrero** Jr.[19] 1 February 1952 and married an unnamed person in Pasadena, Los Angeles Co., California 8 July 1978.

    17   iv.   Miguel Antonio **Guerrero**[20] 31 March 1956 and married Cynthia Ann **Severe** there 14 September 1985.

+   18   v.   Martha Irene **Guerrero** 19 March 1957.

    19   vi.   Dennis Alberto **Guerrero**[21] 7 August 1958 and married Letitia **Damien** there 4 April 1993.

    20   vii.   George Jose **Guerrero**[22] 18 December 1959 and married Anna Maria **Pacheco** in Baldwin Park, Los Angeles Co., California 10 February 1990.

    21   viii.   Liana Margarita **Guerrero**[23] 22 December 1963 and married John **Langstaff** in Whittier 17 October 1987.

FOURTH GENERATION

18. **Martha Irene**[4] **Guerrero** (Leoncio Francisco[3], Miguel Lucio[2], Dr. Jose DeLa[1] LuzCoverrero)[24] was born in Los Angeles, Los Angeles Co., California 19 March 1957 and married **Larry Joseph Drotzman** in Las Vegas, Clark Co., Nevada, 20 March 1982. Larry,[25] son of Edwin LeRoy **Drotzman** and Patricia Ellen **Whipple**, was born in Yankton, Yankton Co., South Dakota 2 September 1955 and died there 23 January 1995 at 39 years of age. He is buried in Yankton's Sacred Heart Cemetery. After Larry's death, Martha moved back to California to be near her family.

Martha Irene **Guerrero** and Larry Joseph **Drotzman** had the following children born in Sioux Falls, Minnehaha Co., South Dakota:

    22   i.   Jason Ryan[5] **Drotzman**[26] 17 February 1987.

    23   ii.   Laura Ann **Drotzman**[27] 28 May 1990.

GUERRERO FAMILY ENDNOTES

1. through 24. Delfa Clemencia Rodriquez Guerrero to Blaine Whipple. Letter dated 7 March 1995 at 11426 Allerton St., Whittier, Calif. 90606. In possession of Whipple (2005).
25. through 27. Pat (Whipple) Drotzman to Blaine Whipple. Letter dated 25 Aug. 1990 at 703 E. 18th, Yankton, SD 57078. In possession of Whipple (2005). She is the author's sister.

JOSE RODRIQUEZ ABT 1867 TO LAURA ANN DROTZMAN 1990

(Rodriquez lineage of Laura Ann Drotsman Generation 13, No. 7396, Larry J. Drotzman, her father.)

FIRST GENERATION

1. **Jose**[1] **Rodriquez**[1] was born in Nicaragua abt 1867 and died there 9 February 1929 at 61 years of age. He married **Delfa Clemencia Cabezas** in Nicaragua. She was born in Nicaragua 23 November 1897 and died 23 February 1970 in Whittier, Los Angeles, Co., California at 72 years of age.[2]

Jose **Rodriquez** and Delfa Clemencia **Cabezas** had the following children born in Manaqua, Nicaraqua:

	2	i.	Margarita[2] **Rodriquez**[3] 23 March 1914 and married Thomas E. **Sparks** Jr. in Los Angeles, Los Angeles Co., California 28 December 1959.
	3	ii.	Jose **Rodriquez**[4] abt 1919 and married Isabel Rivera there 30 April 1943.
	4	iii.	Maria S. **Rodriquez**[5] abt 1920 and died there 9 August 1920, at less than 1 year of age.
	5	iv.	Miguel Angel **Rodriquez**[6] abt 1922 and died there 15 October 1923, at 1 year of age.
	6	v.	Aramando **Rodriquez**[7] abt January 1923 and died there 5 February 1923, at less than 1 month of age.
+	7	vi.	Delfa Clemencia **Rodriquez** 26 March 1924.
	8	vii.	Martha Irene **Rodriquez**[8] abt 1928 and died there in 1930, at 2 years of age.

SECOND GENERATION

7. **Delfa Clemencia**[2] **Rodriquez** (Jose[1])[9] was born in Manaqua, Nicaraqua 26 March 1924 and married **Leoncio Francisco Guerrero** in Los Angeles, Los Angeles Co., California 14 February 1946. Leoncio,[10] son of Miguel Lucio **Guerrero** and Esther Sampson **Osorio,** was born in Leon, Dept. De Leon, Nicaraqua 19 August 1919.

Delfa Clemencia **Rodriquez** and Leoncio Francisco **Guerrero** had the following children born in Los Angeles:

	9	i.	Sylvia S.[3] **Guerrero**[11] 19 November 1947 and married Ray C. **Boone** Jr. in Temple City, Los Angeles Co. 1 July 1967.
	10	ii.	Esther Emma **Guerrero**[12] 12 August 1949 and married Michael Leigh **Jones** in Whittier, Los Angeles Co. 30 August 1975.
	11	iii.	Leoncio Francisco **Guerrero** Jr.[13] 1 February 1952 and married an unnamed person in Pasadena, Los Angeles Co. 8 July 1978.
	12	iv.	Miguel Antonio **Guerrero**[14] 31 March 1956 and married Cynthia Ann **Severe** there 14 September 1985.
+	13	v.	Martha Irene **Guerrero** 19 March 1957.
	14	vi.	Dennis Alberto **Guerrero**[15] 7 August 1958 and married Letitia **Damien** there 4 April 1993.
	15	vii.	George Jose **Guerrero**[16] 18 December 1959 and married Anna Maraia **Pacheco** in Baldwin Park, Los Angeles Co 10 February 1990.
	16	viii.	Liana Margarita **Guerrero**[17] 22 December 1963 and married John **Langstaff** in Whittier, Los Angeles Co. 17 October 1987.

THIRD GENERATION

13. **Martha Irene**[3] **Guerrero** (Delfa Clemencia[2] Rodriquez, Jose[1])[18] see No. 18 p. 1671.

RODIQUEZ FAMILY ENDNOTES

1. through 18, Delfa Clemencia Rodriquez Guerrero to Blaine Whipple. Letter dated 7 March 1995 at 11426 Allerton St., Whittier, CA 90606. In possession of Whipple (2005).
19. Pat (Whipple) Drotzman to Blaine Whipple. Letter dated 25 Aug. 1990 at 703 E. 18th, Yankton, SD 57078. In possession of Whipple (2005). She is the author's sister..
20. and 21. Ibid.

{ G 1699 }

APPENDIX G-7

PEDER MADSEN ABT 1838 TO INES MAY PETERSON 1929-

(Peterson lineage of Ines Mae Peterson, Generation 12, No. 6209, wife of Robert Blaine Whipple.)

FIRST GENERATION

1. **Peder**[I] **Madsen**[1] was born in Denmark abt 1838 and married **Johanne Rasmusdatter** in Oster Ulslev, Maribo Co., Denmark 17 October 1858. Johanne,[2] daughter of Rasmus **Christiansen** and Marem **Pedersdatter**, was born in Oster Ulslev 13 March 1838 (christened 1 May) and died in Denmark.[3]

Peder **Madsen** and Johanne **Rasmusdatter** had the following children born in Oster Ulsev:

2	i.	Rasmus[2] **Pedersen**[4] 29 October 1858 (christened 1 February 1859).
3	ii.	Mads **Pedersen**[5] 1 September 1861 (christened the day of birth). Died in infancy
4	iii.	Mads **Pedersen**[6] 12 January 1863 (christened 26 April 1863).
+5	iv.	Jens Christian **Peterson** 20 January 1866.
+6	v.	Peter T. **Peterson** 2 April 1869.
7	vi.	Frederick **Pedersen**[7] 30 June 1877 (christened 5 August 1877).

SECOND GENERATION

5. **Jens Christian**[2] **Peterson** (Peder[I] Madsen)[8] was born in Oster Ulslev, Maribo Co., Denmark 20 January 1866 (christened 18 February) and married **Emma L. (__)**. She was born in Indiana abt 1870.[9]

Jens Christian **Peterson** and Emma L. (__) had the following children born in Panama, Lancaster Co., Nebraska:

8	i.	Ernest W.[3] **Peterson** abt 1892.[10]
9	ii.	Clifton B. **Peterson**[11] abt 1894.
10	iii.	Roy **Peterson** abt 1896.[12]
11	iv.	Lucy M. **Peterson** abt 1898.[13]

{ G 1700 }

6. **Peter T.**[2] **Peterson** (Peder[1] Madsen)[14] was born in Oster Ulslev, Maribo Co, Denmark 2 April 1869 (christened 17 May) and died 6 July 1940 in Portland, Multnomah Co., Oregon, at 71 years of age. He married **Agnes Faye Frye** in Panama, Lancaster Co., Nebraska 29 September 1892. Agnes, daughter of Henry Abraham **Frye** and Helen M. **Diamon**, was born in Peoria, Peoria Co., Illinois 20 February 1876 and died 11 December 1962 in Portland, at 86 years of age. Pete and his older brother Chris arrived in New York City from Copenhagen, Denmark aboard the *SS Circassea* on 22 March 1887 after an 11 day voyage. Arch Campbell was the ship's Master and the ship apparently picked up additional passengers at Glasgow, Scotland after leaving Copenhagen. The ship's burthen was 2,769 tons. Their passage was in No. 5 Steerage. Pete was listed as No. 539 on the Passenger List, age 17, a laborer from Denmark with one piece of luggage. Chris was No. 545, age 20, laborer from Denmark, one piece of luggage. Both indicated it was their intent to become citizens of the U.S. Their surname was spelled Pedersen.[15]

Pete must have been an industrious fellow because 17 months after he arrived in the U.S. and four months shy of his 20th birthday, he bought from the U. S. government on 10 November 1888 for $438.30 the northeast one-fourth of Section 4, Township 12, Range 7. He sold it to Oscar Johnson of Saunders Co., Nebraska in 1902 for $21,500 of which he accepted $10,000 in the form of a mortgage.[16] A marriage license was issued to Peter, 23, and Agnes, 16, both of Panama, 21 September 1892. The certificate included a notation that Agnes' mother gave her consent "in open Court." They were married 29 September by Rev. W. G. Whitaker. Witnesses were Mrs. Marion (Alcy) Frye and Miss Lillie Atkinson. The *Hickman Enterprise* of Hickman, Lancaster Co. reported in its issue of 21 February 1902 that "Pete Peterson sold his farm and held a stock sale. He will load a car for Monmouth, Polk Co. Oregon next week. Mrs. Frye, Mrs. Peterson's mother, will accompany them." He was then just shy of his 33rd birthday.

Pete's *Petition for Naturalization* (No. 85405) presented to the Circuit Court of Polk County, Oregon was dated 5 February 1912.[17] He stated he left Copenhagen, Denmark, about 11 March 1887 and that on 1 October 1890 in Lincoln in the District Court of Lancaster Co., Nebraska, he declared his intention to become a citizen of the U.S., that he was not a polygamist,

Peter and Agnes, Portland, Oreg.

{ G 1701 }

Peterson farm home, Parker, Polk Co., Oreg.

that he was attached to the principles of the Constitution of the United States, that it was his intention to become a citizen of the United States, that he renounced his allegiance to Frederick VIII, King of Denmark, that it was his intention to reside permanently in the United States, that he resided at Independence, Polk Co., Oregon, and that he had lived in Oregon since 10 March 1902. His witnesses were Alfred P. Erickson and Frank Johnson, laborers, residing at Dallas, Polk Co., Oregon. His *Certificate of Naturalization,* No. 136547, was issued by the Polk County Circuit Court at Dallas 3 June 1912. He was described as being age 43, 5' 6" tall, color, white, complexion, light, color of eyes, blue, color of hair, brown, and no visible distinguishing marks. The Certificate noted he had "in all respects complied with the law in relation [to becoming a citizen] and that he was entitled to be so admitted [and] it was thereupon ordered by the said Court that he be admitted as a citizen of the United States of America." The Certificate named the following and their place of residence: Wife, Agnes Faye, 36, Oscar H., 17, Owen D., 17, Guy L., 16, Isabell, 12, Winnegene, 9, Peter Lynn, 6, and Caroline A., 4, all residing at Independence. Peter signed the Certificate.

{ G 1702 }

The Peterson farm was on Parker Road in south Polk County (the farm home is now identified as Box 8435 Parker Rd.) To find the farm, drive south of Monmouth on Hwy. 99W until you come to the Helmick State Park (on the west side of the highway and north of the Luckiamute river). Drive east on Old Fort Road for approximately one mile then south on Parker Road approximately .9 of a mile, cross the railroad track and the old Peterson place is the first house on the left. Peter and Agnes are buried at the Hilltop (IOOF) Cemetery which is approximately three miles south of Independence on Corvallis Road #9. Their graves are on the north side of the most southerly road in the cemetery. The family plot is east of a large Oak tree. Also buried here are daughters Caroline and Lenore and Helen Frye, mother of Agnes.

Peter T. **Peterson** and Agnes Faye **Frye** had the following children:

+	12	i.	Owen Diamon[3] **Peterson** 1 December 1894.
+	13	ii.	Oscar H. **Peterson** 1 December 1894.
+	14	iii.	Guy L. **Peterson** 27 May 1896.
+	15	iv.	Isabelle Hope **Peterson** 5 September 1899.
	16	v.	Lenore **Peterson** 1 October 1901 and died 22 January 1903 at 1 year of age. Buried in the Hilltop (IOOF) Cemetery.
+	17	vi.	Winnogene Marie **Peterson** 17 June 1903.
	18	vii.	Peter Lynn **Peterson**[18] born in Parker 12 September 1905 and died 8 February 1978 in Portland, at 72 years of age. He married Mrs. Velma Grace **Turner** in Portland 22 August 1947. Velma was born in Sedgwick, Sedgwick Co., Colorado 24 March 1910.[19] She married (1) Bruce R. **Turner** in Portland 6 June 1925. They were divorced in Portland in 1940.
+	19	viii.	Caroline A. **Peterson** 31 December 1907.
	20	ix.	Genevieve **Peterson**[20] born in Parker 24 May 1914 and died 16 October 1978 in Portland, at 64 years of age. She married Joseph **Stoll** in Portland in March 1937.
+	21	x.	Eldon Edgar **Peterson** born 3 June 1919.

THIRD GENERATION

12. **Owen Diamon**[3] **Peterson** (Peter T.[2], Peder[1] Madsen)[21] was born in Panama, Lancaster Co., Nebraska 1 December 1894 and died 28 October 1943 in Portland, Multnomah Co., Oregon, at 48 years of age. He married **Josephine Berniece Bartruff** in Corvallis, Benton Co., Oregon 14 February 1924. Jo,[22] daughter of Charles Jacob **Bartruff** and Anna Mary **Loeb**,

{ G 1703 }

Center row standing in bib overalls, twins Owen and Oscar Peterson.

was born in Marion Co., Oregon on the Bartruff family's 140 acre farm on Silverton, Road 21 March 1901 and died 14 February 1995 in Portland, at 93 years of age.

Owen attended Parker Grade School and Buena Vista High School. Following high school he farmed and worked for the Southern Pacific Railroad on a bridge building crew. He enlisted for four years (unless sooner discharged) in the U.S. Navy 14 December 1917 at Portland. He

Owen and Oscar on each side of their teacher.

{ G 1704 }

Josephine B. (Bartruff) Peterson.  Owen, late 1930s or early 1940s

entered with the rank of Fireman Third Class at pay of $24.20 per month. He served briefly at Mare Island, San Francisco, California and Norfolk, Virginia, before being assigned Engineman duty on the Battleship *USS Ohio* 31 March until 30 September 1918 and the *USS El Sol* from 31 December 1918 to 15 September 1919. On 4 August 1919, he requested a change in status from U.S. Navy to duration of war. The request was granted and he was discharged 26 September 1919 at the Naval Yard in Puget Sound, Washington. By then he was an Engineman First Class earning $55 a month. At discharge he was paid $97.61 and a travel allowance of $13.75 to return home to Parker. He was issued the Oregon State Victory Medal 27 May 1921.[23]

Junior Captain Owen Diamon Peterson, second from right. Portland Fire Department personnel. Picture probably taken 1943.

{ G 1705 }

Wayne, Ines, and Norman.

 He moved to Portland and worked as an iron worker in the Portland shipyard until 30 September 1921 when he was appointed a Fire Fighter with the Portland Fire Department. He was assigned to Engine 7 at SE 11th and Stark streets until 16 December 1924 when he became an Assistant Engineer assigned to Engine 20 at the station at SE 13th and Tenino streets. His next transfer was to Engine 4 at the station at SW 4th and Montgomery streets on 30 November 1930. He was promoted Junior Captain 14 January 1943 and assigned to Engine 5 at the station at SW

Harbor Drive and Gibbs streets. He drove the fire truck and operated the pumper.[24]

Owen died in the Veterans Administration Hospital in Portland two days after being admitted. Cause of death was "intestinal obstruction; acute with general peritonitis." The appendicitis occurred while he was on a deer hunting trip in Eastern Oregon. His funeral was at the Holman & Lutz Chapel in Portland; Rev. E.A. Fogg officiated. He was buried 1 November 1943 at Lincoln Memorial Cemetery, Portland.

Owen Diamon **Peterson** and Josephine Berniece **Bartruff** had the following children born in Portland:

+ 22 i. Wayne Allen[4] **Peterson** 1 October 1924.

23 ii. Owen Norman **Peterson**[25] 21 November 1925 and died 30 October 1992 in Junction City, Lane Co., Oregon, at 66 years of age. He married twice. (1) Ramona **Kilday** 29 August 1959. They were divorced. (2) Marjorie E. **Reetz** in Reno, Washoe Co., Nevada 30 May 1971. Norm was a veteran serving in the Army of Occupation in Germany following WWII. While in the Army, he traveled extensively in Europe and was able to visit Peterson relatives in Denmark. Following his discharge, he returned to Oregon and entered the Oregon Technical Institute at Klamath Falls, Klamath Co. where he was trained in diesel mechanics. His career was varied and included working in an iron works in Portland, serving on the Anchorage, Alaska Fire Department, and working for the U.S. Forest Service near Oregon's Crater Lake National Park. He was hired by the Rosboro Lumber Co. of Springfield, Lane Co., Oregon in 1964 where he worked on the line until his retirement in 1987. He and Marjorie were avid square dancers and were members of several clubs and attended various dance festivals annually throughout the Pacific Northwest. He loved to hunt — chukars, pheasant, duck, geese, deer, and elk — and fish — salmon and steelhead in coastal waters and kokanee in Oregon high lakes — and went on annual hunting trips with brothers Wayne and Bob. He and Marjorie owned a fifth wheeler and following retirement spent winter months in Southern California and Arizona and summer months in Alaska. Norm's Memorial Service was 7 November 1992 at the United Methodist Church in Junction City. He was buried at Rest-Haven Memorial Park, Eugene, Lane Co., Oregon. His grave is marked showing his veteran status

+ 24 iii. Ines Mae **Peterson** 24 September 1929.
+ 25 iv. Robert Charles **Peterson** 21 October 1936.

13. **Oscar H.**[3] **Peterson** (Peter T.[2], Peder[1] Madsen)[26] was born in Panama, Lancaster Co., Nebraska 1 December 1894 and died of cancer 10 November 1946 in Portland, Multnomah Co., Oregon at 51 years of age. He married **Anna Robbins** in Portland. Oscar adopted Anna Robbins' daughter Jerry and gave her the Peterson surname. She was born in Portland and married Donald **Pearson**.

Oscar H. **Peterson** and Anna **Robbins** had the following child:
+   26   i.   Margaret Fay[4] **Peterson** born 17 October 1929.

14. **Guy L.**[3] **Peterson** (Peter T.[2], Peder[1] Madsen)[27] was born in Panama, Lancaster Co., Nebraska 27 May 1896 and died of cancer 23 May 1966 in Youngstown, Maricopa Co., Arizona, at 69 years of age. He married twice. (1) **Elva Blanchard**. (2) **Lorene (__)**.

Guy L. **Peterson** and Elva **Blanchard** had the following children:
   27   i.   Lorene[4] **Peterson**.
   28   ii.   Lucille **Peterson**.

15. **Isabelle Hope**[3] **Peterson** (Peter T.[2], Peder[1] Madsen)[28] was born in Panama, Lancaster Co., Nebraska 5 September 1899 and died 1 April 1958 in Portland, Multnomah Co., Oregon, at 58 years of age. Buried at Portland's Riverview Cemetery. She married **Daniel McEwen** in Portland 15 May 1919. He was born in Paisley, Scotland 28 October 1887 and died 4 March 1950 in Portland, at 62 years of age.[29] Buried at Lincoln Memorial Cemetery.

Isabelle Hope **Peterson** and Daniel **McEwen** had the following children:
+   29   i.   Donald Wallace[4] **McEwen** born 5 June 1920.
+   30   ii.   Carol Ruth **McEwen** born 8 May 1922.

17. **Winnogene Marie**[3] **Peterson** (Peter T.[2], Peder[1] Madsen)[30] was born in Parker, Polk Co, Oregon 17 June 1903 and died 25 February 1998 in Newberg, Yamhill Co., Oregon, at 94 years of age. She married **Ellis Howard Baker** in Parker at the farm home of her parents 1 August 1926. Ellis,[31] son of Thomas Howard **Baker** and Lillie May **Cummings**, was born in Butteville, Marion Co., Oregon 12 August 1896 and died 24 April 1976 in Newberg, at 79 years of age. Ellis was a veteran of WWI serving with the Coast Artillery Unit at Ft. Warden, Grant Co., Washington. Ellis and Winnogene met in Dundee, Yamhill Co., Oregon where she was a teacher and he drove the school bus. After their marriage they purchased a farm in the red hills of Dundee where their primary crops were

plums, nuts, and berries. Ellis was also a Rural Mail Carrier in the Dundee-Newberg area for 42 years, retiring in 1964. They sold the farm in 1947 and lived in Newberg for four years before returning to Dundee. Both are buried at Valley View Cemetery, Newberg. After almost 17 years raising her sons, Winnogene returned to teaching at the Dundee school in 1943. She returned to college and received a Degree in Education from Oregon College of Education (now Western Oregon College) in Monmouth, Polk Co. in 1957. She retired from teaching in 1968.

Winnogene Marie **Peterson** and Ellis Howard **Baker** had the following children:
+ 31 i. Lynn Maurice[4] **Baker** born 5 August 1927.
+ 32 ii. Ronald Ellis **Baker** born July 2, 1933.

19. **Caroline A.**[3] **Peterson** (Peter T.[2], Peder[1] Madsen)[32] was born in Parker, Polk Co., Oregon 31 December 1907 and died 12 July 1976 in Salem, Marion Co., Oregon, at 68 years of age. She married **Clifford Jack Cox** in Salem 18 July 1924. Jack,[33] son of Alfred **Cox** and Laura **Johnson**, was born in Grass Valley, Wasco Co., Oregon 5 November 1905 and died 6 June 1994 in Portland, Multnomah Co., Oregon, at 88 years of age. Caroline is buried in the Hilltop (IOOF) Cemetery south of Independence, Polk Co., Oregon.

Caroline A. **Peterson** and Clifford Jack **Cox** had the following child:
+ 33 i. Eleanor[4] **Cox** born 26 December 1928.

21. **Eldon Edgar**[3] **Peterson** (Peter T.[2], Peder[1] Madsen)[34] was born in Dallas, Polk Co., Oregon 3 June 1919 and married **Mary Ann Gimarelli**. Mary,[35] daughter of Vincent **Gimarelli** and Grace **Mash**, was born in Portland, Multnomah Co., Oregon 22 December 1918. Eldon's life work was as a Purchasing Agent with Blake, Moffitt and Towne Paper Co. for 14 years after which he was a Sales Representative for A. Smith Office Products for 25 years. Both were located in Portland. He and Mary live in Tigard, Washington Co., Oregon. (2005)

Eldon Edgar **Peterson** and Mary Ann **Gimarelli** had the following children born in Portland:
34 i. Lona[4] **Peterson**[36] 9 May 1941.
+ 35 ii. Peter Thomas **Peterson** 25 May 1943.
+ 36 iii. Grace **Peterson** 22 March 1947.

FOURTH GENERATION

22. **Wayne Allen**[4] **Peterson** (Owen Diamon[3], Peter T.[2], Peder[1] Madsen)[37] was born in Portland, Multnomah Co., Oregon 1 October 1924 and married twice. (1) **Jacqueline Marie Mohland** in Vancouver, Clark Co., Washington 18 May 1957. Jackie,[38] daughter of Walter George **Mohland** and Marie **Simmons**, was born in Portland 30 October 1925 and died of cancer 14 February 1992 in Portland, at 66 years of age. She was buried in the Willamette National Cemetery, Portland. Jackie was a Legal Secretary for most of her working career. (2) **Shirley Brace** in Lake Tahoe, Placer Co., California 8 July 1997. Shirley,[39] daughter of George Ransom **Brace** and Mary Clay **Cooley**, was born in Walla Walla, Walla Walla Co., Washington 23 July 1924. She married (1) **Eugene Brian Valdemi** in Portland 30 January 1949 (divorced in La Habra, Orange Co., California in 1965). (2) **Frank Joseph Hamnesfahr** in Las Vegas, Clark Co., Nevada 30 September 1972 (divorced in 1993). After graduating from Portland's Benson High School, Wayne entered the U.S. Navy in July 1943 and served until February 1946. He attained the rank of Radarman Second Class and served in California and Florida. Upon discharge, he joined the Portland Fire Bureau retiring 31 years later as a Lieutenant. For years he was a firetruck driver. Upon becoming a Lieutenant, he was in charge of one piece of equipment in the station with a 3-4 man crew working under him. Following retirement, he has traveled extensively in the U.S. and abroad. His overseas trips have taken him to the Hawaiian Islands, China, Korea, Japan, England, Germany, France, Austria, Italy, Spain, Norway, Sweden, and the Netherlands. He and Shirley live in a retirement community in Tigard, Washington Co., Oregon. (2005)

Wayne Allen **Peterson** and Jacqueline Marie **Mohland** had the following children born in Portland:
+ 37 i. Deborah Sue[5] **Peterson** 26 January 1959.
+ 38 ii. Mark Allen **Peterson** 16 February 1962.

24. **Ines Mae**[4] **Peterson** (Owen Diamon[3], Peter T.[2], Peder[1] Madsen) was born at Portland Sanitarium Hospital in Portland, Multnomah Co., Oregon 24 September 1929.[40] The family then lived at 1251 S.E. 20th. She married twice. (1) **Harold Steele** in Portland 24 February 1951. Harold, son of Bruce C. **Steele** and Lena **Matzke**, was born in Portland 10 April 1929 and died there of cancer 2 September 1962, at 33 years of age. Buried in Riverview Abbey Mausoleum, Portland. (2) **Robert Blaine Whipple** in Portland, Washington Co., Oregon 6 August 1966. Blaine,[41] son of Lucien Blaine **Whipple** and Pearl Julia **Scott**, was born at 11:50 a.m. in a

log cabin, the family home, in Martin, Bennett Co., South Dakota 22 February 1930.

Ines Mae **Peterson** and Harold **Steele** had the following children:
+   39   i.   Judith Lynn[5] **Steele** born 30 January 1952.
+   40   ii.   Robert Bruce **Steele** born 15 March 1960.

(For a continuation of the Peterson lineage, see Generation 5, No. 15, Judith Lynn Steele and No. 16, Robert Bruce Steele, in the Steele Family included in this appendix.)

Judith, Sunset High School graduation, Beaverton Oreg.

Ines Mae **Peterson** and Robert Blaine **Whipple** had the following child born in Portland:
+   41   iii.   Blaine Scott **Whipple** 27 December 1968.

(For a continuation of the Peterson lineage through Blaine Scott, see Generation 13, No. 7399 in the main Genealogical Section.)

25. **Robert Charles**[4] **Peterson** (Owen Diamon[3], Peter T.[2], Peder[1] Madsen)[42] was born in Portland, Multnomah Co., Oregon 21 October 1936 and married **Diane Janice Varney** there 27 June 1964. Diane,[43] daughter of Vearl Vernon **Varney** and Lois Ruth **Anderson**, was born in San Diego, San Diego Co., California 12 August 1941. Bob was graduated from Oregon State University, Corvallis, Benton Co., Oregon and spent his working career as a U. S. Forest Service Ranger. Following retirement, he worked summers as an inspector for private contractors building and repairing U. S. highways in Montana and Idaho. He is an avid hunter and fisherman. Diane worked for the U. S. West Telephone Co.

Robert Charles **Peterson** and Diane Janice **Varney** had the following children:
+   42   i.   Sandra Denise[5] **Peterson** born 30 September 1965.
+   43   ii.   John Robert **Peterson** born 7 October 1969.
+   44   iii.   James Michael **Peterson** born 29 May 1972.

{ G 1711 }

26. **Margaret Fay**[4] **Peterson** (Oscar H.[3], Peter T.[2], Peder[1] Madsen)[44] was born in Portland, Multnomah Co., Oregon 17 October 1929 and married **Warren Messick** in Vancouver, Clark Co., Washington 15 December 1947. They were divorced in Portland in 1953.

Margaret Fay **Peterson** and Warren **Messick** had the following child born in Portland:
    45   i.   Linda Fay[5] **Messick**[45] 13 July 1949.

29. **Donald Wallace**[4] **McEwen** (Isabelle Hope[3] Peterson, Peter T.[2], Peder[1] Madsen)[46] was born in Seattle, King Co., Washington 5 June 1920 and died 15 January 2000 in Oregon, at 79 years of age. He married **Jean Oldham** in Gallatin, Sumner Co., Tennessee 5 April 1943. Jean,[47] daughter of Sam **Oldham** and Laura Eugenia **Avert**, was born in Hartsville, Trousdale Co., Tennessee 25 July 1921. Donald moved to Portland, Multnomah Co., Oregon as a child and was graduated from Roosevelt High School. He attended Linfield College in McMinnville, Yamhill Co., Oregon before joining the U. S. Army in 1940. He fought with the 6th Armored Division in Europe for two years during WWII. He met Jean while stationed at Fort Knox, Hardin Co., Kentucky and was graduated from Willamette University College of Law at Salem, Marion Co., Oregon in 1949. He began the practice of law in Portland as an Assistant U.S. Attorney and was a partner in the McEwen, Gisvold, Rankin, Carter and Streinz law firm from 1955 until his death. The Oregon Legislature created the Council on Court Procedures in 1977 composed of 13 lawyers and 10 judges. Donald was its first chair. The Council drafted new rules for Oregon civil trials including a requirement that lawyers identify expert witnesses and disclose expert testimony to opposing lawyers before trials. He was named Oregon Distinguished Trial Lawyer of the Year by the Oregon Chaper of the American Board of Trial Advocates in 1991 and received the Multnomah Bar Association's Professionalism Award in 1993. The Oregon State Bar honored him with the Owen M. Panner Professionalism Award in 1999. He died while on a hunting trip in Eastern Oregon and was interred in Portland's Willamette National Cemetery.

Donald Wallace **McEwen** and Jean **Oldham** had the following children:
+   46   i.   Carol Jean[5] **McEwen** born 22 March 1944.
+   47   ii.   Robert Bruce **McEwen** born 11 November 1953.
    48   iii.   Jamie Wallace **McEwen**[48] born in Portland 18 May 1957 and married Nona **Olivas** in New York, N.Y. They were living in New York City in 1999.

30. **Carol Ruth**[4] **McEwen** (Isabelle Hope[3] Peterson, Peter T.[2], Peder[1] Madsen)[49] was born in Seattle, King Co., Washington 8 May 1922 and married **Berton Kenton Lawson Jr.** in Portland, Multnomah Co., Oregon 29 November 1952. Berton,[50] son of Berton Kenton **Lawson** and Jordan Belle **Lilly**, was born in Cottage Grove, Lane Co., Oregon 5 May 1911 and died 4 April 1976 in Portland, at 64 years of age.

Carol Ruth **McEwen** and Berton Kenton **Lawson** Jr. had the following children born in Portland:
- + 49 i. Wallace Kenton[5] **Lawson** 2 November 1954.
- 50 ii. Barbara Anne **Lawson**[51] 15 February 1957.

31. **Lynn Maurice**[4] **Baker** (Winnogene Marie[3] Peterson, Peter T.[2], Peder[1] Madsen)[52] was born in McMinnville, Yamhill Co, Oregon 5 August 1927 and died 16 May 1999 in Portland, Multnomah Co., Oregon, at 71 years of age. He married **Janet JoAnn Abelson** in Portland 17 August 1951. Janet,[53] daughter of Martin **Abelson** and Josephine Amanda **Jacobson**, was born in Portland 19 May 1929. They were divorced in Portland in 1976. Jan was graduated from Western Oregon College at Monmouth, Polk Co., Oregon in 1950 and taught school until 1961 when their first child was born. Maurice served in the Marine Corp for nine months following graduation from high school then earned an Engineering Degree from Oregon State College (now Oregon State University) at Corvallis, Benton Co., and worked for the U.S. Army Corps of Engineers, the Atomic Energy Commission, and Pacific Power and Light Co. for several years. He was also a Consulting Engineer and became a stockbroker in Portland in 1963. In addition to his daughters, he was survived by seven grandchildren. His funeral was 21 May 1999 at the Lincoln Memorial Park & Funeral Home and he was buried in Willamette National Cemetery, Portland. His obituary appeared in the Portland Oregonian of 20 May 1999.

Lynn Maurice **Baker** and Janet JoAnn **Abelson** had the following children:
- + 51 i. Kyle Ann[5] **Baker** born 21 April 1961.
- + 52 ii. Kristen Sue **Baker** born 28 February 1963.
- + 53 iii. Alison Lee **Baker** born 14 November 1965.

32. **Ronald Ellis**[4] **Baker** (Winnogene Marie[3] Peterson, Peter T.[2], Peder[1] Madsen)[54] was born in Portland, Multnomah Co., Oregon July 2, 1933 and married **Nora Leone McCart** in Lake Grove, Clackamas Co., Oregon 25 May 1962. Nora,[55] daughter of Warren **McCart** and Leona Helena **Kasch**, was born in Oregon City, Clackamas Co., Oregon 4

October 1938. Ron was in the U.S. Army for two years 1953-55, stationed in Korea during part of that time. After discharge he joined Consolidated Freightways in Portland where he worked for 35 years before retiring in 1992. He became one of their computer programmers in 1959 making him an early participant in the growing industry of computers and data processing. Ron met Nora at Consolidated where she also worked. They lived in Lake Oswego, Clackamas Co., Oregon until 1994 when they built their retirement home in Tigard, Washington Co., Oregon.

Ronald Ellis **Baker** and Nora Leone **McCart** had the following children born in Portland:

    54   i.   Jeffrey Ronald[5] **Baker**[56] 28 December 1964 and was graduated from the U. of Oregon at Eugene, Lane Co. in 1989.

    55   ii.   Lisa Marie **Baker**[57] 18 February 1967 and married Stephen Christopher **Petersen** in Cannon Beach, Clatsop Co., Oregon 17 August 1996.

33. **Eleanor**[4] **Cox** (Caroline A.[3] Peterson, Peter T.[2], Peder[1] Madsen)[58] was born in Hoskins, Benton Co., Oregon 26 December 1928 and married twice. (1) **John Koos** in Corvallis, Benton Co., Oregon 26 January 1949. John,[59] son of John **Koos**, was born in Albany, Linn Co., Oregon 17 March 1924. They were divorced in Albany in 1971. (2) **Roger Williams** in Salem, Marion Co., Oregon 13 February 1977. He was born in Fargo, Cass Co., North Dakota 3 October 1936.[60]

Eleanor **Cox** and John **Koos** had the following children in Salem, Marion Co., Oregon:

    56   i.   Roger C.[5] **Koos**[61] 20 August 1949.

    57   ii.   Marsha L. **Koos**[62] 16 September 1950.

+   58   iii.   Ronald L. **Koos** 3 June 1952.

35. **Peter Thomas**[4] **Peterson** (Eldon Edgar[3], Peter T.[2], Peder[1] Madsen)[63] was born in Portland, Multnomah Co., Oregon 25 May 1943 and married **Sharon Lea Johnson** in Eugene, Lane Co., Oregon 15 March 1969. Sharon,[64] daughter of Harold Victor **Johnson** and Betty Jo **Adair**, was born in Tampa, Hillsborough Co., Florida 3 January 1946.

Peter Thomas **Peterson** and Sharon Lea **Johnson** had the following children born in Eugene:

+   59   i.   Devon Thomas[5] **Peterson** 21 March 1971.

60 ii. Kimberly Ann **Peterson**[65] 2 August 1974 and married Richard Arnold **Daniels** there 16 December 1995. Richard,[66] son of Richard Craig **Daniels** and Cynthia Fay **McClane**, was born in Eugene 23 July 1974.

36. **Grace**[4] **Peterson** (Eldon Edgar[3], Peter T.[2], Peder[1] Madsen)[67] was born in Portland, Multnomah Co., Oregon 22 March 1947 and married **Walter Sanders** there 19 March 1966. Walter,[68] son of Calvin **Sanders** and Amy **Judd**, was born in Portland 30 August 1945.

Grace **Peterson** and Walter **Sanders** had the following children born in Portland:

61 i. Tiffany[5] **Sanders**[69] 9 April 1969 and married Jason **Taylor** there 18 March 1994. Jason,[70] son of Glenn **Taylor** and Kathy **Meisner**, was born in Portland 12 November 1971.

62 ii. Trevor **Sanders**[71] 28 June 1971 and married Amy **Eisenhardt** 14 August 1999. Amy,[72] daughter of James **Eisenhardt** and Kay (__), was born 26 March 1974.

FIFTH GENERATION

37. **Deborah Sue**[5] **Peterson** (Wayne Allen[4], Owen Diamon[3], Peter T.[2], Peder[1] Madsen)[73] was born in Vancouver, Clark Co., Washington 26 January 1959 and married **Gary D. Smith** in Portland, Multnomah Co., Oregon 27 June 1981. Gary,[74] son of Roger **Smith** and Carol **Tittle**, was born in Portland 25 February 1959. He earned a Business Administration degree from Oregon State University at Corvallis, Benton Co., and is owner of Construction Equipment Co. of Tualatin, Washington Co., Oregon. (2005) The company builds equipment to crush and screen rock. Debbie attended Portland's Wilson High School and earned a B.S. in Nursing at the Oregon Health Sciences University in Portland. She was a nurse at Portland's Meridian Park Hospital.

Deborah Sue **Peterson** and Gary D. **Smith** had the following children born in Portland:

63 i. Lauren Marie[6] **Smith**[75] 19 October 1989.

64 ii. Tyler Davis **Smith**[76] 29 September 1993.

38. **Mark Allen**[5] **Peterson** (Wayne Allen[4], Owen Diamon[3], Peter T.[2], Peder[1] Madsen)[77] was born in Portland, Multnomah Co., Oregon 16 February 1962 and married **Charlene Webb** in Stafford, Clackamas Co., Oregon 20 August 1988.

{ G 1715 }

Mark Allen **Peterson** and Charlene **Webb** had the following children born in Portland:
    65   i.   Amber[6] **Peterson**[78] 17 December 1982.
    66   ii.   Ashley **Peterson**[79] 28 June 1991.

42. **Sandra Denise**[5] **Peterson** (Robert Charles[4], Owen Diamon[3], Peter T.[2], Peder[1] Madsen)[80] was born in Portland, Multnomah Co., Oregon 30 September 1965 and married twice. (1) **Donald Dodson** in Reno, Washoe Co., Nevada 18 October 1986. They were divorced in Portland in March 1992. (2) **Craig Gearheart** in Welches, Clackamas Co., Oregon 26 September 1998. Craig,[81] son of James **Gearheart** and Susan **Raymen**, was born in Portland 4 January 1971. Sandra is an Emergency Medical Technican and Craig works in construction. (2005)

Sandra Denise **Peterson** and Donald **Dodson** had the following child born in Portland:
    72   i.   Jamie Nicole[6] **Dodson**[82] 21 June 1990.

Sandra Denise **Peterson** and Craig **Gearheart** had the following child born in Gresham, Multnomah Co., Oregon:
    73   ii.   Hunter James **Gearheart** 11 August 2000.[83]

43. **John Robert**[5] **Peterson** (Robert Charles[4], Owen Diamon[3], Peter T.[2], Peder[1] Madsen)[84] was born in Portland, Multnomah Co., Oregon 7 October 1969 and lives with **Jessica Bailey** as domestic partners.

John Robert **Peterson** and Jessica **Bailey** had the following child born in Portland:
    74   i.   Jenna Beverly[6] **Peterson** 29 November 1999.[85]

44. **James Michael**[5] **Peterson** (Robert Charles[4], Owen Diamon[3], Peter T.[2], Peder[1] Madsen)[86] was born in Portland, Multnomah Co., Oregon 29 May 1972.

James Michael **Peterson** and Anna Marie **Raymond** had the following child born in Gresham, Multnomah Co., Oregon:
    75   i.   Lacy Marie[6] **Peterson**[87] 1 September 1996.

46. **Carol Jean**[5] **McEwen** (Donald Wallace[4], Isabelle Hope[3] Peterson, Peter T.[2], Peder[1] Madsen)[88] was born in Portland, Multnomah Co., Oregon 22 March 1944 and married **Erik Lund** there. Erik,[89] son of Raoul **Lund**, was born in California. They were divorced in Portland.

Carol Jean **McEwen** and Erik **Lund** had the following children born in Portland:

    76   i.   Britta (Lund)[6] **McEwen**[90] 22 April 1973. Following her parent's divorce, Britta had her surname changed to McEwen. She is a graduate of Scripts College, Claremont, Los Angeles Co., California. She was a Fullbright Scholar in 1999 in Vienna, Austria where she studied European history.

    77   ii.   Erik McEwen **Lund**[91] 21 February 1975. He is graduate of Pomona College, Claremont, California in 1997 and played professional basketball in Norway and Denmark beginning in 1997.

47. **Robert Bruce**[5] **McEwen** (Donald Wallace[4], Isabelle Hope[3] Peterson, Peter T.[2], Peder[1] Madsen)[92] was born in Portland, Multnomah Co., Oregon 11 November 1953 and married **Kathryn Burke**.

Robert Bruce **McEwen** and Kathryn **Burke** had the following child born in San Francisco, San Francisco Co., California:

    78   i.   Ian[6] **McEwen**[93] in 1983.

49. **Wallace Kenton**[5] **Lawson** (Carol Ruth[4] McEwen, Isabelle Hope[3] Peterson, Peter T.[2], Peder[1] Madsen)[94] was born in Portland, Multnomah Co., Oregon 2 November 1954 and married **Jane Manson** there 21 September 1985. Jane,[95] daughter of Robert **Manson** and Sylvia **(__)** , was born in New York, N.Y. 29 December 1954. They were divorced in Portland in 1994.

Wallace Kenton **Lawson** and Jane **Manson** had the following children born in Portland:

    79   i.   Miles McEwen[6] **Lawson**[96] 17 April 1987.
    80   ii.   Sean Thomas **Lawson**[97] 9 May 1989.

51. **Kyle Ann**[5] **Baker** (Lynn Maurice[4], Winnogene Marie[3] Peterson, Peter T.[2], Peder[1] Madsen)[98] was born in Corpus Christi, Nueces Co., Texas 21 April 1961.

Kyle Ann **Baker** had the following child born in Portland, Multnomah Co., Oregon:

    81   i.   Roland Laszlo[6] **Benes**[99] 20 August 1999. His father is Richard **Benes**.

52. **Kristen Sue**[5] **Baker** (Lynn Maurice[4], Winnogene Marie[3] Peterson, Peter T.[2], Peder[1] Madsen)[100] was born in Bell Fourche, Butte Co., South Dakota 28 February 1963 and married **Ilias Bakouros** in Portland, Multnomah Co., Oregon in October 1980. Ilias was born in Greece 20 April 1954.[101]

Kristen Sue **Baker** and Ilias **Bakouros** had the following children born in Portland:

    82   i.   Sotiri Ilias[6] **Bakourus**.[102]
    83   ii.   Lela Elizabeth **Bakourus**.[103]
    84   iii.   Apostoli Ilias **Bakourus**.[104]

53. **Alison Lee**[5] **Baker** (Lynn Maurice[4], Winnogene Marie[3] Peterson, Peter T.[2], Peder[1] Madsen)[105] was born in Portland, Multnomah Co., Oregon 14 November 1965 and married **Timothy Colhouer** 29 December 1993. He was born 27 January 1964.[106]

Alison Lee **Baker** and Timothy **Colhouer** had the following children born in Portland:

    85   i.   Jacob Lynn[6] **Colhouer**[107] 16 November 1994.
    86   ii.   Austin Nash **Colhouer**[108] 17 December 1995.

58. **Ronald L.**[5] **Koos** (Eleanor[4] Cox, Caroline A.[3] Peterson, Peter T.[2], Peder[1] Madsen)[109] was born in Salem, Marion Co., Oregon 3 June 1952 and married twice. (1) **Kathleen White** in Albany, Linn Co., Oregon in June 1972. Kathi,[110] daughter of B. J. **White** and Barbara (_), was born 5 April 1952. (2) **Jerri Moersch** in Corvallis, Benton Co., Oregon in December 1989.

Ronald L. **Koos** and Kathleen **White** had the following children born in Albany:

    87   i.   Ryan C.[6] **Koos**[111] 9 January 1981.
    88   ii.   Tyler L. **Koos**[112] 15 April 1983.

59. **Devon Thomas**[5] **Peterson** (Peter Thomas[4], Eldon Edgar[3], Peter T.[2], Peder[1] Madsen)[113] was born in Eugene, Lane Co., Oregon 21 March 1971 and married **Nicole Marie Schmauder** in Vancouver, Clark Co., Washington 14 December 1997. Nicole,[114] daughter of John Melvin **Schmauder** and Janice Marie **Gismervig**, was born in Ellensburg, Kittitas Co., Washington 11 November 1968.

Devon Thomas **Peterson** and Nicole Marie **Schmauder** had the following child born in Vancouver:

    89   i.   Cole Thomas[6] **Peterson**[115] 7 June 1999.

PETERSON FAMILY ENDNOTES

1. *Oster Ulslev Parish Registers, Maribo Co., Denmark* (Salt Lake City, UT: Family History Library, Film #0049792), p. 265. (Hereafter Denmark, *Parish Registers*).
2. Ibid., p. 112.
3. The Family History Library Locality Catalog include a Gazetteer which alphabetically lists all record-keeping jurisdictions in the Library. The July 1997 microfiche version includes the Oster Ulslev Parish in Maribo county. Additional research on this family should begin with the 1870 census of Oster Ulselev Parish which should include the ages and birth places of the family members. If the census shows Peder and Johanne were born in the same Parish, birth records should be searched covering years before and after the ages at marriage listed in the census. Because Denmark used the patronymic naming system, we know Peder's father's first name was Mads (Mats) and Johanne's father's first name is Rasmus.
4. Ibid., p. 37, #14.
5. Ibid., p. 47, #10.
6. Ibid., p. 51, #1.
7. Ibid., p. 12, #5.
8. Ibid., p. 57, #1.
9. through 13. 1900 U.S. Census, Population Schedule, Panama District, Lancaster Co., Nebr. (Hereafter 1900, *U.S. Census*).
14. Denmark, *Parish Registers,* p. 65, No. 3.
15. National Archives, *Microfilm Publication M237,* Roll 504, page 11, Line 539 and 545.
16. Landcaster County *Land Records*, Court House, Lincoln, Nebr.
17. The Naturalization Petition is in Volume 1, page 17, Sub, Volume 6455, page 7.
18. and 19. Interview, Velma G. Peterson, 16901 SE Division, Portland, Oreg. 97236, with Blaine Whipple, 6 September 1999 Transcript in possession of Whipple (2005). (Hereafter Velma G. Peterson, *Interview*).
20. Interview, Eldon E. Peterson, 900 NE Francis, Space 49, Gresham, Oreg. 97030, with Blaine Whipple, 7 September 1999. Transcript in possession of Whipple (2005). (Hereafter Eldon E. Peterson, *Interview*).
21. Personal knowledge of daughter, Ines Mae (Peterson) Whipple of 236 NW Sundown Way, Portland, OR 97229-6575 1999; and Owen Diamon Peterson, Death Certificate State File No. 4198, Multnomah Co. Registar's No. 4195, 30 Dec. 1946, Oregon State Board of Health, Division of Vital Statistics, Salem, Oregon.
22. Personal knowledge of daughter, Ines Mae (Peterson) Whipple, and Owen D. Peterson & Josephine B. Bartruff, Marriage Certificate, 13 Feb. 1924, N.S. No. 2152, Vol. 59: 46, County Clerk's Office, Multnomah County, Oregon.
23. Oregon War Records - Personal Military Service, Archives, State of Oregon, Salem, Oregon.
24. Letter to the author dated 18 Sept. 1982 at 6120 S.W. 41st, Portland, Oreg. from Wayne Allen Peterson, Owen's oldest son. In possession of Whipple (2005).
25. Personal knowledge of Ines Mae Peterson and Wayne Allen Peterson, brother and sister of Norm.
26. Interview, Margaret Fay (Peterson) Moilanen, 4617 N. Lombard, Portland, Oreg. 97203, with Blaine Whipple, 7 September 1999. Transcript in possession of Whipple (2005). (Hereafter Margaret Moilanen, *Interview*).
27. Eldon E. Peterson, *Interview.*
28. and 29. Mrs. Carol Lawson to Blaine Whipple. Letter dated 3 Sept. 1998 and interview 28 Aug. 1999 at 4737 SW 42nd Ave., Portland, Oreg. 97221-3630. In possession of

Whipple (2005). Family Group Sheet included. (Hereafter Lawson to Whipple, *Letter and Interview*).

30. and 31. Winnogene Peterson-Ellis Baker Family Group Sheet, supplied 20 Sept. 1998 and 13 Nov. 2000 by Ronald Ellis Baker, 14697 SW Woodhue St., Tigard, OR 97224. No documentation. Information on his and his parents families is based on personal knowledge. (Hereafter Peterson-Baker, *Family Group Sheet*).
32. and 33. Interview Caroline (Cox) Williams, 4120 NE 125th, Portland, Oreg. 97230, with Blaine Whipple, 7 September 1999. Transcript in possession of Whipple (2005). (Hereafter Caroline (Cox) Williams, *Interview*).
34. through 36. Eldon E. Peterson, *Interview*.
37. and 38. Wayne Allen Peterson - Jacqueline Marie Mohland Family Group Sheet, supplied 2 Nov. 1998 by Wayne Allen Peterson, 16296 SW 126th Terrace, Tigard, Oreg. 97224. This sheet cites no documentation and represents the personal knowledge of the submitter. (Hereafter Peterson - Mohland, *Family Group Sheet*).
39. Interview, Shirley (Brace) Peterson, 16296 SW 126th Terrace, Tigard, Oreg. 97224, with Blaine Whipple, 6 Sept. 1999. Transcript in possession of Whipple (2005).
40. Ines Mae Peterson, Birth Certificate State File No. 3187, Multnomah Co. Registrar's No. 3219, State Bureau of Vital Statistics, Salem, Oregon.
41. Robert Blaine Whipple, Birth Certificate No. 344742, Registry Book 725, South Dakota State Board of Health, Division of Vital Statistics, Pierre, S. Dak.
42. and 43. Robert C. Peterson-Diane J. Varney Family Group Sheet, supplied 21 May 1999 with additions supplied 10 Sept. 2000 by Diane (Varney) Peterson, 49001 SE Highway 26, Sandy, Oreg. 97055. This sheet represents the personal knowledge of the submitter. (Hereafter Peterson-Varney, *Family Group Sheet*).
44. and 45. Margaret Moilanen, *Interview*.
46. through 51. Lawson to Whipple, *Letter and Interview*.
52. through 57. Peterson-Baker, *Family Group Sheet*.
58. through 62. Caroline (Cox) Williams, *Interview*.
63. through 65. Peter Thomas (Tom) Peterson to Blaine Whipple. E-mail dated 19 Oct. 1999 at TPeter1005@aol.com. in possession of Whipple (2005). (Hereafter T. Peterson to Whipple, *E-Mail 19 Oct. 199*).
66. Ms. Lona Peterson to Blaine Whipple. Letter dated 27 Sept. 1999 in possession of Whipple (2005). (Hereafter Peterson to Whipple, *Letter, 09/27/1999*).
67. through 72. Grace Peterson-Walter Sanders Family Group Sheet, supplied 14 Sept. 1998 by Grace (Peterson) Sanders, 167 SW Hartley, Gresham, Oreg. 97030. No documentation provided. The information is from personal knowledge of her own family. (Hereafter Peterson - Sanders, *Family Group Sheet*).
73. through 79. Peterson - Mohland, *Family Group Sheet*.
80. through 87. Peterson-Varney, *Family Group Sheet*.
88. through 97. Lawson to Whipple, *Letter and Interview*.
98. through 108. Peterson-Baker, *Family Group Sheet*.
109. through 112. Caroline (Cox) Williams, *Interview*.
113. through 115. T. Peterson to Whipple, *E-Mail 19 Oct. 1999*.

HENRY ABRAHAM FRYE 1836-1890 TO AGNES FAYE FRYE 1876-1962

(Frye lineage of Ines Mae Peterson, Generation 12, No. 6209, wife of Robert Blaine Whipple.)

FIRST GENERATION

1. **Henry Abraham[I] Frye[I]** was born in Peoria, Peoria Co., Illinois 19 September 1836 and died 23 September 1890 in Lancaster Co., Nebraska, at 54 years of age. He was buried in the Cemetery 1 mile west and 1 mile south of the Town of Panama. He married twice. (1) **Amy Ellen Gheen** in Zanesville, Muskingum Co., Ohio 17 April 1856. Amy was born in Zanesville 12 August 1835 and died 20 January 1873 in Peoria, at 37 years of age.[2] (2) **Helen M. Diamon** who was born in New York State 23 September 1835 and died in Oregon 20 March 1915, at 79 years of age.[3] She is buried in the Hilltop (IOOF) Cemetery, south of Independence, Polk Co., Oregon.

After completing common school Henry began farming in Illinois. He enlisted in the 11th Illinois Cavalry in 1865 and participated in several Civil War skirmishes. He returned to the Illinois farm after military service until the spring of 1881 when he moved to Lancaster Co. where he purchased 160 acres in Section 25, Panama Precinct. Since the farm was only slightly improved, he developed it and sold it in 1882 and bought the northwest quarter of Section 23 and the northeast quarter of Section 22, Panama Precinct, which he developed into a well improved and valuable farm which he operated until his death. He was a member of the Grand Army of the Republic in Panama.[4]

The *Daily Nebraska State Journal*

Agnes Faye Frye.

{ G 1721 }

of Lincoln reported on 24 September 1890 that Henry committed suicide on his farm about 8 miles east of Panama. The death occurred about 10 a.m. in an outhouse with a shot gun "that blew the whole of his head from his body." No suicide note was found and he left no will. Helen was appointed administratrix on 29 September.

He owned a total of 400 acres of land in Sections 14, 22, and 23 which was appraised at $7,400. His personal property consisted of $213.85 cash, two milch cows, 37 fat hogs, a dun colored pony, a team of sorrel horses, a spring wagon, and a set of double harness. He held notes from sons Marion and Alonzo and from George W. Atwood and Charles Wilson. The personal property was appraised at $2,153.36. His heirs were Helen, daughters Flora A. Dickinson, 32, of Alta, Peoria Co., Illinois, Emma E. Wilson, 23, of Adams, Gage Co., Nebraska, Agnes, 14, Lenore, 12, and sons Marion K., 30, and Alonzo H., 28, the first and the last four named of Panama. Helen was allowed by law the two milch cows valued at $44, the dun colored pony, $40, a sorrel horse named Billy, $85, and hogs worth $31. The estate had costs of $795.23 including $93.50 to bury Henry, $55.93 for the support and maintenance of Agnes and Lenore, and $540 owed to Abraham Frye.[5]

Henry Abraham **Frye** and Amy Ellen **Gheen** had the following children born in Peoria:

	2	i.	Flora F.[2] **Frye** abt 1856 and married (__) **Dickinson**.
+	3	ii.	Marion Kingsley **Frye** 14 December 1859.
	4	iii.	Alonzo H. **Frye** abt 1862. He moved to Montana.
	5	iv.	Emma **Frye** abt 1867[6] and married C. F. **Wilson** in Lancaster Co. 2 December 1885.[7] C F., son of J. L. **Wilson** and H. S. **Broll**, was born in Iowa abt 1861.

Henry Abraham **Frye** and Helen M. **Diamon** had the following children born in Peoria:

+	6	v.	Agnes Faye **Frye** 20 Februry 1876.
+	7	vi.	Lenore **Frye** in May 1878.

SECOND GENERATION

3. **Marion Kingsley**[2] **Frye** (Henry Abraham[1])[8] was born in Peoria, Peoria Co., Illinois 14 December 1859 and died 12 February 1942 in Lancaster Co., Nebraska, at 82 years of age. He married twice. (1) **Salome Hedges** 6 March 1884. Salome,[9] daughter of Ira **Hedges** and Elizabeth **Duryea**, was born in Keithsburg, Mercer Co., Illinois in 1866. (2) **Alcy**

Kathcart in Lancaster Co. 26 March 1887. Alcy,[10] daughter of William **Kathcart** and Mary **Cochlin**, was born in Wapakoneta, Auglaize Co., Ohio 28 October 1870. After completing school, Marion worked on his father's Illinois farm until 1880 when he moved to Panama (arriving 21 May). His father and the balance of the family followed a year later. Marion began working for Cooper & Canfield, large cattle dealers of Bennet, Lancaster Co. in 1882. After a year he began working for his father until 1887 when he rented a farm near Panama which he operated until 1891. His father's estate was settled that year and he became the owner of 80 acres of good land in Section 22 which he farmed until 1901 when he sold the place and bought the southeast quarter of Section 29, Nemaha Township. He farmed the new place until December 1915 when he sold and moved into Panama. He was a member of the Board of School District No. 26 for nine years, a Presbyterian, a member of Panama Camp No. 2227, M.W.A., in which he held a number of offices, and was a registered Democrat.[11]

Marion Kingsley **Frye** and Salome **Hedges** had the following child born in Lancaster Co.:

    8   i.   Leota[3] **Frye** 23 February 1885 and married Jacob O. **Craig**.

Marion Kingsley **Frye** and Alcy **Kathcart** had the following children born in Lancaster Co.:

    9   ii.   Nellie Maude **Frye**[12] 24 January 1888 and died there in February 1889, at 1 year of age.

    10   iii.   Marion Merle **Frye**[13] 28 October 1892 and married Claude **Gardner**.

    11   iv.   Ellis Kingsley **Frye**[14] 26 May 1894 was graduated from Peru State Normal College, Peru. Nemaha Co., Nebraska and in 1914 and became Principal of the high school at Syracuse, Otoe Co., Nebraska.

6. **Agnes Faye**[2] **Frye** (Henry Abraham[1]) was born in Peoria, Peoria Co. Illinois 20 Februry 1876 and died 11 December 1962 in Portland, Multnomah Co., Oregon, at 86 years of age. She married **Peter T. Peterson** in Panama, Lancaster Co., Nebraska 29 September 1892. Pete,[15] son of Peder **Madsen** and Johanne **Rasmusdatter**, was born in Oster Ulslev, Maribo Co., Denmark 2 April 1869 (christened 17 May) and died 6 July 1940 in Portland, Multnomah Co., Oreg., at 71 years of age.

(For a continuation of the Frye lineage see Agnes Faye Frye's descendants in the Peterson lineage above.)

7. **Lenore**[2] **Frye** (Henry Abraham[1]) was born in Peoria, Peoria Co., Illinois in May 1878[16] and married **George Conn** in Lancaster Co., Nebraska 2 January 1895. George, son of Reuliar **Conn** and Maggie **Kistler**,[17] was born in Indiana in September 1873.[18] Under the title "Panama News," the *Hickman Enterprise*, Hickman, Lancaster, Panama Co., Nebraska in the issue of 6 September 1901 reported that George Conn will have a public sale next week and start for Oregon about 30 September. The issue of 20 September reported that George Conn, Chris Peterson, and O. L. McClum each loaded a car this week and left for Oregon.

Lenore **Frye** and George **Conn** had the following children born in Lancaster Co.:

    22   i.   Edna[3] **Conn**[19] in September 1895.

    23   ii.   Helen **Conn**[20] in June 1897.

FRYE FAMILY ENDNOTES

1. *Lincoln The Capital City and Lancaster County, Nebraska,* 2 vols. Chicago, Ill.: The S.J. Clarke Publishing Co., 1916, 2:286-7. (Hereafter Lincoln, NE, 1916).
2. Ibid., 2:289.
3. Helen Fry entry, 1900 U.S. Census, Lancaster County, Nebraska, Enum. Dist. 79, p. 9, line 100. (Hereafter Helen Frye, *1900 Nebraska*); and Helen Frye entry, 1885 State Census, Lancaster County, Panama Precinct, Nebraska, Enum Dist 494, p. 11, line 19, dwelling 96, family 98. (Hereafter Helen Frye, *1885 State Census*).
4. Lincoln, NE 1916.
5. *Probate Records,* Lancaster Co. Court House, Lincoln, Nebr.
6. Helen Frye, *1885 State Census.*
7. C. F. Wilson & Emma E. Frye, Marriage License, 2 December 1885, State of Nebraska, Office of the County Judge, Lancaster County.
8. Lincoln, Neb. 1916, 2:286-90.
9. and 10. Ibid., 2:289.
11. Ibid., 2: 288-90.
12. through 14. Ibid., 2:289.
15. *Oster Ulslev Parish Registers, Maribo Co., Denmark* (Salt Lake City, UT: Family History Library, Film #0049792), p. 65, No. 3.
16. George Conn entry, 1900 U.S. Census, Lancaster County, Panama Precinct, Nebraska, Enum. Dist 79, p. 5, line 23. (Hereafter George Conn, *1900 U.S. Census.*)
17. George Conn & Lenore Frye, Marriage License, 29 December 1894, State of Nebraska, Office of the County Judge, Lancaster County.
18. through 20. George Conn, *1900 U.S. Census.*

{ G 1724 }

FRIEDERICH LUDWIG BARTRUFF 1826-1902 TO JOSEPHINE BERNIECE BARTRUFF 1901-1995

(Bartruff lineage of Ines Mae Peterson, Generation 12, No. 6209, wife of Robert Blaine Whipple.)

FIRST GENERATION

1. **Friederich Ludwig**[1] **Bartruff**[1] was born in Winzerhausen Oberamt Marbach, Germany 6 June 1826 and died 16 January 1902 in Jonesboro, Union Co., Ilinois, at 75 years of age. He married **Katharina Frederika Spangler** in Wuerttemberg, Germany in 1847. Catherine was born in Lauffen am Neckar, Germany 28 September 1832 and died 29 June 1899 in Jonesboro, at 66 years of age. Both are buried in the Ebenezer German Cemetery south of Jonesboro. From the Jonesboro Town Square drive 3.2 miles south on State Highway 127, turn left on Ebenezer Church Road and drive 1.2 miles to the Ebenezer Methodist Church. The cemetery is adjacent to the church. The birth and death dates are on his tombstone and her name is spelled Catherine Frederica Bartruff on her tombstone.[2] The author has a copy of Friederich's obituary published in German in a German-American newspaper. Neither the name of the paper or its date is known. The obituary was translated by L.H. Bauer in January 1980. Friederich and Frederika emigrated to the U.S. in 1852 and their son Gottlieb Fredrick was born in Portsmouth, Scioto Co., Ohio before the end of 1852 and they were living in Piketon, Pike Co., Ohio by 1857. They were farming near Jonesboro, Union Co., Illinois by 1861. Friederich's Jonesboro's farm was in Section 9, Township 13, Range 1 West. Their post office address in 1865 was Anna, Union Co., Illinois.[3]

Friederich's birth year of 1826 and the immigration year to the U.S. of 1852 are confirmed in the 1900 U.S. Population Schedule for Jonesboro, Union Co., Illinois. He was a widower in 1900 and was living in the home of his daughter Theresa and son-in-law Charles Adam Bauer and their 5-year-old daughter Esther and 3-year-old son Rudolph in Household No. 303 found on sheet 16 in the Jonesboro Precinct of the census. According to the census he could speak English and read and write. It also stated he had not worked for the 12 months previous to the June date the census was taken.

The origin of the Bartruff family name is in question. Though they moved to the U.S. from Germany, the name does not sound Tuetonic and the family religion was "Evaangelische." not Catholic or Luthern. A family tradition suggests they were descendants of French Huguenots. The *Eng-*

{ G 1725 }

lish-German Dictionary compiled by Ernest Thode has nothing on the "-truff" suffix but indicates the "-troff" suffix is a "French place-name suffix meaning Village." The *Lexikon deutscher Hugenottenorte* (lexicon of German places where Huguenots lived) states that Huguenots were connected with Hausen an der Zaber where some Bartruffs lived. Whether these circumstances confirm that the name Bartruff is of French derivation is yet to be proved. Friederich lived in Winzerhausen Oberamt Marbach. A "Winzer" is a vine-grower. Anyone interested in exploring the French Huguenot connection may want to engage Dr. Lutz Jacob and Katharina Kahlert who specialize in the origins and meaning of German names. They may be reached at Gohliser Strasse 1, D-04105 Leipzig, Germany.

The *Wuerttemberg Emigratioin Index* by Trudy Schenk and Ruth Froelke lists several Bartruff emigrants, four of whom spell the name with only one "f." Seven were from the Oberamt of Brackenheim, six from the Oberamt of Heilbronn, one from the Oberamt of Weinsberg and one, Gottlob Bartruff, born in Winzerhkausen, Oberamt of Marbach as was Friederich. Gottlob's birth was 15 August 1834 and his emigration application dated in August 1868 listed North America as his destination (original microfilm # 834609). Few people with the name Bartruff live in Germany in 2005. The majority live in the old Wuerttemberg City of Heilbronn, some in the City of Saarlouis in the German state of Saarland, and a few scattered in other places.

Friederich Ludwig **Bartruff** and Katharina Frederika **Spangler** had the following children:

	2	i.	Gottlieb Fredrick[2] **Bartruff**[4] born in Portsmouth, Scioto Co., Ohio 12 December 1852 and died in infancy.
+	3	ii.	Charles Jacob **Bartruff** born 10 January 1854.
+	4	iii.	Frederick **Bartruff** born 9 September 1856.
+	5	iv.	John **Bartruff** born 13 February 1857.
+	6	v.	Eva Katherine **Bartruff** born 17 June 1859.
+	7	vi.	Jacob E. **Bartruff** born 7 July 1861.
	8	vii.	Mary Anna **Bartruff**[5] born 26 January 1863. She married Philip **Foehr** in Jonesboro, 30 October 1883.
+	9	viii.	Wilhelmina Fredericka **Bartruff** born 4 September 1865.
	10	ix.	Mathis **Bartruff**[6] born 9 September 1866 and died in infancy.
+	11	x.	Joseph E. **Bartruff** born 6 November 1868.
+	12	xi.	William **Bartruff** born 17 July 1871.
+	13	xii.	Theresa Race **Bartruff** born 1 February 1875.
	14	xiii.	Samuel **Bartruff**[7] born in Jonesboro 13 December 1886 and died there 6 January 1893, at 6 years of age.

SECOND GENERATION

3. **Charles Jacob**[2] **Bartruff** (Friedrich Ludwig[1])[8] was born in Portsmouth, Scioto Co., Ohio 10 January 1854 and died 31 January 1936 in Salem, Marion Co., Oregon, at 82 years of age. He married twice. (1) **Anna Mary Loeb** in Jonesboro, Union Co., Illinois 6 September 1882. Anna,[9] daughter of Casper **Loeb** and Elizabeth **Dukshied**, was born in Cobden, Union Co. 6 October 1863 and died 29 March 1911 in Salem, at 47 years of age. Charles and his brother John married sisters Anna Mary and Katherine Loeb. (2) **Mary Bauer** in Jonesboro in 1912. Mary was born there in March 1872 and died 1 June 1945 in Portland, Multnomah Co., Oregon, at 73 years of age.[10] Her parents were born in Germany. She married (1) **Joseph E. Bartruff** in Jonesboro 8 January 1894. Mary was the widow of his brother Joseph. Charles owned a general merchandise store in Jonesboro where he sold dry goods, groceries, and hardware. He moved the family to a farm approximately six miles northeast of Salem in 1890 or 1891. The farm fronted Silverton Road and eventually became Route 7. The move was motivated by a visit to Oregon by Robert Loeb, Mary's brother who, upon his return to Illinois, convinced his sister and brother-in-law that Oregon held a better future for them and their family. Charles sold the store and contacted through a land agent to buy the 80-acre farm which included a small stand of Douglas fir, a prune orchard, and apple, cherry, and pear trees. The move was made by train with Charles renting a boxcar to transport the family and their furniture and other possessions. Their new home was a 2-story farm house with two bedrooms and an attic upstairs and a living room, dining room, two bedrooms, kitchen, and pantry on the main level. It had a front and back porch and outbuildings including a horse barn, cow barn, and chicken coop. Several years later the home was badly burned and was rebuilt larger, including indoor plumbing. The house was furnished, except for the stoves, with things brought from Illinois. The living room had a couch, center table with claw feet, a couple of rockers, some side chairs, and pump organ. The dining room had a table and chairs and a shelf above the wood stove which held "Dad's Bible when he wasn't reading it." The windows had shades and lace curtains. There was a woodburning cook stove in the kitchen and a woodburning heater in both the living and dining rooms. There was no heat upstairs so the kids didn't dawdle much in the winter mornings. They got down to the warm stove as soon as possible.

The parents slept in one of the downstairs bedrooms, the younger kids in the other. The larger bedroom had a closet and highboy chest with five or six drawers. The girls slept in the larger upstairs bedroom in two double beds. They had a two-drawer Princess dresser with mirror but no closet

{ G 1727 }

Bartruff farm home on Silverton Rd, Marion Co., Oreg.

which was not a problem since they didn't have any extra clothes. The boys had the other upstairs bedroom furnished with with one double bed and a small dresser. The hired hands who slept in the attic had a straw tick.

There was no sink in the kitchen but it had a work table with two deep drawers for sugar and flour. The large pantry held most of the food, pots, pans, and other utensils. Two shelves over the kitchen table held other items. Water was heated in a cistern on the cook stove. It came from a well on the back porch.

Charles began his farming career by raising wheat, oats, hay, and harvesting prunes. They had a driving horse for the buckboard and one team of draft horses. He later acquired 60 adjoining acres — some of it heavily timbered with first growth fir — a small dairy herd and a second draft team. They developed a milk route on Silverton Road and sold milk and cream. They usually milked eight to 10 cows and this job fell to Elmer and Margaret who made good use of their time by developing singing voices during their twice-a-day milking times. Margaret said her voice was "so-so soprano" and Elmer had a "beautiful baritone voice." They were good enough to be invited to sing at church and school functions.

Charles hired extra hands for harvest. Some slept in the bunkhouse near the timber on the new acreage, others in the attic in their home. A neighbor with a binder was hired to cut the grain. Fruit from the apple, cherry, and pear trees and prune orchard was sold to commerical packers in Salem. The income from the prune orchard always covered the property taxes. He hired cutters in the fall and sold large quantities of cord wood to large commercial accounts in Salem. It was a self-sufficient family with large garden, fruit, chickens, cows, hogs, and timber supply. A noon dinner was the main meal followed by an evening supper. The hired hands often ate with them which the kids enjoyed because they were someone new to talk to. The kids went to Middle Grove School and walked the mile each way. It was a 1-teacher, 1-room school with grades 1-8. Most of the kids didn't go beyond eight grade.

Charles was approximately 5' 7" with an average build for his height. He had blue eyes, auburn hair, and wore a full beard which was reddish before turning gray. He was a religious man who conducted daily family prayers and read the Bible to the children following breakfast. He eventually became a deacon or trustee in a Salem church. He completed the eighth grade and took a business course at night school in Illinois. Both Charles and Mary spoke German and they subscribed to a German language newspaper from Illinois. Other than the paper and the Bible there wasn't much to read in the home. Charles told the children stories about the Civil War and how notorious Confederate General John Hunt Morgan and his Raiders made skirmishes to their area of southern Illinois to steal horses and other livestock. When they heard Morgan was in the area, Charles had to hide their horses in some nearby timber until the Raiders left. He also told the children about seeing President Lincoln's Funeral Train on the way to Springfield for burial. Mary was about 5' '6" with gray eyes and black hair and had an eighth grade education. She and Charles sang German songs to the children who didn't understand the words but they learned them and sang along. Mary was was extremely overweight and suffered poor health for much of her adult life. An excellent cook and baker, she was unable to stand or be near the stove toward the end of her life. She died suddenly of a heart attack.

About a year after Mary died, Charles returned to Jonesboro to marry

Middlegrove School, Silverton Rd. Younger children attended first through eight grades here.

his brother Joseph's widow and returned with her and her daughters, Lillian and Theresa, and sons, Erick, Louis, and Ed. Mary's oldest son George was married and remained in Illinois. The step-mother-aunt was never accepted by Charles' children.[11] Charles' obituary appears in the Salem *Capital Journal* of 31 January 1936. He was buried at Howell Cemetery in the same plot as his first wife, Mary and their daughter Gertrude. Mary's grave had a stone but neither Charles or Gertrude did. In 1998 a number of his grandchildren and great grandchildren installed a stone with the names of all three. Howell Cemetery, established in 1843, is .2 mile north of Silverton Road on 64th Place N.E. The Bartruff plot is at the north end of the Cemetery in the second row from 64th Place.

Charles Jacob **Bartruff** and Anna Mary **Loeb** had the following children:

+ 15 i. Lydia Helen[3] **Bartruff** born 7 July 1883.
+ 16 ii. Daniel Edward **Bartruff** born 22 August 1884.
+ 17 iii. Anna Elizabeth **Bartruff** born 25 March 1886.
   18 iv. Rosa Katherine **Bartruff**[12] born in Jonesboro 31 December 1888 and died unmarried 1 January 1974 in Salem, at 85 years of age. Buried in Salem's Lee Mission Cemetery. She attended Middle Grove Grade School, was graduated from Salem High School, and studied nursing at the Salem Hospital Training School for Nurses. She also studied at the U. of California and took a course in Hospital Administration at Seattle College in Seattle, King Co., Washington. She was inducted into the U. S. Nurse Corp in Salem in October 1918 and was stationed at Camp Dodge, Des Moines, Polk Co., Iowa, St. Louis, Independence Co., Missouri., and Plattsburg, Clinton Co., New York where she was discharged in September 1919.
+ 19 v. Elmer Walter **Bartruff** born 27 December 1890.
   20 vi. Margaret Elfreda **Bartruff**.[13] Born in Salem 12 May 1893 and died 22 March 1983 in Mt. Angel, Marion Co., Oregon, at 89 years of age. She married Andrew Lyman **Bunch** in Portland 3 July 1919. He was born 1 July and died 28 April 1962 at 61 years of age.[14] Margaret remembers the Bartruff home as a place where God was honored — "especially by Dad" who had so much joy in serving God and greeted friends with a "God Bless You." She remembers her father telling her that his parents were married at Wurttemberg, Germany and that they came to America shortly after being married about the time of the Crimean War when many young German men left to

avoid conscription. Her mother told her that her mother (__) Metz (Margaret's grandmother) and aunt came to America from Germany together. Margaret remembers that her mother taught her the scale and chords on the organ when she was about 7. She says she wasn't tall enough to sit on the stool to play so had to stand and play. She enjoyed practicing and eventually got good enough to play at school and church functions. She said the Bartruff kids didn't have a lot of scheduled activities as children but there was the occasional birthday party and special occasion but they were not allowed to go to dances, movies, or other "racy" things. But, we always had a nice tree at Christmas and were remembered with gifts.[15] Margaret and Andrew were childless and are buried in the Lee Mission Cemetery in Salem.

21   vii.   Gertrude Matilda **Bartruff**[16] born in Salem 1 April 1895 and died there 18 February 1898, at 2 years of age. Buried at Howell Cemetery with her parents.

22   viii.   Lois Mabel **Bartruff**.[17] Born in Salem 9 December 1897 and died there 21 June 1974, at 76 years of age. She married Grant **Wycoff** in Salem 24 November 1921.[18] Grant is buried beside Lois at Salem's Lee Mission Cemetery. Lois was graduated from Salem High School. One of her most precious memories was her mother's cheerful outlook on life. "No matter what the disappointment, she would try to find something for me to be glad about. She knew she was dying but never talked about it in front of we children. I would hear her saying quietly to herself, 'Praise the Lord.' I don't believe she had any idea anyone heard her." Lois and Grant were childless.

+   23.   ix.   Josephine Berniece **Bartruff** was born 21 March 1901.

24   x.   Ruth Mildred **Bartruff**[19] born in Salem 13 October 1904[20] and died 27 March 1998 in Portland, at 93 years of age.[21] She married Willard **Walter** in Portland 5 April 1931. They were divorced. Both worked for the federal government in Washington, D. C. following the election of President Franklin D. Roosevelt. No issue. Ruth is buried in Lee Mission Cemetery.

    4. **Frederick**[2] **Bartruff** (Friederich Ludwig[1])[22] was born in Portsmouth, Scioto Co., Ohio 9 September 1855[23] and died 1 January 1921 in Anna, Union Co., Illinois, at 64 years of age. He married **Mary J. Schaefer** 16

{ G 1731 }

September 1879. Mary was born in Illinois 20 June 1861[24] and died 3 January 1922 in Anna, at 60 years of age.[25] According to the 1880 federal census of Union County, Town of Jonesboro, Fred was a 24-year-old farmer born in Ohio whose parents were born in Germany. Mary was an 18-year-old housekeeper born in Illinois whose parents were born in Germany. They rented a farm for a share of the production. The farm had a value of $150 and included 15 acres of tilled land, 14 of which were devoted to wheat and produced 90 bushels in 1879. Farm implements were valued at $10, and livestock at $120. They owned one horse, one milking cow, one "other" cow and one calve was "dropped" during the year. The 20 poultry in the barnyard produced 50 eggs in 1879. Total value of goods produced in 1879 was $95. Both are buried in Ebenezer German Cemetery in Jonesboro.

Frederick **Bartruff** and Mary J. **Schaefer** had the following children:
+ 25 i. Joseph Ernest[3] **Bartruff** born 3 September 1881.
+ 26 ii. Emma Ester **Bartruff** born 6 May 1884.
   27 iii. Samuel **Bartruff**[26] born in Anna 13 December 1886 and died 6 January 1893, at 6 years of age.[27]
+ 28 iv. Rudolph E. **Bartruff** born 29 April 1889.
+ 29 v. Huldah Freeda **Bartruff** born 6 April 1893.
+ 30 vi. Elda **Bartruff** born 30 July 1894.
+ 31 vii. Walter Benjamin **Bartruff** born 7 February 1897.
+ 32 viii. Carl William **Bartruff** born 15 September 1899.

5. **John**[2] **Bartruff** (Friederich Ludwig[1])[28] was born in Piketon, Pike Co., Ohio 13 February 1857[29] and died 29 November 1929 in Salem, Marion Co., Oregon, at 72 years of age. He married **Katherine Loeb** in Jonesboro, Union Co., Illinois in 1881. Katherine, daughter of Casper **Loeb** and Elizabeth **Dukshied**, was born in Kentucky in January 1857[30] and died 27 January 1931 in Salem, at 74 years of age. Brothers John and Charles married sisters Katherine and Mary Loeb. John lost his hand in a corn sheller and almost lost his mind constantly thinking that worms were chewing on his hand in the dark earth where it was buried. Finally, one of his brothers dug up the hand, placed it in a glass jar, and reburied it. From then on John was okay and was seen using a hook and doing almost everything he had been able to do before the accident.[31] Both are buried in Howell Cemetery.

John **Bartruff** and Katherine **Loeb** had the following child:
+ 33 i. John Robert[3] **Bartruff** born 18 January 1883.

6. **Eva Katherine**[2] **Bartruff** (Friederich Ludwig[1])[32] was born in Piketon, Pike Co., Ohio 17 June 1859 and died died 10 April 1955 in Salem, Marion Co., Oregon, at 95 years of age. She married **Frank Scharf** in Jonesboro, Union Co., Illinois 12 May 1885. Frank,[33] son of August **Scharf** and Appolonia **Duerekheimer**, was born 28 May 1861 and died 17 November 1942 in Salem, at 81 years of age.

Frank and Kate and their family moved to Oregon in September 1907 from Jonesboro. Both are buried in Howell Cemetery.

Eva Katherine **Bartruff** and Frank **Scharf** had the following children born in Jonesboro:

- \+ 34 i. William Harry[3] **Scharf** 17 September 1886.
- \+ 35 ii. Rose Katherine **Scharf** 23 November 1887.
- \+ 36 iii. August Frederick Ludwig **Scharf** 7 June 1889.
- \+ 37 iv. John Edward **Scharf** 3 June 1891.
- \+ 38 v. Joseph Elmer **Scharf** 5 November 1893.
- \+ 39 vi. Daniel Peter **Scharf** 15 August 1896.
- \+ 40 vii. Esther Freda **Scharf** 8 February 1899.

7. **Jacob E.**[2] **Bartruff** (Friederich Ludwig[1])[34] was born in Jonesboro, Union Co., Illinois 7 July 1861 and died there 12 August 1940, at 79 years of age. He married **Anna Bauer** in Jonesboro 16 July 1892. Anna was born 15 August 1869 and died 16 March 1940 in Jonesboro, at 70 years of age.[35]

Brothers Jacob and Joseph married sisters Theresa and Mary Bauer. In 1865 Jacob's farm was in Section 7, Township 13, Range 1 West. His post office address was Jonesboro.[36]

Jacob E. **Bartruff** and Anna **Bauer** had the following children born in Jonesboro:

- \+ 41 i. Ernest Frederick[3] **Bartruff** 19 May 1893.
- 42 ii. Herbert Edward **Bartruff**[37] 14 August 1896 and died 23 March 1957, at 60 years of age. He married Virgie E. **Brown** in Jonesboro 23 July 1922. She died in Anna, Union Co., 22 July 1960.
- \+ 43 iii. Clara Augusta **Bartruff** 1 April 1898.
- \+ 44 iv. Adolph Benjamin **Bartruff** 21 March 1900.
- \+ 45 v. Paul Martin **Bartruff** 28 May 1902.
- \+ 46 vi. Lydia Rosetta **Bartruff** 6 March 1904.
- 47 vii. Olva **Bartruff**[38] 6 June 1906 and married Helen Marie **Bauer** in Anna 3 November 1929.
- \+ 48 viii. David Leo **Bartruff** 25 March 1909.
- \+ 49 ix. Gilbert James **Bartruff** 25 July 1912.

9. **Wilhelmina Fredericka**[2] **Bartruff** (Friederich Ludwig1)[39] was born 4 September 1865 and died 17 February 1930 in Jonesboro, Union Co., Illinois, at 64 years of age.[40] She married **Phillip E. Weiss** who was born in Germany in 1864 and died 11 February 1920 in Jonesboro, at 55 years of age.

Philip, a naturalized citizen, was a day laborer. The Jonesboro U.S. census for 1900 gives his birth as April 1863. Minnie and her brother William married Weiss siblings, Phillip and Elizabeth.

Wilhelmina Fredericka **Bartruff** and Phillip E. **Weiss** had the following children born in Jonesboro:

    50   i.   Susan Ida[3] **Weiss**[41] 21 October 1886 and died 28 February 1922 at 35 years of age. She married Frank **Casey**

+ 51   ii. Effin Mary **Weiss** 9 January 1888.

+ 52   iii. Arthur Peter **Weiss** 15 July 1891.

+ 53   iv. Louis **Weiss** 4 October 1891.

    54   v. Rudolph Benjamin **Weiss**[42] 9 August 1894[43] and died 12 July 1966 in Denver, Denver Co. Colorado, at 71 years of age. He married Grace **Hull** in Louisville, Jefferson Co. Kentucky.

    55   vi. Samuel **Weiss**[44] 15 June 1895[45] and married twice. (1) Blanch **Weaver** in Jonesboro 9 January 1918. She died 28 May 1966 in Jonesboro.[46] (2) Susan **Ecker** in Jonesboro 19 January 1967.

+ 56   vii. Clara K. **Weiss** 1 December 1896.

    57   viii. Anna C. **Weiss**[47] 28 December 1899[48] and died 13 March 1932 in Anna, Union Co., at 32 years of age. She married O. Oswald **Cerney**.

    58   ix. William R. **Weiss** 6 December 1900 and married Irene **Thiess** in Jonesboro 1 October 1923.

11. **Joseph E.**[2] **Bartruff** (Friederich Ludwig1)[49] was born in Jonesboro, Union Co., Illinois 6 November 1868 and died there 18 April 1909, at 40 years of age.[50] He married **Mary Bauer** in Jonesboro 8 January 1894. Mary was born in Jonesboro in March 1872[51] and married (2) **Charles Jacob Bartruff** there in 1912. She died 1 June 1945 in Portland, Multnomah Co., Oregon, at 73 years of age. Her parents were born in Germany. Joseph was a farmer. His birth month is given as March in the 1900 U.S. Census for Jonesboro (sheet 15, household 318) conducted 9 June by Paul W. Baker.

Joseph E. **Bartruff** and Mary **Bauer** had the following children:

    59   i.   George Andrew[3] **Bartruff**[52] 11 August 1894[53] and died 1 November 1967 in Washington State, at 73 years of age. He married Sarah Opal **Ellis** in Jonesboro 25 November 1916.

+	60	ii.	Louis Mathis **Bartruff** 29 November 1896.
+	61	iii.	Eric Edwin **Bartruff** 27 December 1898.
+	62	iv.	Edward Jona **Bartruff** 21 June 1900.
+	63	v.	Teresa Ellen **Bartruff** 6 April 1902.
	64	vi.	(Daughter) **Bartruff** 27 June 1905 and died the day of birth.[54]
+	65	vii.	Lillian Viola **Bartruff** 1 March 1907.

12. **William**[2] **Bartruff** (Friedrich Ludwig[1])[55] was born in Jonesboro, Union Co., Illinois 17 July 1871 and died there 14 November 1934, at 63 years of age.[56] He married **Elizabeth Weiss** there 16 January 1893. She was born in Illinois in March 1876 and died 15 March 1952 in Jonesboro, at 76 years of age. Her parents, names unknown, were born in Germany.

William **Bartruff** and Elizabeth **Weiss** had the following children born in Jonesboro:

+	66	i.	Susan Katherine[3] **Bartruff** 18 December 1895.
+	67	ii.	Samuel Andrew **Bartruff** 24 August 1897.
	68	iii.	Lulu Mabel **Bartruff**[57] 21 June 1899[58] and married James Herman **Stilly** 1 July 1922.
	69	iv.	Benjamin William **Bartruff**[59] 27 November 1902 and died 10 June 1926 at 23 years of age.
	70	v.	Laura Augusta **Bartruff**[60] 17 October 1905 and married Doyle **Lipe** there 29 May 1926.
	71	vi.	Glenn LaVerne **Bartruff**[61] 26 January 1908 and died 8 July 1964 at 56 years of age. He married Agnes **Ingram** in Jackson, Kansas City Co., Missouri 7 October 1939.
+	72	vii.	Arthur Watson **Bartruff** 10 September 1911.

13. **Theresa Race**[2] **Bartruff** (Friedrich Ludwig[1])[62] was born in Jonesboro, Union Co., Illinois 1 February 1875 and died there 21 September 1969, at 94 years of age. She married **Charles Adam Bauer** in Jonesboro 18 August 1895. Charles, an Engineer, was born in Illinois in March 1872.[63] His parents are unknown but according to the 1900 U.S. Jonesboro Census, his father was born in Illinois and his mother in Ohio.

Theresa Race **Bartruff** and Charles Adam **Bauer** had the following children born in Jonesboro:

+	73	i.	Esther[3] **Bauer** 8 September 1895.
+	74	ii.	Rudolph **Bauer** 25 July 1897.
+	75	iii.	Frederick Joe **Bauer** 16 January 1902.

THIRD GENERATION

15. **Lydia Helen**[3] **Bartruff** (Charles Jacob[2], Friederich Ludwig[1])[64] was born in Jonesboro, Union Co., Illinois 7 July 1883 and died 7 July 1960 in Salem, Marion Co., Oregon, at 77 years of age. She married twice. (1) **Omer George Bewley** in Salem 17 June 1903.[65] They divorced there abt 1932. He died 1 March 1952 in Salem. (2) **Thomas L. Ross**, a farmer and resident of Salem for 60 years, in Salem 11 May 1942. He was born in Kentucky 8 February 1873 and died 3 April 1952 in Salem, at 79 years of age.[66] They lived at 1050 N. 19th St. His funeral services were at the Howell-Edwards Chapel and he was buried at the IOOF Cemetery. In addition to Lydia, he was survived by son Claude of Tillamook, Tillamook Co., Oregon, grandson Robert Ross of Portland, Multnomah Co., and granddaughter Mrs. Herman Schlappi of Corvallis, Benton Co., Oregon.

Lydia remembers that her mother had premonitions about many different events. She especially remembers when she was about 5 and Dan was 4 and they were staying with their grandmother Elizabeth (Dukshied) Loeb at Cobden, Union Co., Illinois their mother had a vision one night that they were in serious trouble. She caught the train to Coben the next morning and found the children had pulled up a board on the cistern and were lying on their stomachs spilling in the cistern. Grandma Loeb was in the garden tying up tomatoes and unaware of what the kids were doing. Mother believed we would have fallen in and drown if she hadn't come to check.

Lydia Helen **Bartruff** and Omer George **Bewley** had the following children:
- \+ 76 i. Helen Lola[4] **Bewley** born 9 August 1904.
- \+ 77 ii. Gladys Elizabeth **Bewley** born 19 April 1906.
- \+ 78 iii. Carl Omer **Bewley** born 13 January 1911.

16. **Daniel Edward**[3] **Bartruff** (Charles Jacob[2], Friederich Ludwig[1])[67] was born in Jonesboro, Union Co., Illinois 22 August 1884 and died 1 August 1938 in Dayton, Yamhill Co., Oregon, at 53 years of age. He married **Laura Humphrey** in Salem, Marion Co., Oregon 29 November 1916. Laura was born in 1888 and died 2 February 1958 in Salem, at 69 years of age.[68] Daniel attended Middle Grove School and Dallas College. Both are buried in Howell Cemetery east of Salem.

Daniel Edward **Bartruff** and Laura **Humphrey** had the following children born in Salem:
- \+ 79 i. Cordelia[4] **Bartruff** 16 June 1918.
- \+ 80 ii. Rosa Winifred **Bartruff** 22 December 1920.
- \+ 81 iii. Wallace Lynn **Bartruff** 2 March 1925.

17. **Anna Elizabeth**[3] **Bartruff** (Charles Jacob[2], Friederich Ludwig[1])[69] was born in Jonesboro, Union Co., Illinois 25 March 1886 and died 31 January 1969 in Salem, Marion Co., Oregon, at 82 years of age. She married **Herbert McDonough** in Salem 8 May 1907. He died 2 November 1963 in Salem.[70] Both are buried in City View Cemetery.

Anna Elizabeth **Bartruff** and Herbert **McDonough** adopted the following child:
+ 82 i. Delbert Leroy[4] **McDonough** born 16 May 1920.

19. **Elmer Walter**[3] **Bartruff** (Charles Jacob[2], Friederich Ludwig[1])[71] was born in Jonesboro, Union Co., Illinois 27 December 1890 and died 28 June 1946 in Coos Bay, Coos Co., Oregon, at 55 years of age.

He married **Lonie Melvin Peoples** in Salem, Marion Co., Oregon 12 October 1917. Lonie,[72] daughter of Oliver Mason **Peoples** and Gracie **Inge**, was born in Morgan Co., Missouri 7 February 1895 and died 28 June 1946 in Coos Bay, at 51 years of age. She lived in the LaComb, Linn Co., Oregon area 29 years before her death. She was survived by her father, Oliver, two sisters, Mrs. Esther Chritcher and Mrs. Lyda Keebough, three brothers, Lacy M., Ralph W. and Frank O., and a stepbrother Carl T. Morris.

Elmer attended Oregon State College in Corvallis, Benton Co., Oregon. He and Lonie drowned in Coos Bay when their fishing boat overturned. Her body was found about a week later when it washed ashore. A double funeral service was conducted at the Howe-Huston chapel in Lebanon on 3 July. She was buried in the Lacomb Cemetery. Separate grave side rites were read for him after his body was recovered.

Elmer Walter **Bartruff** and Lonie Melvin **Peoples** had the following children born in LaComb:
+ 83 i. Grace Velma[4] **Bartruff** 13 November 1918.
+ 84 ii. Victor Leon **Bartruff** 26 March 1921.
+ 85 iii. Bryce Oliver **Bartruff** 6 February 1926.
+ 86 iv. Marion Elizabeth **Bartruff** 14 April 1930.

23. **Josephine Berniece**[3] **Bartruff** (Charles Jacob[2], Friederich Ludwig[1])[73] was born in Marion Co., Oregon 21 March 1901 and died 14 February 1995 in Portland, Multnomah Co., Oregon, at 93 years of age. She married **Owen Diamon Peterson** in Corvallis, Benton Co., Oregon 14 February 1924. Owen,[74] son of Peter T. **Peterson** and Agnes Faye **Frye**, was born in Panama, Lancaster Co., Nebraska 1 December 1894 and died 28 October 1943 in Portland, at 48 years of age.

Jo was born on the Bartruff family's 140 acre farm east of Salem on Silverton, Road. Today the farm home is known as 5963 Silverton Rd., S.E., Salem. She attended grades one through eight at Middle Grove School (the corner of Silverton and Cordon Roads) and walked the 1.4 mile each way. She completed the ninth and tenth grades at a Salem High School where she sang soprano in the chorus. While in the ninth grade, she lived in Salem with her sister Lydia (18 years her senior) and brother-in-law Omer Bewley. She was back home for her sophomore year and got to and from school by horse and buggy. Her 16th birthday stands out because a boy friend invited her to a movie and her parents said she could go — it would be her first. But they didn't go to a movie. He drove into Salem and right back to her home where the house was full of family and friends who were having a surprise party for her. "I don't remember any of the gifts but I sure remember the occasion," she said. Times were tough so her parents decided she had enough schooling and she spent the next year-and-a-half on her brother Elmer's farm in LaComb, Linn Co., Oregon where she did house work, general farm work, and milked cows. In 1918 she and her cousin Esther Scharf spent six months at a logging camp in Yacolt, Clark Co., Washington working in the cook house and waiting tables. When the camp closed for the winter season, she moved to Portland and lived with Lydia and Omer who had moved there with their three children — Helen, Gladys, and Carl. She worked for her board and room and later became a live-in domestic for the Russell family who lived in Portland's Ladd's Addition. She enrolled in a nurse's training course at Sellwood Hospital in Portland sometime in 1920 and lived at the Hospital for three years while in training and gaining practical nursing experience. Students received board and room and $5 a month spending money. She was graduated as a Registered Nurse but didn't practice, marrying shortly after graduation.

Jo and Owen met on a blind date in the summer of 1923. It was a picnic-swimming date on the Willamette River, "the first real date I ever had and he was the only real boy friend I ever had." After we were married, he always gave me the same gift every anniversary — a box of chocolates. "Funny, the box kept getting smaller the longer we were married." They were married in Corvallis, Benton Co., Oregon in a Parsonage by Rev. S.M. Wood, an Evangelical preacher. After the ceremony they went to Albany, Linn Co., Oregon for a luncheon hosted by her sister Anna (Mrs. Herbert McDonough) and her family. From there they drove to the Peterson farm at Parker, Polk Co. Oregon to tell his folks about the surprise wedding, then returned to Portland. Owen's twin brother Oscar was best man and Jo's younger sister Ruth, a freshman at Oregon State College in Corvallis, was maid of honor. They rented the Portland home of Jo's sister Margaret and her husband Andrew L. Bunch who were working in a logging camp. Wayne and Norm were born when they lived in this Montavilla Park home. Wayne was born at St. Vincents Hospital and Norm in the Women's Maternity Home. Jo was in the hospital with each for two weeks after they born. The cost was $90 plus the doctor's bill. Ines and Bob were born in the Portland Adventist Hospital. They had to give up the house when the Bunch's returned and rented a house in Ladd's Addition. They purchased a home at 6123 SE 21st in the Westmoreland District of Portland in 1927 and Jo lived there for the next sixty years. Almost new, the house cost $5,200. They borrowed $2,000 from the First National Bank for the down payment and got a mortgage from the State Veteran Home Loan Program. The payment was $15 a month. Jo's memories of her mother, who died when Jo was 10, are limited. She did not get along with her step-mother-aunt and after her father's second marriage so most of the family socializing was with the Petersons. Her relationship with her mother-in-law Agnes Frye Peterson was close. "I loved her like I would a mother." The family spent some holidays and summer time at the Peterson farm in Parker but it was an all-day trip so they didn't get to go as often as they would have liked. They were also frequent visitors to the Dundee farm of Owen's sister and brother-in-law, Winnogene and Ellis Baker. While the family lived frugally, they always owned a car and were able to take annual vacations to places like Long Beach, Pacific Co., Washington where they did a lot of claming and to various fishing lakes in central and eastern Oregon. One summer in the 1930s, they motored to Yellowstone National Park. Owen loved fishing and was on the Willamette and Clackamas rivers on most of his days off during fishing season. "We always had our share of salmon and to his everlasting credit he always cleaned the fish." Owen did most of the food preparation at the fire station and became an excellent cook. Jo said he was a great helpmate, cooking and baking, diapering the kids, helping with the wash, etc. He was also a good mechanic and always took care of their cars. The family usually spent Christmas at home, many times without Owen as he was on duty. Limited finances made it impossible to give the kids the presents they wanted but they always got at least one toy. The older boys got bikes that Owen fixed and repainted. Turkey, which Owen won at a turkey shoot, was the usual Thanksgiving and Christmas meal. When the kids were small, Jo cut their hair and made most of their clothes. She also knit Argyle socks. Disciplining the kids fell mostly to her. The kids had the usual childhood diseases. Owen enjoyed good health but Jo had frequent bouts with pleurisy and pneumonia. She was on the verge of a nervous breakdown in the early 1940s but thyroid treatments helped overcome that problem.

 Jo was a "Born Again Christian" who attended tent revival meetings as a youngster. "Believe in the Lord Jesus Christ and thy shall be saved," was her creed. She was a long-time member of the Moreland Presbyterian Church but eventually left that Church and joined the Lents Evangelical Church, feeling the Presbyterians had become too modern and no longer satisfied her basic Christian needs. She attended Wednesday Bible classes and Sunday services and purchased bonds to help the Lents Church in its building program. She gave each of her grandchildren a $1,000 church bond.

About two years after her husband died, Jo began a 12-year career as a cook in the cafeteria at Cleveland High School. She left that job to become a clerk at the Portland State University Book Store for 10 years. By the time of her retirement at age 68, she was in charge of her shift's receipts and for depositing the money in a night depositary. After retirement, she and her sister Ruth visited Israel, Egypt, Syria, and Greece. In later years she visited Taiwan, Japan, Alaska, and Hawaii with various friends. She developed cataracts in her 70s (age) and operations on each eye a year apart greatly improved her vision. She was still driving her car in her mid-80s.[75] Her granddaughter Rev. Judith L. Steele officiated at her Memorial Service 2 March 1995 at the Virgil T. Golden Chapel in Salem. Her grandson Scott Whipple delivered the eulogy. Pallbearers were her grandchildren: Mark, James, and John Peterson, Deborah (Peterson) Smith, Sandra (Peterson) Dodson, Kelly Reitz, Robert B. Steele, and Scott Whipple. She was buried in Salem's Lee Mission Cemetery. Her sisters Ruth Walter, Margaret Bunch, Rosa Bartruff, and Lois Wycoff are in adjacent graves as are her brothers-in-law Andy Bunch and Grant Wycoff.

Josephine Berniece **Bartruff** and Owen Diamon **Peterson** had the following children born in Portland:

+   87   i.   Wayne Allan **Peterson**.
     88   ii.   Norman Owen **Peterson**.
+   89   iii.   Ines Mae **Peterson**.
+   90   iv.   Robert Charles **Peterson**.

(See Peterson Family above, Generation 3, for a continuation of the Bartruff lineage.)

25. **Joseph Ernest**[3] **Bartruff** (Frederick[2], Friederich Ludwig[1])[76] was born in Ware, Union Co., Illinois 3 September 1881[77] and died 20 February 1953 in Salem, Marion Co., Oregon, at 71 years of age. He married **Christina Carolyn Duerckheimer** in Union Co. 20 January 1903. She was born in Jonesboro, Union Co. 25 February 1880 and after an illness of two years died 25 October 1957 in Salem, at 77 years of age.[78] She was buried in Salem's City View Cemetery. Joe and Christine moved to Oregon from Illinois in 1917 and lived in the Hazel Green area of Marion

county for two years before moving to the Keizer, Marion Co. area where he was a farmer.

Joseph Ernest **Bartruff** and Christina Carolyn **Duerckheimer** had the following children:

    91   i.   Elton Valentine[4] **Bartruff**.[79]

    92   ii.   Maria Magdalena **Bartruff**.[80]

    93   iii.   Verna Elizabeth **Bartruff**[81] married (__) **Byerly**. She lived at Albany, Linn Co., Oregon.

    94   iv.   Nina Louise **Bartruff**[82] married (__) **Stesmey**. She lived in Salem.

    95   v.   May Margaret **Bartruff**[83] married (__) **Poole**. She lived at Annapolis, Sonoma Co., California.

    96   vi.   Joseph Sydney **Bartruff**.[84]

    97   vii.   Chris Martin **Bartruff**.[85]

    98   viii.   Muriel Carolyn **Bartruff**[86] and married (__) **Zumer**. She lived in Salem.

26. **Emma Ester**[3] **Bartruff** (Frederick[2], Friederich Ludwig[1])[87] was born in Anna, Union Co., Illinois 6 May 1884[88] and died 3 March 1928 at 43 years of age. She married **Walter Carl Hileman** 21 August 1904. Walter,[89] son of Jacob **Hileman** and Mary E. **Kimmel**, was born in Union Co. 10 May 1882 and died 13 February 1965 in Anna, at 82 years of age. They are buried in Mission Chapel Cemetery, Anna.

Emma Ester **Bartruff** and Walter Carl **Hileman** had the following children born in Anna:

    99   i.   Owen Warren[4] **Hileman**[90] 5 October 1904 and died there 21 January 1915, at 10 years of age.

    100   ii.   Fredrick Jacob **Hileman** 6 February 1906 and married Nellie **Eddleman** 16 March 1930.

+   101   iii.   Floyd Lester **Hileman** 23 May 1907.

    102   iv.   Elmer Raymond **Hileman** 17 December 1908. He never married.

    103   v.   Mary Helen **Hileman**[91] 13 October 1911 and died 22 February 1988 at 76 years of age. She married George **Sivia** in 1935.

    104   vi.   Lela Irene **Hileman**[92] 25 March 1914 and died 7 May 1948 at 34 years of age. She married Bud **Settlemoir** 2 July 1932. Bud was born in 1871 and died in 1940, at 69 years of age.[93]

    105   vii.   Everett Woodrow **Hileman**[94] 4 April 1917 and died 18 June 1983 at 66 years of age. He married Gertrude **Farlie**.

106 viii. Naomi LaVerne **Hileman**[95] 11 August 1922 and died 27 December 1950 at 28 years of age. She married Edward **Snyder**.

28. **Rudolph E.**[3] **Bartruff** (Frederick[2], Friederich Ludwig[1])[96] was born in Jonesboro, Union Co., Illinois 29 April 1889[97] and died 21 November 1964 in Anna, Union Co., at 75 years of age. He married **Rose Pauline Zeller** in Anna 16 September 1913. She was born in 1889 and died 5 January 1973 in Anna, at 83 years of age.[98]

Rudolph E. **Bartruff** and Rose Pauline **Zeller** had the following children:
  107 i. Dennis Harold[4] **Bartruff**.[99]
  108 ii. Frances Viola **Bartruff**.[100]
  109 iii. Robert Lee **Bartruff**.[101]
  110 iv. Georgia Lorne **Bartruff**.[102]

29. **Huldah Freeda**[3] **Bartruff** (Frederick[2], Friederich Ludwig[1])[103] was born in Jonesboro, Union Co., Illinois 6 April 1893[104] and died 1 January 1925 in Anna, Union Co., at 31 years of age. She married **William Otis Brown** in Anna 11 August 1911.

Huldah Freeda **Bartruff** and William Otis **Brown** had the following children:
  111 i. Clifford Otis[4] **Brown**.[105]
  112 ii. Lester Paul **Brown**.[106]
  113 iii. Bon Richard **Brown**.[107]
  114 iv. Berniece Mae **Brown**.[108]

30. **Elda**[3] **Bartruff** (Frederick[2], Friederich Ludwig[1])[109] was born in Anna, Union Co., Illinois 30 July 1894[110] and died 15 February 1961 in Illinois, at 66 years of age. She married **William E. Freeman** there 30 January 1916.

Elda **Bartruff** and William E. **Freeman** had the following children:
  115 i. William Frederick[4] **Freeman**.[111]
  116 ii. Wilma Jean **Freeman**.[112]

31. **Walter Benjamin**[3] **Bartruff** (Frederick[2], Friederich Ludwig[1])[113] was born in Anna, Union Co., Illinois 7 February 1897[114] and died there 6 February 1950, at 52 years of age. He married **Lela Jerrell** in Anna 25 April 1918.

Walter Benjamin **Bartruff** and Lela **Jerrell** had the following children:
  117 i. June Maxine[4] **Bartruff**[115] married Olen **Osman** who was born 27 June 1927.

+ 118 ii. Wayne Watson **Bartruff** born 15 October 1919.
119 iii. Courtney Belmont **Bartruff**[116] born 19 April 1922.
+ 120 iv. Harold Eugene **Bartruff** born 13 December 1924.

32. **Carl William**[3] **Bartruff** (Frederick[2], Friederich Ludwig[1])[117] was born in Anna, Union Co., Illinois 15 September 1899[118] and died 11 December 1964 in Salem, Marion Co., Oregon, at 65 years of age. He married **Martha Ammann** in Salem 18 November 1926.

Carl William **Bartruff** and Martha **Ammann** had the following child born in Salem:
121 i. Carl Eugene[4] **Bartruff**.[119]

33. **John Robert**[3] **Bartruff** (John[2], Friederich Ludwig[1])[120] was born in Jonesboro, Union Co., Illinois 18 January 1883[121] and died 29 November 1927 in Salem, Marion Co., Oregon, at 44 years of age. He married **Lena Maude Knupp** in Wetaug, Pulaski Co. Illinois 4 October 1906. She was born in Wetaug 14 October 1885 and died in 1958 in Salem, at 72 years of age. She lived at 6102 Silverton Rd. NE at the time of her death. She was a member of the Middle Grove Evangelical United Brethren Church. Her funeral services were at the Virgil T. Golden Chapel and she was buried at Howell Cemetery east of Salem. In addition to her children, she was survived by a brother, John Cecil Knupp of St. Louis, Independence Co., Missouri, three sisters, Mrs. Minnie Lichiliter, Mrs. Vera Goodman, and Mrs. Bertie Misenheimer, all living in Illinois, 19 grandchildren and seven great grandchildren. Robert and Lena moved to Salem from Illinois in 1910. He farmed and worked for the Marion County Road Department.

John Robert **Bartruff** and Lena Maude **Knupp** had the following children:
122 i. Frieda LaWanda[4] **Bartruff**[122] married (__) **Schwab**. She was living in Portland, Oregon in 1959.
123 ii. Cecil Paul **Bartruff**[123] was living in San Angelo, Tom Green Co., Texas in 1959.
124 iii. Helen Roberta **Bartruff**[124] married (__) **Crocker**. She was living in Monument, Grant Co., Oregon in 1959.
125 iv. Emery David **Bartruff**[125] was living in Salem in 1959.
126 v. George Zacharius **Bartruff**[126] was living in Salem in 1959.
127 vi. Robert James **Bartruff**[127] was living in Renton, King Co. Washington in 1959.
+ 128 vii. John Omer **Bartruff** born 17 June 1907.
+ 129 viii. Virginia Rosa **Bartruff** born 3 May 1911.

34. **William Harry**[3] **Scharf** (Eva Katherine[2] Bartruff, Friederich Ludwig[1])[128] was born in Jonesboro, Union Co., Illinois 17 September 1886 and died 12 July 1962 in Salem, Marion Co., Oregon, at 75 years of age. He married **Lydia Caroline Herndon** in Salem 24 November 1915. She died in February 1976 in Salem.[129]

William Harry **Scharf** and Lydia Caroline **Herndon** had the following children:
+ 130 i. Mary Katherine[4] **Scharf** born 26 August 1916.
+ 131 ii. William Harry **Scharf** Jr. born 25 March 1920.

35. **Rose Katherine**[3] **Scharf** (Eva Katherine[2] Bartruff, Friederich Ludwig[1])[130] was born in Jonesboro, Union Co., Illinois 23 November 1887 and died 2 May 1978 at 90 years of age. She married **Frank Crane** in Salem, Marion Co., Oregon, 24 December 1908.

Rose Katherine **Scharf** and Frank **Crane** had the following children:
132 i. Myrtle[4] Crane.[131]
133 ii. Owen Crane.[132]
134 iii. Laura Crane.[133]
135 iv. Lucille Crane.[134]

36. **August Frederick Ludwig**[3] **Scharf** (Eva Katherine[2] Bartruff, Friederich Ludwig[1])[135] was born in Jonesboro, Union Co., Illinois 7 June 1889 and died 2 March 1972 in Salem, Marion Co., Oregon, at 82 years of age. He married **Irene McClellan** in Portland, Multnomah Co., Oregon 19 November 1913. Irene was born in Chicago, Cook Co., Illinois and died 23 July 1972 in Salem, at 82 years of age.[136]

August Frederick Ludwig **Scharf** and Irene **McClellan** had the following child born in Salem:
136 i. Genevieve Ruth[4] **Scharf**[137] 17 February 1918 and married Gerald **Jaffe**.

37. **John Edward**[3] **Scharf** (Eva Katherine[2] Bartruff, Friederich Ludwig[1])[138] was born in Jonesboro, Union Co., Illinois 3 June 1891 and married **Ruth C. Bollier** in Salem, Marion Co., Oregon 27 September 1917. She died 19 December 1974, at 82 years of age.[139]

John Edward **Scharf** and Ruth C. **Bollier** had the following children:
137 i. Robert Edward[4] **Scharf**.[140]

138 ii. Dorothy Florence **Scharf**.[141]
139 iii. Kenneth Lloyd **Scharf**.[142]

38. **Joseph Elmer**[3] **Scharf** (Eva Katherine[2] Bartruff, Friederich Ludwig[1])[143] was born in Jonesboro, Union Co., Illinois 5 November 1893 and died 6 November 1920 in Salem, Marion Co., Oregon, at 27 years of age. He married **Ruby Pearl Hill** in Salem 8 November 1917. She was born in Hebo, Tillamook Co, Oregon 11 December 1895 and died 6 November 1979 in Klamath Falls, Klamath Co., Oregon, at 83 years of age.[144] She married (2) **George Benton Wolfe**.

Joseph Elmer **Scharf** and Ruby Pearl **Hill** had the following children:
+ 140 i. Gertrude Helen[4] **Scharf** born 26 August 1918.
+ 141 ii. Loween Vivian **Scharf** born 4 October 1919.

39. **Daniel Peter**[3] **Scharf** (Eva Katherine[2] Bartruff, Friederich Ludwig[1])[145] was born in Jonesboro, Union Co., Illinois 15 August 1896 and married **Thelma Blanton** in Salem, Marion Co., Oregon 11 October 1930.[146] She died 24 February 1972 in Salem.

Daniel Peter **Scharf** and Thelma **Blanton** had the following children:
142 i. Joan Grace[4] **Scharf**.[147]
143 ii. Janice Ray **Scharf**.[148]

40. **Esther Freda**[3] **Scharf** (Eva Katherine[2] Bartruff, Friederich Ludwig[1])[149] was born in Jonesboro, Union Co., Illinois 8 February 1899 and died 3 June 1964 in Salem, Marion Co., Oregon, at 65 years of age. She married **John M. VanLaanen** in Salem 13 March 1921.

Esther Freda **Scharf** and John M. **VanLaanen** had the following children:
144 i. Joan Esther[4] **VanLaanen**.[150] Died in infancy.
145 ii. Norma Jean **VanLaanen**[151] married William **Massey**.
146 iii. Dale Vernon **VanLaanen**[152] married Jessie (__).

41. **Ernest Frederick**[3] **Bartruff** (Jacob E.[2], Friederich Ludwig[1])[153] was born in Jonesboro, Union Co., Illinois 19 May 1893 and died 23 November 1958 in Edwardsville, Madison Co., Illinois, at 65 years of age. He married **Leona Irvin** in Anna, Union Co., 16 November 1915.

Ernest Frederick **Bartruff** and Leona **Irvin** had the following children:
147 i. Merrill Blain[4] **Bartruff**.[154]
148 ii. Ernest Lowell **Bartruff**.[155]

149	iii.	Velma Lorene **Bartruff**.[156]
150	iv.	Norma Jean **Bartruff**.[157]
151	v.	Ralph Leon **Bartruff** born 10 October 1927 and[158] died 20 September 1954 at 26 years of age.[159] Ralph was a sergeant in the 135th Engineer Combat Battalion.

43. **Clara Augusta**[3] **Bartruff** (Jacob E.[2], Friederich Ludwig[1])[160] was born in Jonesboro, Union Co., Illinois 1 April 1898 and died 23 September 1977 at 79 years of age. She married **Barney Wall** in Jonesboro 16 December 1946.

Clara Augusta **Bartruff** and Barney **Wall** had the following child:
| 152 | i. | Anna May[4] **Wall**.[161] |

44. **Adolph Benjamin**[3] **Bartruff** (Jacob E.[2], Friederich Ludwig[1])[162] was born in Jonesboro, Union Co., Illinois 21 March 1900 and died 29 July 1959 in Pekin, Tazewell Co., Illinois, at 59 years of age. He married **Alda Brecher** in Pekin 20 December 1927.

Adolph Benjamin **Bartruff** and Alda **Brecher** had the following child:
| 153 | i. | Raymond Adolph[4] **Bartruff**.[163] |

45. **Paul Martin**[3] **Bartruff** (Jacob E.[2], Friederich Ludwig[1])[164] was born in Jonesboro, Union Co., Illinois 28 May 1902 and married **Charline Cleo Young** in Gadwin, Michigan 23 June 1929.

Paul Martin **Bartruff** and Charline Cleo **Young** had the following children:
| 154 | i. | Doris Marie[4] **Bartruff**.[165] |
| 155 | ii. | Carolyn Jean **Bartruff**.[166] |

46. **Lydia Rosetta**[3] **Bartruff** (Jacob E.[2], Friederich Ludwig[1])[167] was born in Jonesboro, Union Co., Illinois 6 March 1904 and married **Leo K. Bernhard** in Metropolis, Massac Co., Illinois 6 March 1934. Leo died 20 May 1969 in Marion, Williamson Co., Illinois.[168]

Lydia Rosetta **Bartruff** and Leo K. **Bernhard** had the following children:
156	i.	Betty[4] **Bernhard**.[169]
157	ii.	William Leo **Bernhard**.[170]
158	iii.	Robert Edward **Bernhard**.[171]
159	iv.	Maxine Franziska **Bernhard**.[172]

48. **David Leo**[3] **Bartruff** (Jacob E.[2], Friederich Ludwig[1])[173] was born in Jonesboro, Union Co., Illinois 25 March 1909 and married **Reba Cox** 2 February 1931.

David Leo **Bartruff** and Reba **Cox** had the following children:
    160   i.   Wesley Eugene[4] **Bartruff**.[174]
    161   ii.   Norman David **Bartruff**.[175]
    162   iii.   Mary Ruth **Bartruff**.[176]
    163   iv.   Patricia Ann **Bartruff**.[177]

49. **Gilbert James**[3] **Bartruff** (Jacob E.[2], Friederich Ludwig[1])[178] was born in Jonesboro, Union Co., Illinois 25 July 1912 and married **Louise Kies** in Alton, Madison Co., Illinois 21 December 1944.

Gilbert James **Bartruff** and Louise **Kies** had the following children:
    164   i.   Donna Jean[4] **Bartruff**.[179]
    165   ii.   Barbara Ann **Bartruff**.[180]

51. **Effin Mary**[3] **Weiss** (Wilhelmina Fredericka[2] Bartruff, Friederich Ludwig[1])[181] was born in Jonesboro, Union Co., Illinois 9 January 1888[182] and died there 3 July 1945, at 57 years of age. She married **Douglas Weaver** there 12 November 1905. He died there 3 July 1937.[183]

Effin Mary **Weiss** and Douglas **Weaver** had the following children:
    166   i.   Fred[4] **Weaver**.[184]
    167   ii.   Helen **Weaver**.[185]
    168   iii.   Lorene **Weaver**.[186]

52. **Arthur Peter**[3] **Weiss** (Wilhelmina Fredericka[2] Bartruff, Friederich Ludwig[1])[187] was born in Jonesboro, Union Co., Illinois 15 July 1891[188] and died 13 March 1968 at 76 years of age. He married **Pearl Neely** 1 February 1914.

Arthur Peter **Weiss** and Pearl **Neely** had the following children:
    169   i.   Karl Arthur[4] **Weiss**.[189]
    170   ii.   Martha J. **Weiss**.[190]
    171   iii.   Donald E. **Weiss**.[191]

53. **Louis**[3] **Weiss** (Wilhelmina Fredericka[2] Bartruff, Friederich Ludwig[1])[192] was born in Jonesboro, Union Co., Illinois 4 October 1891[193] and died 13 May 1976 in Salem, Marion Co., Oregon, at 84 years of age. He married twice. (1) **Marnie Korb** in Salem 15 January 1916. (2) **Elizabeth**

May McAllister in Eugene, Lane Co., Oregon 14 February 1944. Louis is buried at Howell Cemetery, Marion County.

Louis **Weiss** and Marnie **Korb** had the following child:

    172   i.   Guy Alford[4] **Weiss**.[194]

56. **Clara K.**[3] **Weiss** (Wilhelmina Fredericka[2] Bartruff, Friederich Ludwig[1])[195] was born in Jonesboro, Union Co., Illinois 1 December 1896[196] and died there 19 April 1969, at 72 years of age. She married **Jefferson E. Slicker** in Jonesboro 4 September 1915. He died there 1 March 1966.[197]

Clara K. **Weiss** and Jefferson E. **Slicker** had the following children:

    173   i.   Minnie J.[4] **Slicker**.[198]
    174   ii.   Lucille **Slicker**.[199]
    175   iii.   Ruth E. **Slicker**.[200]
    176   iv.   Helen L. **Slicker**.[201]
    177   v.   Jefferson E. **Slicker**.[202]

60. **Louis Mathis**[3] **Bartruff** (Joseph E.[2], Friederich Ludwig[1])[203] was born in Jonesboro, Union Co., Illinois 29 November 1896[204] and married **Mildred Irene Williamson** in Salem, Marion Co., Oregon 13 June 1931.

Louis Mathis **Bartruff** and Mildred Irene **Williamson** had the following child:

    178   i.   Jeanette Delores[4] **Bartruff**.[205]

61. **Eric Edwin**[3] **Bartruff** (Joseph E.[2], Friederich Ludwig[1])[206] was born in Jonesboro, Union Co., Illinois 27 December 1898[207] and died 9 November 1949 in Eugene, Lane Co., Oregon, at 50 years of age. He married **Jessie Gladys Edwards** in Portland, Multnomah Co., Oregon 28 August 1920.

Eric Edwin **Bartruff** and Jessie Gladys **Edwards** had the following child:

    179   i.   Eric Edwin[4] **Bartruff** Jr.[208]

62. **Edward Jona**[3] **Bartruff** (Joseph E.[2], Friederich Ludwig[1])[209] was born in Jonesboro, Union Co., Illinois 21 June 1900[210] and died 22 June 1949 in Trent, Spokane Co., Washington, at 49 years of age. He married **Lois Margaret McGowen** in Longview, Cowlitz Co., Washington 27 January 1932.

Edward Jona **Bartruff** and Lois Margaret **McGowen** had the following children:
- 180   i.   Shirley Mae[4] **Bartruff**.[211]
- 181   ii.   Lowell Milton **Bartruff**.[212]
- 182   iii.   Merrill Blaine **Bartruff**.[213]

63. **Teresa Ellen**[3] **Bartruff** (Joseph E.[2], Friederich Ludwig[1])[214] was born in Jonesboro, Union Co., Illinois 6 April 1902 and married **Roy Lee Brown** in Salem, Marion Co., Oregon 26 September 1922.

Teresa Ellen **Bartruff** and Roy Lee **Brown** had the following child:
- 183   i.   Ronald Leroy[4] **Brown**.[215]

65. **Lillian Viola**[3] **Bartruff** (Joseph E.[2], Friederich Ludwig[1])[216] was born in Jonesboro, Union Co., Illinois 1 March 1907 and married **Richmond Pearson Rankin** in Vancouver, Clark Co., Washington 30 June 1928. He died 11 May 1957 in Portland, Multnomah Co., Oregon.[217]

Lillian Viola **Bartruff** and Richmond Pearson **Rankin** had the following children:
- 184   i.   Wayne Edwin[4] **Rankin**.[218]
- 185   ii.   Elaine Marie **Rankin**.[219]

66. **Susan Katherine**[3] **Bartruff** (William[2], Friederich Ludwig[1])[220] was born in Jonesboro, Union Co., Illinois 18 December 1895[221] and died there 28 October 1956, at 60 years of age. She married **Carl Fowler** there 21 March 1917.

Susan Katherine **Bartruff** and Carl **Fowler** had the following children:
- 186   i.   Gilbert[4] **Fowler**.[222]
- 187   ii.   Vesta **Fowler**.[223]
- 188   iii.   Lewis Carl **Fowler**.[224]
- 189   iv.   Mabel Elaine **Fowler**.[225]

67. **Samuel Andrew**[3] **Bartruff** (William[2], Friederich Ludwig[1])[226] was born in Jonesboro, Union Co., Illinois 24 August 1897[227] and died 30 December 1937 at 40 years of age. He married **Jennie Hoag** 4 July 1925.

Samuel Andrew **Bartruff** and Jennie **Hoag** had the following child:
- 190   i.   Elizabeth Jane[4] **Bartruff**.[228]

72. **Arthur Watson**[3] **Bartruff** (William[2], Friederich Ludwig[1])[229] was born in Jonesboro, Union Co., Illinois 10 September 1911 and married **Hazel Guthrie** in September 1937.

Arthur Watson **Bartruff** and Hazel **Guthrie** had the following children:
- 191　i.　Carol Ann[4] **Bartruff**.[230]
- 192　ii.　Linda Lou **Bartruff**.[231]
- 193　iii.　Thomas Frederick **Bartruff**.[232]

73. **Esther**[3] **Bauer** (Theresa Race[2] Bartruff, Friederich Ludwig[1])[233] was born in Jonesboro, Union Co., Illinois 8 September 1895[234] and died there 20 August 1973, at 77 years of age. She married **Carl Henry Shaefer** in Anna, Union Co., Illinois 29 November 1922. He died 20 August 1962 in Jonesboro.[235]

Esther **Bauer** and Carl Henry **Shaefer** had the following children:
- 194　i.　Thomas[4] **Shaefer**.[236]
- 195　ii.　David **Shaefer**.[237]

74. **Rudolph**[3] **Bauer** (Theresa Race[2] Bartruff, Friederich Ludwig[1])[238] was born in Jonesboro, Union Co., Illinois 25 July 1897[239] and married **Essie Reams** there 30 July 1921.

Rudolph **Bauer** and Essie **Reams** had the following children:
- 196　i.　Roy Rudolph[4] **Bauer**.[240]
- 197　ii.　Carl Victor **Bauer**.[241]
- 198　iii.　John Charles **Bauer**.[242]
- 199　iv.　Jean **Bauer**.[243]
- 200　v.　Eloise **Bauer**.[244]

75. **Frederick Joe**[3] **Bauer** (Theresa Race[2] Bartruff, Friederich Ludwig[1])[245] was born in Jonesboro, Union Co., Illinois 16 January 1902 and married **Norma Lorrance** in Anna, Union Co. 11 November 1922.

Frederick Joe **Bauer** and Norma **Lorrance** had the following children:
- 201　i.　Frederick Earl[4] **Bauer**.[246]
- 202　ii.　Bruce Britton **Bauer**.[247]

FOURTH GENERATION

76. **Helen Lola**[4] **Bewley** (Lydia Helen[3] Bartruff, Charles Jacob[2], Friederich Ludwig[1])[248] was born in Salem, Marion Co., Oregon 9 August 1904 and died there 6 October, 2000 at 96 years of age. She married **M. Henry Sim** in Dallas, Polk Co., Oregon 28 April 1923. He died in 1963.

Helen Lola **Bewley** and M. Henry **Sim** had the following child:
+   203   i.   Daryle[5] **Sim** born 1 April 1926.

77. **Gladys Elizabeth**[4] **Bewley** (Lydia Helen[3] Bartruff, Charles Jacob[2], Friederich Ludwig[1])[249] was born in Miles, Lincoln Co., Washington 19 April 1906 and married twice. (1) **Alden "Red" Wilson** in Monmouth, Polk Co., Oregon 26 August 1926. (2) **Hersil Marvin Acuff** in Vancouver, Clark Co., Washington 23 April 1942.

Gladys Elizabeth **Bewley** and Alden "Red" **Wilson** had the following child:
+   204   i.   Barbara Jean[5] **Wilson** born 30 April 1928.

78. **Carl Omer**[4] **Bewley** (Lydia Helen[3] Bartruff, Charles Jacob[2], Friederich Ludwig[1])[250] was born in Portland, Multnomah Co., Oregon 13 January 1911 and married **Lorraine P. Acuff** in Vancouver, Clark Co., Washington 15 April 1933.

Carl Omer **Bewley** and Lorraine P. **Acuff** had the following children:
+   205   i.   Sharon Lee[5] **Bewley** born 20 September 1933.
+   206   ii.   Stanley Carl **Bewley** born 23 October 1934.
     207   iii.   Stephenie Lorraine **Bewley**[251] born 8 November 1937. She married (__) **Flora**.

79. **Cordelia**[4] **Bartruff** (Daniel Edward[3], Charles Jacob[2], Friederich Ludwig[1])[252] was born in Salem, Marion Co., Oregon 16 June 1918 and married **Harry Tompkins** 23 August 1935.

Cordelia **Bartruff** and Harry **Tompkins** had the following children:
     208   i.   Edward Eugene[5] **Tompkins**.[253]
     209   ii.   Rebecca Sue **Tompkins**.[254]

80. **Rosa Winifred**[4] **Bartruff** (Daniel Edward[3], Charles Jacob[2], Friederich Ludwig[1])[255] was born in Salem, Marion Co., Oregon 22 December 1920 and married **Alva Huntley** 2 June 1940.

Rosa Winifred **Bartruff** and Alva **Huntley** had the following children:
- 210 i. Allan Rodger[5] **Huntley**[256] born 10 September 1947.
- 211 ii. Mary Jo **Huntley**[257] born 28 June 1951.

81. **Wallace Lynn**[4] **Bartruff** (Daniel Edward[3], Charles Jacob[2], Friederich Ludwig[1])[258] was born in Salem, Marion Co., Oregon 2 March 1925 and married **Mary Bishop** in McMinnville, Yamhill Co, Oregon 13 August 1948.

Wallace Lynn **Bartruff** and Mary **Bishop** had the following child:
- 212 i. Gwendolyn Kay[5] **Bartruff**.[259]

82. **Delbert Leroy**[4] **McDonough** (Anna Elizabeth[3] Bartruff, Charles Jacob[2], Friederich Ludwig[1])[260] was born in Portland, Multnomah Co., Oregon 16 May 1920 and died at home of lung cancer 30 September 2003 in Salem, Polk Co., Oregon, at 83 years of age. He married **Octiva Elizabeth Bauer** in Riverside, Riverside Co., California 8 December 1940. Octiva,[261] daughter of George Matt **Bauer** and Julianna **Meyer**, was born in Glen Ullin, Morton Co., North Dakota 2 October 1920. Octiva's parents moved to Salem in the early 1930s and she was graduated from Salem High School the same year (1938) as Del. She was employed by the Salem School System as a Secretary from 1957 to 1970 and by the Oregon Legislature until 1981 when she retired. Delbert was adopted by Herbert and Anna McDonough on 14 December 1921. He was the son of Josephine B. Bartruff, unmarried, who "duly and properly relinquished said child and [gave] her consent that the said petitioners should be granted his adoption." The Court found the petitioners to be "competent and have sufficient means and ability to furnish said minor with proper education and support, proper environment, and a good home."[262] His father was Claude Cox, 19, who farmed with his father in Lacombe, Linn Co., Oregon Josephine, also 19, was a housekeeper for her brother in Lacombe.

Del was graduated from Salem High School in 1938 (Salem had only one high school then) and enlisted in the U.S. Army following graduation. He spent three years on active duty and more than 20 years in the Air Force Reserve. Following discharge from active duty he became a trainman with Southern Pacific Railroad and retired from SP 37 years later.

Delbert Leroy **McDonough** and Octiva Elizabeth **Bauer** had the following children:
- + 213 i. Anne Elizabeth[5] **McDonough** born 25 June 1941.
- + 214 ii. Susan Lee **McDonough** born 9 February 1944.
-   215 iii. Michael Gene **McDonough**[263] born in Salem 5 November 1946.

83. **Grace Velma**[4] **Bartruff** (Elmer Walter[3], Charles Jacob[2], Friederich Ludwig[1])[264] was born in Lacomb, Linn Co, Oregon 13 November 1918. She married **Ruben Len Edwards** there 17 April 1938. He was born in Lacomb 21 May 1917.[265]

Grace Velma **Bartruff** and Ruben Len **Edwards** had the following children:
    216 i.   Nancy[5] **Edwards**.[266]
+ 217 ii. Roxie Ann **Edwards** born 7 March 1944.
+ 218 iii. Tracy Lee **Edwards** born 1 March 1946.
+ 219 iv. Dixie Louise **Edwards** born 19 September 1949.
+ 220 v. Nancy Renee **Edwards** born 17 October 1950.

84. **Victor Leon**[4] **Bartruff** (Elmer Walter[3], Charles Jacob[2], Friederich Ludwig[1])[267] was born in Lacomb, Linn Co, Oregon 26 March 1921 and died there 21 November 1950, at 29 years of age. He married **Juanita Keebaugh** in Beaverton, Washington Co., Oregon 17 January 1947. Juanita,[268] daughter of William Perry **Keebaugh** and Nona Ionia **Andrews**, was born in LaCenter, Clark Co., Washington 23 May 1926. She married (2) **Arthur Melville Collins** in Lebanon, Linn Co., Oregon 23 May 1976. Victor lived in LaComb all his life except for service in the Navy during WWII. A 1939 graduate of Lebanon High School, he owned and operated a mint farm and was a member of the LaComb Baptist Church. A day after going to work for a logging company as a choke setter, he was killed in an accident at Snow Peak Camp. The crew was fighting a hangup on the hillside when the logs from the tangle began rolling, pinning him between them. He is buried at the LaComb Cemetery.

Victor Leon **Bartruff** and Juanita **Keebaugh** had the following children:
+ 221 i. Victor Leon[5] **Bartruff** Jr. born 1 October 1947.
+ 222 ii. Cynthia **Bartruff** born 3 September 1950.

85. **Rev. Bryce Oliver**[4] **Bartruff** (Elmer Walter[3], Charles Jacob[2], Friederich Ludwig[1])[269] was born in Lacomb, Linn Co, Oregon 6 February 1926 and married **Harriet Alice Snyder** in Lebanon, Linn Co., Oregon 20 December 1946. Harriet was born in Roseland, Adams Co., Nebraska 30 April 1926 and died 4 May 2005 in Albany, Linn Co., Oregon. She was a Registered Nurse at Portland's Woodland Park Hospital for 30 years.[270]

Bryce Oliver **Bartruff** and Harriet Alice **Snyder** had the following children:
    223 i.   Mary Kristine[5] **Bartruff**[271] born 7 November 1948 and married (___) **Horton**.
    224 ii. Bryce Duane **Bartruff**[272] born 24 August 1950.

{ G 1753 }

86. **Marion Elizabeth**[4] **Bartruff** (Elmer Walter[3], Charles Jacob[2], Friederich Ludwig[1])[273] was born in Lacomb, Linn Co, Oregon 14 April 1930 and married **Robert Spooner** in Lebanon, Linn Co., Oregon 22 July 1948. Bob was born in Havana, Sargent Co., North Dakota 26 July 1919 and died 4 March 1998 in Terrebonne, Deschutes Co., Oregon, at 78 years of age.[274] He is buried at Deschutes Garden, Bend, Deschutes Co.

Marion Elizabeth **Bartruff** and Robert **Spooner** had the following children:

- 225   i.   Clifford[5] **Spooner**[275] born in Lebanon 22 October 1949.
- \+ 226   ii.   Vivian **Spooner** born 22 September 1951.
- 227   iii.   James **Spooner**[276] born in Lebanon 25 May 1953 and married twice. (1) Jacqueline **Shadone** in Lebanon 26 June 1982. (2) Nadine **Slone** in Crooked River, Jefferson Co., Oregon 24 May 1986.
- \+ 228   iv.   Virginia **Spooner** born 20 January 1955.

101. **Floyd Lester**[4] **Hileman** (Emma Ester[3] Bartruff, Frederick[2], Friederich Ludwig[1])[277] was born in Anna, Union Co., Illinois 23 May 1907 and died 23 April 1989 in Dongola, Union Co., at 81 years of age. He married **Lovena Fisher** in Dongola 24 February 1934. Lovena,[278] daughter of Lee **Fisher** and Addie **Aden**, was born in Dongola 19 December 1913 and died there 15 January 1968, at 54 years of age. They are buried in the American Legion Cemetery in Dongola.

Floyd Lester **Hileman** and Lovena **Fisher** had the following children:

- \+ 237   i.   Jo Ann[5] **Hileman** born 17 September 1934.
- 238   ii.   Patsy Jean **Hileman**[279] born. 26 July 1939 and married Harley Gene **Rhodes** 27 January 1962.

118. **Wayne Watson**[4] **Bartruff** (Walter Benjamin[3], Frederick[2], Friederich Ludwig[1])[280] was born in Anna, Union Co., Illinois 15 October 1919 and died 13 October 1968 in St. Louis, Independence Co., Missouri, at 48 years of age. He married **Florence Brasel** in Cobden, Union Co., Illinois 7 May 1947. Florence,[281] daughter of Charles **Brasel** and Mary Elizabeth **Hartley**, was born in Anna 29 November 1916. Wayne is buried in the Anna Cemetery.

Wayne Watson **Bartruff** and Florence **Brasel** had the following children:

- \+ 239   i.   Linda A.[5] **Bartruff** born 11 December 1947.
- 240   ii.   Joyce A. **Bartruff**[282] born in Anna 10 February 1952.
- \+ 241   iii.   Sharon K. **Bartruff** born 28 August 1955.

120. **Harold Eugene**[4] **Bartruff** (Walter Benjamin[3], Frederick[2], Friederich Ludwig[1])[283] was born 13 December 1924 and married **Joann (__)**.

Harold Eugene **Bartruff** and Joann (__) had the following children:
    242   i.   Terry[5] **Bartruff**.[284]
    243   ii. Brian **Bartruff**.[285]

128. **John Omer**[4] **Bartruff** (John Robert[3], John[2], Friederich Ludwig[1])[286] was born in Jonesboro, Union Co., Illinois 17 June 1907 and died in 1959 in Salem, Marion Co., Oregon, at 52 years of age. He married twice. (1) **Bertha Young** in Salem in 1930. She died there in 1951. (2) **Dorothy Richardson** in Salem in May 1952.

John Omer **Bartruff** and Bertha **Young** had the following children born in Salem:
    244   i.   Ronald[5] **Bartruff** living in Salem at the time of his father's death.
    245   ii. Steven **Bartruff** living in Salem at the time of his father's death.
    246   iii. Ralph **Bartruff** living in Texas at the time of his father's death.
+   247   iv. Celesta **Bartruff**.

129. **Virginia Rosa**[4] **Bartruff** (John Robert[3], John[2], Friederich Ludwig[1])[287] was born in Salem, Marion Co., Oregon 3 May 1911 and died 31 October 2002 in Woodburn, Oregon, at 91 years of age. She married **Jake Fryberger** in 1946. He died in 1999. Virginia served in the Women's Army Corp during WWII and was a founding member of the Order of Amaranth Cherry Court in Salem. She worked in the commercial banking industry and for the state of Oregon for 15 years.

Virginia Rosa **Bartruff** and Jake **Fryberger** had the following children:
    248   i.   Linda[5] **Fryberger**[288] married (__) **Mosher**.
    249   ii. Sarah **Fryberger**.

130. **Mary Katherine**[4] **Scharf** (William Harry[3], Eva Katherine[2] Bartruff, Friederich Ludwig[1])[289] was born in Salem, Marion Co., Oregon 26 August 1916 and married twice. (1) **Erling N. Thompson** in Salem 9 June 1939. He was born in Portland, Multnomah Co., Oregon 24 October 1911 and died 17 November 1985 in McMinnville, Yamhill Co., Oregon, at 74 years of age.[290] (2) **Carl E. Hanson**.

{ G 1755 }

Mary Katherine **Scharf** and Erling N. **Thompson** had the following children:
- \+ 250 i. Eldon[5] **Thompson** born 12 June 1941.
- \+ 251 ii. Carl **Thompson** born 6 March 1944.
- \+ 252 iii. Elinor **Thompson** born 24 April 1948.

131. **William Harry**[4] **Scharf Jr.** (William Harry[3], Eva Katherine[2] Bartruff, Friederich Ludwig[1])[291] was born in Salem, Marion Co., Oregon 25 March 1920 and died there of lung cancer in 1987, at 67 years of age. He married **Ella Mae Stotler** in Salem in 1942. William is buried at the Rest Lawn Cemetery in Polk Co., Oregon.

William Harry **Scharf** Jr. and Ella Mae **Stotler** had the following children:
- \+ 253 i. Harry Lee[5] **Scharf** born 18 June 1942.
- \+ 254 ii. Dennis **Scharf** born 6 November 1944.
- \+ 255 iii. Roger **Scharf** born 16 June 1948.

140. **Gertrude Helen**[4] **Scharf** (Joseph Elmer[3], Eva Katherine[2] Bartruff, Friederich Ludwig[1])[292] was born in Salem, Marion Co., Oregon 26 August 1918 and married **Leonard Nelson Porterfield** in Parkdale, Hood River Co., Oregon 29 June 1946.

Gertrude Helen **Scharf** and Leonard Nelson **Porterfield** had the following child:
- \+ 256 i. Marla Jo[5] **Porterfield** born 25 November 1947.

141. **Loween Vivian**[4] **Scharf** (Joseph Elmer[3], Eva Katherine[2] Bartruff, Friederich Ludwig[1])[293] was born in Salem, Marion Co., Oregon 4 October 1919 and died 6 November 1971 in Klamath Falls, Klamath Co., Oregon at 52 years of age. She married **Marvin Benton Cook** in Salem 4 October.

Loween Vivian **Scharf** and Marvin Benton **Cook** had the following children:
- \+ 257 i. Marvin Benton[5] **Cook** Jr. born 11 October 1947.
- 258 ii. Alvin **Cook**[294] born in Salem 22 April 1949 and married Kathy **Perman**.

FIFTH GENERATION

203. **Daryle**[5] **Sim** (Helen Lola[4] Bewley, Lydia Helen[3] Bartruff, Charles Jacob[2], Friederich Ludwig[1])[295] was born 1 April 1926.

Daryle **Sim** had the following child:
  259 i. Steven[6] **Sim** born 30 May 1952.

204. **Barbara Jean**[5] **Wilson** (Gladys Elizabeth[4] Bewley, Lydia Helen[3] Bartruff, Charles Jacob[2], Friederich Ludwig[1])[296] was born 30 April 1928 and married **Charles Jones** in Vancouver, Clark Co., Washington 30 April 1945.

Barbara Jean **Wilson** and Charles **Jones** had the following children:
  260 i. Monti Lu[6] **Jones** born 12 November 1946.
  261 ii. Charles **Jones** Jr. born 28 August 1947.
  262 iii. Lynn **Jones** born 30 January 1949.
  263 iv. Kathy **Jones** born 17 November 1953.
  264 v. Jill **Jones** born 12 December 1954.

205. **Sharon Lee**[5] **Bewley** (Carl Omer[4], Lydia Helen[3] Bartruff, Charles Jacob[2], Friederich Ludwig[1])[297] was born 20 September 1933 and married **Jerry Payne** in Vancouver, Clark Co., Washington 7 February 1950.

Sharon Lee **Bewley** and Jerry **Payne** had the following children:
  265 i. David[6] **Payne** born 24 November 1950.
  266 ii. Lurinda **Payne** born 21 May 1956.

206. **Stanley Carl**[5] **Bewley** (Carl Omer[4], Lydia Helen[3] Bartruff, Charles Jacob[2], Friederich Ludwig[1])[298] was born 23 October 1934 and married **Shirley Smith** in Vancouver, Clark Co., Washington 25 August 1955.

Stanley Carl **Bewley** and Shirley **Smith** had the following children:
  267 i. Carol Ann[6] **Bewley** born in September 1956.
  268 ii. Bruce Arlen **Bewley** born 23 November 1957.
  269 iii. Ricky Gene **Bewley** born 30 December 1958.

213. **Anne Elizabeth**[5] **McDonough** (Delbert Leroy[4], Anna Elizabeth[3] Bartruff, Charles Jacob[2], Friederich Ludwig[1])[299] was born in Riverside, Riverside Co., California 25 June 1941 and married **Jay Alan Thompson** in Salem, Marion Co., Oregon 25 August 1962. Jay,[300] son of Willard **Thompson** and Myrna (__), was born in Salem 25 April 1939.

Anne Elizabeth **McDonough** and Jay Alan **Thompson** had the following children:
 + 270 i. Sarah Anne[6] **Thompson** born 10 December 1969.
  271 ii. Leslie Suzanne **Thompson**[301] born in Portland, Multnomah Co., Oregon 27 March 1973.

214. **Susan Lee**[5] **McDonough** (Delbert Leroy[4], Anna Elizabeth[3] Bartruff, Charles Jacob[2], Friederich Ludwig[1])[302] was born in Salem, Marion Co., Oregon 9 February 1944 and married **Craig Lamont Clark II** there 20 August 1966.

Susan Lee **McDonough** and Craig Lamont **Clark** II had the following children:
- 272   i.   Craig Lamont[6] **Clark** III[303] born in Portland, Multnomah Co., Oregon 7 June 1968.
- 273   ii.   Jennifer **Clark**[304] born in Eugene, Lane Co., Oregon 11 July 1972.

217. **Roxie Ann**[5] **Edwards** (Grace Velma[4] Bartruff, Elmer Walter[3], Charles Jacob[2], Friederich Ludwig[1])[305] was born in Salem, Marion Co., Oregon 7 March 1944 and married twice. (1) **Patrick Portlock** in Salem 25 March 1966. (2) **Lawrence Oglesby** in Salem 1 June 1974.

Roxie Ann **Edwards** and Patrick **Portlock** had the following child:
- 274   i.   Stephany Lynne Oglesby[6] **Portlock**[306] born in Westminster, Orange Co., California 28 November 1968 and married David **Boyle** in Hawaii 9 October 1995.

218. **Tracy Lee**[5] **Edwards** (Grace Velma[4] Bartruff, Elmer Walter[3], Charles Jacob[2], Friederich Ludwig[1])[307] was born in Salem, Marion Co., Oregon 1 March 1946 and married **Blair Wasson** there 22 December 1965.

Tracy Lee **Edwards** and Blair **Wasson** had the following children:
- +   275   i.   Sean Craig[6] **Wasson** born 6 September 1975.
- 276   ii.   Tara Tiffany **Wasson**[308] born in Salem 8 May 1978.

219. **Dixie Louise**[5] **Edwards** (Grace Velma[4] Bartruff, Elmer Walter[3], Charles Jacob[2], Friederich Ludwig[1])[309] was born in Salem, Marion Co., Oregon 19 September 1949 and married twice. (1) **Gordon Patterson**. (2) **Dan Sims** in Wenatchee. Washington 17 January 1981.

Dixie Louise **Edwards** and Gordon **Patterson** had the following children born in Salem:
- 277   i.   Tye Louis[6] **Patterson**[310] 26 January 1976.
- 278   ii.   Brent Len **Patterson**[311] 10 February 1978.

220. **Nancy Renee**[5] **Edwards** (Grace Velma[4] Bartruff, Elmer Walter[3], Charles Jacob[2], Friederich Ludwig[1])[312] was born in Salem, Marion Co., Oregon 17 October 1950 and married **Robert Emrick** in Salem 10 June 1972.

Nancy Renee **Edwards** and Robert **Emrick** had the following child:
> 279   i.   Ginger LaVonne[6] **Emrick**[313] born in McMinnville, Yamhill Co., Oregon 26 June 1980.

221. **Victor Leon**[5] **Bartruff Jr.** (Victor Leon[4], Elmer Walter[3], Charles Jacob[2], Friederich Ludwig[1])[314] was born in Lebanon, Linn Co., Oregon 1 October 1947 and married **Carolyn Jean Jelden** in Salem, Marion Co., Oregon 8 June 1968.

Victor Leon **Bartruff** Jr. and Carolyn Jean **Jelden** had the following children born in Lebanon:
> 280   i.   Victor Leon[6] **Bartruff** III[315] 22 May 1970.
> 281   ii.   Elizabeth Ann **Bartruff**[316] 18 January 1973.

222. **Cynthia**[5] **Bartruff** (Victor Leon[4], Elmer Walter[3], Charles Jacob[2], Friederich Ludwig[1])[317] was born in Lebanon, Linn Co., Oregon 3 September 1950 and married **David Roger Ludeman** 18 December 1976. David,[318] son of Louis **Ludeman** and Luella **Muhmel**, was born in Portland, Multnomah Co., Oregon 11 March 1951.

Cynthia **Bartruff** and David Roger **Ludeman** had the following children:
> 282   i.   Rebecca Lynn[6] **Ludeman**[319] born 30 March 1979.
> 283   ii.   Timothy David **Ludeman**[320] born 2 July 1981.

226. **Vivian**[5] **Spooner** (Marion Elizabeth[4] Bartruff, Elmer Walter[3], Charles Jacob[2], Friederich Ludwig[1])[321] was born in Lebanon, Linn Co., Oregon 22 September 1951 and married twice. (1) **Kenneth McCord** in January 1972. He was killed in an automobile accident 25 December 1981[322] and is buried in Eugene, Lane Co., Oregon. (2) **Greg Allen** 3 March 1985. They were divorced in December 1988.

Vivian **Spooner** and Kenneth **McCord** had the following child:
> 284   i.   Carrie[6] **McCord**[323] born in Springfield, Lane Co., Oregon in 1977.

Vivian **Spooner** and Greg **Allen** had the following child:
> 285   ii.   Ryan **Allen**[324] born in Eugene, Lane Co., Oregon in 1986.

228. **Virginia**[5] **Spooner** (Marion Elizabeth[4] Bartruff, Elmer Walter[3], Charles Jacob[2], Friederich Ludwig[1])[325] was born in Lebanon, Linn Co., Oregon 20 January 1955 and married **Cleve Knabe** in Albany, Linn Co., Oregon 21 July 1973.

Virginia **Spooner** and Cleve **Knabe** had the following children born in Albany:
   286 i. Ginia[6] **Knabe**[326] 6 September 1977.
   287 ii. Janeie **Knabe**[327] 5 May 1979.

238. **Jo Ann**[5] **Hileman** (Floyd Lester[4], Emma Ester[3] Bartruff, Frederick[2], Friederich Ludwig[1])[328] was born in Dongola, Union Co., Illinois 17 September 1934 and married **Howard Lynn Day** 12 June 1955. Howard,[329] son of Albert Enos **Day** Sr. and Lois Mabel **Bankson**, was born in Union, Mc Henry Co., Illinois 18 April 1930.

Jo Ann **Hileman** and Howard Lynn **Day** had the following child:
+ 301 i. Wayne Allan[6] **Day** born 6 December 1955.

239. **Linda A.**[5] **Bartruff** (Wayne Watson[4], Walter Benjamin[3], Frederick[2], Friederich Ludwig[1])[330] was born in Carbondale, Jackson Co., Illinois 11 December 1947 and married **Edward Boyd** in Cobden, Union Co., Illinois 24 January 1970. Edward,[331] son of Walker Turner **Boyd** and Edna **Epperson**, was born in Rogers, Benton Co., Arkansas 12 September 1947. Linda is a Nursing Instructor at Three Rivers College in Sikeston, Scott Co., Missouri and Ed is an Electrician at the Sikeston Power Plant. (1999)

Linda A. **Bartruff** and Edward **Boyd** had the following children born in Sikeston:
   302 i. Valerie Lynne[6] **Boyd**[332] 21 November 1973 and married John David **Bollinger** there 8 November 1997. John was born 15 March 1974.[333] Valerie is an Occupational Therapist at a hospital in Killeen, Bell Co., Texas. (1999)
   303 ii. Edward E. **Boyd** Jr 23 August 1977.

241. **Sharon K.**[5] **Bartruff** (Wayne Watson[4], Walter Benjamin[3], Frederick[2], Friederich Ludwig[1])[334] was born in Anna, Union Co., Illinois 28 August 1955 and married **John Philip Hileman** in Mill Creek, Union Co., Illinois 6 November 1976. John,[335] son of Carl **Hileman** and Susie **Poole**, was born in Mill Creek 23 October 1956. Sharon is a Secretary at the Jonesboro, Union Co. Elementary School and Phil is a Mortician who owns the Hileman & Parr Funeral Home in Jonesboro with Dan Parr. (1999)

{ G 1760 }

Sharon K. **Bartruff** and John Philip **Hileman** had the following children born in Carbondale, Jackson Co., Illinois:

    304   i.   Justin Philip[6] **Hileman**[336] 4 February 1983.
    305   ii.   Megan Elizabeth **Hileman**[337] 26 September 1986.

247. **Celesta**[5] **Bartruff** (John Omer[4], John Robert[3], John[2], Friederich Ludwig[1]) was born in Salem, Marion Co., Oregon and married **Loyd William Saul** in Vancouver, Clark Co., Washington 14 Fanuary 1955. Loyd,[338] son of Adam William Michael **Saul** and Mary Elizabeth **Powell**, was born in Gregory, Gregory Co., South Dakota 12 May 1930. Celesta was living in Turner, Marion Co., Oregon at the time of her father's death.

Celesta **Bartruff** and Loyd William **Saul** had the following children:

 +   306   i.   Karen Elizabeth[6] **Saul** born 9 December 1957.
 +   307   ii.   Kathleen Ann **Saul** born 20 July 1959.
 +   308   iii. Jeffrey Loyd **Saul** born 25 November 1961.
 +   309   iv. Ronda June **Saul** born 26 June 1965.

250. **Eldon**[5] **Thompson** (Mary Katherine[4] Scharf, William Harry[3], Eva Katherine[2] Bartruff, Friederich Ludwig[1]) was born in Heppner, Morrow Co., Oregon 12 June 1941 and married **Lois Berry** in McMinnville, Yamhill Co., Oregon.

Eldon **Thompson** and Lois **Berry** had the following children born in San Diego, San Diego Co., California:

    310   i.   Eric[6] **Thompson**[339] 19 March 1974.
    311   ii.   David **Thompson**[340] 24 September 1975.

251. **Carl**[5] **Thompson** (Mary Katherine[4] Scharf, William Harry[3], Eva Katherine[2] Bartruff, Friederich Ludwig[1])[341] was born in McMinnville, Yamhill Co., Oregon 6 March 1944 and married **Leslie Miller** there.

Carl **Thompson** and Leslie **Miller** had the following children:

 +   312   i.   Kimberly[6] **Thompson** born 15 July 1967.
 +   313   ii.   Corey **Thompson** born 23 February 1969.

252. **Elinor**[5] **Thompson** (Mary Katherine[4] Scharf, William Harry[3], Eva Katherine[2] Bartruff, Friederich Ludwig[1]) was born in McMinnville, Yamhill Co., Oregon 24 April 1948 and married **Gregory Smith** there. They were divorced in 1978.

Elinor **Thompson** and Gregory **Smith** had the following children:
- 314 i. Walter[6] **Smith**[342] born in Salem, Marion Co., Oregon 5 December 1969.
- 315 ii. Gwyn **Smith**[343] born 17 May 1971 and married Everett **Schneider** in Big Sky, Gallatin Co., Montana 20 September 1997.

253. **Harry Lee**[5] **Scharf** (William Harry[4], William Harry[3], Eva Katherine[2] Bartruff, Friedrich Ludwig[1])[344] was born in Salem, Marion Co., Oregon 18 June 1942 and married **Karan Fleshman** there.

Harry Lee **Scharf** and Karan **Fleshman** had the following children:
- \+ 316 i. Kimberly[6] **Scharf**.
- \+ 317 ii. Shelly **Scharf**.

254. **Dennis**[5] **Scharf** (William Harry[4], William Harry[3], Eva Katherine[2] Bartruff, Friedrich Ludwig[1]) was born in Salem, Marion Co., Oregon 6 November 1944 and married twice. (1) **Linda (__)**. They were divorced. (2) **Suzanne (__)**. They were divorced.

Dennis **Scharf** and Linda (__) had the following child:
- 318 i. Toni[6] **Scharf**.[345]

Dennis **Scharf** and Brenda **Pardum** had the following child:
- 319 ii. K.C. Dean **Scharf**.[346]

255. **Roger**[5] **Scharf** (William Harry[4], William Harry[3], Eva Katherine[2] Bartruff, Friedrich Ludwig[1])[347] was born in Salem, Marion Co., Oregon 16 June 1948 and married twice. (1) **Cheryl Blake**. They were divorced. (2) **Sandra (__)**.

Roger **Scharf** and Cheryl **Blake** had the following child:
- 320 i. Danielle[6] **Scharf**.[348]

256. **Marla Jo**[5] **Porterfield** (Gertrude Helen[4] Scharf, Joseph Elmer[3], Eva Katherine[2] Bartruff, Friedrich Ludwig[1])[349] was born in Hood River, Hood River Co., Oregon 25 November 1947 and married **Jeffrey Bellis** in Parkdale, Hood River Co., Oregon 4 August 1973.

Marla Jo **Porterfield** and Jeffrey **Bellis** had the following child:
- 321 i. Tyler[6] **Bellis**[350] born in Beaverton, Washington Co., Oregon 4 November 1981.

257. **Marvin Benton**[5] **Cook** Jr. (Loween Vivian[4] Scharf, Joseph Elmer[3], Eva Katherine[2] Bartruff, Friederich Ludwig[1])[351] was born in Salem, Marion Co., Oregon 11 October 1947 and married **Cathy Sheeley** in Hermiston, Umatilla Co., Oregon.

Marvin Benton **Cook** Jr. and Cathy **Sheeley** had the following children born in Portland, Multnomah Co., Oregon:
- 322   i.   Geoffry Aaron[6] **Cook**[352] 2 February 1972.
- 323   ii.   Jeremy **Cook**[353] 3 March 1978 and died 24 November 1996 at 18 years of age.

SIXTH GENERATION

270. **Sarah Anne**[6] **Thompson** (Anne Elizabeth[5] McDonough, Delbert Leroy[4], Anna Elizabeth[3] Bartruff, Charles Jacob[2], Friederich Ludwig[1])[354] was born in Portland, Multnomah Co., Oregon 10 December 1969 and married **Fred Schroedl** there 12 August 1995. Fred, son of Michael **Schroedl**, was born in Portland 11 December 1969.

Sarah Anne **Thompson** and Fred **Schroedl** had the following child born in Portland:
- 324   i.   Max Thompson[7] **Schroedl** 12 July 2000.[355]

275. **Sean Craig**[6] **Wasson** (Tracy Lee[5] Edwards, Grace Velma[4] Bartruff, Elmer Walter[3], Charles Jacob[2], Friederich Ludwig[1])[356] was born in Salem, Marion Co., Oregon 6 September 1975 and married **Elizabeth Lynn Smith** in Monmouth, Polk Co., Oregon 10 August 1997.

Sean Craig **Wasson** and Elizabeth Lynn **Smith** had the following child born in Salem:
- 325   i.   Ian Conner[7] **Wasson**[357] 24 July 1998.

301. **Wayne Allan**[6] **Day** (Jo Ann[5] Hileman, Floyd Lester[4], Emma Ester[3] Bartruff, Frederick[2], Friederich Ludwig[1])[358] was born in Paducah, McCracken Co., Kenucky 6 December 1955 and married **Patricia Hannaford** in Senatobia, Tate Co., Mississippi 3 October 1981. Patricia,[359] daughter of Leon E. **Hannaford** and Bobbie Jean **Bowden**, was born in Senatobia 9 March 1952.

Wayne Allan **Day** and Patricia **Hannaford** had the following children:

 326 i. Bryan Allan[7] **Day**[360] born in Fort Worth, Tarrant Co., Texas 6 February 1987.

 327 ii. Mary Kathryn **Day**[361] born in Jackson, Madison Co., Tennessee 24 April 1992.

306. **Karen Elizabeth**[6] **Saul** (Celesta[5] Bartruff, John Omer[4], John Robert[3], John[2], Friederich Ludwig[1])[362] was born in Salem, Marion Co., Oregon 9 December 1957 and married **Mark Alan Stayer**. Mark,[363] son of John Steven **Stayer** and Naomi Marie **Johnson**, was born 4 April 1954.

Karen Elizabeth **Saul** and Mark Alan **Stayer** had the following child born in Portland, Multnomah Co., Oregon:

 328 i. Mary Elizabeth[7] **Stayer**[364] 6 April 1990.

307. **Kathleen Ann**[6] **Saul** (Celesta[5] Bartruff, John Omer[4], John Robert[3], John[2], Friederich Ludwig[1])[365] was born in Salem, Marion Co., Oregon 20 July 1959 and married **Joel Garrett** in Houston, Harris Co., Texas 5 September 1982. Joel,[366] son of Earl **Garrett** and Margaret (__), was born in Fremont, Dodge Co., Nebraska 8 January 1954.

Kathleen Ann **Saul** and Joel **Garrett** had the following children:

 329 i. Matthew[7] **Garrett**[367] born 8 October 1991.

 330 ii. Ann Elizabeth **Garrett**[368] born 24 April 1993.

 331 iii. Jonathan **Garrett**[369] born 21 March 1995.

 332 iv. Benjamin **Garrett**[370] born 23 May 1998.

308. **Jeffrey Loyd**[6] **Saul** (Celesta[5] Bartruff, John Omer[4], John Robert[3], John[2], Friederich Ludwig[1])[371] was born in Salem, Marion Co., Oregon 25 November 1961 and married **Catherine Marie Bartels** there 22 May 1992. Catherine,[372] daughter of Ronald Ray **Bartels** and Judith Catherine **Hansel**, was born in Seattle, King Co., Washington 26 December 1966.

Jeffrey Loyd **Saul** and Catherine Marie **Bartels** had the following children born in Portland, Multnomah Co., Oregon:

 333 i. Stephanie Marie[7] **Saul**[373] 1 September 1998.

 334 ii. Phillip **Saul**[374] 3 August 2001.

309. **Ronda June**[6] **Saul** (Celesta[5] Bartruff, John Omer[4], John Robert[3], John[2], Friederich Ludwig[1])[375] was born in Salem, Marion Co., Oregon 26 June 1965 and married **Michael Edward Traeger** in Lake Tahoe, Nevada

29 December 1993. Michael is the son of James Raymond **Traeger** and Dorothy Alice **Edwards**.[376]

Ronda June **Saul** and Michael Edward **Traeger** had the following children:
- 335   i.   Megan[7] **Traeger**.[377]
- 336   ii.   Michael **Traeger**.[378]
- 337   iii.   Alex **Traeger**.[379]

312. **Kimberly**[6] **Thompson** (Carl[5], Mary Katherine[4] Scharf, William Harry[3], Eva Katherine[2] Bartruff, Friedrich Ludwig[1])[380] was born in McMinnville, Yamhill Co., Oregon 15 July 1967 and married **Brett Langer** in Beaverton, Washington Co., Oregon.

Kimberly **Thompson** and Brett **Langer** had the following children born in Tualatin, Washington Co., Oregon:
- 338   i.   Parker[7] **Langer**[381] 27 July 1995.
- 339   ii.   Harrison **Langer**[382] 13 March 1998.

313. **Corey**[6] **Thompson** (Carl[5], Mary Katherine[4] Scharf, William Harry[3], Eva Katherine[2] Bartruff, Friedrich Ludwig[1]) was born in McMinnville, Yamhill Co., Oregon 23 February 1969 and married **Laura Cabrea** in Phoenix, Maricopa Co., Arizona.

Corey **Thompson** and Laura **Cabrea** had the following child born in Scottsdale Maricopa Co., Arizona:
- 340   i.   Elsie Katherine[7] **Thompson**[383] 15 November 1997.

316. **Kimberly**[6] **Scharf** (Harry Lee[5], William Harry[4], William Harry[3], Eva Katherine[2] Bartruff, Friedrich Ludwig[1])[384] birth date unknown, married **Jeffry Welty**.

Kimberly **Scharf** and Jeffry **Welty** had the following children:
- 341   i.   Ashley[7] **Welty**[385] born 14 June 1990.
- 342   ii.   Austin **Welty**[386] born 25 September 1993.

317. **Shelly**[6] **Scharf** (Harry Lee[5], William Harry[4], William Harry[3], Eva Katherine[2] Bartruff, Friedrich Ludwig[1])[387] birth date unknown, married **Rick Sellers**.

Shelly **Scharf** and Rick **Sellers** had the following child:
- 343   i.   Akota[7] **Sellers**.[388]

BARTRUFF FAMILY ENDNOTES

1. Delbert L. McDonough, great grandson of Friederich L. and Katharina Frederika (Spangler) Bartruff, to Blaine Whipple. Letters dated 12 Nov. 1992, 1 October 1999, and 31 Aug. 2000 at 1035 Chestnut, NW, Salem, OR 97304. In possession of Whipple (2005). (Hereafter McDonough to Whipple, *3 Letters*); *Union County, Illinois Cemeteries* (Carterville, Ill 62918: The Genealogy Society of Southern Illinois, 1990), 1:73. (Hereafter Cemeteries, *Union Co, Ill.*); and 1900 U.S. Census, Population Schedule, Jonesboro Precinct, Union Co., Illinois, enumerated by Paul W. Baker 8, 9, and 11 June. FHL film. (Hereafter Jonesboro Precinct 1900, *U.S. Census*).
2. McDonough to Whipple, *3 Letters*; and Cemeteries, *Union Co, Ill.*, 1:73.
3. George E. Parks, comp., *History of Union County, Illinois With Some Genealogy Notes* vol. 2, published by Parks, 405 S. Main, Anna, Ill. 62906, 1983 (Hereafter *History of Union Co.*).
4. through 7. Friederich L. Bartruff-Katharina Frederica Spangler Family Group Sheets, supplied 10 April 1999 by Howard Lynn Day, 3571 Maxon Rd., Paducah, Ky. 42001-9501. No documentation provided. (Hereafter Bartruff - Spangler, *Family Group Sheets*).
8. Interview with Margaret E. (Bartruff) Bunch, 341 Calico St. NW, Salem, Oreg. 97304, by Blaine Whipple, 25 Feb. 1981 Transcript in possession of Whipple (2005). (Hereafter Margaret E. (Bartruff) Bunch, *Interview*); and Charles J. Bartruff, Death Certificate State Registered No. 03, 11 March 1987 (A true, full, and correct copy of the original certificate on file in the Vital Records Unit of the Oregon State Health Division.), Oregon State Health Division Vital Statistics Section, Salem, Oreg.
9. Margaret E. (Bartruff) Bunch, *Interview*; and Anna Mary (Loeb) Bartruff, Death Certificate Registered No. 937, 14 Nov. 1986. (A true, full, and Correct Copy of the Original Certificate on File in the Vital Records Unit of the Oregon State Health Division.), Oregon State Board of Health Bureau of Vital Statistics, Salem, Oreg. (hereafter cited as Anna Mary Bartruff, *Death Certificate*).
10. Bartruff - Spangler, *Family Group Sheets*.
11. Margaret E. (Bartruff) Bunch, *Interview*.
12. through 19. Margaret E. (Bartruff) Bunch, *Interview*.
20. Ruth M. Bartruff, Birth Certificate Decree for Registration of Birth, a correct transcript of the original as the same appears on record in Book 1, page 47, 14 April 1943, Circuit Court of the State of Oregon for the County of Multnomah, Portland, Oreg.
21. Ruth Mildred Walter, Death Certificate ID Tag No. H-11106, 2 April 1998, Oregon Health Division Center for Health Statistics, Oregon Department of Human Resources, Salem, Oreg.
22. Bartruff - Spangler, *Family Group Sheets*.
23. Cemeteries, *Union Co, Ill.*, 1:73; and Jonesboro Precinct 1900, *U.S. Census*, enumerated 8 June 1900, Sheet 14, household 388.
24. Jonesboro Precinct 1900, *U.S. Census*, enumerated 8 June 1900, Sheet 14, household 388.
25. Cemeteries, *Union Co, Ill.*, 1:73.
26. Bartruff - Spangler, *Family Group Sheets*.
27. Cemeteries, *Union Co., Ill.*, 1:73.
28. Bartruff - Spangler, *Family Group Sheets*.
29. and 30. Jonesboro Precinct 1900, *U.S. Census*, enumerated 8 June, Sheet 14, household 296.
31. and 32. Source: Stephenie Lorraine Bewley, Salem, Oreg.
33. Ibid.; and Katherine Hanson to Blaine Whipple. letter dated 6 July 1999 at 1549 Morgan Lane, McMinnville, Oreg. 97128. In possession of Whipple (2005). (Hereafter Hanson to Whipple, *Letter, 6 July 1999*).
34. Bartruff - Spangler, *Family Group Sheets*.

35. Cemeteries, *Union Co, Ill.*, 1:74.
36. *History of Union County.*
37. through 39. Bartruff - Spangler, *Family Group Sheets.*
40. Cemeteries, *Union Co, Ill.*, 1:72.
41. and 42. Bartruff - Spangler, *Family Group Sheets.*
43. Jonesboro Precinct 1900, *U.S. Census*, enumerated 11 June, Sheet 16, household 338.
44. Bartruff - Spangler, *Family Group Sheets.*
45. 1900, *U.S. Census* enumerated 11 June, Sheet 16, household 338.
46. and 47. Bartruff - Spangler, *Family Group Sheets.*
48. Jonesboro Prencict 1900, *U.S. Census* enumerated 11 June, Sheet 16, household 338.
49. Bartruff - Spangler, *Family Group Sheets.*
50. Cemeteries, *Union Co, Ill.*, 1:75.
51. and 52. Bartruff - Spangler, *Family Group Sheets.*
53. 1900, *U.S. Census* enumerated 9 June, Sheet 15, household 318.
54. Cemeteries, *Union Co, Ill.*, 1:75.
55. Bartruff - Spangler, *Family Group Sheets.*
56. and 57. 1900, *U.S. Census* enumerated 8 June, Sheet 14, household 302.
58. 1900, *U.S. Census* enumerated 8 June, Sheet 14, household 302.
59. through 62. Bartruff - Spangler, *Family Group Sheets.*
63. 1900, *U.S. Census*, Sheet 16, household No. 303.
64. Margaret E. (Bartruff) Bunch, *Interview.*
65. and 66. Bartruff - Spangler, *Family Group Sheets.*
67. and 68. Margaret E. (Bartruff) Bunch, *Interview.*
69. and 70. McDonough to Whipple, *3 Letters.*
71. Margaret E. (Bartruff) Bunch, *Interview*; and Elmer Walter Bartruff-Lonie Peoples Family Group Sheet, supplied 11 June 1999 by Bryce Bartruff, 2732 Foxglove Loop S.E., Albany, OR 97321. Source is personal knowledge. (Hereafter Bartruff - Peoples, *Family Group Sheet*).
72. Bartruff - Spangler, *Family Group Sheets*; and Bartruff - Peoples, *Family Group Sheet.*
73. Personal knowledge of daughter, Ines Mae (Peterson) Whipple, 236 NW Sundown Way, Portland, Oreg. 97229-6575. 1999; and Owen D. Peterson & Josephine B. Bartruff, Marriage Certificate, 13 Feb. 1924, N.S. No. 2152, Vol. 59: 46, County Clerk's Office, Multnomah County, Oregon.
74. Personal knowledge of daughter, Ines Mae (Peterson) Whipple 1999.; and Owen Diamon Peterson, Death Certificate State File No. 4198, Multnomah Co. Registar's No. 4195, 30 Dec. 1946, Oregon State Board of Health, Division of Vital Statistics, Salem, Oregon.
75. Interview by the author with Jo Peterson 31 May and 19 June 1982.
76. Bartruff - Spangler, *Family Group Sheets.*
77. 1900, *U.S. Census* enumerated 8 June, Sheet 14, household 388.
78. through 87. Bartruff - Spangler, *Family Group Sheets.*
88. 1900, *U.S. Census* enumerated 8 June, Sheet 14, household 388.
89. through 96. Bartruff - Spangler, *Family Group Sheets.*
97. Cemeteries, *Union Co, Ill.*, 1:74; and 1900, *U.S. Census*, Census enumerated 8 June 1900 by Paul W. Baker. Sheet 14, household 388.
98. Bartruff - Spangler, *Family Group Sheets.* Cemeteries, Union Co, Ill., 1:74.
99. through 103. Bartruff - Spangler, *Family Group Sheets.*
104. 1900, *U.S. Census* enumerated 8 June, Sheet 14, household 388.
105. through 109. Bartruff - Spangler, *Family Group Sheets.*
110. 1900, *U.S. Census* enumerated 8 June, Sheet 14, household 388.

111. through 113. Bartruff - Spangler, *Family Group Sheets*.
114. 1900, *U.S. Census* enumerated 8 June, Sheet 14, household 388.
115. and 116. Bartruff - Spangler, *Family Group Sheets*.
117. Ibid.; and Jonesboro Precinct, 1900 *U.S. Census,* Sheet 14, Household 388.
118. 1900, *U.S. Census* enumerated 8 June, Sheet 14, household 388.
119. and 120. Bartruff - Spangler, *Family Group Sheets*.
121. 1900, *U.S. Census* enumerated 8 June, Sheet 14, household 296.
122. through 127. Bartruff - Spangler, *Family Group Sheets*.
128. Ibid.; and Hanson to Whipple, *Letter, 6 July 1999*.
129. Hanson to Whipple, *Letter, 6 July 1999*.
130. through 142. Bartruff - Spangler, *Family Group Sheets*.
143. Ibid.; and Joseph Elmer Scharf-Ruby Pearl Hill *Family Group Sheets*, supplied 23 August 1999 by Gertrude Scharf Porterfield, 4110 Post Canyon Dr., Hood River, Oreg. 97031. The family group sheets represent her personal knowledge. (Hereafter Scharf, *Family Group Sheets*).
144. Bartruff - Spangler, *Family Group Sheets*; and Hill - Scharf, *Family Group Sheets*.
145. through 149. Bartruff - Spangler, *Family Group Sheets*.
150. Ibid.; and Hanson to Whipple, *Letter, 6 July 1999*.
151. and 152. Bartruff - Spangler, Family Group Sheets; and Hanson to Whipple, *Letter, 6 July 1999*.
153. through 157. Bartruff - Spangler, *Family Group Sheets*.
158. and 159. Cemeteries, *Union Co, Ill.*, 1:75.
160. through 181. Bartruff - Spangler, *Family Group Sheets*.
182. 1900, *U.S. Census* enumerated 11 June, Sheet 16, household 338.
183. through 187. Bartruff - Spangler, *Family Group Sheets*.
188. 1900, *U.S. Census* enumerated 11 June, Sheet 16, household 338.
189. through 192. Bartruff - Spangler, *Family Group Sheets*.
193. 1900, *U.S. Census* enumerated 11 June 1900, Sheet 16, household 338.
194. and 195. Bartruff - Spangler, *Family Group Sheets*.
196. 1900, *U.S. Census* enumerated 11 June, Sheet 16, household 338.
197. through 203. Bartruff - Spangler, *Family Group Sheets*.
204. 1900, *U.S. Census* enumerated 9 June 1900, Sheet 15, household 318.
205. and 206. Bartruff - Spangler, *Family Group Sheets*.
207. 1900, *U.S. Census* enumerated 9 June, Sheet 15, household 318.
208. and 209. Bartruff - Spangler, *Family Group Sheets*.
210. 1900, *U.S. Census* enumerated 9 June, Sheet 15, household 318.
211. through 220. Bartruff - Spangler, *Family Group Sheets*.
221. 1900, *U.S. Census*, enumerated 8 June. Sheet 14, household 302.
222. through 226. Bartruff - Spangler, *Family Group Sheets*.
227. 1900, *U.S. Census*, enumerated 8 June. Sheet 14, household 302.
228. through 233. Bartruff - Spangler, *Family Group Sheet*s.
234. 1900, *U.S. Census*.
235. through 238. Bartruff - Spangler, *Family Group Sheets*.
239. 1900, *U.S. Census*.
240. through 259. Bartruff - Spangler, *Family Group Sheets*.
260. and 261. McDonough to Whipple, *3 Letters*.
262. and 263. Order by Judge W.R. Bilyeu in the County Court of the State of Oregon for the County of Linn; dated 14 Dec. 1921.
264. Bartruff - Spangler, *Family Group Sheets*; Bartruff - Peoples, Family Group Sheet; and Ruben Len Edwards-Grace Velna Bartruff Family Group Sheets, supplied 17 August

1999 by Grace V. Edwards, 7016 River Road S., Salem, OR 97306. These sheets represent the personal knowledge of Grace V. Edwards. (Hereafter Edwards - Bartruff, *Family Group Sheets*).
265. Edwards - Bartruff, *Family Group Sheets*.
266. Bartruff - Peoples, *Family Group Sheet*.
267. Bartruff - Spangler, *Family Group Sheets*; and Bartruff - Peoples, *Family Group Sheet*.
268. Juanita (Bartruff) Collins to Blaine Whipple. letter dated 19 July 1999 at 250 "D" St., Lebanon, OR 97355-2535. In possession of Whipple at 236 NW Sundown Way, Portland, OR 97229-6575 (2005). (Hereafter Collins to Whipple, *Letter, 7 July 1999*).
269. Bartruff - Spangler, *Family Group Sheets*; and Bartruff - Peoples, *Family Group Sheet*.
270. Obituary, *The Oregonian*, 10 May 2005, B-6, col. 1. Portland, Oreg.
271. and 272. Bartruff - Peoples, *Family Group Sheet*.
273. through 276. Marion Elizabeth Bartruff-Robert Spooner *Family Group Sheets*, supplied 26 Aug. 1999 by Marion E. (Bartruff) Spooner, 350 Pearl St., Eugene, Oreg. 97401. The sheets contain information that is personally known to the submitter. (Hereafter Spooner - Bartruff, *Family Group Sheets*).
277. through 279. Bartruff - Spangler, *Family Group Sheets*.
280. Ibid.; and Wayne Watson Bartruff-Florence Brasel *Family Group Sheet*, supplied 26 April 1999 by Florence (Brasel) Bartruff, 412 N. Main St., Anna, Ill. 62906. This sheet represents personal knowledge of the submitter. (Hereafter Brasel - Bartruff, *Family Group Sheet*).
281. Brasel - Bartruff, *Family Group Sheet*.
282. and 283. Bartruff - Spangler, *Family Group Sheets*.
284. and 285. Brasel - Bartruff, *Family Group Sheet*.
286. Bartruff - Spangler, *Family Group Sheets*.
287. Ibid.; and Obituary of Virginia R. (Bartruff) Fryberger, *Oregonian*, Portland, Oreg. (7 Nov. 2002).
288. Fryberger Obit, *Portland Oregonian*.
289. Bartruff - Spangler, *Family Group Sheets*; and Hanson to Whipple, *Letter, 6 July 1999*.
290. Hanson to Whipple, *Letter, 6 July 1999*.
291. Bartruff - Spangler, *Family Group Sheets*; and Hanson to Whipple, *Letter, 6 July 1999*.
292. through 294. Hill - Scharf, *Family Group Sheets*.
295. through 298. Bartruff - Spangler, *Family Group Sheets*.
299. through 304. McDonough to Whipple, *3 Letters*.
305. through 313. Edwards - Bartruff, *Family Group Sheets*.
314. Bartruff - Peoples, *Family Group Sheet*; and Collins to Whipple, *Letter, 7 July 1999*.
315. and 316. Collins to Whipple, *Letter, 7 July 1999*.
317. through 320. Cynthia Bartruff-David Ludeman *Family Group Sheet*, supplied 4 Aug. 1999 by Cynthia Bartruff Ludeman, 16446 SE Stephens Ct., Portland, Oreg. 97233. Information on this sheet is based on personal knowledge. (Hereafter Bartruff - Ludeman, *Family Group Sheet*).
321. through 327. Spooner - Bartruff, *Family Group Sheets*.
328. and 329. Bartruff - Spangler, *Family Group Sheets*.
330. Ibid.; and Brasel - Bartruff, *Family Group Sheet*.
331. through 333. Brasel - Bartruff, *Family Group Sheet*.
334. Bartruff - Spangler, *Family Group Sheets*.
335. through 337. Brasel - Bartruff, *Family Group Sheet*.
338. Loyd and Celesta Saul to Blaine Whipple. E-mail dated 20 Oct. 2002 at lwsaul@nehalemtel.net. In possession of Whipple (2005). Information is based on personal knowledge. (Hereafter Saul to Whipple, *E-mail 20 Oct. 2002*).

339. through 348. Hanson to Whipple, *Letter, 6 July 1999.*
349. through 353. Hill - Scharf, *Family Group Sheets.*
354. and 355. McDonough to Whipple, *3 Letters.*
356. and 357. Edwards - Bartruff, *Family Group Sheets.*
358. through 361. Bartruff - Spangler, *Family Group Sheets.*
362. through 379. Saul to Whipple, *E-mail 20 Oct. 2002.*
380. through 388. Hanson to Whipple, *Letter, 6 July 1999.*

JOHN STEELE 1822 TO BREANNA JO STEELE 1990-

(Steele lineage of Miles Bruce and BreAnna Jo Steele, Generation 13, No. Robert Bruce Steele, their father.)

FIRST GENERATION

1. **John**[1] **Steele**[1] was born in Scotland in 1822 and married **Catherine (__)** there in 1852. She was born in Scotland 16 May 1837.[2]

John **Steele** and Catherine (__) had the following children born in Central City, Lawrence Co., South Dakota:

	2	i.	Robert[2] **Steele**.[3]
	3	ii.	Annabelle **Steele**.[4]
+	4	iii.	James LaRue **Steele** 16 July 1851.

SECOND GENERATION

4. **James LaRue**[2] **Steele** (John[1])[5] was born in Scotland 16 July 1851 and died 16 July 1917 in Central City, Lawrence Co., South Dakota, at 66 years of age. He married twice. (1) **Emma (__)** who was born abt 1853 and died 12 August 1872 in Central City, at 19 years of age.[6] (2) **Clara Mae Cook** in Toledo, Lucas Co., Ohio. She was born 14 February 1875 and died 11 November 1918 in Central City, at 43 years of age.[7] Clara was 24 years younger than her husband and the move from Ohio to Dakota Territory was a culture shock for her. She died of the flu one day after her son Vernard died of the same disease. James was a Stationary Engineer with the Homestead Gold Mine in Deadwood, Lawrence Co.

It is believed the family lived in Blancherd, Newfoundland before moving to the U.S. He died on his birthday.

{ G 1770 }

James LaRue **Steele** and Emma **(__)** had the following child:

    5   i   Harry **Steele**.[8]

James LaRue **Steele** and Clara Mae **Cook** had the following children:

    6   ii.   Vernard[3] **Steele**[9] died of the flu 10 November 1918 in Central City. His mother died of the flu the next day.
    7   iii.   Robert **Steele**.[10]
    8   iv.   Gladys **Steele**.[11]
    9   v.   Grace **Steele**.[12]
+ 10   vi.   Bruce C. **Steele** born 24 May 1906.
+ 11   vii.   Gordon **Steele** born 29 April 1914.

THIRD GENERATION

9. **Bruce C.**[3] **Steele** (James LaRue[2], John[1])[13] was born in Central City, Lawrence Co., South Dakota 24 May 1906 and died 1 March 1986 in Salem, Marion Co., Oregon, at 79 years of age. He married **Lena Matzke** in Portland, Multnomah Co., Oregon 28 June 1927. Lena,[14] daughter of Wilhelm Carl **Matzke** and Ernestine Henrietta Louise **Hardt**, was born in Portland 1 June 1902 and died there 27 May 1981, at 78 years of age. Bruce was in the restaurant business most of his adult life and was an investor in stocks and real estate. He loved to travel and fish the Columbia river

Bruce Steele with 47 pound Salmon.

Bruce and Lena Steele. Photos courtesy of Robert B. Steele.

{ G 1771 }

and Tillamook Bay, Tillamook Co., Oregon. After retirement, he and Lena would spend part of the winter in California and Arizona. They eventually acquired a motor home to travel in and a second home in Garibaldi, Tillamook Co., Oregon near Tillamook Bay. He died of causes relating to stroke and age. The final distribution and closing of Bruce's estate was filed 3 August 1987 in the Circuit Court of Oregon, Multnomah County Department of Probate. The case file # is 8603-90524. It was entered in the *Journal* 9 September 1986, Book 1506, page 1206. They are buried in Riverview Abbey Mausoleum, Portland.

Lena and Harold.

Bruce C. **Steele** and Lena **Matzke** had the following child:
+   12   i.   Harold[4] **Steele** born 10 April 1929.

10. **Gordon**[3] **Steele** (James LaRue[2], John[1])[15] was born in Central City, Lawrence Co., South Dakota 29 April 1914 and died 9 May 1981 in Salem, Marion Co., Oregon, at 67 years of age. He married **Marguerite Elizabeth Huntington** in Buffalo, Harding Co., South Dakota 21 September 1933. Marguerite was born in Missouri Valley, Harrison Co., Iowa 10 November 1907.[16]

Gordon **Steele** and Marguerite Elizabeth **Huntington** had the following child:
+   13   i.   Corale[4] **Steele** born 25 February 1935.

FOURTH GENERATION

12. **Harold**[4] **Steele** (Bruce C.[3], James LaRue[2], John[1])[17] was born in Portland, Multnomah Co., Oregon 10 April 1929 and died there of cancer 2 September 1962, at 33 years of age. He is buried in Riverview Abbey Mausoleum, Portland. He married **Ines Mae Peterson** in Portland 24 February 1951. They were married at 8 p.m. at the Valley Community United Presbyterian Church, 7850 S. W. Brentwood Ave., West Slope. Rev. H. A. Armstrong officiated. The bride, given away by her brother Wayne, wore a white satin dress with lace trim. Her three-quarter length

Ines and Harold 24 February 1951.

Harold and Ines with friend.

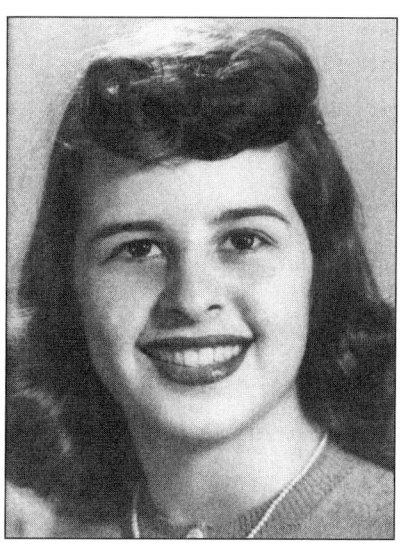

Ines, Washington Hight School graduation.

Judith and Bob.

veil was held by a white satin hat and she carried an orchid bouquet. Mrs. Robert O. Williams was Matron of Honor. Bridesmaids were Shirlee Spring, Pauline Pappas, and Carol Jonson. A church reception followed.

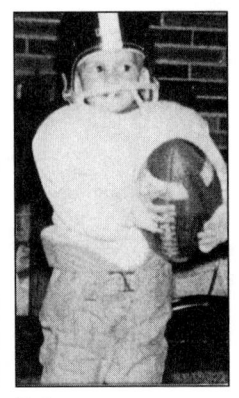

Bob.

Bob with Santa.

Harold.

Harold **Steele** and Ines Mae **Peterson** had the following children born in Portland:
+   14   i.   Judith Lynn[5] **Steele** 30 January 1952.
+   15   ii. Robert Bruce **Steele** 15 March 1960.

13. **Corale**[4] **Steele** (Gordon[3], James LaRue[2], John[1])[18] was born in Rapid City, Pennington Co., South Dakota 25 February 1935 and married **George Carl Goesch** in Hot Springs, Fall River Co., South Dakota 23 May 1954. George was born 6 January 1936.

Corale **Steele** and George Carl **Goesch** had the following children:
+   16   i.   Samuel Tope[5] **Goesch** 7 December 1954.
+   17   ii.   Joel Hans **Goesch** 17 December 1955.
+   18   iii. Tamara Dawn **Goesch** 6 June 1957.
+   19   iv.   Rosemary Mae **Goesch** 28 September 1961.
    20   v.   George Kurt **Goesch**[19] born in Salem, Marion Co., Oregon 17 October 1972 and married Sarah Jennifer **Moritz** there 23 March 1992. Sarah was born in Salem 31 March 1973.[20]

FIFTH GENERATION

14. **Judith Lynn**[5] **Steele** (Harold[4], Bruce C.[3], James LaRue[2], John[1])[21] was born in Portland, Multnomah Co., Oregon 30 January 1952 and married . (1) **William Rudolph Long** in Menlo Park, San Mateo Co., Cali-

fornia 4 June 1977. William, son of Frederick Harold **Long** and Jean Marie **Vontobel**, was born in Stamford, Fairfield Co., Connecticut 15 May 1952. They were divorced in Salem, Marion Co., Oregon 1 October 2001. Judith is a graduate of Sunset High School, Washington Co., Oregon;

Sydney and Will.

Will.

Sydney.

Seattle Pacific University, Seattle, King County, Washington; and Gordon Conwell Seminary, Hamilton, Essex Co. Massachusetts. She has also completed graduate study toward a Ph.D. degree. She has been a pastor at Presbyterian churches in Oregon and Kansas, a chaplain in the Oregon State Prison system, and is a pastor for the Marion Co. Hostice program. (2005)

Judith Lynn **Steele** and William Rudolph **Long** had the following children:
  21 i. Sydney Lynn[6] **Steele-Long**[22] born in Palo Alto, Santa Clara Co., California 13 May 1982. She weighted 8 lbs 8 oz and was 20.5 inches long. She was graduated from the U. of Oregon at Eugene, Lane Co. in June 2004 cum laude and

{ G 1775 }

Will, South Salem High School graduation 2005.

Sydney, graduation, U of Oregon 2004. Double major, English and Journalism, Phi Beta Kappa, Cum Laude, and honors in English.

>   Phi Beta Kappa with double majors in English and Journalism. She works for Kirshenbond & Partners, a nationally known advertising firm in New York City (2006)
>
> 22   ii.   William Scott **Steele-Long**[23] born in Portland 27 February 1987. He was graduated from South Salem High School in June 2005 and will attend Colgate University in Hamilton, Hamilton Co., New York beginning in August 2005.

15. **Robert Bruce**[5] **Steele** (Harold[4], Bruce C.[3], James LaRue[2], John[1])[24] was born in Portland, Multnomah Co., Oregon 15 March 1960 and married **Tamera J. Hunt** there 6 December 1986. Tamera[25] daughter of James Jefferson **Hunt** and Betty Jo **Martinson**, was born in Portland 7 February 1962. She is a Certified Medical Assistant. Bob weighed 8 pounds 7 ounces at birth and was 4'2" and weighed 65 pounds on his eighth birthday; 4' 10 3/8" and 93 pounds on his 12th; and 5' 7 3/8" and 158 pounds on his 17th birthday. A 1979 graduate of Sunset High School, Washington Co., Oregon, he was a three-year letterman in football and track. He was a volunteer coach of soccer and baseball teams at the elementary school level and is an avid sports enthusiast of the Oregon Ducks and Oakland Raiders football teams. He has worked for Costco

BreAnna and Miles Steele.

{ G 1776 }

Tami, Bob, BreAnna, and Miles.

Miles and Bob with Santa Blaine Whipple.

{ G 1777 }

Foods in Beaverton, Washington Co., for the past 16 years with experience in all departments. He is a lead merchandiser in the food department (2006). He enjoys camping and fishing with his family and finds great satisfaction in working in his yard. He and Tamera separated in December 2004.

BreAnna, 15.   Miles, 17.

Robert Bruce **Steele** and Tamera J. **Hunt** had the following children born in Portland:

    23   i.   Miles Bruce[6] **Steele**[26] 15 January 1988. He was graduated from at Sunset High School. (2006)

    24   ii.   BreAnna Jo **Steele**[27] 19 January 1990. She is a Sophomore at Sunset High School. (2006)

16. **Samuel Tope**[5] **Goesch** (Corale[4] Steele, Gordon[3], James LaRue[2], John[1])[28] was born in Rapid City, Pennington Co., South Dakota 7 December 1954. He married **Victoria Elizabeth Fink** in Seattle, King Co., Washington 1 May 1982. Victoria was born in Portland, Multnomah Co., Oregon 4 August 1957.[29]

Samuel Tope **Goesch** and Victoria Elizabeth **Fink** had the following children born in Salem, Marion Co., Oregon:

    25   i.   Kurt Samuel[6] **Goesch**[30] 28 October 1985.
    26   ii.   Eric Donald **Goesch**[31] 15 August 1987.
    27   iii.   Alan Carl **Goesch**[32] 19 April 1991.
    28   iv.   Bret Alexander **Goesch**[33] 3 June 1994.

17. **Joel Hans**[5] **Goesch** (Corale[4] Steele, Gordon[3], James LaRue[2], John[1])[34] was born in Rapid City, S. Dak. 17 December 1955 and married **Alice Margaret Moffitt** in Longview, Cowlitz Co., Washington 28 March 1982. Alice was born in Travis Air Force Base, Solano Co., California 12 November 1960.[35]

Joel Hans **Goesch** and Alice Margaret **Moffitt** had the following children:
- 29   i.   Nathan Joel[6] **Goesch**[36] born in Portland, Multnomah Co., Oregon 19 May 1983.
- 30   ii. Thomas Prescott **Goesch**[37] born in Yakima, Yakima Co., Washington 17 September 1988.

18. **Tamara Dawn**[5] **Goesch** (Corale[4] Steele, Gordon[3], James LaRue[2], John[1])[38] was born in Rapid City, Pennington Co., South Dakota 6 June 1957 and married **Christian Peter Stehr**. He was born in Germany 11 September 1942.[39]

Tamara Dawn **Goesch** and Christian Peter **Stehr** had the following child born in Corvallis, Benton Co., Oregon:
- 31   i.   Sophia Lizbeth[6] **Stehr**[40] 21 August 1987.

19. **Rosemary Mae**[5] **Goesch** (Corale[4] Steele, Gordon[3], James LaRue[2], John[1])[41] was born in La Grande, Union Co., Oregon 28 September 1961 and married **Samuel Oliver Grieser** in Salem, Marion Co., Oregon 27 December 1988. Samuel was born in Albany, Linn Co., Oreg. 4 December 1960.[42]

Rosemary Mae **Goesch** and Samuel Oliver **Grieser** adopted the following children:
- 32   i.   Abigail Mary[6] **Grieser**[43] born in Custer, Custer Co., South Dakota 29 June 1991.
- 33   ii.   Mandy Christina Rose **Grieser**[44] born in Salem, Marion Co., Oregon 24 May 1993.
- 34   iii. Jeremiah Jesse **Grieser**[45] born in Tampa, Hillsborough Co., Florida 9 February 1996.

STEELE FAMILY ENDNOTES

1. through 12. Corale Goesch to Blaine Whipple. Letter dated 9 May 1996 at 179 Hazelbrook Dr., N., Keizer, Oreg. 97303. (Hereafter Goesch to Whipple, *Letter, 9 May 1996*).
13. Personal knowledge of Ines Mae (Peterson) (Steele) Whipple, 236 N.W. Sundown Way, Portland, Oreg. 97229, daughter-in-law of Bruce C. Steele.

14. Gertrude (Matzke) Wilmoth to Blaine Whipple. Letter dated 31 August 1992 at 4734 NE Going, Portland, Oreg. 97219. In possession of Whipple (2005). (Hereafter Wilmoth to Whipple, *Letter, 31 Aug. 1992*).
15. and 16. Goesch to Whipple, *Letter, 9 May 1996*.
17. Personal knowledge of Ines Mae Peterson, his wife.
18. through 20. Goesch to Whipple, *Letter, 9 May 1996*.
21. through 23. Personal knowledge of Judith Lynn Steele, 548 22nd St. N.W., Salem, Oreg 97301.
24. Personal knowledge of Robert Bruce Steele, 95 SW 104th, Portland, Oreg. 97225
25. Tamera J. (Hunt) Steele to Blaine Whipple. Letter dated 9 July 1991 at 95 SW 104th, Portland, Oreg 97225. In possession of Whipple (2005).
26. and 27. Personal knowledge of Robert Bruce Steele.
28. through 45. Goesch to Whipple, *Letter, 9 May 1996*.

KARL WILHELM MATZKE ABT 1845 TO LENA MATZKE 1981

(Matzke lineage of Lena Matzke, mother of Harold Steele Generation 12, No. 6209, first husband of Ines May Peterson, wife of Robert Blaine Whipple.)

FIRST GENERATION

1. **Karl Wilhelm**[I] **Matzke**[I] was born in Germany and married **Ernestine (__)** there. She was born in Germany.[2]

Karl Wilhelm **Matzke** and Ernestine (__) had the following child:
+ 2 i. Wilhelm Carl[2] **Matzke** born 9 October 1867.

SECOND GENERATION

2. **Wilhelm Carl**[2] **Matzke** (Karl Wilhelm[I])[3] was born in Braunsfort, Germany 9 October 1867 and died 25 May 1940 in Beaverton, Washington Co., Oregon, at 72 years of age. He married **Ernestine Henreitta Louise Hardt** in Portland, Multnomah Co., Oregon 3 June 1894. Ernestine,[4] daughter of August **Hardt** and Justine **Pautz**, was born in Hermelsdorf, Germany 12 February 1871.

Wilhelm Carl **Matzke** and Ernestine Henreitta Louise **Hardt** had the following children:

+ 3 i. Martha[3] **Matzke** born 27 March 1895.
+ 4 ii. Hattie **Matzke** born 20 July 1898.
  5 iii. Ida **Matzke**[5] born in Portland and died of diphtheria abt 1916 in Beaverton, at approximately 17 years of age.
+ 6 iv. Carl **Matzke** born 3 April 1900.
+ 7 v. Lena **Matzke** born 1 June 1902.
  8 vi. Bertha Ernestine **Matzke**[6] born in Beaverton 24 August 1906 and died 2 January 1975 in Vancouver, Clark Co., Washington, at 68 years of age. She married Gabe **Waldorf** in Stevenson, Skamania Co., Washington 19 July 1937. He was born in North Dakota in 1894 and died in 1975, at 81 years of age.[7]
  9 vii. William Edward **Matzke**[8] born in Beaverton 30 July 1908, died 5 November 2005 in Hillsboro, Washington Co., Oregon, at age 97 years, and married Mabel **LaFond**. She was born in Minnesota 23 January 1910 and died 30 May 1981 in Beaverton, at 71 years of age.[9]
  10 viii. Alma Marie **Matzke**[10] born in Beaverton 23 May 1910 and died 19 June 2002 in Portland, at 92 years of age. She married Howard **Leiberich** in Beaverton 3 August 1935. Howard was born in Chicago, Cook Co., Illinois 4 June 1911.[11] He is living in Portland in 2006.
+ 11 ix. Gertrude **Matzke** born 2 April 1914.

THIRD GENERATION

3. **Martha**[3] **Matzke** (Wilhelm Carl[2], Karl Wilhelm[1])[12] was born in Portland, Multnomah Co., Oregon 27 March 1895 and died 24 April 1978 in Milwaukie, Clackamas Co., Oregon, at 83 years of age. She married **Alfred Andreas Nielsen** in Portland 15 January 1921. Alfred was born in Ronne, Denmark 24 December 1892 and died 28 April 1962 in Portland, at 69 years of age.[13]

Martha **Matzke** and Alfred Andreas **Nielsen** had the following children born in Portland:

+ 12 i. Alfred Andreas[4] **Nielsen** Jr. 7 October 1921.
  13 ii. Richard William **Nielsen**[14] 12 September 1924 and died in 1980 at 55 years of age. He married Eileen **Kelly** in Portland 17 November 1947. She was born in 1917.[15]
+ 14 iii. Elaine Ernestine **Nielsen** born 16 March 1926.

{ G 1781 }

4. **Hattie**[3] **Matzke** (Wilhelm Carl[2], Karl Wilhelm[1])[16] was born in Portland, Multnomah Co., Oregon 20 July 1898 and died there 21 May 1978, at 79 years of age. She married **Victor Alexander Arrowsmith** in Portland 23 June 1923. He was born in Essex, England 9 October 1897 and died in 1960 in Portland, at 62 years of age.[17]

Hattie **Matzke** and Victor Alexander **Arrowsmith** had the following children born in Portland:
    15 i. Mary Ida[4] **Arrowsmith**[18] 23 April 1924. She is living in Portland in 2005.
+ 16 ii. Vivian **Arrowsmith** 22 September 1927.

6. **Carl**[3] **Matzke** (Wilhelm Carl[2], Karl Wilhelm[1])[19] was born in Portland, Multnomah Co., Oregon 3 April 1900 and died in 1956 in Elmonica, Washington, at 56 years of age. He married **Mary Bolliger** in Stevenson, Skamania Co., Washington 2 April 1935.

Carl **Matzke** and Mary **Bolliger** had the following children born in Portland:
    17 i. Carol[4] **Matzke**[20] 13 December 1935 and married Vern **Gale**.
    18 ii. William **Matzke**[21] 3 May 1942.

7. **Lena**[3] **Matzke** (Wilhelm Carl[2], Karl Wilhelm[1])[22] was born in Portland, Multnomah Co., Oregon 1 June 1902 and died there 27 May 1981, at 78 years of age. She married **Bruce C. Steele** in Portland 28 June 1927. Bruce,[23] son of James LaRue **Steele** and Clara Mae **Cook**, was born in Central City, Lawrence Co., South Dakota 24 May 1906 and died 1 March 1986 in Salem, Marion Co., Oregon, at 79 years of age.

Lena **Matzke** and Bruce C. **Steele** had the following child:
+ 19 i. Harold[4] **Steele** born 10 April 1929.

(For a continuation of the Matzke lineage see Harold Steele, Generation 4, No. 12, in the Steele lineage above.)

11. **Gertrude**[3] **Matzke** (Wilhelm Carl[2], Karl Wilhelm[1])[24] was born in Beaverton, Washington Co, Oregon 2 April 1914 and married **Gurnie Wilmoth** in Vancouver, Clark Co., Washington 28 September 1939. Gurnie was born in Dobson, Surry Co., North Carolina 1 October 1915 and died 6 March 1997 in Portland, Multnomah Co., Oregon, at 81 years of age.[25]

Gertrude **Matzke** and Gurnie **Wilmoth** had the following children:
    20 i. David Franklin[4] **Wilmoth**[26] born in Dobson 6 January 1943.

+	21	ii.	Linda Ann **Wilmoth** born 7 July 1944.
+	22	iii.	Nancy Jean **Wilmoth** born 30 October 1945.
+	23	iv.	Janet Louise **Wilmoth** born 2 January 1948.

FOURTH GENERATION

12. **Alfred Andreas**[4] **Nielsen** Jr. (Martha[3] Matzke, Wilhelm Carl[2], Karl Wilhelm[1])[27] was born in Portland, Multnomah Co., Oregon 7 October 1921 and died there 22 August 1969, at 47 years of age.

He married **Clara Mae Johnson** in Portland 30 April 1943. Clara was born in Portland 8 October 1921.[28]

Alfred Andreas **Nielsen** Jr. and Clara Mae **Johnson** had the following children born in Portland:

| + | 24 | i. | Thomas Alfred[5] **Nielsen** 3 July 1949. |
| + | 25 | ii. | Brian Carl **Nielsen** 28 October 1953. |

14. **Elaine Ernestine**[4] **Nielsen** (Martha[3] Matzke, Wilhelm Carl[2], Karl Wilhelm[1])[29] was born in Portland, Multnomah Co., Oregon 16 March 1926 and married **Bert Cornelius** there 27 May 1944. He was born in Altoona, Blair Co., Pennsylvania 23 January 1923.[30]

Elaine Ernestine **Nielsen** and Bert **Cornelius** had the following children:

+	26	i.	Richard Bird[5] **Cornelius** born 7 March 1945.
+	27	ii.	Robin Dee **Cornelius** born 11 December 1946.
+	28	iii.	Debra Jean **Cornelius** born 16 June 1951.

16. **Vivian**[4] **Arrowsmith** (Hattie[3] Matzke, Wilhelm Carl[2], Karl Wilhelm[1])[31] was born in Portland, Multnomah Co., Oregon 22 September 1927 and married **Glenn Wesley Moore** there in July 1946.

Vivian **Arrowsmith** and Glenn Wesley **Moore** had the following children:

+	29	i.	Annette Marie[5] **Moore** born 8 June 1947.
+	30	ii.	Kristy Lee **Moore** born 29 July 1949.
+	31	iii.	Marlene Glenda **Moore** born 27 October 1953.

21. **Linda Ann**[4] **Wilmoth** (Gertrude[3] Matzke, Wilhelm Carl[2], Karl Wilhelm[1])[32] was born in Dobson, Surry Co., North Carolina 7 July 1944 and married **Rudy Meier** in Germany 6 June 1969. Rudy was born in Poland 26 November 1940.[33]

{ G 1783 }

Linda Ann **Wilmoth** and Rudy **Meier** had the following children born in Austria:

    34   i.   Kurt David[5] **Meier**[34] 26 August 1971.
    35   ii.   Lisa Ann **Meier**[35] 18 October 1974.
    36   iii.   Stephen Timothy **Meier**[36] 1 May 1977.
    37   iv.   Suan Ruth **Meier**[37] 8 July 1978.

22. **Nancy Jean**[4] **Wilmoth** (Gertrude[3] Matzke, Wilhelm Carl[2], Karl Wilhelm[1])[38] was born in Dobson, Surry Co., North Carolina 30 October 1945 and married **Roy Allen Danielson** in Portland, Multnomah Co., Oregon 2 October 1968. Roy was born in Ohio 14 August 1945.[39]

Nancy Jean **Wilmoth** and Roy Allen **Danielson** had the following children:

    38   i.   Ruth Ann[5] **Danielson**[40] born in Santa Ana, Orange Co., California 3 July 1971.
    39   ii.   Robert Allen **Danielson**[41] born in Twenty-Nine Palms, San Bernardino Co., California 7 November 1974.
    40   iii.   Karen Jean **Danielson**[42] born in Mountlake Terrace, Snohomish Co., Washington 26 October 1977.

23. **Janet Louise**[4] **Wilmoth** (Gertrude[3] Matzke, Wilhelm Carl[2], Karl Wilhelm[1])[43] was born in Portland, Multnomah Co., Oregon 2 January 1948 and married **Grant Kenneth Hunter** 19 January 1973. Grant was born in Bremerton, Kitsap Co., Washington 18 January 1954.[44]

Janet Louise **Wilmoth** and Grant Kenneth **Hunter** had the following children born in Vanouver, Clark Co., Washington:

    41   i.   Valerie Yvonne[5] **Hunter**[45] 5 May 1978.
    42   ii.   Julie Anna **Hunter**[46] 9 March 1980.
    43   iii.   Laurie Jean **Hunter**[47] 6 October 1982.

FIFTH GENERATION

24. **Thomas Alfred**[5] **Nielsen** (Alfred Andreas[4], Martha[3] Matzke, Wilhelm Carl[2], Karl Wilhelm[1])[48] was born in Portland, Multnomah Co., Oregon 3 July 1949 and married **Sandra Jean Young** there 10 August 1969. She was born in Portland 28 June 1949.[49]

Thomas Alfred **Nielsen** and Sandra Jean **Young** had the following children:

    44   i.   Eric[6] **Nielsen**[50] born 23 December 1971.

    45   ii.   Shawn **Nielsen**[51] born 2 April 1974.
    46   iii.   Laurie **Nielsen**[52] born 17 November 1976.

25. **Brian Carl**[5] **Nielsen** (Alfred Andreas[4], Martha[3] Matzke, Wilhelm Carl[2], Karl Wilhelm[1])[53] was born in Portland, Multnomah Co., Oregon 28 October 1953 and married **Virginia Nevarro** there in 1978. She was born in California 14 February 1954.[54]

Brian Carl **Nielsen** and Virginia **Nevarro** had the following children:
    47   i.   Brenda[6] **Nielsen**[55] born 17 August 1973. Adopted.
    48   ii.   Angela **Nielsen**[56] born 11 September 1975. Adopted.
    49   iii. Stacy **Nielsen**[57] born 31 July 1979.

26. **Richard Bird**[5] **Cornelius** (Elaine Ernestine[4] Nielsen, Martha[3] Matzke, Wilhelm Carl[2], Karl Wilhelm[1])[58] was born in Portland, Multnomah Co., Oregon 7 March 1945 and married **Joyce Betruchi** there 14 August 1965.

Richard Bird **Cornelius** and Joyce **Betruchi** had the following children born in Portland:
    50   i.   Michael Leon[6] **Cornelius**[59] 25 November 1965.
    51   ii.   Cheri Kim **Cornelius**[60] 4 November 1970.

27. **Robin Dee**[5] **Cornelius** (Elaine Ernestine[4] Nielsen, Martha[3] Matzke, Wilhelm Carl[2], Karl Wilhelm[1])[61] was born in Los Angeles, Los Angeles Co., California 11 December 1946 and married **Dwain Phillip Munyan** in Portland, Multnomah Co., Oregon 17 November 1967. Dwain was born in Portland 10 May 1946.[62]

Robin Dee **Cornelius** and Dwain Phillip **Munyan** had the following children born in Portland:
    52   i.   Shelli Marie[6] **Munyan**[63] 14 October 1972.
    53   ii.   Natasha Nicole **Munyan**[64] 6 July 1978.

28. **Debra Jean**[5] **Cornelius** (Elaine Ernestine[4] Nielsen, Martha[3] Matzke, Wilhelm Carl[2], Karl Wilhelm[1])[65] was born in Vancouver, Clark Co., Washington 16 June 1951 and married **Gary Earl Jensen** in Portland, Multnomah Co., Oregon 2 February 1974. Gary was born 11 October 1946.[66]

Debra Jean **Cornelius** and Gary Earl **Jensen** had the following children:
    54   i.   Joshua Allan[6] **Jensen**[67] born in Portland 14 May 1977.
    55   ii.   Jennlee Ahram **Jensen**[68] born in Korea 25 November 1988. Adopted.

29. **Annette Marie**[5] **Moore** (Vivian[4] Arrowsmith, Hattie[3] Matzke, Wilhelm Carl[2], Karl Wilhelm[1])[69] was born in Portland, Multnomah Co., Oregon 8 June 1947 and married **Fred Thompson**.

Annette Marie **Moore** and Fred **Thompson** had the following children:
- 56 i. Derek[6] **Thompson**.[70]
- 57 ii. Daryl **Thompson**.[71]

30. **Kristy Lee**[5] **Moore** (Vivian[4] Arrowsmith, Hattie[3] Matzke, Wilhelm Carl[2], Karl Wilhelm[1])[72] was born in Portland, Multnomah Co., Oreg. 29 July 1949 and married **Kenneth Harrington**.

Kristy Lee **Moore** and Kenneth **Harrington** had the following children:
- 58 i. Carrie[6] **Harrington**.[73]
- 59 ii. Jill **Harrington**.[74]

31. **Marlene Glenda**[5] **Moore** (Vivian[4] Arrowsmith, Hattie[3] Matzke, Wilhelm Carl[2], Karl Wilhelm[1])[75] was born in Walla Walla, Walla Walla Co., Washington 27 October 1953 and married **Daniel Placencia.**

Marlene Glenda **Moore** and Daniel **Placencia** had the following children:
- 60 i. Michael[6] **Placencia**.[76]
- 61 ii. Jamie **Placencia**.[77]

MATZKE FAMILY ENDNOTES

1. through 22. Gertrude (Matzke) Wilmoth to Blaine Whipple. Letter dated 31 August 1992 at 4734 NE Going, Portland, Oreg. 97219. In possession of Whipple (2005). (Hereafter Wilmoth to Whipple, *Letter, 31 Aug. 1992*).
23. through 31. Personal knowledge of Ines Mae (Peterson) (Steele) Whipple, 236 N. W. Sundown Way, Portland, Oreg. 97229. Wife of Harold Steele whose mother was Lena Matzke.
32. through 77. Wilmoth to Whipple, Letter, 31 Aug. 1992.

LYDER INGEMAND OTEJUS' MARTINSON ABT 1910 TO BREANNA JO STEELE 1990-

FIRST GENERATION

1. **Lyder Ingemand Oteljus**[1] **Martinson**[1] was born in Norway and died 6 April 1956 in Warrenton, Clatsop Co., Oregon at 47 years of age. He married **June Glendora Pape** 6 October 1934. June,[2] daughter of George William **Pape** and Elizabeth Jane **Peterkin**, was born in Morrison, Whiteside Co., Illinois 17 June 1908 and died 13 June 1993 in Portland, Multnomah Co., Oregon at 84 years of age. She married (2) **George Leroy Higgs** in Portland, in 1977.

Lyder Ingemand Oteljus **Martinson** and June Glendora **Pape** had the following children:

+   2   i.   Betty Jo[2] **Martinson** born 12 June 1942.
     3   ii.   Janet **Martinson**[3] born in Astoria, Clatsop Co., Oreg. 7 December 1950.

SECOND GENERATION

2. **Betty Jo**[2] **Martinson** (Lyder Ingemand Oteljus[1])[4] was born in Portland, Multnomah Co., Oregon 12 June 1942 and married twice. (1) **James Jefferson Hunt** in Portland in 1960. They were divorced in Portland in 1964. He was born in Vernon, Oregon 5 April 1940.[5] He married (2) **Karen Faulk** in Vancouver, Clark Co., Washington in 1968. Betty married (2) **Charles N. Kessinger** in Vancouver, Clark Co., Washington 6 July 1973. They were divorced in Portland in 1979.

Betty Jo **Martinson** and James Jefferson **Hunt** had the following children born in Portland:

     4   i.   Kimberly Jo[3] **Hunt**[6] 6 November 1960 and married Rob **Fairbanks** in Las Vegas, Clark Co., Nevada 4 August 1999.
+   5   ii.   Tamera J. **Hunt** 7 February 1962.

THIRD GENERATION

5. **Tamera J.**[3] **Hunt** (Betty Jo[2] Martinson, Lyder Ingemand Oteljus[1])[7] was born in Portland, Multnomah Co., Oregon 7 February 1962 and mar-

{ G 1787 }

ried **Robert Bruce Steele** in Portland 6 December 1986. Bob, son of Harold **Steele** and Ines Mae **Peterson**, was born in Portland 15 March 1960. Tamera is a Certified Medical Assistant.

Tamera J. **Hunt** and Robert Bruce **Steele** had the following children born in Portland:

    6   i.   Miles Bruce[4] **Steele** 15 January 1988. He was graduated from Sunset High School in Washington Co., in 2006.

    7   ii.   BreAnna Jo **Steele** 19 January 1990. She is a Sophomore at Sunset High School in 2006.

MARTINSON FAMILY ENDNOTES

1. Tamera J. (Hunt) Steele to Blaine Whipple. Letter dated 9 July 1991 at 95 SW 104th, Portland, Oreg. 97225. In possession of Whipple. (2005.).
2. Ibid.
3. Ibid.
4. Ibid.
5. Vernon is an historical town which no longer exists. Author is unaware of the county in which it was located.
6. Ibid.
7. Ibid.

JOHN PAPE 1828 TO BREANNA JO STEELE 1990-

FIRST GENERATION

1. **John**[I] **Pape**[I] was born in Yorkshire, England 30 September 1828 and died 28 November 1874 at 46 years of age. He married **Melvina Green** 6 December 1860. Melvina,[2] daughter of Jonathan **Green** and Susan **Mullen**, was born in Johnstown, Licking Co., Ohio 2 January 1842 and died 18 August 1917, at 75 years of age. Although no documentation has been found, it is believed John arrived in the U.S. around 1852. His brother George and wife Cordelia Wilson landed in the U.S. 2 February 1852. George and Cordelia's oldest child, Sarah, was born the day they arrived. Their other children were John, Hannah Elizabeth, and Dora. John and Melvina lived on a farm near Ulric, Meigs Co., Ohio. He was a 33rd

degree Mason and left a pregnant widow and five children. Melvina was known for helping neighbors during their times of sickness. She was a midwife who traveled to the deliveries by buggy or sleigh, depending on the weather. She was usually paid in goods such as material to make clothes. She was known as Aunt Vine.

John **Pape** and Melvina **Green** had the following children:

+	2	i.	Mary[2] **Pape** 2 March 1861.
+	3	ii.	Jane **Pape** 15 April 1864.
+	4	iii.	Noah **Pape** 26 December 1866.
+	5	iv.	George William **Pape** 12 April 1868.
+	6	v.	Minnie **Pape** 27 December 1871.

SECOND GENERATION

2. **Mary**[2] **Pape** (John[1])[3] was born 2 March 1861 and died 20 October 1911 at 50 years of age. She married **Samuel Hawk** who died 6 September 1932.[4]

Mary **Pape** and Samuel **Hawk** had the following children:

+	7	i.	Laura[3] **Hawk**.
+	8	ii.	Edna **Hawk**.
+	9	iii.	George **Hawk**.
	10	iv.	LeRoy **Hawk**.[5]
+	11	v.	Clarence **Hawk**.

3. **Jane**[2] **Pape** (John[1])[6] was born 15 April 1864 and died 15 February 1942 at 77 years of age. She married **William Mitchell** 23 February 1882. He died 6 December 1928.[7]

Jane **Pape** and William **Mitchell** had the following children:

	12	i.	Albert E.[3] **Mitchell**[8] married Edith **Allen** 20 September 1905.
+	13	ii.	Mary Alyce **Mitchell**.
+	14	iii.	Minnie **Mitchell**.
+	15	iv.	Maude **Mitchell**.
+	16	v.	Cecil **Mitchell**.

4. **Noah**[2] **Pape** (John[1])[9] was born 26 December 1866 and died 8 November 1948 at 81 years of age. He married **Date Dyson** 5 January 1888.

{ G 1789 }

Noah **Pape** and Date **Dyson** had the following children:
- \+ 17 i. Blanche[3] **Pape**.
- \+ 18 ii. Lepha **Pape**.
- \+ 19 iii. Lee **Pape**.
- \+ 20 iv. Zelma **Pape**.
- \+ 21 v. Floyd **Pape**.
- \+ 22 vi. Cloy **Pape**.

5. **George William**[2] **Pape** (John[1])[10] was born in Johnstown, Licking Co., Ohio 12 April 1868 and died 21 January 1914 at 45 years of age. He married **Elizabeth Jane Peterkin**. She was born in Illinois 23 September 1878 and died 1 April 1955 in Portland, Multnomah Co., Oregon, at 76 years of age.[11] The Peterkins were from Peterhead, Scotland.

George William **Pape** and Elizabeth Jane **Peterkin** had the following children:
- \+ 23 i. Lloyd[3] **Pape**.
- 24 ii. Lyle **Pape**[12] married Martha **Schultz**.
- \+ 25 iii. Forrest **Pape**.
- \+ 26 iv. Frances **Pape**.
- \+ 27 v. June Glendora **Pape** born 17 June 1908.

6. **Minnie**[2] **Pape** (John[1])[13] was born 27 December 1871 and died 8 February 1948 at 76 years of age. She married **Frank Milnes** 24 February 1891. Frank was born 22 July 1870 and died 26 December 1928 at 58 years of age.[14]

Minnie **Pape** and Frank **Milnes** had the following children:
- \+ 28 i. Vernabelle[3] **Milnes**.
- \+ 29 ii. Harold **Milnes**.
- \+ 30 iii. Clifford **Milnes**.
- 31 iv. Lavon **Milnes**[15] died in infancy.
- \+ 32 v. Winnie **Milnes**.
- \+ 33 vi. Ruby **Milnes**.
- \+ 34 vii. Maud **Milnes**.
- \+ 35 viii. Sidney **Milnes**.

THIRD GENERATION

7. **Laura**[3] **Hawk** (Mary[2] **Pape**, John[1])[16] birth date unknown, married **Jesse Sager**.

Laura **Hawk** and Jesse **Sager** had the following children:
- 36   i.   Clarence[4] **Sager**.[17]
- 37   ii.   Wilbur **Sager**.[18]
- 38   iii.   Harold **Sager**.[19]
- 39   iv.   George **Sager**.[20]
- 40   v.   Lois **Sager**.[21]
- 41   vi.   Arthur **Sager**.[22]

8. **Edna**[3] **Hawk** (Mary[2] Pape, John[1])[23] birth date unknown, married **Edward Dean**.

Edna **Hawk** and Edward **Dean** had the following children:
- 42   i.   Clifford[4] **Dean**.[24]
- 43   ii.   LaVern **Dean**.[25]

9. **George**[3] **Hawk** (Mary[2] Pape, John[1])[26] birth date unknown, married **Irene Pringle**.

George **Hawk** and Irene **Pringle** had the following child:
- +   44   i.   Gene[4] **Hawk**.

11. **Clarence**[3] **Hawk** (Mary[2] Pape, John[1])[27] birth date unknown, married **Fern Burch** 11 November 1920.

Clarence **Hawk** and Fern **Burch** had the following children:
- 45   i.   Marily[4] **Hawk**.[28]
- 46   ii.   Jimmy **Hawk**[29] born abt 1930 and died 31 March 1946 at 16 years of age.

13. **Mary Alyce**[3] **Mitchell** (Jane[2] Pape, John[1])[30] birth date unknown married **Donald Carpenter** 23 August 1911.

Mary Alyce **Mitchell** and Donald **Carpenter** had the following children:
- +   47   i.   Paul[4] **Carpenter**.
- +   48   ii.   Genevieve **Carpenter**.
- +   49   iii.   Clyde **Carpenter**.
- +   50   iv.   Russell **Carpenter**.
- +   51   v.   Pauline **Carpenter**.
- +   52   vi.   Paula **Carpenter**.

14. **Minnie**[3] **Mitchell** (Jane[2] Pape, John[1])[31] birth date unknown, married **Albert Siewert** 31 December 1914.

Minnie **Mitchell** and Albert **Siewert** had the following children:
    53   i.   Wilmer R.[4] **Siewert**.[32]
    54   ii.   Jennie Marie **Siewert**.[33]

15. **Maude**[3] **Mitchell** (Jane[2] Pape, John[1])[34] birth date unknown, married **Ben Wagner** 26 September 1916. The family lived in Thomson, Carroll Co., Illinois.

Maude **Mitchell** and Ben **Wagner** had the following children:
+   55   i.   Mary[4] **Wagner**.
    56   ii.   William **Wagner**[35] married June **South**. They lived in Bensenville, DuPage Co., Illinois.

16. **Cecil**[3] **Mitchell** (Jane[2] Pape, John[1])[36] birth date unknown, married **Lela Atherton** 8 September 1921.

Cecil **Mitchell** and Lela **Atherton** had the following children:
    57   i.   Roland[4] **Mitchell**.[37]
+   58   ii.   Lauren **Mitchell**.
+   59   iii.   Lyle **Mitchell**.
    60   iv.   Eva **Mitchell**.[38] Died in infancy.
    61   v.   Vernon **Mitchell**.[39] Died in infancy.
    62   vi.   Clyde **Mitchell**.[40] Died in infancy.

17. **Blanche**[3] **Pape** (Noah[2], John[1])[41] birth date unknown, married **Earl Frederick**.

Blanche **Pape** and Earl **Frederick** had the following child:
    63   i.   Betty[4] **Frederick**.[42]

18. **Lepha**[3] **Pape** (Noah[2], John[1])[43] birth date unknown, married **Joseph Larson**.

Lepha **Pape** and Joseph **Larson** had the following children:
    64   i.   Babe[4] **Larson**.[44]
    65   ii.   Lucille **Larson**.[45]
    66   iii.   Charlene **Larson**.[46]

19. **Lee**[3] **Pape** (Noah[2], John[1])[47] birth date unknown, married **Louise Jacobs**.

Lee **Pape** and Louise **Jacobs** had the following child:
    67   i.   Merrill[4] **Pape**.[48]

20. **Zelma**[3] **Pape** (Noah[2], John[1])[49] birth date unknown, married **Russell Edlund**.

Zelma **Pape** and Russell **Edlund** had the following children:
    68   i.   Gardner[4] **Edlund**.[50]
    69   ii.   Arlene **Edlund**.[51]
    70   iii.   (Infant) **Edlund**.[52]

21. **Floyd**[3] **Pape** (Noah[2], John[1])[53] birth date unknown, married **Mynda Lechti** 26 January 1911.

Floyd **Pape** and Mynda **Lechti** had the following children:
    71   i.   Opal[4] **Pape**.[54]
+   72   ii.   Dellwin **Pape**.
+   73   iii.   Marion **Pape**.
    74   iv.   Marian **Pape**[55] married Edward **Kaminski**.

22. **Cloy**[3] **Pape** (Noah[2], John[1])[56] birth date unknown, married **Lizzie Worley** 2 February 1911.

Cloy **Pape** and Lizzie **Worley** had the following children:
    75   i.   Iola[4] **Pape**.[57]
    76   ii.   Milford **Pape**.[58]
    77   iii.   Warren **Pape**.[59]
    78   iv.   Glenn **Pape**.[60]

23. **Lloyd**[3] **Pape** (George William[2], John[1]) birth date unknown, had the following children:
    79   i.   June[4] **Pape**.[61]
    80   ii.   Mary Ann **Pape**.[62]
    81   iii.   George Lee **Pape**.[63]
    82   iv.   Kenneth Lloyd **Pape**.[64]

25. **Forrest**[3] **Pape** (George William[2], John[1])[65] birth date unknown, married **Vera Belhm**.

Forrest **Pape** and Vera **Belhm** had the following children:
    83   i.   Frances[4] Pape.[66]
    84   ii.   June Pape.[67]
    85   iii.   Nancy Lee Pape.[68]

26. **Frances**[3] **Pape** (George William[2], John[1])[69] birth date unknown, married **Oscar Nixon**.

Frances **Pape** and Oscar **Nixon** had the following children:
- 86   i.   Corliss[4] **Nixon**.[70]
- 87   ii.   Virginia **Nixon**.[71]
- 88   iii. Virginia **Nixon**.[72]
- 89   iv.   Margery **Nixon**.[73]
- 90   v.   Donald **Nixon**.[74]

27. **June Glendora**[3] **Pape** (George William[2], John[1])[75] was born in Morrison, Whiteside Co., Illinois 17 June 1908 and died 13 June 1993 in Portland, Multnomah Co., Oregon, at 84 years of age. She married twice. (1) **Lyder Ingemand Oteljus Martinson** 6 October 1934. He was born in Norway and died 6 April 1956 in Warrenton, Clatsop Co, Oregon, at 47 years of age.[76] (2) **George Leroy Higgs** in Portland in 1977.

June Glendora **Pape** and Lyder Ingemand Oteljus **Martinson** had the following children:
- + 91   i.   Betty Jo[4] **Martinson** born 12 June 1942.
-   92   ii.   Janet **Martinson**[77] born in Astoria, Clatsop Co., Oregon 7 December 1950.

28. **Vernabelle**[3] **Milnes** (Minnie[2] Pape, John[1])[78] birth date unknown, married **Miles Miller**.

Vernabelle **Milnes** and Miles **Miller** had the following children:
- + 93   i.   Isabelle[4] **Miller**.
- + 94   ii.   Donna Jean **Miller**.

29. **Harold**[3] **Milnes** (Minnie[2] Pape, John[1])[79] birth date unknown, married **Marian Annon**. Her surname may be **Annan**.

Harold **Milnes** and Marian **Annon** had the following children:
-   95   i.   (Infant)[4] **Milnes**.[80]
- + 96   ii.   Gene **Milnes**.

30. **Clifford**[3] **Milnes** (Minnie[2] Pape, John[1])[81] birth date unknown, married **Gladys Stralow**.

Clifford **Milnes** and Gladys **Stralow** had the following child:
- + 97   i.   Ronald[4] **Milnes**.

32. **Winnie**[3] **Milnes** (Minnie[2] Pape, John[1])[82] birth date unknown, married **William Bechtel** 10 September 1913.

Winnie **Milnes** and William **Bechtel** had the following children:
- \+ 98 i. Lucille[4] **Bechtel**.
- \+ 99 ii. Everett **Bechtel**.
- \+ 100 iii. Glenn **Bechtel**.

33. **Ruby**[3] **Milnes** (Minnie[2] Pape, John[1])[83] birth date unknown, married **Clifford Duward** 21 January 1914.

Ruby **Milnes** and Clifford **Duward** had the following children:
- \+ 101 i. Leslie[4] **Duward**.
- \+ 102 ii. Merle **Duward**.
- \+ 103 iii. Lois **Duward**.
- \+ 104 iv. LaVeda **Duward**.
- \+ 105 v. Vera **Duward**.
- \+ 106 vi. Clifford **Duward**.

34. **Maud**[3] **Milnes** (Minnie[2] Pape, John[1])[84] birth date unknown, married **Harry Montgomery** 1 January 1921.

Maud **Milnes** and Harry **Montgomery** had the following child:
- \+ 107 i. Arvilla[4] **Montgomery**.

35. **Sidney**[3] **Milnes** (Minnie[2] Pape, John[1])[85] birth date unknown, married twice. (1) **Pearl L. Witmer**. (2) **Edna Swanson** 17 December 1925.

Sidney **Milnes** and Edna **Swanson** had the following children:
- \+ 108 i. LaVelle[4] **Milnes**.
- \+ 109 ii. Vernon **Milnes**.
- \+ 110 iii. Virgil **Milnes**.
- \+ 111 iv. Beulah **Milnes**.

FOURTH GENERATION

44. **Gene**[4] **Hawk** (George[3], Mary[2] Pape, John[1])[86] birth date unknown, married **Francella Kramer**.

Gene **Hawk** and Francella **Kramer** had the following children:
    112   i.   John[5] **Hawk**.[87]
    113   ii.   Janice **Hawk**.[88]

47. **Paul**[4] **Carpenter** (Mary Alyce[3] Mitchell, Jane[2] Pape, John[1])[89] birth date unknown, had the following child:
    114   i.   Paula Jane[5] **Carpenter**.[90]

48. **Genevieve**[4] **Carpenter** (Mary Alyce[3] Mitchell, Jane[2] Pape, John[1])[91] birth date unknown, married **Les Wiess**.

Genevieve **Carpenter** and Les **Wiess** had the following children:
    115   i.   Michael James[5] **Wiess**.[92]
    116   ii.   Larry Allen **Wiess**.[93]
    117   iii.   Dennis Lee **Wiess**.[94]

49. **Clyde**[4] **Carpenter** (Mary Alyce[3] Mitchell, Jane[2] Pape, John[1])[95] birth date unknown, married **Fern Emmert** 20 November 1941.

Clyde **Carpenter** and Fern **Emmert** had the following children:
    118   i.   Donald Clyde[5] **Carpenter**.[96]
    119   ii.   Joyce Elayne **Carpenter**.[97]

50. **Russell**[4] **Carpenter** (Mary Alyce[3] Mitchell, Jane[2] Pape, John[1])[98] birth date unknown, married **Dorothy (__)** 16 September 1947.

Russell **Carpenter** and Dorothy (__) had the following children:
    120   i.   Alice[5] **Carpenter**.[99]
    121   ii.   Naomi **Carpenter**.[100]

51. **Pauline**[4] **Carpenter** (Mary Alyce[3] Mitchell, Jane[2] Pape, John[1])[101] birth date unknown, married **Gerald VanKampen** 14 February 1953.

Pauline **Carpenter** and Gerald **VanKampen** had the following children:
    122   i.   Steve Allan[5] **VanKampen**.[102]
    123   ii.   Vernon James **VanKampen**.[103]

52. **Paula**[4] **Carpenter** (Mary Alyce[3] Mitchell, Jane[2] Pape, John[1])[104] birth date unknown, married **Marvin Anderson** 22 January 1965.

Paula **Carpenter** and Marvin **Anderson** had the following child:
    124   i.   Cathy Sue[5] **Anderson**.[105]

55. **Mary**[4] **Wagner** (Maude[3] Mitchell, Jane[2] Pape, John[1])[106] birth date unknown, married **John Root**.

Mary **Wagner** and John **Root** had the following children:
  125 i. Allan[5] **Root**.[107]
  126 ii. Karen **Root**.[108]

58. **Lauren**[4] **Mitchell** (Cecil[3], Jane[2] Pape, John[1])[109] birth date unknown, married **LeVona Potter**.

Lauren **Mitchell** and LeVona **Potter** had the following child:
  127 i. Rolland Lee[5] **Mitchell**.[110]

59. **Lyle**[4] **Mitchell** (Cecil[3], Jane[2] Pape, John[1])[111] birth date unknown, married **Anna Mae Wiebenga**.

Lyle **Mitchell** and Anna Mae **Wiebenga** had the following children:
  128 i. Donna Jean[5] **Mitchell**.[112]
  129 ii. Roberta Lee **Mitchell**.[113]
  130 iii. Raymond Cecil **Mitchell**.[114]

72. **Dwllwin**[4] **Pape** (Floyd[3], Noah[2], John[1])[115] birth date unknown, had the following children:
  131 i. Hart[5] **Pape**.[116]
  132 ii. David Ellis **Pape**.[117]

73. **Marion**[4] **Pape** (Floyd[3], Noah[2], John[1])[118] birth date unknown, had the following children:
  133 i. Bobbie[5] **Pape**.[119]
  134 ii. Shirley **Pape**.[120]

91. **Betty Jo**[4] **Martinson** (June Glendora[3] Pape, George William[2], John[1])[121] was born in Portland, Multnomah Co., Oregon 12 June 1942 and married twice. (1) **James Jefferson Hunt** in Portland in 1960. They were divorced in Portland in 1964. He was born in Vernon,[122] Oregon 5 April 1940 and married (2) **Karen Faulk** in Vancouver, Clark Co., Washington in 1968. (2) **Charles N. Kessinger** in Vancouver, Clark Co. 6 July 1973. They were divorced in Portland in 1979.

Betty Jo **Martinson** and James Jefferson **Hunt** had the following children born in Portland.
- 135   i.   Kimberly Jo[5] **Hunt**[123] 6 November 1960 and married Rob **Fairbanks** in Las Vegas, Clark Co., Nevada 4 August 1999.
+ 136   ii.   Tamera J. **Hunt** 7 February 1962.

93. **Isabelle**[4] **Miller** (Vernabelle[3] Milnes, Minnie[2] Pape, John[1])[124] birth date unknown, married **David Crotts**.

Isabelle **Miller** and David **Crotts** had the following children:
- 137   i.   Diana Elaine[5] **Crotts**.[125]
- 138   ii.   David **Crotts**.[126]
- 139   iii.   Miles **Crotts**.[127]

94. **Donna Jean**[4] **Miller** (Vernabelle[3] Milnes, Minnie[2] Pape, John[1])[128] birth date unknown, married **Wayne Seldon**.

Donna Jean **Miller** and Wayne **Seldon** had the following children:
- 140   i.   Lisa[5] **Seldon**.[129]
- 141   ii.   Tony **Seldon**.[130]

96. **Gene**[4] **Milnes** (Harold[3], Minnie[2] Pape, John[1])[131] birth date unknown and married **Jean Oncken**.

Gene **Milnes** and Jean **Oncken** had the following children:
- 142   i.   Susan[5] **Milnes**.[132]
- 143   ii.   Patricia **Milnes**.[133]

97. **Ronald**[4] **Milnes** (Clifford[3], Minnie[2] Pape, John[1])[134] birth date unknown, married **Virginia Bowen**.

Ronald **Milnes** and Virginia **Bowen** had the following children:
- 144   i.   Ricky Lee[5] **Milnes**.[135]
- 145   ii.   Daniel Clifford **Milnes**.[136]
- 146   iii.   Debra Marie **Milnes**.[137]

98. **Lucille**[4] **Bechtel** (Winnie[3] Milnes, Minnie[2] Pape, John[1])[138] birth date unknown, married **Lyle Nice**.

Lucille **Bechtel** and Lyle **Nice** had the following children:
- 147   i.   Elwin[5] **Nice**.[139]
- 148   ii.   Marjorie **Nice**.[140]

99. **Everett**[4] **Bechtel** (Winnie[3] Milnes, Minnie[2] Pape, John[1])[141] birth date unknown, married **Carlene McKee**.

Everett **Bechtel** and Carlene **McKee** had the following children:
- 149   i.   Gary[5] **Bechtel**.[142]
- 150   ii.   Bonnie **Bechtel**.[143]

100. **Glenn**[4] **Bechtel** (Winnie[3] Milnes, Minnie[2] Pape, John[1])[144] birth date unknown, married **Rhea Green**.

Glenn **Bechtel** and Rhea **Green** had the following children:
- 151   i.   Glenda[5] **Bechtel**.[145]
- 152   ii.   Scott **Bechtel**.[146]
- 153   iii.   Ellen **Bechtel**.[147]
- 154   iv.   Carol **Bechtel**.[148]
- 155   v.   Brad **Bechtel**.[149]

101. **Leslie**[4] **Duward** (Ruby[3] Milnes, Minnie[2] Pape, John[1])[150] birth date unknown, married **Ines Whipple**.

Leslie **Duward** and Ines **Whipple** had the following children:
- 156   i.   Diana Dee[5] **Duward**.[151]
- 157   ii.   Gayle **Duward**.[152]
- 158   iii.   John **Duward**.[153]
- 159   iv.   Cynthia **Duward**.[154]

102. **Merle**[4] **Duward** (Ruby[3] Milnes, Minnie[2] Pape, John[1])[155] birth date unknown, married **Lucille Hunter**.

Merle **Duward** and Lucille **Hunter** had the following children:
- 160   i.   Larry[5] **Duward**.[156]
- 161   ii.   Merle **Duward**.[157]
- 162   iii.   Sandra Lee **Duward**.[158]
- 163   iv.   Marjorie **Duward**.[159]

103. **Lois**[4] **Duward** (Ruby[3] Milnes, Minnie[2] Pape, John[1])[160] birth date unknown, married **Irwin Larson**.

Lois **Duward** and Irwin **Larson** had the following children:
- 164   i.   Peggy Lee[5] **Larson**.[161]
- 165   ii.   LaVerne **Larson**.[162]

104. **LaVeda**[4] **Duward** (Ruby[3] Milnes, Minnie[2] Pape, John[1])[163] birth date unknown, married **Vernon Alexander**.

LaVeda **Duward** and Vernon **Alexander** had the following children:
- 166   i.   Raymond Vernon[5] **Alexander**.[164]
- 167   ii.   Keith James **Alexander**.[165]
- 168   iii.   Larry Lee **Alexander**.[166]
- 169   iv.   Karen Sue **Alexander**.[167]

105. **Vera**[4] **Duward** (Ruby[3] Milnes, Minnie[2] Pape, John[1])[168] birth date unknown, married **Lysle Foltz**.

Vera **Duward** and Lysle **Foltz** had the following children:
- 170   i.   Judith Ann[5] **Foltz**.[169]
- 171   ii.   James Duward **Foltz**.[170]
- 172   iii.   Dennis Lyle **Foltz**.[171]
- 173   iv.   Gary Leigh **Foltz**.[172]
- 174   v.   Ronald Alan **Foltz**.[173]

106. **Clifford**[4] **Duward** (Ruby[3] Milnes, Minnie[2] Pape, John[1])[174] birth date unknown, married **Norma Cate**.

Clifford **Duward** and Norma **Cate** had the following children:
- 175   i.   Randall Scott[5] **Duward**.[175]
- 176   ii.   Scott Jay **Duward**.[176]
- 177   iii.   Andrew Steward **Duward**.[177]

107. **Arvilla**[4] **Montgomery** (Maud[3] Milnes, Minnie[2] Pape, John[1])[178] birth date unknown, married **Clair Pickens**.

Arvilla **Montgomery** and Clair **Pickens** had the following children:
- 178   i.   Allen Dale[5] **Pickens**.[179]
- 179   ii.   Keith Arlyn **Pickens**.[180]

108. **LaVelle**[4] **Milnes** (Sidney[3], Minnie[2] Pape, John[1])[181] birth date unknown, married **Harold Peterson**.

LaVelle **Milnes** and Harold **Peterson** had the following children:
- 180   i.   Glenn Harold[5] **Peterson**.[182]
- 181   ii.   LaVon Fern **Peterson**.[183]
- 182   iii.   Ray Dean **Peterson**.[184]

109. **Vernon**[4] **Milnes** (Sidney[3], Minnie[2] Pape, John[1])[185] birth date unknown, married **Rhea D. Clary**.

Vernon **Milnes** and Rhea D. **Clary** had the following children:
- 183   i.   Peggy Ann[5] **Milnes**.[186]
- 184   ii.   Janet Lee **Milnes**.[187]
- 185   iii. Vernon Sidney **Milnes**.[188]
- 186   iv.   Melvin Faye **Milnes**.[189]
- 187   v.   Carol Dene **Milnes**.[190]
- 188   vi.   Sharon Kay **Milnes**.[191]

110. **Virgil**[4] **Milnes** (Sidney[3], Minnie[2] Pape, John[1])[192] birth date unknown, married **Lorraine Rick**.

Virgil **Milnes** and Lorraine **Rick** had the following children:
- 189   i.   Gary Faye[5] **Milnes**.[193]
- 190   ii.   Terri Lee **Milnes**.[194]

111. **Beulah**[4] **Milnes** (Sidney[3], Minnie[2] Pape, John[1])[195] birth date unknown. married **Stephen F. Recker**.

Beulah **Milnes** and Stephen F. **Recker** had the following children:
- 191   i.   Andrya Marie[5] **Recker**.[196]
- 192   ii.   Mark Stefan **Recker**.[197]
- 193   iii. Alayna Patricia **Recker**.[198]

FIFTH GENERATION

136. **Tamera J.**[5] **Hunt** (Betty Jo[4] Martinson, June Glendora[3] Pape, George William[2], John[1])[199] was born in Portland, Multnomah Co., Oreg. 7 February 1962 and married **Robert Bruce Steele** in Portland 6 December 1986. Robert, son of Harold **Steele** and Ines Mae **Peterson**, was born in Portland 15 March 1960. Tamera is a certified medical assistant. They separated in December 2004.

Tamera J. **Hunt** and Robert Bruce **Steele** had the following children born in Portland:
- 194   i.   Miles Bruce[6] **Steele** 15 January 1988.[200]
- 195   ii.   BreAnna Jo **Steele** 19 January 1990.[201]

PAPE FAMILY ENDNOTES:

1. through 120. Tamera J. (Hunt) Steele to Blaine Whipple. Letter dated 9 July 1991 at 95 SW 104th, Portland, OR 97225. In possession of Whipple (2005). (Hereafter Steele to Whipple, *Letter, 1 July 1991*).
121. Vernon is an historical town and no longer exists. Author does not know in which county it was located.
122. through 201. Steele to Whipple, *Letter, 1 July 1991*.

JAN PETRUS ZOERINK CA 1840 TO LORNA JO (ZOERINK) WHIPPLE 1966-

(Zoerink lineage of Lorna Jo Zoerink, Generation 13, No., wife of Blaine Scott Whipple.)

FIRST GENERATION

1. **Jan Petrus**[1] **Zoerink** birth date unknown, married **Jajeticita Maria Nahum** and had the following child:

+ 2 i. Johan Michael[2] **Zoerink** born 16 July 1866.

SECOND GENERATION

2. **Johan Michael**[2] **Zoerink** (Jan Petrus[1])[1] was born in Hoerde Gelderland, Netherlands 16 July 1866 and died 7 April 1931 in Lynden, Whatcom Co., Washington at 64 years of age. He married **"Nellie" Neeltje Kramer** in Orange City, Sioux Co., Iowa, 3 December 1890. Nellie,[2] daughter of "Henry" Hendrik Martens **Kramer** and "Jessie" Jitske Teakes **Boersma**, was born in St. Jacobiparochie, Friesland, Netherland 29 April 1870 and died 24 September 1962 in Bellingham, Whatcom Co., Washington, at 92 years of age. Nellie arrived in the U.S. abt 1889 and settled in the Orange City area.

According to family legend, Johan was the youngest child in his family and came to the U. S. by himself at age 19. His mother was a full-blooded Jew from Russia. Johan was a shoemaker and harness maker and was said to be "very tall and ugly . . . and could stare down dogs, most of whom were afraid of him." Johan and Nellie moved from Sioux Center, Sioux Co., Iowa to Lynden in 1922. After Johan died, Nellie lived with her daughter Jessie in Lynden.

Johan Michael **Zoerink** and Nellie Neeltje **Kramer** had the following children born in Sioux Center:

	3	i.	Maria[3] **Zoerink**[3] 18 November 1891 and died 8 June 1980 in Lynden, at 88 years of age. She married Jacob **Van Zwol** 4 October 1911.
+	4	ii.	Jessie **Zoerink** 1 October 1892.
+	5	iii.	John Peter **Zoerink** 30 April 1898.
+	6	iv.	Ella **Zoerink** 25 March 1902.
+	7	v.	Henry **Zoerink** 11 June 1907.

THIRD GENERATION

4. **Jessie**[3] **Zoerink** (Johan Michael[2], Jan Petrus[1])[4] was born in Sioux Center, Sioux Co., Iowa 1 October 1892 and died 23 January 1993 in Lynden, Whatcom Co., Washington, at 100 years of age. She married **John Snapper** in Hull, Sioux Co., Iowa, 16 February 1917. John was born in Putten, Gelderland, Netherlands 9 June 1898 and died in September 1971 in Lynden, at 73 years of age.[5] Jessie was a school teacher. Both are buried in Lynden's Monument Cemetery.

Jessie **Zoerink** and John **Snapper** had the following children:

+	8	i.	John Nelson[4] **Snapper** born 13 March 1920.
	9	ii.	Marion **Snapper**[6] born in Lynden 9 June 1922 and married Nella **Louws**.
	10	iii.	Theodore **Snapper**[7] born in Lynden 4 November 1924 and married Doris (__).

5. **John Peter**[3] **Zoerink** (Johan Michael[2], Jan Petrus[1])[8] was born in Sioux Center, Sioux Co., Iowa 30 April 1898 and died there 8 May 1973, at 75 years of age. He married **Minnie Groen** in Sioux Center 7 November 1918. Minnie,[9] daughter of Jacob **Groen** and Tetje **Schaap**, was born in Sioux Co., Iowa 7 December 1897 and and died 11 December 1969 in Sioux Center, at 72 years of age. She worked at the Rexall Drug Store and John was manager of the lumber yard in Hull, Sioux Co. They are buried in the Hull Cemetery.

John Peter Zoerink and Minnie Groen had the following children:

+	11	i.	Matilda[4] **Zoerink** born 26 January 1919.
+	12	ii.	Mitchell John **Zoerink** born 7 February 1921.
+	13	iii.	Ivan **Zoerink** born 12 July 1923.
+	14	iv.	Nelva Leone **Zoerink** born 25 August 1925.
+	15	v.	Mary Ann **Zoerink** born 8 November 1927.

{ G 1803 }

+	16	vi.	Iola Mae **Zoerink** born 21 July 1930.
+	17	vii.	Gail **Zoerink** born 23 November 1936.
+	18	viii.	Wayne **Zoerink** born 21 May 1938.
	19	ix.	Merna Jean **Zoerink**[10] born in Hull 13 May 1941. She was living in Bellflower, Los Angeles Co. California in 2005.

6. **Ella**[3] **Zoerink** (Johan Michael[2], Jan Petrus[1])[11] was born in Sioux Center, Sioux Co., Iowa 25 March 1902 and married **Peter Tolsma Jr.** in Inwood, Lyon Co., Iowa 11 February 1924. Peter,[12] son of Peter **Tolsma Sr.** and Alice **Robyn** was born in Larchwood, Lyon Co., Iowa 6 November 1896 and died 25 April 1976 in Inwood, at 79 years of age.

Ella **Zoerink** and Peter **Tolsma Jr.** had the following children:

+	20	i.	Alyce Evandna[4] **Tolsma** born 1 January 1926.
+	21	ii.	Don Jacques **Tolsma** born 14 February 1927.
	22	iii.	Peter Verick **Tolsma**[13] born in Canton, Lincoln Co., South Dakota 10 October 1934 and died in October 1944 in Inwood, at 10 years of age.
+	23	iv.	Dudley Jerome **Tolsma** born 11 November 1939.
	24	v.	Peter **Tolsma**[14] born in Canton 18 October 1945.

7. **Henry**[3] **Zoerink** (Johan Michael[2], Jan Petrus[1])[15] was born in Sioux Center, Sioux Co., Iowa 11 June 1907 and died 2 February 1992 in Lynden, Whatcom Co., Washington, at 84 years of age. He married **Dena Stuurmans** in Lynden 4 March 1931. Dena,[16] daughter of Peter **Stuurmans** and Gertrude **De Jong**, was born 10 May 1910.

Henry **Zoerink** and Dena **Stuurmans** had the following children:

	25	i.	(Daughter)[4] **Zoerink**[17] born in Everson, Whatcom Co., Washington 10 June 1932 and died the day after birth.
+	26	ii.	J. Marshall **Zoerink** born 7 February 1934.
+	27	iii.	Greta Mae **Zoerink** born 9 July 1936.
+	28	iv.	Nelda Marie **Zoerink** born 13 November 1938.
+	29	v.	Phyllis Ann **Zoerink** born 9 September 1942.

FOURTH GENERATION

8. **John Nelson**[4] **Snapper** (Jessie[3] Zoerink, Johan Michael[2], Jan Petrus[1])[18] was born in Hull, Sioux Co., Iowa 13 March 1920 and married **Frances R. Stadt** in Lynden, Whatcom Co., Washington 16 February 1944.

John Nelson **Snapper** and Frances R. **Stadt** had the following children:
- 30   i.   Kirt[5] **Snapper**.[19]
- 31   ii. David **Snapper**.[20]

11. **Matilda**[4] **Zoerink** (John Peter[3], Johan Michael[2], Jan Petrus[1])[21] was born in Sioux Center, Sioux Co., Iowa 26 January 1919 and died 11 October 1992 in Joilet, Will Co., Illinois, at 73 years of age. She married **Allen Russell Pierce** in Moline, Rock Island Co., Illinois. Allen was born in Davenport, Scott Co., Iowa 2 August 1918 and died 15 July 1995 in Joilet, at 76 years of age.[22]

Matilda **Zoerink** and Allen Russell **Pierce** had the following children born in Chicago, Cook Co., Illinois:
- + 32   i.   Sherrie Kay[5] **Pierce** 6 January 1955.
- + 33   ii. Janice **Pierce** 2 January 1957.
-   34   iii. Dianne **Pierce**[23] and married Burt **Peterson**.

12. **Mitchell John**[4] **Zoerink** (John Peter[3], Johan Michael[2], Jan Petrus[1])[24] was born in Sioux Center, Sioux Co., Iowa 7 February 1921 and died 25 March 1994 in LeMars, Plymouth Co., Iowa, at 73 years of age. He married **Gertrude Henrietta Berkenpas** in LeMars 7 October 1942. Gertrude,[25] daughter of Henry **Berkenpas** and Anna **Tamminga**, was born in Bemis, Deuel Co., South Dakota 27 November 1921.

Mitchell John **Zoerink** and Gertrude Henrietta **Berkenpas** had the following children born in LeMars:
- + 35   i.   Dennis Mitchell[5] **Zoerink** 29 April 1943.
- + 36   ii. Dean Allen **Zoerink** 8 January 1947.

13. **Ivan**[4] **Zoerink** (John Peter[3], Johan Michael[2], Jan Petrus[1])[26] was born in Sioux Center, Sioux Co., Iowa 12 July 1923 and married **Jeanette** (__) 21 December 1942. She was born in Chicago, Cook Co., Illinois 8 April 1920.[27]

Ivan **Zoerink** and Jeanette (__) had the following children born in Chicago:
- 37   i.   Sharon[5] **Zoerink**[28] 25 August 1944 and married Dean **Robson**.
- 38   ii. Karen **Zoerink**[29] 1 August 1945 and married Carl **Barone**.
- 39   iii. Richard **Zoerink**[30] 9 January 1947.
- 40   iv. Sally **Zoerink**[31] and married John **Miezala**.
- 41   v.   Michael **Zoerink**.[32]
- 42   vi. Scott **Zoerink**[33] and married Debbie (__).

43	vii.	Bruce **Zoerink**[34] and married Martha (__).
44	viii.	Pat **Zoerink**[35] and married Fina (__).
45	ix.	Holly **Zoerink**[36] 8 December 1954 and married Pete **Dedes**.
46	x.	Glenn **Zoerink**[37] 3 June 1956 and married Janet (__).
47	xi.	Wes **Zoerink**[38] 14 November 1958 and married Anita (__).

14. **Nelva Leone**[4] **Zoerink** (John Peter[3], Johan Michael[2], Jan Petrus[1])[39] was born in Hull, Sioux Co., Iowa 25 August 1925 and married **William G. Metros**. William was born in Murphysboro, Jackson Co., Illinois 26 July 1917 and died 17 February 1988 in Santa Maria, Santa Barbara Co., California, at 70 years of age.[40]

Nelva Leone **Zoerink** and William G. **Metros** had the following child:

| 48 | i. | Timothy William[5] **Metros**[41] born in Santa Maria, Santa Barbara Co., California 25 September 1957 and married Madeline (__) 9 August 1993. |

15. **Mary Ann**[4] **Zoerink** (John Peter[3], Johan Michael[2], Jan Petrus[1])[42] was born in Hull, Sioux Co., Iowa 8 November 1927 and married **Charles William Van Meetern** in Sheldon, O Brien Co., Iowa, 26 December 1947. Charles,[43] son of Peter **Van Meetern** and Rena **Woudstra**, was born in Sheldon 12 June 1926 and died there 13 February 1993, at 66 years of age.

Mary Ann **Zoerink** and Charles William **Van Meetern** had the following children born in Sheldon:

| + | 49 | i. | Brian Kurt[5] **Van Meetern** 11 September 1960. |
| + | 50 | ii. | Beth Renae **Van Meetern** 10 October 1966. |

16. **Iola Mae**[4] **Zoerink** (John Peter[3], Johan Michael[2], Jan Petrus[1])[44] was born in Hull, Sioux Co., Iowa 21 July 1930 and married **Henry Moss** there 1 June 1955. He was born in Carmel, Sioux Co., Iowa 5 April 1925.[45]

Iola Mae **Zoerink** and Henry **Moss** had the following children:

+	51	i.	Carl[5] **Moss** born 7 March 1956.
	52	ii.	Marcia Fay **Moss**[46] born in Sioux Center, Sioux Co., Iowa 20 June 1957 and died 25 May 1977 in Valley Springs, Minnehaha Co., South Dakota at 19 years of age.
+	53	iii.	Denise **Moss** born 11 January 1959.
+	54	iv.	Nora Kay **Moss** born 16 May 1960.
+	55	v.	Tylene Joy **Moss** born 30 June 1962.
+	56	vi.	Jolene **Moss** born 19 July 1963.

57 vii. John Harlan **Moss** born in Luverne, Rock Co., Minnesota 8 March 1965.[47]

17. **Gail**[4] **Zoerink** (John Peter[3], Johan Michael[2], Jan Petrus[1])[48] was born in Hull, Sioux Co., Iowa 23 November 1936 and married **Tom Craven** in Costa Mesa, Orange Co., California 2 August 1958. He was born in Mobridge, Walworth Co., South Dakota 6 November 1931.[49]

Gail **Zoerink** and Tom **Craven** had the following children born in Costa Mesa:

58 i. Thomas A.[5] **Craven**[50] 25 February 1962.
59 ii. Carol **Craven**[51] 1 November 1964.

18. **Wayne**[4] **Zoerink** (John Peter[3], Johan Michael[2], Jan Petrus[1])[52] was born in Hull, Sioux Co., Iowa 21 May 1938 and married **Beverly Jean Gerritson** in Bellflower, Los Angeles Co., California 20 August 1964. Alex,[53] daughter of John **Gerritson** and Greta **Van der Naald**, was born in Inwood, Lyon Co., Iowa 23 November 1943. She had her name legally changed to Alex Andrea in Ft. Collins, Larimer Co., Colorado 17 March 1989. Wayne is retired from the Kodak corporation and he and Alex live in Palm Harbor, Pinellas Co., Florida. (2006.)

Wayne **Zoerink** and Beverly Jean **Gerritson** had the following children:
+ 60 i. Lorna Jo[5] **Zoerink** born 1 December 1966.

Alex and Wayne Zoerink. Photo courtesy of L. J. Whipple.

{ G 1807 }

Lorna Jo Zoerink high school graduation.

Connie Rae Zoerink. Photos courtesy of L. J. Whipple.

        61   ii.   Connie Rae **Zoerink**[54] born in Lakewood, Los Angeles Co., California 8 July 1968. Living in Denver, Denver Co., Colorado in 2005.

        62   iii.   David Wayne **Zoerink**[55] born in Greeley, Weld Co., Colorado 23 June 1978. Living in Palm Harbor 2005.

David Wayne Zoerink.

20. **Alyce Evandna**[4] **Tolsma** (Ella[3] Zoerink, Johan Michael[2], Jan Petrus[1])[56] was born in Inwood, Lyon Co., Iowa 1 January 1926 and married **Dean S. McNeil** 29 May 1950.

Alyce Evandna **Tolsma** and Dean S. **McNeil** had the following children:
+   63   i.   Diane[5] **McNeil**.
+   64   ii.   David **McNeil**.
     65   iii. Daniel **McNeil**.[57]
+   66   iv. Dean **McNeil**.

21. **Don Jacques**[4] **Tolsma** (Ella[3] Zoerink, Johan Michael[2], Jan Petrus[1])[58] was born in Inwood, Lyon Co., Iowa 14 February 1927 and married **Dona Mae Palmer**.

Don Jacques **Tolsma** and Dona Mae **Palmer** had the following child:
+   67   i.   Dirk Jeffrey[5] **Tolsma** born in 1956.

23. **Dudley Jerome**[4] **Tolsma** (Ella[3] Zoerink, Johan Michael[2], Jan Petrus[1])[59] was born in Canton, Lincoln Co., South Dakota 11 November 1939 and married **Ruth Brumage**.

Dudley Jerome **Tolsma** and Ruth **Brumage** had the following children:
       68   i.   Dawndra[5] **Tolsma**.[60]
       69   ii.   Kenneth **Tolsma**.[61]

26. **J. Marshall**[4] **Zoerink** (Henry[3], Johan Michael[2], Jan Petrus[1])[62] was born in Everson, Whatcom Co., Washington 7 February 1934 and married **Yvonne Stap** in Lynden, Whatcom Co., Washington 11 June 1954. Yvonne,[63] daughter of John **Stap** and Alice **De Jong**, was born in Lynden 30 June 1934.

J. Marshall **Zoerink** and Yvonne **Stap** had the following children born in Bellingham, Whatcom Co., Washington:
+   70   i.   Arvin Louis[5] **Zoerink** 20 June 1956.
       71   ii.   June Marlys **Zoerink**[64] 12 October 1958 and died there 14 April 1961, at 2 years of age.
+   72   iii.   Marlin Jay **Zoerink** 11 July 1963.
+   73   iv.   Marlys Joy **Zoerink** 11 July 1963.
       74   v.   Luanne Kay **Zoerink**[65] 6 January 1966 and married Darren Jay **Lagerway** there 4 September 1987.

27. **Greta Mae**[4] **Zoerink** (Henry[3], Johan Michael[2], Jan Petrus[1])[66] was born in Everson, Whatcom Co., Washington 9 July 1936 and married **Donald Bruce Elsbree** in Lynden, Whatcom Co., Washington 22 July 1955. Donald,[67] son of Alonzo Forrest **Elsbree** and Alice **Dickinson**, was born in Bellingham, Whatcom Co., Washington 21 December 1932.

Greta Mae **Zoerink** and Donald Bruce **Elsbree** had the following children born in Bellingham:
+   75   i.   Douglas Brian[5] **Elsbree** 4 June 1956.

{ G 1809 }

	76	ii.	Duane Bruce **Elsbree**[68] 25 November 1959 and married Sonje Dee **Bajema** in Cedar Springs, Washington 18 August 1984. They were divorced in January 1988.
+	77	iii.	Delayne Michelle **Elsbree** 10 May 1966.

28. **Nelda Marie**[4] **Zoerink** (Henry[3], Johan Michael[2], Jan Petrus[1])[69] was born in Lynden, Whatcom Co., Washington 13 November 1938 and married **Raymond Lee Stuit** there 2 October 1959. Raymond,[70] son of Peter **Stuit** Jr. and Frances **LeFebre**, was born in Hettinger, Adams Co., North Dakota 28 November 1936.

Nelda Marie **Zoerink** and Raymond Lee **Stuit** had the following children born in Bellingham, Whatcom Co., Washington:

+	78	i.	Randall Lee[5] **Stuit** 23 September 1961.
+	79	ii.	Ryan Lane **Stuit** 10 May 1963.
	80	iii.	Kendall Ray **Stuit**[71] 25 December 1965.
	81	iv.	Kevin Dale **Stuit**[72] 6 December 1968.
	82	v.	Steven Ladd **Stuit**[73] 18 January 1970 and died in a motorcycle accident 8 June 1980 in Lynden, at 10 years of age.

29. **Phyllis Ann**[4] **Zoerink** (Henry[3], Johan Michael[2], Jan Petrus[1])[74] was born in Lynden, Whatcom Co., Washington 9 September 1942 and married **Sherman Lee Polinder** there 21 August 1963. Sherman was born in Bellingham, Whatcom Co., Washington 21 February 1942.[75]

Phyllis Ann **Zoerink** and Sherman Lee **Polinder** had the following children born in Bellingham:

+	83	i.	Sheri Lynn[5] **Polinder** 31 January 1965.
	84	ii.	Jayson Lee **Polinder**[76] 27 March 1968 and married Carleen F. **Terpstra** in Lynden 2 August 1991.
	85	iii.	Barbara Ann **Polinder**[77] 31 January 1972.
	86	iv.	Jeff Henry **Polinder**[78] 11 October 1973.

FIFTH GENERATION

32. **Sherrie Kay**[5] **Pierce** (Matilda[4] **Zoerink**, John Peter[3], Johan Michael[2], Jan Petrus[1])[79] was born in Chicago, Cook Co., Illinois 6 January 1955 and married **Ben Daniel Basham II** 15 December 1973.

Sherrie Kay **Pierce** and Ben Daniel **Basham** II had the following children:

	87	i.	Jessica[6] **Basham**[80] born 21 May 1976.

  88 ii. Ben Daniel **Basham** III[81] born 9 March 1977.

33. Janice[5] **Pierce** (Matilda[4] Zoerink, John Peter[3], Johan Michael[2], Jan Petrus[1])[82] was born in Chicago, Cook Co., Illinois 2 January 1957 and married **Joe Aimaro** there 10 July 1976.

Janice **Pierce** and Joe **Aimaro** had the following children:
  89 i. Allen[6] **Aimaro**.[83]
  90 ii. Anna Marie **Aimaro**.[84]

35. Dennis Mitchell[5] **Zoerink** (Mitchell John[4], John Peter[3], Johan Michael[2], Jan Petrus[1])[85] was born in LeMars, Plymouth Co., Iowa 29 April 1943 and married **Patricia Ann Luense** there 12 November 1966. She was born in LeMars 17 August 1944.[86]

Dennis Mitchell **Zoerink** and Patricia Ann **Luense** had the following children born in Cedar Rapids, Linn Co., Iowa:
  91 i. Michelle Ann[6] **Zoerink**[87] 24 May 1972.
  92 ii. Todd **Zoerink**[88] 23 March 1978.

36. Dean Allen[5] **Zoerink** (Mitchell John[4], John Peter[3], Johan Michael[2], Jan Petrus[1])[89] was born in LeMars, Plymouth Co., Iowa 8 January 1947 and married **Ellen May Bartlett** in Grimes, Polk Co., Iowa 7 August 1971. Ellen was born in Des Moines, Polk Co., Iowa 5 January 1950.[90]

Dean Allen **Zoerink** and Ellen May **Bartlett** had the following children:
  93 i. Sarah[6] **Zoerink**[91] born 30 April 1978.
  94 ii. Matthew **Zoerink**[92] born 23 June 1980.

49. Brian Kurt[5] **Van Meetern** (Mary Ann[4] Zoerink, John Peter[3], Johan Michael[2], Jan Petrus[1])[93] was born in Sheldon, O Brien Co., Iowa 11 September 1960 and married **Beth Dykstra** in Hull, Sioux Co., Iowa, 4 June 1982. Beth,[94] daughter of Leroy **Dykstra** and Henrietta **Scholten**, was born in Hull 21 July 1961.

Brian Kurt **Van Meetern** and Beth **Dykstra** had the following children:
  95 i. Emilee Cynthia[6] **Van Meetern**[95] born in Pocahontas, Pocahontas Co., Iowa 5 January 1988.
  96 ii. Hannah Mary **Van Meetern**[96] born in Fort Dodge, Webster Co., Iowa 20 March 1993.
  97 iii. Faith Elizabeth **Van Meetern**[97] born in Spencer, Clay Co., Iowa 28 January 1997.

50. **Beth Renae**[5] **Van Meetern** (Mary Ann[4] Zoerink, John Peter[3], Johan Michael[2], Jan Petrus[1])[98] was born in Sheldon, O Brien Co., Iowa 10 October 1966 and married **Frank Van Der Wilt** there 8 December 1990. Frank,[99] son of Gerrit **Van Der Wilt** and Eunice **Youstra**, was born in Sioux Center, Sioux Co., Iowa 11 February 1964.

Beth Renae **Van Meetern** and Frank **Van Der Wilt** had the following child born in Orange City, Sioux Co., Iowa:
  98 i. Garret Charles[6] **Van Der Wilt**[100] 14 September 1995.

51. **Carl**[5] **Moss** (Iola Mae[4] Zoerink, John Peter[3], Johan Michael[2], Jan Petrus[1])[101] was born in Sioux Center, Sioux Co., Iowa 7 March 1956 and married **Cindy Scholten** in Valley Springs, Minnehaha Co., South Dakota 1 September 1975. Cindy was born in Luverne, Rock Co., Minnesota 27 January 1956.[102]

Carl **Moss** and Cindy **Scholten** had the following children born in Luverne:
  99 i. Amy Sue[6] **Moss**[103] 24 May 1977.
  100 ii. Angela Leone **Moss**[104] 1 August 1979.
  101 iii. Staci Ann **Moss**[105] 28 November 1983.

53. **Denise**[5] **Moss** (Iola Mae[4] Zoerink, John Peter[3], Johan Michael[2], Jan Petrus[1])[106] was born in Sioux Center, Sioux Co., Iowa 11 January 1959 and married **Alvin Rozeboom** in Valley Springs, Minnehaha Co., South Dakota 2 July 1976. Alvin was born in Luverne, Rock Co., Minnesota 1 October 1957.[107]

Denise **Moss** and Alvin **Rozeboom** had the following children born in Luverne:
  102 i. Jared Lee[6] **Rozeboom**[108] 14 November 1976.
  103 ii. Marie **Rozeboom**[109] 4 June 1978.

54. **Nora Kay**[5] **Moss** (Iola Mae[4] Zoerink, John Peter[3], Johan Michael[2], Jan Petrus[1])[110] was born in Luverne, Rock Co., Minnesota 16 May 1960 and married **Donald Halverson** in Valley Springs, Minnehaha Co., South Dakota 23 June 1977. He was born 29 April 1956.[111]

Nora Kay **Moss** and Donald **Halverson** had the following children born in Luverne:
  104 i. Derek Alan[6] **Halverson**[112] 18 June 1978.
  105 ii. Ryan Byron **Halverson**[113] 15 January 1980.
  106 iii. Nicole Mae **Halverson**[114] 8 December 1981.

55. **Tylene Joy**[5] **Moss** (Iola Mae[4] Zoerink, John Peter[3], Johan Michael[2], Jan Petrus[1])[115] was born in Luverne, Rock Co., Minn. 30 June 1962 and married **Clifford Goembel** in Valley Springs, Minnehaha Co., South Dakota 18 June 1983. Clifford was born in Luverne 2 September 1962.[116]

Tylene Joy **Moss** and Clifford **Goembel** had the following child born in Luverne:
    107   i.   Misty Rae **Goembel**[6] 26 February 1989.[117]

56. **Jolene**[5] **Moss** (Iola Mae[4] Zoerink, John Peter[3], Johan Michael[2], Jan Petrus[1])[118] was born in Luverne, Rock Co., Minnesota 19 July 1963 and married **Burdell Jansma** there 17 September 1982. BJ was born in Luverne 17 March 1963.[119]

Jolene **Moss** and Burdell **Jansma** had the following children:
    108   i.   Gregory Wayne[6] **Jansma**[120] born in Mankato, Blue Earth Co., Minn. 28 February 1983.
    109   ii.   Tami Lynn **Jansma**[121] born in Luverne 20 May 1986.
    110   iii.   Megan Jo **Jansma**[122] born in Luverne 6 March 1988.

60. **Lorna Jo**[5] **Zoerink** (Wayne[4], John Peter[3], Johan Michael[2], Jan Petrus[1])[123] was born in Lakewood, Los Angeles Co., California 1 December 1966 and married **Blaine Scott Whipple** in Turner, Marion Co., Oregon 14 August 1998. Scott,[124] son of Robert Blaine **Whipple** and Ines Mae **Peterson**, was born at 12:24 p.m at Bess Kaiser Hospital in Portland, Multnomah Co., Oregon 27 December 1968. He was 20 and 1/2 inches long and weighed 8 pounds 2 ounces. At age 4 he was 3' 2 1/2" and weighted 50 pounds; at 8, 4' 11 1/4" and 77 pounds; at 12, 5' 5 3/4" and 131 pounds; at 18 6'4" and 240 pounds. He earned varsity letters in football and wrestling at Sunset High School in Washington Co., Oregon. He was graduated from Grinnell College, Grinnell, Poweshkiek Co., Iowa in June 1990 with a major in Economics and was both a football (four years) and basketball (three years) letterman and Captain of both teams his senior year. He was awarded a Doctor of Jurisprudence Degree by the U. of Oregon at Eugene, Lane Co. and inducted into the Order of the Coif in May 1998. He worked in the Trust Department of a major bank in Chicago (1990-92) and as an Underwriter with Standard Insurance Co. of Portland (1993-95). He is trial lawyer and partner with the Portland law firm of Schwabe, Williamson, and Wyatt (2006).

    L. J. earned an Associate of Arts degree from Colorado Northwestern Community College at Rangely, Rio Blanco Co., Colorado in 1987. She attended on a basketball scholarship and was Captain of both the basketball and volleyball teams both years. She was awarded a B.S. degree from Colorado State University, Fort Collins, Larimer Co. in 1993 where she majored in Human Development and Family Studies. She has worked as an Education Assistant in Special Ed classes in Portland and for the Child Center (a day treatment center) in Eugene. In the latter position she worked in schools and with families with children (ages 7-12) who have behavorial problems. She joined the Portland School System in 2001 while simultaneously working for a Masters of Education Degree from Portland State University.

Lorna Jo **Zoerink** and Blaine Scott **Whipple** had the following children born in Portland, Washington Co.:

  111 i. Spencer Blaine[6] **Whipple**[125] at St. Vincent's Hospital at 10:42 p.m. 15 October 2001. He weighed 6 pounds and was 21 inches long.

  112 ii. Turner Collins **Whipple**[126] at St. Vincent's Hospital at 1:24 a.m. 8 May 2004. He weighed 7 pounds 2 ounces and was 18 1/2 inches long.

63. **Diane**[5] **McNeil** (Alyce Evandna[4] Tolsma, Ella[3] Zoerink, Johan Michael[2], Jan Petrus[1])[127] birth date unknown, married **David Doty**.

Diane **McNeil** and David **Doty** had the following children:

  113 i. Vanya[6] **Doty**.[128]
  114 ii. Timothy **Doty**.[129]
  115 iii. Shannon **Doty**.[130]
  116 iv. Ella **Doty**[131] and married John **Dietrick**.

64. **David**[5] **McNeil** (Alyce Evandna[4] Tolsma, Ella[3] Zoerink, Johan Michael[2], Jan Petrus[1])[132] birth date unknown, and married **Karen (__)**.

David **McNeil** and Karen (__) had the following children:

  117 i. David Michael[6] **McNeil**.[133]
  118 ii. Gracie Jean **McNeil**.[134]
  119 iii. Ian **McNeil**.[135]
  120 iv. Gracian **McNeil**.[136]

66. **Dean**[5] **McNeil** (Alyce Evandna[4] Tolsma, Ella[3] Zoerink, Johan Michael[2], Jan Petrus[1])[137] birth date unknown, married **Marcia (__)**.

Dean **McNeil** and Marcia (__) had the following child:

  121 i. Ruby[6] **McNeil**.[138]

{ G 1814 }

67. **Dirk Jeffrey**[5] **Tolsma** (Don Jacques[4], Ella[3] Zoerink, Johan Michael[2], Jan Petrus[1])[139] was born in 1956 and was killed in an auto accident in 1986 at 30 years of age. He married twice. (1) **Rita Menage**. (2) **Julie Jacobsen**.

Dirk Jeffrey **Tolsma** and Rita **Menage** had the following child:
    122   i.   Danielle Joy[6] **Tolsma**.[140]

Dirk Jeffrey **Tolsma** and Julie **Jacobsen** had the following children:
    123   ii.   Dustin Jed **Tolsma**.[141]
    124   iii.   Tina Melanie **Tolsma**.[142]

70. **Arvin Louis**[5] **Zoerink** (J. Marshall[4], Henry[3], Johan Michael[2], Jan Petrus[1])[143] was born in Bellingham, Whatcom Co., Washington 20 June 1956 and married **Bridget Joan Vlas** 31 August 1979.

Arvin Louis **Zoerink** and Bridget Joan **Vlas** had the following children born in Bellingham:
    125   i.   Nathan Andrew[6] **Zoerink**[144] 16 January 1981.
    126   ii.   Leisha Rachelle **Zoerink**[145] 31 January 1987.
    127   iii.   Michael Arvin **Zoerink**[146] 5 April 1990.

72. **Marlin Jay**[5] **Zoerink** (J. Marshall[4], Henry[3], Johan Michael[2], Jan Petrus[1])[147] was born in Bellingham, Whatcom Co., Washington 11 July 1963 and married **Tracy Ann Temple** 20 April 1991. They were divorced in Bellingham 22 May 1993.

Marlin Jay **Zoerink** and Tracy Ann **Temple** had the following child born in Bellingham:
    128   i.   Travis Tyler[6] **Zoerink**[148] 22 April 1989.

73. **Marlys Joy**[5] **Zoerink** (J. Marshall[4], Henry[3], Johan Michael[2], Jan Petrus[1])[149] was born in Bellingham, Whatcom Co., Washington 11 July 1963 and married **Kenneth John Lange** there 10 February 1984.

Marlys Joy **Zoerink** and Kenneth John **Lange** had the following children born in Bellingham:
    129   i.   Christy Marie[6] **Lange**[150] 23 November 1978.
    130   ii.   Heather Kay **Lange**[151] 23 November 1978.

75. **Douglas Brian**[5] **Elsbree** (Greta Mae[4] Zocrink, Henry[3], Johan Michael[2], Jan Petrus[1])[152] was born in Bellingham, Whatcom Co., Wash-

ington 4 June 1956 and married **Randi Sue Kayser** in Lynden, Whatcom Co., Washington 9 December 1978. She was born in Dayton, Columbia Co., Washington 26 June 1961.[153]

Douglas Brian **Elsbree** and Randi Sue **Kayser** had the following children born in Bellingham:
    131   i.   Erica Dawn[6] **Elsbree**[154] 10 June 1979.
    132   ii.   Stacy Jo **Elsbree**[155] 10 July 1983.
    133   iii.   James Douglas **Elsbree**[156] 10 January 1987.

77. **Delayne Michelle**[5] **Elsbree** (Greta Mae[4] Zoerink, Henry[3], Johan Michael[2], Jan Petrus[1])[157] was born in Bellingham, Whatcom Co., Washington 10 May 1966 and married **Dean Vander Haak** in Lynden, Whatcom Co., Washington 20 July 1984.

Delayne Michelle **Elsbree** and Dean **Vander Haak** had the following children born in Bellingham:
    134   i.   Taylor Dean[6] **Vander Haak**[158] 25 November 1987.
    135   ii.   Jessa Llayne **Vander Haak**[159] 10 March 1990.
    136   iii.   Abby Mae **Vander Haak**[160] 17 June 1991.

78. **Randall Lee**[5] **Stuit** (Nelda Marie[4] Zoerink, Henry[3], Johan Michael[2], Jan Petrus[1])[161] was born in Bellingham, Whatcom Co., Washington 23 September 1961 and married **Margaret Mary Houweling** in Lynden, Whatcom Co., Washington 28 August 1980.

Randall Lee **Stuit** and Margaret Mary **Houweling** had the following children:
    137   i.   Benjamin Lee[6] **Stuit**[162] born in Bellingham 3 March 1981.
    138   ii.   Leah Marie **Stuit**[163] born in Bellingham 16 April 1982.
    139   iii.   Jesse Ladd **Stuit**[164] born in Bellingham 26 August 1984.
    140   iv.   Stephanie R. **Stuit**[165] born in Sumas, Whatcom Co., Washington 15 March 1988.
    141   v.   Lane J. **Stuit**[166] born in Sumas 25 May 1990.
    142   vi.   Levi Peter **Stuit**[167] born in Bellingham 25 November 1991.

79. **Ryan Lane**[5] **Stuit** (Nelda Marie[4] Zoerink, Henry[3], Johan Michael[2], Jan Petrus[1])[168] was born in Bellingham, Whatcom Co., Washington 10 May 1963 and married **Donna Lynn Baldwin** in Lynden, Whatcom Co., Washington 3 October 1992. She was born in San Antonio, Bexar Co., Texas 29 October 1971.[169]

Ryan Lane **Stuit** and Donna Lynn **Baldwin** had the following child born in Bellingham:

    143   i.   Austin Ray^6 **Stuit**^{170} 9 April 1993.

83. **Sheri Lynn**^{5} **Polinder** (Phyllis Ann^4 Zoerink, Henry^3, Johan Michael^2, Jan Petrus^1)^{171} was born in Bellingham, Whatcom Co., Washington 31 January 1965 and married **Steven J. Groen** in Lynden, Whatcom Co., Washington 30 March 1984.

Sheri Lynn **Polinder** and Steven J. **Groen** had the following children born in Bellingham:

    144   i.   Corby Steven^6 **Groen**^{172} 24 March 1987.
    145   ii. Brielle Nichole **Groen**^{173} 16 September 1989.

(For a continuation of the Zoerink line, see Generation 13, No. 7399, Lorna Jo Zoerink, wife of Blaine Scott Whipple.)

ZOERINK FAMILY ENDNOTES

1. Arlene B. Kramer, comp., *Kramer Family Tree*, Grand Forks, ND, 915 Park Dr., 58201, 1996. Copy in the home of L. J. (Zoerink) and Blaine Scott Whipple, 12155 N. W. McDaniel Road, Portland, OR 97229 in 2005. (Hereafter Arlene B. Kramer, *Kramer Family Tree*), 3.
2. Ibid., 2-3.
3. Ibid., 3, 5.
4. Ibid., 3, 42.
5. Ibid., 42.
6. Ibid., 42, 44.
7. Ibid., 42, 45.
8. through 10. Ibid., 3, 46.
11. Ibid., 3, 77.
12. through 14. Ibid., 77.
15. Ibid., 3, 85.
16. and 17. Ibid., 85.
18. Ibid., 42-3.
19. and 20. Ibid., 43.
21. Ibid., 46-47.
22. Ibid., 47.
23. Ibid., 47, 50.
24. Ibid., 47, 51.
25. Ibid., 51.
26. Ibid., 46, 54.
27. Ibid., 54.
28. Ibid., 54-55.

{ G 1817 }

29. Ibid., 54, 56.
30. Ibid., 54.
31. Ibid., 54, 57.
32. Ibid., 54.
33. Ibid., 54, 58.
34. Ibid., 54, 59.
35. Ibid., 54, 60.
36. Ibid. 54, 61.
37. Ibid., 54, 62.
38. Ibid., 54, 63.
39. Ibid., 46, 64.
40. Ibid., 64.
41. Ibid., 64, 65.
42. Ibid., 46, 66.
43. Ibid., 66.
44. Ibid., 46, 69.
45. and 46. Ibid., 69.
47. Ibid., 46, 75.
48. through 50. Ibid., 75.
51. Ibid., 46, 76.
52. through 54. Ibid., 76.
55. Ibid., 77-78.
56. Ibid., 78.
57. Ibid., 77.
58. Ibid., 77, 84.
59. and 60. Ibid., 84.
61. Ibid., 85-86.
62. and 63. Ibid., 86.
64. Ibid., 86, 90.
65. Ibid., 85, 91.
66. Ibid., 91.
67. Ibid., 91, 93.
68. Ibid., 85, 95.
69. through 72. Ibid., 95.
73. Ibid., 85, 98.
74. Ibid., 98.
75. Ibid., 98, 100.
76. and 77. Ibid., 98.
78. Ibid., 47-8.
79. and 80. Ibid., 48.
81. Ibid., 47, 49.
82. and 83. Ibid., 49.
84. Ibid., 51-52.
85. through 87. Ibid., 52.
88. Ibid., 51, 53.
89. through 91. Ibid., 53.
92. Ibid., 66-67.
93. through 96. Ibid., 67.
97. Ibid., 66, 68.
98. and 99. Ibid., 68.

{ G 1818 }

100. Ibid., 69-70.
101. through 104. Ibid., 70.
105. Ibid., 69, 71.
106. through 108. Ibid., 71.
109. Ibid., 69, 72.
110. through 113. Ibid., 72.
114. and 115. Ibid., 68, 73.
116. Ibid., 69-74.
117. through 120. Ibid., 74.
121. Lorna Jo Zoerink, Certificate of Live Birth District Certificate #7097-114661, 27 Dec. 1966, Register-Recorder/ County Court, County of Los Angeles, Los Angeles, Calif.
122. Blaine Scott Whipple & Lorna Jo Zoerink, Marriage License, Local File No. 651005, 17 Aug. 1998, Lane County Oregon Court House, Eugene, Oreg.
123. Spencer Blaine Whipple, Birth Certificate Local File No. 005848, 30 October 2001, County Registrar, Washington County, Hillsboro, Oreg.
124. Personal knowledge of his grandfather, Blaine Whipple, who was in the hospital to meet and greet him a few hours after birth.
125. and 126. Arlene B. Kramer, Kramer Family Tree, 78-79.
127. through 129. Ibid., 79.
130. Ibid., 78.
131. through 134. Ibid., 80.
135. Ibid., 78.
136. Ibid., 80.
137. Ibid., 82-3.
138. Ibid., 82.
139. and 140. Ibid., 83.
141. Ibid., 86-87.
142. through 144. Ibid. 87.
145. Ibid., 86.
146. Ibid., 89.
147. Ibid., 86, 89.
148. and 149. Ibid., 89.
150. Ibid., 91-2.
151. through 154. Ibid., 92.
155. Ibid., 91, 94.
156. Ibid., 95-96.
157. and 158. Ibid., 94.
159. Ibid., 95-96.
160. through 165, Ibid., 96.
166. Ibid., 95, 97.
167. and 168. Ibid., 97.
169. Ibid., 98-9.
170. through 173. Ibid., 99.

{ G 1819 }

APPENDIX G-8

HAROLD GEORGE WM. JASPERSON 1908-1944 TO EMILY JANE JASPERSON - 1992-

(Jasperson lineage of Emily Jane Jasperson Generation 13, No. 7402, David Blaine Jasperson, her father.)

FIRST GENERATION

1. **Harold George William**[1] **Jasperson** was born in Tracy, Lyon Co., Minnesota 25 August 1908 and died there 14 January 1944, at 35 years of age. He married **Evelyn Helgemo** in Tracy 25 January 1927. Elevyn,[1] daughter of Ole **Helgemo** and Ida **Pederson**, was born in Tracy 28 July 1910 and died there 6 September 2004, at 94 years of age.[2] She married (2) **Jens Hibbard** in Tracy 17 March 1948. He was born 17 February 1897 and died in Tracy 5 February 1991, five days shy of his 94th birthday.

Harold George William **Jasperson** and Evelyn **Helgemo** had the following child:

+ 2 i. Donald J.[2] **Jasperson** born 11 November 1931.

SECOND GENERATION

2. **Donald J.**[2] **Jasperson** (Harold George William[1])[3] was born in Tracy, Lyon Co., Minnesota 11 November 1931 and married twice. (1) **Nancy Jane Whipple** in Tracy 30 July 1950. Nancy,[4] daughter of Lucien Blaine **Whipple** and Pearl Julia **Scott**, was born in Ryder, Ward Co., North Dakota 5 January 1932 at 10:35 p.m. at home. The attending physician was H. O. Graangaard, M.D. and her grandmother Nellie Scott was midwife. She died 26 December 1987 in Glencoe, McLeod Co., Minnesota, at 55 years of age. (2) **Barbara (Shipp) Bruns** in Glencoe 6 October 1990.

Obituary: Funeral services for Nancy J. Jasperson, 55, of Glencoe were held 29 December 1987 at Christ Lutheran Church in Glencoe with the Rev. Chester Hoversten officiating. Organist was Peggy Hatlestad. Music selections were "The Lord is My Shepherd," "The King is Coming," "Lead On, Oh King Eternal," and "Amazing Grace." Pallbearers were Maurice Stromswold, Ray Swanson, Rolland Olson, Paul Soule, Don McKee, and Robert Tibbets. The Glencoe Ambassadors served as hon-

Don and Nancy's wedding 30 July 1950 in Tracy, Minn. Pat Whipple Drotzman, maid of honor and Bernie Jasperson, best man. Tracy Luthern Church.

Barb and Don with Don's grandchildren. Rear: Amanda, Katie, and Sarah Ebert and Jeff Barney, and Luke and Steffanie Schmidt. Yankton, SD. 15 August 2004.

{ G 1821 }

orary bearers. Internment in the Glencoe Cemetery.

Nancy Jane was baptized in Douglas, Ward Co., North Dakota and confirmed in Bismarck, Burleigh Co., North Dakota. Her family lived in various communities before moving to Tracy in 1946 where she graduated from High School. She and Don were married at the Tracy Lutheran Church. They lived in Tracy, LeMars, Iowa, and Marshall and Appleton, Minnesota before coming to Glencoe. She was active in her church as President of the ALCW and taught Sunday school in Marshall and was Superintendent of Sunday School in Appleton. She worked as a Nurses' Aid and held varied department store clerking jobs. As well as being a loving wife and mother, she was active in the Homemakers Club and she liked to fish, golf, play bridge, crochet, and do needle work. She died at the Glencoe Area Health Center following a lengthy battle with cancer.

Surviving are her husband, Donald, three daughters, and one son: Terri Ebert (husband Charles) of Luverne, Minnesota; Donna Barney of Appleton; David Jasperson, (wife Jan) of Rochester, Minnesota; and Molly Jasperson of Glencoe; five grandchildren, Katie, Sarah, and Amanda Ebert and Jeff and Leah Barney; mother, Pearl Whipple of Glencoe; brothers, Blaine Whipple (wife Ines) of Portland, Oregon and Richard Whipple of Eagan, Minnesota; two sisters, Patricia Drotzman of Yankton, South Dakota and Mary Ann McPherson (husband Bill) of Littleton, Massachusetts; mother-in-law Evelyn Hibbard (husband Jens) of Tracy; and half-sister Mrs. Elaine West (husband Stephen) of Mt. Vernon, Iowa; as well as nieces and nephews. She was preceded in death by her father. Visitation was held 28 December at Johnson-McBride Funeral Chapel in Glencoe.[5]

Donald was graduated from Tracy High School and worked at the Tracy J. C. Penny Store after schools. Following graduation he was employed full time by Penny's, eventually becoming a store manager in Iowa and Minnesota. He was managing the store at Appleton when Penney's decided to close it and

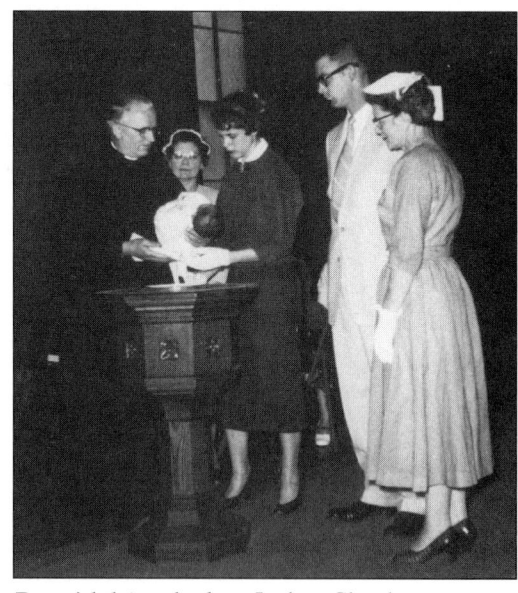

Donna's babtism, Appleton Luthern Church, minister, Evelyn Jasperson, Mary Ann, Bob, and Pearl Whipple

{ G 1822 }

instead of remaining with the chain, he opened the Jasperson Department Store in Appleton which he and Nancy operated for several years. After eventually closing the store he became an insurance salesman for a short period of time before becoming the manager of the Glencoe Chamber of Commerce. Since retirement he and Barb spend winters at Mesa, Maricopa Co., Arizona and summers on a lake in Minnesota. (2006)

Donald J. **Jasperson** and Nancy Jane **Whipple** had the following children:

+ 3 i. Terri Lynn[3] **Jasperson** born 11 October 1951.
+ 4 ii. Donna Marie **Jasperson** born 10 May 1955.
+ 5 iii. David Blaine **Jasperson** born 7 November 1959.
+ 6 iv. Molly Jane **Jasperson** born 23 November 1966.

THIRD GENERATION

3. **Terri Lynn**[3] **Jasperson** (Donald J.[2], Harold George William[1])[6] was born in Tracy, Lyon Co., Minnesota 11 October 1951 and married **Charles Jacob Ebert** in Appleton, Swift Co., Minnesota 20 September 1975. Chuck,[7] son of Vance Leroy **Ebert** and Doris Helen **Warner**, was born in Clearlake, Deuel Co., South Dakota 26 January 1951 and died 14 June 2002 in Luverne, Rock Co., Minnesota, at 51 years of age.

O b i t u a r y : Charles (Chuck) Jacob Ebert, age 51 of Luverne, Minn. passed away on Friday, June 14, 2002 at the Luverne Hospice Cottage. When Chuck was in grade school in Clear Lake, S. Dak. he moved with his family to Luverne where he graduated from High School in 1969. He continued his education at Winona State College and worked as a Marketing Man-

Chuck, Terri, Katie, Sarah, and Amanda.

{ G 1823 }

ager at CWG-Tri State Insurance in Luverne. Over the years he continued with his insurance education and received the following titles and degrees: CPCU, CIC, ARM, AU, and ALCM. Chuck will be lovingly rememberd by his wife Terri of Luverne; his daughters Katie of Luverne, Sarah and Amanda of Marshall, Minn.; his parents Vance and Doris Ebert of Luverne; his brothers Jim (Mary) of Bemidgi, Minn. and

Terri.

Paul (Dyan) of Elk River, Minn; his nieces Jessica (Ethan) Harvey of Little Falls, Minn. and Laurin Ebert of Elk River; his nephew Jake Ebert of Truman, Minn. His grandparents preceded him in death. Funeral services were 17 June at the Grace Luthern church; burial in Maplewood Cemetery, Luverne. Donations can be given to the First Farmers & Merchants Bank of Luverne for the Ebert Family Scholarship which will be awarded at the Pheasants Forever banquet. Chuck was a member of Grace Lutheran Church in Luverne. He served as Past President of the Jaycees, Past President of the Luverne Toastmasters, Past Treasurer for the Music Boosters, Board Member for the Green Earth Players, Scorekeeper for the Gymnastics Team, and current Treasurer for Pheasants Forever. Above all, Chuck cherished the time he could spend with his family.[8]

Amanda, Luverne High School graduation 1999.

Terri attended grades two through eleven at Marshall, Lyon Co., and was graduated from Appleton High School. She was graduated from Alexandria,

Blaine Whipple autographing a copy of his book on John Whipple of Ipswich, Massachusetts for his grand niece Katie. 14 August 2004.

Sarah, 14 August 2004, Yankton, S. Dak.

Douglas Co., Minnesota Technical College (a 2-year course) and spent a year and a half at Moorhead State College in Moorhead, Clay Co., Minnesota. She worked in the Registrar's Office during the day and attended night classes. Following college she clerked for her parents at the Jasperson Department Store in Appleton and had an afternoon radio program on KBMO.

Terri and Chuck met while both were vacationing in Hawaii. After the family moved to Luverne, she joined the Rock County Sheriffs Department in August 1983 and is the Dispatch Supervisor/Administrative Assistant to the Sheriff (2006). The job includes managing the 911 system, supervising/training dispatchers, giving drug tests to pris-

Amanda, Terri, and Sarah Ebert with Matt and Katie (Ebert) Mostad 27 Nov. 2004, Luverne, Minn.

oners, transporting prisoners and mental patients to and from court/jail/prison. She trains Deputies on how to write reports, give drug tests, and how to use the fingerprint machine. She also works closely with the County Attorney and Family Services. She is President of the Communication Supervisors Organization for the fifth Minnesota District.

She was a cast member of the musical "Oklahoma" in high school and began serious acting with the Luverne Readers Theater productions where she has played leads in a number of productions. She also helped with makeup, costumes, and props and is on the Board of the Green Earth Players. She taught Sunday School and Confirmation Classes, served communion, and has been a Reader in Luverne's Grace Lutheran Church.

Terri Lynn **Jasperson** and Charles Jacob **Ebert** had the following children:

    7   i.   Katherine Marie[4] **Ebert**[9] born in Stevens Point, Wisconsin 7 December 1977 and married Matthew A. **Mostad** in Luverne 27 November 2004. Their ceremony at the Grace Luthern Church was followed by a dinner reception at Beaver Creek Golf Course, Beaver Creek, Rock Co., Minnesota. Matthew son of Manferd **Mostad** and Mary **Gratton**, was born in Thief River Falls, Pennington Co., Minnesota 7 September 1973.

{ G 1826 }

8	ii.	Sarah Elizabeth **Ebert**[10] born in Fridley, Anoka Co., Minnesota 17 September 1979.
9	iii.	Amanda Louise **Ebert**[11] born in Fridley 4 May 1981.

4. **Donna Marie**[3] **Jasperson** (Donald J.[2], Harold George William[1])[12] was born in Tracy, Lyon Co., Minnesota 10 May 1955 and died 16 November 1989 in Appleton, Swift Co., Minnesota, at 34 years of age. Funeral services were held 19 November at Appleton's Zion Lutheran Church and internment was in the Appleton City Cemetery. She married **Gerald Dean Barney** in Appleton 22 July 1973. Jerry, son of Christian **Barney** and Hattie **Van Heurulan**, was born in Willmar, Kandiyohi Co., Minnesota 11 March 1944. They were divorced in Appleton in 1982.

In 1982, Donna, 27, recently divorced, raising two children, and working as Legal Secretary in Appleton was diagnosed with a giant aneurysm on her brain stem. Four days after entering the hospital and after the doctors had tied off the

Donna Jasperson and Jerry Barney.

L. to R. David Blaine, Donald, Nancy Jane, Donna Marie, Molly Jane, Gerald Dean Barney, Terri Lynn Jasperson, Appleton, Minn. 22 July 1973. Photos courtesy of Blaine Whipple.

{ G 1827 }

Elaine West and Blaine Whipple with grand nephew Jeff Barney, 14 August 2004, Yankton, SD. Photo courtesy of Michael J. Drotzman.

aneurysm, she had a stroke which robbed her of her ability to walk and altered her memory (she couldn't remember the previous three years). She had limited use of her vocal chords, enhanced by a trachea tube, and had to be fed by a stomach tube. In short, she had lost the ability to take care of herself and had to re-learn independent living skills.

She began a long recovery period which led to her acceptance at Courage Residence in Golden Valley, Hennepin Co., Minnesota in September 1984. Courage Residence is a live-in transitional rehabilitation facility where individuals 16 and older with disabilities learn independent living skills. When she first arrived she needed "hands-on" support but within a year had progressed to a point of needing little help. She made a successful transfer to using a walker as well as a wheel chair, learned to use her vocal chords,

Leah and Jeffrey Barney. Photo courtesy of Blaine Whipple.

{ G 1828 }

memory strategies, and how to cook. Her progress was such she was able to move into an apartment retrofitted for her disabilities in the fall of 1985. It was a long process but with grit and determination, she achieved a level of independence that allowed her to return to her Appleton home and to help raise her two children.[13] Jerry teaches high school at Appleton.

Donna Marie **Jasperson** and Gerald Dean **Barney** had the following children born in Appleton:

    10   i.   Jeffrey Dean[4] **Barney**[14] 16 November 1975. Following graduation from Lac Qui Parle Valley High School at Appleton, Jeff was graduated from the U. of Minnesota where he attended with a golf scholarship. He has traveled extensively in Europe and is living in Minneapolis, Minn. where he is a mortgage broker in 2005.

    11   ii.   Leah Marie **Barney**[15] 5 February 1979 was graduated from Lac Qui Parle Valley High School and earned a degree from the School of Pharmacy at the University of Minnesota in 2002 and received a Doctorate Degree in Pharmacy from the same institution in 2004. She is working in The Twin Cities area of Minn. 2005.

    5. **David Blaine**[3] **Jasperson** (Donald J.[2], Harold George William[1])[16] was born in Marshall, Lyon Co., Minnesota 7 November 1959 and married **Jan C. Knobbe** in Waukegan, Lake Co., Illinois 29 September 1984. Jan, daughter of Joseph William **Knobbe** and Jeanette Hildagaard **Caraver**, was born in Waukegan 2 September 1957. Following graduation from High School in 1975, Jan attended Saint Teresa College in Winona, Winona Co., Minnesota where she received a B.S. in Nursing in 1979. She was awarded an M.A. in Management and Health & Human Services from Saint Mary's University, Rochester, Olmsted Co., Minnesota in 1996. She worked as the Neuro Staff Nurse at St. Mary's Hospital in Rochester 1979-84; Assistant Head Nurse 1984-90; and Nurse Manager of the Neuro ICU beginning in 1990. She is also an Adjunct Faculty Member of Saint Mary's University of Minnesota where she is a Systems Analyst, S&P-MICS Implementation Team. (2005).

Dave was graduated from the Appleton, Swift Co., Minnesota High School (1978) where he was quarterback of the football team, won the award as Outstanding Basketball Player as a senior, and the WCCO Young Achiever Award. He attended Concordia College in Moorhead, Clay Co., Minnesota where he earned a B.A. in Business Administration & Communications (1982), and completed a course at Winona State University (1994) which led to a Parent Educator's Teaching License from the state of Minnesota. He was awarded an M.A. in Management from Saint Mary's University of Minnesota (1995). As a consequence of his thesis research, he developed the Father-Friendly Assessment Tool now used by managers and employees in the workplace. He later modified it so it can also be used as the Family-Friendly Assessment Tool.

He was Senior Credit Analyst with First Bank Systems, Inc., Rochester 1982-86; Executive Director of the Olmsted, Minnesota County Historical Society 1986-90; Parent Educator with Parents are Important in Rochester (PAIIR), 1990-92; and worked in the early childhood family education program in the Rochester School District with fathers, immigrants, incarcerated parents, non-English speaking parents, and first time parents. He joined the Mayo Clinic Health Information Program as a memeber of the Wellness Team in February 2004 when he joined its Lifestyle Coaching team. In July 2005 he became a Behavioral Counseling Supervisor with the Health Information Program in charge of the Tobacco Quitline.

David, Jan, and Emily Jasperson. Photo courtesy of Blaine Whipple.

David Blaine **Jasperson** and Jan C. **Knobbe** had the following child born in Rochester:

    12   i.   Emily Jane[4] **Jasperson**[17] 30 June 1992.

6. **Molly Jane**[3] **Jasperson** (Donald J.[2], Harold George William[1])[18] was born in Marshall, Lyon Co., Minnesota 23 November 1966 and married **Kurt Roger Schmidt** at Christ Lutheran Church in Glencoe, McLeod Co., Minnesota 8 May 1993. Kurt, son of Roger **Schmidt** and Marilyn **Wirtz**, was born in Glencoe 13 November 1967.[19] He joined the Army after graduating from Glencoe High School in June 1986 serving for two

years. Upon discharge he attended Moorhead State University Moorhead, Clay Co., Minnesota for two years and then worked in the millwork department for Plato Millwork in Plato, McLeod Co., Minnesota. In June of 1994 he completed a two year course in Mechanical Drafting at Rochester Technical College, Rochester, Olmsted Co., Minnesota and was hired to design and draw custom spiral staircases for Custom Iron in Zumbrota, Goodhue Co., Minnesota. He worked for Nigon Woodworks in Rochester designing kitchens, entertainment centers, and fireplace mantels from March 1997 until June 2005 when he and Craig Hill started Maple Leaf Custom Cabinetry LLC to design, construct and install cabinets.[20]

Molly, Kurt, Luke, and Stephanie Schmidt. Photo courtesy of Blaine Whipple.

Blaine Whipple autographing a copy of his book on John Whipple of Ipswich, Massachusetts for his grand niece Stephanie Schmidt. 14 August 2004, Yankton, SD. Photo courtesy of Michael J. Drotzman.

{ G 1831 }

Molly completed the first ten grades of school in Appleton, Swift Co., Minnesota, a small town in southwest Minnesota. The family moved to Glencoe in 1983 where she was graduated from High School in 1985. She completed her freshman year of college at Concordia College then transferred to Moorhead State University where she earned a Bachelor of Science Degree in Mass Communications in December 1991. Both colleges are located in Moorhead.

She took a year off between her sophomore and junior years to help care for her mother who was dying of breast cancer. During that year she also worked as a Secretary for Cargilll Corporation at Minnetonka, Hennepin Co., Minnesota, an easy drive from her Glencoe home. She worked directly for the Cargill family in the Waycross Division. She returned to college after her mother's death in December 1987.

She completed her Public

Stephanie and Luke Schmidt. Photo courtesy of Blaine Whipple.

Relations Internship at St. Luke's Hospital in Fargo, Cass Co., North Dakota and worked in the marketing department for a custom cabinet manufacturer in Plato during the summer. Upon graduation she became the Public Relations Coordinator for the Southeastern Minnesota Private Industry Council, part of the Minnesota Department of Economic Security, in Rochester. In December 2000 she was hired as the Marketing and

Molly and Stephanie, 14 August 2004. Photo courtesy of Michael J. Drotzman

Communications Director for the Rochester Area Economic Development, Inc. where she is currently employed. (2005)

Molly Jane **Jasperson** and Kurt Roger **Schmidt** had the following children born in Rochester:

    13   i.   Stephanie Lynn[4] **Schmidt**[21] 8 March 1996.

    14   ii.   Luke Anthony **Schmidt**[22] 25 April 1998. Seven pounds 11 ounces, 18 1/4 inches long. Born at 3:21 p.m.

JASPERSON FAMILY ENDNOTES

1. Blaine Whipple, comp., *Scott, A Name Worth Looking Into, a History-Genealogy of the Scott Family of Quebec Province, Canada and Minnesota and allied lines*. The "Tanguay Dictionary" was the main source for the French Canadian information. Personal letters from the children of Ben and Nellie (Dolan) were the main sources of information for those lines. Copies available at the Library of Congress, Minnesota Historical Society, and North Dakota Historical Society. The work has been updated by hand since publication. Sources of the updates are letters from various individuals involved who provided birth, marriage, death, and other pertinent information. (Portland, Oreg: Self published, 1981), 48 (Hereafter *Scott Genealogy*).
2. E-mail dated 8 Sept. 2004 from Molly (Jasperson) Schmidt (mollyjschmidt@qwest.net) informing the author that her Grandmother Evelyn (Helgmo) Jasperson had died the evening of 6 Sept. 2004 at the Tracy (Minnesota) Nursing home. Her funeral was Friday 10 September.
3. *Scott Genealogy* 48.
4. Ibid.; and Nancy Jane Whipple, Birth Certificate State File No. 12502, 3 February 1932, North Dakota Department of Health, Bismarck, N. Dak.
5. McLeod County Chronicle, Glencoe, Minn., 6 Jan. 1988.
6. and 7. Terry Lynn (Jasperson) Ebert to Blaine Whipple. Letter dated 26 April 1989 at 619 W. Main, Luverne, Minn. 56165. In possession of Whipple (2005.) She is a niece of the author. (Hereafter Ebert *Letter*.)
8. *Argus Leader*, Sioux Falls, S. Dak. 16 June 2002.
9. through 11. Ebert *Letter*.
12. *Scott Genealogy*, 48.
13. *McLeod County Chronicle*, Glencoe, Minn., 6 Jan. 1988 p. 3, col. 1-3; includes her picture using her walker.
14. and 15. *Scott Genealogy* 48.
16. and 17. David Blaine Jasperson to Blaine Whipple. Letter dated 30 May 2004 at 445 17th St. S.W., Rochester, Minn. 55902. In possession of Whipple (2005). (Hereafter Jasperson to Whipple, *Letter, 30 May 2004*). He is a newphew of the author.
18. *Scott Genealogy*, 49.
19. through 22. Molly Jane (Jasperson) Schmidt to Blaine Whipple. E-mail dated 24 July 2000 and 23 July 2005 at mollyschmidt@qw; (mail address 708 Bonner Ct., S.E., Stewardville, Minn. 55976). In possession of Whipple (2005). She is a niece of the author.

APPENDIX G-9

MACE R. MCPHERSON TO MELISSA ANN MCPHERSON 1959-

(McPherson lineage of Billie June and Melissa Ann McPherson, Generation 13, No. 6212, Mary Ann Whipple, wife of Billie Nathaniel McPherson.)

FIRST GENERATION

1. **Mace R.**[1] **McPherson** birth date unknown, married **Icie Bell**.[1]

Mace R. **McPherson** and Icie **Bell** had the following child:
+   2   i.   Rev. Frank[2] **McPherson**.

SECOND GENERATION

2. **Rev. Frank**[2] **McPherson** (Mace R.[1])[2] was born in Ireland and married **Elizabeth (__)** bef 1859. She was born in Ireland.

Rev. Frank **McPherson** and Elizabeth (__) had the following child:
+   3   i.   Rease Alvin[3] **McPherson** born 4 March 1859.

THIRD GENERATION

3. **Rease Alvin**[3] **McPherson** (Rev. Frank[2], Mace R.[1])[3] was born in Idaho 4 March 1859 and died 23 September 1917 in Nawata, (town apparently no longer exists) Oklahoma at 58 years of age. He married **Maggie Baker** bef 25 September 1907.[4]

Rease Alvin **McPherson** and Maggie **Baker** had the following children:
+   4   i.   Nathaniel Leroy[4] **McPherson** born 25 September 1907.
     5   ii.   Walter **McPherson** born in 1913.[5]

FOURTH GENERATION

4. **Nathaniel Leroy**[4] **McPherson** (Rease Alvin[3], Rev. Frank[2], Mace R.[1])[6] was born in Springfield, Greene Co., Missouri 25 September 1907 and died

21 April 1983 in Vista, San Diego Co., California at, 75 years of age. He was buried 27 April 1983 in Dennard, Van Buren Co., Arkansas. He married **Thelma Viola Thornsberry** in Marshall, Searcy Co., Arkansas 13 May 1928.[7] Thelma, daughter of William Tilton **Thornsberry** and Annie Vinetty **Crow**, was born in Leslie, Searcy Co., Arkansas 24 March 1912 and died 25 March 2005 at Concord, Middlesex Co., Massachusetts, at 93 years of age.

Nathaniel Leroy **McPherson** and Thelma Viola **Thornsberry** had the following children:

	6	i.	Nathaniel Leroy[5] **McPherson** Jr. born in Leslie 14 October 1929 and died there in February 1931, at 1 year of age.[8]
+	7	ii.	Billie Nathaniel **McPherson** born 2 February 1932.
+	8	iii.	Robert Waymond **McPherson** born 17 July 1934.
+	9	iv.	Betty Jo **McPherson** born 17 October 1937.
+	10	v.	Jerry Dewanne **McPherson** born 17 March 1942.
+	11	vi.	Charles Edward **McPherson** born 12 March 1944.

FIFTH GENERATION

7. **Billie Nathaniel**[5] **McPherson** (Nathaniel Leroy[4], Rease Alvin[3], Rev. Frank[2], Mace R.[1])[9] was born in Waltonville, Jefferson Co., Illinois 2 February 1932 and married **Mary Ann Whipple** in Yankton, Yankton Co., South Dakota 21 August 1955. They were married in the first Methodist Church built when Yankton was a part of Dakota Territory.[10] Mary, daughter of Lucien Blaine **Whipple** and Pearl Julia **Scott**, was born in Bismarck, Burleigh Co., North Dakota 8 December 1937.[11]

Mary Ann and Bill McPherson on the Greek Island of Andros, July 2005. Photo courtesy of Mary Ann McPherson

Billie Nathaniel **McPherson** and Mary Ann **Whipple** had the following children:

+	12	i.	Billie June[6] **McPherson** 16 June 1956.
+	13	ii.	Melissa Ann **McPherson** 10 August 1959.

{ G 1835 }

8. **Robert Waymond**[5] **McPherson** (Nathaniel Leroy[4], Rease Alvin[3], Rev. Frank[2], Mace R.[1])[12] was born in Smallette, Douglas Co., Missouri 17 July 1934, died 25 September 1980 in Tempe, Maricopa Co., Arizona at 46 years of age, and was buried in Green Acres Memorial Gardens in Scottsdale, Maricopa Co., Arizona. He married three times. (1) **Beth Smith** in Russellville, Pope Co., Arkansas in 1956. (2) **Thelma Hall**. (3) **Susan Carol Schwartz** in Las Vegas, Clark Co., Nevada 16 May 1972.[13] Susan, daughter of Andrew **Schwartz** and Adeline **Becker**, was born in Melrose Park, Cook Co., Illinois.[14]

Robert Waymond **McPherson** and Beth **Smith** had the following child born in Russellville:
    14   i.   Christopher Brian[6] **McPherson** 30 May 1964.[15]

Robert Waymond **McPherson** and Susan Carol **Schwartz** had the following child in Tempe:
    15   ii.   Charles Andrew **McPherson** 17 July 1974.[16]

9. **Betty Jo**[5] **McPherson** (Nathaniel LeRoy[4], Rease Alvin[3], Rev. Frank[2], Mace R.[1])[17] was born in Leslie, Searcy Co., Arkansas 17 October 1937 and married **James Wayne Hightower** in Yankton, Yankton Co., South Dakota 17 July 1955.[18] James, son of Elmer **Hightower** and Millie **Bayless**, was born in Oakland, Marion Co., Arkansas 17 November 1933.[19]

Betty Jo **McPherson** and James Wayne **Hightower** had the following children:
    16   i.   James Wayne[6] **Hightower** Jr. in Long Beach, Los Angeles Co., California 4 February 1957.[20]
    17   ii.   Jeffery Dean **Hightower** in Orange, Orange Co., California 27 May 1961.[21]
    18   iii.   Tracy Lynn **Hightower** born in Orange 26 April 1963.[22]

10. **Jerry Dewanne**[5] **McPherson** (Nathaniel LeRoy[4], Rease Alvin[3], Rev. Frank[2], Mace R.[1])[23] was born 17 March 1942 and married twice. (1) **Jeanette Marie Lindeman** in California. (2) **Cinnie Mae Zitzow** in Garden Grove, Orange Co., California 16 August 1971.

Jerry Dewanne **McPherson** and Jeanette Marie **Lindeman** had the following children born in Santa Anna, Orange Co., California:
    19   i.   Jerry Dewanne[6] **McPherson**, Jr.,[24] 4 September 1966.
    20   ii.   Elizabeth Ann **McPherson**[25] 13 June 1972.

11. **Charles Edward**[5] **McPherson** (Nathaniel Leroy[4], Rease Alvin[3], Rev. Frank[2], Mace R.[1])[26] was born in Russellville, Pope Co., Arkansas 12 March 1944 and married twice. (1) **Carole Dean Nelson** in Santa Ana, Orange Co., California 2 February 1963. Carole, daughter of Roy Dean **Nelson** and Mary Lee **Stephens**, was born in Pryor, Mayes Co., Oklahoma 25 January 1945. They were divorced in Vista, San Diego Co., California in December 1980. (2) **Susan Fortier** in Las Vegas, Clark Co., Nevada.[27]

Charles Edward **McPherson** and Carole Dean **Nelson** had the following children born in Orange Co., California:

21   i.   Patrick Edward[6] **McPherson** 28 September 1964.[28]
22   ii.   Tiara Louise **McPherson** 19 October 1965.[29]
23   iii.   Daniel Lee **McPherson** 25 May 1967.[30]

SIXTH GENERATION

12. **Billie June**[6] **McPherson** (Billie Nathaniel[5], Nathaniel Leroy[4], Rease Alvin[3], Rev. Frank[2], Mace R.[1])[31] was born in Russellville, Pope Co., Arkansas 16 June 1956 and married **Robert Leon Mauro Jr.** in Westford, Middlesex Co., Massachusetts 28 August 1982.[32] Bobby, son of Robert Leon **Mauro** and Toby K. **Krasiuk**, was born in Concord, Middlesex Co., Massachusetts 9 January 1956.[33]

Jayme-Lee and Gregory Mauro.

Jayme-Lee Mauro. Photos courtesy of Blaine Whipple.

Billie June **McPherson** and Robert Leon **Mauro Jr.** had the following children born in Concord, Mass.:

> 24 i. Jayme-Lee Jenkins[7] **Mauro** 16 April 1983 and weighted 7 lbs., 8 3/4 oz. and was 21" long.[34]
>
> 25 ii. Gregory Robert **Mauro** 19 February 1986 and weighed 8 lbs., 3 oz. and was 22" long.[35]

Greg Mauro, Littleton High School graduation, 2004. Photo courtesy of Blaine Whipple

13. **Melissa Ann**[6] **McPherson** (Billie Nathaniel[5], Nathaniel Leroy[4], Rease Alvin[3], Rev. Frank[2], Mace R.[1])[36] was born in Fayettville, Washington Co., Arkansas 10 August 1959 and married **George Nicholas Giambanis** in St. Nicholas Greek Orthodox Church in Lexington, Middlesex Co., Massachusetts 30 August 1980.[37] George, son of Nicholas John **Giambanis** and Mary **Mastoris**, was born in Piraeus, Greece 17 November 1959.[38] Following graduation from High School Melissa was graduated from a 2-year course at Johnson & Wales Culinary School in Providence, Providence Co., R. I. She worked weekends at various cafes and restaurants and met George, at the school. Their son Nicholas enrolled in the school in the fall of 2002 following graduation from High School. George co-owns and operates a restaurant in Cherry Hill, Camden Co., N.J.[39]

Melissa and George Giambanis. Photo courtesy of Melissa Giambanis.

Melissa Ann **McPherson** and George Nicholas **Giambanis** had the following children born in Marlton, Burlington Co., N.J.:

26   i.   Nicholas Nathaniel[7] **Giambanis** 7 June 1983.[40]

27   ii.   Amy Nichole **Giambanis** 27 February 1985.[41]

Nicholas and Amy Giambanis. Photo courtesy of Mary Ann McPherson.

MCPHERSON FAMILY ENDNOTES

1. through 30 Mary Ann (Whipple) McPherson to Blaine Whipple. Letter dated 26 March 1996 at 87 Goldsmith, Littleton, Mass. 01460. In possession of Whipple (2005.) She is the author's sister.
31. through 35. Billy June (McPherson) Mauro to Blaine Whipple. Letter dated 30 March 1989 at Robinwood Rd., Littleton, Mass. 01460. In possession of Whipple (2005). She is the author's niece.
36. through 41. Melissa Ann (McPherson) Giambanis to Blaine Whipple. Letter dated 11 June 1993 at 141 Autumn Lane, Cherry Hill, N.J. 08003. In possession of Whipple (2005). She is the author's niece.

ROBERT THORNBROUGH-THORNSBERRY TO
MELISSA ANN MCPHERSON 1959-

(Billie June and Melissa Ann McPherson Thornborough (Thornsberry) lineage Generation 12, No. 6212, Mary Ann Whipple, wife of Billie Nathaniel McPherson.

FIRST GENERATION

1. **Robert**[1] **Thornbrough** birth date unknown, married **Sarah Jackson**.[1]

Robert **Thornbrough** and Sarah **Jackson** had the following child:
+   2   i.   Edward[2] **Thornbrough**.

{ G 1839 }

SECOND GENERATION

2. **Edward**[2] **Thornbrough** (Robert[1]) birth date unknown, married **Jean** (__). He was one of three brothers who immigrated to the American colonies from Ireland between 1714 and 1725. That he was in the United States by 1725 is known by the certificate from the Lurgan meeting of Ireland[2] he presented to the Kennett monthly Quaker meeting in Pennsylvania on 16 September 1725.[3]

Edward **Thornbrough** and Jean (__) had the following child:
+   3   i.   Joseph[3] **Thornbrough** born abt 1730.

THIRD GENERATION

3. **Joseph**[3] **Thornbrough** (Edward[2], Robert[1]) was born in Pennsylvania abt 1730, died 25 June 1800 in North Carolina at 69 years of age, and was buried in New Garden, (town no longer exists) North Carolina. He married **Nancy Ann Armfield** in Pennsylvania abt 1755 and they moved to North Carolina shortly thereafter.[4]

Joseph **Thornbrough** and Nancy Ann **Armfield** had the following children born in North Carolina:

     4   i.   Jane[4] **Thornbrough**.[5]
     5   ii.   Edward **Thornbrough**.[6]
+   6   iii.   Joseph **Thornbrough** 29 February 1759.
     7   iv.   Ann **Thornbrough**.[8]
     8   v.   Mary **Thornbrough**.[9]
     9   vi.   Margaret **Thornbrough**.[10]
    10   vii.   Elizabeth **Thornbrough**.[11]
    11   viii.   Isaac **Thornbrough**.[12]

FOURTH GENERATION

6. **Joseph**[4] **Thornbrough** (Joseph[3], Edward[2], Robert[1]) was born in North Carolina 29 February 1759 and died 13 May 1842 in Indiana at 83 years of age. He married **Rachel Brown** in at the Crane Creek monthly meeting in Orange Co., North Carolina 14 February 1782. Rachel, daughter of William **Brown** and Hannah **Moon**, was born in Orange Co. 2 October 1754 and died 14 March 1842 in Rush Co., Indiana at 87 years of age.[13]

{ G 1840 }

Joseph **Thornbrough** and Rachel **Brown** had the following children born in North Carolina:

	12	i.	William[5] **Thornbrough**.[14]
+	13	ii.	John **Thornbrough** 14 March 1784.
	14	iii.	Joseph **Thornbrough** Jr.[15]
	15	iv.	Edward **Thornbrough**.[16]
	16	v.	Joel **Thornbrough**.[17]
	17	vi.	Isaac **Thornbrough**.[18]
	18	vii.	Hannah **Thornbrough**.[19]

FIFTH GENERATION

13. **John**[5] **Thornbrough** (Joseph[4], Joseph[3], Edward[2], Robert[1]) was born in North Carolina 14 March 1784 and died aft April 1850 in Miller Co., Missouri. He married **Christiana Ann Beals**. John changed his name to Thornsberry. For additional information on John, see the article "The Chicken Crows" in Judge Jenkins, *History of Miller County, Missouri*.[20]

John **Thornbrough** and Christiana Ann **Beals** had the following children:

	19	i.	William[6] **Thornsberry**.
	20	i.	Lewis[6] **Thornsberry**.[21]
	21	ii.	Peter **Thornsberry**.[22]
	22	iii.	William Thomas **Thornsberry**.[23]
	23	iv.	Perth **Thornsberry**.[24]
+	24	v.	John **Thornsberry** born in 1821.
	25	viii.	Elizabeth **Thornsberry**.[25]

SIXTH GENERATION

24. **John**[6] **Thornsberry** (John[5] Thornbrough, Joseph[4], Joseph[3], Edward[2], Robert[1]) was born in North Carolina in 1821 and married **Martha Ann Perkins** in Miller Co., Missouri 22 August 1847.[26]

John **Thornsberry** and Martha Ann **Perkins** had the following children:

	26	i.	Miara[7] **Thornsberry**.[27]
	27	ii.	John F. **Thornsberry**.[28]
	28	iii.	Louis **Thornsberry**.[29]
	29	iv.	Sterling P. **Thornsberry**.[30]
+	30	v.	William Benjamin **Thornsberry** born in 1849.[31]

{ G 1841 }

SEVENTH GENERATION

30. **William Benjamin**[7] **Thornsberry** (John[6], John[5] Thornbrough, Joseph[4], Joseph[3], Edward[2], Robert[1]) was born in Missouri in 1849 and married **Millie Caroline Heaton** abt 1875.[32]

William Benjamin **Thornsberry** and Millie Caroline **Heaton** had the following children:

	31	i.	Patima Elizabeth[8] **Thornsberry**.[33] Known as Timy.
	32	ii.	Johnager Benjamin **Thornsberry**.[34] Known as J. B.
+	33	iii.	William Tilton **Thornsberry** 10 September 1876.

EIGHTH GENERATION

33. **William Tilton**[8] **Thornsberry** (William Benjamin[7], John[6], John[5] Thornbrough, Joseph[4], Joseph[3], Edward[2], Robert[1]) was born 10 September 1876 in Marionville, Lawrence Co., Missouri and died 23 June 1958 in Russellville, Pope, Co. Arkansas and was buried in the Dennard Cemetery, Dennard, Van Buren Co., Arkansas. He married twice. (1) **Mandy Presley** in Boone Co., Arkansas 2 August 1901. Mandy was the daughter of William Benjamin **Presley** and Millie Caroline (__). (2) **Annie Vinetty Crow** in Boone County 20 July 1906. Annie, daughter of Ervin Russett **Crow** and Tulula Upton **Powell**, was born 3 June 1890 in Leslie, Searcy Co., Arkansas.[35]

William Tilton **Thornsberry** and Mandy **Presley** had the following child born in St. Joe, Searcy Co., Arkansas:

	34	i.	Troy Thomas[9] **McPherson**, 9 June 1903, died 21 July 1979 in Battle Creek, Calhoun Co., Michigan, and was buried in Dennard. He married Frances Modrelle **Richie** 16 October 1926 in Searcy Co.[36]

William Tilton **Thornsberry** and Annie V. **Crow** had the following children born in Leslie.:

	35	ii.	Roy Clifford **Thornsberry** 5 December 1907 and died 1 June 1963 at Garden Grove, Orange Co., California He married Pauline **Bratton** 30 August 1930 in Leslie.[37]
+	36	iii.	Joe Dickens **Thornsberry** 28 May 1909.
+	37	iv.	Thelma Viola **Thornsberry** 24 March 1912.
	38	v.	Opal Faye **Thornsberry** 4 September 1914 and married Eugene J. **Fincke** 31 August 1940 in San Antonio, Bexar Co., Texas.[38]

{ G 1842 }

39 vi. Elmo Irvin **Thornsberry** 14 June 1917; married 22 April 1941 at Dardanelle, Arkansas.[39]

40 vii. Lula Juanita **Thornsberry** 15 September 1919 and married M. Leonard **Jennings** 15 June 1941 in Marshall, Searcy Co., Arkansas.[40]

41 viii. Wanda Lee **Thornsberry** 4 September 1924 and married Ernest **Dietzmann** 26 August 1943 in San Antonio.[41]

NINTH GENERATION

36. **Joe Dickens**[9] **Thornsberry** (William Tilton[8], William Benjamin[7], John[6], John[5] Thornbrough, Joseph[4], Joseph[3], Edward[2], Robert[1]) was born in Leslie, Searcy Co., Arkansas 28 May 1909 and married twice. (1) **Velma Marie Horton** in Leslie 4 March 1931. (2) **Connie Chadwick** in Oxley, (author unable to find this town in current records) Oklahoma.[42]

Joe Dickens **Thornsberry** and Velma Marie **Horton** had the following child:
42. Arma Jean[10] **Thornsberry** born 22 June 1932 and married (__) **LeBeau**.[43]

Joe Dickens **Thornsberry** and Connie **Chadwick** had the following children:
43 i. Richard Lee **Thornsberry**.[44]
44 ii. Frances Louise **Thornsberry**.[45]
45 iii. Marsha Jo **Thornsberry**.[46]
46 iv. Ella **Thornsberry**.[47]
47 v. Marlene Gaye **Thornsberry**.[48]

37. **Thelma Viola**[9] **Thornsberry** (William Tilton[8], William Benjamin[7], John[6], John[5] Thornbrough, Joseph[4], Joseph[3], Edward[2], Robert[1]) was born 24 March 1912 in Leslie, Searcy Co., Arkanas and died 25 March 2005 at Concord, Middlesex Co., Massachusetts, at 93 years of age. She married **Nathaniel Leroy McPherson** in Marshall, Searcy Co., Arkansas 13 May 1928.[49] Nathaniel, son of Rease Alvin **McPherson** and Maggie **Baker**, was born 25 September 1907 in Springfield, Greene Co., Missouri and died 21 April 1983 in Vista, San Diego Co., Calif., at 75 years of age. He was buried in Dennard, Van Buren Co., Arkansas.[50]

Thelma Viola **Thornsberry** and Nathaniel Leroy **McPherson** had the following children:
48 i. Nathaniel Leroy[10] **McPherson** Jr. born in Leslie 14 October 1929 and died there in February 1931, at 1 year of age.[51]

+	49	ii.	Billie Nathaniel **McPherson** born 2 February 1932.
+	50	iii.	Robert Waymond **McPherson** born 17 July 1934.
+	51	iv.	Betty Jo **McPherson** born 17 October 1937.
+	52	v.	Jerry Dewanne **McPherson** born 17 March 1942.
+	53	vi.	Charles Edward **McPherson** born 12 March 1944.

TENTH GENERATION

49. **Billie Nathaniel**[10] **McPherson** (Thelma Viola[9] Thornsberry, William Tilton[8], William Benjamin[7], John[6], John[5] Thornbrough, Joseph[4], Joseph[3], Edward[2], Robert[1]) see Fifth Generation, No 7 p. 1807.

50. **Robert Waymond**[10] **McPherson** (Thelma Viola[9] Thornsberry, William Tilton[8], William Benjamin[7], John[6], John[5] Thornbrough, Joseph[4], Joseph[3], Edward[2], Robert[1]) see Fifth Generation No. 8 p. 1807-1808.

51. **Betty Jo**[10] **McPherson** (Thelma Viola[9] Thornsberry, William Tilton[8], William Benjamin[7], John[6], John[5] Thornbrough, Joseph[4], Joseph[3], Edward[2], Robert[1]) see Fifth Generation No. 9 p. 1808.

52. **Jerry Dewanne**[10] **McPherson** (Thelma Viola[9] Thornsberry, William Tilton[8], William Benjamin[7], John[6], John[5] Thornbrough, Joseph[4], Joseph[3], Edward[2], Robert[1]) see Fifth Generation No. 10 p. 1808.

53. **Charles Edward**[10] **McPherson** (Thelma Viola[9] Thornsberry, William Tilton[8], William Benjamin[7], John[6], John[5] Thornbrough, Joseph[4], Joseph[3], Edward[2], Robert[1]) see Fifth Generation No. 11 p. 1808-1809.

THORNBERRY FAMILY ENDNOTES

1. Mary Ann (Whipple) McPherson to Blaine Whipple. Letter dated 26 March 1966 at 87 Goldsmith, Littleton, Mass. 01460. In possession of Whipple (2005). Mary Ann is the author's sister. (Hereafter McPherson Letter.)
2. Lurgen Ancestry is a site developed by genealogy enthusiasts in Lurgan, Northern Ireland. www.lurganancestry.net/.
3 through 51. McPherson Letter.

ALFONSO MAURO TO GREGORY ROBERT MAURO 1986-

(Mauro lineage of Jamye Lee and Gregory Robert Mauro Generation 13, No. 7404, Billie June McPherson, wife of Robert Leon Mauro, Jr.)

FIRST GENERATION

1. **Alfonso**[1] **Mauro** birth date unknown and wife unnamed had the following child:[1]
+   2   i.   Francesco[2] **Mauro** born 1 June 1885.

SECOND GENERATION

2. **Francesco**[2] **Mauro** (Alfonso[1]) was born in Naples, Italy 1 June 1885 and died 14 February 1961 in South Acton, Middlesex Co., Massachusetts at 75 years of age. He married **Angela Maria Palmo** bef 1929.[2] Angela, daughter of Ralph **Palmo**, was born in Naples 10 August 1888 and died 20 March 1967 in South Acton at 78 years of age.[3]

Francesco **Mauro** and Angela Maria **Palmo** had the following child:
+   3   i.   Robert Leon[3] **Mauro** born 11 April 1929.

THIRD GENERATION

3. **Robert Leon**[3] **Mauro** (Francesco[2], Alfonso[1]) was born 11 April 1929 and married **Toby K. Krasiuk** in Massachusetts 5 July 1953. They were divorced 20 January 1976.[4] Toby, daughter of Nickolas **Krasiuk** and Katherine **Kuruta**, was born in Newmarket, Rockingham Co., New Hampshire 31 January 1931.[5] Nickolas was the son of Amufry **Krasiuk** and Helen **Sukorski**.

Robert Leon **Mauro** and Toby K. **Krasiuk** had the following children:
+   4   i.   Robert Leon[4] **Mauro** Jr. born 9 January 1956
     5   ii.   Wayne Neal **Mauro** born in Concord, Middlesex Co., Massachusetts 6 May 1957 and died 27 April 1993 in Boston, Suffolk Co., Massachusetts, at 35 years of age.[6]
     6   iii.   Susan Katherine **Mauro** born in Concord 15 January 1959.[7]

{ G 1845 }

7   iv. David Frank **Mauro** born in Ayer, Worcester Co., Massachusetts 25 September 1967 and married Marilyn **McClatchey** 1 May 1993.[8]

FOURTH GENERATION

4. **Robert Leon**[4] **Mauro Jr.** (Robert Leon[3], Francesco[2], Alfonso[1]) was born in Concord, Middlesex Co., Massachusetts 9 January 1956 and married **Billie June McPherson** in Westford, Middlesex Co., Massachusetts 28 August 1982.[9] Billie, daughter of Billie Nathaniel **McPherson** and Mary Ann **Whipple**, was born in Russellville, Pope Co., Arkansas 16 June 1956.[10]

Robert Leon **Mauro** Jr. and Billie June **McPherson** had the following children born in Concord:

8   i. Jayme-Lee Jenkins[5] **Mauro** 16 April 1983 and weighted 7 lbs, 8 3/4 oz and was 21" long.[11]

9   ii. Gregory Robert **Mauro** 19 February 1986 and weighed 8 lbs, 3 oz and was 22" long.[12]

MAURO FAMILY ENDNOTES

1. through 12. Billie June (McPherson) Mauro to Blaine Whipple. Letter dated 30 March 1989 at Robinwood Rd., Littleton, Mass. 01460. In possession of Whipple (2005.) She is the author's niece.

DIMITRIOS GIAMBANIS TO AMY NICHOLE GIAMBANIS 1985-

(Giambanis lineage of Nicholas Nathaniel and Amy Nichole Giambanis Generation 13, No. 7405, Melissa Ann McPherson, wife of George Nicholas Giambanis.)

FIRST GENERATION

1. **Dimitrios**[1] **Giambanis** was born in Greece and married **Anna Lontorfos** in Greece.[1]

{ G 1846 }

Dimitrios **Giambanis** and Anna **Lontorfos** had the following child:
+   2   i.   John Dimitrios **Giambanis** was born 10 September 1895.

SECOND GENERATION

2. **John Dimitrios**[2] **Giambanis** (Dimitrios[1]) was born in Rogo Andros, Greece 10 September 1895 and died 29 April 1967 in Athens, Greece at 71 years of age. He married **Elenh Loussides** in Greece 4 February 1930.[2] Elenh, daughter of Dimitrios **Loussides** and Ellisavet **Apostolou**, was born in Bouni Andros, Greece 15 April 1908.[3]

John Dimitrios **Giambanis** and Elenh **Loussides** had the following child:
+   3   i.   Nicholas John **Giambanis** born 26 August 1934.

THIRD GENERATION

3. **Nicholas John**[3] **Giambanis** (John Dimitrios[2], Dimitrios[1]) was born in Rogo Andros, Greece 26 August 1934 and married **Mary Mastoris** in Greece 15 December 1958.[4] Mary, daughter of George James **Mastoris** and Marigoula **Pantajis**, was born in Athens, Greece 2 April 1937.[5]

Nicholas John **Giambanis** and Mary **Mastoris** had the following child:
+   4   i.   George Nicholas **Giambanis** born 17 November 1959.

FOURTH GENERATION

4. **George Nicholas**[4] **Giambanis** (Nicholas John[3], John Dimitrios[2], Dimitrios[1]) see Sixth Generation No. 13 p. 1809-1810.

GIAMBANIS FAMILY ENDNOTES

1.   through 5. Melissa Ann (McPherson) Giambanis to Blaine Whipple. Letter dated 11 June 1993 at 1410 Autumn Lane, Cherry Hill, NJ 08003. In possession of Whipple (2005). She is the author's niece.

DIMITRIOS MASTORIS, 1850 TO AMY NICHOLE GIAMBANIS 1985-

(Mastoris lineage of Nicholas Nathaniel and Amy Nichole Giambanis Generation 13, No. 7405, Melissa Ann McPherson, wife of George Nicholas Giambanis.)

FIRST GENERATION

1. **Dimitrios**[1] **Mastoris** was born in Hones Andros, Greece in 1850 and died in 1929 at 79 years of age. He married **Maroulio Glynos** in 1882.[1] Maroulio was born in Gianiseo Andros, Greece in 1860 and died in May 1942 in Chicago, Cook Co., Illinois at 81 years of age.[2]

Dimitrios **Mastoris** and Maroulio **Glynos** had the following child:
+ 2 i. George James[2] **Mastoris** born 19 July 1886.

SECOND GENERATION

2. **George James**[2] **Mastoris** (Dimitrios[1]) was born in Hones Andros, Greece 19 July 1886 and died 29 October 1972 in Bellmawr, Camden Co., New Jersey at 86 years of age. He married **Marigoula Pantajis** in Greece 26 April 1933.[3] Marigoula, daughter of Dimitrious **Pantazis** and Irene **Tatieris**, was born in Ormos Korthion, Greece 9 September 1900.[4]

George James **Mastoris** and Marigoula **Pantajis** had the following child:
+ 3 i. Mary[3] **Mastoris** born 2 April 1937.

THIRD GENERATION

3. **Mary**[3] **Mastoris** (George James[2], Dimitrios[1]) was born in Athens, Greece 2 April 1937 and married **Nicholas John Giambanis** in Greece 15 December 1958.[5] Nicholas, son of John Dimitrios **Giambanis** and Elenh **Loussides**, was born in Rogo Andros, Greece 26 August 1934.[6]

Mary **Mastoris** and Nicholas John **Giambanis** had the following child:
+ 4 i. George Nicholas[4] **Giambanis** born 17 November 1959.

FOURTH GENERATION

4. **George Nicholas**[4] **Giambanis** (Mary[3] Mastoris, George James[2], Dimitrios[1]) was born in Piraeus, Greece 17 November 1959 and married **Melissa Ann McPherson** at St. Nicholas Greek Orthodox Church in Lexington, Middlesex Co., Massachusetts 30 August 1980.[7] Melissa, daughter of Billie Nathaniel **McPherson** and Mary Ann **Whipple**, was born in Fayettville, Washington Co., Arkansas 10 August 1959.[8]

George Nicholas **Giambanis** and Melissa Ann **McPherson** had the following children born in Marlton, Burlington Co., New Jersey:

 5 i. Nicholas Nathaniel[5] **Giambanis** 7 June 1983.[9]
 6 ii. Amy Nichole **Giambanis** 27 February 1985.[10]

MASTORIS FAMILY ENDNOTES

1. through 10. Melissa Ann (McPherson) Giambanis to Blaine Whipple. Letter dated 11 June 1993 at 1410 Autumn Lane, Cherry Hill, N. J. 08003. In possession of Whipple (2005).

APPENDIX G-10

WHIPPLE VITAL RECORDS[1]

IPSWICH BIRTHS

WHIPLE
Johanna, d. Mathew, Sr. and Johanna, July 22, 1692.
Martha, d. John, 3rd, bp. April 21, 1771.

WHIPPLE
Aaron, s. John, 3rd, bp. Sept. 15, 1782.
Amos, s. Will[ia]m, bp. Dec. 20, 1741.
Anna, d. John, Jr., Oct. 29, 1675.
Anna, d. Joseph and Sarah, July 29, 1695.
Anna, d. John, 6th, bp. Oct. 10, 1779.
Appleton, s. Mathew, Sr. and Johanna, Oct. 19, 1693.
Archelaus, s. Joseph and Mary, March 26, 1692.
Benja[min], s. Francis, bp. July 2, 1727.
Benja[min], s. Benja[min], bp. July 18, 1784.
Bethiah, d. Matthew and Bethiah, April 29, 1705.
Bethiah, d. Sam[ue]ll, bp. Feb. 12, 1726-7.
Betsy, d. wid. Anna, bp. Sept. 28, 1777.
Betsy, d. Thomas, Jr., bp. Nov. 23, 1788.
Bridget, d. John, Jr., bp. April 21, 1782.
Catherine, d. William, bp. Oct. 30, 1785.
Charles, s. Benja[min], bp. March 19, 1786.
Ciprian, s. Jo: Jan. 17, 1671.
Cyprian, s. Cyprian and Dorothery, 10: 4 m: 1697.
Dan[ie]ll, s. James, bp. Aug. 2, 1713.

Ebenezer, s. John and Mary, bp. Sept. 26, 1713.
Edward, s. John, 3rd, bp. Nov. 15, 1771.
Edward, s. John, 3rd, bp. June 25, 1780.
Edwards, s. Jonathan, bp. June __, 1722.
Elizabeth, d. Jonathan, bp. April 16, 1786.
Elizabeth, d. John, 3rd, 12: 10 m: 1661.
Elizabeth, d. John and Katherine, March 1, 1649.
Elizabeth, d. Joseph and Mary, Dec. 9, 1696.
Elizabeth, d. Joseph, bp. May 23, 1736.
Elizabeth, d. Capt. John, March __, 1740.
Esther, d. Joseph, bp. Sept. 23, 1733.
Eunice, d. John, 5th, bp. Jan. 26, 1783.
Francis, s. Jona[than] and Frances, bp. Nov. 4, 1705.
George Albert, s. Hervey and Martha B., bp. July 5, 1846.
Hannah, d. John, 3rd, and Hannah, June 30, 1692.
Hannah, July 22, 1692.
Hannah, d. John, Nov. 30, 1738.
Hannah, d. Nath[anie]ll and Mary, April 17, 1747.
Hannah, d. Jonathan, bp. Oct. 19, 1788.
Hannah Dean, d. Thomas, Jr. bp. Oct. 28, 1792.
Irene, d. John, 4th, bp. Nov. 27, 1785.
Jacob, s. James and Mary, May 26, 1707.
James, s. James and Mary, April 12, 1705.

{ G 1850 }

Jemima, d. John, 3rd [4th] and Dorothy, Aug. 23, 1740.
Jerusha, d. John, 4th, bp. May 30, 1773.
John, s. John, Jr., July 15, 1657.
John, s. John, 3rd, March 30, 1660.
John, s. Mathew, Sr. and Johanna, July 2, 1689.
John, March 27, 1690.
John, s. John, Jr. and Hannah, Dec. 16, 1695.
John, s. John (s. Maj. Matthew) and Hannah, June 25, 1717.
John, s. John 4th [6th] bp. May 5, 1776.
John, s. W[illai]m, bp. June 13, 1779.
John, s. Benja[min] bp. Jan. 25, 1789.
Jona[than], s. John, 3rd, bp. Nov. 23, 1724.
Joseph, s. Cornet John, March 6, 1664.
Joseph, s. John, 3rd, Sept. 17, 1665.
Joseph, s. Joseph, Nov. 1, 1665.
Joseph, s. John, Jr., June 8, 1666.
Joseph, s. Cornet John, 8: 4 m : 1666.
Joseph, s. Joseph, Oct. 31, 1666.
Joseph, s. Mathew and Martha, July 31, 1701.
Joseph, s. Matthew and Dorcas, Aug. 2, 1707.
Joseph, s. Joseph of the Hamlet, Aug. 3, 1738.
Joseph, s. John 4th, bp. Nov. 6, 1791.
Joseph, s. John, 4th, bp. Nov. 6, 1791.
Kathrine, d. John and Kathrine, Aug 25, 1685.
Lucinda, d. Jonathan, bp. Sept. 18, 1791.
Lucy, d. Francis, bp. Jan. 5, 1728-9.
Lucy, d. Hervey and Martha B., bp. July 5, 1846.
Margery, d. Joseph, Aug. 28, 1668.
Martha, d. John, Jr., April 1, 1682.
Martha, d. Matthew and Martha, Jan. 7, 1704.
Martha, d. Lt. John, bp. Nov. 30, 1735.
Martha, d. Capt. John, bp. May 20, 1739.
Martha, d. John, 3rd, bp. July 11, 1742.
Martha, d. Jonathan, bp. Aug. 24, 1783.
Mary, d. John, 3rd, May 11, 1667.
Mary, d. Joseph, Dec. 25, 1674.
Mary, d. Joseph and Mary, Feb. 15, 1698-9.
Mary, d. James, bp. Jan. 20, 1616-17.
Mary, d. Lt. John and Martha, bp. Feb. 13, 1726 [1736?].
Mary, d. Samuel, Oct. ___ 1728.
Mary, d. John, Jr., Feb. 12, 1736.
Mary, d. Nath[anie]ll and Mary, Oct. 29, 1745.
Mathew, s. Mathew, Dec. 20, 1658.
Mathew, s. John, May 29, 1664.
Mathew, s. Joseph, Nov. 25, 1672.
Mathew, s. Mathew and Jemima, Oct. 20, 1685.
Matthew, s. William, June ___, 1740.
Mercy, d. John and Katherine, Feb. 7, 1697-8.
Nabby Dane, d. Thomas Jr., bp. Oct. 17, 1790.
Nathan, s. Matthew and Dorcas, Feb. 7, 1705.
Nathaniel, s. Cornet Matthew and Martha, bp. 2: 7 m: 1711.
Nathaniel, s. John (s. Maj. Matthew) and Hannah, Oct. 7, 1721.
Nathaniel, s. Jonathan, bp. April 18, 1779.
Nathan[ie]ll, s. (twin to Sarah) John and Sarah, bp. March 27, 1715.
Oliver, s. William, bp. Oct. 26, 1788.
Parker, s. Samuel, bp. July 1, 1792.
Paul, s. John, bp. Jan. 20, 1722-3.
Paul, s. John, 4th, bp. July 18, 1773.
Polly, d. John, 3rd, bp. Sept. 7, 1777.
Priscilla, d. Joseph, joiner, and Mary, March 6, 1700.
Robert, s. Robert, bp. Dec. ___, 1724.
Robert, s. Joseph, March ___, 1740.

Robert, s. Joseph of the Hamlet, June 20, 1741.
Ruth, d. of Joseph and Sarah, Oct. 27, 1692.
Sally, d. Thomas, bp. Dec. 2, 1781.
Sally, d. John, 4th, bp. May 4, 1788.
Sally, d. William, bp. May 15, 1791.
Salome, d. John, 4th, bp. April 12, 1778.
Salomia, d. John, 4th, bp. June 25, 1780.
Samuel, s. Zipporan and Dorothy, Sept. 13, 1702.
Samuel, s. Sam[ue]ll, bp. Dec. 18, 1730.
Samuel, s. Benja[min], bp. Aug. 11, 1782.
Sarah, d. Joseph, March 29, 1670.
Sarah, d. Cornett John, Sept. 2, 1671.
Sarah, d. John and Kathrine, Dec. 16, 1692.
Sarah, d. Joseph and Mary, May 14, 1693.
Sarah, d. (twin to Nathaniel) John and Sarah, bp. March 27, 1715.
Sarah, d. John, 6th, bp. May 21, 1721.
Sarah, d. James, Jr., bp. Jan. 11, 1729-30.
Sarah, d. Joseph of the Hamlet, June 1, 1746.
Sarah, d. Benja[min], bp. Sept. 9, 1792.
Sarah, d. Hervey and Martha B., July 5, 1846.
Solomon Smith, s. Matthew, bp. April 5, 1789.
Stephen, s. John (s. M[atthe]w), bp. Nov. 19, 1727.
Stephen, s. John, 4th, May 30, 1773.
Stephen, s. Jonathan, bp. March 11, 1781.
Susa Clark, d. John, 3rd, bp. March 20, 1774.
Susanna, d. Joseph and Mary, Feb. 22, 1698-9.
Susannah, d. John, Sr. and Katherine, April 3, 1696
Thomas, s. Matthew and Bethia, Oct. 1, 1701.
Tho[ma]s, s. Francis, bp. 24: 8 br: 1731.
Thomas, s. William, Aug.)), 1738.
William, s. Matthew, Sr. and Johannah, Feb. 28, 1695-6.
William, s. John (s. Maj. Matthew) and Hannah, Dec. 15, 1727.
William, s. William, bp. May 25, 1777.
William, s. wid. Anna, bp. Sept. 28, 1777.
William, s. Matthew, bp. Aug. 5, 1787.
Zebulon, s. Samuel and Bethiah, bp. Sept. 17, 1732.
_____, s. Daniel, and Adeline, b. Hamilton, Oct. 26, 1848.

IPSWICH MARRIAGES

WHIPPLE

Amos and [Mrs. int.] Mary Bowles, both of the Hamlet, May 8, 1770.
Anna, Mrs., and Adam Brown, int. May 9, 1770.
Anna, Mrs. and Nathan Poland, int. Jan. 17, 1767.
Anna, and Edmund Patch, May 5, 1778.
Benja[min], and Sarah Tutle, Dec. 14, 1780.
Bethiah, (Mrs.. int.] and Oliver Appleton, Jr., Jan. 9, 1728.
Bethiah, Mrs. and Jonathan Lampson, Jr., int. Feb. 19, 1768.
Cyprian, s. Lt. John, and Dorothy Symonds, d. William, Dec. 19, 1695.
Dorothy, and Mark Perkins, int. June 4, 1721.
Elizabeth, and Thomas Puttnam [of Salem int.], April 10, 1705.
Eliza[beth], and Nath[anei]l Emerson, int. Nov. 19, 1715.

Elizabeth, and Joseph Gilbert, int. Sept. 17, 1739.
Elizabeth, "Ms." and Solomon Smith, Jr., int. Dec. 11, 1762.
Francis and Abigail Lamson, May 11, 1727.
Hannah, and John Whipple, June 7, 1714.
Hannah, Mrs. and Antipas Dodge, int. May 24, 1755.
Hannah, Mrs. and Nathan Patch, int. Dec. 14, 1756.
Hannah, Mrs. and David Harradine, Jr of Gloucester, int. Jan. 16, 1768.
Hannah, and Israel Dodge of Wenham, Feb. 22, 1781.
Hannah, and Matthew Lamson, Aug. 2, 1782.
Hervey, of Hamilton, and Martha P. Brown, Jan. 1, 1835.
James, and Mary Fuller of Salem, at Salem, Jan. 12, 1704.
James [Jr. int.] and Sarah Adams, Jan. 9, 1728-9.
Jemima, Mrs. and Sam[ue]l Adams, int. Dec. 6, 1766.
Jemima, and Nath[anie]l Abot of Beverly, Dec. 18, 1768.
John, and Elizabeth Woodman, May 5, 1659.
John, Capt., and Mrs. Elizabeth Paine, June 28, 1680.
John and Kathrin Layton, June 16, 1681.
John [Jr., int.], and [wid. int.] Joanna Pottar, April 14, 1703.
John, and Mary Fairfeild of Wenam, int. 10: 12 m: 1710.
John, and Hannah Whipple, June 7, 1714.
John [5th. int.], and Elizabeth Annable, April __ 1719.
John, 3rd [4th int.], and Dorothy Moulton, Aug. 18, 1737.
John, 4th, and Mrs. Martha Cogswell, int. Dec. 6, 1766.
John, 3rd, Capt., and Mrs. Sarah Adams, int. April 23, 1767.
John, 5th, and "Ms." Deliverance Dodge, int. May 28, 1768.
John, 7th, and Anna Lamson, June 27, 1774.
John, 4th, and Jane Jewett of Rowley, int. Dec. 20, 1781.
Jonath[an], and Frances Edwards, July 14, 1702.
Jonathan, and Martha Whipple, int. Nov. 15, 1777.
Joseph, and Mary Symonds, Dec. 10, 1697.
Joseph, and Esther Batchelder of Wenham, at Wenham, Jan. 5, 1731.
Joseph, and Ruth Treadwell, int. Dec. 31, 1762.
Lucy, and Benja[min] Peck, March 2, 1779.
Lucy A., and John Tuttle, Jr., both of Hamilton, June 12, 1823.
Martha, Mrs. and Richard Brown, Jr. of Newbury, at Newbury, April 22, 1703.
Martha, Mrs. and Edwards Lampson, int. Nov. 23, 1759.
Martha, and Jonathan Whipple, int. Nov. 15, 1777.
Martha, and John Safford, Dec. 30, 1784.
Mary, and Richard Jacob, Jan. 15, 1673.
Mary, and Increase How, int. April 23, 1709.
Mary, Mrs., and Maj. Symond Epes, int. March 26, 1715.
Mary, Mrs., and Benja[min] Crocker, int. 12: 10 m: 1719.
Mary, and John Jones, Aug. 20, 1734.
Mary Ann, of Hamilton, and John Cleveland Kimball, Dec. 28, 1823.
Matthew, and Mrs. Martha Thing, June 11, 1697.
Matthew, and Martha Cogswell, int. Sept. 23, 1710.

{ G 1853 }

Matthew, and Elisabeth Smith, Oct. 2, 1785.
Mercy, and Stephen Caldwell, Jr., Jan. 4, 1787.
Minah, and John Annable, Jan. 18, 1787.
Nath[anie]ll, and Mary Appleton, int. Nov. 10,. 1744.
Paul, and Susanna Woodbury, int. Oct. 29, 1743.
Samuel, and Bethiah Patch, June 20, 1726
Samuel, of Danvers, and Elisabeth Burnam, Jan. 19, 1773.
Sam[ue]l, [Ens. int], and Hannah Dodge, July 12, 1789.
Sarah, and Joseph Goodhue, July 13, 1661.
Sarah, Mrs. and Francis Wainwright, March 12, [1690?]
Sarah, wid., and Walter Fairfeild, int. 14: 2 m: 1711.
Sarah, Mrs. and Robert Anable, Jr., int. Dec. 27, 1766.
Sarah, and Ezeliel Adams, Jr., Jan. 14, 1773.
Sarah, [Mrs. int.], and Joseph Poland [Jr., int.], Dec. 15, 1774
Stephen, and Anne Woodbury, int. April 4, 1747.
Susanna, and John Laine of Billerica, at Salem, 20: 10 m: 1683.
Susanna, Mrs., and John Rogers, int. Sept. 6, 1718.
Susanna, and Joseph Burnam, int. Aug. 2, 1760.
Susanna, and Natha[nie]l Poland, Jr., Oct. 31, 1765.
Thomas, and Mrs. Mary Furnace, int. Nov. 23, 1759.
Thomas, Jr., and Molly Elenwood, Nov. 15, 1787.
William, and Mary Adams, April 11, 1738.
William, 3rd, and Katherine Appleton, May 29, 1776.
William, 3rd, and Sarah Lovering, April 16, 1782.

IPSWICH DEATHS

WHIPLE
Marthy, Capt., Jan. 8, 1743., a. 70 y.

WHIPPLE
Aron, s. John, 3rd, ricket, July 16, 1783, a. 10 m.
Cyprian, s. Cyprian and Dorothy, Feb. 8, 1698-9.
Dorcas, w. Matthew, Jr., May 11, 1735.
Dorcas, d. wid. Susanna, consumption, Feb. 7, 1773, a. 15 y.
Dorothy, w. Capt. John, 3rd, Sept __, 1766.
Edward, s. John, 3rd, canker, Jan. 8, 1773, a. 1 y.
Elisabeth, d. John and Cathrine, ____, 1688.
Elizabeth, d. John and Kathrine, Jan. 2, 1695.
Elisabeth, pulmonic consumption, April 12, 1783, a. 20 y.
Esther, d. Joseph, bur. Oct. __, 1736.
Hanna, "last of" Aug. 1692.
Hannah, w. John, Jr., Oct. 20, 1701.
Hannah, w. Capt. John, Jan. 24 17[58], in her 66th y.
Jemima, bur. Oct. __, 1737.
Johanna, d. Mathew, Sr. and Johanna, Aug. 31, 1692.
John, Lt., Nov. 22, 1695.
John, Capt. June 11, 1722.
John, Maj., Esq., "he went to bed well at Night & was found dead in the morning," June 12, 1722. [in his 65th y.]
John [3rd], killed by felling a tree in

{ G 1854 }

Cheba Woods," Jan. 19, 1738.
John, Jr., Capt., Jan. 16, 1769.
John, 5th, second s. William and Katharine, Jan. 10, 1797, in his 18th y.
Joseph, s. Cornet John, Aug. __, 1665.
Joseph, s. Joseph, Nov. 12, 1665
Joseph, May 11, 1699.
Joseph, joiner, Dec. 14, 1729.
Joseph, old age, June 20, 1781, a. 76 y.
Katharine, d. John and Katharine, Aug. 16, 1702, in her 17th y.
Katherine, w. Maj. John, Esq., Jan. 15, 1720-21, a. 62 y. 7 m.
Leverett A., only s. Hervey, Jan. 7, 1845, a. 4 y.
Martha, w. Capt. John, Feb. 24, 1679.
Martha, d. Matthew and Martha, Jan. 30, 1704.
Martha, w. Maj. Mathew, Esq., and d. John Dennison, only s. Maj. Daniel, Sept. 12, 1728, in her 60th y.
Martha, wid., consumption, Aug. 7, 1774, a. 84 y.
Mary, wid. Joseph, June 20, 1703.
Mary, wid. Joseph, joiner, June 16, 1734.
Mathew, Oct. 20, 1658.
Mathew, s. Lt. John, bur. May __, 1738.
Mathew, Dea., Jan. 24, 1764.
Matthew, of the Hamlet, weaver, May 28, 1736.
Matthew, bur. Jan. __, 1737.
Matthew, Capt., bur. Nov __, 1737
Matthew, Esq., Jan. 28, 1738, a. 80 y.
Mina, d. John, 3rd, sore throat, Sept. 20, 1748.
Nathaniel, s. Dea. Nathaniel, convulsion fits, Nov. 2, 1771, a. abt. 12 y.
Oliver, s. Nath[anie]l, March __, 1762, a. 9 y.
Paul, "Extream Heat," Aug. 6, 1771.
Robert, of the Hamlet, Jan. 1, 1759.
Sarah, w. John, June 14, 1658.
Sarah, w. Joseph, July 16, 1676
Sarah, d. Joseph and Mary, May 14, 1695.
Sarah, d. Maj. John and Catherine, July 4, 1713, a. 20 y. 6 m.
Susan, consumption , Oct. 24, 1772, a. abt. 26 y.
Sarah, wid., consumption, July 4, 1787, a. 25.
Susanna, d. Joseph and Mary, Feb. 22, 1698-9.
Susanna, wid., consumption, Oct. 14, 1773, a. 47 y.
William, June 29, 1784, in his 57th y.
_____, mother of Appleton, consumption, Sept. 14, 1696.
_____, ch, Francis, bur. Oct. __, 1730.
_____, ch. Joseph, bur. Aug. __, 1731.
_____, ch. Joseph, bur. July __, 1736.
_____, w. Dea., bur. June __, 1737.
_____, w. Capt. John, malster, Jan. 24, 1758.
_____, wid. Matthew, "back Hambt.," May 7, 1761.
_____, d. Matthew, July 15, 1786, a. 1 h.
_____, wid., Dec. 31, 1799.
_____, s. Daniel, oct. 5, 1845, a. 1 y.

NOTES

1. *Vital Records of Ipswich, MA to the end of 1849*, Vol. I. The Essex Institute. (Salem, 1910). pp. 390-94.

{ G 1856 }